Valuing Contaminated Properties

An Appraisal Institute Anthology

Readers of this anthology may also be interested in the following books published by the Appraisal Institute.

- *The Appraisal of Real Estate*, 12th edition
- *Real Estate Damages: An Analysis of Detrimental Conditions*
- *Real Estate Valuation in Litigation*, 2d edition
- *A Business Enterprise Value Anthology*

Valuing Contaminated Properties

An Appraisal Institute Anthology

Richard J. Roddewig, MAI, CRE, Editor

Reviewers: Richard Marchitelli, MAI
Michael S. MaRous, MAI, SRA
John A. Schwartz, MAI
Vice President, Educational Programs and Publications: Larisa Phillips
Director, Publications: Stephanie Shea-Joyce
Supervisor, Book Design/Production: Michael Landis
Production Specialist: Lynne Mattick Payne
Book Editor: Mary Elizabeth Geraci
Book Coordinator: Colette Nicolay

For Educational Purposes Only

The material presented in this text has been reviewed by members of the Appraisal Institute, but the opinions and procedures set forth by the author are not necessarily endorsed as the only methodology consistent with proper appraisal practice. While a great deal of care has been taken to provide accurate and current information, neither the Appraisal Institute nor its editors and staff assume responsibility for the accuracy of the data contained herein. Further, the general principles and conclusions presented in this text are subject to local, state, and federal laws and regulations, court cases, and any revisions of the same. This publication is sold for educational purposes with the understanding that the publisher is not engaged in rendering legal, accounting, or other professional services.

Nondiscrimination Policy

The Appraisal Institute advocates equal opportunity and nondiscrimination in the appraisal profession and conducts its activities in accordance with applicable federal, state, and local laws.

© 2002 by the Appraisal Institute, an Illinois not for profit corporation. All rights reserved. No part of this publication may be reproduced, modified, rewritten, or distributed, either electronically or by any other means, without the express written permission of the Appraisal Institute.

Printed in the United States of America

Library of Congress Cataloging-in-Publication Data

Valuing contaminated properties : an Appraisal Institute anthology / Richard J. Roddewig, editor
    p. cm.
  Includes bibliographical references and index.
  ISBN 0-922154-71-6
  1. Real Property—Valuation—United States. 2. Brownfields—United States. 3. Hazardous waste sites—United States. 4. Liability for hazardous substances pollution damages—United States. I. Roddewig, Richard J. II. Appraisal Institute (U.S.)

HD1389.5.U6 V36 2002
333.33'6—dc21

2002066597

Table of Contents

Foreword ix

About the Editor xi

Preface xiii

Acknowledgments xvii

Chapter 1.   The Evolution of Appraisal Methods: Where Did We Begin and Where Are We Now?

Valuing Partial Losses in Contamination Cases by Joseph A. Campanella
The Appraisal Journal (April 1984) 2

Valuation of Contaminated Properties by Peter J. Patchin, MAI
The Appraisal Journal (January 1988) 5

How North American Appraisers Value Contaminated Property and Associated Stigma
by William N. Kinnard Jr., MAI, SRA, PhD and Elaine M. Worzala, PhD
The Appraisal Journal (July 1999) 15

Chapter 2.   Contaminated Properties and the Real Estate Appraisal Process: Articles of General Applicability

Environmental Pollution: Valuation in a Changing World by John D. Dorchester, Jr., MAI, CRE
The Appraisal Journal (July 1991) 29

Contaminated Properties—Valuation Solutions by Anthony J. Rinaldi, MAI, ASA
The Appraisal Journal (July 1991) 42

The Impact of Hazardous Materials on Property Value by Bill Mundy, MAI, PhD
The Appraisal Journal (April 1992) 47

Issues in the Valuation of Contaminated Property by James A. Chalmers, PhD, and Scott A. Roehr
The Appraisal Journal (January 1993) 54

The Environmental Opinion: Basis for an Impaired Value Opinion by Albert R. Wilson
The Appraisal Journal (July 1994) 67

Emerging Approaches to Impaired Property Valuation by Albert R. Wilson
The Appraisal Journal (April 1996) 83

Choosing the Right Analytical Tool for the Job by Richard J. Roddewig, MAI
The Appraisal Journal (July 1998) 103

The Impact of Detrimental Conditions on Property Values by Randall Bell, MAI
The Appraisal Journal (October 1998) 111

Valuing Contaminated Properties

Chapter 3. Inspections, Disclosures, Environmental Site Assessments and Remediation Processes

Environmental Audits: Real Estate's Newest Transaction Safeguards by Thomas R. Kearns
The Appraisal Journal (July 1991) 127

The ASTM Standards on Environmental Site Assessments for Commercial Real Estate Transactions
by Robert V. Colangelo, CPG, and Ronald D. Miller, Esq.
Chapter 3 in *Environmental Site Assessments and Their Impact on Property Value: The
Appraiser's Role* (Appraisal Institute: 1995) 131

The New URAR and Environmental Hazards by Danny J. Martin
The Appraisal Journal (January 1995) 139

Agency Standards and Industry Guidance on Addressing Environmental Hazards
by Robert V. Colangelo, CPG, and Ronald D. Miller, Esq.
Chapter 2 in *Environmental Site Assessments and Their Impact on Property Value: The
Appraiser's Role* (Appraisal Institute: 1995) 146

Getting the Lead Out: New Regulations Require Disclosure and Evaluation by Donald E. Kelly
Valuation Insights & Perspectives (First Quarter 1997) 152

Contaminated Properties and Guide Note 8: Questions, Answers, and Suggestions for Revision
by Richard J. Roddewig, MAI
The Appraisal Journal (January 1998) 156

Environmental Challenges Can Create Work for Real Estate Appraisers by Steven A. Levine, CERS, CERA
Valuation Insights & Perspectives (Third Quarter 1999) 165

Class VIII—Environmental Conditions by Randall Bell, MAI
Chapter 8 in *Real Estate Damages: An Analysis of Detrimental Conditions* (Appraisal Institute: 1999) 169

Chapter 4. Understanding, Analyzing and Estimating Stigma

Contaminated Properties—Stigma Revisited by Peter J. Patchin, MAI, ASA, CRE
The Appraisal Journal (April 1991) 194

Stigma and Value by Bill Mundy, MAI, PhD
The Appraisal Journal (January 1992) 199

Stigma, Environmental Risk and Property Value: 10 Critical Inquiries by Richard J. Roddewig, MAI
The Appraisal Journal (October 1996) 205

Classifying the Level of Risk and Stigma Affecting Contaminated Property by Richard J. Roddewig, MAI
The Appraisal Journal (January 1999) 219

The Dose Makes the Poison: Environmental Phobia or Regulatory Stigma? by Wayne C. Lusvardi
The Appraisal Journal (April 2000) 225

Chapter 5. Contaminated Properties and the Three Traditional Approaches to Value

Estimating Value Diminution by the Income Approach by Richard A. Neustein, MAI, SRA
The Appraisal Journal (April 1992) 241

The Impact of Hazardous and Toxic Material on Property Value: Revisited by Bill Mundy, MAI, PhD
The Appraisal Journal (October 1992) 245

The Valuation of Defective Properties: A Common Sense Approach by Scott B. Arens, MAI, SRA
The Appraisal Journal (April 1997) 252

Mortgage-Equity Analysis in Contaminated Property Valuation by Thomas O. Jackson, MAI
The Appraisal Journal (January 1998) 259

Adjusting Environmental Case Study Comparables by Using an Environmental Risk Scoring System
by Richard J. Roddewig, MAI, CRE
The Appraisal Journal (October 2000) 270

The Analysis of Environmental Case Studies by Thomas O. Jackson, PhD, MAI, and Randall Bell, MAI
The Appraisal Journal (January 2002) 274

Table of Contents

Chapter 6.   Mortgage Lenders and Contaminated Properties

Lenders' Perspectives on Environmental Issues by Patricia R. Healy and John J. Healy, Jr., MAI
The Appraisal Journal (July 1992) 288

Investor & Lender Reactions to Alternative Sources of Contamination
by Elaine M. Worzala and William N. Kinnard, Jr., CRE
Real Estate Issues (August 1997) 293

Lender Attitudes Toward Source and Nonsource Impaired Property Mortgages
by Albert R. Wilson and Arthur R. Alarcon, SRA
The Appraisal Journal (October 1997) 300

Mortgage Lenders and the Institutionalization and Normalization of Environmental Risk Analysis
by Richard J. Roddewig, MAI, CRE, and Allen C. Keiter, MAI
The Appraisal Journal (April 2001) 305

Chapter 7.   Appraising Properties Affected by Various Types of Environmental Contamination
Asbestos
Probable Financial Effect of Asbestos Removal on Real Estate by Albert R. Wilson
The Appraisal Journal (July 1989) 317

Effects of Asbestos on Commercial Real Estate: A Survey of MAI Appraisers
by Jeffrey D. Fisher, PhD, George H. Lentz, PhD, and K.S. Maurice Tse, PhD
The Appraisal Journal (October 1993) 329

LUSTs
Liquidity Loss and Delayed Transactions with Leaking Underground Storage Tanks
by Robert A. Simons, PhD, and Arthur Sementelli
The Appraisal Journal (July 1997) 343

The Price and Liquidity Effects of UST Leaks from Gas Stations on Adjacent Contaminated Property
by Robert A. Simons, PhD, William M. Bowen, PhD, and Arthur J. Sementelli, PhD
The Appraisal Journal (April 1999) 350

EMFs, Radon, and Radiation
Electromagnetic Radiation Field Property Devaluation by Michael Rikon
The Appraisal Journal (January 1996) 360

The Effects on Residential Real Estate Prices from Proximity to Properties Contaminated
with Radioactive Materials by William N. Kinnard, Jr., CRE, and Mary Beth Geckler
Real Estate Issues (Fall/Winter 1991) 365

Groundwater Contamination
The Causes of Loss in Value: A Case Study of a Contaminated Property by Robert W. Hall, CRE
Real Estate Issues (April 1994) 381

Contaminated Properties and the Sales Comparison Approach by Peter J. Patchin, MAI
The Appraisal Journal (July 1994) 388

Groundwater Contamination and Residential Property Values by Mark Dotzour, PhD
The Appraisal Journal (July 1997) 398

Landfills
Landfills Aren't All Bad: Considerations for Real Estate Development
by Michael L. Robbins, CRE, Michele Robbins Norman, and John P. Norman
Real Estate Issues (Fall/Winter 1991) 406

Sick Buildings
Sick Commercial Buildings: What Appraisers Need to Know by Krisandra Guidry, PhD
The Appraisal Journal (January 2002) 421

Chapter 8.   Contaminated Properties and the Tax Assessment Process
Impact of Hazardous Waste Sites on Property Value and Land Use: Tax Assessors' Appraisal
by Michael Greenberg, PhD, and James Hughes, PhD
The Appraisal Journal (January 1993) 430

Toxic Tax Assessments: The Ad Valorem Taxation of Contaminated Property
by Robert P. Carver, Esq., and Anthony W. Crowell, Esq.
Real Estate Issues (Fall 1999) 439

Valuing Contaminated Properties

Chapter 9. Superfund Sites, Hazardous Waste Disposal Sites, Brownfield Initiatives, and Risk-Based Assessments

How Clean is Clean? by Robert Simons, PhD
The Appraisal Journal (July 1994) 454

The EPA's Brownfield Initiative: Will It Improve the Market for Contaminated Properties?
by Richard J. Roddewig, MAI, CRE
Valuation Insights & Perspectives (Third Quarter 1997) 468

Impact of a Toxic Waste Superfund Site on Property Values by Alan K. Reichert, PhD
The Appraisal Journal (October 1997) 474

The Lesson of Love Canal by Anthony P. Girasole, Jr.
Valuation Insights & Perspectives (First Quarter 1999) 488

The Persistence of Contamination Effects: A Superfund Site Revisited by Alan Reichert, PhD
The Appraisal Journal (April 1999) 493

Chapter 10. Environmental Insurance and Environmental Indemnities and Guarantee Programs

Seattle-Kent Good Neighbor Program by Gary Zarker, Director
Final Report January 1990 Seattle Engineering Department 508

Using the Cost of Environmental Insurance to Measure Contaminated Property Stigma
by Richard J. Roddewig, MAI
The Appraisal Journal (July 1997) 522

Mitigating Factors in Appraisal & Valuation of Contaminated Property
by Allan E. Gluck, Donald C. Nanney, and Wayne C. Lusvardi
Real Estate Issues (Summer 2000) 528

Chapter 11. Legal Issues and Valuation in Litigation Settings

Current Legal Issues Raised by Environmental Hazards Affecting Real Estate by Ralph W. Holmen
Real Estate Issues (Fall/Winter 1991) 540

Will New Environmental Laws Redefine Just Compensation? by Bowen P. Weisheit, Sr.
The Appraisal Journal (January 1992) 550

Temporary Stigma: Lessons from the Exxon Valdez Litigation by Richard J. Roddewig, MAI
The Appraisal Journal (January 1997) 558

Settlement of an Oil Pipeline Leak with Contaminated Residential Property: A Case Study
by Robert A. Simons
Real Estate Issues (Summer 1999) 565

Junk Science, Environmental Stigma, Market Surveys, and Proper Appraisal Methodology:
Recent Lessons from the Litigation Trenches by Richard J. Roddewig, MAI
The Appraisal Journal (October 1999) 571

Defending an Oil Company Against Litigation for Environmental Contamination (A Case Study)
by Jack P. Friedman, CRE
Real Estate Issues (Winter 1999/2000) 580

The Federal Rules of Evidence and *Daubert:* Evaluating Real Property Valuation Witnesses
by John D. Dorchester, Jr., MAI, CRE
The Appraisal Journal (July 2000) 588

Addenda

• Excerpts from Fannie Mae Guidelines 611

• Related Discussion from *The Appraisal of Real Estate,* 12th edition 623

• International Association of Assessing Officers (IAAO) Standards 631

• Guide Note 8 664

• Advisory Opinion AO-9 671

• Bibliography 674

Foreword

In the past 20 years, the Appraisal Institute has been a significant contributor to the development of appropriate methods and professional standards for the valuation of properties affected by environmental contamination. As the world's largest publisher of real estate appraisal literature, the Appraisal Institute has also been the leading source of educational materials on the effects of contamination, stigma, and risk on the marketability and value of real estate. In the pages of *The Appraisal Journal, Valuation Insights & Perspectives,* and *Real Estate Issues* (published by the Counselors of Real Estate), leading real estate professionals have investigated, illustrated, and debated professional approaches to the challenges posed by contaminated properties. The best of their work as well as significant contributions of related professionals are published in this volume, which chronicles the evolution of the concepts and techniques put forth by appraisers, developers, lenders, and other business professionals and points the way toward improved strategies for dealing with environmentally compromised properties in the future.

Thomas A. Motta, MAI, SRA
2002 President
Appraisal Institute

About the Editor

Richard J. Roddewig, MAI, CRE, is president of Clarion Associates, Inc., an appraisal and real estate and land use consulting firm with offices in Philadelphia, Cincinnati, Chicago, and Denver. Mr. Roddewig began his professional career as a land use and zoning attorney but has been a real estate counselor and appraiser since 1978. Much of Mr. Roddewig's real estate appraisal and consulting work is as an expert witness in litigation and administrative proceedings. He works nationally out of Clarion's Chicago office and his areas of appraisal expertise include valuing special purpose properties, determining the value and real estate market impacts of contamination and other types of environmental risks, and measuring the damages in eminent domain and regulatory taking situations. Mr. Roddewig is the regular environmental columnist for *The Appraisal Journal* and won the 1996 Sanders A. Kahn Award for his article "Stigma, Environmental Risk and Property Value: 10 Critical Inquiries" (October 1996), which is included in this book. He also has developed a number of Appraisal Institute seminars, including two seminars on valuing contaminated properties, which he has taught all across the United States.

Preface

Twenty years ago there were no established techniques for directly valuing contaminated properties or properties indirectly affected by their proximity to contaminated sites. The situation has changed so dramatically that the twelfth edition of *The Appraisal of Real Estate* states that "currently a diverse array of techniques are being used to value contaminated properties, and the evolution of a standardized approach to the challenges presented by such assignments is unlikely."

This anthology traces that 20-year evolution. It does so primarily through *The Appraisal Journal* articles, yet key topics are also explored in articles taken from *Valuation Insights & Perspectives,* also published by the Appraisal Institute, and *Real Estate Issues,* published by the Counselors of Real Estate. Also included are chapters from two books published by the Appraisal Institute that deal with contaminated property. The articles have been arranged by topic. Within each topic they have been organized chronologically from oldest—in this case with two exceptions no earlier than 1991—to most recent. Surprisingly, a review of even the articles from the 1980s indicates that their content is still as relevant today as it was then.

In collecting the articles to be considered for this book, it became apparent that a few topics have generated more interest among appraisers than others. Not surprisingly, how to define, evaluate, and account for the presence or absence of "stigma" over and above the direct costs to remediate contaminated properties has been perhaps the most popular subject. Most of the articles in this collection deal with that issue either as their primary focus (see Chapter 4) or as part of a more general discussion. Other topics of particular interest to many appraisers have included attitudes of mortgage lenders to contamination and its risks (see Chapter 6) and the applicability of the developing body of valuation techniques to various specific types of properties (see Chapter 7).

By contrast, some topics have not yet received the attention they deserve. The relationship between the Uniform Standards of Professional Practice and our particular responsibilities as appraisers in using the various evolving concepts, techniques, and methods has been addressed directly in only one article and in passing in an Appraisal Institute book (see Chapter 3). Nevertheless, USPAP issues are significant, and the addenda contains the text of Guide Note 8 as well as Advisory Opinion AO-9, first promulgated in 1992 and modified in 1998. As this book goes to press, the Appraisal Standards Board is again dealing with the need for further delineation of the responsibilities of real estate appraisers and the appropriate techniques they should employ. And, as some of the articles in Chapter 11 on emerging legal issues make clear, the relationship between innovative appraisal techniques and standards of professional practice is beginning to be tested in the courts as well. The resulting court decisions will have future implications for this area of appraisal practice.

Other topics are just beginning to get the attention they merit, for example, how the wider availability of environmental insurance, the content of environmental indemnities, or publicly funded programs to guarantee property values (see Chapter 10) can either quantify some risks in terms of hard dollar amounts or offset some level of risk. This topic, however, is so significant that a program booklet about Seattle's home price guarantee program in one neighborhood affected by methane gas contamination has been included in this anthology.

Many assignments involving appraisal of properties directly or indirectly affected by contamination and environmental risks also directly or indirectly involve real estate "counseling" or "consulting," and USPAP continues to deal with the difference between "appraisal" and "appraisal consulting" assignments. Therefore, the inclusion in this anthology of articles from *Real Estate Issues,* the professional publication of the Counselors of Real Estate, is particularly appropriate.

Because this anthology focuses on contaminated properties, it does not include articles on related types of detrimental conditions such as proximity to powerlines, airports, and other noise sources, or sources of dust or odor. However, the bibliography contains references to many articles on these topics. The Appraisal Institute's recent book *Real Estate Damages: An Analysis of Detrimental Conditions* by Randall Bell, MAI, deals with many of these proximity issues.

Each chapter in this anthology has a short introduction designed to highlight key points raised in each group of articles and the way they relate to one another. Although we have categorized the articles for better organization, many of the articles deal with multiple topics and could be properly included in more than one topic area. So, at the end of each chapter we have included a brief "cross-reference" section designed to alert readers to other articles in the anthology that discuss the chapter's main topic.

The addenda contains other important reference material, including a comprehensive bibliography, applicable USPAP provisions, and the section of the twelfth edition of *The Appraisal of Real Estate* that focuses on environmental liabilities. The bibliography has been compiled from the following sources: all articles published in *The Appraisal Journal;* sources footnoted or cited in articles published in *The Appraisal Journal;* sources cited in other publications of the Appraisal Institute; and bibliographies published by other appraisal professionals, including a comprehensive bibliography contained in "Stigma and Property Values—A Summary and

Preface

Review of Research," which was presented by William Kinnard at an Appraisal Institute symposium in 1997. We have tried to arrange the bibliography by topic, but again, many of the sources contained in the bibliography cover a variety of issues of interest to appraisers and other real estate professionals.

The publication of this anthology is timely for a number of reasons. There is now a significant body of published articles that can and should be collected in one book for easy access and reference. More importantly, however, is the fact that *The Appraisal Journal,* together with USPAP, the twelfth edition of *The Appraisal of Real Estate,* and the courses and seminars of the Appraisal Institute constitute the body of accepted appraisal practice and methodology. Appraisers who want to understand the evolution of appraisal techniques for the consideration of environmental risks affecting real estate, and who want to learn appraisal techniques practiced by other appraisal professionals, should familiarize themselves with the content of published *Appraisal Journal* articles. The Appraisal Institute hopes this anthology will help them do that.

Acknowledgments

Thanks are first due to each and every author of an article about the valuation of contaminated properties that has appeared in *The Appraisal Journal* and *Valuation Insights & Perspectives* since 1984. Unfortunately, it has not been possible to include them all in this anthology, and the selection process has required that many fine articles be omitted. During the past 20 years, I have gotten to know many of the authors included in this anthology and have learned much from them.

The appraisal profession is deeply indebted to the early pioneers in this appraisal subject area—those who first dealt with these complex valuation issues during the late 1980s and early 1990s—particularly Peter Patchin, Bill Mundy, Don Dorchester, and Jim Chalmers, all of whom had the courage to venture boldly into a world where few appraisers had previously gone. We also must recognize the important contributions of appraiser-academics such as Jeff Fisher, PhD, Robert Simons, PhD, Alan Reichert, PhD, Tom Jackson, PhD, and most significantly, Bill Kinnard, MAI, SRA, PhD, recently deceased; they have challenged us to evaluate the ways in which innovative and non-traditional techniques, such as regression analysis, affect our work as appraisers.

Special acknowledgment must be given to Appraisal Institute staff, especially Director of Publications Stephanie (Tep) Shea-Joyce for thinking of this anthology. She and Book Coordinator Colette Nicolay showed endless patience in the face of my many missed deadlines. But others on the Appraisal Institute staff also must be thanked, especially Heather Crego and Donna O'Loughlin, current and past managing editors of *The Appraisal Journal*, and Debbie Katz, former managing editor of *Valuation Insights & Perspectives*. Without their dedication and editorial expertise, this anthology would not have been possible. I would also like to acknowledge three Clarion staffers: research associates Daniel Farrell and Erin Smith, who contributed to the collection and editing of the work and prepared the bibliography, and my Clarion business associate of almost 20 years, Gary R. Papke, MAI, CRE, AICP, an important sounding board and reviewer for virtually every one of my Appraisal Institute publications.

Finally, I must thank Noreen Roddewig for her constant support of my writing and publishing penchant, especially this time, when my time was especially needed at home.

The Evolution of Appraisal Methods: Where Did We Begin and Where Are We Now?

CHAPTER 1

Editor's Introduction

The articles in this first chapter trace the history of the appraisal profession's investigation into and analysis of the valuation of contaminated properties. Campanella's 1984 article is the first published Appraisal Journal *article dealing with contaminated properties. He summarizes many of the constants that still characterize this area of appraisal practice 20 years later, including the typical need to compare values "before and after" considering the contamination situation, the difficulties in finding truly comparable sales or leases of contaminated properties, the constant search for verifiable evidence that eliminates subjectivity in our analysis and conclusions, and the highly case-specific nature of the quantification of lost value.*

Kinnard and Worzala show us how far we have come and how we have gotten to where we are today, from Patchin's first article discussing stigma in 1988, to the focus on income capitalization analysis in 1990–1992, and eventually to the development of reliable sales transactions. Based on 86 responses to a questionnaire sent to real estate appraisers and counselors, Kinnard and Worzala concluded that American and Canadian appraisers are "generally quite experienced in the valuation of contaminated properties." They summarize the "diversity of (valuation) methods (currently) employed and the differences of opinion about how best to employ them" as evidenced by the survey responses.

Valuing Partial Losses in Contamination Cases

by Joseph A. Campanella

Joseph A. Campanella is a fee appraiser and consultant with C. Gordon Gilbert Associates, Inc., and a principal of Property Development Advisors, Inc., a consulting and development firm in Baltimore, Maryland. Previously a hazardous waste consultant, Mr. Campanella is a graduate of the Wharton School of the University of Pennsylvania. He is also a member of the board of directors of the Baltimore City Chapter of the Home Builders Association of Maryland, a guest lecturer at the University of Baltimore, and a licensed Realtor in the State of Maryland.

This article originally appeared in the April 1984 issue of The Appraisal Journal.

If you have never had a client seeking an award for losses to his real estate from some form of contamination, the chances are you will over the next 10 years. As a result of contaminants, property losses are running into the billions of dollars. This is only the tip of the iceberg. Ground water pollution alone is likely to touch a great many American families because, according to a study done by the Environmental Protection Agency in the late 1970s, about 50% of the surface impoundments in the country are over known aquifers and have no effective liners.

Legal counsel in the Jacksonville, Florida, area found it necessary to be aware of the special valuation problems encountered in contamination assignments. The valuation experts in the special case believed it was important to further the dialogue on some of the difficult issues relating to the valuation of partial losses attributable to contamination. The following discussion is designed to help the legal community identify potential weaknesses in reports generated for or against their clients.

The traditional approach to valuing partial takings in condemnation is in some ways similar to the approaches taken in the valuation of damages sustained as a result of contamination. The property value is appraised as though the contaminant never existed and then reappraised in its current condition. Any difference is then estimated to be the value lost as a result of the contaminant. The problems arise in the estimate of value "after contamination" because the traditional approaches may become very subjective or at best very difficult to substantiate.

It is important to reaffirm that the job of an appraiser is to predict how people will act in relation to property and then to substantiate that prediction with some verifiable evidence. The valuation of contaminated properties may become very subjective. Findings may be very difficult to substantiate even for those appraisers with experience in this field. Almost all appraisers agree that this is one of the most difficult areas in the valuation field.

Chapter 1: *Valuing Partial Losses in Condemnation*

The sales comparison approach will often become the appraiser's most convincing indication of value in an ordinary assignment. In contamination cases it is very rare to find good, arms-length comparable sales of contaminated properties. This is especially true for commercial office, institutional, and industrial properties. Contaminated properties sell very rarely; when they do, great care must be taken to compare only those properties of similar uses, which are contaminated by a similar pollutant and in a similar manner. One would be hard-pressed to derive a meaningful discount for a restaurant that has a benzene-contaminated well by comparing it to a residence with urea formaldehyde insulation in the attic. How does one compare the damage sustained by a retail property where PCB is found in the drains with an office building insulated with asbestos? Is the loss in value for a farm contaminated with dioxin similar to the loss in value sustained by residences whose private wells test too high in iron and phosphates? Will a city residence contaminated with lead paint suffer the same loss in value before the pending legislation as after? The appraiser must be careful to draw comparisons from those sales where the level of "threat" was similar to that facing the typical buyer of the subject property.

The income capitalization approach to value is limited in its reliability for the same reasons. Even when there is a lease made on a contaminated property, the appraiser must be sure to check if the type, quantity, and location of the pollution add up to the same threat facing the typical tenant in the subject property. The appraiser is now forced to seek similarity between the utility of the properties in an expanded context.

The principle of substitution leads many contamination assignments to rely on the "cost-to-cure approach." The extent of the losses are equal to the cost of curing the contamination problem. For certain types of contamination this approach can provide a convincing indication of the losses sustained as a result of the contamination. In many cases, however, the cost-to-cure is reduced to a "broad brush" approach to the solution. Flat percentage or dollar amounts become deductions purporting to reflect the true loss in property value. All this is done under the guise of the typical, unsophisticated buyer's approach to the solutions.

Picture yourself as the typical buyer faced with the opportunity to buy a small commercial property where the groundwater is contaminated. How do you solve the problem? The engineers and equipment vendors you speak with all assure you that their solution to the problem is the best. As a layman you are forced to decide among charcoal filtration, digging deeper wells, building a cistern and pumping system on site, or setting up cross easements to pipe clean water from a nearby uncontaminated well. To confuse matters the local regulatory authority will not commit itself to accepting any one of the solutions until after its operation.

The appraiser faces all these issues when attempting to quantify the losses in the cost-to-cure approach. If the property is small and the profit opportunity for the buyer is minimal, then perhaps a flat discount from the sale price is warranted since it does not benefit the prospective buyer to spend money chasing the best solution. If the property is much larger with substantial profit incentive available then a refinement of the alternative solutions would be warranted.

Whatever approach to value the appraiser finally chooses, he or she may consider attempting to quantify other strata of diminution in value.

Each right of the bundle of rights is subject to restriction or revocation, alone or in a myriad of configurations. Quantifying lost value in these scenarios is a highly case-specific task.

The following list may be helpful for the preparation of direct or cross-examination in the event an appraiser experienced in contamination issues is not available:

> "Chilling Effect"—Loss in value because of past negative publicity, the reduction on local commercial activity, the prospect of future negative impacts due to additional contamination, negative publicity, and inconvenience. Usually confined to those properties actually contaminated or in the immediate vicinity depending on the nature of the contaminant. The "chilling effect" can often be substantiated by the reduction in gross sales experienced by local merchants, the leveling off of rents, the increase in vacancy rates, and reduction in quantity or price for residential sales.

Other more subjective deductions in the value of the contaminated property may be attributed to

> The loss of insurability
> The loss of mortgageability
> Restrictions on density rights
> Nonissuance of building permits
> Nonissuance of revocation of occupancy permits
> Restrictions on the transfer of title
> Restrictions on the transfer of leasehold interests
> Restrictions on the transfer of easement interests
> Restrictions on water rights
> Restrictions on mineral rights
> Restrictions on air rights

As the public becomes more aware of various contaminants they will become more aware of the threats and solutions associated with various types of contamination. Their preferences will become more predictable as buyers and sellers. Technically sophisticated, contaminant-specific solutions will be more readily available. Regulators will eventually begin to form guidelines concerning the acceptability of specific solutions and the appraisal community will not be able to argue for the "broad brush" discounts that tend to be more subjective. Until then the legal and appraisal communities together need to develop fresh new ideas. Clients depend on appraisers to navigate successfully the waters around the iceberg headed their way.

Valuation of Contaminated Properties

by Peter J. Patchin, MAI

Toxic contamination has a major impact on the values of the properties it affects. The costs of the cleanup, along with liability to the public and stigma, often eliminate or significantly reduce a property's value.

Until recently, very few buyers, sellers, lenders, or appraisers gave much thought to the impact of toxic contaminants on a property's value. Until about 15 years ago, many industries simply disposed of hazardous wastes on-site. There was little, if any, concern for the fact that ecologic and economic time bombs were being created.

The enactment of the so-called "superfund" or Comprehensive Environmental Response Compensation and Liability Act of 1980 (CERCLA)[1] by the federal government and similar legislation passed by various state governments have had a dramatic effect on both the use and valuation of properties that are contaminated or subject to contamination. The basic provisions of these laws call for the following:

1. The party who placed the contamination in the ground must bear the costs of cleanup as directed by either the federal or state agency having jurisdiction.

2. If the parties originally responsible for the contamination are no longer financially solvent or no longer exist, the responsibility falls on successors in the chain of title; most likely, the existing or present property owner. A leading court case held that a present owner who had no part in placing the contamination on the site was liable for the costs of cleanup.[2]

3. Other parties associated with the title to a contaminated property may also be held responsible for the costs of cleanup. A recent court case held that a bank that foreclosed on a property must pay for the costs of cleanup because previous owners were judgment-proof (financially insolvent or no longer in existence).[3] Consequently, the bank was held liable for cleanup costs in the aggregate amount of $460,000, when the total amount of the loan foreclosed was only $335,000.

Peter J. Patchin, MAI, is a fee appraiser and president of Peter J. Patchin & Associates, Inc., Burnsville, Minnesota. He specializes in valuing commercial and industrial real estate, as well as business enterprises. He has previously contributed to The Appraisal Journal.

This article originally appeared in the January 1988 issue of The Appraisal Journal.

1. 42 U.S.C. Sec. 9601-9657 (1982).
2. *State of New York* v. *Shore Realty Corp.*, 759 F. 2d 1032 (2d. Cir. 1985).
3. *United States* v. *Maryland Bank and Trust Co.*, 16 E.I.R. 20557 (D. Md. April 9, 1986).

In October 1986, CERCLA was amended to clarify the intent of Congress that under certain circumstances one who acquires property without knowledge or reason to know of contamination cannot be held liable for hazardous wastes. This amendment established standards of due diligence for prospective property buyers. The new owner must demonstrate that he or she had no reason to know that the property was contaminated and "appropriate inquiry" was made into the background of the property. Because National Priority List properties and less contaminated properties can be clearly identified through public information disseminated by federal and state environmental protection agencies (EPAs), prospective buyers are relatively well protected against purchasing properties already evaluated as contaminated. However, if a buyer takes a title with the knowledge that the property is contaminated, he or she is subject to the inherent liabilities. The intent of the amendment to CERCLA is to protect innocent buyers in those cases in which no contamination is detected at the time of the sale. The amendment may help buyers, but it does not help properties that have already been evaluated as contaminated.

As a result of the superfund laws and the body of case law that is developing around these laws, buyers, sellers, and lenders are developing a new awareness of both the environmental and economic affects of toxic or hazardous waste contamination. Many informed corporate buyers now require a diligent inquiry into the possibility of contamination for each property they purchase. Many of the larger lenders now have a standard clause in their loan commitment forms that nullifies the loan commitment if toxic contamination is discovered.

When toxic contamination is found and a cleanup mandated by federal or state authorities, conflicts frequently arise between existing and previous owners as to who pays the bill. Once a property has been cleaned up to the extent physically possible, the questions of contingent future liability to the public and stigma must be dealt with.

The most seriously contaminated properties are graded for their toxicity and danger to the public by the U.S. EPA. Properties that score 28.5 or higher on the Hazardous Waste Ranking System (HRS) test are placed on the National Priority List in the Federal Register. This list of the most toxic-contaminated properties is commonly known as the "Superfund List." At the time this article was written, there were 734 such properties on the National Priority List. The number grows each time the list is published, which is every six months. Obviously these properties must be entered into a cleanup program immediately to protect public safety. I have encountered several instances in which the costs of the cleanup have far exceeded the fair market value of the property without contamination.

Thousands of other properties are contaminated to a lesser extent, and while not on the superfund list are still supervised and monitored by state and federal agencies. Quite frequently these less-contaminated properties are not required to clean up, at least for the present. Government agencies reserve judgment until further information is gathered. If it is determined that the property will be hazardous at a later time, a cleanup will then be ordered. Consequently, the threat of cleanup costs hangs over the owners of these properties like a dark cloud.

At this point one might ask what these contaminated properties are worth, and how one goes about such a valuation.

Chapter 1: *Valuation of Contaminated Properties*

The development of techniques for valuing contaminated properties is still in its infancy. I have completed 10 such appraisals. The purpose of this article is to share the knowledge I have gained thus far, as well as the valuation theories that I have developed.

When I accepted my first assignment to value a contaminated property, some four years ago, I approached it with the idea of discounting the value of the property before considering the contamination. This notion was quickly dispelled when I found that there was little, if any, market data on contaminated properties. The reasons for this lack of market data became evident when I interviewed corporate real estate personnel who had dealt with the problem. These individuals were practically unanimous in voicing the opinion that a seriously contaminated property will not sell at any price. More than one stated the old adage "don't buy trouble." Others cited the principle of substitution wherein it would not be wise to purchase a contaminated property when so many non-contaminated substitutes are readily available. One manager of a large corporate real estate department stated that his board of directors had made a resolution never to sell a group of properties in which toxic contamination is even suspected, to eliminate as much contingent future liability to the public as possible.

The first thing I concluded from this series of interviews was that seriously contaminated properties are generally unmarketable.

The unmarketability of a superfund list property is dramatically illustrated in a case I recently handled. A large industrial property had been listed for sale for over three years. During that period six written purchase offers had been received. All but one offer was rescinded on disclosure of the contamination. The one remaining offer is that of the local county government, which is seeking to buy the property for less than one quarter of the asking price. This buyer has the capability of solving the indemnity problems for the future chain of title.

The courts have explicitly recognized the unmarketability of contaminated property. One court decision stated that "it seems beyond dispute that designation of property as having a problem serious enough to warrant E.P.A. & Superfund clean up will mark that property as an unmarketable pariah for years to come."[4]

Such a decision leads to a mixed bag of consequences for valuation. For example, only a moderate decline in value may occur for a contaminated property that can still be utilized under its originally intended use. On the other hand, a property that can no longer be utilized for its originally intended use may be subject to total loss of value.

After interviewing corporate real estate personnel who had experience with contaminated properties, I interviewed buyers and sellers of properties in which toxic contamination was relatively mild or perhaps just suspected, but not yet proven. The market's attitude toward these properties was something less than total unmarketability, however, the overall attitude was one of extreme caution. For example, a large city had an otherwise very desirable 40-acre tract of industrial land for sale. The site had been previously used by the city waterworks department for disposal of filtrate sediments from its water treatment plant. There was no proof that these contaminants were in any way toxic. Nonetheless, the market of buyers was extremely wary on the basis that the site could be designated as

4. *SCA Services of Indiana, Inc.* v. *Thomas,* 634 F. Supp. 1355 (N.D. Ind. 1986) at 1364.

hazardous in the future. Most local appraisers were in agreement that the site was worth no less than $2.00 per square foot if not contaminated. After several years of effort, the city finally sold the site for $1.00 per square foot. In addition, the city had to include an indemnity of up to $800,000 for contingent future liabilities. The indemnity was of greater importance in making the deal than the apparent discount in value.

I found a limited amount of additional market data on mildly contaminated properties. In almost every case, the buyer insisted that the seller bear the cleanup costs, as well as some sort of indemnity for future liabilities.

On the basis of the information I obtained, I concluded that property that is mildly contaminated or suspected of contamination has limited marketability. This marketability is limited by cleanup costs, availability of an indemnity, higher equity yield demands to compensate for risk, and possibly higher financing costs because fewer lenders are willing to consider the property.

Indemnities

Because securing an indemnity is often a key step in marketing a contaminated property, the subject of indemnities must be included in any discussion of contaminated property values.

An indemnity, in the case of contaminated properties, is a financial guarantee against future claims and costs arising from contamination. To be effective, an indemnity must usually be issued by a financially secure organization whose performance, in the event of a claim, can be guaranteed many years into the future. Consequently, very few sellers of contaminated properties have the requisites to issue an indemnity that will be acceptable in the marketplace. Even the largest business organizations can experience financial difficulties and are subject to the possibility of failure. An indemnity offered by a AAA credit corporation may look good today, but can become utterly worthless if the corporation becomes insolvent or goes out of business 20 years from now.

Generally speaking, the only indemnities acceptable in the market are those underwritten by large insurance or bonding companies; or in some instances, underwritten as a general obligation of large governmental organizations. In most private transactions it is necessary to secure an indemnity insurance policy or bond.

Like so many areas of casualty insurance underwriting today, indemnity insurance for contaminated property is frequently difficult to obtain. When such coverage is obtainable, it is almost never available on properties that have a proven record of contamination. A contaminated property can be cleaned up to the best levels technology will allow, and it will still be impossible to obtain an indemnity policy.

My experience in recent cases has shown that an indemnity policy against future liabilities to the public cannot be obtained for even mildly contaminated properties. However, it is possible to obtain a bond that insures payment of future cleanup costs if ordered by the appropriate authorities. In these situations, the insuring company carefully reviews engineering reports on the property before issuing the bond.

In my experience many sales of contaminated property have involved an indemnity issued by a large governmental organization that has taken

Chapter 1: *Valuation of Contaminated Properties*

title sometime prior to the sale. Fairly large municipalities acquire a contaminated property and then grant an indemnity to aid in getting the property back into useful production in the community. More of this type of urban renewal may be seen in the future.

Financing

Lenders are understandably wary of contaminated properties. If a bond insuring cleanup costs can be secured, as is the case for some mildly contaminated properties, a major obstacle has been overcome. However, some lenders refuse to advance funds on such a property, bond or not, strictly as a matter of policy. Usually a limited number of lenders can be found for mildly contaminated sites.

There is virtually no chance of obtaining mortgage financing for a seriously contaminated property. Several lenders that I surveyed stated that they were still formulating their policies on contaminated properties.

Causes of Market-Value Loss

In my experience with contaminated properties, the causes of market-value loss have generally fallen under three broad categories:

1. Costs of cleanup
2. Liability to the public
3. Stigma after cleanup

Costs of Cleanup

Cleanup procedures are usually specified by either federal or state EPAs, at which time the owner of the property or the EPA, if the owner is unable or unwilling, retains the services of one or more engineering firms to explore cleanup methods and costs. Frequently, more than one way is found to do the job. In some cases, the EPA will give conditional approval to a less expensive method with the understanding that if it fails, the more expensive method must be implemented. In one case that I appraised, the total property value before contamination was about $20 million. The least costly method for total removal of the contaminants was $26 million, thereby wiping out the value of a very large industrial facility. As a compromise, the state EPA allowed a containment wall to be constructed around the contaminated area at a cost of about $4 million. However, the state EPA withheld final approval of the containment wall with the understanding that if it was ever found to be inadequate, the more expensive method of total removal would have to be implemented.

One misconception that some persons have with respect to cleanup costs is that the superfund will pay for them, thus relieving innocent present owners of this responsibility. Superfund monies are to be expended only for those cleanups in which no one financially capable of covering them can be found, and the cleanup must proceed on a timely basis to protect public interests.

In the case of properties with moderate or mild contamination, the EPA may find no present threat to public health. The cleanup may be deferred until such time as new information indicates a public hazard. Thus the mildly contaminated property may have no immediate cleanup costs, with contingent liability for future costs.

Valuing Contaminated Properties

A discussion of cleanup costs is incomplete without mentioning monitoring costs. Monitoring costs usually involve the maintenance of test wells and the analysis of materials drawn from them. The annual costs of these services must be paid by those responsible for the property. In my experience, monitoring costs have ranged from a low of $1,500 to a high of $30,000 per year.

Liability to the Public

Liability to the public as a cause of property-value loss to contaminated properties stems from the possibility of the property owner having to defend lawsuits because of the release of toxic contaminants onto surrounding properties. In cases in which the contamination has penetrated the water table used for public drinking supply, these types of lawsuits are bound to occur. Publicity surrounding the discovery of contamination on a property and the EPA enforcement of cleanup measures further exposes the owners to legal actions from the public.

In most cases I have observed, no lawsuits were filed against the property owner. The potential threat of such legal exposure is usually a sufficient deterrent when considering purchase of the property.

Stigma After Cleanup

One of the most difficult concepts to understand when considering the effect of contamination on property value is that a physical cleanup does not usually eliminate the value loss resulting from the stigma. Obviously this cause of market-value loss is related to the issue of liability to the public.

I have observed several cases in which physical cleanups were accomplished to the full limits of available technology. The toxic contaminants were removed until their presence tested positive under EPA minimums. Despite cleanup to the satisfaction of the EPA, potential buyers remained reluctant. This reluctance has to do with all the risk and financing problems previously discussed. The result is that even a cleaned up property may suffer from reduced marketability.

In one case in Minnesota, a jury awarded $1.5 million for reduced property value after the cleanup costs had been taken into consideration.[5]

In another recently concluded case, a jury awarded $2.6 million to a landowner for personal injuries, loss in property value, and punitive damages.[6] On review, the presiding judge set aside the jury award except for the loss in property value. An important factor was that the defendant had already paid for a complete cleaned up of the property.

Valuation Techniques

As previously stated, the tendency of most appraisers in valuing contaminated property is to approach the problem on the basis of discounting the value before contamination. Such a method is difficult, if not impossible, to support with market data. What market research will disclose is that contaminated properties suffer from varying degrees of reduced marketability or total unmarketability.

In some valuations of contaminated property that I have observed, the appraiser has concluded that the property is unmarketable. From this conclusion, he or she jumped to a second conclusion that the property is

5. *Onan Corporation* v. *Boise Cascade Corp.,* (D. Minn. 1984)

6. *Woyke* v. *Tonka Corporation,* (D. Minn. 1987)

Chapter 1: *Valuation of Contaminated Properties*

totally worthless. Such a value conclusion is unreasonable when the property is still being utilized by its present owner for some useful purpose. It is even more unreasonable when the property is still being utilized for its originally intended purpose.

Previously in this discussion I have reviewed data on increased risks of ownership, difficulties in financing, and so forth. A valuation tool that utilizes all of these factors is the capitalization rate. Consequently, with its mortgage-equity measurement techniques the capitalization rate appears to offer a means of valuing contaminated property.

In reviewing the basic requirements of the Ellwood capitalization method, one can see that the capitalization rate is dependent on three major factors:

1. Equity yield rate
2. Mortgage terms available
3. Anticipated future appreciation or depreciation

If a property is no longer marketable, anticipation of appreciation or depreciation is not applicable. If a property cannot be mortgaged, there is no leverage available to the investor in terms of borrowing capital. Thus, in the case of an unmarketable property, the primary component of the capitalization rate is equity yield.

For properties with reduced marketability, the three components of the capitalization rate remain intact but are altered because of changing risk factors as perceived by both the investor and lender. Consequently, the capitalization rate for such properties can be adjusted to suit the circumstances at hand, some of which would be as follows:

1. Extent and nature of contamination—resulting in unmarketability or reduced marketability
2. Type of property involved—industrial, commercial, office, special purpose, and so forth
3. Presence of assumable financing
4. Demand for alternative uses

The following three scenarios illustrate the various situations that an appraiser might encounter in valuing contaminated property.

Scenario 1

An industrial property is severely contaminated with toxic substances and is regarded as unmarketable. The original owner is continuing to utilize the property for its originally intended use and plans to do so into the foreseeable future. The property has a substantial "value in use" to the existing owner, even though it can no longer be sold or mortgaged.

In valuing the property before the contamination, the following information was obtained:

Market net rental for present use	$100,000 per year
Equity yield for similar properties	17%
Mortgage obtainable	11.25% interest for 70% of property value with a 25-year amortization, 10-year balloon

Valuing Contaminated Properties

Indicated market appreciation	3% per year
Estimated cleanup costs presently ordered by the local EPA	$200,000
Capitalization rate using the Ellwood method	10%

The indicated before-value

$$\frac{\text{Net income}}{\text{Cap rate}} =$$

$$\frac{\$100,000}{.10} = \qquad\qquad \$1,000,000$$

After consideration of the contamination, the property is evaluated as unmarketable and unable to be mortgaged, leaving the equity yield as the primary component of the capitalization rate. After contamination, the equity yield not only bears its normal market rate (17% in this case), but an additional risk factor for contingent future liabilities. An illiquidity factor for lack of marketability should also be considered. Thus, a 20% equity yield is designated after the contamination.[7] This equity yield then becomes the capitalization rate, and the after-value may be calculated as follows:

$$\frac{\text{Net income}}{\text{Cap rate}} \qquad \frac{\$100,000}{.20} = \qquad\qquad \$500,000$$

Summary:

Before-value	$1,000,000
After-value	$500,000

Indicated damages

Without cleanup costs	$500,000
Less cleanup costs	$200,000
Property value after contamination	$300,000

Scenario 2

This scenario involves the same property and information, except that the contamination is mild enough to allow limited marketability. Cleanup costs have been estimated by an engineering study. However, the EPA has not required a cleanup because presently the contamination is not regarded as a public threat; a cleanup could be enforced at a later date. Currently the EPA is requiring only that the owners pay for the $1,500 per year monitoring cost. A bond can be obtained to pay for the costs of a cleanup, if one is enforced, at a rate of 2% per year of the estimated costs, which are $200,000. The issuing of a bond removes many of the hazards perceived by lenders, and a limited number of lenders will consider the property at a 12% interest rate; the balance of the terms are the same as in the first scenario. The equity yield will demand an extra risk factor, but not as high as 20% as in the previous scenario. An 18% equity yield is selected.

7. The assignment of an extra risk factor to the equity yield is a subject in itself. Considering the circumstances, the 20% rate in the example is conservative.

Chapter 1: *Valuation of Contaminated Properties*

When the above data are incorporated into the Ellwood method, a capitalization rate of 10.9% is indicated. The after-contamination value of the property can be calculated as follows:

Net income before contamination		$100,000
Less monitoring costs	$1,500	
Cost of cleanup bond $200,000 \times 2\% =$	$4,000	
		$5,500
Net income after contamination		$94,500
Indicated capitalization rate—10.9%		

$$\frac{\text{Net income}}{\text{Cap rate}} =$$

$$\frac{\$94,500}{.109} = \qquad \$867,000$$

Summary:

Before-value (same as in Scenario 1)	$1,000,000
After-value	$867,000
Indicated damages including consideration of cleanup costs	$133,000

The contrast between the results in scenarios 1 and 2 for the same property with the same value before contamination is startling. The only differences are the nature and extent of the contamination. It is obvious that the valuation of contaminated property cannot be approached in the same manner in each instance. The factors involved in each situation must be carefully analyzed before the exact valuation method can be selected.

The wide difference in values found in the two scenarios should clearly demonstrate the dangers of simply selecting a discount percentage when valuing contaminated property.

Scenario 3

In some cases the presence of toxic contamination may force a change in the property's highest and best use. A 10-acre parcel of vacant land is severely contaminated with toxic substances. Before consideration of the contamination, the site was regarded to be ripe for small office development because it has excellent highway access. Comparable land sales in the neighborhood for the same purpose indicate a value of about $100,000 per acre.

Because the contamination is severe enough to render the property unmarketable, its subdivision under its apparent highest and best use is no longer possible. One of the few purposes for which the site could be used after contamination, and that would yield the highest value, would be open storage, such as an industrial yard. Comparable sales of land used for this purpose indicate a value of about $40,000 per acre.

The state EPA has ordered an immediate cleanup to protect public interests. Because of technological limitations, the site will still have a high degree of contamination after cleanup. The engineering report estimates cleanup costs at $300,000.

The value of the analysis would proceed as follows:

Before contamination—10 acres at $100,000 per acre =		$1,000,000
After contamination—10 acres at $40,000 per acre =	$400,000	
Less costs of cleanup	$300,000	
		$100,000
Indicated damages due to contamination		$900,000

Conclusion

The development of valuation techniques for contaminated property is still in its infancy. The appraisal profession and the public are just now becoming aware of the seriousness of the problem. I expect that with an increase in appraisal and case law experience in this field, far more comprehensive valuation techniques will be developed than presented here. There is no quick fix to appraising contaminated property. The results are very dependent on individual circumstances. The extent and nature of the contamination are the crucial factors in estimating the after-value of a contaminated property.

How North American Appraisers Value Contaminated Property and Associated Stigma

by William N. Kinnard, Jr., MAI, SRA, PhD, and Elaine M. Worzala, PhD

Since 1984, a rich and diverse body of literature has developed in U.S. and Canadian journals suggesting how properties with known or suspected on-site contamination should be valued. Only a few papers have also shown the application of the author's recommended methodology, using case examples based on actual market data, however.[1]

At the same time, a parallel series of papers has appeared on the subject of stigma.[2] They contain multiple and wide-ranging definitions of stigma, but generally agree on the procedures appropriate to identify its existence and measure it.[3] Two general sources of stigma have been identified in U.S. and Canadian research, as well as in work from New Zealand and in the United Kingdom: (1) uncertainty and risk of diminished property value after completion of any required program of remediation applied to on-site contamination, and (2) uncertainty and risk of diminished property value from proximity to any perceived hazard to human health and safety, or to property value, from an off-site source.[4]

In valuing properties with on-site contamination that require remediation, or properties stigmatized either from being designated as a contaminated site or from proximity to off-site contamination (or both), appraisers are confronted with a two-part problem: Is there a verifiable negative impact on the value or market price of any such property? If so, how can that negative impact be measured?

The literature on valuing contaminated properties reflects primarily what author-researchers say should be done, might be done, or (occasionally) has been done in one or a few cases. To date, however, no known study has systematically surveyed the actual practices of appraisers experienced in the valuation of properties known or suspected to contain on-site contamination. The only published methodological reviews have reported how analysts do identify and measure the impact of proximity to known or suspected sources of contamination, on nearby property value.[5] The survey results reported in this article identify what U.S. and Canadian appraisers currently do when confronted with an assignment to value

William N. Kinnard, Jr., MAI, SRA, PhD, *is president of the Real Estate Counseling Group of Connecticut, Inc., and professor emeritus of finance and real estate, University of Connecticut, Storrs. His practice includes valuation of contaminated properties, estimation of post-remediation stigma and proximity impact studies. He testifies frequently on the results of his research findings. Dr. Kinnard has published frequently in* The Appraisal Journal, *and other professional and academic journals in the United States, Canada, the United Kingdom, New Zealand, and Australia. Contact: recgc@mail.snet.net.*

Elaine M. Worzala, PhD, *is associate professor of finance and real estate at Colorado State University, Fort Collins. Her research interests include institutional investments, international real estate investments, valuation issues, and the professional behavior of real estate appraisers. She has published on these and related topics in* The Appraisal Journal, *and other professional and academic journals in the United States, Australia, and the United Kingdom.*

> *This article originally appeared in the July 1999 issue of* The Appraisal Journal.

1. Leading examples of such articles are provided in the "References" section. Similar articles, papers, and texts have appeared in the United Kingdom and New Zealand. For details, consult Sandy G. Bond and Paul J. Kennedy, "The Valuation of Contaminated Land: New Zealand and United Kingdom Practice Compared." Paper presented at the European Real Estate Society Conference, Maastricht, Netherlands, June 1998.

2. Randall Bell, "The Impact of Detrimental Conditions on Property Values," *The Appraisal Journal* (October 1998): 380–391.

3. Bond and Kennedy.

4. Bell identifies the reaction to increased risk associated with on-site contamination as "market resistance," which subsumes stigma, onus, taint, or impairment.

5. For details, see William Kinnard, Jr., "Stigma and Property Values: A Summary and Review of Research and Literature." Paper presented at the Appraisal Institute Symposium, Washington, D.C., June 1997.

Valuing Contaminated Properties

a contaminated property or a property that is formally and officially declared to have been remediated. It is important to understand that remediation is rarely a synonym for "cleanup." Under Environmental Protection Agency (EPA) regulations, and those of most state departments of environment protection (DEP) regulations, remediation is activity designed to reduce the actual level of specified on-site contaminants to or below the maximum contaminant level (MCL) established by the EPA for the contaminants in question. On the other hand, cleanup would be the result of removing virtually all contaminants from the site and reducing its presence to approximately zero parts per milllion. This is frequently not technically possible, and usually not financially feasible.

Objectives of the Current Research

There were three related objectives to this survey research:

1. To summarize the major U.S. and Canadian literature that addresses recommended valuation procedures for estimating the market value of some specified ownership interest (most commonly, the unencumbered fee interest) in either a property known or suspected to be contaminated, a property known or assumed to have been remediated, or a property near a known or suspected source of contamination

2. To identify valuation procedures and techniques actually applied by U.S. and Canadian appraisers experienced in the valuation of properties affected by contamination

3. To compare actual practice with recommended valuation procedures and techniques contained in the literature

Contaminated Property Valuation Literature

The literature on the effects of on-site contamination on real property in the United States dates from approximately 1984, when Joseph Campanella's article was published in *The Appraisal Journal*.[6] Thereafter, only a handful of articles and papers appeared before 1991. In one of them, Peter Patchin first introduced the concept of stigma to the valuation of properties with on-site contamination, and noted a dearth of comparable sales of contaminated properties:

> Corporate real estate personnel...were practically unanimous in voicing the opinion that a seriously contaminated property will not sell at any price... More than one stated the old adage "Don't buy trouble"... The first thing I concluded from the series of interviews was that seriously contaminated properties are generally unmarketable.[7]

Thus, the importance of marketability, especially when market value is to be estimated, was recognized and introduced.

Patchin also indicated that "lenders are understandably wary of contaminated properties...There is virtually no chance of obtaining mortgage financing for a seriously contaminated property."[8] This finding was reinforced by Bill Mundy[9] in his first reported survey of institutional lenders. Respondents generally reported aversion to and avoidance of lending on properties either known or suspected to be contaminated. Such market behavior indicates the existence of elevated levels of risk perceived by market participants, especially potential buyers and lenders.

6. Joseph A. Campanella, "Valuing Partial Losses in Contamination Cases," *The Appraisal Journal* (April 1984): 301–304.

7. Peter J. Patchin, "Valuation of Contaminated Properties," *The Appraisal Journal* (January 1988): 9.

8. Ibid., 11.

9. Bill Mundy, "Survey Cites Impacts of Contaminants on Value and Marketability of Real Estate." News release, American Society of Real Estate Counselors, Chicago, Illinois, November 1988.

Finally, Patchin identified the causes of price-value loss experienced by contaminated properties as falling under three broad categories: cost of cleanup, liability to the public, and stigma after cleanup. In discussing stigma after cleanup, Patchin observed that:

> A physical cleanup does not usually eliminate the value loss resulting from stigma...I have observed several cases in which...potential buyers remained reluctant. This reluctance has to do with all the risk and financing problems previously discussed. The result is that even a cleaned up property may suffer from reduced marketability.[10]

Reiterating the virtual lack of market sales transactions data for contaminated properties, Patchin concludes:

> A valuation tool that utilizes all of these [foregoing] factors is the capitalization rate, [which] is dependent on three major factors: (1) equity yield rate, (2) mortgage terms available, and (3) anticipated future appreciation/depreciation.[11]

Reliance on Income Capitalization Analysis

The early valuation literature of 1990–1992[12] emphasized the necessity to use the framework of income capitalization to identify the *deductions* from unimpaired market value (i.e., market value as if noncontaminated) in order to estimate the impaired market value of contaminated property. That general framework persists as of this writing. An appraiser estimates unimpaired market value of the property and then deducts the following elements:

- The present worth of the estimated cost to remediate (typically obtained from environmental engineers or technicians);
- The present worth of reduced revenues, stemming from a combination of reductions in occupancy and rentals;
- The present worth of increased operating expenses, including increased insurance premiums, increased interest on debt, and monitoring costs anticipated after remediation; and
- The present worth of holding costs (e.g., insurance, property taxes, repairs, and maintenance) that would otherwise have been covered by the reduced revenues.

Present worth is calculated as a function of the anticipated duration of the remediation period plus the marketing period (for sale or rental) anticipated when remediation is completed. Over that total period of time, the discount rate (or, sometimes, the capitalization rate) that is applied to the anticipated income is adjusted upward to reflect the perception that increased risk is associated with the existence, or even suspicion, of on-site contamination. These risk rates are further increased by the likelihood of having to pay higher interest on debt (when debt financing is available at all) or relying on a higher proportion of equity investment (which requires a higher rate of return). Negative cash flows associated with anticipated losses or necessary expenses, on the other hand, are appropriately discounted at an applicable safe rate.

A further deduction from impaired market value is then made for post-remediation stigma. Initially, stigma was reflected in further increases in the risk rates applied to the reduced revenue.[13] In more recent years, sales transaction information has become available to indicate the percentage

10. Patchin, 12.

11. Ibid., 13.

12. See especially, Bill Mundy, "Stigma and Value," *The Appraisal Journal* (January 1992a): 7–13; "The Impact of Hazardous Materials on Property Value," *The Appraisal Journal* (April 1992b): 155–163; "The Impact of Hazardous and Toxic Material on Property Value: Revisited," *The Appraisal Journal* (October 1992c): 463–471; Peter J. Patchin, "Contaminated Properties—Stigma Revisited," *The Appraisal Journal* (April 1991a): 167–172; "Valuing Contaminated Properties: Case Studies," Measuring the Effects of Hazardous Materials Contamination on Real Estate Values: Techniques and Applications (Chicago, Illinois: Appraisal Institute, 1992); Anthony J. Rinaldi, "Contaminated Properties—Valuation Solutions," *The Appraisal Journal* (1991): 377–381; William N. Kinnard, Jr., "Measuring the Effects of Contamination on Property Values," *Environmental Watch* (Winter 1992): 1–4.

13. See, for example, James A. Chalmers and Scott Roehr, "Issues in the Valuation of Contaminated Property," *The Appraisal Journal* (January 1993): 28–41; Mundy (1992a,b,c); and Patchin (1988; 1991a); "The Valuation of Contaminated Properties," *Real Estate Issues* (Fall/Winter 1991b): 50–54.

Valuing Contaminated Properties

difference between the sales price of a remediated property with "closure" from a regulatory body (or indemnification from a reliable, financially responsible seller) and the estimated unimpaired market value of that property, as of the same date. Thus, contaminated property market sales transactions data have become sufficiently numerous and available as direct market evidence to be utilized in estimating post-remediation stigma.[14]

Therefore, there is growing evidence for, and emphasis on, the use of sales of similarly contaminated properties following completion of remediation (with and without indemnification and/or closure) to identify and measure post-remediation stigma. Nevertheless, most U.S. authors still recommend increasing the capitalization rate or discount rate. This latter procedure recognizes the increased risk associated with marketing a property known to have been contaminated (for sale or lease). However, as the volume of available sales transactions data increases and becomes generally known, it is anticipated that this more "objective" evidence will become the major source of identifying and measuring post-remediation stigma.

Alternative methods of identifying and quantifying stigma continue to be suggested. For example, Bruce Weber utilizes Monte Carlo techniques to develop a probability estimate of post-remediation stigma.[15]

In addition, there are situations in which neither market sales nor market rental information relating to contaminated properties is available. In those circumstances, some authors (academics and practitioners alike) recommend the use of opinion survey research.[16]

Survey of Appraiser Practice

During the summer of 1998, a four-page mail questionnaire was sent to a targeted, preselected group of 208 appraisers in the United States and Canada. The target group consisted of 192 appraisers in the United States and 16 in Canada. After five mail packages were returned as undeliverable, and nine were returned blank, a total of 194 potential respondents remained (183 in the United States and 11 in Canada). From this group, 86 usable responses were received: 81 from U.S. appraisers and five from Canadian, resulting in a 43% response rate. The survey questionnaire (see figure 1) was adapted from a lengthier, more detailed interview form developed by Paul J. Kennedy of Nottingham Trent University in England. The Kennedy questionnaire also served as the basis for a slightly shorter survey questionnaire developed by S. G. Bond at Massey University in New Zealand.[17]

Characteristics of Respondents

The first few survey questions identified the respondent's professional background and level of experience. Responses came from 29 U.S. states and two Canadian provinces. All but two of the U.S. respondents were licensed or certified in one or more states. Sixty-three (73%) of the respondents held the Appraisal Institute's MAI designation, followed by 43 who held the Counselors of Real Estate designation, 11 with the Appraisal Institute's SRA designation (some of whom were dually designated as MAIs), nine with the American Society of Appraisers designation, and three with the AACI designation conferred by the Appraisal Institute of Canada. Over half of the respondents (54%) reported more than 10 years' experience in appraising contaminated properties. Moreover, approximately

14. Bell, 380–391; Peter J. Patchin, "Contaminated Properties and the Sales Comparison Approach," *The Appraisal Journal* (July 1994): 402–409; Albert R. Wilson, "Emerging Approaches to Impaired Property Valuation," *The Appraisal Journal* (April 1996): 155–170.

15. Bruce R. Weber, "Stigma: Quantifying Murphy's Law," *Urban Land* (June 1998): 12.

16. Victoria Adams and Bill Mundy, "Attitudes and Policies of Lending Institutions Toward Environmental Impairment," *Environmental Watch* (Winter 1993): 1–4; "Environmentally Impaired Properties and the SIOR," *SIOR Professional Report* (Fall 1995): 2–4; Sandy G. Bond, William N. Kinnard, Jr., Elaine W. Worzala, and Steven D. Kapplin, "Market Participants' Reactions Toward Contaminated Property in New Zealand and the U.S.A.," *Journal of Property Valuation and Investment*, v. 16, no. 3 (1998): 251–272; Kinnard and Worzala (1996); "Evolving Attitudes and Policies of institutional Investors and Lenders Toward On-Site and Nearby Properties Contamination." Paper presented at "The Cutting Edge" Conference sponsored by the Royal Institution of Chartered Surveyors, Bristol, England, 1996; "Investor and Lender Reactions to Alternative Sources of Contamination," *Real Estate Issues* (August 1997): 42–48; Mundy (1995); "Contamination, Fear, and Industrial Property Transactions," *SIOR Professional Report*, (1993); Urban Land Institute, "Mortgage Industry Suffering from Fears of Environmental Problems," *Land Use Digest*, v. 28, no. 8 (1995); Albert R. Wilson and Arthur R. Alarcon, "Lender Attitudes Toward Source and Nonsource Impaired Property Mortgages," *The Appraisal Journal* (October 1997): 396–400. The great majority of these surveys have focused primarily on the attitudes and perceptions of lenders, brokers, and appraisers.

17. Bond and Kennedy.

Chapter 1: *How North American Appraisers Value*

FIGURE 1 Survey of Valuation Practice for Contaminated/Stigmatized Property: June 1998

PART A. PRACTICE INFORMATION AND PROFESSIONAL QUALIFICATIONS

1. In which state is your office located?_____

2. In how many states are you certified or licensed?_____

3. Appraisal/counseling designations:

	ARA ❑	ASA ❑	CRA ❑
CRE ❑	IFA ❑	MAI ❑	SRA ❑
SREA ❑	SRPA ❑	Other _____	

4. Years of experience appraising contaminated properties:

   0–2 ❑   3–5 ❑   6–10 ❑   Over 10 ❑

5. Years of experience measuring stigma:

   0–2 ❑   3–5 ❑   6–10 ❑   Over 10 ❑

6. Types of contaminated properties regularly appraised: (Please check all that apply.)

   Vacant land: Residential ❑   Commercial/retail ❑   Industrial ❑   Agricultural ❑

   Improved: Residential ❑   Commercial/retail ❑   Industrial ❑   Public ❑

   Other _____

PART B. THE VALUATION OF CONTAMINATED PROPERTY

7. When contamination exists on a property you are valuing, do you:
   a. Value the property as if noncontaminated only, and include disclaimer to this effect?   Yes ❑   No ❑
   b. Value the property as contaminated?   Yes ❑   No ❑
   c. Decline the appraisal assignment?   Yes ❑   No ❑
   d. Other (Please specify.)_____

8. When valuing a property, what sources do you investigate to determine the presence of contaminants? (Please check all that apply.)
   a. State list of contaminated properties   ❑
   b. EPA list of Superfund sites   ❑
   c. Environmental reports from the owner/occupant/mortgagee   ❑
   d. Phase I reports as a precondition to appraising property   ❑
   e. Other (Please specify.) _____

9. Do you carry out the above procedure(s) for all properties valued, or only for those suspected to be contaminated?

   All properties valued ❑   Only those suspected to be contaminated ❑

10. When valuing a contaminated property, which valuation procedure(s) do you regularly attempt to use? (Please check all that apply.)
    a. Sales comparison approach (Other similarly contaminated properties)   ❑
    b. Income capitalization approach   ❑
       i.   Reduced rental income   ❑
       ii.   Increased capitalization rate   ❑
       iii. Increased debt interest rate   ❑
       iv.   Reduced loan-to-value ratio   ❑
       v.   Reduced loan amortization period   ❑
       vi.   Increased equity yield rate   ❑
       vii. Increased equity dividend rate   ❑
       viii. Increased discount rate   ❑
       ix.   Decreased occupancy (increased vacancy rate)   ❑
       x.   Other_____
    c. Value as if noncontaminated, *less* forecast cost to remediate
       [including investigation and monitoring]   ❑
    d. Value as if noncontaminated, *less* present worth of forecast cost to remediate   ❑
    e. Value as if noncontaminated, *less* both present worth of forecast cost to remediate,
       and a percentage reduction for stigma   ❑

11. Over the past three years, approximately what percentage of your appraisals of contaminated properties have included:

	0%	Under 25%	25%–75%	Over 75%	100%
a. Sales comparison approach	❑	❑	❑	❑	❑
b. Income capitalization approach:					
i. Direct capitalization	❑	❑	❑	❑	❑
ii. Discounted cash flow	❑	❑	❑	❑	❑
c. A separate, additional deduction for stigma	❑	❑	❑	❑	❑

Valuing Contaminated Properties

FIGURE 1 Survey of Valuation Practice for Contaminated/Stigmatized Property: June 1998 *(continued)*

12. What, if any, causes of temporary interruptions in net operating income flows (including increased vacancy) have you encountered that result from on-site contamination? (Please check all that apply.)
    a. Site investigations:
    b.   i.   Phase I ❑
           ii.   Phase II ❑
    c. Remediation activities ❑
    d. Monitoring activities ❑
    e. Legal actions (litigation, regulatory orders) ❑
    f. Lease-up after remediation ❑
    g. Sales marketing after remediation ❑
    h. Other (Please specify.)_____

13. How, if at all, do you account for anticipated gaps or interruptions in net operating income from remediation, when valuing contaminated property? (Please check all that apply.)
    a. No adjustment ❑
    b. Enter reduced/zero *NOI* for specified periods in DCF model ❑
    c. Increase discount rate ❑
    d. Increase capitalization rate ❑
    e. Other (Please specify.)_____

14. How do you account for anticipated or forecast remediation costs in valuing contaminated property? (Please check all that apply.)
    a. Ignore ❑
    b. Deduct total costs estimated by environmental experts from unimpaired value ❑
    c. Deduct present worth of total costs estimated by environmental experts from unimpaired value ❑
    d. Develop independent estimate of value loss resulting from contamination ❑
    e. Other (Please specify.)_____

15. Do you regularly estimate remediation costs independently of those provided by licensed environmental engineers and technicians?
         Yes ❑   No ❑   Sometimes ❑
    a. If "yes" or "sometimes," on what sources do you rely?_____

16. Do you regularly accept, without independent verification, the remediation cost and duration estimates provided to your client by licensed environmental engineers and technicians?
         Yes ❑   No ❑   Sometimes ❑

17. On which of the following information sources do you base your assessment of environmental risks and uncertainties (stigma) associated with cash flow estimates for a contaminated property? (Please check all that apply.)
    a. Experience ❑
    b. Comparable market sales or lease evidence for:
         i.   Noncontaminated properties similar in location to the subject property ❑
         ii.   Contaminated properties similar in location but not type(s) of contamination ❑
         iii.   Contaminated properties similar in type(s) of contamination but not location ❑
         iv.   Contaminated properties similar in both location and type(s) of contamination ❑
    c. Cash flow risk analysis (based on anticipated variance from forecast cash flow) ❑
    d. Phase I reports ❑
    e. Phase II reports ❑
    f. Other (Please specify.)_____

18. How do you commonly incorporate this adjustment into your valuations of contaminated property? (Please check all that apply.)
    a. Increase the yield or discount rate ❑
    b. Increase the capitalization rate ❑
    c. Reduce cash flow estimates ❑
    d. Reduce sales comparison value estimates ❑
    e. Other (Please specify.)_____

19. How do you typically identify and measure stigma? (Please check all that apply.)
    a. Ignore ❑
    b. Experience ❑
    c. Market sales data ❑
    d. Buyer/seller/broker opinion ❑
    e. Other (Please specify.)_____

Please use the space below to describe any characteristics of your approach to the valuation of contaminated property, or the identification and measurement of stigma, not addressed in your answers to the preceding questions.

Chapter 1: *How North American Appraisers Value*

40% indicated more than 10 years' experience in identifying and measuring stigma. In brief, the respondents were both professionally qualified and experienced appraisers of contaminated property. It was therefore concluded that the sample of respondents and their responses could reasonably be accepted as representative of current practice in the United States (and Canada).

Approaches Used

As shown in Table 1, a large number of respondents (65, or 80%) reported that they used the sales comparison approach whenever required data were available. (The percentage reported here and shown in the tables are calculated as the number of "yes" responses divided by total responses (n) to each particular question.) Moreover, respondents' comments indicated that many felt that the required data were generally available. Many respondents also indicated that they supplement the findings based on sales comparison analysis with opinion survey research, preferably with buyers and lenders.

A large number of respondents reported using the income capitalization approach (64, or 79%). When asked for more details, 56 respondents (72%) reported that they used the direct capitalization technique, while 50 (64%) indicated that they applied discounted cash flow (DCF) models. Nearly 60% (49) reduced rental income to account for on-site contamination. At the same time, however, some comments indicated that a noticeable number of respondents found no impact on the rental income of contaminated properties that were used for commercial, retail, or industrial purposes. Several additional comments indicated that some

TABLE 1 Methods of Valuing Contaminated Property

Valuation Format Used	Number of Respondents Indicating "Yes"	Percent of Respondents Indicating "Yes"*
Valuation approach used (n = 81)		
Sales comparison approach	65	80%
Income capitalization approach	64	79%
Adjustments to income capitalization		
Increased capitalization rate	57	70%
Increased discount rate	54	67%
Reduced rental income	49	60%
Increased equity yield rate	40	49%
Increased vacancy rate	38	47%
Reduced loan-to-value ratio	34	42%
Increased equity dividend rate	32	40%
Increased debt interest rate	30	37%
Reduced amortization period	24	30%
Type of income capitalization (n = 78)		
Direct capitalization	56	72%
Discounted cash flow	50	64%
Value as if noncontaminated with a disclaimer (n = 82)	45	55%
Less total cost to remediate (n = 81)	42	52%
Less present worth cost to remediate (n = 81)	28	35%
Less present worth cost to remediate and percent deduction for stigma (n = 81)	51	63%
Value as contaminated (n = 82)	71	87%
Decline assignment (n = 82)	0	0%

* Total number of "yes" responses divided by total responses (n).

respondents also used increased operating expenses when valuing a contaminated property.

Finally, the consensus of respondents (including information provided in the "Comments" section) was that it is most appropriate to value a contaminated property both with and without contamination present (unless specifically requested by a client not to do so).[18] Most respondents (51, or 63%) calculate and deduct from unimpaired value the present worth of the cost to remediate plus a percentage deduction for stigma. At the same time, 42 (52%) indicated that on occasion they have deducted the total estimated cost to remediate without any discount. However, the latter procedure has been disfavored by state courts in the United States. One example is the *Inmar* decision in New Jersey.[19] The comments of several respondents indicated that a property would not be marketable, and therefore have market value of zero, if the present worth of the cost to remediate exceeded the estimated market value as if uncontaminated.

None of the respondents indicated that they would refuse an assignment to value a contaminated property, reflecting their experience with such properties. Nearly 55% (45 of 82) indicated that they sometimes valued a property as if uncontaminated only, while including a disclaimer to this effect.[20] The great majority (82%) stated that they applied "as if contaminated" procedures to only those properties known or suspected to be contaminated. Most striking was the fact that 71 respondents (87%) indicated that they would value the property "as contaminated."

Most respondents indicated that they use as many sources of information as are available to them (see Table 2). The most frequently mentioned source of information about on-site contamination (74, or 90%) was reported to be the property owner or tenant, with the state list of contaminated properties second (70%).

Treatment of Disruptions in *NOI*

Table 3 indicates that 60 respondents (85%) reported on-site remediation activities as the major cause of any reduction or disruption in net operating income (*NOI*). This answer was followed by legal actions (69%) and post-remediation marketing (50%).

In measuring anticipated temporary gaps or interruptions in *NOI*, 70% of the respondents indicate that they would enter a reduced or zero *NOI* for specified periods in their DCF models. Less than half indicated that they usually increase the capitalization rate or discount rate (or both). This was substantially less than the number who indicated that they would increase one or both rates in valuing a contaminated property.

Treatment of Remediation Costs

All but one of the respondents said they would *not* ignore anticipated or forecast remediation costs in valuing contaminated properties. Some 60% indicated that they would deduct the present worth of total remediation costs estimated by environmental experts. That is reasonably consistent with the earlier answer to a similar question, in which 63% gave the same answer. Also, slightly over half of the respondents (52%) indicated that they occasionally deduct total estimated remediation costs from unimpaired value without taking into account the duration of the remediation process.

18. Those respondents who were identified as members of the Appraisal Institute would be subject to its Guide Note 8, which became effective January 1, 1991. This guide note requires all members of the Appraisal Institute to report the limited scope of an appraisal that estimates value "as if noncontaminated," as well as "an appropriate statement of purpose and properly qualified conclusions." See Appraisal Institute, "Guide Note 8: The Consideration of Hazardous Substances in the Appraisal Process," Standards of Professional Appraisal Practice (Chicago, Illinois: Appraisal Institute, 1997): D-25.

19. Frank E. Ferruggia, "Valuation of Contaminated Property: New Jersey's Inmar Decision," *Assessment Digest* (March/April 1991): 2–6.

20. Guide Note 8, D-24.

Chapter 1: *How North American Appraisers Value*

TABLE 2 Handling of Environmental Risks/Uncertainties (Stigma)

	Number of Respondents Indicating "Yes"	Percent of Respondents Indicating "Yes"*
How to adjust for stigma (n = 77)		
Increase yield (discount) rate	47	61%
Increase capitalization rate	51	66%
Reduce cash flow estimates	44	57%
Reduce sales comparison value estimate	56	73%
Information sources (n = 76)		
Experience	42	55%
Comparable sales/lease evidence for:		
Noncontaminated, similar location	53	70%
Contaminated, similar location	37	49%
Contaminated, similar contaminants	45	59%
Contaminated, similar location and similar contaminants	57	75%
Cash flow risk analysis	33	43%
Phase I reports	31	41%
Phase II reports	40	53%
Basis for stigma identification and measurement (n = 77)		
Ignore	2	3%
Experience	39	51%
Market sales data	64	83%
Buyer/seller/broker opinion	39	51%

* Total number of "yes" responses divided by total responses (n).

TABLE 3 Causes and Measures of Temporary Interruptions in *NOI*

	Number of Respondents Indicating "Yes"	Percent of Respondents Indicating "Yes"*
Causes (n = 71)		
Phase I investigation	24	34%
Phase II investigation	30	42%
Remediation activity	60	84%
Monitoring activity	30	42%
Litigation, regulatory orders	49	69%
Post-remediation marketing		
Leasing	35	49%
Sales	36	51%
Measures (n = 79)		
No adjustment	7	9%
Reduced/zero *NOI* in DCF model	61	77%
Increased discount rate	33	42%
Increased capitalization rate	35	44%

* Total number of "yes" responses divided by total responses (n).

Only about one-fourth of the respondents indicated that they can or would develop their own independent estimates of remediation costs. Indeed, nearly 80% reported that they accept, without independent verification, the estimates provided by licensed environmental engineers and technicians.

Identification and Measurement of Post-Remediation Stigma

While 73% of respondents report that they occasionally make a separate deduction for stigma, only 26% indicate that they do so as often as 75%

of the time. The uncertainties and risks associated with cash flows from a contaminated property are most frequently reflected in decreased estimates of value via sales comparison analysis (73%), followed by an increased capitalization rate (66%) or an increased yield, or discount, rate (61%)—see Table 3.

Respondents most frequently base their assessments of risk and uncertainty (stigma) on comparable sales evidence for properties both in similar locations and with similar contaminants (75%), followed by their own experience (55%) and Phase II environmental reports (53%). Further, many respondents' comments indicated that they adjust value for stigma "by all methods that the available data will allow." A substantial minority included comments that reductions in rental revenues were not necessary for commercial, retail, and industrial properties because (in their experience) such tenants are typically not affected by fear of on-site contamination (past or present).

Finally, only two respondents (3%) indicated that they ignore stigma entirely. The great majority (64, or 83%) rely on market sales transactions data to quantify stigma, while 51% rely on their experience. Over half seek the opinions of buyers, sellers, and brokers. Additional comments indicated that some respondents also rely on the opinions of lenders.

Identifying and measuring stigma was the most frequently mentioned concern of respondents providing comments. Nearly all respondents who made comments anywhere on the questionnaire want more and better market sales transactions data to support their estimates of stigma.

Conclusion

U.S. and Canadian appraisers are generally quite experienced in the valuation of contaminated properties. Moreover, they believe that the necessary market data are available to enable them to base their estimates of value as if contaminated (impaired value) on market sales transactions data, market rental data, and market-derived capitalization rates and discount rates. They are also remarkably self-confident about their skills and abilities to estimate the market value of contaminated properties competently and convincingly.

At the same time, respondents are inclined to rely heavily on licensed professional environmental engineers and technicians for estimates of both cost to remediate, and the duration, timing, and magnitude of the remediation process.

Few respondents who are experienced in the valuation of contaminated properties appear to believe that there is (or, indeed, should be) a single, standardized approach that is universally appropriate and recommended. This is indicated by the diversity of methods employed and the differences of opinion about how best to employ them, coupled with comments made throughout the questionnaire responses. Because of their strong belief in the efficacy of real estate markets, these respondents typically make it clear that they apply whatever methods or procedures can be applied by using whatever market data are available to them in any given assignment. Generally, they believe that sufficient transactions data are available for effective use both in estimating the market value of contaminated properties and in measuring stigma. Nevertheless, they would like to see more and better data.

Finally, the U.S. and Canadian respondents generally believe in the existence of post-remediation stigma although many have reservations on specific points. A large proportion believe that stigma declines over time and is greatest when the on-site contamination is first discovered. Many respondents also believe that informed users tend to disregard the risks of post-remediation stigma whenever the property is continued in the same industrial or commercial use after the completion of remediation. Despite these beliefs, respondents mentioned the identification and measurement of stigma most frequently as an issue requiring further investigation and research.

Most appraisal practitioners who responded to the survey questionnaire are reasonably content with the procedural tools and techniques at their disposal. Faced with the necessity to communicate their findings to others (most particularly clients and courts), they appear to recognize that methodological nicety and "sophistication" are often achieved at the cost of reduced understanding on the part of decision-makers seeking to use the results of the appraiser's analyses. The fine and fragile line between statistical, conceptual, and perceptual purity on the one hand and cost-effective usefulness on the other is apparently recognized and acknowledged by those who practice the art of valuation/appraisal. It needs to be appreciated as well by those who critique, evaluate, and add to the ever-expanding kit of tools potentially available to the practitioner.

References

Appraisal Institute. "Measuring the Effects of Hazardous Materials Contamination on Real Estate Value: Techniques and Applications." Papers and proceedings of the 1991 Appraisal Institute Symposium, Philadelphia, Pennsylvania, 1992.

Campanella, Joseph A. "Valuation of Environmentally Impaired Assets." Paper presented to Conference on Brownfields Redevelopment, Washington, D.C., March 23, 1995.

Chalmers, James A., and Thomas O. Jackson. "Risk Factors in the Appraisal of Contaminated Property," *The Appraisal Journal* (January 1996): 44–58.

Elliot-Jones, Michael. "Real Estate Value and Toxic Sites," *The Digest of Environmental Law* (July 1992): 89–92.

_____ "Valuation of Post-Cleanup Property: The Economic Basis for Stigma Damages," *Bureau of National Affairs Toxics Law Reporter* (February 1995): 944–945.

Healy, Patricia R., and John J. Healy, Jr. "Lenders' Perspectives on Environmental Issues," *Real Estate Issues* (Fall/Winter 1991): 1–4.

Kinnard, William N., Jr. "Analyzing the Stigma Effect of Proximity to a Hazardous Materials Site," *Environmental Watch* (December 1989): 4–7.

Wilson, Albert R., Maxwell Ramsland, Thomas Wilhelmy, and Roger Groves. "Ad Valorem Taxation and Environmental Devaluation Part I: An Overview of the Issues and Processes," *Journal of Property Tax Management* (Summer 1993): 1–32.

Valuing Contaminated Properties

CHAPTER 1 Cross-References

Related article in Chapter 2: John D. Dorchester, Jr., MAI, CRE, "Environmental Pollution: Valuation in a Changing World" *The Appraisal Journal* (July 1991), 31, 37–39.

Related article in Chapter 11: John D. Dorchester, Jr., MAI, CRE, "The Federal Rules of Evidence and *Daubert*: Evaluating Real Property Valuation Witnesses" *The Appraisal Journal* (July 2000), 590–595.

Contaminated Properties and the Real Estate Appraisal Process: Articles of General Applicability

CHAPTER 2

Editor's Introduction

Dorchester's 1991 article sets the stage for this chapter with a discussion of factors that contribute to a rising concern for valuation techniques applicable to contaminated properties. The article also gives an overview of some of the legal and scientific issues involved.

Rinaldi, like Patchin, gives us a more detailed account of the potential impacts costs to cure, additional operating expenses, lost rental income, and deferred sales have on value.

Mundy summarizes and critiques statistical studies of the late 1980s and early 1990s. He finds that the results have been inconclusive and the models "of real and perceived risk" relied on are "difficult to integrate with actual market behavior." Mundy then suggests an alternative model for determining the impact of contamination, which indicates a temporary but significant impact on value followed by a gradual recovery as remediation occurs and market stigma is eliminated.

Chalmers and Roehr build on both the Patchin and Mundy analyses but with "an important clarification" as to the importance of stigma as well as direct remediation costs to the potential impact of the environmental situation on value.

Wilson, a real estate analyst and engineer, approaches the problem from a different perspective and has contributed a number of important articles to the literature. In his 1994 article, he dispels a number of myths, including the myth that the presence of an environmental risk automatically results in a decrease in property value in the marketplace. Wilson also effectively argues that stigma, when it exists, actually consists of a number of components that should be separately considered. He also argues that stigma has an important timeframe component that must also be considered. In his 1996 article, Wilson explores the significance of expected versus actual remediation costs in determining the level of stigma, and why it is more difficult to estimate remediation costs in some situations than in others.

Roddewig argues that the assumption that an appraisal of a contaminated property is a typical assignment involving an estimate of value at a single point in time is often incorrect. The changing character of stigma over time due to many factors he describes may necessitate something quite different than an appraisal, such as a market study or highest and best use analysis.

Finally, Bell firmly squares the changing character of the contaminated property value model put forward by Patchin, Mundy, Chalmers, and Roddewig with other types of "detrimental condition" situations in which there are also stages and cycles that affect the value conclusion.

Environmental Pollution: Valuation in a Changing World

by John D. Dorchester. Jr., MAI, CRE

Over the past 20 years, concern about environmental pollution has increased at an unprecedented rate throughout the world. While philosophers and analysts may examine this question from various perspectives according to their particular interpretations of society and nature, several inescapable facts underlie any analysis of environmental issues:

- We have only one world, and its resources are finite.
- It is now possible to scientifically quantify effects on the environment that once were subject to debate and conjecture.
- We have paid, and will continue to pay, a terrible price for progress through the costly and in some cases irreparable damage inflicted on the planet by the methods of the Industrial Age.
- Many less well-developed countries face the same economic and moral dilemmas faced years ago by the more developed countries. With better knowledge of the effects environmental abuse, they must frequently decide between economic growth and preservation of our planet.
- Each of the more economically advantaged countries faces equally distressing moral and economic questions: Who will pay for the sins of the past? How will current problems be remedied while economic equilibrium is maintained? What can reasonably be done to avoid compounding the problems of our environment in the future?
- Although scientists have greatly broadened the understanding of environmental problems over the past 20 years, we are still just beginning to comprehend the relationship between the nature of our environment and the critical issue of human survivability.
- Because the environmental deterioration caused by our abuses simply quickens the pace of the existing natural entropy, it becomes increasingly difficult to establish some level of control.

These comments may seem more appropriate for a scientific meeting of socially conscious citizens' action group. Understanding these points,

John D. Dorchester, Jr., MAI, CRE, is currently president of Real Estate SCIENCES International, Inc., in Winnetka, Illinois. He received a BA as well as an MA from the University of Oklahoma. Mr. Dorchester is a past president of the American Institute of Real Estate Appraisers and has previously published in The Appraisal Journal.

This article originally appeared in the July 1991 issue of The Appraisal Journal.

Adapted from a speech presented to The International Assets Valuation Standards Committee and the Japanese Association of Real Estate Appraisers on September 21, 1990, in Tokyo.

however, is central to our ability to function as professionals in the field of real estate valuation.

- If project developers sometimes focus too narrowly on the profitability of their developments rather than the question of the cost to society (and future ownerships) of their projects, might not valuers also focus too narrowly in their valuations?
- If site development and building costs are increased by efforts to maintain the environment, if not to improve it, what are the effects on value estimates? How are these effects measured in a changing world?
- If land has economic utility but contains hazardous or toxic contamination, and if buildings are functionally suitable to their purpose, in economic demand, but pose health hazards to their occupants, what are the responsibilities—and the corresponding processes—of professional appraisers?

These questions will not all be answered in this article. Instead, the focus will be an exploration of some contemporary environmental problems within the context of a brief historical framework. Steps that appraisers can take in response to these problems will then be listed.

Brief Historical Background

Thoreau's statement, "Things do not change; we change," applies to environmental concerns dating back to antiquity. When modern scientific understanding did not exist, the earliest human beings moved their "sewage treatment" away from living areas and food stores. Even water sources were protected, and petroglyphs show death as the penalty for contamination.

The planning of Greek and Roman cities as well as many other examples of early town planning show an understanding of relationships among land uses and a sensitivity to the handling of potable water, sewage, waste, and human burial. The "ancient ones"—the Anasazi Indians of the American Southwest—and their ancestors, demonstrated high-rise, group living developments more than 1,000 years ago. Their cliff houses featured zoned separation of living functions and sophisticated handling of their environment.

More detailed study of environmental problems and responses to them in each country reveals that the problems have similar roots, but unique local solutions. These tend to vary according to differences in historical events, cultural heritage, the natural environmental setting, the extent and nature environmental setting, the extent and nature of land use development, legal and related societal systems, and other factors. The common root is the question: What are the direct and indirect effects of environmental action and inaction on human beings today and in the future?

Specifically, these problems involve the handling of trash and sewage, selection of construction materials, analysis of air quality, control and disposition of hazardous substances, preservation of life forms, consideration of the global warming or "greenhouse effect," analysis of water supplies above and below ground, and many other factors.

While some of these questions may be beyond the concern of daily appraisal practice, they are not beyond our concern as neighbors on a shrinking planet. Broad understanding, sensitivity, and the application of general knowledge to specific appraisal assignments are required.

Chapter 2: *Environmental Pollution*

A Case Study: The United States

By examining only relatively recent history and using the United States as a case study, it is possible to see how identification of environmental problems has come about, how some of the problems have developed, and what professional appraisers are now doing about them.

After World War II, the U.S. population turned its attention to a massive overhaul of its physical, social, and economic systems. Both the war and the preceding disastrous economic and political times left the nation functionally obsolete while at the same time faced with dramatic financial and economic opportunity. In response, the government instituted massive rebuilding programs for its worn-out center cities ("urban renewal"), developed new public and private housing programs to better house its citizens and a growing population of immigrants, created a new federal highway system, overhauled many economic systems, and achieved new levels of socially concerned legislation.

Looking back, many argue that the price of success was frequently more than the value contributed. It is certain that early in this period the emphasis was on individual freedoms and economic growth, with little official regard for the environment as a whole. During the 1940s and 1950s the nation's focus was economic recovery and growth, while during the 1960s attention shifted to heightened social reform, including avoidance of discrimination based on race, religion, or national origin. In the 1970s the focus was individuals and the role of government, with increasing concern about general environmental issues. In addition, awareness of the international community increased dramatically in the 1980s.

Until recently appraisers have tended not to question the impact of dumping raw chemicals into nearby streams or rivers when valuing industrial plants. Clearly, however, assessment of the cleanup costs for the damage caused by such properties is one of an appraiser's responsibilities. What is the value effect in countries that have not reached this level of concern and enforcement?

Until recently appraisers have tended to examine only past values when appraising land adjacent to oceans or other major waterways. What is their responsibility if global warming occurs (the United States government recently reported that there is a 99% chance that we are entering such a period), and the shoreline rises substantially over the foreseeable future? Are values affected now? Should disclosures of this potential effect be made by appraisers in their reports and in client discussions?

Until recently appraisers have tended to examine comparable sales rather then cost when appraising properties frequently traded in the open market. Such comparisons may not be adequate when valuing a new property that has a 15% higher cost attributable to sophisticated air-handling systems, new materials that are not environmentally destructive, and design characteristics that reflect concern for the lifestyles of those who will occupy the building.

Unfortunately, appraisers' attention has predominately been focused on existing environmental problems rather then the equally important matter of environmental problem *avoidance*. While appraisers are now deeply involved in dealing with existing environmental problems, this involvement is largely a phenomenon of the past 5 years rather than the past 50 years, which parallels the pace of the growth of environmental awareness in general.

Environmental concerns have been heightened over the past 20 years by better information from the scientific community, greater public and private involvement, and better communication of the issues. If these are positive reasons for positive results, positive results have also developed from negative events.

In 1978 the residents of the Love Canal area in New York, became aware of the unusually high incidence of infants born with birth defects. It was found that the area was built on a toxic waste dump and was subject to further hazardous chemical contamination from discharges into the waterways serving the community. Massive effort and investment have been required to remedy the problems, and the social costs can never be repaid.

In 1979 a nuclear plant at Three Mile Island, Pennsylvania, experienced a partial nuclear meltdown that resulted in the release of nuclear contamination into the atmosphere. In addition to the damage to properties (and life) in the vicinity, this incident focused attention on nuclear plants in general, and began an era in which many nuclear plants have been closed, while planned or partially completed nuclear facilities have been abandoned.

In 1982 it was discovered that the town of Times Beach, Missouri, had been completely contaminated by the widespread distribution of PCBs (PolyChlorinated Biphenyls) into the soil. PCBs are associated with dioxins, which are chemicals known to be cancer–causing agents. In short, an entire town had become poisoned by uncontrolled distribution of a toxic substance. The town was abandoned and is now undergoing a massive cleanup in an attempt to make it habitable once again.

In 1983 an electrical transformer explosion occurred in an office building occupied by governmental agencies of the state of New York. The transformer contained PCBs. Measurements after the explosion revealed that the PCBs had been chemically altered into dioxins by the heat of the explosion, and that these dioxins had been carried into various areas of the building. It was abandoned and still is not in use.

Each of these negative events contributed to public awareness and, in a perverse way, has helped in the definition and treatment of environmental problems.

Were appraisers who made valuations immediately prior to these events without taking the environmental problems into consideration wrong? While they could not have foreseen the events, could they have understood the underlying causes or foreseen the effects that such potential problems would have on "value as the present worth of future benefits" of each of the properties? What were the responsibilities of these appraisers? What are appraiser responsibilities today?

Environmental Issues: The United States Today

In 1970 the United States government created the Environmental Protection agency (EPA). The EPA was charged with safeguarding the environment and human health. Among other missions, it regulates the use and disposal of toxic substances in air, water, and land.

Since its inception the EPA has been the nation's watchdog and regulator of environmental issues. While its activities have been heavily criticized on political grounds, the EPA has been given stronger legal and financial capacity over time.

Chapter 2: *Environmental Pollution*

Some major, relevant federal laws and their principal areas of concern include the following:

- *Clean Air Act*—Approved in 1970 and amended in 1977 and 1990, this act imposes requirements for attainment and maintenance of air quality standards. It includes specific deadlines by which federal and state governments as well as industry must reduce air pollution, and provides for control of specific sources of air emissions.

- *Clean Water Act*—This act, approved in 1974, imposes requirements for attainment and maintenance of water quality standards. It strictly regulates the level of pollutants discharged from any "point source" to waters of the United States, including those discharged from municipal and industrial wastewater treatment plants. Control of discharges is imposed through a federally sanctioned permit from the U.S. Army Corps of Engineers that specifies the amount and specific contents of discharges.

- *National Emissions Standards for Hazardous Air Pollutants (NESHAP)*—Through the NESHAP program, amended in 1984, the EPA regulates emission standards for hazardous air pollutants judged to increase mortality or serious irreversible or incapacitating illness. Pollutants from asbestos mills and from various manufacturing and fabricating operations are included. The use of asbestos in roadway surfacing and in insulation materials is regulated, as is the disposal of asbestos-containing material (ACM), and most uses of sprayed asbestos are banned. These standards also require specific work practices to be used during demolition and renovation operations involving asbestos materials.

- *Toxic Substances Control Act of 1976 (TSCA)*—TSCA regulates the manufacturing, processing, and distribution of hazardous chemical substances and mixtures that present an unreasonable risk of injury to health or the environment.

- *Resource Conservation and Recovery Act (RCRA)*—RCRA was enacted to protect human health and the environment from improper wastes management practices. It authorizes the EPA to develop and enforce regulations governing hazardous waste management. It also sets forth a process by which states can be authorized to administer the RCRA program.

  This program is designed to prevent more uncontrolled hazardous waste sites from springing up across the country. RCRA, a body of federal regulations governing the management of hazardous wastes, was authorized in 1976 and amended in 1980 and 1984. The regulations are designed to protect public health and the environment so that hazardous wastes cause as little damage as possible. RCRA establishes many technical and safety standards for the generation, treatment, storage, transportation, and disposal of hazardous wastes.

- *Comprehensive Environmental Response Compensation and Liability Act (CERCLA)*—Approved in 1980, CERCLA authorizes the president to react to the release or threatened release of any hazardous substance or pollutant that may present an imminent and substantial danger to the public. CERCLA allows the EPA to clean up abandoned hazardous waste sites. It allows a purchaser to be charged with the cost of cleaning up hazardous material even though the purchaser may not have been responsible for depositing it on the property.

- *Hazardous and Solid Waste Amendment (HSWA)*—Passed in 1984, HSWA greatly expands the EPA's authority to deal with hazardous wastes. According to these amendments, the EPA must phase out the land disposal of hazardous wastes and induce industry to reduce the amount of waste it creates.

- *Asbestos Hazard Emergency Response Act of 1986 (AHERA)*—AHERA provides that school buildings must be inspected for friable asbestos-containing material and, depending on the condition of the ACM, that certain actions be taken in response. AHERA also establishes an accreditation program for inspectors, contractors, and laboratories.

- *Superfund Amendments and Reauthorization Act of 1986 (SARA)*—This law includes, under Title III, the Emergency Planning and Community Right-to-Know Act, which requires committees across the country to set up local committees to plan responses to chemical emergencies. It also requires a variety of notifications and reports to state and local government concerning chemical inventories, uses, and releases.

  SARA contains an "innocent purchaser exemption" that exempts persons from liability if they acquired property after the disposal or placement of hazardous substances on, in, or at the property, and at the time of acquisition did not know or have reason to know that the property was contaminated. To establish exemption from liability, the purchaser must have made appropriate inquiry into the previous ownership and uses of the property consistent with good commercial or customary practice.

At the state level, New Jersey has passed a law, the Environmental Cleanup Responsibility Act (ECRA), which requires sellers of industrial sites to perform an environmental audit at the site prior to sale, and to submit an engineer's declaration that no adverse environmental contamination exists, or to provide a cleanup plan to the state and the purchaser. Illinois has passed a similar law, requiring a "negative declaration" statement.

Connecticut has adopted a version of ECRA that allows transfers to be completed prior to state approval, but imposes strict liability for failure to clean up contaminated property to the satisfaction of the state. Colorado, Iowa, and Missouri require an environmental official's approval prior to the transfer of certain sites.

Property markets consisting of buyers, sellers, and professionals have proceeded from inaction on environmental issues, to reaction, to overreaction, to new levels of understanding and awareness. For example, ACMs in buildings caused numerous scientific studies and EPA commentaries in the 1970s and early 1980s. However, it was not until the mid-1980s that real estate markets began to react to ACM concerns. In the past five years, the issue of ACM has been subject to the entire inaction/reaction/overreaction/new awareness cycle. A speaker at a recent pension fund conference in New York observed:

> It is difficult to understand why asbestos should be removed from an office building in New York when ambient air measurements show that there is

more asbestos from vehicle brake linings to be breathed when walking on the streets of New York than there is from being in the typical office building that has ACMs.[1]

This new awareness places new responsibilities and strains on real estate practitioners and professionals and illustrates that environmental concerns are subject to change. Greater appraiser understanding and involvement are required so that appropriate responses can be devised.

Eleven states have "super lien" laws that enable government to clean up hazardous or toxic environmental problems if the property owner will not, and to place a lien against the property to be satisfied when it is sold. "Superfund" laws that provide for the cleanup of environmentally sensitive problems and for punitive damages when applicable exist in 39 states.

A new profession has arisen to meet the inspection and testing requirements of these laws: environmental consulting. Many such businesses feature engineers and others trained in inspection, assessment, and measurement of the materials and conditions involved. Others deal with legal liabilities and business concerns. Environmental law is now the fastest growing sector of the legal profession. Related court cases involve billions of dollars in claims and thousands of defendants and plaintiffs.

To determine the presence (or absence) of pollution problems, it is customary to use an environmental real estate survey (or audit). This is usually a two-tier process, with the second tier only becoming necessary if the results of the first tier study reveal a need for quantitative measures. These tiers are as follows:

- *First tier*—A qualitative study, this phase typically includes interviews, historical research, title search, zoning history analysis, aerial photo studies, and site inspections. The purpose is to trace the history of a site's use to its original native state, and to determine whether there are any indications of uses or substances that would pose potential environmental problems.

- *Second tier*—In this quantitative type of study, specific scientific measurement and analysis is performed for each of the areas of concern identified in the first-tier research. This typically involves the taking of core drillings, building material samples, and air testing: both on–site and off–site measurements may be taken as appropriate.

There are various levels of precision for each of these two tiers of research depending on the application. Standards are being developed to overcome any confusion that such differences might cause.

General considerations for the first-tier study (sometimes referred to as a "preliminary survey") include:

Site Inspections
- *Topography*—What land uses drain onto and off of the site; what are the implications for construction on-site and possible poolings of environmentally sensitive materials; what is the relationship of the site with its surroundings; what are the implications for specific land uses?

- *Discoloration*—Is there discoloration that might indicate previous dumpings, burials, storage, or other problems?

1. Phillip B. Rogers, senior vice president, Grubb & Ellis, Philadelphia, speaking at the New York University Pension Fund Investment and Real Estate Conference on May 15, 1990, in New York City.

- *Oil sheen*—Do waterways indicate any discharges leaving or entering the site?
- *Depressions*—Are there indications of previous land uses that no longer exist; are there evidences of buried materials?
- *Hazardous waste*—Is there a known previous or current use of substances identified to be hazardous?
- *Groundwater*—Do any of the previous or current processes on-site have an impact on underground waterways or resources; are the on-site resources affected by other properties?
- *Wetlands*—Will any land use result in a net reduction of or effect on existing wetlands?
- *Soil/rock content*—Are there naturally appearing materials on-site that must be handled in a special way, or that might limit or preclude the use of the site?
- *Off-site considerations*—Are there any specific conditions on-site that have special relevance to other property off-site, or vice versa?

Building Inspections
- *Radon*—Do potentially hazardous levels of this toxic gas exist or might they be affected by the design and use of improvements?

    Radon is a natural gas that comes from earth. Its existence is observable in various building circumstances and is apparently compounded in areas with limited air circulation, tobacco smoking, or proximity to certain types of geological soil structures.

    A Philadelphia industrial worker was recently arrested and accused of stealing nuclear materials because he set off radioactive sensors at his workplace. It was found that he was not a thief, but had set off the sensors because of the high level of radon gas in his home through which he had become contaminated.
- *Lead*—Are potentially hazardous levels of lead present in pipes, paint, or elsewhere?

    Still with low levels of public concern and understanding of remedial needs and methods, lead is now a major target of the nation's public housing programs. Brochures have been developed to explain how corrective measures can be taken.
- *PCBs*—Do they exist on-site; if so, are there plans for removal? If they are not to be removed or replaced immediately, are there special plans in the event of fire or other PCB discharges?

    U.S. laws require a ban on the general industrial use of PCBs by October 1990. They have been subject to a phase-out program, but are still found in many electrical transformers and elsewhere. When the presence of PCBs is discovered, separate testing of compounds is required. Scientific controversy exists over the method and level of measurements that should be applied.
- *Air quality*—What is the nature, capacity, and effect of heating, ventilation, and air-conditioning (HVAC) systems? Is there evidence of worker-related diseases or trauma?

    This is another area of rapidly developing concern, particularly among building tenants. The General Services Administration has been sued by government workers who claim they have become ill

Chapter 2: *Environmental Pollution*

because of government buildings' poor air-handling systems. It is likely that additional building analysis standards will be developed to assist with the "old building syndrome."

- *Asbestos*—Does the building contain ACM; what is the location, nature, and condition of these materials; what mitigation (if any) is required immediately; what will be required upon major renovation or demolition of the property; how do the market and tenants react to these conditions?

    Efforts during the past year to develop a consensus on this issue among mortgage bankers, building managers, and union laborers were largely unsuccessful. It is likely that the EPA will be looked to for additional guidance and as a source of new laws to be passed by Congress.

This brief survey, while generalized and incomplete, should at least help to define the nature of the problems we face.

William K. Reilly, the administrator of the EPA, recently said that the current controversy over asbestos in our schools and public buildings is "an excellent example of a clash between real risks and public perceptions." He commented in a public address on June 12, 1990, that "middle-class enthusiasms" should not be the basis for environmental policy, and that we should instead rely on scientific data and principles. He said, "Based on recent meetings I have held with school officials, on decisions with members of Congress, and on a recent update of inaccurate and sometimes tendentious articles and columns in the news media, it's clear to me that a considerable gap has opened up between what EPA has been trying to say about asbestos and what the public has been hearing." He further explained that what EPA has been "saying" about asbestos is that it can be safely managed in place if the material is undisturbed and will remain that way, and that the unnecessary removal of asbestos-containing material may pose a greater risk than leaving it alone.[2]

The EPA has recently published an operations and maintenance guide to expand on earlier guides they have produced. In addition to offering building owners detailed and up-to-date instructions for operation and maintenance programs, the document also informs owners, lenders, and insurers that such programs can in many cases be as appropriate for an asbestos control strategy as removal.

The example of the asbestos reaction/overreaction/revision cycle is paralleled by cycles of concern about other environmental issues. While careful management may reduce such extreme fluctuations, these cycles can be expected to continue.

Dealing with Environmental Issues

Appraisers may meet environmental problems at any of three phases of the cycle of ownership: 1)before acquisition or construction, 2)during an investor's ownership period, or 3)when sale of the property occurs. Before an appraiser's role is examined more directly, the general concerns pertaining to each phase will be examined.

Before Acquisition or Construction

The best way to avoid a problem is never to face the situation. Thus, a full understanding of potential problems is a direct aid in avoiding them.

2. EPA News Release, June 12, 1990

Acquisition or development of property today requires a team of specialists. Occasionally two or more skills may be provided by a single source. Such a team can be drawn from the ranks of architects, engineers, or surveyors; environmental lawyers; specialists with finance and market experience; real estate appraisers, consultants, and managers; and (on occasion) environmental specialists. When environmental problems are to be taken on through purchase of property, it is particularly important that experienced management be present.

Prior to acquisition, a competent preliminary environmental site survey is most important. This inspection will require analysis of the factors discussed earlier as well as a consideration of the effects of other nearby properties. Occasionally, the off-site questions may extend even beyond the immediate neighborhood.

Building materials and construction types must be identified and thoroughly understood. As changing standards develop, new materials must be tested against their ability to meet either specific or general performance requirements.

If environmental problems exist, it is necessary to quantify the costs and value implications associated with them. Under federal law, once an owner steps into the chain of title he or she may become totally liable for all costs of cleanup and damages to others—a cost that may far exceed the value of the property if no problem existed.

Finally, once there is a specific quantification and analysis of the problems it is necessary to make an investment decision. The feasibility of purchase when environmental problems exist will depend heavily on the management program developed before the purchase to avoid, mitigate, or remedy the problems.

During Ownership

Trained specialists are also needed over the period of ownership, because it is important to identify, quantify, and manage each specific risk component.

Usually environmental problems require the continuing use of consultants, with testing and retesting of the condition(s). Ownership liability can be reduced through planning and implementation of special programs such as firefighting and evacuation plans when PCBs are present, or tenant notices when air quality or asbestos are problems.

Some risks can be insured against, but it is necessary to understand both the realties associated with known problems and the risks that new problems will be identified. Legal requirements and the potential for financial penalties, costs associated with the problem(s) and their related effects on returns, the attitudes and reactions of the marketplace, and the ultimate question of investment risk should be eveluted.

When Sale Occurs

In the United States, laws generally provide for continuing liability for environmental matters beyond the period ownership. Recent statistics indicate that 25% of properties with environmental problems offered for sale will fail to sell. About 80% of lenders now require at least a preliminary environmental survey, up from less than 25% only three years ago.

Only two states have the "negative disclosure statement" requirement that in effect requires the seller to say that if there was a problem, it no longer exists. Many advisors tell owners that it is in their best interest to clean up environmental problems and to sell property as free from environmental concern as possible.

Each of these phases offers substantial opportunities for professionals in the real estate field, but also requires knowledge and training beyond typical appraisal education and experience.

Appraisers: Professional Responsibilities

Although this article has largely addressed broader concepts, environmental issues ultimately involve areas of scientific concern that are far beyond the typical qualifications of appraisers. In the same sense that appraisers do not certify the tensile strength of materials used in construction, instead relying on other experts in that field, appraisers are also not environmental specialists and must rely on qualified professionals.

Appraisers must, however, deal with the effects of environmental concerns, and are responsible for handling them in a manner consistent with the standards of the profession. In general this will entail:

- Continued education, to enable appraisers to become better acquainted with the issues, and to stay abreast of new developments;
- Advice to clients, to assure them that they have the benefit of appraiser experience and market observations, particularly when seeking appropriate expert advice from other specialists;
- Appraisals and appraisal reports that meet standards and that assist in client decisions; and
- Clear unequivocal separation of the valuation function from that of environmental specialists in such a way that the market understands the function of appraisers and can properly use our services.

In the latter regard, there are at least two areas of particular concern to appraisers:

- *"Findings" of environmental problems*—If an appraiser reports that a particular property contains asbestos, for example, he or she has made a finding. This may not only be potentially misleading (has the appraiser actually made the scientific measurements to determine that the material is asbestos, or is that merely a presumption?), but it may subject the appraiser to unnecessary liability as well. If an appraiser is supposedly competent to identify one environmentally sensitive material, shouldn't the client or users of the services assume that an observation (or finding) of one environmental concern will imply, in the absence of comment on others, that other environmental concerns do not exist? As is pointed out in Guide Note No. 8 of the Appraisal Institute's *Standards of Professional Appraisal Practice*, "The typical appraiser does not have the knowledge or experience required to detect the presence of hazardous materials or to measure the quantities of such material. The appraiser, like the buyers and sellers in the open market, typically relies on the advice of others in matters that require special expertise."[3] Further, the following sample report disclosure is suggested in Guide Note No. 8:

> It is reported that asbestos is present within the subject property. The presence of asbestos may have a negative influence on the value of the

3. Appraisal Institute, Guide Note No. 8, *Standards of Professional Appraisal Practice of the Appraisal Institute* (Washington, DC: The Appraisal Foundation, 1990): D-21

subject property, but the consideration of the effects of asbestos on the value of the subject property is beyond the purpose and scope of this appraisal. The appraiser cautions against the use of this appraisal without knowledge of the intended purpose and limited scope of the appraisal.[4]

- *Special assumptions in the engagement*—A client may request a valuation "as though there were no environmental hazards." It is still necessary for the appraiser to determine to the extent possible any contamination that is actually known or suspected before accepting the engagement. It is also necessary that any service performed not performed in a way that would confuse or mislead either the client or any third party affected by that appraisers services. In some instances it may be necessary to decline the engagement to avoid these problems.

When handling environmental contaminated properties, professional appraisers must determine whether they are competent to deal with the specific problem. If not, they must deal with the engagement (or it refusal) as required by valuation standards.

When an environmentally sensitive assignment is accepted, the letter of engagement should clearly state the purpose and application of the appraisal, any special instructions of the client, and any restrictions to be placed on the services or the report and the reasons for those restrictions. Whether the value estimate is to include the effects of the environmental conditions or whether they are to be handled in some other way, the client's knowledge of known or suspected environmental conditions as well as other experts involved should also be mentioned.

It is particularly important that this letter be extensive in its coverage. The client must fully understand the nature of the appraiser's services and the scope, purposes, and limitations of the services to be provided must be established. The appraiser must also determine that performance of the engagement will in no way result in a violation of professional standards.

If an appraiser encounters situations that suggest outside expert environmental advice is required, it may be necessary to interrupt an appraisal while separate studies are performed. This eventuality should be provided for in the letter of engagement. Because many valuations are quite time sensitive, delays in investment decisions or reporting can be a major problem for the client. Thus, early involvement of the client in the issues to be considered is important. Usually is it considered best that an environmental experts be hired by the client.

How environmental problems should be handled in the appraisal process and report is beyond the scope of this article; however, the market must be considered paramount in these studies. Categories of concern aid in organizing research and thought processes, but they should not be substituted for market evidence.

In Guide Note No. 8 of the *Standards of Professional Appraisal Practice,* the Appraisal Institute has published the following clause:

Unless otherwise stated in this report, the existence of hazardous substances, including without limitation asbestos, polychlorinated biphenyls, petroleum leakage, or agricultural chemicals, which may or may not be present on the

4. Ibid., D-23

property, or other environmental conditions, were not called to the attention of nor did the appraiser become aware of such during the appraiser's inspection. The appraiser has no knowledge of the existence of such materials on or in the property unless otherwise stated. The appraiser, however, is not qualified to test such substances or conditions. If the presence of such substances, such as asbestos, urea formaldehyde foam insulation, or other hazardous substances or environmental conditions, may affect the value of the property, the value estimated is predicated on the assumption that there is no such condition on or in the property or in such proximity thereto that it would cause a loss in value. No responsibility is assumed for any such conditions, nor for any expertise or engineering knowledge required to discover them.[5]

If hazardous substances are in fact known to exist, this statement obviously cannot be made, or if made could only be stated with appropriate limitations on the appraisal and its report. If the engagement involves such substances, this statement must be modified accordingly, and an appropriate explanation should be included in the accompanying valuation report.

Guide Note No. 8 also emphasizes that, "The value of a property impacted by environmental hazards may not be measurable simply by deducting the apparent costs of losses from the total value as if 'clean.' The possibility of other changes affecting value, such as a change in highest and best use or even the marketability, should be considered."[6] This supports the idea that is necessary to discuss actual valuation methodologies.

Conclusion

The problems of understanding, measuring the effects, and dealing with environmental pollution are expanding and complex. The effect on the appraisal profession and on the ownership and use of real estate in general will become increasingly profound.

Human as well as professional concerns and responses have been suggested in this article, because the professional response of appraisers will likely be improved by the range of their general understanding if not involvement, in the issues of environment.

The three valuation approaches, the meanings of compiled data, property inspection techniques, analyses, and reporting should be reexamined. Knowledge placed in the context of professional endeavor and objectivity is essential to a proper handling of client engagements.

It is of particular importance that general standards, mandated at the international level through The International Assets Valuation Standards Committee, be adopted and implemented in each country. Although there are provincial concerns that must be locally addressed, the principles are common to us all.

5. Ibid., D-23
6. Ibid., D-22

Contaminated Properties— Valuation Solutions

by Anthony J. Rinaldi, MAI, ASA

Anthony J. Rinaldi, MAI, ASA, is president and principal owner of Miller-Rinaldi & Co., an appraisal and consulting firm with offices in New Jersey and New York. Mr. Rinaldi has given extensive expert testimony in state and federal courts and has previously published and lectured on real estate matters.

This article originally appeared in the July 1991 issue of The Appraisal Journal.

In recent years countless articles have been published about hazardous materials and contaminated properties—including a few horror stories. Appraisers are increasingly required to deal with contaminated properties, especially those appraisers who practice a significant amount of industrial appraisal work. Despite this, however, little has been published that addresses the problems of appraising such properties.

Contaminated properties involve complex issues. There are many types of contamination that affect property, its use, and its value. Contaminants take various forms, including oil, chemicals, toxic matter, nuclear waste, and asbestos. All of these can affect a property's utility and, therefore, its value.

This article is not intended to be a comprehensive study of every problem associated with contamination. Rather, it is intended to present an overview of how the appraisal of contaminated properties should be approached. In this article, solutions are proposed for two frequently encountered contaminated property appraisal problems. For the purposes of illustration, simple appraisals are presented in which the methodology can be easily described and demonstrated.

The appraisal of contaminated properties involves first the valuation of the property as if uncontaminated, and then an analysis of the loss in value caused by the contamination. Because contamination is a loss in value, it is a form of depreciation, which must be viewed as a reduction from the value as if uncontaminated.

Little or virtually no reliable market data exist that can be properly used within the three approaches to value and directly applied to contaminated properties. This is because properties generally cannot be sold, rented, or conveyed in a contaminated condition. It is also highly unlikely that any knowledgeable buyer would be willing to take on the burden of contamination. Finally, the degree of contamination is so specific to a particular property that it would be almost impossible to make a meaningful comparative analysis between a sale of any other contaminated prop-

Chapter 2: *Contaminated Properties—Valuation Solutions*

erty and the subject property. Accordingly, transactions that involve contaminated properties are suspect and tend to be unsuitable for comparative analysis.

In addition, it is difficult to imagine a situation in which a client would need to know only the contaminated value and not the uncontaminated value. Clearly, any meaningful discussion of the property with the client should involve both values.

When appraising the property as if uncontaminated, the approaches and procedures that would normally be used are applied and then reconciled with out any consideration given to the contamination.

Analysis of Cleanup Requirement

An understanding of the required cleanup is paramount to the valuation solution. It is essential for an appraiser to interview the engineer who preformed the cleanup study and categorize the cleanup requirements according to their impact on the property. All cleanup requirements result in costs that fall into one of the following three categories:

- Cost to cure;
- Deferred utility; and
- Excess operating expenses.

Cost to Cure

The most obvious costs are the costs both to remove the contaminated material and to restore the property to its usable condition. Although these cost estimates will be provided by the firm that will perform the cleanup, the cost estimate should be analyzed in terms of whether they are adequate or too excessive for the job. Cost manuals, comparative analyses, and consultations with other contractors are helpful in this regard. It is important to determine whether the projected costs provide for adequate disposal of the contaminated materials.

The timing of the cleanup is also significant. In certain situations, a cleanup can be deferred until the eventual demolition of the improvements. In the meantime, there may be some value in the use of the property.

Deferred Utility

An often overlooked consideration is the time required to implement the cleanup and obtain the necessary approvals from environmental agencies. During this period the property may not be used, either entirely or partially. This deferred use is, in effect, a reversion of the use (and therefore value). As the reversion is a future value, is must be discounted to the present. If only a portion of the property is affected, then a prorartion must be estimated.

Excess Operating Expenses

There are two types of excess operating expense to be considered. The first is the usual expense for repairs, maintenance, property taxes, and security that will be incurred during the period of deferment. These can be deducted as a lump sum if they extend over a period of less than a year, or discounted if they cover a period of more than a year.

The other category of expense encompasses those future costs that may be required to monitor the cleanup and maintain the property at an un-

Valuing Contaminated Properties

contaminated level. The period for which the recurring expenses will be required must first be estimated, and then their present value be deducted as a loss in value. In either case, because there are excess operating expenses, they must be reduced by the marginal income tax rate. Two problems that illustrate different scenarios for the same property follow.

Problem A

Assume the subject property is a 100,000-square-foot industrial building valued at $25 per square foot, or $2,500,000 as if uncontaminated. There are three well defined sections with a combined area of 10,000 square feet in which the concrete floors are impregnated with PCBs.

A cleanup company has provided a bid of $300,000 to break up the floor, remove and dispose of the contaminated concrete, and replace the floor with new concrete. Further, the nature of the cleanup will require that the plant be closed for one year. During this time, opersting expenses of $75,000 will be incurred for maintenance, secruity, and property taxes. Finally, after the cleanup the plant will be inspected and tested annually for a period of ten years, at an annual expense of $20,000. The solution is illustrated in Table 1.

Problem A represents the situation that will likely be encountered most frequently. It presents the three elements of value loss: 1) cost to cure, 2) deferred utility, and 3) excess operating expenses. When no significant loss of utility and no excess operating expenses exist, however, it may only be necessary to deduct the cost to cure.

TABLE 1 Solution to Problem A

Value as if uncontaminated	$2,500,000
Value deferred one year (× .8850 present-value factor)*	$2,212,500
Less cost to cure	$(300,000)
Less interim operating expenses (x.60)	$(45,000)
Less present value of excess operating expenses ($20,000 × .60** × 6.148)***	$(77,016)
	$1,790,484
Value as contaminated (rounded)	$1,790,000

*   13%/1-year present-value factor
**   1–.40 tax rate
*** 9%/10-year present-value annuity factor

Problem B

Assume the same 100,000-square-foot industrial building is valued at $2,500,000 as if uncontaminated. However, in this situation the cleanup will cost $2,600,000, require the demolition of the building, and will effectively render the property worthless on a current market-value basis. Although the company cannot sell the property without a cleanup, it can continue operating, but must eventually clean up the property when operations cease. What, therefore, is the value in use?

The property as if uncontaminated has a market rent of $250,000 net per annum and, although the building has a remaining useful life of 20 years, operations can reasonably be expected to continue for 15 years. The current cleanup costs are expected to increase at an annual rate of 4%, as is the value of the vacant land, which is currently valued at $275,000 as if uncontaminated. (See Table 2.)

Chapter 2: *Contaminated Properties—Valuation Solutions*

TABLE 2 Solution to Problem B

Present value of net rent $250,000 × 6.142 present-value annuity factor*	$1,535,500
Less present value of future cleanup cost $4,682,000** × 0.1401 present value factor***	$(655,948)
	$879,552
Plus present value of land reversion $495,000† × 0.2394 present-value factor‡	$118,503
	$998,055
Value as contaminated (rounded)	$1,000,000

*   14%/15-year present-value annunity factor

** $2,600,000 increased at 4% per annum for 15 years

***   14%/15–year present-value factor

† $275,000 increased 4% per annum for 15 years

‡   10%/15–year present-value factor

Explanation

Both Problem A and Problem B are the same property: however, in the case Problem B, the cost to cure is so extensive that on a market-value basis the property is rendered valueless. In this particular example, however, the property is allowed to continue operating as long as title is retained by the same owner.

Of particular importance in this problem is the application of different interest rates for different purposes. It is also important to point out that discount rates should generally be higher than those normally attributed to uncontaminated properties because of the risk and uncertainties involved.

One of the key elements of Problem B is the determination of the specific period over which operations may continue. An appraiser must be guided by the on going operation, and keep in mind that the duration of the operation may depend more on the life of the assembled equipment than on the life of the real estate improvements. Even for a vacant land site or a land site with minimal improvements this method is appropriate, provided that a reasonable time period can be established. In this regard, it is suggested that the typical life of an industrial process (approximately 20 years to 35 years) be used. One effect of discounting is that the present value of any period beyond 35 years to 40 years will not significantly change. Frequently, although a building may contain asbestos, for example, the building can continue to be used and demolition can be deferred until the end of its useful life.

Another important aspect of this problem is the determination of the annual rental. In the example given, the market rent was readily available. Often this may not be the case, because marketability of the property may be limited even if uncontaminated. In such a situation an economic annual rental charge must be determined.

This can be derived by applying an amortization charge to provide for the capital recovery cost of the improvements (as if uncontaminated) and an annual ground rent. In table 2, the building has a depreciated cost of $2,225,000 and a land value of $275,000. Applying the amortization factor to the building, plus an annual ground rental, results in the following required economic charge for the subject property:

Building requirement	$2,225,000 × .1391*	$309,498
Land requirement	$275,000 × .09**	$24,750
Annual economic rental charge		$334,428

*   11%/15-year amortization factor

**   Land interest rate

Conclusion

Although the preceding problems do not present all possible contaminated situations, they do illustrate the methodology that should be employed to solve the problem of appraising contaminated properties. While there are variations of these solutions, the underlying methodology is the same.

One factor not considered is the "stigma" of contamination. Contaminated properties, especially those with major problems, unquestionably have a stigma attached to them. Informed purchasers are understandably reluctant to consider buying a contaminated property until it is certain that the property is free of contaminants. In many cases, the results of the cleanup effort cannot be assured until after its completion and the final inspection and approval by the authorities. An allowance that provides for the stigma of contamination might be helpful, although this may be only a partial solution. While the existence of the stigma is a certainty, the precise measure of the loss in value caused by the stigma is elusive.

In summary, it is critical to distinguish between value in exchange and value in use. Appraisal must focus on the loss in value created by the three elements of cost to cure, deferred utility, and excess operating expenses. All costs associated with these three elements as well as the timing of such costs must be considered. Only this level of analysis will enable appraisers to measure the impact of contamination and solve these appraisal problems.

The Impact of Hazardous Materials on Property Value

by Bill Mundy, MAI, PhD

The issue of safe handling, storage, and disposal of hazardous and toxic materials is becoming a significant national problem. On an economic basis alone, the known environmental risk to real estate from hazardous and toxic materials is estimated to be $2 trillion.[1]

Community opposition to the handling, storage, or disposal of wastes in proximity to human or wildlife populations is high, and the "not in my backyard" syndrome is widespread. One reason for this high level of concern is the fear of a negative impact on property value. This is especially true if a property is in proximity to a generating, handling, disposal, or storage site. This fear relates to both real and perceived health risks.

While models of real and perceived risk exist, they lack empirical content and applicability to real estate. These models are thus difficult to integrate with actual market behavior. Further, the effects of hazardous and toxic materials on a wide range of independent variables (e.g., actual costs to monitor risk and to clean up wastes, or soft costs such as a stigma that adversely affects the financing of property) are unknown. Clearly, however, market behavior does influence real property value.

The Public's Response to Contamination

Research reveals that approximately two decades ago, the general public was not overly concerned about the presence of hazardous and toxic materials or the health risks these materials posed. In two surveys two years apart, Louis Harris documented that in the late 1970s the focus of concern about nuclear power facilities changed dramatically. While previously people had been concerned about a catastrophic accident, by 1980 people were principally concerned with storage of hazardous waste.[2] Rankin[3] and Forcade[4] have also used survey research techniques to document how concern about hazardous and toxic materials has been changing over time. It thus can be seen that the public response to contamination has a time dimension.

Bill Mundy, MAI, PhD, is president and senior analyst at Mundy and Associates in Seattle. He received a BA in agriculture from Washington State University as well as an MA in urban economics and a PhD in market research and urban economics from the University of Washington. He has made numerous presentations to Appraisal Institute groups on the topic of contamination and property values.

This article originally appeared in the April 1992 issue of The Appraisal Journal.

The author would like to express appreciation to the Real Estate Consulting Group of America, Inc., for their thoughtful suggestions and financial support.

1. *Focus,* September 1990.
2. Louis Harris, *Public Opinion* (April/May 1980): 26.
3. William L. Rankin and Barbara D. Melber, *Public Perceptions of Nuclear Waste Management Issues* (Seattle, Washington: Battelle Memorial Institute Human Affairs Research Centers, 1980).
4. Bill S. Forcade, "Public Participation in Siting," *Hazardous Waste Management in Whose Backyard?*, M. Hearthill, ed. (Colorado: Westview Press, 1984).

Valuing Contaminated Properties

5. James R. Webb, "Nuclear Power Plants: Effects on Property Values," *The Appraisal Journal* (April 1980): 230-235.

6. Chris Zeiss and James Atwater, "Waste Facility Impacts on Residential Property Values," *Journal of Urban Planning and Development* v. 115 (1989): 123-134.

7. Joseph Havlicek, Jr., Robert Richardson, and Lloyd Davies, "Measuring the Impacts of Solid Waste Disposal Site Location on Property Values," *University of Chicago Urban Economics Report No. 65* (November 1971; unpublished c. 1972).

8. G. Rudzitis and E.G. Hwang, "The External Costs of Sanitary Landfills," *Journal of Environmental Systems* v. 7, no. 4 (1977-1978): 301-308.

9. Hays B. Gamble, R.H. Downing, J.S. Shortle, and D.J. Epp, "Effects of Solid Waste Disposal Sites on Community Development and Residential Property Values," *Final Report for Bureau of Solid Waste Management*, Dept. of Environmental Resources, Commonwealth of Pennsylvania (Institute for Research on Land and Water Resources, Pennsylvania State University, November 1982).

10. Hays B. Gamble and Roger H. Downing, "Effects of Nuclear Power Plants on Residential Property Values," *Journal of Regional Science* v. 22, no. 4 (1982).

11. Jon P. Nelson, "Three-Mile Island and Residential Property Values: Empirical Analysis and Policy Implications," *Land Economics* (August 1981): 363-372.

12. Glenn Blomquist, "The Effect of Electrical Utility Power Plant Location on Area Property Value," *Land Economics* (February 1974): 97-100.

13. Francis J. Egar, "Air Pollution and Property Values in the Hartford Metropolitan Region," unpublished PhD dissertation Fordham University (1973).

14. Gary H. McClelland, William D. Schulze, and Brian Jurd, "The Effect of Risk Beliefs on Property Values: A Case Study of a Hazardous Waste Site," *Risk Analysis*, in press.

15. Michael R. Greenberg and Richard F. Anderson, *Hazardous Waste Sites: The Credibility Gap* (New Brunswick, NJ: Center for Urban Policy Research, 1984).

16. Ronda K. Hageman, "Nuclear Waste Disposal: Potential Property Impacts," *Natural Resources Journal* (October 1982): 789-810.

17. Zeiss and Atwater, 123-134.

18. Howard Kunreuther, William H. Desvousges, and Paul Slovic, "Nevada's Predicament," *Environment* (October 1988): 16-33.

The response to hazardous materials also is affected by a distance dimension. Webb[5] conducted interviews with residents who lived at varying distances from a nuclear power plant and found that the perceived impact of a power plant on property values lessened significantly as the distance from the power plant increased. Clearly, perceptions of hazards are changing over time and depend on distance from the source of the hazard.

Real Estate Value Impact Caused by Contamination

A significant amount of research has been done in an attempt to quantify the effects of various types of contamination on property value. While such statistical models as hedonic price models, multiple regression, and PROBIT have been used in this research and such contamination sources as nuclear power plants, sanitary landfills, and air pollution have been studied, the results have been inconclusive.

Six studies have used multiple regression in their analyses. Both Zeiss[6] and Havlicek,[7] for example, studied the effect sanitary landfills have on property values. Zeiss's research indicates that in six cases property value decreased, in eight no significant change occurred, and that value increased in one case, while Havlicek's research also found that property value impact varied according to distance from and degrees away from a downwind line from the site. However, Rudzitis[8] reanalyzed Havlicek's data, brought in new data, and concluded that such factors had no effect of any consequence on property value. In addition, Gamble[9] studied ten landfill sites and found no value effect.

The impact that nuclear power plants have on property value has been researched by both Gamble[10] and Nelson.[11] Gamble analyzed 540 single-family residential sales near four nuclear power plants and found no effect, while Nelson obtained the same result from studies of sales and listings in the vicinity of Three Mile Island. Blomquist,[12] however, found that proximity to a power plant did have an effect on property values and Egar[13] found a moderate relationship between the amount of air pollution and changes in property value.

Other researchers have used different research techniques with results that are just as confusing. For example, McClelland[14] used ordinary least squares and PROBIT in the analysis of 178 real estate transactions and found a significant correlation between selling price and neighborhood risk associated with hazardous waste sites. On the other hand, Greenberg found that "Property value and rent in 189 dump site communities appreciated more than those of the remainder of their counties."[15] Hageman[16] used a hedonic price model based on survey research to study nuclear power plants and found little effect. He predicted, however, that with the public becoming more sensitive to incidents and litigation, property value may be affected to a larger extent in the future.

Interesting research has been conducted to discover ways to allay people's concerns about property value impacts. One way is to guarantee residents that the value of their property will not decrease. In interviewing 117 households, Zeiss[17] found that people would not accept guarantees. To determine whether residents were willing to allow hazardous waste site in "their backyard," Kunreuther[18] conducted both a national and statewide survey (in Nevada) and found that if assured that the hazardous waste site was safe, residents would accept compensation and agree to allow the site to be located near them. Smith[19] surveyed 609 households in an attempt to determine whether people were willing to pay to decrease risk. His study was not directly related to real estate value, however, and the results of his research were inconclusive.

These researchers used many statistical techniques to determine whether risk associated with various types of hazardous and toxic material has an impact on property value. A review of this research leads to several conclusions. First, an adequate general theory of how contamination affects property value has not been developed. A link has not been established between a general theoretical model and a site-specific model. Second, property values are affected by many complex events over time. While both the severity and the persistence of contamination have an effect, these factors are not necessarily related. Third, the statistical models have not been properly used. Data sets are too small, and the variables are neither properly specified nor adequate. That is, they do not reflect important moderating variables, such as lender/lending institution attitudes, which have substantial effects on the marketability and value of property.

How Contamination Influences Property Value: A Theory

The impact a contaminating material has on the value of a property can be traced on a time continuum. Initially, a clean property has a value equal to full market value. In many cases a dirty (i.e., contaminated) property that is perceived as clean can also have a value equal to full market value. When the public, or an influential part of it (e.g., a scientist, the media) becomes aware that a contaminated property poses a health or financial risk (either real or perceived), the property is transformed into a problem property, which will affect value.

When the market[20] perceives a property as a problem, value will be significantly affected in several ways. A disclosure requirement by the sales agent or seller, concern on the part of the lender, and appraiser uncertainty all may have a noticeable effect on the marketability of the property. When a property loses its marketability, it also loses its value. Considerable uncertainty may occur at this stage as people involved in the transaction attempt to understand the magnitude of the problem.

When the problem is understood, uncertainty is lessened and the value of a property should then increase to a point at which the difference between its contaminated value and its market value is the sum of the cost to control[21] the problem plus any residual stigma. When the contamination is controlled, the value of the property would be expected to increase to full market value if the public believes scientists and public health experts.

Whether this actually occurs is debatable, however, because the public does not necessarily agree with the scientific community. This difference between cured value and full market value is the residual uncertainty caused by stigma, and should decrease with time as the public's perception of risk subsides—assuming there is no further contamination.

The factor of persistence concerns the time between the onset of a problem and the decrease in stigma to the point at which full market value is again reached. The length of time is a function of the severity of the problem and varies with the type and amount of contamination, time to cure as well as how the cure is accomplished, media exposure, real and perceived health risk, and visibility, among other things.

19. V. Kerry Smith and W.H. Desvousges, "An Empirical Analysis of the Economic Value of Risk Changes," *Journal of Political Economy* v. 95, no. 11 (1987).

20. The market is broadly defined as the various actors who are involved in a real estate transaction, such as the buyer, seller, real estate agent, appraiser, lender, title insurer, soils engineer, and so on.

21. The appraisal literature typically refers to this as the cost to cure. However, as Al Wilson, president of Environmental Assessment and Valuation, appropriately points out, we seldom know if the contamination problem is completely cured. (Appraisal Institute Symposium, Philadelphia, October 3 and 4, 1991.)

Valuing Contaminated Properties

For an income-producing property such as an apartment, this process has two value-influencing components. The first is the impact the hazard has on the marketability of a property. This process is illustrated in Figure 1. The second is the effect the hazard has on the property's income-producing ability, which is shown in Figure 2. For non-income-producing property the income effect would be the lost utility of the property.[22]

FIGURE 1 Marketability Effect

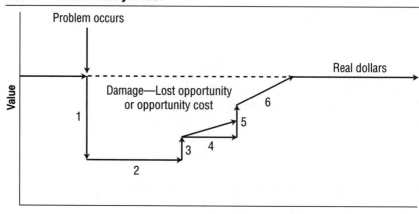

1 = Loss in value as a result of diminished marketability. Public becomes aware of the problem. How buyers and intermediaries perceive risk (unknown & dread factors).
2 = Duration. Time to understand relationship between hazard and risk.
3 = Amount of improvement in value resulting from knowledge (scientific) of hazard and effect knowledge has on perceived risk.
4 = Duration as hazard remains. Value may change as perceived risk changes.
5 = Increased value caused by removal of hazard (i.e., cost to cure).
6 = Stigma remaining after hazard removed. A period of uncertainty related to uncontrollable, involuntary, unknown, unobservable character of the hazard.
Damage—Related to opportunity. Lost opportunity is an opportunity cost measured by the diminished value over the duration of the event at a market rate.

FIGURE 2 Income Effect

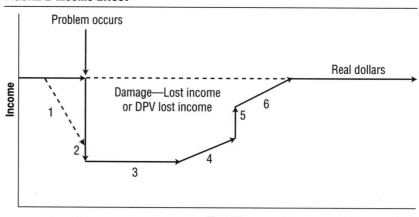

1 = Possible decrease in income if hazard is observable, known.
2 = Decreased income when problem becomes publicly known: Perceived risk becomes a major factor affecting rent, occupancy, expenses.
3 = Duration: Time the hazard remains.
4 = Improved income as people become accustomed to the hazard.
5 = Improved income caused by removal of hazard.
6 = Stigma.
Damage—Related to lost income. Estimated by discounting present value of lost income over duration of event at market interest rate, in the uncontaminated condition, at a risk rate in the uncontaminated condition.

22. The multivariate technique conjoint measurement may offer promise in quantifying, in dollar terms, the lost utility.

Chapter 2: *The Impact of Hazardous Materials*

Because contaminants affect both income and marketability, it is necessary to measure each separately.

Income effect

This is the present value of the difference between the property value as if uncontaminated and the property value as if contaminated, and is related to lost income. The damage is estimated by discounting the present value of lost income over the duration of an event—at a market interest rate in the uncontaminated condition, and at a risk rate in the contaminated condition.

$$\text{Damage} = V_C - V_D$$

where

$$V_C = \text{Value clean}$$
$$V_D = \text{Value dirty}$$
$$V_C = \sum_{t=1}^{n} \frac{NOI_C}{(1 + i_m)^t} + \frac{NOI_C}{(1 + i_m)^n}$$

where

$$NOI_C = \text{Net operating income (clean)}$$
$$i_m = \text{Market rate}$$
$$V_D = \sum_{t=1}^{n} \frac{NOI_D}{(1 + i_r)^t} + \frac{NOI_D}{(1 + i_r)^n}$$

where

$$NOI_D = \text{Net operating income (dirty)}$$
$$i_r = \text{Risk rate as a result of contamination}$$

Marketability effect

This part of the analysis quantifies the damage directly related to the lost opportunity to fully use the affected property. The situation is analogous to that which occurs when an owner of a frozen asset, while able to enjoy the income the asset generates (although the income may be less than expected), cannot sell the asset or use it for collateral. In such a case, an asset can actually become a liability, thus encumbering other assets.

The damage is related to lost opportunity, and this cost is measured by the present value of the diminished value over the duration of the event at a market rate.[23]

Figure 1 can be expanded to clarify the marketability impact. Figure 3 shows, on a year-by-year basis, how the value for real estate may be influenced by contamination. The damage may be quantified as follows.

$$\text{Damage}^{24} = [\sum_{i=1}^{n} PV_{r_r}(V_C - V_D)(r_m) + \sum_{i=1}^{n} PV_{r_r}(\text{cleanup cost})] +$$
$$[\sum_{i=0}^{n} FV_{r_r}(V_C - V_D)(r_m) + \sum_{i=0}^{-n} FV_{r_r}(\text{cleanup cost})]$$

where

$$n = \text{Annual periods}$$
$$V_C = \text{Value clean}$$
$$V_D = \text{Value dirty}$$
$$r_m = \text{Market rate}$$
$$PV = \text{Present value}$$
$$r_r = \text{Risk rate}$$
$$FV = \text{Future value}$$

23. One needs to be careful when quantifying income and marketability value effects to make sure double counting does not occur. When only income or marketability has been affected, double counting will not be a problem. When both are affected, an analyst must make sure each is quantified independently of the other.

24. The formula on the left side of the plus sign quantifies the historical opportunity costs.

FIGURE 3 Quantifying the Marketability Impact

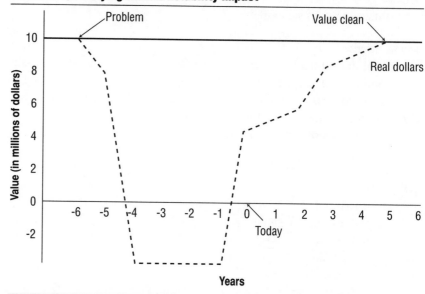

1 = Loss in value as a result of perceived risk and stigma.
2 = Uncertainty as research on contamination proceeds.
3 = Scope of problem and level of risk becomes known. Scientific risk does not necessarily equal perceived risk.
4 = Cost to cure contamination plus risk (stigma) impact.
5 = Cleanup process.
6 = Residual stigma.

TABLE 1 Calculation of Damage to Marketability

Year	Loss in Value ($000,000)	Market Rate*	Opportunity Cost ($000,000)	Misc. Cost ($000)	Cleanup Cost ($000)	Risk Rate**	Total Damage (Present Value in $000)
-6	$0.0	10%	$0.00	$0	$0	15%	$0.0
-5	$2.0	10%	$0.20	$0	$0	15%	$402.3
-4***	$12.0	10%	$1.20	$0	$0	15%	$2,098.8
-3	$12.0	10%	$1.20	$0	$0	15%	$1,825.1
-2	$12.0	10%	$1.20	$0	$0	15%	$1,587.0
-1	$12.0	10%	$1.20	$4.0	$0	15%	$1,384.6
Today 0	$7.0	10%	$0.70	$10.0	$0	15%	$710.0
+1	$6.0	10%	$0.60	$20.0	$100	15%	$626.1
+2	$4.0	10%	$0.40	$15.0	$100	15%	$389.4
+3	$1.5	10%	$0.15	$2.0	$20	15%	$113.1
+4	$1.0	10%	$0.10	$2.0	$0	15%	$58.3
+5	$0.5	10%	$0.05	$1.0	$0	15%	$25.4
Total damage, marketability							$9,220.1

* Rate as if clean. The normal return one would receive on this class of asset. Equivalent to annual rate from market evidence.
** Rate reflecting added risk caused by known contamination. The rate might be equated to a junk bond rate.
*** Includes $2.0 million personal liability.

An example of how such damage could be calculated is shown in Table 1. As an example, assume a non-income-producing property is located near a source of contamination such as a landfill. Contaminated ground water and methane gas have migrated to the subject property, and a cleanup is required. The public became aware of this problem five years ago, when the market value of the property was $21.8 million. Market evidence applied to both the market and income approach reveals that the value of the property has decreased by 55%, or $12 million. Therefore, five years

Chapter 2: *The Impact of Hazardous Materials*

ago there was a value decrease for two-twelfths of the year ($200,000), and the decrease is applied to the entire fourth year ($12 million).

The owner of the property is entitled to a market rate of return on the investment, which might be 10%, or $2,180,000, for the entire property and $ 1,200,000 for the damaged part. This is the owner's opportunity cost—the cost of having the asset frozen. The $1.2 million opportunity cost occurred four years ago. The present value, using a 15% risk rate (because the property and the property owner are jointly and severally liable for damages) is $402,300. This set of circumstances concerns historical damages.

Currently, the property owner may have completed preliminary site testing and may know the extent of contamination. Because uncertainty is diminished, the loss in property value is diminished. Substantial engineering and testing, legal, and appraisal costs are being incurred, however, which are estimated at $10,000 this year and $20,000 next year. These are shown as miscellaneous costs. Next year (year + 1) cleanup will begin at $100,000. Therefore, in year + 1 costs will be:

Opportunity cost on lost value	$600,000
Miscellaneous costs	$20,000
Cleanup costs	$100,000
Total (year + 1)	$720,000

The present value of these costs, discounting at the 15% risk rate, is $626,087, which is rounded to $626,100. In year + 4, these are nominal miscellaneous costs ($2,000), but a lingering stigma effect still has a $1 million impact on the property's value. Over the entire ten-year period the present value of the costs, which includes opportunity and out-of-pocket costs, is $9.22 million, which is a measure of the damage suffered by the property owner as a result of lost marketability. For an income-producing property, the damage would be increased by the present value of the lost *NOI*.[25]

25. For an income-producing property the analysis becomes more complex. Factors that need to be considered include the risk rate (when applied to the income stream), which may account for the lost marketability. Also, debt and collateral will affect the amount the property owner has at risk. The author is presently working on a method to quantify these damages.

Issues in the Valuation of Contaminated Property

by James A. Chalmers, PhD, and Scott A. Roehr

James A. Chalmers, PhD, is a partner in the financial advisory services practice of Coopers & Lybrand in Phoenix, Arizona. A designated member of the American Society of Real Estate Counselors, Mr. Chalmers received a PhD in economics from the University of Michigan and is a candidate in the Appraisal Institute.

Scott A. Roehr is a managing associate in the financial advisory services practice of Coopers & Lybrand in Phoenix, and is a Certified Public Accountant (CPA). Mr. Roehr received a BS in business administration from the University of Southern California and specializes in the valuation of closely held businesses, intangible assets, and real estate.

This article originally appeared in the January 1993 issue of The Appraisal Journal.

Valuation of contaminated property poses a challenge to scientific and engineering knowledge, to economic analysis and appraisal methods, and to the very definitions of value that underlie our legal system. This article begins with a conceptual framework to analyze the effect of contamination on property value. This is followed by a general valuation model appropriate to a contaminated, income–producing property. The model clarifies the definition of stigma and shows how the effect of stigma on the value of a property changes over time as contamination is discovered and subsequently remediated. The remainder of the article addresses specific measurement techniques and a number of issues that arise in the definition of value of contaminated property, particularly in the condemnation and ad valorem tax contexts.

How Contamination Affects Value

The effect of contamination on property value must be examined within a much broader framework than might at first be thought. Figure 1 presents such a framework and shows that the value of contaminated property ultimately depends on

- The extent of the contamination
- The way in which the contamination is perceived or evaluated
- The remediation and indemnification responses to the contamination
- The effect of these responses on utility and marketability
- The appropriate standard of value

In evaluating a contaminated property, the first issue centers on the nature of the problem. Is the property physically contaminated? That is, is it affected by hazardous substances present in, on, or near the subject property in measurable quantities? Perhaps the property is affected by nonphysical contaminants such as noise or visual pollution, which can

Chapter 2: *Issues in Valuation*

FIGURE 1 Conceptual Framework: How Environmental Contamination Affects Value

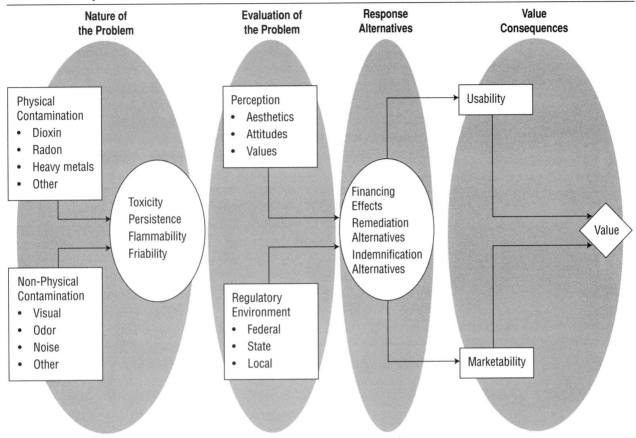

also influence value. The extent of the contamination (e.g., its toxicity, persistence, flammability, friability), must then be documented.

Once the nature of the contamination is clarified, how it is perceived or evaluated by relevant segments of the public must be understood. These segments include, at a minimum, the regulatory authorities as well as the participants in the market in which the value of a subject property is determined. Their perceptions are relevant because it is not actual contamination but the perception of the contamination by the market (or regulators) that is of concern.

Three major areas of response must then be considered. To what extent has the contamination affected the financeability of the property? How may the contamination be remediated? For which of the risks associated with the property may indemnification be obtained? In the case of each of these questions, issues of timing, costs, and liability are paramount.

Once financing, remediation, and indemnification questions are answered, it will be possible to determine the utility and marketability of a property. For example, is it leasable in its contaminated condition? If so, at what rates can it be leased? Can it be marketed in its "as is' condition? Considerations of utility and of marketability will in turn allow an assessment of a property's value-in-use and value-in-exchange (i.e., market value).

This framework focuses attention on the following factors that are unique to contaminated property valuation.

- The high degree of reliance on sophisticated technical/scientific analysis of the problem and of the ways in which it can be remediated
- The importance of the "perceived reality" in determining value
- The enhanced risk and uncertainty, with their attendant impacts on the cost of attracting capital
- The potential for significant divergence of value-in-use from value-in-exchange

A General Valuation Model

The seminal article by Peter Patchin, "Valuation of Contaminated Property,"[1] outlines the importance of remediation costs, indemnification, and stigma in valuing contaminated property, showing how capitalization and yield rates can be adjusted to account for the effects on contamination on the financeability and marketability of property. In "Contaminated Properties—Stigma Revisited,"[2] Patchin further defines stigma and discusses how it can best be measured. These contributions were followed by two important articles by Bill Mundy. In "Stigma and Value,"[3] he focuses on real and perceived risk in determining the stigma attached to a contaminated, or previously contaminated, property. In "The Impact of Hazardous Materials on Property Value,"[4] a generalized theory is presented of how the value of a contaminated property would change over time as uncertainty with respect to its condition changes and as it is, in fact, cleaned up. Additional insight is provided by Richard Neustein in "Estimating Value Diminution by the Income Approach,"[5] who shows how the income impairment of contaminated property and the risk premium necessary to attract capital to it combine to determine the value discount of a contaminated property relative to an uncontaminated property.

These ideas have been developed in a generally consistent fashion and ultimately express the general proposition that value reflects an anticipated future stream of benefits discounted at a return necessary to attract investors to that opportunity. In the case of contaminated property, both are affected. The future benefit stream is depressed and required returns increase. As emphasized by Mundy,[6] these effects occur over time and the pattern they establish has to be accounted for in establishing the value of, or damages to, the impaired property.

The model outlined in the next section makes an important clarification with respect to the definition of stigma. The analysis offered here argues that the value of contaminated property differs from the value of uncontaminated property for one of two reasons—direct costs or stigma. Direct costs refer to any effect of the contamination on the net cash flow to the owner. These can stem from a variety of causes including lowered effective income flows, remediation costs, and insurance costs. Stigma refers to impacts on value stemming from the increased risk associated with the property and the effect of this on marketability and financeability.

As such, stigma does not refer exclusively to the difference between the value of an uncontaminated property and the value of an otherwise identical, but once contaminated, property that is fully remediated and indemnified. Stigma is a much more general concept and refers to the discount, beyond direct costs, required to compensate investors or lenders for the risks associated with the property. Stigma can exist, therefore, at any time after contamination is discovered—before remediation, during

1. Peter J. Patchin, "Valuation of Contaminated Property," *The Appraisal Journal* (January 1988): 7–16.
2. Peter J. Patchin, "Contaminated Properties—Stigma Revisited," *The Appraisal Journal* (April 1992): 167–172.
3. Bill Mundy, "Stigma and Value," *The Appraisal Journal* (January 1992): 7–13.
4. Bill Mundy, "The Impact of Hazardous Materials on Property Value," *The Appraisal Journal* (April 1992): 155–162.
5. Richard A. Neustein, "Estimating Value Diminution by the Income Approach," *The Appraisal Journal* (April 1992): 283–287.
6. Mundy, "The Impact of Hazardous Materials on Property Value."

remediation, or after remediation. In fact, Mundy argues that uncertainty, and therefore stigma, are likely to be largest soon after contamination is discovered when little may be known about its extent or the true cost of its remediation.

The Model

In general terms, the relationships can be defined as follows:

$$V_U = \sum_{t=1}^{n} \frac{NOI_t}{(1 + i_u)} \text{ and}$$

$$V_C = \sum_{t=1}^{n} \frac{NOI - (LI_t + R_t + I_t)}{(1 + i_c)^t}$$

where

V_u = Value uncontaminated

V_c = Value contaminated

NOI = Net operating income of the property uncontaminated in year t

LI = Lost income resulting from contamination in year t

R = Remediation costs resulting from contamination in year t

I = Indemnification costs resulting from contamination in year t

i_u = Market discount rate appropriate to an uncontaminated property

i_c = Risk-adjusted discount rate appropriate to a contaminated property

The variables necessary to estimate V_C are each discussed briefly as follows:

- Net operating income (*NOI*)—The starting point of the valuation is the anticipated net income stream of the property in its uncontaminated condition.

- Lost income (*LI*)—In general lost income can be the result of diminished market demand for the property that shows up in lower rents or lower occupancy. It can also result from physical interference of contamination with use of the property, or from the interference of testing, remediation, or monitoring with use of the property. Reductions in income from these causes can be expected to differ before remediation, during remediation, and after remediation.

- Remediation (*R*)—A second cost associated with a contaminated property is the cost of remediation. This can include costs related to testing, clean up, disposal, and subsequent monitoring.

- Indemnification (*I*) A property owner usually seeks indemnification with respect to the effectiveness of the remediation process. He or she may also seek indemnification from any costs or liability from previously unidentified contamination of the property. Fortunately, insurance policies are increasingly available in the market which, after appropriate testing, will insure against previously undisclosed contamination. The ERIC Group, Inc., in Englewood, Colorado, for example, specializes in insuring against environmental risk.

Valuing Contaminated Properties

- Risk-adjusted discount rate (i_c)—The intrinsic value of any investment can be measured by the cash flows it is expected to generate discounted at a rate of return commensurate with the risk of those cash flows being achieved. The cash flows of contaminated property will often be perceived to be less certain as a result of concerns that include
  - Adequacy of projections of remediation costs and timing
  - Changes in technology or regulation that affect the property or its cleanup
  - Impact of contamination/remediation on absorption and *NOI*
  - Potential for legal costs and liabilities

As Mundy emphasizes,[7] the uncertainty related to the cash flows of a specific property will vary over time. Typically, uncertainty is highest when a problem is first discovered. As engineering studies are completed and the nature and extent of the contamination is ascertained, uncertainty decreases. This uncertainty continues to decrease as remediation strategies are evaluated and implemented. Finally, when remediation and indemnification are completed, further decreases will occur. The risk-adjusted discount rate (i_c) must ultimately reflect the way in which the market evaluates these risks over time.

An Example

These relationships can be demonstrated by considering the simple example illustrated in Tables 1, 2, and 3. Assume that a property is contaminated and that it will take three years to prepare the remediation plan. Remediation then takes place over the three-year period from years 4 to 6.

Summary of Key Factors

Net Operating Income (*NOI*)	
• Uncontaminated (per year)	$200,000
Lost income (*LI*)	
• Preremediation (per year, years 1–3)	$10,000
• During remediation (per year, years 4–6)	$25,000
• Postremediation (per year, years 7+)	$5,000
Remediation (*R*)	
• Planning costs preremediation (per year, years 1–3)	$5,000
• Remediation costs (per year, years 4–6)	$100,000
• Postremediation monitoring (per year, years 7+)	$5,000
Indemnification	
• Postremediation (per year, year 7+)	$4,000
Discount Rate	
• Uncontaminated	12%
• Contaminated (before remediation)	20%
• Contaminated (during remediation)	17%
• Contaminated (after remediation)	13%
Inflation	4%
Capitalization rate (uncontaminated)	8%
Capitalization rate (uncontaminated, after remediation)	9%

7. Ibid.

Chapter 2: *Issues in Valuation*

TABLE 1   Valuation of Contaminated Property

		Direct Costs			
Year	NOI	LI	R	I	NOI – (LI + R + I)
1	$208,000	$10,400	$5,200	$0	$192,400
2	$216,320	$10,816	$5,408	$0	$200,096
3	$224,973	$11,249	$5,624	$0	$208,100
4	$233,972	$29,246	$116,986	$0	$87,739
5	$243,331	$30,416	$121,665	$0	$91,249
6	$253,064	$31,633	$126,532	$0	$94,899
7	$263,186	$6,580	$6,580	$5,264	$244,763
8	$273,714	$6,843	$6,843	$5,474	$254,554
9	$284,662	$7,117	$7,117	$5,693	$264,736
10	$296,049	$7,401	$7,401	$5,921	$275,325
11	$307,891	$7,697	$7,697	$6,158	$286,338

TABLE 2   Calculation of Present Value of Cash Flows with Variable Discount Rate[1]

Year	Annual Cash Flow NOI – (LI + R+I)				One-Year PV Factor	
10	$3,456,864[2]	+	$0 = $3,456,864	×	.8849558[3] =	$3,059,172
9	$264,736	+	$3,059,172 = $3,323,908	×	.8849558 =	$2,941,511
8	$254,554	+	$2,941,511 = $3,196,065	×	.8849558 =	$2,828,376
7	$244,763	+	$2,828,376 = $3,073,139	×	.8849558 =	$2,719,592
6	$94,899	+	$2,719,592 = $2,814,491	×	.8547009[4] =	$2,405,548
5	$91,249	+	$2,405,548 = $2,496,797	×	.8547009 =	$2,134,015
4	$87,739	+	$2,134,015 = $2,221,754	×	.8547009 =	$1,898,935
3	$208,100	+	$1,898,935 = $2,107,035	×	.8333333[5] =	$1,755,862
2	$200,096	+	$1,755,862 = $1,955,958	×	.8333333 =	$1,629,965
1	$192,400	+	$1,629,965 = $1,822,365	×	.8333333 =	$1,518,638

Present value of cash flows or value contaminated
$1,518,638

---

1. Because the discount rate changes, the cash flow must be brought back, one year at a time, starting with year 10. This is done by taking the year 10 cash flow, discounting it one year at 13%, adding it to the year 9 cash flow, discounting that at 13% and so on.

2. Equals year 10 net cash flow of $275,325 plus reversion of $3,181,533.

3. One-year *PV* factor for 13%.

4. One-year *PV* factor for 17%.

5. One-year *PV* factor for 20%.

TABLE 3   Stigma: Change in Value Resulting from Risk

Year	Cash Flows NOI – (LI + R + I)	i_u	i_c
1	$192,400	12%	20%
2	$200,096	12%	20%
3	$208,100	12%	20%
4	$87,739	12%	17%
5	$91,249	12%	17%
6	$94,899	12%	17%
7	$244,763	12%	13%
8	$254,554	12%	13%
9	$264,736	12%	13%
10	$3,456,864	12%	13%

Present value of cash flows @ i_u = $2,185,097

Present value of cash flows @ i_c = $1,518,638 (see Table 2)

Stigma $666,459

It is further assumed that even after remediation and indemnification, the market requires a permanent risk premium of 1% because of the history of the property. Table 1 shows the relevant cash flows for the property in its contaminated state.

The year 11 net cash flow of $286,338 is then capitalized at 9%, indicating a value of $3,181,533 assumed to occur at the end of year 10. The present value of the cash flows is then determined by discounting them at the variable rate i_c as shown in Table 2.

The value of the property in its contaminated condition is only about $1.5 million based on the lost income, remediation costs, and indemnification costs together with the yield premium necessary to compensate an investor for the uncertainties associated with these projections.

If the value uncontaminated is calculated from Table 2 by capping year 11 *NOI* at 8% and then discounting the cash flows at 12%, a value of $2.6 million is indicated. This suggests value diminution caused by contamination of about $1.1 million. The following sections disaggregate this effect into two components—stigma and direct costs.

Stigma Defined

Stigma is defines here as the reduction in value caused by contamination resulting from the increased risk associated with the contaminated property. In the pervious analysis, the considerations of risk as a result of incertainties with respect to the projected cash flows and future liabilities are all summarized by i_c. If we define $\Delta i_c = i_c - i_u$ as the yield premium necessary to compensate for the risk of the contaminated property, there will be stigma effects on value as long as Δi_c is positive.

Figure 2 shows the pattern of Δi_c assumed in the example. Risk is assumed to be highest in the early, preremediation period. Once remediation begins, it can be assumed that the contractor is bonded for performance and that the risk associated with the property diminishes. After remediation is complete, the property has been certified "clean," and the owner is properly indemnified against future liability, the risk falls still further. It is assumed, however, that the market will see some modest, continuing risk associated with the property because of its history.

Illustrating this concept with the previous example, stigma (*S*) will be defined formally as:

$$S = \sum_{t=1}^{n} \frac{NOI_t - (LI_t + R_t + I_t)}{(1 + i_u)^t} - \sum_{t=1}^{n} \frac{NOI_t - (LI_t + R_t + I_t)}{(1 + i_c)^t}$$

Table 3 shows that the impact of risk, that is, the impact of discounting the cash flow at i_c as opposed to i_u, is $666,459. In other words, as the contaminated property is valued at the beginning of year 1, $666,459 of its loss in value is a result of stigma.

This definition of stigma allows the isolation of the other component of value dimimution caused by contamination, which is referred to as the direct costs (*DC*) of contamination.

$$DC = \sum_{t=1}^{n} \frac{NOI_t}{(1 + i_u)^t} - \sum_{t=1}^{n} \frac{NOI_t - (LI_t + R_t + I_t)}{(1 + i_u)^t}$$

FIGURE 2 Yield Premiums Resulting from Risk

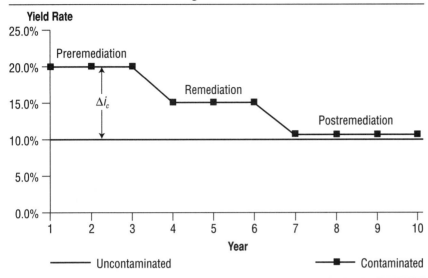

The first term is the value uncontaminated while the second term is the contamination-affected cash flows discounted at a market rate, not a risk rate. As shown in Table 3:

$$\text{Present value of } NOI - (LI + R + I) \text{ at } i_u = \$2,185,097, \text{ and}$$
$$\text{Present value of } NOI \text{ at } i_u = \$2,600,000$$
$$\text{Direct costs of contamination} = \$414,903$$

In other words, $414,903 of the value diminution is caused by changed cash flow from the contaminated property and $666,459 is caused by increased risk. It follows that:

$$V_u = V_c + DC + S \text{ or}$$
$$\$2,600,000 = \$1,158,638 + \$414,903 + \$666,459$$

Changes in Value, Direct Costs, and Stigma Over Time

After a contaminated property at the beginning of the year 1 has been valued and the relationship between V_u, V_c, DC, and S has been shown, it is instructive to observe how these value components change if the property is valued at the beginning of years 2, 3, or 4. Figure 3 shows the three components of value diminution and how they can be expected to change over time. It should be noted that stigma continues to be a residual concept (i.e., the risk-related loss in value after direct costs are accounted for), but that stigma is significantly associated with the highly uncertain, preremediation stages of a property. As remediation is begun, V_c has risen to about $1.9 million from $1.5 million in year 1 and $2.7 million after remediation.

Specific Measurement Techniques

The previous section outlines an approach to the valuation of contaminated property based on the difference between the value of the property uncontaminated and the various costs necessary to make it equivalent to a property that has never been contaminated. The usefulness of this ap-

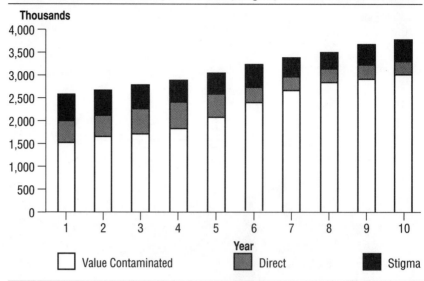

FIGURE 3 Value Contaminated, Direct Costs, Stigma, and Value Uncontaminated

proach depends on the extent to which it is possible to measure loss of income caused by contamination, the timing and cost of remediation, costs of indemnification, and increased cost of capital as a result of the risks associated with contaminated property. Frequently, each of these costs is defined well enough that contaminated property can be usefully valued.

Important circumstances may occur, however, that make other measurement techniques more appropriate. In general, these involve direct valuation of a property in its as is contaminated state. Two approaches are discussed here. The first is regression analysis, which is effectively a modification of the sales comparison approach. The second is the contingent valuation approach.

Regression Analysis

One of the first consequences of contamination is impaired marketability. The difficulty of measuring market response is further complicated by the unique circumstances that may accompany each individual property. Conditions relating to underground storage tanks or asbestos may occasionally be sufficiently common that traditional sales comparison techniques can be used to directly value properties in their contaminated state, but even this is rare. More usually, sufficient market information does not exist to allow the use of the sales comparison approach. An important exception exists, however, with respect to the impacts of hazards on residential property.

In an increasingly large number of valuation arenas, it is necessary to understand how an environmental condition has affected residential property value. Such conditions include overhead electric transmission lines, airport noise, freeway noise, air quality, odor, insect swarms, view impairment, waste dumps, nuclear waste dumps or transport routes, gas pipelines, accident or spill sites, surface or groundwater contamination, and radon. In these cases, the question is whether there is any evidence of a systematic effect of the identified contaminant or hazard on property values.

Because of the relatively large number of residential transactions. this question is frequently amenable to statistical investigation using multiple

Chapter 2: *Issues in Valuation*

regression analysis. This effectively allows the different elements of a conventional sales adjustment matrix to be estimated based on the useful ability of regression analysis to isolate the efforts of one variable independent of the effects of other variables. These techniques are the foundation for mass appraisal models as well as for the increasingly large body of statistical analysis carried out by economists and appraisers. Representative applications of this technique include Zeiss and Atwater[8] as well as Smith and Desvouges[9] applied to waste disposal sites; Gamble and Downing[10] applied to nuclear power plants; Nelson[11] applied to airport noise: Kinnard and Geckler[12] applied to radioactive contamination; and Kirshner and Moore[13] applied to water quality.

In each of these cases, the goal is to first identify those characteristics of properties, of their locations and neighborhoods, of times of sale, and of other important variables that may affect value. Once these have been determined, it is possible to statistically investigate whether proximity to a hazard, to a point-source emitter of pollution, to noise, or to other sources of contamination are systematically associated with value. These techniques are particularly relevant in litigation when property value diminution is alleged with respect to residential property. Because property value diminution claims are arising more frequently around Comprehensive Environmental Response, Compensation, and Liability Act of 1980 (CERCLA) and other high-profile contaminated sites, regression-based attempts to directly measure the consequence of contamination or hazard on market value will become increasingly common.

Contingent Valuation Methodology

Contingent valuation methodology (CVM) constitutes a second direct approach to valuing property in its as is contaminated state. CVM has become increasingly prominent in the context of natural resource damage claims under CERCLA and has been recognized as an appropriate measure of value when other, more traditional approaches do not work.[14]

As Patchin remarks[15] there may be more relevant information associated with transactions that do not occur that with those that do. Appraisers have long recognized the relevance of careful interviews with market participants in developing their opinions. In the context of contaminated property, interviews of informed buyers, sellers, brokers, and lenders frequently become critical because of the absence of relevant transaction data. CVM pushes these techniques forward in two important respects. First, it uses formal rather than informal procedures to select interviewees, to determine the number of interviewees, and to set other interview conditions. This allows subsequent statements to be made with respect to the reliability of the statements. Second, much effort has been expended to develop questioning techniques in terms of a hypothetical choice that will have maximum reliability for actual choices. The essence of this work is to make the hypothetical as real and understandable as possible for the respondent. Research in this area is well summarized by Cummings et al.[16]

CVM can be appropriately applied in real property cases that involve contamination. A recent case in point involved a master-planned community centered around a four-acre lake. Expensive lots had been sold around the lake and equally expensive homes built to enjoy the view of snow-capped mountains across the open water. Unfortunately, there was

8. Chris Zeiss and James Atwater, "Waste Facility Impacts on Residential Property Values," *Journal of Urban Planning and Development,* v. 115 (1989): 123–124.

9. V. Kerry Smith and William H. Desvouges, "The Value of Avoiding a LULU: Hazardous Waste Disposal Sites," *The Review of Economics and Statistics,* v. 68 (1986): 293–299.

10. Hays B. Gamble and Roger H. Downing, "Effects of Nuclear Power Plants on Residential Property Values," *Journal of Regional Science,* v 22, no. 4 (1982); 457–478.

11. Jon P. Nelson, "Airport Noise, Location Rent, and the Market for Residential Amenities," *Journal of Environmental Economics and Management,* v. 6 (1979): 320–331.

12. William N. Kinnard, Jr., and Mary Beth Geckler, "The Effects on Residential Real Estate Prices from Proximity to Properties Contaminated with Radioactive Materials, *Real Estate Issues* (1991): 25–36

13. D. Kirshner and Deboral Moore, "The Effect of San Francisco Bay Water Quality on Adjacent Property Values," *Journal of Environmental Management,* v. 27 (1989): 263–274.

14. See *Ohio v. U.S. Department of the Interior,* 800 F.2d 432 (1989). These issues as they apply to natural resource damage assessment are discussed at length in "Department of Interior, 43CFR Part 11, Natural Resource Damage Assessments, Notice of Proposed Rulemaking," *Federal Register,* v. 56, no. 82 (April 29, 1991): 19752–19773.

15. Patchin, "Contaminated Properties—Stigma Revisited."

16. Ronald G. Cummings, David S. Brookshire, and William D. Schulze, *Valuing Public Goods, The Contingent Value Method* (Totowa, N.J.:Rowman & Allanheld Publishers, 1986).

little water. The lake leaked and frequently managed to hold only enough water to breed huge swarms of sewer midges, expose an unattractive lake bed, and generate noxious odor. The intensity of the landowners' ire was substantial and the developer continually assured the residents that the problem would be rectified. After five years, and little progress, suit was brought by the landowners.

Some limited market evidence did exist suggesting that damages to the landowners were small or nonexistent. It was clear, however, that the apparent ability of the properties to maintain their value was illusory. Landowners were resolute that, despite the fact they were being damaged each year, they would not capitulate and discount their property. They were determined to hold out and find a solution to the problem with the lake. In fact, there were even a few buyers who apparently believed that the situation was temporary and bought at precontamination prices. This, however, in our view could not be considered as evidence of the absence of damages.

To demonstrate this, a survey of knowledgeable recreational property brokers was conducted. They were provided a set of visual materials that clearly illustrated the distinction between the impaired and the unimpaired condition and were asked their opinion of the discount required to sell the impaired property assuming permanent impairment. They found this an easy hypothetical to deal with, as did the jury. The brokers concluded that a typical impaired property would have to be discounted by $40,000 if it were to be permanently located next to the malfunctioning lake. If a 10% discount rate is applicable to the future stream of benefits (or disamenities received from this kind of property, the implied, annualized damages are $4,243 per year assuming the property has a 30-year life. This estimate can then be applied to the number of years each property owner had been affected, independent of whether the lake might be repaired in the future.

In this instance, the market evidence was ambiguous and counterintuitive, while the CVM evidence was straightforward, easy to understand, and probably as good a measure as could be obtained of the loss of enjoyment offered by the landowners.

Issues

The preceding sections show that although contamination presents both conceptual and empirical challenges, the valuation profession is making progress on both fronts. Perhaps the most perplexing issue for appraisers is development of a clear definition of the value concept they are trying to estimate. Confusion with respect to a value definition is well illustrated both in the context of condemnation of contaminated property and in the context of the assessment of contaminated property for purposes of ad valorem taxation. In both cases, much of the problem stems from the fact that with contaminated property there can be a large disparity between value-in-use and value-in-exchange.

Condemnation of Contaminated Property

Condemnation actions frequently involve properties adjacent to transportation routes. As a result, condemnation actions involving contaminated property are frequent, particularly within larger metropolitan areas. In a worst-case scenario, assume a landowner owns an improved commercial property of 20,000 square feet on two acres of land. Assume further a zero-inflation environment in which the property generates $100,000 of *NOI* annually and that similar properties have sold at cap rates of 10%, suggesting a value of $1 million. The owner has just retired and is living off the cash flow from his property. He has no debt on the property and no inclination to sell it.

Unexpectedly, the local mass transit authority routes a new subway line across the property that requires taking the entire property. As part of the acquisition process, test drilling on the property reveals serious soil and groundwater contamination from a previous use of the land unknown to the landowner. The previous user no longer exists. The condemnor receives estimates from its environmental and engineering consultants that remediation will cost $1.2 million. Based on this, they conclude the property has zero market value and proceed to take the property with offered compensation of zero dollars. If this property had to face a true market test, the seriousness of its contamination may well indicate zero market value.

There is more in the bundle of fee simple property rights, however, than the right to sell. There are the right to use and the right to lease. What are those worth? Assume the landowner contacts an environmental attorney, the local regulatory body, and environmental engineers, and they conclude that it is highly unlikely that remediation would be required on the site for a period of 10 years. Further, experts indicate that the remediation can be carried out for $600,000 to a standard sufficient to sell the property. If the next most attractive investment with similar risk characteristics for the landowner yielded 10%, the center can be valued from the condemnee's perspective. Assuming $100,000 *NOI* annually for 10 years, with $600,000 of remediation in year 10, all discounted at 10%, and then a sale in year 11 with a cap of 10%, with the reversion discounted at a rate at 10%, the value to the condemnee is about $768,674. The condemnor and the condemnee obviously have different perspectives on value became their remediation program have different timing and different costs.

Case law and legislative statute create a supposition that favors market value as the measure of just compensation. As Jay Dushoff and Denise Henslee,[17] among others, have argued, however, it is hard to escape the implication of the Fifth Amendment that the landowner be made whole. To make this landowner whole, compensation of $768,674 is sought. This obviously does not leave the condemnor very happy. This $768,674 is for the site as is so $1.2 million still has to be spent to clean it. The result is a total bill of about $2 million for a property everyone thought had a market value of $1 million in an uncontaminated state.

There is no relevant case law to the authors' knowledge on this issue, although several cases are moving forward in the courts. Condemnors are well served to recognize that the condemnee may have a legitimately different perspective on value from their own. In many cases the difference will not be great and accommodation can be easily reached. When the divergence is great, however, decisions need to be made with full understanding of the differences between the points of view of the two parties.

Valuation of Contaminated Property for Ad Valorem Taxation

Unlike eminent domain, for which there is little judicial guidance at this time, the tax courts have a broadening (if not enlightening) record of valuing con-

17. Jay Dushoff and Denise Henslee, "When Eminent Domain 'Working Rules' Don't Work," *The Appraisal Journal* (July 1991): 429–435.

taminated property for the purposes of ad valorem taxation. The record has been well summarized in the writing of Gladstone,[18] Dunmire,[19] and McMurray and Pierce.[20]

The issues here, while they include the value-in-use and value-in-exchange questions discussed previously in the context of eminent domain, go on to add a significant emphasis on "liability or fault" as part of the determination of value. The courts are understandably reluctant to sanction tax reductions for parties that have fouled their own property, but this has put them in a difficult position with respect to owners who clearly have no responsibility for the contamination. Gladstone characterizes the courts as trying mightily to avoid the basic valuation issue while trying to maintain the local property tax base and to avoid rewarding polluters.[21] This is not an unreasonable set of goals but is unlikely to be a tenable strategy over the long run. He foresees an ad hoc evolution of the case law with a gradual move to a discounted cash flow (DCF) analysis of the sort discussed earlier in this article.

Conclusion

This article argues that valuation of contaminated property is a complex process that requires an understanding of 1) the nature of the problem; 2) how the problem is perceived; 3) the remediation, indemnification, and financing responses that can address the problem; and 4) the ultimate effect of these on the utility and marketability of the property.

Within this general framework, a specific valuation model was proposed in which the consequences of contamination were segregated into direct costs (e.g., loss of income, remediation, indemnification) and stigma. Stigma is defined to represent all of the risk, hazard, and uncertain consequences of contamination, which increase the costs of attracting capital to a contaminated or previously contaminated property.

Although a DCF framework frequently provides the most useful approach to the valuation of contaminated property, multiple regression and contingent valuation techniques increasingly allow appraisers to directly address the value of the contaminated property.

Judicial ambivalence between notions of value-in-use and market value are the source of considerable confusion in the valuation of contaminated property. This is evident in the determination of just compensation in condemnation proceeding as well as in the valuation of real property for ad valorem taxation. Because of the particularly distorting effect contamination has on market value, value-in-use is likely to become increasingly important in valuing contaminated property.

18. Robert A. Gladstone, "Contaminated Property: A Valuation Perspective," *Toxics Law Reporter* (November 1991): 798–802.

19. Thea D. Dunmire, "Real Estate Tax Valuations: Factoring in Environmental Impacts," *Environmental Finance* (1992): 461–472

20. Robert I. McMurray and David Pierce, "Environmental Remediation and Eminent Domain," *ALI-ABA Eminent Domain Seminar* (January 1992): 105–146

21. Gladstone, 798–802.

The Environmental Opinion: Basis for an Impaired Value Opinion

by Albert R. Wilson

Over the past several years the subject of how to value an environmentally impaired property has been discussed from a number of perspectives. The Appraisal Institute has issued "Guide Note 8" to the *Standards of Professional Appraisal Practice,* which advises appraisers not to exceed their training and expertise when appraising properties whose values may be adversely affected by environmental factors.

A number of related terms and phrases that have come into common use appear to have precise meanings but upon examination are anything but precise. In addition, the very legal and regulatory foundations of how environmental issues are resolved appear to be illogical and unfair. How can appraisers reasonably function under such conditions?

This article is the distillation of a number of years of experience both on the author's part and on the part of many environmental and appraisal professionals with whom the author has had extensive contact. The goal is to present a comprehensive view of what an environmental opinion must provide to support the appraisal opinion.

Myths

The following list dispels some of the myths associated with environmentally impaired property values.

1. The presence of an environmental risk devalues a property.

While this is often true, the mere presence of an environmental risk does not automatically imply devaluation. To devalue a property the environmental risk must: 1) result in a cost to remediate the problem; 2) result in an increased operating cost; and/or 3) result in a perception in the marketplace that the property is less desirable than a property without that environmental risk present. It should be noted that the presence of some environmental risks may enhance value in the proper circumstances. For example, a wetland, when preserved and utilized as a part of the amenities of a development, may tend to enhance value.

Albert R. Wilson is a specialist in the development of valuation opinions for the assignment of environmental impairment damages to real property and businesses. He received a BS in materials science and engineering form Northwestern University in Chicago, Illinois, and an MBA from Bowling Green State University in Bowling Green, Ohio. Mr. Wilson lectures, writes, and testifies regularly on the value impacts of environmental impairments on property.

This article originally appeared in the July 1994 issue of The Appraisal Journal.

2. Environmental risks that affect value are regulated.

This is patently false. Probably the simplest example is that of underground storage tanks (UST)—less than 35% of all USTs are regulated. Remediation costs, however, can be imposed on a property whether the tank from which the leak originated is regulated or not. In fact a regulated tank may impose less of a value penalty than an unregulated tank because state insurance funds may assist in the remediation of a leak from a regulated tank. Such funds may not be available for an unregulated tank.

3. The impaired value can be established through the use of the sales comparison approach.

Unfortunately, this is not the case. Each environmental impairment to value is as unique as a fingerprint, and generally in ways that are not obvious or amenable to adjustments. As an example consider two commercial office buildings built to the same structural plan, both containing spray-on asbestos applied to the same specifications, but in different political jurisdictions. One building was built for a single tenant, the other for speculative rental. There would likely be more walls, phone lines, and power lines in the second building than in the first, and it would not be unusual to find a lower level of maintenance in the second than in the first. The net result would be that the present value of the cost to deal with the asbestos would more heavily affect the second building. If the different political jurisdictions had different asbestos treatment rules, then the value would reflect this fact also.

4. An environmental risk in location A is also an environmental risk in location B.

This may not be true for two reasons. First, the political jurisdiction in which A is located may have developed more stringent requirements than B. Under the existing laws a city may have more stringent rules and regulations than the state, and state regulations may be more stringent than federal regulations. Second, an environmental risk is defined by the total risk system as outlined later in this article. The specific circumstances resulting in a threat to human health or the environment in one physical location may not be present in another location. More likely, the environmental risk may be present in both locations but not to the same degree, resulting in vastly different remediation plans and costs.

5. A Phase I audit will establish a purchaser as an "innocent purchaser."

This is a pleasant idea that dies hard. To the best of this author's knowledge and that of all of his associates, a purchaser of industrial or commercial property has never been held by the courts or the U. S. Environmental Protection Agency (EPA) to be an innocent purchaser. The innocent purchaser concept is thus far a "safe harbor with no water." The reason is that there is no established standard for what constitutes "all appropriate inquiry" under the Comprehensive Environmental Response, Compensation and Liability Act (CERCLA, Superfund).

6. A Phase I audit will provide absolute assurance that a property is "clean."

Like the idea of innocent purchaser, the idea that any Phase 1 audit will provide absolute assurance that a property is clean is a myth. An environmental investigation is an attempt to prove the unprovable, to prove that the needle is not in the haystack. It is logically and scientifically impossible to prove a negative hypothesis and regardless of how much time, energy, or resources are expended, absolute assurance is impossible.

7. The Phase I audit will provide the required information to establish the impaired value.

This is absolutely false except in the single case when the Phase I audit indicates that the property is unlikely to contain an environmental risk and the impaired and unimpaired values are therefore identical. The Phase I audit does not, cannot, and will not contain the information necessary to establish the impaired value.

Definitions

As stated, definitions in the environmental field are fuzzy at best, and certainly are subject to legal and professional controversy. For the purposes of this article I propose the following definitions.

Phase I environmental value assessment (Phase I EVA).

The Phase I EVA is designed to answer two questions: Is there a reasonable basis to suspect the presence of an environmental risk (the subject matter of the classic Phase I audit)? Are there environmental restrictions on the use of the property?[1]

Phase II EVA.

The Phase II EVA, given that the Phase I EVA has found a reasonable basis to suspect the presence of an environmental risk, is designed to demonstrate, to a reasonable degree of scientific certainty, whether the suspected environmental risk is or is not present. The reasonableness of the level of remaining uncertainty is a client decision. This definition follows the classic Phase II audit definition.

Phase III EVA.

If the phase II EVA has demonstrated the presence of an environmental risk, the Phase III is designed to accomplish the following objectives; 1) to quantify the type and extent of the environmental risk; 2) to develop a remediation plan that will be acceptable under the National Contingency Plan (NCP) or other governing rules and regulations; 3) to develop budget estimates for the implementation of the remediation plan; and 4) to identify any restrictions on use or incremental operating costs required to prevent or minimize future environmental liabilities. The first three items are normal parts of Phase III audits. Item 4 is specific to valuation and is rarely, if ever, a part of a traditional Phase III audit.

Environmental risk.

An environmental risk has four components parts: risk source, primary control mechanism, transport/secondary control mechanism, and target. Each of these components must be evaluated according to a specific set of protocols outlined in the NCP (a part of CERCLA) in order to determine if a risk exists and the appropriate response plan if so.

- The risk source is the source of potential damage to human health or the environment.

1. This was written prior to publication of the American Society for Testing and Materials (ASTM), "Standard Practice for Environmental Site Assessments," (ASTM E 1527-93), *Standards for Phase I Environmental Site Assessments* (Washington, D.C.: American Society for Testing and Materials, 1993). Within limits these standards directly address the questions outlined here.

- The primary control mechanism is the means by which the risk source is maintained under control to prevent damage to human health or the environment.
- The transport/secondary control mechanisms are the available means by which the risk source, given a failure of the primary control mechanism, may be transported to the immediate vicinity of the target. Secondary control mechanisms are natural or man-made obstructions contained within the transport mechanism that may retard the movement of the risk source.
- The target(s) may be human beings or sensitive environments such as nature preserves, wetlands, or endangered plant or animal species.

Environmental impairment (to value).
Assuming that an environmental risk exists, an environmental impairment to value may exist if the risk 1) restricts the use of the property; 2) imposes incremental ownership costs on the property; and/or 3) makes the property less desirable in the marketplace.

Uncertainty.
In a condition of uncertainty, an event cannot be assigned a probability of occurrence.

Risk.
In a condition of risk, an event can be assigned a probability of occurrence. Therefore, risk can be quantified while uncertainty cannot be quantified (although attempts can be made to estimate the magnitude or range of values for an uncertain event).

FIGURE 1 Environmental Risk System

Risk Source ⟶ Primary Control Mechanisms ⟶ Transport/Secondary Control Mechanism ⟶ Target(s)

Stigma.
The value impact of uncertainties. For the purposes of this discussion stigma shall refer to the value impact of environmentally related uncertainties—uncertainties resulting from the presence or assumed presence of an environmental risk.

Unimpaired value.
The unimpaired value of a property is the value considering all restrictions on use and costs of ownership other than those imposed by the presence of an environmental risk.

Impaired value.
The impaired value is derived from the unimpaired value according to the following relationship. It is the value giving due consideration to the impact of environmental risks known or assumed to be present:

$$I = U - C_{NCP} - C_R - C_F - M_U$$

where

I = Impaired value

$U =$ Unimpaired value

$C_{NCP} =$ Cost to implement the NCP-defined remediation plan

$C_R =$ Cost of restrictions on use and/or environmental liability prevention

$C_F =$ Impaired financing cost

$M_U =$ Intangible market factors

It should be noted that C_{NCP} will be the environmental equivalent of the "typical" construction cost. Many courts have held that the only recoverable environmental costs from a third party are those costs defined by application of the NCP.

Remediation.

Remediation as defined in the NCP and common usage can consist of one or more of the following methods for dealing with a specific environmental situation.

- *Do nothing.* This is not to be taken literally. The "do nothing" option consists of a determination that specific physical action is not required at the present time, but that continuous observation (as with an operations and maintenance program) may be required to identify changed circumstances that may require implementation of another method in the future to protect human health and/or the environment.

- *Repair.* The restoration of the primary control mechanism(s) to a functional state whereby the risk source may be maintained such that human health and/or the environment are protected.

- *Operations and maintenance program.* A specific, written program of daily functions, training, equipment, and discipline intended to provide observation of the environmental risk and the maintenance of the primary and man-made secondary control mechanisims.[2]

- *Isolation.* The prevention of access to a risk source except possibly by trained and equipped personnel. Isolation may be accomplished by something as simple as a fence, or by something as complex as a controlled-atmosphere structure.

- *Encapsulation.* The construction or application of a physically (to the risk source) impermeable membrane. The purpose of the encapsulation is to isolate the risk source from the transport mechanism and thereby from the targets.

- *Enclosure.* The construction of a physically impermeable and structurally sound barrier around the risk source and its primary control mechanism. The difference between encapsulation and enclosure is in the structural strength of the barrier.

- *Removal with disposal.* The physical removal of the risk source, usually involving the destruction of the primary control mechanism, and the disposal of the risk source in another location.[3]

- *Removal with destruction.* Destruction means the reduction or transformation of the risk source to non-risk elements or form. If it can be accomplished, the destruction of the risk source after removal is the only method for cutting off future liability, although it will do

2. Under the Occupational Safety and Health Administration's (OSHA) Worker Protection Rules an operations and maintenance program is now virtually required for almost any organization coming under OSHA or OSHA-equivalent jurisdiction.

3. Removal with disposal does not end the owner's (at the time of removal) financial risk; it freezes title to the risk source with that owner for as long as the risk source may exist in its new location. This may involve that owner in later Superfund liabilities even if the risk source is relatively benign.

Valuing Contaminated Properties

nothing about any liabilities associated with the past presence of the risk source or the actual removal and destruction activities. Generally removal with destruction is technically difficult and expensive.

Cost to control/cost-to-cure.
Especially with respect to soil, surface water, and groundwater contamination, the concept of a "cure" for an environmental impairment is essentially meaningless, at least over any reasonable economic time frame such as several decades. For this reason the use of the phrase "cost to cure" can be extremely misleading and the more accurate phrase "cost to control" should be applied to remediation activities. A careful examination of the major environmental laws such as CERCLA or the Resource Conservation and Recovery Act (RCRA) will clearly indicate that control is the objective, cure being implicitly if not explicitly recognized as a usually unattainable goal.

Impaired Value Opinion Development

In these definitions a new phrase was introduced—EVA. After much experience and research it has become obvious that the existing Phase I, II, and III audits, and even the new Phase I Environmental Site Assessment by the American Society for Testing and Materials (ASTM),[4] do not address the needs of appraisers. While they deal with specific environmental laws, rules, and regulations, only rarely do they address the issues of how environmental concerns will influence the costs of ownership, the highest and best use, or the restrictions on use that are the major concerns of appraisers. Value covers a much broader range of concerns than the environmental laws.

The ASTM Phase I Environmental Site Assessment is a case in point. A standard for an environmental site assessment to meet the requirements of "all appropriate inquiry " to establish "innocent purchaser" status under CERCLA is a welcome and highly important step toward regularizing commercial transactions. There should be no doubt that property owners informed that Superfund liability applies to a newly acquired property will have their whole day ruined, and certainly the value of the property will change if it becomes a listed site under Superfund. (Technically, the site will be a CERCLIS site until it has achieved a Hazard Ranking Score of 28.5 or greater, at which point it becomes a National Priorities List [NPL][5] or Superfund site.) Even without Superfund status, however, a property may be rendered substantially less valuable without a particle of a hazardous substance present because of environmentally driven restrictions on use. This is one issue among many other value issues only glancingly dealt with by the ASTM standards.

The ASTM standards also define a time in the past (1940) before which investigation, while recommended if information is readily available, is not required. While this may limit liability under CERCLA, the property owner may still face large remediation costs and an unmarketable property because of something that occurred earlier than the cutoff date. The major point, however, is that all parties must recognize that a Phase I assessment cannot develop the detailed information required to establish the impaired value of a property. The balance of this article will outline the data requirements for establishing the impaired value, and the likely sources of these data.

4. ASTM E 1527-93.

5. CERCLIS (Comprehensive Environmental Response, Compensation and Liability Index of Sites) listing means that there is some basis to believe that the site may contain an uncontrolled or threatened uncontrolled release of a hazardous substance. CERCLIS is a precursor to NPL status. A site on the NPL is a site eligible for remediation under Superfund, a highly undesirable status for any property owner.

Chapter 2: *The Environmental Opinion*

Development of the Unimpaired Value Opinion (*U*)

The unimpaired value opinion is the basis for the development of an impaired value opinion, should one be required. An experienced appraiser with extensive local knowledge is best equipped for this task. It can be accomplished in much the same way as value opinions are typically developed, using the sales comparison, the income, and the cost approaches, but with some cautions.

The cost approach is probably the least vulnerable to distortions resulting from environmental impairments provided that it is recognized that typical construction may be considerably different from what has previously been considered typical in the marketplace. Assume, for example, that an industrial facility is to be constructed on virgin land in a municipality. The local publicly owned treatment works (POTW, or sewage plant to most of us) will have a National Pollution Discharge Elimination System (NPDES) permit that allows it to accept and handle specific quantities and types of wastes. If the industrial plant will discharge wastes other than those the POTW is permitted to handle, or in quantities greater than those allowed, then the typical construction of the industrial facility will have to include a pretreatment works that will be required to have its own NPDES permit. If the facility will be processing liquid hazardous materials it may need to have a stainless steel floor drain system and special overflow catch basins. It also may need to pretreat storm water and have a specially constructed area for the storage of solid and liquid hazardous substances and wastes. All of these items would be considered typical construction in light of current environmental rules.

It is possible that the POTW may place a restriction on the commercial or industrial facility by not having sufficient capacity to accept additional sewage of any type. In 1990, the Ohio Environmental Protection Agency (EPA) prohibited any new connection to Dublin, Ohio's, sewer system until its capacity problems were resolved, a situation that lasted almost a year.

Establishing the unimpaired value with the income approach is more complicated. Specifically, the existing income and expense streams may be influenced by the presence of hazardous substances through depressed rental rates or inflated expenses. Ideally, the expenses associated with environmental issues in the operation of a property should have their own line item in the budgets and financial records, for example for the operations and maintenance program noted previously. Unfortunately owners do not yet recognize the usefulness of specific identification of environmental costs as a liability-reduction device, both for themselves and their lenders.[6] This of course assumes that an owner is responding properly to the presence of an environmental risk. Appraisers must exercise care to ensure that these income offsets and expense increases are identified and adjustments are made to arrive at the unimpaired value. Otherwise the impaired value opinion may include a second adjustment for the same items, effectively lowering the value of the property twice for the same concerns.

The sales comparison approach may cause the most problems in establishing the unimpaired value because comparables may not be comparable. How is it possible to know for sure whether the comparable sale prices have an adjustment, downward or upward, for an undisclosed envi-

6. In June 1993 the Securities and Exchange Commission published "Staff Accounting Bulletin 93," *Federal Register,* v. 58 (Washington, D.C.: Department of the Treasury, Office of the Comptroller of the Currency, June 14, 1993): 32843, requiring disclosure of environmental liabilities and the methods for developing the amount to be disclosed.

ronmental problem? An owner may be reluctant to reveal that a plume of contaminated groundwater underlies a property to anyone other than a buyer, and the buyer may be motivated to pay a premium price for the property because it is the buyer's plume. If the environmental problem were known without detailed information on the specific cost to remediate that specific problem, it should be obvious that an adjustment to sale price would be difficult to make unless one of the parties to the transaction were willing to reveal the amount of the adjustment.

A knowledgeable local appraiser is critical to establishing the unimpaired value of a property, especially when the local marketplace's reaction to an environmental concern tends to be strong or the local authorities are contemplating a change in the environmental criteria for properties and the sales comparison approach is to be used. The unimpaired value opinion must be just that—the value of the subject as if no environmental impairments exist. If it is not, the relationship for establishing the impaired value opinion will be compromised.

The Cost of Remediation as Established Through the National Contingency Plan (C_{NCP})

It would be nice to be able to provide a single impaired value opinion for a property as opposed to a range of impaired values. Unfortunately this is not going to be possible unless a client is prepared to pay for Phase III-level work and to wait a period of months—if then. Short of Phase III work it is only possible to provide a range of values that, depending on the quality of the Phase I and II work, may be relatively broad. This is a result of the uncertainties involved in developing estimates based on incomplete information in a number of critical areas, as will be discussed next. Prior to a Phase III, the situation is roughly equivalent to asking a contractor to estimate the cost of a building before the specific site is known or the floor plan or structural/ architectural design has been implemented.

The NCP[7] sets forth the protocols for determining how the human health/environmental risks will be mitigated. Generally these protocols require the following steps.

- Characterization of the environmental risk. Specifically, this means the identification of each of the risk sources present; the identification of the primary control mechanisms and their current and likely future status with respect to the protection of human health or the environment; the analysis of the transport and secondary control mechanisms to determine their efficiency in bringing the risk source and the targets into proximity to each other; and the identification of targets, whether human or sensitive environments.

- Analysis of the environmental risks to determine if an actual threat to human health or the environment exists as well as the extent or severity of that threat.

- Identification of the Applicable and Relevant and Appropriate Requirements (ARARs) that will govern the objectives and methods for site remediation. Simply identifying the federal, state, and local remediation requirements is a major task and may consume hundreds of hours of risk assessment and site engineering work and require large quantities of analytical data. In the simplest cases of the

---

7. The National Contingency Plan (NCP) is set forth in the *Code of Federal Regulations* at 40 CFR, Part 300.

remediation of asbestos in commercial office buildings or the remediation of leaking underground storage tanks, the need formally identify the ARARs has been dealt with through codification of the responses required for these common situations. The uncommon situations require far more highly specialized analysis from health risk professionals, engineers, attorneys, and others.

- Development of risk/benefit estimates and implementation budgets for each of the available remediation alternatives.

- Selection of the most appropriate remediation strategy based on the following objectives in order of priority.

1. Protection of human health or the environment
2. Technological feasibility
3. Economic feasibility
4. Local considerations developed through public hearings or specialized requirements such as the capabilities of the local POTW or landfill

From the appraisal viewpoint this process is critical and produces the value of C_{NCP} needed in the impaired value relationship. From the owner's viewpoint something even more important may result. If litigation for recovery of remediation costs is even remotely contemplated it will be necessary to demonstrate that this process has been used to establish the methods and thereby the recoverable costs for remediation.

The NCP process will provide several key items of information to an owner and an appraiser. First, it provides the estimated costs and timing for remediation activities from which a present value of remediation costs can be calculated. Second, the process should provide a clear outline of restrictions on use resulting from the presence of an environmental risk at all stages of the projected remediation—before, during, and after. Third, the process should reveal some specialized areas of concern for an owner and an appraiser, particularly in the evaluation of marketplace uncertainties. This may include the possibility of litigation against the owner for contamination of neighboring properties or damage to individuals or natural resources.

As mentioned, the development of the value C_{NCP} is equivalent to the specification of the typical cost of an improvement, and all other remediation costs are either deficient or superadequate for the purposes of an appraisal. The value of C_{NCP} can only be developed through the formal consideration of the NCP for the specific site, called a Remedial Investigation/Feasibility Study (RI/FS), or through a less formal analysis that nevertheless considers all of the same issues. The minimum information required to develop C_{NCP} is normally that produced through the Phase III analysis of the subject property—Phase I or II data will be insufficient for anything other than an approximation over a broad range because of the large degree of uncertainty.

Cost of Restrictions on Use (C_R)

The number and type of environmental restrictions on use is large and increasing. The Clean Air Act provides for a system of discharge permits that in certain local jurisdictions may extend to the local body shop or drycleaner and specify the annual quantity of particular substances that the facility may release into the atmosphere. If the facility exceeds the permitted level, either technological means must be employed to reduce emissions below the specified level, the facility must purchase from another facility additional discharge capacity, or the facility must restrict its operations. The permit itself thus takes on a value related to the demand for the right to discharge the substance and the cost of the technology to reduce discharges of that substance. If the cost of discharging is high, the highest and best use of the property may be restricted to some upper limit of discharge capacity, and thereby some upper limit of productive use.

In a similar vein although without the tradability aspects, the NPDES permits may significantly restrict the upper capacity limit of a property's highest and best use, or preclude certain uses altogether as a result of a lack of discharge capacity for liquid wastes. In a different category, the ability of a firm to dispose of its solid waste may be severely limited by the capacity of landfills or other storage facilities to accept the waste. The local environmental lobby may also provide limiting factors on the use to which a specific property may be put, with or without formal regulatory restrictions.

Restrictions on use also may take the form of wetlands or sensitive environment concerns, and these limitations may be in the form of permanent or semipermanent impediments to development. The cost of development of a property containing a wetlands will be significantly greater than the cost of development for a property without wetlands if the wetlands must be disturbed in any way. The cost of simply obtaining a 404 Dredge and Fill Permit from the Army Corps of Engineers can be substantial in terms of both direct engineering costs to support an application and the delay in development time. If the wetlands are to be destroyed, mitigation in the form of the construction of replacement wetlands at a ratio of from 1:1 to greater than 1:3 (area destroyed versus area constructed as a replacement) may be required, depending on the jurisdiction and type of wetlands. Replacement may not be possible, thereby precluding the intended use. Replacement wetlands may also carry an ongoing maintenance cost to the owner of the original wetlands property that can be both substantial and perpetual. Endangered species may totally preclude development. It should be remembered that endangered species include both fauna and flora.

The Clean Water Act, the Clean Air Act, the Solid Waste Disposal Act, the Endangered Species Act, the National Environmental Policy Act if Federal Funds are involved, the Toxic Substance Control Act, and others may all place restrictions on how a property can be operated and its ultimate productive capacity. The RCRA will impose operating restrictions on businesses generating a quantity, sometimes a surprisingly small quantity, of hazardous substances or wastes as defined in that law.

Each of these laws, and others that while not specifically environmental laws have environmental components, may generate a need to provide long-term preventative measures. This is especially the case in light of the fact that insurance to cover environmental problems is generally not available, necessitating the accrual of a self-insurance fund to cover this contingency. Whether such a fund should be treated as a business expense or as a capital investment is an accounting and tax decision, but the need for the fund is obvious and the present value of this reasonably anticipated future expenditure will have an influence on the value of the property.

Chapter 2: *The Environmental Opinion*

The Impact of Marketplace Uncertainties

To this point the analysis has concerned issues that are presumably quantifiable. They are only partially quantifiable, however, for reasons to be explained shortly. Until remediation has been accomplished there are a great number of areas mentioned previously where only rough estimates can be provided regardless of the amount of time spent in investigation or analysis. It is for this reason that Peter Patchin and others have argued that prior to the completion of remediation the marketplace may extract a premium over the estimated cost of remediation of as much as 100% to 200% of that estimated cost . The premium is based on the esitmated cost of remediation, not on the unimpaired value of the subject. There is no relationship between the cost of remediation and the unimpaired value of the property and an appraiser is well advised to keep this principle in mind.

Market factors may also indicate that the impact of the estimated costs is not as great as the estimate because of offsetting factors such as the demand for the subject in the local marketplace, the availability of substitutes, the perceived quality of cost estimates, or the perceived value of indemnifications and warranties by the seller, and not infrequently the degree of familiarity in the local marketplace with respect to the specific environmental condition. These factors may all work toward reduction of the total impact on value.

Stigma, as the term has been used by other writers in the field,[8] implies a negative. This may be the case in some situations, but the term "market factors" used here is intended to imply that positive offsets may be possible.

With respect to stigma, or the negative side of offsetting market factors, several points arising from recent field experience should be made. First, stigma resulting from environmental impairments does exist and is supported by excellent data in specific cases. Second, the basic concept of stigma is being badly abused, particularly by buyers of properties in an effort to obtain lower prices from the sellers. Third, the positive market factors are often ignored in developing an opinion concerning stigma. Based on what is currently known, market factors may be broken down into a series of component factors that must be dealt with in the appraisal of an impaired property. These are:

$$M_U = f(U_E,\ U_R,\ U_M,\ U_F,\ C_t)$$

Read $M_U = f(\ )$ as: Market factors are a function of the variables inside the parentheses, where

U_E = Uncertainty concerning engineering estimates of cost to control

U_R = Uncertainty concerning regulatory requirements, present and future

U_M = Uncertainty concerning the marketplace's reaction to the presence of an impairment in a given condition. This may result in a positive or negative offset

U_F = Uncertainty concerning the financial marketplace's reaction to the presence of an impairment in a given condition

C_t = Change in the marketplace's reaction to the presence, or past presence, of an impairment over time

8. James A. Chalmers and Scott A. Roeher, " Issues in the Valuation of Contaminated Property," *The Appraisal Journal* (January 1993): 28–41; Bill Mundy, "The Impact of Hazardous Materials on Real Property Value," *The Appraisal Journal* (April 1992): 155–162; Bill Mundy, "Stigma and Value," *The Appraisal Journal* (January 1992): 7–13; Bill Mundy, " The Impact of Hazardous and Toxic Material on Property Value: Revisited," *The Appraisal Journal* (October 1992): 463–471; Peter J. Patchin, "Valuation of Contaminated Properties," *The Appraisal Journal* (January 1988): 7–16; Peter J. Patchin, " Contaminated Properties—Stigma Revisited," *The Appraisal Journal* (April 1991): 167–172; and O.R. Colan Associates, Inc., *The Effect of Contamination on the Market Value of Property* (Research report prepared under contract to the Federal Highway Administration and currently in an unreleased draft form).

Valuing Contaminated Properties

U_E—The uncertainty concerning engineering estimates for the cost to control or cure. Although an amazing number of appraisers do not wish to hear about this, refusing to hear about it unfortunately will not make the problem go away. The problem is that the engineering estimate is not for the cost to build a building. Typically a remediation project, especially one involving soils or groundwater, is actually conducted on the basis of "dig until there is nothing to dig." Punching a few holes in the ground in an effort to determine where the contamination is will not provide more than an approximation of the true final volume of soils to be removed and treated, for example. Therefore stigma must contain an element that represents this uncertainty in the engineering estimate versus the audited, after-completion cost.

U_R—In addition to the uncertainty concerning engineering estimates there is uncertainty concerning regulatory decisions that govern a specific situation. Unfortunately, regulatory decisions are not based on pure science, but on science, politics, and sometimes the individual reaction of the specific regulator assigned to the case. Further, regulations change with time, generally to a more stringent view of what is clean. This may necessitate a change in the scope of remediation work or a complete overhaul of the work. Also, regulatory decisions are contingent, not final, decisions. Clients often ask whether a regulatory agency will issue a "clean bill of health" after the work has been completed to the agency's specifications, and unfortunately the answer is always no. The impact of regulatory uncertainty on the value of the property thus must be considered.

U_M—The uncertainty concerning the marketplace's reaction to the presence (past or present) of an environmental impairment is the most often discussed component of stigma. Some may, with justice, argue that it *is* stigma, and is comparable to the reaction of the marketplace to a deficiency. This view may overlook the importance of the other factors identified here.

Marketplace uncertainty is generally a function of several factors: 1) the strength of demand for the subject property in the marketplace (stronger demand, less uncertainty); and 2) the knowledge of the buyer relative to the environmental impairment (greater familiarity, less uncertainty).

U_F—There is also uncertainty concerning the financial marketplace's reaction to the presence of an environmental impairment. As reported by a number of studies, most notably those performed by Mundy & Associates, the financial marketplace has a widely varying reaction to the presence of an environmental impairment. The reaction appears to depend on a number of objective and subjective factors including 1) the financial strength of the institution; 2) the status of the subject property's local economy and market demand (U_M); 3) the type and extent of the environmental impairment; 4) the perceived quality of the technical analysis of the environmental impairment (U_E); 5) the perceived status of the regulatory attitudes toward the impairment (U_R); and 6) the visibility and quality of the impairment's remediation.

C_t—The impact of stigma on the value of a property has a strong time-dependent relationship. Both Peter Patchin and Bill Mundy have been exploring this relationship in various articles and presentations over the past few years, and understanding of the time-dependent nature of stigma is growing. In Figure 2, this is summarized using a graph that follows Bill Mundy's work.[9]

9. See Mundy, "The Impact of Hazardous and Toxic Material on Property Value: Revisited."

Assume for the purposes of discussion that a property has an unimpaired value of U at time t_o and that some time later it is discovered that the property has a case of the polygoshawfuls. Ignoring the issues of C_R and C_F for the moment to simplify the discussion, at first the marketplace finds itself unfamiliar with polygoshawful and the severity of the contamination is not known, so no one is willing to purchase or finance the property. The new market value I_1 at this time t_1 cannot be greater than zero (no willing buyer, possibly no willing seller, and no financing, therefore at least no *market* value). This may be thought of as a pure stigma effect, S_1, and primarily depends on the marketplace's reaction to all of the uncertainties.

Figure 2 Impaired Value Versus Time

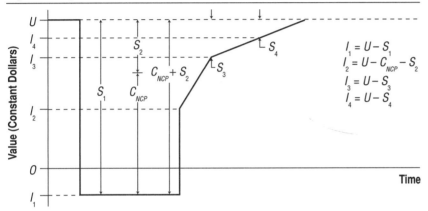

This condition will extend for some period of time, generally until the extent of the problem has become reasonably quantified (e.g., until the cost for remediation under the NCP has been established). At this point the value of the property becomes I_2. I_2 is greater than I_1 because some of the uncertainty has been resolved (e.g., the estimated cost to deal with the problem, C_{NCP}, is known).

In general, it should be noted that I_2 is still less than the unimpaired value U minus the estimated cost to deal with the problem C_{NCP}. The difference is accounted for as the new stigma amount, S_2. The reason for the difference is that while some of the uncertainties have been resolved, other uncertainties continue to exist. The marketplace still does not know whether the actual cost to deal with the problem has been correctly estimated (U_E); whether the regulators will approve the remediation program (U_R); whether the property will be truly clean of if the definition of clean will change, rendering the property once again unclean (U_R again); whether lenders will lend or on what terms (U_F); and so on.

When the remediation activity required under the NCP has been completed, a new market value is established, I_3. This new value is likely to be greater than $I_2 + C_{NCP}$ because again some of the residual uncertainties will have been resolved, particularly the uncertainty in the engineering estimate (U_C) and some (although not all) of the uncertainty in the regulatory reaction (U_R). The uncertainty in the marketplace's reaction to the contamination (U_M), even though cleanup has been affected, will still remain to some extent, as will the uncertainty concerning financing (U_F), resulting in a new stigma amount, S_3. From this time t_3 to a point in time

t_4 in the future, these uncertainties appear to dissipate and the property achieves a new market value of I_4 that, while not quite back to the original unimpaired value U, is close to that value leaving a new stigma of S_4. Indications are that the time required to achieve this status is three to five years after the completion of remeditaion.

After time t_4 the property will probably gradually close the gap between the value I_4 and the unimpaired value U. That is, the magnitude of S_4 will shrink toward zero. This gap may never completely close, however, if there is an incremental transaction cost levied against the property for increased "due diligence" on the part of each new buyer because of the past existence of an environmental risk. There may be other factors influencing the magnitude of stigma, but it is hoped that this paints a somewhat detailed picture of the manner in which stigma operates in influencing the impaired value of a property.

As noted, stigma is only one aspect of the market factors. The forces of demand for the subject, the perception of the quality of indemnifications, and the degree of the public's familiarity with the environmental concern may operate to offset the negative implications of stigma.

Impaired Financing Cost (C_F)

At this point an appraiser should be able to establish or estimate any financing cost penalties associated with the property. The report of the environmental experts and a knowledge of the unimpaired financing cost should provide the basis for developing a clear and accurate picture of how financing institutions are likely to view the situation. In light of the new lender liability rules promulgated by the EPA, the position of the lender is beginning to clarify, although not necessarily to the extent that lenders would like, and some assurances regarding lender liability have been provided. The key parameter is that if a lender does not become overly involved in the management of the debtor's business to the extent that the management of environmental risks is influenced, the lender can be reasonably assured of maintaining the "secured creditor" exemption offered under Superfund.[10]

While the lender liability rule and the *Nurad* decision are important, credit concerns may be more important in lender decisions. The provision of several key items of information developed in the foregoing C_{NCP} and C_R analyses may positively influence the credit decision and the financing costs. For example, if the lender knew that the debtor's budget planning included provisions for the remediation of existing environmental risks, provisions for protection against future additional environmental risks, a self-insurance fund to provide financing for emergencies, and similar information, a more positive response may be forthcoming. It is even possible that the more forward-thinking lenders may choose to assist in the financing of such programs and may at least recognize that the development and implementation of these specific budgets can provide key information on what a lender must not disturb if involvement in the debtor's financial operations should become necessary.

In any event, the willingness of lenders or others in the financial marketplace to finance and environmentally risky situation, and the terms of that financing compared to the terms of financing for a similar but nonrisky situation, will allow for the development of the last key piece of informa-

10. *Nurad, Inc. v. William E. Hooper & Sons, Co.,* CA 4, No. 91-1775, as reported in Bureau of National Affairs, *Toxics Law Reporter* (Washington, D.C.: Bureau of National Affairs, November 20, 1991): 757.

tion necessary to the establishment of the impaired value opinion—the incremental cost of financing. Both debt and equity holders have a significant role in this part of the analysis as both may demand increased rates of return to compensate for increased risks. An appraiser should seek to quantify and document this area to the greatest extent reasonable under the circumstances.

Conclusion

The impaired value opinion, defined as:

$$I = U - C_{NCP} - C_R - C_F - M_U$$

will be a difficult and complex appraisal assignment if something more than a broad range of value possibilities is to be provided to the client, and much of the information required is simply not within the area of normal appraisal data development. An appraiser must rely heavily on complex technical assessments performed by other experts who are not generally familiar with the broad scope of information required to establish value. To deal with these concerns it would seem that appraisers should follow several practices with respect to both clients and the suppliers of information on environmental impacts.

With respect to clients, appraisers should make the following points clear from the beginning.

- An unimpaired value opinion can be rendered subject to the quality of verifiable data available within each of the approaches used to establish value.

- A so-called Phase I audit will not allow an appraiser to express an impaired value opinion and is unlikely to provide critical information about restrictions on the highest and best use resulting from environmental restrictions on use. Further, the Phase I audit and even the ASTM Phase I Environmental Site Assessment are only part of the basic information required to determine whether an environmental impairment to value exists.

- Environmental experts must be retained by the client, and analytical investigations must be conducted to a level of assurance acceptable to the client that will provide reasonable quantitative estimates of the remediation plan, budgets, and use restrictions on the subject property. Without these plans, budgets, and use restrictions it is not possible to provide a reasonable range of estimated impaired values for the subject property.

- Until the completion of remediation it will only be possible to specify a range of values, possibly with a most likely value, for the impaired value opinion. The breadth of the range of values will totally depend on the quality and completeness of the environmental expert's work, and is not within the control of an appraiser.

To support the development of C_{NCP} to cover expenditures for existing environmental impairments, C_R to cover future expenditures, C_F to estimate the incremental cost of financing, and S to estimate the impact of uncertainties on the marketplace's perception of value, an environmental expert must provide to an appraiser the following key assurances and information based on that expert's work.

- Assurance that all reasonable efforts have been expended within the constraints of time, available resources, and defined scope of work as set forth by the client to identify the environmental risks associated with the property, and all reasonably identifiable environmental constraints on the use or operation of the property.

- Assurance that at least an informal analysis of the existing situation has been performed in reasonable conformance with the NCP or its applicable equivalent, and that the expert's budgets and recommendations reasonably conform with the NCP requirements.

- A budget, including expenditure timing that may extend 20 to 30 years into the future, which covers the planned response actions for dealing with the existing environmental impairments.

- A budget for the operations and maintenance program that will almost certainly be required for any commercial or industrial property. This may be limited in form to the costs for the owner to reasonably ensure that tenants are complying with all applicable environmental laws. Because the owner of the property is the first party that will be held responsible without regard to who actually created the problem, however, this is a reasonable cost of ownership.

- A budget to accrue funds for emergency response to environmental problems. This is essentially the provision of a self-insurance fund and will be highly dependent on the specific property situation and use.

- A budget for the implementation of needed upgrades to the property to bring it into compliance with applicable environmental laws and regulations and to minimize future liabilities. This will generally be a capital expenditure budget and may be an integral part of the construction costs for a new facility. An appraiser's concern will be to recognize whether these expenditures are now a necessary part of the typical improvement under the specific circumstances.

With respect to market factors, environmental experts should provide quantitative information on the sensitivity of their estimates to changes in fundamental assumptions such as the quantity of materials to be remediated, changes in remediation costs or restrictions on use if the contaminated is more or less severe than indicated, the probability of the acceptance of the remediation plan by the governing authorities, and an estimate as to the possibility that at the completion of remediation no further contamination will be discovered at a later date or that the rules governing the cleanliness of the site will change in a manner that will result in re-remediation. It should be remembered that these will be expressions of uncertain future events; at best they will be highly qualified and qualitative, and an appraiser will have to form an opinion as to how the value of the property will be perceived by the marketplace under these circumstances. Not to be ignored are the market factors that may act to mitigate the negative aspects.

Emerging Approaches to Impaired Property Valuation

by Albert R. Wilson

Since the late 1980s, a number of papers have focused on techniques for the valuation of real property having environmental impairments. This paper examines current thought on this subject and provides some background on related concepts. The "engineering impaired value model" is introduced as both a complement to the case study approach,[1] and a quantitative business value impact assessment tool. Topovalue mapping as applied to a neighboring property and other geographically dependent value analysis problems is also introduced.

In order that the valuer may acquire a fuller understanding of the issues related to the valuation of properties having environmental impairments, the following definitions are provided.

Environmental Impairment: An environmental impairment results when the presence of an environmental risk has a negative economic impact on property. The impact of an environmental risk need not be negative. For example, if a wetland is used as an amenity in a development, the wetland may enhance the value of the subject and simultaneously present an environmental risk.

Environmental Risk: An environmental risk results when four components interact in a manner that results in a substantive risk to human beings or sensitive environments. The environmental risk system may be described as follows:

Risk Source: A risk source is something that, if allowed to come into sufficient proximity to the target, may damage it. Risk sources include hazardous substances, hazardous wastes, and human activities. Human activities are a particular concern with respect to endangered species and sensitive environments.

Primary Control Mechanism: A primary control mechanism acts to prevent the risk source from entering the transport mechanism and becoming an actual—as opposed to a potential—threat to the target.

Transport/Secondary Control Mechanisms: A transport mechanism is the means by which a risk source may come into proximity to the target. A

Albert R. Wilson of Parker, Colorado, is a specialist in the development of valuation opinions for the assignment of environmental impairment damages to real property. He holds a BS in materials science engineering from Northwestern University, Evanston, Illinois, and an MBA from Bowling Green State University, Ohio.

This article originally appeared in the April 1996 issue of The Appraisal Journal.

---

1. Peter J. Patchin, MAI, "Contaminated Properties and the Sales Comparison Approach," *The Appraisal Journal* (July 1994): 402–409.

FIGURE 1 Environmental Risk System

Risk Source $\longrightarrow$ Primary Control Mechanism $\longrightarrow$ Transport/Secondary Control Mechanisms $\longrightarrow$ Target

secondary control mechanism may operate within the transport mechanism to retard or prevent movement.

Target: The target is an entity that may be damaged by the risk source. A target can be a human being, an endangered species, or a wetland for example.

Example of an Environmental Risk System: Suppose there is an above-ground fuel oil storage tank on a hill overlooking a river. The fuel oil is the risk source; the tank is the primary control mechanism; a transport mechanism is gravity; a secondary control mechanism is the dike surrounding the tank; and a target is the river. Note that under the Comprehensive Environmental Response, Compensation and Liability Act (CERCLA, or Superfund), fuel oil is not a hazardous substance, and under the Resource Conservation and Recovery Act (RCRA), fuel oil is not hazardous waste. A risk source need not be legally defined as a hazardous substance or a hazardous waste although it is still a source of environmental risk according to the definition used in this paper.

With respect to impact on property values, environmental risks may be analyzed in terms of three categories of impairment. Each category has a different set of value-impacting characteristics and frequently requires different valuation approaches.

Contained Impairments: These are environmental risks wholly contained within well-defined and easily recognized boundaries. Probably the best-known example would be asbestos in a commercial office building. For valuation purposes, the key characteristics are that the environmental risk can be measured quite accurately, and an estimate of the mitigation cost can be developed that will closely approximate the actual mitigation cost.

Uncontained Impairment: These are environmental risks not contained within distinct, well-defined, and easily identified boundaries. An example would be a hazardous substance that has contaminated soils and groundwater. For valuation purposes, the key characteristic is that the extent of the environmental risk cannot be estimated with precision resulting in a possibly very wide variance between estimated and actual remediation costs. Further, it is almost impossible to achieve total mitigation of the condition, particularly over a short period of time.

Indirect Impairments: Value impacts, if any, result when a target is in proximity to a known risk source. No risk source is present on the subject property. An indirect impairment is generally a function of marketplace reactions.

Two additional definitions are essential.

Unimpaired Value: The unimpaired value is the value of the subject, assuming no environmental risks are present. The unimpaired value may be established using the three approaches to value as long as the valuer screens the comparables, income and expense, and cost data to ensure that environmental offsets are not included in the data.

Impaired Value: This is the value of the subject, given the presence of the environmental risk. The Impaired Value is related to the Unimpaired Value through the following general relationship.

Impaired Value = Unimpaired Value LESS Remediation Costs and Stigma

Chapter 2: *Emerging Approaches*

To complete the background, it is necessary to understand several additional points. First, the reaction of the marketplace to the presence of an environmental risk is not always rational. Fear of damage may not be based on a rational assessment of the situation but can, nevertheless, negatively influence the value of a property. In contrast, buyers may ignore rational assessments of environmental risks and their possible consequences and pay a price approximating unimpaired market value for property having significant risks. These reactions are in large part a function of demand for the subject, the buyer's familiarity with the environmental risk, and a lack of understanding of the financial and environmental consequences of the presence of the risk, among other factors.

Another important point to understand is the unusual nature of ownership of an environmental risk. An environmental risk, or more properly, the risk source, belongs to at least one of the following entities, possibly simultaneously:

- The owner of the risk source at the time of release.
- The owner of the property on which the risk source was released.
- The property on which the risk source was released.

The last statement may require some explanation. If title to the property is transferred, then title to the risk source passes to the new owner. But note that title to the risk source is also shared with previous owner(s) on a strict joint and several basis under CERCLA. If the risk source is partially removed then title to the risk source as it relates to the portion removed becomes frozen with the owner(s) at the time of removal, and a new owner of the property will acquire title to only that portion of the risk source remaining on the subject.

Note also the phrase "...on which the risk source was released." If a risk source is released on a parcel but a portion later migrates or moves to another parcel, liability for the risk source present on the second parcel remains with the first. Under CERCLA, at the time of release a "facility" was created. A facility[2] is defined to include all of the air, soils, and waters contaminated by the risk source. A new owner of the originating property also acquires the facility. Put another way, title to the facility runs with the source property.

This fact gives rise to two additional definitions.

Source Property: A source property is the property on which the release of the risk source occurred. The source property has strict joint and several liability under CERCLA for the remediation costs of the facility created by the release without regard to legal parcel boundaries.

Non-Source Property: A nonsource property may contain a part of the facility created by the release of a risk source, but the owner of the nonsource property does not generally have liability for the costs of remediation.

The valuer would do well to keep these two definitions in mind whenever dealing with impaired property as the consequences of the existence of the impairment on value are very different between source and nonsource properties. Unfortunately the literature, case studies, and "comparable" property data have not always clearly identified whether a given property is a source or nonsource property.

This complex risk source and facility ownership situation is frequently misunderstood. An owner of a nonsource property, which nevertheless contains a part of a facility but having no their relationship to the risk source, does not generally have any financial liability with respect to remediation.

---

2. "Facility" is defined broadly to include, *inter alia*, "any site or area where a hazardous substance has...come to be located." 42 USC 9601 (9)(B). In construing the term "facility," courts have emphasized repeatedly that Congress intended this term to be interpreted broadly. See, e.g., *U.S. v. Northeastern Pharmaceutical and Chemical Co.,* (NEPACCO) 810 F.2d 726,743; 25 ERC 1385 (CA 8, 1986) cert. denied, 484 U.S. 848, 26 ERC 1856 (1987). The cases concerning this issue uniformly state that as long as a hazardous substance is present at a site in question, the site will be considered a facility. EDDG 101.3(a).

There may be other impacts on the nonsource property owner, but direct responsibility for the cost of cleanup is not one of them. Virtually all of the discussion that follows is directed toward the source property, and many issues associated with the liability imposed on the source property are not germane to the nonsource property.

As a last set of background points, note that the liability associated with the presence of an environmental risk can only rarely be discharged in the sense of a mortgage or tax lien, and indemnification of a buyer by the seller may only be partially successful. CERCLA explicitly provides that the federal government is not obligated to recognize any private liability transfer mechanism such as warranties, indemnifications and hold-harmless agreements. Note also that the courts have held that CERCLA liability is perpetually retroactive and prospective. Further, no agency will absolutely and unconditionally certify that a property is free of an environmental liability, particularly in the case of uncontained impairments, even though extensive remediation work indicates successful removal of the risk source.[3]

Contained Impairment Valuation Techniques

In many respects, valuing a property having a contained impairment is relatively straightforward and generally within the range of appraisal experience. Suppose that during the course of examining the subject the appraiser notices a large cracked beam apparently supporting a portion of the structure. The presence of the cracked beam would drive the property's value down because most purchasers would require the seller to repair the beam or insist on having funds reserved from the unimpaired value to cover the estimated cost of repairs.

Except for certain kinds of risk sources—such as PCBs which have a tendency to penetrate the building materials—many forms of contained environmental risks are hardly different from the cracked beam for valuation purposes. It is necessary to obtain a competent estimate of the cost of remediation and to adjust the unimpaired value accordingly. Provided that the risk source is one with which the marketplace is familiar and to which it has become adjusted, little more is required.

The use of comparable sales should, however, be viewed cautiously. The cost of dealing with asbestos may be very different from one building to the next. The cost of removal is primarily a function of labor cost, and removing asbestos from steel decks is much less time consuming than doing so from bar joists or poured concrete.

One must also consider the issue of "stigma," or the negative impact of intangible factors. There are a number of sources for intangible impacts—for example, the unusual nature of ownership of a risk source. If asbestos is removed from a building the owner at the time of removal will forever hold title to the removed asbestos. If the removed asbestos ends up in a site that must be remediated under CERCLA, the owner at the time of removal will be asked to contribute toward the cost of the site remediation because of the asbestos. This perpetual liability risk can influence value.

In general, intangible impacts are a function of several factors such as the following:

- The demand for the subject in the marketplace and its corollary, the availability of substitutes. (The stronger the demand and the fewer the number of available substitutes, the weaker the impact will be.)

3. As an example, consider the following form of the letter used by the Broward County, Florida, Department of Natural Resources Protection: "The Broward County Department of Natural Resource Protection (DNRP) has received and reviewed the (type of report) __ dated __ for the above referenced site. The __ is acceptable. This case has been reclassified to inactive based solely on information submitted by your consultant...Should additional information become available which indicates that the site status has changed, DNRP reserves the right to reclassify the site to active and to require further investigation and/or remediation as appropriate."

Chapter 2: *Emerging Approaches*

- The degree of familiarity of the marketplace with the condition. (Generally, the more common the condition, the less impact the condition will have.)

- The level of confidence the marketplace will have in remediation cost estimates. (In general, the higher the confidence level that the estimates accurately reflect the remediation cost, the less impact the condition will have.)

- The perception in the marketplace of the stability of regulatory decisions concerning the impairment. (If the regulatory agencies' remediation requirements are perceived as being unclear or changeable, or if the agencies are perceived to commonly reopen cases to which they have given prior approval of completed remediation work, the impact will be greater.)

- The availability of financing, given the presence of the impairment. (If financing is readily available at terms equivalent to those associated with unimpaired properties, then the impact will generally be less. Because lenders often do not understand the distinction between source and nonsource properties, the nonsource properties may be subjected to unnecessary penalty.)

- The possibility of "toxic torts" and other forms of public liability arising from the condition. (The less likely the possibility, the smaller the impact on value.)

Uncontained Impairments

Uncontained impairments are inherently not comparable. For instance, a recent case involved two gas stations on opposite sides of the same intersection, each having essentially the same unimpaired value. Both experienced leaking underground storage tanks. Station A has an expected remediation cost of $450,000, but Station B has an expected remediation cost of $1,300,000. The difference is that Station B overlies an old streambed that allowed the gasoline to travel over a greater distance, contaminating a very large volume of soils and groundwater. Station A was built on clay that restricted the movement of the gasoline to a very small volume immediately underlying the station property itself.

In general, uncontained impairments are as unique as fingerprints and must be evaluated using newly developed methods such as the case study approach and the engineering impaired value model (EIVM).

Case Study Approach

The case study approach was described in a recent article[4] and is only briefly discussed here.

Fundamentally, this approach entails careful analysis of several cases analogous to the subject property. Frequently these are properties that were once on the market but did not sell. A factual relationship between these properties and the subject is identified, and an inference is drawn about the likely offset to the unimpaired value that would apply to the subject. This offset is generally stated as a percentage reduction in the unimpaired value.

The offset to value may cover a range of value-impacting factors, including the costs of remediation, costs of restriction on use resulting from the condition, incremental costs of financing, value of probable recover-

4. Patchin, 402–409.

Valuing Contaminated Properties

ies, and the intangible factors. The result is a gross offset to the value based on the analogous cases.

The case study approach has the advantage of being based on market data and, in the hands of an experienced valuer, may provide a significant indication of the impaired value of the subject. It does not and generally cannot provide several kinds of information that may be important to the analyst.

First, the case study approach lacks detailed, property-specific quantitative information. Detailed information is normally not available in typical case data to allow for a direct comparison of the case environmental impairment to the subject impairment. This is not a fault of the technique, but a common problem of the data available to the valuer; owner are very reluctant to reveal detailed and specific information on their environmental condition. Even if they were willing to do so, the amount of data to be analyzed would be staggering.

Second, a gross percentage offset to value will not allow for an analysis of certain areas of financial impacts that may be of great importance to both the buyer and the seller. The supervisory financial analyst of the Federal Reserve Board's division of banking supervision and regulation, Stanley B. Redinger stated, "...[B]ankers should also think about 'solvency risk'—the risk that borrowers may have trouble paying back a loan because of an environmental problem they have, even if the bank itself has no liability."[5] Environmental remediation expenditures tend to come in lump sums that can create negative cash flows. These may jeopardize the financial viability of the subject property both for the debt and equity interests. Detailed cash flow information is generally not available through the case study approach.

Third, if the subject property is likely to be owned by a registrant under the Securities and Exchange Acts, some reporting requirements may need to be addressed as a point of concern for the owner. In 1993, the Securities and exchange Commission (SEC) published Staff Accounting Bulletin 92 (SAB 92)[6], which outlined the environmental liability reporting requirements for registrants. In part, those requirements state that for material environmental liabilities the registrant must disclose the following:

- The estimated amount of the liability, even if that estimate is known only over a range or the liability would be experienced only on sale, disposal or abandonment of the underlying asset. (If only a range is known, the most likely value within the range must be disclosed; if no one value is more likely than another, the minimum of the range must be disclosed. If sale, disposal, or abandonment is not planned, it must be assumed.)

- The discount rate to be used in evaluating a future liability must be a safe rate of return.

- Liabilities may not be netted against possible recoveries.

Fourth, the recent IRS Revenue Ruling 94-38[7] contains provisions important to the balance sheet, profit and loss, and cash position of many owner or buyers. This ruling at least partially reverses earlier IRS policy by allowing the deduction of some remediation costs as expenses against current income. However, investments in remediation equipment such as groundwater pump and treatment facilities, remediation of asbestos, re-

5. BNA, *Environmental Due Diligence Guide* (April 1994): 29.

6. Securities and Exchange Commission, *Staff Accounting Bulletin 92,* 17CFR Part 211, (SAB 92) 58 FR 32843 (June 14, 1993).

7. Internal Revenue Service, Revenue Ruling 94-38 (June 1994).

Chapter 2: *Emerging Approaches*

moval of underground storage tanks, and *remediation costs for contaminated property purchased by the taxpayer* [emphasis added] must generally be capitalized. The type of analytical data necessary to evaluate these factors is generally not available through the case study approach.

Even though these issues most frequently come up in business enterprise valuation, they should never be ignored. The SEC and IRS positions provide valuation guidance. The valuer should consider at least these specific points: Some remediation costs are expenses of operation; other costs must be capitalized, including capitalization against nondepreciable assets such as land; future costs should be conservatively discounted; and recoveries are sufficiently speculative that they should be separately evaluated.

The timing of remedial actions is another common concern of the valuer. The longer major remediation expenditures can be delayed, the less the impact on present worth. However, the major environmental laws are "strict joint and several." It would be misleading to say that remediation need not be undertaken before some governmental action has taken place. The Washington Supreme Court recently ruled that "Environmental statutes that feature strict liability...impose liability on polluters without further governmental action..."[8] In the proposed amendments to CERCLA currently before Congress are a number of provisions designed to encourage voluntary remediation.

If these and other issues specific to the subject property are important in valuing the subject, the case study approach by itself will rarely provide sufficient quantitative data for analysis of their specific impacts. In any event, two indications of value are generally better than one as some situations may simply have no analogous cases, hence the need for a second approach—the engineering impaired value model (EIVM).

EIVM

The EIVM was briefly introduced by the author in a published article written more than two years ago.[9] Since then, significant improvements in the model have been made, important additional information has been gathered, and the model has been successfully applied in litigation and negotiations.

Expected cost of remediation

CERCLA contains a set of provisions generally known as the National Contingency Plan (NCP).[10] The NCP defines the methodology for evaluating an environmental risk and selecting appropriate remedial actions at a Superfund site.[11] The courts have uniformly held that the recovery of costs for remedial actions from a third party or Superfund can occur only when those actions have been consistent with the requirements of the NCP. Other state and federal laws contain similar provisions for the evaluation and selection of remedial actions.

The point is that these laws and regulations form, in essence, a set of environmental building codes that define the "typical" cost of remediation. The EIVM will refer to the expected costs developed in conformance with these rules and regulations as C_{NCP} in honor of the NCP, even when CERCLA is not involved in the specific situation.

In proposed amendments to CERCLA recently presented before Congress is a provision designed explicitly to recognize a concept already in effect in some states: Different levels of cleanliness are required based on

8. *Weyerhouser v. Aetna Casualty and Surety Co.,* 61000-2 (Wash. Sup. Ct. 1994).

9. Albert R. Wilson, "The Environmental Opinion: Basis for an Impaired Value Opinion." *The Appraisal Journal* (July 1994): 410–423.

10. Comprehensive Environmental Response, Compensation and Liability Act, 40 CFR Part 300, National Oil and Hazardous Substance Pollution Contingency Plan; Final Rule, March 8, 1990.

11. There is a legal difference between a remedial action and a removal action. That difference will be ignored here, but it can be very important in certain circumstances.

highest and best use. Michigan, for example, distinguishes between three levels of cleanliness based on whether the site has a residential, commercial or industrial use. A change in the cleanliness requirements can increase or decrease remediation costs significantly and C_{NCP} may therefore be at least partially dependent on the highest and best use.

Expected cost of restrictions on use

An environmental risk may result in a change in the highest and best use. In one case, a site had an unimpaired highest and best use "...for light industrial development" and was valued at $1.75 per square foot. However, because the site was a former municipal solid waste landfill, subsidence and methane gas generation concerns would increase construction costs to achieve this highest and best use so significantly that an altogether different highest and best use would be indicated. The impaired highest and best use was determined to be for "...outdoor storage" and the indicated value was $0.75 per square foot. The difference, $1.00 per square foot, is the cost of a restriction on use resulting from the presence of the environmental risk.

The presence of an environmental risk may also restrict the use of a property in terms of income generation. For example, revenue may decrease because a portion of the available space had to be dedicated to remediation activities. (Examples of this would be a floor of a building dedicated for asbestos removal or a portion of the land for a pump and treat facility.) The costs resulting from a change in highest and best use, and those resulting from other restrictions on use are addressed in the EIVM as C_R.

Incremental financing costs

The presence of an environmental risk may prompt debt and equity participants to change financing terms and conditions. The debt participant may require a lower loan-to-value ratio, a shorter term, increased reporting requirements, increased closing costs, and, possibly, increased interest rates. Occasionally debt participation may not be available at all.

Equity participants may seek a higher rate of return. It has been reported that in some instances equity sought 25% to 50% rates of return. An article in the *Denver Business Journal* (November 11, 1994) reported that the Cherokee Real Estate and Environmental Fund, an active investor in contaminated properties, sought an 8% to 10% incremental rate of return over a "normal" real estate return of 8% to 10%. The difference between the costs of financing an unimpaired property and financing the property as impaired (e.g., the incremental 8% to 10%) is addressed in the model as CF, the incremental cost of financing.

In addition, there is the cost of financing the remediation project itself. This cost may require financing from pure equity sources or from the working capital of the organization and may carry risk rates of return, significantly adding to the total costs of remediation.

Most likely cost

In the literature, the term "stigma" is often used to identify environmentally related offsets to value. Usually what is referred to as stigma is the impact of the risks and uncertainties associated with the environmental problem as perceived by the marketplace. These risks and uncertainties result from two factors: (1) the risk that the estimated costs will understate the actual remediation costs (i.e., the total cost as identified after all work has been completed), and (2) uncertainty as expressed through the intangible factors to be addressed separately under "Market Factors."

The author has conducted two surveys of environmental remediation experts[12] and is currently engaged in a third survey. The purpose of these surveys is to obtain a measurement, based on experience, of the relationship between the expected remediation cost[13] developed at a specific state of knowledge for a specific type of environmental risk, and the actual remediation cost. State of knowledge refers to the knowledge available from investigative work performed before the estimate was developed, such as after completion of an ASTM Phase I Environmental Site Assessment, or after completion of a Remedial Investigation/Feasibility Study (RI/FS) under CERCLA.

Figure 2 provides the survey results for two extreme situations: expected cost of asbestos remediation formed after a thorough engineering survey of the building (a contained impairment with a high level of confidence in the estimate), and the expected cost of soil/groundwater remediation after an ASTM Phase I Environmental Site Assessment (an uncontained impairment with a low level of confidence in the estimate). Note the axes of the graph are strength of belief versus the ratio of expected to actual cost. If the ratio of expected to actual cost is 2, then the experts believe the actual cost will be twice the expected cost developed at a given state of knowledge. The ratio between actual and expected cost will be referred to in the model as the k_X factor, with one k_X factor for each of the C_X components introduced above. The combined factor, $k_X * C_X$ is the most likely cost.

The two vertical straight lines are labeled "Contained k_{NCP}" and "Uncontained k_{NCP}." Contained and uncontained refer to the earlier definitions. Note that for the contained impairment the experts have indicated a high level of confidence that the estimate will accurately reflect the actual cost while for the uncontained impairment the experts have indicated a low level of confidence. These same ideas and similar data can be applied to the costs of restrictions on use and financing.

Suppose that the expected remediation cost were $100,000. Then:

1) For the contained impairment the actual cost will most likely be $100,000 (most likely cost calculated as (Contained k_{NCP} = 1.00) × $100,000) with a range from $95,000 (minimum likely cost) to $105,000 (maximum likely cost).

FIGURE 2 Illustration of the Cost of Remediation for a Given State of Knowledge and Condition

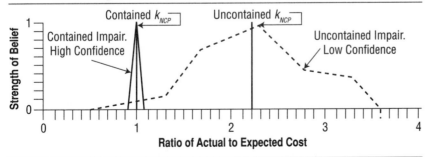

12. Defined as individuals active in the management of remediation projects for at least the past five years in the private sector.
13. Expected cost is defined as the estimated cost multiplied by the probability that the cost will occur as estimated.

2) For the uncontained impairment the actual cost will most likely be $220,000 (most likely cost calculated as (Uncontained $k_{NCP} = 2.2$) $\times$ $100,000) with a range from $50,000 (minimum likely cost) to $350,000 (maximum likely cost).

The difference between the most likely and the maximum likely cost of remediation assumes great importance as one of the major contributing elements of stigma. The buyer who is well informed or well advised will recognize that the most likely cost of remediation, restrictions on use, or incremental cost of financing is soundly based on the best available, current information, but that it may be and has in the past been an understatement of the actual costs. The risk that the cost will be greater is properly a component of stigma and the difference between the most likely and the maximum likely cost is a quantitative measure of the amount of exposure. Market forces may exaggerate or diminish the impact of this difference on the impaired market value, but the fact that the risk exists and its magnitude will be given serious consideration by the buyer and is a component of stigma.

Recoveries from third parties

There may be number of possible sources for the recovery of remediation costs for the current owner of a property. Such sources may include public or private insurance funds and other potentially responsible parties to the release. First, it should be noted that these sources of funding may be limited to the recovery of the direct cost of remedial activities conducted in accordance with the requirements of the NCP, the amount already identified as C_{NCP} in the model. When so limited the owner will remain exposed to the other cost factors without a source of third-party funding. In addition, some sources of funding may only be available to the owner at the time of release, not to a successor, or may require a difficult and lengthy process, including the possibility of protracted litigation in order to effectuate recovery.

For these reasons, the SEC in SAB 92 clearly states that recoveries should not be netted against the environmental liability—the amount, timing and success of recovery of remediation costs is often problematical. From the point of view of the marketplace, any possible recovery will be tempered by consideration of these and other factors, including the cost of the litigation required to recover from a third-party and the present worth of delayed recoveries. The net most likely amount of possible recoveries is addressed in the model as $k_{REC}*R_{REC}$ where R_{REC} is the present worth of the net amount of the possible recovery and k_{REC} is the probability of the successful recovery of that amount.

Market factors (a portion of "stigma")

A knowledge of the costs is important, but the intangible factors exert a strong, and sometimes contrary, influence. Take, for example, two gas stations having similar unimpaired value and very similar environmental conditions resulting from leaking underground tanks with contamination offsite under neighboring commercial property. Both stations had an unimpaired value of $420,000, and after thorough investigation, both had an estimated remediation cost of $350,000. Station A sold for $430,000, and the neighboring commercial property owner believes—

Chapter 2: *Emerging Approaches*

with good reason—that its value is unaffected. Station B and the adjoining commercial property cannot be sold at all. The differences lie in two areas:

- The oil marketing firm that owned Station A undertook aggressive remedial actions perceived to be, and that indeed are highly effective; offered substantial indemnifications and warranties to the purchaser, the purchaser's lender, and any successor purchaser or lender; and publicly acknowledged responsibility. The firm that owned Station B did none of the above.

- The properties associated with Station A are in high demand, with relatively few available substitutes; Station B does not enjoy these advantages.

- The point is that the intangible factors may act to offset, partially or totally, the impact of the objectively defined costs associated with the environmental risks, or they may act to multiply the impact depending on the specific circumstances of the marketplace and the situation. These market factors will be referred to in the model as M_F.

The model statement

The EIVM may be stated as follows:

$$I = U - k_{NCP}*C_{NCP} - k_R*C_R - k_F*C_F + k_{REC}*R_{REC} \pm M_F$$

Where

I = Impaired value

U = Unimpaired value

$k_{NCP}*C_{NCP}$ = Most likely cost of remediation

k_R*C_R = Most likely cost of restrictions on use

k_F*C_F = Most likely incremental cost of financing

$k_{REC}*R_{REC}$ = Most likely net present worth of recoveries

M_F = Net impact of intangible market factors (stigma)

An alternative statement of the EIVM would be as follows:

"The impaired value is equal to the unimpaired value less: (1) the most likely cost of remediation in accordance with the appropriate or relevant and applicable requirements; (2) the most likely cost of restrictions on use; (3) the most likely incremental cost of financing; plus the most likely net present worth of any recoveries from third parties; tempered by the influence of the market factors."

It is worth noting that the predictions made of the impaired value using the EIVM have, whenever sales data has been available, proven to be quite accurate. Generally, the sale price has been within 20% of the predicted impaired value, with results falling on both sides of the prediction.[14] The EIVM has proven to be particularly useful in the evaluation of business enterprise impacts and for exposition in a litigation setting.

EIVM example

To illustrate, suppose that after an ASTM Phase I Environmental Site Assessment and some limited testing, an environmental remediation expert makes the following statements concerning a gas station site: (Note that the underlined portions of the statements are not often explicitly provided, but are always present.)

14. See the article by Gene Dilmore, MAI, SREA, "Appraising Houses," *The Real Estate Appraiser* (Chicago: Society of Real Estate Appraisers, July–August 1974): 21–32. Depending on appraisal methodology used, 100% of the appraisals of houses would be within 24% of the sale price with an average error of up to 6.1%. The author knows of no comparable study of commercial or industrial property that would be more analogous to the application of the EIVM.

Valuing Contaminated Properties

- Two underground storage tanks (UST) require removal. A flat fee contract of $30,000 for removal can be obtained.
- The removal and disposal of 400 cubic yards of soils as petroleum contaminated at an estimated cost of $20,000 will be required with a high likelihood of occurrence as estimated.
- A groundwater pump and treatment system at an estimated present value cost of $100,000 will be required with a high likelihood of occurrence as estimated.
- Given the limited amount of analytical data available, only a low level of confidence in the estimates accurately reflecting the actual cost can be expressed.

The expected cost of remediation, based on the author's survey results and on the above statements, is developed in Table 1. Note that the probabilities are for illustration purposes only and should not be used in an actual analysis.

The estimated cost for dealing with this situation, given the current state of knowledge, is $150,000. The expect cost, including the data concerning the probability that events will proceed as currently estimated, is $130,800. The $130,800 is the C_{NCP} in the EIVM. If no additional information were applicable, C_{NCP} would be the most likely cost of remediation.

TABLE 1   Expected Cost of Remediation

Activity	Estimated Cost	Likelihood	Probability	Expected Cost
Tank removal	$30,000	Certain	1.00	$30,000
Soil removal	20,000	High	0.84	16,800
Pump and treat	100,000	High	0.84	84,000
Total	$150,000			$130,800

However, the expert states that the level of confidence is low that the current estimate will accurately reflect the actual cost, an issue that becomes critically important in the analysis. With regard to soils and groundwater contamination problems, the experts have indicated a broad range of actual-to-expected cost ratios for the low confidence case, from 0.50 to 3.5 times the expected cost (see Figure 2). The central tendency of the data indicates that the most likely ratio is 2.2. Based on this information, the most likely cost of remediation would be developed as shown in Table 2.

The most likely cost of remediation in this situation, the $k_{NCP}*C_{NCP}$ value in the EIVM, is $251,760. If there were no influences on the value of the subject from restrictions on use, incremental financing costs, recoveries, or the market factors, the impaired value would be:

$$I = U - \$251,760$$

Naturally, a seller would argue for the minimum likely cost as the offset to value, while the buyer would argue for the maximum likely cost absent any other factors or conditions of concern. Assuming the conditions of market value,[15] the bargaining should result in an offset approximating the best available knowledge and information concerning the most likely cost, the $k_{NCP}*C_{NCP}$ value as calculated above. The entire analytical process is shown in Figure 3.

15. "Market value" means: (1) the most probable price which a property should bring in a competitive and open market under all conditions requisite to a fair sale, the buyer and seller, each acting prudently, knowledgeably, and assuming the price is not affected by undue stimulus. Implicit in this definition is the consummation of a sale as of a specified date and the passing of title from seller to buyer under conditions whereby: (a) buyer and seller are typically motivated; (b) both parties are well informed or well advised, and each acting in what he or she considers his or her own best interest; (c) a reasonable time is allowed for exposure in the open market; (d) payment is made in terms of cash in U.S. dollars or in terms of financial arrangements comparable thereto; and (e) the price represents the normal consideration for the property sold and unaffected by special or creative financing or sales concessions granted by anyone associated with the sale.
(2) Adjustments to the comparables must be made for special or creative financing or sales concessions. No adjustments are necessary for those costs that are normally paid by sellers as a result of tradition or law in a market area; these costs are readily identifiable since the seller pays these costs in virtually all sales transactions. Special or creative financing adjustments can be made to the comparable property by comparisons to financing terms offered by a third-party institutions lender that is not already involved in the property or transaction. Any adjustment should not be calculated on a mechanical dollar-for-dollar cost of the financing or concession, but the dollar amount of any adjustment should approximate the market's reaction to the financing or concessions based on the appraiser's judgment. See Office of Thrift Supervision, OTS Regulation 564.2(f).

Chapter 2: *Emerging Approaches*

TABLE 2 Most Likely Cost of Remediation

Activity	Expected Cost (C_{NCP})	Level of Confidence	Most Likely Ratio (k_{NCP})	Most Likely Cost ($k_{NCP}*C_{NCP}$)	Minimum Likely Cost	Maximum Likely Cost
Tank removal	$30,000	Certain	1.0	$30,000	$30,000	$30,000
Soil removal	16,800	Low	2.2	36,960	8,400	58,800
Pump and treat	84,000	Low	2.2	184,800	42,000	294,000
Total	$130,800			$251,760	$80,400	$382,800

The area between the minimum likely cost and the most likely cost has been identified as the area of "buyer risk," while the area between the most likely cost and the maximum likely cost has been identified as the area of "seller risk." The reason is simple. If the buyer deducts from the unimpaired value an amount less than the most likely cost, the buyer is taking increasingly greater risks with decreasing purchase price compensation that the actual cost will exceed the compensation. The opposite is true for the seller.

The area of seller risk is also the area of the contribution to stigma resulting from the risk that the actual cost will exceed the most likely cost. To the extent that the marketplace will allow, the buyer will naturally seek to transfer this risk to the seller by demanding a greater offset to the unimpaired value.

There is always a danger in illustrating a situation like this. Readers tend to assume that because the data for a particular situation is illustrated, that data is equally applicable to all other situations. This is not the

Figure 3 Development of the Most Likely Cost of Remediation

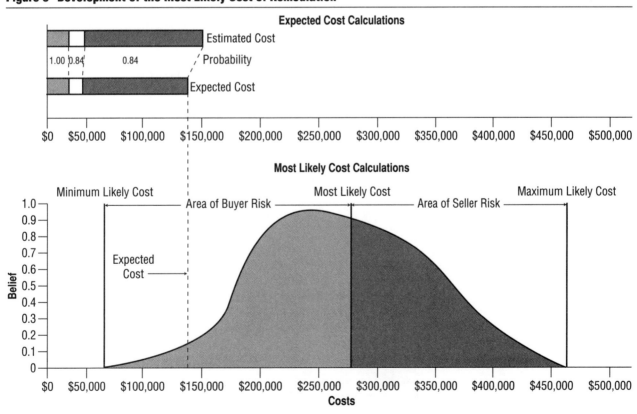

case in environmental analyses. The surveys show that very different k_x values apply to different situations as shown in Figure 2. Asbestos in buildings, underground storage tank remediation, and general soils and groundwater remediation all have very different k_x values and these values further diverge, depending on the level of confidence in the estimate (high, moderate, or low). In addition, governmental remediation appears to have larger k_x values compared to privately funded remediation.

Section Summary

Two approaches to value for the uncontained impairment case are gaining acceptance—the case study approach and the EIVM. Whenever possible, both should be used and a conclusion drawn based on the indications. It will not always be possible to apply the case study approach simply because there may be no comparable cases sufficiently analogous to the subject to allow reasonable inferences to be drawn. The EIVM is always available but requires a high level of technical expertise and a relatively large quantity of technical data concerning the environmental risk. Generally, the EIVM requires the combined experience of the appraiser and the environmental impact expert. In cases where cash flow, profit and loss, and balance sheet information is needed, the EIVM can supply the necessary data.

Stigma

An additional word about stigma and environmental impairments in general is warranted. Their impacts on value are highly time dependent. As already noted, the remediation cost is dependent on the state of knowledge at a particular point in time. Stigma exhibits an apparently greater time dependency because it is related to market perceptions as well as the state of knowledge concerning the remediation costs.

Stigma may, in fact, have three distinct time-dependent phases or parts. These might be thought of as:

(1) Post-remediation stigma or the impact on value after remediation has been completed and resulting from such factors as the uncertainty generated by the example Broward County, Florida, reclassification letter quoted earlier. This stigma impact may dissipate to an undetectable level over time.

(2) Pre-remediation stigma, or the influence of the post-remediation stigma plus the impact of the risks associated with the possible difference between estimated and actual costs plus other market factors.

(3) During-remediation stigma, an interim or transition phase stigma impact that is generally less then pre-remediation but more than post-remediation stigma impacts.

Remediation costs are also time dependent given that increasing knowledge generally accrues with time, allowing greater confidence in the estimates accurately reflecting the actual costs. Further, as time passes, more of the actual remediation costs become known as the work is performed, reducing the amount of the estimated cost remaining and subject to the risk of error.

Obviously great care in the analysis of stigma and remediation costs is required, paying particular attention to the state of knowledge associated with the environmental condition on the date of valuation and the difference between source and nonsource liability exposures.

Chapter 2: *Emerging Approaches*

Indirect Impairments

One of the most frequent situations involving environmental impairments is the case of a property value allegedly influenced by a nearby known environmental risk such as a Superfund site. The indirect impairment case is usually the most difficult analytical situation of all and one in which popular perceptions are frequently not supported by the data. An analysis of cases involving indirect impairments indicates the following:

- The impairments are generally not as great as commonly believed.
- The impairments are generally much more geographically restricted than commonly believed.
- The actual degree of the impairment is much more difficult to establish quantitatively due to limitations in the data and the analytical techniques normally employed.

None of the foregoing implies that indirect impairments do not occur. They do, and with some frequency. They simply do not seem to occur to the extent that popular belief would indicate. Further, indirect impairments, by definition, occur only on nonsource properties.

To date, several techniques have been used to attempt to quantify the indirect impairment. These have included multiple regression on values in segmented areas radiating outward from the known environmental risk site; study techniques adapted from market analysis, such as multifactor purchasing studies; and analyses of the sale price and time on the market for individual properties offered in the assumed impact area versus a control area. All of these have met with varying degrees of success, and all have offered some insight into the dynamics of the indirect impairment.

Assuming the environmental risk is obvious to the participants in the marketplace, meaning clear indications of the impairment can be seen, smelled, heard, or are well documented to the potential purchaser, the studies generally indicate that those properties immediately adjoining the problem site may have impaired values. In some limited cases, the next property away from the risk may also be impaired. In a very limited number of cases where the risk is particularly obvious over a distance, a reduction in value in decreasing amounts with greater distance has been indicated.

The type of environmental risk also seems to be an influencing factor. Well-known risks, such as a closed landfill, seem to have a lesser influence on value[16] when they are compared with, for example, the presence of a nuclear facility with a history of problems. However, an event such as the destruction of a home by a methane explosion apparently emanating from a nearby landfill is likely to alter this relationship.

Beyond generalizations such as the above, it is difficult to quantify indirect impairments using the analytical tools with which the valuer is generally familiar. There is, however, a set of mathematical tools that may offer significant quantitative insight into the situation. These tools are based on the mathematics of geostatistics, a branch of statistics developed for the economic analysis of ore bodies in mining.

To analyze the indirect impairment the factors associated with the real estate adage of "location, location, location" must be measured. Geostatistics makes several assumptions that are pertinent. First, it assumes that the available data is from randomly located points in space.

16. In at least one case, a partially closed landfill has been cited as a positive amenity.

Valuing Contaminated Properties

Second, it assumes that the relationship between the values at two points is partially dependent on an inverse (declining) relationship to increasing distance between the points, except when a sample point lies very close to another point—the "nugget" effect. Third, because of the inverse relationship with distance, geostatistics assumes that beyond some distance, one data point no longer has a detectable influence on another.

In a test of geostatistics applied to real estate, the author analyzed commercial office space rental rate data for the northern half of Franklin County (Columbus), Ohio, based on published listings from spring 1989. One of the outputs of a geostatistical analysis is a map of likely values. This map looks very much like a topographic map with the lines of equal value representing, in this case, the rental rate per square foot (see Figure 4), with the topovalues lines overlying a street map for orientation. Note that this map can also be developed in a three-dimensional format, portraying the "lay of the land" with respect to value even more clearly than the two-dimensional map shown.

Suppose we slice through the rental rate hills and valleys and examine the resulting rental rate profiles along the section lines N-S and W-E. The graphs of the rental rate profiles along these section lines are shown in Figures 5 and 6.

These rental rate profiles lie approximately along High Street and Broad/Main Streets in Columbus. The intersection of Broad and High is in the heart of the central business district (CBD) where the state capital building stands on the southeast corner of the intersection. The immediate downtown area of Columbus is the site of a number of newer Class A office buildings, including the headquarters of Nationwide Insurance, BankOne, Borden Chemical, and Huntington Banks.

FIGURE 4 Commercial Rental Rate Topovalue Map

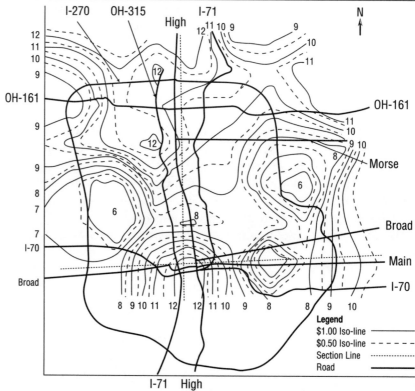

The trend lines drawn in Figures 5 and 6 start roughly at the Broad and High intersection. The trend line that measures the rate of change in rental rate going north from Broad and High (shown in Figure 5) indicates a rate of decline of $1.00 per square foot per mile. Although not shown here, a related map of occupancy rates was available at the same scale and indicated that occupancy declined from 90% in the CBD to 50% at the low point in rental rates just north of the CBD. The trend line going east from Broad and High (shown on Figure 6) has a rate of decline of $0.83 per square foot per mile although lower rental rates eventually are found in an area where the occupancy rate is 40%.

Compare this to the physical reality. If the valuer goes north on High from Broad, he or she will have first passed through an area being redeveloped into Class A commercial office space and anchored on the north by the new Nationwide Insurance headquarters buildings. Immediately after the Nationwide complex however, an area of rundown storefronts located across from the old rail yards is encountered, followed by a stretch of older commercial buildings eventually leading to the main campus of The Ohio State University. Thereafter, the quality of the area and buildings increases gradually to the high-quality professional area of Worthington.

Going east from Broad and High for the first mile or so are the headquarters of BankOne and Borden Chemical and new high-rise office buildings. Then comes an area of mansions converted into high-quality office space and smaller Class A and B office buildings, declining to an area of older industrial properties, some of them abandoned. Increasingly attractive areas are then encountered and stretch to the outer belt expressway where major new commercial office space is under development.

FIGURE 5 Rental Rate Profile, Section N-S

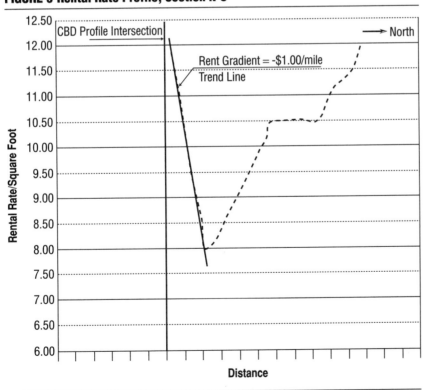

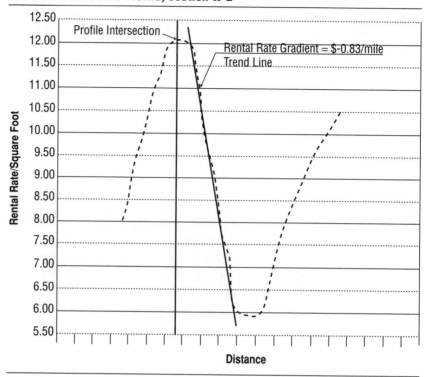

FIGURE 6 Rental Rate Profile, Section W-E

How would one measure the impact of the old rail yards on the commercial rental rate? It seems that the gross impact is the incremental rate of decline in rental rate per square foot of $0.17 per mile—the difference between going east on Broad where no equivalent to the rail yards exists for several miles and going north on High where the rail yards are located within a mile. On a larger-scale topovalue map, the impact can be more closely estimated, especially when other influences are examined by using topovalue data from other areas in the city to eliminate influences such as building quality or proximity to especially high-valued residential areas.

A similar study of residential properties found that major arterial street frontage tends to reduce value. No surprise there. However, if attractive sound barriers are placed between the street and the houses, the effect is much the same as if the street were replaced with a park. Surprised?

Conclusions

Contained Impairments: Generally, contained impairments are the simplest to deal with and the most amenable to standard appraisal practice. While caution must be exercised, particularly in the application of the sales comparison approach or when an unusual risk source is involved, practical appraisal experience may well serve the needs of the valuer.

Uncontained Impairments: Uncontained impairments generally present a very different valuation situation from the contained impairment case. First, the unusual nature of the ownership characteristics of the risk source presents new legal and intellectual problems for the valuer. Although these same problems generally exist for any impaired property, they are particularly important in the uncontained case because they are essentially a new stick in the bundle of rights that must be analyzed, with respect to the facility. The ownership characteristics affect the value of the property from which the risk source originated (the source property) and the value of the source property may be directly and strongly influenced by the presence of that risk source on other properties (the nonsource properties). In a sense, the source property "owns" the facility created by the risk source and is explicitly responsible for its remediation, even when it is not on the source property.

Second, given a specific state of knowledge, there can be a very large spread in the possible costs of remediation, leading to greater risks and uncertainty. Often the risks and uncertainties result in value offsets much greater than the estimated costs of dealing with the facility.

Third, standard appraisal techniques will not work adequately in most uncontained impairment situations. The new techniques of case study analysis and the engineering impaired value model must be employed, all of which frequently require expertise not normally within the appraiser's domain.

Indirect Impairments: Quantifying the amount of an indirect impairment is the most difficult task in the field. A number of techniques have been tried with varying degrees of success and the application of geostatistics shows promise.

In general, popular perceptions of the amount and geographic extent of an indirect impairment impact are usually exaggerated. The geographic range of impact appears very short. In residential cases, the detectible impact may not extend even to the property immediately adjoining the site of the impairment. If the impairment is notorious, meaning well publicized in the media, or can be clearly identified by sight, smell, or sound or otherwise explicitly called to the attention of the participants in the marketplace the impact may extend to the adjoining property or beyond. If the impairment lacks these characteristics, demonstrating an impaired value becomes difficult or simply not possible. In the case of commercial and industrial properties, the range of impact generally appears to be isolated to the source property although there are some exceptions, particularly if local lenders do not adequately understand the environmental rules and regulations.

Source Versus Nonsource Properties: The magnitude of the impact of an environmental risk on a source property is significantly different from the impact of that same environmental risk on a nonsource property, even if the nonsource property contains a part of the facility created by the release of the risk source. Some of the differences are:

- The source property has strict joint and several liability for the remediation of the total facility, including that portion that may lie on the nonsource property. The nonsource property does not have this liability and the most likely cost of remediation tends toward zero although there may be restrictions on use cost impacts (which may be recoverable from the source property).

- Because the nonsource property does not have remediation liability, the more sophisticated lenders tend not to penalize the nonsource property in the provision of debt financing, hence the incremental financing cost tends toward zero.

- Depending on the financial resources of the source property owner or the party responsible for remediation and insurance coverage for example, indemnifications or sources of recovery may be available to the nonsource property owner that tend toward making that owner whole.

These and other factors result in a strong need to distinguish clearly between the value impacts of an environmental risk on a source versus a nonsource property.

Choosing the Right Analytical Tool for the Job

by Richard J. Roddewig, MAI

Appraisers with little experience evaluating the impact of environmental risks on real estate and real estate markets are often at a loss when approached by potential clients with a contaminated property assignment. Of course, if the appraiser has little or no experience with contaminated property, the appraiser must consider the applicability of the Competency Provision of the *Uniform Standards of Professional Appraisal Practice* (USPAP) and, among other questions, ask, "What steps must I take to complete this assignment competently?"[1]

But in taking on an assignment involving contaminated property or other kinds of environmental risks, an even more fundamental question arises under the Competency Provision of USPAP, "What is the most appropriate technique to address the real estate problem involved?" The Competency Provision of USPAP recognizes that the very first thing the appraiser must do before entering into any assignment is properly identify the problem to be addressed.

Many appraisers automatically assume that performing an appraisal is the only way to handle every real estate problem presented to them. For whatever reason, whether force of habit, inexperience with real estate consulting, uncertainty about the applicability of USPAP to consulting assignments, etc., they automatically structure the assignment as an appraisal of a specific piece of property at a particular date in time. Far too often, however, in dealing with contaminated properties and other forms of environmental risks, an "appraisal" is precisely what the client does not need and the assignment does not demand. In many situations involving environmental risks, it may actually do the client a disservice and potentially be misleading to perform an "appraisal" when another analytical technique, such as "consulting," market analysis, or a highest and best use study, is more appropriate. This may be especially true in many types of litigation-related assignments.

Richard J. Roddewig, MAI, is president of Clarion Associates, with offices in Chicago, Denver, and Philadelphia. He codeveloped the Appraisal Institute's seminar, "Environmental Risk and the Real Estate Appraisal Process," and has taught the seminar nationwide. He is a regular contributor to The Appraisal Journal on environmental issues, and has been an adjunct lecturer on real estate valuation at DePaul University, Chicago.

This article originally appeared in the July 1998 issue of The Appraisal Journal.

---

1. For more discussion about the relationship between the Competency Provision and assignments involving environmental risk analysis, see Richard J. Roddewig, "Contaminated Properties and Guide Note 8: Questions, Answers, and Suggestions for Reform," *The Appraisal Journal* (January 1998): 99–105. See also, The Appraisal Foundation, *Uniform Standards of Professional Appraisal Practice* (Washington, D.C.: The Appraisal Foundation, 1998), 5.

Valuing Contaminated Properties

Classification of Environmental Risk Assignments Commonly Encountered by Appraisers

The assignments in which appraisers may be asked to analyze the impact of environmental risks on property values and real estate markets can be broadly characterized by type of client; date, dates of valuation, and evaluation; and intended use of the appraiser's report. Once the assignment is properly characterized, the type of analytical approach—whether appraisal, consulting, market analysis, highest and best use analysis, or some combination of all of those approaches—will be more readily apparent.

The most common types of clients encountered in this practice field are current or potential lenders; past owners, current owners, or potential buyers; governmental units and public agencies; and attorneys and their clients.

The analytical problem may require consideration of the real estate at a single point in time or on a series of dates on which the contamination or environmental risks are to be considered. The potential consideration dates include: (1) consideration of one particular retrospective date, on the current (or near-current) date, and on a particular prospective date, and (2) consideration of a series of retrospective dates, on the current (or near-current) date, and on a prospective date or a series of prospective dates.

The use of the analysis can be broadly characterized as being for lending/collateralization decisions, purchase/sale/hold decisions, public policy decisions (e.g., zoning approvals, regulatory proceedings, administrative hearings, policy analysis, legislative processes, etc.), and estimating damages in litigation. Of course, the nature of the contamination or risk affecting or potentially affecting the property may also be a key consideration in classifying the assignment and selecting the method of analysis.

Cleanup Costs, Stigma, Temporary Impacts, and Fluctuating Values

If each type of contamination and environmental risk permanently and uniformly affected all property types in every location on every date, then the proper analytical technique would be uniformly the same in virtually every assignment—an appraisal of the value of the property as of a specific date. As appraisers have learned, however, over the past two decades, it is not that simple, and a host of factors combine in a thousand different ways to make every contamination situation slightly different. But in every one of these situations, three essential questions emerge: (1) What will it cost to investigate and remediate the site? (2) How long will the environmental site assessment/remediation process last? (3) What is the stigma, if any, associated with the uncertainties that accompany the environmental site assessment and remediation process? Stigma may most simply be defined as the impact on value over and above the direct remediation costs.[2] It may or may not be present, and has been discussed in numerous *Appraisal Journal* articles.[3] The stigma impact can rise and fall in harmony with a variety of cycles.[4]

The basic stigma model shows that the property's market value typically takes a sudden plunge when contamination is discovered (see Figure 1). Once remediation begins, the property's market value often starts to recover to its original level. However, even after remediation is completed, the market value may not have recovered to its precontamination level. In this model, environmental stigma is shown as the difference between the

---

2. Stigma is "an adverse effect on the market's perception of the value of property containing an environmental risk even after cleanup costs have been expended or considered an estimating value." See Appraisal Institute, "Environmental Risk and the Real Estate Appraisal Process," seminar (Chicago, Illinois: Appraisal Institute, 1994), 128.

3. Peter J. Patchin, "Valuation of Contaminated Properties," *The Appraisal Journal* (January 1988): 7-16; Peter J. Patchin, "Contaminated Properties—Stigma Revisited," *The Appraisal Journal* (April 1991): 167–172; Bill Mundy, "Stigma and Value," *The Appraisal Journal* (January 1992): 7–13; and Mark Dotzour, "Groundwater Contamination and Residential Property Values," *The Appraisal Journal* (July 1997): 279–285.

4. Richard J. Roddewig, "Stigma, Environmental Risk and Property Value: 10 Critical Inquiries," *The Appraisal Journal* (October 1996): 375–387.

FIGURE 1 Basic Environmental Stigma Model

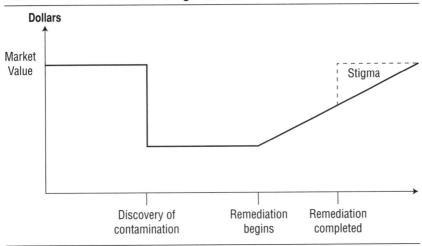

value of the property uncontaminated and the value of the property after remediation is completed. But even this oversimplified model shows that the level of environmental stigma can change over time (in this case, decrease) as the market value of the property gradually increases after remediation is completed.

In reality, the environmental stigma model is typically much more complex. Figure 2 shows how variables often present in environmental risk situations can complicate a situation: First, property values may decline slightly after the contamination is initially discovered, and then show a more precipitous decline until the full extent of the remediation cost is known.[5] Second, the value of the property can be reduced to less than zero if the remediation cost exceeds the value of the property disregarding the contamination.[6] Third, stigma is a component of the impact on value even during the remediation process. In other words, the value of the property may be even less than simply the difference between its uncontaminated value and the cost of the cleanup.

Of course, the trend lines representing the impact of contamination on property value and eventual recovery in value are usually not nice and straight in many environmental risk situations. Perceptions, prices, and therefore values may move in fits and starts in response to the complex interplay between various forces and cycles, including the remedial investigation and cleanup cycle, the legal, regulatory, and legislative cycle, the amount of attention in the media, and the degree of lenders' concerns about loans involving environmental risks. Often the more complex model will look like a stock market trend line, with peaks and valleys scattered along the general upward or downward pattern of movement.

As that model clearly shows, the stigma associated with the presence of contamination or environmental risk can change dramatically over time. Stigma can decline—and therefore property value increase—as site investigation and remediation proceed. Although in many situations, there is a lingering stigma even after cleanup, it too can dissipate over time or be suddenly eliminated in response to such factors as environmental insurance policies, seller indemnities, "no further action letters" from state or federal regulators, or simply market acceptance of any lingering risk.

5. In some situations, the reverse may also occur. Property values may drop precipitously when contamination is first discovered in expectation of substantial remediation costs, and then partially recover if the completed investigation reveals that a less costly remediation program is possible.
6. See Appraisal Institute, "Guide Note 8: The Consideration of Hazardous Substances in the Appraisal Process" in the Standards of Professional Appraisal Practice (Chicago, Illinois: Appraisal Institute, 1998): D23–D27. This guide note specifically recognizes that environmental contamination can create negative value.

Valuing Contaminated Properties

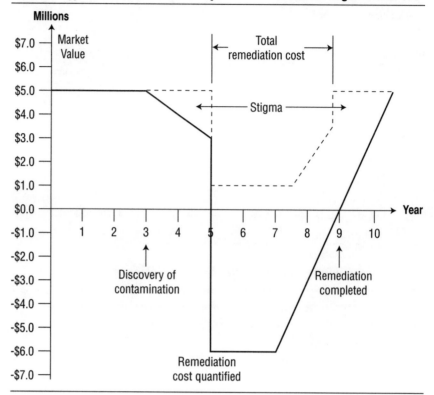

FIGURE 2 Typical Conditions That Complicate Environmental Stigma Situations

Tailoring the Analysis to the Situation

The following examples represent the types of environmental risk assignments that appraisers may be asked to evaluate.

Assignment 1: An electric utility company proposes an extension of an existing high-voltage power line. Residents in a new subdivision adjacent to one stretch of the proposed new right-of-way become concerned about the potential impact of the proposed line on the value of their property. There are 200 homes in the existing subdivision, including 20 immediately adjacent to the new power line corridor. Some residents even one-quarter mile away in the subdivision express concern that the corridor will adversely affect the value of their homes. The line must be approved by a state utility commission before it can be constructed. A group of concerned residents retains a real estate appraiser to analyze the potential impact of the proposed power line on home value in the subdivision. The electric utility company does the same.

Assignment 2: A real estate development company has recently completed the purchase of a piece of property for $1.0 million. The improvements on the property generate some income now, but the intention of the developer is to combine it with an adjacent site for redevelopment at its highest and best use. The developer investigated the property prior to acquisition and discovered some contamination that it believed could be readily remediated at a small cost. After acquisition, more extensive testing by an environmental assessment firm reveals much more significant contamination than was first believed. The *estimated* cost of total cleanup is now at $4.0 million–$7.0 million, depending on the remediation program and cleanup level achieved, and it is not clear yet whether state regulators will require the entire site to be cleaned or if something less than complete cleanup will be needed under the state's new "brownfield" program. More onsite testing is necessary to better qualify the appropriate remedial technique, cleanup timetable, and cost. Before starting a complete site investigation to determine the full nature and extent of contamination and the costs of remediation, the developers approach an appraiser for assistance in understanding the impact of the contamination on the property's value for advice on what to do with the property.

Assignment 3: An attorney calls on an appraiser to be an expert witness in complicated environmental litigation involving a hotel property. The contamination was discovered 10 years earlier, at a time when the then-owners of the hotel were in the process of negotiating a sale of the property. The hotel market at the time was extremely strong, and the sale had a high probability of being completed at a low capitalization rate and a high value. When the contamination was discovered, however, the potential buyer refused to sign the purchase contract that had been negotiated.

The hotel owners then started the long process of investigating the site and dealing with state regulatory agencies to discern the degree of cleanup that would be required or needed. Shortly after the discovery of the contamination, the national hotel market crashed. Prices that were paid for hotels in this market and nationwide plummeted in response to overbuilding, high vacancies, declining room rates, and lack of mortgage financing for hotel acquisitions. Occupancy and income at this hotel suffered along with other hotels in the same marketplace.

Attempts to sell the hotel were unsuccessful until recently when three things happened to change the situation: First, environmental investigations and state-mandated remediation were completed. Second, state environmental regulators issued a "no further action" letter clarifying that future owners of this property would not be responsible for any further environmental remediation so long as the existing use continued and no further disturbance of the site occurred. Third, the hotel market recovered to the point that buyers were once again interested and mortgage financing became available.

As a result of the changed market conditions and the completed remediation, the hotel was recently sold, but at a price substantially lower than the price negotiated 10 years before the contamination was discovered.

The hotel owners have recently sued the owners of a nearby property that was the source of the underlying contamination. One count of the claim is for damages to real estate. The attorneys for each side need a real estate analyst to evaluate the real estate damages, if any.

Each of the three case studies involves valuation issues, but in none is an appraisal in the traditional sense and format necessarily the best analytical solution. In assignment 1 involving the proposed power line, it might be possible to prepare an appraisal of the prospective value of the homes after the date of completion of the proposed new transmission line right-of-way. However, there are 200 homes in the subdivision, and to appraise them all and estimate the impact, if any, of the proposed power line on each one could be a time-consuming and expensive undertaking.

Valuing Contaminated Properties

For example, it could be that the potential impact, if any, might depend on the type of power line and the poles and pole configuration, the width of the right-of-way, setbacks, and prospective views of the poles from different locations in the subdivision. Each of those factors, among others, would have to be considered for each house.

This power line assignment is clearly one in which consulting rather than appraising is the better technique. USPAP defines consulting as "the act or process of providing information, analysis of real estate data, and recommendations or conclusions on diversified problems in real estate, other than estimating value."[7] Determining the potential impact, if any, of the proposed power line might also involve market analysis defined by USPAP as "the study of real estate market conditions for a specific type of property."[8] Both the homeowners and the power company are most likely interested in two central questions: (1) Will the proposed line have any impact on the market value of nearby property values? (2) If the proposed line will adversely impact nearby residential property values, which properties will be affected, how far from the power line will that impact extend, and what will be the likely percentage impact on home values?

Case studies of other subdivisions near power lines could be conducted, and adjustments made as necessary to account for locational and situational differences. Each of the appraisers involved could estimate the percentage impact, if any, likely to be experienced by homes near the power line, and their findings could be reviewed. The analysis could discuss whether such factors as the type of power line, view lines, type and price point of the homes, etc., make a difference. In any event, the assignment could be completed without estimating the market value of a specific house before and after considering the proposed power line.

In assignment 2, the full nature and extent of the contamination are not yet known, nor complete site investigation completed. Further, a remediation plan still has to be prepared and approved by regulatory authorities. However, the appraiser can prepare the following for the developer client at this early stage:

- He or she can prepare an estimate of the highest and best use and market value of the property disregarding the contamination. This can then be compared to the range of estimated cleanup costs.

- Next, the appraiser can compare the range of cleanup costs to the property's market value at its highest and best use or value in current use. The appraiser might also provide consulting to the developer on the types of stigma and the potential magnitude of the stigma (expressed as a percentage of market value) that people might associate with the property before, during, and after an approved remediation.

It may be premature for the appraiser to estimate the exact market value of the property considering the contamination, unless the market value uncontaminated was less than the likely cost of remediation, in which case the property would have "negative value."

Assignment 3 may be the most difficult of the three for the typical appraiser accustomed to valuing property at one particular point in time. The case is coming to trial 10 years after the discovery of the contamination. Even though it may be tempting for an appraiser to estimate the market

7. USPAP, 9.
8. USPAP, 10.

Chapter 2: *Choosing the Right Tool*

value as of one particular point in the past "before and after" considering the contamination, doing so may lead to an inaccurate estimate of the true damages resulting from the discovery of the contamination. For example, if, on the second of the two previous stigma models presented, an appraiser picks year 4 as the key point and looks only at market value before and after considering the contamination, he or she might conclude that the damages are only $1.0 million. The same analysis process done one year later in year 5 may result in a damage estimate of $8.0 million. If year 9 is selected, the damage estimate may be only $5.0 million.

Values are changing over time in harmony with the total interplay between market forces and the environmental investigation and remediation process. It may be best for the appraiser in this situation to step back and ask, "What are the components of the damages to the property owner?" What the owner has lost as a result of the entire process of discovery, investigation, remediation, and eventual resale might include:

- Proceeds from the sale of the property before the discovery of the contamination and lost income in the net proceeds of that sale.
- An opportunity to sell the property due to the collapse of the hotel market that occurred after the discovery of the contamination.
- The difference between net income from the operation of the hotel before and after the discovery of the contamination and the subsequent downturn in the hotel market. (The income was lower than before the discovery of the contamination because occupancies, room rates, and net operating income were lower due to the downturn in the hotel market.)
- An inability to refinance at lower interest rates.
- Expenditures on environmental investigation and remediation.
- An inability to construct site improvements and hotel additions that would disturb the existing condition of the site.
- Additional marketing costs to find buyers.
- Upon the hotel market's recovery, the difference between the prediscovery price and the eventual sale price.
- Interest on the difference between the two prices and on the other losses.

The owner's gains might include:

- An increase in value due to remediation expenditures, completion of remediation process, and issuance of a "no further action letter"
- Interest on the positive net operating income, if any, that was generated

In litigation, all the losses and gains would need to be tallied as of the date of the trial in which damages are to be determined. Of course, underlying legal principles will determine which of the elements of measurable potential damage are recoverable, given underlying law, the particular jurisdiction, and type of case.

In other situations somewhat similar to assignment 3, it may be possible to measure damages by looking forward and undertaking discounted present value calculations to arrive at an estimate of damages on a particular date before the completion of all remediation and before full market value recovery.

Conclusion

Measuring the impact of contamination and environmental risks on property values and property markets is not always simple. The complex interplay between the forces and factors at work in the marketplace usually means that estimating environmental stigma is like shooting at a moving target. In some situations, it is perfectly appropriate to select one particular date in time and compare the market value that considers the contamination to the market value that disregards all environmental risks. In other situations involving environmental risks and real estate, it may do the client little good to fix on one point in time or even on one particular property. It may be in conflict with established legal principles for measuring damages. When the appraiser has the advantage of looking back at a completed contamination investigation and remediation, the pattern of market value or sales price impacts may be more discernible than if the appraiser has to look forward from a vantage point before the remediation is completed. What all appraisers must do in these types of assignments is clear: They must understand the nature of the real estate assignment and correctly apply the appropriate technique to complete the analysis in a professional manner.

The Impact of Detrimental Conditions on Property Values

by Randall Bell, MAI

There are over 200 detrimental conditions (DCs) that can affect real estate values. They include temporary easements, airport noise, construction defects, serious toxic waste, geotechnical issues, and natural disasters. Determining the diminution in property value brought about by a DC requires the application of specialized methods, procedures, and formulas. In fact, contamination and geotechnical issues present some of the most involved problems in real estate valuation.

All DCs can be classified into 10 categories, each having unique patterns and attributes that can be illustrated on a graph. Further, a DC's impact on value can vary from case to case. A DC could even be completely benign. Therefore, each situation must be independently and competently analyzed. The Bell Chart[1] defines each classification and graphs the relationship between property values and typical events (see Figure 1).

Detrimental Conditions Model

All DCs involve some or all of six basic elements that lead to an understanding of: the costs or losses associated with the assessment of the condition, the repair or remediation costs, any ongoing conditions, and any residual market resistance to the condition. The DC Model[2] illustrates the costs before, during, and after the actual remediation (see Figure 2). These costs are shown as A or the value as if unaffected by the DC; B, the value upon the realization that a DC exists; C, the value upon assessment of the situation; D, the value upon repair or otherwise resolved; E, the value upon the consideration of any ongoing costs; and F, the impact of any market resistance.

The value patterns of any DC will involve some or all of these six basic elements. For example, Classes III through VI generally utilize only components of this model, as may Classes VI and IX although they may have all the elements of the model. The point is that all elements must be considered in any DC assignment.

Randall Bell, MAI, directs the real estate damages practice of PricewaterhouseCoopers in Costa Mesa, California. He specializes in the valuation of properties affected by detrimental conditions, and is the developer and an instructor of the Appraisal Institute's seminar, "Valuation of Detrimental Conditions." His book on the same subject, titled "Real Estate Damages," was released in 1999. Mr. Bell earned an MBA from the University of California, Los Angeles.

This article originally appeared in the October 1998 issue of The Appraisal Journal.

1. Randall Bell, "The Ten Standard Categories of Detrimental Conditions," *Right of Way* (July 1996): 14–16.
2. Randall Bell, "Quantifying Diminution in Value Due to Detrimental Conditions: An Application to Environmentally Contaminated Properties," *Environmental Claims Journal* (October 1996): 135.

Valuing Contaminated Properties

FIGURE 1 The Bell Chart: The 10 Classifications of Detrimental Conditions

Class		Detrimental Conditions	Analysis	Result
I	No Detrimental Condition (DC) or Benign Condition	Any DC if No Impact Sales Arrangement at Market *(If Over Market: II or If Under: IV)* Sale-Leaseback/Land Contract Build-to-Suit/Tenant Purchase Threat of Condemnation/Auction First Right-of-Refusal/Double Escrow	There are hundreds of Detrimental Conditions (DCs) that may impact property values. The analysis of property damages starts with the DC Model, which illustrates the array of related issues. All six elements of the DC Model should be considered in every analysis. This can yield a variety of valuation patterns based upon the inclusion, exclusion, and timing of each element.	DCs have a variety of impacts which, upon analysis, vary on a case-by-case basis.
II	Non–market Premium	Special Buyer Motivation Assemblage/Expansion Redevelopment Project Feng Shui Short-Term Windfall		
III	Market Condition	Economy/Supply & Demand Recession/Depression Lease Option/Rolling Option Exercise of Option/Takedown		
IV	Temporary Condition	Distress Sale*/Tragedy** Bulk-Portfolio Sale/Business Inc. High Vacancy/Temp. Easement Deferred Maintenance/Legal * Bankruptcy/Probate-Estate-Short Sale US Marshall/REO/Private REO/FDIC/RTC ** Crime Scene/Accident/Disease/Riot/Fire		
V	Imposed Condition	Neighboring Issue* Eminent Domain/Bond/Tax Deed Restriction/Ground Lease Leasehold/Leased Fee Physical Depreciation/Historical *Sewage-Power-Nuclear Plant/Blight Illegal Use/Jail/EMF/Traffic-Airport Noise	Damages are benchmarked against the *Unimpaired Value*. In determining the impact on value, it is critical that a distinction be made between the DC and unrelated issues. For example, market conditions may be responsible for a change in value that is unrelated to the condtion being studied.	
VI	Building Construction Condition	Construction Defect Building Code Violations Poor Workmanship/Leaks ADA Non-compliance Functional Depreciation	The impact of DCs on property values is ultimately an empirical question that requires the application of one or more of the three traditional approaches to value: 1. The Sales Comparison Approach utilizing market data with and without the DC. 2. The Income Capitalization Approach utilizing income and risk factors with and without the DC. 3. The Cost Approach utilizing data with and wihout the costs and losses associated with a DC. The DC Model, coupled with the three approaches to value, provides the fundamental framework for the analysis of DCs.	
VII	Soil or Geotechnical Construction Condition	Soil Construction Drainage/Tunneling Foundation/Cut & Fill Retaining Wall or Slope Grading/Soil Compaction		
VIII	Environmental Condition	Soil Contamination Building Contamination Hydrocarbons/Metals/Solvents Asbestos/Radioactive Groundwater/Landfill/LUST		
IX	Natural Condition	Natural Disasters Natural Habitat Flood/Earthquake/Volcano Tornado/Landslide/Soil Types Infestation/Sulfates/Wetlands		
X	Incurable Condition	Applicable to many DCs in severe situations where a complete loss or net liability exists		

Detrimental Condition Model

Key to Graphs
- - Unimpaired Value   —— Value With DC
A: Unimpaired Value
B: DC Occurs or Discovered
C: Assessment Stage
  Cost & Responsibility
  Use
  Uncertainty Factor (Risk)
D: Repair Stage
  Cost & Responsibility
  Use
  Project Incentive (Risk)
E: Ongoing Stage
  Cost & Responsibility
  Use
F: Market Resistance (Risk)

© 1996–1998 by Randall Bell, MAI

Chapter 2: *The Impact of Detrimental Conditions*

FIGURE 2 Detrimental Condition Model

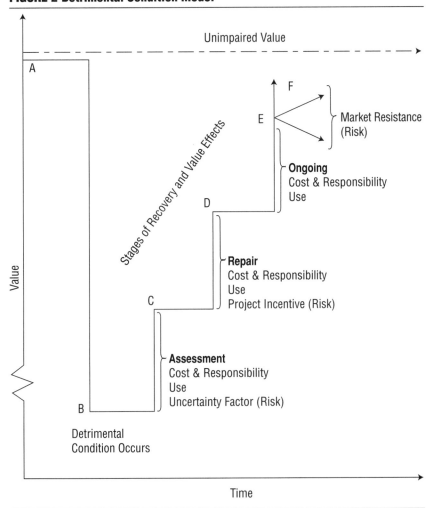

© 1996, 1997, by Randall Bell, MAI. Used by permission.

Six Basic Elements

Valuation as if no detrimental condition. The first step of a DC assignment is to value the property as if there were no DC. This establishes a benchmark for the following studies.

Assessment costs. These encompass all the costs associated with monitoring and assessing the DC before any repairs or remediation, including the Phase I and II studies, soils and geotechnical studies, and other monitoring costs. These costs are provided by the engineering firms that do such monitoring, and because requests for this work are commonplace, the cost estimates are generally well established.

Remediation costs. The remediation costs represent all costs associated with the actual repairs, cleanup, and correction of the condition. A vast spectrum of costs could be included, depending on the remediation method chosen. The costs would also include any agency oversight, engineering, legal review, permits, sampling, improvement demolition, improvement reconstruction, additional scientific analysis, and backfill. Again, these costs are often provided by the engineers of the firm contracted to conduct the remediation. However, special care should be taken in reviewing the completeness of such estimates because the original cost estimates are often exceeded. The firm providing the estimates should clearly set forth whether the costs are *best case, expected case,* or *worst case* scenarios—an important point for implementing the next step.

As stated, remediation costs can exceed their original estimates. For this reason, a contingency factor may be required to adjust remediation costs to reflect a complete and reasonable cost estimate, so that the real estate market is reasonably assured that *all* reasonable remediation costs are accounted for in the estimates provided. It is important to note that the contingency factor applied to the remediation costs relates to the hard costs of remediation and should not be confused with intangible losses, such as onus or stigma. Because informed potential buyers must be reasonably assured that they have a clear indication of their potential cash liability, it is essential that the total remediation costs accurately reflect the total reasonable repair costs, not just a cursory and optimistic estimate.

Carrying costs must also be considered. During the remediation process, there may be disruptions to the property's use, resulting in a loss of rental revenues or the utility of the property. In addition, operating expenses, which may be paid by the tenant under the terms of a net lease, would also be considered.

The final element of the repair process is the project incentive. This is the entreprenuerial profit required for a buyer to purchase damaged property and make the repairs.

Ongoing costs. Some damaged properties incur ongoing costs even after repairs or remediation is completed. For example, a contaminated property may undergo continued monitoring. Formally damaged or contaminated properties may have difficulty in obtaining financing. Lenders may not consider financing an unremediated site and may also be reluctant to finance a property that has been remediated, usually due to concerns that government agencies do not permanently certify a site as clean. The result could be an environmental review of the property, additional loan points, a higher interest rate, or a lower loan-to-value ratio. In the end, the property owner could pay additional financing costs.

A damaged property may also incur restrictions in use. For example, a formally contaminated site may be limited to industrial uses, even if it had previously been a commercial or residential use. This issue must be individually studied for any damaged property.

Market resistance. At this point, the total costs and losses are subtotaled, and an adjustment is made for the overall market resistance to the property, if any. This adjustment reflects the market's post-repair resistance to purchase the property when similar properties without a history of defectiveness are available.

Valuation as is. To derive the value, as is, all the above issues must be addressed, quantified, and deducted from the value as if no DC exists. The total losses attributable to a DC can range from being nominal to exceeding the Class I value. Additionally, the costs of remediation may actually be minor compared with all the associated costs.

DC Classifications

Class I—No Detrimental Conditions or Benign Condition. Class I is the most straightforward because it involves an absence of DCs. Many DC assignments include the initial step of determining the market value as if no DC exists. The formulas relating to the concepts of Classes I through X are summarized in Figure 3.

This class also involves situations in which an act or event occurs, but the issue has no effect on value. Such cases can involve any one of the DC Classes II through IX. This concept is straightforward, but it can be the grounds for litigation.

For example, a plaintiff may contend that some condition affected his or her property value, while the defendant claims that the event had no impact on value. One way to determine if an issue is, in fact, a DC is with a paired-sales analysis. In this process, market data that is clearly unaffected by the issue is collected and then compared with similar market data that is affected. If a legitimate DC exists, there will likely be a measurable and consistent difference between the two sets of market data; if not, there will likely be no significant difference between the two sets of data. When a published study about a neighborhood adjacent to a well-designed landfill in the Los Angeles area was compared with comparable neighborhoods some distance from the landfill, the results indicated no significant difference between the two neighborhoods in either current prices or appreciation rates.[3]

FIGURE 3 Detrimental Condition Valuation Formulas

DC Cost Approach
Unimpaired Value
− Assessment Stage Value Effects
    Cost & Responsibility
    Use
    Risk (Uncertainty Factor)
− Repair Stage Value Effects
    Cost & Responsibility
    Use
    Risk (Project Incentive)
− Ongoing Stage Value Effects
    Cost & Responsibility
    Use
    Risk (Market Resistance)
= Impaired Value

DC Sales Comparison Approach
Control Area Market Data (No DC, Point A)
− Test Area Market Data (With DC, Points B, C, D, E, or F)
= Diminution in Value

DC Income Capitalization Approach

$$\text{Value}(V) = \frac{\text{Net Operating Income (I)}}{\text{Capitalization Rate (R)}}$$

Cost Effects ⎫
Use Effects ⎭ Impacts Income (I)

Risk Effects } Impacts Rate (R)

---

3. Donald H. Bleich, M. Chapman Findlay, III, and G. Michael Phillips, "An Evaluation of the Impact of a Well-Designed Landfill on Surrounding Property Values," *The Appraisal Journal* (April 1991): 247.

Class II—Non-market Premium. Class II includes asemblage, redevelopment zones, and other situations where the buyer paid a premium. This is a detrimental condition in terms of the higher price being paid by the buyer.

Class III—Market Condition. Class III includes the normal cycle of the real estate market when values increase, decrease, or remain level over a specific period of time. These patterns of value are simply the effects of the general economy coupled with real estate supply and demand. This is a significant classification because a certain condition might be suspected to have affected the value when, in fact, the DC was benign, and the market conditions caused the loss or gain in value.

In addition, each of the other graphs depicting the common characteristics of the impact of various DCs on value is based on level market conditions. In reality, market conditions may have an added impact in and of themselves, thereby requiring adjustments for market conditions with any one of the various classifications of DCs.

One way of measuring Class III conditions may be to study several comparable sales that resold at a later date. By comparing the initial and subsequent sales dates and values, a determination can be made about the market trends. Graphically, Class III simply reflects increased, decreased, or level market conditions over time.

Class IV—Temporary Condition. Because this class describes DCs that are only temporary in nature, the loss in value is limited to the disruption caused by the temporary condition. The most common Class IV situation involves temporary construction easements in which a portion of a property is used by another party while adjoining construction is underway. Upon the completion of construction, the full use of the property is returned to its original state.

This temporary disruption can affect value. For example, if temporary construction disrupts the traffic patterns of a shopping center, the diminution in value may be extracted from the lost revenues, higher vacancy rates, and other related losses. The diminution in value would be in addition to the rental rate of the land being used during the temporary construction. Further, while the effects of bankruptcy are often a benign Class I DC, this situation may be a Class IV DC if there is substantial deferred maintenance or there are other temporary conditions that affect the value.

Another type of Class IV DC involves absorption losses. For example, if a particular condition causes a major tenant to vacate the building abruptly, the property value would drop upon the tenant's departure and then increase over time as the vacant space is absorbed. Absorption losses specifically include lost rents, leasing commissions, and tenant improvements.

Class IV conditions may also be the result of a crime scene or other tragic event. Media coverage of the incident might negatively influence the market's perception. Interviews with brokers and agents indicate that, when disclosed, a violent crime committed within a residence adversely affects value.[4] As depicted by the graphs, these types of conditions may either have a brief effect only or have a long-lasting effect that could diminish with time. In some extreme situations, the memories caused by

4. Sheila A. Little, "Effects of Violent Crimes on Residential Property Values," *The Appraisal Journal* (July 1988): 342.

Chapter 2: *The Impact of Detrimental Conditions*

the tragedy may be so unpleasant that the improvements are eventually demolished; however, the stigma tends to impact the site continuously.

Measuring Class IV DCs often involve comparing the subject property to other properties in similar Class IV situations and subsequently sold to buyers informed of the tragic event. (A lower sales price is often required to entice buyers to purchase these properties.)

The Class IV graphs may reflect only a short and temporary drop in value if the condition is minor and forgotten by market participants quickly. It may also reflect a sudden drop with a gradual increase in value as the market eventually becomes more accepting of the situation.

Class V—Imposed Condition. Adverse external factors, eminent domain, undesirable acts, or forced events by another person or entity constitute Class V conditions. Specifically, the DCs can be imposed governmental conditions such as down-zoning, special bond assessments, or the designation of a property as a historic site. Examples of adverse external factors are dumps, landfills, factories that produce noise and bad odors, neighbors that allow their property to deteriorate, and transmission lines.[5] They may also include the discovery that improvements were illegally constructed, or the development of surrounding nuisances (or perceived nuisances) such as a sewer treatment plant, airport noise, or a prison. For example, published studies illustrate that there is a measurable impact on values due to international airport noise.[6] In addition, Class VI DCs apply to eminent domain situations, especially a partial taking, and to willful acts of the property owner, such as entering into a ground lease.

In some situations, the effects of an imposed condition may be relatively easy to assess. In other cases, the imposed condition may be unclear and require special studies to predict how the market will change. Upon full investigation and assessment, the uncertainties are eliminated and the value of the property generally increases.

Graphically, Class V often reflects a sudden drop in value upon the occurrence of the DC and a permanent loss in value as a result of the imposed condition. In a situation involving diminishing effects, such as a ground lease, the leasehold value gradually decreases over time.

Class VI—Building Construction Condition. The basic premise of both Class VI and VII DCs is that they are manmade, which means that they can often be repaired. Class VI DCs involve construction issues above grade. As such, they are relatively easy to assess, and often result in the restoration of the property's full value upon completion of the repairs. Typically, the problems are self-evident, and no special studies are required to determine the scope of the problem; however, all potential losses should be addressed.

To quantify these types of DCs, the appraiser must study the cost of repairs, engineering, related services such as relocating the tenant, free rent for the tenant while repairs are being made, post-repair cleanup, and so forth. Some tenant relocation costs can partially, if not entirely, be mitigated simply by waiting until the property is vacant to make the repairs.

Depicted on a graph, a Class VI situation may show a drop in value upon the discovery of the condition and a return to full value upon the repair of the condition. In unusual circumstances, there may be an ongo-

5. Hsiang-te Kung and Charles F. Seagle, "Impact of Transmission Lines on Property Values: A Case Study," *The Appraisal Journal* (July 1992): 413.

6. Marvin Frankel, "Airport Noise and Residential Property Values: Results of a Survey Study," *The Appraisal Journal* (January 1991): 96–110.

Valuing Contaminated Properties

ing condition that remains because it is not physically or economically possible to cure, thereby resulting in a permanent loss in the value of the improvements. For example, if a construction defect cannot be economically repaired, it may be a situation similar to inadequate insulation or asbestos abatement. The most noteworthy example of this situation is asbestos-containing materials which, because they may be impractical to remove from a building, are an ongoing condition. Air monitoring may be required throughout the life of the improvements and special handing and disposal costs would be incurred if the building is eventually demolished.[7] Under this condition, the graphic illustration reflects a permanent loss of value because the condition remains, or is perceived to remain, unchanged over time.

Class VII—Soil or Geotechnical Construction Condition. These DCs, which involve construction issues below grade, are more difficult to assess and repair than Class VI conditions because of the challenges of assessing conditions below grade and the associated drilling, coring, and excavation. This category of DCs could include site grading; soil cut, fill, and compacting; slopes; drainage; tunneling; or retaining walls.

Often, Class VII DCs can be assessed and repaired even if the foundation must be reinforced or the improvements underpinned. Like Class VI DCs, calculating the diminution in value would involve the review of the functional utility of the property, repairs that are necessary to prevent a loss to life or property, repair costs, engineering costs, disruption to the property, etc. These conditions are manmade and can usually be corrected although in some extreme conditions, they cannot be repaired and an ongoing condition may remain, affecting the value if the functional utility of the property is diminished or the market perceives the ongoing issue to impact the value. Thus, the functional use of the property and the necessary repairs must be carefully reviewed.

For example, if a site has fill soil that is up to 100 feet deep and differential settlement occurs, it may not be economically or physically possible to install piles and extra building foundations to the bedrock to support the improvements and fully mitigate the situation. As a result, it may be reasonable to expect that the property will be more prone to earthquake damage and continued settlement damage. In this type of condition, the value of the property may be permanently impaired and beyond the other Class VI and VII categories.

On the other hand, some Class VI and VII DCs do not have any effect on the rental rates paid by tenants, or the property's liability or utility and may, therefore, be questionable as Class VI or VII DCs at all, if the capitalization rate is also unaffected.

For example, if improperly compacted shallow soils cause some minor settlement cracks on the floor of a warehouse building, and similar settlement cracks are commonly found in comparable properties with no known soils problems, the issue may not have any impact on value. This is particularly true if the tenants' use of the property is unaffected by the condition and the marketability of the space is comparable to that of similar properties.

The Class VII graph indicates a loss in value when the condition is discovered and a return to the non-impacted value upon the assessment

7. Randall Bell, "The Impact of Asbestos on Real Estate Values," *Right of Way* (October 1994): 10–21.

Chapter 2: *The Impact of Detrimental Conditions*

and repair of the condition. As stated, in some unusual conditions, there may be a residual market resistance remaining even after repairs are made.

Class VIII—Environmental Condition. Class VIII involves environmental contamination such as hydrocarbons, asbestos, radioactive waste, solvents, and metals. In these situations, remediation costs must be analyzed carefully. There may be a variance between estimated and actual remediation costs.[8] However, in recent years, this concern has subsided somewhat due to the introduction of cost cap insurance and increased use of indemnifications by responsible parties. In addition, if the property is contaminated, there may be continued and justified concerns about problems and issues resurfacing in the future. The Environmental Protection Agency maintains a list of problem sites, including those yet to be investigated. These lists are available on request, and if a problem arises, a Freedom of Information Act officer can be contacted.[9] No government agency will irrevocably certify a site as clean even if the site has undergone remediation and has *site closure* status.[10] In fact, once contaminated, a site is always on *a list* and, as a result, may be reexamined in the future. Further, it is difficult to prove that all contaminants were removed and no longer exist. In other words, it is logically and scientifically impossible to prove a negative hypothesis and regardless of how much time, energy, or resources are expended, absolute assurance is impossible.[11] Figure 4 shows the general flow of activity related to a contaminated site and the possible circular nature of this process:[12] In recent years, "letters of nonresponsibility" and other mitigation techniques have elevated many of these concerns.

As shown on the chart, even with *site closure,* the sale, refinancing, or new use of a property may trigger a Phase I survey, which in turn could lead to a Phase II study. This, of course, could result in another review of the property by the government regulatory agency, with possible new political agendas or other factors altered since the previous *site closure* was issued. This means that, in rare instances, a formerly contaminated site could be subjected through the site assessment and remediation process again.

Stigma-related losses can be nonexistent, nominal or, in extreme situations, virtually destroy a property's value.[13] When environmental features are viewed as repulsive, upsetting, or disruptive, they are stigmatized as undesirable.[14] While engineering experts may possess the expertise to judge that a specific situation is not a cause for concern, the non-engineer, who is also often the potential buyer and lender, may view a formerly damaged property with skepticism. In contamination cases, the reduction in value results from the increased risk associated with the contaminated property.[15] Such ongoing concerns may create market resistance—sometimes referred to as stigma, onus, taint, or impairment—against properties that have a history of problems and have potentially incurred future liabilities or hidden cleanup costs, as well as against the general hassle involved with owning the property. With source contamination properties, all elements of the DC Model should be considered.

Class IX—Natural Condition. Class IX involves curable natural conditions that may be economically and physically repaired. These would include earthquakes, tornadoes, floods, landslides, endangered species, and other natural conditions.

8. Albert R. Wilson, "Emerging Approaches to Impaired Property Valuation," *The Appraisal Journal* (April 1996): 156.

9. Ralph K. Olsen, "Hazardous Waste Sites," *The Appraisal Journal* (April 1989): 234.

10. Wilson, 158.

11. Albert R. Wilson, "The Environmental Opinion: Basis for an Impaired Value Opinion," *The Appraisal Journal* (July 1994): 441.

12. Randall Bell, "Quantifying Diminution in Value Due to Detrimental Conditions: An Application to Environmentally Contaminated Properties," *Environmental Claims Journal* (October 1996): 135.

13. Peter J. Patchin, "Contaminated Properties and the Sales Comparison Approach," *The Appraisal Journal* (July 1994): 408.

14. Bill Mundy, "Stigma and Value," *The Appraisal Journal* (January 1992): 10.

15. James A. Chalmers and Scott A. Roehr, "Issues in the Valuation of Contaminated Property," *The Appraisal Journal* (January 1993): 33.

Valuing Contaminated Properties

FIGURE 4 Environmental Contamination: Flow of Events

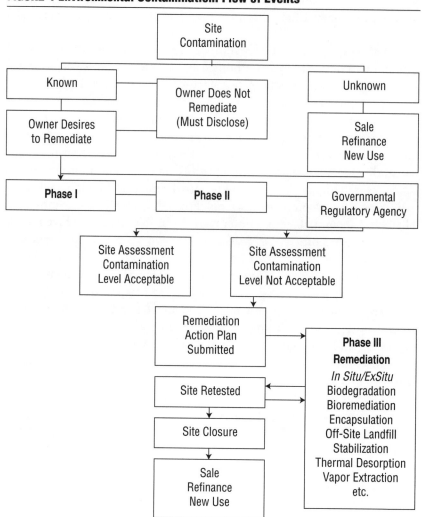

These DCs may involve a significant safety issue to the occupants of the property. If the DC can be fully assessed and repaired, the property value may return to the previous level before the condition existed. However, if there is still a question about the effectiveness of the repair or remediation, there may be a residual loss of value. Again, the impact on value involves the costs to clean up or fortify the site, incidental costs, and any residual conditions. All the elements of the DC Model should be considered.

Class X—Incurable Condition. This class represents the most serious cases, for the property may not be economically or physically remedied, resulting in considerable or total loss in property value. The property may be a liability if the condition creates a serious hazard or the cost to repair exceeds the property value.

Examples of Class X DCs would include extreme toxic or hazardous waste issues and major landslides—situations that pose a risk to life, health, and property, and cannot be economically and physically repaired.

Even if the DC is curable, it would still be considered Class X because the problem cannot be cured by the property owner. For example, if a landslide originates in an adjoining canyon, the property owner cannot make repairs to the affected property because it belongs to another person or entity.

Class X conditions bring about a total or an overwhelming loss in value upon the discovery of the condition and are so severe that property becomes worthless or even a liability if the costs to correct the DC exceeds the property's Class I value.

Methodologies to Quantify Diminution in Value

General research sources. Regardless of the method used in quantifying the impact of a DC, market data must be collected and analyzed. The challenge is that comparable information on DCs is often not provided in typical appraisal reports. For this reason, specialized research methods must be employed. For example, if the DC is soils subsidence, a search may be conducted for all articles published on the topic. From this information, property owners and brokers may be contacted and interviewed. Also, government agencies, environmental engineers, and soils engineers often have logs of completed remediation projects from which specific projects may be identified and studied. Of course, brokers and sales agents often provide excellent leads on properties affected by DCs. Comps Infosystems, Inc., based in San Diego, California, now publishes market data nationwide that is categorized by the Bell Chart.

Paired-sales analysis. This process involves comparing sales affected by a DC with similar sales not affected by a DC. For example, a group of properties under the flight path of an airport can be compared with similar properties not located under the flight path.

Resale analysis. To conduct this analysis, the appraiser would study sales comparables and the subsequent resales of the same properties, usually to determine the increase, decrease, or level conditions of market values, or to determine the impact of a DC by comparing values before and after the DC is discovered. For example, if there is a discernible pattern to the selling prices of a specific property type, the effects and direction of the market can be determined.

Cost-to-remediate analysis. Conducting this analysis means studying the costs to remediate a DC, including engineering, tenant relocation, lost rents, demolition, repair, cleanup, new tenant improvement buildout, leasing commissions, carrying costs, etc.

Market data analysis. This analysis consists of studying the effects of DCs on other properties. Although the unique characteristics of every DC makes direct comparison difficult, market data can help support the appraiser's conclusions. A study designed to cross-reference remediation and stigma costs and losses illustrates the wide range of effects of DCs and provides market data on conditions of sales comparables (see Table 1).

Direct capitalization analysis. This process capitalizes permanent lost rents brought about by a DC. For example, if a property leases for a certain rate before the construction of an adjoining sewage treatment plant and then leases for less upon the completion of the plant, the difference in the net

Valuing Contaminated Properties

TABLE 1 Soils Contamination Survey

Number	Property	Value Uncontaminated	Value Pre-remediation	Estimated Remediation	Project Incentive and Market Resistance	Actual Remediation	Estimated Versus Actual
1	Industrial	$1,100,000	$700,000	$100,000 (B)	30%	$150,000	50%
2	Service station	$550,000	$390,000	$500,000 (S)	29%	n/a	n/a
3	Subdivision	$3,800,000	$3,800,000	$250,000 (S)	0%	$100,000	-60%
4	Retail site	$9,142,368	$9,142,368	$10,000,000 (S)	0%	$20,000,000	100%
5	Industrial	$1,000,000	$400,000	$175,000 (B)	51%	n/a	n/a
6	Industrial	$700,000	$580,000	$100,000 (S)	n/a	n/a	n/a
7	Subdivision	$2,000,000	$1,268,000	$150,000 (S)	n/a	n/a	n/a
8	Auto repair	$655,000	$500,000	$100,000 (B)	10%	$30,000	-70%
9	Service station	$750,000	$340,000	$200,000 (B)	38%	$700,000	250%
10	Industrial	$500,000	$330,000	$30,000 (B)	30%	n/a	n/a

(S) = Seller paid remediation costs.

(B) = Buyer paid remediation costs.

Stigma losses computed on estimated remediation costs.

1 Project incentive and market resistance losses computed by (value uncontaminated − projected remediation) / post-remediation value.

2 Remediation still in progress at the time of interview.

3 Remediation completed by seller without a contractor, reported a savings of $150,000 on this basis.

4 The seller paid all remediation costs. The property had no value contaminated.

5 Remediation not started at time of interview.

6 Sold remediated, with $150,000 in monitoring costs.

9 Buyer purchased property believing remediation costs would be low. In actuality, they were much higher than expected.

10 Remediation not started at time of interview.

Sources: COMPS InfoSystems, Inc., San Diego, California; Orell C. Anderson of PricewaterhouseCoopers, Costa Mesa, California; and Joseph B. Haeussler, MAI, Mason & Mason, Montrose, California.

operating income may be capitalized to determine the permanent impact of the DC. If the income and risks (capitalization or discount rates) are affected, the situation must be addressed, using specific methods.[16]

Discounted cash flow analysis. This analysis involves the calculation of the net present value of a stream of income that reflects an affected property's various costs and fluctuating revenues. If a property is undergoing asbestos abatement or soils remediation, the cash flow study would incorporate all the costs cited in the cost-to-repair approach. In addition, the cash flow would include air or groundwater monitoring costs and, if some contaminants remain, any future demolition, disposal, or cleanup costs. Further, the discount rate may be increased to account for the perceived risks of property ownership, if supported by the market.

Modified cash flow studies are also required to measure the impact of a ground lease on leasehold estates. These leasehold advantage studies involve the calculation of market and contract ground rents and the computation of the net present value of any difference.

Analyzing Detrimental Conditions

The basic guidelines for analyzing DCs are summarized in the following:

1. Always use market data when quantifying the impact of DCs on value. Quantifying damages based *solely* on experience and professional judgment is reckless and probably unethical, particularly when market data exists for virtually all DCs. In the absence of direct market data, surveys may be used.

Failing to research and apply relevant market data is the single most common flaw in DC analysis. Some individuals tend to lump all DCs together when discussing or writing about various condi-

16. Richard A. Neustein, "Estimating Value Diminution by the Income Approach," *The Appraisal Journal* (April 1992): 283–287.

Chapter 2: *The Impact of Detrimental Conditions*

tions. Be careful to understand the limitations of such information, as there are distinct traits for each classification of DCs.

2. Be cautious in using market data from one DC classification when attempting to quantify the diminution in value of another DC category. This is the basic concept of comparing apples to apples. The common characteristics of each class of DCs are graphically distinct. Some DCs involve repairs and some do not; some involve permanent residual conditions while others diminish over time; some involve engineering studies and others do not, and so forth.

3. An appraiser should never go beyond his or her area of expertise. It is unethical for appraisers to go beyond their area of expertise, such as assessing soils conditions, making engineering calculations, identifying contaminants, estimating the extent of damages or contamination, or estimating the time to remediate.[17]

4. Consider the reliability of remediation estimates. It is not uncommon for remediation projects to incur cost overruns. Many issues and questions should be considered, such as: Does the contractor have a contract clause that allows for additional costs? Is the property indemnified against cost overruns? Are the estimates best case, most likely, or worst case scenarios? Do bonds, cost capitalization insurance, or indemnifications exist that shift the liability overruns to the contractor, insurance company, or other party? Are the estimates itemized to reveal any additional incidental costs? Is the site assessment comprehensive enough to yield a realistic cost estimate?[18]

5. Always review the remediation costs and related engineering costs for "reasonableness." While real estate appraisers and analysts are generally not also engineers, it is not only possible but appropriate that these costs be reviewed for basic reasonableness.[19]

6. Consider all the associated repair costs. The actual cost of repair can often be relatively minor compared with all the associated costs, such as engineering costs, tenant relocation, lost rents, demolition, repair, clean-up, tenant improvement buildout, leasing commissions, and absorption. All costs should be itemized, categorized, and analyzed.

7. Never attempt to quantify damages based solely on the Bell Chart. The chart is in no way intended to quantify any loss in value. This can be accomplished only by a comprehensive study by a qualified expert. However, the Bell Chart does show the general issues, typical value patterns, and relative impact on values for various classifications.

8. Exceptions do exist, but usually only in more extreme circumstances. These charts reflect the common characteristics of DCs, but exceptions do exist. For example, a construction defect may be so major that it takes many years to repair. This situation may involve considerable disruptions to the tenants and even create media attention. In these types of conditions, the property value may be impacted by negative market reactions to the problems even after the repairs are fully completed.

9. Study the functional utility and mitigation issues carefully. The issues related to the DC's actual impact on the utility of a property

17. Appraisal Institute, "Guide Notes to The Standards of Professional Appraisal Practice, Guide Note 8—The Consideration of Hazardous Substances in the Appraisal Process" (Chicago, Illinois: Appraisal Institute, 1991): D21.

18. Ibid., Guide Note 6—Reliance on Reports Prepared by Others, D14.

19. Ibid.

must be addressed. For example, some DCs do not require immediate repair, and the costs may be significantly mitigated by merely waiting for a naturally occurring tenant vacancy before repairing the problem. Other DCs may affect the property, but the rents, occupancy, and resale value remain unaffected. In these cases, the DC may, in fact, be benign. How the DC has had a real or perceived impact on the day-to-day use of the property must be considered. For example, a few years ago asbestos abatement was considered a necessity by many. Today the perception that asbestos is a health risk has diminished.

10. Recognize the various dimensions of using the Bell Chart. The applications for using the standard Bell Chart classifications are far-reaching. In fact, it is possible that one property issue will involve the use of three or more classifications.

   A property owner may contend that an adjoining development caused his or her property value to decline when market conditions are actually to blame. The property owner might inappropriately use the Class V criteria and presume an impact on value, but the proper analysis would involve a Class I analysis to demonstrate that the condition is benign. Class III would be used to illustrate the real cause of the declining value. By properly classifying DCs, selecting the appropriate method, and following these basic rules, each individual situation may be more effectively and accurately studied. Relevant market data can then be researched and the proper methods applied.

Conclusion

Quantifying the value diminution of property affected by a detrimental condition can be a challenging appraisal assignment. The appraiser must recognize six basic issues: (1) the value as if the property is unaffected by the DC; (2) the value upon the DC's occurrence or its discovery; (3) the necessity for a proper and thorough assessment of the situation; (4) the determination of value upon completion of repairs—i.e., the condition is otherwise resolved; (5) the necessity for the value conclusion to take into account any ongoing costs; and (6) the need to examine the impact of any market resistance. In other words, the appraiser must examine the full spectrum of events—before remediation, the remediation process itself, post-remediation, and any post-repair market resistance caused by the situation. The result should be a meaningful and accurate assessment of how a detrimental condition has affected the value.

Inspections, Disclosures, Environmental Site Assessments, and Remediation Processes

CHAPTER 3

Editor's Introduction

Many appraisers do not want to appraise a property if it is contaminated or use a sale as an unimpaired comparable if it is actually affected by contamination or an environmental risk. They do, however, want to understand their legal and professional duties, responsibilities, and liabilities when they encounter an assignment involving a property affected by contamination or environmental risk.

The articles in this chapter deal with these issues from a variety of viewpoints. The Kearns article provides a good summary of the events that prompted state and federal lawmakers to adopt requirements for site investigation and disclosure of contamination on a property. The article also summarizes the effects of contamination on the financial and appraisal industries. For many years, the appraisal profession has lobbied vigorously to ensure that federal and state regulators do not mistakenly impose a legal responsibility on appraisers to detect the presence of environmental contamination. Many of the articles in this chapter carefully note the differences between the job of the real estate appraiser and that of the trained environmental site inspection expert. The first extract from the Colangelo and Miller book and the Bell material summarize the site assessment process, and Bell provides additional information on types of contaminants and remediation processes.

The Kearns article explains how Guide Note 8, clarifying the duties of appraisers to note environmental conditions, emerged in response to these developments in state and federal law. The second Colangelo and Miller extract, as well as the Roddewig and Martin articles, summarize (and evaluate) relevant standards of professional appraisal practice. Martin, like Colangelo and Miller, describes the requirements for proper completion of the URAR form to report on observed environmental conditions. Kelly summarizes the appraisal implications of regulations requiring disclosure and remediation of lead-based paint when residences are sold.

Levine asserts, however, that appraisers can build on their knowledge of real estate by becoming environmental site assessment specialists and adding Phase I site assessments to the services they can provide potential clients. The

Appraisal Institute in recent years has cooperated with Mr. Levine's organization of professional site assessment specialists by developing joint educational programs and exploring avenues for professional growth and business development for real estate appraisers in the site assessment field.

Environmental Audits: Real Estate's Newest Transaction Safeguards

by Thomas R. Kearns

Environmental protection is one of this country's highest social goals. Public opinion polls rank environmental protection foremost on the list of public concerns—and with good reason.[1] The mishandling of hazardous substances and wastes by industrial and commercial establishments has wreaked havoc on uninformed employees and has interfered with millions of citizens' rights to peace and tranquility. The spilling of such a small amount as one gallon of trichlorethylene, an organic solvent used principally in the dry cleaning industry, into a public water supply can sicken thousands of people, and cost millions of dollars and take many years to remedy.

The press is quick to report horror stories such as the Exxon Valdez oil spill in Alaska; the disaster in Bhopal, India, where the release of methyl isocyanate (MIC) from a Union Carbide plant killed and injured thousands of people and animals; and the infamous tragedy at Love Canal, where the indiscriminate disposal of hazardous wastes in the Niagara Falls area resulted in hundreds of cases of physical and emotional illness. In fact, almost any contemporary magazine or newspaper contains an article about an environmental catastrophe involving hazardous substances.

Strong public demand has resulted in thousands of laws nationwide to control pollution. At first, these laws were at the federal level and were primarily designed to protect rivers and air. In response to the use of hazardous substances in the workplace and elsewhere, however, regulatory laws became increasingly sophisticated. The establishment of a large fund was authorized to pay for the identification and cleanup of environmental problems as well as to ensure that the responsible parties pay for such cleanups.

Eventually, state legislatures became proactive by enacting laws that are even stricter than federal laws. Some of these laws regulate activities that had not been considered necessary to regulate in the 1960s and 1970s. For example, the New Jersey Environmental Cleanup Responsibility Act (ECRA) requires those who sell industrial or commercial property to ob-

Thomas R. Kearns *is president of Environmental Appraisers, Inc., in Langhorne, Pennsylvania, which specializes in Phase 1 audits of industrial and commercial property. He received a BA in psychology from West Chester State University in Pennsylvania and an MA in public administration from Arizona State University. Mr. Kearns is an MAI candidate with the Appraisal Institute.*

This article originally appeared in the July 1991 issue of The Appraisal Journal.

---

1. The Roper Organization, Inc., *The Environment: Public Attitudes and Individual Behavior* (Commissioned by S.C. Johnson & Son, Inc., July 1990), v, 1.

tain an environmental clearance form the state prior to the sale of the property. If contamination exists, the owner or operator of the property must remedy the problem prior to the sale. Because cleanup costs may reach into the millions of dollars, prudent real estate companies and lenders currently require an environmental review before the consummation of an industrial or commercial sale.

Environmental Audits

These environmental laws have created a new area of economic growth. When a real estate transaction takes place, environmental appraisals (otherwise known as environmental audits or Phase 1 Audits) and remediation services are now commonly required to specify the parties responsible for paying pollution cleanup costs.

In this litigation-oriented society, it pays to be prudent when buying or selling real estate. Lender, buyers, real estate brokers, and title companies are insisting that environmental audits occur at the time the real property is sold. Formerly, the only lender-imposed requirements were that the purchaser perform a market appraisal and a termite inspection. Now lenders are mandating radon tests, engineering inspections of the total structure, and detailed environmental inspections to ascertain the extent of any hazardous substances and wastes.

Innocent Landowner Defense

The impetus for these environmental inspections is largely from the original federal Superfund law. Known as the Comprehensive Environmental Response, Compensation and Liability Act, Superfund mandates that current owners of property contaminated with hazardous substances be strictly, jointly, and severally liable for conducting and financing cleanup of such substances. It is not necessary that the owner be linked to the placement of the hazardous substances on the property in order to be held responsible. In other words, the purchaser of contaminated property is as liable as the party that caused the contamination. Amendments to the Superfund Law have attempted to clarify this anxiety-laden issue. The Superfund Amendments and Reauthorization Act of 1986 (SARA) established what has become known as the "innocent landowner" defense.

To invoke the innocent landowner defense, a purchaser must not know or have reason to know that any hazardous substances were disposed on, in, or at the facility. To establish that the purchaser had no reason to know, the purchaser must have undertaken an appropriate inquiry into the previous ownership and uses of the property at the time of the acquisition, consistent with good commercial or customary practice. The establishment of appropriate inquiry minimizes liability for the lender and purchaser.

A bill known as HR 2787, sponsored by Representative Curt Weldon (R-Pennsylvania), is currently before Congress. The bill is an attempt to define what exactly may be considered an appropriate inquiry to qualify for the innocent landowner defense. An appropriate inquiry, or Phase 1 Audit, must be performed by an environmental professional and includes the following steps.

- A review of the recorded chain-of-title documents, including all deeds, easements, leases, restrictions, and covenants for a period of 50 years;

- A review of aerial photographs taken over time (e.g., 1950, 1965, and 1985);
- A search for existing recorded environmental cleanup liens;
- A review of reasonably obtainable federal, state, and local government records;
- An inspection of the property to determine the potential for environmental hazards at the site; and
- The development of a detailed report.

The report to the client should indicate whether there are potential environmental concerns at the site that should be precisely delineated through detailed sampling and analysis.

Lenders in particular need to pay attention to the appropriate inquiry requirement. At the time of a mortgage application for the purchase or refinancing of commercial or industrial real property, a lender should contract for an environmental audit. This environmental appraisal will eventually become as familiar to the commercial and industrial sector as termite inspections for residential homes are to the residential sector.

Judicial, Legislative, and Executive Activities

Several government actions that affect lender liability are worth noting. In *United States v. Maryland Bank & Trust Co.*,[2] the court held the bank liable for the substantial cleanup costs required on a property. The mortgagee defaulted on the loan and the bank subsequently foreclosed on the property. Under Superfund, the bank was viewed as the owner of the property and was therefore found liable. With a payment of $400,000, the bank settled the claim with the government.

The recent decision in *United States v. Fleet Factors Corp.*[3] broadens the potential liability of financing institutions. Decided May 23, 1990, it holds that a secured creditor could incur Superfund liability, even without foreclosure, if the lender participates in the financial management of the borrower's business. There are no guidelines to clarify what the court deemed "the financial management of the borrower's business."[4]

Two recently introduced federal bills, HR 4494 and S 2319, attempt to provide the necessary guidelines for limiting lender liability for environmental cleanup costs. They are a result of the confusion created by the Superfund lender liability court decisions, most notably the *Fleet Factors* decision. Both bills provide an exemption from liability when a depository institution or mortgage lender acquires property through foreclosure or manages property in a fiduciary capacity. However, the Senate bill requires lenders to "develop and implement adequate procedures to evaluate potential environmental risks that may arise from lending and fiduciary activities."[5]

The United States Environmental Protection Agency (EPA), also reacting to pressure from the banking industry, has drafted a rule to clarify Superfund lender liability. The "interpretative" rule is currently being reviewed by the Office of Management and Budget. It allows private and government lending institutions as well as successors-in-interest holding a security interest in a facility to perform activities related to a borrower's facility while protecting their security interest, without sacrificing the exemption. The draft requires lenders to take "actions consistent with pro-

2. 632 F. Supp 573 (D. Md. 1986).
3. 905 F. 2d 1550 (11th Cir. 1990).
4. Ibid.
5. HR 4494 was introduced by U.S. Representative John J. LaFalce (D-New York), and S 2319 was introduced by U.S. Senator Jack Garn (R-Utah). Both were introduced in 1990.

tecting the security interest, possibly including cleanup of the property prior to or during the life of the loan and permission for the lender to periodically or regularly monitor or inspect both the collateral (including site inspections) or the borrower's business and financial condition."[6] As is to be expected, lenders have no interest in becoming the environmental police force of the 1990s and are therefore opposed to monitoring a borrower's environment-related activities.

Effect on Appraisers

How do the ramifications of these laws affect market appraisers during real estate appraisals? Guide Note No. 8 of the *Standards of Professional Appraisal Practice*[7] provides guidance for those who appraise real estate affected by hazardous substances. It states that an appraiser should note in the report any condition observed during the inspection of the subject property or through the normal research involved in performing the appraisal that would lead the appraiser to believe that hazardous substances may be present in or on the property. An appraiser should also note any data at variance with information or descriptions provided by others.

An appraiser may accept an assignment that involves the consideration of hazardous substances without having the required specialized knowledge and experience provided he or she discloses such lack of knowledge and experience to the client before accepting the assignment and arranges to complete the assignment competently. This may entail reliance on professional reports prepared by those reasonably believed to have such necessary knowledge and experience.

Conclusion

Real estate appraisers can minimize potential environmental problems by analyzing or having an expert analyze property to ascertain the use or misuse of hazardous substances at the time of the real estate transaction. This analysis, in the form of a Phase 1 Audit, can make a realtor, lender, appraiser, or purchaser less subject to liability.

Real estate appraisers are obligated to tackle the issue of hazardous substances, either by relying on knowledgeable professionals or by formally noting the limitation of the scope of the assignment in appraisal reports.

6. Mary Anne Reilly, "EPA, Congress Moving Toward Lender Liability Rule Under CERCLA," *Hazmat World* (December 1990): 14–15.

7. Appraisal Institute, Guide Note No. 8, *Standards of Professional Appraisal Practice of the Appraisal Institute* (Washington, DC: The Appraisal Foundation, 1990), D-21.

The ASTM Standards on Environmental Site Assessments for Commercial Real Estate Transactions

by Robert V. Colangelo, CPG, and Ronald D. Miller, Esq.

ASTM (formerly the American Society for Testing and Materials) is a not for profit organization that provides a forum and set of procedures for the development of industry standards. After recognizing the need to standardize environmental assessment procedures, major real estate trade organizations such as Fannie Mae, Freddie Mac, National Association of Home Builders, National Apartment Association, American Bankers Association, and the Independent Bankers Association formed a committee under the jurisdiction of ASTM.

While the group initially set out to develop a single standard for Phase I ESAs, the group recognized a need for a procedure that can be utilized by someone other than an environmental professional to prescreen properties for environmental hazards. The Transaction Screen consists of a series of questionnaires that call for "objective observation" as opposed to the "subjective evaluation" of an environmental professional in a Phase I ESA. Therefore, because it requires no technical training or experience, the ASTM Transaction Screen is a valuable tool for the appraiser.

Scope, Purpose, and Design of the ASTM Standard Practices

The stated purpose of the ASTM Standard Practices for Environmental Site Assessments is to define "good commercial or customary practice for conducting an environmental site assessment" on commercial real estate. The intent is to identify "recognized environmental conditions," which are defined as the presence, or likely presence, of any hazardous substances or petroleum products on a property under conditions that indicate a release into the structure, groundwater, surface water, or soils. This does not include "de minimis conditions" that do not present a material risk of harm to public health or the environment and that generally would not be the subject of an enforcement action if brought to the attention of government agencies.

Robert V. Colangelo, CPG, *is managing director and cofounder of the Environmental Planning Group, Inc., which provides strategic consulting and capital markets services to the environmental industry.*

Ronald D. Miller, Esq. *is an attorney with extensive experience in the area of environmental risk in real estate transactions.*

The material was originally published in Environmental Site Assessments and Their Impact on Property Value: The Appraiser's Role (Chicago: Appraisal Institute, 1995).

The objectives of the ASTM Standard Practices are to

1. Synthesize, in writing, "good commercial and customary practice" for ESAs for commercial real estate
2. Facilitate high-quality standardized ESAs
3. Ensure that the standard of "all appropriate inquiry" is practical and reasonable
4. Clarify an industry standard for appropriate inquiry in an effort to guide legal interpretation of Superfund's Innocent Landowner Defense

With the notable exception of petroleum products, the scope of the ASTM standards is generally limited to hazardous wastes and materials defined under CERCLA. Therefore, these environmental hazards are *not* covered:

- Radon
- Asbestos and asbestos-containing materials
- Lead-based paint
- Lead in drinking water
- Wetlands and other environmentally sensitive lands

Although these issues may be of concern to a real estate purchaser or lender, they are outside the scope of ASTM's two ESA standards. Accordingly, it is the responsibility of environmental professionals and their clients to negotiate a scope of work that addresses these items.

The ASTM Standard Practice for Environmental Site Assessments consists of two related practices: the Transaction Screen Process (E 1528) and the Phase I Environmental Site Assessment Process (E 1527). Each is intended to meet the standard of appropriate inquiry necessary to qualify for the Innocent Landowner Defense under CERCLA. It is the user's option to commence the inquiry with either practice. Note that multifamily residential buildings and single-family homes are not included within the term "commercial real estate transactions" and, accordingly, fall outside the scope of both ESA standards. However, because environmental hazards are often of concern to purchasers of residential properties, ASTM specifically states that the user may elect to perform an environmental site assessment consistent with either the Transaction Screen or Phase I Environmental Site Assessment process.

Other important principles of the ASTM standards are helpful in exercising the discretion accorded to users or environmental professionals performing an ESA or Transaction Screen. First, the ASTM standards note that no ESA can wholly eliminate uncertainty about *potential* environmental conditions on a particular property. Therefore, the performance of either ASTM practice is intended to reduce, not necessarily eliminate, uncertainty with regard to the environmental integrity of a subject property.

As is the case in any environmental investigation, the purpose of the ASTM practices is to identify a balance between 1) the competing goals of limiting cost and time demands in performing an environmental assessment and 2) reduction of uncertainty about unknown environmental hazards. Accordingly, there may be a point at which the cost of information obtained, or the time required to gather it, outweighs the usefulness of the information and may be a material detriment to the efficient completion of real estate transactions. The standards allow the user to determine when the information to be obtained is more costly or time-consuming than its respective benefit, recognizing that not every property warrants the same level of assessment. Therefore, the scope of work can be modified according to the type of subject property, the expertise and risk tolerance of the user, and the information developed in the course of the inquiry. Subsequent environmental site assessments should not be considered valid standards to judge the appropriateness of any prior assessment based on hindsight, new information, or use of developing technology or analytical techniques.

The ASTM Transaction Screen Process

The Transaction Screen Process is designed for completion by those who have limited or no formal training in the identification of environmental hazards. It may be conducted by the user—including an agent, independent contractor, employee, or appraiser hired by the user—or the user may elect to perform the Transaction Screen Process through an environmental professional. However, the process is designed so that the judgment of an environmental professional is not required.

In completing the Transaction Screen Process, the user may conclude that 1) no further inquiry into recognized environmental conditions on the property is needed for the purposes of appropriate inquiry or 2) further inquiry is needed to assess recognized environmental conditions. The further inquiry may be limited to specific issues identified as of concern, or it may proceed to a full Phase I ESA. For example, if the Transaction Screen Process indicates that 55-gallon storage drums are located on the property, the user may elect to limit further inquiry to the contents of and soil conditions around the drums. However, if the user elects to perform a full Phase I ESA, it must be performed by a qualified environmental professional.

The basic components of the Transaction Screen Process are

1. A questionnaire for completion by owners and occupants of the property to be filled out at the time of the site inspection
2. A site inspection checklist
3. Limited research regarding government environmental records
4. Historical fire insurance maps or contacting a local fire department to determine potential for historical uses of the property involving hazardous materials

A guide is included to assist the user in completing the Transaction Screen Questionnaire.

In performing the Transaction Screen, the user should employ good faith efforts to determine appropriate answers. While the person conducting the Transaction Screen has an obligation to ask the questions set forth, in many instances the parties to whom the questions are addressed have no obligation to answer. The user is only required to obtain information to the extent it is "reasonably ascertainable." If the user does not receive responses, or only partial answers, the questions will be deemed to have been answered, provided appropriate telephone and written records have been kept.

If any of the questions in the Transaction Screen Questionnaire are answered in the affirmative, the user must document the reason. If any of the questions are not answered or the answer is unknown, this should be documented and evaluated based on other information obtained. If the user decided that no further inquiry is warranted after receiving no response, an answer of "unknown," or an affirmative response, the user must document the reason for such conclusion because a presumption exists that further inquiry is necessary if not otherwise explained. To overcome this presumption, the user should evaluate the information obtained from other components of the Transaction Screen to determine whether sufficient information has been obtained for a conclusion of no further inquiry.

The persons qualified to answer the owner/occupant questionnaire include

1. The current owner of the property
2. Any major occupant of the property, or if the property does not have any major occupants, at least 10% of the occupants of the property
3. In addition to the current owner and occupants identified above, all occupants likely to possess or use hazardous substances or petroleum products on the property

A major occupant is any occupant using at least 40% of the leasable area of the property, or an anchor tenant when the property is a shopping center. For a multifamily property with both residential and commercial uses, the preparer does not need to ask questions of the residential occupants. The preparer should ask each person to answer all questions to the best of their actual knowledge and in good faith.

ASTM Phase I Environmental Site Assessment Process

The ASTM Phase I Environmental Site Assessment must be performed by an environmental professional. However, the user has some basic responsibilities. First, the user has responsibility for checking land title records for environmental liens. Specifically, ASTM suggests that the user check land title records at the appropriate place (where land titles are normally recorded). Alternatively, the user may engage a title company or other title professional to check land title records for environmental liens currently recorded against the property. In the event that there are such liens, this information must be communicated to the environmental professional prior to the performance of the Phase I ESA. Additionally, if the user is aware of any specialized knowledge or experience that is material to the potential for contamination on the property, the user is responsible for communicating this information to the environmental professional. Finally, if the user has actual knowledge that the sale price of the property is significantly less than the sale price of comparable properties, the user should try to identify an explanation for the lower price and make a written record of such explanation, which then becomes part of the Phase I ESA.

Basic components of the ASTM Phase I ESA are

1. Records review, including government environmental records and historical information sources
2. Site reconnaissance

Chapter 3: *The ASTM Standards*

3. Interviews with current owners and occupants of the property as well as interviews with local government officials

4. A report summarizing the investigation

The records review, site reconnaissance, and owner-occupant interviews are to be used in concert with each other to corroborate evidence of the property's environmental integrity.

Records Review

The objective of the records review is to help identify environmental hazards on, or in close proximity to, the property. Standard government environmental record sources and approximate search distances are summarized in Figure 3.1.

FIGURE 3.1 Phase I ESA: Standard Environmental Record Sources

Record Source	Search Distance
Federal NPL [National Priorities List]	1.0 miles
Federal CERCLIS list	.5 miles
Federal RCRA TSD facilities lists	1.0 miles
Federal RCRA generators list	Property and adjoining property
Federal ERNS list	Property only
State lists of hazardous waste sites identified for investigation or remediation (NPL and CERCLIS equivalents)	1.0 miles
State landfill and/or solid waste disposal site lists	.5 miles
State leaking UST lists	.5 miles
State registered UST lists	Property and adjoining properties

Source: ASTM E 1527, Sec. 7.2.1.1

In addition, other state or local sources (such as county health departments, municipal departments, and building departments) may be checked at the discretion of the environmental professional to enhance and supplement the federal and state sources in Figure 3.1. Local records may include

- Lists of landfill and solid waste disposal sites
- Lists of hazardous waste and contaminated sites
- Lists of registered underground storage tanks
- Records of emergency release reports (under SARA Section 304)
- Records of contaminated public wells
- Records of PCB-containing transformers

Potential sources for local environmental records include the

- Health department's environmental division
- Fire department
- Planning department
- Building permit/inspection department
- Local or regional pollution control agency
- Local or regional water quality agency
- Local electric utility companies (for records relating to PCBs)

In addition, the ASTM Phase I ESA requires incorporation of a current U.S. Geological Survey 7.5-minute topographic map showing the area in which the property is located. Other physical setting information, including hydrogeologic, hydrologic, or soil conditions of the site, may be obtained at the discretion of the environmental professional.

Historical Use Information

Consulting historical sources on previous uses or occupancies of the property and surrounding areas can help identify past uses or occupancies that may pose current environmental risks. Identifying prior property uses is a two-tiered process under the ASTM standard.

1. Uses of the property are identified from the present back to 1940 using as many standard historical sources as necessary.

2. Uses prior to 1940 (until a time when the property was not yet developed) are identified using at least one standard historical source.

To meet the requirements of the ASTM standard, at least one of these standard historical sources must be consulted:

- Aerial photographs
- Historical fire insurance maps
- Property tax files
- Recorded land title records
- Historical USGS topographic maps
- Local street directories
- Building department records
- Zoning or land use records
- Any other historical sources that are credible to a reasonable person that identify past uses or occupancies of the property

In addition to the history of the subject site, a history of the properties in the surrounding area may be researched at a search distance and time period determined by the environmental professional.

Site Reconnaissance

During the site reconnaissance the environmental professional visits the property and visually and physically observes the property and any structures located on it to the extent not obstructed by bodies of water, adjacent buildings, or other obstacles. The property's periphery and interiors must be inspected.

The environmental professional must document the specific grid patterns or other systematic approaches used for large properties. To the extent that physical observation is obstructed, the environmental professional must document such obstructions in the report. The environmental professional should observe the current uses and conditions and indications of historical uses and conditions of the subject property and adjoining properties. Observations of the surrounding area should be made on the site visit or while going to or from the property for the site visit.

Specific items to be observed during the Phase I ESA site inspection include:

- Storage tanks (above or below ground)
- Strong, pungent, or noxious odors

Chapter 3: *The ASTM Standards*

- Pools of liquid
- Drums
- Hazardous substance and petroleum products containers
- Unidentified substance containers
- PCBs (electrical or hydraulic equipment known to contain PCBs)
- Heating or cooling systems (including the fuel source)
- Stains or corrosion
- Drains and sumps
- Pits, ponds, or lagoons
- Stained soil or pavement
- Stressed vegetation
- Solid waste
- Wastewater
- Wells (including dry wells, irrigation injection, or abandoned wells)
- Septic systems

Interviews with Owners and Occupants

The objective of the owner-occupant interviews is to obtain information from current owners or users about the potential for environmental problems. The interview may be conducted in person, by telephone, or in writing. Interviewees include the key site manager, occupants, and anyone having knowledge about the current or past uses of the property. In addition, the environmental professional should ask questions about helpful documents that might be available, including previous environmental site assessment reports, environmental audit reports, environmental permits, registrations, or correspondence with environmental agencies.

The ASTM Phase I ESA Standard also requires interviews with local government officials, including fire department and health agency personnel. In many instances, these persons (including local government officials) may have no obligation to answer questions. If the person conducting the interviews does not receive answers, or receives only partial answers, records must be kept documenting the attempt.

Evaluation and Report Preparation

The ASTM Phase I ESA Standard includes a recommended report format to document results of inquiries consistently. Documentation to support the analyses, opinions, and conclusions should be included. All sources, including those that did not reveal findings, should be sufficiently documented to facilitate reconstruction of the research at a later date. The report should include all matters and issues included in the research for the report.

The report must identify the environmental professional(s) involved in conducting the Phase I ESA and the qualifications of the person responsible for the performance of the ESA. The standard also requires the environmental professional's opinion of the impact of any and all recognized environmental conditions identified in connection with the property. A findings and conclusion section then states one of the following:

1. "We have performed a Phase I Environmental Site Assessment in conformance with the scope and limitations of ASTM Practice E 1527 of the property. Any exceptions to, or deletions from, this prac-

Valuing Contaminated Properties

tice are described in Section _ of this report. This assessment revealed no evidence of recognized environmental conditions in connection with the property."

2. "We have performed a Phase I Environmental Site Assessment in conformance with the scope and limitations of ASTM Practice E 1527 of the property. Any exceptions to, or deletions from this practice are described in Section _ of this report. This assessment has revealed no evidence of recognized environmental conditions in connection with the property except the following," with an appropriate list provided.

All additions, deletions, and deviations from the practice are to be listed individually and in detail. The ASTM Phase I Environmental Site Assessment Process is reprinted in Appendix E.

The ASTM Standards go a long way toward facilitating the efficient consideration of environmental hazards in commercial real estate transactions. Because the ASTM Standards are subject to continued amendment and modification, readers with an ongoing interest in this area are advised to join ASTM Committee E-50 on Environmental Site Assessment.[1]

1. Membership information can be obtained from ASTM at 1916 Race St., Philadelphia, PA 19103 (215) 299-5400.

The New URAR and Environmental Hazards

by Danny J. Martin

As of January 1, 1994, a new version of the Uniform Residential Appraisal Report (URAR) is required for all loan purchases made by the Federal National Mortgage Association (Fannie Mae). The form's newly revised comments section specifically requires that an appraiser comment on "adverse environmental conditions (such as, but not limited to, hazardous wastes, toxic substances, etc.) present in the improvements, on the site, or in the immediate vicinity of the subject property."[1] This addition clarifies an appraiser's responsibility to report what he or she discovers during the inspection of the property and the normal research involved in performing an appraisal. All appraisers thus are now required to address environmental issues.

Successful completion of the URAR comments section requires a basic understanding of environmental issues; it requires more than answering "none noted" and relying on a limiting condition. It is, however, much less cumbersome than it appears.

The new comments section is comprehensive in scope, requiring an appraiser to note "obvious" environmentally hazardous risks in the improvements, site, and vicinity. "Obvious" environmental conditions are those conditions that a layperson exercising reasonable care would uncover. In addition, limited research or screening of public records for "known" environmental hazards is necessary to determine if a site or proximate sites are known to have environmental hazard risks. Environmental hazards that would require intrusive investigation or scientific testing to detect are clearly outside of a layperson's level of expertise, and an appraiser is considered a layperson in these matters.

USPAP Requirements

Standards Rule 1-1 (a) of the *Uniform Standards of Professional Appraisal Practice* (USPAP) provides the authority for appraisers to upgrade their personal knowledge and understanding of all new appraisal issues and techniques. The standard states:

Danny J. Martin is a commercial fee appraiser in Garden Grove, California. He is a member of the E50 Committee of the American Society for Testing and Materials (ASTM). Mr. Martin's published works include numerous articles, environmental training manuals, and environmental database systems.

This article originally appeared in the January 1995 issue of The Appraisal Journal.

---

1. Federal National Mortgage Association (Fannie Mae), Uniform Residential Appraisal Report (Form 1004) (Washington, D.C.: Fannie Mae, 1993), 1.

In developing a real property appraisal, an appraiser must be aware of, understand, and correctly employ those recognized methods and techniques that are necessary to produce a credible appraisal.[2]

USPAP Standards Rule 1-1 (b) states:

In developing a real property appraisal an appraiser must not commit a substantial error of omission or commission that significantly affects an appraisal.[3]

The USPAP comment for this standard provides clear authority that:

An appraiser must be certain that the gathering of factual information is conducted in a manner that is sufficiently diligent to ensure that the data that would have a material or significant effect on the resulting opinions or conclusions are considered.[4]

USPAP Standards Rule 1-3(a), which deals with the preliminary analysis, selection, and collection of data, states:

In developing a real property appraisal, an appraiser must observe the following appraisal guidelines: consider the effect on the use and value of the following factors: existing land use regulations, reasonably probable modifications of such land use regulations, economic demand, the physical adaptability of the real estate, neighborhood trends, and the highest and best use of the real estate.[5]

Standards Rule 3 sets forth a list of factors that affect use and value. Since adverse environmental conditions can exist in the areas listed within this standard, an appraiser must investigate and consider issues affecting a site, improvements, and neighborhood.

Clearly, the need to understand the environmental issues that affect real estate has always existed. The USPAP and revised URAR bring this requirement to the forefront.

Client Requirements

Appraisers who have been in the profession for some time will remember the original Fannie Mae Form 1004. It standardized residential appraisal requirements and reporting. In the mid-1980s the URAR was introduced. Since the form's introduction, new issues have evolved and user requirements have changed; environmental hazard risk is one of many such issues. Lenders need credible environmental information because environmental hazards affect both human health and property values. The bottom line is that users of appraisal services want environmental information and analysis so they can make informed decisions.

"But I'm Not an Expert"

When it comes to environmental investigations, most appraisers would agree on two matters. First, appraisers are not environmental experts. Second, many feel that they do not need to address environmental issues and instead choose to rely on disclaimers and limiting conditions. (A third item some appraisers might confess to is the wish that the whole issue would just go away!)

With regards to the first statement, no one would expect an appraiser to be an environmental expert nor even ask that he or she become one.

2. The Appraisal Foundation, *Uniform Standards of Professional Appraisal Practice* (USPAP) (Washington, D.C.: The Appraisal Foundation, 1994), 9.

3. Ibid.

4. Ibid.

5. Ibid., 11.

Chapter 3: *The New URAR*

The second issue, however, is much more complex. If the USPAP require an appraiser to investigate and consider issues affecting a site, improvements, and neighborhood, disclaimers such as those found in the Appraisal Standards Board (ASB) Advisory Opinion G-9 and the new limiting condition contained in Fannie Mae's Form 439 will not serve to eliminate the requirements to investigate, consider, and report adverse environmental conditions.

Why All the Confusion?

An environmental investigation should not be confused with the requirements made of an environmental expert, but rather those of a layperson exercising "reasonable care."

Users of appraisal services are best served when appraisers investigate environmental risks and report the findings in an appraisal report, as occurs when appraisers investigate and report zoning, flood, or other geological considerations. If adverse conditions are found to exist, a user is put on notice and advised to seek expert consultation.

With a basic level of proficiency in performing environmental due diligence, an appraiser can estimate adjustments for environmental risks if cost data or market information are available. An appraiser cannot, however, be expected to make adjustments for cleanup costs, location, or stigma without first identifying the basic physical and neighborhood characteristics. Failure to perform due diligence may result in nondisclosure of known public facts and an unreliable value estimate.

Checklists and a Word of Caution

Many mortgage lenders have been and will be requesting appraisers to explain adverse environmental findings with expanded comments or completion of an environmental checklist. The Appraisal Institute has responded to the need for standardized checklists by releasing the Property Observation Checklist, which was developed with the assistance of the American Society for Testing and Materials (ASTM). The checklist was approved in July 1993 at the Appraisal Institute's national meeting in Reno, Nevada, and was published in the Summer 1993 issue of *Environmental Watch.*[6] Appraisers may wish to use this form as the guide to environmental screening or actually include it in the addenda section of a report. The Appraisal Institute's Task Force on Appraisers' Environmental Liability should be commended for its efforts.

The checklist is divided into three parts. Section I, titled "Extent of Appraiser's Inspection of the Property," deals with the scope of the inspection. An appraiser simply states the scope of the investigation he or she conducted. Section II, "Environmental Issues Observed by the Appraiser," is well designed and easy to use. All of the questions can be answered by a layperson. Sections I and II are thorough and will limit an appraiser's liability.

Section III, titled "Environmental Issues Reported by Others," asks the question: "Have you been informed, verbally, or in writing, of any of the following?"[7] Six of the nine items following the question deal with issues that are useful to a client only if an appraiser searches the public records. A client could infer that a "no" response to any of these questions means no environmental hazards exist; in reality, the response may mean only

6. "Final Report on the Task Force on Appraisers' Environmental Responsibility," *Environmental Watch* (Summer 1993): 2.

7. Appraisal Institute, Property Observation Checklist (Chicago: Appraisal Institute, 1993).

that an appraiser was not informed of any existing hazards because he or she did not check the public records.

If at a later date your testimony is required in a court of law, would you rather respond, "No, Your Honor, I don't know. No one informed me," or "Yes, Your Honor, I checked the following public records and here are my findings?"

It should be remembered that an appraiser typically meets an owner or a representative at the property. When was the last time a property owner informed you about the toxic waste dump up the street or the leaking tank next door, or, for that matter, any other property defect? There are tens of thousands of known hazardous sites. Don't be the appraiser who overlooks the site next door, or worse, the subject property.

Basic Environmental Screening

Professional real estate appraisers will be pleased to note that the same basic investigative techniques used in the appraisal process can be applied to the environmental screening process. Environmental hazards relating to the improvements or site can be investigated during the physical inspection of the property. Remember, the intent of the physical inspection is to detect *obvious* environmental hazards, not to tear out walls or perform soil corings.

Obvious environmental concerns relating to the immediate vicinity (i.e., hazardous waste facilities, dumps, factories, gas stations) can be uncovered during a neighborhood investigation. In many instances, an appraiser can now conveniently search from the office for publicly reported locations of known environmentally hazardous sites by ordering an electronic search from an environmental information provider.

Risks Present in the Improvements

Improvement-related risks refer to any environmental hazard within the improvements. Some of these items are quite obvious; others are concealed or out of sight. Unfortunately, the items appraisers are most frequently requested to address are concealed items such as asbestos, urea-formaldehyde insulation, PCBs, lead paint, and radon gas. None of these items falls into the "obvious" category.

Asbestos

Asbestos was first regulated in 1972, with many construction applications severely restricted by law. In 1979 further restrictions eliminated its use in residential construction. Therefore, buildings constructed before 1979 have a much higher probability of having asbestos materials. The likelihood that a structure built after 1979 contains asbestos is very limited.

The most common occurrences of asbestos in residential structures include:

- *Sprayed-on acoustic ceiling material.* This resembles stucco and is commonly referred to as "cottage cheese." A finer, granular variation of this material was commonly used for interior fireproofing materials for walls. Though these materials were used until the late 1970s, the majority of builders adopted the use of cellulose-based acoustic ceiling materials, which have a spongy texture compared with the rock-like hardness of asbestos.

- *Floor tiles.* Asbestos was used in some tiles predating 1980, and it was even more common in floors predating the introduction of vinyl flooring. Tiles that are most likely to contain asbestos are typical in homes built before 1970. The tiles require wax to maintain a shine and have a faux-marble or "grocery store" look.
- *Heating, ventilation, and air-conditioning (HVAC) systems and boiler systems.* The most common place asbestos might be is the furnace vent pipe, which may have the appearance of a cement pipe.

If a structure was built after 1980, the probability of finding asbestos is limited; if a house predates 1980, keep your eyes open for the common occurrences just listed.

Urea-formaldehyde insulation

Urea-formaldehyde insulation is a foam sprayed between wall cavities. The use of urea-formaldehyde insulation was short-lived, beginning in about 1970 and ending with a ban in 1982. Its most common use was as a retro-fit insulation during the oil shortage years of the 1970s. If an appraiser suspects the presence of the foam, he or she should check the exterior walls for evidence of its installation, specifically patched holes about two inches in diameter. Be aware, however, that cellulose insulation (i.e., shredded newspaper) was installed in a manner similar to formaldehyde insulation and would therefore leave the same signs. If a structure was not built between 1970 and 1982, the probability of finding urea-formaldehyde is limited. Always ask whether a house is insulated, and if so what type of insulation was used. If the answer includes the word "foam," investigate further.

PCBs

If a property has underground utilities an appraiser need not worry about PCBs, because PCB contamination would most likely occur from a leaking transformer attached to an overhead utility pole. If a property has a pole with a transformer, check the ground under the transformer for any signs of oily residue. If a residue is present, tell the homeowner to contact the electrical utility company for an inspection.

Lead-based paint

Lead is the agent that affects the drying and hardening of paint. Some painters swear by the use of lead paint and still acquire lead additives through black-market channels; they continue to use them, even though lead-based paint was banned several years ago. Appraisers should note that the older the house, the more likely it is that lead-based paint was used. The bottom line: It requires scientific testing to detect lead.

Radon

The United States Environmental Protection Agency's (EPA) Statewide Radon Survey, which is available in most states, is a statewide summary of test results actually conducted within houses and can be a useful screening source to locate known areas where radon gas frequently occurs.[8] This report can be used as a general overview, but appraisers should remember that the only way to detect the presence of radon gas is to test for it.

8. United States Environmental Protection Agency (EPA), *Statewide Radon Survey* (Washington, D.C.: EPA, 1990).

Risks Present on the Site

Site-related risks can include an array of potentially hazardous conditions such as underground storage tanks; stained soils; stressed vegetation; 55-gallon drums; sewage treatment; on-site storage of paints, chemicals, or petroleum products; and piled debris. In suburban tract developments, these risks rarely occur, so concern is typically not required. In rural or older urban settings, these hazards occur more frequently. Remember, be alert for the obvious. As a rule of thumb, if it doesn't look right it probably isn't.

Risks Present in the Vicinity

A diligent visual inspection of a neighborhood will uncover obvious environmental hazards. But what about those environmental hazards one cannot see? A search of public records for known environmental hazards becomes necessary. The information uncovered in the records search may be critical to a neighborhood analysis or surrounding-area analysis. Information uncovered in a public records search may determine or explain location adjustments.

The purpose of a public records search is to determine if a site or any proximate site is a publicly reported environmental hazard. Findings can be disclosed as is done for zoning, flood, and other geological considerations.

What Public Records Should Be Searched?

To begin, an appraiser should consult ASTM standards; their Transaction Screen Process is the industry benchmark. The process focuses on three main areas, including a list of questions an appraiser would ask of the subject property's current owner or operator and a search of government records.[9] The screening process is the basis for the Appraisal Institute's Property Observation Checklist and is widely accepted by the lending community. Completion of the screening process requires that an appraiser search the following eight databases:

- National Priorities Sites List (NPL)
- Comprehensive Environmental Response, Compensation and Liability Index of Sites (CERCLIS)
- Resource Conservation and Recovery Act (RCRA) Treatment, Storage, and Disposal (TSD)
- Superfund Liens List
- State equivalent of the NPL
- State equivalent of CERCLIS
- State list of leaking underground storage tanks
- State list of landfill sites

Environmental databases come in a variety of reporting formats including "street-listings," which require street-by-street searches, and the more convenient "zip code sorts" for searching defined areas.

The databases just listed include sites that are publicly reported environmental hazards. Other available databases cover potential environmental hazards (e.g., permitted underground storage tanks, dry cleaners). An analogy that would be familiar to appraisers is to consider ASTM's eight suggested databases as "closed sales" and potential environmental hazards as "listings," or potential future events. Therefore, in the context of the

---

9. For more information on the Transaction Screen Process, see William H. Ethier, "The ASTM Standards on Environmental Assessments for Commercial Real Estate," *Environmental Watch* (Spring 1994): 1–3.

environmental screening process, an appraiser should focus on the publicly reported environmental hazards and leave potential environmental hazards to experts performing Phase I Environmental Site Assessments (ESAs).[10]

To access federal databases (e.g., NPL, CERCLIS, RCRA TSD, Superfund Liens), the regional office of the U.S. EPA should be contacted. EPA representatives can also help locate state agency contacts for obtaining environmental information in a particular state. In addition, many private firms package and resell databases or provide individual search services.

Conclusion

Professional appraisers see environmental issues as evolutionary and are willing to assume appropriate environmental inspection responsibilities as they are developed. Fannie Mae has recognized appraisers as logical participants to perform the environmental screening process since appraisers are trained to make physical site and neighborhood inspections. This is a vote of confidence for the appraisal profession, and appraisers should make every effort to perform this service competently.

Reference

American Society for Testing and Materials (ASTM), *Standard Practice for Environmental Site Assessment: Transaction Screen Process,* E1528 (Philadelphia: ASTM, 1993).

10. For more information on the different levels of environmental assessment, see Albert R. Wilson, "The Environmental Opinion: Basis for an Impaired Value Opinion," *The Appraisal Journal* (July 1994): 410–423.

Agency Standards and Industry Guidance on Addressing Environmental Hazards

by Robert V. Colangelo, CPG, and Ronald D. Miller, Esq.

Robert V. Colangelo, CPG, *is managing director and cofounder of the Environmental Planning Group, Inc., which provides strategic consulting and capital markets services to the environmental industry.*

Ronald D. Miller, Esq. *is an attorney with extensive experience in the area of environmental risk in real estate transactions.*

The material was originally published in Environmental Site Assessments and Their Impact on Property Value: The Appraiser's Role *(Chicago: Appraisal Institute, 1995).*

As financial, government, and related regulatory bodies recognize the increasing impact of environmental hazards on real estate transactions, some groups are imposing new requirements on appraisers. Such requirements may redefine the appraiser's role in the environmental hazard identification process. To address industry concerns, government agencies, the secondary mortgage market, and appraisal associations are issuing documents that variously attempt to clarify the appraiser's responsibility toward environmental issues. This chapter summarizes some of the current standards and guidelines in the area that directly impact appraisal practice. In addition, summation of a related court case is provided.

Appraisal Standards Board Advisory Opinion G-9

In December 1992 the Appraisal Standards Board (ASB) of The Appraisal Foundation issued Advisory Opinion G-9, "Responsibility of Appraisers Concerning Toxic or Hazardous Substance Contamination." Advisory Opinion G-9 notes that while an appraiser is a trained and experienced observer of real estate, "recognizing, detecting or measuring contamination is often beyond the scope of the appraiser's expertise." Should an appraiser be requested to complete a checklist as part of the process for recognizing contamination, "the appraiser should only respond to questions that can be answered competently by the appraiser within the limits of his or her particular expertise in this area. In each situation, the competency provision of USPAP [Uniform Standards of Professional Appraisal Practice] outlines the responsibility of the appraiser."

Guide Note 8. Standards of Professional Appraisal Practice of the Appraisal Institute

Guide Note 8 of the Standards of Professional Appraisal Practice of the Appraisal Institute is titled "The Consideration of Hazardous Substances in the Appraisal Process."[1] The guide note was written to provide direction to appraisers on how to approach hazardous substances in the ap-

1. Originally adopted by the Governing Council of the American Institute of Real Estate Appraisers in May 1989, Guide Note 8 was adopted by the Board of Directors of the unified Appraisal Institute in January 1991.

praisal process. While recognizing that the typical appraiser is not qualified to detect or measure hazardous materials, the document outlines a basis for proper consideration of hazardous substances and includes the following language:

- When there are no known hazardous substances it is recommended, as a matter of standard practice, for the appraiser to issue a disclaimer or limiting condition to the effect that the appraisal is predicated on the assumption that hazardous substances do not exist. No property can be assumed to be uncontaminated.

- For an appraisal that accounts for the effects on value of hazardous substances, the typical appraiser would require the assistance of an environmental professional.

- If the property being appraised is known to be affected by hazardous substances, or if there is reason to believe that it may be so affected, the appraiser cannot exclude the consideration of such materials without limiting the scope of the appraisal.

- The valuation of the property, as if unaffected by hazards that are known to be present or are suspected of being present, would be predicated on an extraordinary assumption and therefore subject to S.R. 2-1(c) without exception.

- The appraiser should note in the report any condition that is observed during the inspection of the subject property, or becomes known to the appraiser through the normal research involved in performing the appraisal, that would lead the appraiser to believe that hazardous substances may be present in or on the subject property, or is at a variance with information or descriptions provided by others.

Fannie Mae

The Federal National Mortgage Association (Fannie Mae) has set forth environmental requirements for appraisers according to three residential categories.

Multifamily Residential

In Chapter 5 of the Fannie Mae delegated underwriting standards for conventional selling of multifamily residential property mortgages, Fannie Mae sets out specific environmental requirements. This document, published August 1, 1988, is credited with coining the term "Phase I Assessment."

Fannie Mae's multifamily standards require that Phase I site assessments normally be provided by environmental consultants and engineers. It is important for appraisers to recognize that this responsibility has been delegated in the underwriting process. While the responsibility for identifying environmental hazards is placed on environmental professionals, appraisers may encounter Phase I site assessments that identify some environmental hazard. Accordingly, an appraiser may be asked to determine how an identified hazard impacts a property's value.

Condominiums and Cooperatives

In addition to its underwriting guidelines for multifamily apartment buildings Fannie Mae also addresses the identification of environmental hazards in section 801.02 of its project standards guidance specifically for condominium and cooperative projects. This standard states that lenders generally hire a qualified environmental consultant to conduct a Phase II site assessment. However, it does not specify whether environmental professionals must perform a Phase I site assessment.

An appraiser may be called on to evaluate the impact of an identified hazard on the value of a condominium or cooperative project.

Single-Family Residential

After years of discussion and debate, Fannie Mae issued its revised Uniform Residential Appraisal Report (URAR) on June 30, 1993. The new URAR (Fannie Mae Form 1004B) requires the appraiser to comment on "adverse environmental conditions (such as, but not limited to, hazardous wastes, toxic substances, etc.) present in the improvements, on the site, or in the immediate vicinity of the subject property."

As Edmund P. Coffay III has noted in a detailed explanation of the URAR revisions,

> Recent developments within the residential mortgage market affecting the way loans are originated and underwritten have increased the reliance on the appraiser as the primary source of relevant information on the subject property. Growth in wholesale and correspondent lending operations has resulted in underwriters placing substantial reliance on the appraisal report when determining if the property is acceptable collateral for the mortgage loan amount. It has become increasingly important for appraisal reports to address all relevant factors that affect value. By including the environmental hazards section on the URAR, any questions about the necessity to report this information for the property being appraised have been removed.[2]

However, recognizing that the typical appraiser is not an expert in the field of environmental hazards, Fannie Mae has included language that qualifies the appraiser's responsibility in identifying environmental hazards on single-family residential properties. Limiting Condition Number 6 states that

> The appraiser has noted in the appraisal report any adverse conditions (such as needed repairs, depreciation, the presence of hazardous wastes, toxic substances, etc.) observed during the inspection of the subject property or that he or she became aware of during the normal research involved in performing the appraisal. Unless otherwise stated in the appraisal report, the appraiser has no knowledge of any hidden or unapparent conditions of the property or adverse environmental conditions (including the presence of hazardous wastes, toxic substances, etc.) that would make the property more or less valuable, and has assumed that there are no such conditions and makes no guarantees or warranties, express or implied, regarding the condition of the property. The appraiser will not be responsible for any such conditions that do exist or for any engineering or testing that might be required to discover whether such conditions exist. Because the appraiser is not an expert in the field of environmental hazards, the appraisal report must not be considered as an environmental assessment of the property.

Nonetheless, knowledge of an environmental hazard can be gained through the property inspection or the normal research involved in performing the appraisal. When the appraiser has knowledge of any environ-

2. Edmund P. Coffay III, "The Revised URAR: Clarifying the Appraiser's Role in Reporting Environmental Hazards," *Environmental Watch* (Summer 1993), 1, 6–8. Coffay is the manager of Mortgage Standards for Fannie Mae.

Chapter 3: *Agency Standards and Industry Guidance*

mental hazard (in or on the subject property or on any site within the property's vicinity), he or she must note the hazardous condition on the appraisal and comment on any influence the hazard has on the value and marketability of the property (if it can be measured through an analysis of comparable market data as of the appraisal's effective date).

Accordingly, Fannie Mae has also modified the Appraiser's Certification on the URAR regarding personal inspection of the subject property (Certification Number 8). The appraiser certifies that

> I have noted any apparent or known adverse conditions in the subject improvements, on the subject site, or on any site within the immediate vicinity of the subject property of which I am aware and have made adjustments for these adverse conditions in my analysis of the property value to the extent that I had market evidence to support them. I have also commented about the effect of the adverse conditions on the marketability of the subject property.

The 1993 modifications to the URAR are consistent with Section 303 ("Properties Affected by Environmental Hazards") of the Fannie Mae Selling Guide. The section addresses environmental hazards affecting conventional mortgages secured by one- to four-family properties and VA mortgages secured by two- to four-family properties. Section 303 states that when the "appraiser has knowledge of any hazardous condition (whether it exists in or on the subject property or any site within the vicinity of the property. . . . he or she must note the hazardous condition on the appraisal report and comment on any influence that the hazard has on the property's value and marketability. . . . and make appropriate adjustments in the overall analysis of the property's value." Section 303 specifies that the appraiser is not an expert in the field of environmental hazards and that the "typical residential real estate appraiser is neither expected nor required to be an expert in this specialized field."

Federal Deposit Insurance Corporation

The Federal Deposit Insurance Corporation (FDIC) has an extensive Environmental Risk Checklist, which was developed for use during a preforeclosure property assessment to provide for consistency and uniformity in appraisal reports. However, the checklist is lengthy and requires an analysis typically seen in a Phase I environmental site assessment. Appraisers should proceed with caution if asked to complete this lengthy and complex document.

Farm Credit Administration

On November 20, 1992, the Farm Credit Administration (FCA) issued a final rule that established collateral evaluation requirements for Farm Credit System (FCS) institutions engaged in lending and leasing. Collateral evaluations apply to FCA transactions that require the services of a state licensed or state certified real estate appraiser, as well as those that require the services of an evaluator.[3] The rule imposes some environmental responsibility on those performing collateral evaluations. Under FCA regulation, all collateral evaluations must "identify potential liabilities, including those associated with any hazardous waste or other environmental concerns."

In the preamble to its final rule, the FCA states that the appraiser or evaluator is not required to complete an environmental analysis of the prop-

3. Evaluator is the term used by the FCA for persons who perform collateral evaluations on projects which do not meet minimum criteria requiring a licensed or certified real estate appraiser.

erty. Rather, the appraiser is required to "identify any obvious environmental concerns in the appraisal or evaluation report on the real property collateral. Once an environmental concern has been documented in the appraisal or evaluation report, it is the institution's responsibility to engage an expert to conduct an analysis to ascertain: 1) the impact of the environmental concern; 2) the associated cost of any necessary cleanup; and 3) the effect of the environmental concern on the market value of the subject property."

Department of Housing and Urban Development

The Department of Housing and Urban Development (HUD) issued a final rule on August 3, 1993, on "HUD Systems for Approval of Single-Family Housing in Subdivisions."

In this final rule, HUD eliminated the Appraiser/Underwriter Checksheet offered in its proposed rule. The checksheet would have applied in cases where HUD provides mortgage insurance on home loans for newly constructed individual dwellings in a subdivision. The proposed checksheet placed some environmental responsibility on the appraiser by asking the appraiser to consider noise, explosion/flammable material storage hazards, airport runway clear zones, and toxic waste hazards. The appraiser could have rejected a property "if, in his or her opinion, any of these hazards would adversely affect 1) the health or safety of the mortgagors or 2) the continued marketability of the property." HUD eliminated the checksheet in response to real estate industry concerns.

HUD's final rule on subdivisions expands on an existing form, the HUD 92541 Builder's Certification. The certificate is prepared by the subdivision builder for the limited purpose of alerting the lender and HUD about possible problems, including environmental ones, that might warrant further exploration as part of the underwriting process. The Builder's Certification is to be furnished to the appraiser for reference in performing the property appraisal. The appraiser is then responsible for providing "comment on any apparent discrepancy between the site conditions observed and the statements included in the Builder's Certification."

Title XI of FIRREA

In 1989 Congress passed the Financial Institutions Reform, Recovery and Enforcement Act (FIRREA). Title XI of this act mandated numerous changes for appraisers engaged in federally related transactions. Under FIRREA states have established a system of state licensing and certification programs for real estate appraisers. In addition, Title XI requires the federal financial institutions regulatory agencies and the Resolution Trust Corporation (RTC) to establish standards for appraisals in accordance with standards promulgated by the Appraisal Standards Board of The Appraisal Foundation. The federal financial institutions regulatory agencies are the Board of Governors of the Federal Reserve System (FRS), Federal Deposit Insurance Corporation (FDIC), Office of the Comptroller of the Currency (OCC), Office of Thrift Supervision (OTS), and National Credit Union Administration (NCUA).

These agencies issued regulations implementing Title XI in 1990. While these regulations, and subsequently issued amendments, do not directly address environmental concerns, the regulations do mandate that for federally related transactions appraisers shall, at a minimum, "disclose any steps that are necessary to comply with the Competency Provision of the Uniform Standards of Professional Appraisal Practice (USPAP)." The Competency Provision of USPAP requires the appraiser to either 1) have the knowledge and experience necessary to complete a specific appraisal assignment competently or 2) disclose his/her lack of knowledge or experience to the client and take all steps necessary or appropriate to complete the assignment competently.

Common Law: A Critical Court Case

The potential liability that can be imposed on appraisers with regard to environmental hazards was made evident in a 1991 decision by the Court of Appeals in the State of Wisconsin in the case of *Horicon State Bank v. Kant Lumber Company, Inc.* (478 N.W. 2d 26 [Wis. App 1991]). The Horicon State Bank purchased a mortgaged property at a sheriff's sale for $10,000 on June 13, 1989. Before the sale, the bank's appraiser estimated the property's value at $6,000. Subsequently, the bank learned that the property had been contaminated with petroleum, resulting in extensive cleanup costs. In defending against liability for the cleanup, the bank argued that it was mistaken regarding the condition of the property and therefore the sale should be nullified. The bank further argued that it was inequitable to impose cleanup costs on the bank rather than on the parties that originally owned the land.

The trial court determined that the bank's appraiser should have seen the evidence of oil storage tanks on the property. The court stated that "the fuel pump, the fill pipe, and vent pipe were all there for the appraiser to see when he viewed the lots and took the picture." The trial court concluded that the appraiser was the bank's "agent" and that his knowledge was therefore imputed to the bank. Upon appeal, the court rejected the bank's contention that its bid was based on mistake. The Appellate court stated that "had the bank examined the property before the sheriff's sale, it would have seen.... what its appraiser ought to have seen. Had it done so, the risk of pollution would have been apparent." Accordingly, it seems that courts are willing to impose liability on the appraiser's client where the appraiser should have noted obvious environmental hazards such as above ground tanks and vent pipes.

Getting the Lead Out: New Regulations Require Disclosure and Evaluation

by Donald E. Kelly

Donald E. Kelly *is vice president of Washington Operations for the Appraisal Institute. As a former House Banking Committee staff member, Kelly maintains contacts on Capitol Hill and with the federal agencies in Washington, D.C. He is the Appraisal Institute's principal liaison with industry-related groups such as Fannie Mae, Freddie Mac, and the American Bankers Association.*

This article originally appeared in Valuation Insights & Perspectives *(First Quarter 1997).*

The Environmental Protection Agency (EPA) and the Department of Housing and Urban Development (HUD) have published a final rule, "Lead: Requirements for Disclosure of Known Lead-Based Paint and/or Lead-Based Paint Hazards in Housing." Published on March 6, 1996, the final rule requires persons selling or leasing most residential housing built before 1978 to provide purchasers and renters with a federally approved lead hazard information pamphlet and to disclose known lead-based paint and/or lead-based paint hazards. For owners of more than four residential dwellings, the requirements became applicable on September 6, 1996, and for owners of one to four residential dwellings, the requirements were effective December 6, 1996.

These regulations are based on Federal Law P.L. 102-550, known as the Residential Lead-Based Paint Hazard Reduction Act of 1992. Title X of this act mandates a comprehensive effort to find and reduce lead-based paint hazards in residential housing to prevent childhood lead poisoning. The requirements of Title X focus attention on hazards in housing units built before 1978. That is the same year that the federal Consumer Product Safety Commission banned the use of lead in residential house paint. Appraisers need to be aware of these regulations, as existence of lead-based paint on a property may impact a value determination.

Hazards of Lead-Based Paint Poisoning

Lead ingestion is hazardous to all humans. Various researchers have observed effects of lead poisoning to include colic, neurological difficulties and dysfunction, and adverse hematological effects. The effects of lead on children can be particularly severe and include decreased intelligence, learning disabilities, and impaired neurobehavioral development. For adults, the primary effects include neurological problems such as dizziness, fatigue, and changes in the cardiovascular and reproductive systems.

Lead-based paints are still available for industrial, military, and marine usage. In addition, according to the National Center for Lead-Safe Housing, approximately 79% of all privately owned housing built before 1978 contains lead-based paint. Children and adults may ingest flaking or chipping paint or paint dust generated through impact or friction. Adults can ingest lead-contaminated paint if they are exposed to rehabilitation, renovation, and abatement activities without proper protection.

The Alliance to End Childhood Lead Poisoning estimates that of the 93 million occupied housing units in the United States, 72 million units were built before 1978. A report states that, according to HUD estimates, 57 million of these units contain lead-based paint. Furthermore, 38% of the housing units were built before 1950. Paint manufactured before 1950 contained higher concentrations of lead than paint manufactured from 1950 to 1977. Consequently, the hazards in pre-1950 housing are potentially more severe.

Where Are These Units?

The American Housing Survey estimates that the majority of pre-1978 housing units are located in central cities or urbanized suburbs of metropolitan statistical areas. It is believed that 75% of all housing containing potential lead hazards—some 62.1 million units—are located in urbanized areas. The 1989 survey shows that the largest share of pre-1978 units are located in the Southern region of the United States, comprising 32% of pre-1978 units. As a percentage of all housing stock in the area, however, the Northeast and Midwest regions have the largest numbers of pre-1978 housing stock. These regions are generally considered to have the highest incidences of lead poisoning, largely because their housing stock is older and therefore more deteriorated.

Title X Programs

Title X is the latest national legislative response to the dangers of lead poisoning. It is intended to focus attention and national resources on lead-based paint hazards and to evaluate and reduce these hazards before a child is lead poisoned. Under the act, a lead-based paint hazard is any condition that causes exposure to lead in sufficient amounts to cause adverse human health effects. Section 1004 of Title X defines six such conditions:

1. "Deteriorated lead-based paint" is any interior or exterior lead-based paint that is peeling, chipping, chalking, or cracking, or is located on any surface or fixture that is damaged or deteriorated.

2. Lead-based paint on any "friction surface," defined as an interior or exterior surface subject to abrasion or friction, such as painted floors and friction surfaces on windows.

3. Lead-based paint on any "impact surface," defined as an interior or exterior surface subject to damage by repeated impacts, such as parts of doorframes.

4. Lead-based paint on any "accessible surface," defined as an interior or exterior surface accessible to a young child to mouth or chew, such as a windowsill.

5. "Lead-contaminated dust" is defined as surface dust in residential dwellings that contains an area or mass concentration of lead in excess of the standards to be established by the EPA.

6. "Lead-contaminated soil" is defined as bare soil on residential property that contains lead in excess of the standards to be established by the EPA.

In any home built before 1978, the possibility that one of these conditions exists is high.

Appraisal Requirements

Title X, along with extending notice requirements to private dwellings, also requires HUD to publish new regulations for notice and abatement of lead-based paint in federally assisted housing. In the HUD proposed rule, real estate appraisers will be responsible for a visual evaluation of all painted surfaces to identify deteriorated paint. Responding to this draft regulation, Appraisal Institute Government Relations Committee Chair Woodward S. Hanson, MAI, commented that a requirement "to inspect all painted surfaces within a dwelling is overly broad...and extends the traditional role of the appraiser." In the comment letter, Hanson seeks further clarification from HUD on the extent of this requirement so as to properly limit the appraisers' liability exposure.

Lingering Liability

Under the regulations, borrowers are not given recourse against the appraiser for failure to report lead paint. However, appraisers could possibly be liable under common law negligence. Damages could include compensation for lead poisoning and the likely decrease in property value due to unreported lead contamination. In addition to common law actions, many states are enacting legislation designed to address lead poisoning and notice requirements. Faced with evolving legal duties, federal regulations, and state statutes, landlords, sellers, brokers, and appraisers should document any disclosures given regarding lead-based paint hazards. If faced with a lawsuit, such documentation will make it easier to prove that the regulations have been complied with and proper action taken.

Appraisal Industry Role

A Lead-Based Paint Hazard Reduction and Financing Task Force has been mandated by Title X and is comprised of 39 individuals representing a diversity of constituencies. The task force represents various organizations including HUD, the Farmer's Home Administration, Fannie Mae, Freddie Mac, private lending institutions, low income housing organizations, and state and local lead poisoning prevention facilities. The report of the task force articulates its view of the role of the appraiser in these matters:

"Appraisers have an important role in real estate transactions and the availability of financing. The role is limited, however, in identifying and controlling lead-based paint hazards. Lenders use appraisals in underwriting decisions to establish the appropriate size of a loan in relationship to the estimated value of a property. In addition, an appraisal helps lenders to understand how much they can recoup in the market if a property owner defaults on a loan. Appraisers typically make visual inspections and then assess a property's value, based on both the market values of comparable properties and the cost to build.

"The function of appraisers as it relates to lead-based paint is limited for several reasons. First, appraisers are not technically competent to make judgments about the presence or absence of lead-based paint hazards, nor do they perform paint tests or evaluate the underlying conditions of a property. Second, it is the appraiser's job to reflect market value, not to

Chapter 3: *Getting the Lead Out*

create it. If the market places less value on properties with lead-based paint hazards, appraisers will eventually reflect this fact in their estimates of value, but they cannot be expected to lead the market or create values based on their own opinions or knowledge. Third, appraisal reports are not completed until after the contract of sale is final; so appraisals are likely to come too late to affect the buyer's decision to purchase.

"Despite its limited role, the task force believes it is important for appraisers to be sensitive to and knowledgeable about lead-based paint hazards and their potential effects on value. With sufficient understanding and training, the task force hopes that appraisers will be able to quickly recognize changes in value attributable to consumer concerns about lead-based paint hazards and appropriately reflect these changes in their appraisals."

The task force goes on to recommend that "initial and continuing training for appraisers include information about lead-based paint hazards, the Title X required lead-based paint notification and disclosure, and state and local hazard control requirements."

Find Out More about Lead-Based Paint Hazards

For information and government pamphlets on lead-based paint hazards contact:

- The National Lead Information Clearinghouse (NLIC) at (800) 424-LEAD. You may also send your request by fax to (202) 659-1192 or e-mail to ehc@cais.com. The NLIC can be located on the Internet at http://www.nsc.org/nsc/ehc/ehc.html.

- Bulk copies of the pamphlet are available from the Government Printing Office at (202) 512-1800. The GPO stock number is 055-000-00507-9.

- The EPA pamphlet and rule are available electronically and may be accessed through the Internet. Gopher: gopher.epa.gov:70/11/Offices/PestPreventToxic/Toxic/lead_pm or WWW: http://www.epa.gov/docs/lead_pm and http://www.hud.gov

For state rules on lead-based paint matters call your local jurisdiction.

State/Region	Number	State/Region	Number
AL	(205) 242-5661	MT	(406) 444-3671
AK	(907) 465-5152	NE	(402) 471-2451
AR	(501) 661-2534	NV	(702) 687-6615
AZ	(602) 542-7307	NH	(603) 271-4507
CA	(510) 450-2424	NJ	(609) 633-2043
CO	(303) 692-3012	NM	(505) 841-8024
CT	(203) 566-5808	NY	(800) 458-1158
DC	(202) 727-9850	NC	(919) 715-3293
DE	(302) 739-4735	ND	(701) 328-5188
FL	(904) 488-3385	OH	(614) 466-1450
GA	(404) 657-6514	OK	(405) 271-5220
HI	(808) 832-5860	OR	(503) 248-5240
ID	(208) 332-5544	PA	(717) 782-2884
IL	(800) 545-2200	RI	(401) 277-3424
IN	(317) 382-6662	SC	(803) 935-7945
IA	(800) 972-2026	SD	(605) 773-3153
KS	(913) 296-0189	TN	(615) 741-5683
KY	(502) 564-2154	TX	(512) 834-6600
LA	(504) 765-0219	UT	(801) 536-4000
MA	(800) 532-9571	VT	(802) 863-7231
MD	(410) 631-3859	VA	(800) 523-4019
ME	(207) 287-4311	WA	(206) 753-2556
MI	(517) 335-8885	WV	(304) 558-2981
MN	(612) 627-5498	WI	(608) 266-5885
MS	(601) 960-7463	WY	(307) 777-7391
MO	(314) 526-4911		

Contaminated Properties and Guide Note 8: Questions, Answers, and Suggestions for Revision

by Richard J. Roddewig, MAI

Richard J. Roddewig, MAI, is president of Clarion Associates, Inc., in Chicago and Denver. He codeveloped the Appraisal Institute's seminar, Environmental Risk and the Real Estate Appraisal Process, and has taught the seminar nationwide. He is an adjunct lecturer on real estate valuation at DePaul University, Chicago.

This article originally appeared in the January 1998 issue of The Appraisal Journal.

When appraising a property affected by contamination, hazardous substances, or other types of environmental risks,[1] the appraiser must give careful consideration to appraisal standards. In terms of the Appraisal Institute's *Standards of Professional Appraisal Practice,* it is important to understand Advisory Opinion AO-9 titled "Responsibility of Appraisers Concerning Toxic or Hazardous Substance Contamination," and "Guide Note 8: The Consideration of Hazardous Substances in the Appraisal Process."[2]

Advisory Opinion AO-9 covers in a general way much of the same material as is in the more detailed Guide Note 8.

Guide Note 8

This guide note, adopted by the Appraisal Institute Board of Directors in 1994, is the touchstone for all Appraisal Institute members appraising contaminated properties. The significant components of the guide note include the following:

- An introduction that includes a definition of the term "hazardous substances," an explanation that negative values can result from the appraisal process involving contaminated properties, and the technical limitations of the guide note

- A discussion of the Competency Provision of the *Uniform Standards of Professional Appraisal Practice* (USPAP)[3] as it applies to this practice area

- A section titled "Basis for Proper Evaluation," which includes a discussion of such practice issues as understanding the potential existence of stigma over and above remediation costs, acknowledging those providing significant professional assistance, complying with the Departure Provision when issuing "limited" appraisals that acknowledge but disregard the presence of hazardous substances, and using standard environmental disclaimers when no hazardous substances are present

- A summary of five specific "unacceptable practices"

---

1. For the purposes of this article, the terms "contamination," "hazardous substances," and "environmental risks" are used interchangeably. As explained in the text, the precise definitions of these terms may differ from one appraisal assignment to another.

2. Appraisal Institute, "Guide Note 8: The Consideration of Hazardous Substances in the Appraisal Process," *Standards of Professional Appraisal Practice* (Chicago, Illinois: Appraisal Institute, 1997), D23-D27. Also applicable are Guide Note 6: "Reliance on Reports Prepared by Others," D15-D17, and the Appraisal Institute's Property Observation Checklist, developed and adopted in 1995.

3. The Appraisal Foundation, *Uniform Standards of Professional Appraisal Practice* (Washington, D.C.: The Appraisal Foundation, 1997).

Chapter 3: *Contaminated Properties and Guide Note 8*

Types of Hazardous Substances Covered in Guide Note 8

The term "hazardous substances" is broadly defined in Guide Note 8:

> For the purpose of this guide note the term "hazardous substances" covers any material within, around or near a property that may have a negative impact on its value. Accordingly, the principles discussed in this guide note apply equally to hazardous substances that may be contained within the property and external hazardous substances.

Note that this definition applies to any *material.* Although one does not customarily think of radiation or electromagnetic fields as a "material," the intent of the guide note is to cover these forms of energy—to the extent that they affect value. This is a key point for, in effect, it says that a hazard is not defined in terms of its actual or potential health effects, but in terms of its potential impact on value. One can extrapolate from this overly broad definition that an ugly building or eyesore across the street from a property being appraised may affect the value of the appraised property. The eyesore meets the definition of "material" in this guide note, but would it typically be considered a hazardous substance? Certainly not. The meaning of the guide note would be clearer if the term "environmental risks" rather than "hazardous substances" were used. The Appraisal Institute's video and seminar on this practice area are very careful to use this more general term.[4]

The guide note covers offsite as well as onsite hazardous substances. The key words are "within, around or near a property," but there is no further description as to how far away a material potentially affecting value must be before its potential impact can be disregarded. The Appraisal Institute's Property Observation Checklist gives some guidance on this thorny issue.[5]

Negative Value

One of the more significant statements in Guide Note 8 is the acknowledgment that the presence of hazardous substances within, around, or near a property may so affect its value that the property has "negative" value. For many appraisers, the concept of "negative market value" may be elusive. Most owners simply would not put a property on the market if they believed that the property had no market value, or if the transfer of the property would require them to, in effect, give away the property for free *and* sweeten the transaction by giving the prospective buyer some cash to take the property. That is what the concept of negative value is all about: Some properties may be so adversely affected by environmental risks of various sorts that *if the property were placed on the market,* there would be no potential buyers unless a pot of cash were offered to make buying the property, along with its associated risks and responsibilities, economically worth while. Indeed, there are situations in which a current owner or a potential purchaser needs to quantify in dollars the magnitude of such market risks.

Competency Provision

The introduction to Guide Note 8 contains a warning to appraisers about its intended purpose. It is not intended "to provide technical instructions or explanations concerning the detection or measurement of the effect of hazardous substances." This raises one of the most vexing problems for

---

4. Appraisal Institute, *Hidden Factors: Environmental Risk Evaluation and the Real Estate Appraiser* (Chicago, Illinois: Appraisal Institute, 1992), videotape; and *Environmental Risk and the Real Estate Appraisal Process,* seminar.

5. See footnote 2.

appraisers in this practice area: How much responsibility does an appraiser have for detecting potential environmental risks that might affect value? The discussion in the guide note about the Competency Provision of USPAP directly answers this question, but also leaves some unanswered questions. Three critical points emerge from this section:

- First, even if an appraiser has no previous experience in appraising contaminated properties, he or she can accept such an assignment but must comply with the four requirements of the Competency Provision (e.g., disclose the inexperience to the client, complete the work competently through learning and/or association with others, describe the lack of experience in the appraisal report, and describe in the report the steps taken to complete the assignment competently).

- Second, because most appraisers, like most buyers and sellers, do not have the necessary experience to measure or detect hazardous substances, they must rely on the "advice of others" for such information. Most appraisers, therefore, need professional assistance from environmental specialists to complete an appraisal assignment that considers the impact of hazardous substances on value.

- Third, appraisers more technically skilled in analyzing the presence of contamination may be held to a higher standard of care in completing the appraisal. The guide note is addressed to those appraisers *who are not qualified to detect or measure the quantities of hazardous substances.* However, the guide note fails to state what makes an appraiser so qualified: Does extensive experience in appraising contaminated property make an appraiser so qualified, or is it a matter of technical education and nonappraisal environmental investigation experience, such as can be gained by performing Phase I, Phase II, or Phase III environmental assessments? The guide note also does not say what the higher standard of care or professional responsibility might be for those appraisers who are technically qualified.

Reports Prepared by Technical Environmental Specialists

As already indicated, Guide Note 8 is addressed to the "typical" appraiser and recognizes that the typical appraiser is not technically qualified to detect contamination or the presence of hazardous substances. Yet, the guide note is very clear in saying that it has become an "accepted practice in the marketplace" to hire a trained and experienced professional to conduct an environmental investigation in transactions involving commercial, industrial, or vacant properties that are actually or potentially affected by contamination. What responsibility does the appraiser have for reviewing these reports, and when can the appraiser rely on the results of the investigation?

Those are among the most frequently asked questions by appraisers new to the contaminated property practice area. Guide Note 8 gives little detailed guidance other than to say that one must comply with the mandates of Standards Rules 2-3 and Standards Rules 5-3, which require that the names of any individuals providing significant professional assistance be disclosed in a written appraisal report: "Accordingly, environmental engineers, inspectors and other professionals who prepare reports, furnish advice or make findings that are used in the appraisal process must be named in the certification."

Chapter 3: *Contaminated Properties and Guide Note 8*

However, another part of the Standards, Guide Note 6, "Reliance on Reports Prepared by Others," provides specific guidance on appraisers' responsibilities to review the reports prepared by technical specialists. Guide Note 6, when read in conjunction with other language in Guide Note 8, makes two points very clear:

- The level of review and critical analysis that must be given to a technical environmental report depends on the type of environmental report and the qualifications of the author.
- Also, appraisers with no technical environmental training must practice a minimum level of due diligence.

Guide Note 6 defines four categories of reports on which an appraiser may rely: (1) general informational, (2) reports prepared by licensed or certified nonreal estate appraisal professionals, (3) those prepared by other nonreal estate appraisal professionals, and (4) other reports. Each category requires different levels of review and verification from the appraiser. The fourth category, "other reports," creates the highest level of review responsibility and the first category, "general informational reports," the least.

"Environmental studies" as well as "engineering services" and "other reports related to matters beyond the scope of an appraiser's expertise" are specifically listed under category 2, a type of report prepared by licensed or certified nonreal estate appraisal professionals. The standard of care in relying on these reports is stated as:

> Absent reasonable doubt, these reports usually can be accepted conditioned upon the qualification that they were prepared by recognized professionals. Should observed or apparent material discrepancies exist between the appraiser's investigation and the submitted report prepared by a licensed or certified nonreal estate appraisal professional, such material discrepancies must be disclosed (emphasis added).

What does that mean in our everyday use of these reports? At a minimum, it means that the appraiser should take the following steps:

- Determine whether the principal author of the report is licensed or certified as an engineer or environmental specialist. It should be sufficient to check the statement of qualifications in the report to determine if the technician is *state licensed* or certified anywhere.
- Be wary if the technician is certified but not state licensed. Guide Note 6 does not define the types of licensing or certification that is sufficient for our reliance. However, as in any profession, there are significant differences among professional organizations that certify professionals with a designation. Some impose minimum experience and technical education requirements while others impose stringent requirements. While appraisers cannot be expected to pass judgment on the relative merits of one environmental inspection designation versus another, they may assume the responsibility at least to ask a specialist who is certified but not state licensed to explain the requirements for the certification that he or she does have.
- Read the report prepared by the environmental specialist. While the typical appraiser is not expected to understand it all, he or she should know enough about the environmental conditions that affect the

property being appraised to be able to meet the responsibilities under Guide Note 6, and spot any "observed or apparent *material* discrepancies" between what is stated in the technical report and what the inspection reveals.

- Ask questions if there seem to be inconsistencies between the environmental report and actual site conditions. This is especially true if something appears to be evidence of contamination but is not discussed in the environmental study. Appraisers should talk to the environmental specialist who prepared the report. There may be sound reasons for the discrepancy. If the discussion with the environmental specialist does not resolve concerns, appraisers should talk to their clients and seek clarification as to the scope of the assignment, given the unresolved concerns.

Appraisers must be careful to comply with all the Guide Note 6 requirements for referencing the environmental study in an appraisal report. While Guide Note 8 simply requires a list of any reports used, Guide Note 6 goes well beyond that, requiring that the appraisal report identify the report relied on, the "specifics" in the technical report that were relied on, the author, and the date of the environmental report.

Inconsistent Environmental Assessment Reports

The section of Guide Note 8 titled "Basis for Proper Evaluation" also raises a number of challenging but unanswered questions. For example, the guide note recognizes that appraisers typically will be provided with an environmental assessment prepared by technical specialists who have analyzed the environmental situation affecting the property. In fact, the appraiser may be provided with more than one report, and there may be inconsistencies in the reports on such points as the amount and type of contamination affecting the property, "the level of cleanup required, the appropriate method of that cleanup, or the cost." This is frequently true in litigation involving contaminated property. What should the appraiser do when confronted with widely divergent technical assessments? After all, appraisers are not technical specialists and the typical appraiser is not sufficiently adept at the technical aspects to test the property for contamination.

The answer is that appraisers must do what the marketplace of buyers and sellers would do: review the conflicting technical assessments, and if the situation allows it—often in litigation it is inappropriate to talk directly with experts on the other side—discuss the findings in the various reports with the various technical specialists involved. Sometimes it may be possible to interview other technical experts or persons knowledgeable about the property's environmental situation and have them provide a critical comparison of the bases for the conclusions in each of the conflicting technical reports. If the technical studies contain widely divergent estimates of the cost of remediation, the appraiser will have to stand in the shoes of the typical buyer in the marketplace and determine how such a buyer would discount the price that would be offered based on the uncertainty associated with cleanup costs.

Usually, if the appraiser takes the time to read the conflicting reports carefully, he or she will begin to find some basis for giving one of the reports more credibility. An appraiser does not need to be a technically qualified environmental specialist to be able to do such things as the following:

Chapter 3: *Contaminated Properties and Guide Note 8*

- Compare the conflicting reports on the level or amount of testing that supports the technical conclusions about cleanup methods or costs—a Phase II analysis is typically more reliable than a Phase I or preliminary environmental assessment. A report supported by extensive on-site or off-site testing may be more supportable than one based on only spot testing. A report based on a number of years of monitoring or a larger number of samples is usually more reliable than one based on out-of-date data or a small number of samples.

- Compare the reports on the cleanup standard that is assumed to apply. Often a critical reading of the conflicting reports will reveal that widely divergent cleanup cost estimates may actually result from widely divergent assumptions about the appropriate cleanup standard that applies to the property. A review of the regulatory standards that apply, or a determination of the regulations that have a reasonable probability of applying—highest and best use analysis frequently requires appraisers to do the same thing with other types of land use and zoning laws—and even interviews with local, state, or federal environmental agencies may help the appraiser understand which of the cleanup standards would be considered by the marketplace of buyers and sellers to be applicable.

- Compare the reports on the amount of the property that is assumed must be remediated. This is an analysis in which the appraiser's real estate experience and instincts can be very helpful. In many situations involving larger properties and some types of contaminants, it may be possible to plan the future use of the site so that some or all of the troublesome materials can be left in place without removal or remediation. For example, trouble spots on the property may be able to be devoted to parking lots or required open space, or buildings and foundation supports can be located in such a way as to avoid pockets of hazardous substances. It may be up to the appraiser to make those kinds of determinations based on all the elements of a highest and best use analysis.

Measuring Stigma

Of course, the appraiser's job does not end once the remediation cost issue has been addressed. Guide Note 8 specifically recognizes that there is much more that must be considered:

> The appraiser is cautioned that the value of a property impacted by hazardous substances may not be measurable simply by deducting the typical remediation cost, or discovery cost from the total value, as if "clean." The possibility of other changes affecting value, such as a change in highest and best use, marketability, and stigma should be considered.

Thus, Guide Note 8 recognizes that stigma can exist over and above direct remediation costs. Unfortunately, the guide note gives little guidance on how to measure stigma in the marketplace. The only statement in the guide note is that "the loss of value attributable to hazardous substances is sometimes measurable using the same methods and techniques that are used to measure depreciation from other causes. In other cases, more specialized techniques are indicated." Guide Note 8 does not explain what the "more specialized techniques" are but warns appraisers that they "must correctly employ those recognized methods and techniques that are necessary to produce a credible appraisal."

But if Guide Note 8 does not set out any specific methods and techniques, where does one find information about them? It is not enough simply to use *any* method or technique — it must be a "recognized" technique and one "necessary" to produce a credible appraisal. How does one know if a method or technique has become "recognized?" Appraisal Institute courses, seminars, and publications provide guidance to its members on recognized methods and techniques.[6]

Departure Provision and Appraising Properties Affected by Known Contamination

Guide Note 8 also has a very important discussion of what to do if an appraiser knows or suspects that a hazardous substance exists that may affect value and the client either does not know or the client asks to have the impact of the hazardous substance on value disregarded. The four central rules of Guide Note 8 are:

- Rule 1: If an appraiser knows or has reason to know that contamination may affect value, an Appraisal Institute member cannot exclude the potential impact of contamination on value unless he or she invokes the Departure Provision and limits the scope of the appraisal report.
- Rule 2: Even if an appraiser is excluding the potential impact of the contamination from the appraisal analysis, he or she must *nevertheless disclose the known or suspected existence of the hazardous substance.*
- Rule 3: The exclusion of consideration of contamination must be prominently stated as an extraordinary assumption throughout the appraisal report.
- Rule 4: An appraiser must also indicate the likely impact on value if the contamination was indeed to be considered.

The third rule is derived from Standards Rules 2-1(c), which makes it clear that it is not enough simply to state in the assumptions and limiting conditions section of the appraisal that hazardous substances are being excluded from consideration. A statement describing a known hazardous substance and indicating that the known contamination is not being considered must be included "with statements of each opinion or conclusion that is affected." The guide note also requires a statement in the body of the report, specifically in the statement of purpose. That seems to mean that such qualifying statements should appear, at a minimum, in the following places in the appraisal report: cover letter, summary of significant facts and conclusions, statement of assumptions and limiting conditions, body of the report in the statement of the purpose of the appraisal, highest and best use conclusion, conclusion concerning the value of the property by each of the approaches used, and the final value reconciliation and conclusion section.

What does Rule 4, requiring a statement concerning the impact of the contamination on value, mean? How detailed does the statement have to be? Does this mean an appraiser must actually quantify the impact on value, a requirement that would be inconsistent with all the other provisions of the guide note allowing the exclusion of the contamination as long as he or she complies with the Departure Provision? The guide note

---

6. See *Hidden Factors* videotape and Environmental Risk seminar; also the book, *Environmental Site Assessments and Their Impact on Property Value: The Appraiser's Role,* 1995, and the technical report, *Measuring the Effects of Hazardous Materials Contamination on Real Estate Values: Techniques and Applications,* 1992. *The Environmental Watch* newsletter can also be a good information source although it is no longer published.

gives an example of a proper disclosure statement limiting the scope of the assignment. The example simply recognizes that the presence of the hazardous substance (in this example, friable asbestos) "may have a negative influence on the value of the subject property."

Standard Disclaimers and the Uncontaminated Property

Finally, Guide Note 8 contains a detailed discussion of the types of standard disclaimers that appraisers should use when "there is no reason to believe that the property is affected by hazardous substances." Most appraisers have been using such disclaimers for years. Take some care, however, to compare your standard language to that in the suggested disclaimer statements. Three things stand out from a reading of this section of Guide Note 8:

- Such standard disclaimers are not required by USPAP.
- Including such statements does not turn the assignment into a limited appraisal requiring departure unless an appraiser knows or has reason to know that there is contamination that affects the property and elects to disregard it.
- If a Phase I, Phase II, or Phase III environmental assessment finds no evidence of possible contamination, it is best to mention that fact and do so in such a way as to comply with Guide Note 6.

Suggestions for Revising Guide Note 8

While Guide Note 8 answers many questions that appraisers had before it was issued in 1991 and amended in 1994, it leaves many issues unresolved and raises some new questions that also need to be answered. Among the more significant issues that should be addressed in future revisions of the guide note are the following:

- Since offsite environmental risks may affect value, what responsibilities does the appraiser have in investigating potential sources of contamination or environmental risk in proximity to the appraised property? Exactly what does "in the proximity" mean? The Property Observation Checklist has entries for the appraiser to describe "adjoining properties" but there is no such reference in Guide Note 8. The guide note should be made consistent with the Property Observation Checklist if indeed appraisers are obligated to undertake such an inspection of properties in proximity.
- The revision should clear up the confusing terminology by replacing the term "hazardous substance," as applied in Guide Note 8, with the broader term "environmental risks." Guide Note 8 should conform with the related seminar and videotape of the Appraisal Institute.
- The inconsistencies between Guide Note 8 and Guide Note 6 need to be corrected. Guide Note 6 clearly distinguishes between reports that an appraiser would "use" and reports he or she would "rely on." Guide Note 8 blurs that distinction in inelegant language that implies that appraisers must mention every technical environmental report they would use rather than those on which they would actually rely.
- More practical examples and illustrations should be added to the guide note. These would be especially helpful in such areas as the meaning

of such terms as "knowledge," "obvious to the untrained person," "specifically communicated through a reasonably reliable source," and "indicate its impact on value."

- A cross reference to Advisory Opinion AO-9 and an explanation of any additional obligations, if any, imposed by Guide Note 8 are needed.

- A better explanation is needed as to why the typical "knowledgeable buyer" of commercial, industrial, or vacant property is expected to have completed a Phase I, Phase II, or Phase III environmental assessment before a transaction is completed. The reason is that most commercial lenders now require at least a Phase I (or at least a pre-Phase I environmental screening process) before making a mortgage loan. But it mentions nothing of commercial, industrial, and vacant land on which there is no mortgage loan or that is going into a real estate investment trust, or anything regarding a typical single-family home buyer. Single-family buyers are not expected to have undertaken the same kind of environmental assessment and the completion of residential form reports raises an additional set of issues not addressed by Guide Note 8.

- Finally, Guide Note 8 should supplement and expand Guide Note 6's coverage on the issue of relying on reports prepared by others. Just how extensive are appraisers' responsibilities to check the credentials of the authors of environmental assessments, and just how far should they go in reading and reviewing those studies?

Environmental Challenges Can Create Work for Real Estate Appraisers

by Steven A. Levine, CERS, CERA

With the onset of the new millennium, the need to balance economy and ecology has become an integral part of business decisions that will ensure the planet's sustainability. Earlier practices developed during the industrial revolution permitted the ferocious exploitation of the earth without regard to environmental degradation.

Since the 1960s professions of all kinds have responded to this change. It is now commonplace to describe some of these specialists as "environmental" attorneys, engineers, health and safety experts and scientists. Real estate appraisers also have a role to play in this megatrend. This article discusses the current legal and regulatory environmental pressures on appraisers and the resultant opportunities.

Challenges

The First Quarter 1999 issue of *Valuation Insights and Perspectives* featured an excellent article on this subject by David W. Craig, MAI, CRE, titled "The Environmentally Impacted Property Assignment: The best approach is a good defense." In the article he describes three environmental situations in which appraisers can find themselves:

- where a property has a problem that is not obvious and the appraiser is uninformed;
- where there is a problem, the extent of which is unknown; and
- where the appraiser is aware of remediation steps and estimated costs for clean-up.

In all cases, Craig says "it is important to attempt to place yourself in the position defined as the 'innocent landowner defense' where the appraiser would have no 'reason to know' of a site's contamination."

In the first scenario he discusses how it's the appraiser's responsibility to make appropriate inquiries and observations regarding any known environmental problems and to "make note that this was done in the report."

Steven A. Levine, CERS, CERA, *has been involved with NAERA since its inception in 1988 and has been its Executive Vice President since 1995. He has extensive experience in the Federal Emergency Management Agency's Disaster Assistance Program and began studying environmental damages to properties during the Times Beach, Mo., disaster of 1982.*

Levine has served as a consultant to federal and state agencies in developing and presenting real estate training programs and represents NAERA in ongoing cooperative educational initiatives with the Appraisal Institute and the Center for Advanced Real Estate Analysis. He has a B.A. with honors in political science from the University of Cincinnati and studied government and public administration at The George Washington University.

This article originally appeared in Valuation Insights & Perspectives *(Third Quarter 1999).*

In the second instance he discusses the appraisal of a property as if unimpacted by environmental damages; compliance with Standards Rule 2-1(c) of the Uniform Standards of Professional Appraisal Practice (USPAP) covering "disclosure of this extraordinary assumption;" Appraisal Institute Guide Note 8, which addresses treatment of hazardous substances; and the need to retain qualified environmental professionals as due diligence.

He explains in the third case about increased environmental awareness in the marketplace, liability issues, stigma, the potential unreliability of cost-of-cure estimates vis-à-vis diminution in value and possible remediation, and alternative usages for contaminated properties such as landfills and brownfields. The Comprehensive Environmental Response, Compensation and Liability Act (also known as Superfund) made potentially responsible parties (PRPs) liable for environmental clean-up costs whether or not they caused the contamination. The Superfund Amendment and Reauthorization Act made PRPs liable for all costs unless they are eligible for the innocent land-owner/purchaser defense. In order to avoid liability, those doing environmental work must support that the pollution was caused by a third party, the property was acquired after the fact, they had no actual or constructive knowledge of the problem and that due care was exercised. Due care is defined as "all appropriate inquiry." HR 2787 defines all appropriate inquiry as "a Phase One Environmental Site Assessment" performed by an environmental professional.

Appraisers Not Immune

According to Craig "the Superfund sets forth items that would take an appraiser out of the 'innocent landowner defense.' These are the following: specialized knowledge, knowledge of a recent price significantly below market value, ignoring reasonably ascertainable information and/or disregarding contaminants which could be detected by appropriate inspection."

Federal agencies have also addressed appraisers' environmental responsibilities. Fannie Mae says the "appraiser has a responsibility to note in the appraisal report any adverse conditions that were observed during the inspection of the subject property or report any information that he or she became aware of through the normal research involved in performing an appraisal."

According to Freddie Mac "ignorance is not acceptable" and the "appraiser must consider any known contaminated sites or hazardous substances that affect the subject property or the neighborhood." The U.S. Department of Housing and Urban Development has stated that "there are a number of environmental factors that by law and/or regulation must be considered by every appraiser and underwriter on every property."

Lenders are subject to corresponding requirements. The Office of Thrift Supervision warned member institutions of the dangers of environmentally contaminated properties and requires lenders to establish due diligence in all real estate transactions.

The Federal Deposit Insurance Corporation requires banks to develop and implement an Environmental Risk Management Program for all types of transactions, including residential and commercial real estate loans and trust operations.

Chapter 3: *Environmental Challenges*

Appraisers are Excellent Candidates

There is growing demand by industry and consumers to determine if properties are environmentally safe at a reasonable cost. Having properties inspected by highly trained environmental engineers or assessors can satisfy these needs. However, these services can cost a great deal of money. Also, the number of these professionals is so small that they cannot handle the amount of inspections that will likely need to be performed in the foreseeable future. Some of this gap in the market can be filled by appraisers.

Retaining a properly trained and certified Environmental Risk Screener (ERS) is one solution, although real estate appraisers are excellent candidates for this work. They already analyze on-site information and are trained to interpret real estate data from national, regional, local and neighborhood sources.

Certified screeners are qualified to screen properties to identify potential environmental risks. Several national environmental database firms provide practitioners one-stop shopping for public environmental disclosures in communities throughout the nation. Public agencies and associations can also be contacted individually.

The screen is typically limited to an on-site above-grade visual inspection to identify apparent indications that the property may have some environmental problems. Items screened for include asbestos, polychlorinated biphenyls (PCBs), formaldehyde, lead, air pollutants, radon and contamination in underground storage tanks, waste disposal, waste sites and other hazards. Depending on clients' desires screening may also be expanded to include a records and regulatory review and personal interviews. It has been used for both residential and commercial properties.

However, given increasing consumer awareness of home-related environmental health and safety issues and recent Federal Housing Administration initiatives, the demand for this service is expected to increase in the months and years ahead. Residential practitioners are well suited to add this service to their menu.

Users must be aware that not all problems may be apparent. It is better to report these problems rather than nothing at all, which is often the only course available for those who do not want to pay for a very expensive study. The extremes of requiring either an engineer's/assessor's report or no report at all are not satisfactory. Usage of ERSs and increased awareness of their services can provide the protection needed by buyers, sellers, lenders and others with an interest in the property.

Environmental due diligence needs can also be satisfied by retaining a properly trained and certified Environmental Risk Assessor (ERA) to perform Phase I Environmental Site Assessments (ESAs). The ERA has completed advanced training and is qualified to perform complex assessments on commercial, industrial, agricultural and special purpose properties. This involves evaluation of the present and past condition of the site and likelihood of a spillage, discharge, seepage, uncontrolled loss or filtration of a hazardous substance. The steps include a site investigation, neighborhood search, records and regulatory review and personal interviews. If the Phase I ESA uncovers the possibility of contamination, or suggests that a release may have occurred, a Phase II ESA is recommended. There is no testing in the Phase I process.

The Phase II ESA is a technical study designed to deny or confirm the presence of hazardous substances. It is performed by environmental pro-

In 1990 the National Association of Environmental Risk Auditors (NAERA) developed the first national guidelines for this work. In 1993 the American Society for Testing and Materials finalized national standards. NAERA designations are the standards of excellence in the real estate environmental industry, primarily because prerequisites include rigorous experience, training, testing and formal demonstration report writing requirements, as well as adherence to a Code of Ethics and Standards of Professional Practice.

NAERA is working with the Appraisal Institute to provide members the one-day Environmental Awareness seminar and the three-day Certified Environmental Risk Screener precertification program, both of which will be offered soon in cooperation with Appraisal Institute chapters. NAERA and the Center for Advanced Real Estate Analysis are cooperating to present the five-day Certified Environmental Risk Assessor precertification program and the Certificate Program in Appraising Environmentally Damaged Properties.

For information regarding membership, training and designation programs, contact NAERA, 6645 Colerain Avenue, P.O. Box 53185, Cincinnati, Ohio 45253 or call 513-674-1109; fax: 513-674-0680.

fessionals with understanding and knowledge of analytical and sampling processes and often entails complex on-site environmental sampling and laboratory analysis.

Most states require licensing for those working with radon, lead, underground storage tanks, hazardous materials and asbestos. Many designated ERSs and ERAs have aligned with other qualified specialists to provide competent services. Others have pursued licensing.

The Phase III ESA is performed to determine the rate, degree and extent of contamination and to evaluate the potential impact on health and safety. Investigations can be quite complex and may involve soil, groundwater, surface water, air and relevant hydrologic and geologic information.

Remediation and cost estimates typically take place during the Phase III process.

Develop a Skill Set

It is clear that appraisers face potential environmental liabilities in the normal course of their professional practices. To summarize Craig's article, appraisers are not generally considered environmental experts. Nonetheless, they must support the innocent landowner defense to produce a credible report on which users can rely. This requires at least awareness of environmental hazards. Appraising properties "as-if-clean" with a disclaimer and no environmental due diligence may result in a USPAP violation, dangerous exposure and potentially disastrous financial liability.

Real estate appraisers now have the opportunity to develop the skills and expertise necessary to avoid environmental liability in their existing work and to provide additional career-building services to their clients. Transaction Screens and Phase I ESAs are the best ways to treat environmental issues as a constructive part of the real estate transaction process, rather than as an obstacle to be overcome later.

Class VIII—Environmental Conditions

by Randall Bell, MAI

Class VIII involves curable, man-made environmental conditions that may be economically and physically repaired. These conditions may affect the improvements, site, subsurface, or even air space. They range from archaeological sites to contamination in soil and groundwater to asbestos-containing materials (ACMs), radon, or lead-based paints. Contamination can result from a variety of pollutants being emitted in a number of ways. Some contaminants are released into the air through factory or vehicle emissions. Other are discharged or spilled onto the ground or directly into oceans, lakes, or rivers.

Modern society depends upon many hazardous substances. Fuels are needed for automobiles and to heat buildings. Solvents are necessary for manufacturing processes and also to dry-clean clothes. Other chemicals are needed to control agricultural pests and weeds, to ensure that paint goes onto surfaces smoothly, or to make a plastic bag that keeps food fresh. In years past, society was largely ignorant of the health effects of hazardous materials, but as more was learned, it became apparent that contaminants are directly responsible for a variety of serious diseases and health problems. These and other revelations have prompted new laws and regulations, many of which impose severe financial burdens on property owners, lenders, and tenants.

Laws and Regulations

While environmental laws have been established for many decades, the public was jolted into awareness of the detrimental effects of contamination in the early 1960s with the publication of *Silent Spring* by Rachel Carson, in which the author reported on how the insecticide DDT entered the food chain and caused the thinning of egg shells, which in turn would cause eggs to break before hatching. That book is generally acknowledged as a catalyst for the creation of the modern environmental movement, which spawned a network of new federal, state, and local laws and regulations, as shown in Exhibit 8.2. Two of the more recent acts

Randall Bell, MAI, is an expert in property damage issues and the author of Bell's Guide: The Real Estate Encyclopedia. *He has an MBA in real estate from UCLA and a BS in finance and accounting from BYU.*

This material was originally published in Real Estate Damages: An Analysis of Detrimental Conditions *(Chicago: Appraisal Institute, 1999).*

Valuing Contaminated Properties

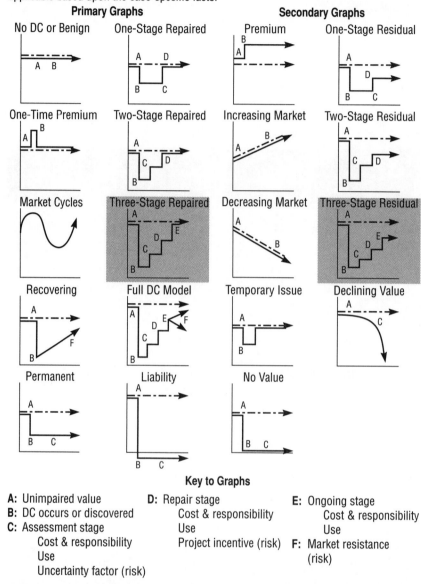

EXHIBIT 8.1 Class VIII—Environmental Conditions

The graphs for DC Class VIII have been highlighted here; however, DCs have a variety of impacts which, upon analysis, vary on a case-by-case basis. Ultimately any graph may be applicable based upon the case-specific facts.

Source: *Bell's Guide: The Real Estate Encyclopedia*

deserve special attention because they and their derivative regulations established many of the terms and precedents that are almost universally used today. They are the Resource Conservation and Recovery Act (RCRA) of 1976 and the Comprehensive Environmental Response, Compensation, and Liability Act (CERCLA) of 1980, which is commonly referred to as the Superfund Act. The intent of all these laws is to protect human health and the environment from harm caused by hazardous materials.

Resource Conservation and Recovery Act (RCRA)

Under the RCRA of 1976, when a party generates hazardous waste, it must be labeled, manifested, placarded, and shipped by an approved transporter to a permitted storage or disposal facility. The waste remains the

Chapter 3: *Class VIII—Environmental Conditions*

EXHIBIT 8.2 Chronology of Selected Environmental Acts, Laws, Regulations, and Cases

Year	Act, Law, Regulation, Policy, or Case
1899	**Rivers and Harbors Act (The "Refuse Act")** Designed to protect navigable waters, especially the Mississippi River system, from floating debris that constituted hazards to navigation.
1947	**Federal Insecticide, Fungicide, and Rodenticide Act (FIFRA)**
1948	**Federal Water Pollution Control Act (Old Clean Water Act)**
1954	**Atomic Energy Act**
1956	**Clean Water Act**
1963	**Clean Air Act (CAA)**
1966	**National Historic Preservation Act**
1967	**Clean Air Act Revision**
1969	**National Environmental Policy Act**
1972	**Marine Protection, Research, and Sanctuaries Act**
1972	**Federal Coastal Zone Management Act**
1972	**Federal Water Pollution Control Act Amendments (Clean Water Act)**
1973	**Federal Endangered Species Act**
1974	**Safe Drinking Water Act**
1976	**Resource Conservation and Recovery Act (RCRA)** Defined what was hazardous and drew a distinction between hazardous material and hazardous waste.
1976	**Toxic Substances Control Act (TSCA)**
1977	**Clean Water Act Amendments**
1978	**Uranium Mill Tailings Radiation Control Act**
1979	**Hazardous Liquid Pipeline Safety Act**
1980	**Comprehensive Environmental Response, Compensation, and Liability Act (CERCLA) "Superfund"** Intended to take care of cleanups at sites that were no longer being operated.
1984	**Hazardous and Solid Waste Amendments**
1985	**Supreme Court Support of Adjacent or Isolated Wetlands as "Waters of the U.S."**
1986	**Safe Drinking Water and Toxic Enforcement Act (California Proposition 65)**
1986	**Superfund Amendment and Reauthorization Act (SARA)**
1986	**Maryland Bank and Trust** Superfund liability can attach to a lender that takes title to a property through foreclosure.
1987	**Federal Water Quality Act**
1987	**Air Toxics "Hot Spots" Information and Assessment Act**
1990	**Oil Pollution Act**
1990	**Pollution Prevention Act**
1990	**Hazardous Waste Operations and Emergency Response Act**
1990	**Fleet Factors** A lender doesn't even have to hold title to have liability under CERCLA. If the lender exerts control over a business, then it may become liable.
1992	**OSHA Process Safety Management Standards**
1992	**Title X Housing and Community Development Act (lead-based paint)**
1992	**EPA Issues Lender Liability Rule** Attempted to protect lenders, etc., and struck down by Appeal Court 2/4/94.
1994	**ASTM Standard Practice for Site Assessment**
1995	**EPA Officially Begins Brownfields Programs** Contaminated Aquifer Policy Prospective Purchaser Agreements Comfort Letters
1995	**EPA Issues Lender Liability Policy** Attempts to protect still unconvinced lenders.

property of the generator, and the generator remains liable for it, even when it is stored elsewhere. This has been termed *cradle to grave* responsibility. RCRA also provides for sizable daily penalties for knowingly violating its strictures.

A material is defined as hazardous if it has at least one of the four characteristics of *ignitability, corrosivity, reactivity,* or *toxicity,* or if it appears on one of the lists maintained by the Environmental Protection Agency (EPA). Ignitability and toxicity are the characteristics that most often qualify a waste material as an RCRA hazardous waste. If a material spontaneously catches fire at a temperature below 140° F, then it is considered to be hazardous because of ignitability.

EXHIBIT 8.3 Lists of Hazardous Materials (or Wastes) Maintained by EPA

EPA List Code	Characteristic	Description
D001	Ignitability	Flashpoint <140° (spontaneously catches fire)
D002	Corrosivity	pH is less than 2.0 (acid) or more than 12.5 (base)
D003	Reactivity	Reacts violently or generates pressure
D004-D017	Toxicity	Toxic at specified concentrations
F List	Listed wastes	Listed wastes from non-specific sources
K List	Listed wastes	Wastes from listed sources or processes
P List	Listed wastes	Specific substances
U List	Listed wastes	Off-spec or discarded products and/or residues

The hazard characteristics are so significant that they are the basis of a commonly seen, diamond-shaped sign on nearly every building that contains hazardous materials. The sign, as shown in Exhibit 8.4, was devised by the National Fire Protection Association (NFPA) as a way to quickly inform firefighters about the nature of the materials within a building and the appropriate firefighting techniques to use. Real estate professionals would also find the knowledge of the risks posed by a building's contents useful.

Superfund Act

Some of the most seriously contaminated sites in the U.S. are the result of what were accepted business practices in the distant past. Some of these sites have posed dangers to resident populations while the parties who contributed to the contamination are no longer around or not easily found. CERCLA, the Superfund law, was enacted in 1980 to marshal the forces needed to clean up the worst of these sites and to get those who are responsible to pay the bill. Originally, the worst 400 sites were going to be cleaned up. These were placed on a National Priority List (NPL), which at one time grew to over 1,100 sites.

CERCLA conferred extraordinary powers on regulators by providing for swift response to emergency situations and by defining liability broadly to fall on generators (those with whom the contaminants originated), transporters (those who carried the materials to the site), operators (those who accepted the materials at the site), and owners of the site.[1] Those who are considered likely to be responsible under CERCLA are termed *potentially responsible parties* (PRPs). Often, a group of PRPs will band together in order to handle a regional problem they all contributed to because costs can quickly run into the millions of dollars as they fund the steps in the Superfund process. The basic steps in the process are shown in Exhibit 8.5.

1. These terms have very specific definitions under the statutes and as they have been interpreted by the courts. There is no intent here to provide a formal or exhaustive definition.

Chapter 3: *Class VIII—Environmental Conditions*

EXHIBIT 8.4 NFPA Hazard Identification System

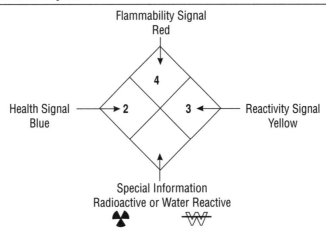

Identification of Health Hazard	Identification of Flammability	Identification of Reactivity
Color Code: Blue	**Color Code: Red**	**Color Code: Yellow**

Signal	Type of Possible Injury	Signal	Susceptibility of Materials to Burning	Signal	Susceptibility to Release of Energy
4	Materials that on very short exposure could cause death or major residual injury even though prompt medical treatment were given	4	Materials that will rapidly or completely vaporize at atmospheric pressure and normal ambient temperature or which are readily dispersed in air and which will burn readily	4	Materials that in themselves are readily capable of detonation or of explosive decomposition or reaction at normal temperatures and pressures
3	Materials that on short exposure could cause serious temporary or residual injury even though prompt medical treatment were given	3	Liquids and solids that can be ignited under almost all ambient temperature conditions	3	Materials that (1) in themselves are capable of detonation or explosive reaction but require a strong initiating source or (2) must be heated under confinement before initiation or (3) react explosively with water
2	Materials that on intense or continued exposure could cause temporary incapacitation or possible residual injury unless prompt medical treatment is given	2	Materials that must be moderately heated or exposed to relatively high ambient temperatures before ignition can occur	2	Materials that (1) in themselves are normally unstable and readily undergo violent chemical change but do not detonate or (2) may react violently with water or (3) may form potentially explosive mixtures with water
1	Materials that on exposure could cause irritation but only minor residual injury even if no treatment is given	1	Materials that must be preheated before ignition can occur	1	Materials that in themselves are normally stable but that can (1) become unstable at elevated temperatures or (2) react with water with some release of energy but not violently
0	Materials that on exposure under rare conditions would offer no hazard beyond that of ordinary combustible material	0	Materials that will not burn	0	Materials that in themselves are normally stable, even when exposed to fire, and that do not react with water

173

EXHIBIT 8.5 Steps in the Superfund Process

Name of Step	Comments
Preliminary assessment	Initial reconnaissance to ascertain whether there is a need for emergency action.
Emergency removal action	If needed, materials that pose an immediate threat to human health or the environment are removed.
Site inspection	This is a more thorough inspection in order to get a better idea of the problem and to better plan the investigations to come.
Hazard ranking	The hazard ranking score (HRS) is computed for the known conditions at the site in order to see whether the property should be added to the National Priority List. If the HRS is 28.5 or greater, then the property gets listed.
Remedial investigation (RI)	This involves both field and laboratory investigations and is usually done iteratively with the feasibility study until the site is sufficiently characterized.
Feasibility study (FS)	Based upon information from the remedial investigation, various technologies are studied in order to select those that will achieve the remediation goals most cost effectively.
Remedial action plan (RAP)	This is the plan to remediate the problem. It brings together scientific, engineering, regulatory, and community concerns into a unified program.
Record of decision (ROD)	This is the formal document that accepts and records the remedial action plan.
Remedial design	The systems and procedures to implement the plan are designed.
Remedial action	The contamination is remediated according to the RAP.

Source: Environmental Protection Agency

Source, Non-Source, and Adjacent Properties

One of the fundamental issues related to contamination and liability under the law is whether a property is the source of a release that poses a risk (the source site) or is a property onto or into which the contamination has migrated (a non-source site). This is a fundamental distinction for contaminated properties and one that is especially important to liability under CERCLA. Under the Superfund Law, a *source property* has strict joint and several liability for all costs to remediate the entire area affected by the problem. The affected area, called a *facility* for Superfund purposes, is defined to include all the air, soils, and waters contaminated by the risk source, and the facility may include any number of legal parcels.

A *non-source property* may contain a part of the facility created by the release of the risk source, but the owner of the non-source property does not generally have liability for the costs of remediation. An *adjacent property* is not a part of the facility, but adjoins either a source or non-source property. It is not directly affected by the release at the facility and has no liability for any part of the remedial process. Clearly it is imperative that this distinction be made in any valuation analysis, as the category could have a profound effect on value. Exhibit 8.6 illustrates these three various types of fundamental property classifications.

Geology and Hydrogeology

The sciences of geology and hydrogeology enable environmental engineers to understand the structure of the subsurface and how groundwater and contaminants move through that structure. The reason that these

EXHIBIT 8.6 Environmental Contamination (Source, Non-source, and Adjacent)

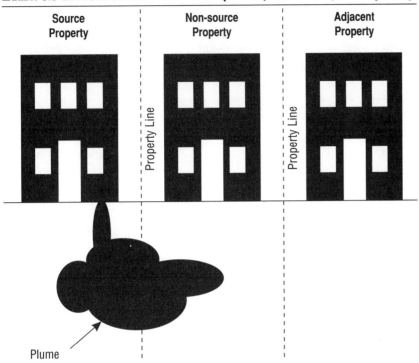

Plume

sciences are important is that one of the focal points of environmental engineering is protection of drinking water resources. Groundwater is a major source of the water used for drinking and irrigation, and it accounts for 40% of the water consumed in the United States.[2]

When contamination enters a site, it typically first sinks into the soil. There, gravity prompts the contaminant to continue its downward path. Most contaminants move more quickly through porous layers like sand and gravel and are slowed by clays, but they generally continue their descent under gravity's influence. When a descending plume of contaminant runs into an aquifer, its direction of travel may change significantly. Movement of water within the aquifer is generally to the side, not downward. Thus, when the plume reaches the aquifer, it makes a turn and starts to migrate to the side, towards the property of others. Once the moving plume crosses a property line, it has carried contamination into the property of others.

Floating and Sinking Contaminants

Water is known as the universal solvent because it dissolves most contaminants and many hydrocarbons. A dissolved contaminant is said to be in the *aqueous phase*. Once the water has dissolved all it can, the contaminant then begins to develop a separate layer of undissolved material, a non-aqueous phase liquid (NAPL). Materials that are less dense than water are called light non-aqueous phase liquids (LNAPLs) and float and accumulate near the upper water surface. This makes LNAPLs relatively easy to find. In contrast, some contaminants sink in water, as they are more dense than water. These dense non-aqueous phase liquids (DNAPLs) are usually harder to find and treat than LNAPLs.

2. United States Geological Survey, Water Supply Paper 2220.

Toxicology

Toxicology is often called the science of poisons, or the study of the harmful effects of chemicals on living things. Within the context of contamination, it is more rightly viewed as a way to define and quantify the adverse effects of chemicals in order to establish safe human exposure levels. This latter definition is more appropriate because our society has chosen to live with a broad spectrum of chemicals, some of which have the potential to cause harm or death. An important distinction exists between the terms *hazardous* and *toxic*. For example, table salt is generally not considered hazardous, but if ingested at high levels it becomes toxic. Likewise, gasoline is a hazardous substance but is considered toxic, again, only if ingested at certain levels. A hazardous material is considered toxic only if it becomes *bioavailable*, meaning that harmful levels come into contact with humans.

A particularly important set of safe exposure levels was put forward by the EPA in the Drinking Water Standards in publication EPA 822-B-96-002 (October 1996). The government document lists over 250 elements or compounds and has maximum contaminant levels (MCLs) for about 100 of them. The MCL is the maximum concentration of a substance allowed in drinking water, usually expressed as milligrams or micrograms per liter (mg/L or ug/L) or parts per million or per billion (ppm or ppb). Because one of the primary goals of environmental policy is to protect drinking water resources, MCLs often play important parts in establishing cleanup goals.

Types of Contaminants
Lead

Lead may be found in paints, car batteries, dust, pipes and solder, and drinking water. When exposure is excessive, lead can accumulate in the blood, tissues, and bones. As a result, there may be damage to the brain, kidneys, male reproductive organs, and nervous systems. Lead accumulation can cause learning disabilities, decreased IQ, and behavioral problems.

The two most common sources of lead are paint and water. The Environmental Protection Agency estimates that lead-based paints were used in about two-thirds of the homes built before 1940, one-third of the homes built between 1940 and 1960, and in some homes built after 1960. Beginning in 1978, the federal government required that paints for home use contain less than 0.06% lead. Paints for other uses, such as industrial, military, marine, and other situations, may have lead contents much higher than this. For this reason, a home owner should only use a paint intended for residential properties when painting a house.

Any home that was painted before 1978 has the potential to contain lead-based paint. If home paints contain lead, they may be covered by more recent layers of non-lead paint or by wallpaper or paneling. A test called x-ray fluorescence (XRF) can now distinguish if any of the paint layers contain lead and, if so, which layers. Removing the paint in some ways, such as sanding, may actually increase the risk of exposure to lead in the form of inhaled or ingested dust.

Lead may enter the drinking water via lead pipes or lead solder used on copper pipes. Lead pipes are usually found only in homes built before 1930, and lead soldering materials have been banned since 1988. Since

Chapter 3: *Class VIII—Environmental Conditions*

October 1996, the EPA's MCL action level for lead in drinking water has been 0.015 mg/L, or 0.015 parts per million (ppm) or 15 parts per billion (ppb). If lead is found within drinking water, then the plumbing system may need to be renovated, filters may be employed, or only bottled water used. If any reason exists to suspect that lead is in paints or water, laboratory testing of samples should be conducted. If lead concentrations above MCL are detected in any samples, then corrective measures need to be taken.

Formaldehyde

Formaldehyde is a colorless gas emitted from a variety of products and categorized as a probable carcinogen (i.e., a cancer-causing substance) by the EPA. Household products that possibly contain formaldehyde include wood-pressed products such as particleboard, urea-formaldehyde foam, insulation, fabrics, paints, plastics, photographic materials, and resins. Two main areas of concern are materials used in mobile homes and wood-pressed products, though formaldehyde may also be produced by improperly vented gas or kerosene heaters. Newer products are more likely to emit formaldehyde gas than older ones.

Formaldehyde exists in the outside air at levels ranging from 0.0002 to 0.050 ppm. Many people experience throat or eye irritation at levels of 0.1 ppm or above. The only way to determine if formaldehyde levels are excessive (over the outdoor air levels) is through laboratory testing of air samples. Gas levels, if excessive, may be reduced by removing the materials that contain formaldehyde and generally increasing air circulation.

Radioactive Contamination

Radioactive materials emit high speed particles or energetic photons, collectively called *ionizing radiation.* Ionizing radiation includes alpha and beta particles, gamma rays, x-rays, neutrons, and heavy ions. Nearly all of human exposure to radiation comes from natural background radiation (81%) or medical tests (14%). Contrary to some perceptions within the real estate market, nuclear power plants actually emit only a small amount of radiation, which is sometimes even less than coal- or oil-powered plants. Neutrons, x-rays, and gamma rays can penetrate deeply into the human body. Alpha and beta particle sources cause damage mainly if they are inside the body from being inhaled, ingested, or directly applied to the skin. Radioactive particles move at velocities that approach the speed of light—186,000 miles per second. It is theorized that these fast moving particles can break up or alter molecules, thereby causing cancer.

Among the Japanese atom bomb survivors, a carefully monitored group of 8,500 people were exposed to doses of radiation measured at 100,000 to 600,000 millirem. To date, there have been 200 (2.4%) cases of excess cancers amongst this group (i.e., 2.4% more cases than the normal probability). Another study followed British medical patients exposed to unusually high levels of radiation. About 14,000 British patients received x-ray doses averaging 300,000 millirem, resulting in 100 excess cancers (0.7%).[3]

As related to real estate, by far the most problematic source of radioactive exposure is from radon, as can be seen in Exhibit 8.7. Radon is a colorless and odorless naturally occurring radioactive gas that forms when

3. American Council on Science and Health.

EXHIBIT 8.7 Sources of Radiation

Radiation Source	Dose (Millirem/Year)	Percent of Total
Natural indoor radon	200	54%
Natural cosmic radiation	100	27%
Medical procedures	53	14%
Nuclear bomb testing	6	2%
Other man-made (soot, dust)	10	3%
Nuclear power plant	0.1	0%
Totals	369	100%

Source: American Council on Science and Health

EXHIBIT 8.8 Radon

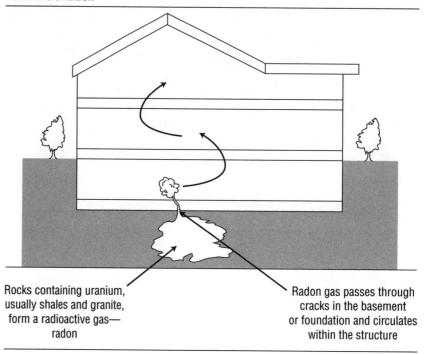

Rocks containing uranium, usually shales and granite, form a radioactive gas—radon

Radon gas passes through cracks in the basement or foundation and circulates within the structure

radioactive uranium and radium decay within rocks, as shown in Exhibit 8.8. The gas has been determined by the EPA to be a carcinogen. It accumulates in areas closest to the source, usually the ground or basement levels. Smokers are impacted more by radon, although the effects may take over 20 years to become apparent. The EPA recommends that action be taken if radon levels are over 4 picocuries per liter of air (pCi/L). In addition to gases, radon may also enter the water system, particularly when water comes from wells. Water treatment for radon includes a granular-activated carbon unit (GAC) or an aeration unit.

Radon gas is unpredictable and may affect one property and not the one next door. If any reason exists to suspect radon gases may be present, only a special laboratory test will provide conclusive answers. Often, a modestly priced system of fans and ducts provides sufficient ventilation to disperse radon and reduce its concentration to acceptable levels.

Hydrocarbons

Hydrocarbons is a general term for all carbon-based chemicals. These include methane gas, gasoline, oils and greases, asphalt, solvents, pesticides, plastics, and even DNA. Most contamination matters have been concerned

Chapter 3: *Class VIII—Environmental Conditions*

with only the categories of fuels and solvents, many of which are considered hazardous because of their flammability or toxicity characteristics.

The fuel hydrocarbons of most concern have been the four ubiquitous components of gasoline: benzene, toluene, ethylbenzene, and xylene, known collectively as BTEX. One of the most hazardous of these is benzene, a known carcinogen. Many sites that have had a gasoline tank have some BTEX in the soil and perhaps even in the groundwater. Once viewed with great alarm, BTEX contamination in soil is now treated as a fairly routine matter, although it is still considered very dangerous if a drinking water supply is threatened.

Asbestos

Although asbestos and asbestos-containing materials (ACMs) have been used in building construction since they were introduced by the Romans and Greeks in the first century A.D., their days of being considered staple building materials are clearly over. Asbestos is a naturally formed fibrous material with properties that suit it well to building uses. It is non-combustible, has high tensile strength, and has outstanding thermal, electrical, and acoustical insulating properties. According to some studies, it also has been shown to pose health risks. Accordingly, its use has been mostly discontinued and it has been removed from some buildings.

In the past, the use of asbestos in the building industry was tremendous. The EPA estimates that of the 30 million tons of asbestos used from 1900 to 1980, 60% to 70% was in the construction industry. (The United States produced 25% of the asbestos it consumed and imported 97% of the remainder from Canada.) Two terms frequently used when referring to ACMs are *friable* and *non-friable*. Friable simply means that the ACMs can be pulverized or crushed with hand pressure. Non-friable ACMs are formed into solid building materials and cannot be crushed with hand pressure. Examples of friable uses are sprayed acoustical ceilings and sprayed fireproofing on structural steel. Non-friable materials include vinyl flooring, insulating bricks, and roofing materials. Typical locations of ACMs in buildings include sprayed surfaces such as thermal insulation on structural steel, sprayed acoustical ceilings or walls, pre-formed block insulation surrounding furnaces, insulation on boilers and hot water tanks, drywall, pipe wrap, patching compounds, texture paints, vinyl floor tiles, and floor sheeting.

While asbestos was widely used for centuries, in the early 1970s it was declared a health risk. No safe threshold has ever been established for exposure to asbestos. ACMs in and of themselves do not pose a health hazard, but asbestos fibers released by disturbance, destruction, or decay can cause serious health problems. There are about six diseases attributed to asbestos, the two most common being mesothelioma, a lung cancer, and asbestosis, a chronic lung disease. Because of these health risks, the federal government has intervened and restricted asbestos use. As would be expected, the demand for ACMs has fallen dramatically, with the 1989 use level approximately 15% of what it was in 1979. The EPA estimates that as many as 31,000 schools and 733,000 public and commercial buildings contain friable ACMs. ACMs can be found in approximately 20% of the 3.6 million commercial properties in the United States.

Valuing Contaminated Properties

The office building above was photographed just a few weeks before an asbestos abatement program was initiated. Asbestos abatement, like many remediation processes, can be highly intrusive and result in the demolition of the tenant improvements.

Following is a summary of the legal limitations placed on ACMs used in new construction or products:

1973	All sprayed ACMs that contain an amount of 1% asbestos by weight or volume.
1978	All friable ACMs.
1989	A phased-in ban of virtually all ACMs.
1990	Phase I includes roofing and flooring felt, sheeting, tile, and clothing.
1993	Phase II includes brake linings, transmission components, clutches, and other friction products.
1996	Phase III includes floor coatings, paper, brake blocks, pipes, and shingles.

With the exception of school buildings, ACMs in existing buildings were not affected by the EPA bans and regulations.

EXHIBIT 8.9 Asbestos in the Home

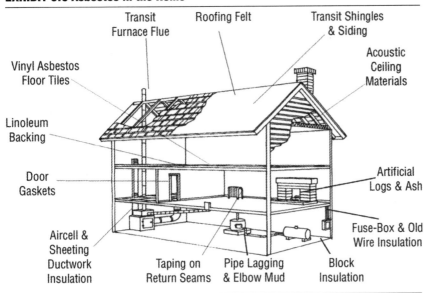

EXHIBIT 8.10 Asbestos in the Office

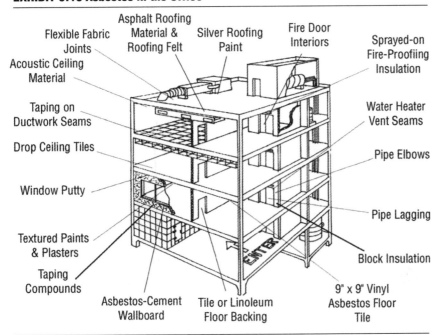

In ascertaining whether or not a building contains ACMs, the first consideration is the construction date. Properties constructed prior to 1979 are more likely to have ACMs. Friable or sprayed construction materials are also a warning sign that there may be ACMs within a building. It is important to review building records of any building in question, but the only way to be certain of the presence of ACMs is to test air and building material samples.

Air sampling, as the name implies, means taking samples of the air for laboratory testing. The air is tested in the laboratory for fiber counts using one of three microscopy methods. The Occupational Safety and Health Administration (OSHA) has established an action level of 0.1 fibers per cubic centimeter of air. Samples of building materials are often taken in conjunction with air sampling. For the study, small amounts of various building materials are collected for laboratory testing. Building materials are considered an ACM if the lab analysis indicates that the materials contain 1% or greater of asbestos (by either volume or weight). Asbestos sampling is usually unobtrusive and can be done without causing any risk of exposure to the building occupants.

Attitudes towards asbestos have changed dramatically since the 1970s and 1980s. The high profits that attracted many contractors to the asbestos abatement business in the 1980s have fallen, and contractors now number approximately 1,600, which is down 27% from 1989.[4] Abatement revenues fell from $3.9 billion to $3.2 billion in 1989 and 1990 respectively, yet asbestos will continue to be an important issue in the real estate industry with an estimated $75 billion in asbestos-related cleanup costs remaining over the next 25 years.

In 1990, the EPA issued the *Green Book,* which recommends various means of treating or managing ACMs. As a result of this and other studies, most banks do not require ACM removal as a condition of financing.

Solvents

A variety of solvents used for cleaning and manufacturing purposes are usually carcinogenic materials that do not biodegrade easily. They often are compact, dense molecules that may move fairly quickly through soil and sink through groundwater to the bottom of an aquifer, where they may be difficult to remediate.

Contamination and its Impact on Real Estate

When dealing with contamination that impacts a specific property, two broad categories must be considered, building contaminants and soil contaminants. Building contaminants include those hazards that are part of or contained within the improvements, such as asbestos, radon, lead paint, and formaldehyde. Soil contaminants include hydrocarbons, solvents, chemicals such as pesticides and herbicides, and other toxins that threaten the environment. It is entirely possible for the same contaminant to be found in both buildings and soils. For example, lead-based paints can be found in many buildings, and lead in the drinking water is a soils condition. Also, although asbestos is most commonly associated with asbestos-containing building material, it is also possible for asbestos to contaminate soil.

Contaminants in Building Improvements

Several contaminants are most commonly found within the improvements on a property, as seen in Exhibit 8.11. These include asbestos, radon, lead paint, formaldehyde, and others. The risk associated with these hazardous materials as part of, or within, the improvements is that there may be direct human contact. A child may eat lead paint chips, asbestos fibers may be inhaled by the occupants of an office building, or radon gas or formaldehyde fumes may be inhaled by a family in their home.

A laboratory analysis is virtually always required to determine the presence and concentrations of these contaminants. An assessment is easier for improvements than it is for soils contamination because the materials

4. United Press International, "New Attitudes and Litigation Over Asbestos," *Los Angeles Times* (September 22, 1993): Business section, 7.

EXHIBIT 8.11 Environmental Conditions Within Building Improvements

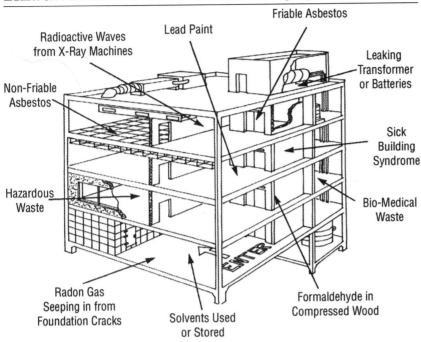

are easily accessed, as opposed to having to drill in the soil. All the work is above-grade, so remediation is easier.

When dealing with a property that has contaminants within the improvements, there are various alternatives, including encapsulation, enclosure, immediate removal, staged removal, or an operations and management program with removal at demolition.

Encapsulation

Encapsulation is a term used when sealants are sprayed onto the contaminant. The sealants surround, coat, and bond the contaminant and prevent any particles from being released into the air. A simple analogy would be the hard coating surrounding the soft chocolate in M&M candies. Encapsulation may be less expensive than removal or, in many cases, enclosure, but it has disadvantages as well. The added weight of the encapsulating materials may hasten the decay of the contaminant, and encapsulated contaminants are more difficult to remove than if they had not been treated at all. Encapsulation is usually considered a temporary solution. It is currently not recommended as being a viable abatement choice, except in special circumstances.

Enclosure

Enclosure involves the construction of air-tight walls that surround the building contamination materials (BCMs). Often this means that the BCMs are surrounded with drywall. This is an effective technique and is less expensive than removal, although it has important engineering considerations because of the added weight of the enclosures. Additionally, access is not always available to all the areas within buildings that contain BCMs. Like encapsulation, enclosure is also considered only a temporary solution, as all BCMs must be removed from a building prior to demolition.

Removal

As the name indicates, this method involves removing the BCMs from the building. It has permanent results, but the process is usually expensive, with asbestos removal costs often ranging from $10 to $70 per square foot. (In actual abatement projects, costs are not calculated on gross building area but rather on *reflective* area, which refers only to the areas within the building that have BCMs.) With removal, the building owner retains legal ownership, and thus liability, for up to 40 years for any disposed materials, even when taken to a landfill or storage site. Another negative aspect of removal is that, according to a study by the Energy and Environmental Policy Center at Harvard University, removal may actually increase asbestos exposure for building occupants because of the disruption of the asbestos.

There are three alternatives for removing BCMs:

1. Immediate or initial removal
2. Staged removal over a period of time
3. Removal at the end of the economic life (demolition) of the building

Operations and Management

Another option for dealing with BCMs is an *operations and management* (O&M) program. This means that the BCMs in good condition are simply left alone while the situation is monitored to ensure that there are no health hazards to the occupants of the building. According to the EPA, a good O&M program is 95% as effective as a non-asbestos building. The EPA recommends an O&M program over removal when the BCMs are in good condition.

When implementing an O&M program, the building owner or manager hires a qualified O&M consultant, who in turn trains the building management, engineers, custodians, and occupants concerning the handling of BCMs. The consultant may also conduct routine air sampling and building inspections to ensure that no fibers are released into the air through disturbance. The O&M program is generally continued until the BCMs are removed or the building is eventually demolished. Even with an O&M program, BCMs must be eventually removed, whether initially, staged removal over a number of years, or at the end of the building's economic life. In the event that the BCMs are removed at demolition, special BCM handling and disposal can double the demolition costs.

Soil and Groundwater Contamination

Soil contamination is a general term that sometimes includes the contamination of both soil and groundwater. The contamination may consist of materials in a variety of locations, such as on or near the surface, as is often the case with heavy metals or asbestos. Gases or vapors can form from volatile materials in the subsurface. They can also be found within the subsurface soils, which is usual for leaking underground storage tanks (LUSTs). In these cases, they may impact the groundwater, either dissolved, as a separate phase, or both. Various forms of soil contamination are illustrated in Exhibit 8.12

The danger with some contaminants, such as lead or asbestos, is that they are on the surface and can be ingested by humans or animals. If a

EXHIBIT 8.12 Contamination in the Soil

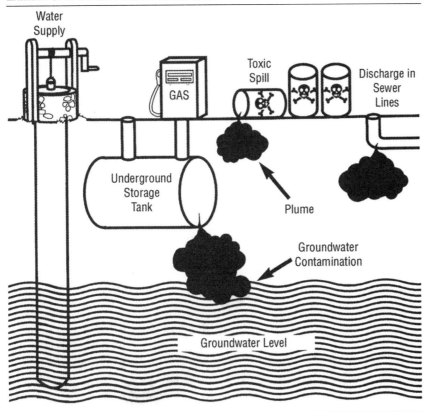

contaminant is capable of being absorbed downward into the soils, the concern is the risk to the groundwater, aquifers, or the water supply. If the groundwater is contaminated, then the contaminants may be ingested by humans, animals, or plants and cause a variety of health-related problems. When mixed with groundwater, some contaminants dissolve, some float on the surface, and some sink to the bottom, much in the same way that salad dressing separates. These attributes create additional problems in terms of assessing and remediating the contamination.

Site Assessment
Properties that have been impacted by soils contamination undergo a four-phased process of a preliminary site assessment (Phase I), an intrusive site investigation involving subsurface exploration to ascertain whether contamination in fact exists (Phase II), systematic testing to fully describe (or "characterize") the nature and extent of the contamination (Phase III), and the remediation of the contaminants (Phase IV).[5]

Phase I: Surface and Records Review
A Phase I study is an initial review of a site to determine if there is any reason to suspect that there is contamination. It may also address compliance with environmental or OSHA laws and regulations. This study is done by a trained environmental engineer or assessor who inspects the site and reviews aerial photographs to determine if there were any historical uses that might be linked with contamination, such as a manufacturing facility or agricultural uses with pesticides. Records of such agencies as

---

5. It is important to note that many professionals combine Phases II and III, effectively creating a three-phased process where the final phase is remediation.

Valuing Contaminated Properties

the Fire, Health, Planning, Building and Safety, and Public Works Departments may be reviewed to see if any historical uses, permits, or records exist of underground tanks, special manufacturing permits, or other issues that may warrant further investigation. Agencies such as the EPA and Air and Water Quality Control Boards are also contacted, and their lists are reviewed to determine if there are any records reflecting historical or current contamination issues related to the property. Current and former tenants may be interviewed to learn of any actions taking place on the property associated with contamination.

Nearly all regulatory agencies maintain databases of properties that are somehow connected with contamination. There are lists of properties with suspected contamination, contamination that is still to be cleaned up, sites that have been remediated and approved, sites that are partly remediated and contain residuals, and so forth. Usually when a property is put on a list, it remains on that list permanently. Some recent programs provide for listings to be removed as certain goals are met. With databases being maintained by federal, state, and local agencies, a single agency will likely have two or more overlapping databases, particularly if it enforces regulations for two or more programs. Nearly every database or list is available to the public, and the EPA and many state agencies have Internet sites that can be a helpful research source. There are even environmental research services that charge a very modest fee to tap into all applicable lists, produce a summary report and map for any address, and fax and mail the report to a caller.

If the Phase I study indicates that no reason exists to suspect contamination, then no other studies may be necessary. However, if evidence indicates that the site may be contaminated, then a Phase II study may be required.

Phase II: Subsurface Study

The goal of the Phase II study is to establish whether contamination exists at a site. A Phase II assessment may include collecting samples of soil, groundwater, surface water, sediment, soil vapor, and even building materials. Samples are usually taken near likely sources (tanks and plumbing) and from suspicious areas such as discolored soil and standing puddles of unidentified fluids.

The EPA and other agencies have prescribed sampling techniques and laboratory analyses to be done for a broad spectrum of contaminants. Often samples must be kept cool or frozen and must be delivered to a certified lab in a timely manner. Chain of custody is documented, and the labs have quality control and assurance programs that must be strictly followed. These assure that the samples have not been altered by activities in the field or in the lab.

The Phase II study may find no contamination or concentrations that are below regulatory action limits. These are usually seen as positive findings because the property is then deemed to be unimpaired by contamination. If contamination is found and is present at levels that require remediation, then a Phase III investigation will be necessary.

Phase III: Characterization

Before a cleanup plan can be designed, it is necessary to define the nature and extent of the contamination. For a groundwater plume, for example, this involves knowing the three-dimensional shape of the plume—its length, width, and depth as well as the direction and speed at which it is moving. These studies are more often referred to as *remedial investigations* (RI) than Phase III studies and are necessary before the effectiveness and cost of various remedial alternatives can be examined in feasibility studies (FS).

The culmination of the site assessment process is the development of the remedial action plan (RAP). This plan is subject to careful review by the regulatory agencies involved and must be approved by them. It is the blueprint for the schedule and the methods to be applied, and the results to be achieved in the cleanup process. An approved RAP sets the stage for the start of the actual remediation process.

Phase IV: Remediation

The remediation process is the actual cleanup of the released material. Its goal is not necessarily to return the property to an uncontaminated state but to remedy the problem to the satisfaction of the regulatory authorities. Parts of the property may be excavated and refilled, piping may be extended into the soil, and wells may be used to reach and treat groundwater. Numerous remediation technologies are available, depending upon the specific mix of contaminants and where they are found. The choices of remedial technologies for various categories of contaminants are summarized in Exhibit 8.13. In many cases, a succession of technologies is used as concentrations change in order to get the most remedial efficiency.

EXHIBIT 8.13 Remedial Technology Choices for Various Contaminants

Remediation Method or Process	Aqueous Solutions		Organic Liquids	Sludges and Slurries	Solids
	Inorganic	Organic			
Adsorption		√	√		
Bioremediation		√	√	√	
Dewatering	√		√	√	
Distillation			√		
Drying			√		
Emulsion Breaking		√	√		
Extraction		√	√	√	
Incineration		√	√	√	√
Landfarming		√	√	√	
Landfill/Landspreading				√	√
Neutralization	√	√		√	
Oxidation	√	√	√	√	√
Precipitation	√				
Solidification	√				
Stabilization	√			√	√
Steam Stripping		√	√		
Surface Impoundments	√	√		√	
Wastewater Treatment	√	√		√	

All remedial options fall under one of two categories, *in situ* and *ex situ*. In situ remediation means that the treatment of the soils or groundwater are completed with them in place. In other words, they are not excavated as they are with ex situ remediation measures. In situ processes are less disruptive and less expensive than ex situ methods. However, they may

Valuing Contaminated Properties

take longer and are often not as thorough as when soil is excavated for treatment.

In Situ Remediation Methods

There is a variety of in situ procedures:

- Bioremediation and bioventing involve the injection of oxygen or oxygen-releasing compounds through pipes into the soils or groundwater. The oxygen injected in this process stimulates aerobic biodegradation of the carbon-based contaminants.

- Biodegradation is a process where the microorganisms that are mixed and added to soils break down contaminants within the soils or groundwater.

- Soil vapor extraction (SVE) is a process whereby fresh air is drawn into the ground with a vacuum pump. The air mixes with the contaminant's vapors and is then vacuumed back to the surface. The mix of air and contaminants is filtered, incinerated, or otherwise treated.

- Passive biodegradation involves the concept of natural attenuation, allowing the natural biodegradation of contaminants by the microbes that are already in the soil.

- Groundwater treatment involves boring wells or driving pipes down to the contaminated groundwater tables and pumping the subsurface contaminated groundwater to the surface, much like a regular water well. The contaminated water is filtered or otherwise treated and then, according to permit, is either discharged as waste or pumped back down into the ground through an injection well. An alternative treatment, called air sparging, involves injecting air into the groundwater to stimulate aerobic degradation and microbial activity and to promote migration of contaminants to the remedial process.

Ex Situ Remediation Processes

There is also a variety of ex situ remediation methods:

- Excavation and off-site disposal, sometimes called *scoop and haul,* is the simplest concept. Contaminated soil is merely excavated, exported, and disposed of in an approved off-site landfill. Then the soil is replaced with imported clean soils. While conceptually straightforward, this process is relatively costly, and there may be a lingering liability associated with the contaminated soils that were shipped off-site.

- A variation of this idea is to excavate the soils, treat them on- or off-site, and then put them back into the excavation. One way of treating excavated soils, either on- or off-site, is by incineration where the contaminants are simply burned. In a process known as *on-site low temperature thermal desorption,* the soils are heated to vaporize and release the contaminants, which are then collected and treated.

- Bioremediation, biomounding, and land farming all involve excavating contaminated soils, adding nutrients or bacteria to stimulate microbes already in the soil, and perhaps adding microbes as well, all in order to facilitate biodegradation. The soils are spread by a bulldozer over a lined treatment area or kept in mounds. The soils are tilled from time to time to stimulate the process.

Chapter 3: *Class VIII—Environmental Conditions*

Most people traveling on and around this service station may never notice the small enclosed area near the corner. However, a closer investigation reveals a vapor extraction unit that has been installed to remediate the contaminants located in the soils.

- Fixation or encapsulation involves the excavation of contaminated soils and the addition of fixation materials that stabilize, enclose, and/or encapsulate contaminants.
- Capping is used when it is considered best not to disturb the subsurface material but there is still a chance that rain or other water moving through the soil could promote contaminant migration. Some contaminants may be removed and an impermeable cap is placed over the contamination and prevents water from moving down into the site, thereby halting any movement of the contaminants.

Site Closure
When all the remedial goals are met, the responsible government agency generally confirms that fact in writing. The written document is often called a *closure letter* or a *no further action letter* (NFA letter), which states that the case is closed or that no further action is required. An NFA letter

is a positive step, as it is evidence that regulators are satisfied for the time being. It may also signal that a listing of the property has been moved from one publicly available database to another one with less onerous connotations. This may reduce the potential risks of property ownership and is often viewed favorably by potential lenders. Nevertheless, an NFA letter does not mean that a property is free of contamination, that it poses no further risks, that all of the contamination has even been found, or that there will not be additional, future investigations interfering with property use. The letter simply means that no further action is required on the project for which the letter was issued. No governmental agency will irrevocably certify a site as clean, even if the site has undergone remediation and has *site closure* status; however, while a technical risk may exist, the market perceptions may be such that no material risk exists at that point. Of course market data must be used to make such a determination.

Chapter 3: *Class VIII—Environmental Conditions*

CHAPTER 3 Cross-References

Related article in Chapter 1: William N. Kinnard, Jr., MAI, SRA, PhD and Elaine M. Worzala, PhD, "How North American Appraisers Value Contaminated Property and Associated Stigma" *The Appraisal Journal* (January 1999), 16.

Related articles in Chapter 2: John D. Dorchester, Jr., MAI, CRE, "Environmental Pollution: Valuation in a Changing World" *The Appraisal Journal* (July 1991), 35–37; Albert R. Wilson, "The Environmental Opinion: Basis for an Impaired Value Opinion" *The Appraisal Journal* (July 1994), 68–69, 71–72, 74–75; Albert R. Wilson, "Emerging Approaches to Impaired Property Valuation" *The Appraisal Journal* (April 1996), 89; Richard J. Roddewig, "Choosing the Right Analytical Tool for the Job" *The Appraisal Journal* (July 1998); and Randall Bell, MAI, "The Impact of Detrimental Conditions on Property Values" *The Appraisal Journal* (October 1998), 113–114.

Related articles in Chapter 4: Peter J. Patchin, MAI, ASA, CRE, "Contaminated Properties— Stigma Revisited" *The Appraisal Journal* (April 1991); Richard J. Roddewig, "Stigma, Environmental Risk and Property Value: 10 Critical Inquiries" *The Appraisal Journal* (October 1996), 209, 211–212, 213–214; Richard J. Roddewig, "Classifying the Level of Risk and Stigma Affecting Contaminated Property" *The Appraisal Journal* (January 1999), 219–220, 221–223; and Wayne C. Lusvardi, "The Dose Makes the Poison: Environmental Phobia or Regulatory Stigma?" *The Appraisal Journal* (April 2000), 235–237.

Related article in Chapter 5: Scott B. Arens, MAI, SRA, "The Valuation of Defective Properties: A Common Sense Approach" *The Appraisal Journal* (April 1977), 253.

Related articles in Chapter 6: Patricia R. Healy and John J. Healy, Jr., MAI, "Lenders' Perspectives on Environmental Issues" *The Appraisal Journal* (July 1992), 290–291; and Richard J. Roddewig, MAI, CRE and Allen C. Keiter, MAI, "Mortgage Lenders and the Institutionalization and Normalization of Environmental Risk Analysis" *The Appraisal Journal* (April 2001), 308.

Related articles in Chapter 7: Albert R. Wilson, "Probable Financial Effect of Asbestos Removal on Real Estate" *The Appraisal Journal* (July 1989); and Jeffrey D. Fisher, PhD, George H. Lentz, PhD, and K.S. Maurice Tse, PhD, "Effects of Asbestos on Commercial Real Estate: A Survey of MAI Appraisers" *The Appraisal Journal* (October 1993), 329–331.

Related article in Chapter 10: Allan E. Gluck, Donald C. Nanney, and Wayne Lusvardi, "Mitigating Factors in Appraisal & Valuation of Contaminated Property" *Real Estate Issues* (Summer 2000), 529, 531–534.

Related articles in Chapter 11: Ralph W. Holmen, "Current Legal Issues Raised by Environmental Hazards Affecting Real Estate" *Real Estate Issues* (Fall/Winter 1991), 545–547; and Jack P. Friedman, CRE, "Defending an Oil Company Against Litigation for Environmental Contamination (A Case Study)" *Real Estate Issues* (Winter 1999/2000), 582, 583.

Understanding, Analyzing and Estimating Stigma

CHAPTER 4

Editor's Introduction

As some of the earlier articles in this anthology make clear, determining the stigma that may or may not affect a property over and above the cost of remediation or following completion of remediation is one of the most vexing problems facing real estate appraisers. This chapter deals with the development of the definition of "stigma," the variety of techniques now used to determine its presence, and its impact on value.

Patchin's 1988 article (see Chapter 1) first purported that there can be a lingering stigma following cleanup. His 1991 article in this chapter is the first Appraisal Journal *piece to explore the causes of stigma in detail.*

While Patchin explored the meaning and causes of stigma from a real estate market point of view, Mundy presents seven criteria of stigma from the viewpoint of the social scientist and psychologist rather than that of the marketplace of competing buyers and sellers.

Roddewig's award-winning 1996 article says stigma can fluctuate in relation to a complex interplay between various cycles that appraisers should consider and evaluate. His 1999 article explores how case studies can be used to derive a stigma adjustment factor based on classifying contaminated property sales as low-risk, high-risk, or changing-risk situations.

Lusvardi discusses how the difference between "phobia" (persistent and irrational fear of unlikely health impacts) and real estate "stigma" (assessment of the true risk for real estate values) affects the appraisal process in actual situations.

Contaminated Properties—Stigma Revisited

by Peter J. Patchin, MAI, ASA, CRE

Peter J. Patchin, MAI, ASA, CRE, *is president of Peter J. Patchin and Associates, Inc., in Burnsville, Minnesota. Mr. Patchin is a 1956 graduate of Kansas State University, and is affiliated with several professional associations. He has published articles in* The Appraisal Journal *as well as in other real estate-related journals.*

This article originally appeared in the April 1991 issue of The Appraisal Journal.

In "Valuation of Contaminated Properties," which appeared in the January 1988 issue of *The Appraisal Journal*, I explored the potential negative effect on market value of the stigma attached to contaminated properties, after all cleanup costs and related tangible factors have been considered. The term "stigma" was used to represent a variety of intangible factors from possible public liability and fear of additional health hazards to the simple fear of the unknown. In the more than two years since this article appeared, I have been repeatedly questioned on the issue of stigma. Many who inquired either stated directly or implied that perhaps the concept of stigma was a figment of this writer's imagination.

With the passage of time, however, a greater awareness of the extreme threat toxic contamination poses to real estate values has begun to inform the market. Indeed, a recent environmental publication estimated that the aggregate loss could well exceed 10% of the total U.S. real estate value.[1] With increased market awareness, data are now being developed that conclusively prove that in many cases stigma does indeed exist.

For example, in the 1990 sale of an industrial property formerly owned by a Fortune 500 company, serious soil contamination had been discovered in 1983. The large corporate owner signed a consent order and the cleanup was begun. Seven years later, the local environmental protection agency considered the cleanup complete. It is important to note that if any future cleanup were deemed necessary the corporate owner would be held responsible for such costs. Another Fortune 500 company was an intermediate holder of title in this property and stood second in line to pay for cleanup costs if the first owner failed to pay for any reason. Consequently, liability for present and future cleanup costs simply was not an issue in the sale of this property. Any discount from its unimpaired value would thus be attributable strictly to the stigma factor. Several local appraisers and the assessor agreed that the unimpaired value of the property was about $2,000,000. After an 8-month sales effort, the property was sold for $95,000 cash. The indicated discount, caused solely by the effect of stigma, was over 95%.

---

1. *Focus—The Bulletin of Environmental Risk Evaluation And Management,* (Columbus, Ohio: Hazardous Materials Institute, March 30, 1990) 6.

Chapter 4: *Contaminated Properties—Stigma Revisited*

In this article, specific stigma-related market data will be discussed, and some of the many components of this phenomenon will be identified.

One problem that many appraisers have in dealing with the notion of stigma is their expectation that there should be a rational or logical cause for any loss in value. Appraisers must recognize that there are many irrational factors in the marketplace. If there is a general perception in the market that a hazard from contamination exists, a value loss could result whether the market perception is rational or not. An appraiser's job is simply to interpret market reactions in terms of value, not to establish whether that market reaction is rational. Property owners may be certain that there is a greater chance of being struck by lightning than of being harmed by toxic contamination after a cleanup has been completed, and on a technical basis these owners are probably correct. But if the market does not reflect this awareness, the stigma still exists.

It may be helpful to think of stigma as a negative intangible. This intangible is likely to be caused by one or a combination of the following factors.

Fear of Hidden Cleanup Costs

If a cleanup has not yet begun, it is difficult to assure buyers that estimated cleanup costs are adequate. As David Houston points out, "If the estimated cleanup cost is 'X',...the typical buyer will deduct '2X' from his purchase offer."[2] For this reason clients should be advised to complete all known cleanup costs before attempting to market the property.

Even after the cleanup has been completed and a certification has been obtained from an environmental expert that the property is now in compliance, resistance may still be encountered in the marketplace. In some cases this resistance is well founded. For example, a contaminated site was restored and received a "clean bill of health" in 1983. In 1989, however, further contamination from the same source was discovered and the cleanup process was repeated.

The Trouble Factor

Many comparable sales exist in which the costs of correction are well defined, yet the decline in market value is shown as a fixed dollar amount in addition to the costs to cure. This is particularly true in cases of single-family residential properties, when contamination may dictate such improvements as the renovation or demolition of a building, or the drilling of a new water well. When these properties sell before a cure is undertaken, the difference between the unimpaired value and the actual selling price may be substantially greater than the cost to cure. Analysis of this disparity typically indicates that in addition to the costs to cure, such approximate amounts as $10,000 or $20,000 are often deducted. The rationale for these deductions is that although buyers are aware of the costs to cure, they feel they should also be compensated monetarily for the trouble of making the necessary improvement.

Fear of Public Liability

In many cases, stigma has little relationship to cleanup costs. The property may have been cleaned up to the extent that present-day technology

2. American Society of Real Estate Counselors, *Seminar on Toxic Contamination in Real Estate,* (November 1989), statement by speaker—David Houston, CRE.

Valuing Contaminated Properties

allows, and a well-financed indemnity for the benefit of future owners may have been offered to pay for any future cleanup costs. Yet the property still may not sell.

To illustrate this point, in 1989 a four-year-old, hi-tech industrial building and site had received its clean bill of health from an environmental consultant. The original owner and contaminator of the site possessed a well-endowed environmental protection fund that had paid for the original cleanup and stood ready to pay for any further cleanup costs. In addition, the large city in which the property was located had agreed to pay for cleanup costs not covered by the original owner's environmental protection fund. In effect, the property carried a double indemnity with regard to cleanup costs. The city also offered to finance the sale of the property under one of its bonding programs. After being exposed on the market for less than six months the property attracted an offer from a Fortune 500 company that was within 7% of its unimpaired appraised value. A few days before closing, the buyers backed out of the deal because of the site's contamination history, stating that they "just felt compelled to consider other alternatives."[3]

This property continues to be offered on the market and has not yet attracted further offers. The principle of substitution thus comes into play as buyers seek an equally desirable substitute property without the contamination problem.

Lack of Mortgageability

The inability to obtain financing, either for the sale of a property or its future development, is one of the most frequent causes of stigma-related value loss. Since January 1988, lenders have become increasingly aware of the risks of mortgaging contaminated properties. The vast majority of lenders will not even consider a property until it has been cleaned up and tests within required limits. This reluctance to lend applies not only to superfund sites, but to sites with comparatively low levels of contamination. The net result of the loss of mortgageability is that the property is held off the market until the cure has been accomplished. Time thus becomes an important factor in the measurement of value loss.

In the case of development lands, the value loss caused by a long waiting period off the market is particularly apparent. For example, a client owns an 80-acre parcel of land ready for development. In the past two years he has signed two purchase agreements, both for approximately $3,000,000 cash. Both purchase agreements failed when it was disclosed that an electronics plant across the road is responsible for a plume of contaminated ground water that extends under 2 of the 80 acres. Both purchasers declined to close the sale on the basis that they could not receive financing for their development projects because of the contamination. According to environmental consultants who have thoroughly studied this spill, to make the site conform to acceptable standards would take about three years (not a major problem as contamination cures go). Unfortunately, the contamination has already kept the property off the market for two years and remediation of the site has not yet begun, while litigation proceeds. Consequently, the property will be off the market for five years even if remediation were to start immediately (two years already elapsed, plus three years remediation). If a nominal 12% yield rate is as-

3. "3M Corporation" *Minneapolis Star Tribune,* (November 30, 1989) 7D.

sumed, the loss in value caused by excess time delays may be illustrated as follows:

Present worth if remediation starts as soon as possible
$3,000,000 × .7118 (3-year 12% present worth factor) = $2,135,000

Present worth if remediation starts 2 years later
$3,000,000 × .5674 (5-year 12% present worth factor) = $1,702,000

Difference $433,000

Thus, by their delaying tactics the defendants have created an additional $433,000 liability for themselves. The defendants' legal counsel should weigh this type of value loss when considering their strategy.

In the preceding example, the stigma loss caused by a three-year cleanup period is $865,000 ($3,000,000 less $2,135,000). This figure does not account for cleanup costs, which are a separate issue.

Residential versus Commercial

Data are beginning to reveal that in some instances, the market reaction to contamination differs according to whether the property is residential or commercial. Several cases were examined in which residential drinking water wells were contaminated by nearby landfills or industries. The comparables studied contained, in aggregate, several hundred single-family residential properties, and consequently the results appear to be meaningful. The market reaction in these cases may be briefly summarized as follows.

- Sharp drops in value occur during the first year or two following disclosure of contamination.
- Stigma begins to disappear when local officials announce plans for an alternative water supply (e.g., municipal water lines are extended, new wells are drilled for affected properties, carbon filters are installed).
- Once the cure is actually in place, the stigma seems to disappear altogether. The one exception may be when residences have carbon filters and no promise of an alternative water supply. This situation appears to cause a slight stigma to remain.
- A survey of lenders indicates little, if any, discrimination against such properties.

How Clean Is Clean?

The major issue now confronting those working with contaminated properties is: How clean must the site become to be marketable once again? Many appraisers and clients seem to be under the impression that a government agency makes this judgment. Such is not the case. Both the federal and state environmental protection agencies have the protection of the public health as their primary objective. It is not their job to declare any particular site clean so that it may become marketable. A clean bill of health for a site must be obtained from a private environmental assessment professional rather than a public agency. Such persons have widely varying opinions, as do appraisers. Frequently, the only way to settle these differences of opinion is to litigate—just as is the case when appraisers have differences. Consequently, a clean bill of health may not be perceived as such by either the market or the courts.

As increasing numbers of properties become unmarketable, the comprehensive plans of urban areas are likely to be disrupted. Already many cities have a patchwork of these unmarketable properties covering their maps. As a result, pressure will mount to compel government agencies to decide: How clean is clean?

A major question facing environmental experts is thus which standard is applicable when judging whether a property is clean enough. For instance, if a drinking water supply is threatened, the U. S. Environmental Protection Agency (EPA) drinking water standards apply. If skin contact is the only hazard, however, the Occupational Health & Safety Administration (OSHA) standards apply.

For example, in the case of a gasoline spill (a common occurrence), the maximum allowable limits for benzene are indicated as follows:

EPA standard	5 parts per billion
OSHA standard	1,000 parts per billion

Obviously, the costs to reach the level of the EPA standard are far higher than to reach the OSHA standard. The difference in the costs to cure may well decide the property's future marketability. Cleanups are often ordered to meet the EPA drinking water standards when drinking water supply does not appear to be involved. While such professional judgments must be accepted, few environmental assessment experts seem to give much consideration to the economic consequences of their actions.

A simplified example of the consequences of the cleanup standard on property value is as follows:

Commercial Site:

Unimpaired market value	$3.00 per sq. ft.
Costs of cleanup—OSHA standard	$1.00 per sq. ft.
Costs of cleanup—EPA standard	$6.00 per sq. ft.

Clearly, if the EPA standard is considered most appropriate, the property is likely to become unmarketable, unless the contaminator or someone in the chain of title can be compelled to pay for the cleanup. As long as the property does not present an immediate public health threat, the cleanup is frequently deferred and the property becomes another unmarketable blot on the landscape.

Such problems are becoming far more pervasive. In time, the situation may overwhelm many urban areas. Eventually, someone in authority is going to have to define the limits of an acceptable standard.

Conclusion

The market has become significantly more aware of the impact of toxic contamination on real estate values. With this awareness, market data are being developed that either confirm or deny the presence of stigma in a particular situation. Appraisers will seldom find this type of market data in recorded transactions and it may be necessary to conduct extensive research to disclose the relevant information. The reasons for sales that did not go through can be more important than the sales that actually did occur. In the majority of cases, appraisers clearly cannot do a thorough job by merely deducting the cost to cure from a property's unimpaired value.

Stigma and Value

by Bill Mundy, MAI, PhD

The real estate valuation literature is only beginning to address the effects contamination has on the value of real estate. Recently, several articles have appeared concerning various methods of dealing with the impact that contamination has on value.[1] These articles deal with quantifying variables on which data are relatively easy to obtain, such as the cost to remove or encapsulate asbestos and the cost to clean soil contaminated by a leaking underground storage tank. In addition, quantitative techniques such as market research are used to estimate the change in value caused by contamination.[2] The literature indicates that often a mathematical derived conclusion regarding an effect may not correspond with the opinion of the public at large. In other words, real risk may not be synonymous with perceived risk.

The value paradigm of value before contamination minus value after contamination equals compensation can be restated to apply to contaminated property.

$$V_b - V_a = \text{compensation}$$

where

$$V_b = \text{Value before contamination}$$
$$V_a = \text{Value after contamination}$$

or

$$V_c - V_d = \text{damage}$$

where

$$V_c = \text{Value clean}$$
$$V_d = \text{Value dirty}$$

From a mathematical perspective, damage should equal the cost to cure.[3] However, if a contaminated property were valued using two different methods to determine damage, the conclusions would probably not agree. For example, in one instance damage might be considered equivalent to the cost to cure, while in a second instance damage might be estimated

Bill Mundy, MAI, PhD, is president and senior analyst of Mundy & Associates in Seattle, Washington. He received a BA in agriculture from Washington State University as well as an MA in urban economics and a PhD in market research and urban economics from the University of Washington. Mr. Mundy has made numerous presentations to Appraisal Institute groups on the topic of contamination and property values.

This article originally appeared in the January 1992 issue of The Appraisal Journal.

1. See, for example, Peter J. Patchin, "Valuation of Contaminated Properties." *The Appraisal Journal* (January 1988): 7–16; Albert Wilson, "A Valuation Model for Environmental Risk." *Focus* (January 15, 1990): 17–20; Albert Wilson, "Environmental Risk Evaluation." *Focus* (March 30, 1990): 6–29; and Maxwell O. Ramsland, Jr., "An Asbestos Assessment Model: A Valuation Methodology for Appraisers." *Environmental Watch* (Spring 1990): 2–4.

2. William N. Kinnard, Sr., "Analyzing the Stigma Effect of Proximity to a Hazardous Materials Site." *Environmental Watch* (December 1989): 4–7.

3. Albert Wilson, president of the Hazardous Materials Institute, would argue that the term "cost to cure" is inappropriate because we never really know if a problem is cured. Generally what is accomplished is the problem is controlled. Speech at the Appraisal Network and Real Estate Counseling Group of America, Inc., meeting in Orlando, Florida. February 28, 1991.

using multiple regression in which a dummy variable represents damages. Using a carefully developed data set (e.g., two neighborhoods similar in all respects except in their levels of contamination) and a well-specified model in which multi-collinearity is zero and the R^2 is 1.00, the damage estimate would probably be found to be greater if the latter technique is used than if the cost-to-cure method is used. The reason for this inconsistency is that the damage is the sum of the cost to cure plus a stigma effect. Examples of this dichotomy are discussed in Peter Patchin's article, "Contaminated Properties—Stigma Revisited," in which he notes that "In many cases, stigma has little relationship to cleanup costs."[4]

Stigma influences are beginning to be recognized by the courts. In a recent ruling by the Washington Board of Tax Appeals, the board agreed that certain variables that influence value, such as a capitalization rate, can be affected by an environmental stigma.[5] What is an environmental stigma? What is its origin? Can such a stigma affect two equally contaminated properties differently? How can the amount of stigma be quantified? These are some of the questions this article attempts to address.

What is Stigma?

The characteristics of social stigma may be summarized as follows.

> It is the essence of the stigmatizing process that a label marking the deviant status is applied, and this marking process typically has devastating consequences for emotions, thought, and behavior. Many words have been applied to the resulting status of the deviant person. He or she is flawed, blemished, discredited, spoiled, or stigmatized...
>
> The mark may or may not be physical: It may be embedded in behavior, biography, ancestry, or group membership. It may also be possible to conceal it. The mark is potentially discrediting and commonly becomes so when it is linked through attributional processes to causal dispositions, and these dispositions are seen as deviant. Furthermore, the discredit becomes more consequential when the deviant dispositions are judged to be persistent and central and, therefore, part of the marked person's identity.[6]

Environmental stigma is the result of an undesirable event that disrupts the balance of an environmental system.[7] This disruption may cause blame to be associated with it. The following seven criteria are used to evaluate and determine the degree of stigma.[8]

1. *Disruption*—Would the contamination alter a given person's normal day-to-day behavior? The examples of a leaking underground storage tank (LUST) and the Exxon Valdez oil spill in Prince William Sound, Alaska, will be used to contrast some of the criteria. If the LUST does not cause off-site problems and alternative sites from which to obtain fuel are readily available, the LUST will probably cause little, if any, disruption. In contrast, the oil spill caused tremendous disruption to fisherman and Alaskan natives in Prince William Sound.

2. *Concealability*—The old bromide "out of sight, out of mind" applies to stigma. A LUST cannot be seen, smelled, or felt. In contrast, the Prince William Sound spill was highly visible to the world through extensive television coverage.

4. Peter J. Patchin, "Contaminated Properties—Stigma Revisited." *The Appraisal Journal* (April 1991): 169.

5. Washington Board of Tax Appeals, *Northwest Cooperage Company, Inc.* v. *Ruthe Ridder, King County Assessor.* Tax Lexis 208, July 12, 1990. #36278-36280.

6. Edward E. Jones, Amerigo Farina, Albert H. Hastorf, Hazel Markus, Dale T. Miller, and Robert A. Scott. *Social Stigma: The Psychology of Marked Relationships* (New York: W.H. Freeman and Co., 1984): 4–7.

7. Michael R. Edelstein. *Contaminated Communities: The Social and Psychological Impacts of Residential Toxic Exposure* (Boulder, Colorado: Westview Press, 1988): 6.

8. Ibid., 14.

3. *Aesthetic effect*—To what extent does the contamination visibly alter the environment? The LUST is out of sight; however, rocks along the shoreline and marshes still show the effects of the oil spill.

4. *Responsibility*—To what extent was an individual or an entity responsible for the contamination? Research shows that the more direct the association between the stigmatizing event and the responsible party, the greater the stigma effect that will accrue to both the event and the responsible party.

5. *Prognosis*—The prognosis for contaminated property contains two elements: 1) the severity of the contamination; and 2) the persistence of the contamination. For instance, PCB contamination from a transformer may not be severe and may affect only a small area, but because of its chemical characteristics, it will persist for many years.

6. *Degree of peril*—Peril is multidimensional—a contamination event can affect the health of humans, wildlife, and fauna. In other words, peril is viewed broadly as affecting the entire environment. For a LUST, a worst-case scenario might be a contaminated aquifer. In the case of the Prince William Sound spill, the entire food chain of native Alaskans living in the areas affected by the spill has been disrupted.

7. *Level of fear*—Aaron Wildavsky, in his article, "No Risk is the Highest Risk of All," describes this phenomenon:

> How extraordinary! The richest, longest lived, best protected, most resourceful civilization, with the highest degree of insight into its own technology, is on its way to becoming the most frightened.
>
> Is it our environment or ourselves that have changed? Would people like us have had this sort of concern in the past?. . . Today, there are risks from numerous small dams far exceeding those from nuclear reactors. Why is the one feared and not the other? Is it that we are just used to the old or are some of us looking differently at essentially the same sorts of experience?[9]

When environmental features are viewed as repellent, upsetting, or disruptive, they are stigmatized as undesirable. One source of stigma is technologies such as petroleum processing, nuclear power plants, and high voltage or transmission lines. A second source of environmental stigma is activities like the transportation of hazardous materials, the development of hazardous storage sites, or the underground storage of petroleum products. The third source of stigma is within the products themselves, including petroleum–based products and agricultural products associated with a health risk, such as the Alar used by the Washington apple industry.

The consequences of environmental stigma can be direct or indirect. Examples of direct consequences of various stigmas are an increasing incidence of cancer, lower work quality as a result of air or noise pollution, decreased occupancy in an apartment building, or lower market price or increased marketing time for single-family residences located adjacent to sanitary landfill. Consequences can also be indirect, however. The exodus of residents from an area affected by contamination, such as the Love Canal area of New York, or the negative economic impact on the apple industry in general caused by the few producers that used Alar, are two examples.

9. Aaron Wildavsky. "No Risk Is the Highest Risk of All" *American Science* (Vol. 67, 1979): 35.

Valuing Contaminated Properties

An environmental stigma results from perceptions of uncertainty and risk. It may be relatively easy to quantify the cost to remedy a simple contamination problem, such as a leaking underground storage tank. However, as the complexity of the contamination increases the level of uncertainty and perceived risk rises.

Uncertainty

The level of uncertainty or risk associated with a hazard or contamination is influenced by the amount of knowledge people have about it. When a contamination problem becomes known, there is generally a period of heightened uncertainty during which the magnitude and character of the problem are researched and documented. During this period of heightened uncertainty, risk is much greater, therefore value discounts are greater. As research progresses, and a better understanding of the magnitude, character, and possible solutions to the problem is reached, uncertainty decreases. The market's ability to predict the possible value effects and the probability of whether those effects will be realized become more certain. Even though the risk of a catastrophe may be high, the degree of uncertainty about it is low at this point, and an analyst will be able to calculate the value changes resulting from the hazard more easily. Consequently, time is an important consideration in determining the degree of uncertainty.[10]

Perception of Risk

Risk can be differentiated based on whether it is real or perceived.[11] The effect of real risk can be quantified with a high degree of confidence. For example, a water hydrologist's statement concerning risk might be that "The site generating water contamination has been contained and there is no more migration of contaminating substances moving through the soil." An environmental engineer may estimate that the cost to soil farm a site that has a leaking underground storage tank will be $15,000.

Perceived risk is the risk seen by the public in the marketplace. It is an individual's disinclination to believe that a source of contamination is safe.

The perception of risk varies with the nature of an event's cause. For example, the risk associated with illness from drinking well water contaminated by an undetected source such as a landfill or LUST is greater than the risk associated with living downriver from a dam because the former is involuntary while the latter is voluntary.

Another factor that affects the level of perceived risk is whether the source of risk might result in a catastrophic accident. For example, the level of risk associated with a nuclear reactor is higher than the risk of living in a home where radon gas is present.

Finally, the level of risk associated with contamination varies according to the level of familiarity with the particular contamination. Because people are relatively unfamiliar with PCBs, greater risk is associated with them than with smoking cigarettes. Ironically, however, many more people die every year from the results of smoking than from the results of PCBs. This illustrates the discrepancy between real and perceived risk.

Another example of the difference between real and perceived risk is revealed in research that the author recently concluded involving a sanitary landfill. From a scientific standpoint, the landfill was contained. However in a survey of 25 lending institutions in the Pacific Northwest in

10. For a good discussion of the difference between uncertainty and risk from a financial standpoint see Lawrence Schall and Charles Haley, *Introduction to Financial Management,* 6th ed. (New York: McGraw Hill. 1990): 173–218 and 326–361.

11. Paul Slovic. "Perception of Risk," *Science* (Vol. 236, 1987): 280–285.

which the precise scientific status of the landfill was explained, 50% of the lenders indicated they would not make a loan on an adjacent property for an average of ten years into the future.

Risk Amplification

As previously illustrated, the level of perceived risk can vary depending on the nature of the event; that is, whether it is involuntary, unfamiliar, or catastrophic.[12] In addition, the same type of risk can vary depending on certain "amplification" traits, including media exposure. If an incident receives a great deal of television, radio, or newspaper exposure, its level of risk may be elevated in comparison with a similar incident that receives little, if any, media exposure.

A second amplification trait is the extent to which blame can be attributed to a person or entity; that is, the extent to which the entity or person responsible for the event acted carelessly, incompetently, or irresponsibly. One of the reasons that the Exxon Company was so severely criticized after the Prince William Sound oil spill was because the press revealed that Captain Hazelwood was below deck, drunk (carelessness); that the third mate was piloting the ship (incompetence); and that Exxon had allowed Captain Hazelwood to pilot the Exxon Valdez in spite of his rather questionable background (irresponsibility).

A final factor that affects the amplification of perceived risk for a particular incident is the innocence of the victim. If a victim is innocent (e.g., an office worker in an asbestos-contaminated building), the level of risk associated with that property can be expected to be much greater than in a situation in which the victim is not innocent (e.g., a homeowner knowingly living in a house that has asbestos insulation and asbestos-wrapped hot water lines).

Stigma and Marketability

The value of real estate is based on the premise that it is marketable. A number of people take part in the transaction process who can have an influence on a property's marketability. Different sets of buyers may act differently. For example, the buyer of an apartment building located adjacent to a sanitary landfill may want a price discount or an indemnification agreement from the operator of the landfill to offset risk. If the buyer is not able to obtain these concessions he or she may not be willing to acquire the property. On the other hand, some segments of the real estate market are more willing to accept risk—for example, companies in which a byproduct of the production process is soil contamination. Transactions involving the acquisition and disposition of oil refineries, oil terminals, and tank farms when the transaction is on a "within industry" basis are examples of situations when risk would not significantly concern the buyer.

Buyers and intermediaries in the acquisition process perceive risk differently. While an individual may be willing to buy a property that is contaminated or has the possibility of being contaminated, the lending institution may not be willing to provide financing for the acquisition.

Quantifying Stigma

In a perfect world, stigma would be quantified on a direct basis. We do not operate in a perfect world however, and therefore we must frequently

12. Ibid.

rely on indirect measures. In a perfect world, or alternatively with a good-quality set of market data, stigma might be expected to have the following influences on market behavior as measured through the income approach.

- *Rent*—For a stigmatized property rent could be less than for the same property unstigmatized. This is a simple market demand phenomenon.

- *Occupancy*—Occupancy would also be expected to be less as a result of such stigma.

- *Expenses*—For such a property, higher operating expenses could be expected for such items as marketing to maintain rent and occupancy levels and professional services to determine whether contamination persists.

- *Rate*—The capitalization or discount rate could be influenced by lending institutions' desire to alter the loan-to-value ratio, interest rate, or term of the loan to offset perceived risk.

For many properties, though, the stigma influence may be so subtle that its effect would be completely explained by the error term in our analysis.[13] However, careful multiple regression analysis may measure the stigma influence if such an influence does in fact exist.

Indirect Approaches

A number of indirect approaches to quantifying the effects of stigma are potentially useful. One of these is contingent valuation, which is a survey research technique used to determine the value of noneconomic goods (e.g., the value of a public beach).[14]

A second technique is trade-off (conjoint) analysis, which can be used to determine the relative importance of variables that contribute to the value of a home. Trade-off analysis is another survey research technique that quantifies, through nonparametric statistical techniques, the relative utility (or value) of the individual attributes that compose a product.[15]

Conclusion

Property that is directly or indirectly affected by sources of contamination may suffer a diminution in value from two factors. The first is real risks that can be scientifically quantified, such as the cost to cure or manage a risk. An additional factor is perceived risks, which are much more difficult to quantify. The level of perceived risk varies with the characteristics of the contamination, such as whether it has catastrophic effects, is unfamiliar, or is involuntary. Risk also varies depending on the level of media exposure, whether blame can be attributed to an individual or entity, and the innocence of the victim.

The challenge of quantifying the damaging effect contaminants have on real estate has only recently, since the passage of the Comprehensive Environmental Response, Compensation and Liability Act of 1980 (CERCLA or Superfund), become a major valuation problem. This article has indicated the complexity of the issue and has suggested some things to observe. In addition, this article has offered methods that may prove useful in determining the impact of various forms of contamination on real property value.

13. Gene Dillman, speaking at the February 28, 1991, meeting of the Real Estate Counseling Group of America, Inc., in Orlando, Florida.

14. Robert Cameron Mitchell and Richard T. Carson, "Using Surveys to Value Public Goods: The Contingent Valuation Method." *Resources for the Future* (1988): 2–17.

15. Gilbert A. Churchill, *Marketing Research: Methodological Foundations* (Chicago: Dryden Press, 1987): 364–376.

Stigma, Environmental Risk and Property Value: 10 Critical Inquiries

by Richard Roddewig, MAI

Over the past two decades, real estate appraisers have gained considerable experience in valuing property affected by environmental risk . In fact, many in the appraisal community are now so comfortable analyzing those impacts on property markets and market values that some now specialize in environmental risk analysis. The increased comfort level of both the marketplace and appraisers with this type of analysis is, in part, a result of improved techniques for environmental assessment, wider availability of data about the numbers, types and locations of properties likely to be affected by environmental risks, better information about health risks posed by some environmental conditions, and enhancements in removal/remediation techniques. The simple passage of time has also helped. It has allowed real estate owners, developers, lenders, buyers, sellers, and appraisers to become familiar with processes for the appropriate analysis of the potential impact of environmental risks on property.

The Appraisal Institute and its predecessor organizations have been instrumental in this process as well. For example, since 1985, *The Appraisal Journal* has published at least 70 articles dealing with environmental topics.[1] In addition, the Appraisal Institute launched a new publication called *Environmental Watch* in 1988. This newsletter concentrated on environmental issues pertinent to appraisers.[2] In 1989, the American Institute of Real Estate Appraisers adopted Guide Note 8 which dealt with "The Consideration of Hazardous Substances in the Appraisal Process." That note was adopted in 1991 in its entirety by the Appraisal Institute. In 1992, the Appraisal Institute Board of Directors appointed a special Appraisers' Environmental Responsibility Task Force that subsequently promulgated a voluntary Property Observation Checklist, which appraisers may use when inspecting property likely to be affected by environmental risks. In 1993 the Appraisal Institute published a video titled *Hidden Factors: Environmental Risks and the Real Estate Appraiser,* that gives special attention to the environmental site assessment process. In 1994, the Appraisal Institute introduced a new seminar titled "Environmental Risk and the Real Estate Appraisal Process," which has been taught in many loca-

Richard Roddewig, MAI, is president of Clarion Associates, Inc., in Chicago and Denver. He co-developed the Appraisal Institute's seminar, "Environmental Risk and the Real Estate Appraisal Process," and has taught the seminar nationwide. He is adjunct lecturer of real estate valuation in the Department of Finance at DePaul University, Chicago.

This article originally appeared in the October 1996 issue of The Appraisal Journal.

1. See, for example, Danny J. Martin, "The New URAR and Environmental Hazards." *The Appraisal Journal* (January 1995): 47–52; Peter J. Patchin, "Contaminated Properties and the Sales Comparison Approach." *The Appraisal Journal* (July 1994): 402–409; Robert Simons, "How Clean is Clean?" *The Appraisal Journal* (July 1994): 424–438; and Albert R. Wilson, "The Environmental Opinion: Basis for an Impaired Value Opinion." *The Appraisal Journal* (July 1994): 410–423.

2. Appraisal Institute, *Environmental Watch* (Chicago: Appraisal Institute). Publication of this newsletter was terminated in 1995 because of the increased availability of information on environmental issues from other sources.

tions across the country. The essence of many of the articles published in *The Appraisal Journal* and *Environmental Watch,* and the information in the *Hidden Risks* video, and the seminar course can be distilled to 10 critical inquiries that every real estate appraiser should bear in mind in assignments involving contaminated properties.

Stigma and Environmental Risk: What Are They?

The concept of environmental risk as applied to real estate is broad and covers a range of substances, events and land use activities. We may typically think of environmental risk as emanating from such things as groundwater contamination or soil contamination by hazardous substances. But it can be generated in many other ways as well, for example, by air pollution or movement of airborne contaminants on the wind, by pollution of lakes or streams, by contamination of drinking water distribution systems, or even by noise such as might emanate from a busy expressway or an airport. An event, such as a marine oil spill or a railroad derailment involving tank cars carrying chemicals, may create temporary environmental risks until cleanup is completed. Also, certain types of land uses, such as power plants, electrical transmission lines, landfills, waste incinerators, chemical or radioactive material storage facilities, may be perceived in some locations as creating environmental risk for adjacent or nearby real estate.

In analyzing environmental risk, however, real estate appraisers must carefully bear in mind the following points. Not every use of a hazardous substance results in contamination. Not every use of a hazardous substance that does result in contamination necessarily creates an environmental risk. And not every use of a hazardous substance that results in contamination and results in environmental impact and environmental risk necessarily results in a real estate market impact.[3]

The Appraisal Institute emphasizes that environmental risk should be evaluated in the context of a system. The substance itself may be a big part of the risk, but the amount of real estate impact, if any, depends on many other systemic factors such as how the substance is controlled, how it is spread, how many people are potentially affected by the risk, and the degree to which people may be affected.[4]

Stigma, as it applies to real estate affected by environmental risk, is generally defined as "an adverse public perception about a property that is intangible or not directly quantifiable."[5] It is an additional impact on value, over and above the cost of cleanup or remediation. Stigma can occur on sites that once contained contaminants and have been cleaned up, on sites undergoing cleanup, or on sites that were never contaminated but neighbor a property that contains or once contained contaminants.

In many appraisal assignments, the costs of cleanup or remediation are known or have been reasonably quantified by technical environmental assessment specialists. The appraiser's principal task may be to provide an opinion of the additional impact, if any, arising from the "stigma" associated with the site in the marketplace before, during, or after the cleanup process.

Question 1: What Type of Risk or Contamination is Present?

Not every contaminant or hazardous substance creates the same level of health risk. And not every contaminant creates the same level of risk of

---

3. Appraisal Institute, *Environmental Risk and the Real Estate Appraisal Process,* Seminar Workbook, Chap. 1 (Chicago: Appraisal Institute, 1994), 21.

4. Ibid. See also *Hidden Factors: Environmental Risk Evaluation and the Real Estate Appraiser,* video, Appraisal Institute, Chicago, 1992.

5. *Environmental Risk and the Real Estate Appraisal Process,* 128.

Chapter 4: *Stigma, Environmental Risk and Property Value*

impact on property values or markets. Therefore, for the appraiser to do his or her job effectively, the character of the contaminant and its technical environmental impacts and potential health impacts should be understood.

What types of information about the substance should the appraiser obtain in order to understand the real estate impact risks? They can be summarized as follows: the most likely locations, typical transport media, typical transport mechanisms, types of environmental impact and potential health effects, and accepted remediation techniques.

An appraiser needs to know about the typical or most common sources of the substance or risk. Are they widespread or localized? Are the locations well known and carefully documented, or of uncertain extent? How does the substance get into the environment? Does it get into soil, air, groundwater, surface water? Does it get into the food chain? Does it result from natural processes, such as with radon emissions? Or does it get into the environment only as a result of human processes, such as with PCBs?

How does it move through the environment? For example, is it transported by erosion, water, air currents, human or animal activities? The speed at which it moves and the distance it can travel can be affected by such factors as topography, soil type, geology, hydrology, or even wind and air patterns. How do such factors as temperature and humidity affect its movement and presence?

What are the known or suspected impacts on human health? Is the substance a known carcinogen or only suspected of contributing to cancer? How conclusive is the scientific evidence about the link between the substance and health impacts? At what stage is the research on the health effects? These are all things an appraiser may need to know something about because they may be at the core of the real estate marketplace reaction to owning property containing or affected by proximity to the substance or risk.

Knowledge of the appropriate remediation techniques is also crucial to the appraiser's inquiries. Some substances and risks can be easily controlled or remediated, while others cannot. Remediation techniques may include physical removal, on-site treatment, or encapsulation. On-site treatment techniques may vary depending on the nature of the substance, the degree of contamination, or the media in which the substance is located, such as in groundwater or soil. Appropriate remediation techniques may vary from one substance or risk to another. For example, physical removal of some substances, like PCBs, may be the only appropriate technique while on-site encapsulation is appropriate for others like urea-formaldehyde insulation or some types of asbestos.

Question 2: How Do the Five Critical Cycles Affect Perceptions of the Risk?

Every appraiser experienced with evaluating environmental risks soon notices discernible stages in the market concern about environmental impacts of any particular substance. To understand how this works, consider the history of the concern about asbestos as a hazardous substance. Asbestos was widely used in the construction industry in the 1950s and 1960s. Use grew substantially in the early 1970s as well until studies began to conclusively document that asbestos fibers could get into the lungs and cause asbestosis, a potentially fatal condition. Between 1972 and 1975, the Environmental Protection Agency (EPA) issued a series of regulations about the use of asbestos, in many cases banning its use in construction.

Newspapers in the early 1970s had extensive coverage of the asbestos health risks,[6] causing near panic in some sectors of the real estate marketplace. Many properties containing asbestos were stigmatized, becoming unmarketable virtually overnight when many major lenders and financial institutions adopted policies against lending on any property containing asbestos, and some prospective tenants adopted policies against leasing in buildings containing asbestos.[7] By the early 1990s, however, the situation was completely changed. Buildings in which asbestos had been removed, and even buildings with asbestos in place, were routinely bought and sold in the marketplace, and most lenders and tenants were quite comfortable in evaluating the risks.

What happened in the intervening 20 years that so dramatically changed the situation? The marketplace simply got more comfortable in evaluating the risks associated with ownership of a building containing or once containing asbestos. This naturally occurred as a result of the normal evolution of five critical cycles that affect the market for properties affected by environmental risk: the health risk cycle, the remediation cycle, the public relations (media) cycle, the regulatory cycle, and the lending cycle. All of these five cycles are interrelated. In fact, they may more properly be considered as part of one larger systemic cycle that repeats itself over and over again with each new substance or environmental risk that gets attention in the real estate marketplace. To evaluate the impact of environmental risk on real estate, the appraiser needs to understand each component and how the five cycles fit into a larger pattern.

The Health Risk Cycle

The health risk cycle typically begins with the publication of a groundbreaking study linking some common substance in the environment with a health effect. This initial study typically finds some correlation between the substance and a serious disease or condition, often an increased incidence of cancer in persons exposed to the substance. Appearance of the first study typically begets additional studies showing the same effects or focuses attention on other earlier studies showing the same results.

Soon, however, a scientific dialogue emerges, as additional studies critically evaluate the results of the initial studies, poke holes in the methodology, or refine the analysis to better clarify the situations in which health impacts may or may not be likely. This is typically accompanied by better measurement and understanding of the concentrations necessary to create health risks, better data about the locations of sources of the substance, and information on simple ways to limit exposure to the contaminant.

With most of the significant environmental risks that have initially been considered to have widespread impacts on the real estate marketplace in recent years—consider asbestos, PCBs, radon, and electromagnetic fields, for example—the result has been the same: As more scientific information becomes available, general alarm and concern in the real estate community abates and becomes more narrowly focused on a smaller pool of properties than first suspected.

6. See, for example, "Perilous Particle: Tiny Asbestos Fibers Pose a Health Threat to Workers," *The Wall Street Journal* (June 8, 1972): col. 1, 1.

7. See, for example, Janis L. Kirkland, "What's Current in Asbestos Regulation," *University of Richmond Law Review*, v. 23 (Spring 1989): 375–402, citing Adams and Baker, "Sale or Lease of Asbestos-Contaminated Buildings: Legal and Marketplace Issues," 4 *National Asbestos Council Journal* (1986): 50, 53.

Chapter 4: *Stigma, Environmental Risk and Property Value*

The Remediation Cycle

Once the potential health risk posed by a substance becomes a factor in the real estate marketplace, the real estate community immediately begins to seek information about techniques to remediate or lessen the risk. One reason why a marketplace may shut down, as it did in the wake of early concerns about asbestos in commercial buildings, is due to lack of information about types and costs of remediation techniques. As time passes, however, if the market gets more information about remediation, the stigma typically decreases.

Attention given to developing remediation techniques is often directly proportional to the perceived magnitude of the health risks and the number of properties potentially affected by the environmental risk. Remediation techniques are proposed, evaluated, and tested. Results of the tests are publicized, leading to further refinements. A remediation "industry" may actually develop to apply appropriate techniques to the problem properties. Initially, remediation costs may be high, but as more research is done, and more competitors for remediation business enter the marketplace, the cost of remediation is driven down. Eventually, the real estate marketplace becomes more comfortable with its ability to estimate remediation costs for particular types of environmental risks in a variety of settings. Over time, that often means a decrease in the component of stigma caused by uncertainty about remediation techniques and costs.

The Public Relations (Media) Cycle

The old conundrum about falling trees, noise, and human ears applies to the publication of articles about the health effects of substances commonly found in the environment. If it is published only in the scientific or technical literature, and gets no mention in the popular press or at least in professional real estate publications, the substance may have little effect on real estate markets.

Consider the recent concern about the impact of electromagnetic fields emitted by power lines on property values. The first U.S. epidemiological study showing a possible relationship between power lines and some forms of cancer was published in 1979.[8] It was not until a decade later that this study received serious attention. This was the result of an article published in *The New Yorker* magazine by an author whose book, published a year later, put the issue before the general public for the first time.[9]

The popular media treatment of environmental risks typically runs in three phases. In the first phase of the cycle, there is extensive newspaper and electronic media reporting of studies asserting some adverse health effect associated with a substance, building material, or land use previously perceived by the public as being of no environmental concern. This first phase of the cycle also typically involves allegations that the substance, material, or land use creates a widespread risk of serious magnitude, and includes interviews with concerned citizens and environmental groups emphasizing possible dangers from exposure. As the first phase continues, government authorities promise investigation and response, and promise new regulations, if necessary, to lessen the risk.

The second phase of the cycle typically begins with the publication of information on ways of avoiding, remediating, ameliorating, or limiting exposure to the potential problem, publication of additional studies indi-

8. See N. Wertheimer and E. Leeper, "Electrical Wiring Configurations and Childhood Cancer," *American Journal of Epidemiology,* v. 109, no. 3 (March 1979): 273–284.

9. See Paul Brodeur, "Annals of Radiation: The Hazards of Electromagnetic Fields," *The New Yorker* (June 12, 1989): 51–88; (June 19, 1989): 47–73; and (June 26, 1989): 39–68, later published as *Currents of Death: Power Lines, Computer Terminals and the Attempt to Cover Up Their Threat to Your Health* (New York City: Simon and Shuster, 1989). See also Gary Taubes, "Fields of Fear," *The Atlantic Monthly* (November 1994): 94, for a discussion of the sequence of publications and public inquiry into the issue.

cating that the health effects are not as conclusive or as serious as first reported, or at least not likely to be as widespread or occur as frequently as first suspected.

In the second phase also, the media begin to report on technologies and techniques for control, cleanup, remediation, or avoidance of the risk. As this information becomes more widely available, the costs associated with the techniques become better understood and more easily quantifiable. Information also becomes available about the situations in which the risks are likely to be high and those in which exposure or proximity to the risk is limited. Much of the information resulting from this second phase comes as a result of the government process of investigating the existence and seriousness of the risk and determining if there is any need for new regulation of the causes.

In the third phase of the cycle, the market has completely digested the information and makes more informed decisions about the level of risk, if any, and the costs of avoiding or ameliorating it. In this third phase, initial perceptions about potential impacts may be greatly diminished. When the potential impacts relate to property values, the concerns of the marketplace about the number and type of properties potentially affected may also be greatly reduced. And with respect to some types of risks, the market may no longer perceive any adverse impact on property values.

The Regulatory Cycle
There is also a cycle in the way regulators and lawmakers respond to public concerns about possible environmental risks. It typically follows the same pattern as the three phases of the media cycle. In the first phase, lawmakers and regulators respond with cries of concern and alarm, and promises to investigate and "do something" about the problem, if there is one. In the second phase, they launch investigations of the problem, and perhaps hold public hearings to determine its seriousness and garner different points of view. Regulators publish technical studies and propose new regulations or improved laws to control the problem. In the third phase, the new laws are put into practice and then monitored to determine if they are having the intended effect, or whether the laws themselves are creating unforeseen problems and need to be adjusted.

If the laws enacted are very strict, they may have unintended consequences. That is exactly what has happened as a result of some of the Superfund program and the state programs modeled on it. In some older industrial areas, so-called "brownfields," so many properties have contamination problems that qualify or potentially qualify for federal or state Superfund programs, that the real estate market, in some cases, has virtually evaporated. In other markets, it simply creates further impetus for suburban rather than inner-city development. Federal and state regulators are now trying to modify and streamline regulations in order to eliminate some of these regulatory impediments to sale and redevelopment, now reversing past trends for ever-tighter environmental regulations.

The Lending Cycle
The lending community has also gone through a cycle in the way it has reacted to environmental risk, and now has institutionalized and regularized its procedures for dealing with those risks. In the early 1980s, lenders

were so nervous about environmental risk and the real estate marketplace that even the hint of a contamination problem might cause entire categories of properties to be unmortgageable.

That attitude has changed dramatically. Lenders have become more comfortable in evaluating environmental risks. Some of this is the result of the institutionalization of the environmental site assessment process as part of customary mortgage lending practice. Some of it is the result of changes in laws and regulations that clarify when mortgage lenders are, and are not, responsible for cleanup costs. Some of it results from the Federal Deposit Insurance Corporation (FDIC) guidelines issued in February 1993, outlining the steps that member banks should take to implement a proper program for analysis of environmental risk.[10] One of the recommendations of the FDIC is that every institution should appoint a designated senior officer to be responsible for environmental program implementation. Some of it is the simple result of lenders gaining more knowledge about comparative risks created by various environmental conditions.

Question 3: Has There Been an Environmental Site Assessment?

Thanks to the cycle that has occurred in the lending community, a new industry in environmental site assessment has developed since 1986. Most major lenders now routinely insist on some kind of environmental analysis on commercial properties before making a loan, and the standard Uniform Residential Appraisal Report (URAR) form specifically requires an appraiser to comment on "adverse environmental conditions (such as, but not limited to, hazardous wastes, toxic substances, etc.) present in the improvements, on the site, or in the immediate vicinity of the subject property."[11]

The purpose of the analysis is to gather as much information as possible about existing or potential environmental conditions that might affect value and the security of the mortgage loan. Site assessments are undertaken in stages, typically known as Phase I, Phase II, and Phase III site assessments. Phase I assessments usually consist of four areas of research and inquiry: (1) interviews with current owners/operators and inspection of owner or operator documents and records; (2) search of the chain of title for any evidence that past owners, operators, or tenants undertook activities that might have resulted in discharges of contamination; (3) inquiry to government agencies for information about past discharges or storage of potential contaminants on site or nearby; and (4) actual onsite inspection.

If the Phase I work results in some evidence of possible surface or subsurface contamination or past or present violations of environmental laws and regulations, a Phase II assessment may be undertaken. The purpose of this second phase is to confirm the presence or absence of contamination, and document the types, amounts and locations, and possible rates of migration through soil or groundwater. Soil testing and even groundwater testing may be undertaken during the Phase II investigation. Following completion of the Phase II assessment, there may be a Phase III assessment that further analyzes the site and better defines the amount, location, and control or cleanup techniques and costs.

The information gathered in the environmental site assessment process can be very significant to the potential mortgage lender, the real estate

10. See *Environmental Watch*, v. 6, no. 1 (Spring 1993): 1, for a discussion of these FDIC guidelines.

11. Federal National Mortgage Association (Fannie Mae), Uniform Residential Appraisal Report Form 1004 (Washington, D.C.: Fannie Mae, 1993), 1. For additional commentary on this requirement, see Danny J. Martin, "The New URAR and Environmental Hazards," *The Appraisal Journal* (January 1995): 47–52.

marketplace, and therefore the appraiser in estimating value. The site assessment process pinpoints the location and amount of any contaminants, and, if it proceeds into a Phase II or Phase III assessment, the appropriate control or remediation techniques and their costs. The availability of accurate information about the levels of contamination and the costs and duration of control or cleanup can cut down dramatically on the risk associated with ownership of property affected by environmental risk.

Question 4: Is It a Designated Federal or State Superfund Site?

The federal program known as "Superfund" was established by the Comprehensive Environmental Response, Compensation and Liability Act of 1980, known better by its acronym, CERCLA.[12] The principal focus of the program is to identify abandoned and inactive hazardous waste sites and stimulate their cleanup. The Superfund itself is the pot of money appropriated by Congress to clean up specifically designated sites.

As of the end of 1994, just over 38,000 sites all over the country had been brought into the program. However, only about 1,300 of these sites are actual Superfund sites with cleanup programs in process. These 1,300 properties are on the National Priority List (NPL), and have been selected from the larger group of sites based on a scoring system that evaluates many factors, including relative toxicity of substances on site, location, size of the population at risk, potential for groundwater contamination, and potential threat to air quality. The larger database from which NPL sites is drawn is called the Comprehensive Environmental Response, Compensation and Liability Information System (CERCLIS). Qualifying sites can be brought to the attention of the EPA in many ways, including as a result of actual government monitoring of reported releases of hazardous substances at the site, citizen complaints, or government investigations.[13]

Inclusion of a property in either the CERCLIS or NPL lists can often have significant consequences for the value of the property and even the value of adjacent properties.[14] The principal reason is that the EPA can undertake a remedial cleanup plan and hold current or past owners or operators of NPL sites liable for reimbursement of those cleanup costs.[15] A current or past owner or operator can be liable whether or not it had any involvement in the handling, disposal, or treatment of the hazardous substance on the site.[16] And because cleanup responsibility is "joint and several," each current or former owner or operator can be held liable for the entire costs of cleanup. That means the owner or operator with the deepest pockets is often the one pursued hardest, even when that entity made no contribution to the problem.

Those factors by themselves might be enough to create significant market stigma for many Superfund sites. But there is another reason also. Lenders are extremely reluctant to make a loan on a site that is or potentially could be part of the Superfund program because as the law is currently being applied by the courts, in some circumstances a lender can be declared to be an owner or operator—and therefore a party potentially responsible for cleanup—even in the absence of a foreclosure action.[17]

One way a buyer or prospective operator of a site included in the CERCLA program can avoid liability for cleanup costs is to meet the legal definition of an "innocent landowner."[18] That exception is available when an owner did not know at the time of purchase, or had no reason to know,

---

12. 42 U.S.C., sec. 9601 et seq.

13. 42 U.S.C., sec 9603(a) and (c), 9604(b), 9659(a).

14. According to EPA administrator Carol M. Browner, "The mere fact that these sites have remained in CERCLIS has caused potential developers to shy away from them and many lending and real estate investment communities have denied loans for businesses in or near CERCLIS sites as a matter of policy." Statement of Carol M. Browner, Administrator, U.S. Environmental Protection Agency before the Commerce, Trade, and Hazardous Materials Subcommittee, Committee on Commerce, U.S. House of Representatives, March 16, 1995.

15. EPA's policy is not to seek cleanup costs from residential property owners unless those owners caused the contamination. See Policy Towards Owners of Residential Property at Superfund Sites, OSWER Directive No. 9834.6, July 3, 1991.

16. Most courts have found an exception for state government. See, for example, *United States* v. *Dart Indus., Inc.*, 847 F.2d 144 (4th Cir. 1988).

17. When CERCLA was first adopted, lenders thought they were exempted from the strict liability rule for cleanup. However, a series of court cases, culminating in *United States* v. *Fleet Factors Corp.*, 724 F.Supp. 955 (S.D. Ga. 1988), 901 F.2d 1550 *reh'g denied, en banc,* 911 F.2d 742 (11th Cir. 1990), held that in some limited circumstances, a mortgage lender could be held to be an "operator" and therefore potentially liable for cleanup costs. In the wake of the Fleet Factors decision, the U.S. EPA, at the urging of the lending community, adopted a regulation that specifically exempted lenders from strict liability for cleanup. However, that regulation was eventually struck down by the courts on the basis that it exceeded the agency's rulemaking authority.

18. 42 U.S.C., sec. 9607(b)(3).

Chapter 4: *Stigma, Environmental Risk and Property Value*

that hazardous substances were on the property. The proof is evidence that before the purchase the buyer made all reasonable inquiries consistent with good commercial or customary practice, thus, the impetus for Phase I and Phase II environmental assessments.

At least 35 states[19] have adopted their own programs modeled on the federal Superfund concept. Some states may have their own equivalent of the CERCLIS list, the scoring system, and the NPL list of properties with the highest priority for cleanup.[20] Also, many of these properties may not otherwise qualify for the federal Superfund program. State listing too may create responsibilities for cleanup, with the same kind of joint and several "no fault" liability.[21]

All of this means, however, that an appraiser should carefully evaluate the potential for a property to be part of the Superfund program. Information about existing properties on the CERCLIS or NPL lists can be obtained from regional offices of the EPA. It may even provide maps. State environmental protection agencies can also provide information on either federal or state equivalent listings.

But the regulatory environment is changing quickly. Early in 1995, the EPA removed about 25,000 sites from CERCLIS. These were generally sites that had been investigated by the EPA and found no longer to be of federal interest either because they were found to contain no or little contamination or were being cleaned up under state programs. The intention was to remove some of the stigma that accompanies inclusion in CERCLIS, and encourage more sale and redevelopment of brownfields, which are typically in the Northeast and Midwest. And Congress has before it a number of legislative initiatives that would clarify and limit the responsibility of lenders for cleanup, help identify portions of contaminated sites that do not require cleanup, and match the appropriate remediation technique to "reasonably expected future land uses at sites."[22] All of these pending changes may, in the future, reduce the amount of stigma associated with Superfund site listing.

Question 5: Is There an Approved or Completed Remediation Plan?

There are many different types of control and cleanup techniques and methods. In fact, there are many different definitions of the word "remediation." It can have a technical, legal term that can carefully differentiate some types of control or cleanup activities from others, for example, by differentiating a "remedial action" from a "removal action."[23]

Under Superfund and its state-level surrogates, a federal or state environmental protection agency typically undertakes a remedial investigation and feasibility study to determine type of contamination, extent, possible cleanup technologies and options, and likely costs. The same kind of investigation is undertaken in some other types of environmental programs, for example, under state programs requiring removal of underground storage tanks.[24] A common element in these types of programs is that a federal, state or local agency with environmental responsibility eventually approves a plan for action to lessen the risk of a release of a contaminant or assure cleanup to an appropriate standard.

The approval of such a plan, therefore, can eliminate some of the environmental risk associated with owning a contaminated, site. The basis of the action plan is a site investigation. The testing and monitoring pro-

---

19. The following states either do not have their own Superfund legislation, or have more limited legislation: Alabama; Connecticut (state only has authority to act under CERCLA and has no independent state provision); Washington, D.C.; Georgia; Nebraska; Nevada (very limited CERCLA-like provisions); Ohio (state has no independent liability provisions); Rhode Island (no clear liability standards of its own); South Dakota; West Virginia (no liability provision of its own); Wisconsin (limited CERCLA-like provisions); and Wyoming.

20. See, for example, Wisconsin Stat. Ann., sec, 144.442(4), and Utah Code Ann., sec. 19-6-311.

21. See, for example, New Jersey Stat. Ann., sec. 58.10-23.11g(c); Or. Rev. Stat., sec. 466.567 and 466.640; and Pennsylvania Stat. Ann. sec. 60320.702.

22. See, generally, the testimony of Carol Browner, supra.

23. "Remedial action" has been defined, in part, as follows: "Those actions consistent with permanent remedy taken instead of, or in addition to, removal action in the event of a release or threatened release of a hazardous substance into the environment, to prevent or minimize the release of hazardous substances so that they do not migrate to cause substantial danger to present or future public health or welfare or the environment."

"Removal action" has been defined as follows: "Short-term immediate actions taken to address releases of hazardous substances that require expedited response." See Thomas F.P. Sullivan, ed., *Environmental Regulatory Glossary*, 6th ed. (Rockville, Maryland: Government Institutes, Inc., 1093): 469–471.

24. See, for example, Florida Stat. Ann. Ch. 376-3071(5).

vides data about the nature and extent of the problem that allows selection of the appropriate technology for cleanup and a quantification of the cost. But most importantly, approval of the plan by a government agency often defines the legal cleanup responsibility of parties involved with the property and the cleanup attainment standard that must be met. All of that narrows risk.

As part of this inquiry the appraiser should ask the following questions:

- Is there an approved remediation plan?
- Who has approved it and how?
- How certain is the remediation approval?
- Is there any risk of additional remediation being ordered after completion?
- What is the approved remediation technique?
- How long will the remediation process take?
- What will be the level of cleanup after remediation?
- Does the remediation require ongoing monitoring? If so, for how long, and who pays for monitoring costs?
- What will the remediation cost?
- Who will pay the cost of remediation?
- Is there a federal or state program to reimburse for remediation costs?

Question 6: How Does the Contamination Affect Current Use?

Some uses may be more affected by contamination or environmental risk than others. For example, a use that sits above a contaminated aquifer and needs unpolluted groundwater for on-site drinking water may be more affected than a use on the same site that does not need to use the groundwater.

So the appraiser has to undertake a highest and best use analysis, taking into account the presence of the environmental risk. A careful analysis should be undertaken to determine if the current use has, in any way, been affected by the risk. If it has not been affected, and the current use is the highest and best use and is likely to continue indefinitely, then many times there may be little or no stigma from the contamination or risk.

Sometimes, for example, in litigation, the appraiser may be asked to consider the highest and best use of the property both before and after considering the environmental risk. In some situations, the current use may not be the highest and best use of the property when the value of the property is considered free and clear of the contamination. However, an analysis of the past operations of the current use may indicate that it can continue indefinitely even with the contamination in place. If so, there may be some continuing use of the property after considering the contamination, and that use may indeed be the highest and best use.

Question 7: How Does the Contamination Affect Surrounding Uses?

This inquiry may be important in two contexts. First, the appraiser may be valuing property adjacent to a source of potential contamination or risk, for example, property next to a landfill or adjacent to overhead transmission lines or a service station with a leaking underground storage tank. Second, the appraiser may be valuing the property that is itself the source of potential contamination or risk, but trying to determine the implications of actual or possible off-site migration or transmission on the value of the source property.

In either context, perceptions in the marketplace may be as important as the reality of whether the contamination or substance is actually physically affecting surrounding property. But the appraiser must take care to determine real market impacts on adjacent property from mere allegations of market impact. The appraiser's job is to investigate the market for evidence that indicates an impact on value, and if so, how far the off-site impact extends.

The starting point for the inquiry is usually the factual basis of any off-site migration or physical effects. What do the technical assessments and off-site testing show about the actual location and intensity of off-site impacts? Does the extent of the off-site migration vary, depending on such factors as soil conditions, slopes, wind patterns, etc.? How have local governments with land use and zoning authority responded? Have they imposed, or are they likely to impose in the future, development moratoria, limitations on use, special hearing requirements, or other land use regulations around the source of the risk?

Many types of uses, such as sanitary landfills, power plants, transmission lines, airports, expressways, and hazardous waste sites have been studied in a variety of settings to determine their off-site impacts, if any.[25] The appraiser may be able to use these other case studies as evidence of the actual or potential impact of similar uses in other settings. Care must be taken, however, to make adjustments as appropriate when considering case studies from other locations or based on past events or different contamination or risk situations.

Actual or potential impact on surrounding uses may affect the value of the source property. The risk of owning the property that is the source of the contamination may be increased if there is the possibility of impact on surrounding properties as well.

Question 8: Are There Government Programs to Offset Risks?

Many states have been assisting the private sector in cleaning up contaminated properties. Other states have been trying to limit the exposure of property owners to damage claims as a way of encouraging the redevelopment of older industrial areas. These programs, when effective, can go a long way to offsetting the risk associated with owning some types of properties affected by environmental risk.

For some types of environmental cleanup, there is special state funding available to reimburse cleanup expenditures. This is most frequently available for the removal of leaking underground storage tanks and the remediation of soil or groundwater contamination problems that may have resulted. Often "Petrofund" programs, they are typically paid for by a special tax on gasoline sales,[26] and may go far to offsetting the impact of environmental risk on the value of the properties that qualify for the program.[27]

In some states, regulatory agencies will issue various "letters" to relieve property owners of their anxiety regarding environmental risk on their properties. Among the types of letters are the "no action" letters, which are intended to assure future buyers that once a plan for cleanup has been approved, no further cleanup actions will be required. "No association" or

25. For a good summary of many of these studies and articles, see *Environmental Risk and the Real Estate Appraisal Process*, Addenda N and O.

26. See generally, Nebraska Rev. Stat., sec. 81-15 and Wisconsin Stat. Ann., sec. 101.43.

27. In some states, there may be limits on the amount of money that can be allocated to any one particular site. For example, in Arkansas the fund will reimburse an owner, after he has expended $25,000, up to the maximum amount of $1.0 million per occurrence. Arkansas Code Ann., sec. 8-7-907(a). In other states, such as Illinois, while there may be a "Petrofund" program on the books, funding is so limited that the program is ineffective, and property owners in effect pay their own cleanup costs.

"good neighbor" letters state that if an owner did not cause the original contamination and has voluntarily undertaken approved testing and cleanup on the property, there is no liability for further cleanup.[28]

The EPA has a number of programs in the works to "help remove the barriers to property transfer and revitalization"[29] of contaminated sites in the CERCLIS and NPL programs. These are the so-called brownfield initiatives, designed to encourage the reuse of older contaminated, manufacturing sites in major urban areas. As a result of one of the initiatives, the EPA has promised to develop "guidance" to "reassure lenders and prospective purchasers of the safety of their investments, and to thereby encourage the cleanup and redevelopment of contaminated properties."[30] As these brownfield initiatives develop, the perceptions of risk associated with actual or potential Superfund listing may be significantly reduced for some properties.

Question 9: Are There Guarantee or Insurance Programs for Buyers?

With some types of environmental risks, it has become quite common for property owners to provide an indemnity to purchasers and even neighbors against liability for future cleanup costs and other potential impacts of the contamination. This has become quite common, for example, when major oil companies sell service station/convenience store sites. It also has become common practice among major landfill operators to provide property value guarantee programs as part of the process of seeking government approval for expansion or construction of landfills.[31]

Such a guarantee program can offset some or all of the stigma risk associated with owning a previously contaminated property, or owning a property adjacent to a source of environmental risk. There are some critical questions that the appraiser should ask about the guarantee or indemnity, including the following:

- What does the guarantee cover? Are all cleanup costs, including testing, monitoring and consultants fees covered? Are only future cleanup costs covered, or are other types of impacts such as potential stigma impact on value also covered?
- How long does the guarantee run?
- Does it extend to third parties, such as future owners and tenants?
- What is the credit rating of the company providing the guarantee? Is it a large national concern with significant assets?
- Is the guarantee structured to survive merger, sale, or acquisition of the company?
- What is the track record of the guarantor? Do they stand behind their promises? Do they cooperate when claims are made for indemnification on environmental risk guarantees?

Availability of environmental insurance should also be explored by the appraiser. True "environmental impairment liability" policies are available to provide site-specific coverage for some types of land uses that may create environmental risks, for example, landfills, hazardous waste storage and treatment facilities, and manufacturing sites where potential pollutants are used in or produced as a by-product of the manufacturing process.[32] These policies generally provide third-party, bodily injury and property damage coverage for loss, along with cleanup costs and legal expenses

---

28. For a discussion of one of the recent programs, in Minnesota, see "Minnesota's Superfund Shield," Planning (June 1995): 22–23.

29. See the testimony of Carol M. Browner, supra.

30. Ibid. Administrator Browner's testimony indicated that some of the focus will be on "soil screening guidance" to help identify appropriate portions of contaminated properties that do not need remediation, as well as on modifying remediation standards to fit the most likely land use that a property will be devoted to in the future.

31. See, for example, discussion of such programs in "Report of the Subcommittee on Land Use and Solid Waste," The Urban Lawyer, v.23, no. 4 (Fall 1991): 773–784.

32. See, generally, Evelyn Hall, "EIL Is Poised for Growth," Best's Review—Property & Casualty (April 1995): 40–43.

generated by pollution accidents.[33] Policy premiums can be expensive—$200,000 per year for simple third-person property damage and bodily injury coverage to $2.0 million or more for facilities that produce or store vast quantities of potential pollutants. As new insurers enter the marketplace, premium costs are expected to decrease substantially.[34] An appraiser's job is to observe the marketplace's response to the availability of such insurance programs. If the marketplace begins to consider it a standard operating expense item for certain types of property, then an appraiser may have to make an adjustment to operating expenses or to market value to reflect the costs. That may, in turn, affect the appropriate capitalization or discount rate on income-producing property.

Question 10: How Good Are the "Comparable" Sales?

As the appraisal profession becomes more comfortable with valuation of properties affected by environmental risk, it is developing a better database of sales transactions and market studies involving property affected by environmental risk. This sales information is typically collected by appraisers in one of four ways:

- From inquiries to appraisers who specialize in valuation of properties affected by environmental risk
- As a result of a notice in the Appraisal Institute's newsletter, *Appraiser News*,[35] requesting sales or other market data involving a particular risk
- From independent research into contaminated property sales, beginning with data about properties included in various federal or state lists of contaminated properties

Even the best sales information about properties affected by environmental risk obtained from a reliable source may not fit the standard definition of a comparable sale. The appraisal profession typically thinks of a comparable as property similar in many respects to the property being appraised. Often, the best the appraiser may be able to do when evaluating stigma impact of environmental risk is to find sales of other property affected by a different type of intensity of contaminant, in a different location, and for a different use. Is that a comparable? Probably not in the strict definition of the term. Nevertheless, it may be quite helpful in arriving at an opinion on the impact of stigma on value. It should properly be considered as a case study rather than a comparable sale.

When collecting sales information from other appraisers about stigma-affected properties, it is more important than ever to verify the accuracy of the information. Valuation of property affected by environmental risk is such a new area of appraisal practice that the thoroughness of data collection practices vary considerably from one appraiser to another.

As part of the evaluation of the comparable sale or case study, the appraiser may have to compare and contrast that sale with the property being appraised on many points that might affect the appraiser's conclusion regarding the amount of stigma, including the following factors:

- Type of environmental risk, contamination or event creating potential for stigma, including comparison on such points as toxicity, persistence, amount or physical extent of contamination (for example, on-site or off-site migration)

---

33. Ibid. Usually, coverage only applies to pollution that is accidental and sudden and which takes place onsite. For an additional premium, some insurers will include first-party, offsite cleanup or coverage for non-sudden and gradual pollution.

34. Ibid., 42–43.

35. The publication of *Appraiser News* was terminated after its December 1995 issue and its contents have been merged with *Valuation Insights & Perspectives*, a quarterly magazine, which debuted in February 1996.

- Regulatory framework affecting the risk or substance
- Physical characteristics of the site
- Amount and quality of the testing, assessment, and monitoring (meaning the extent and reasonable accuracy of the data)
- Type and level of cleanup
- Date of sale, especially considering the importance of the five cycles
- Location
- Media coverage
- Conditions of the sale, including availability of an indemnity or insurance program
- Use of the property
- Motivations of buyers and sellers
- Lenders' attitudes

Conclusion

It is not enough for an appraiser today simply to conclude that if a property is contaminated, there is no market for it. That may still be true for some types of properties, but the number of such totally stigmatized properties is relatively small. It is also not good enough for the appraiser to expect that he or she will always be able to assume away the presence of the contamination and appraise the property as if unaffected by environmental risk. While there may still be times when such an approach is absolutely the right thing to do, more and more users of appraisal services want answers to tough questions about the actual impact, if any, of specific types of environmental risk on property values, and will go to another vendor of appraisal services if their usual appraiser rejects the assignment.

But in valuing property affected by environmental risk, appraisers have to ever alert to the nuances of the marketplace. Our job, as always, is to look to the marketplace to see how it actually prices property and determines value. As the marketplace adjusts to risks and prices the real estate product to reflect changing perceptions, so too must old appraisal theory give way to new professional practice techniques that incorporate those changes in the marketplace.

That is especially true today in the rapidly changing practice area involving contaminated properties and other forms of real estate affected by environmental risk. The appraiser's job is to ask the right questions and then listen to the market as it reveals its reasons for acting the way it does. Only if the appraiser does that can he or she gain enough understanding of the market to apply that knowledge to other appraisal situations correctly.

Classifying the Level of Risk and Stigma Affecting Contaminated Property

by Richard J. Roddewig, MAI

Every year the appraisal profession and the real estate marketplace become more comfortable in evaluating the impact of environmental contamination on the market value of real property. As appraisers in this practice area have learned, the impact of contamination on the market value of property depends on a number of factors including, but not limited to:

- The type/intensity of contamination;
- The type of property (e.g., commercial, industrial, residential);
- The extent to which contamination interferes with current use or most probable future use during and after remediation;
- Site topographical conditions and characteristics;
- Geographic location;
- The status of the site investigation/environmental assessment and the extent of information about the location of the contamination on site;
- The source of the contamination (e.g., on-site, off-site, groundwater, air pollution);
- The applicable regulatory review process and the degree to which additional remediation is mandated by law or regulation;
- The stage of cleanup or remediation plan approval;
- Appropriate past, present, or future cleanup or monitoring methods and costs;
- The availability and strength of available environmental indemnities, if any;
- The availability and cost of environmental insurance policies and programs, either private or public;
- The availability of mortgage financing for properties undergoing similar types of investigation, remediation, and ongoing environmental monitoring; and

Richard J. Roddewig, MAI, is president of Clarion Associates, with offices in Chicago, Denver, and Philadelphia. He codeveloped the Appraisal Institute's seminar, "Environmental Risk and the Real Estate Appraisal Process," and has taught the seminar nationwide. He is a regular contributor to The Appraisal Journal *on environmental issues, and is an adjunct lecturer on real estate valuation in the Finance Department at DePaul University, Chicago.*

This article originally appeared in the January 1999 issue of The Appraisal Journal.

- Perceptions of the public and knowledgeable buyers in the property's marketplace.

When faced with a new contaminated property assignment, an appraiser should, of course, evaluate the new situation against the factors that determine the impact of contamination on market value. These factors have been addressed over the past decade in many articles in *The Appraisal Journal*[1] and in the *Environmental Risk and the Real Estate Appraisal Process* seminar of the Appraisal Institute. Many of these articles and the seminar materials recommend the use of case studies as one of the appropriate methods for determining the impact of contamination, especially the stigma impact of contamination, on market value.[2] Appraisers who regularly specialize in this practice area compile extensive case study information from their investigations when appraising a piece of contaminated or formerly contaminated (but now remediated) property.

What the various articles and seminar materials have not yet addressed in detail, however, is how to classify the case studies and the subject property in order to compare the contamination at the subject property with the indicated impact on value, if any, or the stigma impact identified in the case study research. Classification may also be especially helpful in some types of real estate decision making; for example, portfolio review or evaluation, or buy/sell decisions. Some major institutional investors and underwriters are beginning to develop their own standardized due diligence checklists and evaluation forms that allow them to analyze the environmental risks on properties or portfolios as part of a systematic underwriting process. Institutional investors may be heading toward a numerical scoring or rating system for environmental risks (more on this in a future edition of this environmental column) but a standardized system has not yet emerged.

In the meantime, appraisers can begin to develop their own internal evaluation systems and forms to assure analytical rigor and internal consistency from one assignment to the next in estimating the impact of contamination on market value. These evaluation systems can be used in two ways: first, as a way of pigeonholing each new case study or contamination comparable into a consistent analytical framework; second, as a way of then comparing the property being appraised to the outcomes of past assignments involving contaminated or potentially stigmatized property.

Use of Case Studies to Estimate Environmental Stigma

The appropriate method for appraising property affected by contamination varies from one valuation situation to another, depending upon the particular set of factors from the list above that apply. Using sales of contaminated properties as direct evidence of the value of property after considering contamination is often difficult. This is because of the small number of such transactions and the problems involved in making proper adjustments to reflect distinguishing factors.

When contaminated property sales are not available or not truly comparable, analyzing case studies of contaminated properties to discern implications for market value arising from contamination is appropriate. Case study analysis is specifically recognized as an appropriate valuation technique by the Appraisal Institute in *Environmental Risk and the Real Estate Appraisal Process,* the Appraisal Institute's official seminar on the valuation of contaminated property.

1. See, for example, Peter J. Patchin, "Valuation of Contaminated Properties," *The Appraisal Journal* (January 1988): 7–16; Peter J. Patchin, "Contaminated Properties—Stigma Revisited," *The Appraisal Journal* (April 1991): 167–172; Bill Mundy, "Stigma and Value," *The Appraisal Journal* (January 1992): 7–13; Mark Dotzour, "Groundwater Contamination and Residential Property Values," *The Appraisal Journal* (July 1997): 279–285; Richard J. Roddewig, "Stigma, Environmental Risk and Property Value: 10 Critical Inquiries," *The Appraisal Journal* (October 1996): 375–387; and Randall Bell, MAI, "The Impact of Detrimental Conditions on Property Values," *The Appraisal Journal* (October 1998): 380–391.

2. See Appraisal Institute, "Environmental Risk and the Real Estate Appraisal Process," Seminar (Chicago: Appraisal Institute, 1994), 126. Also see Randall Bell, MAI, "The Impact of Detrimental Conditions on Property Values," *The Appraisal Journal* (October 1998): 388.

Chapter 4: *Classifying Risk and Stigma*

Environmental stigma is "an adverse effect on the market's perception of the value of property containing an environmental risk even after cleanup costs have been expended or considered in estimating value." (Appraisal Institute, *Environmental Risk and the Real Estate Appraisal Process,* Chapter 6).

Indeed, in some situations, previously contaminated properties may suffer a diminution in value as a result of past contamination even after cleanup. This may also be true of some clean properties located in proximity to known contaminated property.

Stigma is not uniform, however, and is not always present. Factors such as type of contamination and type of property affect the possible presence and effect of stigma, if any. Buyer concerns about environmental stigma typically arise due to risks they may fear will result from the presence of contamination, including the risks of:

- Additional site investigation costs;
- Additional remediation costs;
- Additional environmental monitoring costs;
- Additional legal or administrative costs associated with ownership of the property;
- Potential adverse changes in regulations concerning required levels of investigation, remediation, and monitoring;
- Higher vacancies or lower rents due to tenant concerns or interference with occupancies and use by tenants;
- Potential inability to obtain mortgage financing;
- Third-party claims against future property owners due to health or property value risks related to past occupancy or use; and
- Potential delays in ability to resell the property or potential inability to resell the property in the future.

Appraisers who have conducted a number of assignments involving contamination and potential stigma may begin to discern a pattern or patterns emerging from the case study research. What may at first appear to be a somewhat random collection of case studies showing no stigma in some fact situations and significant stigma in others, can, upon further analysis, be systematized. While every appraiser can come up with his or her own approach to classifying case studies, each of these contamination/stigma case studies can be placed into at least three basic categories: "high risk/high stigma" situations, "low risk/low stigma" situations, and "changing risk/changing stigma" situations.

Typical Characteristics of High Risk/High Stigma Situations

Each of these types of risk/stigma relationships has a typical set of characteristics. The typical characteristics of high risk/high stigma situations are:

- Little or no site investigation has been completed as of the date of sale or offering.
- Site investigation that has been done indicates property-wide presence of contamination in relatively high concentrations.
- Remediation costs are unknown, unquantifiable, or hard to determine.
- The type of remediation plan and program likely to be required by regulators is uncertain.

- There are no federal, state or local programs to pay for some or all of the potential investigation, remediation, and monitoring costs.
- The length of the likely remediation program and monitoring is undetermined or uncertain.
- Prior owners or parties responsible for the contamination do not recognize a cleanup responsibility and have not indicated willingness to pay for remediation costs or potential stigma impacts, or to provide indemnities to future owners to offset potential risks.
- The property fails to qualify for private sector or public sector environmental risk insurance programs.
- The contamination situation at the particular property has received considerable adverse media attention emphasizing the severity of the problem or risks.
- Uncontaminated or remediated portions of the whole property cannot be subdivided and sold separately.
- Lenders indicate considerable unwillingness to make loans on this property or type of property.

Typical Characteristics of Low Risk/Low Stigma Situations

Some of the typical characteristics of low risk/low stigma situations are as follows:

- Thorough site investigation has been completed.
- Remediation costs are known with considerable certainty.
- A remediation plan has been prepared, submitted for regulatory review, and approved by appropriate regulators.
- The approved remediation plan has been implemented.
- Regulators have issued "no further action" or "closure" letters indicating prospective future purchasers/owners will not be subject to any additional cleanup costs as long as specific requirements for future use of the property are followed.
- Prior owners or parties responsible for the contamination have recognized their cleanup responsibilities, paid for their appropriate share of remediation costs, and provided indemnities to current or future owners to offset potential remaining risks.
- The property qualifies for private sector or public sector environmental risk insurance programs.[3]
- Media attention has focused on the diminished contamination and risks associated with the property.
- Uncontaminated portions of the property can be subdivided and separately sold.
- Lenders indicate ready willingness to make loans on this property or type of property.

In many situations, as site investigation, regulatory review, remediation, and environmental monitoring continues, an initially high risk/high stigma property may later become a low risk/low stigma property. Of course, lots of gradients exist between high risk/low stigma and low risk/low stigma properties.

3. For a discussion of utilization of environmental insurance cost estimates in the appraisal process, see Richard J. Roddewig, MAI, "Using the Cost of Environmental Insurance to Measure Contaminated Property Stigma," *The Appraisal Journal* (July 1997): 304–308.

Chapter 4: *Classifying Risk and Stigma*

Fact Situations Showing High Risk/High Stigma Changing to Low Risk/ Low Stigma

Sometimes, case studies reveal that risks and stigma have changed with the passage of time. As environmental investigation, regulatory review, remediation, and environmental monitoring continues, properties that once had significant stigma may evolve into ones with little or no stigma. Finding and evaluating such case studies may be important in some valuation situations, especially in many litigation assignments. For example, an appraiser might be asked to provide an opinion concerning damages over time or the likelihood that risks and stigma may change if particular changes in the underlying facts are assumed.

A Form for Classifying the Case Studies and the Property Appraised

Based on the review of the respective contamination and environmental remediation/monitoring situations, using Table 1 an appraiser can "score" each case study and the property being appraised on the set of factors that distinguish a property as low risk/low stigma or high risk/high stigma. By tallying the number of "yes" and "no" answers, the appraiser can categorize the case study and the subject property properly within the risk/stigma universe.

As a check on the comparison of the appraised property with the case study, the appraiser might also want to undertake a risk evaluation of the subject property. In Table 2, most of the various risks associated with owning a contaminated or remediated property have been included. Those types of risks are the essential elements of stigma.

Using the Scorecards

Once the scorecards have been completed, an appraiser can use them as a point of comparison. The appraiser can compare the number of "yes" and "no" answers for a case study on the risk/stigma scorecard with the "yes" and "no" answers for the property being appraised. If analysis of the case study or case studies with the pattern of "yes" and "no" answers closest to the appraised property indicated a stigma impact of 5.0 to 10.0%, then there would be support for (all other things being equal) a deduction of 5.0 to 10.0% against the market value of the appraised property to account for stigma impact.[4] The second scorecard indicating the low/medium/high risks for the appraised property serves as a check on the results of the first analytical approach.

Conclusion

This system is only one possible approach to systematizing the analysis of stigma impacts on contaminated or remediated properties. There are many others. Appraisers with considerable experience with contaminated properties may want to assign points or otherwise weight the various answers in the scorecards based on what their expertise and the marketplace tell them about the relative significance of each factor in contributing to stigma. But even the simplest of scorecards such as those shown here can help provide consistency in appraisers' efforts to understand stigma and how it may vary from one contaminated property situation to another.

4. Of course, the appraiser also has to be aware that the comparison tables do not account for all of the potential differences between a case study and the appraised property.

Valuing Contaminated Properties

TABLE 1   Analysis of Risks Associated with Contaminated Real Property

Characteristic of Low Risk/Low Stigma Property	Property Address		Comments
Thorough site investigation completed	Yes	No	
Remediation costs are known with considerable certainty	Yes	No	
Remediation plan prepared, submitted for review, and approved	Yes	No	
Regulators have issued no further action or closure letter	Yes	No	
Prior owners or other parties take responsibility and provide indemnity	Yes	No	
Property qualifies for private/public environmental risk insurance	Yes	No	
Media attention has focused on diminished contamination/risks	Yes	No	
Portions of the property little contaminated and can be subdivided & sold	Yes	No	
Lenders indicate ready willingness to make loans	Yes	No	
Total low risk/low stigma "yes" answers			
Total low risk/low stigma "no" answers			

Characteristic of High Risk/High Stigma Property	Property Address		Comments
Little or no site investigation completed	Yes	No	
Site investigation conducted indicates property-wide contamination	Yes	No	
Remediation costs are unknown, unquantifiable, or hard to determine	Yes	No	
Type of remediation plan required by regulators is uncertain	Yes	No	
No federal, state or local programs to pay for investigation/remediation	Yes	No	
Length of likely remediation/monitoring undetermined	Yes	No	
Prior owners/others do not accept responsibility and/or no indemnity	Yes	No	
Property does not qualify for private/public environmental risk insurance	Yes	No	
Considerable adverse media attention	Yes	No	
Uncontaminated portions of the property cannot be subdivided and sold	Yes	No	
Lenders indicate considerable unwillingness to make loans	Yes	No	
Total high risk/high stigma "yes" answers			
Total high risk/high stigma "no" answers			

TABLE 2   Degree of Potential Risks Associated with Future Ownership

Risks	Low	Med	High	Comments
Additional site investigation costs				
Additional remediation costs				
Additional environmental monitoring costs				
Risk of additional legal/administrative costs				
Potential adverse change in regulations				
Higher vacancy or lower rents due to environmental issues				
Inability to obtain mortgage financing				
Third-party claims				
Delays in ability to resell the property or inability to resell				
Totals				

"The Dose Makes the Poison:" Environmental Phobia or Regulatory Stigma?

by Wayne C. Lusvardi

New federal and state laws require appraisers to meet more rigorous evidentiary standards for expert testimony when dealing with the use of scientific evidence related to environmental hazards identified with real estate. In addition, emerging literature in the field of environmental risk assessment and epidemiology (cause and effect studies) is now calling into serious question the likely harmful effects resulting from minute exposures to purportedly harmful environmental substances associated with real estate.

This article offers what is believed to be a needed antidote to the often unquestioned literature that has developed in the last decade in the field of real estate appraisal regarding the imputed effects of environmental hazards on real estate values. It applies the scientific tests required under the 1993 U.S. Supreme Court decision in *Daubert v. Merrell Dow Pharmaceuticals*[1] (i.e., the *Daubert* rule) to some of the most notorious environmental hazards affecting real estate such as radon, lead, asbestos, electromagnetic fields, and hazardous waste sites (Superfund). The degree to which property damages and so-called stigma result from a rational reaction to actual or potential health hazards associated with the aforementioned environmental conditions, or from an irrational fear of insignificant risks, is deduced from a review of the scientific literature.

Background

Richard W. Hoyt and Robert J. Aalberts have discussed how the *Daubert* case has changed the reliance that expert witnesses can make on scientific information used in the courts of 27 states and the federal government.[2] Hoyt and Aalberts relate how the *Daubert* rule is causing a "Copernican revolution" in real estate appraisal-related cases involving damages from natural or environmental causes, construction defect liability, investment fraud, damages in eminent domain partial acquisitions, and other potentially harmful conditions impacting property values. Even where the market reaction to purported environmental conditions can be reliably esti-

Wayne C. Lusvardi *is senior real estate representative with The Metropolitan Water District of Southern California. Mr. Lusvardi holds a BA degree in demography from Aurora University and a certificate in real estate appraisal from the University of California, Los Angeles, School of Business, Engineering, and Management. The views expressed in this article do not reflect those of any employer or associate appraiser. Contact: WLusvardi@MWD.Dst.CA.US; Fax (213) 217-7650.*

This article originally appeared in the April 2000 issue of The Appraisal Journal.

1. *Daubert v. Merrell Dow Pharmaceuticals, Inc.*, 509 U.S. 579, 113 S. Ct. 2786, 125 L. Ed. 2d 469 (1993) incorporated into Federal Rules of Evidence 702.

2. Richard W. Hoyt, and Robert J. Aalberts, "New Requirements for the Appraisal Expert Witness," *The Appraisal Journal* (October 1997): 342–349.

Valuing Contaminated Properties

mated, the courts are refusing such evidence if there is no underlying likelihood of health risk or rational fear thereof.[3] Reaffirming and extending the *Daubert* decision, the *U.S. Supreme Court in Kumho Tire Company, Ltd., et. al.* v. *Carmichael et al.* has ruled that the scientific standard applies not only to expert testimony based on "scientific knowledge," but also to testimony based on technical, specialized, experience-based, or skill-based knowledge of nonscientists and nonengineers, such as real estate appraisers. The point of this case law is to cut down on lawsuits becoming legal lotteries where causation and harm are irrelevant to judgment and real damages. This new body of case law reflects the ancient Latin legal dictum *de minimus non curat lex* (the law does not concern itself with trivial or inconsequential matters).

The *Daubert/Kumho* cases shift the role of the judge in a courtroom proceeding from passively allowing the testimony of expert witnesses to actively serving as a "gatekeeper" for what is admissible evidence according to four nonexhaustive factors: testability and falsification, peer review, error rates, and scientific acceptance. Under *Daubert* v. *Merrell Dow Pharmaceutical, Inc.,* incorporated into *Federal Rules of Evidence 702,* a trial judge must determine whether the proposed testimony is both reliable and relevant.[4] When an issue requires testimony based on scientific knowledge, the testimony is judged reliable if it is grounded in the methods and procedures of science. It is judged relevant if the "reasoning or methodology properly can be applied to the facts in issue." Moreover, it must be demonstrated that the "act complained of probably, or more likely than not, caused the subsequent disability (i.e., damage)."[5] The major change mandated in the law as it applies to the valuation of real estate is the shift to proper research design and empirical testing from reliance on subjective judgment, anecdotal testimony, the clinical appraisal method, and the reputation of an appraiser.

Paralleling these legal trends is the rise of seller and broker disclosure laws in real estate. But to properly value real estate, appraisers must be able to identify not just the presence or absence of environmental risks but their magnitude. To do this requires college-level scientific knowledge and environmental risk assessment.

Literature Review

To understand the relationship between environmental regulations and the true health risks of imputed environmental hazards, I present a brief scientific review of some of the most notorious environmental risks associated with real estate. Rather than attempt an impractical comprehensive review of the literature, seven recent books have been selected that summarize the relevant environmental science and regulatory policies. It is believed these books avoid selection bias because they do not rely on the analysis of environmentalists, industrial scientists, or regulatory scientists.[6]

Radon[7]

Radon is a form of natural gas created by the nuclear decay of uranium in rocks and soil. The gas is present in the earth virtually everywhere in the United States, but is potentially harmful only when concentrated in "hot spots." Radon is unavoidable and is part of the air we breathe. It is the radioactivity from radon that evokes fear. Actually radon itself is harm-

3. *San Diego Gas & Electric Co.* v. *Superior Court of the State of California for the County of Orange.* Respondent, Martin Covalt and Joyce J. Covalt, parties of interest, August 22, 1996, Ct. Appeal 4/3 No. G216256. A reasonable fear is one that is predicated on knowledge, corroborated by reliable medical and scientific opinion, that it is "more likely than not" that the feared consequence of exposure to environmental hazards will develop in the future.

4. Kurtis B. Reeg and Cawood K. Bebout, "What's It All About, *Daubert?*," *Journal of the Missouri Bar* (November-December 1997): 1–13.

5. Steven J. Milloy, "Expert's Testimony Excluded Under Daubert As Irrelevant, Unreliable, Ninth Circuit Says," *Westlake Solutions.* http://junkscience.com/news/daubert/html, 1997): 1.

6. Aaron Wildavsky, *But, Is It True? A Citizen's Guide to Environmental Health and Safety Issues* (Cambridge, Massachusetts: Harvard University Press, 1995); Roger Bate, editor, *What Risk?* (Oxford, England: Butterworth-Heimemann, 1997); Cassandra Chromes Moore, *Haunted Housing: How Toxic Scare Stories Are Spooking the Public Out of House and Home* (Washington, D.C.: Cato Institute, 1997; M. Alice Ottoboni, *The Dose Makes The Poison: A Plain Language Guide to Toxicology,* 2nd ed. (New York, New York: Van Nostrand Reinhold, 1997); Kenneth R. Foster, David E. Bernstein, and Peter W. Huber, *Phantom Risk: Scientific Risk and the Law* (Cambridge, Massachusetts: Massachusetts Institute of Technology Press, 1993; Ronald E. Gots, *Toxic Risks: Science, Regulation and Perception* (Ann Arbor, Michigan: Lewis Publishers, 1993; H. W. Lewis, *Technologic Risk* (New York, New York: W. W. Norton, 1990).

7. Except where otherwise noted the following discussion draws from: "Radon: The Spectral Evidence" in Moore, 9–78.

Chapter 4: *The Dose Makes the Poison*

less, but the chain of radioactive particles released from radon poses the potential risk. Uranium miners who breathe huge amounts of radon suffer extraordinarily high rates of lung cancer. But the poison is in the amount of the dosage. Working in confined areas, such as mines, magnifies a miner's exposure to radon which can then overwhelm the human body's multilayered defense system.

Using studies of uranium miners, the Environmental Protection Agency (EPA) has concluded that radon causes 5,000 to 30,000 lung cancer deaths per year.[8] The underlying assumption of these studies is that if massive amounts of radon can kill, so can very small amounts. The use of these studies exaggerates the incidence of health problems in the general population due to radon gas because they improperly extrapolate the miner data to household data. Nonetheless, the U.S. Congress in 1994 enacted the *Radon Awareness and Disclosure Act.*

Studies that compare high-radon exposure with low-radon exposure households indicate that there is no greater prevalence of lung cancers in high-radon homes. These studies are glossed over by the National Research Council (NRC), Environmental Protection Agency (EPA), and the Board on the Effects of Ionizing Radiation (BEIR). The EPA, NRC, and BEIR claim that none of the control and comparison studies have large enough samples to statistically prove there is no radon health risk from exposure levels found in homes. But the scientific method cannot prove a negative (i.e., there is no harm). Moreover, the comparison and control studies have superior research designs to the linear nonthreshold studies on which the NRC, EPA, and BEIR rely. The largest known control and comparison study from Finland ($N = 2,500$) concluded, "Our results suggest no important public health impact for indoor radon exposure."[9] Major studies of radon exposure reported in the December 1994 issue of the National Cancer Institute's journal and the August 1994 issue of the *American Journal of Epidemiology* found no significant elevation of lung cancer in areas with high household radon. The Health Physics Society, a nonprofit and nonpoliticized organization for the protection of people and the environment from the effects of radiation, has stated that the risks from radon are "too small to be observed or nonexistent" with the "likely possibility of zero adverse health effects."[10]

The linear extrapolation model relied on by the EPA, BEIR, and NRC contrasts with the S-shaped, dose-response curves and threshold levels found by researchers in most cause and effect studies (see Figure 1). Leonard Cole has stated that "virtually every scientific report on the subject (recognizes) that the effects of radon levels commonly found indoors are specu-

8. Ibid., 27.

9. Michael Fumento, "Time To Overthrow The Radonistas." www.townhall.com/edpage/columnists/fumento/fume040198.html.

10. Health Physics Society, "Radiation Risk In Perspective." *Position Statement,* McLean, Virginia, Health Physics Society, 1996.

FIGURE 1 Relative Carcinogenic Risk of Substances Compared to Woburn, Massachusetts Well Water

Substance	Toxic Substance	Relative Risk	Risk Multiple
1 sleeping pill	Phenobarbitol	16	26,667 x
1 glass of beer	Ethyl alcohol	2.8	4,667 x
1 apple	Cafeic acid	0.10	166.7 x
1 peanut butter sandwich	Aflatoxic	0.03	50.00 x
2 slices white bread	Furfural	0.002	3.333 x
1 liter tap water (U.S. Avg.)	Chloroform	0.001	1.667 x
1 liter Woburn well water	Trichloroethylene (267 ppb)	0.0006	(base line)

Source: DeLong, see footnote 43.

Valuing Contaminated Properties

lative."[11] Despite this, home testing continues. It is estimated that it will cost between $10 billion-$20 billion to inspect every home in the U.S. for radon. The cost of mitigation will range between $50 billion to $1 trillion.

Instead of the government using its resources to identify the geological radon hot spots and then assisting the local governments of these areas with soil testing and the creation of new building and zoning codes, it has elected to mandate a costly nationwide disclosure and abatement program.

The general conclusion that can be drawn from Moore's review of the scientific literature on radon is that the EPA's regulatory policy is excessive with regard to radon's potential harm. It also broadly targets all households instead of focusing attention on those most likely to be affected by dangerously high radon levels. The type of soil under a building and the type of ventilation it has are all culprits that can raise a building's radon level. Radon accumulates where air stagnates or is confined. Ironically, newer environmental energy conservation standards that mandate sealed windows, open-ceiling modular office furniture, and modern ventilation systems that restrict the intake of fresh air can result in sick building syndrome. Such regulations promote the buildup of toxins like radon, airborne asbestos fibers, and synthetic chemicals from carpeting and other building supplies.[12] It seems we have forgotten the wisdom of past generations. When people lived with wood-burning stoves and heaters, it was well known that airtight rooms promoted illness. Radon buildup is an example of how an environmental program created to solve one problem (saving fuel) has created another and possibly more serious problem (poor indoor air quality).

Lead[13]

Lead, a natural occurring element, is a neurotoxin when taken into the body in high concentrations but is not currently considered to be a carcinogen.[14] In the past, lead was used as an additive in paint and gasoline, as solder for tin cans, and in plumbing pipes and pumps. It also entered the environment in industrial emissions. In 1970 concern for increasing levels of lead contamination resulted in the EPA's restricting the level of lead used in gasoline. The Clean Air Act further mandated the elimination of lead in all gasoline by 1995. Today the amount of lead emitted into the air from automobiles has been reduced by 97% since 1970. In addition, the U.S. Department of Housing and Urban Development (HUD) banned the use of lead in plumbing, soldering, and pumps by 1994. Today blood lead levels in children have dropped sixfold. Despite its continued regulation, lead is no longer a universal public health problem. The most enduring source of contamination is in lead-based house paint.

Lead exposure is measured in micrograms (mg) of a deciliter (dl) or 1 part per 100 million. Historical rates of lead exposure have plummeted from 60 per mg per dl of blood in 1970 to 10 mg per dl in 1990. The major source of scientific disagreement is whether 10 mg per dl of blood adversely affects children. No credible studies have shown harmful health effects from exposure to lead of 25ug per dl or lower. Nonetheless, the Center for Disease Control lowered the level of concern from 25 to 10 ug

11. Leonard Cole, *Element of Risk: The Politics of Radon* (Washington, D.C.: AAAS Press, 1993): 29.

12. Ottobani, 57–162.

13. Except where otherwise noted, the following discussion draws from Moore, 79–158; and Gots, 223–246.

14. Lewis, 134.

Chapter 4: *The Dose Makes the Poison*

per dl, with an estimated cost of additional regulation and litigation between $200 billion–$500 billion.

Pressed to show actual harm to children from lead exposure, Herbert Needleman, a professor of child psychiatry and pediatrics, wrote an article for the *New England Journal of Medicine* in 1979 purporting to prove that children with high lead blood levels had measurably lower IQ scores and poor school performance. At the prompting of the Office of Scientific Integrity at the National Institutes of Health, the University of Pittsburgh Hearing Board concluded in 1992 that Needleman's work reflected "deliberate misrepresentation of the procedures actually used in the conduct of the study as reported in 1979 and thereafter." Needleman's research ignored "confounding effects" from socioeconomic status, parental education, household violence, etc. In addition, scientific reviewers could not replicate Needleman's graphs from his raw data. Yet, journalists have, for the most part, continued to report only the most sensationalistic stories about lead poisoning. For example, in 1995 journalist Jane Brody of *The New York Times* wrote an infamous, unscientific article linking lead to male juvenile delinquency.

As Ronald E. Gots has stated:

> [T]he story of lead toxicity has in recent years taken on the qualities of a soap opera drama. It represents the struggle between classes: residents in the inner city versus wealthy landlords. Sociologists have claimed that poverty and educational disadvantage can be blamed solely upon lead poisoning. Politicians are running on lead platforms. New lead abatement industries have sprung up to sell over-priced remediation services that capitalize on the fears of middle- and upper-middle-class parents.[15]

Yet, the reduction of lead in our environment to naturally occurring "background levels" from dust and soil has not resulted in measurably improved health or higher school performance in disadvantaged children.

Despite the success of lead reduction programs, the effort to reduce lead in the environment has been counterproductive. It has diverted funds from more serious health threats to children. The culprit is reported to be the fallacy that the dose response to lead is linear and doses must be reduced to zero or an unrealistically low threshold. The EPA and other federal agencies do not recognize a curvilinear model whereby the risk from lead exposure has for all intents and purposes reached its limit of effectiveness. As Ronald E. Gots states:

> The data connecting such (high lead) levels to adverse health effects are essentially nonexistent and what data do exist, do not confirm these dire estimates. People are worried, and I fear that our regulatory machinery has, in this case, contributed to false perceptions and intensified unnecessarily those fears.[16]

Additionally, an unintended consequence of the effort to eliminate lead from the air has been the widespread contamination of drinking water, groundwater, and surface water by methyl tertiary butyl ether (MTBE), a fuel additive that leaks from underground storage tanks, fuel pipelines, and other sources.[17] MTBE is the engine "anti-knock" agent that replaced lead in gasoline. MTBE also serves as a reported "marker" in gasoline to trace leaks from underground storage tanks, a necessary "ingredient" for lawyers pursuing toxic tort lawsuits.

15. Gots, 223.
16. Ibid., 238.
17. Joe Pomento, "Clean Air-Clean Water: At What Cost?," *Aqueduct* (Metropolitan Water District of Southern California, November 1, 1998): 2, 14.

Asbestos[18]

Asbestos is a naturally occurring fibrous silicate mineral found in rocks. It exists in two forms that are important to toxicologists: amphiboles ("white asbestos" pointed at each end) and chrysotile ("blue" or "brown" asbestos with flexible structure). Asbestos is not a toxin or an allergen. It is simply an inert substance and an irritant. Natural exposure to asbestos occurs when rocks weather and the fibers disperse into the atmosphere. Asbestos has valuable properties such as noncombustibility and resistance to moisture, microorganisms, chemical attack, and decay. It can serve as an insulator from fire, heat, noise, electricity, and wear and tear. The flexibility of its fibers makes it adaptable to many uses. Historically, it has been incorporated into pottery, textiles, building materials, and automobile parts. It has also been used in appliances, for strength, insulation, and fire retardation. The superior fire retardant properties of asbestos are nearly irreplaceable. Countless lives have been saved from building fires because of its use. Prior to 1970, asbestos could be found in use nearly everywhere: in modern homes, commercial and public buildings, and factories.

Although asbestos has been used for centuries, it was not until 1924 that the medical literature reported the first clear cases of death due to pulmonary fibrosis from exposure to asbestos. The formation of plaque in the chest cavity can occur from decades of asbestos exposure. Asbestos can cause death by cutting off oxygen to the body, blocking blood flow in the lungs thus causing cardiac arrest, or playing a part in the development of lung cancer. The incidence of asbestosis disease increases with the length and extent of exposure, as well as the type of fiber. Chrysotile ("white") asbestos fibers are short and thin and penetrate less deeply into the lung than Amphibole ("blue/brown") asbestos fibers which are long and needle-shaped. The main occupations at risk from asbestos exposure are miners; textile workers; construction workers; automobile assemblers; and more recently, asbestos removal technicians. Asbestos workers who smoke have a ninetyfold greater risk of developing lung cancer compared to workers who have neither been exposed to asbestos nor smoked. While the most severe health problems associated with asbestos have been occupational rather than real estate related, asbestos is no longer used in theater curtains, home or school insulation, or linoleum floor tiles.

The impact of asbestos on real estate mainly affects commercial and public buildings. Schools built or renovated before 1973 were required to use asbestos for fire insulation. The EPA implemented a complete ban on asbestos in 1978. In that same year, the National Cancer Institute (NCI) projected that in the next three decades over 2 million cancer deaths (17% of all cancer deaths) would be due to asbestos. This estimate did not go unchallenged, however. The then-editor of *Science* magazine reported that the research paper from which such estimates were made was widely condemned by scientists. Epidemiologists estimate that environmental carcinogens from all sources maximally cause only 1% of all cancers, casting serious doubt on the 17% figure given for asbestos alone. Despite this, the government implemented the Asbestos School Hazard Detection and Control Act in 1980. It led to a nationwide asbestos removal program in all schools. The commercial real estate sector soon had to follow suit with its own asbestos removal programs. Despite these massive programs, Aaron Wildavsky sums up the health data on asbestos exposure by stating that

18. Except where otherwise noted, the following discussion is drawn from Wildavsky, 185–200.

Chapter 4: *The Dose Makes the Poison*

"the danger of contracting asbestosis at the low level exposures normally found in schools is nil."[19] Hammond and Selikoff are reported to have found that only 1 of 73 deaths in a sample of 2,066 asbestos insulation workers was possibly related to asbestos exposure. The other 72 deaths were related to a combination of smoking and asbestos exposure.[20] In general, lung cancer is not as common as believed in non-smoking asbestos workers. Summarizing studies in the United States, France, and Great Britain, researchers have reported that "fiber concentrations in buildings are comparable to levels in outdoor air, a point surely relevant to assessing the health risk of asbestos in buildings."[21] Asbestos exposure in school buildings is reported at less than one thousandth of the limit that the Occupational Safety and Health Administration (OSHA) places on workplace exposures.[22]

Common sense and scientific consensus dictates the obvious: The health risk from intact asbestos insulation and floor tiles in schools or commercial buildings is minute except when disturbed. *The Report of the Royal Commission on Matters of Health and Safety Arising from the Use of Asbestos in Ontario* (1984) stated that "asbestos in building air will almost never pose a health hazard to building occupants."[23] As Wildavsky states:

> In our opinion there is no hazard in classrooms with asbestos fibers unless there is a lot of flaking. The reason there appears to be any hazard at all is that analysts have adopted lose-dose linearity, that is, the idea that damage is proportional to the dose and that even the tiniest dose must be rated above zero and assumed to have some effect.[24]

Physicist H. W. Lewis has aptly stated, "The reason many schools and businesses are removing old asbestos is fear of later litigation, not fear of asbestos."[25]

Electromagnetic Fields[26]

Once mankind learned how to use, generate, and transmit electricity, exposure to electromagnetic fields began to increase. Yet, there was never a time when a "zero dose" condition existed. The human body produces its own electrical currents, some of which create electromagnetic fields millions of times greater than those created by power lines. Then there is the natural magnetic field of the earth to consider. It is hundreds of times greater than that produced by electrical power plants. No one fears these naturally occurring energy fields. It is the manmade electromagnetic fields that create concern even though electricity typically is transmitted through encased copper or fiber optic wires. Electromagnetic fields (EMFs) occur only when electric current is flowing. EMFs refer to fields of electromagnetic energy extending into the air space surrounding electric power lines and appliances, television and radio stations, or wireless telephone and data transmission systems. EMFs transmitted through the air from radio and TV broadcasting or wireless telephone systems are generally believed to be harmless due to their extremely low power and frequency. The greatest source of concern is high-voltage power lines and power substations located near schools or residences with children. It is feared that the electromagnetic fields they generate may cause cancer, particularly in children. A consideration of the facts brings this assumption into question. The maximum energy field within the right of way of an electric transmission line

19. Ibid., 193.
20. Moore (1997): 168.
21. Wildavsky, 198.
22. Lewis, 166.
23. Wildavsky, 197.
24. Ibid., 199.
25. Lewis, 167.
26. Except where otherwise noted, the following discussion is drawn from Moore, 209–252.

Valuing Contaminated Properties

is 100 mG (100 milligauss or 0.1 gauss). This is 50 times less than the level naturally found in the human body. Measurements taken just 10 meters (± 33 feet) from a distribution line show that the fields drop off to between 2 mG–10 mG. If one moves further away to the edge of the right of way, the measurement continues to weaken to 1 mG–10mG. This is 500–2,500 times less than the 5G level of current naturally occurring in the body. As one continues to move further away, the exposure drops to a negligible level. By comparison, the energy field of household appliances is reported to vary from 0.2 mG–1G.[27]

The Panel on Public Affairs of the American Physical Society's publication concludes that there is no established link between EMFs and cancer. The paper concludes, "The ELF (or EMF) cancer link, if any, should be extremely difficult to detect because of its small, if any, magnitude."[28] The American Physical Society in a review of 16 studies, stated that the link between EMFs and cancer was "either a truly small or nonexistent risk, or else a measure of the confounders of different lifestyles, chemical exposures, etc."[29] In another paper, the APS stated "the studies have generally not shown dose response relationships. When power frequency fields are actually measured, the correlation vanishes."[30] The APS states that evidence for a positive correlation with incidence of leukemia is mostly anecdotal.[31] The literature warns of confusing weak correlation with causation.

In sum, EMFs are unproven to be associated with harmful health effects and any regulation to zero risk would be impossible. The cost estimated for regulation of EMFs is estimated at $1 billion per year, excluding lowered property values, health research, litigation, and the staggering costs of retrofitting all electric power transmission and distribution systems.[32]

Abandoned Hazardous Waste Sites (Superfund)[33]

In 1980, the U.S. Congress passed the Comprehensive Environmental Response, Compensation, and Liability Act (CERCLA, also known as "Superfund"). The Federal Superfund program is reported to target 1,200 abandoned former industrial, military, or local governmental sites for cleanup of hazardous wastes. Superfund is designed to "make the polluter pay." On the Federal level, the Environmental Protection Agency has jurisdiction. The program identifies "Principal Responsible Parties" (PRPs) who are liable for the sites' cleanup costs. A backstop "Public Superfund" program is used when responsible parties cannot be found or are unable to pay cleanup costs. This is principally funded by a special tax on the chemical industry passed through to consumers in the form of higher prices for chemical products. Legal liability has also been extended to insurance companies, banks, and local governments.

Under CERCLA, the EPA defined as hazardous any waste that "may cause or significantly contribute to serious illness or death, or that poses a substantial threat to human health or the environment when improperly managed."[34] Wastes are considered hazardous if they are ignitable, corrosive, reactive, or toxic. Historically, waste material was disposed of in open dumps, containers buried in landfills, ground surface bulk containers, and in sludge ponds. The Superfund program identified two classes of hazards: materials requiring "emergency removal" and those requiring long-

27. Ibid., 240-241.
28. Ibid., 223.
29. Ibid., 215.
30. Ibid., 224.
31. Ibid., 227.
32. Ibid., 209.
33. Except where otherwise noted, the following discussion is drawn from Wildavsky, 81–125, 126–152; and 153–184.
34. Ibid., 155.

Chapter 4: *The Dose Makes the Poison*

term "remediation." Sites were identified that required emergency removal of ignitable metal drums after a couple of high-profile fires. The "emergency removal" part of CERCLA was a focused response to a "readily discernible hazard." However, the vast majority of Superfund sites involved unmanaged properties with perceived chronic exposure threats that were believed to cause cancers, birth defects, miscarriages, and mutations. The remedial program was based on two underlying untested assumptions: (1) low doses of a variety of industrial chemicals had already exposed or could expose the surrounding population, (2) such exposures could cause cancers and other maladies.

After the implementation of the Superfund program, scientific studies were undertaken, mainly by the government, to search for adverse health effects from waste sites. The initial evidence of actual effects on public health from chronic exposure to waste sites was scant and counter to media explanations. A review of six studies by the Congressional Research Service revealed that adverse health effects were "none" and "unknown" at six waste sites. The definitive study, "Health Aspects of the Disposal of Waste Chemicals: A Report of the Executive Scientific Panel,"[35] was conducted in 1986 by the Universities Associated for Research and Education in Pathology. Unlike other studies that relied on anecdotal evidence, this study was conducted with a variety of research designs and was extensively peer reviewed. The conclusion was that there was no support for the hypothesis that a causal link exists between exposure to chemicals at a nonemergent hazard disposal site and latent or delayed harmful health effects.

U.S. Supreme Court Justice Stephen Breyer describes how the cleanup policies for toxic waste sites also are not based on science. Breyer describes a case of the forced cleanup of a toxic waste site in the State of New Hampshire where the site was already 90% clean.[36] Without cleaning up the last 10% of toxic material in the soil, a child could eat small amounts of dirt for 70 days each year without significant harm. One half of the chemicals on the property would have evaporated in 15 years, reducing the toxic level to 5%. But the site was a remote swamp without any foreseeable likelihood of residential development. Moreover, development could have been prevented by local land use controls. Nonetheless, the property owner was required to pay $9.3 million to "protect nonexistent dirt eating children" from the last 10% of toxic material in the soil.

The infamous events surrounding the evacuation of two communities due to purported chemical hazards are also illuminating. Love Canal, New York, the community synonymous for the term "chemical tragedy," was declared an emergency in 1978. Approximately $300 million was spent for evacuation, relocation, mass purchase of homes, research, remediation, and litigation due to the presence of toxic substances. In hindsight, it all was uncalled for.[37] Today the community has been re-populated, and no serious illness has ever been attributed to living adjacent to Love Canal. It was a case in which overwhelming media coverage and literature distorted the facts. Countering this trend in popular media, the June 3, 1980 issue of *Science* magazine contained an article that summed up the real tragedy: "Love Canal: False Alarm Caused by Botched Study."[38]

Likewise, the evacuation of the community of Times Beach, Missouri, due to the presence of dioxins was reported as a "textbook example of hype, panic, and the use of science for political purposes." It was caused

35. Ibid., 160.

36. Stephen Breyer, *Breaking the Vicious Circle: Toward Effective Risk Regulation* (Cambridge, Massachusetts: Harvard University Press, 1993): 12.

37. Allan Mazur, *A Hazardous Inquiry: The Rashomon Effect At Love Canal* (Cambridge, Massachusetts: Harvard University Press, 1998):142–161.

38. Wildavsky, 146.

Valuing Contaminated Properties

by people's inability to understand what a "safe" dose of dioxin might be.[39] The initial coverage of the Times Beach incident by the media evoked fear and panic. The fact that these initial reports were later recanted could not undo the real damage of evacuation and site abandonment.

The more recent Woburn, Massachusetts, toxic tort trial against the W. R. Grace Company made famous by the book and movie titled *A Civil Action*[40] is perhaps more fiction than fact.[41] The case is based on events that occurred between 1972 and 1986 when 12 cases of leukemia were diagnosed in Woburn allegedly due to contaminated well water. The case claimed that the W. R. Grace Company was responsible for the contamination. The major substance identified as toxic was trichloroethylene (TCE), a common industrial solvent. But a city-hired consulting engineer had already reported in 1958 that the groundwater in the area was "too polluted to be used for public water supply. This was two years before the W. R. Grace Company began business operations in the area.[42] In addition, the EPA studies identifying TCE as causing tumors in animals do not include leukemia. Also, the preponderance of other studies have found no such link.[43] Moreover, Bruce Ames, professor of biochemistry and molecular biology at the University of California, and probably the most eminent cancer scientist in the world, estimates that the carcinogenic risk from drinking one liter of water containing the same concentration of TCE discovered at Woburn is less than the risk presented by the intake of cafeic acid contained in one carrot.[44] A comparative ranking of the risk of cancer presented from the well water in Woburn is shown in Figure 1.

As James V. DeLong, attorney and former editor of the Harvard Law Review, has stated:

> In general, despite the general alarm over toxic chemicals, the heavy-duty tools of medicine and epidemiology have never linked any human harm to long-term exposure to chemicals discarded into the environment. Not at Times Beach, not at Love Canal…and not at Woburn. The Superfund program is part disaster and part joke, pouring hundreds of billions of dollars into cleaning up sites that present no discernible risk to humans as long as some elementary, and cheap, methods of containment are practiced.[45]

Wildavsky summarizes the evidence of chronic health risks from waste sites as follows:[46]

1. There are thousands of inactive waste sites around the country where waste chemicals have to some degree migrated into the surrounding environment. At many of these sites, chemicals have made their way into underlying aquifers.

2. There is no peer-supported epidemiolgical evidence of inactive waste sites having caused chronic illnesses such as cancer in surrounding communities.

3. There is no occupational-study evidence of serious illness stemming from chemical exposure levels as low as those associated with waste sites.

4. Administered as dosages thousands of times higher than would be encountered by populations in the vicinity of waste sites, some common waste chemicals have caused cancer in mice and rats.

Any hazards posed by waste sites become threatening mainly if new residential neighborhoods are developed on or adjacent to such sites and

39. Ibid., 107.

40. Jonathan Harr, *A Civil Action* (New York, New York: Vintage Books, 1995).

41. Civil Action Skeptic can be reached at http://members.tripod.com/OlsonW/civilact.html.

42. Timothy Lynch, "The Woburn Controversy: What We Know," *Regulation*, v.21, no. 4 (1998): 56.

43. James V. DeLong, "A Civil Action or a Civil Fiction?," *Competitive Enterprise Institute* (January 1999): 4. www.cei.org/civilaction.html.

44. Bruce N. Ames and Lois Swirsky Gold, "The Causes and Prevention of Cancer: The Role of the Environment," in Ronald Bailey, editor, *The True State of the Planet* (New York, New York: The Free Press, 1995): 141, 161-163.

45. DeLong, 5.

46. Wildavsky, 183.

use water from local groundwater basins rather than local water companies. This worst-case scenario is unlikely and is easily prevented by local zoning ordinances and oversight by regional water quality control boards. Despite the popular perception to the contrary, such examples reflect regulatory failure not "market failure." Except for a few waste sites initially requiring urgent removal that were remedied long ago, or wells for residential water supply over old landfills, the overwhelming fact of waste sites is that the toxic substance is too far from people, the transmission pathway is too improbable, and the amount of potentially harmful substances is too small to do substantial harm.

Conclusion

A review of summaries of the scientific literature concludes that the level of environmental regulation and media response is highly disproportionate to the actual probable health risks from the most well-known trace environmental hazards identified with real estate. The proverb by the 15th century Swiss physician Paracelsus, "the dose makes the poison" (small doses are typically not harmful), is closer to the scientifically supported real level of risk from most environmental conditions identified with real estate. The exposure levels of most trace environmental substances associated with real estate are far below what would be accepted by a consensus in the scientific or medical community or admissible in a court of law under the *Daubert* rule as harmful to public health. In sum, there are no toxic substances, only toxic levels.

The implications for real estate appraisal from the above are as follows:

1. Fear and risk should not be identified as the same factor in evaluating environmental conditions impacting real estate.

2. The market response to many of the most notorious environmental conditions affecting real estate is phobia not stigma.[47] By definition, phobia is a persistent and irrational fear. Irrational fear or panic cannot be considered to reflect the legal definition of market value (i.e., knowledgeable parties).

3. Real estate markets typically look to real estate appraisers to have a more accurate assessment of environmental risks than a real estate broker or the market participants themselves. Real estate brokers only must disclose the presence or absence of environmental conditions affecting real estate. However, to conduct accurate assessments of environmental risks impacting real estate value, appraisers must be knowledgeable of the magnitude of such risks. This presumes a minimum of scientific literacy by appraisers as to the true risks of environmental conditions associated with real estate.

4. Appraisers cannot rely on the exaggerated response of media or the overregulation by government environmental protection agencies as substitutes for assessment of the true risks of environmental conditions on real estate. In particular, environmental risk studies or experts using "zero dose," "no threshold," or "extremely low" threshold scientific standards do not meet rigorous scientific standards and thus should not be relied upon by appraisers.[48]

5. Because the true risk from most trace environmental substances is negligible or nonexistent, the source of risk from many trace envi-

47. Lewis, 22, 107.
48. Peter VanDoran, *Chemicals, Cancer and Choices: Risk Reduction Through Markets* (Washington, D.C.: Cato Institute, 1999) 5–24.

Valuing Contaminated Properties

ronmental conditions is "regulatory stigma" that results from fear of an environmental lawsuit, fine, excise tax, forfeiture, or violation, rather than some real threat to health or property values.

6. Appraisers do not have to become their own scientists or engineers to evaluate environmental risks. Common sense and professional judgment is necessary to evaluate many risks. For example, it is common sense that intact asbestos insulation is not likely to be hazardous. Similarly, poorly ventilated buildings may present health problems. Also, houses located a normal distance from electric transmission lines are unlikely to be exposed to higher concentrations of electromagnetic fields than already found in the home. To state that appraisers should rely solely on the findings and conclusions of trained, experienced, and skilled experts in the environmental field is to deny that appraisers can exercise sound judgment and common sense. Of all the professionals dealing with environmental risk issues impacting real estate, it is strange that real estate appraisers seem to miss the truth that it is fear of the impact of such conditions on residential property values, not health risk, that drives most of the reaction of the market.[49] Appraisers who use such terms as "detrimental conditions" and "stigma" are implying a false expertise that assumes trace environmental conditions are harmful to health and safety. A minimum of environmental literacy is required to determine the source and magnitude of environmental risk affecting property values.

7. Critics of the rational scientific approach to environmental risk assessment, state that risk is associated with perception more than substance. Some real estate appraisers assert that market value is entirely subjective, including the market's assessment of environmental risks. Although the legal definition of market value contains a subjective (perceptual) element, it precludes an irrational element. Many notorious risks associated with trace environmental substances or emissions are not only infinitesimally small but are often likely to be zero.[50] Assessing the mere presence of trace environmental substances embedded in or proximate to real estate as representing a substantial health risk is irrational. To meet new legal evidentiary standards for expert witnesses (i.e., *Daubert* tests), appraisers need to distinguish between risks that are really high and those that are highly discussed.

8. Appraisers must recognize that the standard of health and safety contained in environmental protection regulations is not science based but mainly furthers wealth redistribution and wealth-protection policies.[51] These political objectives often are meant to enfranchise the nonpropertied against the propertied, lessees over lessors, buyers over sellers, inner city occupants over absentee landlords, workplace occupants over employers or insurance companies, and incumbent residential property owners over nearby vacant landowners or commercial property owners. This creates a practical and ethical dilemma for appraisers who traditionally serve as impartial arbiters and evaluators of property value. Appraisers, who unknowingly rely on government environmental standards of health and safety, may be taking a biased, but albeit legal, position for one side against another in

49. Mazur, (1998), 210.
50. Bruce N. Ames and Lois S. Gold, "Pollution, Pesticides, and Cancer Misconceptions," in *Bate*, 187.
51. Tom Bethell, *The Noblest Triumph: Property and Prosperity Through the Ages* (New York, New York: St. Martin's Press, 1998): 308-309; Richard Pipes, *Property and Freedom* (New York, New York: Alfred A. Knopf, 1999): 208–292.

Chapter 4: *The Dose Makes the Poison*

a real estate transaction. Environmental regulations provide a rationale for buyers or tenants to discount transaction prices, or for even mere occupants of workplace buildings to extract substantial value from real estate via "sick building syndrome" lawsuits. This is a modern sophisticated version of an old ploy used by buyers to find fault with a property for sale to pick it up on the cheap. The only way for appraisers to remain neutral where such public policies conflict with the legal definition of fair market value is to accurately report the source of any value diminution as "regulatory stigma," not some false notions of "detrimental conditions" or "environmental stigma." Real estate appraisers should identify the true source of any environmental risks: media effects, overbearing regulations, the apprehension of surrounding property owners, the reaction of non-market occupants, or the actual behavior of effected market participants.[52]

52. Ibid., 308–309.

CHAPTER 4 Cross-References

Related articles in Chapter 1: Peter J. Patchin, MAI, "Valuation of Contaminated Properties" *The Appraisal Journal* (January 1988), 10; and William N. Kinnard, Jr., MAI, SRA, PhD and Elaine M. Worzala, PhD, "How North American Appraisers Value Contaminated Property and Associated Stigma" *The Appraisal Journal* (January 1999), 15, 17.

Related articles in Chapter 2: Anthony J. Rinaldi, MAI, ASA, "Contaminated Properties— Valuation Solutions" *The Appraisal Journal* (July 1991), 46; James A. Chalmers, PhD and Scott A. Roehr, "Issues in the Valuation of Contaminated Property" *The Appraisal Journal* (January 1993), 56–57, 60–61; Albert R. Wilson, "The Environmental Opinion: Basis for an Impaired Value Opinion" *The Appraisal Journal* (July 1994), 70, 77–80; Albert R. Wilson, "Emerging Approaches to Impaired Property Valuation" *The Appraisal Journal* (April 1996), 86, 90–91, 95, 96; and Richard J. Roddewig, MAI, "Choosing the Right Analytical Tool for the Job" *The Appraisal Journal* (July 1998), 104–106.

Related article in Chapter 3: Richard J. Roddewig, "Contaminated Properties and Guide Note 8: Questions, Answers, and Suggestions for Revision" *The Appraisal Journal* (January 1998), 161–162.

Related articles in Chapter 5: Scott B. Arens, MAI, SRA, "The Valuation of Defective Properties: A Common Sense Approach" *The Appraisal Journal* (April 1977), 253–254; Richard J. Roddewig, MAI, CRE "Adjusting Environmental Case Study Comparables by Using an Environmental Risk Scoring System" *The Appraisal Journal* (October 2000), 270–271, 273–274; and Thomas Jackson, PhD, MAI, and Randall Bell, MAI, "The Analysis of Environmental Case Studies" *The Appraisal Journal* (January 2002).

Related articles in Chapter 7: Robert A. Simons, PhD, William M. Bowen, PhD, and Arthur J. Sementelli, PhD, "The Price and Liquidity Effects of UST Leaks from Gas Stations on Adjacent Contaminated Property" *The Appraisal Journal* (April 1999), 353; Robert W. Hall, CRE, "The Causes of Loss in Value: A Case Study of a Contaminated Property" *Real Estate Issues* (April 1994), 384; and Peter J. Patchin, MAI, "Contaminated Properties and the Sales Comparison Approach" *The Appraisal Journal* (July 1994), 391, 395–397.

Related article in Chapter 8: Robert P. Carver, Esq. and Anthony W. Crowell, Esq., "Toxic Tax Assessments: The Ad Valorem Taxation of Contaminated Property" *Real Estate Issues* (Fall 1999), 440.

Related article in Chapter 9: Anthony P. Girasole, Jr., "The Lesson of Love Canal" *Valuation Insights & Perspectives* (First Quarter 1999), 491.

Related articles in Chapter 10: Richard J. Roddewig, "Using the Cost of Environmental Insurance to Measure Contaminated Property Stigma" *The Appraisal Journal* (July 1997), 522–523, 525–527; and Allan E. Gluck, Donald C. Nanney, and Wayne Lusvardi, "Mitigating Factors in Appraisal & Valuation of Contaminated Property" *Real Estate Issues* (Summer 2000), 528, 531–535.

Related articles in Chapter 11: Richard J. Roddewig, "Temporary Stigma: Lessons from the Exxon Valdez Litigation" *The Appraisal Journal* (January 1997), 558–559; Richard J. Roddewig, MAI, "Junk Science, Environmental Stigma, Market Surveys, and Proper Appraisal Methodology: Recent Lessons from the Litigation Trenches" *The Appraisal Journal* (October 1999), 575–578; and Jack P. Friedman, CRE, "Defending an Oil Company Against Litigation for Environmental Contamination (A Case Study)" *Real Estate Issues* (Winter 1999/2000), 586–587.

Contaminated Properties and the Three Traditional Approaches to Value

CHAPTER 5

Editor's Introduction
Many of the articles included in Chapters 2 and 4 proposed using regression analysis, case studies, market surveys, and other innovative techniques as tools for understanding the potential impacts of environmental risks and stigma on value. Many writers, however, have asserted that all of this can be done within the context of the three traditional approaches to value.

Neustein's 1992 article was the first Appraisal Journal *article to explore in detail the way in which the income approach to value can be used to compare value unaffected by contamination to value affected by contamination. His article was based on research into the differences in rental rates, occupancy rates, and risk premiums between contaminated and uncontaminated industrial properties in the Los Angeles marketplace. Arens, in a much later article, shows how net income can be reduced to account for lost rent or increased vacancy. He also demonstrates how expenses can be increased to account for remediation costs and capitalization rates can be increased to account for any additional "risk premium" in the traditional direct capitalization of income approach to value.*

Jackson and Mundy say much the same thing but in the context of income, cap rates, and discount rates applicable to a discounted cash flow income approach. Jackson goes further than Mundy by investigating this in relation to traditional mortgage-equity analysis using the Ellwood technique.

Both the Roddewig and Jackson/Bell articles investigate the applicability of the traditional sales comparison approach to the valuation of contaminated properties. Both articles propose a way in which various sales of property affected by contamination and its associated risks can be systematically evaluated and compared to the property being appraised. Roddewig suggests that the case studies can be "scored" to derive a stigma adjustment factor to apply to the unaffected value of the appraised property. Jackson and Bell recommend that when there are lots of potential case studies available, care should be taken to select the most "comparable" case studies by reference to such factors as property characteristics, contamination/discharge issues, and other comparative factors such as the presence or absence of an identified party responsible for cleanup, the risk of third-party liabilities, and written indemnifications or environmental insurance policies.

Estimating Value Diminution by the Income Approach

by Richard A. Neustein, MAI, SRA

When an income-producing property is affected by a condition that causes value to decrease, the sales comparison approach is often the primary means of estimating value diminution. The incorporation of the income approach depends on whether sufficient data are available to support the analyses. A new formula that relies on data that are frequently available from the market may make inclusion of the income approach simpler, however.

The fundamental relationship for measuring diminution of value is:

$$D = \frac{V_U - V_A}{V_U}$$

where

D = Diminution of value, expressed as a decimal fraction of the value in the unaffected condition

V_U = Value in the unaffected condition

V_A = Value in the affected condition

From the direct capitalization method of the income approach, V_U and V_A may be expressed as:

$$V_U = \frac{I_U}{R_U} \qquad\qquad V_A = \frac{I_A}{R_A}$$

where

I_U = Net operating income (NOI) in the unaffected condition

R_U = Overall capitalization rate in the unaffected condition

I_A = NOI in the affected condition

R_A = Overall capitalization rate in the affected condition

When the *NOI* in the affected condition is divided by the *NOI* in the unaffected condition, the result is a lowered income ratio, L. Thus:

$$L = \frac{I_A}{I_U}$$

Richard A. Neustein, MAI, SRA, is the principal of R.A. Neustein & Associates in Los Angeles, where he specializes in the appraisal of unusual and problem properties with a focus on litigation. He received a B.S. in mechanical engineering from Northrop University in Los Angeles and an MBA from the University of California in Los Angeles.

This article originally appeared in the April 1992 issue of The Appraisal Journal.

If the *NOI* of a property is normally \$10,000 and the condition affecting the property has reduced the net income to \$9,000, the $L = 0.9$ (\$9,000/\$10,000).

A rearrangement of the equation for L expresses I_A in terms of I_U:

$$I_A = I_U \times L$$

When the subject property is an industrial property for which the rents are net, and if rental rates have not been affected, the ratio between occupancy rates of affected and unaffected properties may be substituted for *NOI*s.

The other factor necessary to estimate the amount of value diminution is the risk premium required by buyers to induce them to buy property in the affected condition. This is a mark-up premium (*RISK*) that is applied to the overall capitalization rate. Thus:

$$R_A = R_U \times (1 + RISK)$$

If the normal cap rate were 10% and the risk premium were 20%, the risk-modified cap rate would be 10% x 1.2 or 12%.

When the formula for V_A is restated to incorporate L and *RISK*, the result is:

$$V_A = \frac{I_A}{R_A} = \frac{I_U \times L}{R_U \times (1 + RISK)} = \frac{I_U}{R_U} \times \frac{L}{1 - RISK}$$

Substituting the restated V_A in the fundamental equation for value diminution yields:

$$D = \frac{V_U - V_A}{V_U}$$

$$= \frac{\dfrac{I_U}{R_U} - \dfrac{I_U}{R_U} \times \dfrac{L}{1 + RISK}}{\dfrac{I_U}{R_U}}$$

$$= \frac{\dfrac{I_U}{R_U}}{\dfrac{I_U}{R_U}} - \frac{\dfrac{I_U}{R_U} \times \dfrac{L}{1 + RISK}}{\dfrac{I_U}{R_U}}$$

$$D = 1 - \frac{L}{1 + RISK}$$

Table 1 and Figure 1 exhibit value diminution for a wide range of reduced income and risk premiums. These were developed for the entire range of *NOI* reduction, including the complete elimination of all net income. Before a condition reduces a property's income to this point, however, the need for a change in property use is likely to become apparent.

Chapter 5: *Estimating Value Diminution*

TABLE 1 Value Decline as a Function of Income Decline and Cap Rate Risk Premium

Risk Premium on Cap Rate	\multicolumn{11}{c}{Affected-Condition Income as a Percentage of Unaffected-Condition Income}
	100.00%	90.00%	80.00%	70.00%	60.00%	50.00%	40.00%	30.00%	20.00%	10.00%	0.00%
500.00%	83.33%	85.00%	86.67%	88.33%	90.00%	91.67%	93.33%	95.00%	96.67%	98.33%	100.00%
450.00%	81.82%	83.64%	85.45%	87.27%	89.09%	90.91%	92.73%	94.55%	96.36%	98.18%	100.00%
400.00%	80.00%	82.00%	84.00%	86.00%	88.00%	90.00%	92.00%	94.00%	96.00%	98.00%	100.00%
350.00%	77.78%	80.00%	82.22%	84.44%	86.67%	88.89%	91.11%	93.33%	95.56%	97.78%	100.00%
300.00%	75.00%	77.50%	80.00%	82.50%	85.00%	87.50%	90.00%	92.50%	95.00%	97.50%	100.00%
250.00%	71.43%	74.29%	77.14%	80.00%	82.86%	85.71%	88.57%	91.43%	94.29%	97.14%	100.00%
200.00%	66.67%	70.00%	73.33%	76.67%	80.00%	83.33%	86.67%	90.00%	93.33%	96.67%	100.00%
150.00%	60.00%	64.00%	68.00%	72.00%	76.00%	80.00%	84.00%	88.00%	92.00%	96.00%	100.00%
100.00%	50.00%	55.00%	60.00%	65.00%	70.00%	75.00%	80.00%	85.00%	90.00%	95.00%	100.00%
90.00%	47.37%	52.63%	57.89%	63.16%	68.42%	73.68%	78.95%	84.21%	89.47%	94.74%	100.00%
80.00%	44.44%	50.00%	55.56%	61.11%	66.67%	72.22%	77.78%	83.33%	88.89%	94.44%	100.00%
70.00%	41.18%	47.06%	52.94%	58.82%	64.71%	70.59%	76.47%	82.35%	88.24%	94.12%	100.00%
60.00%	37.50%	43.75%	50.00%	56.25%	62.50%	68.75%	75.00%	81.25%	87.50%	93.75%	100.00%
50.00%	33.33%	40.00%	46.67%	53.33%	60.00%	66.67%	73.33%	80.00%	86.67%	93.33%	100.00%
40.00%	28.57%	35.71%	42.86%	50.00%	57.14%	64.29%	71.43%	78.57%	85.71%	92.86%	100.00%
30.00%	23.08%	30.77%	38.46%	46.15%	53.85%	61.54%	69.23%	76.92%	84.62%	92.31%	100.00%
20.00%	16.67%	25.00%	33.33%	41.67%	50.00%	58.33%	66.67%	75.00%	83.33%	91.67%	100.00%
10.00%	9.09%	18.18%	27.27%	36.36%	45.45%	54.55%	63.64%	72.73%	81.82%	90.91%	100.00%
0.00%	0.00%	10.00%	20.00%	30.00%	40.00%	50.00%	60.00%	70.00%	80.00%	90.00%	100.00%

FIGURE 1 Decline in Income Value

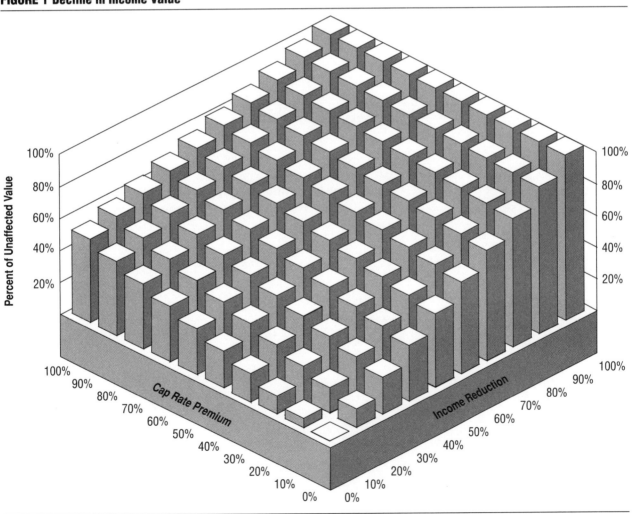

Valuing Contaminated Properties

Testing the Formula

This formula was derived in connection with a case that involved hazardous material contamination of an industrial property in the Los Angeles area. In addition to data researched by the author, the market data developed by Peter J. Patchin, who pioneered the estimation of value diminution caused by hazardous contamination,[1] were employed in this case. Sales comparison analysis of these market data indicates that the diminution of the subject property's value ranged between 20% and 25% of its value in the uncontaminated condition.

Because the subject property was an industrial property leased on a net basis, the gross and net operating incomes were the same. In such a situation, the reduction in occupancy rate may be substituted for the reduction in net income.

Two properties were found in the Los Angeles area for which occupancy rates in the contaminated condition were measurably reduced. The marketing time for these properties had lengthened; however, the rental rates achieved were essentially at market levels. The occupancy level of one property was reduced to between 91.2% and 95.5% of normal occupancy in the uncontaminated condition.

The other property exhibited an occupancy rate that was 92.73% of the average occupancy of surrounding properties, as measured by CB Commercial.[2] The correlation between these two reduced occupancy rates is strong. The reduced occupancy that was selected for use in the analysis was 93%. Thus, $L = 0.93$.

Only one contaminated property with a risk premium was found. The overall rate for this property was specifically raised from 8.9% to 10.44%, an increase of 17.3%. Thus, $RISK = 0.173$.

When these values of L and $RISK$ are used in the formula, the resulting estimate of value diminution is:

$$Diminution = 1 - \frac{0.93}{1.173}$$

The 20.7% value diminution indicated by the formula correlates well with the 20% to 25% range indicated by sales comparison and serves as a validation of the formula:

$$Diminution = 1 - \frac{L}{1 + RISK}$$

1. Peter J. Patchin, "Valuation of Contaminated Properties," *The Appraisal Journal* (January 1988): 7–16; and Peter J. Patchin, "Contaminated Properties—Stigma Revisited," *The Appraisal Journal* (April 1991): 167–172.

2. *CB Commercial Industrial Space Real Estate Market Bulletin, South Bay of Los Angeles County,* (First and second quarters, 1991), published by CB Commercial Real Estate Group.

The Impact of Hazardous and Toxic Material on Property Value: Revisited

by Bill Mundy, MAI, PhD

In "The Impact of Hazardous and Toxic Materials on Property Value," I presented a theory about the ways in which contaminants influence property value as well as a method to quantify such influences.[1] The value of property may be affected both by an impact on the income stream and by an impact on its marketability. The income effect (i.e., damage) is measured as follows:

$$Damage = V_U - V_I$$

$$V_U = \sum_{t=1}^{n} \frac{NOI_U}{(1+i_m)^t} + \frac{NOI_U}{(1+i_m)^n} \quad (1)$$

$$V_I = \sum_{t=1}^{n} \frac{NOI_I}{(1+i)^t} + \frac{NOI_I}{(1+i)^n}$$

where

V_U = Value unimpaired

V_I = Value impaired

NOI_U = Net operating income, unimpaired

NOI_I = Net operating income, impaired[2]

i_m = Market rate

i_r = Risk rate

The marketability effect, or the loss in the opportunity to use a property as a result of its contaminated condition, is synonymous with the effect of a frozen asset. The marketability effect was measured as follows:[3]

$$Damage = [\sum_{i=1}^{n} PV_{r_r}(V_U - V_I)(r_m) + \sum_{i=1}^{n} PV_{r_r}(\text{cleanup cost})] +$$

$$[\sum_{i=0}^{n} FV_{r_r}(V_U - V_I)(r_m) + \sum_{i=0}^{n} FV_{r_r}(\text{cleanup cost})] \quad (2)$$

where

r_r = Risk rate

r_m = Market rate

V_U = Value unimpaired

V_I = Value impaired

Bill Mundy, MAI, PhD, *is president and senior analyst at Mundy & Associates in Seattle. He received a BA in agriculture from Washington State University as well as an MA in urban economics and a PhD in market research and urban economics from the University of Washington, and is a member of the American Society of Real Estate Counselors. Dr. Mundy would like to acknowledge research support provided by the Real Estate Counseling Group of America, Inc.*

This article originally appeared in the October 1992 issue of The Appraisal Journal.

---

1. Bill Mundy, "The Impact of Hazardous and Toxic Materials on Property Value," *The Appraisal Journal* (April 1992): 155–162.

2. The prior article referred to an uncontaminated property as clean (NOI_c) and a contaminated property as dirty (NOI_D). Preferable terms are unimpaired and impaired. Thanks to comments by Al Wilson, President, Environmental Assessment and Valuation.

3. This model was discussed at the Appraisal Institute's symposium in Philadelphia, Pennsylvania, on October 3 an 4, 1991. The model was originally presented at the Weimer School for Advanced Study in Real Estate and Land Economics in January 1991 and subsequently in January 1992. This model is an outgrowth of these presentations. Jeffrey Fisher, PhD, Indiana University, was particularly helpful in reformulating the model. In addition, the author would like to thank the insights and challenge presented by Max Derbes, III, MAI, New Orleans. The author is a fellow at the Weimer School.

PV = Present value

FV = Future value

The opportunity cost is the difference between the value unimpaired and the value impaired of a property if the owner could fully use it; for example, if 100% of its value is used as collateral, and if the risk rate in Equation 1 does not also take into consideration the marketability opportunity cost. This seldom reflects reality, however. Because most real estate is encumbered with debt, an owner does not have the entire value of the property at his or her disposal. Also, such other factors as liens against the property may restrict its use as collateral.

The value of a property, unimpaired, is shown in Figure 1, which represents an income-producing property. For an income-producing property—for example, a single-family, owner-occupied residence or vacant land—it would be necessary to estimate an income stream.

Mathematically, the process used to determine the present value of that income stream is as follows:

$$V_U = \sum_{t=1}^{n} I_U (1 + r_m)^n$$

For the impaired property the following factors may influence the income stream and value and therefore the impaired value.

- Factors that affect the net operating income:
  1. A decrease in rent.
  2. A decrease in occupancy.
  3. An increase in operating expenses.
- Factors that affect the rate:
  4. An increase in risk to the equity. For example, the amount and accessibility of the collateral in a property may change as a result of changing level of risk.
  5. An increased risk to the debtor's position. For example, the monthly debt service or annual debt service may change if the property must be refinanced during that part of the holding period in which contamination is present.

The increases in risk both to the equity and debt can be accounted for in the discount rate for the contaminated property. The rate would reflect all forms of risk to the property, including the opportunity cost from the impaired collateral. Figure 2 represents the income stream for the contaminated property.

The following formula can be used to calculate the value of the property.

$$V_I = \sum_{t=1}^{n} I_I (1 + r)^n$$

where

I_I = Income impaired

The damage is therefore the difference between the value unimpaired and the value impaired, or

$$D = V_U - V_I$$

The difficult task for appraisers is to quantify the changes in rent, occupancy, expenses, risk to the equity, and risk to the debt. One method

Chapter 5: *Impact of Hazardous and Toxic Material*

FIGURE 1 Property Income Stream—Unimpaired

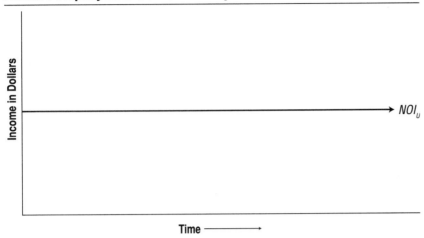

FIGURE 2 Property Income Stream—Impaired

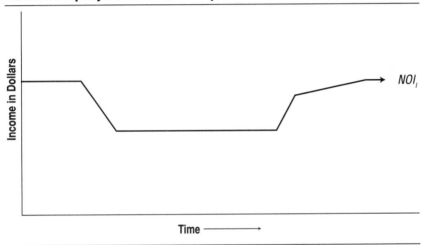

for quantifying the impact on those variables is explained in the following section. Table 1 shows the income, vacancy, expense characteristics, and present value of a hypothetical unimpaired property whose value is $21.9 million.

Changes in Rent
The change in rent might be quantified by comparing an impaired property to similar replica properties that do not have the impairment. In addition, it may be possible to track the rent of the impaired property with control properties before, during, and after the contamination problem occurs.

Changes in Occupancy
For changes in occupancy, a method similar to that discussed for changes in rent could be followed.

Changes in Expenses
Careful interviews should be conducted with the subject property owner to learn how the subject property's expenses have changed. In addition,

Valuing Contaminated Properties

TABLE 1 Property Value: Unimpaired

	Year	Gross Income	Vacancy at 5%	Effective Gross Income	Expense Ratio 30%	Net Operating Income	Market Rate (i_m)	Present Value
	-6	$2,475,000	$123,750	$2,351,250	$705,375	$1,645,875	10%	$2,915,768
	-5	$2,475,000	$123,750	$2,351,250	$705,375	$1,645,875	10%	$2,650,698
	-4	$2,475,000	$123,750	$2,351,250	$705,375	$1,645,875	10%	$2,409,726
	-3	$2,475,000	$123,750	$2,351,250	$705,375	$1,645,875	10%	$2,190,660
	-2	$2,475,000	$123,750	$2,351,250	$705,375	$1,645,875	10%	$1,991,509
	-1	$2,475,000	$123,750	$2,351,250	$705,375	$1,645,875	10%	$1,810,463
Today	0	$2,475,000	$123,750	$2,351,250	$705,375	$1,645,875	10%	$1,645,875
	1	$2,475,000	$123,750	$2,351,250	$705,375	$1,645,875	10%	$1,496,250
	2	$2,475,000	$123,750	$2,351,250	$705,375	$1,645,875	10%	$1,360,227
	3	$2,475,000	$123,750	$2,351,250	$705,375	$1,645,875	10%	$1,236,570
	4	$2,475,000	$123,750	$2,351,250	$705,375	$1,645,875	10%	$1,124,155
	5	$2,475,000	$123,750	$2,351,250	$705,375	$1,645,875	10%	$1,021,959
							Total value	$21,853,859
							Rounded to	$21,900,000

this should be verified if possible with other properties that have also been impaired as a result of contamination. Repair and maintenance expense, professional fees (e.g., attorneys, environmental engineers), and insurance costs may change if there are risks to those who use the property.

Rate

In Table 1, a market rate of 10% was used to determine the discounted present value of the unimpaired property. For an impaired property, the task is to determine an appropriate rate that reflects the risk associated with the particular level of contamination. It is difficult to obtain data to determine the appropriate rate to use in an impaired analysis. Sales of income-producing contaminated property, interviews with investors, or some type of analog can be used to generate data.

In this case, the differential between rates of return on corporate AAA bonds and junk bonds is used—a differential of approximately 500 basis points. For prior years, the 500 basis points are deducted from the market rate and for future years a premium is added for discounting purposes. The process is shown in Table 2. The variables that change are rent and vacancy, with expenses associated with an impairment such as professional fees and cleanup costs also accounted for. In this example, the damage caused by the contamination is estimated at $7 million (value unimpaired of $21.9 million less value impaired of $14.9 million).

Because of the difficulty in obtaining direct and reliable rate data, it is recommended that analysts use multiple methods as a part of the income approach.

Equity

An appraiser could attempt to determine whether, for income-producing properties that have been sold, there was a change in the equity yield rate. This may seem like looking for a needle in the haystack, and probably would be as difficult.

A second method is to conduct interviews in a well-controlled environment with investors in properties similar to the subjects, while a third method is to quantify the change in collateral available as a result of the

Chapter 5: *Impact of Hazardous and Toxic Material*

TABLE 2   Property Value: Impaired (present value based on risk rate)

	Year	Gross Income	Vacancy Rate	Vacancy	Effective Gross Income	Expense Ratio at 30%	Costs Resulting from Impairment Professional Fees	Clean-up	Net Operating Income	Risk Rate (i)	Present Value
	-6	$2,475,000	5%	$123,750	$2,351,250	$705,375			$1,645,875	5%	$2,205,630
	-5	$2,351,250	10%	$235,125	$2,116,125	$634,838			$1,481,288	5%	$1,890,540
	-4	$2,227,500	15%	$334,125	$1,893,375	$568,013			$1,325,363	5%	$1,610,986
	-3	$1,980,000	20%	$396,000	$1,584,000	$475,200			$1,108,800	5%	$1,283,575
	-2	$1,732,500	25%	$433,125	$1,299,375	$389,813			$909,563	5%	$1,002,793
	-1	$1,856,250	20%	$371,250	$1,485,000	$445,500	$4,000		$1,035,500	5%	$1,087,275
Today	0	$1,980,000	15%	$297,000	$1,683,000	$504,900	$10,000		$1,168,100	15%	$1,168,100
	1	$2,103,750	10%	$210,375	$1,893,375	$568,013	$20,000	$100,000	$1,205,363	15%	$1,048,141
	2	$2,227,500	10%	$222,750	$2,004,750	$601,425	$15,000	$100,000	$1,288,325	15%	$974,159
	3	$2,351,250	10%	$235,125	$2,116,125	$634,838	$2,000	$20,000	$1,459,288	15%	$959,505
	4	$2,475,000	10%	$247,500	$2,227,500	$668,250	$2,000		$1,557,250	15%	$890,363
	5	$2,475,000	10%	$247,500	$2,227,500	$668,250	$1,000		$1,558,250	15%	$774,726

Total value $14,895,792

Rounded to $14,900,000

increased risk. The latter method can be used as a validation tool or as an independent method in itself, but also has its drawbacks in terms of easily obtained, reliable data. The following process can be used.

1. Estimate the unimpaired value.
2. Estimate the impaired value using a market rate (r_m) rather than a risk rate (r). This will account for changes in income, occupancy, and expenses as shown in Table 3. In this case the change in value is $4.5 million, which excludes risk to the equity and debt.
3. Estimate the impact on the equity interest. This will account for the impairment or lost opportunity to take advantage of one's equity in the property.
4. Estimate the impact on the debt position in the property.

Debt

For many properties debt will not be affected. If it is necessary to refinance the impaired property during the period of impairment, however, there can be significant risk. For example, it may not be possible to refinance the property, or if the property can be refinanced the terms and conditions under which it will be financed may reflect the increased level of risk to the lender. This could affect the loan amount, term call provisions, and rate.

An example that shows the impact on value resulting from a change in equity and debt service is presented in Table 4. The impact on the equity and debt position (i.e., opportunity cost) is $2.5 million. This, added to the impact on the income stream ($4.5 million), is a second estimate of the damage, or $7 million.

Conclusion

The impact of contamination can have an influence on both the income-generating ability of a property and the level of risk associated with the asset itself. As indicated, rents may decrease, occupancy may decrease,

Valuing Contaminated Properties

TABLE 3   Property Value: Impaired (present value based on market rate)

Year	Gross Income	Vacancy Rate	Vacancy	Effective Gross Income	Expense Ratio at 30%	Costs Resulting from Impairment Professional Fees	Clean-up	Net Operating Income	Risk Rate (i)	Present Value
-6	$2,475,000	5%	$123,750	$2,351,250	$705,375			$1,645,875	10%	$2,915,768
-5	$2,351,250	10%	$235,125	$2,116,125	$634,838			$1,481,288	10%	$2,385,628
-4	$2,227,500	15%	$334,125	$1,893,375	$568,013			$1,325,363	10%	$1,940,463
-3	$1,980,000	20%	$396,000	$1,584,000	$475,200			$1,108,800	10%	$1,475,813
-2	$1,732,500	25%	$433,125	$1,299,375	$389,813			$909,563	10%	$1,100,571
-1	$1,856,250	20%	$371,250	$1,485,000	$445,500	$4,000		$1,035,500	10%	$1,139,050
Today 0	$1,980,000	15%	$297,000	$1,683,000	$504,900	$10,000		$1,168,100	10%	$1,168,100
1	$2,103,750	10%	$210,375	$1,893,375	$568,013	$20,000	$100,000	$1,205,363	10%	$1,095,784
2	$2,227,500	10%	$222,750	$2,004,750	$601,425	$15,000	$100,000	$1,288,325	10%	$1,064,731
3	$2,351,250	10%	$235,125	$2,116,125	$634,838	$2,000	$20,000	$1,459,288	10%	$1,096,384
4	$2,475,000	10%	$247,500	$2,227,500	$668,250	$2,000		$1,557,250	10%	$1,063,623
5	$2,475,000	10%	$247,500	$2,227,500	$668,250	$1,000		$1,558,250	10%	$967,551
									Total value	$17,413,466
									Rounded to	$17,400,000

and expenses may increase. Because these changes may take place over time, to quantify the impact of the contamination an analyst can discount the *NOI* to a present value, taking into consideration the unimpaired and impaired nature of the income stream.

The rate at which the income stream is discounted may be a market rate or a risk rate. If it is a risk rate, the implication is that the effect on the equity and debt is accounted for by the rate differential (i.e., difference between the market rate as if unimpaired and the risk rate under the impaired condition).

Alternatively, the impact on the level of risk associated with an asset, and consequently its marketability, can be estimated by determining the change in the equity yield rate over the holding period. This is also true with regard to the change in the debt constant. The former reflects the opportunity cost incurred as a result of the inability to use the collateral in the property.

TABLE 4 Opportunity Cost of Impaired Collateral

Year	Value Unimpaired* V_u	Value Impaired* V_i	Value Change* V_{chg}	Value of the Debt** V_d	Value of the Equity* V_e	Loan-to-Value Ratio L/V	Value of the Collateral* $V_c = V_e*L/V$	Ratio of Collateral to Value V_c/V_u	Lost Collateral (LC) $V_{chg}*V_c/V_u$	Rate Differential**	Rate on Lost Collateral*	Change in Debt Service***	Present Value of Opportunity Cost
-6	$16,459	$10,973	$5,486	$9,875	$6,584	75%	$4,938	30%	$1,646	5%	$82		$110
-5	$16,459	$9,875	$6,584	$9,875	$6,584	75%	$4,938	30%	$1,975	5%	$99		$126
-4	$16,459	$8,836	$7,623	$9,875	$6,584	75%	$4,938	30%	$2,287	5%	$114		$139
-3	$16,459	$7,392	$9,067	$9,875	$6,584	75%	$4,938	30%	$2,720	5%	$136		$157
-2	$16,459	$6,064	$10,395	$9,875	$6,584	75%	$4,938	30%	$3,119	5%	$156		$172
-1	$16,459	$6,903	$9,555	$9,875	$6,584	75%	$4,938	30%	$2,867	5%	$143		$151
Today 0	$16,459	$7,787	$8,671	$9,875	$6,584	75%	$4,938	30%	$2,602	5%	$130		$130
1	$16,459	$8,036	$8,423	$9,875	$6,584	75%	$4,938	30%	$2,527	5%	$126		$120
2	$16,459	$8,589	$7,870	$9,875	$6,584	75%	$4,938	30%	$2,361	5%	$118		$107
3	$16,459	$9,729	$6,730	$9,875	$6,584	75%	$4,938	30%	$2,019	5%	$101	$441	$468
4	$16,459	$10,382	$6,077	$9,875	$6,584	75%	$4,938	30%	$1,823	5%	$91	$441	$438
5	$16,459	$10,388	$6,070	$9,875	$6,584	75%	$4,938	30%	$1,821	5%	$91	$441	$417
												Total value	$2,536
												Rounded to	$2,500

* In thousands

** Assumes the equity owner can earn 5% net on borrowed capital

*** For simplicity a nonamortizing loan is assumed. Debt assumptions are as follows:

	Unimpaired	Impaired
Interest rate	10.0%	12.5%
Term in years	30	15
Constant	0.1061	0.1508
Debt service ($000)	$1,047.7	$1,489.1

The Valuation of Defective Properties: A Common Sense Approach

by Scott B. Arens, MAI, SRA

Scott B. Arens, MAI, SRA, is owner of the Arens Group, Real Estate Appraisal and Consultation, in San Diego. He earned a BS in architectural design from Arizona State University and specializes in appraising defective properties.

This article originally appeared in the April 1997 issue of The Appraisal Journal.

Defective properties as discussed here are those with significant physical problems, such as contamination or construction defects (cracked slabs, soil problems, etc.). These problems generally require expensive remediation and create significant market aversion.

The valuation model described here is logical and systematic, with strong links to the sales comparison approach. It presents no theoretical breakthroughs or secret formulas, nor is it applicable to every defective property situation. However, when used with sound judgment, it has proven to be a reliable way to extract the more elusive diminution elements, particularly stigma. The strength of this method is its simplicity and applicability. With slight variations, this basic model has proven useful in valuing problem properties ranging from single-family homes with cracked slabs to severely contaminated commercial centers.

Basic Valuation Model

The basic model for this analysis begins with the classic before condition/after condition equation, indicated as follows:

$$\text{Before condition} = \text{After condition} + \text{Diminution in value}$$

Diminution in value is divided into two distinct loss groups. Category I losses are those not directly derived from comparable sales. These losses are unique to and are a function of the subject's specific situation. They might include cost to remediate, additional vacancy, additional financing and insurance costs, and monitoring costs associated with contamination. Sources include cost experts, engineers, loan brokers, insurance agents, etc.

Category II losses are those derived from comparable sales and tend to be much more subjective. The benefit of this valuation model is the isolation of these losses, which may include stigma, buyer contingency, and buyer's entrepreneurial incentive.

Chapter 5: *Valuation of Defective Properties*

Diminution of value is comprised of both categories of losses. Thus, the equation representing this valuation model is as follows:

$$A = B - \text{Diminution in value}$$
$$A = B - (\text{Category I losses} + \text{Category II losses})$$
$$A = B - \{[C_R + AV + AC_F + AC_I] + [S + BC + EI]\}$$

where,

A = After condition

B = Before condition

C_R = Cost to remediate

AV = Additional vacancy

AC_F = Additional costs of financing

AC_I = Additional cost of insurance

S = Stigma

BC = Buyer contingency

EI = Buyer's entrepreneurial incentive

The major motivation of this method is to isolate Category II losses; therefore, the final form of the equation and a description of each item follows:

$$[S + BC + EI] = B - A - [C_R + AV + AC_F + AC_I]$$

Before condition (BC): The value with no problems or *before* acknowledgment of the problems. Sources include offers made before problems were known, opinions of principals, and analysis of similar nondefective sales.

After condition (A): This is the "as is" value or *after* acknowledgment of the problems and is typically what the appraiser is looking for.

Category I Losses

Cost to remediate (C_R): Whether the property is a single-family home with a cracked slab or a contaminated industrial park, one of the first questions buyers ask is "what will it cost to fix?" No reasonable after-condition estimate can be made without a qualified opinion of cost. Also, comparable sales of problem properties have little use without these costs. For comparables sold before remediation, anticipated costs are used. Eventual actual costs are ignored because perceptions at sale dictate purchase price. For properties that are not feasible to remediate, it is important to extract the Category II amounts from comparables that are also not feasible to remediate.

The cost of remediation will depend on the scope of the work. Certainty level is the perception of how adequate the remediation is in light of the problems. It is not uncommon to find that remediation costs reported by different sources can vary by as much as 100%, particularly in litigation. This wide range is typically the result of experts assuming (or being told to assume) different certainty levels. Certainty levels refer to the certainty that the problem will not occur again and is classified on a scale of 1 through 5, with 5 being most certain and 1 the least. It is important to recognize where a particular fix is on the scale because it can have a significant effect on stigma. Helpful questions are "what are [will be] the chances of recurrence?" and "what more could be done that is not being done?"

Additional vacancy (AV): If work to be completed makes the property unrentable for some period, an additional vacancy factor will be considered by buyers. For owner-occupied properties, alternative rental costs should be considered. Using estimates of construction periods and rental rates, a reasonable additional lump-sum vacancy figure can be derived.

Additional cost of financing (AC$_F$): Financing plays a major role in the marketability of problem properties. In fact, many appraisers consider financing the primary factor and the key element in valuation.[1] Whatever conclusions are reached about additional financing costs, they can be converted into a cash-equivalent dollar figure.

Additional cost of insurance (AC$_I$): As with additional financing costs, the cash equivalent lump-sum cost of additional insurance is used here.

Category II Losses

Stigma (S): Of all loss elements, stigma is probably the most elusive and debated. However, arguments are more often than not due to different definitions. As used here, stigma is defined as the discount resulting from a property's bad reputation from having once been defective. It is the discount that buyers demand in relation to properties with no history of problems.

More than anything else, stigma is a function of uncertainty. "When the problem is understood, uncertainty is lessened and the value of a property should then increase."[2] Logically then, the certainty level of a fix and the resultant stigma are very strongly linked. As such, accurate appraisals should derive stigma from sales with similar certainty levels, not those with similar remediation work. Conceptually, the type and extent of work performed should not affect stigma other than in reference to its certainty level. The reason is that the marketplace has mixed, offsetting feelings about any scope of remediation. While an extensive fix is comforting, it tends to indicate that the problem was extensive. A minor one, on the other hand, tends to indicate that the problem was minor, but the smaller scope of the fix is bothersome. What should and does concern informed buyers is the *perception* of how the scope of the fix relates to the problem. If the certainty level of the cure is very high, stigma can approach zero.

Consider the case of a buyer who purchases a new building, finds large cracks in the slab, and sues the builder for damages. In court, the seller's expert recommends a minor epoxy fix, using the argument that it should stop any future problems. The buyer's attorney, on the other hand, recommends replacing the entire slab, using the argument that although epoxy may work, the buyer purchased a new property with a defect-free slab and therefore deserves one. The appraiser should not be drawn into this moral argument. However, the different levels of these fixes would be analyzed differently. If it is assumed that the property gets the new slab, the stigma must be estimated appropriately and would likely be much lower. It would be improper to place most of the weight on a sale that also got a new slab because of major soil problems. It is very possible that the comparables fix was mandatory and possibly inadequate. As a result, the comparable would likely indicate much higher stigma than is appropriate for the subject despite the fact that the scope of the work on the two properties is the same.

Buyer contingency (BC): Buyer contingency is the discount required by buyers for taking the risk of remediation cost overruns. It applies when

1. Peter J. Patchin, "Valuation of Contaminated Properties," *The Appraisal Journal* (January 1988): 7–18.
2. Bill Mundy, "The Impact of Hazardous Materials on Property Value," *The Appraisal Journal* (April 1992): 158.

Chapter 5: *Valuation of Defective Properties*

the buyer is to pay for the work or when the seller guarantees only a fixed amount of money for repairs rather than a full cure.

Buyer entrepreneurial incentive (EI): Buyer entrepreneurial incentive is the reward for the time, trouble, and risk associated with managing the work. "Buyers feel they should be compensated monetarily for the trouble of making the necessary improvement."[3] It applies when buyers are responsible for doing the work but do not necessarily have to pay for it. Even with indemnification, buyers may have to orchestrate work or at least be nuisanced by it and generally require some compensation.

Case Study

Assume a multitenant retail property which had previously contained leaking gasoline tanks. Although the tanks were removed, the current owners discovered that the ground was still contaminated. Their attorney requested the appraisal to be used to support an "as is" estimate in litigation against the seller. The property is 100% leased with tenants all paying basically market rents.

According to experts, the contaminated soil can be dug up and removed, but would require demolishing a portion of the rear building. Costs to remove the contaminated dirt, properly dispose of it, replace with clean dirt, and repair the rear building are estimated at $285,000. The front building would not be affected by the construction in any significant way, but two of the rear units would have to be vacated for about three months, resulting in about $15,000 in lost rents. Financing for the property was available but would involve higher points and a slightly higher interest rate than normal as a result of the contamination. Estimated additional financing costs are $27,000. Insurance rates are estimated to be about $6,000 higher as a result of the contamination. In addition, the appraiser is informed of a recent offer of $650,000 for the subject, which was made without knowledge of the contamination. Based on sales and discussions with brokers, this is a reasonable before-condition estimate.

Although many contaminated sales would likely be used for this analysis, only four are presented and are intended to illustrate a full range of scenarios. The contaminated sales need not be comparable to the subject in the typical valuation sense, but it is important that they are similar in terms of the problem. In choosing these sales, the following factors should be considered:

- Demand levels should be similar (i.e., if a property is in a particularly desirable location or has a unique, desirable zoning, buyers may be willing to accept lower stigma discounts).
- Consequences of recurrence should be similar. Even if a cure has a high degree of certainty and recurrence would be catastrophic, it will likely indicate a much higher stigma level than one in which recurrence would be less extensive.
- Sales should be recent in terms of developments and changes in market perception. If additional technology, knowledge, or exposure about the particular problem has occurred since that sale, stigma can change considerably.
- Property types should be similar as certain concerns may affect one property type much differently from others (e.g., a cracked slab in a

---

3. Peter J. Patchin, "Contaminated Properties—Stigma Revisited," *The Appraisal Journal* (April 1991): 169.

Valuing Contaminated Properties

single-family home may create a much different market reaction than one in an industrial building).

- No change in use occurred as a result of problems. When use changes, a significant part of the loss could be attributed to that change, which is an indirect result of the problem. Using these sales to derive stigma will often result in high stigma estimates.

For the purposes of this case study, assume that the four sales meet all the above criteria. Each sale is discussed as follows and summarized in Table 1.

Sale 1

This center had been built over a gas station site, which was later identified as having severe contamination. The purchase price was $1.3 million, and the buyer had spent about $250,000 in cleanup work even though he had anticipated spending only about $200,000. At the time of purchase, the buyer recognized that even extensive cleanup may not completely cure the problem because of the high water table. Portions of the property had to be vacated, which the buyer estimated cost him about $30,000. Financing was available, but about $49,000 more was paid due to the problems. The buyer indicated that additional insurance cost him about $8,000. Based on a prior, predisclosure offer, a before condition estimate is made at $2.4 million.

Because the buyer anticipated that the cure may not be completely successful, a cure level of 1 is used in the grid/matrix. Because the buyer was responsible for all the work, both entrepreneurial effort and buyer contingency apply. Stigma also applies.

Sale 2

A retail center had been built over an industrial property with contaminated soil from chemical dumping that took place years ago. The buyer purchased the property for $615,000, and the seller guaranteed $150,000 of the cleanup costs. According to engineers, this would probably accomplish a complete fix to the point that the governing agency would issue a "no further action" letter, indicating that, as far as it was concerned, the issue was closed. The buyer indicated that eventual costs were slightly higher. The financing costs were reportedly about $23,000 higher, but no additional insurance costs were incurred. A before-condition estimate is made at $860,000 based on recent sales in the area.

TABLE 1 Contamination Grid/Matrix

	Subject	Sale 1	Sale 2	Sale 3	Sale 4
Before condition	$650,000	$2,400,000	$860,000	$420,000	$1,350,000
– Sale price (after condition)	—	$1,300,000	$770,000	$380,000	$1,285,000
– Cost to remediate	$285,000	$200,000	$0	$0	$0
– Additional vacancy	$15,000	$30,000	$0	$0	$16,000
– Additional financing cost	$27,000	$49,000	$23,000	$7,000	$0
– Additional insurance cost	$6,000	$8,000	$0	$3,000	$0
= Total Category II discount	—	$813,000	$67,000	$30,000	$49,000
Category II discount (%)	—	34%	8%	7%	4%
Certainty level of fix	3	1	3	3	4
Stigma	■	■	■	■	■
Entrepreneurial effort	■	■	■	□	□
Buyer contingency	■	■	■	■	

Chapter 5: *Valuation of Defective Properties*

The buyer anticipated that the site would probably be adequately cleaned; thus, a certainty level of 3 is used in the grid/matrix. Although remediation costs were paid by the seller, the buyer contingency is appropriate as he took the risk of cost overruns. Entrepreneurial effort applies because the buyer did the work. Stigma applies.

Sale 3

This convenience store had been built on a gas station site that had contained leaking tanks. After completion of the store, test samples indicated that the contamination was still present. Sellers guaranteed up to $50,000 in cleanup and agreed to engage the contractors and monitor the work. According to the engineer, the scope of the work would probably be adequate to obtain a "no further action" letter. No vacancy loss would be experienced, but the seller indicated that the financing costs were about $7,000 higher and the insurance costs about $3,000 higher.

A certainty level of 3 is used on the grid/matrix as the work was perceived as probably being adequate. Stigma and buyer contingency apply since the buyer takes on the risk of cost overruns. Entrepreneurial effort applies partially since the buyer will not be responsible for most of the work but will be nuisanced by it. This is indicated by an empty box in the matrix.

Sale 4

This center is contaminated from a prior dry cleaners tenant, which went bankrupt. The seller, a local bank, indemnified all costs of cleanup necessary to obtain a no further action letter. At the time of the sale, the owner anticipated experiencing slightly higher vacancy as a result of the work in progress, which would take several months. Based on figures provided, additional lost rent is computed at about $16,000. The buyer stated that no additional cost of financing or insurance was experienced. The sale price was $1.285 million and a before-condition value is estimated at $1.35 million.

A certainty level of 5 is used in the grid/matrix due to the indemnification by the bank. Although the buyer did not need a contingency since all costs would be paid, some entrepreneurial effort is considered due to the hassle and possible problems. A lower level of entrepreneurial effort would be required because the buyer would not have to monitor the work but would be nuisanced by it. Stigma applies.

Case Study Conclusion

This is an as is estimate for the subject, indicating that stigma, entrepreneurial effort, and buyer contingencies all apply. Of the four comparables, Sale 2 most closely resembles the subject, with a level 3 fix and all three Category II losses applying. Sale 1 has a Category II loss of 34%, which is logically higher than the others, reflecting that the site will probably never be completely cleaned and may require monitoring costs. Sale 3 is similar to Sale 2 in that it has a certainty level of 3 and both stigma and buyer contingency apply. Entrepreneurial effort is only partially applicable as the buyer did not have to do the work. As such, it is logical that the buyer would demand a slightly lower discount compared with the subject in which all the work would be the buyer's responsibility. Sale 4 is 4% lower but had no risk of cost overruns and minor entrepreneurial effort. This sale is a logical lower limit for the subject.

Based on these sales, Category II losses are estimated at 8% of the before-condition value. Using this percentage, which equates to $52,000 ($650,000 × 8%), the subject's as is value is estimated as follows:

Before condition	$650,000
Cost to remediate	− 285,000
Additional vacancy	− 15,000
Additional financing cost	− 27,000
Additional insurance cost	− 6,000
Category II losses	− 52,000
After condition	$265,000

Additional Step

The above results in a total decrease in value of 59%. The higher the total decrease, the more plausible it becomes that some individuals will purchase the property without intentions of curing the defects (if legal). Assume in the case study that there are two sales of properties purchased with defects and with the purchaser not intending to cure the problems. Further assume that these sales indicate total discounts of 75% and 80%. This would be evidence that the highest and best use of the subject, in the after condition, is to proceed with the cure, accepting the 59% discount. If, however, non-cured sales indicate discounts lower than 59%, it is possible that the highest and best use of the subject is not to cure the defects and continue to operate the property in its defective state for the remainder of its economic life.

In this case study, which involved soil contamination, it could be argued that Category II losses should be analyzed against land value only. In cases involving asbestos or other problems of the building, it may be appropriate to analyze them on the basis of improvement value only. The method presented here is appropriate for any or all these variations. The appraiser's judgment in each situation will dictate how it is used.

Conclusion

The methodology discussed in this article provides a way for appraisers to analyze problem properties directly from the marketplace, minimizing the need to make theoretical assumptions. In a single-family home appraisal, this may be the sole method used. For income properties, an additional income approach model is typically warranted (possibly using the same comparables). This method does not represent a cure-all, nor will it apply to all problem scenarios, but it is another useful method in the appraiser's toolbox.

References

Mundy, Bill. "The Income Approach and Environmentally Impaired Property: A Response," *Environmental Watch* (Fall 1994): 2–4.

Patchin, Peter J. "Contaminated Properties and the Sales Comparison Approach," *The Appraisal Journal* (July 1994): 402–409.

Phillips, Beverly S., Peter D. Bowes, and John Reiss. "Environmental Issues and Diminution of Value: A Case Study," *Environmental Watch* (Winter 1994): 1–4.

Wilson, Albert R. "Emerging Approaches to Impaired Property Valuation, *Environmental Watch* (Summer 1994): 1–3.

Mortgage-Equity Analysis in Contaminated Property Valuation

by Thomas O. Jackson, MAI

Mortgage-equity analysis provides a framework that allows for adjustments to the key parameters necessary for estimating the effects of contamination on real property value. This framework offers a mechanism to address one of the most difficult tasks and a primary concern of appraisers in analyzing contaminated property, the quantification of risk and stigma.[1] Other contamination-related effects on property value, such as any reduction in value due to remediation costs, require the expertise of nonappraisers such as environmental engineers. Appraisers typically do not estimate these costs, but can usually measure their effect on value in a relatively straightforward manner as a capital expenditure.

Risk quantification, on the other hand, involves the complexities of measuring the perceptions of market participants. Adverse changes in these perceptions produce a stigma effect. For income-producing properties, key market participants include mortgage lenders and equity investors. Uncertainties regarding regulatory compliance requirements, the cost and duration of contamination cleanup and potential lost property income during remediation are reflected in changes in investor return requirements and loan underwriting criteria. In some cases, these uncertainties are offset by indemnifications from the party responsible for the contamination. These indemnifications, if properly structured and enforced, would hold other parties harmless from future remediation costs and other potential liabilities. It is important to note that market perceptions may or may not accurately reflect realities concerning the extent and cost of the contamination. These perceptions do, however, influence property values.

By incorporating lending and equity investment parameters, mortgage-equity analysis can be used to quantify the effect of contamination-related risk and uncertainty on commercial and industrial property values. In addition, this technique can quantify risk and property value diminution for undeveloped land through the land residual approach. In this approach, the improved property value is estimated through risk-adjusted capitalization or yield rates, which, after deducting development costs and risk-

Thomas O. Jackson, MAI, is director in the financial advisory services practice of Coopers & Lybrand, LLP, Houston, Texas, where he specializes in the valuation and analysis of contaminated properties for litigation and transactions. He is also a visiting lecturer at Texas A&M University, College Station. Mr. Jackson has previously published articles in The Appraisal Journal as well as other real estate publications. He earned an MA in regional planning from the University of North Carolina at Chapel Hill.

This article originally appeared in the January 1998 issue of The Appraisal Journal.

---

1. James A. Chalmers and Thomas O. Jackson, "Risk Factors in the Appraisal of Contaminated Property," The Appraisal Journal (January 1996): 44–57.

adjusted entrepreneurial profit, leaves a land residual value that reflects the contamination. The sales comparison approach could also be useful in analyzing risk and stigma, but most often is severely hampered by the lack of sufficient data. The cost approach is least useful, and by itself does not offer a clear vehicle for estimating contaminated property value diminution.

Market Characteristics

The recent market for contaminated property can be characterized by an emerging group of knowledgeable investors who understand the risks associated with this property type; lenders who are more willing to finance transactions involving these properties; and a more flexible regulatory environment with risk-based cleanup standards and brownfields programs.[2] The risk and return requirements of equity investors, who purchase contaminated property prior to remediation and hold it through cleanup and closure, provide benchmark information for valuing contaminated property. Lenders may make adjustments to their underwriting standards to compensate for the increased risk involved in a contaminated property, or, in some cases, may deny a loan altogether. The property value effects of the perceptions and reactions of these market participants can be quantified through mortgage-equity analysis.

Equity Investors

The perceptions and requirements of equity market participants are important determinants in developing any analysis of real estate value, and are particularly important in the quantification of risk-related effects on property value due to contamination. As noted, the recent and emerging market involving contaminated property has attracted a group of knowledgeable investors who seek out contaminated property and hold it through remediation until resale.[3] Accordingly, their investment return is dependent on the resale, or reversion, of the property after completion of the remediation. This suggests that yield capitalization, which specifically considers future changes in income and value, would be an appropriate valuation framework.

The risk factors that vary the return requirements of these investors include the completeness of the characterization of the level and extent of the contamination; the existence and strength of indemnifications provided by responsible parties against future liabilities; compliance status with respect to the appropriate state and/or federal regulations; the strength of the appropriate regulatory framework; the cost and timing of the remediation effort; and the market for the future use of the property, considering any use restrictions that may be imposed as a condition of regulatory compliance. In general, the more uncertainty, the higher the required return, the lower the value, and the greater the diminution in property value due to the contamination.

In the income capitalization approach, the increased equity return requirement, over the market return for an uncontaminated but otherwise similar property, can be measured as a risk premium adjustment to the equity yield rate. Through the mortgage-equity framework, this can be translated into changes to the overall yield rate and the overall capitalization rate.

2. Thomas O. Jackson, Mark E. Dobroski, and Trevor E. Phillips, "Analyzing Contaminated Real Estate in a Changing Market," *The Journal of Real Estate Finance* (Fall 1997): 67–72.

3. Thomas O. Jackson, "Investing in Contaminated Real Estate," *Real Estate Review* (Winter 1997): 38–41.

Chapter 5: *Mortgage-Equity Analysis*

Mortgage Lenders

Transactions involving contaminated property, like other real estate transactions, are typically leveraged in that they have a debt component. For contaminated property, and the additional risk involved, lenders may adjust their underwriting standards by reducing the loan-to-value ratio, increasing the interest rate, or shortening the amortization period. Further, and perhaps more frequently, lenders will require an increased level of personal guarantees from the borrower and/or indemnifications from the borrower or other responsible party with respect to future environmental liabilities. These reactions vary considerably by region and the specifics of the contamination and the property. The analysis of lender perceptions, therefore, should be done on a property- and location-specific basis.

Nevertheless, generalizations from surveys and experience indicate that the most likely underwriting standard to change is the loan-to-value ratio.[4] The least likely is the interest rate. Lenders may also adjust the amortization period for the loan. Overall, though, the most frequent lender reaction to the mortgageability of contaminated property is a yes/no decision, without any adjustment to the credit underwriting standards. This, of course, is equivalent to reducing the loan-to-value ratio to zero.

Brownfields

Brownfields programs target underutilized urban properties that have some environmental impairment. The remediation and return of these properties to productive use serves several public policy objectives by promoting the efficient use of downtown and other existing urban areas. In concept, the catalyst for the remediation and redevelopment of brownfields properties would be some form of incentives, such as assurances or at least regulatory streamlining, by the public sector. The incentives could reduce environmental risk, and perhaps result in a property meeting the investor return requirements. A critical point with respect to this currently popular initiative is that the local real estate market must be capable of supporting the end use of the remediated property. The brownfields incentives, although important, would be ineffective without sufficient underlying market demand for the redevelopment use.

Measuring Value Diminution

As explained above, reductions in property value due to contamination are a function of the market's perception of the additional risks involved in a contaminated property that would not be present in an uncontaminated but otherwise similar property. The key sets of market participants are equity investors, lenders, and users. The contamination-related risks may be reflected in increased equity investor return requirements, changes in lenders' underwriting criteria, and reduced income due to lowered occupancies or rents that may result from the concerns of tenants or other property users. The framework presented here focuses on investors and lenders.

Investor and lender risk adjustments can be reflected in corresponding changes in income and yield capitalization rates. The disaggregation of capitalization rates into mortgage and equity components allows for adjustments in the key mortgage and equity parameters that reflect the increased risk from contamination perceived by these market participants.

4. Patricia R. Healy and John J. Healy, Jr., "Lenders' Perspectives on Environmental Issues," *The Appraisal Journal* (July 1992): 394–398.

Valuing Contaminated Properties

As capitalization rates are adjusted upward to reflect this increased risk, property value decreases. Investors will pay less for the same cash flow in order to achieve a higher return, or yield, and lenders will seek a more secure position through credit underwriting adjustments, thereby increasing the cost of capital, and reducing property value.

In adjusting the mortgage-equity parameters to reflect the increased risks associated with the contamination, environmental factors must be reviewed on a property-specific basis. As noted, these factors include the level of characterization of the contamination; the regulatory status of the site, cost, and length of the remediation effort; approvals and financing of the remediation plan; effects on the use of the property during remediation; the availability of indemnifications by financially sound responsible parties; and any post closure property use restrictions. Once this information has been assembled and reviewed, the mortgage and equity adjustments can be determined either through comparative sales/case studies or through surveys of investors and lenders.

If sales/case studies are used, they must be carefully analyzed for comparability to the subject on each of the relevant environmental risk factors. In addition, the sales of contaminated property must be matched against another set of sales of similar but uncontaminated property in order to extract market-based risk adjustments. In the second method, lenders and investors are surveyed as to their investment and lending criteria applicable to the property as if uncontaminated. After a review of the relevant environmental risk factors and remediation assumptions, they are asked about any changes to these criteria as a result of the contamination. The differences in the two sets of survey responses provide the adjustments necessary for the mortgage-equity analysis.

Estimating Value Diminution Through the Ellwood Procedure

Mortgage-equity analysis has traditionally been accomplished through the Ellwood procedure, a technique originally developed by L. W. Ellwood.[5] The Ellwood technique estimates the overall capitalization rate (R_O) on the basis of assumptions concerning mortgage and equity requirements, including the required equity yield (Y_e); total change in income (D_i) and value (D_O) over the holding period; and the anticipated pattern of income change—constant ratio (compound annual growth), J-factor change, or straight-line change. Real estate investor surveys indicate that the most typical expectation is for changes in income to occur at a compound annual growth rate. This pattern would be reflected in the constant ratio assumption and the K-factor adjustment in the Ellwood framework.

Table 1 presents a mortgage-equity analysis of a hypothetical property with and without the effects of contamination. The resulting difference in the final property value estimates indicate the value diminution resulting from the contamination. The uncontaminated, or baseline, assumptions in this analysis include a 2% annual increase in income and value, a 9% mortgage interest rate (Y_m), a 70% loan-to-value ratio $(LTVR)$, a 20-year loan amortization period, and a Y_e of 17% over a 10-year holding period. This analysis produces four estimates of R_O. Excluding the level income assumption, they range from 10.14% to 10.19%. Applying the R_O estimated with the constant ratio income pattern of 10.17% to the property's net operating income (NOI) of $600,000 produces an esti-

---

5. Appraisal Institute, *The Appraisal of Real Estate*, 11th ed. (Chicago, Illinois: Appraisal Institute, 1996): 748–762.

Chapter 5: *Mortgage-Equity Analysis*

TABLE 1 Property Value Diminution Analysis Through Ellwood Procedure

General Mortgage-Equity Formula:

$$R_0 = \frac{Y_e - M(Y_e + P\,1/SFF - R_m) - D_0\,1/SFF}{1 + D_i\,J \text{ or } K\text{-factor}}$$

As if uncontaminated		With contamination	
Mortgage:			
M or $LTVR$	0.7000	Mortgage or loan-to-value ratio	0.5000
Y_m	9.00%	Mortgage interest rate	9.00%
Amortization period:	20	Years	20
Equity:			
Y_e	17.00%	Equity yield rate	22.00%
Additional inputs:			
D_0	0.2190	Change in value during period	0.5750
D_i	0.2190	Change in income during period	0.2190
Projection period:	10	Years	10
Interim calculations:			
P	0.296968	Percent paid off during period	0.296968
SFF	0.044657	Sinking fund factor at Y_e	0.034895
R_m	0.109546	Mortgage constant	0.109546
J	0.3012	J-factor, Ellwood premise	0.2457
J	0.3255	J-factor, straight-line premise	0.2959
K	1.0681	K-factor	1.0618

Overall capitalization rate (R_0) by income pattern

Pattern	Adjustment factors	Estimated R_0	Adjustment factors	Estimated R_0
Level income	n/a	10.86%	n/a	13.95%
Constant-ratio	1.0681	10.17%	1.0618	13.14%
Ellwood	0.3012	10.19%	0.2457	13.24%
Straight-line	0.3255	10.14%	0.2959	13.10%

Value estimates

Net operating income (NOI)	$600,000		$6,000
Overall capitalization rate (R_0)	10.17%		13.14%
Value as if uncontaminated (V_0)	$5,900,249		
Value with contamination (V_c)			$4,565,957
Property value diminution (PVD)			**$1,334,292**

Note: Mortgage parameters calculated on an annual payment basis.

mated value, without the effects of contamination (V_0), of $5.9 million. This is also referred to as the unimpaired value, and establishes a baseline from which to estimate property value diminution (PVD).

As noted, Table 1 also presents an analysis in which the lending and investing criteria have been adjusted to reflect increased contamination risks. In this analysis, the equity investment criteria have been adjusted to reflect an increase in Y_e of 500 basis points, and the mortgage component has been adjusted to reflect a decrease in the $LTVR$ from 70% to 50%. In this example, value increases more rapidly than income due to the reduction in risk following remediation. As can be seen, these risk adjustments result in an R_0 range of 13.10%–13.24%, excluding the level income assumption, which will be reconciled at 13.14%, consistent with the constant-ratio income pattern. Applying this adjusted R_0 to the property's NOI of $600,000, which is assumed to be unaffected by the contamination, results in an estimated impaired value (V_c) of $4.6 million. This equates to a PVD of $1.3 million, or 29% of the unimpaired value.

Valuing Contaminated Properties

Estimating Value Diminution Through the Discounted Cash Flow Procedure

The Ellwood procedure has been criticized as too complex, requiring many difficult calculations, and as being limited in that only a few prescribed income patterns can be accommodated.[6] Ellwood's critics note that his formula and tables were developed before the inexpensive computers and software that now make discounted cash flow (DCF) techniques easier.[7] However, most DCF analyses are not primarily concerned with estimating value on the basis of mortgage and equity interests, and adapting them for mortgage-equity analysis significantly increases their complexity. The real advantage of DCF analysis over Ellwood is greater accuracy when there is an anticipation of an irregular income stream over the holding period, such as an increasing NOI followed by a decrease.

Table 2 presents a mortgage-equity analysis through a DCF procedure that is comparable to, and based on the same assumptions as, the Ellwood analysis in Table 1.[8] This DCF model discounts the property NOI by Y_e and adjusts for annual debt service and loan repayment at the end of the holding period through the use of R_m and percent of the loan paid during the period (P), also factors in the Ellwood formula. Reversion is based on the aggregate change in value (D_O), assumed to change proportionate to the aggregate change in income over the period. As with the previous illustration, this change equals 21.9%. As can be seen, the resulting un-

6. Wayne Kelly, Donald R. Epley, and Phillip Mitchell, "A Requiem for Ellwood," *The Appraisal Journal* (July 1995): 284–290.

7. The analyses in Table 1 are from a spreadsheet model, with the interim calculations based on the equations in the addenda to *The Appraisal of Real Estate*, 11th ed., and in Charles B. Akerson, *Capitalization Theory and Techniques* (Chicago, Illinois: American Institute of Real Estate Appraisers, 1984): 153–156.

8. This DCF procedure is similar to the illustration presented in Wayne Kelly, Donald R. Epley, and Phillip Mitchell, "A Requiem for Ellwood," *The Appraisal Journal* (July 1995): 288.

TABLE 2 Baseline (As If Uncontaminated) DCF Analysis

Year	Cash Flow (NOI)	Debt Service Adjustment (see below)	Present Value Factor @ Y_e	PV of Debt Service Adjusted @ Y_e	PV of NOI @ Y_e	Cash Flow (NOI and Reversion)	Present Value @ Y_o	PV of Cash Flow @ Y_o
1	$600,000	0.076683	0.8547	0.065541	$512,821	$600,000	0.8915	$534,907
2	$612,000	0.076683	0.7305	0.056018	$447,074	$612,000	0.7948	$486,413
3	$624,240	0.076683	0.6244	0.047878	$389,757	$624,240	0.7086	$442,315
4	$636,725	0.076683	0.5337	0.040922	$339,788	$636,725	0.6317	$402,215
5	$649,459	0.076683	0.4561	0.034976	$296,226	$649,459	0.5632	$365,751
6	$662,448	0.076683	0.3898	0.029894	$258,248	$662,448	0.5021	$332,592
7	$675,697	0.076683	0.3332	0.025550	$225,139	$675,697	0.4476	$302,440
8	$689,211	0.076683	0.2848	0.021838	$196,275	$689,211	0.3990	$275,021
9	$702,996	0.076683	0.2434	0.018665	$171,112	$702,996	0.3557	$250,088
10	$717,056	0.076683	0.2080	0.015953	$149,174	$717,056	0.3172	$227,415
11	$731,397							

Property reversion: $7,192,370   0.3172 $2,281,070

Equity reversion: −0.726872   0.2080   −0.15217

Change (D_O): 0.2190

Sum: 0.206017 $2,985,614

Value as if uncontaminated (V_O): $5,900,226   Value ($V_O$): $5,900,226

$$V_O = \frac{\text{Sum of } PV \text{ of } CF @ Y_e}{(1=M) + (\text{Sum of } PV \text{ of } DS \text{ adjusted } @ Y_e)}$$

Equity yield rate (Y_e): 17.00%   Overall yield rate (Y_o): 12.17%

Mortgage interest rate (Y_m): 9.00%   Going-in cap rate (R_o) (from Ellwood model): 10.17%

Mortgage constant (R_m): 0.109546

Terminal cap rate (R_t) (applied to year 11 NOI): 10.17%

Percent paid off during period (P): 0.296968

Mortgage ratio (M or $LTVR$): 0.7000

Debt service adjustment calculations:

    for equity cash flow DS adjustment = $(M \times R_m)$

    for equity reversion DS adjustment = $-((1 + D_O) - (M \times (1 - P)))$

Note: Income growth at 2% per year.

Chapter 5: *Mortgage-Equity Analysis*

impaired property value of $5,900,226 is nearly identical to that produced by the Ellwood model, with minor rounding errors.

The information in Table 2 can also be used to estimate an equivalent Y_O through an internal rate of return (*IRR*) routine. This is calculated at 12.17%. Reversion in this context is estimated by capitalizing the year 11 *NOI* by the 10.17% capitalization rate estimated through the Ellwood model. This assumes that the going-in and terminal rates are the same. Accordingly, the property cash flow (equity and reversion) is discounted at Y_O in the right side of Table 2 to produce an identical estimate of the unimpaired value (V_O) at $5.9 million.

Table 3 presents a corresponding DCF analysis of the same property with the equity and mortgage contamination risk adjustments. As with the previous examples, the analysis reflects two adjustments: an increase in the Y_e of 500 basis points, or from 17% to 22%; and a decrease in the *LTVR* from 70% to 50%. The *PVD* effect is to decrease value from $5.9 to $4.6 million, or by 29%. This was the same result produced by the Ellwood model. This similarity is due to the income and value growth assumptions. Income growth is based on a 2% compound annual growth rate in the DCF model, and is reflected in the Ellwood model through the constant-ratio (*K*-factor) adjustment. The 57.5% increase in value used in both models reflects the application of the unadjusted R_O of 10.17% to

TABLE 3   Property Value Diminution Analysis Through DCF Procedure

Year	Cash Flow (*NOI*)	Debt Service Adjustment (see below)	Present Value Factor @ Y_e	PV of Debt Service Adjusted @ Y_e	PV of *NOI* @ Y_e	Cash Flow (*NOI* and Reversion)	Present Value @ Y_O	PV of Cash Flow @ Y_O
1	$600,000	0.054773	0.8197	0.044896	$491,803	$600,000	0.8572	$514,338
2	$612,000	0.054773	0.6719	0.036800	$411,180	$612,000	0.7348	$449,724
3	$624,240	0.054773	0.5507	0.030164	$343,773	$624,240	0.6299	$393,227
4	$636,725	0.054773	0.4514	0.024725	$287,417	$636,725	0.5400	$343,828
5	$649,459	0.054773	0.3700	0.020266	$240,299	$649,459	0.4629	$300,634
6	$662,448	0.054773	0.3033	0.016612	$200,906	$662,448	0.3968	$262,867
7	$675,697	0.054773	0.2486	0.013616	$167,971	$675,697	0.3402	$229,844
8	$689,211	0.054773	0.2038	0.011161	$140,434	$689,211	0.2916	$200,970
9	$702,996	0.054773	0.1670	0.009148	$117,412	$702,996	0.2500	$175,723
10	$717,056	0.054773	0.1369	0.007498	$98,165	$717,056	0.2143	$153,647
11	$731,397							
Property reversion:						$7,192,370	0.2143	$1,541,149
Equity reversion :		−1.223484	0.1369	−0.167494				
Change (D_O):		0.5750						
Sum:				0.047391	$2,499,361			
Value with contamination (V_O):					$4,565,950	Value (V_O):		$4,565,950

Value (V_O) $= \dfrac{\text{Sum of } PV \text{ of } CF @ Y_e}{(1 - M) + (\text{Sum of } PV \text{ of } DS \text{ adjusted } @ Y_e)}$

Equity yield rate (Y_e):   22.00%

Mortgage interest rate (Y_m):   9.00%

Mortgage constant (R_m):   0.109546
Percent paid off during period (*P*):   0.296968
Mortgage ratio (*M* or *LTVR*):   0.5000
Debt service adjustment calculations:
  for equity cash flow *DS* adjustment $= (M \times R_m)$
  for equity reversion *DS* adjustment $= -((1 + D_O) - (M \times (1 - P)))$

Overall yield rate (Y_O):   16.65%
Going-in cap rate (R_O) (from Ellwood model):   13.15%
Terminal cap rate (R_t) (applied to year 11 *NOI*):   10.17%

Value (V_O): $5,900,226
Value (V_c): $4,565,950

Property value diminution: $1,334,276

Note: Income growth at 2% per year

Valuing Contaminated Properties

the year 11 *NOI* for reversion. The DCF analyses in Tables 2 and 3 also show the corresponding increase in the overall yield rate (Y_O), from 12.17% to 16.65%, reflect the contamination risk adjustments.

Value Diminution Relationships

The foregoing conceptual and methodological framework can be used to illustrate more generalized relationships between contamination-related risk adjustments and *PVD*. As explained, the contamination-related loss in property value is a function of the risks perceived by market participants. These risk perceptions may result in a higher equity yield rate, more conservative credit underwriting, or both. More conservative credit underwriting could be through a lowered *LTVR*, shorter amortization period, increased interest rate, or loan denial.

The generalized effect of adjusting equity return requirements on value diminution is illustrated in Figure 1. This figure is based on the unimpaired mortgage and equity parameters for the hypothetical property presented in Tables 1, 2, and 3. Figure 1 shows the increase in *PVD*, measured as a percentage and in dollars, corresponding to increases in the equity yield requirement, as reflected in the equity risk premium over the unimpaired Y_e of 17%. For example, a 300-basis point risk adjustment to Y_e, indicating an adjusted Y_e of 20%, corresponds to a 7.2% reduction in the property's unimpaired value. The upper end of the risk range, with a 1,000-basis point adjustment, produces a value diminution of over 20%.

Figure 2 depicts the relationship between the most frequently adjusted mortgage parameter, the *LTVR*, and *PVD*, again measured as a percentage and in dollars. The figure shows the decline in *PVD* as the *LTVR* approaches the assumed market level, applicable to a similar but uncontaminated property, of 70%. At the other end of the scale, the *LTVR* of 0% corresponds to the denial of a loan on the property due to the risk associated with the contamination. This total lack of mortgageability results in a *PVD* of nearly 25%. Value diminution would be independent of any additional reductions due to increased equity yield requirements.

Figures 3 and 4 depict the effects of the same range of equity and mortgage risk adjustments on R_O, and again on *PVD*. The overall capitalization rate is a key measure of risk and return in real estate valuation, and is

FIGURE 1 Effect of Equity Risk Premiums on Property Value Diminution

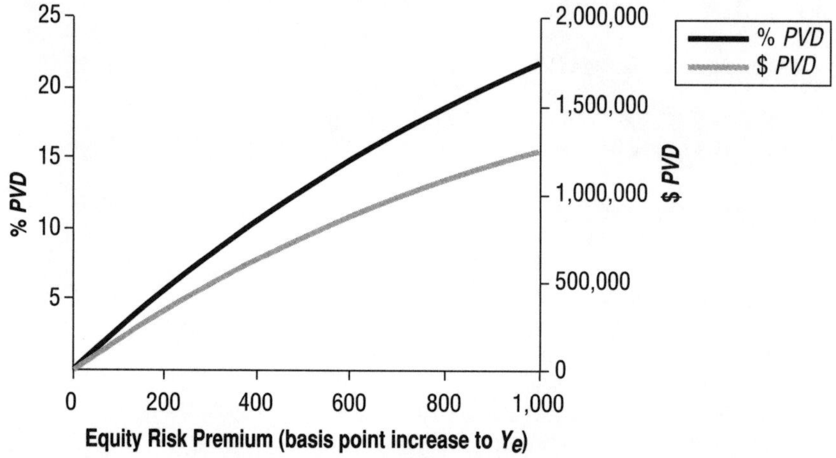

Note: *PVD* relative to unimpaired value of $5.9 million

Chapter 5: *Mortgage-Equity Analysis*

FIGURE 2 Effect of Loan-to-Value Ratio Adjustments on Property Value Diminution

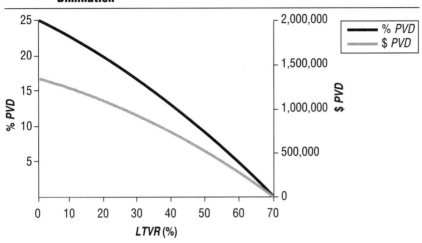

Note: *PVD* relative to unimpaired value of $5.9 million

FIGURE 3 Effect of Equity Risk Premiums on Property Value Diminution and Overall Capitalization Rate

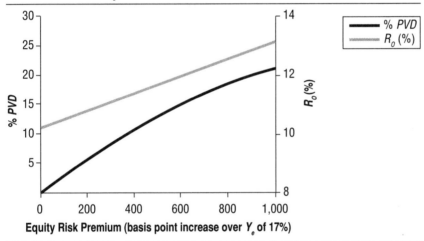

Note: *PVD* relative to unimpaired value of $5.9 million

FIGURE 4 Effect of Loan-to-Value Ratio Adjustments on Property Value Diminution and Overall Capitalization Rate

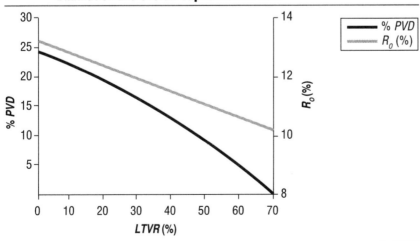

Note: *PVD* relative to unimpaired value of $5.9 million

a commonly used gauge of market expectations and perceptions with respect to a property or property class. As was shown in Table 1, the unimpaired R_O, reflecting the base level of risk and return for the property without any contamination-related effects, was 10.17%. The market's perception of the contamination-related risk effects, resulting in increases in the required equity yield and in reductions in the *LTVR*, is ultimately reflected in corresponding increases in the applicable R_O at each successive risk level. In Figure 3, the upper end of the range of equity risk premiums, at a 1,000-basis point increase to Y_e, corresponds to an adjusted R_O of approximately 13% and a *PVD* of over 20%. Figure 4 shows that the loss of financing, with an *LTVR* of 0%, corresponds to a *PVD* of nearly 25%.

The information in Figures 1 through 4 depicts the effect of *PVD* from changes in either Y_e or the *LTVR* independently. In seriously contaminated properties, both the mortgage and equity parameters will be adjusted. The examples in Tables 1 and 3 had adjustments to both sets of parameters. Figure 5 visually depicts the combined effect of adjusting Y_e and the *LTVR* simultaneously. The analysis in this figure is again based on the hypothetical property and its specific characteristics that have been analyzed heretofore. The reader is cautioned that the results displayed in the tables and figures in this article would vary, depending on the particular characteristics of the property under study.

Accordingly, Figure 5 shows the *PVD* effects of varying the *LTVR* from 70% to 0%, while at the same time varying the equity risk premium from 0 to 1,000 basis points, equating to a Y_e from 17% to 27%. These ranges of contamination risk adjustments result in a reduction in property value of over 50%. This maximum *PVD* corresponds to a Y_e of 27% and the

FIGURE 5 Effects of Equity Risk Premiums and Loan-to-Value Ratio Adjustments on Property Value Diminution

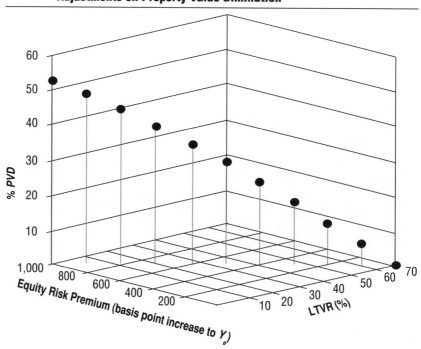

Chapter 5: *Mortgage-Equity Analysis*

loss of financing altogether. A set of adjustments in the middle of the ranges for the two variables: a risk premium of 400 to 600 basis points and an *LTVR* of 30% to 40%, resulting in a *PVD* of nearly 30%. (This can be determined by following a horizontal line from the data point to the *y*-axis.)

Conclusion

Investors, lenders, and the courts are more frequently asking appraisers to analyze the effects of environmental contamination on property value. This is due, in part, to the changing nature of the market for contaminated properties, with increased investor interest, greater availability of financing, and a more flexible regulatory environment. It is also due to the significant amount of litigation involving the market effects of contamination on property value. The key question in approaching this type of analysis is how to measure the unique risks associated with this property type.

These risks are reflected in the reactions and perceptions of key market participants. The analyses presented herein focused on two sets of key participants: equity investors and mortgage lenders. In this context, an old technique known as mortgage-equity analysis provides a powerful and entirely appropriate framework. This technique, pioneered by Ellwood, provides a vehicle for adjusting the key valuation parameters to reflect the perceptions and requirements of market participants more accurately, and measure the effect of contamination-related risk on real estate value.

Appropriate risk adjustments, derived through surveys of investors and lenders with respect to the environmental history of the property under study or through extraction from sales of comparable contaminated properties, are input into the mortgage-equity model. This results in an adjusted set of income and yield capitalization rates, which reflect the contamination-related risks, and can be used to estimate the value of the property and its value diminution from an unimpaired baseline condition.

This approach was illustrated through two mortgage-equity procedures. The first technique, referred to as the Ellwood procedure, estimates the overall capitalization rate on the basis of assumptions concerning income and value growth, equity yield requirements, and financing parameters. The Ellwood model can accurately estimate appropriate capitalization rates in most circumstances, except when the anticipated income pattern over the holding period is irregular. In these cases, DCF analysis, if properly modified, can be used to measure value diminution.

Toward this end, a modified DCF model, incorporating many of the same elements of the Ellwood technique, was presented. These modifications to the DCF framework allow for the same mortgage and equity adjustments as Ellwood, without any limitations on the income patterns that can be accommodated. The application of this DCF model in valuing contaminated property was then demonstrated, with results nearly identical to those produced by Ellwood. Lastly, the graphics show generalized relationships between the mortgage and equity risk adjustments and corresponding *PVD* effects.

Adjusting Environmental Case Study Comparables by Using an Environmental Risk Scoring System

by Richard J. Roddewig, MAI

Richard J. Roddewig, MAI, is president of Clarion Associates, with offices in Chicago, Denver, Philadelphia, and Cincinnati. He co-developed the Appraisal Institute's seminar, "Environmental Risk and the Real Estate Appraisal Process," and has taught the seminar nationwide. He is a regular contributor to The Appraisal Journal on environmental issues and is an adjunct lecturer on real estate valuation in the finance department at DePaul University, Chicago.

This article originally appeared in the October 2000 issue of The Appraisal Journal.

1. See, for example, Richard J. Roddewig, MAI, "Classifying the Level of Risk and Stigma Affecting Contaminated Property," The Appraisal Journal (January 1999): 98–99; and Richard J. Roddewig, MAI, "Choosing the Right Analytical Tool for the Job," The Appraisal Journal (July 1998): 324.

2. Ibid., 324.

3. True uncontaminated "comparables" as traditionally defined are used to estimate the market value of the appraised property disregarding contamination. To then arrive at the market value considering the contamination situation and accompanying environmental risks, if any, "adjustments" are made to the value disregarding contamination and risks. Adjustments to the uncontaminated comparables may be necessary for such items as remaining costs of environmental investigation and remediation, insurance or other administrative or legal costs, or for stigma.

Comparables, Case Studies, and Stigma Adjustment Factors

As frequently mentioned in this column over the past few years, environmental risk/stigma is typically estimated based upon case studies of other properties affected by environmental risk.[1,2] The case study is not a "comparable" in the way we as appraisers typically think of comparables. It is not intended, for example, to provide an indication of price per square foot or price per acre that can then be applied (after adjustments) to the area of the property being appraised. Instead, the case study becomes the source of the "adjustment factor" for stigma that we apply to the market value of the appraised property, disregarding contamination[3] to estimate the market value of the property when considering the environmental contamination and associated risks affecting it.

But how do we as appraisers, based on the case study information, arrive at the appropriate stigma adjustment factor for the property being appraised? We typically use a three-step process. First, we investigate the case study situation to determine the market-based stigma affecting the case study property. Second, we analyze the sources and causes of the stigma affecting the case study property. Third, we analyze the property being appraised to determine if the same sources of stigma are present in the market situation in question. This is done by comparing and contrasting the case study and the property being appraised to determine the appropriate stigma adjustment factor to apply to the market value, disregarding contamination and environmental risks.

Using Rating or Scoring Systems to Compare Risk/Stigma

An earlier *Environment and the Appraiser* column suggested evaluating various types of environmental risks according to a low, medium, or high rating system to compare the risks associated with the case studies to those risks associated with the property appraised. The same article mentioned that many institutional real estate investors have developed "standardized due diligence checklists and evaluation forms that allow them to analyze

Chapter 5: *Adjusting Environmental Case Study Comparables*

the environmental risks on properties and portfolios." Some have even been "heading toward a numerical scoring or rating system for environmental risks."[4]

While evaluating environmental risk/stigma as low, medium, or high may be enough in many, if not most, situations to arrive at an appropriate stigma conclusion, there may be times when more precision is necessary. Using a risk/stigma scoring system can provide that additional precision. It allows the appraiser to evaluate case studies more thoroughly, comparing one against another and against the risks/stigma involved in purchasing or owning the property being appraised. Using a scoring system may allow an appraiser to select a specific numerical stigma percentage with more confidence. It may also allow the appraiser to give more or less weight to some risk factors by comparing them to other risk factors. In a marketplace constantly dealing with risks, risk/stigma factors can change over time and be more or less significant depending upon a variety of property-specific and market-specific factors.

Elements of an Appropriate Scoring System

A proper scoring system has three essential characteristics:

- First, it contains a list of the potential sources and causes of risk/stigma;
- Second, it specifies a score—assigns points—to be applied when considering each of the potential sources of risk/stigma; and
- Third, it is applied consistently from one case study to the next case study being evaluated.

There are a wide variety of possible scoring system models, and appraisers have considerable flexibility to devise one that works best for them. The key to making such a system effective is to devise one that considers all of the potential sources of stigma, and then applies the scoring system consistently when evaluating case studies and the property being appraised.

Using a Scoring System: A Hypothetical Example

Consider the following hypothetical situation to understand how a numerical scoring system can be of significant help.

> Hydrocarbon contamination from leaking underground storage tanks (removed three years earlier) on a vacant site being appraised has already been remediated to the extent required by a state environmental protection agency as part of a state-approved remedial action plan. However, the state requires that on-site monitoring wells must remain in place on 50% of the site until groundwater quality levels reach a specified level. Precisely when that will occur is not clear, but given present trends from most recent sampling, groundwater quality will reach acceptable levels in the next three to five years. The past property owner has accepted responsibility for all ongoing monitoring and sampling costs, and has provided an indemnity against additional remediation costs for all future owners. The state has an established program that is working well and will provide a "no further action" letter to potential purchasers.

You investigate ten other contaminated property sales and conclude the one you are appraising is most like the three that show a stigma adjustment factor in the marketplace between 5% and 12%, a relatively low

4. Richard J. Roddewig, MAI, "Classifying the Level of Risk and Stigma Affecting Contaminated Property," *The Appraisal Journal* (January 1999): 99.

Valuing Contaminated Properties

level of risk/stigma. What do you do? Provide a range in market value considering the risk/stigma situation that is 5% to 12% lower than the market value disregarding the environmental situation? Select the midpoint of the range? Subjectively analyze the three most significant case studies and decide which one should be given the most weight?

If the purpose of the assignment and the use to which the appraisal will be applied require more precision than a range in value, you may prefer to compare and contrast the three case studies to your property's situation and arrive at a specific percentage stigma adjustment factor and conclusion. A scoring system may help you achieve that goal.

Assume that the scoring system you use classifies risk/stigma as either low, medium, or high and within each classification assigns the following numerical scores: from 0 to 3 for a low level of risk; from 4 to 6 for a medium level of risk; and from 7 to 9 for a high level of risk. For example, a score of 4 (the medium category) for the risk of additional administrative costs means that for that particular item, this property is at the low end of the medium range for stigma/risk.

Total scores in the low stigma range would be between 0 and 33 points, in the medium range between 44 and 66 points, and in the high stigma range would be between 77 and 99 points. Potential scores and stigma percentage ranges are classified as follows:

Low Stigma

Total Point Range	0 to 33 points
Indicated Stigma Level	0 to 15%

Medium Stigma

Total Point Range	44 to 66 points
Indicated Stigma Level	15% to 40%

High Stigma

Total Point Range	77 to 99 points
Indicated Stigma Level	40% to 100%

Your analysis of the case studies indicates that they sold at prices between 5% and 12% less than their price/value regardless of their environmental situation. By separately analyzing the risk/stigma characteristics of each case study and assigning a risk/stigma score to each source and cause, you are then in a position to compare the case studies to each other and to the property you are appraising.

Your analysis results in the following stigma/risk score sheet (Table 1).

As shown in the score sheet, you have concluded that the appropriate stigma adjustment to apply to the market value of the property appraised is 6%.

Note that in the above scoring system, each source and cause is given equal weight. It may be that your experience with contaminated or remediated properties indicates that one or more of the sources and causes of potential stigma is given more or less weight by buyers in the marketplace than other sources and causes. In that case, it may be necessary when comparing the scores to also consider the relative weight that should be given to each case study based upon the weight the buyer places on its sources and causes of stigma. Alternatively, it may be possible to assign more points to those sources and causes that are given more weight by buyers in the marketplace.

Chapter 5: *Adjusting Environmental Case Study Comparables*

TABLE 1 Sample Stigma/Risk Score Sheet

Risk/Stigma Source/Cause	Case Study 1			Case Study 2			Case Study 3			Subject Property		
	Lo	Med	Hi	Lo	Med	Hi	Lo	Med	Hi	Lo	Med	Hi
Additional site investigation costs	1			2			2			2		
Additional remediation costs	0			2			2			0		
Additional environmental monitoring costs	1			2			1			1		
Additional legal/administrative costs	0			1				4		2		
Inconvenience during investigation/remediation	1			2				4			4	
Adverse change in regulations	1			0			0			0		
Higher vacancy or lower rents from tenants	0			2			1			0		
Difficulty in obtaining mortgage financing	2			1			3			1		
Third party claims or additional insurance costs	1			3				4		1		
Additional future marketing costs to resell	1			2			2			1		
Additional marketing time to resell in future	1			2			3			1		
Total points		9			19			26			13	
Market stigma factor		5%			8%			12%			6%	

The dates of sale of each of the case study properties compared to the date of valuation for the subject property may also be important. If each of the case study properties (and the subject property) has been assigned a risk/stigma score as of its particular date of sale, and the marketplace has generally shown more comfort with buying, selling, and financing properties affected by environmental risk since the date of the particular case study sale, then the range of indicated stigma factors from the case studies may also have to be lowered to reflect changes in market conditions since their dates of sale.

Conclusion

Over the past 15 years, the appraisal profession has made great strides in its ability to understand and analyze the impact of environmental risks on market value. Utilization of case studies has become an accepted technique for deriving a "stigma adjustment factor" to apply to market value regardless of environmental risk factors.

However, the analytical tools necessary to assist us in properly evaluating risk/stigma case studies are continuously evolving. A risk/stigma score sheet can be a helpful tool, as long as it includes all of the sources and causes of stigma, and is consistently applied by each appraiser using the technique. The score sheet can be applied to each case study analyzed as well as to the subject property, or, if you prefer, to one or more case studies, or only to the property appraised.

At this time, there is no universally accepted scoring system, nor does there necessarily need to be one common model. The score sheet simply provides a systematic and consistent process for arriving at an appropriate and supportable stigma adjustment factor. As long as the case study data is reliable information derived from the marketplace is accurately reported, properly investigated, and appropriately confirmed, the appraiser can apply any one of many tools. The score sheet is the only possible tool for comparing and adjusting the market-derived stigma indicators to the appraisal situation at hand.

The Analysis of Environmental Case Studies

by Thomas Jackson, PhD, MAI, and Randall Bell, MAI

Thomas O. Jackson, PhD, MAI, CRE, AICP, *is the president of Real Property Analytics, Inc. in Bryan, Texas, where he specializes in the analysis of real property damages due to environmental contamination and other sources. In addition, he teaches real property valuation in the land economics and real estate program of the Lowry Mays College & Graduate School of Business at Texas A&M University, and is a member of the Appraisal Standards Board of The Appraisal Foundation.* Contact: (979) 823-5243; email: tomjackson@real-analytics.com.

Randall Bell, MAI, *is an applied economist specializing in real estate damage valuation. He is the author of the Appraisal Institute's textbook* Real Estate Damages *as well as the Detrimental Conditions and Real Estate Disclosure seminars, which he frequently instructs. He is also on the Advisory Board of the Bureau of National Affairs. Mr. Bell has an MBA Degree from UCLA and is the CEO of Bell Anderson & Sanders LLC in Laguna Beach, California.* Contact: (949) 497-7600; email: Bell@RealEstateDamages.com.

This article originally appeared in the January 2002 issue of The Appraisal Journal.

Determining the impacts of environmental contamination on property value requires real estate analysts to address a number of factors and elements not considered in the more typical sales comparison analysis of non-impacted or unimpaired properties. These factors may be considered or analyzed using case studies.

The first step in a case study analysis involves research into the subject property and a determination of the key factors that impact that property. Then, in an effort to determine any effect on value, case studies are developed from other properties that are similarly situated with respect to the subject property and its environmental condition. Like any valuation technique, case study analysis can be properly applied or it can be misused. In order for the analysis to be reliable and valid, the case studies must follow the simple "apples to apples" analogy. This means that the case studies being utilized must have similar property, market, *and* environmental characteristics to the subject property. Because of the complexity of topics surrounding environmental contamination, these characteristics are not always straightforward. Therefore, their applicability must be carefully examined.

Appraisal methodologies ultimately fall within one of the three traditional approaches to valuation: the cost approach, the sales comparison approach, and the income capitalization approach. Case study analysis involves situations where similar properties have been impacted by similar conditions. Thus, the analysis of case studies is an extension of the sales comparison approach. However, in addition to the typical elements of comparison such as property type and location, valid and reliable environmental case studies must consider additional elements and property characteristics. These elements are outlined in the following pages. Like any application of the sales comparison approach, it is difficult, and in some situations impossible, to find comparables that are identical in all respects to the subject property. Nonetheless, certain key characteristics should be similar for resulting inferences and conclusions to be reliable, valid, and not misleading.

Chapter 5: *Analysis of Environmental Case Studies*

Generally, case studies are utilized when there is a lack of direct market data or where analyses of direct market data need additional support. For example, if the impact of a landfill on surrounding properties were being studied, the most pertinent approach would involve actual sales of the surrounding properties. In the event that no direct market data is available, the case studies approach utilizing market data derived of other landfill-proximate sales would become relevant. Although case studies are useful any time there is available and relevant data, they have a secondary role if there is direct market data available at the subject site. Of course, like any assignment involving appraisal practice, the *Uniform Standards of Professional Appraisal Practice* (USPAP) have an essential role to play in the analysis of case studies. A properly developed case study analysis must comply with applicable USPAP standards addressing competency, ethics, and and reporting of assignment results.

Case Study Framework

An environmental case study must take into consideration property characteristics, contamination/discharge issues, and remediation lifecycle/detrimental condition stages if the study is to provide a meaningful comparison to the subject property. These characteristics, as well as other significant factors, are shown in Table 1 and are discussed in detail in the remainder of this article.

Like a market data grid in the sales comparison approach, a case study comparison chart organizes and compares the characteristics or elements of the case study to the subject property. As in any type of sales comparison analysis, the subject property and case studies should ideally be similar in all respects. However, in reality this does not always occur. Problems arise if a significant number of issues differ substantially from the subject property conditions, then a question may arise as to whether the case study is really comparable at all. For example, case studies involving accidental discharges are not comparable to situations where the discharge was legally permitted. Further, a source site case study may not be comparable to a non-source site subject property, except to establish an upward limit of damage. For example, if a source site case study indicates no stigma or market resistance, then it is unlikely that non-source sites would have such damage. On the other hand, using an impacted source site case study to estimate impacts for a non-source site may be misleading, since identifiable impacts derived from source site case studies usually overestimate impacts to non-source subject properties. Remediation, as explained in the following pages, should also match. After selecting an appropriate set of case studies, a relative comparison analysis can be performed, leading to a net comparison ranking for each case study relative to the subject.[1]

The example in Table 1 includes case studies that match on the permitted/accidental discharge elements of comparison. While the subject property is industrial, the case studies include both commercial and industrial properties. Residential properties would not be comparable for purposes of this environmental case study analysis. In calculating the impact on value for each of the case studies, a series of paired sales analyses could be used. In this approach, otherwise similar unimpaired comparables in the market areas of the case studies would be matched to the impaired properties and impact on sales price would be estimated. Before calculating

1. Appraisal Institute, *The Appraisal of Real Estate*, 12th ed. (Chicago: Appraisal Institute, 2001): 459–467.

TABLE 1 Case Study Comparison Chart

	Subject Property	Case Study A	Case Study B	Case Study C	Case Study D	Case Study E	Case Study F	Case Study G
Property characteristics								
Property type*	Industrial	Industrial	Industrial	Commerical	Industrial	Commercial	Industrial	Industrial
Market conditions	Stable	Stable	Stable	Stable	Stable	Declining	Declining	Declining
Contamination/discharge issues								
Source, non-source, adjacent, proximate	Source	Source	Source	Source	Non-source	Source	Source	Source
Permitted vs. accidental discharge**	Accidental	Accidental	Accidental	Accidental	Accidental	Accidental	Accidental	Accidental
Type of contaminant	Chlorinated solvents	Hydrocarbon	Chlorinated solvents	Chlorinated solvents	Chlorinated solvents	Hydro-solvents	Hydro-solvents	Hydro-solvents
Level of contamination/discharge	Medium	Medium	Medium-high	Medium-high	Medium	Medium	Medium-high	Medium-high
Area-bioavailability/risk exposure	Low risk	Low	Low	Low-medium	Low	Low	Medium-high	Medium
Remediation lifecycle/detrimental condition stages								
Before cleanup/assessment stage	Contamination has been characterized	Characterized	Characterized	Characterized	Characterized	Characterized	Not fully	Characterized
During cleanup/repair or remediation stage	No Remedial Action Plan (RAP)	No RAP	RAP	No RAP	No RAP	RAP	No RAP	RAP
After cleanup/ongoing stage	Does not have a No Further Action (NFA) letter	No NFA	No NFA	No NFA	No NFA	NFA	No NFA	No NFA
Other/ related issues								
Costs and responsibility	Seller	Seller	Seller	Buyer	Seller	Buyer	Buyer	Buyer
Scale of project	Medium	Medium-low	Medium-high	Medium-high	Medium	Medium	Medium-high	Medium
Impacts on use and use limitations	Minimal impact	Minimal	Medium	Medium-high	Minimal	Medium	Medium-high	Medium
Third party liabilities	Low risk	Low	Low	Low	Low	Medium	Medium-high	Low
Indemnifications	Idemnified	Idemnified	No indem.	No indem.	Indemnified	No indem.	No indem.	No indem.
Insurance	Cost cap – reopener	None	None	None	Cost cap – reopener	None	None	Cost cap – reopener
Time frame and market experience	Current	Similar	Similar	Similar	Similar	Similar	Similar	Similar
Impact on value	To be determined	No impact	5% Discount	12% Discount	No impact	No impact	15% Discount	No impact

* Income-producing properties are not comparable to residential properties.

** Denotes issue that is essential for comparability.

Chapter 5: *Analysis of Environmental Case Studies*

the impact on value for each of the case studies, the sales prices of the source site contaminated comparables should be adjusted to remove the effect of future remediation costs where such costs have been reliably estimated. This can be accomplished by adding the estimated costs to be paid by the buyer from property cash flows to the nominal sales price. This would leave a price that reflects the risk-related effects of the case study property's environmental condition on its price as of its date of sale.

The second step of this two step procedure is to reconcile the value impacts for each of the case studies to the subject property, based on their comparability of the elements listed in Table 1.[2] As noted, a relative comparison analysis would be appropriate for this purpose. As explained in *The Appraisal of Real Estate,* 12th ed., in this type of analysis each element could be compared and assigned a ranking of superior, inferior, or similar. An overall ranking could then be made after considering each of the individual comparisons. This overall ranking or net comparison derived from the case studies provides the basis for reconciling a range of indicated impacts on value. This is usually the final step in the case study analysis.

An additional step, applicable for certain assignments, would be to deduct the subject property's estimated future remediation costs that are to be borne by property cash flows, and not by the seller or another source, such as environmental insurance. This step provides a final, adjusted estimate of the subject property's impaired value. Care should be taken, though, not to double count remediation cost effects and risk related effects, since risk effects may in part be related to uncertainties about future remediation cost estimates and requirements.

Property Characteristics
Property Type
An important similarity between the subject property and the case study is the general property type. For example, the differences between a residential property and a service station are so vast that there is simply no comparison. Perceptions, pricing criteria, and the market context of a homeowner are different from a service station owner, whose primary objective is generating income. Likewise, the value of income-producing commercial and industrial properties cannot be estimated on the basis of owner-occupied residential comparables or case studies. Not only does this make sense, it is also consistent with accepted methods for sales comparison analysis. Environmental issues will impact these property types differently. Accordingly, the subject property and case studies should be of the same general property type category. For example, these categories could include: service stations and auto repair facilities, commercial, industrial, and residential properties. At a minimum, owner-occupied residential properties should be compared to residential properties, and income-producing properties should be compared to other income-producing properties.

Market Conditions
It is a well-known attribute of the real estate market that when the market is increasing, many prospective buyers are prone to be more forgiving of certain conditions as compared to periods of market declines. Strong market conditions have a mitigating effect, while poor market conditions tend to exacerbate issues. A case study conducted in a declining market may not

2. A similar sales comparison approach is illustrated in Thomas O. Jackson, "The Effect of Previous Environmental Contamination on Industrial Real Estate Prices," *The Appraisal Journal* (April 2001): 200–210.

be as relevant where the market is now strong, or vice versa. This is consistent with formal research on the effects of environmental contamination on real estate prices, which shows that strong market conditions tend to reduce or mitigate detrimental impacts on real estate prices while weak market conditions increase or exacerbate detrimental impacts.[3] These effects are illustrated in Figure 1. This figure is based on a national survey of more than 200 lenders conducted in 1999. As depicted in Figure 1, nearly 60% of the survey respondents indicated that weak market conditions increase risk. On the other hand, more than 30% indicated that strong market conditions reduce risk. These statistically significant results confirm the general direction and effect of market conditions as intervening factors affecting environmental risk and its impact on value.

Contamination/Discharge Issues
Source/Non-Source/Adjacent/Proximate Site (SNAP)

A critical issue in evaluating environmentally contaminated property is identifying whether it is a source, non-source, adjacent, or proximate site (SNAP).[4] A "source site property" is defined as the site from which the contamination was released. An example of a source site is a service station with a leaking underground storage tank. A non-source property is contaminated, but the contamination emanated from another property (the source site)—for example, a doughnut shop next to a contaminated service station where contamination has migrated off-site and under the doughnut shop property. An adjacent property is not contaminated, but it shares a property line with a property that is. A proximate property is not contaminated and is not adjacent to any contaminated property; however, it is in the same general neighborhood of a contaminated, source site property. These distinctions are critical in evaluating contaminated properties because the risks vary considerably between the categories. Source sites have a much different set of environmental risk factors than non-source or adjacent properties.

3. Thomas O. Jackson, "Environmental Risk Perceptions of Commercial and Industrial Real Estate Lenders," *Journal of Real Estate Research* (Nov–Dec, 2001); 271–288.
4. Orell C. Anderson, "Environmental Contamination: An Analysis in the Context of the DC Matrix," *The Appraisal Journal* (July 2001): 322–332.

FIGURE 1 Effect of Market Conditions on Environmental Risk

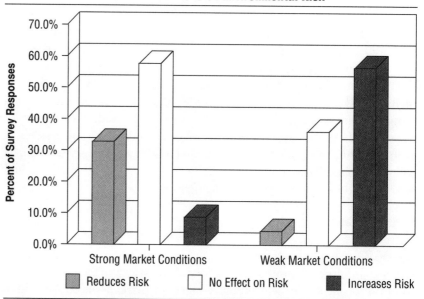

Source: Thomas O. Jackson, "Environmental Risk Perceptions of Commercial and Industrial Real Estate Lenders," *Journal of Real Estate Research* (Nov–Dec, 2001): 271–288.

Generally, the source property owners or prior owners are responsible for the remediation of the contamination. The costs and risks of cleanup and regulatory oversight are far greater than any other category, so comparing a source case study to a non-source, adjacent, or proximate property could be misleading. Accordingly, if the subject property were the source of the contamination, then source site case studies would provide the most meaningful comparisons. Inferences drawn from source site case studies relative to a non-source site subject may be biased toward an overestimate of environmental impacts.

Permitted vs. Accidental Discharges

A reality of the industrialized world is that there are vast quantities of contaminants produced every day. However, contaminants that are a "permitted discharge" should be distinguished from those emanating from an accidental discharge. A permitted discharge includes governmentally allowed releases such as industrial discharges into a body of water, automobile exhaust, washing machine discharges, landfills, and deep soil discharges or storage. Accidental or illegal discharges include leaking underground storage tanks, oil tanker spills, improper dumping, and so forth.

There are critical distinctions between the two types of discharges. One category is permitted and legal, while the other is not. Permitted discharges do not generally involve any level of remediation, while an accidental discharge may require remediation if the quantity of contamination rises above the actionable levels set by governmental agencies. Accidental discharges may be subject to fines and sanctions and permitted discharges generally are not. These are two vastly different sets of circumstances. The release of a potentially hazardous substance that is done under a legally authorized permit with regulatory oversight has a much different set of risk characteristics than an accidental release of hazardous materials from an unplanned or accidental explosion, leak, etc. Risk perceptions of the market are related to unknown information and an accidental release has many more unknowns (cleanup costs, off-site impacts) than a planned release of materials that has been reviewed and permitted by the appropriate regulatory authority. Accordingly, a reliable case study analysis should only use case studies that are identical in this regard.

Type of Contaminant

There are literally hundreds of contaminants, and they can fall into one of several categories: hydrocarbons, including crude oil and refined petroleum; asbestos, a naturally formed rock that can be crushed and used as a building material; solvents, which may be used for dry cleaning or manufacturing; radioactive materials, including radon; metals, such as lead, chrome, or arsenic; and biologicals, such as sewage and medical waste. Research has shown that the type of contamination or hazardous substance has a significant effect on the market's perception of risk, and, in turn, property value diminution.[5]

Ideally, the type of contaminant is the same for both the subject property and the case study. This is important because different contaminants may invoke different responses from the marketplace. A real estate analyst must use caution before comparing a case study that involves a contaminant that differs from the contaminant found at the subject property. It

5. Elaine M. Worzala and William N. Kinnard, Jr., "Investor & Lender Reactions to Alternative Sources of Contamination," *Real Estate Issues* (August 1997): 42–47.

would be improper, for example, to compare a case study involving the effects of petroleum hydrocarbon contamination from a leaking underground storage tank to a subject property impacted by asbestos or radon. However, there are situations where a study is comparable, even though the contaminants differ slightly. For example, it might be worthwhile to compare a shopping center that has soil contamination from a service station's leaking underground storage tank with another shopping center that has soil contamination from dry-cleaning solvents. Careful analysis is required in this situation.

Level of Contamination

While perhaps initially startling to some, virtually all air, water, and soil are "contaminated" at some level. This is a simple reality of an industrialized society. Car emissions alone contaminate the air, water, and soil. Asbestos is a naturally occurring substance, and everyone breathes some asbestos fibers daily. Sewer pipes often leak and contaminate soils. These low-level situations are termed "background contamination." The critical factors in this regard are the standards established by the appropriate regulatory authority. Various governmental agencies set "actionable levels" providing that when some contaminants meet or exceed a certain level, there must be action on the part of the responsible party to remediate the condition. Many agencies tailor the standards to the property type and risk exposure characteristics of the property and surrounding area. These are typically tied to risk-based cleanup action (RBCA) requirements that have been adopted by many states. Thus, rather than asking, "Is a property contaminated?" a more valid question is, "What level is the contamination?" While it would be virtually impossible to find case studies that have exactly the same measured quantities of contaminants as the subject property, certainly it is important that the general level of contamination be comparable.

Area Bioavailability/Risk Exposure

There are six areas of a property that may become contaminated. These are: air, water, building improvements, surface/shallow soils, ground water aquifers, and deep soils. These categories are relevant because of the concept of "bioavailability." Bioavailability is the extent to which a contaminant becomes available to humans or the biota, generally. Air pollution would be considered to have a relatively high level of bioavailability, while contaminants that are restricted to deep soils may have no bioavailability. These categories are regarded quite differently by regulatory agencies due to their differing levels of health risk exposure. Simply, where there is no exposure risk, there should be no environmental risk that reduces the value of the real property. Newer risk-based cleanup standards recognize this by treating sites at which there is limited exposure differently from sites at which the exposure is more immediate and of more serious concern. For example, hazardous materials that are trapped thousands of feet underground are different in kind from sites with hazardous materials in the shallow groundwater or in exposed soil. The risk levels, the level of market concern, and the resulting effects on property value are much different. Thus, the risk exposure for the case study properties and the subject property should be similar for a valid case study analysis.

Chapter 5: *Analysis of Environmental Case Studies*

Remediation Lifecycle/Detrimental Condition Stages

This is perhaps the most important set of factors in determining the effects of environmental contamination on real estate prices and market value.[6] Similarly this element is a critical requirement for a valid and reliable case study analysis. The case study property should be in the same stage of remediation (before, during, or after cleanup) at the time of its sale as is the subject property at its date of value. Research has shown that the risks perceived by the market change dramatically as a property moves though the remediation cycle. Before cleanup, risks and property value diminution attributable to environmental condition are greatest. These decline as remediation is underway pursuant to an approved cleanup plan. After cleanup and regulatory closure, property value impacts are minimal and, in most cases, disappear.[7] Bell outlines three condition stages: assessment, repair, and ongoing stages.[8] Similarly, Jackson analyzes the changes in environmental risk and impacts on property value in three categories: before, during, and after cleanup.[9] Within each category or stage, the costs, use, and risks associated with an environmental condition vary and will impact real estate differently.

The generalized effect of the three remediation stages on environmental risk is illustrated in Figure 2. This figure is based on the 1999 lender survey previously discussed. As shown, over 90% of the lenders surveyed indicated that before cleanup of a contaminated source site, property risks would be very high. During cleanup most of the lenders indicated higher than normal risk, while after cleanup, more than 60% indicated that environmental risks would be normal, and loans would be provided at typical rates and terms. In the survey, very high risk was equated to a situation in which a mortgage loan would not be provided due to excessive environmental concerns. Higher than normal risk indicated that a mortgage loan would be provided, but with some adjustments to the loan amount, rate, amortization, term, or conditions. All of the changes in risk perceptions were statistically significant at the 0.05 level, and the survey sample was a probability-based, representative national sample of mortgage lenders.[10]

The Before Cleanup/Assessment Stage

Prior to being assessed, there may be great uncertainty about the environmental condition of the subject property, thereby generating uncertainty and a discount to account for the unknown characterization of the property's condition. Upon assessment, this uncertainty is reduced. The principle underlying this effect is that risk is directly related to uncertainty about, and potential variance in, future cash flows. If there is little known about an environmental problem that might later require substantial expenditures for remediation, then future cash flows are less predictable and the investor would require a higher rate of return to compensate for this unknown risk and uncertainty. Indeed, there may be a level at which risk and uncertainty are so high that a property is unmarketable until greater knowledge becomes available. For contaminated properties, greater knowledge involves the nature and extent of the contamination, as well as the requirements, costs, and timing of the remediation effort.

The During Cleanup/Repair or Remediation Stage

Upon being assessed, a contaminated property typically goes through a remediation phase where the contaminants are removed, treated, enclosed,

6. Anderson, 322–332.

7. Jackson, 200–210.

8. Randall Bell, *Real Estate Damages: An Analysis of Detrimental Conditions* (Chicago: Appraisal Institute, 1999): 8-10.

9. Jackson, 271-288.

10. *Ibid.*

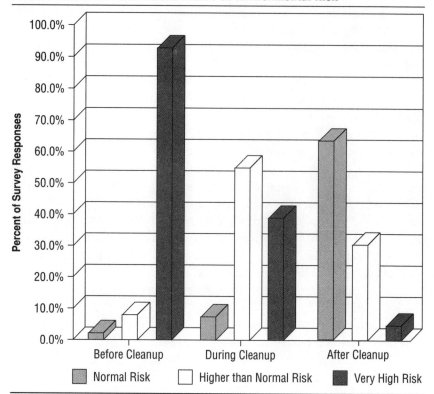

FIGURE 2 Effect of Remediation Status on Environmental Risk

Source: Thomas O. Jackson, "Environmental Risk Perceptions of Commercial and Industrial Real Estate Lenders," *Journal of Real Estate Research* (Nov–Dec, 2001): 271–288.

or left to "bioremediation" through a more passive cleanup strategy. Often there are significant costs associated with a remediation project, and like any property that requires rehabilitation, there is risk associated with these efforts. The assessment of risk during this stage considers whether the cleanup plan has been approved by the appropriate regulatory authority and is being conducted in compliance with the provisions of such a plan. If a property is sold in an assessed but unremediated state, there may be a discount to account for project risk. This can be considered the "project incentive" required by the buyer, if the buyer is responsible for the cleanup. Otherwise, the risk could be termed "market resistance" if another party is responsible for the cleanup costs and related activities. It is likely that there is some combination of these two categories of risk operative at this stage.

The After Cleanup/Ongoing Stage

Research shows that lenders are generally willing to provide mortgage loans after property has been remediated, has achieved a "no further action" status with the appropriate regulatory agencies, and the property value impacts have dissipated (Figure 2).[11] More specifically, the research presented in Figure 2 shows that the perceptions of environmental risk by lenders and investors declines significantly as property is remediated, and that most lenders and investors perceive no additional risk after cleanup to applicable standards and the achievement of "no further action" status. In addition, sales price analyses have shown a similar pattern, with no statistically significant effect on prices after remediation due to previous environmental contamination.[12] Even in situations where there may be

11. *Ibid.*
12. Jackson, 200–210.

Chapter 5: *Analysis of Environmental Case Studies*

ongoing monitoring, operations and monitoring (O&M) programs, and other issues, any residual risk, termed "market resistance," may be eliminated through indemnification, cost cap insurance, secured creditor insurance, value assurance programs, re-opener insurance or other factors.

In a case study analysis, special attention must be paid to the specific status and condition of the subject property within the remediation lifecycle as of its date of value. Case studies in a similar remediation stage should be selected, as these would be most reflective of the subject's environmental impacts. Clearly, the risks associated with a contaminated property that has not yet been assessed are greatly different from risks associated with property that has been fully assessed, fully remediated, and is in the after cleanup stage of its lifecycle. Identifying the specific lifecycle stage is critical for a valid and reliable analysis.

Other/Related Issues
Costs and Responsibility for Remediation

The issue of responsibility for cleanup costs has profound implications if remediation is necessary and the subject property is evaluated in a non-remediated state. Whether or not the potentially responsible party (PRP) is known, has assumed responsibility for the environmental contamination, and has offered or provided indemnities to other parties and property owners makes a significant difference in the market's environmental risk perception. A site for which the PRP has not been identified or for which the PRP does not accept responsibility for remediation will be more adversely impacted than an otherwise similar site for which the PRP accepts responsibility and has fully financed the cleanup plan. In addition, the financial strength of the party responsible for site remediation affects the market's perception of environmental risks. Much of the risk associated with contamination is centered on who is going to have to pay for cleanup and whether or not the responsible party is financially solvent.

For example, consider two service station sites that have been sold with leaking underground storage tank issues. A major oil company, which has assumed all responsibility for cleanup costs, owns Service Station A. The company is solvent and financially responsible. Furthermore, not only will the oil company remediate the site, but it will also provide a full written indemnification to future owners of the property whereby it accepts any future liability associated with the contamination it caused. On the other hand, consider an otherwise similar Service Station B that has been owned by a now retired husband and wife who have moved out of state. The property has changed hands on several occasions, and it is uncertain who is responsible for the releases. Furthermore, all the potentially responsible parties deny any responsibility and have limited financial resources. Clearly, the impact of contamination on the value of Service Station A will not be comparable with Service Station B.

Scale of Project

Simply stated, some projects are quite large and some are quite small. For example, some of the largest contamination cases in history have involved radioactive contamination in the Marshall Islands (from nuclear testing on the Bikini Atoll) and Chernobyl. The dynamics of these cases obviously differ substantially from a radon case in a single-family residence or a leaking underground storage tank near a commercial property. While an extreme example, the same concept applies. Valid case studies should be generally similar to the subject property in terms of the scale of the project.

Impacts on Use and Use Limitations

Whether or not a property's utility has been impacted is another key factor. A situation where the contamination has resulted in the property being vacated is clearly different from a situation where the remediation is non-intrusive and the user can continue operations with little or no disruption. In addition, this element should capture the effects of risk-based cleanups, as previously discussed. Risk-based cleanups typically allow remediation standards to be tailored to specific risk exposures and can allow for regulatory closure without removal of all constituents. For example, an industrial property would be remediated to industrial standards, rather than more costly residential standards. There would then be a future use restriction on such a property, perhaps allowing only industrial uses or land uses with similar risk profiles. This restriction is typically recorded as a deed restriction. Deed restrictions may have an impact on use if the prohibited uses represented have a real and material impact on the use of the property, such as a restriction to develop homes where residential uses would otherwise have been the highest and best use. On the other hand, a historic museum that is always expected to remain a museum would not likely suffer any material impact from a deed restriction for school, daycare, hospital, or residential use.

Third Party Liabilities

Where contaminants have migrated off site from a source property, there may be the risk of litigation from the non-source property owners. Some non-source or adjacent property owners may litigate, even though they have not been impacted in any material way. This risk to the source property owner must be considered, even though the merits of the case may be questionable. If a contaminant plume migration causes a market-recognized concern from a publicized incursion into the groundwater providing potable water in a residential neighborhood, there may be significant risk. In addition, employees or tenants of the contaminated property may pursue claims for personal injury and this may have a detrimental effect. In sum, third-party claims, especially from off-site migration of groundwater contamination, pose an additional risk factor that must be evaluated in a case study analysis. Surrounding property types and neighborhood characteristics are important in this evaluation.

Time Frame and Market Experience

The sale of the case study property ideally should have occurred during the same period as the subject property's date of value. Due to the rapidly changing nature of the market and its experience and ability to deal with environmental risks in real estate transactions, contaminated properties sold many years ago may not be appropriate for more current dates of value. Brownfields programs, more flexible regulations, risk-based cleanup standards, and the increased experience of lenders and investors with environmental issues have all resulted in a lessening of the impacts of contamination on real estate values.[13]

13. Thomas O. Jackson, "Investing in Contaminated Real Estate," *Real Estate Review* (Winter 1997): 38–43.

Chapter 5: *Analysis of Environmental Case Studies*

Indemnification and Insurance

An indemnification is the written assurance of the responsible party that they will incur all costs associated with the contamination. Where an indemnifying party is financially solvent and willing to pay for all required remediation costs, the risk is reduced or may be eliminated altogether. Also, many risks can be insured. For example, remediation cost overruns, third-party liability, loss in property value, agency "re-openers" and other concerns may be virtually eliminated by insurance.

Summary and Conclusions

Case studies can be useful in valuing environmentally impacted properties. However, a case study, like any comparable, should be similar to the subject property being studied. For example, case studies involving leaking underground storage tanks (LUSTs) should include other situations with LUSTs. Asbestos situations should utilize case studies with asbestos. Oil spills should be considered with other oil spills. Ideally, case studies are similar with respect to the type of contaminant and the other issues set forth in this paper. The best and most comparable case studies would be similar to the subject property in terms the SNAP issues, being an accidental versus a permitted discharge, and remediation lifecycle stage. Other elements can be addressed through a sales comparison type analysis, with market-derived quantitative adjustments or qualitative comparisons. With this framework, case studies may be a useful addition to the tools for assessing the effects of adverse environmental conditions and other detrimental conditions on real property. Indeed, the case studies framework outlined herein could be applied to the analysis of a variety of detrimental conditions, although the elements of comparison would be different.

Valuing Contaminated Properties

CHAPTER 5 Cross-References

Related articles in Chapter 1: Joseph A. Campanella, "Valuing Partial Losses in Contamination Cases" *The Appraisal Journal* (April 1988), 3; Peter J. Patchin, MAI, "Valuation of Contaminated Properties" *The Appraisal Journal* (January 1988), 11; and William N. Kinnard, Jr., MAI, SRA, PhD and Elaine M. Worzala, PhD, "How North American Appraisers Value Contaminated Property and Associated Stigma" *The Appraisal Journal* (January 1999), 17–18, 21–22.

Related articles in Chapter 2: Anthony J. Rinaldi, MAI, ASA, "Contaminated Properties—Valuation Solutions" *The Appraisal Journal* (July 1991), 42–43; Albert R. Wilson, "The Environmental Opinion: Basis for an Impaired Value Opinion" *The Appraisal Journal* (July 1994), 68, 73–74; and Albert R. Wilson, "Emerging Approaches to Impaired Property Valuation" *The Appraisal Journal* (April 1996).

Related article in Chapter 7: Peter J. Patchin, MAI, "Contaminated Properties and the Sales Comparison Approach" *The Appraisal Journal* (July 1994).

Related article in Chapter 11: John D. Dorchester, Jr., MAI, CRE, "The Federal Rules of Evidence and *Daubert:* Evaluating Real Property Valuation Witnesses" *The Appraisal Journal* (July 2000), 595.

Mortgage Lenders and Contaminated Properties

Editor's Introduction

Lenders play a critical role in the real estate marketplace. By lending or refusing to lend on a particular property type or by simply increasing interest rates, debt coverage ratios, loan-to-value ratios, or due diligence and underwriting standards for a particular class of real estate asset, they can have a serious impact on demand and price, and therefore market values. They also serve as intermediaries in determining the impact, if any, environmental risks have on property values. The articles in this chapter document the clear evolution of lender attitudes toward lending on contaminated or remediated properties.

The Healys report on the results of their 1990 lender survey, which clearly indicated significant concerns about lending on contaminated or remediated properties. Worzala and Kinnard found in 1996 that lenders were learning to differentiate between various types of contamination situations, and were willing to lend on some types of contaminated properties while avoiding others. They also found that the attitudes of lenders and investors toward contaminated properties differed significantly.

Wilson and Alarcon found from their survey that lenders are more willing to make loans on normal terms than indicated by the results of previous surveys. They recommend that survey questionnaires be structured with a detailed set of facts to elicit a meaningful response about lender willingness to make mortgage loans on contaminated properties.

Roddewig and Keiter report on the reasons lenders are now generally more willing to make loans on contaminated and remediated properties. They then summarize the survey activities by the Environmental Bankers Association that indicate the lending industry's improved sophistication in evaluating the level of risk that accompanies a loan on a contaminated or remediated property.

Lenders' Perspectives on Environmental Issues

by Patricia R. Healy and John J. Healy, Jr., MAI

Patricia R. Healy *is a principal of the Hanford/Healy Companies and is a licensed real estate broker in the state of California. Her academic activities include guest lectures at the University of Virginia and the American Institute of Banking and previous service as a faculty member of St. Mary's College.*

John J. Healy, Jr., MAI, *is a founding principal of the Hanford/Healy Companies, a national firm specializing in real estate appraisal, consulting, asset management, and advisory services. He is a designated member of the American Society of Real Estate Counselors.*

This article originally appeared in the July 1992 issue of The Appraisal Journal.

Reprinted with permission. © 1991 Patricia R. Healy and John J. Healy, Jr.

1. The 25 largest banks were identified in the American Bankers Association 1991 listing of U.S. banks.

2. The 15 largest banks in California did not include banks that had previously qualified as national banks in the book of lists for San Francisco and California.

In the fourth quarter of 1990, The Hanford/Healy Companies (HHC) conducted a survey of major real estate lenders. The purpose of the survey was to quantify lenders' perceptions of environmental risks and the degree to which these perceptions affect underwriting policy. Individuals from 57 institutions were interviewed, including the largest 25 banks in the country,[1] the largest 15 banks in California,[2] and the largest five foreign bank branches in the United States.

It should be noted that more than one person from some of the larger institutions were interviewed, namely a lending/credit officer and an officer from the appraisal/environmental services area. The survey percentages reported in this article consequently do not always reflect the number of institutions contacted. Survey percentages also vary because some lenders did not have an opinion about a specific survey question or felt that more than one response was appropriate or individuals from the same institution had differing opinions.

The survey consisted of eight questions, each of which had multiple parts (see Exhibit 1).

Questions 1 through 3 of the survey addressed the lenders' relative concern about specific environmental issues, such as underground storage tanks and unencapsulated asbestos. Questions 4 and 5 addressed environmental audits and the use of outside environmental consultants. Question 6 linked environmental issues to the appraisal process, while the last two questions focused on underwriting standards.

The results of the survey were compiled in an in-depth report. As it would be impossible to duplicate all of the results herein, this article highlights some of the more significant responses to the survey questions.

Groundwater Contamination: The Greatest Concern

Of all banks responding, 41% believed groundwater contamination was the greatest concern among five specified environmental issues: underground tanks, unencapsulated asbestos, encapsulated asbestos, ground-

Chapter 6: *Lenders' Perspectives*

EXHIBIT 1 Hanford/Healy Companies' Environmental Risk Survey Questions

1. Would your institution lend on a property knowing it:
   a. Had underground storage tanks.
   b. Contained unencapsulated asbestos.
   c. Contained encapsulated asbestos.
   d. Was surrounded by contiguous parcels with environmental problems.
   e. Had tenants that might use toxic materials.
   f. Previously had some contaminations but has been cleaned up.
2. On a 1 to 5 scale, rank the following environmental issues according to their concern, with 1 being the least worrisome and 5 being the most worrisome:
   a. Underground tanks.
   b. Unencapsulated asbestos.
   c. Encapsulated asbestos.
   d. Groundwater contamination.
   e. A tenant who stored toxic materials.
3. Regarding the above environmental issues:
   a. Which issue is the greatest concern to your institution?
   b. Which issue is the least concern to your institution?
4. In regard to environmental audits:
   a. When is a Phase I audit required?
   b. Does the lender or borrower order, deliver and pay for the Phase I audit?
   c. If the borrower orders a Phase I audit, must the environmental consultant be approved by the lender?
   d. If the lender orders the audit, which banking area issues the order and who is responsible for the interpretation of the audit?
   e. Do you have any loans on property where an environmental cleanup is being conducted—other than property containing asbestos?
   f. If so, did your institution lend the money for the cleanup?
5. Does your institution hire outside consultants to aid in review of environmental audits?
   a. What types of consultants?
   b. When are they retained (under what circumstances)?
   c. Do you hire different consultants depending on the nature of the environmental problem?
6. With regard to appraisals:
   a. If the presence of contamination has been proved, do you ask appraisers to consider the known contamination in the appraisal process?
   b. Who is responsible for informing the appraisers of the contamination?
   c. In your opinion, have appraisals of previously contaminated properties that have been cleaned up reflect any loss in value?
7. Are the following underwriting standards on loans adjusted when a property has a potential or an actual environmental problem?
   a. Loan to value ratio.
   b. Borrower indemnification.
   c. Personal liability.
   d. Interest rates.
8. Have your underwriting standards been changed since the *Fleet Factor* court decision?

water contamination, and toxic inventories (see Table 1). Unencapsulated asbestos was a distant second, with 14% of the banks ranking it as their primary environmental concern. Not one bank categorized groundwater contamination as the least disturbing issue. In fact, when rating the five specified environmental issues on a scale of 1 (least worrisome) to 5 (most worrisome), 87% of the banks believed groundwater contamination rated 4 or above.

Conversely, 46% of the banks believed that encapsulated asbestos was the least worrisome vis-à-vis the other environmental issues. On the 1 to 5 scale of risk, 71% of the banks rated encapsulated asbestos at 3 or below.

Valuing Contaminated Properties

TABLE 1   Issues Identified as Greatest Environmental Concerns by Financial Institutions

	Underground Tanks (%)	Unencapsulated Asbestos (%)	Encapsulated Asbestos (%)	Groundwater Contamination (%)	Toxic Inventories (%)	All Are of Equal Concern (%)
National banks	11	21	0	44	8	16
California banks	16	6	6	28	22	22
Foreign banks	0	0	0	75	0	25
Total	12	14	2	41	12	19

SOURCE: The Hanford/Healy Companies.

Less than 40% of the banks would consider lending on a property located contiguous to a parcel that was environmentally contaminated, as shown in Table 2. Not one of the foreign banks was interested in lending to such a borrower, and only 22% of the California banks would consider lending on a property with this risk.

While 61% of the banks said they would lend on a property with an underground storage tank, approximately 66% gave the caveat that the property must pass a Phase I environmental analysis and be on an ongoing monitoring program. (As an aside, 81% of the national banks said they would lend on a property with underground tanks.)

Finally, and of most significant interest, were the survey results related to previously contaminated property after successful remediation. More than 84% of the banks reported that they would have no problem lending on such a project; the perceived stigma of prior contamination consequently does not appear to be significant.

Phase I Audits a Requirement

Seventy-two percent of all national banks (and 100% of all foreign banks) would require a Phase I audit on any loan secured by real property. While only 22% of the California banks would require a Phase I audit on any loan for real property, 78% would require an audit if contamination were known or likely. (There may be some bias in these responses as, on average, the exposure to contaminated properties by California banks may be limited by their overall smaller size vis-à-vis foreign and national banks.)

Eighty-one percent of the banks would require a Phase II audit if the Phase I work indicated that there might be some environmental concerns. The remaining banks indicated that they would not undertake further due diligence if a Phase I report was unfavorable.

TABLE 2   Environmental Issues Affecting Lending

	No. Institutions Represented	Yes Responses (%)	No Responses (%)	Maybe Responses (%)
Would your institution lend on a property knowing it had...				
Underground storage tanks	54	61	28	11
Unencapsulated asbestos	56	36	48	16
Encapsulated asbestos	56	57	27	16
Contiguous contamination	55	38	40	22
Toxic inventories	55	45	35	20
Ongoing cleanup	55	40	52	8
Previous contamination	56	84	3	13
Weighted average	56	52	33	15

SOURCE: Hanford/Healy Appraisal Company.

The national banks were again the most progressive in granting loans on properties that were being cleaned up (other than those that were removing asbestos). Fifty percent of the national banks reported their institutions made loans on such properties, compared with 24% of the California banks and 20% of the foreign institutions. Of those institutions that had loans on properties under remediation, 61% said that their institutions had lent the money for cleanup of some of that property.

It appears that the borrower, not the lender, orders the Phase I audit (68% of all responses), receives the document (66%), and pays for the audit (85%). However, 80% of the banks required that the environmental consultant conducting the audit be approved by the lender, and 57% considered using an outside consultant to aid in the audit review. The consultant most often identified was an engineer, and the engineer most often would be involved when major environmental problems were present or when special technical expertise was required.

Appraiser's Role

If the presence of contamination was proved, 61% of the banks would instruct the appraiser to consider contamination in the appraisal process. The banks would not necessarily require the appraisal to assess the cost of a cleanup (and its implication on the value of the property) but the appraisal should indicate the presence of such contamination in the property description and note that the appraiser did not assess the impact of the contamination on the property's value.

Almost 50% of the banks did not believe there was any loss in current value on properties that had been contaminated but subsequently had been cleaned up; 37% were unsure of the effect on value or had never been faced with that issue. Again, contrary to common perceptions, only 19% of the institutions perceived that there was a stigma on property that had been previously contaminated.

Underwriting Standards Adjusted

On properties with an actual or potential environmental problem, 66% of the banks would require additional indemnification from the borrower; 46% would consider adjusting the loan-to-value ratio; 60% of the institutions would require personal guarantees (or some personal liability). Conversely, only 21% would consider an interest rate adjustment.

The *Fleet Factor* case, which raised uncertainty about the exemption of a lender from liability for cleaning up environmental hazards, is considered a landmark. Nevertheless, survey respondents were divided on whether it affected underwriting standards; 47% believed the case did affect standards and 45% believed it did not. Effectively 100% of the individuals who were aware of the decision believed that regardless of the actual impact, the court ruling had heightened the lending community's level of concern about environmental issues.

Summary

The results of the survey demonstrate a significant level of knowledge about environmental issues among lenders. Although environmental contamination does not appear to discount a bank's interest in lending on a specific property, in all cases it does require a significantly more stringent due diligence process.

As is true in most industries, active involvement in certain aspects of the business results in specialization. Clearly, some banks that are more actively involved in environmental issues have become more comfortable with environmental risk, perceived or actual, than others. Nonetheless, the survey shows that no single environmental issue would result in a blanket rejection of a loan on a contaminated property by an institution. That, in and of itself, appears to be noteworthy to us.

Investor & Lender Reactions to Alternative Sources of Contamination

by Elaine M. Worzala and William N. Kinnard, Jr., CRE

During the 1980s, the prospect of finding an investor to buy or a lender to finance a piece of contaminated property was commonly considered daunting and sometimes virtually impossible. The "word on the street" was, if contamination was even remotely possible, then being on the chain of title to the property should be avoided like the plague. Results from recent research, however, have indicated that attitudes toward property with environmental problems have been evolving and there appear to be some types of contaminants which institutional investors and lenders, in particular, ignore or discount in making investments and loans (Healy and Healy 1991, Mundy 1992, Kinnard and Worzala 1996).

From a 1996 survey of investors and lenders, we have identified some contaminants which will be tolerated and some which professional real estate market participants still consider "taboo." The hierarchy is based on responses to a mail questionnaire to which 78 equity investors and 69 lenders replied, for a total of 145 useable responses.[1]

Attitude Towards Specific On-Site Locales of Contamination

A series of questions focused on the investors' and lenders' attitudes toward property known to be contaminated with various kinds of contamination. Our intent was to identify the hierarchy of attitudes toward different types or sources of contamination which influence investor and lender decisions on whether to commit funds or to avoid doing so.

The first question covered three basic locales of on-site contamination. It read: *Do you/would you invest/lend on a property that had 1). groundwater contamination; 2). soil contamination; and 3). building contamination?* Results show clearly that building contamination is the least feared, followed by soil contamination and then groundwater contamination (most avoided). As illustrated in *Exhibit 1,* of the 115 respondents who answered the question 77.6% indicated that either they would definitely or sometimes invest or lend on a property that had building contamination; 69.6% would possibly make the investment or loan if the soil was contaminated; and only

Elaine M. Worzala, Ph.D., is assistant professor of finance and real estate at Colorado State University. She has published numerous articles on market studies in both the U.S. and Europe, in professional as well as academic journals. In 1995-96, she was a visiting assistant professor of real estate at the University of Connecticut. Dr. Worzala has worked as a commercial real estate appraiser and market analyst with firms in San Francisco and London, England.

William N. Kinnard, Jr., Ph.D., CRE, SREA, MAI, is president of the Real Estate Counseling Group of Connecticut, Inc. He is also professor emeritus of finance and real estate at the University of Connecticut. His practice includes analysis and testimony concerning the market effects of contamination on demand for, and the value of, contaminated properties. Dr. Kinnard has published on this and related topics in both academic and professional journals. He was co-recipient of the 1991 William S. Ballard Award.

This article originally appeared in the August 1997 issue of Real Estate Issues. *Reproduced with the permission of* Real Estate Issues; *published and © by the Counselors of Real Estate (a not for profit organization), Chicago, IL. All rights reserved. Further reproduction/distribution is prohibited without the written permission of* Real Estate Issues.

---

1. To develop the hierarchy shown in this paper, we focused on only 4 questions in the survey. See Kinnard and Worzala (1996) for a complete description of the sample, response rate, and results of the survey.

EXHIBIT 1

Responses Toward the Question: *Do you/would you invest on a property with:*

Panel A: Aggregate Responses

Locale of Contamination	n*	"Yes"(%)	"Sometimes"(%)	"No"(%)
Groundwater contamination	115	7.8	48.7	43.5
Soil contamination	115	11.3	58.3	30.4
Building contamination	116	12.9	64.7	22.4

Panel B: Investors' Responses

Groundwater contamination	56	8.9	50.0	41.1
Soil contamination	56	16.1	58.9	25.0
Building contamination	57	17.5	61.4	21.1

Panel C: Lenders' Responses

Groundwater contamination	59	6.8	47.5	45.8
Soil contamination	59	6.8	57.6	35.6
Building contamination	59	8.5	67.8	23.7

*n equals number of respondents
Source: Survey results

56.5% would possibly make the investment or loan if the contamination was in the groundwater. This was a similar result in the Healy and Healy survey (1991) where groundwater contamination was found to be of the greatest concern for lenders. Looking at absolute negative responses, 22.4% would not commit funds if the building were contaminated, 30.4% would not if the soil were contaminated, and close to half (43.5%) would not if the groundwater was known to be contaminated.

Comparing investor attitudes with those of lenders in all three cases, we found that investor respondents were less averse to investing, than were lenders, and more likely to answer "yes" rather than "sometimes." The hierarchy remained the same with groundwater contamination that most avoided (41.1% of the investors and 45.8% of the lenders would not consider these properties); soil contamination in the middle; and building contamination the most tolerable (78.9% of the investors and 76.3% of the lenders provided a positive response towards this type of contamination). Not surprisingly, lenders were more likely to answer "no" than investors.

Attitude Toward Property Known to Contain Different Sources of Contamination

The second question examined seven different sources of contamination or contaminants. It read: *Do you/would you invest/lend on a property known to be contaminated with 1). an underground storage tank; 2). volatile chemicals; 3). toxic chemicals; 4). petroleum products or derivatives; 5). radioactive materials; 6). asbestos; or 7). tenants that may contaminate the property?* Respondents were asked to indicate how they would react to these contaminants on the following 5-point scale: "yes, "probably," "maybe," "probably not," and "no." Our a priori judgment, based on earlier reports of similar surveys, was that few investors or lenders would be willing to work with any of the types of contamination, with the possible exception of asbestos, as previous surveys had identified some tolerance for this environmental problem. Therefore, the results shown in *Exhibit 2* were somewhat surprising.

Chapter 6: *Investor & Lender Reactions*

EXHIBIT 2

Responses Toward the Question: *Do you/would you invest in property known to be contaminated with:*

Panel A: Aggregate Responses

Type of Contamination	n*	"Yes"(%)	"Probably"(%)	"Maybe"(%)	"Probably Not"(%)	"No"(%)
Underground Storage Tank	115	13.0	15.7	40.9	15.7	14.8
Volatile Chemicals	115	2.6	2.6	23.5	34.8	36.5
Toxic Chemicals	115	2.6	1.7	26.1	31.3	38.3
Petroleum Products	115	3.5	13.9	42.6	20.0	20.0
Radioactive Materials	115	0.9	0.0	8.7	27.0	63.5
Asbestos	115	16.5	20.0	46.1	8.7	8.7
Tenants	116	8.6	6.0	44.8	16.4	24.1
Panel B: Investors' Responses						
Underground Storage Tank	56	12.5	19.6	44.6	14.3	8.9
Volatile Chemicals	56	1.8	3.6	23.2	39.3	32.1
Toxic Chemicals	56	1.8	1.8	23.2	41.1	32.1
Petroleum Products	56	1.8	19.6	39.3	25.0	14.3
Radioactive Materials	56	0.0	0.0	5.4	23.2	71.4
Asbestos	56	19.6	23.2	37.5	8.9	10.7
Tenants	56	7.1	8.9	42.9	19.6	21.4
Panel C: Lenders' Responses						
Underground Storage Tank	59	13.6	11.9	37.3	16.9	20.3
Volatile Chemicals	59	3.4	1.7	23.7	30.5	40.7
Toxic Chemicals	59	3.4	1.7	28.8	22.0	44.1
Petroleum Products	59	5.1	8.5	45.8	15.3	25.4
Radioactive Materials	59	1.7	0.0	11.9	30.5	55.9
Asbestos	59	13.6	16.9	54.2	8.5	6.8
Tenants	60	10.0	3.3	46.7	13.3	26.7

*n equals number of respondents
Source: Survey results

Exhibit 2 indicates that both investors and lenders were willing to make investments in or loans on properties with different sources of contamination in the following order:[2] properties with asbestos (not surprisingly, 36.5%); underground storage tank (28.7%); petroleum products or derivatives (17.4%); and tenants who might contaminate the property (14.6%). Quite a few also replied "maybe" with respect to these contaminants, which could also be viewed as a positive response to the given source of contamination. When the "maybe" category is included, the order switches slightly with an additional 46.1% considering investing or lending when asbestos is present; 44.8% when a tenant might contaminate the property; 42.6% for petroleum products; and 40.9% if the source of contamination were an underground storage tank.

Respondents clearly indicated they would avoid commitments on properties contaminated with radioactive materials (63.5% explicitly said "no" and another 27% said "probably not," for a total of 90.5% responding negatively). Volatile chemicals and toxic chemicals were also viewed primarily negatively, with 71.3% and 69.6%, respectively, responding with either a "no" or "probably not."

The responses by type of respondent basically mirrored the aggregate findings, although lenders seemed to reply "no" more frequently than the investors. Yet, for the most toxic of contaminants, the radioactive materials, 71.4% of the investors answered "no," as opposed to only 55.9% of lenders. Lenders were also more likely to reply with a definite "yes" except

2. Throughout our analysis, we judged a "yes" or "maybe" answer to be a positive response to the question. Each exhibit indicates the actual number responding to each component of each question so the number of respondents for each question does vary.

Valuing Contaminated Properties

in the case of asbestos contamination, where 19.6% of the investors and only 13.6% of the lenders would definitely advance funds.

Attitude Toward Property *Alleged* to Contain Sources of Contamination

After ascertaining the attitudes of investors and lenders toward known contamination and contaminants, we asked a similar question about properties *alleged* to be contaminated with the categories of contamination.[3] *Exhibit 3* summarizes the results for the five different types of contaminants: volatile chemicals, toxic chemicals, petroleum products, radioactive materials, and asbestos. (Underground storage tanks and contaminating tenants were omitted.)

As with the properties known to be contaminated, a hierarchy of willingness to invest or lend on properties with different types of contamination emerged. Asbestos was the least avoided, with 33.7% of the 107 respondents indicating a "yes" or "probably" for this source of contamination. Another 38.3% responded with a "maybe," suggesting that almost three-quarters of the respondents were somewhat positive (or at least not negative) toward properties containing asbestos. This is followed by petroleum products where 19.8% answered "yes" or "probably" and another 29.2% said "maybe."

As for highly negative reactions, the order was similar to that found when contamination was stated to be "known." Radioactive materials had the greatest negative response: 61.3% said "no" and another 26.4% said "probably not." Toxic chemicals elicited a 43.9% "no" response with 29% who indicated "probably not." Volatile chemicals were the third most negatively regarded source of alleged contamination: 43% said "no" and 29.9% said "probably not." It is interesting to note that "alleged" petroleum contamination produces more negative results than "known" contamination

3. In a few cases, respondents commented that they would verify to determine if the allegation were true and then skipped the question. We received 107 responses to this question, as compared with 116 replies when the contamination was *known* to exist.

EXHIBIT 3

Responses Toward the Question: *Do you/would you invest in property* alleged *to be contaminated with:*

Panel A: Aggregate Responses

Type of Contamination	n*	"Yes"(%)	"Probably"(%)	"Maybe"(%)	"Probably Not"(%)	"No"(%)
Volatile Chemicals	107	1.9	4.7	20.6	29.9	43.0
Toxic Chemicals	107	3.7	1.9	21.5	29.0	43.9
Petroleum Products	106	2.8	17.0	29.2	21.7	29.2
Radioactive Materials	106	0.9	0.0	11.3	26.4	61.3
Asbestos	107	13.1	20.6	38.3	11.2	16.8

Panel B: Investors' Responses

Type of Contamination	n*	"Yes"(%)	"Probably"(%)	"Maybe"(%)	"Probably Not"(%)	"No"(%)
Volatile Chemicals	52	1.9	7.7	19.2	32.7	38.5
Toxic Chemicals	52	3.8	1.9	19.2	36.5	38.5
Petroleum Products	51	2.0	21.6	25.5	29.4	21.6
Radioactive Materials	51	0.0	0.0	9.8	23.5	66.7
Asbestos	52	19.2	19.2	32.7	9.6	19.2

Panel C: Lenders' Responses

Type of Contamination	n*	"Yes"(%)	"Probably"(%)	"Maybe"(%)	"Probably Not"(%)	"No"(%)
Volatile Chemicals	55	1.8	1.8	21.8	27.3	47.3
Toxic Chemicals	55	3.6	1.8	23.6	21.8	49.1
Petroleum Products	55	3.6	12.7	32.7	14.5	36.4
Radioactive Materials	55	1.8	0.0	12.7	29.1	56.4
Asbestos	55	7.3	21.8	43.6	12.7	14.5

*n equals number of respondents
Source: Survey results

Chapter 6: *Investor & Lender Reactions*

did, with over 50% indicating "no" or "probably not." By type of respondent, lenders were once again much more negative toward all sources of contamination, except radioactive materials. There, 68.7% of the investors responded with a definite "no" but only 56.4% of the lenders did. As for positive reactions, investors were more favorably inclined than lenders toward both asbestos and petroleum products.

Attitudes Toward Property Located Within 300 Feet of Contaminated Property

To test the judgment that investors and lenders are also concerned enough to limit their investing in and lending on properties located in close proximity to a source of contamination, the following question was asked: *Do you/would you invest in/lend on property within 300 feet [of 9 different contaminants]?* Again, the five response choices included "yes," "probably," "maybe," "probably not," and "no." Results are summarized in *Exhibit 4*, and the frequency of responses is ranked both for all of the respondents and by type of respondent: investor or lender.

EXHIBIT 4

Responses Toward the Question: *Do you/would you invest in property within 300 feet of:*

Panel A: Aggregate Responses

Type of Contamination	n*	"Yes"(%)	"Probably"(%)	"Maybe"(%)	"Probably Not"(%)	"No"(%)
A contaminated groundwater plume	114	3.5	7.0	53.5	30.7	5.3
High-voltage electricity lines	115	15.7	27.0	33.0	18.3	6.1
An industrial landfill (hazardous, toxic)	116	0.9	2.6	22.4	43.1	31.0
A high-traffic street or highway	115	55.7	33.0	10.4	0.9	0.0
A high-pressure natural gas line	115	24.3	34.8	33.9	6.1	0.9
A radioactive materials handling facility	116	0.0	6.0	20.7	33.6	39.7
An oil refinery or petrochemical plant	115	3.5	10.4	30.4	30.4	25.2
A landfill (non-hazardous, non-toxic)	115	7.8	16.5	46.1	20.9	8.7
Land contaminated by radioactive materials	115	0.0	0.9	13.9	29.6	55.7

Panel B: Investors' Responses

Type of Contamination	n*	"Yes"(%)	"Probably"(%)	"Maybe"(%)	"Probably Not"(%)	"No"(%)
A contaminated groundwater plume	57	5.3	7.0	49.1	36.8	1.8
High-voltage electricity lines	57	17.5	19.3	35.1	22.8	5.3
An industrial landfill (hazardous, toxic)	57	1.8	1.8	21.1	47.4	28.1
A high-traffic street or highway	57	61.4	26.3	12.3	0.0	0.0
A high-pressure natural gas line	57	28.1	29.8	36.8	5.3	0.0
A radioactive materials handling facility	57	0.0	5.3	12.3	29.8	52.6
An oil refinery or petrochemical plant	57	3.5	8.8	24.6	29.8	33.3
A landfill (non-hazardous, non-toxic)	57	14.0	17.5	43.9	19.3	5.3
Land contaminated by radioactive materials	57	0.0	1.8	8.8	24.6	64.9

Panel C: Lenders' Responses

Type of Contamination	n*	"Yes"(%)	"Probably"(%)	"Maybe"(%)	"Probably Not"(%)	"No"(%)
A contaminated groundwater plume	57	1.8	7.0	57.9	24.6	8.8
High-voltage electricity lines	58	13.8	34.5	31.0	13.8	6.9
An industrial landfill (hazardous, toxic)	59	0.0	3.4	23.7	39.0	33.9
A high-traffic street or highway	58	50.0	39.7	8.6	1.7	0.0
A high-pressure natural gas line	58	20.7	39.7	31.0	6.9	1.7
A radioactive materials handling facility	59	0.0	6.8	28.8	37.3	27.1
An oil refinery or petrochemical plant	58	3.4	12.1	36.2	31.0	17.2
A landfill (non-hazardous, non-toxic)	58	1.7	15.5	48.3	22.4	12.1
Land contaminated by radioactive materials	58	0.0	0.0	19.0	34.5	46.6

*n equals number of respondents

Source: Survey results

Valuing Contaminated Properties

A high traffic street or highway had the least negative impact. Over three-quarters of all respondents (89.7%) indicated either that they would ("yes") or they might ("probably") invest/lend on property located within 300 feet of a piece of property. A high-pressure natural gas line was second most frequently cited as being no deterrent to investment (58.9%). Both high-voltage electricity lines (42.7%) and a non-toxic landfill (24.3%) were also not regarded as serious bars to investment. When the "maybe" responses were added in, a contaminated groundwater plume is included in the potential list with 64% indicating that "yes," "probably," or "maybe" they would lend or invest if it were within 300 feet of a site. This compares to a high-traffic street/highway (99.1%), high-pressure gas lines (93%), high-voltage electricity lines (75.7%), and non-hazardous landfills (70.4%).

When negative responses are considered, radioactive materials continue to rank highest on the list of contaminants that respondents would avoid ("no" or "probably not"). For a property located within 300 feet of land contaminated with radioactive materials, 55.7% of the respondents indicated they would not lend or invest. When the "probably not" responses are included, total negative reactions were 85.3%. A radioactive materials handling facility was the second most frequently listed "no" response (39.7%), followed by hazardous industrial landfill (31%). When the "probably not" responses are considered, these two contaminants have almost identical negative response ratings. Proximity to an oil refinery or petrochemical plant was the fourth most negatively mentioned contaminant, with 25.2% indicating "no" and another 30.4% responding "probably not."

When the most negatively regarded contaminants are examined, investors were more likely than lenders to say "no" for property contaminated by radioactive materials (64.9% vs. 46.6%); a radioactive materials handling facility (52.6% vs. 27.1%); and an oil refinery or petrochemical plant (33.3% vs. 17.2%). On the other hand, the lenders were more likely to say "no" for the hazardous landfill (33.9% vs. 28.1%).

Conclusion

A major finding from this study is that there are some sources of contamination which investors and lenders are willing to tolerate. Building contaminants such as asbestos and underground storage tanks were more acceptable than many of the other sources of contamination. In particular, radioactive materials were high on the list of contaminants that investors and lenders alike avoid, and generally will not consider. For the most part, investors were more definite and pronounced about their aversion than lenders. While reactions to the different sources of contamination varied when the contamination problem was *alleged,* rather than *known,* the hierarchy of aversion remained basically the same. When investors and lenders were asked about contamination on properties in close proximity to a subject property, very strong negative reactions toward radioactive materials persist. Furthermore, investors were again much more concerned than lenders.

Although there is obviously a large degree of aversion to investor or lender liability from several types of both on-site and off-site (but proximate) contaminants, the results of this study provide some good news to owners and would-be purchasers of commercial and industrial property since a lot of institutional grade investment property is already known or suspected to be contaminated by asbestos or underground storage tanks, rather than by radioactive materials. Therefore, for the marketplace, these results suggest that many of the environmental "problem" properties actually do have a market that is somewhat broader than has previously been believed. Moreover, a not insignificant proportion of investors and lenders appear willing to invest or lend with some of the contaminants so the previous "word on the street" should be revised.[REI]

References

Healy, Patricia R., and John E. Healy, "Lenders' Perspectives on Environmental Issues," *Real Estate Issues,* Fall/Winter 1991. (Reprinted in The Appraisal Journal, July 1992.)

Kinnard, William N., Jr., and Elaine M. Worzala, *Attitudes and Policies of Institutional Investors and Lenders Toward On-site and Nearby Property Contamination.* Paper presented at American Real Estate Society Annual Meeting, South Lake Tahoe, CA, March 1996.

Mundy, Bill, "Stigma and Value," *The Appraisal Journal,* January 1992.

Lender Attitudes Toward Source and Nonsource Impaired Property Mortgages

by Albert R. Wilson and Arthur R. Alarcon, SRA

Albert R. Wilson, of Parker, Colorado, is a specialist in the development of valuation opinions for the assignment of environmental impairment damages to real property. He earned a BS in materials science engineering from Northwestern University, Evanston, Illinois, and an MBA from Bowling Green State University, Ohio.

Arthur R. Alarcon, SRA, is the owner of ARA & Associates, Denver, Colorado. He received a BA in business administration from the University of Texas, El Paso.

This article originally appeared in the October 1997 issue of The Appraisal Journal.

The results of a number of general surveys of lender policies and attitudes concerning environmentally impaired property have been published over the past several years.[1] In general, those surveys indicate that lenders have adopted policies addressing the environmental condition of a property. They also indicate that lenders tend to avoid lending when such property is to be used as collateral or to lend at incrementally higher premiums or at terms, and conditions that increase the borrower's costs as a way of offsetting lender perceptions of higher risks.

A sample of mortgage lenders were surveyed on specific circumstances involving a source and a nonsource property. A source property is defined as the property on which a release of a hazardous substance occurred. Therefore, the owner of a source property is assumed to have liability under the *Comprehensive Environmental Response, Compensation and Liability Act* (CERCLA). A nonsource property is one that has been contaminated by a release of a hazardous substance on another property having no ownership or operating relationship to the subject. The sampling was conducted in two market areas, south Florida and Chicago.

The results of the sampling indicated that lenders were not a priori adverse to mortgage lending on either the source or the nonsource property at unimpaired market terms and conditions, given the situations that were described to them in the sampling. This result is somewhat at odds with what one might expect from earlier, more general published surveys of lender attitudes. Part of the apparent difference may be attributed to the normal respondent reactions to a general inquiry versus a specific case on which to base answers.

Sampling Description

Both samplings were conducted in an identical manner. Lenders were selected based on the premise that the lender was in the market area of the subject property and had a designated member of the Appraisal Institute on staff, or a designated member in the area knew of the lender's activities.

1. See Bill Mundy, "The Impact of Hazardous Material on Real Property Value," *The Appraisal Journal* (April 1992): 155–162; "Stigma and Value," *The Appraisal Journal* (January 1992): 7–13; "The Impact of Hazardous and Toxic Material on Property Value: Revisited," *The Appraisal Journal* (October 1992): 463–471; and John J. Healy and Patricia R. Healy, "Lenders' Perspectives on Environmental Issues," *The Appraisal Journal* (July 1992): 394–398.

Chapter 6: *Lender Attitudes*

Each lender was contacted to identify within its organization the individual most capable of providing experienced lending officer responses, given the type of property involved. That individual was then contacted by an appraiser with expertise in obtaining lender data and underwent several specific screening criteria. To prevent bias, the interviewer was not the person who constructed the questionnaire and was not acquainted with the respondent.

The screening criteria were number of years of experience in commercial and/or industrial property mortgage origination, and specific experience in environmentally impaired properties. If the individual did not have at least five years of experience lending to commercial and/or industrial properties and experience dealing with environmentally impaired properties, the interview was terminated.

As an additional qualification criterion, the individual was questioned about the lender's policy on environmental screening of property before granting a mortgage and was asked to provide an outline of the policy. If the lender did not have a written or an unwritten policy, or the individual could not provide a policy outline, the interview was terminated.

Case Descriptions

Once the screening procedure was cleared, a specific case was described to the individual. The following descriptions of the cases were read to the respondent:

Source property case description

"The subject property is a small (12,000-square-foot) industrial building approximately 20 years old in reasonable condition for its age. It is of masonry and steel frame construction with approximately 1,000 square feet of office space included within the building and located in an industrial park containing similar buildings with a high occupancy rate. An appraisal performed by a well-respected, experienced MAI concluded that the market value of the subject was $475,000, assuming the building is ready for occupancy. According to the appraisal report, estimated gross annual rental income would be $51,570 with an estimated net income of $46,323 in 1991. Assume that all of the information is the same today as in 1991."

Nonsource property case description

"The property is a neighborhood shopping center with a strong positive cash flow more than sufficient to cover debt service, and an ownership that has successfully managed both the subject property and several similar properties for more than ten years. The property is held in a partnership and the net worth of the partners is in excess of ten times the amount requested. Individual guarantees by the partners are available.

"The subject property was appraised in 1990 and the value opinion was $3.15 million. For purposes of this analysis, the 1990 value is assumed to be the current market value subject to confirmation by an appraisal. The existing loan has been successfully serviced since origination, but carries a higher than current market rate. The owners, therefore, feel it is desirable to obtain a replacement loan at contemporary rates. They are requesting a loan with a loan-to-value ratio of 70%, seven-year term, 15-year amortization with a balloon payment."

After the case description had been read, the respondent was given an opportunity to clarify his or her understanding of the information. The questions asked by the respondent were recorded along with the interviewer's response to the questions. The interviewer had been briefed on the most likely questions and was required to provide responses within his understanding of the case.

The respondent was then asked specific questions about his or her organization's willingness to lend on the subject property, given the case description, and—in the source property case—the probable terms of any mortgage financing available. These responses were recorded in terms of recourse versus nonrecourse loan types, loan-to-value ratios, amortization schedules, call dates, interest rates, and likely closing costs.

The respondent was then informed that certain environmental conditions existed on the property and was given the following information:

Source property environmental condition

"An environmental issue of concern has been revealed by an American Society for Testing and Materials (ASTM) Phase I Environmental Site Assessment and additional data. As a result of the conditions identified, a competent, experienced environmental consultant has reviewed the available records. The following is a summary of findings and opinions:

"A review of the governing agency records indicates that the tenant of the property at the time the *Resource Conservation and Recovery Act* (RCRA) was first in effect had filed a request for RCRA Part A and Part B permits. Those permits were granted on an interim basis by the governing agencies.

"After an investigation and post-issuance review, the governing agencies notified the tenant to formally request a withdrawal of the permits because the tenant neither stored hazardous material nor generated hazardous waste. Thus, the permits should not have been issued as the tenant was not an RCRA facility. The governing agency asked the tenant to send the appropriate paperwork withdrawing the RCRA permits. Because the tenant moved and went out of business, the administrative step for withdrawal of the permits was not completed. Accordingly, the permits are still present on the records.

"Small quantities of several common industrial substances were also identified in the soils on the subject property. These substances are of unknown origin. It is the considered opinion of the environmental expert that the substances will not require remediation due to low concentrations and lack of threat to human health and/or the environment. A requirement by the governing agencies to remediate the solvents is unlikely. The governing agency staff is aware of the situation and has expressed no interest in pursuing the matter."

Nonsource property environmental condition

"The environmental issue of concern has been revealed by an ASTM Phase I Environmental Site Assessment and additional data. It is summarized as follows:

"Adjacent to the subject property is a major brand gasoline station with underground storage tanks. Leaks and spills are likely to have occurred on the station property. The property owner and the operator have jointly undertaken investigative work that outlined the extent of the problem. Further, they have acknowledged responsibility for any leaks or spills originating on their property. Based on available information, it appears that some of the refined petroleum products entered the groundwater and migrated under the subject. The subject and surrounding properties do not use the groundwater, having full municipal water and sewer services.

"There are not now and have never been as far as can be determined any underground storage tanks on the subject. Remediation of the groundwater

Chapter 6: *Lender Attitudes*

underlying the subject will be wholly financed by the station owner and operator, who have sufficient financial resources to complete the work. The remediation activities should not disturb the subject's use, occupancy, or revenues. There is no evidence of any impact on the subject property's buildings nor is any expected."

The respondent was then given an opportunity to clarify his or her understanding of the environmental condition on the same basis as before. Having answered the respondent's questions about the case, the interviewer then asked the identical mortgage lending questions regarding the availability of funds for this situation and the terms and conditions associated with those funds, given the environmental description.

Sampling Results

Table 1 indicates the respondents' average number of years of experience and loan-to-value ratios. The ranges of other responses are also shown. Note that the nonsource property sampling was conducted before the United States Environmental Protection Agency (EPA) issued its "EPA Policy Toward Owners of Property Containing Contaminated Aquifers" on May 25, 1995. This policy should improve the lending environment for the nonsource property case. The policy was summarized as follows:

> As part of the Agency's Administrative Reform and Brownfields Initiatives, EPA is issuing a new policy toward certain owners of property to which hazardous substances have migrated in an aquifer from a source outside the property. Based on EPA's interpretation of CERCLA, the Agency will not pursue such property owners to perform cleanups or for reimbursement of response costs and will consider *de minimis* settlements with such owners where necessary to protect them from third-party contribution suits.[2]

Analysis of Results

One of the first points to keep in mind is that the results of the sampling may be biased in the sense that lenders appear to be more wary of commercial property than of industrial property. To the extent that this is an underlying phenomenon, it may be worthwhile to examine the nonsource property sampling absent the two respondents who were unwilling to lend because the loan was too small. All of the lenders expressed concern over the tenants of the commercial property and, in particular, were interested in whether or not a major retail anchor tenant was in place with a remaining lease term at least equal to the call date of the proposed mortgage. This issue obviously has nothing to do with the environmental condition of the property. In a similar vein, the industrial property lenders were very interested in owner occupancy and several stated that they would not lend to a property unless it was owner-occupied. Again, this bias has nothing to do with the environmental condition.

Given these concerns, the results of the sampling indicate that a majority of lenders are prepared to provide mortgage financing on the same terms and conditions whether or not the property is affected by environmental conditions so long as those environmental conditions do not appear to create a financial threat to either the borrower or the lender. Put another way, the results indicate clearly that it is improper to characterize a contaminated property as "non-financeable" without careful, in-depth analysis and evaluation of the facts and circumstances of the case. While

2. Environmental Protection Agency, "EPA Policy Toward Owners of Property Containing Contaminated Aquifers," *Environmental Due Diligence Guide* (1996): 501:1425 et seq.

Valuing Contaminated Properties

TABLE 1 Summary of Sampling Responses

	Nonsource Property Responses	Source Property Responses	Data Description
Number of respondents	10	5	
Years of lending experience (average)	10.9	11.4	
Experience with impaired properties:			
Number of properties	2,918+	229+	
Number successfully placed	61%	75%	
Unimpaired case:			
Willing to lend?			
Yes	8	5	
No	2	0	
Reason for not lending:			
Too small	2	0	
Terms of lending:			
Recourse	7	4	
Nonrecourse	1	1	
Loan to value	NA	75%	
Amortization (years)	NA	20–25	
Call (years)	NA	3–5	
Rate:			
Fixed	NA	7.875%–8.875%	
Variable	NA	2%–3% over T-bill	
Closing costs	NA	2% + appraisal fee	
Impaired case:			
Willing to lend (of those willing to lend in the unimpaired case)?			
Yes	7	5	
No	1	0	
Reason for not lending:			
Environmental condition	1	0	
Terms of lending:			
Recourse	6	4	
Nonrecourse	1	1	
Loan to value	NA	75%	
Amortization (years)	NA	20–25	
Call (years)	NA	3–5	
Rate			
Fixed	NA	7.875%–8.875%	
Variable	NA	2%–3% over T-bill	
Closing costs	NA	2% + appraisal + environmental review costs	
Additional conditions of lending:			
Cleanup performance bond	5	No	
Owner guarantee of cleanup	6	No	
Hold-harmless	6	No	
Other	NFA	NFA	

NA = Not asked in the survey.

NFA = "No further action" letter from the governing environmental agencies or a "no further action" opinion by a reputable environmental expert.

additional due diligence—with its attendant costs—may be reasonably anticipated by the borrower and those additional costs may be sufficient to decrease the property value to a minor extent ($5,000 to $15,000), the sampling suggests that no other incremental costs imposed by debt financing are likely.

Mortgage Lenders and the Institutionalization and Normalization of Environmental Risk Analysis

by Richard J. Roddewig, MAI and Allen C. Keiter, MAI

Real Estate Markets, Uncertainty, Environmental Risk, and the Real Estate Appraiser

Buyers and sellers of real estate, whether a personal residence, an income-producing investment, or a property used in a trade or business, understand intuitively that owning real estate involves accepting risks. For example, home buyers accept risks related to such things as the condition of building systems that are hidden behind walls or floors, the friendliness of their neighbors, the quality of the local school system, or the future state of the marketplace when it comes time to sell the property.

As appraisers, we too know that owning real estate, or lending on it, is accompanied by willing acceptance of some types of risks. Although the level of risk can be reduced by laws or regulations requiring disclosure of specific types of information—and by customary "due diligence" by typical buyers, sellers, or lenders in a marketplace—acceptance of some risk is inherent in the process of real estate acquisition and lending. Acceptance of some risk is a fundamental and normal component of the typical marketplace of buyers, sellers, and lenders who are reasonable, knowledgeable, and willing.

One of our functions as real estate appraisers and analysts is to determine, from the marketplace itself, what level of risk the marketplace is willing to accept. Appraisers, in the normal course of their work, become experienced in the identification and evaluation of what risks the marketplace is willing to accept. Market prices paid for similar properties with similar degrees of risk lead us to our market value conclusions, and, in the case of income producing properties, we further evaluate risks based upon the accepted rates of return for properties carrying similar levels of risk.

The history of the American real estate marketplace over the last 100 years is a story of constant change and innovation. New types of property concepts, new types of regulations, new types of uses for real estate, and new types of ways to own and finance real estate are constantly being added to the factors that the marketplace must incorporate into the trans-

Richard J. Roddewig, MAI, is president of Clarion Associates, Inc., with offices in Chicago, Denver, Philadelphia, and Cincinnati. He co-developed the Appraisal Institute's environmental seminar, "Environmental Risk and the Real Estate Appraisal Process," as well as the revised seminar due to be released later in 2001. He is a regular contributor to The Appraisal Journal on environmental issues.

Allen C. Keiter, MAI, is a senior real estate analyst in the Chicago office of Clarion Associates. Before joining Clarion, he was a senior real estate appraiser and risk manager with ABN AMRO in Chicago, and served as a staff review appraiser with NATIONSBANK in Palm Beach, Florida.

This article originally appeared in the April 2001 issue of The Appraisal Journal.

actional process. Change creates uncertainty, and every time there is uncertainty some level of risk is introduced that must be analyzed and dealt with by the marketplace. With time, the market becomes comfortable with the new uncertainty and any early impact on price due to its novelty diminishes.

The environmental awakening of the 1970s was just such a fundamental change, creating considerable uncertainty in the real estate marketplace. New information about the toxic effects of some types of chemicals and the extent of these chemicals in the environment, as well as new laws and regulations limiting emissions and imposing cleanup responsibilities, had to be assimilated into the real estate marketplace.

Over the past 15 years or so, the American real estate marketplace has become increasingly comfortable evaluating and handling environmental risks. This is due to a variety of factors, including the development of the technical and scientific expertise to identify the presence and extent of contamination, the creation of a remediation industry and cost-effective cleanup techniques, the clarification of legal responsibilities, and the infusion into the marketplace of the information and techniques necessary to evaluate those risks and quantify them into hard dollars and cents.

Consider, for example, the evolution of environmental science as a profession. Twenty-five years ago, environmental science was not a common university curriculum. Today, it is a well-recognized science field with a clear career path. Many environmental professionals—whether employed by a government agency, a lending institution, or an independent consulting office preparing environmental reports—have master's degrees in science. An increasing number of these technical professionals have been involved in the environmental field for 10 to 20 years or more. Today's environmental profession and industry utilize reliable techniques and cost-effective procedures to detect environmental contamination and to implement reasonable cleanup.

Lenders and the Internal Institutionalization of Environmental Risk Analysis

As the marketplace has evolved, all of the players in the marketplace have grown in their sophistication in understanding and evaluating environmental risks. This is especially true of the lending community, one of the most critical players. The attitude of the lending community toward environmental risk has changed dramatically over the past 25 years.

Mortgage lenders have incorporated techniques for evaluating environmental risks into their mortgage lending, business lending, trust, and real estate acquisition and disposition processes. The impetus for this has come from several sources, including:

- case law such as the *Fleet Factors* case[1] that initially made mortgage lenders potentially responsible for cleanup and other liabilities associated with classification as "potentially responsible parties" (PRPs) unless they could successfully invoke the "innocent purchaser" defense by having utilized good commercial due diligence practice before making a mortgage loan;

- guidance comments from lending industry regulators that "encourages" lenders to add environmental professionals to their staffs and to adopt acceptable procedures to gauge environmental risks before making some types of decisions;[2] and

---

1. *United States v. Fleet Factors Corp.*, 724 F.Supp. 955 (S.D. Ga. 1988), 901 F.2d 1550, *reh'g denied, en banc,* 911 F.2d 742 (11th Cir. 1990).

2. Among the agencies issuing such "guidance" notes were the OTS in 1989, Fannie Mae/Freddie Mac in 1991, the Federal Reserve in 1991, and the FDIC and OCC in 1992.

Chapter 6: *Institutionalization and Normalization of Risk*

- the natural inclination of lenders to develop systematic and efficient ways to handle risks associated with real estate lending and ownership.

An astute lender recognizes that all real estate and business transactions involve acceptance of some risk. To competently lend, a lender must first identify the risk, then identify the extent of the risk, and finally identify ways of managing the risk. Lenders can take on the risk themselves or to transfer some or all of the risk to another entity—by requiring or securing environmental insurance, for example. Some larger banks with a risk management culture have responded by hiring environmental professionals to provide professional guidance to the loan committee on environmental issues and risks.

Surveys Show Changing Lender Attitudes Over Time

During the late 1980s and early 1990s, lender attitudes about making loans on contaminated properties evolved quickly. Spurred on by a number of policy and regulatory initiatives, lenders gradually developed techniques and procedures for incorporating environmental risk analysis into their lending decisions. Adding to the pressure was a movement by state and federal lawmakers to clarify the situations in which mortgage lenders would be characterized as "innocent purchasers" who could avoid potential liability for the costs of environmental remediation.[3] The resulting change in lender attitudes toward lending on properties affected by environmental risks has been documented in surveys conducted by appraisers.

Patricia and John Healy, Jr., MAI, reported in *The Appraisal Journal* in 1992 the results of their 1990 fourth quarter survey of major lenders on issues related to environmental risk. The purpose of the survey was "to quantify lenders' perceptions of environmental risks and the degree to which these perceptions affect underwriting policy."[4] They contacted 57 institutions, including the 25 largest banks and a number of international banks. The survey was relatively short and to the point, comprising only eight questions, two of them vaguely worded queries about which environmental problems these lenders believed were most significant.[5]

The Healys' most significant questions involved bankers' attitudes about lending on contaminated property, previously contaminated property, or property adjacent to contaminated property, as well as their question concerning underwriting standards on properties affected by environmental risk.

More than 84% of the bankers said they would have no problem lending on a previously contaminated property after remediation. About 50% of the national banks said they made loans on properties that were in the process of being remediated. But fewer than 40% would consider making a loan on a property contiguous to a contaminated parcel. As to properties that had once been contaminated but were subsequently remediated, almost 50% of the bankers interviewed did not believe there was any loss in market value, 37% of the bankers were not sure if there was a loss in market value, and 19% perceived a "stigma" effect on market value as a result of the previous contamination.

The bankers in the Healys' survey considered various types of underwriting techniques when contamination was a concern. About 66% said they would require additional indemnification—60% would require some form of personal guarantee—while 46% would consider adjusting the loan-to-value ratio, and 21% would consider an interest rate adjustment.

3. See, for example, Thomas R. Kearns, "Environmental Audits: Real Estate's Newest Transaction Safeguards," *The Appraisal Journal* (July 1991): 348–352.

4. Patricia R. Healy and John J. Healy, Jr., MAI, "Lenders' Perspectives on Environmental Issues," *The Appraisal Journal* (July 1992): 394–398, at 398.

5. Question 2 stated "On a 1 to 5 scale, rank the following environmental issues according to their concern, with 1 being the least worrisome and 5 being the most worrisome: a. underground storage tanks. b. unencapsulated asbestos. c. encapsulated asbestos. d. groundwater contamination. e. a tenant who stored toxic materials." This question did not clearly establish the basis for the worry—personal concern on the part of the survey respondent? Institutional concern, and, if so, how established? Societal concern? Concern in terms of difficulties to clean up, or concern in terms of lending decisions? Question 3 was similarly ambiguous: "Regarding the above environmental issues: a. Which issue is the greatest concern to your institution? b. Which issue is the least concern to your institution?" Again, the meaning of "concern to your institution" was not defined for the survey respondent. Of great concern because the institution had made loans on properties in the past with that type of environmental problem? Concern because it is the most serious problem facing the country? Concern because the institution does not have the expertise to evaluate the risks associated with lending on a property so affected?

Valuing Contaminated Properties

Another appraisal firm that surveyed lenders about the same time as the Healys found an increasing concern about environmental issues among the lenders surveyed in the late 1980s, but decreasing concern about these issues in the early 1990s. Mundy & Associates found that the percentage of surveyed lenders with formal policies about contaminated properties increased from 41% in 1987 to 88% in 1991, and to 90% in 1992.[6] But at the same time, this survey found that while 42% of the lenders surveyed in 1991 believed that environmental problems would continue to increase, only 27.5% of survey respondents in 1992 shared that belief.

The Mundy & Associates 1991 survey found that despite the bankers' belief that environmental issues had become more acute during the 1980s, the vast majority of banks were ready and willing to consider making loans on property with known or suspected contamination. About 88% of the respondents to the 1991 survey said loans on property with known or suspected contamination were only occasionally, rarely, or never declined solely due to the contamination. Only 12% said such loan applications were often declined.

Changing Lender Attitudes as Evidenced by Revised Internal Loan Policy Procedures

Lenders have gradually reduced the amount of environmental review necessary before making many types of lending and transactional decisions, further evidence that lenders perceive that the environmental risks associated with many types of properties are decreasing. In the 1980s and early 1990s, many lenders required full Phase I environmental site assessments before making most types of real estate lending decisions.[7] Today, most national and regional banks use *risk-based criteria* to decide if a full Phase I site assessment is necessary. The criteria are based on property type and loan amount. For example, the threshold for a Phase I assessment may be set on a specific loan amount; many banks set this at a million dollars. (For a shopping center, this threshold may be set somewhat higher.) Transactions that do not trigger a Phase I assessment may be subject to "ASTM transactional screens."[8] As banks frequently use less rigorous rubrics when first reviewing most loan, trust, and acquisition decisions, there are now in effect two levels of less-detailed review and risk analysis that are frequently used by lenders before a full Phase I environmental assessment is triggered.

Scaling back of the due diligence process is evidence of the increasing comfort of the lending community in evaluating environmental risks. Lenders have evolved due diligence techniques that have shorter turnaround times and are less expensive—about $800 for an ASTM screen, and only $200 for a typical non-ASTM-compliant screen—a sure indication that they feel more comfortable with risk analysis, and that the perceived risks attached to many types of properties have decreased dramatically. Lenders today feel much more comfortable with their ability to analyze and manage environmental risks at a much lower cost.

The Environmental Bankers Association and the External Institutionalization of Environmental Risk Analysis

Another telltale sign that the environmental industry has matured in its evaluation of environmental risk is the development of a national organization of lending professionals involved in environmental risk analysis.

---

6. Victoria Adams and Bill Mundy, MAI, "Attitudes and Policies of Lending Institutions Toward Environmental Impairment," *Environmental Watch* (6:4, 1993). *Environmental Watch* is a discontinued publication of The Appraisal Institute.

7. See, for example, Albert R. Wilson, "The Environmental Opinion: Basis for an Impaired Value Opinion," *The Appraisal Journal* (July 1994): 410–423. The American Society for Testing and Materials (ASTM), founded in 1898, is the largest voluntary consensus standards developing organization in the world. It provides the standards for both Phase I and Phase II audits. See *Standard Guide for Environmental Site Assessments: Phase 1 Environmental Assessment Process* (ASTM order number E1527-00) and *Standard Guide for Environmental Site Assessments: Phase 2 Environmental Assessment Process* (ASTM order number E1903-97). ASTM's web site is www.ASTM.org.

8. ASTM's Standard Practice for Environmental Site Assessments: Transactional Screen Process (Standard No. E1528) requires the 28-question "transaction screen" and an on-site inspection. Industry-wide, this is commonly called an "ASTM transaction screen," while the plain term "transaction screen" refers only to the 28-question computer printout.

Chapter 6: *Institutionalization and Normalization of Risk*

The Environmental Bankers Association (EBA) is a non-profit group that represents the financial services industry, including banks, insurers, and asset management firms.[9] Its membership comprises lending institutions, insurers, environmental engineers, consultants, and attorneys. The EBA was established to heighten sensitivity to environmental risk issues, and to highlight the need for environmental risk management and due diligence policies and procedures in financial institutions. The membership includes environmental officers employed in some of the largest financial institutions in the nation.

Founded in 1994 with a membership of about 25 banks, the EBA today has a roster of 38 regional banks. Its main functions are to:

- keep members informed about new developments in environmental policy, banking policy, legislative and regulatory trends, and other emerging environmental issues on both a state and national level;

- provide input about new benchmarks for environmental due diligence procedures and risk-based decision making for appropriate levels of environmental inquiry to financial transactions;

- periodically update information on environmental insurance programs and ways to utilize insurance to quantify the cost of environmental risks;[10]

- interface with banking and environmental regulatory officials;

- provide industry training and round table discussions at twice-yearly conferences; and

- conduct periodic surveys of EBA members about their procedures for handling environmental risks.

Since 1995, the EBA has undertaken two surveys of its members. The first survey was conducted in 1995 and had 30 questions, some with a number of subsections. It was sent to member financial institutions, and 32 responded. All respondents had net asset values in excess of $1 billion.[11] The second, conducted over the course of 1999 and 2000, had 35 questions (again some had a number of subsections), and 25 member banks responded.[12] Both surveys addressed many of the same questions, though the second survey was more extensive. The first survey was designed to address "Environmental Due Diligence policy and procedures for real estate property taken, or considered for collateral, ownership and fiduciary assets."[13] According to the EBA, the second survey conducted in 1999/2000 was designed to "provide insights about trends relative to how environmental policies are being employed, how the due diligence process is evolving, what are the average cost and time frames for conducting due diligence, and what additional risk management tools are being used, such as environmental insurance for real estate transactions."[14]

A comparison of the results of the two surveys provides a number of important insights about the real estate lending industry and its increasing ability to institutionalize environmental risk evaluation and management procedures. Among them are the following:

- There is a growing trend toward written environmental review policies adopted on a corporate-wide basis. In 1995, for example, 93% of the surveyed institutions responding had written environmental policies addressing real estate secured lending/credit risks, a figure

9. The Environmental Bankers Association has an administrative staff of two. It can be contacted at *www.envirobank.org* and is headquartered in Alexandria, Virginia.

10. Based on comments of the bankers who attended the EBA's conference in Santa Fe, New Mexico, in February 2001, many of them now view environmental insurance as the ultimate way to quantify environmental risk and stigma in hard dollars and cents and to transfer that risk from the property itself to an insurance carrier. For more information on environmental insurance programs and their relevance to the appraisal process, see Richard J. Roddewig, MAI, "Using the Cost of Environmental Insurance to Measure Contaminated Property Stigma," *The Appraisal Journal* (July 1997): 304–308.

11. Eight of the responding banks had net assets between $1 billion and $10 billion, while six had net assets in excess of $100 billion. The remaining 18 had net assets between $10 billion and $100 billion.

12. Two banks had more than one representative return a survey form, so the 1999/2000 had 27 total responses.

13. Environmental Bankers Association, Inc., *January, 1995 Environmental Due Diligence Survey:* 1.

14. Environmental Bankers Association, Inc., *1999/2000 Environmental Due Diligence Survey:* 1.

Valuing Contaminated Properties

that rose to 100% by 1999/2000. In 1995, only 29% had a single corporate-wide environmental policy, while 60% reported such a policy in the 1999/2000 survey.

- Lenders are increasingly appointing full-time environmental risk managers or environmental policy managers to designated internal departments or groups responsible for implementation and overview of environmental due diligence. These professionals are increasingly likely to be trained environmental professionals (65% in 1995 compared to 80% in 1999/2000) rather than "converted" bankers (48% in 1995 compared to 20% in 1999/2000), and are increasingly likely to be located in either their credit policy, real estate, or appraisal areas of business.

- Lenders are becoming more likely to provide internal environmental risk training programs (90% in 1995, increasing to 96% in 1999/2000).

- Lenders seem to be more skilled at quickly differentiating between potentially risky environmental situations without automatically requiring environmental due diligence. In 1995, for example, 93% of the respondents required environmental due diligence before purchasing a facility or a property, but only 76% required this in 1999/2000. In 1995, 92% of the respondents said they required environmental due diligence prior to acceptance of a trust asset/account, compared to only 56% in 1999/2000.

- While member institutions continue to establish thresholds for requiring environmental due diligence, the threshold seems to be getting lower. For example, in 1995, 79% of the respondents reported that they did not require environmental due diligence when lending on one- to four-unit residential properties. In 1999/2000, only 56% automatically exempted such properties. In 1995, 14% automatically exempted properties valued under $100,000 and 53% automatically exempted properties under $250,000, but by 1999/2000, the percentages were 28% and 24%, respectively.

- Institutions are generally employing a wider variety of environmental due diligence procedures. The percentage of respondents using each of the eight types of due diligence procedures listed in the 1995 survey increased dramatically in five of the eight categories specified again in 1999/2000.[15]

- The costs and completion times associated with inspections, screenings, and Phase I environmental site assessments are decreasing, and it is the borrower who now tends to order the work (40% in 1995, compared to 60% in 1999/2000).

The 1999/2000 EBA survey included a number of new questions. Many of these dealt with issues related to environmental insurance, an increasingly popular tool for lenders to quantify the costs associated with environmental risks. In 1995, only 6% of the respondents indicated that they used "environmental impairment/transaction insurance" as a due diligence technique. By 1999/2000, "forty percent (40%) of the respondents said that they used environmental insurance for real estate secured lending and 32% for commercial and/or industrial transactions..."[16] A number of the banks were using environmental insurance as a substitute for guaran-

15. The only exceptions were "environmental inspections" (81% in 1995 and 72% in 1999/2000), environmental compliance audits (50% in 1995 and 48% in 1999/2000), and environmental site assessments (100% in both surveys).

16. Environmental Bankers Association, Inc., *1999/2000 Environmental Due Diligence Survey:* 12.

tor or borrower environmental indemnities, and the two most prevalent types of insurance policies and coverage were secured creditor policies (48% of respondents) and "cost cap/stop loss coverage" (36% of respondents).

Conclusion
Implications for Appraisers in the Evolution of Lender Attitudes About Environmental Risk

This internal and external institutionalization of environmental risk analysis by lenders has a number of significant implications for appraisers and the appraisal community.

First, it indicates that appraisers must increasingly expect to review and understand various types of environmental issues and reports, because lenders are routinely producing such reports and analyses as part of their internal due diligence and risk-analysis procedures. Just appraisers are expected to consider the title reports produced by the potential mortgage lenders as part of our process of estimating highest and best use and market value, we may increasingly be expected to do the same with environmental reports.

Second, the surveys indicate that the lending community is increasingly comfortable and sophisticated in its analysis of environmental risk, is making loans on contaminated or remediated properties, and is far less likely today than it was in the late 1980s to have blanket policies against lending on properties affected by environmental risks. Lenders are analyzing environmental risks on a case-by-case basis and are finding fewer situations in which they will not lend or must impose penalties in the form of lower loan-to-value ratios, higher interest rates, personal guarantees, or other means to offset perceptions of the presence of environmental risks. They now have customary techniques for evaluating those risks, dealing with them, and quantifying them, increasingly through environmental insurance or other means when any significant risks are present. They, like the marketplace as a whole, have also become accustomed to accepting many kinds of environmental risk in the same manner as the other types of risks that accompany an ownership or secured creditor position in real estate.

Third, the evolving attitude of the lending community to a particular condition can often be central to understanding the actions of the "typical" buyer and seller in the marketplace and therefore, in many situations, to the impact of environmental risks on market prices and values. Lenders are in some ways an "indicator species," and the attitude of the lending community toward properties affected by environmental risk has evolved dramatically in the past 25 years. From their early-1980s position of generally refusing to loan on properties affected by environmental risk, lenders now routinely lend on such properties.

Finally, the institutionalization and normalization of environmental risk analysis by the lending community demonstrates that the marketplace is indeed dealing with environmental risks on a day-to-day basis, and that prices in the marketplace increasingly reflect reasonable and knowledgeable consideration of environmental risk. Lenders are involved in marketplace transactions because of the prevalence of mortgage financing as a customary part of the way American real estate is owned and held. Buyers and sellers of many types of properties in the United States have customarily relied on lenders to perform a due diligence function. Consider title searches and title insurance—because secured lenders require a title search before making a mortgage loan, the buyer customarily relies on that title search in analyzing title issues. There is little if any need for the buyer to duplicate the activity of the lender in scrutinizing title issues because the knowledge gathered by the lender is transmitted to the buyer and seller and is therefore appropriated by the buyer and the seller.

More and more often, the same holds for issues related to environmental risks. The mortgage lender routinely undertakes an environmental due diligence effort as part of the mortgage lending process. In many types of transactions, buyers rely on the lender's environmental due diligence as the first level of assessment of potential environmental issues. If the lender is comfortable with the environmental risks, the buyer usually concurs. If the lender determines that the price accurately reflects the presence or absence of environmental risks, then the price negotiated more likely than not represents the reasoned result of a transaction between a knowledgeable buyer and seller. In other words, the marketplace relies on the knowledge and expertise that the mortgage lending industry is increasingly bringing to the table in evaluating and dealing with environmental risks, and their potential (and actual) impacts on market prices and values.

Lenders have traditionally contributed to making the typical buyer a "knowledgeable" buyer, as that term is understood in the definition of market value used by the appraisal profession. Lenders with set environmental due diligence guidelines and trained environmental officers ensure that a "knowledgeable" person was part of the purchase process. Certainly, the presence of a lender's environmental due diligence review is not a necessary prerequisite to establishing that the marketplace has acted knowledgeably and reasonably; buyers and sellers have other sources of information on environmental issues and different opportunities for assistance and advice. But the changing attitude of lenders helps appraisers understand how the marketplace as a whole has become more comfortable with evaluating and accepting environmental risks, and how levels of risk—and therefore potential sources of marketplace stigma—have generally been reduced over the last 15 or 20 years.

There are, of course, situations in which environmental stigma is present, and there are still other situations where mortgage lenders will refuse to lend or will require significant extra costs to the borrower. But the marketplace as a whole, including buyers and sellers individually as well as lenders, has become more knowledgeable about the proper evaluation of environmental risks and more comfortable in evaluating those risks. As a result, the prices established in today's real estate marketplace can increasingly be relied on to reflect a reasoned evaluation of environmental risks affecting real estate.

Chapter 6: *Institutionalization and Normalization of Risk*

CHAPTER 6 Cross-References

Related articles in Chapter 1: Peter J. Patchin, MAI, "Valuation of Contaminated Properties" *The Appraisal Journal* (January 1988), 9; and William N. Kinnard, Jr., MAI, SRA, PhD and Elaine M. Worzala, PhD, "How North American Appraisers Value Contaminated Property and Associated Stigma" *The Appraisal Journal* (January 1999), 16.

Related article in Chapter 2: Albert R. Wilson, "The Environmental Opinion: Basis for an Impaired Value Opinion" *The Appraisal Journal* (July 1994), 80–81.

Related articles in Chapter 3: Danny J. Martin, "The New URAR and Environmental Hazards" *The Appraisal Journal* (January 1995), 139, 141; Robert V. Colangelo, CPG and Ronald D. Miller, Esq., "Agency Standards and Industry Guidance on Addressing Environmental Hazards," Chapter 2 in *Environmental Site Assessments and Their Impact on Property Value: The Appraiser's Role,* Appraisal Institute: 1995, 147–149; and Steven A. Levine, CERS, CERA, "Environmental Challenges Can Create Work for Real Estate Appraisers" *Valuation Insights & Perspectives* (Third Quarter 1999), 166.

Related articles in Chapter 4: Peter J. Patchin, MAI, ASA, CRE, "Contaminated Properties—Stigma Revisited" *The Appraisal Journal* (April 1991), 196–197; and Richard J. Roddewig, MAI, "Stigma, Environmental Risk and Property Value: 10 Critical Inquiries" *The Appraisal Journal* (October 1996), 210–211.

Related articles in Chapter 5: Scott B. Arens, MAI, SRA, "The Valuation of Defective Properties: A Common Sense Approach" *The Appraisal Journal* (April 1997), 254; and Thomas O. Jackson, MAI, "Mortgage-Equity Analysis in Contaminated Property Valuation" *The Appraisal Journal* (January 1998), 261.

Related articles in Chapter 7: Jeffrey D. Fisher, PhD, George H. Lentz, PhD, and K.S. Maurice Tse, PhD, "The Effects of Asbestos on Commercial Real Estate: A Survey of MAI Appraisers" *The Appraisal Journal* (October 1993), 339; Robert A. Simons, PhD and Arthur Sementelli, "Liquidity Loss and Delayed Transactions with Leaking Underground Storage Tanks" *The Appraisal Journal* (July 1997), 344–346, 348; Robert A. Simons, PhD, William M. Bowen, PhD, and Arthur K. Sementelli, PhD, "The Price and Liquidity Effects of UST Leaks from Gas Stations on Adjacent Contaminated Property" *The Appraisal Journal* (April 1999), 352–353; and Robert W. Hall, CRE, "The Causes of Loss in Value: A Case Study of a Contaminated Property" *Real Estate Issues* (April 1994), 385.

Related article in Chapter 8: Robert P. Carver, Esq., and Anthony W. Crowell, Esq., "Toxic Tax Assessments: The Ad Valorem Taxation of Contaminated Property" *Real Estate Issues* (Fall 1999), 440.

Related article in Chapter 9: Richard J, Roddewig, MAI, CRE, "EPA's Brownfield Initiative: Will It Improve the Market for Contaminated Properties?" *Valuation Insights & Perspectives* (Third Quarter 1997), 471.

Related article in Chapter 11: Jack P. Friedman, CRE, "Defending an Oil Company Against Litigation for Environmental Contamination (A Case Study)" *Real Estate Issues* (Winter 1999/2000), 585–586.

Appraising Properties Affected by Various Types of Environmental Contamination

CHAPTER 7

Editor's Introduction

Many of the articles in this anthology discuss valuation issues in relation to a generic "contaminated property." Appraisers, however, must not ignore the fact that valuation techniques may need to be modified from one type of contamination situation to another. This chapter addresses specific issues related to a few of the more common types of environmental contamination, including asbestos, leaking underground storage tanks (LUSTs), electromagnetic radiation fields (EMFs), radon and radiation, groundwater contamination, solid waste landfills, and "sick" buildings.

Both the Wilson article and the Fisher, Lentz, and Tse article explore the effect that the presence of asbestos-containing materials (ACMs) may have on property value. Wilson analyzes the methodology used to determine the impact that ACMs have on market value, while Fisher, Lentz, and Tse provide the results of a survey of MAI-designated appraisers giving the reader insight into the importance of ACM considerations in the valuation of a property.

Simons and Sementelli explore the actual performance of LUST sites in the private market and find that these sites are less likely to sell than comparable, uncontaminated sites are. They also find that it is harder for buyers of LUST sites to obtain financing for their purchases. Building on these findings, Simons, Bowen, and Sementelli then probe the more specific case of the effects that gas station LUSTs have on neighboring properties, again determining that these properties are less likely to be sold and sell for prices lower than comparable, "clean" sites do.

EMFs, radon, and radiation are similar in some ways (e.g., invisible) but dissimilar in others (e.g., the health impacts of radon and radiation are firmly established while those caused by EMFs are subject to considerable debate). Rikon discusses the ramifications that the Criscuola v. Power Authority of the State of New York *decision might have in the valuation of property in proximity to EMFs, claiming that this decision contributes to restricted resale prospects for these sites. Kinnard and Geckler present a comprehensive case study of three early-1980s New Jersey Superfund sites and the impact that they* had on single-family property sale prices in the surrounding area. They found that the market's response to this known contamination varied directly with the speed and apparent effectiveness of any remediation efforts.

Hall uses the single case study of groundwater contamination at the Shadyside Apartments to present the reader with his list of nine factors—ranging from clean-up costs and liability to stigma and loss of marketability—that appraisers must consider when dealing with an environmentally impaired property. Similarly, Patchin states that sales of contaminated properties, although once unheard of, were beginning to rise. He then uses multiple case studies to illustrate his main point that, with the rise in contaminated sales, the sales comparison approach to valuation was again a viable tool for the appraiser. Dotzour uses the example of groundwater contamination in Wichita, Kansas, as the basis for his model to assess the price changes associated with the discovery of this type of contamination. Surprisingly, he finds that the discovery did not affect home prices in the area.

Sometimes, as in the case of solid waste or hazardous waste landfills, a property can have considerable value precisely because it is an approved location for storage of contaminated materials. While landfills can be valued for their continuing use, more difficult issues are often involved when the question is the value of a landfill after closure. Robbins, Norman, and Norman describe the modern landfill in detail and explain the features that make it a viable site for future development; they then summarize a few of the types of development best suited to a landfill site.

Over the past 30 years the national press has reported a number of incidents of alleged "sick building" syndrome, in which many occupants in the same building reported mysterious illnesses or other physical symptoms such as rashes or headaches. The outbreak of Legionnaire's Disease at a Philadelphia hotel may be the most famous example of this problem. Guidry first defines the types of indoor air pollution that can cause the syndrome and the documented causes. Causes include insufficient, inefficient, or malfunctioning ventilation systems, toxic gases and chemicals in synthetic carpeting or furnishings, and biological contaminants such as molds, viruses, and bacteria in air-conditioning and humidity-control systems, carpeting, ducts, or spaces behind walls. Guidry then explores diagnostic techniques, the costs to building owners, and the implications for the appraisal process.

Probable Financial Effect of Asbestos Removal on Real Estate

by Albert R. Wilson

To analyze the probable effects of asbestos on a possible purchase or sale of a property, a model was constructed based on historical data available from an existent small commercial structure. The owners in this model desired a 13% rate of return on investment. It was decided to ignore all issues peculiar to real estate and examine the property's rate of return as if it were generated by a normal business enterprise; that is, to look only to the normal discounted cash flows (DCFs) that would result from owning and operating the property. Although the tax laws indicate a longer depreciation term, a 19-year term was used. This article focuses only on the consequences of the existence of asbestos in a property and the three available strategies for dealing with it; namely, immediate removal, staged removal over time, and careful maintenance and control until removal at a much later date.

Asbestos removal costs were estimated by a highly competent contractor in June 1988. Although there are many published figures on removal costs, these costs are extremely volatile. Consequently, any estimate of cost must be considered in terms of the date at which it was made. Also, because published data contain many unspecified assumptions, such information must be used cautiously.

The latter is best illustrated by the fact that published data for removal costs often include an estimation factor per linear foot of pipe for removal of pipe containing asbestos lagging. What is often not stated is that the cost is for a certain diameter of pipe (often not specified) that can be reached without scaffolding or other special equipment, and is in an area that is part of the required negative air enclosure associated with a much larger project. Unless all of these stated and unstated conditions are observed, the estimation factor is meaningless. Therefore, I have chosen to use an estimate provided by a contractor without stating precisely how that estimate was calculated.

It was indicated in the preliminary analysis that the greatest negative effect on property value would result from a decision to remove asbestos

Albert R. Wilson is president of Hazardous Materials Institute, Inc., Columbus, Ohio, which performs research and consulting in hazardous material inspection and management planning. He has an MBA from Bowling Green State University and a BS in engineering from Northwestern University.

This article originally appeared in the July 1989 issue of The Appraisal Journal.

Valuing Contaminated Properties

from the building within the next several years. This decision could result in a value decline from 30% to 50%. A decision to remove asbestos either at a much later date or slowly over time while carefully maintaining the material in a safe condition should result in a lesser decline in value, from 15% to 26%.

Both of these strategies include the probable effects of a decline in revenue resulting from the presence of asbestos in a building. In certain markets, this income reduction could range from 10% to 15% compared with rental rates of space containing no asbestos. These results also include the increased operating costs resulting from proper maintenance of the asbestos materials. This increase in operating costs may range from 5% to 15%, depending on the historic operating costs of the building.

Operating and maintenance costs are based on the experience of schools, which are required by law (Asbestos Hazard Emergency Response Act of 1986, or AHERA) to maintain their asbestos inventories in a safe condition through a specifically defined Operations and Maintenance Program (O&M program). This requirement, embodied in the Code of Federal Regulations (CFR) at 40 CFR 763, will probably be held by the courts to be the minimum stipulation for all buildings, public and private, containing asbestos.

Experience has shown that normal pricing factors for asbestos removal are no longer applicable. Consequently, three asbestos-removal cost scenarios were constructed and used in the evaluation of the alternative removal models.

In the first, the normal cost scenario, it was assumed that the costs for removal were similar to those of any other product or service. Costs are initially high when the product or service is new, but decline over time with the advent of new technology, experience, and the entry of more firms into the marketplace.

In the second scenario, AHERA cost, attempts were made to factor in the very high demand from schools for removal services. Schools want to remove the asbestos as soon as possible regardless of the fact that the federal rules and regulations specifically discourage such action. This has caused a demand for removal services far in excess of both the supply of competent contractors to perform the service and the normal gestation period required to develop improved removal technology that could possibly reduce costs.

In the third scenario, AHERA + mortgage cost, attempts were made to factor in the additional demand generated by the reaction of mortgage lenders (some estimate as many as 37%) who refuse to lend to a party whose building contains a significant amount of asbestos. To the extent that this attitude continues or accelerates, the cost for removal will be driven even higher and remain high for a longer period than indicated by the AHERA cost scenario.

A summary of the analyses is contained in Tables 1 and 2, and Figure 1.

Analysis Methods
Initial Financial Assumptions

Throughout the analysis, a number of financial assumptions were maintained. First, it was assumed that the real estate would be held in a normal, for-profit corporation with all income, expenses, and taxes based on

Chapter 7: *Financial Effect of Asbestos Removal*

TABLE 1 Rate of Return on Investment for Various Sales Prices and Removal Timing and Cost Scenarios (sales prices in $1,000s)

Sales price	800	750	700	650	600	550	500
Base model (%)	**12.9**	**14.7**	16.7	19.2	22.2	26.1	31.0
End removal model (%)							
Normal removal costs	9.6	10.8	**11.3**	**13.9**	16.0	18.7	22.1
AHERA removal costs	9.7	10.8	**12.1**	**13.9**	15.9	18.7	22.1
AHERA + mortgage costs	9.4	10.7	**11.9**	**13.7**	15.8	18.5	21.9
Staged removal model							
Normal removal costs	9.1	10.1	11.3	**12.6**	**14.1**	16.0	18.4
AHERA removal costs	8.6	9.6	10.6	**12.0**	**13.6**	15.5	18.0
AHERA + mortgage costs	7.8	8.7	9.8	11.0	**12.6**	**14.3**	16.8
Initial removal model	8.0	8.8	9.7	10.5	11.7	**12.9**	**14.2**

Note: The percentages in boldface bracket the desired rate of return (13%).

TABLE 2 Required Sales Prices for a 13% Rate of Return

Model or Scenario	Sales Price ($)
Base model	800,000
End removal model	
Normal cost	678,000
AHERA cost	676,000
AHERA + mortgage cost	671,000
Staged removal model	
Normal cost	639,000
AHERA cost	620,000
AHERA + mortgage cost	589,000
Initial removal model	549,000

FIGURE 1 Effect of Asbestos Abatement Strategies on Property Value

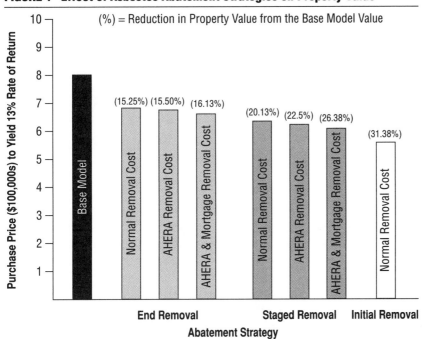

that assumption. A straight-line depreciation schedule of 19 years to a zero salvage value was assumed, as was a tax rate of 34% with unlimited tax-loss carry-forward. The purpose of this set of assumptions was to separate the analysis from any peculiarities of real estate investment to allow direct comparison of results from all of the models.

Further, it was assumed that the property would increase in value at a compounded real rate of 2% per year, and that normal operating costs would increase at a real rate of 4% per year. Income from rentals is assumed to increase by a compounded rate of 5% per year.

It was also assumed, based on the building's historic data, that 10% of the space was vacant at any one time as a result of the normal turnover of tenants and existent market conditions. This is implicitly included in the initial rental income figures.

The building was renovated in 1985; thus, additional extensive renovation was not immediately required. The cost of future renovation (i.e., the nonasbestos portion of such renovation work) was assumed to increase by a compounded rate of 4% per year.

An initial investigation of the building produced the following data.

- Asbestos is in the form of both sprayed-on fireproofing on structural steel, and thermal insulation on boilers and piping throughout the building.
- The costs for removal and disposal alone will be $70,000, assuming that the materials have been exposed by prior demolition of inner wall and ceiling materials, and that replacement of the wall and ceiling materials will be accomplished under a separate contract.
- The cost of demolition of the existent wall and ceiling materials, functional replacement of the materials containing asbestos, and installation of new wall and ceiling materials and floor coverings will be $140,000.

It was also assumed that renovation costs may be capitalized at the time of occurrence and funded at the rate of 80%, through commercial loans with the same term as the original mortgage. The original mortgage rate was assumed to be 10%, and additional mortgage borrowings would carry the same rate. Any cash operating deficits and cash needed to meet unfunded renovation and asbestos removal costs were assumed to result in additional contributions to capital investment on the part of the owners. The building will be sold in the 20th year.

The renovation costs were assumed to contribute to an increase in building value at the rate of 100% of the cost to renovate, but the cost of asbestos removal was assumed to be an expensed item contributing nothing to the value except the enhancement of the income potential of the space.

Base Model
The base model was constructed from the historic records of the building, and asbestos-related issues were completely ignored. It was determined, using normal DCF techniques, that a sales price of $800,000 would result in a probable rate of return on investment of 13% to new owners. This was considered to be a reasonable rate of return for the market.

In this model, all of the above-mentioned basic assumptions about the appreciation of values, income potential, operating cost behavior, and mortgage costs were used.

Initial Removal Model

The initial removal model was built from the base model in that it was assumed that the new owners would immediately on purchase remove all asbestos and, in so doing, completely renovate the building. Thus, the new owners would forego income from the building for the first year of ownership but would experience normal income and operating costs from that point forward.

The question of which asbestos removal cost scenario is applicable is not an issue in this model. Nevertheless, it was inferred from preliminary analysis that if a delay of a year or two in implementing this strategy occurred, the removal cost scenarios would heavily influence the building's value. From an initial calculation it was found that if the AHERA + mortgage scenario was applied, a delay of two years would reduce the value of the building by more than 50%, as opposed to the 31.38% reduction shown for an immediate implementation of an initial removal action.

The removal timing assumptions, revenue growth, and operating cost assumptions are graphically displayed in Figures 2, 3, and 4.

The Staged Removal Model

The staged removal model is the most complex. Using this model, one assumes that as space becomes vacant (approximately 10% per year) renovation and removal will take place before the space is returned to the market.

In this model, it was assumed that costs are incurred for renovation and removal, with the effects of attendant capitalization, expense, mortgage, and cash flow experienced at various times in the future. Over time, less and less unrenovated space will be made available through tenant turnover, and at some point the vacant space available needing renovation or removal will fall below a minimum level for economic renovation or removal. It was decided to set a limit such that when 20% of the original asbestos-filled space remained, the balance would be vacated and the work completed. This would occur in the 16th year.

FIGURE 2 Revenue for Removal at Purchase

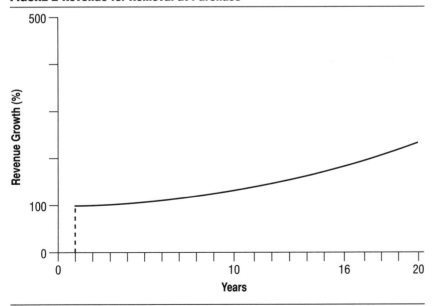

FIGURE 3 Operating Cost for Removal at Purchase

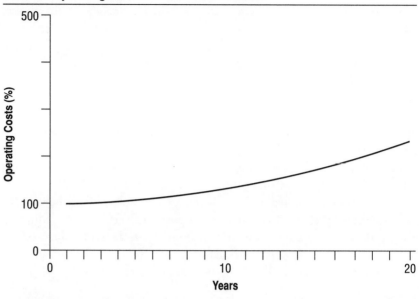

FIGURE 4 Timing for Removal at Purchase

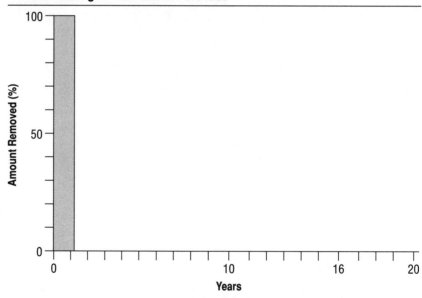

During the period when space containing asbestos remains in the building, the income from that space will be reduced by 12.5%; the operating costs will increase by 10% in recognition of the special requirements of the O&M program.

In this model, like the end-removal model, all three removal cost scenarios were used to analyze their effects on the rate of return on investment.

The removal timing, revenue growth, and operating cost assumptions for the staged removal model are displayed in Figures 5, 6, and 7.

The End Removal Model
With the end removal model, it was assumed that nothing would be done to remove asbestos or renovate space containing asbestos until the 16th year, at which time all of the space would be renovated and the asbestos

FIGURE 5 Revenue for Staged Removal

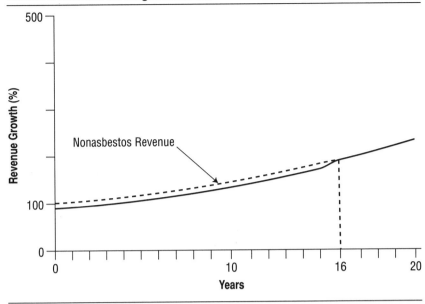

FIGURE 6 Operating Cost for Staged Removal

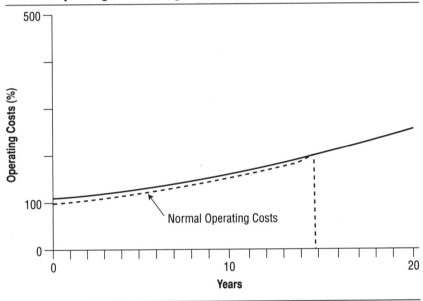

removed. The income from rental, however, would be reduced by 12.5% from normal market rates, and the operating costs would be increased by 10% above normal operating costs for the entire period prior to the 16th year.

The removal timing, revenue growth, and operating cost growth assumptions for the end removal model are shown in Figures 8, 9, and 10.

Removal Cost Scenarios
The removal cost scenarios are based on the following data.

Normal Cost Scenario
Under this cost scenario, the market for asbestos removal services behaves in a fashion similar to that of other new products or services. When a new

FIGURE 7 Timing for Staged Removal

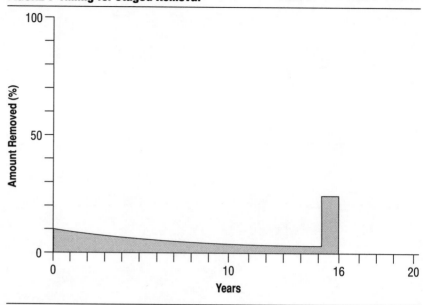

FIGURE 8 Revenue for End Removal

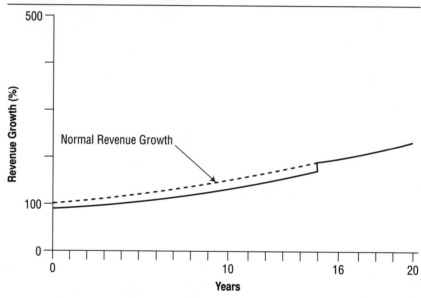

product or service is introduced into the marketplace and it meets with a high level of acceptance, the price is initially fairly high. As demand increases, however, new technology is developed to reduce production costs, experience is gained resulting in more efficient production and less costly distribution, and new competitors appear. All these factors contribute to a decline in real price somewhat equivalent to that shown in Figure 11. This is what could be expected in the cost of asbestos removal services if the market behaved in a normal manner.

AHERA Cost Scenario

In the asbestos removal market over the past several years, cost for removal has increased by 50% to 100% per year. This fact is recognized in the AHERA cost scenario.

FIGURE 9 Operating Cost for End Removal

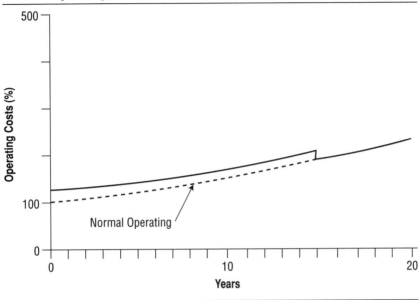

FIGURE 10 Timing for End Removal

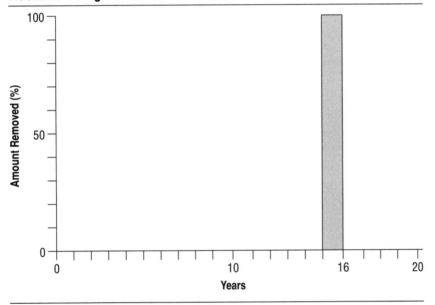

This increase is a result of two major factors. First, an increasing demand for removal services from both the public and private sectors has outstripped the supply of competent contractors. Second, requirements of the new AHERA regulations that went into effect in December 1987 include licensing contractors, workers, and project designers, at least to the extent that they will be permitted to work on school buildings. The regulations also specify the methods and standards under which asbestos removal is to be performed. These factors further restrict the supply of individuals and organizations available to service the demand.

While AHERA rules and regulations apply strictly only to schools, they are viewed by many legal experts as establishing a minimum set of conditions that the courts may reasonably be expected to apply to all building

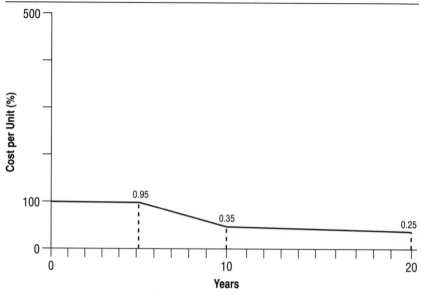

FIGURE 11 Normal Market Cost Behavior Assumption

owners or individuals working with asbestos in whatever capacity. Further, AHERA rules and regulations are commonly misunderstood as requiring, or at least forcing through extensive maintenance and documentation requirements, removal of all materials containing asbestos. These factors act both to accelerate demand for removal services and shorten the time in which new technology, experience, and normal competitive forces have to operate to reduce costs.

The net result of AHERA regulations is shown in Figure 12, which displays a continuing increase in costs for the next several years, followed by a period of level but high costs, and finally a decline over time in a more normal fashion. The exact quantitative amounts of the increases in costs, or the length of time over which they will apply, is the subject of much debate. Nevertheless, the general shape of the cost curve is agreed on by most experts in the field.

The AHERA + Mortgage Cost Scenario

To the extent that data are available, although fragmentary at this time, it is apparent that mortgage lenders are reacting to the issue of asbestos in buildings in one of three general ways. Some are essentially ignoring the issue and proceeding in a normal fashion. Others are increasing the cost of borrowing through the use of higher rates, higher down payments, escrow accounts to cover removal cost risks, or a combination of these and other devices. Another lender reaction is simply to refuse to lend unless all of the materials are immediately removed. Preliminary indications are that the latter two types of reactions are more prevalent.

Lender reaction to asbestos in real estate is a relatively new phenomenon and does not seem yet to have fully affected the cost of removal services. For this reason, the AHERA + mortgage scenario, in which the costs for removal services climb and remain at an even higher level for a longer period than the AHERA cost scenario, appears to be a reasonable projection of future costs. This is shown in Figure 13.

Chapter 7: *Financial Effect of Asbestos Removal*

FIGURE 12 AHERA Driving Force

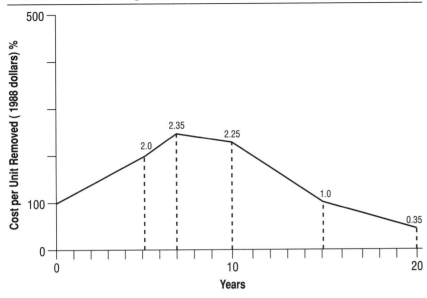

FIGURE 13 AHERA and Mortgage Equity Policy Driving Forces

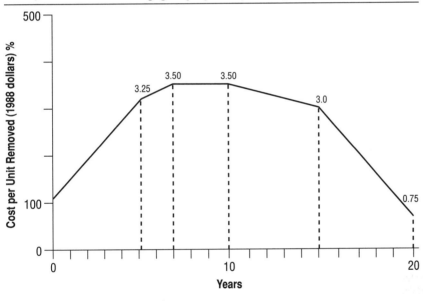

Conclusion

In this analysis, an attempt has been made to determine the financially optimum strategy. For example, no recommendation as to whether removal should be completed before, on, or after the 16th year has been made. In addition, no attempt was made to include elements of liability risk in the analysis. It must be clear that virtually no liability insurance policy covers the risks associated with asbestos in a building.

No costs for examining the building to determine the current condition, extent, or cost-to-cure of any existent asbestos problem have been included in this analysis. Generally, a cost-to-cure analysis of a building will range from $.10 to $.20 per square foot of gross building space. This is particularly the case if the staged or end removal options are selected because of the exacting and detailed documentation of the existent inventory of materials containing asbestos required to operate a successful O&M program.

Without a very exact inventory of the materials present, including careful documentation of the inventory's existent condition, it would be difficult, if not impossible, to prove that an owner is doing all that is reasonable to protect human health and the environment from asbestos-exposure risks. Without such proof, a decision to delay removal is a calculated risk with unfavorable conditions to the owner.

For example, clearly specified in AHERA rules and regulations is the requirement to notify all occupants and short-term workers (telephone repairpersons, plumbers, electricians, etc.) of the existence and location of asbestos and its associated risks. This is nearly impossible without careful initial documentation and a comprehensive, auditable record-keeping system. The simple requirement to notify occupants, unless a positive and creditable risk-control program based on detailed and verifiable data is in place, will probably result in a significant decline in income for a property.

A number of subjects of further research have been outlined by this initial study. The probable future costs of removal services should be investigated. Although the preliminary data from schools regarding the costs of O&M programs are helpful, further data are needed to determine how that experience may apply to commercial space. Of fundamental interest is the development of uniform standards for property inspections that will develop verifiable data for cost-to-cure and O&M program usage.

Finally, a competent examination of a building to develop data for an O&M program is a highly specialized area of property inspection. A number of modern asbestos-free materials look exactly like materials that contain asbestos. AHERA rules specifically require that any material suspected of containing asbestos be assumed to contain asbestos until proved otherwise by specialized sampling and testing techniques. Those not specifically trained to perform this work should not attempt it, both for the sake of their own health and safety and to prevent the possible gross contamination of an otherwise uncontaminated area.

Effects of Asbestos on Commercial Real Estate: A Survey of MAI Appraisers

by Jeffrey D. Fisher, PhD, George H. Lentz, PhD, and K.S. Maurice Tse, PhD

Considerable evidence exists that asbestos-containing materials (ACMs) in buildings do not pose a significant health hazard to building occupants.[1] Nonetheless, the health risks associated with exposure to asbestos fibers give rise to legal (e.g., regulatory and tort) risks for an operator or anyone with an ownership interest in a building. The legal risks that arise from potential health risks from exposure to asbestos have economic implications for owners and operators of property with asbestos.

Under Superfund legislation,[2] the classes of parties who may be declared "potentially responsible parties" include tenants and lenders as well as owners. As operators of the spaces they lease, tenants can become liable for asbestos-related damages. A number of court decisions in the 1980s have held that a lender qualifies as an owner or operator of a property that contains hazardous or toxic substances when, as the result of a foreclosure or a loan workout, the lender becomes the owner or operator of the property.[3] Insurers face potentially huge claims as a result of judgments awarded by the courts to parties found to be injured by exposure to asbestos. Because of the potential problems ACMs pose for lenders and insurers, property owners and tenants of buildings with ACMs may find it difficult to obtain loans and insurance coverage for asbestos-related costs.

In spite of the publicity asbestos has received, there is an apparent lack of consensus about how its presence affects the market value of commercial property. For example, a recent study by Koehn, MacAvoy, and De Silva[4] on the effects of asbestos on commercial property values in Los Angeles found that the presence of asbestos in buildings had no significant effect on values. On the other hand, a recent ruling by a New York trial judge reduced the assessment of a New York City office building because of the presence of asbestos.[5]

Estimating the impact of asbestos on property values is complicated by the fact that in the current overbuilt real estate markets there is no shortage of asbestos-free new buildings. Tenant rejection of older buildings with ACMs may be caused as much by the plentiful supply of relatively cheap new space as by the presence of asbestos.

Jeffrey D. Fisher, PhD, is associate professor of finance and director of the Center of Real Estate Studies in the School of Business at Indiana University, Bloomington, Indiana. He obtained a BSIM from Purdue University, an MBA from Wright State University, and a PhD from Ohio State University. Mr. Fisher has published extensively.

George H. Lentz, PhD, is an associate professor of finance and real estate at California State Polytechnic University in Pomma, California. Mr. Lentz obtained a BA from the University of Santa Clara, an MBA from Indiana University, and a PhD from the University of Arizona, and has written several real estate-related articles.

K.S. Maurice Tse, PhD, is assistant professor of finance, School of Business, Indiana University. Mr. Tse has authored several articles, and received a BSc from Hong Kong University as well as an MS, an MBA, and a PhD from Michigan State University.

This article originally appeared in the October 1993 issue of The Appraisal Journal.

1. Harvard University, *Summary of Symposium on Health Aspects of Exposure to Asbestos in Buildings* (Cambridge, Mass.: Energy and Environmental Policy Center, John F. Kennedy School of Government, Harvard University, 1989). See also B.T. Mossman, J. Bignon, M. Corn, A. Seaton, and J.B.L. Gee, "Asbestos: Scientific Developments and Implications for Public Policy," *Science,* v. 247 (January 19, 1990): 294–301; letters in discussion of this article, "Asbestos, Carcinogenicity, and Public Policy," *Science,* v. 248 (May 18, 1990): 795–802; and "Asbestos and Carcinogenicity," *Science,* v. 249 (August 24, 1990): 844.

2. The original Superfund legislation, called the Comprehensive Environmental Response, Compensation and Liability Act of 1980 (CERCLA), Public Law 96-510, was amended by the Superfund Amendments and Reauthorization Act of 1986 (SARA), Public Law 99-499. The statute, as amended, is located at 42 U.S.C. Section 9601 et seq.

Footnotes continue on next page.

Most of the published information about the effects of asbestos on the value and marketability of commercial property is in the form of case studies.[6] Little general information exists about the effects of asbestos on property values. One reason for the lack of generalized information is that the extent and types of ACMs present in buildings—and thus the costs of removing, controlling, or containing those ACMs—vary considerably from building to building. Further, the exposure to legal risks, the costs of dealing with asbestos, and the real estate market conditions tend to vary by location.

The purpose of the study presented in this article is to obtain from commercial real estate appraisers an assessment of how asbestos affects the value of commercial properties. Probing the collective wisdom of real estate appraisers can increase understanding about how the market value of properties is affected by the presence of asbestos. Selected members of the American Institute of Real Estate Appraisers (AIREA) were thus surveyed during June and July of 1990.

The Ways Asbestos Affects Property Values

The value of a property with asbestos (V_A) can be expressed generally in a present value (PV) framework as follows:

$$V_A = PV \text{ of expected net operating income } (NOI) + PV \text{ of expected net} $$
$$\text{sales price } (NSP) - PV \text{ of expected containment and/or}$$
$$\text{removal costs. (1)}$$

To the extent the presence of asbestos reduces a property's expected net operating income (NOI) and expected net sale price (NSP), increases a property's discount rate, and causes a property owner to incur costs of containment or removal, the value of a property with ACMs is depressed below that of a comparable clean property (i.e., a property without ACMs). The loss in property value (LV) caused by the presence of asbestos can be expressed generally as:

$$LV = PV \text{ of property without asbestos} - PV \text{ of property with}$$
$$\text{asbestos } (V_A). \text{ (2)}$$

Analyzing the adverse impact of asbestos on a property's NOI involves estimating how the presence of asbestos may affect revenue and expense items such as occupancy rates, rental rates, rental concessions, and operating expenses. The property's discount rate may be higher than that of a comparable property without asbestos if equity investors or mortgage lenders perceive the cash flows of the property to be subject to greater economic and legal risks. If ACMs remain in a building at the time of sale, the NSP may be lower because of the reduced NOI and the increased risk anticipated by prospective buyers. The NSP may also be adversely affected by the increase in the transaction costs of the sale, notably the need for environmental audits and surveys of various degrees of complexity.

The three terms on the right-hand side of equation 1 are interrelated insofar as decisions about how to deal with asbestos affect the $PVNOI$ and $PVNSP$. Alternatives for dealing with asbestos thus must be considered before the impact of asbestos on the market value of the property can be estimated. The primary alternatives for dealing with asbestos are 1) im-

---

3. Cases that establish how a lender can face financial liability as an "operator" of property if it acts to protect its security interest in the property include *United States v. Mirable*, No. 84-2280 (E.D. {a/. Sept/ 4. 1985), 15 Envtl. L. Rep. (Envtl.L. Inst.) 20994 (1985), *In re T. P. Long Chemical Co., Inc.*, 45 B.R. 278 (Bkrtcy. 1985), *U.S. v. Maryland Bank and Trust Co.*, 632 F. Supp 573, *Guidice v. BFG Electroplating*, 30 Env't Rep. Cas. 1665 (BNA), and *U.S. v. Fleet Factors Corp.*, CA 11, No. 89-8094, May 23, 1990. However, the economic interests of lenders can be affected even if they do not become owners or operators insofar as the solvency of the borrower and the value of the collateral property are adversely affected by the ACMs. See Johnine J. Brown, "Superfunds and Superliens: Super Problems for Secured Lenders," *BNA's Banking Report*, v. 50, no. 14 (April 4, 1988); Jay Gwin and Judon Fambrough, *The Effect of Environmental Law in Real Estate Transactions*, a technical report of The Real Estate Center (College Station, Texas: Texas A&M University, January 1990); and Walter D. James, III, "Financial Institutions and Hazardous Waste Litigation: Limiting the Exposure to Superfund Liability," *Natural Resources Journal* (Spring 1988); 329–355.

4. Michael F. Koehn, Paul W. MacAvoy, and Harindra De Silva, "Market Responses to Asbestos in Buildings," *Journal of Real Estate Finance and Economics* (September 1990): 213–232.

5. Neil Barsky, "Assessment Cut on Office Building Due to Asbestos," *The Wall Street Journal* (January 23, 1991): B2.

6. Douglas S. Bible, Marshall F. Graham, and Michael T. Newman, "Travis Square: A Study of ACM Removal in a Class A Office Building," *Environmental Watch* (Chicago: Appraisal Institute, Winter 1991); Will McIntosh, "Study of the Southern State Office Building: The Effect of ACMs on Rents and Marketability in a Healthy Market," *Environmental Watch* (Chicago: Appraisal Institute, Winter 1991); Wade R. Ragas and R. Dunbar Argote, "Valuation of Office Buildings with ACMs Using DCF Analysis," *Environmental Watch* (Chicago: Appraisal Institute, Winter 1991); and Albert Wilson, "Probable Financial Effect of Asbestos Removal on Real Estate, " *The Appraisal Journal* (July 1989): 378–391. Two major exceptions are the recent article by Koehn, MacAvoy, and De Silva and the economic analysis of the effects of asbestos in buildings by Donald N. Dewees, *Controlling Asbestos in Buildings: An Economic Investigation* (Washington, DC: Resources for the Future, 1986).

Chapter 7: *Effects of Asbestos*

mediate removal; 2) no removal until demolition of the building; and 3) postponement of removal until a time between immediate removal and demolition of the building.[7]

All alternatives other than immediate complete removal of asbestos require the development and implementation of an operations and maintenance (O&M) plan for the building. O&M procedures are intended to maintain the asbestos in a safe (i.e., nonfriable and nonairborne) condition as long as the building is operated while the asbestos is present.[8] Implementation of these procedures increase operating expenses. Additional costs may be incurred to encapsulate or enclose to safely contain the asbestos in lieu of removal, but the cost of either action is normally significantly less than the cost of removal.

Broadly speaking, efforts to remove ACMs from a building involve both direct costs and indirect costs. The direct costs of removal include all of the expenditures for removing and disposing of the asbestos. The direct costs, in brief, can be regarded as the costs associated with working on the asbestos itself. The indirect costs are the costs associated with the disruption of building operations and the dislocation of a building's occupants while removal takes place. These include the costs of moving and temporarily relocating tenants and the loss of rental revenue resulting from building "down time" while the asbestos is being removed.

If after asbestos is removed from a building the property's *NOI* and discount rate quickly adjust to levels appropriate for comparable buildings without asbestos, then the total cost of removing the asbestos immediately following acquisition of the property should be the ceiling of the loss in value caused by the presence of asbestos. In some situations, however, a building may continue to experience asbestos-related problems that linger past completion of total removal. Lingering costs can result from outstanding contracts that produce lags in the adjustment of rental income and operating expenses to levels appropriate for comparable buildings without asbestos, from overhanging legal liability, or from a taint a building continues to bear for once having contained asbestos. The effect of these lingering costs is to reduce the anticipated benefits from removal.

The Asbestos Survey

The sample of appraisers to whom the survey was distributed consisted of 200 MAI-designated members of AIREA. To maximize the chance of reaching appraisers who had experience appraising properties containing asbestos, the sample was limited to MAI-designated appraisers who belonged to chapters whose memberships were exclusively located in metropolitan areas. Consequently, the sample of appraisers was drawn from five chapters representing AIREA's largest exclusively metropolitan chapters: New York, Philadelphia, Washington, D.C., San Diego, and Houston. Through a form of stratified sampling, 40 MAIs were randomly selected from each of these chapters. A total of 78 members returned questionnaires that were at least partially completed, for a response rate of 39%. Thirteen of the 78, however, were eliminated from the sample because the respondents indicated little or no experience with buildings containing ACMs or because the questionnaires were not sufficiently complete to process. The usable response rate was thus 33%.

7. In Jeffrey D. Fisher, George H. Lentz, and K.S. Maurice Tse, "Valuation of the Effects of Asbestos on Commercial Real Estate," *The Journal of Real Estate Research* (Summer 1992): 331–350, the authors show that an optimal time may exist for removing the asbestos such that the loss in value resulting from ACMs is minimized.

8. Operations and maintenance activities include recording the location and condition of any ACMs in the building, cleaning up any asbestos that may have been released from the ACMs, periodically inspecting and following other procedures for monitoring the condition of the ACMs to determine whether repairs or other corrective action may be warranted, developing procedures for responding to asbestos emergencies, and informing building employees about the location of the ACMs and instructing them about safe methods of working in the vicinity of ACMs.

Valuing Contaminated Properties

TABLE 1   Summary of Responses to Questions 1 and 5

Question 1: How Important are *each* of the following
problems as motivations for removing asbestos?

Response Scale

1 = extremely important	2 = quite important	3 = somewhat important	4 = not very important	5 = not at all important

		Responses	Mean	Median	Mode	Standard Deviation
1-1	Asbestos-containing materials (ACMs) are difficult to safely control	64	2.67	3	3	1.00
1-2	ACMs pose health threat to building occupants	64	2.44	2	3	1.04
1-3	Tenants react adversely	64	2.31	2	2	0.90
1-4	Property is difficult to sell	64	1.95	2	2	0.87
1-5	Insurance coverage is difficult to obtain	64	2.41	2	2	1.03
1-6	Cost of insurance increases	64	2.44	2	2	0.96
1-7	Desired financing is difficult to obtain	64	1.75	2	2	0.75
1-8	Cost of financing increases	64	2.25	2	2	1.02
1-9	Costly regulatory actions are perceived as a future threat	64	2.05	2	2	0.91
1-10	Lawsuits for asbestos-related illness and damages are perceived as potential threat	64	1.92	2	1	0.91
1-11	Presence of asbestos causes bad publicity and image problems	64	2.00	2	2	0.90

Question 5: How often do new owners of a property with
asbestos-containing materials (ACMs) typically pursue *each*
of the following strategies or plans for dealing with the asbestos?

Response Scale

1 = always	2 = usually	3 = sometimes	4 = seldom	5 = never

		Responses	Mean	Median	Mode	Standard Deviation
5-1	Remove all asbestos immediately or as soon as possible after acquisition	57	2.88	3	3	0.94
5-2	Develop a plan to remove the asbestos in stages over time (e.g., in conjunction with tenant turnover)	60	2.58	2	2	0.86
5-3	Postpone removal of the ACMs until a planned renovation of the structure	58	2.86	3	3	0.82
5-4	Postpone removal of the ACMs until just prior to the sale of the property	53	3.60	4	4	0.79
5-5	Postpone removal of the ACMs until demolition	53	3.06	3	2	1.02
5-6	Contain the ACMs by encapsulation or enclosure	56	2.66	3	3	0.71

The Survey Instrument

The survey questionnaire consisted of 24 questions containing a total of 115 response items. Table 1 through Table 5 contain the text of all of the questions in the survey as well as a statistical summary of the responses to each item. The questions can be divided into three broad sets. The first set (questions 1–9) contains questions designed to obtain qualitative assessments of how the market is likely to react to buildings with asbestos (questions 2–4, 6–9) and of how anticipated marketplace reactions are likely to affect the strategies pursued by owners of such buildings (questions 1 and 5). The second set of questions (questions 10–16) requests that appraisers provide quantitative estimates of adjustments for commercial property in general. The third set of questions (questions 17–24) asks for estimates of adjustments for different types of commercial property.

Report of Survey Results

The statistical summary next to each of the question items listed in Table 1 through Table 5 reports the number of responses to the item, the mean,

Chapter 7: *Effects of Asbestos*

TABLE 2 Summary of Responses to Questions 2 through 4 and 6 through 8

Response Scale

1 = always	2 = usually	3 = sometimes	4 = seldom	5 = never

		Number of Responses	Mean	Median	Mode	Standard Deviation
2.	How often do potential purchasers simply refuse to purchase any property containing asbestos?	57	2.79	3	3	0.61
3.	How frequently do potential buyers of a property demand that the seller pay for (or adjust the selling price for) *each* of the following types of property surveys?					
3-1	A preliminary environmental audit to determine the presence or extent of asbestos	55	2.75	3	2	1.13
3-2	A comprehensive engineering survey to diagnose the specific characteristics of the asbestos problem and to estimate the cost to cure or contain	55	2.75	3	2	0.99
4.	How often do purchasers that are willing to buy a property with asbestos-containing materials (ACMs) do *each* of the following when negotiating the purchase?					
4-1	Demand that the asbestos be removed prior to purchase as a condition of the sale	56	2.86	3	3	0.81
4-2	Agree to purchase the property as is, but at a price discount approximately *equal* to the estimated cost to remove all ACMs from the structure	58	2.76	3	2	0.90
4-3	Agree to purchase the property as is, but at a price discount *greater than* the estimated cost to remove all ACMs from the structure	54	2.94	3	3	0.91
6.	How often do *each* of the following adverse effects on a property's income stream remain *even though* all of the asbestos has been removed from the structure?					
6-1	Higher vacancy rates than comparable properties that never had asbestos	51	3.49	4	4	0.75
6-2	Greater difficulty in obtaining the same quality of tenants than comparable properties that never had asbestos	53	3.42	4	4	0.76
6-3	Lower rental rates than comparable properties that never had asbestos	54	3.39	3	3	0.80
6-4	Higher operating expenses than comparable properties that never had asbestos	51	3.63	4	4	0.82
6-5	Higher financing costs than comparable properties that never had asbestos	54	3.37	3.5	4	0.91
7.	Indicate how frequently loans made on properties with asbestos have *each* of the following additional costs, limitations, or requirements:					
7-1	Lending a lesser amount (lower loan-to-value ratio) than similar properties without asbestos	43	3.05	3	3	0.86
7-2	Charging a higher interest rate	43	3.23	3	3	1.01
7-3	Charging higher "points," or loan origination fees	41	3.20	3	4	1.09
7-4	Requiring indemnification guarantees	46	1.93	2	2	0.94
8.	How often do lenders refuse to lend on properties with asbestos?	51	2.47	2	2	0.57

Valuing Contaminated Properties

TABLE 3 Summary of Responses to Question 9

Response Scale

| 1 = always | 2 = usually | 3 = sometimes | 4 = seldom | 5 = never |

	Number of Responses	Mean	Median	Mode	Standard Deviation
9. How often do you and other appraisers make *each* of the following adjustments to reflect the impact of asbestos on the value of affected properties?					
9-1 Decrease the rental rate relative to comparable properties without asbestos	60	3.20	3	4	1.12
9-2 Increase the vacancy rate	59	2.98	3	4	1.08
9-3 Increase the amount of rental concessions to tenants	58	3.24	3	4	1.15
9-4 Increase workletter/buildout allowances	56	2.82	3	2	1.05
9-5 Increase repair and maintenance expenses to reflect the need for asbestos maintenance and monitoring	59	2.34	2	2	1.04
9-6 Increase legal expenses	56	2.86	3	3	1.04
9-7 Increase insurance costs	58	2.64	2	2	0.94
9-8 Reduce the property value by the *direct* costs of asbestos removal (including costs of preparing for removal, physical removal of ACMs, reconstruction of damaged areas, reinstallation of substitute materials, and disposing of the removed asbestos)	62	2.08	2	2	0.90
9-9 Reduce the property value by the *indirect* costs of asbestos removal (including the loss of rental revenue because of the downtime necessary to remove the asbestos, and the costs to move and temporarily relocate tenants while the asbestos is being removed)	60	1.92	2	2	0.78
9-10 Increase the cap rate	58	2.78	3	2	0.97
9-11 Increase the discount rate	57	2.79	3	2	1.00

the median, and the mode responses to the item, and the standard deviation of the response scores for questions 1 through 9 and 17 through 24. For questions 10 through 16, which required open-ended rather than structured responses, the modal response has been replaced by a column indicating the range of responses.

The multiple-item questions attempt to determine whether some factors are considered by the respondents to be more important than others. To analyze the responses, two levels of statistical tests were performed. The one-way analysis of variance (ANOVA) test was performed on questions 1, 4, 5, 6, 7, 9, and 17 through 24.

The null hypothesis,

$$H_0: \mu_1 = \mu_2 = \ldots = \mu_K.$$

is tested against

H_a: the mean responses are not equal,

where

K = the number of items in the question

Conditional on the null hypothesis, the appropriate test is an *F*-test with $(K-1)$ and $(n_k - K)$ degrees of freedom, where nk is the number of responses to the *k*th item in the question. Table 6 presents the ANOVA test results for the previously mentioned questions.

Pair-wise comparison of the means using Tukey's studentized range test was also performed on all item means in multiple-item questions to ex-

Chapter 7: *Effects of Asbestos*

TABLE 4 Summary of Responses to Questions 10 through 16

	Responses	Mean	Median	Mode	Standard Deviation
10. What is the typical range of the *percentage reduction* (or discount) in the *market value* of a property with asbestos relative to similar properties that do not have asbestos?	18	24%	18%	9.98%	13.4%–34.1%
11. When a property containing asbestos is being sold, *how much longer* does it typically take *to sell,* compared to a comparable property without asbestos? Indicate the number of *additional months* on the market.	20	8.28	6	6.12	1–30
12. When leased space in a property containing asbestos becomes vacant, *how much longer* does it take *to acquire* replacement *tenants* than in a comparable property without asbestos? Indicate the additional time, *in months,* it takes to acquire new tenants.	20	4.88	3	4.10	0–12
13. On average, what is the increase in the discount rate (not the cap rate) for a property with asbestos? Indicate *the additional risk premium* added to the discount rate because of the presence of asbestos.	27	1.99%	1.5%	1.88%	0%–4%
14. What is the typical range of the *lump sum cost* of an *environmental audit* to ascertain the presence and the extent of an asbestos problem in a structure?	22	$8,750	$3,875	$16,255	$300–100,000
15. What is the typical range of the *lump sum cost* for a *comprehensive engineering survey* of a structure to diagnose the specific characteristics of the asbestos problem and to estimate the cost to cure or safely contain the asbestos?	16	$13,241	$6,875	$18,907	$1,200–100,000
16. What is the average *increase* in the *effective interest rate* (taking into account the effects of points and other origination fees) of first mortgage loans made on properties with asbestos?	12	0.73%	0.5%	0.86%	0%–3%

plore how the items could be grouped based on significantly different mean levels.

Owner Strategies for Dealing with Asbestos

The mean response scores to question 1 listed in Table 1 indicated that the most significant motive for removal is that desired financing is difficult to obtain for properties with asbestos. The least important motivation is that ACMs are difficult to safely control. All of the motivations had a mean response score lower than 3, indicating that they are considered to be more than "somewhat important" motivations for removal.

The ANOVA *F*-statistic shown in Table 6 indicates that the 11 problems are not all equally important. In accord with Tukey's studentized range test, the problems are arranged into the following three groups representing three statistically distinct levels of motivations:

Most Important
Group I

- Desired financing difficult to get
- Potential lawsuits
- Property difficult to sell

Valuing Contaminated Properties

TABLE 5   Summary of Responses to Questions 17 through 24

Response Scale

1 = no difference	2 = less than 6% difference	3 = 6% through 10%	4 = 11% through 15%
5 = 16% through 20%	6 = 21% through 25%	7 = 26% through 30%	8 = greater than 30%

	Number of Responses	Mean	Median	Mode	Standard Deviation
17. For *each* of the following property types, indicate the average *percentage reduction* in the *stated* (or quoted) *rental rate* for a property with asbestos compared to a property without asbestos.					
17-1 High-rise office building	29	3.86	4	3	2.01
17-2 Low-rise office building	30	3.83	4	4	2.02
17-3 Free-standing retail store	25	3.08	3	3	1.65
17-4 Neighborhood shopping center	25	3.00	3	3	1.60
17-5 Regional shopping center	22	3.41	3	3	1.72
17-6 Warehouse	28	2.54	2	1	1.52
17-7 Light industrial building	27	2.52	2	1	1.57
17-8 Heavy industrial building	26	2.85	3	1	1.77
18. For *each* of the following property types, indicate the average *percentage increase* in *rental concessions,* including workletter or buildout allowances, for a property with asbestos compared to a property without asbestos.					
18-1 High-rise office building	22	2.82	2.5	1	1.72
18-2 Low-rise office building	21	2.62	3	1	1.65
18-3 Free-standing retail store	21	2.00	2	1	1.27
18-4 Neighborhood shopping center	21	2.14	2	1	1.21
18-5 Regional shopping center	19	2.16	2	1	1.14
18-6 Warehouse	21	1.86	2	1	1.04
18-7 Light industrial building	21	1.86	2	1	1.04
18-8 Heavy industrial building	20	1.80	1	1	1.08
19. For each of the following property types, what is the average *increase* in *operating expenses* of a property with asbestos compared to comparable properties without asbestos? (Asbestos operating expenses include expenses for monitoring and maintaining ACMs, additional insurance costs, additional legal expenses)					
19-1 High-rise office building	27	2.93	2	2	1.49
19-2 Low-rise office building	27	2.78	2	2	1.40
19-3 Free-standing retail store	24	2.38	2	2	1.07
19-4 Neighborhood shopping center	24	2.42	2	2	1.08
19-5 Regional shopping center	22	2.73	2.5	2	1.17
19-6 Warehouse	24	2.13	2	2	0.93
19-7 Light industrial building	24	2.13	2	2	0.93
19-8 Heavy industrial building	22	2.23	2	2	1.17
20. For each of the following property types, *how much higher,* on average, is the *vacancy rate* of properties with asbestos relative to comparable properties without asbestos?					
20-1 High-rise office building	26	3.35	3	2	1.86
20-2 Low-rise office building	27	3.26	3	2	1.82
20-3 Free-standing retail store	25	3.12	3	2	1.97
20-4 Neighborhood shopping center	25	3.08	2	2	1.85
20-5 Regional shopping center	24	3.13	2	2	1.99
20-6 Warehouse	26	2.54	2	1	1.84
20-7 Light industrial building	26	2.54	2	2	1.82
20-8 Heavy industrial building	24	2.83	2.5	1	1.99

Chapter 7: *Effects of Asbestos*

TABLE 5   Summary of Responses to Questions 17 through 24 *(continued)*

		Number of Responses	Mean	Median	Mode	Standard Deviation
21.	For each of the following property types, indicate the average *decrease* in *net operating income,* of properties with asbestos, relative to properties without asbestos, as a result of the effects of the presence of asbestos on rental income and operating expenses.					
21-1	High-rise office building	26	3.65	3.5	2	1.92
21-2	Low-rise office building	27	3.48	3	2	1.97
21-3	Free-standing retail store	24	3.00	2.5	2	1.63
21-4	Neighborhood shopping center	25	2.88	2	2	1.61
21-5	Regional shopping center	23	3.09	3	2	1.59
21-6	Warehouse	25	2.72	2	2	1.66
21-7	Light industrial building	25	2.64	2	2	1.67
21-8	Heavy industrial building	23	2.83	2	2	1.95
22.	What is your estimate of the average *reduction* in the *loan-to-value ratio* for first mortgage loans originated on properties with asbestos?					
22-1	High-rise office building	18	3.44	3.5	1	2.14
22-2	Low-rise office building	19	3.32	3	4	2.03
22-3	Free-standing retail store	18	3.11	3	1	2.08
22-4	Neighborhood shopping center	18	3.00	2.5	1	2.08
22-5	Regional shopping center	16	3.13	2.5	1	2.15
22-6	Warehouse	19	2.68	2	2	1.72
22-7	Light industrial building	19	2.68	2	2	1.72
22-8	Heavy industrial building	17	2.71	2	1	1.81
23.	For *each* of the following property types, indicate the average *percentage reduction* in the *value* of a property attributable to the expected *direct* costs of asbestos removal (which include costs for preparing areas for asbestos removal, costs for scrapping, tearing out, or otherwise physically removing the asbestos, costs for reconstructing building areas damaged by the removal, costs associated with reinstalling functional substitutes for the removed ACMs, and costs of properly disposing of the removed asbestos).					
23-1	High-rise office building	20	5.25	5	5	1.55
23-2	Low-rise office building	22	4.82	4.5	3	1.67
23-3	Free-standing retail store	20	4.40	4	3	1.85
23-4	Neighborhood shopping center	20	4.50	4	3	1.86
23-5	Regional shopping center	19	4.63	4	3	1.81
23-6	Warehouse	20	4.00	3	3	1.79
23-7	Light industrial building	20	4.00	3	3	1.82
23-8	Heavy industrial building	18	4.44	5	5	1.89
24.	For each of the following property types, indicate the average *percentage reduction* in the value of a property attributable to the expected *indirect costs* of asbestos removal (which include the loss of revenue during downtime necessary to remove asbestos, and the cost to move and temporarily relocate tenants while the asbestos is being removed).					
24-1	High-rise office building	22	4.00	4	5	1.65
24-2	Low-rise office building	24	3.67	3	2	1.65
24-3	Free-standing retail store	22	3.59	3	2	1.72
24-4	Neighborhood shopping center	22	3.59	3	2	1.78
24-5	Regional shopping center	21	3.76	4	2	1.77
24-6	Warehouse	22	3.14	3	2	1.79
24-7	Light industrial building	22	3.09	3	2	1.83
24-8	Heavy industrial building	20	3.20	2.5	2	1.96

Valuing Contaminated Properties

Table 6 ANOVA Results

Question	Number of Items	Number of Observations	Model DF[a]	Error DF	Between MS[b]	Within MS	F-Value	Probability > F
1	11	700	10	689	5.166	0.890	5.80**	0.0001
4	3	168	2	165	0.484	0.778	0.62	0.5377
5	6	335	5	329	6.830	0.727	9.89**	0.0001
6	5	263	4	258	0.572	0.670	0.85	0.4930
7	4	171	3	167	14.303	0.940	15.21**	0.0001
9	11	642	10	631	10.648	1.033	10.30**	0.0001
17	8	212	7	204	7,801	3.186	2.45**	0.0197
18	8	165	7	157	2.920	1.755	1.66	0.1216
19	8	194	7	186	2.417	1.449	1.67	0.1191
20	8	203	7	195	2.499	3.725	0.67	0.6967
21	8	198	7	190	3.342	3.227	1.04	0.4076
22	8	144	7	136	1.597	4.102	0.39	0.9074
23	8	159	7	151	3.435	3.336	1.03	0.4126
24	8	175	7	167	2.336	3.278	0.71	0.6614

** Indicates that the results are significant at 5% significance level.

DF^a is an abbreviation for degrees of freedom.

MS^b is an abbreviation for mean square.

Group II

- Bad publicity and bad image
- Potential costly regulations
- Increase in cost of financing
- Tenants react adversely

Least Important
Group III

- Insurance coverage difficult to get
- Health threat to occupants
- Increase in cost of insurance
- ACMs difficult to safely control

The mean response scores to question 5 in Table 1 show that the respondents rated the development of a plan for removal in stages as the strategy most frequently pursued by building owners. Containment of ACMs by encapsulation or enclosure is the second most frequently pursued strategy.

The ANOVA result indicates that the six strategies are not all equally likely to be undertaken by new property owners. Tukey's studentized range test allows the separation of four of the six items into the following three statistically distinct groups:

Most Frequent
Group I

- Develop plan to remove asbestos in stages
- Encapsulation or enclosure of ACMs

Group II

- No removal of ACMs until demolition

Least Frequent
Group III

- No removal of ACMs until just prior to sale of property

Market Responses to Buildings with Asbestos

Table 2 summarizes the responses to questions 2 through 4 and 6 through 8. The results for question 2 imply that potential purchasers do not rule out buying buildings with asbestos.[9] Question 3 indicates that prospective buyers may or may not require the seller to pay for both preliminary and comprehensive environmental audits.[10]

Questions 4 and 6 concern whether adverse consequences are expected to linger after ACMs have been completely removed. Question 4 indirectly addresses this issue by asking how the cost of removal is reflected in the negotiations of the sale. If buyers generally accept a price discount approximately equal to the estimated total cost of removal, the implication is that investors are confident that removal of the asbestos will eliminate all associated problems. On the other hand, if buyers demand a price discount greater than the total cost removal, the implication is that they expect adverse consequences to linger after removal is completed. Responses to question 4, however, do not indicate that the latter expectation prevails. The mean response scores for the three buyer demands are similar. The ANOVA F-statistic implies that these demands are equally likely. These results are supported by the responses to question 6, which indicate that appraisers do not expect the adverse consequences listed to occur frequently.

Responses to question 7 indicate that indemnification guarantees are the most frequent of the listed loan requirements imposed by lenders on property with ACMs. The ANOVA F-statistic implies that the four loan requirements are not equally likely. The Tukey's studentized range test allows the arrangement of the four items into two distinct groups.

Most Frequent
Group I

- Requirement of indemnification guarantee

Least Frequent
Group II

- Lower loan-to-value ratio
- Higher "points" or origination fees
- Higher interest rate

Lenders may require indemnification guarantees more frequently than higher loan costs or lower loan amounts because they are unable to accurately price the risks posed to them by asbestos.[11] Responses to question 8 indicate that refusal to lend is fairly common, confirming that many lenders tend to be cautious about lending on buildings with ACMs.[12]

Appraiser Adjustments to Properties with ACMs

Table 3 summarizes the responses to question 9. The responses indicate that the adjustments most frequently made by appraisers are to reduce the property value by the combined direct and indirect costs of asbestos re-

---

9. Comments to this question indicated that a prospective purchaser's reaction depends on who the purchaser is. Institutional investors and government were identified as being the most reluctant to purchase such buildings.

10. Comments to this question indicated that practice varies among buyers and sellers. A few respondents commented that some sellers routinely provide a preliminary type of survey for older buildings (the class of buildings most likely to contain asbestos). Several other responses, however, indicated that it is common for a potential buyer to pay for the preliminary audit. One possible explanation of why buyers pay for the preliminary audit is that a typical buyer may want to be able to show, in accordance with the "innocent party" defense provided in CERCLA, that it exercised due diligence in attempting to detect the presence of ACMs.

11. Comments indicated that other loan costs (not listed in the question) that may be imposed by lenders are required environmental surveys and periodic air sampling. The requirement that surveys, air sampling, and so on be completed before loan origination extends the loan processing time for buildings with ACMs.

12. Comments indicated that lender actions depend on the type of lender making the loan as well as on the amount and condition of the ACMs in the building. It was noted that some institutions (individual insurance companies were specifically cited as examples) have a policy of refusing to lend on properties with ACMs. Yet the general feeling of the respondents was that many lenders will make a loan if the ACMs are adequately controlled.

moval; that adjustments are more likely to be made to the operating expenses of the property than to the rental income; that the most frequent of the operating expense adjustments is to increase repair and maintenance expenses (when O&M expenses are likely to be included); and that adjustments are made to the cap rate and the discount rate with almost equal frequency.

The Tukey's studentized range test allows the arrangement of the adjustments into the following three groups:

Most Frequent
Group I

- Reduction of property value by indirect costs
- Reduction of property value by direct costs
- Increase in maintenance and repair expenses

Group II

- Increase in insurance costs
- Increase in cap rate
- Increase in discount rate
- Increase in workletter/buildout allowances
- Increase in legal expenses

Least Frequent
Group III

- Increase in the amount of rental concessions to tenants
- Decrease in rental rate
- Increase in vacancy rate

Magnitudes of Selected Asbestos Effects

Responses to questions 10 through 16 are presented in Table 4. The mean and median estimates to the questions have the following implications.

- The discount in the market value of properties with ACMs typically ranges from about one-tenth to about one-third of the value of comparable properties without asbestos.
- Properties with ACMs take, on average, 8.2 months longer to sell than comparable properties without asbestos,[13] and rental properties with ACMs take, on average, 4.88 months longer to obtain tenants to fill vacancies than properties without asbestos.[14]
- The average increase in the discount rate for properties with ACMs (i.e., the size of the additional risk premium) is 1.99%.[15]
- The average range in the lump sum cost for an environmental audit to determine whether ACMs are present is $4,091 to $13,432 (the median range is $2,250 to $5,500), and the average range in the lump sum cost for a comprehensive engineering study to determine the extent as well as the specific characteristics of the asbestos present in a building is $5,638 to $20,844 (the median range is $3,750 to $10,000).

13. Some comments indicated that at least a portion of the additional time to sell is caused by the need for environmental surveys and engineering studies, providing further evidence that the transaction costs imposed by the need for asbestos (environmental) audits/surveys/studies include delay costs as well as actual expenditures.

14. Some comments indicated that some of the additional time to re-lease might be attributable to the down time needed to remove asbestos from the leased space.

15. An impression obtained from comments is that some respondents felt that adjustments to the discount rate to reflect the presence of asbestos are difficult to support.

- The average increase in the effective interest rate for mortgage loans made on properties with ACMs is 73 basis points (.73%) and the median increase is 50 basis points.

Income and Value Effects of Asbestos on Different Property Types

Table 5 contains summaries of the responses to questions 17 through 24.[16] With the exception of question 23, a consistent pattern of responses is apparent. This pattern is that commercial properties (e.g., office buildings and shopping centers) are generally perceived to be more adversely affected by ACMs than industrial properties (e.g., warehouses and factories). Further, among the commercial property types office buildings, are perceived to be more adversely affected by ACMs than retail properties. Heavy industrial buildings are generally perceived to be the most severely affected of the industrial property categories.[17] Responses to question 23, the exception, indicate that the value reduction for heavy industrial buildings as a result of the direct costs of removal may be slightly higher than for retail space. This deviation may be explained by the commonly accepted notion that heavy industrial buildings contain a large amount of asbestos.

The mean response scores for questions 17 through 24 imply the following approximate percentage adjustments to properties with ACMs.

- An average decrease in rental rates of 11% to 12% for office buildings, 8% to 10% for retail buildings, and 6% to 7% for industrial properties
- An average increase in rental concessions of 6% to 7% for office buildings, and of less than 6% for both retail and industrial properties
- An average increase in operating expenses of 7% to 8% for office properties, 5% to 7% for retail properties, and 3% to 4% for industrial properties
- An average increase in vacancies of 9% to 10% for office buildings, 8% for shopping centers, and 6% to 7% for industrial buildings
- An average decrease in *NOI* of 10% to 11% for office buildings, 7% to 8% for retail properties, and 6% to 7% for industrial buildings
- An average reduction in the loan-to-value ratio of 9% to 10% for office buildings, 8% to 9% for retail buildings, and 6% to 7% for industrial buildings[18]
- An average reduction in value caused by direct removal costs of 17% to 19% for office buildings, 15% to 16% for retail buildings, and 13% to 15% for industrial buildings
- An average reduction in value caused by indirect removal costs of 11% to 13% for office buildings, 11% to 12% for retail buildings, and 8% to 9% for industrial buildings
- An average loss in value caused by the total cost of removal (i.e., combined direct and indirect costs) of 28% to 32% for office buildings, 26% to 28% for retail buildings, and 21% to 24% for industrial buildings

Apparent congruence can be observed between the results summarized above and the estimates of value reduction provided in question 10. The upper end of the range of the estimates of value reduction provided in

16. The results summarized in Table 5 for questions 17 through 21 must be interpreted with caution. In particular, the average percentage change in the individual components of *NOI* taken together, as indicated by the mean response scores to questions 17 through 20 do not reconcile with percentage change indicated in question 21, the overall percentage change in *NOI*. The reason they do not reconcile is that the percentage calculations are applied to different bases. Questions 17 through 20 are nonetheless useful because they contain information about the effects of asbestos on the individual components of *NOI*.

17. There are several possible explanations of why commercial property types might be more adversely affected by asbestos than industrial property types. One is that commercial properties are more likely than industrial properties to cater to the public. A second reason is that industrial properties are perhaps more likely to be owner-occupied properties, and thus experience less pressure from the marketplace. A third possibility is that industrial properties are more likely to be special-purpose properties used by clientele not as prone to be alarmed by asbestos as clientele of commercial buildings.

18. The less adverse lender reactions to industrial properties than to the other property types may be because loans on industrial properties are based on the credit of the company occupying the space rather than on the value of the property. Moreover, because industrial properties are more likely to be owner occupied, the firm occupying the space may try harder to make a loan work out because of the value "in use" of that space to the company.

question 10 closely corresponds to the total cost of removal for high-rise office buildings indicated. On the other hand, the lower end of the range of estimates may represent buildings in which the value loss associated with the presence of asbestos is less than the total cost to remove it.

Conclusion

Asbestos in buildings clearly remains a problem for many building owners, and thus it must be dealt with in appraisal. The survey of MAI appraisers reported in this article is intended to contribute toward understanding of the costs imposed on real property by environmental problems such as asbestos, and also about how the market and the institutional players in the market are likely to respond to contaminated properties. This questionnaire also can be easily modified to deal with most types of hazardous and toxic valuation problems currently confronted by appraisers.

Obviously, informed opinions (i.e., best judgments) are not the same as real knowledge. In addition, the respondents to this survey may not have dealt with the asbestos problem in sufficient numbers and depth to be able to answer many of the questions knowledgeably. Notwithstanding the limits of the survey, disseminating informed opinions of practicing real estate appraisers can contribute to a better understanding of how asbestos affects the value and marketability of properties with ACMs.

Liquidity Loss and Delayed Transactions with Leaking Underground Storage Tanks

by Robert A. Simons, PhD, and Arthur Sementelli

Urban developers often encounter brownfield-related costs, expense required to clean up environmental contamination from prior land uses. Parties redeveloping brownfield sites also face uncertainty about the degree of remediation, the financial responsibility of polluters and owners, and potential lender uncertainty. This puts urban brownfield developments at a disadvantage when compared with greenfield sites that have not been previously used.

Discovery of potential contamination from leaky underground storage tanks is a common brownfield problem encountered in virtually all jurisdictions in the United States. In 1982, about 6% of the estimated 1.2 million known steel tanks were believed to be leaking.[1] Another estimate from the U.S. Environmental Protection Agency (EPA) places the number of USTs containing petroleum in the millions, with the leak rates as high as 25%.[2] While many releases of toxic liquids from USTs result in modest amounts of contaminated soil confined on site, a substantial portion of cases are more severe and involve groundwater contamination, both on site and off site.

Underground storage tank sites are among the most common types of brownfield. They are more numerous than Superfund or toxic release inventory sites. For example, in Cuyahoga County, the core urban county in the Cleveland primary metropolitan statistical area (PMSA), there were under 30 potential Superfund sites, almost 300 toxic release inventory (TRI) sites, and over 1,300 leaking tank sites known in late 1994.

Many USTs are located in obvious places, including operating or former gas stations, transportation service facilities, industrial plants, government-operated service yards, and along major traffic arteries. Hence, they often have otherwise favorable locations at strategic intersections, making them attractive as fast-food sites or key corner parcels in a larger-site assembly.

When leaking underground storage tanks are encountered by developers, the project may become delayed or abandoned because of the associated costs necessary for remediation. Depending on what is found, par-

Robert A. Simons, PhD, is an associate professor of planning and development at Cleveland State University, Ohio. He consults and conducts research for local governments and developers on real estate effects of contamination on neighboring property and on brownfield issues. He earned his graduate degrees in planning and economics from the University of North Carolina, Chapel Hill.

Arthur Sementelli is a doctoral student with dual emphasis in operations research and organization studies, and holds a joint teaching and research position at Cleveland State University, Ohio. He consults and conducts research for governmental and quasi-governmental agencies on management and human resource issues. Mr. Sementelli earned an MPA with emphasis in organizational behavior from Gannon University, Erie, Pennsylvania, and a BA in history and policy at Carnegie-Mellon University, Pittsburgh.

This article originally appeared in the July 1997 issue of The Appraisal Journal.

1. Darrel Kost and Walter Parish, "Petroleum Recovery Operations in an Urban Area," *Journal of Water Resources Planning and Management,* v. 112, no. 1 (1986): 548.

2. William Page and Harvey Rabinowitz, "Potential for Redevelopment of Contaminated Brownfield Sites," *Economic Development Quarterly,* v. 8, no. 4 (1994): 353.

cels may undergo several months or years of environmental remediation to remove contamination from the site. This potential for additional costs raises several questions about LUST sites under remediation. Can they be sold or financed? Does removing functionally obsolete tanks from a site help? Does the perception of possible leaks stigmatize registered nonleaking tanks (RUST)?

This study augments the growing body of research on redevelopment in lieu of environmental regulation, and extends the recent work of Page and Rabinowitz[3] on groundwater contamination and its effect on property values by examining the relationship between on-site soil and groundwater contamination, property transactions and financing for non-leaking (RUST) and leaking (LUST) sites. It also provides indirect empirical evidence related to Patchin's notion of stigma.[4]

This paper presents evidence from Cuyahoga County on the transaction rates of commercial property, including LUST sites. Once leaks are detected, property owners are expected to cooperate voluntarily with state regulators in mitigating environmental contamination. In Ohio, the regulating agency is the Bureau of Underground Storage Tank Regulations (BUSTR). Its activities include maintaining lists of registered and leaking tank sites, assisting property owners with soil and water testing, engaging consultants, and removing the contaminated soil.

The detection of environmental contamination should depress property value, and there is no assurance that these "sunk" remediation costs would be recaptured upon sale. Known contamination may also have a spillover effect on nearby properties. This uncertainty may prevent the completion of a transaction until the environmental problems are addressed through mitigation, litigation, or both.

In Cuyahoga County, most of the drinking water is provided by the City of Cleveland Water Department directly from Lake Erie. Over 98% of the LUST sites analyzed have municipal drinking water rather than wells, minimizing the potential health risks of LUST incidents in this research. The presence of tanks or documented leak incidents are expected to impede an owner's ability to finance or sell the property. Stigma associated with known contamination could mean that sales activity would not rebound quickly to the levels of uncontaminated properties.[5]

Results based on 77 sales of tank sites indicate that only 4.9% of properties with nonleaking tanks completed transactions over a four-year period compared with 10.4% of comparable, otherwise uncontaminated commercial properties. Only 3.8% of leaking UST sites were sold over the study period, a figure also significantly smaller than for uncontaminated commercial sites. Lower sales volume is considered an indicator of stigma because of the potential loss to the owner's liquidity in the property.

Financing rates and loan-to-value ratios differed for UST sites. While 32.6% of commercial properties without tanks obtained mortgage financing when sold, only 9.3% of sales with nonleaking tanks on site were mortgaged. However, 29.4% of those sites with reported leaks, many of them with tanks removed, received mortgages. Further, loan-to-value ratios for sites with nonleaking tanks were lower. Hence, the presence of tanks on site, with or without a leak, appears to stigmatize properties, impeding access to mortgage capital.

3. William Page and Harvey Rabinowitz, "Groundwater Contamination: Its Effects on Property Values and Cities," *Journal of the American Planning Association* (Autumn 1993): 473–487.

4. Peter Patchin, "Contaminated Properties and the Sales Comparison Approach," *The Appraisal Journal* (July 1994): 402–409.

5. Ibid.

Chapter 7: *Liquidity Loss and Delayed Transactions*

Relevant Literature

Owners wishing to transact contaminated properties face several obstacles, including environmental regulation, real estate market pricing, and financing considerations. Combined, risk and uncertainty about contaminated sites add to sluggish real estate markets that make selling tainted sites difficult.

Real estate transactions occur only when a buyer and a seller agree on a price. A buyer's offer for a property should reflect the present value of the discounted net cash flow stream over time, including remediation, adjusted for risk. In addition to business risk, uncertainty about environmental matters may be substantial enough to kill a transaction. The stigma that potential buyers attach to previously contaminated lands may interfere with the pricing and the time frame of the sale. The risk may also include liability concerns about impact on nearby properties. Lender liability in property financing may be another reason for reduced transaction activity. Potential sellers may have incomplete information about new regulation and may face voluntary compliance for cleanup costs. If they do not fully realize the sunk costs of remediation, they may try to recover cleanup expense by setting a sales price higher than the market can bear. For example, state-mandated environmental regulations on buried construction and demolition debris substantially affected market activity by imposing cleanup costs on the seller/owner.[6]

Page and Rabinowitz support the notion that changing environmental rules themselves can hinder development.[7] They assert that potential liability may affect property value more than actual contamination and that parties are deterred by the threat of delays and potential cleanup costs that could arise while waiting for a relaxation of remediation criteria. Page and Rabinowitz cover two issues pertaining to environmentally contaminated sites in general and leaking USTs in particular. Because property owners could be held accountable for off-site effects resulting from contamination originating from their properties, it is important to consider these situations.

Contamination of Nearby Properties

Known contamination can affect the value of nearby properties. Fear of lawsuits may prevent new buyers from acquiring property with tanks. Proximity to toxic waste sites,[8] landfills,[9] and petrochemical refineries[10] has been known to affect residential property values negatively, diminishing with distance from the subject property. However, when Page and Rabinowitz[11] used a case study design, they found no diminution of value for nearby residential sites attributable to groundwater contamination. Their small sample size (two contaminated homes and five uncontaminated), research design (not all other factors were controlled), and use of assessed value rather than sales price as the value indicator may explain the counter-intuitive result. Further, it's possible that the local assessor did not recognize contamination when setting sales prices.

In another study we conducted, we found that close proximity (in the same city block or within 300 feet) to a registered, leaking underground storage tank reduced residential property values by about 17% of value. Some but not all of these leaking sites had offsite groundwater contamination. Overall, evidence supports the notion that known contamination has a negative effect on nearby properties.

6. Robert Simons, "How Clean is Clean? The Effect of Proposed Governmental Regulations on Vacant and Underutilized Inner-City Land Being Recycled in the Residential Market," *The Appraisal Journal* (July 1994): 424–438.

7. *Economic Development Quarterly,* 354.

8. Katherine Kiel, "Measuring the Impact of the Discovery and Cleaning of Identified Hazardous Waste Sites on House Values," *Land Economics* (November 1995): 428–435. See also: J. J. Kohlhase, "The Impact of Toxic Waste Sites on Housing Values," *Journal of Urban Economics,* v. 30 (1991): 1–26; and R. Michaels and V. Smith, "Market Segmentation and Valuing Amenities with Hedonic Models: The Case of Hazardous Waste Sites," *Journal of Urban Economics,* v. 28 (1990): 223–242.

9. Nelson A. Chris, J. Genereux, and M. Genereux, "Price Effects of Landfills on House Values," *Land Economics* (November 1992): 359–365. See also Alan Reichert, M. Small, and S. Mohanty, "The Impact of Landfills on Residential Property Value," *Journal of Real Estate Research,* v. 7, no. 3 (1992): 297–314.

10. David Clark and Leslie Nieves, "An Interregional Hedonic Analysis of Noxious Facility Impacts on Local Wages and Property Values," Working Paper, Marquette University, Milwaukee, Wisconsin, 1993. See also Patrick Flower and Wade Ragas, "The Effects of Refineries on Neighborhood Property Values," *Journal of Real Estate Research,* v. 9, no. 3 (1994): 319–338.

11. *Journal of the American Planning Association,* 473–487.

Uncertainty, Risk, and Stigma

Even with known cleanup costs, contaminated properties are difficult to transact. The prices of the subject and nearby sites may be reduced. Further, the publicizing of contamination on Superfund sites has a negative effect on residential property in the vicinity.[12]

Austrian and Eichler's[13] survey on brownfields found that of the 46 midwestern respondents, 61% indicated that contaminated sites would only sell at a discount equal to or greater than the cleanup costs. Presumably, part of the discount that is in excess of the cleanup costs would dissipate when a formal assessment of the cleanup costs is done. If not, then the property is likely to incur additional price-reducing stigma. Although real estate markets have been reluctant to recognize the sale of contaminated properties, they are becoming more accustomed to them, with sales usually occurring slowly and with severe discounts.[14]

Lenders may be reluctant to finance properties with USTs, leaking or not. While lenders have long been considered potentially responsible parties (PRPs) under the Comprehensive Environmental Response, Compensation and Liability Act of 1980 (CERCLA), lender safe harbor legislation from UST liabilities has recently been proposed by the EPA. This might make UST properties easier to finance.[15] However, Ohio law did not hold lenders exempt from liability from environmental contamination during the study period.

Given these issues, research investigating if and when contaminated UST properties sell, along with their ability to get financing, are clearly warranted. This study focuses on properties during and after the completion of government-sanctioned remedial procedures.

RUST and LUST Database

The properties used in this research were drawn from registered lists for LUST and RUST incidents in Cuyahoga County, Ohio, dating back to 1988. Of the 1,362 total incidents reported through January 1, 1993, 1,000 incidents having useable street addresses with a unique permanent parcel number (property tax number) were examined. Approximately 120 incidents reported in 1993 or later were excluded. The resulting available information included in this paper was based on 889 LUST sites, 882 RUST sites, and a baseline of 23,700 comparable commercial properties. The ratio of this sample to the overall population of contaminated sites with useable addresses initiated in 1992 or earlier is just under 50%.

Transactions and Financing

The crux of the empirical portion of this research is, what effect does the presence of tanks and a known leak have on transaction activity? The statistical technique used to evaluate this relationship is to compare the sale probabilities of nontank (baseline) commercial properties with commercial properties with RUST properties and contaminated LUST sites.

The decision to use a comparison of the sale probabilities instead of a hedonic pricing model was based, in part, on our other study concerning residential sales near contaminated UST sites. In that study, which employed a hedonic price model, a smaller-than-expected number of sales were found, raising the issue that lower transaction rates could be present near contaminated sites. Thus, that study focuses on the transaction rates

12. Kiel, 428–435.
13. Ziona Austrian and Henning Eichler, "1993 Urban Brownfields Site Survey: Preliminary Analysis," Working Paper, Cleveland State University, Ohio, April 1993.
14. Patchin, 402–409.
15. Jeremy Gibson, "Lender Safe Harbor for Underground Storage Tank Liabilities Proposed by EPA," *Environmental Insights* (June 1994).

Chapter 7: *Liquidity Loss and Delayed Transactions*

rather than the effect of contamination on sales price. It is acknowledged that certain site attributes may affect the sale price of commercial property.

However, a brief evaluation of selected sites and locational characteristics supports the notion that property attributes do not play a main factor in transaction rate differences between the populations studied in this research. Baseline commercial and tank sites are scattered throughout the county, with tank sites often located along major traffic arteries. With respect to key site attributes, the mean square footage of RUST and LUST properties was 3,964, compared with 4,203 for baseline commercial parcels without tanks. The results of a difference-of-means test were not significant at a significance level of 0.1. Differences between baseline and UST means for lot depth and legal frontage were likewise found not to be statistically significant. Thus, site attributes of the baseline and tank groups do not seem to be significantly different.

In the Cuyahoga County study, the number of transactions, quality of title transfer (number of weaker quitclaim deeds), and presence of mortgage financing were considered. Loan-to-value ratios for those properties receiving financing were noted. The study identified the baseline population of all applicable commercial sales in Cuyahoga County over the period 1989–1992, which had the county auditor's land use classification of similar commercial property. This baseline group excludes those properties with known USTs or incidents, properties containing multifamily residences or condominiums, and hotel and office buildings. A total of 23,714 properties was considered. The desired unit of analysis is the site rather than the parcel because some properties have multiple parcels. The "lead" or main parcel of each transaction was chosen, thus avoiding the possibility of double-counting sales. Over the four-year period, 2,472 transactions occurred, a rate of 10.4%.

Expected Outcomes

Because contaminated properties under active mitigation are expected to have lower transaction levels, the percentage that sell should be lower than for the baseline. Fewer mortgage originations and lower loan-to-value ratios are also anticipated.

These hypotheses are tested by comparing each category with the baseline to see if the percentages are different from one another. A binomial probability model was used to test if the transaction levels for LUST and RUST properties are significantly different from those of the baseline population of commercial properties.

Results

A total of 43 properties with registered non-leaking tanks (4.9%) were sold (see Table 1). A total of 34 LUST sites (3.8%) were transacted during the four-year study period. As expected, these percentages are lower than for the baseline commercial population, and this difference is statistically significant at a confidence level of 0.05.

Among baseline properties, 248 sales (10.0%) had quitclaim deeds. The number of quitclaim deeds for tank and leak incident transactions was very small: Only four tank properties sold had this weak form of deed upon transfer (4.7% for RUST sales and 5.9% for LUST). Both UST

Valuing Contaminated Properties

TABLE 1 Incidence of Transactions, "Weak" Deed Transfers and Mortgage Financing for Selected Commercial and UST Sites, 1989–1992 (Properties Sold)

Category	Sample Number	Sale Transactions	Sale Percentage	Quitclaim Deeds	Quitclaim Percentage	Mortgage Financing	Mortgage Percentage
Baseline Commercial Properties[a]	23,714	2,472	10.4%	248	10.3%	805	32.6%
RUST List[b]	882	43	4.9%	2	4.7%	4	9.3%
LUST List[c]	889	34	3.8%	2	5.9%	10	29.4%

Sources: Bureau of Underground Storage Tank Regulations, Cuyahoga County Auditor, and Simons and Sementelli.

(a) Commercial and industrial properties (not on RUST and LUST lists) in Cuyahoga County, less multifamily, residential condominiums, hotels, and office buildings.

(b) List of RUSTs that have not leaked.

(c) List of LUSTs exclusive of those which have received "no further action" letters.

rates are lower than the baseline, suggesting that sellers and buyers recognize that quitclaim deeds do not provide adequate protection from potential liability for site cleanup expenses, especially for owner-operators.

With respect to financing, 32.6% of the baseline properties sold had registered mortgages (secured by the property) that were originated on or around the sale date. However, only four RUST properties (9.3%), and 10 LUST sales (29.4%) obtained financing. This demonstrates a statistically significant difference in financing for RUST properties, but not for LUST. Thus, properties with registered tanks appear less likely to receive a mortgage than clean commercial sales or sites with known contamination.

The low rate of mortgage financing for RUST sites may be attributed to financial institutions for fear of potential liability after the sale. It is possible that sales with tanks obtain unsecured financing instead of secured mortgage loans. But LUST sites with ongoing mitigation may have had tanks removed. The small number of such sites appears to be obtaining financing at a similar rate as baseline properties. Recent case law on lender liability may substantially ease the financing problem.[16] Private environmental liability insurance partially addresses the issue of uncertainty, reducing lender concerns and increasing the property's marketability. Some states, such as Michigan and Illinois, are also moving toward a lender liability exemption for brownfield properties.

Average loan-to-value ratios (LTV) for all nontank commercial properties in Cuyahoga County have decreased from over 0.95 to 0.80 during the 1989–1992 period (average LTV is 0.96), consistent with national financial trends. With these high LTVs, it is plausible that some are seller financed. For the sites with tanks, the loan-to-value ratios were substantially less (0.51 for the four RUST sales). The loan-to-value ratios for sites where incidents occurred were more consistent with current financial trends (0.84 for LUST sales). This reinforces the assertion that lenders are more concerned with uncertainty concerning potential liability than with known liability.

Conclusion

This paper addressed the presence of both leaking and nonleaking underground storage tanks and their effect on property transactions. Properties with tanks, contaminated or not, are transacting in the marketplace. However, these properties transacted at significantly reduced rates (less than half as often) than did baseline commercial properties. Properties that still

16. Ibid.

Chapter 7: *Liquidity Loss and Delayed Transactions*

had tanks on site are also much less likely to obtain secured mortgage financing than properties with no tanks. Also, loan-to-value ratios were substantially lower for properties with nonleaking tanks.

The cumulative reduction of financial liquidity for owners of sites where leak incidents have occurred is substantial. Multiplying the relative proportion of transactions (0.038/0.104) by the likelihood of obtaining secured financing (0.294/0.326) yields 0.33, implying that property owner assets in contaminated sites are less than one half as liquid than for clean commercial sites. (LTV ratios were not considered because the sample size for LUST and RUST sales was very small. There would have been further reduction in liquidity if LTVs had been included.) The figures are even lower for sites with tanks remaining on site, which were only 0.13 as liquid as comparable commercial properties without tanks. These reductions are evidence of the stigma associated with contaminated sites or those tank sites where there is potential for a future environmental event.[17]

The reduction in sales activity can be a problem for appraisers seeking to identify comparable sales for environmentally tainted properties. Having only a few comparables available tends to invalidate traditional market approaches to determining value. This indicates that appraisers should stratify comparables by known versus unknown contamination to get a better idea about arm's length financing for otherwise desirable RUST or LUST sites. By stratifying comparables by known or unknown contamination, appraisers can better differentiate between high- and low-quality sites, limiting the possibility of poor appraisals and their consequences.[18]

Property owners who cannot avoid dealing with or owning a UST site should consider removing tanks not needed for business purposes and then obtain a covenant not to sue (CNTS), if possible. Ideally, this should remove some of the associated stigma, and enable properties to be financed more readily through conventional sources after tank removal. For development properties with tanks still on site, nonsecured financing may be the rule rather than the exception. Since there appears to be reluctance in capital markets to financing contaminated sites, a risk-reducing role for the public sector may be appropriate. If environmental insurance is available, it may be worthwhile to pursue it.

References

Donovan, Brian, and Pat O'Connor. "Underground Storage Tank Update," *Plant Engineering* (June 1989): 60–62.

Nooney, Kathleen. "Criminal Sentencing Guidelines and Corporate Compliance Programs," *Environmental Insights* (January 1994): 1–12.

17. Patchin, 402–409.

18. Patricia Rudolph, "Will Bad Appraisals Drive Out Good?," *The Appraisal Journal* (July 1994): 363–366.

The Price and Liquidity Effects of UST Leaks from Gas Stations on Adjacent Contaminated Property

by Robert A. Simons, PhD, William M. Bowen, PhD, and Arthur J. Sementelli, PhD

Robert A. Simons, PhD, *is an associate professor of real estate and urban planning in the Levin College of Urban Affairs at Cleveland State University in Ohio. He earned his graduate degrees from the University of North Carolina, Chapel Hill. Dr. Simons consults and conducts research on the effects of environmental contamination on real estate values. Other areas include brownfields, housing policy, and government real estate problems. Contact: roby@wolf.csuohio.edu.*

William M. Bowen, PhD, *is an associate professor of urban studies and public administration in the Levin College of Urban Affairs at Cleveland State University. He received his PhD in regional analysis and planning from Indiana University, Bloomington. His interests center on the use of empirical research methods and statistics as applied to decisions in environmental affairs, energy policy, and economic development.*

Arthur J. Sementelli, PhD, *is an assistant professor of political science and geography in the public administration program at Stephen F. Austin State University in Texas. He received his PhD from Cleveland State University, and conducts research on public administration and public policy. Other research areas include management science, environmental policy, and economic impacts of contamination.*

This article originally appeared in the April 1999 issue of The Appraisal Journal.

1. Robert Simons, William Bowen, and Arthur Sementelli, "The Effect of Underground Storage Tanks on Residential Property Values in Cuyahoga County, Ohio," *The Journal of Real Estate Research*, v. 14, no.1/2 (1997): 29–42.

The effects of gas station leaking underground storage tanks (LUSTs) are a concern because petroleum compounds may potentially cause groundwater contamination (especially serious if drinking water is affected), soil contamination, and noxious deleterious fumes in confined areas such as basements. The main hypothesis of this article is that if nearby properties are contaminated by petroleum from LUSTs, their value would be reduced. We address the effects of LUSTs on various market outcomes, including transaction rate, sales price, and ability to obtain financing. The study area was Cuyahoga County, Ohio, with Cleveland as its central city. All analyses were based on public records.

The statistical technique used to analyze each of the different market outcomes depended largely on matching the requirements and capabilities of each of the alternative feasible techniques with the characteristics of the available data for the particular outcome of interest. The main constraint was the small number ($n < 10$) of contaminated properties sold in a property class in any given year. For each type of analysis, we used the technique providing the best match between technique and available data, including predictive regression models in a hedonic framework for individual properties, multivariate analysis of variance (MANOVA), presale/postsale analysis, and difference of proportions analysis. Throughout, we report only those results established at a 95% confidence level or better.

This research approach is complementary to direct surveys of market participants. Though direct surveys are often more detailed and specific about certain hypothetical situations or past experiences, they are often more difficult to employ. Moreover, they often fail to present an overall view of a situation in a real estate market, thereby limiting the ability to generalize any conclusions drawn from them.

The results we present here are consistent with our earlier findings of the effects of registered LUSTs on residential property, which concluded that there was a 17% reduction in sales price.[1] For residential properties in this study, results indicate a statistically significant reduction of up to

14%–16% for those properties sold after contamination becomes known. This is an observable effect from sales only, before consideration of effects on value from any delayed sale or reduced transaction rates. For commercial properties, we find a significant reduction in transaction rates (33% lower), a reduction in sales price of approximately 28%–42%, and more than twice the incidence of seller financing.

The rest of this article covers the literature pertaining to value loss of adjacent property, including a detailed description of the data collection and analysis used in this research, and reports results for residential and commercial property.

Literature Review
Residential Property Affected by Environmental Contamination (Including LUSTs)

The effects of environmental contamination on surrounding residential property are well documented, with important studies noted in the reference section of this article. Studies have been conducted on Superfund toxic waste sites, landfills, and existing hazardous waste sites, as well as high-voltage overhead electrical transmission power lines. Relevant work has also addressed the relationship between groundwater contamination and residential property values.[2] Results from these studies generally support the notion that a negative relationship exists between proximity to these objectionable sites and residential sale values. This relationship diminishes with increasing distance from the site. The type of toxic substance also affects the reduction in values. For example, one would expect to find a larger negative effect for hazardous waste than for nonhazardous environmentally harmful materials. Compared with other forms of contamination, LUSTs would be considered a moderately toxic environmental problem.[3]

Housing markets assimilate publicly available information (e.g., a discovery that contamination at a Superfund site is worse than expected) by capitalizing it into a lower sales price. Homeowners may also perceive separate diminution of value attributable to a nuisance associated with close proximity to a site and more general negative effects related to potential health hazards. Proximity to visually obvious hazardous sites may also deter potential buyers from making offers on homes, thus affecting sales price by reducing demand.

There is a small but growing body of empirical information on the effect of underground storage tank leaks on residential property. Our study finds a 17% reduction in sales price for residential property sold within one block or 300 feet of a registered LUST, where the site continued to have tanks onsite.[4] This result pertains to 1992, a year when recovery from the recession indicated generally soft market conditions. These results also include LUSTs associated with industrial sites that were not gas stations.

Nonresidential Property Affected by LUSTs

There is strong evidence in the literature to support the notion that nonresidential (income-producing) property could be negatively affected by proximity to environmental contamination (of which LUSTs are an important subgroup), even if no sale of the property occurs.[5] Because LUSTs are relatively common, they are often cited as a likely source of contamination appraisers should watch for, or are used as examples of contami-

---

2. Mark Dotzour, "Groundwater Contamination and Residential Property Values," *The Appraisal Journal* (July 1997): 279–285; and G. William Page and H. Rabinowitz, "Groundwater Contamination: Its Effects on Property Values and Cities," *Journal of the American Planning Association* (Autumn 1993): 473–481.

3. Paul Syms, "Perceptions of Risk in the Valuation of Contaminated Land," *The Journal of Property, Valuation and Investment*, v.15, no. 1 (1997): 27–39.

4. Simons, et al., 1997.

5. James A. Chalmers and Scott A. Roehr, "Issues in the Valuation of Contaminated Property," *The Appraisal Journal* (January 1993): 28–41.

Valuing Contaminated Properties

6. Daniel F. Ryan, "Lender's View of Hazardous Substances and Appraiser Responsibility," *The Real Estate Appraiser and Analyst* (Fall 1989):10–12; Richard Roddewig, "Stigma, Environmental Risk, and Property Value: 10 Critical Inquiries," *The Appraisal Journal* (October 1996): 375–387; Albert Wilson, "The Environmental Opinion: Basis for an Impaired Value Opinion," *The Appraisal Journal* (July 1994): 410–423 and "Emerging Approaches to Impaired Property Valuation," *The Appraisal Journal* (April 1996): 155–170.

7. Simons, et al., 1997; Arthur Sementelli and Robert Simons, "Regulation of Leaking Underground Storage Tanks: Policy Enforcement and Unintended Consequences," *Economic Development Quarterly* (August 1997): 236–238.

8. Bill Mundy, "Stigma and Values," *The Appraisal Journal* (January 1992a): 7–13; Peter J. Patchin, "Valuation of Contaminated Properties and the Sales Comparison Approach," *The Appraisal Journal* (January 1988): 7–16 and "Contaminated Properties—Stigma Revisited," *The Appraisal Journal* (April 1991): 167–172.

9. Richard A. Neustein, "Estimating Value Diminution by the Income Approach," *The Appraisal Journal* (April 1992): 283–287; Chalmers and Roeher, 1993; Mundy, 1992a; Bill Mundy, "The Impact of Hazardous Materials on Property Value: Revisited," *The Appraisal Journal* (October 1992b): 463–471; Anthony J. Rinaldi, "Contaminated Properties—Valuation Solutions," *The Appraisal Journal* (July 1991): 377–381; Wilson, 1994 and 1996.

10. Michael V. Sanders, "Post-Repair Diminution in Value from Geotechnical Problems," *The Appraisal Journal* (January 1996): 63–65; Patchin, 1991; B. Christensen, "Can Pollution Contaminate Value?," *The Real Estate Appraiser and Analyst* (Fall/Winter 1987): 53–55; and John D. Dorchester, Jr., "Environmental Pollution: Valuation in a Changing World," *The Appraisal Journal* (July 1991): 289–302.

11. Simons, et al., 1997; Alan K. Reichert, Michael Small, and Sunil Mohanty, "The Impact of Landfills on Residential Property Values," *The Journal of Real Estate Research*, v. 7, no. 3 (1992): 297–314; and William N. Kinnard, Jr., "Tools and Techniques for Measuring the Effects of Proximity to Radioactive Contamination on Single-Family Residential Sales Prices," working paper, Real Estate Counseling Group of Connecticut, Inc., Storrs, 1991.

12. Wilson, 1996.

13. Neustein, 1992; Joseph A. Campanella, "Valuing Partial Losses in Contamination Cases," *The Appraisal Journal* (April 1984): 301–304 and "Commercial Property Values and Toxic Sites," *The California Lawyer* (May 1990); Gerald E. Smolen, Gary Moore, and Lawrence V. Conway, "Hazardous Waste Landfill Impacts on Local Property Values," *The Real Estate Appraiser* (April 1992): 4–11.

14. Smolen, et al., 1992; and Rinaldi, 1991.

15. Mundy, 1992b; Patchin, 1991; Patricia R. Healy and John J. Healy, Jr., "Lenders' Perspectives on Environmental Issues," *The Appraisal Journal* (July 1992): 394–398; Mundy, 1992a; and Simons et al., 1997.

nated property.[6] Further, a substantial portion of LUSTs have been found to have off-site groundwater contamination.[7] Much of the literature pertains directly to contaminated subjects, although the effects may also be applicable to some degree to proximate off-site properties if contamination becomes known, or if the sites are perceived to be contaminated.[8]

Regardless of how this potential value diminution comes to pass, the end result is that value diminution can occur without a sale. It is a form of unrealized capital loss due to a lessened income stream and loss of full use of the property. These losses in value can be attributed to reduced net income streams, delayed transactions, loss in the owner's ability to access equity in the property, higher discount rates to adjust for perceived risk, or reductions to property value due to stigma. Any combination of these factors can result in an overall reduction in value. Through discounted cash flow (DCF) analysis, an appraiser (or other real estate professional) can determine diminished future net income due to lost income, lower expected rents, lower occupancy rates, and higher environmental monitoring costs that depress the present value of income-producing property (including apartment buildings). The DCF approach has been generally accepted by many scholars and experts.[9]

Mechanisms Through Which Loss of Property Value May Occur

Delayed transactions. Contaminated properties are more difficult to sell, experience reduced marketability, or may never reach the market. Thus, lack of sale or a delayed sale is a loss.[10] There is evidence to support the proposition that LUSTs and other types of environmental contamination experience this problem.[11]

A standard for establishing the magnitude of loss in real estate is the hedonic price model. However, hedonic pricing models require a sale. Therefore, it can be argued that hedonic pricing models understate the actual loss because only the most desirable properties get sold, and also because the loss of value attributable to a delayed sale is not considered. A smaller number of sales and a higher percentage of failed transactions indicate that the present value of those properties that do sell would be lower because of the delay. Also, net sales price would be lower because of excess supply. The market clearing price may be harder to establish because buyers and sellers may have different perceptions of the cost to cure contamination.[12]

Reduced net income stream. According to prevailing theory, income can be reduced even if tenants do not move out, because future tenants may pay less rent to compensate for the environmental risk. There could also be a higher vacancy rate, where tenants avoid the building[13] or there is downtime for mitigation to occur. These conditions would apply to an income property affected by offsite contamination from a LUST. Also, any unreimbursed environmental monitoring costs could drive down net revenues for the building by increasing operating costs.[14]

Loss in accessing owner equity. A contaminated property owner may lose the ability to obtain mortgage financing. There is evidence that lenders refuse to provide mortgage loans on contaminated properties, including those with USTs.[15] Such a situation may prevent the owner from obtaining financing and could cause cash flow problems for the business because the structure may not be used as collateral. Hence, the liquidity of the property (i.e., the owner's ability to convert the asset to cash relatively quickly) could be substantially impaired. In certain severe cases, a firm could undergo financial stress severe enough to cause bankruptcy. These issues related to liquidity loss indicate that the owner may have lost the ability to fully use the property or that the asset has been frozen. This liquidity loss includes the inability to refinance and loss of full income potential. Restrictions on future use are also a concern, and may affect both property owners and lenders worried about the value of the real estate as collateral.[16]

Higher discount rate to adjust for actual or perceived risk. A higher discount rate drives down the present value of the property, even if debt structure and revenue do not change. In some cases, upward adjustment in the risk premium component of the discount rate can be substantial. A two-percentage-point increase, or about 20%, was reported in one survey.[17]

Stigma. This term is generally accepted to mean the residual value loss outside of the cost to cure the actual contamination. One important component of stigma is fear or uncertainty about a future recurrence, and another is a chilling effect.[18] The stigma would be greater before remediation, and even after a successful cleanup, the affected property may never regain its full unimpaired value. Failed transactions may be a form of stigma. In addition, the stigma of a bad address should be controlled for by using either regression or matched pairs analysis. Courts have accepted the notion of permanent post-cleanup stigma. Also, courts have considered stigma damages in cases of incomplete repair, where the property has not been totally remediated back to clean standards.[19] This may become more common in the future, given the emergence of risk-based corrective action cleanup strategies.

Overall reduction in value. In summary, the combination of all the mechanisms mentioned here clearly supports the notion that unsold income-producing property can experience substantial diminished value. Both contaminated subjects and nearby property, whether perceived or actually contaminated, could be affected. Limited quantitative evidence exists of this value diminution for subjects and offsite properties.[20] Based on this evidence, the value diminution effects should be larger for offsite nonresidential properties than for offsite residential properties. The amount of loss can also depend on whether it was determined before or after remediation, the timing of market cycles, the severity of contamination, and other factors.[21]

Data Collection and Methods
Identification of Contaminated UST Sites
The first step in the empirical part of this research was to identify properties actually or very likely to be contaminated. In Ohio this was accomplished at the Bureau of Underground Storage Tank Regulations (BUSTR), the state UST regulating agency. BUSTR has a reasonably complete set of files on corrective action sites in Ohio, including well test results, gradient

16. Smolen et al., 1992; Mundy, 1992a; and Sanders, 1996.

17. Neustein, 1992; Smolen et al., 1992; Mundy, 1992b; and Fisher et al., 1993, reported the 20% change.

18. Patchin, 1988; Sanders, 1996; Mundy, 1992b; Patchin, 1991; and Campanella, 1992.

19. Syms, 1996; Patchin, 1994; M. Elliot-Jones, "Stigma Damages and the Bad Address," unpublished paper (1996); B. Hogin, "Post-Cleanup Stigma Claims: The Latest from the War Over Hazardous Waste," *Toxics Law Reporter* (February 1995): 918; and Muldowney and Harrison, "Stigma Damages: Property Damage and the Fear of Risk," *Defense Counsel Journal* (October 1995): 525–538.

20. Page and Rabinowitz, 1993; Patchin, 1994; and Karl Guntermann, "Sanitary Landfills, Stigma and Industrial Land Values," *Journal of Real Estate Research*, v. 10, no. 5 (1995): 531–542.

21. Syms, 1996; Patchin, 1994; Sanders, 1996; and Kinnard, 1991.

Valuing Contaminated Properties

maps, and other materials for more than 200 UST events in Cuyahoga County. The operational definition of contamination refers to the documented presence of the carcinogen benzene and other volatile petroleum compounds in excess of 5 parts per billion (ppb). Due largely to measurement limitations faced by BUSTR engineers responsible for site characterization (most consultant reports stop at the property boundary), a degree of judgment is required in determining whether and to what extent an adjacent site meets this definition. Accordingly, upon review of each file, this research employed a ranking system (1 being the highest, 3 the lowest) based on the degree of confidence we could place in whether that property was actually contaminated. The highest was a "1", where direct evidence (well test results) showed that contamination was present. A property classified as a "2" was adjacent and down-gradient from a contaminated site, or refused to be tested. A "3" was adjacent to a 1 or 2 and also down-gradient, within 50 feet to 100 feet of the edge of contamination. A total of 60 sites were identified as having offsite contamination at level 3 or above. Care was taken to avoid classifying properties as contaminated if they were on the margin of these criteria.

The next step was to verify the parcel numbers of offsite contaminated properties. This was accomplished in Cuyahoga County at the county property tax map room by examining the LUST maps from BUSTR and comparing them to tax maps. Accordingly, 133 contaminated residential properties were identified in Cuyahoga County. Of these, about 100 were existing residential homes. The balance of the residential properties were new construction, all in one new residential subdivision. We similarly identified a total of 154 actually contaminated commercial properties.

Property data. Sales activity and sales price data are available through the county's property tax records. We obtained these records from the Amerestate Corporation (a data vendor) for sales data since 1986 and characteristics on all properties (sold or not) through the first quarter of 1997. This data set was combined with the contaminated property information, thus enabling comparison of the contaminated and uncontaminated properties.

This study focused on a subset of the data from July 1994 through December 1996, after the Ohio residential real estate disclosure form became required but during a relatively stable period in the regulation of and requirements concerning USTs. This time period provides some of the best available data on environmental contamination and property characteristics.[22]

Methods. Subject to the sorts of considerations mentioned previously, the best available analytical techniques were employed. These techniques were driven by quality and availability of property data, number of contaminated properties, if sold, market segmentation, distribution of variables and error terms in statistical models, degree of site remediation, and comparability of commercial property. The overall database permitted construction of hedonic multiple regression models for existing residential properties. Limitations existed due to cross-year pooling and a small number of sales in each year (fewer than 10). These limitations rendered it infeasible to follow a more traditional approach using hedonic models.

22. See Sementelli and Simons, 1997, for more details on the regulatory environment.

Chapter 7: *Price Liquidity Effects of UST Leaks*

Instead, depending on the number of available cases, this research used hedonic models to predict individual property values, MANOVA (multivariate analysis of variance), and sale/resale analysis, as appropriate. (The variables and predictive regression computer models that underlie this research are available from the authors on request.)

Results for Residential Properties
Existing Residential Properties
Given the available data, the best analytical technique for existing residential sales is individual prediction using hedonic multiple regression analysis, with data transformed using the Box-Cox technique. One model was created for each year of sale. Expressing the sales prices in log form helps to correct for lack of normality in their distribution. This technique enables comparison of the predicted sales price with the actual sales price. The difference can be attributed to contamination, holding all other information constant. Table 1 contains the results. The most important information includes the percentage reduction in value between the predicted and observed sales prices.

TABLE 1 Existing Residential Properties Sold After 1994 with Disclosure in Effect

Year Sold	Parcel	Degree of Contamination	Actual Price	Predicted Price	Price Difference	Price Change Predicted
1994	821-18	3	$72,000	$98,280	-$26,280	-26.7%*
1994	312-05	3	$102,000	$131,453	-$29,453	-22.4%*
1995	363-15	2	$103,000	$85,440	$17,560	20.6%*
1995	134-23	2	$20,000	$32,169	-$12,169	-37.8%*
1995	018-04	2	$61,000	$64,467	-$3,467	-5.4%*
1995	018-04	2	$60,000	$60,699	-$699	-1.2%
1995	022-14	2	$53,000	$60,118	-$7,118	-11.8%*
1996	684-01	2	$63,500	$91,780	-$28,280	-30.8%*
1996	131-19	1	$15,000	$21,077	-$6,077	-28.8%*
1996	018-04	1	$48,000	$51,058	-$3,058	-6.0%*
1996	314-21	3	$129,000	$145,129	-$16,129	-11.1%*
Totals			$726,500	$841,670	-$115,170	
					Total Loss:	-13.7%
					Average Loss:	-14.7%

*Significant at 0.05

Eleven existing residential properties were sold after contamination became known, and before remediation was known to be initiated. Comparing the actual sales price with its predicted (market) price among this group, nine have a statistically significant reduction in price, one has a reduction that is not significant, and one has a significant increase in sales price. Aggregating these sales together reveals a 14%–15% reduction in sales price that can be attributed to the LUST contamination, without accounting for delay or other impacts on value.[23] Typically, these properties were under remediation at the time of sale.

Higher-Priced New Residential Units
Higher-priced new construction in one new upper-end subdivision in a desirable neighborhood forms one subset of the sales. The contamination in this subdivision resulted from a leak with a well-documented, extensive

23. A 95% confidence interval around these data would indicate the change to be between -3.6% and -25.8%. If the one positive value is omitted, a 95% confidence interval would be -9.1% to -27.3%. Either way, the confidence interval excludes zero, indicating that the value is negative and the loss is statistically significant.

LUST plume. The event was discovered in mid to late 1994, and partially documented in 1995. By late 1995 and early 1996, residential disclosure forms were known to be in use in marketing these units. Some nicely located and otherwise attractive residential building lots currently remain undeveloped.

Consistent with the notion of price segmentation, these homes were modeled separately from the lower- and middle-priced homes. For these higher-priced sales, MANOVA was used. This technique enables comparison of the sales prices of properties classified as contaminated with those classified as uncontaminated, without violating regression assumptions. Statistical significance tests on bivariate relationships can be used to indicate the marginal difference in sales price attributable to contaminated and otherwise similar uncontaminated properties.

The results, shown in Table 2 and Figure 1, indicate that before contamination became known, the properties in this subdivision were selling at a 5% premium over houses in similar neighborhoods. By 1995, the contaminated sales had experienced a reduction of 2% over the other properties. By 1996, the price reduction was 16% for those contaminated units that sold. These results are statistically significant at a level of 0.05.

TABLE 2 Higher-Priced New Residential MANOVA Results

Year of Sale	Number of Contaminated Sales	Total Number of Sales	Price Range	Model F-statistic	Price Uncontaminated	Price Contaminated	Average Change in Price	Annual Difference
1994	4	117	$300–$450	15.18	$333,830	$352,191	$18,361	5.5%
1995	8	325	$300–$450	14.29	$345,511	$336,990	-$8,521	-2.5%
1996	8	287	$300–$450	15.32	$360,572	$303,983	-$56,589	-15.7%

Notes: Average prices of contaminated properties when compared with uncontaminated properties are statistically different at 0.01. This table is based on 20 contaminated sales over a three-year period.

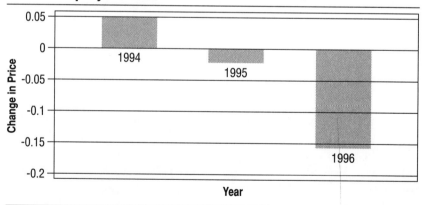

FIGURE 1 Higher-Priced New Residential: Average Change in Contaminated Property Over Time

Commerical Property Results

Three types of analysis can be conducted to determine the effect of LUSTs on contaminated commercial property: transaction rates once contamination becomes known, the likelihood of seller financing on sale, and difference in sales price upon sale.

Chapter 7: *Price Liquidity Effects of UST Leaks*

Transaction Rates of Contaminated Versus Uncontaminated Commercial Properties

This study identified 154 nonresidential properties known to be contaminated. This number was reduced to 122 properties to account for government-owned lands and double counts of properties with multiple parcels. Next, commercial properties sold in the same year or after information about LUST contamination became known were considered. This indicates that commercial properties contaminated by LUSTs transact at a rate of 2.7% per year, compared with 4.0% per year (based on activity of over 32,000 properties) for uncontaminated properties. This is a reduction of 33% in the rate of sales activity. A simple difference of proportions analysis (comparing the average annual sales ratios for contaminated and uncontaminated properties) indicates that the difference between the two groups is statistically significant. This provides evidence that contamination is associated with a significant delay in sales activity.

Financing of Contaminated Commercial Properties

Twenty commercial properties sold in the same year or after the BUSTR file date was initiated. Of these, 30% obtained seller financing registered with the county auditor at time of sale, compared with only 13% for all commercial properties sold since 1988. Differences in these proportions are statistically significant, and this substantiates the notion that owners of contaminated properties have difficulty accessing their equity in the property, and suffer from a type of liquidity loss that further compounds property value loss. These results are shown in Table 3.

TABLE 3 Commercial Properties that Sold After Contamination Was Known to Polluters

Received Financing	— Contaminated — After File Date		—————— All Commercial —————— 1988–1997		1994–1997	
	Number	Percentage	Number	Percentage	Number	Percentage
None	9	45.0	6,687	59.6	2,663	57.9
Seller	6	30.0	1,452	13.0	521	11.3
Bank	4	20.0	3,057	27.3	1,396	30.4
Other	1	5.0	16	0.1	16	0.3
Total	20	100.0	11,212	100.0	4,596	100*

Note: Contaminated properties had a significantly higher proportion of seller financing ($p = 0.0044$) than all commercial properties between 1994 and 1997 and also a significantly higher proportion of seller financing ($p = 0.0234$) than all commercial properties between 1988 and 1997.

* Totals may not add to 100% due to rounding error.

Pre- and Post-Remediation Sales Price Analysis

Because of the variety of commercial properties (e.g., retail, office, freestanding stores) and the small number of sales in each type, regression analyses of these data are not feasible. In addition, in our case resource limitations preclude the possibility of conducting appraisals of each property and comparable sales. Therefore, the best available technique is a presale/postsale comparison. This technique is a form of matched pairs, where each sale serves as its own control. That is, a commercial property is sold, found to be contaminated by a LUST, then resold, with no change to the parcel or substantial alteration to the physical structure.

Valuing Contaminated Properties

TABLE 4 Commercial Building Sale/Resale Analysis

PPN, Land Usage, and Contamination Date	Resale Date	Resale Value	Sale Date	Sale Value	Original Price Change	Original Change	Adjusted Change (2% inflation)	Adjusted Change at Market Rate
013-01 Bowling alley 5/90	4/96	$270,000	11/77	$477,000	-$207,000	-43%	-61%	-82%
449-25 Office building 4/91	12/91	$530,000	2/86	$510,000	+$20,000	+4%	-6%	-36%
396-07 Car wash 4/96	5/96	$200,000	4/78	$225,000	-$25,000	-11%	-38%	-69%
372-18 Bank 7/90	1/95	$1,110,150	10/85	$1,800,000	-$689,850	-38%	-49%	-66%
005-18 Commercial 10/90	11/93	$96,550	1/90	$190,000	-$93,450	-49%	-52%	-58%
140-05 Retail 3/90	3/96	$91,000	5/84	$128,600	-$37,600	-29%	-44%	-64%
Total		$2,297,700		$3,330,600	-$1,032,900	**Average** -28%	**Average** -42%	**Average** -63%
							Weighted average:	-31%

Six properties were eligible for the presale/postsale analysis. Lack of physical changes were confirmed at the county auditor's office. Table 4 shows these results.

Before adjusting for commercial property appreciation trends, five properties experienced a value loss when sold after contamination became known, and one property had a small increase. The average diminution of value was 28%–31% (depending on how the results are weighted). An even more realistic measure would also include the effects of property appreciation trends. Commercial property in Cuyahoga County (as proxied by the value of the property tax duplicate) increased by an annual rate of well over 4% over the study period. Assuming the contaminated properties appreciated at only 2% (less than half the county average), all six properties (as well as the vacant parcel) decreased in real value, and the average reduction was 42%. These results are statistically significant.

Conclusion

Table 5 summarizes the results of this research on the effect of LUSTs from gas stations on nearby properties that were actually contaminated. For residential properties, we found a statistically significant reduction of up to 14%–16% in observed sales price for those properties sold after

TABLE 5 Summary of Results

Property Type	Probability of Transaction	Reduction in Sales Price	Incidence of Seller Financing
Existing residential	N/A	-14% to -15%*	N/A
New higher priced residential	N/A	-16%*	N/A
Commercial	Annual rate for contamininated is 33% lower* (2.7% versus 4.0%)	-28% to -42%*	Contaminated more than twice as likely to be seller financed* (30% versus 11%–13%)

* Statistically significant at a 95% level of confidence.

contamination became known. This does not consider any effects due to reduced transaction rates or delayed sale. These results are consistent with the earlier figure of a 17% reduction in price for residential sales located in close proximity to LUSTs with ongoing nuisance and the potential for future releases.

For commercial properties, we identified several results. There is a significant reduction in transaction rates (33% lower) compared with uncontaminated properties. Further, there is a significant increase (more than double) in the incidence of seller financing. This increase indicates a further loss in value to the owner of contaminated property. For those properties that did sell, a 30%–40% reduction in sales price occurs. These results are consistent with expected relationships evident in the literature.

The overall pattern of these results consistently shows evidence of reduction in price, and (among commercial properties) reduced market transaction rates as a result of delay or other problems as well as difficulty in obtaining financing among properties that are very likely to be actually contaminated. These results and methods can be generalized to Cuyahoga County and potentially to other areas. In the context of other studies, these results provide evidence that properties actually contaminated by LUSTs experience a reduction in value from reduced sales prices and other market effects.

These results confirm that environmental contamination attributable to LUSTs should be a consideration when appraising both contaminated residential and commercial properties. We show that proximity to and actual LUST contamination have a more pronounced effect on commercial than on residential property. This is probably due to the lack of substitutability (and thinner markets) among relatively unique commercial property, whereas residential units are more interchangeable. In addition to reductions in sales price, value reductions for contaminated commercial property should also consider the present value of the loss to the seller from a delayed transaction or longer marketing period, and any favorable seller financing terms beyond normal market conditions.

References

Colwell, Peter and K. Foley. "Electric Transmission Lines and the Selling Price of Residential Property," *The Appraisal Journal* (October 1979): 490–499.

Colwell, Peter. "Power Lines and Lane Value," *Journal of Real Estate Research* (Spring 1990): 117–127.

Delaney, C. and D. Timmons. "High Voltage Power Lines: Do They Affect Residential Property Value?," *Journal of Real Estate Research* (Summer 1992): 315–330.

Kiel, Katherine. "Measuring the Impact of the Discovery and Cleaning of Identified Hazardous Waste Sites on House Values," *Land Economics*, 71 (1995): 428–435.

Kohlhase, J. "The Impact of Toxic Waste Site on Housing Values," *Journal of Urban Economics* (1991): 30, 1–26.

Michaels, R., and V. Smith. "Market Segmentation and Valuing Amenities with Hedonic Models: The Case of Hazardous Waste Sites," *Journal of Urban Economics* (1990): 28, 223–242.

Nelson, A. Chris, J. Genereux, and M. Genereux. "Price Effects of Landfills on House Values," *Land Economics* (November 1992): 359–365.

Thayer, M., H. Albers, and M. Rahmatian. "The Benefits of Reducing Exposure to Waste Disposal Sites: A Hedonic Housing Value Approach," *Journal of Real Estate Research* (Summer 1992): 265–282.

Electromagnetic Radiation Field Property Devaluation

by Michael Rikon

Michael Rikon *is a partner in Goldstein, Goldstein & Rikon, P.C., in New York City. He received a BS in business administration from the New York Institute of Technology, a JD from Brooklyn Law School, and an LLM from New York University, School of Law. Mr. Rikon was a consultant to the New York State Commission on eminent domain procedure law.*

This article originally appeared in the January 1996 issue of The Appraisal Journal.

1. *Criscuola* v. *Power Authority of the State of New York,* 81 NY2d 649,602 NYS2d 588, 621 NE2d 1199 (1993). Also reported, *ATLA Law Reporter* 23, no. 33, 37; *Toxic Law Reporter* 8, no. 20; *Indoor Pollution Law Report* 7, no. 5; *Mealey's Litigation Reports, Toxics Torts* 2, no. 14; *EMF Litigation News* (November 1993); and *Microwave News* (Sept./Oct. 1993, Nov./Dec. 1993, Jan./Feb. 1994).

When New York State's highest court, the Court of Appeals, handed down *Criscuola* v. *Power Authority of the State of New York*[1] last year, many hailed the decision as the missing piece of the puzzle that would provide the means to obtain monetary damages because of diminution of property values caused by proximity to an electromagnetic radiation field (EMF).

One year later, the aggressive use of the holding can be observed in many different types of lawsuits. The *Criscuola* doctrine is also being used in inverse condemnation cases and in a host of other situations as diverse as the fertile imagination of learned counsel would allow.

Much has been written in legal periodicals about *Criscuola* and its potential application to any litigation involving the use of land. It is therefore necessary to carefully explore the decision to consider its application to valuation problems.

Eminent Domain Context

Criscuola arose in the context of a pure eminent domain taking; that is, there was a condemnation of a strip of property through the Criscuola brothers' farm in rural New York. The appropriation was by the Power Authority of the State of New York for a 345-KV power transmission line, involving a 160-foot corridor crossing the property diagonally in an east-west direction approximately midway of its depth.

The claimants filed a claim for damages seeking just compensation, not only for the six acres directly taken for the powerline, but for the loss in value sustained by the remaining 94 acres because of the remainder's loss of market value. Condemnation lawyers refer to these two types of damages in partial takings as direct and consequential.

Claimants alleged that the consequential damages arose as a result of the public's perception of health risks associated with high-voltage powerlines, a fear known as "cancerphobia." One of the owners testified that he never would have bought the property if it had had a high-voltage powerline across it. Claimants' expert valuation witness, an MAI-desig-

Chapter 7: *Electromagnetic Radiation*

nated appraiser, testified that because of the public's cancerphobia, the market value of the remainder was worth half of its prevesting value.

The trial court, the New York State Court of Claims, held that the Criscuolas were only entitled to recover for the direct takings, and awarded $5,400, plus $543 for hardwood trees taken down, a total of $5,943. The court ruled that to recover for consequential damages, the claimant must first prove that powerlines cause health problems by a preponderance of the credible scientific evidence. If scientific proof supported the cancerphobia of the public, the claimant must then also establish that this reasonable apprehension has affected the purchaser's willingness to pay the fair market value of the property.

On appeal, the trial court's decision was affirmed by the Appellate Division.[2] The Appellate Court, in affirming *Criscuola,* relied on a companion case involving another parcel located in a different county that was also taken by the Power Authority for the same Marcy-South powerline that was decided by another appellate court of equal jurisdiction.[3]

Criscuola moved for, and received permission to appeal to New York State's highest court, the Court of Appeals. The Power Authority argued, once again, that existing law required that the claimants must first prove by a preponderance of the evidence that health fears were scientifically reasonable, and that the claimants (who were joined with all other Marcy-South claimants) could not convince the trial judge, who heard a bevy of impressive and certainly expensive expert witnesses, that there was a basis in scientific evidence for a fear of exposure to the fields emitted by powerlines.

New York State Court of Appeals Decision

The Court of Appeals held otherwise, and reversed in a decision by Judge Bellacosa, who stated:

> We are satisfied that there should be no requirement that the claimant, as a separate and higher component of its market value proofs, must establish the reasonableness of a fear or perception of danger or of health risks from exposure to high-voltage powerlines. The issue is a just compensation proceeding (citations omitted). This consequence may be present even if the public's fear is unreasonable. Whether the danger is a scientifically genuine or verifiable fact should be irrelevant to the central issue of its market value impact. Genuineness and proportionate dollar effects are relevant factors, to be sure, but in the usual evidentiary framework. Such factors should be left to the contest between the parties' market value experts, not magnified and escalated by a whole new battery of electromagnetic power engineers, scientists or medical experts. "Adverse health effects *vel non* is not the issue in eminent domain proceedings: full compensation to the landowner for property taken is" (citations omitted). As the Court of Appeals of Kansas has noted, "Logic and fairness...dictate that any loss of market value proven with a reasonable degree of probability should be compensable, regardless of its source. If no one will buy a residential lot because it has a high-voltage line across it, the lot is a total loss even though the owner has the legal right to build a house on it. If buyers can be found, but only at half the value it had before the line was installed, the owner has suffered a 50% loss."[4] Thus, relying on *Willsey,* the Supreme Court of Kansas concluded, and we agree, that evidence of fear in the marketplace is admissible with respect to the value of property taken without proof of the reasonableness of the fear."[5]

2. *Criscuola* v. *Power Authority of the State of New York,* 188 AD2d 951, 592 NYS2d 79 (3d Dept., 1992).

3. *Zappavigna* v. *State of New York,* 186 AD2d 557, 588 NYS2d 585 (2d Dept., 1992).

4. *Willsey* v. *Kansas City Power,* 631 P2d 268, 277-278.

5. *Ryan* v. *Kansas Power & Light Co.,* 815 P2d 528, 533.

Key Holding

In the key holding, once again, the New York Court of Appeals ruled:

- There should be no requirement that the claimant must establish the reasonableness of a fear or perception of danger or of health risks from exposure to high-voltage powerlines, and
- Whether the danger is a scientifically genuine or verifiable fact should be irrelevant to the central issue of its market value impact.

Application to Noncondemnation Cases

It is this marketplace evidence rule that has sparked the plaintiff's bar to apply *Criscuola* to noncondemnation situations. Indeed, *Criscuola* is being applied against the City of New York by homeowners who live in Staten Island and are unable to sell their homes because of the largest landfill in the country. The noxious smell and unsightliness of this mountain of garbage has created a well-publicized fear of cancer to would-be home buyers.

Fear in the real estate marketplace is also argued as a reason for not allowing construction for a CellularOne Tower in Glen Cove, Long Island. Community Board Two in Greenwich Village, New York, uses this reason to oppose the construction of a power substation the Transit Authority plans to build. The State of Connecticut General Assembly's Committee on Transportation is considering the potential EMF property devaluation that may be caused by Amtrak's electrification of railroad lines within the state.

The argument being advanced in these situations is that even though the best-informed experts cannot say for sure that EMF causes cancer, everyone agrees that if a powerline is constructed next door, local real estate values may suffer substantial devaluation.

Litigation is currently proceeding in New York against Consolidated Edison and against the Long Island Lighting Company, seeking damages for inverse condemnation, trespass, and injunctive relief. Similar inverse condemnation claims are being filed across the country. The number of property devaluation claims continues to grow geometrically.

Criscuola Formula

Judge Bellacosa wrote in *Criscuola* that "evidence of fear in the marketplace is admissible with respect to the value of property taken without proof of the reasonableness of the fear."[6]

A claimant, however, is not relieved from giving any proof to establish claims and just compensation damages. *Criscuola* v. *Power Authority of the State of New York* mandates that a claimant must still establish some prevalent perception of a danger emanating from the objectionable condition.

Quoting the *Ryan* decision once again, the Court of Appeals stated that "no witness, whether expert or nonexpert, may use his or her personal fear as a basis for testifying about fear in the marketplace. *However, any other evidence that fear exists in the public about the dangers of high-voltage lines is admissible*" (emphasis added). Judge Bellacosa further stated:

> Claimants should have to connect the market value diminution of the property to the particular fear in much the same manner that any other adverse market effects are shown; e.g., by proffering evidence that the market value

6. *Ryan v. Kansas Power & Light Co.*

Chapter 7: *Electromagnetic Radiation*

of the property across which powerlines have been built has been negatively affected in relation to comparable properties across which no powerlines have been built (citations omitted).

EMF Inverse Condemnation

In an inverse condemnation (i.e., an EMF property devaluation claim), the damage calculation should be the same as if the property were condemned because the public perceives that there is a health risk when one lives in close proximity to a high-voltage power transmission line. This perception among the prospective purchasers of the property results in a substantial loss of value.

This cancerphobia affects the minds of any prospective purchaser, causing a loss of demand, a loss of market value, and thus damage to an EMF-affected property. Indeed, even if a prospective purchaser were certain that there was no risk to health, he or she still would not be disposed to acquire a property with such a limited resale potential.

One thing is certain: whether the danger is a scientifically genuine or verifiable fact is irrelevant to the central issue of its market value impact. Appraisers should be cognizant of not only the change in law, but of the market effect as well.

It should not be difficult to establish that the market value of real property in close proximity to a high-voltage powerline is substantially lower than a comparable property unaffected by a powerline.

The Public's Perception—Cancerphobia

According to an article by Ron Marx,[7] a public poll taken in 1993 by Cambridge Reports/Research showed that 63% of all adult Americans were aware of the EMF issue, up from 31% in 1989. Half responded that they were "extremely worried" about it. The public's perception of a problem is well established.

The reason for the growing awareness has been the increased reporting of residential and school cancer cluster investigations near powerlines, along with numerous studies of occupational exposure showing an increased frequency of cancer in workers who have had higher exposure levels to EMF.

Recently, an article in *The New York Times,* "Power Lines Raise Fears in Home Buyers,"[8] began, "When Marie Trizano takes people to see houses near powerlines, she says sometimes they won't even get out of the car." There have been hundreds of other similar articles in magazines and newspapers across the country.[9]

Homeowners who adjoin high-voltage powerlines have reported that their EMF-affected homes are unsellable at any price. An appraiser should be easily able to connect the market value diminution of the property to the public's fear of an EMF.

Approach to Valuation

The proper approach for an appraiser to take in valuing a parcel of land damaged by the visible presence of a high-voltage powerline will be a before-and-after valuation of similar properties. In other words, comparable unaffected properties will be selected and adjusted, with an appraiser considering location, market conditions, physical characteristics, conditions of sale, time, financing terms, and use. This sales comparison ap-

7. Ron D. Marx, "This ELF Could Be the Next Giant in Environmental Hazards," *Econ the Environmental Magazine for Real Property Hazards* (November 1993): 22.

8. *The New York Times,* "Power Lines Raise Fears in Home Buyers," *The New York Times,* Section 10 (July 11, 1993): 5.

9. See, for example, "Power Lines Short-Circuit Sales, Homeowners Claim," *The Wall Street Journal* (December 8, 1993): B1; *New York Newsday,* "Power Struggle—High-Tension Lines Creating Tension Among Some Buyers," *New York Newsday* (August 14, 1994): *Real Estate,* 1.

proach will provide or indicate a market value for the unaffected (before) property.

The appraiser will then attempt to find comparable sales of parcels similarly situated next to a powerline, if possible. It may be extremely unlikely that any recent sales of EMF-affected properties exist. Assuming that the appraiser's research does indicate some nonforeclosure or other distress sales of property in proximity to a powerline, these sales must be analyzed and compared with the subject property. The after (affected) property value is then subtracted from the before (unaffected) property value, and the difference will be the damages.

Conclusion

It is entirely possible to conclude after an EMF market study that most parcels of EMF-affected property will have a restricted resale value, and thus there will be damages in the full indicated value found by adjusted comparable properties not affected by high-voltage powerlines.

The Effects on Residential Real Estate Prices from Proximity to Properties Contaminated with Radioactive Materials

by William N. Kinnard, Jr., CRE, and Mary Beth Geckler

On December 1, 1983, the U.S. Environmental Protection Agency (USEPA) and the New Jersey Department of Environmental Protection (NJDEP) jointly announced that concentrations of radon gas and levels of onsite gamma radiation were well above regulatory standards in three residential neighborhoods in three adjacent towns in northern New Jersey. The elevated levels of radon and gamma radiation resulted from the presence of radium-contaminated fill material on many lots in the neighborhoods.

The three neighborhoods were placed on the National Priorities List and included in the Superfund program in October, 1984. These three Superfund Site Areas (SSAs) are referred to in this article as Towns A, B and C.

Extensive remediation programs were initiated promptly in Towns A and C; these programs were completed during 1985. In Town B, on the other hand, a program to excavate contaminated fill material (and later to replace the material with clean fill) was only partially completed before it was abandoned in September, 1985. Because a disposal site was not available, NJDEP was forced to place the excavated fill material in sealed drums, which were stored openly on the lawns of vacated houses.

The initial announcement of the elevated radon and gamma radiation on the sites received widespread publicity in both print and electronic media. There also was continuous, daily publicity about the open storage of the contaminated fill material. Danger! Radiation signs and radiation warning symbols were displayed on a fence surrounding the sites on which the drums were stored. The drums of contaminated materials were removed in September, 1987, which also generated considerable publicity, and they eventually were shipped out of state. Not until June, 1990, was a USEPA remediation program approved.

Property owners seeking to sell or lease properties within the three SSAs were required by state law to reveal the most recent radon readings (if any) to any potential buyer or tenant.

William N. Kinnard, Jr., CRE, is president of the Real Estate Counseling Group of Connecticut, Inc. (RECGC). He is professor emeritus in real estate and finance at the University of Connecticut and a principal in the Real Estate Counseling Group of America. He also testifies regularly as an expert witness on methodology for real property and personal property valuation.

Mary Beth Geckler is vice president of RECGC and a licensed general appraiser in Connecticut. She was a commercial real estate lending officer at regional banks in Connecticut for nine years after spending nearly a decade in market research and project advising for clients of public agencies and educational institutions.

This article originally appeared in the Fall/Winter 1991 issue of Real Estate Issues. *Reproduced with permission of* Real Estate Issues; *published and © by the Counselors of Real Estate (a not for profit organization), Chicago, IL. All rights reserved. Further reproduction/distribution is prohibited without the written permission of* Real Estate Issues.

The Research Assignment

In October, 1989, the Real Estate Counseling Group of Connecticut, Inc., (RECGC) was retained to conduct a market research study of all single-family residential property sales within the three SSAs. In addition, RECGC was asked to study all residential property sales within a larger study area that extended one mile beyond the outer limits of each SSA.

The study period extended from July 1, 1980, through June 30, 1989, and it included 67 months of post-announcement sales experience. The analysis identified, reported and measured the actual market sales behavior of buyers and sellers. Both the impact on sales prices and the changes in the volume of sales transactions were analyzed.

Questions To Be Addressed

Statistical tests were conducted on the assembled residential property sales transaction data to answer the following questions:

- What was the pattern of inflation-adjusted sales prices per square foot of single-family residences in each town, within each SSA and within selected distance zones up to one mile from the SSA? What was the pattern in the 41 months preceding the public announcement of the existence of radioactive contamination within the SSAs? What was the pattern in the 67 months that followed the announcement?

- What changes in levels of inflation-adjusted sales prices per square foot of living area were identifiable and measurable after the announcement? How did these prices compare with levels of inflation-adjusted unit sales prices before the announcement?

- What patterns of sales volumes of single-family residential properties were observed during the 41 months before the announcement and over the 67 months afterward? What changes in those patterns occurred before and after the announcement?

- How far distant from the outer boundary of an SSA did a residential sales property have to be before there was no measurable negative impact on the inflation-adjusted sales price per square foot of living area, or on the volume of sales associated with proximity to the SSA?

Research Project Design
Analytical Models

Three categories of analytical, statistical models were utilized. They provided comparisons of inflation-adjusted price levels and of rates of change in those price levels for single-family properties at varying distances from the three SSAs before and after January 1, 1984. They also provided comparisons of sales volumes within the study areas.

- *Comparison of Averages.* Arithmetic means of inflation-adjusted prices were calculated and compared by year for each distance zone.

- *Trends.* Percentage changes in levels of inflation-adjusted prices and in volume of sales were calculated and compared.

- *Multiple Regression.* Sales data were assembled into four data sets: one for each of the three towns and one for the combined total. Dependent and independent variables were entered into regression models in the standard Hedonic Pricing Model format to test the

Chapter 7: *Effects on Residential Real Estate*

influence and statistical significance of time, location (distance from an SSA) and property characteristics on the inflation-adjusted sales price per square foot of living area. Multiple Linear Regression Analysis (MRA) often is used to identify, measure and evaluate the influence, relative importance and statistical significance of all property, transaction and location characteristics that influence sales prices. In this study, it was used to isolate, measure and test the significance of both distance from an SSA by zone *and* the likely effects of post-announcement awareness of radon gas and gamma radiation concentrations within the SSAs.

Data Requirements

Certain categories of information were required to apply the analytical models.

- *Sales Price Data.* Every transaction had to have a recorded sales price to be used in the study. Sales prices were deflated to December, 1983, dollars through the use of the All Urban Households Consumer Price Index. The result of this deflation was the adjusted sales price (ADJSP). Because *size* (square feet of living area) is one of the most important determinants of sales price, the ADJSP was refined to incorporate square footage. The adjusted sales price per square foot (ADJSPSF) was the dependent variable used in this study.

- *Time.* The date of sale was recorded for every sales transaction by year and month. Two measures of time and its possible influence on ADJSP or ADJSPSF were employed. The first was the date of the deed (DDATE), which indicated the year and month of the execution. The

FIGURE 1 List of Variables for Multiple Regression Analysis

Dependent Variables

Inflation-adjusted sales price per square foot	(ADJSPSF)

Independent Variables

Deed date (year, month)	(DDATE)
After January 1984 (Yes-No)	(BEFAFT)
Square feet of living area	(SFLIVARE)
Square feet of lot area	(LOTSIZE)
Age in years at time of sale	(AGE)
Number of stories of residence	(#Stories)
Shingle/wood siding (Yes-No)	(SHINGLES)
Brick exterior finish (Yes-No)	(BRICK)
Stucco exterior finish (Yes-No)	(STUCCO)
Stone exterior finish (Yes-No)	(STONE)
Number of garage/carport stalls	(GARSTALS)
Attached garage (Yes-No)	(ATTACHED)
Detached garage (Yes-No)	(DETACHED)
Carport (Yes-No)	(CARPORT)
Basement garage (Yes-No)	(BASE GAR)
Within Zone A (Yes-No)	(A ZONE)
Within Zone B (Yes-No)	(B ZONE)
Within Zone C (Yes-No)	(C ZONE)
Within Zone D (Yes-No)	(D ZONE)
Within Zone E (Yes-No)	(E ZONE)
Within Zone F (Yes-No)	(F ZONE)
Within Superfund site (Yes-No)	(S ZONE)

Valuing Contaminated Properties

second measure of time (BEFAFT) indicated whether the deed was recorded *before* or *after* January 1, 1984. For the purposes of this study, any deed recorded during December, 1983, was excluded because it did not represent a sale that was affected by the announcement.

- *Property Characteristics.* All properties in the study were single-family residences. Two of the most important influences on the sales prices of residential properties are size (square feet of living area) and age (in years) at the time of sale. Data on size and age therefore were gathered on all sales transactions. Any sales transaction for which either the size or the age of the residence could not be obtained from an official source was excluded from further analysis.

Because it was not possible to identify retroactively the condition of the property at the time of sale, age at the time of sale served as a proxy for the condition of the property. In addition, data on lot size, type of garage, number of parking stalls, number of stories of residence and exterior finish were obtained. Data were not available on the number of rooms, number of bedrooms or number of bathrooms.

- *Location: Distance from the Superfund Site Area.* The focus of the research project was to ascertain any impact from or effect of proximity to the SSAs on sales prices (adjusted for inflation and size). Therefore, particular attention was paid to the location and distance from an SSA for each sales transaction property. The measure of distance was obtained by identifying the distance zone in which each sales property was located.

Data Collection and Data Recording

Data Sources. Listings of all property sales coded as residential were obtained for each fiscal year (July 1–June 30) from 1980-81 through 1988-89. These data came from SRIA forms on which local assessors report all bona fide, arm's-length real estate sales transactions for the year.

Additional information came from Real Estate Data Incorporated (REDI). This subscription service summarizes sales transaction data within communities in northern New Jersey quarterly and monthly. REDI listings provided the street addresses of most sales properties, which were correlated with the block and lot number provided in the SRIA summaries.

The major source of information was assessor's property cards for each of the three townships. The property cards frequently provided corroboration of data obtained from other sources as well. If critical information was missing from the assessor's property cards and could not be obtained from other sources, the property was not included in the database.

Finally, visual inspections of the exterior of all sales properties were conducted to check and verify (or correct, as necessary) the information obtained from REDI and the assessor's property cards.

Mapping and Distance Zone Identification. The distance of each sales transaction property from the pertinent Superfund site in its town had to be identified. Since the Town B Superfund site extends into Town C, some properties that are relatively distant from the Town C Superfund site are actually relatively close to the Town B Superfund site.

Chapter 7: *Effects on Residential Real Estate*

To identify distance from or proximity to each SSA, distance zones were established. (The zone definitions are summarized in Table 1) Every sales transaction property was mapped, and its zone location was recorded.

Data Screening and Usable Data Sets

A total of 2,317 sales were identified from the SRIA forms as likely candidates for analysis. It was necessary, however, to eliminate those sales transactions and properties that did not meet the eligibility standards of the research study.

First, a complete data file was necessary for the sales transaction to be included in the study. Any file without data on square feet of living area, date of construction of the dwelling (to provide age at the time of sale) or the number of families (only single-family residential property sales were usable) had to be eliminated. Table 2 shows that 88 sales transactions were eliminated because of unavailable record data.

Ninety-eight sales were eliminated because more precise measurement on large-scale maps revealed that they were located more than one mile from an SSA. One sale that occurred prior to July 1, 1980, also was eliminated.

TABLE 1 Identification of Distance Zones

Zone	Distance from SSA*
S	Inside SSA
A	1–250 feet
B	251–500 feet
C	501–1000 feet
D	1001–1500 feet
E	1501–2500 feet
F	2501–3500 feet
G (Control area)	3501–5280 feet

* Distance from the SSA is the linear distance of the nearest portion of the sales transaction property to the outer boundary of the closest SSA.

The SRIA reports include both one-family and two-family properties in the "2" property coding for sales transactions. As Table 2 shows, 668 two-family (or other non-one-family) sales had to be removed.

TABLE 2 Summary of Sales Data Screening Process (by Town, by Reason)

	Town A	Town B	Town C	Total
Total unscreened sales	541	831	945	2317
Less: Outside limits of property characteristic parameters				
Located beyond 1 mile	15	13	70	98
Bought before 7/1/80	0	1	0	1
More than 5,500 square feet	4	28	5	37
Not a single-family dwelling	7	316	347	668
Subtotal: Outside limits	26	358	422	804
Balance	515	473	523	1513
Less: Record data missing				
Square foot of living area	21	23	27	71
Year built	7	0	8	15
Number of families	0	1	1	2
Subtotal: Data missing	28	24	36	88
Screened, usable sales	487	449	487	1425

Valuing Contaminated Properties

Finally, no property was included in the final data set if one of three major characteristics was outside the 99% confidence interval around the mean for that characteristic: square feet of living area, age at the time of sale, and lot size. This eliminated another 37 sales as non-representative outliers.

Table 2 shows that the final total usable data set for all three towns contained 1,425 sales. The sales were almost evenly divided among the three towns, with 487 usable sales in both Towns A and C and 449 sales in Town B.

Variables for Multiple Regression Analysis

MRA requires the identification of both a dependent variable and the independent variables that will be used in the analysis. The dependent variable used in this study was inflation-adjusted sales price per square foot of living area (ADJSPSF). In each MRA run, only one time variable was used: either the date of deed (DDATE) or before-after January 1, 1984 (BEFAFT). Figure 1 identifies, explains and lists the dependent variable and independent variables that were used in the MRA models.

Research Findings
Average Property Characteristics

Average of property and transaction characteristic values provided a basis for comparison as well as indications of what is typical or representative of the market.

Inflation-Adjusted Sales Price (ADJSP). The average ADJSP in each zone for each year was compared within the three-town usable sales data set and the data set for each town. A notably consistent pattern of findings emerged. First, during the years 1980-83 (before the announcement), the average ADJSP in Zones S (the SSAs), A and B was typically *lower* than the average ADJSP in more distant zones. Some exceptions were found in Zone B. Although there was no absolute decrease in average ADJSP, rates of increase in Zones S, A and B were lower than those in the other zones after 1984. ADJSP in general was lower in 1989, regardless of zone.

Size of Dwelling (Square Feet of Living Area). In the three-town total, the houses in Zones S, A and B were typically smaller than those in other zones both before and after January 1, 1984. In Town A, the smallest houses were in Zones S, A and B. In Town B, the houses in Zones S and A also averaged the smallest. In Town C as well, the houses in Zones S, A and B were well below average in size. Part of the explanation for lower average ADJSP in Zones S, A and B is the smaller (below-average) size of houses in those zones in each of the three towns. This was true both before and after the December, 1983, announcement.

Age of Dwelling at the Time of Sale. The study areas in the three towns tended to be concentrated in older neighborhoods. The average age of dwellings at the time of sale for the 1,423 total usable sales was 64 years. The *lowest* average age of dwelling at the time of sale was in Zones S and A.

The same general pattern of average age distributions appeared in each of the three towns. Generally, the houses in Zones S, A and B averaged 60

Chapter 7: *Effects on Residential Real Estate*

years old or less. Average ages tended to increase for houses that were more distant from a Superfund site. The one exception was in Town C, where the lowest average ages at the time of sale were in Zones F and G. However, age of dwelling at the time of sale did not help explain the generally lower average ADJSP in Zones S, A and B.

Lot Size (Square Feet of Land Area) The average lot size for the three-town data set was 10,700 square feet. Throughout each of the three towns and in the three-town total, lot sizes in Zones S, A and B were consistently smaller on average; the smallest average sizes usually were in Zone S.

Therefore, in Zones S, A and B (especially Zone S), average house sizes were smallest, and these smaller houses were located on smaller lots. The combination of smaller houses on smaller lots helped to explain in part the lower average ADJSP found in Zones S, A and B both before and after the December, 1983, announcement.

These observable and measurable size and age differences suggested strongly that simple comparisons of averages by zone over time probably would fail to capture enough of the influence of proximity to an SSA on ADJSP. That is why comparisons of averages and of trends were supplemented with multiple regression analysis.

Sales Volume (Number of Sales). One indicator of changing market conditions is a change in the number of sales that occurs in a given area or zone over a specified time period. This reflects changing buyer attitudes toward owning and living in that location. One important way for potential buyers to react negatively to a given market situation is to withdraw from the market and refrain from purchasing.

The sales data in the study showed an overall decline in residential real estate market activity in all three towns (and in the county) after 1985. This is the context within which sales volumes in the three study areas were examined and analyzed.

There was an across-the-board decrease in residential property sales volume after 1985, but there was no perceptible or measurable decrease in sales volume in 1984 and 1985, the two years immediately following the December, 1983, announcement. This suggested that there was no negative reaction to residential property purchase in the three-town total. Moreover, sales volume actually increased in Zones A and B in 1984 and 1985. There was a very modest decline in sales in Zone S in 1984, but sales recovered again in 1985. In 1989, sales volumes in Zones S, A and B declined more than in the more distant zones.

Buyer reactions to proximity to the three SSAs apparently varied considerably from one town (and SSA) to another. Proximity to the Town B SSA appeared to be more of a deterrent to would-buyers than was proximity to the SSA in either Town A or Town C.

Inflation-Adjusted Sales Prices per Square Foot of Living Area. Table 3 shows average inflation-adjusted sales price per square foot of living area (ADJSPSF) by zone and by year for each town studied and for the three-town total data set.

For the three-town total, levels and trends of average ADJSPSF in Zones A through D were roughly similar. Averages were higher in Zone E, espe-

Valuing Contaminated Properties

TABLE 3 Average Inflation-Adjusted Sales Price per Square Foot (by Year, by Zone)

Year	S	A	B	C	D	E	F	G	All
Three-Town Total									
1980	$48.66	$55.30	$37.15	$54.04	$45.83	$41.49	$48.15	$39.37	$45.90
1981	52.78	57.58	48.59	49.68	45.47	45.19	40.36	39.99	46.38
1982	49.40	45.88	49.80	43.37	36.65	48.91	44.74	53.64	47.64
1983	50.27	54.56	47.81	53.39	43.74	57.31	47.18	42.46	48.94
1984	56.53	57.87	61.85	61.20	51.86	55.32	62.12	54.22	56.89
1985	71.25	66.75	72.02	66.75	68.60	64.86	68.97	63.40	67.31
1986	90.25	92.25	87.55	97.49	85.81	89.99	81.60	78.98	87.59
1987	102.50	103.87	103.29	94.97	97.93	101.43	94.06	104.57	100.37
1988	112.75	100.81	106.19	106.90	112.54	116.73	98.92	101.41	107.71
1989	97.50	92.42	90.49	103.25	100.32	129.34	101.77	98.12	104.39
All	74.34	76.43	74.38	76.29	74.77	72.92	68.00	66.99	72.24
Town A									
1980	$52.31	$63.79	$48.01	$65.80	$51.75	$39.68	$43.57	$46.78	$51.42
1981	55.89	61.49	49.19		45.02	55.64	42.73	45.60	52.79
1982	53.97	57.35	64.17	38.25	45.08	53.38	47.87		53.42
1983	54.68	59.35	65.97	63.87	55.78	79.66	49.46	50.53	56.74
1984	61.89	76.74	62.89	132.60	55.29	63.78	61.00	52.44	62.88
1985	81.47	80.23	90.10	66.26	82.89	80.05	79.86	65.59	78.62
1986	103.65	109.48	123.57	102.00	104.47	97.28	102.05	83.83	101.37
1987	104.71	122.80	158.01	108.46	113.99	109.06	101.02	103.02	108.30
1988	116.49	110.61	115.97	114.13	117.50	126.36	99.69	95.72	112.06
1989	108.79		107.37	87.36		108.08	92.81	119.30	106.02
All	81.09	87.48	89.21	86.55	82.18	82.15	72.78	70.39	80.14
Town B									
1980	$22.99	$62.83		$45.86	$30.64	$41.61	$40.31	$37.49	$41.13
1981	35.36			23.58	47.81	39.70	43.70	30.21	38.87
1982	40.36	37.16	$40.23	43.38	43.56	50.75	44.67	54.60	47.85
1983	37.05	39.21	50.46	48.14	38.00	46.16	45.51	39.85	42.17
1984	45.08	47.20	48.87	44.78	48.87	51.79	62.71	46.38	51.35
1985	55.09	46.57	62.07	75.97	47.61	54.79	61.18	65.44	59.64
1986	61.77	79.56	78.73	96.04	80.42	91.14	69.84	65.82	78.54
1987	87.42	82.32	126.54	83.41	70.49	97.67	82.79	89.91	88.17
1988	84.85	91.84			86.54	81.61	96.97	99.12	92.66
1989			59.06	124.95	58.19	136.38	108.23	100.74	106.46
All	52.68	62.77	63.63	68.84	58.66	64.89	64.23	59.71	62.18
Town C									
1980	$46.28	$35.05	$35.34	$50.46	$47.69	$45.99	$60.56	$32.09	$44.74
1981	58.67	38.02	48.41	54.03	40.27	41.38	31.31	44.17	44.99
1982	48.59	47.86		44.64	33.58	40.57	44.20	50.76	44.22
1983	45.86	56.51	43.65	46.85	36.89	40.41	20.13	24.65	42.06
1984	51.48	46.37	67.64	50.21	50.32	47.78	63.29	62.61	55.29
1985	64.33	57.46	70.41	60.51	66.62	64.07	66.68	56.92	63.58
1986	76.12	83.17	82.22	95.00	84.07	79.81	74.94	88.92	83.39
1987	104.80	95.28	92.15	90.57	94.16	98.27	105.43	116.23	100.25
1988	98.67	93.85	100.60	104.19	115.19	122.50	104.80	108.89	109.36
1989	86.21	92.42	92.92	99.32	142.44	136.49	78.44	75.73	101.88
All	69.63	70.09	72.34	75.24	79.34	73.55	67.98	76.15	73.63

Chapter 7: *Effects on Residential Real Estate*

cially in 1988 and 1989. The average for Zone S followed essentially the same pattern as that for every zone except E.

In the individual towns, there was considerably more variation in average ADJSPSF by zone from year to year. There also were gaps for those zones in which no sales occurred during the given years.

The total pattern of levels and variations in average ADJSPSF by zone suggested that some measurable negative impact probably occurred in Zones S, A and B in Town B and possibly in Town C; no such negative impact occurred in Town A.

Before-After Changes

Comparisons of average ADJSPSF and of sales volume by zone and by town before and after January 1, 1984, helped to clarify whether any discernable negative impact on average ADJSPSF or sales volume was evident after the announcement. (The results of these comparisons are presented in Tables 4, 5 and 6.)

Average ADJSPSF by Zone, Before and After January 1, 1984. Table 4 shows the percentage changes in average ADJSPSF by zone.

For the three-town total set of usable sales, Zone A exhibited the lowest percentage increase, suggesting some possible negative impact. The percentage increase in average ADJSPSF for Zone S was approximately equal to the average for all study areas.

Virtually the same pattern in average ADJSPSF by zone was exhibited in Towns A and B. In Town C, on the other hand, the percentage increase after January 1, 1984, was lowest in Zone S. This finding indicated a possible further negative impact.

Number of Sales by Zone, Before and After January 1, 1984. A different pattern was shown for changes in sales volume (Table 5). For the three-

TABLE 4   Inflation-Adjusted Sales Prices per Square Foot (by Zone) Before 1/84 and After 12/83

Time	S	A	B	C	D	E	F	G	All
Three-Town Total									
Before	$50.41	$53.53	$45.75	$50.21	$43.25	$48.87	$45.48	$44.10	$47.45
After	86.91	82.91	84.79	89.49	85.57	83.32	79.35	77.66	83.09
Percent Change	+72	+55	+85	+78	+98	+70	+74	+76	+75
Town A (487 Sales)									
Before	$54.45	$60.82	$56.78	$61.67	$50.55	$60.94	$47.64	$48.18	$54.36
After	96.18	97.23	101.37	97.21	93.13	89.97	86.16	79.76	91.73
Percent Change	+77	+60	+79	+58	+84	+48	+81	+66	+69
Town B (449 Sales)									
Before	$36.28	$46.40	$42.79	$44.14	$41.64	$46.04	$44.09	$42.74	$43.41
After	64.26	68.54	69.58	89.43	68.28	76.21	74.13	71.33	73.19
Percent Change	+77	+48	+63	+103	+64	+66	+68	+67	+69
Town C (487 Sales)									
Before	$48.95	$44.03	$42.73	$49.50	$40.05	$41.31	$44.42	$43.40	$44.24
After	77.05	74.53	83.68	85.65	89.16	84.12	79.28	83.79	82.82
Percent Change	+57	+69	+96	+73	+123	+104	+78	+93	+87

Valuing Contaminated Properties

TABLE 5 Number of Usable Sales (by Zone) Before 1/84 and After 12/83

Time	Zone								
	S	A	B	C	D	E	F	G	All
Three-Town Total									
Before	73	28	28	41	36	77	67	83	433
After	139	99	77	81	105	178	133	178	990
Percent Change	+36	+253	+175	+98	+192	+131	+99	+115	+129
Town A									
Before	47	15	6	9	9	21	25	19	151
After	83	41	16	21	26	57	47	45	336
Percent Change	+77	173	+167	+133	+189	+171	+88	+137	+123
Town B									
Before	12	6	4	15	13	36	30	50	166
After	17	17	14	18	23	60	61	73	283
Percent Change	+42	+183	+250	+20	+77	+67	+103	+46	+70
Town C									
Before	14	7	18	17	14	20	12	14	116
After	39	41	47	42	56	61	25	60	371
Percent Change	+179	+486	+161	+147	+300	+205	+108	+328	+220

town total, the smallest percentage increase was found in Zone S. The largest percentage increase in sale volume occurred in Zone A, and the third-highest percentage increase occurred in Zone B.

A spotty pattern of percentage increase in sales volume by zone appeared when before and after sales volumes were compared from town to town. This pattern suggested that any negative market response was confined to the SSAs themselves.

Percentage Distribution of Number of Sales, by Zone and by Year. Table 6 expresses the number of sales in each zone as a percentage of total sales for that year.

For the three-town total, no consistent pattern of relative change emerged among the zones closest to the SSAs. That inconsistency became even more evident when data for the individual towns were considered. There was substantial variation over time by zone from town to town. Moreover, the evidence suggested a short-term (1984-1985) avoidance of properties in Zone S. The small numbers of sales in individual zones in each town in each year made it both difficult and potentially misleading to draw further general conclusions.

Multiple Regression Analysis

The dependent variable used in all MRA models was inflation-adjusted sales price pre square foot of living area (ADJSPSF). Two time variables were employed: DDATE (date of deed: year and month) and BEFAFT, which indicated whether the deed was recorded before January 1, 1984, or after December 31, 1983. If the recording occurred after December 31, 1983, BEFAFT was assigned a value of 1; if the sale occurred prior to January 1, 1984, the value of BEFAFT was 0.

The price influence of all reported distance zone locations was compared with that of Zone G, the most distant zone from each SSA. Therefore, the values or coefficients for each of the reported seven zone variables (S and A

Chapter 7: *Effects on Residential Real Estate*

TABLE 6 Number of Sales as a Percentage of Each Year's Total (by Zone)

Year	S	A	B	C	D	E	F	G	All
Three-Town Total									
1980	16.25%	8.75%	8.75%	11.25%	8.75%	13.75%	15.00%	17.50%	100.00%
1981	17.31	5.77	8.65	6.73	9.62	23.08	11.54	17.31	100.00
1982	15.24	5.71	4.76	10.48	6.67	20.95	17.14	19.05	100.00
1983	18.06	6.25	4.86	9.72	8.33	13.89	17.36	21.53	100.00
1984	12.43	8.65	7.03	3.78	5.95	23.24	14.59	24.32	100.00
1985	12.39	11.50	7.08	7.52	11.50	19.03	14.60	16.37	100.00
1986	14.03	12.22	9.05	10.41	11.76	14.03	13.57	14.93	100.00
1987	19.14	8.02	5.56	8.02	11.73	16.05	15.43	16.05	100.00
1988	13.43	11.94	8.21	8.21	14.18	17.16	8.21	18.66	100.00
1989	12.90	1.61	12.90	16.13	6.45	19.35	11.29	19.35	100.00
All	14.90	8.92	7.38	8.57	9.91	17.92	14.05	18.34	100.00
Town A									
1980	32.14%	10.71%	3.57%	10.71%	3.57%	10.71%	14.29%	14.29%	100.00%
1981	33.33	12.82	5.13	0.00	7.69	17.95	7.69	15.38	100.00
1982	41.18	5.88	11.76	5.88	5.88	23.53	5.88	0.00	100.00
1983	26.87	8.96	1.49	7.46	5.97	10.45	25.37	13.43	100.00
1984	19.70	9.09	6.06	1.52	6.06	25.76	16.67	15.15	100.00
1985	18.42	17.11	3.95	6.58	11.84	15.79	15.79	10.53	100.00
1986	25.35	14.08	4.23	9.86	5.63	12.68	14.08	14.08	100.00
1987	32.76	8.62	1.72	6.90	10.34	13.79	13.79	12.07	100.00
1988	27.78	12.96	7.41	5.56	5.56	14.81	9.26	16.67	100.00
1989	36.36	0.00	9.09	9.09	0.00	27.27	9.09	9.09	100.00
All	26.69	11.50	4.52	6.16	7.19	16.02	14.78	13.14	100.00
Town B									
1980	3.85%	7.69%	0.00%	11.54%	3.85%	26.92%	15.38%	30.77%	100.00%
1981	11.54	0.00	0.00	3.85	19.23	19.23	23.08	23.08	100.00
1982	5.36	3.57	5.36	10.71	1.79	23.21	23.21	26.79	100.00
1983	8.62	3.45	1.72	8.62	10.34	18.97	12.07	36.21	100.00
1984	5.77	3.85	5.77	1.92	3.85	25.00	21.15	32.69	100.00
1985	6.58	6.58	5.26	6.58	6.58	22.37	19.74	26.32	100.00
1986	5.56	6.94	6.94	11.11	13.89	19.44	19.44	16.67	100.00
1987	10.81	5.41	2.70	5.41	5.41	18.92	29.73	21.62	100.00
1988	4.55	13.64	0.00	0.00	9.09	18.18	22.73	31.82	100.00
1989	0.00	0.00	4.17	8.33	8.33	20.83	20.83	37.50	100.00
All	6.46	5.12	4.01	7.35	8.02	21.38	20.27	27.39	100.00
Town C									
1980	11.54%	7.69%	23.08%	11.54%	19.23%	3.85%	15.38%	7.69%	100.00%
1981	5.13	2.56	17.95	15.38	5.13	30.77	7.69	15.38	100.00
1982	18.75	9.38	0.00	12.50	15.63	15.63	12.50	15.63	100.00
1983	15.79	5.26	26.32	21.05	10.53	10.53	5.26	5.26	100.00
1984	10.45	11.94	8.96	7.46	7.46	19.40	7.46	26.87	100.00
1985	12.16	10.81	12.16	9.46	16.22	18.92	8.11	12.16	100.00
1986	11.54	15.38	15.38	10.26	15.38	10.26	7.69	14.10	100.00
1987	11.94	8.96	10.45	10.45	16.42	16.42	8.96	16.42	100.00
1988	3.45	10.34	12.07	13.79	24.14	18.97	1.72	15.52	100.00
1989	14.81	3.70	22.22	25.93	7.41	14.81	3.70	7.41	100.00
All	10.88	9.86	13.35	12.11	14.37	16.63	7.60	15.20	100.00

through F) represent dollar differences in comparison with the price effects of a Zone G location. A negative coefficient meant that the dollar level of price influence for the zone in question was *lower* than that for Zone G. A positive coefficient meant that it was *higher* than that for Zone G.

Adjusted Sales Price per Square Foot as the Dependent Variable. MRA was applied separately to the three-town total data set and to the Town A, Town B and Town C data subsets.

The results were impressive statistically. The coefficient of multiple determination (R-squared), which indicated the percent of variance in ADJSPSF explained by the independent variables, was at acceptable to high levels. Moreover, the F ratios in the models mean that it was almost totally unlikely that the results occurred by chance.

Both DDATE and BEFAFT were highly significant and *positive*, which indicated a continuing (implicitly linear) increase in ADJSPSF over the entire study period. Lot size and square feet of living area were next most significant, followed by number of garage stalls and age at the time of sale.

In Town A, *none* of the zone variables was statistically significant. Moreover, they all were positive. In Town B, on the other hand, *all* zone coefficients were negative. Coefficients for Zones S, B and D were statistically significant. These results indicated a probable negative influence on ADJSPSF associated with Zones S, B and D (and possibly Zone A) locations relative to Zone G.

In Town C, as in Town A, *none* of the zone variables was statistically significant. The Zone S coefficient was negative in both time models, but there was a high probability that this was a chance occurrence.

In summary, there was no evidence of negative price impacts from locations in Zones S, A and B in Town A; there was a small but almost totally insignificant negative impact in Zone S in Town C. In Town B, on the other hand, the negative influences of proximity to the Superfund site (Zones S, A and B as well as D) were both apparent and statistically significant.

Time-Distance Interactions. The MRA models discussed above took into consideration the separate price influences of both time and distance from the pertinent SSA in each town. Other property and transaction characteristics also were included in the analysis with ADJSPSF as the dependent variable.

RECGC made further tests in an attempt to identify and measure the *combined* or *joint* effects of time and distance zone location on ADJSPSF. Special emphasis was placed on "time" after January 1, 1984.

In MRA models, any existing joint or combined effect can be identified and measured through the use of an interactive variable. In this instance, the interactions of the time and location variables were calculated and tested.

(Table 7 shows the interactions of the deed date with each of the distance zone indicators to produce the seven time-distance interactive variables included in the models. Similarly, Table 8 shows the results of using before-after/distance zone interactive variables. Tables 7 and 8 identify the same highly significant variables: DDATE or BEFAFT, SFLIVARE and LOTSIZE. AGE and GARSTALS also are significant.)

All of the distance zone variables were not significant in the three-town total data set. Similarly, all the time-distance interactive variables were not significant except for D/BEFAFT (which was positive). Only the interactive variable for Zone B in Table 7 was negative; all the others in both models were positive. For the three-town total data set, therefore, no post-announcement negative effect of any consequence on ADJSPSF was associated with proximity to the SSAs.

Very similar results were found for Town A. Only the Zone C/DDATE interactive variable in Table 7 was negative. All others, especially for Zones

Chapter 7: *Effects on Residential Real Estate*

TABLE 7 Comparison of MRA Coefficients and t Values Time-Distance Interactions[1]

Variable	Three-Town Total	Town A	Town B	Town C
SFLIVAREA	-0.01	-0.01	-0.01	-0.03
	(14.67)**	(-6.85)**	(-6.56)**	(-12.49)**
AGE	-0.16	-0.16	-0.25	-0.16
	(-4.47)**	(-2.49)*	(-4.40)**	(-2.56)*
DDATE	8.30	8.14	7.74	7.97
	(15.04)**	(9.21)**	(9.51)**	(7.39)**
LOTSIZE	.0007	.0008	.0007	.0011
	(16.01)**	(4.66)**	(7.68)**	(15.55)**
GARSTALS	6.64	2.60	5.66	9.99
	(5.56)**	(1.37)	(2.74)**	(5.07)**
Zone S	-60.55	-95.68	-113.72	-51.23
	(-0.88)	(-1.06)	(-0.66)	(-0.37)
Zone A	-29.59	-87.86	49.55	-51.03
	(-.34)	(-0.76)	(0.26)	(-0.34)
Zone B	18.66	-111.46	-160.13	50.16
	(0.22)	(-0.78)	(-0.64)	(0.42)
Zone C	-0.05	15.78	-132.78	32.48
	(-.0007)	(0.12)	(-0.90)	(0.26)
Zone D	-100.61	-215.06	151.70	-163.19
	(-1.27)	(-1.53)	(1.08)	(-1.30)
Zone E	-76.04	-162.86	-111.82	-74.62
	(-1.14)	(-1.57)	(-1.08)	(-0.61)
Zone F	-79.97	-234.42	-36.98	-5.23
	(-1.11)	(-2.11)*	(-0.35)	(-0.04)
S*DDATE	0.71	1.13	1.13	0.58
	(0.88)	(1.07)	(0.55)	(0.36)
A*DDATE	0.35	1.09	-0.60	0.59
	(0.35)	(0.81)	(-0.32)	(0.33)
B*DDATE	-0.23	1.36	1.68	-0.56
	(-0.23)	(0.81)	(0.58)	(-0.39)
C*DDATE	0.03	-0.12	1.54	-0.36
	(0.04)	(-0.08)	(0.88)	(-0.25)
D*DDATE	1.16	2.55	-1.91	1.94
	(1.25)	(1.55)	(-1.16)	(1.33)
E*DDATE	0.90	1.96	1.27	0.84
	(1.15)	(1.61)	(1.04)	(0.59)
F*DDATE	0.95	2.77	0.38	0.09
	(1.12)	(2.13)*	(0.31)	(0.05)
R-Squared	0.62	0.69	0.62	0.71
F Ratio	80.91	35.80	24.25	39.18
Standard Error of Estimate	20.75	17.29	21.14	20.19
Durbin-Watson	1.54	1.79	1.58	1.83
Number of Sales	1,403	485	445	473

1. Time is deed date; ADJSPSF is the dependent variable.

2. Numbers in parentheses are t-values

* = Significant at the .05 level

** = Significant at the .01 level

S, A and B, were *positive*. Moreover, only the positive interactive variable for Zone F in Table 7 was statistically significant. None of the BEFAFT interactions was statistically significant.

In Town B, on the other hand, the interactive variables for Zones A and D in Table 7 and for Zones S, A, B and D in Table 8 were all *negative*. All others were positive. None of the interactive variables for Town B was statistically significant, however.

Valuing Contaminated Properties

TABLE 8 Comparison of MRA Coefficients and t values Time-Distance Interactions: Before-After January 1, 1984[1]

Variable	Three-Town Total	Town A	Town B	Town C
SFLIVAREA	-0.01	-0.01	-0.01	-0.03
	(13.78)**	(-5.30)**	(-7.01)**	(-11.41)**
AGE	-0.10	-0.10	-0.23	-0.09
	(-2.36)*	(-1.24)	(-3.54)**	(-1.18)
BEFAFT	30.00	30.36	29.94	26.69
	(9.12)**	(5.06)**	(6.79)**	(3.63)**
GARSTALS	5.88	0.94	6.90	8.23
	(4.14)**	(0.38)	(2.93)**	(3.43)**
LOTSIZE	.0008	.0009	.0008	.0011
	(15.19)**	(4.40)**	(7.22)**	(14.58)**
Zone S	-4.94	-7.74	-19.78	-4.30
	(-1.19)	(-1.22)	(-2.51)*	(-0.44)
Zone A	-1.99	-2.94	-11.80	0.30
	(-0.36)	(-0.37)	(-1.13)	(0.03)
Zone B	-7.29	-3.11	-17.58	-4.01
	(-1.34)	(-0.30)	(-1.41)	(-0.45)
Zone C	-2.02	-1.87	-9.63	-0.15
	(-0.42)	(-0.21)	(-1.35)	(-0.02)
Zone D	-8.75	-5.98	-9.84	-5.41
	(-1.76)	(-0.67)	(-1.29)	(-0.57)
Zone E	-1.37	-0.02	-6.00	-7.35
	(-0.34)	(-0.00)	(-1.13)	(-0.81)
Zone F	-3.43	-3.29	-7.87	-6.65
	(-0.85)	(-1.22)	(-1.42)	(-0.68)
S*BEFAFT	7.12	13.58	-1.08	4.59
	(1.47)	(1.89)	(-0.11)	(0.43)
A*BEFAFT	2.25	7.69	-0.39	0.22
	(0.36)	(0.86)	(-0.03)	(0.02)
B*BEFAFT	9.33	8.96	-1.51	12.02
	(1.47)	(0.75)	(-0.11)	(1.21)
C*BEFAFT	10.35	11.21	10.51	8.43
	(1.81)	(1.06)	(1.13)	(0.84)
D*BEFAFT	11.62	8.74	-2.62	16.78
	(2.02)*	(0.84)	(-0.28)	(1.63)
E*BEFAFT	1.32	3.05	0.09	6.04
	(0.28)	(0.37)	(0.01)	(0.62)
F*BEFAFT	5.81	8.38	3.45	10.70
	(1.18)	(1.03)	(0.50)	(0.95)
R-Squared	0.47	0.49	0.51	0.58
F Ratio	43.37	15.34	15.22	21.47
Standard Error of Estimate	24.60	22.18	24.10	24.51
Durbin-Watson	1.70	1.96	1.66	1.95
Number of Sales	1,403	485	445	473

1. ADJSPSF is dependent variable.

2. Numbers in parentheses are t values

* = Significant at the .05 level

** = Significant at the .01 level

In Town C, only the interactive variables for Zones B and C in Table 7 were negative, but both zones were quite insignificant. *All* interactive variables were positive in Table 8. *No* interactive variable was statistically significant in either Table 7 or 8.

These interactive variable findings showed a clear and reasonably consistent pattern. Any negative effects that could be identified and measured in association with proximity to one of the SSAs *after* January 1,

Chapter 7: *Effects on Residential Real Estate*

1984, were confined to Town B. Even the negative effects in Town B were not statistically significant, however; they could easily have occurred by chance. In Towns A and C, no measurable or discernable negative effect from proximity to the SSA was indicated, especially after January 1, 1984. Moreover, the interactive model results indicated that the passage of time after the announcement did not enhance or exacerbate any negative effects that a location close to the SSA in Town B already had on ADJSPSF.

Summary

A total data set of 1,423 usable sales of single-family residential properties in three towns in northern New Jersey was studied over the period July 1, 1980, through June 30, 1989. Detailed property and sales transaction information was gathered from public records, published sources and field inspections. The location of each sales property was identified by distance zone from the boundaries of a Superfund site (SSA) in each town. Sales within the SSAs themselves, both before and after January 1, 1984, also were included.

The data sets were subjected to a series of statistical tests to provide a basis for reaching judgments about: 1) whether proximity to a known SSA had a negative effect on residential property values in any of the three towns; 2) how far away from the SSA any negative price effect was felt; and 3) how persistently any such negative effect was felt over time. Three statistical procedures were employed:

- Simple comparisons of averages resulted in graphs depicting the movement of average ADJSPSF in different distance zones.

- Percentage changes were calculated by comparing averages of ADJSPSF before and after January 1, 1984. Trends in sales volume were similarly tested and compared. In addition, changes in the percentage mix of sales by zone for each year within each town were compared.

- Multiple regression analysis received major emphasis. ADJSPSF was the focal dependent variable.

Within MRA, the standard Hedonic Pricing Model was applied using two time measures: 1) deed date, a continuous variable; and 2) before-after January 1, 1984, a binary variable. The coefficients for all reported distance zones represented incremental differences from the price of the most distant zone (G) which served as a control.

Finally, the Hedonic Pricing Model was modified to incorporate time-distance interactions of both deed date and before-after time in combination with distance zone.

Conclusions

The results of the statistical tests and their findings led to the following conclusions.

Only in Town B was there any systematic, significant negative effect on ADJSPSF *and* on sales volume for properties close to the SSA. In Towns A and C, where remediation and cleanup were completed promptly, no systematic or significant negative effect was evident except in sales volume in 1989. The period of this decline in sales was too brief to provide a basis for generalization.

After January 1, 1984, patterns of negative effects on ADJSPSF were spotty, unsystematic and generally insignificant. The only consistent negative impacts appeared in Town B, in Zones S, A, B and D. Even there, negative interactive time-distance variables were not significant. Most consistent was a lower rate of increase in average ADJSPSF in Zone S generally and in Zones A and B in Town B.

Sales volumes in the distance zones closest to the SSAs did not decline perceptibly in the years immediately following the December, 1983, announcement. Any decreases that did occur were quite temporary. In 1988 and 1989, however, when the general level of residential sales volume decreased throughout the market area, the declines were much sharper in Zones S, A and B. No direct association with proximity to the SSAs was demonstrated, however.

No measurable negative impact beyond the SSA was evident in Towns A and B. Even there, the post-announcement effects were not significant. In Town B, on the other hand, negative price (and sales volume) effects were found with properties located at least 500 feet from the outer boundary of the SSA through Zone B. It is arguable that the negative impact extended through Zone D (1,500 feet away from the SSA) in Town B, even though the measurable effects in intervening Zone C was *positive*.

Standard MRA using the Hedonic Pricing Model supported and clarified these conclusions based on comparisons of averages and comparisons of trends. Negative statistically significant coefficients associated with location were found in Town B only. There the coefficients for Zones S, A and B were both negative and statistically significant. There was no such impact in Town A or Town C.

The foregoing conclusions also were reinforced when interactive time-distance variables were incorporated into the Hedonic Pricing Model. The negative impacts noted in Zones S, A and B in Town B were generally not significant; nevertheless, there was a continuing negative impact associated with property locations in Zones S, A and B after January 1, 1984, in Town B only, through at least June, 1989.

Any continuing, significant negative price impacts associated with proximity to an SSA were limited to Town B. The SSA within Town B was the site within which barrels of radioactive soil were prominently stored in the open for more than two years with attendant continuing publicity. Several contaminated properties in this town were fenced off, and danger signs warning of radiation hazards were prominently displayed.

The Superfund sites in Towns A and C, on the other hand, were cleaned up expeditiously, and they had none of the adverse publicity that persisted in Town B. As a result, their potential negative impacts were effectively eliminated. Accordingly, no significant negative effects on ADJSPSF or sales volume emerged. Indeed, with the exception of properties within the Superfund site itself in 1988 and 1989, no negative price effect was identified in Towns A and C.

Therefore, the market response to proximity to a known SSA was a direct function of the speed and apparent effectiveness of any remediation or cleanup effort. These results were generally consistent with findings from other, similarly designed and executed statistical studies in other states.

The Causes of Loss in Value: A Case Study of a Contaminated Property

by Robert W. Hall, CRE

A recent counseling assignment our firm undertook involved estimating the loss in value caused by certain contamination at the Shadyside Apartments. The case presented a multifaceted problem which required thinking through the entire valuation process and reviewing the reasons why an investor buys an apartment house in the first place. The identity of the complex has been changed, however, the facts are true.

Background

The subject property is located in a suburban growth area reasonably near a major midwestern city. In this area home ownership is over 70%, and the typical range of single-family housing is about $95,000–$200,000. Apartment rentals range from around $375 to over $600 depending on size, location and amenities offered. The Shadyside Apartments complex is small, of average quality and with sub-normal amenities. There are 32 units with enough land to build 40 more.

The apartments are in two brick buildings of colonial design. Each building has two-story plus basements and 16 units comprised of eight 1-bedroom units and eight 2-bedroom units. The basement areas are devoted to material storage, tenant storage lockers and the complex's management office. There is ample blacktop parking area. The property was built in 1970 and purchased by the present owner in 1972.

At a later date development plans were submitted to the municipality to build 40 more units on the site, and approval was obtained after lengthy negotiations. However, the municipal sewer plant was operating at capacity and plans to expand were being implemented. Consequently, the permits were held in abeyance until the additional capacity would be operational. This did not occur until about 1985.

In late 1987, residents in neighboring homes began to notice gasoline odors in their basements. They complained to the local health authorities who reported the problem to a local pipeline company. After considerable investigation, it was discovered that one of the pipelines had a corrosion

Robert W. Hall, CRE, has been a real estate counselor and appraiser for over 47 years. He has taught appraisal courses, presented seminars and written articles and books on valuation problems including "Real Estate Investment Analysis." His new company, National Market Data Systems, Inc., offers a nationwide industrial database with a copyrighted computer system for searching and analyzing data.

This article originally appeared in the April 1994 issue of Real Estate Issues. Reproduced with permission of Real Estate Issues; published and © by the Counselors of Real Estate (a not for profit organization), Chicago, IL. All rights reserved. Further reproduction/distribution is prohibited without the written permission of Real Estate Issues.

leak, and by the time it was located and corrected, about 100,000 gallons of gasoline had escaped. Unfortunately for our client most of this lost product settled in a geological basin under the apartment buildings.

The pipeline company, working closely with the EPA, made immediate efforts to recover the product. This included drilling of test, monitoring and pumping wells, and the contruction of an aerating tower system for purifying the water table upon which the gasoline was floating. In a period of two years about 60% of the lost product was recovered, and it was planned that operation of the emergency facilities would continue well into the foreseeable future. The EPA advised us that pumping, monitoring and aeration would continue for at least ten years, since the monitoring wells still indicated considerable amounts of benzene, toluene and xylene.

During the weeks and months following the spill, several unpleasant events occurred as Shadyside. Many residents panicked, broke their leases and vacated, especially smokers who were afraid of an explosion in their apartments. Vacancies, previously low, began to mount, and new tenants became very difficult to find because of the publicity the gasoline leak had received in the news media and the very obvious appearance of the aerating tower. Consequently, income decreased while vacancies and expenses increased from cleaning, lawn maintenance and advertising. It became necessary not only to forgo planned rental increases, but to actually reduce rents in order to secure tenants. As the rental rates came down, the grade of tenancy declined and the complex took on a rather seedy appearance.

Meanwhile, the gasoline floating on the water table contaminated several nearby water company wells requiring permanent shutdown and the need to draw water from other resources. This closure raised the water table under the apartments, and in the basements continual flooding occurred ruining all interior finishes. Maintenance costs increased substantially.

Although the pipeline company was trying diligently to remedy the situation, the owner suffered considerable damages without apparent relief in sight. It was a year and a half after the spill that we were engaged by the owner's counsel to estimate the extent of the damages. The law required conducting a before and after study as of the date of the occurrence on the theory that the damages suffered could be measured by subtracting the after value from the before value, exactly like a partial taking in condemnation. This required imagining the property as it existed on the date of the spill before any damage occurred. Even more difficult was visualizing the property as though all the effects of the spill were apparent and measurable as of the same date. Considerable research was done, and a great deal of judgment was exercised. Fortunately, the owner had kept good records which were made available.

A normal appraisal was conducted to determine the before value. The research uncovered many small apartment sales. The market approach generally indicated value around $30,000 per unit plus the value of the excess land for the additional 40 units, which was indicated at $10,000 per unit based on an abundant supply of land sales. That equaled approximately $1,350,000 from the market. This number was pretty well confirmed by the income approach. The owner's rent roll and expenses proved

Chapter 7: *Cause of Loss in Value*

to be in line with market evidence, but some adjustment was needed to reflect proper management charges and to provide for a reasonable reserve. The market data indicated that a capitalization rate of 9% to 9.25% was appropriate. Nine percent was chosen since the property had an unusually good potential in that location, particularly with the opportunity to build additional units. When the extra land was added to capitalized net income, value was indicated around $1.5 million. We believe that apartment houses are purchased for the income they produce, and therefore, the income approach is usually the most significant of the approaches. Thus, the before value was concluded at $1.5 million. So much for the easy part!

While we were generally familiar with contamination issues, little information was available to provide guidance in the measurement of contamination damages. In addition, most of what was written provided a very superficial approach to the measurement of value. The articles consulted implied that the cost to cure is the measure of damages. While, no doubt, this has validity in many cases, it certainly falls far short in the case of Shadyside. After all the physical problems at Shadyside were cured, the owner still lost a bundle of money.

Possible Factors in a Contamination Study

Presented here is a list of nine possible items which we think should be considered by a counselor in any contamination study. The objective in presenting these items is to call attention to those factors which appear to impact the value of contaminated property, rather than to suggest methods and techniques for measuring the effects of those factors. Most professional real estate counselors are well-equipped to devise the necessary methods and techniques once the elements of value are recognized.

1. The Cost of Cleanup

Cleanup should be the major consideration for any contaminated property regardless of the specific cause of the problem. Engineering studies of the particular situation and several estimates of the cost to cure should be obtained and thoroughly reviewed. Great care should be taken in the selection of the estimators, because extreme variance between estimates is often the rule rather that the exception. These studies should be secured by the client rather than by the counselor.

In the Shadyside case the pipeline company only did what was required to recover the gasoline and to purify the water as much as possible. All increased maintenance, repairs and replacements were performed by the owner's staff. Although sizable, these items were actually the smaller elements of damage.

2. Liability to the Public

The owner of any contaminated property could be faced with a lawsuit claiming damages due to unhealthy conditions. Such suits may be brought by tenants, workmen or visitors to the property. Even if such claims are false or fraudulent, they must be defended, and related expenses can be very high. Often awards in these cases bear little relation to either the facts or reality, and the outcome can easily bankrupt a property owner, especially since such loses are often excluded from liability insurance policies. This consideration of contamination must influence a prospective pur-

Valuing Contaminated Properties

chaser of the property, and it can have a decidedly negative impact on market value. After all, why buy somebody else's problems?

3. Stigma After the Cleanup

Admitting your property is or was contaminated is somewhat like admitting to having a venereal disease. Some buyers will have nothing further to do with the property, because they fear the problem is not removed, and still will have to be dealt with. So the usual attitude is either, "Why should I buy a headache?" or else, "I'll discount the price substantially and get a bargain." In either event, value is negatively impacted.

In the case of Shadyside, a very serious prospective buyer ended all negotiations shortly after the damaging incident. In addition, there is no longer any possibility, in the near term, to build the other 40 units. After the dismantling of the aerating tower (10 years or so hence) and after the pumping finally stops, the new construction may be a viable possibility, but certainly not now.

4. Loss of Net income

Since the only real reason to buy an investment property is to make money, the loss of net income can have a drastic effect upon the value of a contaminated property. The income can be affected in three separate ways, and often such a property experiences all three at the same time.

A. Reduced Rental Rates

Many affected properties cannot be rented for rates as high as those for buildings which otherwise are equal but never have been contaminated. This is often the case even after an expensive cure has been administered. However, the condition may be alleviated over time, as people eventually do forget the contamination.

B. Increased Vacancies

The stigma dies hard, and a cured building can easily suffer additional losses from vacancies and increased collection problems, especially since a lower grade of tenant may result.

C. Increased Expenses

Additional testing, monitoring and extra supervisory personnel may be needed in a particular building. Utilities, supplies, advertising and other office expenses, and management and professional fees (engineering studies and appraisal fees) could easily increase, reducing net income and placing the property at a further disadvantage with its competition.

The result is a considerable reduction in net income, at least in the early years after a cure, and if there is less net income to capitalize, there must be lower value.

In the Shadyside case, all three factors came into play: management was forced to drastically reduce rents so old tenants would stay and new tenants would move in; vacancies rose substantially along with the collection problems; and expenses soared. In considering the after value the only logical method of capitalizing income seemed to be a discounted cash flow analysis, since the picture would undoubtedly improve over time. But how much time? How long does it take for people to forget?

Chapter 7: *Cause of Loss in Value*

5. Financing Difficulty or Inability

The tendency for most lenders is to avoid contaminated properties as if they had the bubonic plague. This attitude is quite understandable since several court decisions have held lenders liable for the cost of cleaning up the contaminated properties which were held due to foreclosure on defaulted mortgages, even though the lenders had nothing to do with the contamination process and were only trying to protect their investment. So, why buy trouble? It is much safer to eliminate the problem by refusing to consider a contaminated property as security for a loan (sometimes even a cured property).

Consequently, the increased difficulty or inability to secure mortgage financing creates great hardship on a property owner trying to sell. After all, the number of cash buyers is severely limited and any prospective purchaser will heavily discount the asking price if cash is used for payment. One possible solution is for the seller to provide financing for the buyer, but this also presents a burden on the ownership which is not generally found in clean properties.

At Shadyside, the owner could not find anyone who would have anything to do with the property. The original mortgage balance was fairly well paid down, and refinancing would have been quite helpful to the owner in handling all the increased expenses during the extended rent-up time while income was depressed. The prospective purchaser could not have secured a mortgage even if it was wanted.

Occasionally some lenders will make loans on contaminated properties or properties which have been cured, upon terms more profitable to the lender and consequently more onerous to the property owner. The lender agrees to assume the added risks of lending on a contaminated property in exchange for some added incentive. This may take one or more, or all, of the following forms:

A. Reduced loan-to value ratio

B. Increased interest rate

C. Decreased loan term

D. Shortened call period

E. Extra fees and charges

Thus the financing of a contaminated property is not an easy job and at times is impossible. Substantial loss in value is usually experienced by the owners for this reason.

6. Business Disruption

In owner-occupied properties the loss of rental income is usually not an appropriate consideration. However, during the elimination of hazardous materials, substantial disruption may occur to the business conducted on the property. This can even happen to clean property that is part of an enterprise which owns or leases another property which becomes contaminated. A domino effect can occur.

7. Contingent Liability Forever

Both the Comprehensive Environmental Response, Compensation and Liability Act of 1980 (CERCLA) and the Superfund Amendments and Reauthorization Act of 1986 (SARA) provide that any person in the chain of title to a contaminated property is individually liable forever for hazardous materials removed from a property, regardless of where the materials are stored or disposed, or by whom they were removed. This contingent liability cannot be eliminated, and forever is a long, long time! Some attorneys have commented that SARA should have been named RACHEL, standing for Retroactive Act Claiming How Everybody's Liable. This liability means that if hazardous material was removed from a property and disposed of in a regulated landfill before you bought the property, and years later the landfill began to leak and the materials migrated to adjacent properties, you could be held responsible for the entire cost to alleviate the problem, plus damages. Although such problems may seem remote, the possibility is very real, and sophisticated market participants will insist upon being compensated with a reduced sale price for this added risk.

At Shadyside the property owner had no control over the disposal of the recovered product or its handling, either on or off the property. In fact, he did not know anything about the disposal. Yet, according to the law, he is completely liable and can never get out of this position.

8. Increased Discount Rate

In appraisal literature reward is always equated with risk. If the risk is low, so will be the reward. However, as risk increases the reward must also become greater to properly compensate for the added risk. Reason would dictate that properties which are or were contaminated should provide their owners with a greater reward because risks were assumed (either voluntarily or involuntarily) which are considerably greater than those found in uncontaminated properties. This means that the discount or capitalization rate should be higher in contaminated properties and in those which were cured. And if the rate is higher, the property value is lower.

In the case of Shadyside, the road back to profitability will be long and arduous. The owner will suffer from reduced income, high vacancies, collection problems and extra heavy expenses. He may occasionally have to fund the investment and will probably be unable to secure any new financing. If this kind of investment does not deserve a higher return, what does?

In considering the discounted cash flow analysis for the after value, a 10-year forecast of income and expenses was used which began on the date of the spill. Fortunately, as previously noted, the owner kept very good records, and the increase in vacancies and expenses was documented on a month-by-month basis. We knew what had occurred for the first year-and-a-half.

Our forecast predicted a further decline in income and an increase in vacancies and expenses for an additional year, followed by a very gradual improvement over the remainder of the 10-year term, eventually returning to a situation similar to what existed just before the spill. After careful analysis, an ending capitaliztion rate of 12% was chosen to calculate the reversion. For discounting each annual net cash flow, a rate of 20%, was selected for the first year. This was gradually reduced, so that in year six the rate was 15% where it remained throughout the balance of analysis. This was justified by the assumption that each year the picture would improve somewhat and the involuntary assumed risk would diminish, thus requiring less reward. In estimating the value of the additional land, we forecast that the value 10 years hence, on a per unit basis, would be somewhat greater that at the time the contamination occurred. The future value was discounted back to the effective date of the appraisal. Our estimate of after value indicated that the total loss in value to the property would be about two-thirds of the before value.

9. Loss of Marketability

Any property which is or was contaminated has lost some of its former marketability. This is true regardless of the type of contamination, because the market always becomes thinner when such problems exist, and it becomes progressively smaller as the hazards increase. In a situation where the cost to cure the condition exceeds the value of the cured property, it is no longer marketable and cannot be sold at any price or even given away. And if a property is not marketable, it certainly cannot have a market value. Although the loss in market value may be complete, the property may still provide substantial utility to its owner and thus provide a value-in-use which may be quite sizable.

As already mentioned, a serious prospective purchaser dropped the Shadyside deal like a hot potato once the extent of the problem was recognized. This property has extreme problems, both physical and financial, which will continue into the foreseeable future. Mortgage financing cannot be secured on the property. It appears the property has lost all marketability for the near term and possibly for a very long period. The land for the additional 40 units can only be mowed and only adds to the expenses.

We believe that these nine factors should be considered in any assignment where the measurement of contamination damages is the issue. While it will be a rare case, indeed, where all the factors are involved, there won't be any where some are not important.

Postscript

It has been said (although certainly not by Murphy) that every cloud has a silver lining. It certainly did in the case of Shadyside! A very satisfactory settlement was arranged out of the court in which the owner was paid the full before value of the property and was able to keep the property. Although the credit for such a favorable conclusion belongs to the owner's legal counsel who handled the entire case with considerable skill and expertise, we like to think our careful research and analysis also contributed to the result.

Contaminated Properties and the Sales Comparison Approach

by Peter J. Patchin, MAI

Peter J. Patchin, MAI, *is president of Peter J. Patchin & Associates, Inc., of Burnsville, Minnesota. Also a member of the American Society of Real Estate Counselors, he has been engaged in private appraisal practice for 32 years. Mr. Patchin has been a frequent contributor to* The Appraisal Journal, *and with his coauthor was the 1992 Armstrong Award winner.*

This article originally appeared in the July 1994 issue of The Appraisal Journal.

During the past decade market participants have become increasingly aware of contaminated property and its many problems. As the market has gained experience with environmentally impaired transactions, some of the panic has worn off and these properties have slowly begun to sell once again. Consequently, a small but steadily increasing body of market data concerning the sale of contaminated real estate is now developing.

The vast majority of market data observed so far has been associated with lightly to moderately contaminated properties. Sales of severely contaminated property, such as Superfund sites, while rare, do exist. Severely contaminated property sales are rare primarily because existing owners, perceiving an increased risk of liability, often do not want to relinquish control of these sites.

Appraisers can no longer dismiss the sales comparison approach simply by stating that contaminated properties are not marketable and that therefore there are no sales. While it is difficult to market environmentally impaired properties, they are being sold with increasing frequency as the market becomes more familiar with them.

This trend benefits the appraisal process in that it gives appraisers yet another tool in the measurement of losses in value resulting from contamination. Previous articles on valuation techniques for contaminated properties[1] focused on various forms of income models. While income techniques are still valid and frequently provide the most accurate indication of value, the sales comparison approach now provides a valuable backup for the income approach conclusions. The income methods have often been criticized for being theoretical in nature and for lacking direct contact with the market, particularly when losses in value caused by stigma factors are indicated. Now an appraiser may point to market sales that indicate that stigma is real and not simply a creation of some income model.

As yet there are few contaminated property sales. It is therefore seldom possible to run a sales comparison approach of contaminated sales with properties that would be comparable to a subject property on an unim-

---

1. Peter J. Patchin, "Valuation of Contaminated Property," *The Appraisal Journal* (January 1998): 7–16; Peter J. Patchin, "Contaminated Properties—Stigma Revisited," *The Appraisal Journal* (April 1992): 167–172; Bill Mundy, "Stigma and Value," *The Appraisal Journal* (January 1992): 7–13; Bill Mundy, "The Impact of Hazardous Materials on Property Value," *The Appraisal Journal* (October 1992): 463–471; and Peter J. Patchin, "The Valuation of Contaminated Properties," *Real Estate Issues* (Fall/Winter 1990): 50–54.

Chapter 7: *Contaminated Properties and Sales Comparison*

paired basis. It is frequently possible, however, to perform a sales comparison approach using sales in which the contamination is comparable or analogous to a subject property. It is the objective of this article to help appraisers recognize, assemble, and analyze these contaminated comparables.

How to Find Market Data on Contaminated Properties

In the course of my work, I frequently take consulting assignments in urban areas located long distances from my local practice, and in which I have had little or no previous experience. I have consistently found that I am able to enter unfamiliar urban areas and develop at least a couple of contaminated sales within the first few days—sometimes to the chagrin of local appraisers who had told me that such data did not exist.

When local appraisers are questioned about the availability of contaminated property sale data in their area, the standard reply is that none exist. Further investigation usually reveals that such data are lying right under their noses, but they fail to recognize this. In most cases, a closer look at sales already in a local appraiser's files is a good beginning.

The problem is that appraisers have to educate themselves about what to look for as each new comparable comes across their desks, and before it goes into files. The following steps may help in this process.

- Be aware of the past uses of a property as well as its immediate neighborhood. If these past uses indicate the potential of contamination, set the sales aside for further investigation. Such uses may include wood preservative manufacturing (creosote or penta), bulk oil or gasoline terminals, insecticide manufacturing, electroplating, computer chip or printed circuit board manufacturing, coal gasification plants, sanitary landfills, machine shops with degreasing operations, chemical manufacturing or distribution, and dry-cleaning operations.

- When confirming sales make it a practice to ask buyers, sellers, and brokers if the property was contaminated, and further, if this was an issue in the sale of the property.

- If a property was sold as contaminated, ask the seller or broker if there were purchase offers or agreements that did not go through because of the disclosure of contamination. This step frequently yields the data of the comparable most difficult to obtain—the value as unimpaired by contamination. If a property has been exposed for sale for a long time, it is quite likely that other brokers previously held the listing. Interviews with these brokers may reveal purchase agreements (offers) that failed because of the discovery of contamination. It must be emphasized that the deal that did not happen is often as important as the deal that did happen. Such advice may fly in the face of conventional appraisal wisdom, which downgrades the importance of purchase offers or failed purchase agreements. In these cases, however, such data can yield the best evidence of unimpaired value.

- Obtain a list of contaminated sites from the local state environmental agency. Such a list is frequently referred to as the "State Superfund List." These state lists generally include more properties for a particular state than would be found on the National Superfund List.

Be aware of the extent and nature of these contaminated areas. Newspaper articles are frequently good sources. Be watchful for sales that are located either on or in close proximity to these sites. It is important to interview the parties to these sales even if some other appraiser has already confirmed the sale for general purposes.

- If the selling price of a comparable sale appears to be inexplicably low, this may be an indication of an environmental impairment. For instance, an industrial building with an obvious unimpaired value in the range of $15 to $20 per square foot that is sold for $7 per square foot in what is otherwise a strong or stable market may signal environmental impairment. I am repeatedly appalled that so many appraisers enter such a sale into their files, or report it to their local appraisal data exchange, without further inquiry or comment.

- If you suspect contamination of a comparable, this may be confirmed with the local environmental agency. Usually a phone call identifying the property by owner's name and street address is sufficient to find if the property has an environmental record. Ask the environmental agency to send a copy of the record—this is public information.

Appraisers who follow these steps will develop a small but significant databank of contaminated property sales. A reasonable expectation is a dozen or more such comparables (i.e., case studies) in a large urban area after a year of using these procedures.

Analysis of Contaminated Market Data

A written contaminated comparable tends to be lengthy, particularly when compared with normal, unimpaired comparables. Further, a contaminated comparable may not be comparable to a subject property in the normal valuation sense, but may be comparable only in its contamination problem. It is for this reason that our firm has the policy of calling contaminated comparables "case studies." The term case study acknowledges the lengthy nature of the data and also helps distinguish between such impaired comparables and the unimpaired comparable sales that may appear in the same appraisal report.

Once a sale of contaminated property has been identified, a large volume of information must be assembled to make it into a reliable comparable. A contaminated sale involves far more data than a normal comparable sale. Some questions that must be answered are listed in the next section.

The extent and nature of contamination
- What types of hazardous materials are involved?
- Is there groundwater involvement, or can cleanup only be accomplished through removal/treatment of soils? This information can be of major importance. For instance, a gasoline spill that is remediated through soils removal generally results in little stigma after the cleanup. If groundwater is involved, however, many more unknowns are present and the resulting stigma may be severe.
- Who is responsible for paying cleanup and future monitoring costs? If the seller or other responsible party is under a consent order or

indemnity agreement to pay for all of these costs, the decline in value may be attributable to stigma factors alone. This is particularly true when a seller or responsible party has a strong credit rating and is very likely to fulfill these obligations.

- If the buyer is responsible for all or part of the cleanup costs, what are those costs? Often, the costs estimated at the time of purchase and the ultimate cleanup costs are quite different.

- What is the time period estimated by remediation consultants for the cleanup to be completed? While this time estimate is often difficult for remediation experts to make, it is important for the appraisal process because it frequently indicates when the property may regain all or part of its mortgageability.

- Is it the intent of the cleanup to remediate to local public health recommended allowable limits (RAL)? Frequently, the local environmental protection agency (EPA) will permit a less thorough cleanup than RAL because they do not perceive any public health risk and the cleanup costs are far less. The dilemma is that although the lesser cleanup effort may satisfy the EPA, it may not satisfy the mortgage lenders, with the result that the property may never regain its mortgageability.

- Is the property under the supervision of the U.S. EPA or the state EPA? Is it on either the state or national Superfund list? If so, what is its hazardous ranking score (HRS)?

Evidence of unimpaired market value

- Some of the best evidence is a purchase agreement that failed because of the discovery of the contamination. Generally the only way to obtain this information is through interviews with buyers, sellers, brokers, and attorneys.

- Was there a previous sale of the property before discovery of the contamination?

- An appraisal of the property as unimpaired may exist. Typically the seller obtains such an appraisal before marketing the property.

- What is the assessor's market value? This may be productive in states where there are stringent requirements that assessors' market values be maintained close to actual market values.

Format of market data for an assembled case study

- What is required for court preparation? In general terms, the format should include the establishment of unimpaired value from a pervious sale, a purchase offer prior to discovery of contamination, or an appraisal. The cost of remediation as well as the actual impaired selling price should be deducted.

- What does the remainder signify? It should be remembered that the remainder is an indication of value loss caused by stigma factors alone.

- How should stigma loss be accounted for? Generally, stigma loss should be expressed as a percentage of unimpaired value.

Valuing Contaminated Properties

Sample Case Studies

The following four case studies provide an idea of the format and information contained in a contaminated sale case study, and are included to illustrate the variations that may be encountered.

Contaminated Case Study Property 1

The property is located in a large Midwestern city. The date of sale is P.A. February 1991, with closing in November 1991. The improvement was designed and constructed in 1985 as a supercomputer manufacturing plant. The plant was closed in the summer of 1989 when the parent company chose to not develop and produce supercomputers. The facility has a number of high-tech improvements that are costly to install, maintain, and operate. These include:

- Fiberoptics cable system
- Computer cabling system
- 5,700 square feet of clean rooms, both class 5,000 and 10,000
- Computer floor—one entire wing (17,444 square feet)
- Electro-static discharge floors
- Compressed air system
- Central vacuum system
- Security system, including card-reader door
- Hazardous waste disposal system
- Wet process circuit-board printing system

The reported cost of the building, including these systems, was nearly $20 million in 1985. The property has been purchased with the intention of remodeling the existing building and constructing an additional 220,00-square-foot building. The property will be leased to a firm to serve as a computer operation center. The site area is 903,656 square feet, or 20.745 acres. The gross building area is 121,965 square feet.

The property was situated on a former coking oven site, which leached toxic contamination into the soils and groundwater. The site has been cleaned up and both the primary responsible party (PRP) and the surrounding municipality have signed a consent order to pay for all future monitoring and cleanup costs.

The cleanup was first thought to be complete in 1982. In 1989, a small amount of groundwater contamination from the same source reappeared, and is currently being remediated.

Concerning its unimpaired value, in October 1989 a purchase agreement was signed by a large multinational company for $5.8 million in cash. Subsequently, this company canceled the purchase, stating that it did not wish to contend with any of the liabilities associated with the ownership of a contaminated property—even if the cleanup were fully indemnified by others.

Concerning the impaired value of the property, a large regional construction company, acting as a straw man for a major corporation future occupant, has purchased it. The buyer will remodel and expand the property and execute a long-term net lease to the major corporation user. The sale price is $4,300,000 cash.

Unimpaired sale price	$5,800,000
Impaired sale price	$4,300,000
Indicated stigma	$1,500,000 or 25.9% of unimpaired value

The discount is entirely attributable to stigma value loss. The property cleanup has been completed and paid for. If any further cleanup or monitoring is ordered, it will be funded by PRP first. If the PRP fails to fund cleanup costs, the surrounding municipality will do so. The new buyer has two large, financially strong entities standing in front of it insofar as cleanup costs are concerned. Therefore, all of the value reduction must be attributed to stigma factors.

Contaminated Case Study Property 2

Located in a large Midwestern city, with a sale date of October 4, 1990, this is an industrial, former chemical division property of a large multinational corporation. A complex of 16 buildings consisting of offices (14,175 square feet), engineering offices, warehouses, and manufacturing, its intended use is rental to multiple tenants. The site area is 256,280 square feet, or 5.88 acres, and the gross building area is 153,870 square feet.

The original building was constructed in 1931; additional buildings were constructed in the 1950s and the 1960s. Soil and groundwater contamination occurred during the years between 1947 and 1962. The chemical division of a multinational corporation was sold in the mid-1970s, and this property was part of the going-concern sale. The buyer was a large European conglomerate. Operations at this property were discontinued in the late 1980s for reasons unrelated to contamination.

The original owner had disposed of organics, solvents, and laboratory wastes from 1947 through 1962 onsite. In 1983 the site was tested and assigned an HRS of 39, which placed the property on the National Superfund List. A remedial action plan was submitted to the state EPA and pump-out of groundwater began in 1985. By 1991 the remediation was completed, with monitoring to continue indefinitely.

The assessor's unimpaired market value in 1990 was $1,780,000. This was in a state where the assessor was required to maintain values at not less than 90% of actual values; therefore, the assessor's market value was regarded as meaningful. In addition, there had been an unimpaired value appraisal prior to sale of $1,500,000, consisting of $700,000 in improvements and $800,000 for land.

When sold for its impaired value, the property was purchased by a local real estate developer who intended to convert the property into a multi-tenant industrial facility. The intent was to provide low rental rates for smaller or newer businesses—thus making the property an "incubator" building. The purchase price was $95,000 cash.

Unimpaired value	$1,500,000
Impaired value	$95,000
Indicated stigma	$1,405,000 or 93.7% of unimpaired value

The discount is entirely attributable to stigma value loss. The property cleanup has been completed by the former owner. If any further cleanup or monitoring is ordered by the U.S. EPA or state EPA, those costs will be paid for by the former owner first and the present owner (seller) second.

The buyer has two Fortune 500 companies standing in front of it insofar as cleanup costs are concerned. Therefore, all of the value reduction must be attributed to stigma factors.

When interviewed, the buyer stated that he would not have considered purchasing the property if the cleanup had not been guaranteed by major credit concerns.

Contaminated Case Study Property 3

The property is located in a large Midwestern city, and the sale closed September 19, 1991. The improvement was originally built in 1983 as a semiconductor facility. The plant was closed in 1987 when operations were consolidated out of state. The facility has several high-tech improvements that are extremely expensive to install, maintain, and operate. These include:

- 58,000 square feet of clean rooms
- 11,000 square feet of vibration-controlled, pneumatically supported lab floor
- Tight temperature and humidity controls
- Purity water system
- Electro-static discharge floors
- Compressed air system
- Central vacuum system
- Security system, including card-reader door
- Hazardous waste disposal system

The reported cost of the building, including these systems, was approximately $42 million in 1983. The property has been purchased with the intent to remodel the existing building into a computer operations center at a total cost of $32 million, including acquisition costs. The site area is 1,759,824 square feet, or 40.4 acres, and the gross building area is 248,332 square feet (not including 56,160 square feet of interstitial space above the laboratories).

During 1988 and 1989, it was discovered that the shallow groundwater aquifer was contaminated with TCE. In October 1989, a groundwater recovery and treatment system began operating. The estimated period of remediation was five years.

The unimpaired value is $9,200,000, from an appraisal before discovery of contamination that was used as a basis of settlement of a property tax appeal.

The impaired value is $6,515, 345 (including $400,000 escrow for possible building contamination expense). The buyer was a major national corporation that chose to finance property through corporate bonds rather than mortgage. The buyer's national headquarters was also located in the same neighborhood.

Unimpaired value	$9,200,000
Actual selling price	$6,515,345
Indicated stigma	$2,684,655 or 29.2% of unimpaired value

The discount is entirely attributable to stigma value loss. Property cleanup is being funded by the seller. Once the cleanup is accomplished, monitoring and any required additional cleanup will also be funded by the seller. Therefore, the value reduction must be attributable to stigma factors.

Contaminated Case Study Property 3A

Also in a large Midwestern city, the adjoining case study property 3A is currently being offered (see Case Study 3). This property consists of unimproved land, zoned light industrial, that adjoins case study property 3 on the south side. The site has sewer, water, and storm sewer services. The frontage is a major four-lane arterial road approximately one block from an interchange onto an interstate freeway. Subsoils are solid and suitable for building purposes. The site area is 81 acres.

This site was contaminated from the same source as Case Study 3. The unimpaired value of the site was at issue before the contamination was discovered. The assessor had valued the site at $100,000 per acre. Upon appeal by the owner, a value of $60,000 per acre was settled on. The owner had an appraisal for $60,000 per acre at the time. In late 1990, the owner, a large corporation, declared the site as surplus and listed it for sale, as impaired, at an asking price of $1.5 million, or $18,815 per acre. The site has now been listed for sale for over two years, with a major real estate firm handling the listing, using large onsite signs. At the time this article was written, no offers had been received.

Unimpaired value	$60,000 per acre
Impaired value	$18,815 per acre
Indicated stigma	$41,482 per acre or *at least* 69% of unimpaired value

The same party is responsible for cleanup as for Case Study 3. Consequently, the entire indicated value loss is caused by stigma. The wide disparity between Case Study 3 (29% stigma) and Case Study 3A (69% stigma) is apparent in spite of the fact that they are adjoining properties with the same source of contamination. The primary reason for the large disparity appears to be the principle of substitution. Case Study 3 was improved with an ultra high-tech building that had few substitutes; consequently, the buyer was willing to work with it as contaminated. Case Study 3A, on the other hand, was bare land with many potential substitutes.

Analysis of Case Studies

When an appraiser has assembled a group of contaminated case studies and reviews the results, there are generally a few conclusions that become readily apparent. For instance, the principle of substitution plays a major role in the amount of stigma value loss. Properties that are in demand and are hard to find in the market generally experience less stigma than those with many substitutes. Case studies 1 and 3 are examples of high-demand properties that experienced relatively low amounts of stigma. Few of these properties were on the market; consequently, the buyers felt compelled to work with them in spite of their contamination problems.

Often when an improved property has many alternative substitutes the prospective buyer is not compelled to work with the property. In these cases, contamination problems, similar to those found in case studies 1 and 3, will result in stigma losses as high as 60% to 70%.

Valuing Contaminated Properties

Further, unimproved land generally suffers a greater stigma loss than improved property. This phenomenon is clearly illustrated by a comparison of case studies 3 and 3A. The primary causes of the greater vulnerability of unimproved land are twofold. First, the previously discussed principle of substitution is a significant cause. Second, most improved properties have an income stream or some type of value in use that tends to place a floor under its contaminated value, in spite of marketability or mortgageability problems. This income, or value in use, tends to mitigate the impact of stigma loss. Land parcels that are in extremely high demand or in short supply tend to exhibit less stigma. Once again, the principle of substitution asserts itself.

Application of Market Data to the Appraisal

Contaminated case studies (i.e., comparables) should not be held as comparable to a subject property in terms of physical characteristics or location. The comparability lies in the similarity of their contamination problems. The contamination case studies may be drawn from a widely diverse group of property types, but can still be applicable to a subject property for purposes of estimating its stigma value loss.

Table 1 provides an example of how contaminated market data may be applied in an appraisal. In this example, eight contaminated case studies were developed. The stigma value loss indicated by each of these case studies and their degree of comparability to the subject property's contamination situation is summarized in Table 1.

Comparisons of the contaminated case studies with the subject indicate:

- Case studies 1 and 4 show stigma value losses of 21% to 26% for situations less serious than the subject.

TABLE 1 Contaminated Case Study Summary

Case Study Number	Indicated Percentage of Unimpaired Value Lost to Stigma	Comparison to subject
1	25.9%	Contamination cleanup complete, stigma caused by fear of additional contamination. Less severe than subject.
2	93.7%	Superfund site. More severe than subject.
3	29.2%	Similar cleanup period of 4 years.
3A	69.0%	Vacant land site adjacent to Case Study 3, same source of contamination.
4	20.9%	No cleanup presently mandated—origin is mostly fuel oil. Less severe than subject.
5	45.4%	10-year cleanup period. More severe than subject. Consists of mostly vacant land.
6	35.5%	Site not actually contaminated itself, proximity to other contaminated property reflects pure stigma. Comparable to subject in terms of the mortgageability problems.
7	32.7%	Similar contamination and mortgageability problems.
8	62.5%	Similar contamination problems. Older property, many alternative substitutes in the market. On balance more severe than subject.

- Case studies 2, 5, and 8 show stigma value losses in the range of 45% to 94% for situations more serious than the subject.
- Case studies 3, 6, and 7 show stigma value losses ranging from 29.2% to 35.5% for situations similar to the subject. The average stigma loss indicated by these three case studies is 32.5%.

In sum, the results of the eight case studies appear to support approximately 30% to 35% stigma value loss. The stigma value loss thus indicated for the subject is:

Unimpaired value[2]	$1,000,000
	× 30% to 35%
Indicated stigma value loss	$300,000 to $350,000

Conclusion

The sales comparison approach for contaminated properties is now in its development stage. There appear to be sufficient data on sales of lightly to moderately contaminated properties to at least obtain an indication of a range of stigma value loss. While market data have not yet developed to the extent that this approach can be used as a primary indicator of value in most cases, it has already become useful as a confirming approach to value. As further market data develop, this method may well become the primary approach to valuation of contaminated properties.

2. This is as found by normal appraisal procedures.

Groundwater Contamination and Residential Property Values

by Mark Dotzour, PhD

Mark Dotzour, PhD, is the chief economist of the Real Estate Center at Texas A&M University, College Station. He received his PhD in real estate at the University of Texas at Austin. Dotzour has served on the Publications Committee and the Body of Knowledge Committee for the Appraisal Institute and has had several articles published in The Appraisal Journal.

This article originally appeared in the July 1997 issue of The Appraisal Journal.

Many papers have been written on how discovering environmental contamination influences the value of real estate. Some describe the legal environment that created the problem, and others suggest methods for valuing a contaminated property. Most papers focus on commercial property, and few offer empirical data to support their assertions.

This research measured the impact of groundwater contamination on the value of residential properties located in the contaminated area. A model that measures the impact of contamination on a large residential area is provided, along with empirical evidence on how residential property values were affected by the contamination event. The results should be of interest to many sectors of the real estate industry, including tax assessors, mortgage lenders, appraisers, and property owners.

The Contamination Event

In November 1989 the Kansas Department of Health and Environment (KDHE) publicly announced that groundwater contamination had been discovered in the central core of the city of Wichita. The announcement was made in the local newspaper and television stations. The groundwater, part of an underground river that flows under the city at a rate of approximately one foot per day, was found to be contaminated with several chemicals that the Environmental Protection Agency (EPA) considers hazardous material. Most, if not all, of the properties in the contaminated area are connected to public water and sewer service. Consequently, none of this groundwater is used for drinking water, and no immediate health hazard was identified. The contaminated area included all of the central business district (CBD) and many residential areas immediately south of the CBD.

After the announcement was made, it became apparent that the entire area would become a Superfund site. Lenders immediately ceased lending on any sort of commercial real estate in the identified area. Market activity nearly came to a standstill in the commercial sector.

If the area were to be declared a Superfund site, each property owner in the area could be assessed a portion of the total cost of $22 million to clean up the groundwater problem. Under Superfund legislation, each property owner in the area could be held both jointly and severally liable for the entire cost of the cleanup. However, there is a safe harbor provision in the EPA legislation for property owners who can demonstrate that they did not cause the contamination. Such owners are classified as *de minimis* owners, and their financial liability is limited to no more than 1% of the entire cost of the cleanup.

Expected Impact

Nationally, thousands of contaminated areas are subject to cleanup by Superfund or CERCLA *(Comprehensive Environmental Response, Compensation, and Liability Act of 1980)* legislation. Real estate values in such areas can be influenced by the potential legal and financial liability for cleaning up the problem.[1]

When groundwater contamination is discovered, it is uncertain who will ultimately be responsible for the cleanup. As a result, the values of properties located in these areas are expected to fall as the perceived risk increases. In some situations, the market is entirely disrupted and arm's length transactions are nonexistent. Part of this uncertainty comes from lack of information about whether the site can actually be cleaned up, how much it will cost to do so, and who will pay for it.

Patchin[2] identified three causes of market value loss that can be associated with contamination: cost of cleanup, liability to the public, and stigma after cleanup. Consequently, the value of a contaminated property could be defined by the following equation:

$$
\begin{aligned}
\text{Contaminated Value} = &\ \text{Uncontaminated Value} \\
&- \text{Cleanup Cost} \\
&- \text{Public Liability} \\
&- \text{Stigma} \qquad\qquad\qquad (1)
\end{aligned}
$$

In another article, Patchin[3] further defines stigma to be a negative intangible that may be caused by the following factors: fear of hidden cleanup costs, the "trouble factor," and lack of mortgageability. Other possible components of stigma may have an impact on value.[4] These include disruption, concealability, aesthetic effect, responsibility, prognosis, degree of peril, and level of fear.

If the components of stigma from Patchin and Mundy are inserted into Equation 1, the value of a contaminated property can be determined to be:

$$
\begin{aligned}
\text{Contaminated Value} = &\ \text{Uncontaminated Value} - f(\text{cleanup cost}) \\
&- f(\text{public liability}) - f(\text{hidden costs}) \\
&- f(\text{trouble factor}) - f(\text{mortgageability}) \\
&- f(\text{disruption}) - f(\text{concealability}) \\
&- f(\text{aesthetic effect}) - f(\text{responsibility}) \\
&- f(\text{prognosis}) - f(\text{degree of peril}) \\
&- f(\text{level of fear}) \qquad\qquad\qquad (2)
\end{aligned}
$$

The f in the equation indicates that the penalty to value is not likely to be the exact cost associated with each of the variables in the equation. The actual penalty could be more or less than the estimated actual cost.

1. For an excellent description of enacted legislation that influences contaminated properties, see John D. Dorchester, "Environmental Pollution: Valuation in a Changing World." *The Appraisal Journal* (July 1991): 293–295. For a discussion of early legal decisions that have increased the perceived risk to potential purchasers of contaminated property and lenders, see Peter J. Patchin, "Valuation of Contaminated Properties." *The Appraisal Journal* (January 1988): 7–10.

2. Patchin, 11–13.

3. Peter J. Patchin, "Contaminated Properties—Stigma Revisited." *The Appraisal Journal* (April 1991): 168–169.

4. Bill Mundy, "Stigma and Value." *The Appraisal Journal* (January 1992): 8–9.

"Cleanup costs" are defined as the cost estimated to meet EPA requirements, including any continuing monitoring costs. "Public liability" is the possible financial cost of settling lawsuits brought by surrounding properties that have become contaminated because of a release of toxic chemicals. The fear of "hidden cleanup costs" may be present because it is possible that contaminated properties may need further treatment, even after they have been certified as clean.

The "trouble factor" could be viewed as a penalty to value since the buyer will have to be compensated over and above the actual cleanup costs for the trouble of complying with cleanup requirements. Lack of "mortgageability" due to lenders' reluctance to get involved may diminish the property's marketability. "Disruption" is the degree to which the presence of contamination disrupts the normal daily behavior of people who reside on the site. "Concealability" indicates how highly visible or hidden from public view the contamination is. "Aesthetic effect" is the extent to which the contamination alters the visual environment of the site. "Responsibility" is the extent to which the owners/users of the site are directly responsible for the contamination. "Prognosis" consists of two elements: the severity of contamination and the difficulty of cleaning it up. "Degree of peril" describes the perceived health hazard to human beings, wildlife, and plants. Level of "fear" is the perceived fear in the community regarding the contamination.

Equation 2 captures all the components of stigma described by Patchin and Mundy. The function notation f in the equation recognizes that estimating value may not be a simple matter of estimating each of the sources of depreciation and then subtracting them from the uncontaminated value. These estimates may need to be modified based on the probability that there will be negative effects. For example, a property may have a possible public liability of $500,000, but the depreciation from this source may need to be adjusted to reflect the probability that the property owner will actually be assessed damages to surrounding property owners. If the probability of incurring public liability is small, then even a large potential liability may not greatly diminish property value.

Mundy[5] presents a theoretical model of how property values are expected to react to the discovery of contamination. He proposes that property values should decline steeply when the public first becomes aware of the contamination, and that values will gradually recover to their original, uncontaminated value as the problem is identified and remedied.

Patchin[6] states that buyers in the residential market may react differently to contamination when compared with the market reaction in the commercial market. He suggests that residential values may fall sharply in value during the first year or two after contamination is disclosed, and that values begin to rise when officials announce plans to remedy it. Values then return to precontaminated levels when the cure is completed.

Methodology

The sample data consists of all residential transactions that were reported in the multiple listing service in and around the contaminated area of Wichita. The data is sorted into three groups. The "contaminated area" contains all sales that are located in the designated contamination area. The "east control area" is a control sample of all sales of houses located in

5. Bill Mundy, "The Impact of Hazardous Materials on Property Value." *The Appraisal Journal* (April 1992): 158–161.

6. "Contaminated Properties—Stigma Revisited." 171–172.

Chapter 7: *Groundwater Contamination*

neighborhoods outside, and immediately east of, the contaminated area. The "west control area" is another control sample of all sales of houses located in neighborhoods outside, and immediately west of, the contaminated area.

The data set contains all transactions reported during a 25-month period (12 months before and after November 1989, the date when the contamination was discovered and announced publicly in the local newspaper) for all three groups from November 1988 through November 1990.

An "event study" was used to measure the impact of the discovery of contamination on values in the contaminated area. The average price of houses sold in the contaminated area for the 12 months *after* the discovery of contamination was compared with the average price of houses sold in the same area for the 12 months before the discovery. Most of the market uncertainty over the contamination event was removed in July 1991, when the City of Wichita created a tax increment financing district for the contaminated area to generate funds for studies and remediation actions at the site. In August 1991, the City of Wichita began a program in which purchasers of land in the contaminated area could apply for a "Certificate and Release for Environmental Conditions." This released future purchasers from incurring the costs for environmental investigation and remediation. These developments became public and were implemented well after the time period analyzed in this study.

Consequently, any difference in the average sales price of the "after discovery sample" and the "before discovery sample" can be attributed to the discovery of contamination because housing prices were generally stable in the area during this time period. Multiple regressions were run for each of the control areas to measure general price appreciation in the houses located in the control samples immediately east and west of the contaminated area. The results of these regressions indicate that prices in both the east control area and west control area were unchanged during the time considered in this study (see Appendix A).

TABLE 1 Summary Statistics for Entire Sample

Variable	Sample Mean
Sales price	$42,374
Days on market	90.64
Bedrooms	2.59
Baths	1.27
Age	43.59
Square feet	1,099
Lot size	7,729
Garage (number of spaces)	1.02
Roof (with wood shingle)	0.2%
Basement	51.3%
Finished basement	28.3%
Fireplace	14.5%
Air conditioning	68.1%
Story (one-story design)	85.6%

Number of sales before the discovery (all three areas): 685

Number of sales after the discovery (all three areas): 707

Total sales in the contaminated area: 366

Total sales in the west control area : 645

Total sales in the east control area : 381

The data set includes 1,392 sales (see Table 1). The average price of houses in the entire sample is $42,374; the average age is 43 years; and the average size is 1,099 square feet. The contaminated area and the contiguous control areas are typical of residential areas in the CBD, consisting of small, older homes that are among the least expensive homes in the community.

Table 2 shows the average sales price, sales price per square foot, number of sales, and days on the market for properties that sold the year before and the year after the contamination discovery. The average sales price for the east control area was $46,729 before the event, and $46,183 after the event. The number of sales in this area was 192 before the event, and 189 after. The average sales price for the west control area was $43,007 before the event and $43,701 afterward. The number of sales in this area was 332 before the event, and 313 after the event.

TABLE 2   Sales Activity in All Three Sample Areas

Year Before Contamination Was Discovered:

	East Control Area	Contaminated Area	West Control Area
Number of sales	192	161	332
Mean sales price	$46,729	$36,817	$43,007
Mean price per square foot	$41.68	$36.48	$41.25
Days on market (DOM)	87	105	84

Year After Contamination Was Discovered:

	East Control Area	Contaminated Area	West Control Area
Number of sales	189	205	313
Mean sales price	$46,183	$35,801	$43,701
Mean price per square foot	$41.36	$35.43	$40.16
Days on market (DOM)	91	98	87

The average sales price in the contaminated area was $36,817 before the event, and $35,801 after. The average marketing time (DOM) actually decreased from 105 days before the event to 98 days after. The number of sales actually increased in the year after the discovery of contamination, from 161 before the event to 205 afterward.

The average sales price in the contaminated area was $36,817 before the contamination discovery, and $35,801 afterward. A two-sample t-test was used to see if the mean sales price in the pre-event sample was significantly different from the post-event sample. The results of this test show that there is no significant difference in the average sales price in the year before or year after the event (see Appendix B). The discovery of groundwater contamination and the threat of Superfund listing had absolutely no impact on the value of houses in the contaminated area.

As previously reported, commercial mortgage lending on properties within the contaminated area came to a complete stop as soon as the discovery became public information. However, residential mortgage lending continued. A breakdown of the sources of financing for houses sold in the contaminated area is presented in Table 3. It is interesting to note that less than 10% of the houses in the area were financed with conventional loans. This is not unusual for an area of lower-priced houses in older areas of the community. The results indicate that Federal Housing Administration (FHA) and Department of Veterans Affairs (VA) lenders stayed in

Chapter 7: *Groundwater Contamination*

TABLE 3 Major Sources of Mortgage Financing in the Contaminated Area

Type of Financing	Before Discovery	After Discovery
Owner	8.8%	10.2%
FHA	35.0%	34.8%
VA	11.9%	11.1%
Conventional	6.9%	5.3%
Cash	11.3%	13.5%
Loan assumption	13.6%	11.4%
Other	12.5%	13.7%

the market after the discovery of the contamination. Owner financing and cash sales increased in the period after the discovery.

Conclusion

Environmental contamination can have a dramatic impact on the value of real estate. The discovery of such contamination immediately creates uncertainty in the local market regarding such issues as how large the contaminated area is, what it will cost to clean up the problem, how long it will be before cleanup begins and costs are assessed, who will ultimately pay for the cleanup, and the stigma attached to the pollution event. Because of these uncertainties, lenders are often unwilling to make loans on properties in contaminated areas.

The results of this study indicate that the discovery of contaminated groundwater in this particular instance had no impact on the value of houses in the area. The average sales price of houses in the area, for the period of one year after the discovery was announced, was not significantly different from the average sales price in the year before the discovery. This may indicate that home buyers in the contaminated area implicitly assessed a very low probability that they would be assessed any portion of the cleanup cost, even though theoretically they could be assessed at least 1% ($220,000) of the total cost of the cleanup as a *de minimis* owner. In addition, no immediate threat to health was perceived.

Lenders in the area must have made a similar assessment that the probability of incurring any liability must be very low for single-family property owners. Local lenders immediately withdrew from lending on commercial property in the contaminated area, but continued to lend to residential borrowers in the area. The number of residential sales transactions was actually greater in the year after the discovery when compared with the year before.

In conclusion, previous authors have shown the reasons why the discovery of contamination is likely to have an adverse impact on the value of real estate located in contaminated areas. Many properties across America have experienced substantial reductions in their value due to environmental problems. This research offers empirical evidence that not all properties within a contaminated site may suffer diminished value, but this research also measures only one market's reaction at one period of time to the specific event in one local community. The market reaction in other areas could be different. However, these findings indicate that further research in this area is needed to answer questions such as, is the percentage penalty to value greater for industrial properties than for other land uses such as office, and other commercial or residential land uses in the same contaminated area, and are there specific land uses that generally do not suffer a diminished value even if they are located in a contaminated site?

The results of this study suggest that each situation is likely to be different and that expert appraisal analysis will be required to measure the unique impact on the value of each land use within a contaminated site.

Appendix A
Regression Test for General Price Appreciation in the Uncontaminated Contiguous Neighborhoods

A multiple linear regression is used to test for any general trends in price appreciation over the 25-month time period (October 1988 through November 1990) for both of the control neighborhoods. The model was constructed, such that:

$$LOGSP = f(SQFT, AGE\ LOTSIZE, STORY, GARAGE, \\ BASEMENT, FINISH, FIREPLACE, COOLING, \\ MONTH)$$

where,

$LOGSP$ = Natural log of the sales price reported in the multiple listing service records

$SQFT$ = Size of the house measured in square footage

AGE = Chronological, actual age of the house

$LOTSIZE$ = Size of the lot measured in square footage

$STORY$ = 1, if the house is all on one story
0, if the house is on more than one story

$GARAGE$ = Number of enclosed garage parking spaces

$BASEMENT$ = 1, if the house had a partial or full basement
0, if the house had no basement

$FINISH$ = 1, if the house had a finished basement
0, otherwise

$FIREPLACE$ = Number of wood-burning fireplaces in the house

$COOLING$ = 1, if the house had central air conditioning
0, otherwise

$MONTH$ = Month in which the contract was signed
1 = November 1988   25 = November 1990

A separate regression is used to analyze sales in both of the control areas to determine if the sales price is correlated with the month in which the property was sold. The results presented below indicate that there is no general change in the value of houses over the two-year period in question. The parameter estimate for the MONTH variable is not significantly different from zero in either the west or east control areas. Consequently, the data indicate that the prices are generally unchanged over the two-year period. Since no general price trend is identified in the two control samples, any change in values in the contaminated area can be attributed to the impact of the contamination discovery.

Regression Results for the Control Samples

	West Control Sample		East Control Sample	
	Parameter	**T statistic**	**Parameter**	**T statistic**
INTERCEPT	10.1069	149.37*	10.3055	99.64*
SQFT	0.0003	10.15*	0.0004	8.55*
AGE	- 0.0052	- 10.23*	- 0.0101	- 8.54*
LOTSIZE	0.00001	0.73	0.0001	3.19*
STORY	0.0685	2.40*	- 0.0127	- 0.31
GARAGE	0.0775	6.37*	0.0632	2.97*
BASEMENT	0.0533	2.29*	0.1867	5.39*
FINISH	0.0912	3.38*	0.0569	1.61
FIREPLACE	0.0155	0.63	0.0760	2.31*
COOLING	0.1696	8.58*	0.2036	7.02*
MONTH	0.0002	0.23	- 0.0018	- 0.25
F value	78.564		57.763	
P value	0.0001		0.0001	
Adjusted R-square	0.5606		0.6132	
Sample size	608		358	

* Indicates significance levels exceeding 95%.

Appendix B
Two Sample T Tests of Sales Prices in the Contaminated Area

Mean sales price before announcement: $36,817 ($N = 161$)
Mean sales price after the announcement: $35,801 ($N = 205$)

Test results

Source	Degrees of Freedom	Sum of Squares	F value	P value
Model	1	0.1506	0.84	0.3614
Error	364	65.6331		
Total	365	65.7837		

Landfills Aren't All Bad: Considerations for Real Estate Development

by Michael L. Robbins, CRE, Michele Robbins Norman, and John P. Norman

Michael L. Robbins, CRE, *is an associate professor of real estate and construction management at the University of Denver. His research and consulting interests include the valuation of wilderness and natural lands, the development of computer software for educational and professional use and the application of geographic information systems (GIS) to real estate analysis.*

Michele Robbins Norman, *completed her graduate studies at the University of Wisconsin-Madison, where she studied solid waste management in the civil and environmental engineering department. She is interested in combining her technical, environmental training with real estate analysis.*

John P. Norman, *received his graduate degree in real estate and investment analysis from the University of Wisconsin-Madison. He has assisted Robbins with several projects involving wilderness valuation and recreation feasibility analysis.*

This article originally appeared in the Fall/Winter 1991 issue of Real Estate Issues. Reproduced with the permission of Real Estate Issues; published and © by the Counselors of Real Estate (a not for profit organization), Chicago, IL. All rights reserved. Further reproduction/distribution is prohibited without the written permission of Real Estate Issues.

What? Real estate development on a landfill! Are you crazy? Well, maybe. Building near or especially on a landfill is a challenging idea that requires careful consideration of complex issues such as site use, architectural modification, safety and liability. After describing the basic components of a modern landfill and discussing some common misconceptions about landfill development, this article addresses issues of interest to the real estate developer by answering the following questions:

- Why consider development on a landfill site?
- What types of development work on a landfill?
- When in the life of a landfill is the best time for development?
- What architectural issues need to be addressed?
- What liability comes with owning a landfill property?
- What does the future hold for landfills and their subsequent development?

Components of a Modern Landfill

The term "modern landfill" refers to a facility that has been engineered so waste may be disposed on land at reasonable cost and with minimum environmental impact. A modern landfill differs greatly from an open dump because of its planned, engineered design and the daily compaction and covering of waste materials (see Figure 1).

Solid wastes placed in a landfill undergo a number of simultaneous biological, physical and chemical changes that result in the decay of organic matter.

Gases and liquids are generated throughout the decomposition of organic matter. A modern landfill is designed to control these decomposition byproducts and minimize their environmental impacts. The following paragraphs discuss the typical manner in which gases and liquids in a landfill are controlled.

Gases

Carbon dioxide and methane are the principal gases produced by the decomposition of organic waste. These gases are vented to the atmosphere in small landfills or collected for use as an energy source, which is economical only for large landfills. The movement of landfill gases typically is controlled by installing vents made of materials that are more permeable then the surrounding soils. Gas vent tubes release the gases that are generated within the landfill, and gravel barrier trenches surrounding the landfill vent any laterally moving gas that may migrate off the site (Figure 1).

FIGURE 1 Cross-Section of a Modern Landfill

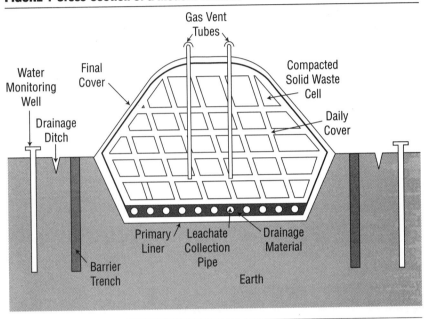

Liquids

The liquid found in landfills is called "leachate," and it arises from the decomposition of wastes and liquid that has entered the landfill from external sources such as surface drainage, percolation from rainfall and groundwater. Leachate usually contains a number of chemical constituents that can pollute groundwater; therefore, a modern landfill is designed to minimize and contain leachate.

The final cover on a landfill is a system of soils that minimizes leachate generation by limiting percolation through the top of the landfill. The final cover typically consists of topsoil which supports vegetation, a middle layer which provides additional rooting depth and a clay layer which protects roots from freezing and thawing.

Under normal conditions, leachate is found in the bottom of landfills; so this is where the major leachate containment measures are constructed. A primary liner of several feet of compacted clay on the base and sidewalls of a landfill reduces or eliminates the percolation of leachate into groundwater.

A layer of drainage material (e.g., sandy gravel) is placed over the primary liner, and a leachate collection system consisting of perforated pipes is built into this material. The leachate collection pipes usually are sloped so the leachate will collect in one low point to facilitate treatment and disposal.

Drainage ditches collect excess surface water and divert it away from the landfill to minimize potential leachate generation. Water monitoring wells around a landfill site are tested regularly to ensure that leachate has not leaked into groundwater.

Common Misconceptions
Refuse Does Not Decompose

Many people believe that waste is simply stored in a landfill and that it does not decompose. Landfills are heterogeneous; decomposition occurs in microenvironments within the landfill (some of which are more conducive to decomposition than others). While it is possible to find isolated pockets of refuse that have not decomposed, the vast majority of refuse in a landfill does decompose. Evidence of decomposition includes the generation of gas, changes in leachate which has percolated through the refuse and contains suspended or dissolved waste and the composition of refuse. Studies have shown that the extent of decomposition is directly related to the amount of moisture in the environment.[1] Thus, waste in landfills in dry, arid climates tends to decompose more slowly than waste in landfills located in temperate or wet climates. It is also important to realize that refuse does not degrade completely because refuse is the result of modern manufacturing techniques which frequently combine degradable materials with non-degradable substances.

Odor

Odor is another attribute that many people associate with completed landfills. However, properly maintained landfills emit little odor. Refuse in a modern landfill is encapsulated within a clay layer, which serves as a protective barrier between the decomposing refuse and the surrounding area and keeps odors within the landfill. Gas vent tubes positioned at regular intervals over a landfill's surface allow methane and carbon dioxide to vent freely. The minimal amount of odor emanating from these vents can be reduced further by placing burners on the vent tubes.

Ugliness

Many people expect a completed landfill to be ugly. However, landfills typically look like hills with short vegetative cover. Gas vent tubes, gas piping leading to a small building, the occasional pump truck and water monitoring wells usually are the only visible features of a completed landfill.

If landfill gas is being collected for use as an energy source, a network of pipes will lead from the landfill to a small building on the site in which the gas will be drawn, compressed and directed to a pipeline. The piping network may be above or below ground. Modern landfills have an underground leachate collection system which must be emptied periodically. The collection system empties the leachate into underground storage tanks or directs it to a nearby sewer system. The only visible aspect of leachate collection is the pump truck that regularly collects the liquid. Water monitoring wells surround the landfill area to determine whether leachate is escaping through the clay base layer and contaminating the groundwater. These wells consist of nothing more than some polyvinyl chloride (PVC) pipe sticking out of the ground.

1. Seppa, Nathan. "Reactor Landfill Study." *Wisconsin State Journal* (September 20, 1990) p.8B.

Chapter 7: *Landfills Aren't All Bad*

Why Consider Development on a Landfill Site?

Landfills constitute a temporary use of land. When carefully constructed, filled and covered, they can become valuable, developed sites. Developers should seriously consider landfill sites for two basic reasons: their location and land cost.

Location

When they are originally constructed, landfills typically are located on the fringe of urban areas, far enough away to be out of sight and mind of the general public but close enough to ensure affordable transportation of wastes. By necessity, landfills are connected with the surrounding community by a network of transportation, utilities and other services; other vacant parcels of land in the area may not have these connections.

As urban areas expand along existing infrastructure, landfill sites often fall in the path of growth and as a result become attractive properties. For example, as a city grows, low density developments and eventually housing extend beyond the urban fringe. While the landfill is in operation, most available surrounding land may be developed for ancillary uses such as shopping malls, churches and parks. As residential density increases, a market may form for an additional shopping center. After waste has decomposed and the landfill has stabilized, the landfill site provides a large parcel of land with transportation, utilities and other linkages.

Views are an important attribute of any real estate development, and the view from the top of a completed landfill should not be disregarded. The landfill siting process is such a time-consuming, laborious and politically ugly process that communities want to go through the procedure as few times as possible. Therefore, communities maximize the life of a landfill by filling it with as much refuse as possible. More garbage can be placed on a site if the elevation of the landfill is increased while the required side slopes (which vary by region) are maintained. The end result of a landfill at capacity (using modern techniques) is a meatloaf-shaped hill rather than a relatively mounded piece of property that blends in with the topography. Consequently, a completed landfill often provides a distant and encompassing view of the area.

Land Cost

As urban land use expands near a landfill, the density of development increases, and land prices rise. At the same time, the availability of vacant land declines. Landfills are considered less desirable than other vacant land and therefore are available at much lower prices. Buyers usually are not interested in landfill property because of fears of liability, concerns about public perception, lack of knowledge about landfill design and refuse decomposition, etc. However, the cost of land is reason enough to consider development of a landfill site as a potential opportunity. All real estate development is risky, and development on a landfill is no exception. However, the money saved on land costs may be used to design and construct a project that takes into account development factors and additional challenges. Consider the following examples:

- In the San Francisco area, land costs range from $500,000 to $750,000 per acre. A developer in Mountain View, California, recently paid approximately $25,000 per acre for a 700-acre parcel that had been the landfilling site for San Francisco's garbage for 13 years. The developer has turned the land into Shoreline Park, which includes a golf course, amphitheater and sailing pond. Revenues from greens fees, theater ticket sales and other park uses are being supplemented by the sale of methane to utility companies.[2]

- Near Columbus, Ohio, a developer is transforming an 80-acre site that includes a 22-acre completed landfill into an industrial park. The proximity of the site to an interstate highway and airport make it an attractive industrial location. Rather than allow the property to remain unused, the city favors development of the landfill site and is contemplating the extension of a road and construction of a bridge to make the property even more accessible to the airport. The developer paid the city $400,000 for the 80 acres ($5,000 per acre) and has nearly recovered his land cost by selling nine acres to an auto parts warehouse operation for $345,000 ($38,000 per acre). Nearby industrial land is selling for between $62,000 and $65,000 per acre.[3]

Just because landfill sites can be purchased for much less cost than nearby property does not necessarily mean that a landfill site is a bargain. Several costs must be considered when acquiring a landfill site, such as the costs of environmental studies, possible cleanup and architectural modifications. Only if the gap between the price of an alternative property and the landfill is larger than these anticipated additional costs will landfill development be advantageous (see Figure 2). It also must be kept in mind that the cost advantage must be large enough to reduce significantly the potential risks associated with landfill property development.

What Types of Development Work on a Landfill?
Development Constraints

When contemplating landfill development, government regulations, waste type and landfill design and condition must be considered. When a landfill

---

2. Pierson, John. "Landfills Become Parks As Refuse Goes Green." *Wall Street Journal* (December 31, 1990) p. 9.
3. Mollard, Beth. "Former Landfill Site Offers Low Price, Special Problems." *Business First, Columbus* (February 11, 1991) pp. 1–8.

FIGURE 2 The Land-Cost Gap

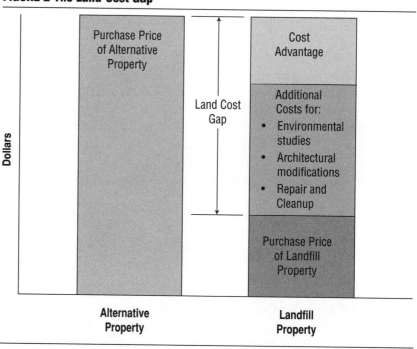

Chapter 7: *Landfills Aren't All Bad*

is closed, it is covered with layers of soil to form a cap. For decomposition to occur as planned, the cap and the underlying refuse cells must remain intact. Accordingly, the purpose of government regulation of closed landfills is to preserve the integrity of the site. In most cases, government agencies require approval of any use of the site other than undisturbed refuse decomposition. Some uses, such as building structures on the site, require special approval by government agencies. Recently, however, governments have been approving a variety of developments on landfill sites.

The type of waste deposited in a landfill also determines the options available for reuse of the site. Municipal waste is subject to biological decomposition within a landfill. During this process, methane is generated by microorganisms as they break down organic material. Methane migrates to permeable areas, and if allowed to collect in those areas, the gas may become explosive. Municipal waste also is subject to settlement. As refuse degrades, the landfill site will settle between 5% and 15%. In cases of poorly compacted refuse, landfill sites have settled as much as 50%.[4] Most settling occurs in the landfill's first five years (in moist climates); however, long-term settling also occurs. Different parts of a landfill are created at different times; so various areas may be undergoing different stages of decomposition simultaneously. These varying stages of decomposition can cause differential settlement.

Other types of waste pose fewer potential development problems. Landfills created with foundry sand, fly ash and demolition debris may be suitable for sophisticated development for two principal reasons. These landfills contain wastes that consist of tightly compacted materials; therefore, they are more stable and less susceptible to settlement, and they have good load-bearing capacities for structures. Also, because the waste they contain has low organic composition, the landfills do not produce methane gas.

Finally, the design and condition of a landfill affect its end use. A real estate developer is always interested in decreasing exposure to risk. One of the most basic forms of risk reduction is to gain more knowledge of the situation. Uncertainty can be reduced if the developer understands the design, construction and maintenance of a landfill site. With an understanding of the design and refuse composition of a particular landfill, a developer can eliminate non-conforming uses and recognize the modifications (and their associated costs) that may be needed for alternative uses.

Various Landfill End Uses

The most common use of a former municipal waste landfill is as open space, often with light recreational facilities such as walking and biking trails, softball and soccer fields and golf courses. Because settlement of a landfill is uneven in the first few years following completion, initial development should require non-permanent and yielding materials. After waste has stabilized, which may take ten years or more, development may include paved areas for parking lots, outdoor storage, tennis courts and roads. The shape of the landfill may be transformed by massive grading and berming efforts using fill so as not to disrupt the integrity of the landfill. Ski hills and toboggan runs have been constructed on transformed landfill sites.

Buildings for residential and commercial use may be constructed on such sites after the land has stabilized and the waste has finished decomposing and ceased producing methane. Depending on the climate, landfill design and other factors, it may take up to 25 years or more for full decomposition.

4. Ham, Robert K. "Landfill Gas, Leachate, and Related Problems." p. 20.

Buildings may be constructed on a recently closed landfill using one of two methods (see Figure 3). First, pilings may be driven down through the landfill to support the structure. Because the pilings will disrupt the integrity of the site, government approval for development and guidance during construction is necessary. Second, virgin soil on which to build may be maintained within the landfill area. This method requires the developer and/or landfill designer to choose the specific area for the development and create the landfill around it.

When building on a recently closed landfill, developers must give serious consideration to land settlement and methane generation. The following is an exciting example of landfill reuse.

> In Albany, New York, a new public works complex was built on a completed landfill using the piling method noted above. The $7 million project consists of a 15,000-square-foot office building and adjoining 49,000-square-foot garage. The complex was built on the south side of the landfill where construction and demolition debris had been deposited. Early borings showed that the landfill was 20 to 25 feet deep and bedrock was encountered at 30 feet. The short distance to bedrock and the inert nature of the fill made this project feasible.
>
> To prepare the site, contractors leveled and compacted the rubble, using a crane to drop 20-ton weights from a height of 60 feet. The weights, dropped ten times in each location, formed a 20-foot grid of approximately ten-foot craters. Bulldozers then packed down two feet of gravel before an ironing compaction pass with wider weights further compressed the upper five feet. The foundation was set with 12-inch diameter concrete piles driven 30 feet down to bedrock.
>
> Constructing the public works complex on the landfill solved two major problems for the city of Albany. First, the cost of the new complex absorbed the $1 million required to close and cap the landfill. Second, the landfill site provided the necessary acreage and linkage[5] to the surrounding area. For years, the department of public works had maintained scattered office space requiring public vehicles to park all over the city. As part of its ongoing capital improvements, Albany sought a new state-of-the art home for the public works department in an ideal location for service to the city.

When in the Life of a Landfill Is the Best Time for Development?

The decomposition process within a landfill suggests that there is no "best time" to develop a landfill site. In general, landfill development should be postponed until the site has been completely capped and vegetation has grown. Good vegetative cover controls erosion and minimizes leachate by

---

5. Nealon, George, and David L. Hansen. "A New Public Works Complex on an Old Landfill." *Public Works* (April 1991) pp. 46–47.

FIGURE 3

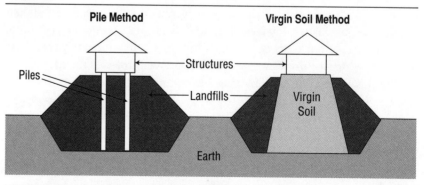

Chapter 7: *Landfills Aren't All Bad*

allowing the plants to utilize moisture on the landfill's surface through evapotranspiration. Vegetation also makes the completed landfill more visually compatible with the surrounding area.

The time to develop such a site depends on the type of development and the type of waste contained in the landfill. Parks and projects that can withstand settlement can pay less attention to timing than more complicated developments. Inert waste (fly ash, foundry sand and demolition debris) may begin soon after landfill closure because these landfills do not settle or generate methane. With municipal waste, however, timing of development is a more difficult issue.

In a municipal waste landfill, waste must undergo several stages of decomposition before methane is generated, creating a lag phase of about six months to two or three years. The duration of active gas generation appears to range from five years in warm, moist climates to 20 years in dry climates.[6] To be as safe as possible, a project should not be started until methane generation has ceased and the refuse is stable. However, these conditions are difficult to judge and may take several decades to occur.

Estimating Decomposition

Two methods may be used to estimate the state of decomposition in a landfill: gas pump tests and cellulose to lignin ratios. Together, these analyses determine how quickly a landfill can be developed for a particular end use.

The gas pump test measures changes in pressure in gas that has been pumped from a landfill to evaluate the potential of the refuse to produce methane or to determine how much more methane the refuse is expected to generate. Data from the pump test must be extrapolated into the future for interpretation, and they are subject to wide variability.

Refuse stability is determined by calculating the cellulose to lignin ratio of refuse samples collected from many different locations and depths in a landfill. Cellulose and lignin are specific organic materials that occur simultaneously in nature and are present in fresh refuse. Cellulose (in the form of paper and paper-related products) is the major chemically identifiable constituent of municipal refuse. Recently, data on the chemical composition of refuse have been published, and these data have been used in a mass balance analysis to calculate a methane potential for each chemical constituent. The results indicate that cellulose and its related hemicellulose fraction account for 91% of the methane potential.[7] Cellulose, therefore, can be expected to degrade during the decomposition process and convert to methane. Lignin does not degrade under the anaerobic (without free oxygen) conditions required for methane production; therefore, the ratio of cellulose to lignin changes with time as waste decomposition occurs. Studies that analyzed refuse samples from landfills across the United States revealed that the cellulose to lignin ratio decreased with time as the waste decomposed. The ratio was approximately 4.0 for fresh refuse, 0.9 to 1.2 for active and partially stabilized landfill and 0.2 for relatively well-stabilized landfill.[8]

A landfill site can be developed in stages that take into account the decomposition process and its associated side effects. The following example shows how this method may be used.

> Salt Meadows Park in Fairfield, Connecticut, is being constructed in stages on 300 acres that contain a wastewater treatment facility, two landfills, a public works garage and a refuse transfer station. The first stage of develop-

6. Ham, Robert K., and Morton A. Barlaz. "Measurement and Prediction of Landfill Gas Quality and Quantity." Paper presented by *ISWA International Symposium, "Process, Technology, and Environmental Impact of Sanitary Landfills."* Cagliari, Sardinia, Italy (October 20–23, 1987) p. 22.

7. Barlaz, Morton A., et al. "Mass Balance Analysis of Anaerobically Decomposed Refuse." *Journal of Environmental Engineering* (December 1989) pp. 1095–1096.

8. Bookter, Todd J., and Robert K. Ham. "Stabilization of Solid Waste in Landfills." *Journal of the Environmental Engineering Division,* ASCE (December 1982) p. 1099.

ment involves constructing walking and bicycling paths (with gravel and stone dust) and picnic areas on the undulating terrain of one of the landfill sites. The next stage involves an outdoor amphitheater that will be terraced with fairly steep, gently sloping and somewhat level grassy areas. Years into the future when the landfill becomes more stable, a stage, bandshell, dressing rooms, storage rooms and restrooms will be added to the amphitheater.[9]

What Architectural Issues Need to Be Addressed?

Any type of development on a landfill requires an architectural design that specifically addresses the characteristics and limitations of the site. Architectural designs must consider such issues as methane generation, settlement, water runoff and long-term care of the site.

Methane

Gases normally diffuse upward. However, since the landfill cover is relatively impermeable due to its high clay content, good compaction and possible wet or frozen conditions, gases travel laterally until they reach an escape location. To prevent methane from moving into structures built on a landfill site, gas barriers and gas channeling devices must be constructed. These gas protection measures may simply involve building a structure on a plastic liner that is positioned over a layer of gravel. Because gravel is permeable, it captures methane that is traveling toward the building. The plastic liner prevents methane in the gravel layer from seeping upward. Gas protection measures also may be quite sophisticated as is shown in the following example.

> The Albany Public Works Complex (mentioned previously) has a unique design for protecting against the release of methane gas. The 15,000-square-foot office area has been constructed over a four-foot crawl space plenum (a space in which the air pressure is greater than that of the outside atmosphere) for venting any methane gas that may escape from the landfill. Gas buildup in the plenum can be detected by manually checking gas detectors. More importantly, a methane concentration that reaches 20% of the gas' explosive limit sounds an alarm and triggers automatic aeration of the plenum to remove the methane within five minutes. Not since the building opened on June 8, 1990, or at any time before, has it been necessary to clear the plenum of gas.
>
> A three-fold system protects the 49,000-square-foot garage area of the complex. Under the garage's concrete floor is a layer of sand that covers a geotextile fabric (a non-woven PVC barrier layer). Below the fabric is a pipe system that collects methane from a one-foot layer of smooth, washed stones. Gas sensors in the layer of stones detect the concentration of methane, and they will sound an alarm if methane reaches 20% of its lower explosive limit. Positive pressure blowers or negative pressure suction then will evacuate the gas within 30 minutes. Beneath the stones is a PVC gas barrier membrane that can stretch 700% before it tears. The PVC layer prevents methane from moving upward. A ring of gas vents at the building's periphery vents any gas that moves laterally.[10]

Settlement

Landfill settlement is another issue that must be addressed in the architectural design of a development. Two foundation methods (piles and the use of virgin soil) for building structures, without waiting for settlement to cease, were described previously. If development can be postponed until

9. Arent, Karen A. "The Creation of a Park." *Public Works* (May 1989) p. 59.
10. Nealon, George, and David L. Hansen. "A New Public Works Complex on an Old Landfill." *Public Works* (April 1991) p. 47.

Chapter 7: *Landfills Aren't All Bad*

the refuse has stabilized, floating foundations may be used. Also, because connections of utilities are subject to shearing from differential settlement, utility couplings must be flexible.

Water Runoff

Water that runs off buildings and parking lots constructed on a landfill should be collected and routed to the sewer system. If not collected and rerouted, the water will slowly seep through the landfill's cap and into the refuse to create excess leachate which is costly to treat and dispose and increases the potential for groundwater contamination.

Long-Term Care

Developments on landfills must be designed and constructed so as not to interfere with the long-term care operations of the site. Typically in the United States a landfill must be monitored and maintained for a 20- to 30-year period after closure. Long-term care involves monitoring groundwater, collecting and treating leachate, monitoring and controlling gas migration as long as necessary and maintaining the slope of and vegetation on the final cover. Development projects must be designed to allow access to particular areas of the landfill, such as leachate storage tanks, water monitoring wells and gas vents, so the long-term care of the landfill can be performed.

What Liability Comes with Owning Landfill Property?

Landfills are designed to accept certain types of refuse. A landfill may accept relatively inert material, such as fly ash or foundry sand, or it may accept only hazardous (or potentially hazardous) materials. Most landfills fall between these two extremes and receive normal community refuse. Today's modern landfills are engineered specifically for the types of waste they receive, and they are designed to minimize potential hazards to the surrounding environment. However, no matter how well-designed and operated, a landfill still may cause surface and subsurface contamination. Waste contained in a properly maintained landfill is not inherently hazardous but may become so under certain circumstances (e.g., excessive settling may cause leachate collection pipes to crack or break, allowing leachate to contaminate the area). If contamination occurs, some party will be held responsible for repair and cleanup costs. Two federal laws are most relevant to the potential liability involved with the investment in, operation on or development of a landfill site.

Resource Conservation and Recovery Act

The Resource Conservation and Recovery Act (RCRA), administered by the U.S. Environmental Protection Agency (USEPA), regulates the generation, transportation, storage and disposal of hazardous wastes. The purpose of this legislation is to protect human beings from the dangers of illegal dumping of hazardous waste. The act applies primarily to businesses that deal with hazardous materials on a daily basis. Under this law, only landfills approved by the USEPA may be used for hazardous waste disposal.

Superfund

The Comprehensive Environmental Response, Compensation and Liability Act (CERCLA), also known as Superfund, was enacted in 1980 (and revised in the Superfund Amendments and Reauthorization Act [SARA] of 1986) to provide funds that state governments and the USEPA can use, in emergency situations, to contain and cleanup hazardous waste contamination. The act authorizes the USEPA to impose cleanup (or remedial action) responsibility on property owners and/or operators. If the cleanup order is ignored, the USEPA can perform the cleanup itself and bill responsible parties for the cost. If cleanup is necessary and the responsible parties cannot be found or forced to do the cleanup at their own expense, the site is placed on the USEPA's National Priority List. Sites on this list are cleaned up in order as determined by the potential harm and human health risk they impose.

Three forms of liability for site remediation exist. Strict liability always exists and is imposed on any entity (e.g., person, partnership or corporation) related to the property as an owner, operator, transporter of or generator of hazardous material. The liability is imposed regardless of whether the entity knew of the problem or was even at fault. If more than one party is responsible, joint liability is imposed. The USEPA can require cleanup costs to be covered by any of the involved parties, including lenders. If a lender has participated in the operation of (or continues to operate after foreclosure) a property that is named by the USEPA , the lender will be a likely target for reimbursement of cleanup costs. This fact has caused many lenders to rethink commercial and industrial loan underwriting policies. Finally, liability is retroactive in that all previous owners and operators of a property may be held liable, even if the problem occurred before the enactment of CERCLA.

Exceptions to Superfund's strict liability are limited. The three exceptions (also known as the "Third Party Defense") are summarized as follows:

1. If the contamination was caused solely by an act of God or war.

2. If contamination "was caused solely by an act or omission of a third party other than an employee or agent of the new owner or other than one whose act or omission occurs in connection with a contractual relationship, existing directly or indirectly with the new owner."

3. If the new owner "establishes by a preponderance of the evidence that he exercised due care with respect to the hazardous substance concerned, taking into consideration the characteristics of such hazardous substance in light of all relevant facts and circumstances, and he took precautions against foreseeable acts or omissions of any such third party and the consequences that could foreseeably result from such acts or omissions."[11]

Given the limited legal defenses against liability, anyone contemplating the purchase or use of a landfill site must do everything possible to protect himself *before committing to anything*.

Suggestions for Risk Reduction

Risk has been defined as the difference between expectations and realizations.[12] Expectations are based on assumptions. The obvious method for reducing the risk of liability is to do everything within legal, financial and time limitations to "assume" as little as possible. In the case of landfill development, the site itself holds a set of specialized assumptions that must be confronted. Therefore, the first step is to learn as much as possible about the assumptions associated with a landfill site. The following is a list of suggested actions.

11. Buonicore, Anthony J. "Environmental Liabilities in Financing Real Estate." *The Real Estate Finance Journal* (Summer 1989) p. 19.

12. Graaskamp, James A., Lecture #1 from the Real Estate Process course at the University Wisconsin-Madison.

Chapter 7: *Landfills Aren't All Bad*

I. Research the site history.

   A. Who were the previous owners?

   B. What were the previous uses? Check to see if any previous use involved the generation, storage (including underground tanks) or disposal of hazardous material listed by the USEPA. If so, were all operations performed according to government regulations? Are there any records of contamination? If so, how was the situation remediated?

II. Find out if the property or surrounding property is (or may be) designated by USEPA or the state as a cleanup site.

III. Review landfill design and construction.

   A. Design.

   1. Who designed the landfill? What is their track record?

   2. Was the landfill designed according to regulations? Were any exceptions made for special conditions?

   3. What type of waste was the landfill designed to handle?

   B. Construction.

   1. Who constructed the landfill? What is their track record?

   2. Did the construction of the landfill follow the design? Were any design revisions necessary?

IV. Review the owner and management history of the site.

   A. Has the owner or manager been cited for any violations regarding the operation or safety of the landfill? For example:

   1. Groundwater contamination?

   2. Improper daily cover?

   3. Complaints about odors?

   4. Violations for accepting wastes other than those types approved for the site (e.g., a municipal landfill taking hazardous waste)?

   B. Are management practices well documented?

   C. What is the owner's and the manager's track record? Have they owned or managed other landfills? If so, how have they performed in the past?

V. Determine long-term care responsibility: Who is currently maintaining the site? Will they continue to do so?

VI. Assess the fit of the project to:

   A. Physical attributes: Is the site suitable for the development, considering such factors as size, shape, slope, topography, soil conditions and drainage characteristics?

   B. Legal/political attributes: Is the property zoned for the intended use? If not, what is the potential for changing the zoning classification? Is there likely to be opposition to the proposed development?

   C. Linkage attributes: Does the site have the necessary access and utilities?

   D. Environmental attributes: How will the proposed project affect the landfill and the surrounding environment? For example, will excess weight disturb the cap? Will runoff from a parking lot overload the surrounding drainage systems?

  E. Dynamic attributes (people's perception): How will the community respond to the proposed development? How will the intended market react to a landfill site?

 VII. Hire a qualified environmental engineer to address the following issues:

  A. Does contamination exist on (or near) the property in the soil, water or air?

  B. If not, what is the potential for contamination from the landfill site and neighboring properties?

  C. If so, what would be the cost of repair according to federal, state and local specifications?

As a final precaution, indemnification clauses, drafted by a lawyer familiar with environmental litigation, should be included in development contracts. Although indemnification clauses do not release owners and operators of the property from the strict liability mentioned above, these clauses can be enforced to recover the cost of cleanup.

What Does the Future Hold for Landfills and Their Subsequent Development?

The function of a landfill will change in the near future due to the practice of integrated waste management, which involves the coordinated use of waste reduction, recycling, treatment and disposal systems to minimize environmental impact and maximize resource utilization at a reasonable cost.[13] One result of integrated waste management is that a landfill will no longer be considered a final resting place for *all* material but a waste decomposition system.

Landfills will always be a necessary component of the integrated waste management system, because there always will be a residue that cannot be recycled, burned or composted. Estimates indicate that if waste were reduced by all possible methods, 50% of the landfill volume still would be needed.[14]

Up to this point, landfills have progressed from the old town dump to today's modern, sanitary landfills because of reactions to environmental problems. It is anticipated that future landfill design will be proactive in nature. Research on refuse decomposition has revealed two principal methods for enhancing decomposition.

Leachate Recycling

Leachate recycling collects leachate from the base of a landfill and pumps it to the landfill's surface where it is injected into the cap. This method maintains a high moisture content throughout the landfill, increasing the rate of waste decomposition. It is expected that leachate recycling will greatly reduce the time necessary for complete decomposition of landfill waste. As a result, development of a landfill site may be possible in 10 to 15 years instead of 20 or 30 years.

Waste Segregation

Some types of waste are more conducive to degradation in a landfill than others. For this reason, future landfills may specialize in specific types of

13. Ham, Robert K. "Sanitary Landfill State-of-the-Art." A paper presented at the *2nd International Landfill Symposium*, Sardinia, Italy (1989) p.1.

14. Ham, Robert K. "Sanitary Landfill State-of-the-Art." A paper presented at the *2nd International Landfill Symposium*, Sardinia, Italy (1989) p. 2.

waste. One kind of landfill may contain inert matter, while another may be like a reactor in which "refuse is kept moist, allowed to decompose, and eventually is dug up and used as compost."[15]

While these enhancement methods have been used in laboratories, they have not yet been applied to full-scale landfills for long-term monitoring and direct evaluation of results. Strict government regulations and liability issues in the United States are impediments to testing and practicing these innovative concepts in landfill disposal. For this reason, Europe is far ahead of the United States in applying modern landfilling techniques and ideas. The lack of research and development funding from federal and state governments and private industry also has curtailed the trial of new ideas regarding decomposition enhancement. Current research and development efforts have improved past design problems, and more rigorous design standards have been developed. Still, future landfill designs (most likely from Europe) will treat landfills as reactors for quickly degrading refuse, promoting gas use, reducing environmental impacts and allowing for faster development of a completed landfill site.

Conclusion

As well-located, developable urban parcels become scarce, landfill sites grow more desirable. Problems associated with the development of landfill sites, such as market perception, lender uncertainty, government regulation and oversight and exposure to liability, are not insurmountable.

This article proposes that modern landfills are temporary land uses and that, following an appropriate period of utilization, redevelopment of a landfill site is not only possible but desirable. Technology is having a significant impact on the duration of the temporary nature of a modern landfill. As the temporary use period is reduced (from 25 or 30 years to less than 10 years), the adaptive reuse considerations of a landfill site fall within the normative time horizons of most large-scale development plans.

With insight, care and craftsman-like diligence, a modern landfill site can be transformed from an underutilized mound of dirt and refuse to an economically efficient real estate asset that is beneficial to the consumer, the community and the developer.

15. Seppa, Nathan. "Reactor Landfills Studied." *Wisconsin State Journal* (September 20, 1990) p. 8B.

Bibliography

Arent, Karen A. "The Creation of a Park." *Public Works* 120 (May 1989): 58–60.

Barlaz, Morton A. et al. "Mass Balance Analysis of Anaerobically Decomposed Refuse." *Journal of Environmental Engineering* 115 (Dec 1989): 1088–1102.

Barlaz, Morton A. et al. "Methane Production from Municipal Refuse: A Review of Enhancement Techniques and Microbial Dynamics." *Critical Reviews in Environmental Control* 19 (1990): 557–584.

Bleich, Donald H. et al. "An Evaluation of the Impact of a Well- Designed Landfill on Surrounding Property Values." *The Appraisal Journal* 59 (Apr 1991): 247–252.

Bookter, Todd J. and Robert K. Ham. "Stabilization of Solid Waste in Landfills." *Journal of the Environmental Engineering Division, ASCE* 108 (Dec 1982): 1089–1100.

Buonicore, Anthony J. "Environmental Liabilities in Financing Real Estate." *The Real Estate Finance Journal* 5 (Sum 1989): 18–25.

Ham, Robert K. "Landfill Gas, Leachate, and Related Problems." 1–23.

Ham, Robert K. "Sanitary Landfill State-of-the-Art." Paper presented at *2nd International Landfill Symposium,* Sardinia, Italy (1989).

Ham, Robert K. and Morton A. Barlaz. "Measurement and Prediction of Landfill Gas Quality and Quantity." Paper presented at ISWA International Symposium, *"Process, Technology, and Environmental Impact of Sanitary Landfills."* Cagliari, Sardinia, Italy (Oct 20–23, 1987).

Harper, Stephen R. and Frederick G. Pohland. "Landfills: Lessening Environmental Impacts." *Civil Engineering* 58 (Nov 1988): 66–69.

Magnuson, Anne. "New Uses for Old Landfills." Waste Age 22 (April 1991): 46–47.

McGregor, Gregor I. "Landowner Liability for Hazardous Waste." *The Journal of Real Estate Development* 4 (Winter 1989): 13–27.

McMahan, John. "Environmental Hazards and Real Estate." Real Estate Issues 14 (Spring/ Summer 1989): 1–6.

Mollard, Beth. "Former Landfill Site Offers Low Price, Special Problems." *Business First, Columbus* 7 (Feb 11, 1991): 1–8.

Nealon, George and David L. Hansen. "A New Public Works Complex on an Old Landfill." *Public Works* 122 (Apr 1991): 46–47.

Norman, Michele R. *Chemical Characterization of Refuse and Leachate and Gas Generation at the Fresh Kills Landfill,* University of Wisconsin-Madison, Dept. of Civil and Environmental Engineering, M.S. thesis (1991).

Olsen, Ralph K. "Hazardous Waste Sites." *The Appraisal Journal* 57 (Apr 1989): 233–236.

Peavy, Howard S., et al. *Environmental Engineering* (New York: McGraw-Hill Book Company, 1985).

Pierson, John. "Landfills Become Parks as Refuse Goes Green." *Wall Street Journal* (Dec 31, 1990): 9.

Seppa, Nathan. "Reactor Landfills Studied," *Wisconsin State Journal* (Sept 20, 1990): 8B.

Tchobanoglous, George, et al. *Solid Wastes Engineering Principles and Management Issues* (New York: McGraw-Hill Book Company, 1977).

Thompson, Stephanie. "Landfill Turned Into Park." *American City and County* 106 (Jan 1991): 22.

Wilson, David G. (ed). *Handbook of Solid Waste Management.* New York: Van Nostrand Reinhold Company, 1977.

Wilson, Sandy. "A Landfill by Any Other Name May Be a Development Site." *The Business Journal, Milwaukee* 7 (Apr 9, 1990): 8–10.

Sick Commercial Buildings: What Appraisers Need To Know

by Krisandra Guidry, PhD

Due to the Arab oil embargo of the 1970s, builders and architects started designing high efficiency work environments in order to conserve energy. Many existing buildings were renovated to meet the new design specifications. As a result, the exchange of indoor air and outdoor air was reduced in many of these buildings. Unfortunately, toxic chemicals (as well as biological contaminants) were present in the building and unable to escape, thus affecting the health of its occupants. These structures and new buildings constructed according to energy conservation specifications are said to be afflicted with "sick building syndrome" (SBS). This form of indoor air pollution[1] is of great concern for property owners, tenants, builders, real estate maintenance firms, and appraisers. It is estimated that 30% of nonresidential buildings suffer from an indoor air quality problem.

What Is a Sick Building?

According to the Environmental Protection Agency (EPA), a building is sick if at least 20% of its occupants suffer persistent headaches and/or eye and mucus membrane irritation that are relieved when they leave the building.[2] Additional symptoms provided through anecdotal evidence include frequent colds, flu and respiratory infections, dizziness, fatigue, short-term memory loss, and hypersensitivity to pollutants. The effect of long-term exposure to a sick building is unknown.

Regulation

It would seem likely that the regulation of commercial indoor air quality would be the domain of the Environmental Protection Agency (EPA)[3] and/or the Occupational Safety and Health Administration (OSHA). However, it is not; there are no specific federal laws governing indoor air quality. OSHA proposed regulations in 1994, but was strongly opposed by many real estate professionals who cited the cost of implementation at close to $8 billion.[4] The American Society of Heating, Refrigerating and Air Conditioning Engineers (ASHRAE) has been the lead professional

Krisandra Guidry, PhD, is an associate professor of finance at Nicholls State University, Thibodaux, Louisiana, teaching real estate courses in the College of Business. She received her PhD from Louisiana State University, Baton Rouge. Her research on various real estate topics has been published in several academic and professional journals. Contact: (985) 448-4232.

This article originally appeared in the January 2002 issue of The Appraisal Journal.

---

1. Other concerns such as asbestos contamination, lead exposure, and radon gas are not discussed in this article.
2. Stanley J. Marks, "Trouble in the Air: Sick Buildings Are a Legal Time Bomb for Landlords," *Los Angeles Business Journal* (April 13, 1992): 14.
3. The EPA lost a $950,000 lawsuit brought by its own employees for poor indoor air quality.
4. Nick Anatasi, "Sick Buildings, Simple Cures," *Long Island Business News* (November 13, 1998): 2.

organization for developing and recommending ventilation standards and guidelines for acceptable indoor air quality in North America. ASHRAE currently recommends (as of 1989) that ventilation systems operate at an exchange rate (exchange of indoor air with outdoor air) of 20 cubic feet per minute (cfm) per occupant. The ASHRAE standard has been upheld by numerous courts and is followed by most construction professionals. However, this standard is not applied retroactively and does not apply to buildings erected prior to 1989.[5]

How Does a Building Become Sick?

The following reasons have been suggested as to why some buildings are afflicted with SBS:

Building Design

Builders and architects design high efficiency buildings to conserve energy. Cracks and crevices are tightly sealed to reduce the loss of airflow, extra heavy insulation is installed, and buildings have few, if any, windows that are operational. Unfortunately, toxic chemicals and biological contaminants, if present in such "tight buildings," are unable to escape. Older buildings are also susceptible to SBS, especially if they have been renovated to include modern energy-saving measures. Indoor air quality problems are even worse in climates with high humidity and in winter when buildings are sealed tighter and indoor air temperatures are higher.

Ventilation Systems

Problems with ventilation systems are often the cause of SBS. These problems include improper operation of the system, outdoor pollution, and inadequate maintenance of the system.

Improper Operation. According to the *Los Angeles Business Journal,* most HVAC systems were designed to provide 15 cfm of outside air for each building occupant. Conservation efforts of the 1970s reduced the amount to 5 cfm.[6] However, long after the energy crisis was over, many building owners, landlords, and real estate management firms have continued to operate their HVAC systems at 5cfm in order to decrease operating expenses and thus increase profits.

Outdoor Pollution. The introduction of outside air into a building through its ventilation system dilutes and flushes out the concentration of indoor contaminants. However, if the outdoor air is also polluted, the indoor air quality problem is exacerbated. Such pollution may be introduced in the following ways: motor vehicle exhausts drawn into outdoor air intakes or through elevator shafts from lower level parking garages, local exhaust ducts or boiler chimneys vented nearby and upwind of outdoor air intakes, failure of flue gases to rise due to strong negative pressures in the building, construction and road work contamination of intake air, gasoline fumes from leaking underground storage tanks and sewer gases, and emissions from pesticides.[7]

Inadequate Maintenance of Systems. Typical HVAC system maintenance deficiencies that may contribute to an indoor air quality problem include contaminated air filters, dirty duct liners and heat transfer coils, clogged

---

5. Thad Godish, *Sick Buildings: Definition, Diagnosis and Mitigation* (Boca Raton, Florida: Lewis Publishers, 1995): 352.

6. Marks, 14.

7. Godish, 81.

Chapter 7: *Sick Commercial Buildings*

condensate drains, dirty air plenum spaces (that foster microbial growth), insufficient water treatment procedures in cooling towers and humidifier systems, and inoperable equipment and controls.[8] Additional factors that may hamper the efficient operation of an HVAC system include placing articles on top of HVAC units and blocking airflow, blocking supply and return grilles with furniture, and accumulating dust and dirt within occupied spaces and on light fixtures.

Indoor Contaminants

Toxic gases and chemicals released from synthetic materials and office equipment may be emitted into a tight building's indoor environment with no place to go. Biological contaminants also cannot escape, and cigarette smoke further complicates matters. Furthermore, inefficient or improperly maintained HVAC systems may be recirculating these contaminants, spreading them to all parts of the building.

Synthetic Materials and Office Equipment. Synthetic materials used to construct and furnish buildings may lead to sick building syndrome. Plywood, paneling, drapes, upholstery, glues, particle board, and fiberboard furniture are particularly susceptible to a process known as "outgassing." They continually release chemicals such as formaldehyde, carbon monoxide, and a mixture of volatile organic compounds (VOCs)[9] into the air. Perhaps the single largest contributor to indoor air pollution is floor covering, which is typically of two types: fabric carpeting or vinyl flooring. These types of floor coverings also outgas due to their composition, but the effect is pervasive and multifold because they are used in such large quantities and have a large surface to volume ratio. Furthermore, the bonding agents used to install such floor covering and the chemicals used to clean them are also toxic.

Office equipment and materials used in the workplace have been documented as contributors to SBS. Copy machines and laser printers release a significant amount of VOCs and ozone into the air. Improper storage of cleaning compounds and chemicals used in office supplies (toners, ink, felt tip markers, etc.) heighten the problem.

Biological Contaminants. Biological contaminants such as mold, bacteria, fungi, and viruses may be spread by humidifiers, air-conditioning units, drip pans, vent pipes, and human-to-human contact. The problem is compounded in buildings with fabric floor coverings—carpets and rugs may provide a harbor for biological contaminants. A variety of illnesses may result, such as hypersensitivity pneumonitis, humidifier fever, Legionnaire's disease, and asthma.

Smoking. "The smoking of tobacco products in indoor environments represents a potentially significant environmental exposure and SBS symptom risk."[10] Several thousand different chemicals have been identified in tobacco smoke, such as carbon monoxide, carbon dioxide, benzene, tar, and nicotine. The detrimental health effects of smoking (on the smoker) are well documented. Furthermore, exhaled smoke and smoke from burning cigarettes expose nonsmokers to the dangers of secondhand smoke.

---

8. Patricia A. Kelsey, "Many Theories are Being Explored for Causes of Sick Buildings," *Air Conditioning, Heating, and Refrigeration News* (November 13, 1989): 4.

9. Volatile organic compounds (VOCs) include aliphatic hydrocarbons; aromatic hydrocarbons; halogenated hydrocarbons (primarily chlorine or fluorine); and oxygenated hydrocarbons such as aldehydes, alcohols, ketones, esters, ethers, and acids. Exposure to VOCs in the range found in many buildings can cause sensory irritation and even neurotoxic effects in humans (Godish, 148, 162.)

10. Godish, 37.

Costs

There are many different costs associated with sick buildings. The most obvious is the cost associated with curing an indoor air quality problem. Depending on the pervasiveness of the problem and the complexity of the solution, a remedy can cost a few hundred dollars to tens of thousands of dollars, or more.[11] However, the costs of curing are small when compared to the loss of profitability associated with sick buildings. Employees in sick buildings suffer from low productivity, increased absenteeism, poor morale, and high turnover. Employers are then faced with increased operating costs in the form of sick leave pay and worker compensation costs.

When a sick building cannot be made healthy, the owner and/or tenant faces the cost of relocating and the possibility of higher rent at the new location. When placing a sick building on the market for sale, an owner should be aware that a potential buyer may require that the building be cured before title changes hands or demand a deep discount from the selling price. Likewise, potential tenants may require concessions and hold the landlord responsible for cleanup.

Legal liability for employee exposure to indoor contaminants would likely involve legal fees, court costs, and punitive damages. Potential defendants in such cases may include owners/operators of the property (landowner, lessee, sub-lessee, and the property management) and those responsible for the design and construction of the building (architects, builders, contractors, and sub-contractors). If the building is judged to have SBS, plaintiffs may claim that the appraiser was negligent and should have discovered the problem during the valuation process.

Appraisers need to know that they too could be the subject of lawsuits brought by clients and/or occupants of the building.[12] Appraisers are obligated to identify a building's problems and make recommendations for remedies to clients and all others who use appraisal report information. Many appraisal forms such as those for Freddie Mac, Fannie Mae, and FHA have sections that ask about environmental hazards; some even have a specific comment requirement regarding excess moisture (a contributor to the growth of mold). According to Knopfler and Robertson, a California law firm involved in environmental cases, potential causes of action against appraisers may include professional malpractice, breach of implied or expressed warranties, breach of contract, fraud, failure to disclose in the sale of property, and as mentioned previously, negligence.[13]

Diagnosing a Sick Building and the Effects Upon the Appraisal Process

An appraiser employed to estimate the value of a property is responsible for discovering and disclosing any problems related to the property, including whether the building suffers from SBS. In order to protect themselves from liability, appraisers should be aware of SBS "symptoms."

The following list of suggested activities could lead an appraiser to a diagnosis of SBS[14] during an inspection of a property:

- Obtain from the building manager and maintenance staff a history of the building, including such information as type of building and its use, age and size of building, dates of any renovations, and location of office equipment.

- Check HVAC system, including layout, air supply, diffusers, returns, and daily operational schedules. Check for obvious impediments to

---

11. Patricia A. Kelsey, "Contractor Administers First Aid to 'Sick' Buildings," *Air Conditioning, Heating, and Refrigeration News* (December 25, 1989): 7.

12. There are no current cases which would indicate liability exposure for an appraiser failing to identify sick building issues. However, in our litigious society, it is probably only a matter of time until a case is brought forth by a property owner and/or tenant.

13. Rich Finigan, "What You Should Know About Mold," Winter 2001, September 9, 2001 <http://www.allstatehomeinspection.com/ know%20mold.html>.

14. Marcia Sawnor, "Avoiding Sick Building Syndrome," June 1995, December 13, 2000 <http://www.isdesignet.com/isdeisnet/Magazine/Jun'95/SickBuilding.html>.

Chapter 7: *Sick Commercial Buildings*

air flow, such as blocked diffusers or returns, the absence of returns, and short circuiting.

- Review the existing HVAC operating and maintenance procedures. Are they up-to-date? Is there proper filter efficiency? Is there proper housekeeping and calibration? What is the condition of the HVAC components? Was the system balanced at start-up?
- Examine the appearance of the air supply system and its location. Is the system rusted? Is it clean? Is there trash around?
- Look for obvious signs of pollutants: water marks, standing water, excessive dust, and excessive garbage.
- Assess the overall appearance of the building's housekeeping. Obtain the building's cleaning schedule and information on the cleaning compounds used.
- Examine the layout of the work spaces: partitions, room height, wall and floor coverings, daily work supplies (markers, inks, glues, solvents) and number of people in the work space.
- Observe the quality of lighting: too dim, too bright?
- Note the overall age of its workforce and the condition of its health.
- Locate designated smoking areas, if any.
- Monitor noise levels: inside traffic, office machines, radios, music, outside traffic noise, and public address system.
- Investigate whether there are factors or activities outside the building, such as a parking lot, highway, road, or building construction that could be affecting the indoor environment.
- Interview the building occupants. If a complaint is made about indoor air quality, note the times when problems are experienced, job responsibilities of the complainant, other activities occurring inside and outside at the same time, and weather conditions.

If the subject property is thought (or perhaps known) to suffer from SBS, contact an indoor air quality specialist. With the help of an expert, the appraiser can draw up an option table to be included in their narrative report. The option table should describe different courses of action that could be taken to alleviate the problem and the associated cost of each (see Sections VII and V for a cursory discussion of these issues).

When a commercial building suffers from SBS, it affects the application of the three approaches to value in the following ways:

- Sales comparison approach: It will be difficult to find truly comparable properties if the subject exhibits SBS. Adjustments for differences in physical condition between healthy and sick buildings may be extremely difficult to quantify.
- Cost approach: It will be difficult to estimate accrued depreciation due to indoor air quality problems.
- Income approach: SBS affects the operating cost of the structure, thus altering net operating income (NOI), an integral part of determining value according to the income approach. Furthermore, development of an overall capitalization rate using market extraction will be difficult for properties with SBS. Other less reliable methods for determining R_o will have to be applied.

Curing a Sick Building

There are several ways to make a sick building "healthy." The key ingredient in most solutions involves the introduction of fresh air. Fresh air dilutes and flushes out the concentration of contaminants. Solutions may be easy or technically difficult to implement. The employment of an environmental engineer or indoor air specialist is necessary to determine the correct course of action.

One of the easiest and certainly least expensive solutions to curing SBS is to open a window. This simple act introduces fresh air into the building and can solve problems such as high carbon dioxide content. This is especially true for older facilities. Newer buildings may not benefit from this; heating and cooling systems may be disrupted and some may not even have windows. Another suggestion regarding recent construction is to let the building remain unoccupied for 30–60 days with the air-conditioning turned on. However, this solution is not only expensive, it is impractical.

Of course, once contaminants are identified, they can be isolated and removed from the building. A suitable substitute for the contaminant needs to be identified and installed. For example (as mentioned previously), fabric carpeting is known to outgas a tremendous amount of formaldehyde. An appropriate response could be to remove all traces of the carpet, its padding and bonding agents, and replace it with wood or ceramic tile flooring.

This same line of reasoning applies to the HVAC system. If the system is the source of illness, it must be thoroughly cleaned or replaced. Proper ventilation is vital to the health of a building and its occupants. Office machines and other supplies releasing volatile chemicals into indoor air must also be properly ventilated.

Avoiding Sick Building Syndrome

Avoiding indoor air quality problems involves the implementation of preventive measures. The following activities can help to avert SBS[15]:

- Inspect HVAC systems annually and clean thoroughly every 5 years.
- Change filters at least 4 times a year.
- Institute a no smoking policy.
- Section off and provide exhaust systems for office equipment which contain volatile chemicals.
- Institute a comprehensive maintenance program for the facility using less toxic or "environmentally safe" cleaning products.
- Improve ventilation. Make sure ventilation systems pull in outside air from as far away as possible from source of pollution such as from high elevations (higher elevations typically have less contaminants).
- Replace carpet and/or vinyl floors with wood or ceramic tile.
- Ban the use of fragrances and other chemical-based grooming products.

Implementing a healthy building plan can be expensive at first, but it makes good business sense. Energy consumption will fall as productivity increases.

---

15. The information presented in this section is primarily drawn from the following sources: George Deter, "A Little Planning Can Go a Long Way Toward Preventing Sick Buildings," *The Business Journal* (February 17, 1992): 16 and James F. Doiron, "Sick Buildings Spell Ills for Risk Managers," *Business Insurance* (March 8, 1999): 17.

Chapter 7: *Sick Commercial Buildings*

Conclusion

Sick building syndrome (SBS), a product of the energy crisis of the 1970s and other combining factors, occurs when 20% of its occupants suffer certain symptoms that are relieved when they leave the building. This form of indoor air pollution is of great concern for property owners, tenants, and other real estate professionals. An appraiser employed to find the value of a property should discover and disclose any problems related to the property, including whether the building suffers from SBS. If a subject property is sick, the appraiser (with the help of an expert) should draw up an option table for the client, describing different solutions and the associated costs of each.

References

Cooper, Joanne K. "Sick Buildings: Some Fresh Remedies." *Business First-Columbus* (May 17, 1993): 20-25.

Gonzalez, Ervin A. *Robles and Gonzalez, P.A. Home Page.* August 30, 1999 <http://www.robles-gonzalez.com/tips/ttsick.html>.

Hayes, Mary. "Energy Conservation Steps of '70s Give Rise to Some 'Sick' Buildings." *The Business Journal* (October 5, 1992): 27.

Valuing Contaminated Properties

CHAPTER 7 Cross-References

Related article in Chapter 1: Joseph A. Campanella, "Valuing Partial Losses in Contamination Cases" *The Appraisal Journal* (April 1988), 2–3.

Related articles in Chapter 2: John D. Dorchester, Jr., MAI, CRE, "Environmental Pollution: Valuation in a Changing World" *The Appraisal Journal* (July 1991), 37; Albert R. Wilson, "The Environmental Opinion: Basis for an Impaired Value Opinion" *The Appraisal Journal* (July 1994); and Randall Bell, MAI, "The Impact of Detrimental Conditions on Property Values" *The Appraisal Journal* (October 1998).

Related articles in Chapter 3: Robert V. Colangelo, CPG and Ronald D. Miller, Esq., "The ASTM Standards on Environmental Site Assessments for Commercial Real Estate Transactions," Chapter 3 in *Environmental Site Assessments and Their Impact on Property Value: The Appraiser's Role,* Appraisal Institute: 1995, 132; Danny J. Martin, "The New URAR and Environmental Hazards" *The Appraisal Journal* (January 1995), 142–144; and Randall Bell, MAI, "Class VIII—Environmental Conditions," Chapter 8 in *Real Estate Damages: An Analysis of Detrimental Conditions,* Appraisal Institute: 1999, 169, 176–182.

Related articles in Chapter 4: Bill Mundy, MAI, PhD, "Stigma and Value" *The Appraisal Journal* (January 1992), 200–201 and Wayne C. Lusvardi, "The Dose Makes the Poison: Environmental Phobia or Regulatory Stigma?" *The Appraisal Journal* (April 2000), 226–232.

Related articles in Chapter 6: Patricia R. Healy and John J. Healy, Jr., MAI, "Lenders' Perspectives on Environmental Issues" *The Appraisal Journal* (July 1992), 288–290; and Elaine M. Worzala and William N. Kinnard, Jr., CRE, "Investor & Lender Reactions to Alternative Sources of Contamination" *Real Estate Issues* (August 1997), 293–294.

Related article in Chapter 8: Robert P. Carver, Esq. and Anthony W. Crowell, Esq., "Toxic Tax Assessments: The Ad Valorem Taxation of Contaminated Property" *Real Estate Issues* (Fall 1999).

Related articles in Chapter 9: Robert Simons, PhD, "How Clean is Clean?" *The Appraisal Journal* (July 1994), 458, 462; Richard J, Roddewig, MAI, CRE, "The EPA's Brownfield Initiative: Will It Improve the Market for Contaminated Properties?" *Valuation Insights & Perspectives* (Third Quarter 1997), 470; Alan K. Reichert, PhD, "Impact of a Toxic Waste Superfund Site on Property Values" *The Appraisal Journal* (October 1997), 474–476; and Alan Reichert, PhD, "The Persistence of Contamination Effects: A Superfund Site Revisited" *The Appraisal Journal* (April 1999), 493–494.

Related article in Chapter 10: "Seattle-Kent Good Neighbor Program: Final Report January 1990" Seattle Engineering Department, Gary Zarker, Director, 508.

Related articles in Chapter 11: Ralph W. Holmen, "Current Legal Issues Raised by Environmental Hazards Affecting Real Estate" *Real Estate Issues* (Fall/Winter 1991), 543-545; Robert A. Simons, "Settlement of an Oil Pipeline Leak with Contaminated Residential Property: A Case Study" *Real Estate Issues* (Summer 1999); and Jack P. Friedman, CRE, "Defending an Oil Company Against Litigation for Environmental Contamination (A Case Study)" *Real Estate Issues* (Winter 1999/2000).

Contaminated Properties and the Tax Assessment Process

CHAPTER 8

Editor's Introduction
Not many articles in The Appraisal Journal, Real Estate Issues, *or* Valuation Insights & Perspectives *have addressed the valuation of contaminated property in the context of property tax assessment or mass appraisal. Greenberg and Hughes report on the results of a two-page survey form sent to every local tax assessor in New Jersey in 1993. Assessors were asked if their town had a hazardous waste site and, if it did, to indicate how the site was impacting property values at various distances from the site. While three-fourths of the respondents said there was no adverse impact due to proximity to the hazardous waste site, some assessors reported significant impacts within a quarter-mile of the site.*

In their 1999 article, Carver and Crowell summarize the reported case law in order to provide "taxing authorities with an analysis of the practical effects that case law may have on methodologies used to value contaminated property for the purpose of ad valorem taxation."

In reading this chapter, please also be aware that the IAAO guidelines to assessors on how to handle contaminated property assessment are included in the addenda to this anthology and should be read in conjunction with the articles in this chapter.

Impact of Hazardous Waste Sites on Property Value and Land Use: Tax Assessors' Appraisal

by Michael Greenberg, PhD, and James Hughes, PhD

Michael Greenberg, PhD, is professor of urban studies and community health at Rutgers University. Mr. Greenberg is also director of the Policy Division of the NSF-Hazardous Substances Management Research Center as well as being a member of the National Research Council Committee on Remedial Action Priorities for Hazardous Waste Sites. He received a PhD from Columbia University.

James Hughes, PhD, is professor of urban planning and policy development at Rutgers University. Mr. Hughes received a PhD from Rutgers University and is director of the Rutgers Regional Report. He has conducted extensive housing and demographic research.

This article originally appeared in the January 1993 issue of The Appraisal Journal.

1. Milton Russell, E. William Colglazier, and Mary English, *Hazardous Waste Remediation: The Task Ahead* (Knoxville, Tenn.: Waste Management Research and Education Institute, 1991).
2. "Hazardous Waste Sites: Priority Health Conditions and Research Strategies—United States," *MMWR*, v. 41, no. 5 (1992): 72–74; National Research Council, *Environmental Epidemiology. v. 1, Public Health and Hazardous Waste* (Washington, D.C.: National Academy Press, 1991).
3. Ibid.
4. Bill Mundy, "Stigma and Value," *The Appraisal Journal* (January 1992): 7–13.

Tens of thousands of abandoned and operating hazardous waste sites are expected to cost the United States $750 billion to remediate from 1990 to 2020.[1] More than 1,200 sites are considered sufficiently dangerous to be on the U.S. Environmental Protection Agency's (EPA) National Priority List (NPL) for cleanup. Approximately 2 million Americans live within a mile of one of these sites and one person in six lives within four miles.[2] The EPA and the Agency for Toxic Substances and Disease Registry (ATSDR) are charged with evaluating the health and environmental impact of hazardous waste sites. Risk assessment studies performed at such sites have proven inconclusive because of data and methods limitations.[3]

Economic impacts are feared because hazardous waste sites can stigmatize neighborhoods. For example, Bill Mundy identified seven criteria including disruption, site visibility, and poor prognosis for remediation that could lead to stigmatization and devaluation of property in "Stigma and Value."[4]

Economic impacts are difficult and costly to assess because an economic study typically requires analysis of every property transaction and data about the hazardous waste site as well as data about local taxes, school systems, and numerous other factors that influence property values. A typical economic analysis can easily cost over $100,000 and require months of research. In light of the political pressure to remediate sites, it would be extremely helpful if a process could be developed to quickly separate hazardous waste sites into those that clearly have affected property values, transactions, and land uses, and those that have not. The clearly affected group would be given priority for more detailed economic studies.

Local tax assessors are in a unique position to make an initial screening; that is, they are the professional group most capable of judging the importance of the factor of hazardous waste compared with the factors of taxes, community services, the business climate, and other characteristics that affect property values, transactions, and land uses. They are charged with the responsibility of assessing value for tax purposes. To properly

Chapter 8: *Impact of Hazardous Waste Sites*

appraise property, tax assessors must keep abreast of transactions and prices and integrate the information represented in hundreds of individual decisions on the part of property owners and buyers about taxes, school systems, and hazardous waste sites. The purpose of the research presented here is to examine the economic impacts of hazardous waste sites through the judgments of local tax assessors.

Expectations About Economic Impacts

There are good reasons to expect hazardous waste sites to reduce property values and deter developments. Numerous national surveys show that the public perceives hazardous waste to be a major threat. The Roper December 1987 and January 1988 surveys for the U.S. EPA reported that 62% and 61% of respondents believed that active and inactive hazardous waste sites are "very serious" problems. Of 28 environmental and occupational issues, these two ranked first and second.[5] Other Roper surveys in 1989 and 1990 as well as Louis Harris polls in 1980 and 1990 confirm the public's aversion to hazardous waste sites.[6] In light of public perception and aversion it is reasonable to expect that people will avoid purchasing homes in proximity to hazardous waste sites, thus exerting a downward effect on values.

At the community level, William Freudenberg asked 100 community groups to rank environmental hazards. Toxic waste dumps were the hazard most often at the top of the list.[7] Michael Edelstein argues that hazardous waste sites can destroy communities. Residents, he says, become chronically depressed, do not allow their children to play in the street, lost faith in their elected officials, worry about the loss of property values, and hope that their homes will burn down so that they can move.[8] Jay Gould was so convinced that hazardous waste sites are detrimental that he classified the quality of life of tens of thousands of zip code areas in the United States on the basis of what he considers to be toxic waste proximity.[9]

Some economic studies support public perception. Gary McClelland, William Schulze, and Brian Hurd; Gregory Michaels and Kerry Smith; and John Hoehn, Mark Berger, and Glenn Blomquist found proximity to toxic sites lowers property values while remediation of such sites increases property values.[10]

There are reasons, however, to expect that not every hazardous waste site will lower property values. One reason is special community circumstances. For example, Anthony Mason studied three communities in New Jersey that are literally surrounded by what normally would be considered noxious facilities. One community is bordered by petroleum tank farms and a small airport on one side, a major highway on a second side, and chemical plants and a chemical landfill on the third and fourth sides. Yet the largely elderly population is satisfied with their location because it protects them from outsiders. In essence, the hazards are a protective moat.[11] Consistent with Mason's results, Milton Russell and colleagues at the University of Tennessee studied ten communities near Superfund sites. While some were adamant about rapid and total cleanup, others were not. The authors suggest that the special circumstances of every site must be understood to comprehend the public reaction.[12]

A second condition that mitigates against economic impacts is the presence of resident populations with limited choices. The United Church of Christ study of hazardous waste sites by zip code areas found that minor-

5. Roper Organization, *Roper Reports* (New York: The Roper Organization, 1987–1990).

6. Louis Harris and Associates, *The ABC-Harris Survey* (New York: The Harris Organization, 1980); and "Public Mood Has Hardened to Advocate Tougher, Stricter Laws on Air Pollution," The Harris Poll (April 1, 1990).

7. William Freudenberg, "Citizen Action for Environmental Health: Report on a Survey of Community Organizations," *American Journal of Public Health*, v. 74 (1984): 444–448.

8. Michael Edelstein, Contaminated Communities: *The Social and Psychological Impacts of Residential Toxic Exposure* (Boulder, Colorado: Westview Press, 1988).

9. Jay Gould, *Quality of Life in American Neighborhoods, Levels of Affluence, Toxic Waste and Cancer Mortality in Residential Zip Code Areas* (Boulder, Colorado: Westview Press, 1986).

10. Gary McClelland, William Schulze, and Brian Hurd, "The Effect of Risk Beliefs on Property Values: A Case Study of a Hazardous Waste Site," *Risk Analysis*, v.10 (1990): 485–497; Gregory Michaels and V. Kerry Smith, "Market Segmentation and Valuing Amenities with Hedonic Models: The Case of Hazardous Waste Sites," *Journal of Urban Economics*, v. 28 (1990): 223–242; and John Hoehn, Mark Berger, and Glenn Blomquist, "A Hedonic Model of Interregional Wages, Rents, and Amenity Values," *Journal of Regional Science*, v. 27 (1987): 605–620.

11. Anthony Mason, *Risk Perception in Communities on the Industrial Margin* (New Brunswick, N.J.: Rutgers University Department of Geography, PhD thesis, 1989).

12. Russell, Colglazier, and English.

Valuing Contaminated Properties

ity population and low socioeconomic status were the two best correlates of the location of hazardous waste sites.[13] People who have limited choices because of racial and economic segregation may not be able to act on their perceptions. Consequently, housing values may not decrease much when a site is identified or appreciate much when it is remediated.

Some sites may not affect property values because they are isolated and uncontroversial. For example, Andrejs Skaburskis found a small percent decrease in sale prices near an inactive, uncontroversial landfill. For these kinds of cases, he argued, it should not be difficult to implement compensation plans or to control negative impacts.[14]

In sum, while it is generally assumed that hazardous waste sites reduce property values, existing published studies are not conclusive. Further, such studies do not routinely investigate other important effects such as the impact of hazardous waste sites on the frequency of real estate transactions as well as on existing and planned land uses and activities. A typical parcel-by-parcel study of changes in property values and a psychometric analysis of property owners' perceptions of impacts require an enormous amount of time, personnel, and monetary resources. While the results of such studies are certainly reliable, they may be too costly and take too long to be feasible for appraisal purposes.

This effort to use the judgments of local tax assessors is a follow-up of a study that attempted to isolate major factors that confound the negative impact of hazardous waste sites on property values.[15] The initial research studied changes of housing sale prices during the period from 1975 to 1988 in 77 towns in New Jersey near hazardous waste Superfund sites. New Jersey is an ideal place to conduct this research because it has more Superfund sites than any other state and maintains a central file of all housing sales. The study found that only communities with populations less than 10,000 or in regions undergoing rapid price increases had statistically significant lower increases in sale prices. For other towns in proximity to such sites, an impact at the community level was not obvious. In addition, the hazard ranking of a particular site calculated by the EPA's hazard-ranking system did not appear to influence sale prices.

Though a useful initial step, the first study had a major geographical scale limitation. Superfund sites may have neighborhood impact without having town, city, or borough-wide impact. In other words, impacts may exist that aggregated town data cannot show. The study presented here emerged from the need to focus on the neighborhood surrounding a site as well as the need to be able to evaluate the relative importance of a hazardous waste site compared with other factors that influence land value, transactions, and land use.

Methods

A two-page survey containing six questions was mailed to the tax assessor of each of New Jersey's 567 minor civil divisions (e.g., boroughs, cities, townships) for which the U.S. Bureau of the Census collects data. For purposes of this article, they are called towns. After defining a hazardous waste site, the first question asked whether a town has or had a hazardous waste site. In towns with multiple sites, assessors were asked to focus on the one with the greatest impact on property values. Using the entire jurisdiction as a basis of comparison, those who responded affirmatively

13. United Church of Christ, Commission for Racial Justice, *Toxic Waste and Race in the United States* (New York: United Church of Christ, 1987).

14. Andrejs Skaburskis, "Impact Attenuation in Conflict Situations: The Price Effects of Nuisance Land Use," *Environment and Planning A*, v. 21 (1989): 375–383.

15. Michael Greenberg and James Hughes, "The Impact of Hazardous Waste Superfund Sites on the Value of Houses Sold in New Jersey," *Annals of Regional Science*, v. 26 (1992): 147–153.

Chapter 8: *Impact of Hazardous Waste Sites*

to the first question were asked to indicate whether the hazardous waste site caused property values to change within one-fourth mile of the site (excluding the impact on the site itself), within one-fourth mile to one mile, and within one mile to three miles. A four-point scale was used:

- 1 = lowered property values a good deal (more than 25%)
- 2 = lowered property values somewhat (5%–25%)
- 3 = no effect on values
- 4 = increased values

An option for expressing uncertainty was also provided. Using the same format, the second part of question 2 asked for similar judgments about real estate transactions.

Question 3 concerned whether existing land uses or activities were harmed when a site was identified, and if so, how they were harmed. Tax assessors were then asked whether a site deterred any new land uses or activities in their jurisdictions, and those who responded affirmatively were asked to provide details.

Question 5 concerned whether a facility had caused the community to change its land-use plans for housing, commerce, industry, recreation, schools, and other public facilities, and if so, what these changes involved. In question 6, respondents were asked to rate the relative importance of 14 factors with the potential to constrain the appreciation of property values in their jurisdictions during the last five years. The 14 factors included:

- Economic recession
- Decline of local industry, agriculture, and commerce
- Remote location without a major highway linkage
- Fully developed area
- State and local planning and environmental policies
- Adjacent areas are more attractive and local services are inferior
- High taxes
- Presence of hazardous waste site

Assessors responsible for towns with hazardous waste sites were asked to answer the sixth question for the mile surrounding the site as well as the entire town. This question provided the opportunity to judge the relative importance of hazardous waste sites and the other 13 factors in towns with such sites. Our hypothesis was that some factors (e.g., economic recession, high taxes) would be important in every town, including towns with hazardous waste sites. On the other hand, hazardous waste sites clearly would only be significant in towns with sites, and especially within one mile of the site.

Responses from towns without sites were used as a statistical control; that is, average scores for question 6 were calculated and *t*-tests were performed to determine whether towns with sites had a higher mean for the hazardous waste variable than towns without sites. The 14 constraints in towns with sites and in towns without them were also ranked and the results were correlated to determine the consistency of the factors in each group of towns.

Results

A total of 200 surveys were returned (35% of 567) within six weeks of the February 28, 1992, mailing. Fifty were not useful because of inadequate

Valuing Contaminated Properties

responses. Some tax assessors responded that they did not feel competent to answer question 6 while others indicated that their towns did not have sites and therefore they could not respond to question 6. A total of 150 useful responses were received. The 26% response rate is higher than expected for most mail surveys.[16]

A good response rate was necessary from the 90 towns that were known to have at least one site on the EPA NPL. In fact, 41% replied (37 of 90). The response rate for towns without Superfund sites was 24% (113 of 477). Nineteen of the 113 without NPL sites indicated that their towns have sites. These included those overseen by the state Superfund program; by the federal RCRA program, which manages active hazardous waste sites; and by the state ECRA program, which requires certification that a site is not contaminated before property can be sold or transferred. Overall, 56 of the 150 respondents' towns have hazardous waste sites while 94 do not.

Table 1 shows that 16 respondents (28%) judged that property values within one-fourth mile of the site were lowered as a result of the hazardous waste site. Five (9%) believed an impact could be observed one-fourth mile to one mile from the site, and only one respondent believed that an impact on property values existed more than one mile away from the site.

The same attenuation of impact with distance was apparent when real estate transactions were considered. Twenty-one percent judged that a negative impact existed within one-fourth mile of the site, 9% at a distance of one-fourth mile to one mile, and 4% at a distance of one mile to three miles. Table 2 shows that new land uses or activities were deterred in 23% of towns, existing land uses or activities were harmed in 16%, and plans were disrupted in less than 10%.

16. J. Wanzer Drane, "Imputing Nonresponses to Mail-Back Questionnaires," *American Journal of Epidemiology*, v. 134 (1991): 908–912.

TABLE 1 Changes in Property Values and Transactions Near Sites (based on 56 towns)

		Distance From Site				
Since 1980 facility has caused:	Within 1/4 mile		1/4–1 mile		1–3 miles	
Property values to be lowered:						
A good deal (>25%)	4	7%	0	0%	0	0%
Somewhat (5–25%)	12	21%	5	9%	1	2%
No impact	37	66%	48	86%	52	93%
Not sure	3	5%	3	5%	3	5%
Number of real estate transactions to be lowered:						
A good deal (>25%)	3	5%	1	2%	1	2%
Somewhat (5–25%)	9	16%	4	7%	1	2%
No impact	40	71%	46	82%	49	88%
Not sure	4	7%	5	9%	5	9%

TABLE 2 Impacts of Site on Jurisdictions' Land Uses and Activities (based on 56 towns)

Impact	Yes		No		Not Sure	
Existing land use or activities harmed	9	16%	35	63%	12	21%
New land uses or activities deterred	13	23%	34	61%	9	16%
Affected jurisdiction's housing plans	4	7%	45	80%	7	13%
Affected jurisdiction's commercial, recreation, school plans	9	16%	36	64%	11	20%

Chapter 8: *Impact of Hazardous Waste Sites*

One reaction to these numbers is to conclude that the claims that sites severely damage property have been exaggerated. Approximately three-fourths of the respondents saw no impact. Yet the responses of the 16 tax assessors in affected towns show that substantial impacts often occurred within one-fourth mile of the site. Some of the tax assessors' responses were:

- We lost a new industrial building near the site. They located in another state, which cost [us] jobs and tax ratable.

- Property owners could not sell and values were down within a mile of the site, no new housing has been built. A nearby recreation area closed because of stream contamination.

- No one wants to build in our area because we are next to [the site].

- We waited two years for a site to be cleaned up. A $17 million project was delayed two years.

- The [site] scared buyers away. Resale of adjacent properties [has been] reduced and [there has been] a significant increase in time to sell and lowering of values. New housing in adjacent areas stopped.

- A high school was proposed for a site nearby—but was deemed to be too close to [the site].

- A housing development was abandoned after contamination was found in an adjacent stream.

- [It] had a drastic impact. No one that I know of would build anything in this area nor would they move into the area. The residents that are there have been there for many, many years and they are all related.

In contrast, other tax assessors' comments suggest that a remote location and the stagnant economy mitigated against impacts in many towns. For example:

- The surrounding area is not conducive to housing anyway.

- The site is not generally known and is remote from the general public.

- The site is on federal land.

- I have been surprised that homes in the area have continued to sell, although no recent sales have occurred, which I would attribute to the overall economy.

Some tax assessors indicated that there has been no impact during the last five years because the causes of such effects have been corrected.

- Existing land uses were hampered for a time. But contaminated wells were replaced by city water, which had been planned anyway. [The site is] no longer a problem.

- The site is cleaned up, and all is back to normal.

Several tax assessors provided anecdotes to support the contention of the majority that hazardous waste sites had not impeded property appreciation or development.

- A new development started within a mile of the site.

- Major new developments and a new school were built within one-half mile of the site.

- One housing development was abandoned, but we have 30% of [the] county's new construction.

Table 3 shows the relative importance of hazardous waste sites as constraints on the appreciation of property values. In the 94 towns without sites, hazardous waste was the least important constraint (averaging 2.35 on a scale of 1 to 9). The average values for the factors of economic recession, state environmental regulations, high taxes, local and state planning policies, adjacent areas being seen as more attractive, and commercial and industrial decline were significantly higher ($P \leq 0.05$).

Forty town assessors reported having hazardous sites in their communities that had no impact on property values. The average for the hazardous waste variable was 1.94, or 13th out of 14. The same eight other variables had statistically significant higher average importance values. Within a mile of the hazardous waste site in these 40 towns, the average was 2.75, or 10th of 14 variables. Only state environmental regulations, the economic recession, high taxes, and local planning policies were statistically significantly more important.

In the 16 towns identified by their assessors as affected, the average importance scale for hazardous waste sites was 3.13 in the towns as a whole and 4.33 within a mile surrounding the site. Only state environmental regulations, the economic recession, and high taxes were considered more important by the assessors within the inner mile, and while hazardous waste ranked only ninth in the towns as whole, none of the higher ranked causes had significantly higher average scale values.

Table 3 illustrates the consistent importance of the economic recession, state environmental regulations (e.g., coastal zone, water connections, wetlands), and high taxes. The Spearman rank correlations between the 14 importance variables in the 94 towns without hazardous waste sites and the 40 towns with sites and no impact was 0.90. The same correlation was 0.89 between the 94 towns without sites and the inner mile surrounding the site in these 40 towns; 0.82 between the 16 towns with sites that caused impacts and the 94 towns without sites; and 0.63 be-

TABLE 3   Factors Constraining the Appreciation of Property Values During the Last Five Years (means are based on a 9-point scale, where 1 = not important, 9 = extremely important)

Factor	With Sites/Impact (N = 16)		With Sites/No Impact (N = 40)		Without Sites (N = 94)
	1 Mile	Town	1 Mile	Town	Town
State environmental regulations	6.08	5.69	5.62*	5.41*	4.69*
Economic recession	4.93	4.47	5.65*	5.71*	5.37*
High taxes	4.36	4.07	4.53*	4.53*	4.67*
Hazardous waste site	4.33	3.13	2.75	1.94	2.35
State planning policies	4.31	3.54	4.16	4.26*	3.78*
Industrial decline	4.07	4.47	3.73	3.83*	3.53*
Local planning policies	3.86	3.86	4.52*	4.29*	4.21*
Commercial decline	3.67	4.13	3.47	3.60*	3.80*
Area too remote	3.07	2.00	2.73	2.20	2.73
Adjacent areas more attractive	3.00	3.53	3.40	3.43*	3.88*
Agricultural decline	2.67	2.20	1.66	1.70	2.87
No major highway linkage	2.27	1.60	2.63	2.40	2.67
Area fully developed	2.13	2.21	3.17	3.23	3.27
Inferior services	1.93**	2.07	2.68	2.34	2.35

* Mean higher than mean of hazardous waste variable at $P < 0.05$.

** Mean lower than mean of hazardous waste variable at $P < 0.05$.

Chapter 8: *Impact of Hazardous Waste Sites*

tween the inner mile in those 16 towns with sites and the 94 towns without sites. All of these correlations were significant at $P \le 0.01$.

The tax assessors' judgments were compared with housing value data for the period from 1985 to 1988 developed from the previous New Jersey study.[17] The focus was 37 towns on the EPA's priority NPL Superfund list. During the period from 1985 to 1988, the average increase in the value of houses sold in the 13 towns affected by a hazardous waste site was 60.8% compared with 61.7% in the 24 towns not affected. These relative changes can be misleading, however, because of variations in regional housing markets. That is, national and regional factors such as the economic recession, state land use and environmental regulations, and taxes can mask local factors like hazardous waste sites. Regional variations were controlled for by subtracting the town percent change from the percent change in the host county. The net housing value appreciation in the affected communities was 2.69% compared with 1.47% for those not affected. Although the difference of means (1.22, 95% confidence limits of -17.1 to 14.7) was not statistically significant at $P \le 0.05$, it was in the direction expected.

Previous research had shown that nearly all the Superfund sites were identified from 1980 to 1985, and in fact the major impact on property values tended to be from 1980 to 1985. Net housing sale values were calculated for the 37 towns for the period from 1980 to 1985 and subtracted from those for the years 1985 to 1988. Housing sale prices should have rebounded more in the 24 unaffected towns than in the 13 affected ones, and they did. The net average difference between the 1985–1988 and the 1980–1985 housing sale values was 14.9% in the 24 unaffected towns and only 6.6% in the 13 affected towns. The net difference, 8.3% (95% confidence limits were -16 to 32.6), was not statistically significant at $P \le 0.05$, but again was in the expected direction.

Conclusion

Tax assessors report that hazardous waste sites have lowered the appreciation of property values, deterred land uses, and affected community plans in about 15% to 20% of the New Jersey towns that report hazardous waste sites. Nearly all of these impacts occur within one-fourth mile of the site. Many town assessors reported no impact because the site is located in a remote location, the problem was slight, or the problem has been solved. In addition, other factors, notably the economic recession, state and local planning and environmental policies, and high taxes are more important or equally important in determining land values.

Three considerations make us cautious about these results. First, results for New Jersey may not be generalizable to the entire United States. New Jersey's population is particularly aware of hazardous waste problems, which is demonstrated by the fact that it is generally recognized as having the strongest hazardous waste management programs in the United States.[18] In other words, New Jersey's citizens may be more sensitive to hazardous waste than the residents of most other areas. Nonetheless, these broad conclusions may be relevant for other states: 1) the existence of a hazardous waste site does not necessarily mean it has a major impact on values; and 2) if there is an impact, it is usually close and specific to the site.

Second, New Jersey experienced a housing price surge from 1980 to 1988, with prices increasing by about 14.5%. But the post-boom period

17. Greenberg and Hughes, 147–153.
18. Bob Hall and Mary L. Kerr, *1991–1992 Green Index* (Washington, D.C.: Island Press, 1991).

produced a dramatic correction. Has the stagnant economy become such an overriding factor that the full property-value and land use consequences of hazardous waste sites are understated in New Jersey at this time? Replication of this study design is needed in different regions of the United States. Third, while this survey approach is a quick and relatively inexpensive way to obtain data on many communities, it cannot replace detailed price estimation and psychometric studies. Based on the results of this study, however, tax assessor judgments can be used to determine which communities may require further in-depth analyses.

Toxic Tax Assessments: The Ad Valorem Taxation of Contaminated Property

by Robert P. Carver, Esq. and Anthony W. Crowell, Esq.

In tax assessment review proceedings involving contaminated property, taxpayers typically contend that property value is substantially impaired or erased by the presence of environmental contamination. Some taxpayers contend contaminated property has no value even when it is fully usable and the taxpayer is liable for the cleanup. These cases present courts with difficult and competing questions of law, equity, and public policy concerning the interplay of *ad valorem* taxation and sound environmental policy. Consequently, the legal premise of *ad valorem* taxation, which is to assess taxes against property at a certain rate upon its value, and the public policy concerning environmental cleanup, namely that the polluter pays, are often seemingly at odds.

Here, the authors review and analyze the reasoning of the courts when addressing these issues in the leading tax assessment review cases involving contaminated property nationwide. The manuscript first addresses issues affecting the marketability of contaminated property in the face of environmental liability statutes. Next, it reviews the methodologies adopted by the courts in adjudicating claims of assessment overvaluation. Finally, it considers the effect of the usability of contaminated property; the cleanup obligation of owners and purchasers of contaminated property; and the public policy concerns of taxing authorities on the outcome in tax assessment review litigation.

Environmental Liability and the Real Estate Market

The impact of environmental liability statutes on the marketability and profitability of contaminated property is central to taxpayer arguments for assessment reductions. It is generally accepted in the legal and appraisal communities that environmental contamination may affect property value. The threat of liability for cleanup imposed on contaminated property owners by the Comprehensive Environmental Response, Compensation, and Liability Act of 1980 (CERCLA)[1] and its state counterparts, cleanup costs, issues of indemnification, and the stigma associated

Robert P. Carver, Esq., and Anthony W. Crowell, Esq., are attorneys at the New York City Law Department and are adjunct faculty members of Brooklyn Law School and Baruch College of the City University of New York. (Note: Any views or opinions expressed in this article belong exclusively to the authors and do not reflect the views or opinions of the City of New York.)

This article originally appeared in the Fall 1999 issue of Real Estate Issues. Reproduced with permission of Real Estate Issues; published and © by the Counselors of Real Estate (a not for profit organization), Chicago, IL. All rights reserved. Further reproduction/distribution is prohibited without the written permission of Real Estate Issues.

1. 42 U.S.C. §§ 9601 *et seq.*

with the actual or perceived risks involved with owning or using contaminated property all yield this conclusion.

CERCLA, commonly known as the Superfund law, is the principal federal statute designed to protect the public and environment from the release of hazardous substances, and to ensure that hazardous substances are cleaned up. Congressional intent behind CERCLA is rooted in the "polluter pays" principle which dictates that: 1). contaminated property which threatens public health and safety be restored to an environmentally acceptable condition; and 2). any parties benefiting from or even involved with the use of hazardous substances that ultimately contaminate property should bear the cost of cleanup, starting though not necessarily ending with the owner or operator of the contaminated property.

CERCLA's liability scheme is strict, joint, several, and retroactive. This means that the entire chain of property owners, including both current and former owners, and other potentially responsible parties, such as lending institutions, other investors and even transporters who carried hazardous substances to property that is contaminated, may be liable for costs associated with restoring that property to an environmentally acceptable state. CERCLA imposes liability on the current owner of contaminated property regardless of whether the owner caused the contamination. And potential liability remains with former owners who sell contaminated property, even in cases where a purchaser agrees to assume the risk of cleanup liability. Thus, acceptance of liability by one party cannot absolve others of potential liability especially in cases where cleanup costs exceed the financial capabilities of the party assuming the risk.

Two decades of experience under CERCLA have proved that it has a stigmatizing effect on property both before and after cleanup of contamination. In economic terms, stigma is a reduction in value caused by the risk inherent in owning a contaminated property. Thus, the level of risk involved in acquiring or even selling a contaminated or formerly contaminated property—including the uncertainties of liability, as well as often unknown cleanup and transaction costs, increased underwriting costs, litigation costs, indemnification, and ultimately the threat of bankruptcy—may outweigh any potential economic benefit of the transaction. Consequently, CERCLA my dramatically affect the marketability and profitability of contaminated property.

Indeed, real estate investors and lending institutions are apprehensive about such purchases and often demand extensive and costly site investigation before investment. And despite recent lender liability reforms enacted by Congress, lenders remain concerned about underwriting contaminated properties because they view those properties as having questionable collateral value even when the property is fully usable.[2] Lenders fear they may be held liable for cleanup in cases of foreclosure. Moreover, some owners of contaminated property, in an effort to avoid public detection of contamination and liability, may decide not to sell their properties at all, sometimes even opting to mothball them. Consequently, the interplay of impaired marketability of contaminated property, with the statutory scheme that obligates specific parties to clean up contamination, has made the adjudication of claims of overassessment particularly vexing.

2. See Asset Conservation, Lender Liability, and Deposit Insurance Protection Act of 1996 (42 U.S.C. §§ 6991(b), 9601, 9607)

Chapter 8: *Toxic Tax Assessments*

Assessment Review Litigation in the Courts

Although the courts have not decided such cases with uniformity, it appears that most if not all courts that have considered the question hold that environmental contamination affects, or at least may affect, property value. Taxpayer challenges to assessments on contaminated property are on the rise, but there are relatively few reported decisions, and those focus on limited legal and policy issues addressing very specific sets of facts. In all the reported decisions reviewed, the taxpayers made one or both of the following arguments: that cleanup costs must be deducted from the value of their property or that their property has no value at all on account of its unmarketability. Some courts have accepted these arguments, while others have rejected them squarely.

The review of the reported decisions below is aimed at providing the real estate community and taxing authorities with an analysis of the practical effects that case law may have on methodologies used to value contaminated property for the purpose of *ad valorem* taxation. Consideration is given to whether these methodologies are mandated by law, or are simply acceptable approaches to value, under the facts of the case, when posited by credible experts. This review looks behind the decisions to discern which facts might be said to dictate the results in the litigation of a tax assessment of a contaminated property, including the cost, timing, and probability of environmental cleanup; the usability of the property in its contaminated condition; the liability, or potential liability, for cleanup of buyers, sellers, and other parties; the stigma associated with a property upon cleanup; and tax and environmental policy.

California: In *Firestone Tire and Rubber Co. v. County of Monterey* (1990),[3] the soil and groundwater were contaminated from chemical spills at the taxpayer's tire manufacturing plant. Soon after the valuation date, the taxpayer closed the plant for reasons unrelated to the contamination. Then the state health authorities apparently prohibited the taxpayer from selling or using the property until it was cleaned.

The court upheld the property's assessment on the ground that a purchaser of the property on the valuation date would not have been aware of the contamination. Accordingly, the court declined to address whether the cleanup expense would be an appropriate measure of value diminution. The court, however, rejected the taxing authority's contention that the value of the property would be unaffected by contamination on account of the taxpayer's liability for cleanup.

Thereafter, *Dominguez Energy, L.P. v. County of Los Angeles* (1997),[4] addressed the treatment of expenses for environmental cleanup. The taxpayer had a property interest in an oil and gas lease and performed and scheduled ongoing remediation of oil contamination, despite no requirement to remediate until a later date.

In valuing the taxpayer's property interest, the taxing authority took the cleanup cost as an expense in the income approach to value, but hypothetically postponed the remediation by allocating the expense to the latest possible date. This approach diminished the effect of the expenses on the present value of the taxpayer's property interest. The court rejected this approach. Under a standard of prudent property management, the court found that the cleanup costs should have been considered when

3. 272 Cal. Rptr. 745 (Cal. Ct. App. 1990)

4. 65 Cal. Rptr. 2d 766 (Cal. Ct. App. 1997)

actually spent by the taxpayer. Additionally, the court noted that it would be poor public policy to adopt a valuation methodology based on imprudent management of environmental cleanup which risked public responsibility for the cleanup.

Iowa: In *Boekeloo v. Bd. of Review of City of Clinton* (1995),[5] the state's highest court rejected the taxpayers' contention that their fully operational tavern was unmarketable on account of groundwater contamination and without value. No government agency required that the taxpayers remediate the contamination, and the cleanup cost was unknown. The court found that the taxpayers failed to meet their burden of proof, since the testimony of the taxpayer's real estate agents suggested that if the cleanup cost were known, the property could in fact be sold.

Massachusetts: In *Reliable Electronic Finishing Co., Inc. v. Bd. of Assessors of Canton* (1991),[6] a chemical spill, from the failure of a secondary containment system, contaminated the taxpayer's property. The taxpayer assumed liability for the cleanup in a consent judgment and had begun some environmental remediation. The state's highest court upheld the assessment on the ground that the taxpayer failed to meet its burden of proof. There was no evidence of the contaminated condition of the property on the valuation date, the anticipated cost of cleanup, or how the contamination would affect the property's value.

The Massachusetts court noted that had the taxpayer established the effects of "proven environmental damage" on value, neither the owner's liability under the consent judgment, nor the owner's culpability, would be relevant factors in determining value for tax assessment purposes.

Michigan: In *Community Consultants, Inc. v. Bedford Township* (1985),[7] the property whose assessment was at issue was a vacant parcel formerly operated as a domestic refuse and industrial waste landfill. The property could not be put to any other use because of the presence of hazardous waste. It was contaminated by PCBs and lead and was ranked one of the state's top three most dangerous environmental contamination sites. The Michigan Tax Tribunal determined that the appropriate way to value the property was through a market approach, but there was no ascertainable market by which value could be examined or extrapolated because of a lack of comparable sales.

The taxpayer contended that the property was unmarketable. The taxing authority conceded, and the Tax Tribunal found, that it could not conceive of any knowledgeable, prospective buyer who would purchase the property. Moreover, the Tribunal determined that the cost of remediating the site "exceeds even the most optimistic value of an uncontaminated site of similar size, location, and zoning." Consequently, the Tribunal found that the property had only nominal value, and established a brightline rule that a nominal value must obtain in cases where former hazardous waste disposal sites remain contaminated on any given valuation date, and cannot be used for any lawful purpose. The Tribunal made clear, however, that this rule should not be construed as an indeterminate exemption for such properties, nor did it apply to hazardous waste disposal sites in current lawful operation.

5. 529 N.W.2d 275 (Iowa 1995)
6. 573 N.E.2d 959 (Mass. 1991)
7. 1985 Mich. Tax LEXIS 10

In *Comerica Bank-Detroit v. Metamora Township* (1989),[8] on the default of the taxing authority, the Tax Tribunal determined that certain agricultural land, which supported crops, had nominal value because of stigma that resulted from uncertainties surrounding the site's contaminated status. The groundwater had been contaminated by some three thousand barrels dumped by unknown parties that leaked PCBs and other toxic substances.

The Tax Tribunal considered the property's inclusion on Michigan's priority list of contaminated sits, which is the state's analog to the federal Superfund National Priorities List. It also considered evidence that cleanup costs would amount to $1.3 million, and that the taxpayer had already spent $393,000 on a cleanup effort. Those factors, the Tribunal found, coupled with "the many unanswered questions pertaining to liability, containment, and future uncertainties involving [the] property, situated as it is within the shroud of toxicity, stereotype it as untouchable even for speculative purpose." Finding the property "uncommonly tainted with stigma certain to adversely affect is marketability," the Tribunal valued the parcels at issue at only $100.

In *Sweepster, Inc. v. Township of Scio* (1996),[9] a fully usable, 47-acre industrial site suffered from groundwater contamination, forcing the closure of one drinking well and the commencement of construction of another. The former owner, Chrysler Corporation, paid for bottled drinking water at the site, as well as the drilling of the new well, pursuant to an indemnity clause in the purchase agreement for the property between Chrysler and the taxpayer.

The taxpayer contended the property had zero value, based on an environmental engineer's testimony that it might cost from $10 million to $20 million to clean up the site, although no amount could be determined with certainty unless further study was done. The taxpayer's value of the property, as if unaffected by contamination, ranged from only $2 million to $3.3 million.

The Tax Tribunal rejected the taxpayer's analysis and affirmed a lower tribunal's adoption of the taxing authority's analysis, which valued the property as follows. From the actual sale price of the property with the indemnity agreement in place, the cost of subsequent improvements to the property was added, and a 10 percent reduction in value for stigma was deducted. The tribunal found that the indemnity clause, which guaranteed cleanup, prohibited any reduction from the purchase price paid by the taxpayer. Any risks of present or future contamination, it reasoned, were reflected by the purchase price.

Minnesota: In *Almor Corp. v. County of Hennepin* (1997),[10] the taxpayer's soil and groundwater were contaminated by wastewater that migrated from a nearby tar plant. The state's highest court rejected a deduction of the cleanup cost from the value of the taxpayer's property to account for the contamination. The court reasoned that no cleanup had been taken or planned, there was no legal requirement to remediate contamination, and a third party was paying for monitoring on the taxpayer's property. The court did, however, approve the lower court's deduction from value for stigma, using the sales comparison approach to value, and a heightened capitalization rate when using the income approach to value.

8. 1989 Mich. Tax LEXIS 12
9. 1996 Mich. Tax LEXIS 26
10. 566 N.W.2d 696 (Minn. 1997)

Valuing Contaminated Properties

However, in *Westling v. County of Mille Lacs* (*Westling III*, 1996),[11] the same court approved the tax court's finding of zero value for property, contaminated by the taxpayer, who used a degreasing chemical in the re-manufacturing of automotive parts. The property was on the state Superfund list and the taxpayer was named a responsible party liable for cleanup by the state Pollution Control Agency. To value the property as of 1992 and 1993, which earned a substantial income, experts for both the taxpayer and taxing authority took a deduction from value for stigma and cleanup costs. The trial court found the taxpayer's deduction, which exceeded the property's value, to be credible, and the high court affirmed.

Previously, in *Westling v. County of Mille Lacs* (*Westling I*, 1994),[12] the high court of Minnesota reversed the tax court's finding of only nominal value for the same property, as of 1991, grounded on testimony that contaminated property was neither marketable nor mortgageable. The high court held that the tax court determination of nominal value was against the weight of the evidence because the property was purchased recently by the taxpayers with money lent by banks for that purchase; the property's continued commercial use generated an annual rental income; the presence of a market for the property was never tested since the taxpayers made no effort to sell the property; and the taxpayers were partly responsible for the property's contamination. The court remanded the case to the tax court to consider these factors, as well as traditional appraisal techniques modified to account for the effects of environmental contamination on value.

On remand the tax court considered but gave little or no weight to the factors itemized by the high court, and adopted the taxing authority's expert's valuation analysis.[13] That analysis deducted the present value of the cost to cure, as well as a 20 percent discount for stigma, from the value of the property as if unaffected by contamination. The resulting values warranted an assessment reduction, but were substantially greater than the nominal values previously found by the tax court. The taxpayer offered no alternative valuation methodology.

New Hampshire: In *re Great Lakes Container Corp.* (1985),[14] presented the high court of New Hampshire with the question of whether a former barrel reconditioning plant that was contaminated with hazardous waste, unusable and the subject of litigation to determine liability for cleanup, was entitled to an assessment reduction. The taxpayer contended that the presence of the contaminants, the pending lawsuit and the threat of liability to a future owner, rendered the property unsalable and thus untaxable. The taxpayer proffered an appraisal report that found zero value for the property and claimed that the circumstances did not allow for the application of conventional methodologies for determining value.

The court held that the contaminated property did not have zero value for several reasons. First, the taxpayer made no good faith attempt to sell the property below its assessed value; in fact, the taxpayer marketed the property for an amount in excess of the assessed value. And second, because the property would be cleaned up in the future, as a result of the litigation, the property had the prospect of some future benefit. In response to the taxpayer's contention that potential liability for cleanup effectively precluded any sale of the property, the court found that the tax-

11. 543 N.W.2d 91 (Minn. 1996)
12. 512 N.W.2d 863 (Minn. 1994)
13. 1994 Minn. Tax LEXIS 19
14. 489 A.2d 134 (N.H. 1985)

Chapter 8: *Toxic Tax Assessments*

payer could have sold the property with title transfer deferred until after any court-ordered cleanup was completed, thus freeing a future owner from potential liability. The taxpayer offered no proof of the present value of the property upon the judicial determination of liability for cleanup. Consequently, the court found the taxpayer's evidence insufficient to find that the assessment was excessive.

New Jersey: The first challenge to a tax assessment of contaminated property to reach a state's highest court was in New Jersey. In *Inmar Associates v. Borough of Carlstadt* (1988),[15] two industrial properties were subject to government-imposed requirements for environmental cleanup—in one instance, CERCLA, and in the other, a state statute (ECRA), that conditioned the sale of property upon environmental cleanup.

To better understand the high court's determination, a review of the procedural history of the case is in order. The trial court disallowed a deduction of the cleanup cost from value on both properties. For the Superfund site subject to CERCLA, the trial court found that "no firm or fixed obligation" for cleanup had been incurred. For the property subject to ECRA (a usable asphalt plant), the trial court found the taxpayer's proof of the cost of compliance with ECRA—mere estimates by the taxpayer-corporation's real estate director—to be insufficient to establish the effect of compliance on value. The state's intermediate appellate court upheld the lower court's disallowance of assessment reductions on, among other things, public policy grounds: to allow an abatement of taxes through a reduced assessment, it reasoned, would contravene the statutory scheme requiring the cleanup of contaminated property.

The state's highest court rejected the appellate court's public policy rationale, reversed and remanded for reconsideration the determination regarding the Superfund site, and affirmed the determination regarding the asphalt plant disallowing an assessment reduction. The court acknowledged that federal and state environmental law may affect the value of contaminated property, but rejected a dollar-for-dollar deduction of the cost to cure from value as a matter of law. Instead, the court left to the appraisal community the measure of whatever "adjustment" to value was necessary to account for the cost of cleanup in the face of environmental regulation. The court further directed that "normal assessment techniques" were to be employed to value properties in use, since they have value to their owners, notwithstanding any legal prohibition of their sale.

Subsequently, in *University Plaza Realty Corp. v. Hackensack* (1993),[16] the state's intermediate appellate court approved a dollar-for-dollar deduction of the cost of asbestos abatement from the value of an office building. The court distinguished this case from *Inmar* on the ground that the asbestos abatement was discretionary, subject only to market forces, and not legally mandated.

New York: In *Commerce Holding Corp. v. Bd. of Assessors of the Town of Babylon* (1996),[17] the soil and groundwater were contaminated by the metal plating operations of a former tenant in the taxpayer's industrial building, which was fully operational. The property was designated a Superfund cleanup site, and the taxpayer entered into a consent order with the Environmental Protection Agency to remediate the contamination.

15. 549 A.2d 38 (N.J. 1988)
16. 624 A.2d 1000 (N.J. App. Div. 1993), cert. den. 634 A.2d 527 (N.J. 1993)
17. 673 N.E.2d 127 (N.Y. 1996)

The state's highest court upheld a lower court's deduction of the present value of the remaining cost to cure the contamination from the value of the property in an uncontaminated state. The court rejected the taxing authority's contentions that public policy considerations and the presence of the consent order precluded such a deduction as a matter of law.

While prescribing no particular methodology to value environmentally contaminated property, the court approved the use of cleanup costs to quantify the diminution in value attributed to contamination. Additionally, the court set forth the following factors to be considered in valuing contaminated property:

> The property's status as a Superfund site, the extent of the contamination, the estimated cleanup costs, the present use of the property, the ability to obtain financing and indemnification in connection with the purchase of the property, potential liability to third parties, and the stigma remaining after cleanup.

The court indicated, however, that property capable of productive use should not have a negative value.

North Carolina: In *Appeal of Camel City Laundry Co.* (1996),[18] the taxpayer's soil and groundwater were contaminated by a prior owner's coal gasification operation. An appellate court rejected a deduction of the present value of the cost to cure from value. That analysis resulted in a zero value, which the court held to be legal error when a property is usable. The court approved the taxing authority's value-in-use approach, which consisted of discounting the unimpaired value of the property for stigma and non-liquidity, through a heightened capitalization rate in the income approach, and also subtracted from value the present value of remediation costs that were amortized over 25 years, which was the useful life of the building on the property.

Ohio: In *Vogelgesang v. CECOS Int'l., Inc.* (1993),[19] the groundwater was contaminated at the taxpayer's hazardous waste facility. There was a history of intervention by federal and state environmental authorities at the site, including a consent order under which the taxpayer was required to build structures designed to prevent groundwater contamination. The costs of building these structures were incurred after the valuation date. Additionally, after the valuation date, the taxpayer closed the facility, lost its operating permits, and entered into another consent order under which the taxpayer would permanently close the facility and retain liability for closure and post-closure costs.

The court rejected the taxpayer's negative value conclusion. The court found that the appeals board below properly declined to deduct from value all the remediation and related closure costs, and costs of compliance with the consent orders, in the absence of evidence of the effect of these costs on value, or evidence of the amount or timing of the costs.

Pennsylvania: In *B.P. Oil Co. v. Bd. of Assessment Appeals of Jefferson County* (1993),[20] the soil and groundwater at a truck stop were contaminated by fuel leaks from underground storage tanks. The lower court upheld the taxing authority's assessment of the property, finding that the taxpayer

18. 472 S.E.2d 402 (N.C. App. 1996)
19. 619 N.E.2d 1072 (Ohio App. 1993)
20. 633 A.2d 1241 (Pa. Commw. 1993)

Chapter 8: *Toxic Tax Assessments*

failed to meet its burden of proof. An appellate court reversed and remanded the case for a new trial. The appellate court held that the taxpayer did meet its initial burden of overcoming the presumptive validity of the assessment through unrebutted expert testimony establishing i). the existence of contamination; ii). the cost and duration of cleanup; and iii). a negative impact on value equal to the cost to cure the contamination.

Earlier, in *Monroe County Bd. of Assessment Appeals v. Miller* (1990),[21] an appellate court affirmed a lower court's finding of a nominal value for property contaminated with benzene. The taxpayer's appraiser testified that the contamination rendered the property unmarketable. The appraiser's testimony was not only unrebutted by the taxing authority, but also corroborated by the taxpayer, who testified that she was forced to abandon her residence on the property, and could neither sell nor even list the property for sale.

Washington: In *Weyerhaeuser Co. v. Easter* (1995),[22] a paper mill required pollution control equipment to continue to operate in compliance with federal and state environmental standards. The mill also contained asbestos and PCBs, which the taxpayer undertook to remediate voluntarily.

The state's highest court held that the anticipated cost of the pollution control equipment represented an item of curable functional obsolescence to be deducted as part of the cost approach to value. The court also allowed a deduction from value of the present value of anticipated remediation costs for the asbestos and PCBs, upon proof of a business necessity for such remediation.

The court set forth the following three factors to be proven by the taxpayer before a claim for pollution control expenses, as a deduction from value, could be considered: 1). the existence of contamination; 2). the existence of a requirement for cleanup; and 3). a reasonably certain estimate of the costs of cleanup, including a formal plan and timetable.

The Washington Board of Tax Appeals had occasion to apply the *Weyerhaeuser* test to determine the value of a shipping terminal in *Salmon Bay Terminals v. Noble* (1996).[23] The terminal, a former plywood manufacturing facility, was contaminated at the time of its purchase by the taxpayer in 1989. The taxpayer negotiated a purchase price that reflected the contaminated condition. Thereafter, pursuant to a consent decree with the Washington Department of Ecology, the taxpayer entered into an environmental agreement with the seller to remediate the contamination.

The Board found that, consistent with *Weyerhaeuser*, the taxing authority was required to consider the environmental contamination in determining value, and had properly done so in valuing the property at issue. The Board adopted the taxing authority's valuation as of 1992, which relied on the 1989 purchase price. To that amount, the cost of capital improvements subsequently undertaken were added, as was the estimated cost of cleanup, which presumably had been undertaken as well.

Previously, in *Fjetland v. Brown* (1990),[24] the Board was presented with a challenge to the assessment of vacant land, used formerly as a log sorting yard, that was contaminated with arsenic, lead, copper, and zinc associated with that former use. The property was designated a Superfund site, was not in use, and would require 10 to 15 years to restore to an environmentally acceptable state at a cost well in excess of the taxing authority's

21. 570 A.2d 1386 (Pa. Commw. 1990)
22. 894 P.2d 1290 (Wash. 1995)
23. 1996 Wash. Tax LEXIS 477
24. 1990 Wash. Tax LEXIS 146

estimate of the property's value in an uncontaminated state. The owner contended that the property was unmarketable and had no value.

The Board found that parties responsible for cleanup other than the owner had been identified and would pay for most if not all of the cleanup. Relying on the principle of anticipation—that value is created by the expectation of benefits to be derived in the future—the Board found that the property could derive income from future use upon cleanup by the responsible parties, and accordingly, had some value in the present. Thus, the court determined the present value of the property by applying a 10 percent discount rate (sufficient to account for the risks and stigma associated with the contamination), for a 15-year period, to an agreed upon future value as if clean. Since that present value was greater than the assessment at issue, the taxpayer failed to sustain its burden of proof and the assessment was upheld.

The Effect of Usability, Liability, and Environmental Policy on the Outcome in Assessment Review Litigation

Usability: Is contaminated property capable of productive use really worth nothing? The case of usable but non-marketable contaminated property presents courts with a dilemma. When the cost of environmental cleanup exceeds the value of the property upon cleanup, a taxpayer may legitimately claim that the property has no market value, which is the usual standard of value for *ad valorem* taxation. If a property is not assessable for taxation, however, it evades responsibility for contribution to the pubic fisc for its impact on public health and the public safety services that the municipality provides, including the police and fire protection that directly benefit the property.

Furthermore, taxing authorities may argue that if a property's value is rendered nominal by virtue of the cost of environmental remediation, the tax abatement resulting from a zero assessment would, in essence, reward the worst polluters most, and penalize careful taxpayers who keep their property free of contamination. Careful taxpayers are not only ineligible for such a "polluter's abatement" of taxes, but are burdened by additional taxes to compensate the municipal treasury for tax revenue lost from the contaminated property.

As described above, the high courts of Iowa and New York, and a North Carolina appellate court, have rejected a zero assessment of contaminated property that is in use, while the high court of Minnesota has approved such a zero assessment. Arguably, the New Jersey and Ohio courts would reject a zero assessment as well, but perhaps not the Pennsylvania courts. The majority that rejects a zero assessment seems to have the better argument.

Historically, the lack of marketability has not precluded the assessment of property for *ad valorem* taxation. For instance, specialty property, which by definition has no market, remains subject to taxation even though there are no buyers for the property. The assessment of specialty property appears to apply the general rule that the market value standard for *ad valorem* taxation applies only when the property, in fact, has a market value.[25] Absent a market for the property, other tests of value must be used.

One such test, promulgated by the International Association of Assessing Officers (IAAO), cited by the North Carolina Court of Appeals, con-

25. 1 Bonbright, *The Valuation of Property*, p. 472 (1937, 1965 reprint)

Chapter 8: *Toxic Tax Assessments*

siders a contaminated property's value in use, in contrast to its market value, or value in exchange:

> [t]here is a tendency to discount [the unencumbered] value based on costs related to remediating or isolating the environmental contamination. Fully deducting the costs may overstate the decline in value, because the value in use concept would then be ignored. Value in use suggests that a property which is still in use, or which can be used in the near future, has a value to the owner. This would be true even if the cost to cure environmental problems exceeds the nominal, unencumbered value.[26]

A value in use methodology sanctioned by the IAAO, and used by the taxing authority's expert at trial in *Appeal of Camel City Laundry Co.,* was approved by the North Carolina court, notwithstanding the market value standard for taxation enunciated in the state statutes. The New Jersey high court said it would approve a value in use approach as well.

Indeed, assessing some tax on a usable property better comports with the design of the real property tax, which provides that each taxpayer contribute equitably to the public fisc. A contrary result seems patently unfair.

Liability: Does liability for cleanup affect the value of contaminated property? The various statutes that govern remediation of contamination often cast a wide net holding multiple parties responsible for cleanup. When a responsible party is solvent, the cleanup cost itself should not lower a contaminated property's value, since a purchaser would not expect to bear that cost in its entirety. However, the value of contaminated property may still be affected by the contamination. Certainly no rational purchaser would pay full price and "buy" a lawsuit against a responsible party, particularly when the purchaser, as a new owner, might also become a responsible party by operation of law. Nevertheless, no rational seller of contaminated property, who is a responsible party, would both sell the property discounted by the cost to cure and also expect to pay for the remediation. Clearly, liability for environmental remediation would affect the amount that willing buyers and sellers would agree to as the sales price for contaminated property, and therefore affect value.

In fact, some environmental statutes preclude the sale of contaminated property altogether. Taxpayers may argue that contaminated property subject to such a statute has no value whatsoever; and taxing authorities, in contrast, may argue that the value of such property is unaffected by contamination, since the property may only be sold upon cure.

But should a tax assessment be affected by the liabilities of particular individuals? The courts have a split of opinion. As described above, the high court of Massachusetts rejected outright consideration of the owner's liability for cleanup in determining the assessment of contaminated property. Similarly, an appellate court in California rejected a taxing authority's contention that the owner's liability for cleanup precluded consideration of the contamination in the valuation of the property.

In the same vein, the high court of Washington approved a deduction of the cost of pollution control equipment from value even though the property owner assumed liability for such costs in a consent order. In essence, this deduction nullified the practical effect of the consent order—the allocation of responsibility for cleanup costs—in the market-

---

26. *Appeal of Camel City Laundry Co.,* 472 S.E.2d 402, 407 (N.C. App. 1996), citing the IAAO "Standard on the Valuation of Property Affected by Environmental Contamination", Clause 4.1 (1992).

place. Similarly, the high court of New York approved a deduction of environmental cleanup costs from value in the face of a consent order under which the owner assumed liability for cleanup; but added that the ability to obtain indemnification in connection with a sale of the property was at least a factor to be considered in determining a tax assessment.

In contrast, the high court of New Hampshire, and the Washington Board of Tax Appeals, have held that when, as a practical matter, the cost of environmental cleanup would not run with the land, a deduction of the cost to cure from value would be unwarranted. The tribunals have upheld assessments that approximated the present value of the contaminated property's value upon remediation by the parties that would pay for the remediation. And the Michigan Tax Tribunal rejected a deduction from value of cleanup costs when the taxpayer had the benefit of an indemnity from the former owner of the contaminated property. There, however, the value found by the tribunal was based on the sale price of the property with the indemnity in place.

Courts have good cause for their reluctance to allow liability for cleanup by particular parties to dictate the value of contaminated property. The real property tax, after all, is assessed on the property, and not on individuals. Ordinarily, value for taxation is based on an objective standard; it is not the value of the property in the hands of any particular taxpayer, or the value of a particular taxpayer's interest in the property. On the other hand, it would be incongruous for courts to ignore the reality of indemnities and liabilities in the marketplace, which lift market values, while approving of zero or nominal values on the ground that property is unmarketable.

Environmental Policy: Should environmental policy override pure appraisal theory? Taxing authorities may argue that reductions in the assessed value of contaminated property that reflect cleanup costs, effectively enable property owners responsible for cleanup to shift the cost of their cleanup obligation to other taxpayers, contrary to the intent of environmental liability statutes to make polluters and other private parties— and not the community—pay for cleanup. In cases where taxpayers seek a nominal or zero tax assessment, which effectively exempts them from taxation, such a result seems perverse, since contaminated property likely poses increased risks to public health as well as an added burden on a taxing authority's public safety resources, such as fire, police, emergency planning and response, and environmental services. Such assessment reductions could be viewed as a reward to owners of contaminated property, some of whom may have caused the contamination. Assessment reductions may also be viewed as a penalty to the public forced to bear these additional burdens. They especially penalize those taxpayers who take responsible measures and make investments to keep their property free from contamination.

A number of courts, including the high courts of New York and New Jersey, have considered these questions of environmental and tax policy and rejected them. While finding that they have some intellectual appeal, these courts have nonetheless held that public policy concerns cannot subordinate statutory and state constitutional requirements to assess property at its "full" or "true" value. Notwithstanding these results in the courts, however, state legislatures may still elect to tax owners of contaminated property whose assessments have been reduced. In Minnesota, for instance, the legislature enacted a novel "contamination tax" based on the amount of value reduction received on account of the presence of contamination.[27]

27. Minn. Stat. §§ 270.91 - .98 (1996); see *Westling v. County of Mille Lacs,* 581 N.W.2d 815 (Minn. 1998) (upholding constitutionality of contamination tax), *cert. denied* 119 S. Ct. 872 (1999)

CHAPTER 8 Cross-References

Related article in Chapter 2: James A. Chalmers, PhD and Scott A. Roehr, "Issues in the Valuation of Contaminated Property" *Appraisal Journal* (January 1993).

Related article in Chapter 9: Richard J, Roddewig, MAI, CRE, "EPA's Brownfield Initiative: Will It Improve the Market for Contaminated Properties?" *Valuation Insights & Perspectives* (Third Quarter 1997), 472.

Superfund Sites, Hazardous Waste Disposal Sites, Brownfield Initiatives, and Risk-Based Assessments

CHAPTER 9

Editor's Introduction

Many of the articles in this anthology emphasize the significant effect the regulatory climate has on the value of contaminated and remediated properties. Roddewig summarizes some of the federal, state, and local initiatives of the 1990s, collectively called the Brownfield Initiative, to remove some of the regulatory and liability barriers that often caused the marketplace to avoid contaminated or remediated properties.

Simons provides the backdrop of Cleveland, Ohio, as it struggled to find innovative ways to encourage and assist the redevelopment of contaminated commercial and industrial properties and nearby residential neighborhoods.

In the 1980s and 1990s the mere designation of a property as a "Superfund" site in some cases created a marketplace stigma. Reichert's 1997 article summarizes many of the academic studies, typically using regression analysis, aimed at understanding the impact of Superfund sites on the value of nearby properties. Reichert then reports on the results of one study conducted in residential neighborhoods around an Ohio Superfund site. His 1999 article provides a follow-up involving the same community and Superfund site.

Girasole traces the long saga of Love Canal near Niagara Falls, New York, the area that prompted the enactment of the federal Superfund program. After a 20-year remediation effort, Girasole reports that the community has been revitalized. More than 250 homes have been remediated and resold at prices "now approximately 90 percent of market value." He believes the history of Love Canal is "a simple lesson in human behavior, people have short memories."

How Clean Is Clean?

by Robert Simons, PhD

Robert Simons, PhD, *is assistant professor of planning and development at the Levin College of Urban Affairs at Cleveland State University. He earned a PhD in planning, an MS in economics, and an MRP in regional planning from the University of North Carolina at Chapel Hill, and a BA in anthropology from Colorado State University. Mr. Simons consults and conducts research for local governments and nonprofit developers.*

This article originally appeared in the July 1994 issue of The Appraisal Journal.

Government mandates on the handling of contaminated material may protect public health and safety, but may also have substantial detrimental effects on the cost of land development. Following federal directives for managing municipal solid wastes, and with hazardous materials standards already in place, the Ohio Environmental Protection Agency (EPA) has set forth regulations regarding the handling and disposal of construction and demolition (C&D) debris. In addition to C&D debris, the proposed regulations also address the issue of asbestos handling in buried debris. The crux of the issue is: How clean is clean for redeveloping urban sites?

This article analyzes the financial effects of stringent enforcement of these regulations on the redevelopment of lightly contaminated inner-city "brownfield" properties, with a wide range of prior land uses, that are being recycled as residential lots in Cleveland, Ohio. The lands available for redevelopment are generally vacant on the surface, with the prior structure buried underneath the ground. Much of the land was previously used for single-family detached or multifamily housing. Other parcels were previously commercial or industrial properties; in addition to having underground structures, they may also have soil contamination or underground tanks. Because of functional or economic obsolescence, location, perceived distance from labor markets, and factor inputs, residential is the highest and best use for these formerly commercial and industrial properties. Regardless of its prior land use, much of the property with redevelopment potential has fallen into government control through property tax foreclosure.

The land recycling issue is analyzed here in the context of a cost-minimizing study of central city residential lot redevelopment, focusing on brownfield costs (i.e., those related to cleanup of previous uses on the property). The focus is thus on the cost side rather than the risk side of the redevelopment problem.

The approach taken in this research is to conduct a case study of an inner-city neighborhood and to create a baseline cost analysis for redeveloping about 120 new residential scattered-site or clustered lots. Existing parcels are grouped into marketable building clusters. Redevelopment costs of formerly residential, multifamily, commercial, and industrial properties are analyzed separately. The baseline estimates show that even before consideration of more stringent environmental regulations, the costs of recycling previously used inner-city land in general and commercial land in particular make it very difficult to recycle as residential land. The expected cost of preparing a buildable residential lot from lands that formerly were commercial and industrial is about $13,000, over double the cost of those lands previously used as single-family detached homes. Brownfield costs represent over 80% of overall redevelopment costs among formerly commercial and industrial properties, compared with a baseline cost of about $6,000 and under 40% of overall redevelopment costs for formerly residential lands.

Stringent enforcement of proposed state environmental regulations regarding handling asbestos during building demolition and removal of buried debris would hit nonresidential properties hard, increasing overall redevelopment costs by about one-third, compared with a 15% rise for formerly residential properties. Thus, the redevelopment costs of nearly all formerly nonresidential lots would exceed their likely market value as land underlying residential homes. Once additional potential costs associated with the enforcement of the asbestos and C&D debris removal are considered, brownfield-related concerns dominate the cost picture to the point where lot redevelopment in its existing form (primarily advocated by the local municipality as owner of large quantities of inner-city land obtained through property tax foreclosure) is threatened. These regulations, if enacted as shown, could have the unintended side effect of substantially deterring redevelopment of inner-city building sites for housing. The balance of this article discusses the local real estate and policy environment and the nature of the study area. It then sets forth in some detail both the environmental and the nonenvironmental cost factors used in the baseline analysis and the baseline estimates of cost by prior land use type. This is followed by a discussion of the proposed regulations and their cost implications.

Local Real Estate, Development, and Policy Environment

Cleveland has experienced substantial population loss over the past three decades. This has caused thousands of residential and commercial lots to fall into property tax foreclosure, and eventually into city ownership through the Land Bank program. Most of the foreclosed lots were too narrow (i.e., functionally obsolete) to be redeveloped individually as residential lots. Further, nearly all structures on lots that appear to be available for redevelopment, whether their former use is single-family, multifamily, commercial, or industrial, have been demolished. Because of the volume of demolitions in Cleveland, nearly all of the demolished structures were simply plowed into the basement rather than hauled away. Therefore, the environmental liability, which now falls on the city's shoulders as property owner, brings the brownfield issue directly into the cost analysis of redeveloping homesites in the city.

The City of Cleveland and Cuyahoga County have been working together in a coordinated fashion for over five years to facilitate land availability for new development in the city. The county had been aggressively pursuing tax-delinquent property owners, with the city obtaining vacant foreclosed properties and putting them into the City Land Bank for future development. In addition to offering developers Land Bank lots for as little as $1, the city provides a "menu" of development assistance, including help with environmental cleanup costs, infrastructure improvements, tax abatement, below-market interest rates on first mortgages, and equity-funding second mortgages.

The Comprehensive Environmental Response, Compensation, and Liability Act (CERCLA) and other environmental regulations, however, cast doubt on the wisdom of municipal ownership of risks associated with fee simple ownership of land. The city is a "potentially responsible party" (i.e., "deep pocket") in the chain of title. Further, research suggests that the perceived risk of redevelopment of contaminated sites may lead to market failure, because investors overvalue the possibility of excessive expense beyond their actual cleanup costs. Hence, there may be a stigma attached to polluted properties beyond actual costs.[1] These issues are peripheral to the focus of this article, which is the cost rather than the risk aspects of redevelopment.[2] While the effects of cleanup of hazardous materials have been discussed, little attention has been devoted to the effects of low levels of contamination on vacant land in the land reuse process.[3]

Study Area Background

The study area is the Wade park section of Cleveland's Glenville neighborhood. Table 1 shows the land use and tax payment status breakdowns of commercial and residential properties in the study area, which is comprised of nearly 1,800 parcels on about 60 city blocks four miles east of downtown Cleveland. A main thoroughfare, Superior Avenue, formerly had streetcars. The area generally has a "first generation" land use pattern, with most structures built on virgin land during the 1910s and 1920s.

The area is predominantly residential (81.8%). Commercially classified properties are twice as likely to be vacant (40.1% versus 20.2% for residential parcels). They are also much more likely to be under public ownership or property tax delinquency (48.3% compared with 30.6%) than residential properties. Only 38.8% of nonresidential parcels are occupied and current on property taxes; thus, over 60% of these lands have atrophied and are candidates for recycling.

1. Peter J. Patchin, "Contaminated Properties—Stigma Revisited," *The Appraisal Journal* (April 1991): 168–172.

2. See Ellen JoAnne Gerber, "Industrial Property Transfer Liability: Reality versus Necessity," *Cleveland State Law Review*, v. 40, (1992): 177–208; and Tex Ann Reid, Edward M. Clar, Anthony M. Diecidue, and Mark F. Johnson, "Assessing a Municipality's Ability to Pay Superfund Cleanup Costs," *Federal Environmental Restoration Conference and Exhibitions* (Washington, D.C.: Federal Environmental Restoration Conference and Exhibitions): 1992.

3. See, for example, Bill Mundy, "The Impact of Hazardous and Toxic Material on Property Value: Revisited," *The Appraisal Journal* (October 1992): 463–471.

TABLE 1   1992 Status of Commercial and Residential Parcels in Cleveland (Wade Park)

1992 Status	Commercial		Residential	
	Number	Percentage	Number	Percentage
Land Use Status				
Vacant land	131	40.1%	296	20.2%
Building present	196	59.9%	1169	79.8%
Total	327	100.0%	1465	100.0%
Property Tax Status				
Publicly owned or in foreclosure	53	16.2%	178	12.2%
Property tax delinquent	105	32.1%	270	18.4%
Vacant land, paying taxes	42	12.8%	75	5.1%
Building, paying taxes	127	38.8%	942	64.3%
Total	327	100.0%	1465	100.0%

SOURCE: Cuyahoga County Auditor, 1992.

Chapter 9: *How Clean is Clean?*

Most of the residential lots and some of the commercial ones are too narrow, however, to be marketable individually. Combining 277 existing lots with adjacent properties to form more marketable residential lots yields up to 190 possible new buildable lots in the study area, in 115 contiguous "strategic" groups. These groups are the overall sample for this analysis.

Residential Demand

To determine demand for new lots, we conducted interviews with several private and nonprofit developers active in the study area. Their past activity includes scattered-site development of 20 units per year. Plans for additional redevelopment call for use of 50 or more additional lots over the next several years. The developers have been marketing single-family detached homes, both stick-built and modular, ranging in price from $60,000 to $150,000. The critical characteristic of lots is their frontage or width. Nearly all of the lots in the study area are 35 to 40 feet wide. With one exception (40-foot corner lots are acceptable), the market is calling for lots with a minimum of 50 feet of frontage. Half of the housing plans, targeting empty nesters, call for at least 62 feet of frontage. Thus existing lots must be combined to form newer, wider lots to effectively access market demand. It should be noted that the relatively long frontage of many commercial lots appears to make them attractive candidates for residential redevelopment, based on this important criterion. We assumed a sustained demand for 30 new residential lots per year in the study area, enough to provide 120 new lots—a total of four years of redevelopment. Both city and county auditor data were used in conducting this analysis.

Baseline Redevelopment Costs

We estimated redevelopment costs for lots identified as part of a strategic lot assembly group (i.e., with two or more contiguous parcels). Costs were calculated for nonenvironmental cost items such as property acquisition, property maintenance, site preparation, replatting, and legal fees.[4] The typical cost per new lot for all of these nonenvironmental items ranges from $2,400 to $4,600, depending on prior land use.

Brownfield-Related Redevelopment Costs

Several brownfield-related costs, such as demolition of standing structures and hauling away and burying debris are considered. For properties with past commercial uses, the remediation costs of disposing of buried underground storage tanks and tainted soil are also considered. Table 2 summarizes the assumptions used for both environmental and nonenvironmental costs.

Demolition Expense

The demolition expense of a standing structure is based on recent experience in Cleveland. In this neighborhood, a residential demolition has been costing about $2,000. Prior to 1992, commercial demolitions were about $6,000, provided no asbestos or other remediation was required. These costs should rise as a result of the proposed asbestos regulations.

Haul Costs

Haul costs for debris include the expenses of hiring a dump truck or pickup truck and transporting debris to a nearby landfill. Assuming typical resi-

4. The source for the cost factors is Robert Simons, "Cost Minimizing and Land Acquisition Strategies for Residential Lot Redevelopment in the City of Cleveland: A Case Study of the Glenville Neighborhood," prepared for the City of Cleveland, Department of Community Development, December 1992.

TABLE 2 Lot Redevelopment Cost Factors

Cost Item	Cost per Lot
Nonenvironmental Costs	
Property acquisition—old lot in land bank	$0
Property acquisition—old lot in foreclosure	$ 700
Property acquisition—long tax delinquency	MV–TD*
Property acquisition—short tax delinquency	MV–TD*
Property acquisition—vacant not tax delinquent	MV*
Lot maintenance/year	$269
Site preparation	$350
Replatting—simple/new lot	$350
Replatting—multiple/new lot	$700
Legal/miscellaneous	$150
Brownfield-Related Costs	
Hauling debris—residential, old lot	$675
Hauling debris—commercial, frontage foot	$50
Debris burial—residential, old lot	$600
Debris burial—commercial, old lot	$1,800
Demolition—residential	$2,000
Demolition—commercial	$6,000
Underground tank removal/tank	$7,500
Removal of tainted soil—petroleum	$10,000
Removal of tainted soil—lot (chromium, lead)	$25,000

*MV— Lot's current market value according to the latest county auditor data.

TD— Lot's outstanding property tax delinquency, according to the latest county auditor data.

NOTE: Some factors, including property maintenance and hauling debris, were based on frontage feet proportionate to the average assumed residential frontage of 40 feet.

dential construction and demolition debris of about 100 cubic yards, this would represent 10 truckloads. At $45 per hour and 1.5 hours per load, this averages out to $675 per old lot with a dwelling in the ground. Because the bulk of multifamily and commercial structures is estimated to be three times that of single-family structures, the lot debris haul expense is based on proportionate frontage, at triple the residential rate, or $50 per front foot, assuming the destination is a C&D landfill.

Debris Burial Costs

This expense represents the cost of burying common construction and demolition debris in a C&D landfill. Such material is typically present after a residential demolition where the structure has been demolished and buried onsite in the basement. The debris is assumed to be clean of garbage, which would instead have to be taken to a sanitary landfill at the additional expense of $10 to $12 per cubic yard.

Standard procedure had been to allow small amounts of asbestos and lead paint normally present in the vintage residential structures in the city to be simply buried along with the C&D debris. This practice may be directly affected by the new asbestos control regulations. The effect of this new policy is discussed in more detail later in this article.

A brief survey of four waste burial firms listed in the Cleveland Yellow Pages indicates that the going rate for burial of C&D material is $5.50 to $6.00 per cubic yard. Assuming 100 cubic yards of debris per old residential lot, burial expense, exclusive of transportation to the site, would be $550 to $600 per old lot. The higher figure is used in the analysis. For multifamily and commercial properties, the burial expense is estimated on a proportionate frontage while the bulk of the demolished structure is

Chapter 9: *How Clean is Clean?*

also considered. As with haul costs, we have assumed that this line item is three times the cost for residentially zoned land.

Soil and Tank Remediation Costs

For lots previously not used for single-family properties, environmental cleaning costs are potentially more volatile. The category of commercial property can be broken down into multifamily investment properties; those with former commercial uses; and those with prior or current use listed as industrial, including gas stations.

To determine the probability of the need for remediation, we conducted a site-by-site analysis of 65 parcel groupings (of a total of 115 groups in this neighborhood) considered prime for redevelopment. Initial estimates indicate that barring environmental "surprises," the average cost to redevelop these lots would be less than $15,000 per lot; therefore, the sample is already reduced to those lots with relatively lower expected redevelopment costs. If redeveloped, these 65 groupings would yield 123 buildable lots, a four-year supply of land for this redevelopment area. The former land use of the sample is about half single-family residential. Sanborn insurance maps of prior land use from 1912 updated to 1944 and 1977 were used to discover the presence of underground storage tanks and prior industrial service land uses on a site-by-site basis.[5] Based on knowledge of the area, subjective probability assessments of the extent of possible soil contamination were then applied.

Table 3 provides the results of the site analysis for the 65 parcel groupings. Ten of these appeared to have potentially expensive soil remediation problems, including two sites with tanks.

With respect to remediation cost factors, we considered available published research, including general case studies on the cost of environmental cleanup.[6] More typical are highly technical reports of specific cleanup cost studies, often of U.S. military bases.[7] We also included case studies of residential cleanup costs where underground tanks, industrial waste, and chromium were found on residential development sites in Cleveland.

Based on these studies, we used $7,500 per underground tank (a weighted average of a simple $5,000 cleanup for a non-leaking tank, with a 10% chance of a larger $25,000 leak, which could extend offsite). We also estimated the additional expense of scraping off, handling, transporting, and disposing of 50 cubic yards of petroleum-tainted soil at a sani-

5. Thanks to Bob Lacock, Planner with the City of Cleveland, Department of Community Development, who conducted the site investigations, June 1993.

6. See, for example, Deborah Cooney, Jocelyn Seitzman, Charles Bartsch, and Carol Andress, *Revival of Contaminated Industrial Sites: Case Studies* (Washington, D.C.: Northeast-Midwest Institute), 1992.

7. Samar Chatterjee and Herman H. Moore, "Remediation of Mercury-Contaminated Soils/Mixed Wastes"; David S. Naleid, "Zen and the Art of Feasibility Study Costing"; and Robert S. Pace, Mark A. Ferdman, and Catain Mike Myers, "Cost Modeling for Environmental Compliance"; all in *Federal Environmental Restoration Conference and Exhibitions* (Washington, D.C.: Federal Environmental Restoration Conference and Exhibitions): 1992.

TABLE 3   Classification of Probability of Contamination Based on Prior Land Uses for Commercial and Residential Redevelopment Parcel Groupings in Cleveland (Wade Park)

	—— Commercial ——		Single-Family —— Residential ——	
	Number	Percentage	Number	Percentage
Type of Environmental Problem				
Underground storage tank(s)	2	6.6%	0	0.0%
Past commercial use*	5	16.7%	0	0.0%
Past industrial use*	3	10.0%	0	0.0%
Multifamily	16	53.3%	0	0.0%
Common 1/2 family debris	4	13.3%	35	100.0%
Total	30	100.0%	35	100.0%

SOURCE: 1992 Cuyahoga County Auditor data, Sanborn Maps, City of Cleveland, Department of Community Development

* This implies a probability of soil contamination.

Valuing Contaminated Properties

tary landfill to be $10,000 per lot. We were prepared to assess a $25,000-per-lot expense for chemically tainted soil (e.g., chromium), but did not find a reasonable likelihood of prior land uses of this type.

Results of Baseline Analysis

Total redevelopment costs to provide the required supply of residential lots, by former land use type, are presented in Table 4. Figures 1 and 2 provide additional detail on the total comparative costs and the percentage of total costs represented by line item. The parcel groupings are sorted by lowest average redevelopment cost per new lot of supply.

For the base case, average redevelopment costs per lot (and total, in parentheses) are estimated to be $6,300 for lands formerly used as single-family detached residential ($357,600), $10,200 for multi-family ($430,000), $12,300 for commercial ($110,800), and $14,000 for industrial ($209,900). Total redevelopment costs for 123 new lots are estimated to be $1.1 million. Expected average baseline costs for formerly commercial and industrial properties are thus about double those of lands that used to be detached housing—a substantial difference.

For the analysis of environmental cost line items, former single-family lots are dominated by nonenvironmental costs (62.0%). Haul and burial costs of common debris represented only an estimated 35.2% of redevelopment costs, a substantial amount but much lower than for other land use types. Lands that used to be multifamily had more than half (54.5%) of expected expense in brownfield-related costs, with haul and burial expense combined representing almost half of the total cost (47.2%). For commercial properties, nonenvironmental costs shrink to less than 20%, with haul, burial, and remediation each approximating one-quarter of costs. For formerly industrial properties, nonenvironmental expenses are only 17.6%, haul and burial combined reflect 34.3%, and expected remediation costs dominate with 45.3%. Further, the percentages of the last three categories reflect larger average cost amounts.

Effect of New Environmental Regulations on Redevelopment Costs

A draft set of regulations pertaining to the handling of C&D debris has recently been set forth by the Ohio EPA as required by state law.[8] These pending rules would also interact with an Ohio state law passed in 1990 on asbestos abatement, and further rely on definitions of asbestos defined by federal regulations and other state laws.[9]

Stringent enforcement of these proposed rules, if enacted, could work in conjunction with existing laws to affect debris burial costs by requiring onsite segregation of asbestos and common debris, or by requiring burial of all debris in a landfill that accepts asbestos rather than a less expensive C&D landfill.[10] This could substantially affect demolition, haul, and debris burial costs. It should be noted that other soil and underground tank remediation costs are not directly affected by the new proposed rules. Contamination of debris by lead paint could be included, however, depending on the concentration levels of lead and whether it is classified as a hazardous material.

The C&D Debris and Asbestos Regulations

As a result of the proposed regulations, C&D landfill operators would be required to refuse admission to vehicles containing forbidden materials,

8. As authorized by Ohio Revised Code Chapter 3714, the document was prepared by the Ohio EPA, *Construction and Demolition Debris Regulations,* OAC-3745-29, April 20, 1992.

9. HB 366 is the Ohio state law regarding asbestos-handling procedures. The federal rules on asbestos are embodied in NESHAP 40 CFR Part 61 Subpart M.

10. According to B.J. Meter of the Cuyahoga County Health Department (September 1993), additional state standards on hazardous waste, including asbestos, are embodied in Ohio Revised Code 37-34. Ohio Administrative Code 37-45-27 pertains to solid waste disposal regulations.

Chapter 9: *How Clean is Clean?*

TABLE 4 Lot Redevelopment Costs for Strategic Groups by Former Land Use Type: Baseline

Group Number	Debris Haul	Debris Burial	Demolition	Remediation Tanks and Contaminated Soil	Subtotal Brownfield	Subtotal* Nonenvironmental Costs	Additional Group Redevelopment Costs	Average Redevelopment Costs per Lot	Number of New Lots	Cumulative Number of New Lots
Formerly Single-Family										
6	$1,232	$1,095	$0		$2,327	$991	$3,318	$3,318	1	1
49	$1,131	$1,005	$0		$2,136	$1,326	$3,461	$3,461	1	2
25	$1,181	$1,050	$0		$2,231	$1,346	$3,577	$3,577	1	3
7	$1,350	$1,200	$0		$2,550	$1,413	$3,963	$3,963	1	4
104	$1,350	$1,200	$0		$2,550	$1,413	$3,963	$3,963	1	5
90	$2,666	$2,370	$2,000		$7,036	$5,213	$12,249	$4,083	3	8
64	$1,755	$1,560	$0		$3,315	$4,899	$8,214	$4,107	2	10
70	$1,637	$1,455	$0		$3,092	$1,152	$4,244	$4,244	1	11
51	$2,126	$1,890	$0		$4,016	$4,547	$8,564	$4,282	2	13
102	$1,350	$1,200	$0		$2,550	$1,742	$4,292	$4,292	1	14
59	$1,215	$1,080	$0		$2,295	$2,059	$4,354	$4,354	1	15
81	$1,266	$1,125	$0		$2,391	$2,079	$4,470	$4,470	1	16
11	$1,316	$1,170	$0		$2,486	$2,100	$4,586	$4,586	1	17
40	$1,013	$900	$0		$1,913	$2,679	$4,591	$4,591	1	18
43	$1,013	$900	$0		$1,913	$2,679	$4,591	$4,591	1	19
15	$1,013	$900	$0		$1,913	$2,793	$4,705	$4,705	1	20
94	$1,181	$1,050	$0		$2,231	$2,521	$4,752	$4,752	1	21
38	$1,013	$900	$0		$1,913	$2,854	$4,766	$4,766	1	22
41	$1,181	$1,050	$0		$2,231	$2,746	$4,977	$4,977	1	23
76	$1,519	$1,350	$0		$2,869	$2,180	$5,049	$5,049	1	24
71	$1,603	$1,425	$0		$3,028	$2,214	$5,242	$5,242	1	25
42	$2,531	$2,250	$0		$4,781	$11,383	$16,164	$5,388	3	28
106	$1,350	$1,200	$0		$2,550	$2,848	$5,398	$5,398	1	29
32	$1,856	$1,650	$0		$3,506	$8,102	$11,608	$5,804	2	31
53	$2,296	$2,371	$0		$4,667	$1,332	$5,999	$5.999	1	32
74	$2,025	$1,800	$0		$3,825	$8,355	$12,180	$6,090	2	34
83	$4,725	$4,200	$0		$8,925	$26,161	$35,086	$7,017	5	39
19	$7,644	$6,795	$0		$14,439	$7,265	$21,705	$7,235	3	42
21	$979	$870	$0		$1,849	$5,940	$7,789	$7,789	1	43
84	$1,215	$1,080	$0		$2,295	$6,035	$8,330	$8,330	1	44
36	$1,856	$1,650	$2,000		$5,506	$11,911	$17,417	$8,709	2	46
9	$2,616	$2,325	$2,000		$6,941	$19,329	$26,270	$8,757	3	49
20	$2,025	$1,800	$0		$3,825	$15,535	$19,360	$9,680	2	51
92	$3,156	$2,805	$2,000		$7,961	$22,108	$30,068	$10,023	3	54
66	$1,350	$1,200	$0		$2,550	$7,738	$10,288	$10,288	1	55
82	$1,772	$1,575	$2,000		$5,347	$16,621	$21,968	$10,984	2	57
Total	$66,505	$59,446	$10,000	$0	$135,951	$221,607	$357,558	$6,273		
Formerly Multifamily										
103MF	$2,941	$3,153	$0		$6,094	$3,006	$9,100	$4,550	2	2
107MF	$4,091	$4,107	$0		$8,198	$3,289	$11,487	$5,743	2	4
72MF	$1,266	$1,125	$2,000		$4,391	$1,379	$5,770	$5,770	1	5
4MF	$2,835	$2,520	$0		$5,355	$877	$6,232	$6,232	1	6
58MF	$5,400	$5,760	$0		$11,160	$9,026	$20,186	$6,729	3	9
50MF	$4,176	$4,504	$0		$8,680	$6,078	$14,758	$7,379	2	11
61MF	$2,700	$2,889	$0		$5,589	$1,813	$7,402	$7,402	1	12
5MF	$12,403	$11,025	$0		$23,428	$6,948	$30,376	$7,594	4	16
63MF	$2,700	$2,880	$0		$5,580	$2,813	$8,393	$8,393	1	17
39MF	$2,700	$2,880	$0		$5,580	$2,813	$8,393	$8,393	1	18
8MF	$3,949	$3,510	$0		$7,459	$2,100	$9,558	$9,558	1	19
62MF	$6,328	$5,625	$0		$11,953	$9,141	$21,094	$10,547	2	21
93MF	$4,860	$4,320	$0		$9,180	$1,846	$11,026	$11,026	1	22
67MF	$3,679	$2,658	$0		$6,337	$16,383	$22,720	$11,360	2	24
110MF	$18,377	$8,350	$2,000		$28,727	$54,732	$83,459	$11,923	7	31
37MF	$7,633	$7,486	$2,000		$17,119	$19,354	$36,473	$12,158	3	34
24MF	$5,063	$4,500	$0		$9,563	$19,773	$29,335	$14,668	2	36
112MF	$6,581	$5,850	$12,000		$24,431	$6,202	$30,634	$15,317	2	38
10MF	$2,728	$2,963	$6,000		$11,691	$4,149	$15,840	$15,840	1	39
60MF	$8,206	$7,905	$8,000		$24,111	$23,722	$47,833	$15,944	3	42
Total	$108,615	$94,010	$32,000	$0	$234,625	$195,442	$430,067	$10,240		

Valuing Contaminated Properties

TABLE 4 Lot Redevelopment Costs for Strategic Groups by Former Land Use Type: Baseline *(continued)*

Group Number	Debris Haul	Debris Burial	Demolition	Remediation Tanks and Contaminated Soil	Subtotal Brownfield	Subtotal* Nonenvironmental Costs	Additional Group Redevelopment Costs	Average Redevelopment Costs per Lot	Number of New Lots	Cumulative Number of New Lots
Formerly Commercial										
73C	$3,106	$3,366	$2,000	$2,500	$10,972	$3,773	$14,745	$7,373	2	2
13MF-C	$4,202	$3,735	$0	$5,000	$12,937	$2,151	$15,088	$15,088	1	3
23C	$3,038	$2,700	$0	$1,250	$6,988	$5,507	$12,494	$12,494	1	4
2MF-C	$12,606	$11,205	$6,000	$15,000	$44,811	$6,275	$51,085	$12,771	4	8
100MF-C	$3,898	$3,465	$0	$6,250	$13,613	$3,773	$17,386	$17,386	1	9
Total	$26,849	$24,471	$8,000	$30,000	$89,320	$21,478	$110,799	$12,311		
Formerly Industrial										
3I	$12,251	$10,890	$6,000	$11,250	$40,391	$16,440	$56,832	$14,208	4	4
22I	$2,325	$2,516	$0	$5,000	$9,841	$3,354	$13,195	$13,195	1	5
1I	$10,226	$9,090	$0	$38,750	$58,066	$6,658	$64,725	$16,181	4	9
105C-I	$9,195	$9,793	$0	$23,000	$41,988	$8,437	$50,425	$10,085	5	14
77C-I	$3,038	$2,700	$0	$17,000	$22,738	$1,979	$24,716	$24,716	1	15
Total	$37,035	$34,989	$6,000	$95,000	$173,024	$36,868	$209,892	$13,993		
Subtotal	$172,499	$153,470	$46,000	$125,000	$496,970	$253,788	$750,758	$11,375		66

* Includes property acquisition, legal/replatting, site preparation, and lot maintenance.

NOTE: I = Industrial, C = Commercial, MF = Multifamily.

FIGURE 1 Lot Redevelopment Costs by Type: Baseline

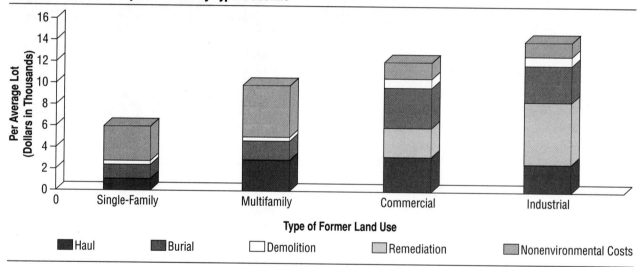

---

[11] See OAC 3745–29–13, subpart G.

[12] Personal interview with Damian Borkowski, February 1992; and telephone interview with Charles Beckles, June 1993; both with the city of Cleveland Demolition Department.

including small amounts of asbestos if they are seen.[11] The proposed rules are unclear, however, as to exactly how clean the C&D debris must be. For example, what if there is both asbestos and lead point seen in the rubble? As a result of this confusion, even in the interim period many commercial demolition jobs in the city have required segregation of asbestos onsite, at substantial increased expense.[12]

If friable asbestos is found in a standing structure, existing legislation requires an EPA permit and use of a certified asbestos contractor. Nonfriable asbestos (e.g., small amounts of duct wrapping) would not necessarily require and asbestos contractor, nor would building materials comprised of less than 1% asbestos. There are three kinds of potential asbestos problems: duct insulation, which is generally nonfriable and can be handled without a certified asbestos contractor by painting then removing, and the more problematic asbestos roof and wall shingles. The latter could be

Chapter 9: *How Clean is Clean?*

FIGURE 2 Lot Redevelopment Costs by Type

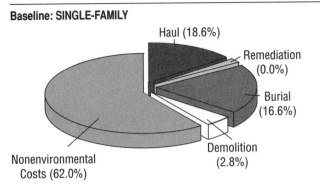
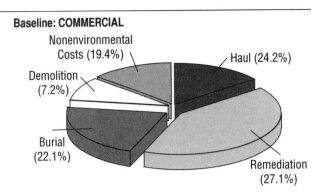
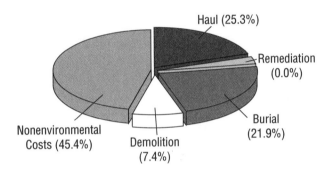
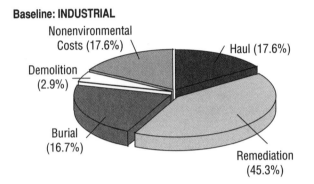
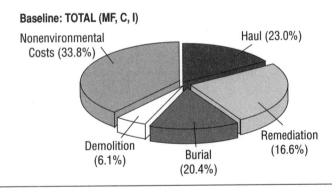

friable and therefore require an EPA permit followed by onsite separation, removal, bagging, and burial in a landfill capable of handling asbestos.

If friable asbestos is found, burial expenses would be much higher: $20 to $35 or more per cubic yard. This would drive the overall weighted average burial cost up from $6 per cubic yard to $18 to $20 per cubic yard, including the possibility of debris segregation onsite. The new regulation is estimated to add about $1,000 to the cost of a residential demolition, an increase of about 50%. For commercial demolitions, the expense is expected to be far greater: We have assumed a two-thirds increase.

For removal of rubble already in the ground where friable asbestos is found, the entire rubble heap would generally be transported several hours away to a landfill capable of handling asbestos. However, not all parcels would experience this problem. We assumed a 33% increase in residential haul costs and a 50% jump in debris burial. For all other former land use types, we assumed a 50% increase in haul costs and a doubling of debris burial expense.[13]

13. According to Bob Lacock, of ten recent demolitions of typical small two-story commercial/multifamily buildings, only two cost less than $10,000, with two others in excess of $60,000. If this is representative of buildings with buried rubble, these assumptions may be conservative.

Valuing Contaminated Properties

Cost Implications of the New Regulations

Total redevelopment costs assuming enactment of the proposed C&D debris and asbestos regulations are presented in Table 5 by former land use type. Figures 3 and 4 provide additional detail on the total comparative costs and percentages of total costs represented by line item. The parcel groupings are sorted by lowest average redevelopment cost per new lot of supply.

After the change in the environmental regulations, average total redevelopment costs per lot (and total percentage increases over the baseline, in parentheses) were estimated to be $7,300 (15.8%) for lands formerly used as single-family detached residential, $12,800 (25.1%) for Multi family, $17,300 (40.5%) for commercial, and $18,000 (28.3%) for industrial.

The cost increases attributable to these proposed regulations are especially onerous for lands formerly used for nonresidential purposes. For example, average costs for redeveloping formerly commercial and industrial properties are more than double those of lands that were formerly detached housing. In addition, only two parcel groupings of formerly com-

TABLE 5 Lot Redevelopment Costs for Strategic Groups by Former Land Use Type After Enactment of Environmental Regulations

Group Number	Debris Haul	Debris Burial	Demolition	Remediation Tanks and Contaminated Soil	Subtotal Brownfield	Subtotal* Nonenvironmental Costs	Additional Group Redevelopment Costs	Average Redevelopment Costs per Lot	Number of New Lots	Cumulative Number of New Lots
Formerly Single-Family										
6	$1,638	$1,643	$0		$3,281	$991	$4,272	$4,272	1	1
49	$1,504	$1,508	$0		$3,011	$1,326	$4,337	$4,337	1	2
25	$1,571	$1,575	$0		$3,146	$1,346	$4,492	$4,492	1	3
7	$1,796	$1,800	$0		$3,596	$1,413	$5,009	$5,009	1	4
104	$1,796	$1,800	$0		$3,596	$1,413	$5,009	$5,009	1	5
90	$3,546	$3,555	$3,000		$10,101	$5,213	$15,314	$5,105	3	8
64	$2,334	$2,340	$0		$4,674	$4,899	$9,574	$4,787	2	10
70	$2,177	$2,183	$0		$4,360	$1,152	$5,512	$5,512	1	11
51	$2,828	$2,835	$0		$5,663	$4,547	$10,210	$5,105	2	13
102	$1,796	$1,800	$0		$3,596	$1,742	$5,338	$5,338	1	14
59	$1,616	$1,620	$0		$3,236	$2,059	$5,295	$5,295	1	15
81	$1,683	$1,688	$0		$3,371	$2,079	$5,450	$5,450	1	16
11	$1,751	$1,755	$0		$3,506	$2,100	$5,605	$5,605	1	17
40	$1,347	$1,350	$0		$2,697	$2,679	$5,375	$5,375	1	18
43	$1,347	$1,350	$0		$2,697	$2,679	$5,375	$5,375	1	19
15	$1,347	$1,350	$0		$2,697	$2,793	$5,489	$5,489	1	20
94	$1,571	$1,575	$0		$3,146	$2,521	$5,667	$5,667	1	21
38	$1,347	$1,350	$0		$2,697	$2,854	$5,550	$5,550	1	22
41	$1,571	$1,575	$0		$3,146	$2,746	$5,892	$5,892	1	23
76	$2,020	$2,025	$0		$4,045	$2,180	$6,225	$6,225	1	24
71	$2,132	$2,138	$0		$4,270	$2,214	$6,484	$6,484	1	25
42	$3,367	$3,375	$0		$6,742	$11,383	$18,124	$6,041	3	28
106	$1,796	$1,800	$0		$3,596	$2,848	$6,444	$6,444	1	29
32	$2,469	$2,475	$0		$4,944	$8,102	$13,046	$6,523	2	31
53	$3,054	$3,557	$0		$6,610	$1,332	$7,942	$7,942	1	32
74	$2,693	$2,700	$0		$5,393	$8,355	$13,748	$6,874	2	34
83	$6,284	$6,300	$0		$12,584	$26,161	$38,745	$7,749	5	39
19	$10,167	$10,193	$0		$20,360	$7,265	$27,625	$9,208	3	42
21	$1,302	$1,305	$0		$2,607	$5,940	$8,547	$8,547	1	43
84	$1,616	$1,620	$0		$3,236	$6,035	$9,271	$9,271	1	44
36	$2,469	$2,475	$3,000		$7,944	$11,911	$19,855	$9,927	2	46
9	$3,479	$3,488	$3,000		$9,966	$19,329	$29,296	$9,765	3	49
20	$2,693	$2,700	$0		$5,393	$15,535	$20,928	$10,464	2	51
92	$4,197	$4,208	$3,000		$11,404	$22,108	$33,512	$11,171	3	54
66	$1,796	$1,800	$0		$3,596	$7,738	$11,334	$11,334	1	55
82	$2,357	$2,363	$3,000		$7,719	$16,621	$24,340	$12,170	2	57
Total	$88,452	$89,169	$15,000	$0	$192,621	$221,607	$414,228	$7,267		

Chapter 9: *How Clean is Clean?*

TABLE 5 Lot Redevelopment Costs for Strategic Groups by Former Land Use Type After Enactment of Environmental Regulations *(continued)*

Group Number	Debris Haul	Debris Burial	Demolition	Remediation Tanks and Contaminated Soil	Subtotal Brownfield	Subtotal* Nonenvironmental Costs	Additional Group Redevelopment Costs	Average Redevelopment Costs per Lot	Number of New Lots	Cumulative Number of New Lots
Formerly Multifamily										
103MF	$3,912	$4,730	$0		$8,641	$3,006	$11,647	$5,824	2	2
107MF	$5,441	$6,161	$0		$11,602	$3,289	$14,890	$7,445	2	4
72MF	$1,683	$1,688	$3,000		$6,371	$1,379	$7,750	$7,750	1	5
4MF	$3,771	$3,780	$0		$7,551	$877	$8,427	$8,427	1	6
58MF	$7,182	$8,640	$0		$15,822	$9,026	$24,848	$8,283	3	9
50MF	$5,554	$6,756	$0		$12,310	$6,078	$18,388	$9,194	2	11
61MF	$3,591	$4,334	$0		$7,925	$1,813	$9,738	$9,738	1	12
5MF	$16,496	$16,538	$0		$33,034	$6,948	$39,981	$9,995	4	16
63MF	$3,591	$4,320	$0		$7,911	$2,813	$10,724	$10,724	1	17
39MF	$3,591	$4,320	$0		$7,911	$2,813	$10,724	$10,724	1	18
8MF	$5,252	$5,265	$0		$10,517	$2,100	$12,616	$12,616	1	19
62MF	$8,416	$8,438	$0		$16,854	$9,141	$25,995	$12,997	2	21
93MF	$6,464	$6,480	$0		$12,944	$1,846	$14,789	$14,789	1	22
67MF	$4,893	$3,987	$0		$8,880	$16,383	$25,263	$12,632	2	24
110MF	$24,441	$12,525	$3,000		$39,967	$54,732	$94,699	$13,528	7	31
37MF	$10,152	$11,229	$3,000		$24,381	$19,354	$43,735	$14,578	3	34
24MF	$6,733	$6,750	$0		$13,483	$19,773	$33,256	$16,628	2	36
112MF	$8,753	$8,775	$24,000		$41,528	$6,202	$47,730	$23,865	2	38
10MF	$3,628	$4,445	$12,000		$20,073	$4,149	$24,222	$24,222	1	39
60MF	$10,914	$11,858	$12,000		$34,771	$23,722	$58,493	$19,498	3	42
Total	$144,458	$141,016	$57,000	$0	$342,474	$195,442	$537,915	$12,808		
Formerly Commercial										
73C	$4,659	$6,732	$3,000	$2,500	$16,891	$3,773	$20,664	$10,332	2	2
13MF	$6,303	$7,470	$0	$5,000	$18,773	$2,151	$20,924	$20,924	1	3
23C	$4,556	$5,400	$0	$1,250	$11,206	$5,507	$16,713	$16,713	1	4
2MF-C	$18,908	$22,410	$12,000	$15,000	$68,318	$6,275	$74,593	$18,648	4	8
100MF-C	$5,847	$6,930	$0	$6,250	$19,027	$3,773	$22,800	$22,800	1	9
Total	$40,274	$48,942	$15,000	$30,000	$134,216	$21,478	$155,694	$17,299		
Formerly Industrial										
3I	$18,377	$21,780	$12,000	$11,250	$63,407	$16,440	$79,847	$19,962	4	4
22I	$3,488	$5,032	$0	$5,000	$13,520	$3,354	$16,873	$16,873	1	5
1I	$15,339	$18,180	$0	$38,750	$72,269	$6,658	$78,928	$19,732	4	9
105C-I	$13,793	$19,586	$0	$23,000	$56,379	$8,437	$64,815	$12,963	5	14
77C-I	$4,556	$5,400	$0	$17,000	$26,956	$1,979	$28,935	$28,935	1	15
Total	$55,553	$69,978	$12,000	$95,000	$232,531	$36,868	$269,399	$17,960		
Subtotal	$240,284	$259,936	$84,000	$125,000	$709,220	$253,788	$963,008	$14,591		66

* Includes property acquisition, legal/replatting, site preparation, and lot maintenance.

NOTE: I = Industrial, C = Commercial, MF = Multifamily.

FIGURE 3 Lot Redevelopment Costs by Type: (after environmental regulations)

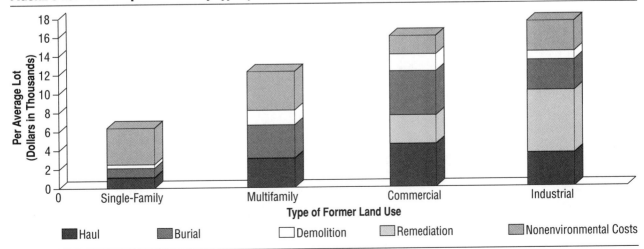

Valuing Contaminated Properties

FIGURE 4 Lot Redevelopment Costs by Type

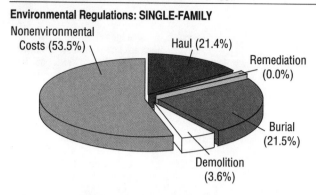
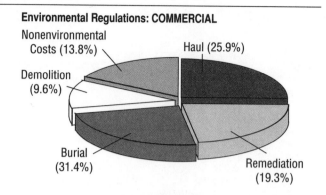
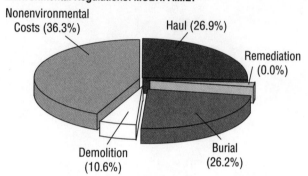
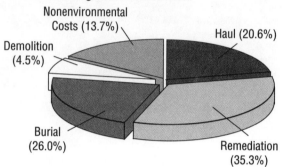
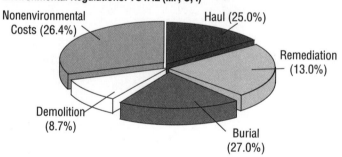

mercial and industrial lands, with a total of seven new lots (about 10% of the sample), have redevelopment costs that are close to or less expensive than available land that was formerly single-family residential. Almost 60% of formerly multifamily properties met this cost-minimizing test. This implies that recycling commercial and industrial parcels as residential land is difficult to justify purely on cost grounds.

For the analysis of environmental cost line items, formerly single-family lots are still dominated by nonenvironmental costs (53.5%). Haul and burial costs of common debris represent only an estimated 42.9% of redevelopment costs, an increase of 21.9% over the baseline. Formerly multifamily lots have almost two-thirds (63.7%) of expected expense in brownfield-related costs; with haul and burial expenses combined representing over half of the total cost (53.1%), up 12.5% over the base. For commercial properties, brownfield-related costs swell to 86.2%, with haul and burial both increasing substantially, while remediation costs are not affected. For formerly industrial properties, brownfield-related costs increase to 86.3% of total costs, haul and burial combined reflect 46.6%, and expected remediation costs drop to 35.3% of total expected costs.

Conclusion

This cost analysis reveals that the effects of the proposed regulations on development costs are substantial—on the order of increases of 15% to 40% depending on prior land use type. Further, recycling formerly commercial and industrial lands in the residential market is difficult to justify based on the cost-minimization criterion alone. Redevelopment costs of these lands are about double those of parcels that were formerly residential, and only about 10% of commercial and industrial lands are competitive purely on a cost basis.

The combined effect of existing asbestos regulations and the proposed C&D regulations would substantially exacerbate an already difficult situation. At best, the additional redevelopment costs of commercial and industrial lands would serve to delay their redevelopment as residential until the available supply of cheaper land has been consumed; in this case, a delay of two to three years or more. At worst, implementation of these proposed government mandates could substantially slow redevelopment of even moderately contaminated inner-city lands, and significantly increase the redevelopment costs in tight fiscal times.

Suggestions for City Land Bank urban developers include the following steps.

- As primary landowner of tax-foreclosed properties, the city should seek to minimize potential brownfield expenses and liability by lobbying for "grandfather" status on stringent enforcement of the asbestos prohibition in the proposed C&D regulations for previously demolished structures. Failing to do so could substantially reduce redevelopment of inner-city land.

- The city should conduct a Phase 1 environmental analysis and systematically evaluate prior land uses before taking control of new properties, especially if they were formerly used for commercial or industrial purposes. Non-fee-simple forms of controlling property should be considered as a way to stay out of the chain of title.

- The city should search for more cost-effective, onsite soil and debris remediation solutions. In light of the large haul, remediation, and burial expense, emerging new technologies (including European soil-washing and electrokinetics for treatment of mercury and other metals) may be appropriate soon.[14]

The more general issue is the importance of finding workable standards for cleaning contaminated lands that can reasonably balance public health and safety with the need for redevelopment of inner-city lands. Even before this latest round of proposed regulations, brownfield-related costs were the major constraining factor in cost-effective redevelopment of inner-city property. What is needed is a workable and precise set of definitions on how clean soil must be before it is considered fit for reuse or burial. Otherwise, perceived and actual financial risks as well as the risk that future regulations could be even more stringent will make redevelopment of inner-city lands very difficult.

14. Consider Michael J. Mann, "European Soil Washing for United States Applications"; and Sibel Pamukcu, J. Kenneth Wittle, and Charles H. Titus, "Electrokinetics: Emerging Technology for In Situ Soil Remediation"; both from the *Federal Environmental Restoration Conference and Exhibitions*, 1992.

The EPA's Brownfields Initiative: Will It Improve the Market for Contaminated Properties?

by Richard J. Roddewig, MAI

Richard J. Roddewig, MAI, *is president of Clarion Associates, Inc., a national real estate appraisal, counseling, and zoning and land use planning consulting firm with offices in Chicago and Denver. Much of his professional work involves "brownfields" and other types of contaminated properties. He is a prolific author and frequent contributor to* The Appraisal Journal—*his October 1996 article on environmental "stigma" won the 1996 Sanders Kahn award. He has also developed two seminars for the Appraisal Institute: Environmental Risk and the Real Estate Appraisal Process and Special-Purpose Properties: The Challenges of Real Estate Appraising in Limited Markets. Roddewig is a land use and zoning attorney and a past chair of the American Bar Association Land Use, Planning, and Zoning Committee.*

This article originally appeared in Valuation Insights & Perspectives *(Third Quarter 1997).*

Over the past two years the U.S. Environmental Protection Agency (EPA) has been implementing a new brownfields initiative, first announced in 1995. The term "brownfields" is a catch-all word for a variety of contaminated sites around the country, typically located in older urban areas. Officially, the EPA defines the term as "abandoned, idled, or under-used industrial and commercial facilities where expansion or redevelopment is complicated by real or perceived environmental contamination." There are between 400,000 and 650,000 such sites across the country. Brownfields typically are not "Superfund" sites, but are other types of properties with less serious contamination problems than properties being remediated under Superfund.

In January 1995, EPA Administrator Carol Browner announced a comprehensive new program to assist state and local governments in redeveloping brownfields. This came in response to intense political pressure from local governments, especially big city mayors, who believed that federal environmental policies were strangling their efforts to create jobs in older industrial and commercial areas. One reason for the dramatic loss of jobs to the suburbs, the urban leaders claimed, has been private sector (and even public sector) fear of the unknowns that accompany acquisition and redevelopment of inner city industrial sites contaminated by past uses.

The EPA's brownfields "Action Agenda," now in full swing, consists of the following components:

- Pilot projects for brownfield clean-ups and redevelopment funded with up to $200,000 in matching EPA grants for two years and intended to demonstrate creative environmental assessment activities that will lead to clean up and redevelopment solutions;

- Clarification of clean-up standards and the liability of prospective purchasers, lessees, and lenders for past and potential future remediation costs and potential future health and damage claims;

- Cooperation between federal agencies in promoting brownfield re-development, and partnership arrangements with state and local governments to turn over more responsibility for remediation approval and cleanup to state government and to foster state initiatives to encourage redevelopment; and
- A grab bag of other initiatives, including job development, training programs, and proposals to modify federal income tax laws to provide brownfield clean-up incentives.

Despite all of the media attention given to federal brownfields initiative, much of the impetus and creative work to assure redevelopment of the more contaminated sites is being done by the states.

Implementation of the Brownfields Initiative: Progress to Date

Pilot Projects: By the end of 1996, 76 pilot projects were up and running. The pilot projects were divided between national pilots selected by U.S. EPA headquarters staff in Washington, DC, and regional pilots selected by regional EPA offices. Among the cities with national pilots are Baltimore, Birmingham, AL, Cleveland, Detroit, Indianapolis, Louisville, Houston, St. Louis, Kansas City, Sacramento, CA, Stockton, CA, and Portland, OR. Regional pilots are underway in, among other places, Buffalo, NY, Atlanta, Clearwater, FL, Miami, Dallas, San Francisco, Chicago, and East St. Louis, IL, as well as Northwest Indiana, Colorado, and Utah.

The pilot projects are of various types. Some are designed to remediate and redevelop specific sites, others aim to enhance databases or site evaluation techniques, while still others are intended to improve cooperation between various public and private interest groups in finding solutions to neighborhood redevelopment problems stemming from contamination concerns.

A few of the pilot projects have been completed, or are nearing completion. An EPA evaluation of the first completed pilot in Cleveland indicates that the initiative leveraged more than $4.5 million in environmental clean-up and property improvements at a bankrupt and abandoned property, resulting in more than 180 new jobs at the site and generating more than $1 million for the local economy. In the Minnesota regional pilot, of the 32 sites that have been targeted for voluntary clean-up, remediation had been completed at 10 of the sites by the spring of 1997. In Buffalo, financing has been secured for redevelopment of a former steel mill site, and buyers have been found for other pilot program properties in Tennessee and Virginia.

Clarification of Clean-up Standards and Liability

This portion of the Action Agenda is the most important to appraisers. Among the significant U.S. EPA policy statements on liability concerns issued since the January 1995 start of the brownfields initiative are the following:

- The Guidance on Agreements with Prospective Purchasers of Contaminated Property;
- EPA's Policy for Owners of Property Containing Contaminated Aquifers;

- The Land Use in the Comprehensive Environmental Response, Compensation, and Liability Act of 1980 (CERCLA) Remedy Selection Process policy guidance;
- The Policy on CERCLA Enforcement Against Lenders and Government Entities that Acquire Property Involuntarily;
- Policy on the Issuance of Comfort/Status Letters.

All five of these policy statements are intended to lessen real estate and lending community fears of potential exposure to Superfund designation in purchasing or lending on contaminated properties that are not yet, but potentially could be, designated as Superfund sites.

The first policy statement expands EPA flexibility in signing specific clean-up agreements with potential buyers, lessees, or operators of property with known contamination. Under the earlier 1989 policy statement on this topic, the EPA was required to receive a substantial benefit from the purchaser, typically an agreement by the buyer to undertake specific site remediation or reimburse the EPA for clean-up costs. While there still must be a public "benefit," the EPA can now take into account "indirect benefits" to the community at large, such as the jobs that will be created after remediation. These clean-up agreements can be very significant to potential buyers because they contain a specific clean-up program and a promise by the EPA not to hold the buyer responsible for any past contamination on the site.

The policy statement relating to contaminated aquifers was issued in November 1995. According to the EPA, about 85% of the sites on the National Priorities List (the Superfund list) contain groundwater contamination, and it is often difficult to trace the groundwater contamination to its source. CERCLA, the Superfund law, requires owners of designated Superfund sites to clean up the groundwater contamination problem whether the source of the contamination was on the site or not, creating considerable uncertainty about clean-up liability for owners of land containing contaminated aquifers. According to the EPA, "(t)his uncertainty makes potential buyers and lenders hesitant to invest in property containing contaminated groundwater." Under the new policy, owners of property with contaminated groundwater will not be held responsible for clean-up costs if 1) the source of the contamination is off-site, and 2) the landowner did not cause, contribute to, or aggravate the problem. In addition, if the owners are threatened with third-party lawsuits as part of complications from a widespread groundwater contamination problem, the EPA will enter into de minimis settlements with the owners if they meet the two criteria.

The third policy statement is a further elaboration of the "risk based corrective actions" (RBCA) concept that tries to match an appropriate remediation program and clean-up standard for Superfund sites with the likely future use of the property. Under the RBCA standard, the cleanup will be more complete, for example, if the property is likely to be used for future residential development for families with small children than if it will continue to be an industrial site. EPA's new land use and Superfund policy statement clarifies the types of information, public inputs, and discussions that are necessary to reach consensus on reasonably anticipated future land uses and therefore on appropriate clean-up goals.

Chapter 9: *The EPA's Brownfield Initiative*

The fourth statement on enforcement of Superfund against lenders, prepared in conjunction with the Department of Justice (DOJ), was issued to give legal weight to the substance of a previously issued EPA rule that had been vacated by the federal courts. The two departments believed this new policy statement was necessary for the following reason: "EPA and DOJ recognize CERCLA's unintended effects on lenders and government entities and the relative concern from these parties regarding the consequences of potential enforcement. In light of these concerns, lenders may refuse to lend money to an owner or developer of a contaminated or potentially contaminated property or they may hesitate in exercising their rights as secured parties if such loans are made. Additionally, government entities that involuntarily acquire property may be reluctant to perform certain actions related to contaminated or potentially contaminated property."

Even more comfort was given lenders when Congress enacted the Asset Conservation, Lender Liability, and Deposit Insurance Protection Act of 1996, further limiting the situations in which lenders will bear Superfund liabilities. Under the new policy statement and legislation, lenders can be more certain that they will not be responsible for Superfund clean-up liabilities simply because they foreclose on a loan on such a site.

The EPA issued further explanation of this fourth policy statement in December 1995 in a quick reference fact sheet titled "The Effect of Superfund on Involuntary Acquisitions of Contaminated Property by Government Entities." In question-and-answer format, this statement clarifies some of the key concerns of state and local governments about their potential Superfund liability if and when they acquire property by such means as tax foreclosure sales, eminent domain, or through bequests.

Finally, the fifth policy statement related to "comfort letters" is designed to give more assurance to purchasers of brownfields that they will not be responsible for costs to clean up contamination resulting from prior uses of the property.

In addition to the various policy statements, the EPA also has taken a significant step in eliminating the uncertainty about potential Superfund clean-up requirements for 27,000 properties around the country. In 1995 and 1996 EPA Administrator Browner removed these properties from the Comprehensive Environmental Response, Compensation and Liability Information System (CERCLIS), the official list of 40,000 properties that might potentially be eligible to become part of the Superfund program. By removing those sites from the CERCLIS list, the EPA is indicating to all potential buyers and lenders that no further federal action is contemplated and hopes to reduce "any stigma associated with federal involvement at these sites and remove potential obstacles to their clean up and redevelopment."

Cooperation with the States

Because most of the hundreds of thousands of brownfield sites are more likely to be subject to state clean-up programs, the U.S. EPA is working with state officials to clarify procedures for eliminating potential duplication of federal and state remediation review and approval. The U.S. EPA formed a work group to devise ways to assure EPA sign-off on more state clean-up programs, thereby eliminating the need for "site-specific federal

Valuing Contaminated Properties

sign-off at sites cleaned up under a state voluntary clean-up program." As a result, the U.S. EPA has recently been more willing to issue either site-specific "comfort letters" indicating no intention to get involved in the clean-up or remediation process or, with a few states, statewide Superfund Memoranda of Agreements ("SMOAs") indicating that the U.S. EPA will not use its Superfund authority at brownfield sites in those states that are cleaned up under the states' voluntary clean-up programs.

These various state initiatives are truly the most important part of the brownfields story since they involve a variety of reform measures to generate new interest in purchase and redevelopment of contaminated properties. Although the state initiatives vary from state to state, most involve one or more of the following features:[1]

- Written agreements with property owners concerning specific clean-up programs;
- Appropriation of additional sources of funds for clean up;
- Expedited consideration of clean-up programs when the private sector pays for agency oversight and management costs;
- "Privatization" of some of the site investigation and remediation oversight responsibilities through licensing of "certified" clean-up specialists who oversee site cleanup in place of state enforcement agency staffs;
- Grants, low-interest loans, property tax abatements, tax credits, and other incentives on selected types of brownfields;
- Lessening of the clean-up and damage liability standard from the onerous retroactive, strict, joint, and severable liability model of Superfund;
- Comfort letters, no further action letters, good neighbor letters, and other types of state assurances that a buyer or lender will not be held responsible for some types of remediation and liability costs and risks; and
- RBCA clean-up standards based upon risks for varying types of future land uses.

Tax Incentives for Clean Up

In 1996 the Clinton Administration proposed changes to the Income Tax Code to reduce the effective after-tax cost of brownfields remediation. Environmental remediation costs in designated economically depressed areas would be deductible in the year in which they were expended. Under current law, such costs must be capitalized over a longer period of time. If and when this legislation is passed, it will further reduce the effective cost of brownfields remediation

Brownfields, Stigma, and the Real Estate Appraisal Process

Real estate appraisers need to monitor and understand these various brownfield initiatives for a number of reasons. All of the federal and state initiatives have a common goal: reduce the legal and regulatory risks associated with owning contaminated sites, thereby encouraging creative approaches to their cleanup and productive redevelopment. In effect, therefore, the brownfield initiatives are intended to reduce the "stigma" associated with owning contaminated properties.[2] Any appraiser who has ap-

---

1. For a good discussion of these various state initiatives, see Jennifer L. Hernandez, Kimberley M. McMorrow, and Laurie G. Ballenger, "Joining the National Brownfields Bandwagon: New Options in Contaminated Property Redevelopment," in *Land Development* (National Association of Home Builders, Fall 1996).

2. For a recent article discussing stigma, see Richard J. Roddewig, MAI, "Stigma, Environmental Risk and Property Value: 10 Critical Inquiries," *The Appraisal Journal* (October 1996): 375–387.

praised a contaminated property, or even a property in close proximity to one, knows that analysis of the degree of stigma that affects the site is a key component of the appraisal process.

What should appraisers be doing? First, check to see if the site you are appraising is subject to any federal or state brownfield initiatives. If the site actually is, or is adjacent to one of the 76 pilot project sites—some of the sites are quite large—there may be a detailed action agenda, and even some financial or tax incentives that can substantially lower the risk for owners of such property.

Even if the property you are appraising is not specifically affected by one of the pilot projects, the risks and therefore the "stigma" associated with its ownership may eventually be reduced by one or more of the other brownfield initiatives. The "archiving" of 27,000 properties from the CERCLIS list is a significant EPA step in reducing the stigma risks associated with owning these properties. If the appraised property has been archived, stigma may have been substantially reduced.

Second, estimate the implications of the new willingness at both the federal and state levels to lessen clean-up standards based on risk-based assessment techniques. Appraisers will have to carefully consider the appropriateness of potential future uses in terms of the higher or lower clean-up costs that might be imposed as part of the analysis of the "legally permissible" and "financially feasible" prongs of highest and best use analysis.

Finally, appraisers need to watch three developments with utmost care. First, keep your eye on Congressional progress in approving the proposed income tax incentive for deduction of clean-up costs. If clean-up costs on some types of properties can be "expensed" rather than "capitalized" it may effectively reduce the capital cost of clean up. On properties with limited clean-up cost risks, it could potentially offset some of the stigma on brownfield properties.

Second, monitor how the lending community is responding to the new brownfield initiatives. To the extent there is an increase in the number of lenders who perceive a reduction in risk and therefore show a greater willingness to loan on some types of brownfield properties, stigma may be dramatically reduced.

But third, and most importantly, become familiar with the state and local programs and innovations implemented in the wake of the EPA's brownfields Action Agenda. The states have generally been much more creative than the U.S. EPA in devising voluntary clean-up programs for contaminated sites, and about 25 states now have such initiatives. Check with state and local environmental officials in the community in which the property you are appraising is located to determine the type of programmatic elements in place and how effective they are in reducing the stigma that often affects the market value of contaminated property.

Impact of a Toxic Waste Superfund Site on Property Values

by Alan K. Reichert, PhD

Alan K. Reichert, PhD, is a professor of finance at Cleveland State University, Ohio, where he teaches banking and real estate as well as conducts research. He is a specialist in statistical valuation models and environmental assessment studies. He earned his PhD in agricultural economics from Ohio State University, Columbus.

This article originally appeared in the October 1997 issue of The Appraisal Journal.

Uniontown, located in the northeast portion of Ohio just north of Canton and a little southeast of Akron, has a population of approximately 10,000. The 30-acre landfill known as the industrial excess landfill (IEL) is about one mile south of the center of Uniontown, close to many residential and commercial properties. The IEL began as a sand and gravel mining operation in the 1950s. From 1966 to 1980, when it was ordered closed, the facility operated as both a municipal and industrial landfill. The landfill accepted a variety of household trash and commercial liquids (latex and organic solvents), sludge, and various solid wastes. The liquid wastes were dumped directly into a large lagoon or mixed with solid wastes.

After a series of fires, the County Board of Health banned the dumping of industrial wastes, but the landfill continued to accept residential trash until 1980. It was soon apparent that toxic waste had begun to contaminate the groundwater, which became a major concern to homeowners who were on well water at the time. In addition, significant accumulations of explosive methane gas were discovered in basements near the landfill. During 1984, the IEL was placed on the EPA's Superfund list and in 1989 a class-action suit was filed on behalf of approximately 1,600 property owners.[1]

Literature Review

The following literature review represents only a small portion of the studies related to contaminated properties found in the literature. The results of these studies, along with the Uniontown results, will be used to illustrate the range of impacts one can expect to find from severely contaminated properties. Further, the combined results of the studies will help identify how property impacts vary by distance.

Kohlhase[2] wrote about the impact of an announcement declaring that a landfill is being placed on the EPA's Superfund list. Eight landfills in the Houston, Texas, area that were placed on the Superfund list by 1985 were analyzed. The study examines the impact on surrounding housing prices

1. In a class-action suit filed on behalf of property owners in Uniontown, the jury awarded the defendants $6.7 million in aggregate damages in December 1994.

2. Janet Kohlhase, "The Impact of Toxic Waste Sites on Housing Values," Journal of Urban Economics (July 1991): 1–30.

Chapter 9: *Impact of Toxic Waste*

in 1976, 1980, and 1985. A linear multiple regression model is estimated that includes a standard set of housing and neighborhood characteristics, plus a measure of distance to the nearest landfill. The model generated an R^2 of 83%. Distance to the landfill was measured in both absolute and quadratic form to allow for decreasing marginal distance effects. A sample of 1,511 homes within seven miles of at least one of the landfills was used in the study. Her research found that Superfund listing creates a market for "safe housing" since nearness to the toxic site was perceived as a disamenity in 1985. The model indicates that housing prices increase at a decreasing rate of up to 6.2 miles from the landfills. For the typical home located at an average distance from each of the landfills, reducing the distance to the landfill by one mile depresses property values by $2,364.

Further, the impact of the landfill is not proportional. Her model estimates that the average value of a home would increase by $4,940 if it were moved from a lot adjacent to the landfill to a location one mile away. If the house were then moved two miles from the landfill, its value would rise by an additional $4,259; an additional $3,476 would be added at three miles; an additional $2,606 would be added at four miles, etc. The maximum increase in value is approximately $17,700 at a distance of seven miles. In addition, while loss estimates varied by site, they seemed to be unrelated to the degree of pollution. To test the robustness of these results, additional analysis was conducted using repeat sales, alternative data sets, and other functional forms. The results were essentially the same.

In 1992, Smolen et al.[3] examined the impact of the Envirosafe landfill located in Oregon, Ohio, on the east side of the Toledo metropolitan area. Envirosafe accepts a low-level category of hazardous waste from a variety of sources across the United States. While the appropriate state and federal environmental regulators indicate that the landfill meets the required safety regulations and is not a health threat, a continuing debate is reported among local residents regarding the long-term safety of the facility. The authors collected data on several housing characteristics for 1,227 property transactions between 1986 and mid-1990. The average selling price for the sample during 1989 was $57,138. Proximity to the landfill was measured in miles for properties located within one of three centroid distance ranges: 0–2.6, 2.61–5.75, or more than 5.75 miles from the landfill. A control sample of 49 properties sold during the 1989–1990 period in a comparable neighborhood located a substantial distance from the landfill was also included. The most consistent results were obtained for properties within 2.6 miles of the landfill. With their eight-variable aggregate model, which generated an R^2 value of 57%, the results indicate that sales prices increased by $8,141 for each additional mile the property is located away from the landfill.

Miller[4] studied the impact of a nuclear waste leak at the Feed Materials Production Facility (FMPC) near Fernald, Ohio, and operated by the U.S. Department of Energy. The case involved leaks of both airborne and groundwater nuclear contaminates. The facility contains over 1,000 acres of rural land in southern Ohio. The subject area was defined as those properties within five miles of the FMPC site. A control area was included in the analysis. Analytical techniques included comparison of price trends, assessed valuations, and turnover rates within the subject and control areas; repeat sales analysis within the subject area; and selected case

3. G. Smolen, G. Moore, and L. Conway, "Economic Effects of Hazardous Waste Landfills on Surrounding Real Estate Values in Toledo, Ohio," *Journal of Real Estate Research* (1991): 283–295.

4. N. Miller, "A Geographic Information System-Based Approach to the Effects of Nuclear Processing Plants on Surrounding Property Values: The Case of the Fernald Settlement Study," Working Paper, University of Cincinnati, March 31, 1992.

studies. The study found that property devaluation was limited to within two miles. For residential properties directly bordering the FMPC, a 35% reduction in value was reported. For properties within one mile, the reduction in property values ranged from 12%–20%. Between one and two miles, the reduction in property values was reported to be in the 5%–12% range.

As previously mentioned, the current study finds that property values within 6,750 feet of the landfill experienced a statistically significant decline in value. The diminution in property values was directly related to proximity to the landfill, with impacts ranging from approximately 5% for the most distant properties to 15% for the closer properties.

With adjustments made to the four individual study findings for differences in surrounding housing values, distance from the landfill, and timing, the range of impact in dollars and percentages is shown in Table 1. Figure 1 plots the percentage diminution in property values against distance to the landfill or source of contamination for each of the aforementioned studies plus the current study results. To help generalize the results, an exponential curve was fitted to the results reported in this paper (labeled "Reichert" in Table 1) and a log regression curve was applied to the Miller results. A linear trend was used to summarize the Kohlhase results, and a kinked linear trend was employed with the Smolen et al. findings.

TABLE 1   Impact in Average Dollars and Percentages for Properties One Mile Away from a Landfill

Kohlhase (Houston, Texas)	$12,728	16.2%
Smolen, Moore, Conway (Toledo, Ohio)	8,141	14.2%
Reichert (Uniontown,Ohio)	7,880	7.6%
Miller (Fernald,Ohio)	7,188	12.0%
Overall average impact	$8,984	12.5%
Standard deviation	$492	3.4%

The range of impacts for the sample of four studies was 7.6%–16.2%, with an average impact of 12.5%. In terms of dollar impacts, the range was $7,188–$12,728, with an average value of $8,894. The standard deviations are $492 and 3.4%, respectively.

In a comprehensive review of the literature, Schultze et al.[5] also found that the reduction in market value for properties located within one mile of a hazardous waste site was approximately $10,000. At the same time, for properties located beyond one mile, the empirical evidence is much less clear. In their words, "The distance (or market size) over which property values may be affected by a disamenity such as a hazardous waste facility is one of the largely unresolved issues in property value studies." The current study provides additional evidence concerning the relevant market size and provides important evidence on the slope of the distance gradient for property values, as suggested by Schultze et al.

Valuation Theory
Property Devaluation

A home represents both a consumption and an investment good that provides a flow of housing services (e.g., safety, shelter, and personal satisfaction) capitalized at an appropriate discount rate when its value is being determined. A negative externality can impact housing values in several

5. W. Schultze, G. McClelland, M. Doane, E. Balistreri, R. Boyce, B. Hurd, and R. Simenauer, *An Evaluation of Public Preferences for Superfund Site Cleanup: A Preliminary Assessment* (Washington, D.C.: U.S. Environmental Protection Agency/Office of Policy, Planning and Evaluation, March 1995): 1–77.

FIGURE 1 Property Impact by Distance

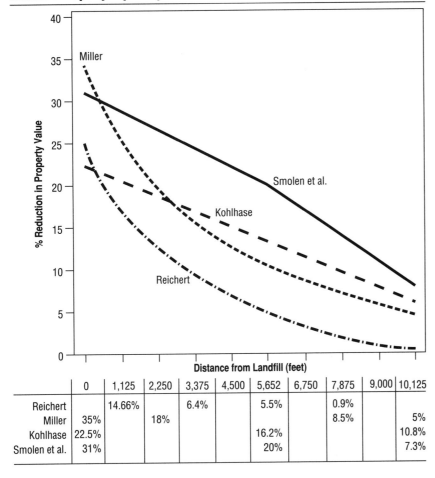

ways. Unpleasant odors, excessive noise, and health and safety concerns can reduce the value of the flow of housing services, for example. From an investment perspective, the difficulty of obtaining financing and the costs associated with meeting health regulations (such as water purification) can increase the rate at which these services are capitalized. Both effects work to reduce the market value of the affected property. In an efficient market, potential home buyers and real estate investors use all available information to estimate the likely decline in the values of these housing services and any potential increase in investment risk. The purchase price will then be discounted accordingly.

When negative news, such as a major toxic leak is announced, the market reaction may take several different forms. First, there may be a temporary liquidity effect as sellers are reluctant to adjust their price expectations downward immediately and as potential buyers attempt to assess the probable long-term impact on market value. Consequently, the market will become less liquid as evidenced by a significant reduction in the volume of sales transactions and a noticeable increase in average "days on the market." Second, a permanent reduction in property values may take place once the market reestablishes a new equilibrium that fully reflects the reduced flow of housing services and/or increased investment risk.

Liquidity Effects

A negative externality may increase the length of time required to sell a given property, imposing significant opportunity costs on property owners. Data was collected on time-on-the-market for properties sold between 1977 and 1991 in both the subject area and a comparable control area. (Because of the difficulty in obtaining reliable days-on-the-market information, the market time analysis was conducted only through 1991. Further, a slightly different control group was used for the market time analysis than that which is used in the price analysis.)

This period was divided into five distinct economic periods. The 1977–1978 period was one of strong housing demand and represents a period that preceded the publicity surrounding the IEL problem. As indicated in Figure 2, the average marketing times for residential properties in both the subject and control areas were almost identical (80 days). The next three years (1979–1982) witnessed a dramatic decline in housing demand caused by a severe recession and very high mortgage rates. Not surprisingly, marketing time increased dramatically in both regions, but the average time on the market was approximately 25 days less in the subject area compared with the control.

Figure 2 indicates that, as the publicity surrounding the IEL developed, the relationship between the two average marketing times reversed, with the average number of days in the control area now less than what was reported in the subject area. This was especially evident during the 1987–1989 period when the average marketing time for the subject area reached approximately 145 days in the subject area compared with only 110 days in the control area. In relation to the 1979-1982 period, this represents a net change of approximately 60 days in favor of the control area (i.e., a shift from a difference of -25 days to a difference of +35 days). During the final period (1990–1991) the two marketing times are once again equal, suggesting that a new and likely lower market equilibrium has been established.

In terms of sales activity, Figure 3 indicates that the annual sales volume for properties located closest to the landfill (Ring 1) and those located in the control area were closely correlated throughout most of the

FIGURE 2 Marketing Time Analysis

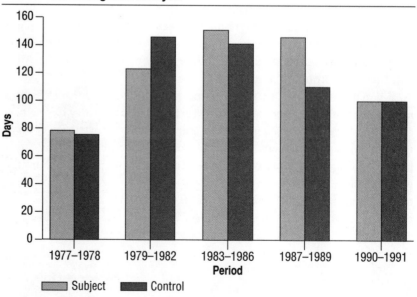

FIGURE 3 Annual Sales Volume: Ring 1 Versus Control Area

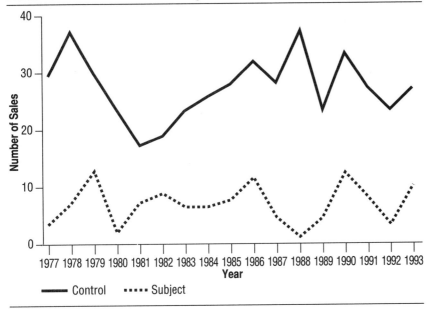

period, with the exception of 1988, which represents the end of the peak publicity period, surrounding the IEL.

Price Effects

Housing prices may differ due to differences in size, style, age, or the presence of various housing amenities. Further, proximity to positive externalities, such as a public park, or negative externalities, such as a landfill, can have a major impact on local property values. In regression analysis, control variables are explicitly included to account for each of these positive or negative housing characteristics. This allows the model to identify the individual influence of any given housing characteristic by holding constant the influence of the remaining factors.

Two alternative functional forms are frequently used in hedonic housing models: the linear and log-linear models. The linear model implies constant partial effects between housing characteristics and selling price, while the log-linear model allows for nonlinear price effects. This study utilizes a Cobb-Douglas[6] exponential log-linear functional form, in which the regression coefficients on the continuous variables represent price elasticities, and the coefficients on the categorical variables indicate the percentage impact on price of that housing characteristic. For example, if a house has a fireplace, the regression coefficient on the categorical fireplace variable (e.g., 0.05) represents the market value of a fireplace measured in percentage terms (5.0% of the total market value). As mentioned, the liquidity effect analysis suggests that a new market equilibrium was established by 1990, meaning that a one-time permanent downward price adjustment took place during the 1988–1989 period. This log-linear model is used to test this hypothesis:

$$lnP = b_o + b_1(lnX_1) + b_2(lnX_2) + \ldots + b_n(lnX_n) + a_oD_o + \ldots + a_mD_m + e \quad (1)$$

where,

  P = Nominal selling price

  $X_1..X_n$ = A series of continuous housing characteristics, such as square footage of living space, age, lot size, etc.

---

6. H. Kang and Alan Reichert, "An Evaluation of Alternative Estimation Techniques and Functional Forms in Developing Statistical Appraisal Models," *The Journal of Real Estate Research* (Fall 1987): 1–29.

Valuing Contaminated Properties

$D_o..D_m$ = Various categorical (dummy) variables such as style, air conditioning, etc.

b, a = Estimated regression coefficients on the continuous and categorical variables, respectively

e = A random error term

Data

Information on homes sold in the Uniontown area were obtained from the multiple listing service (MLS) for January 1977–May 1994. The variables used in the model are listed in Table 2. These variables are common to most statistical real estate appraisal models and are structured in a conventional manner.

TABLE 2   Variables for Log-Linear Model

1. LPRICE = Selling price (nominal terms)
2. LAGE = Age of property at time of sale (years)
3. LSQFT = Square feet of living space
4. FRPL = Presence of a fireplace (1 or 0)
5. CAIR = Presence of central air conditioning (1 or 0)
6. BSMT = Presence of a partial or full basement (1 or 0)
7. POOL = Presence of an in-ground swimming pool (1 or 0)
8. BATHS = Total number of full and half baths
9. BEDRMS = Number of bedrooms
10. NEW = New house (1 or 0)
11. LLOTSIZE = Lot size in square feet
12. GARAGE = Size of garage (square feet)
13. BUNGALOW, BISPLIT, COLONIAL, RANCH (the base) = Style of house (1 or 0)
14. D2250, D4500, D6750, D9000 = Location of the property as measured by one of four concentric circles radiating from the landfill (1 or 0)
15. MAJORRD, MINORRD = Location of property on a high- or medium-traffic road (1 or 0)
16. HSCHOOL = High school district (1 or 0)
17. CTYWATER = Presence of city versus well water (1 or 0)
18. YRxx = Year of sale (1 or 0 for each of 17 years)
19. QTRxx = Season (first, second, third, or fourth quarter)
20. Dddyr = Interaction between year of sale and distance from the landfill (1 or 0)

Control Area

A control area serves as the benchmark against which the price behavior of houses in the subject area are compared. A control group is used to account for various factors that affect housing prices in general. Examples include changes in interest rates, employment, and property taxes. The effects of these general factors are eliminated when the subject area and the control area are compared. To serve as an effective control area, the region should be sufficiently far from the landfill to be unaffected by the toxic emissions and should contain housing of the age and types found throughout the subject area. The property in the control area closest to the landfill is 8,000 feet away. Table 3 provides basic descriptive statistics on several key factors, such as age, size, and style for properties in both the subject and the control areas.

Distance Effects

Distance variables were included in the model. It seems likely that properties closer to the landfill would suffer the largest economic loss, and

Chapter 9: *Impact of Toxic Waste*

TABLE 3 Summary Statistics: Subject Area Versus Control Area (1977–1987)

————————————————— Subject Area —————————————————

Characteristic	Mean	Minimum	Maximum	Standard Deviation
Price	68,243	23,000	155,000	16,350
Building size (square feet)	1,688	660	3,200	342
Lot size (square feet)	23,484	6,956	174,350	13,262
Year built	1973	1907	1987	—

Style	(%)	Bedrooms	(%)	Baths	(%)
Ranch	25.9	1	0.1	1.0	10.8
Colonial	33.2	2	2.9	1.5	20.4
Bi-/split-level	38.6	3	53.7	2.0	24.0
Other	2.3	4	41.3	2.5	42.0
		5	1.8	3.0+	2.8

————————————————— Control Area —————————————————

Characteristic	Mean	Minimum	Maximum	Standard Deviation
Price	65,793	34,000	118,000	12,547
Building size (square feet)	1,660	1,040	2,600	280
Lot size (square feet)	20,397	10,440	54,400	6,859
Year built	1977	1962	1987	

Style	(%)	Bedrooms	(%)	Baths	(%)
Ranch	21.3	1	0.0	1.0	0.0
Colonial	27.0	2	0.7	1.5	22.3
Bi-/split-level	48.6	3	70.3	2.0	29.1
Other	0.8	4	27.7	2.5	33.4
		5	1.3	3.0+	3.0

those farther away might experience a smaller, but still meaningful, impact. To test this relationship, the distance from the nearest edge of the landfill to the middle of each property was measured in 50-foot increments, and each property in the subject area was placed into one of four equal-width concentric distance rings. Thus, Ring 1 includes properties within 2,250 feet of the landfill; Ring 2 includes properties between 2,251 feet-4,500 feet; Ring 3 includes properties between 4,501 feet-6,750 feet; and Ring 4 includes the remaining properties out to 9,000 feet.

Annual Effects

A variety of important developments occurred in the real estate market during the last half of the sample period. For example, in 1989, the EPA released its remediation plan; soil tests continued to provide conflicting evidence regarding the nature and extent of the underground contamination; houses immediately surrounding the IEL were removed; and arrangements were made to bring city water into the area. It can be argued that this information potentially had both positive and negative implications for homeowners. The EPA's proposed remediation plan was viewed as a positive step by certain residents and as grossly inadequate by others. Further, the availability of city water could alleviate the well water contamination problem but at a cost of approximately $6,000 per homeowner to cover assessments and hook-up fees. To capture any potentially beneficial impacts related to the availability of city water, a variable was included in the model to indicate whether the sale took place after the homeowner was hooked up to city water.

While the liquidity analysis suggests that the impact of the landfill was quickly felt, given the variety of potentially positive and negative information reaching the market, a set of annual impact variables was developed. These variables are extremely flexible and would allow for a continuing decline, a potential recovery, or as previously hypothesized, a stabilization in property values. The use of these annual impact variables makes no *a priori* assumptions about a continuation of trends within or between different time periods. In effect, each year is treated as an independent observation. A series of dummy variables is included in the model to indicate the interaction of distance to the landfill as measured by each of the four concentric distance rings and the date of sale.

These interaction variables were formed by taking the product of these annual and distance categorical variables. For example, the categorical variable, D2278, represents the product of the categorical variable year (YR78—not shown in Table 4) times the distance variable, D2250 (i.e., within 2,250 feet of the landfill). These interaction terms are calculated for each year from 1978 to 1994, with 1977 and the control area serving as the base for year of sale and distance, respectively. Thus, the regression coefficient on each of these annual dummy variables indicates how average housing prices in that distance ring for a specific year behave compared with the control area in 1977. For example, if the regression coefficient on D2278 is 0.10, properties within 2,250 feet of the landfill in 1978 sold for 10% more than properties located in the control area during the base year, 1977. All subsequent impacts are measured in relation to housing prices in the control area during 1977. Figures 4 through 6 plot these annual impact coefficients for the entire 17-year period for the first three rings. Given that a relatively small number of sales occurred in each distance ring, it is not surprising that random yearly fluctuations appear throughout the entire period.

Before and After Effects

Initial statistical tests that examined changes in appreciation rates for several submarkets surrounding the IEL confirmed that, by 1988, appreciation rates within the subject area began to decline significantly in relation to appreciation rates in the control area. This period coincides closely with the dramatic increase in negative publicity surrounding the landfill. Thus, the period from 1977 through 1987, called the pre-IEL period, was considered to be free from any statistically significant landfill effects. The period from 1988 through the end of the sample period (May 1994) was considered the post-IEL period.

To reduce the impact of random factors on the annual impact coefficients, the values of the individual annual impact coefficients were averaged over both the pre- and post-IEL subperiods. The bold straight lines depicted in Figures 4–6 graphically represent these two average values. The estimated impact of the IEL for each distance ring is then calculated as the difference between these two average values. A pooled *F*-test was conducted on the difference between the means of the two sets of regression coefficients to identify any statistically significant shifts.

Chapter 9: *Impact of Toxic Waste*

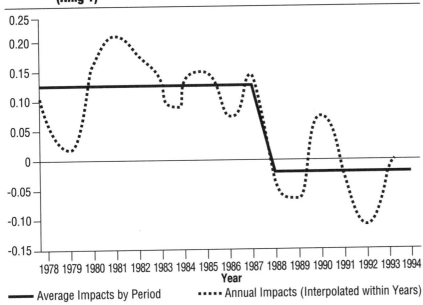

FIGURE 4 Percentage Impact on Housing Prices: Within 0–2,250 Feet of IEL (Ring 1)

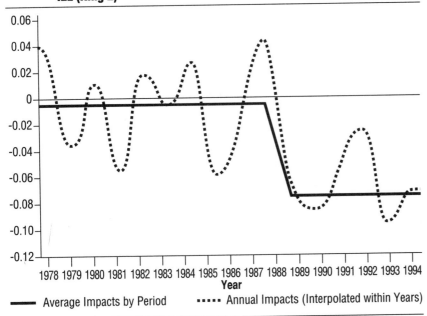

FIGURE 5 Percentage Impact on Housing Prices: Within 2,251–4,500 Feet of IEL (Ring 2)

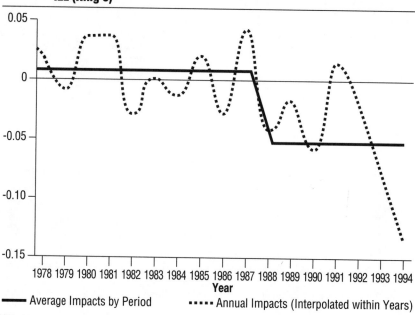

FIGURE 6 Percentage Impact on Housing Prices: Within 4,501–6,750 Feet of IEL (Ring 3)

Regression Results

A set of partial regression results illustrating the impact on properties located in Ring 1 is presented in Table 4. The model generated an adjusted R^2 of approximately 84%, and an overall F-value of 67.2. (Tests for autocorrelation, heteroscedasticity, and multicollinearity generally indicate that the model is adequately specified and that the data are not severely ill conditioned.) All the physical characteristic variables in the model were statistically significant and had the expected signs with the exception of minor road (MINORRD) and city water (CTYWATER). For example, the three most significant variables in the model are log of square feet of living space (LSQFT), log of the age of the house at time of sale, and log of the number of baths (BATHS). The regression coefficient on LSQFT is 0.347, which indicates that, on average, a 10% increase in square feet will generate a 3.47% increase in selling price. The coefficient on age (-0.092) indicates that a 10% increase in age would generate a 0.9% reduction in market value.

As already mentioned, the regression coefficient on the categorical variables is a direct measure of the percentage impact on market value. Thus, the results indicate that the presence of central air conditioning adds 5.2% to the value of a home, while an in-ground pool typically adds 5.6% to market value. On the other hand, homes located on a busy street sold at an average discount of 6.3% compared with identical houses located elsewhere. In terms of style, the results indicate that the least expensive homes for a given square footage are bungalows and bi-/split-levels. The coefficients on the three quarterly variables reflect seasonality in housing prices. The results indicate that houses selling during the third and fourth quarters command a price averaging 4%–5% above the first quarter base.

The regression coefficients on the yearly dummy variables measure the annual rate of price appreciation across the entire sample in relation to the

Chapter 9: *Impact of Toxic Waste*

TABLE 4 Partial Set of Regression Results Illustrating Impacts on Ring 1*

Dependent Variable: LPrice $\quad$ N: 1,394 $\quad$ Multiple R: 0.922
R^2: 0.849 $\qquad\qquad\quad$ $\bar{R}^2$: 0.837 $\quad$ Standard Error of Estimate: 0.105

Variable	Coefficient	Standard Error	T	P (2 Tail)
CONSTANT	7.335	0.167	43.982	0.000
BEDRMS	0.022	0.006	3.489	0.001
BATHS	0.080	0.007	10.831	0.000
LSQFT	0.347	0.022	15.951	0.000
LAGE	-0.092	0.006	-14.490	0.000
NEW	-0.102	0.014	-7.153	0.000
LLOTSIZE	0.071	0.009	7.715	0.000
FRPL	0.045	0.008	5.366	0.000
CAIR	0.052	0.007	7.876	0.000
GARAGE	0.039	0.009	4.194	0.000
BSMT	0.030	0.011	2.838	0.005
BUNGALOW	-0.073	0.017	-4.285	0.000
BISPLIT	-0.071	0.009	-8.026	0.000
COLONIAL	-0.039	0.010	-3.776	0.000
MAJORRD	-0.063	0.020	-3.169	0.002
MINORRD	0.003	0.012	0.217	0.828
HSCHOOL	-0.045	0.015	-2.936	0.003
POOL	0.056	0.020	2.793	0.005
CTYWATER	-0.007	0.033	-0.198	0.843
QTR2	0.025	0.008	3.016	0.003
QTR3	0.040	0.009	4.500	0.000
QTR4	0.050	0.009	5.433	0.000
D2250	-0.051	0.056	-0.908	0.364
D4500	0.048	0.026	1.841	0.066
D6750	0.010	0.028	0.345	0.730
D9000	0.049	0.012	4.194	0.000
D2278	0.106	0.071	1.487	0.137
D2279	0.300	0.066	0.458	0.647
D2280	0.164	0.096	1.715	0.087
D2281	0.205	0.073	2.801	0.005
D2282	0.175	0.071	2.445	0.015
D2283	0.109	0.074	1.481	0.139
D2284	0.151	0.074	2.046	0.041
D2285	0.118	0.072	1.645	0.100
D2286	0.073	0.066	1.109	0.268
D2287	0.147	0.079	1.862	0.063
D2288	-0.023	0.122	-0.192	0.848
D2289	-0.052	0.080	-0.660	0.509
D2290	0.063	0.066	0.965	0.335
D2291	-0.007	0.071	-0.104	0.917
D2292	-0.106	0.080	-1.321	0.187
D2293	0.012	0.068	0.174	0.862

* The annual dummy variables are not shown. Upon request, the author will provide a full set of regression results. Call (216) 687-6958 or e-mail sumbreeze@aol.com.

base year, 1977. The coefficients indicate the rapid appreciation during the late 1970s and the slowdown during 1981–1983. The coefficients on the four distance ring variables (D2250, D4500, D6750, and D9000) show how the average prices of properties in the four distance rings compare with the prices in the control area throughout the entire sample period. The remaining set of interaction variables shows the impact of both location and time on housing values in the subject area compared with housing values in the control area.

Damage Calculations

The results of the regression model are used to calculate the average annual impact on properties less than 75 years old. (Damages on residential properties older than 75 years are calculated using tax assessment data.) For properties that sold after 1987, losses were calculated at time of sale by using the regression model to predict a property's market value in the presence of the landfill. The value of the property in the absence of the landfill was then calculated by dividing this estimated price by one minus the impact coefficient calculated for the appropriate distance ring and year of sale. These losses were then adjusted for changes in the Consumer Price Index between the year of sale and May 1994.

For properties that did not sell in the post-IEL period, the damages as of 1994 were calculated by comparing the predicted market value of these properties in the presence of the landfill and their predicted "but for" values as of May 1994. Property damages for individual properties in the subject area were then totaled to provide an estimate of aggregate damages for the entire class.

The impact on residential properties older than 75 years old, vacant lots, and commercial properties with a residential component (e.g., multifamily properties, apartments, and small office buildings) were determined, using the most recent market value estimates for these properties as determined by the county tax assessor's office. The appropriate distance-related percentage impacts previously discussed were then applied to these market value calculations to establish losses. No attempt was made to quantify the impact of the landfill on agricultural land and structures, nonresidential commercial properties, or a wide variety of special-use properties such as, schools, churches, recreational parks, etc.

Damages are calculated for only the first three distance rings (within 6,750 feet from the landfill) where the F-test results indicated a high level of statistical significance. The average percentage loss and their associated level of statistical significance for each of the distance rings are indicated in Table 5. The impact coefficients represent the average effect experienced by all properties in each ring. Properties closest to the landfill in each distance ring more than likely suffered a larger impact than did properties toward the outer edge of any given ring. (See the results of fitting an exponential curve to the ring-specific impact coefficients depicted in Figure 1.)

TABLE 5   Impact and Statistical Tests

Ring	Impact %	F-test**	Probability
1	-14.66%	26.5	0.00
2	-6.40%	21.0	0.00
3	-5.48%	15.3	0.00
4	-0.97%*	0.7	0.80

*   Decrease is not statistically significant.

** Test of equality of mean regression coefficients between the pre- and post-IEL periods using a pooled F-test.

Damage estimates in 1994 dollars for residential properties less than 75 years old are summarized in Table 6. The average percentage loss in market value for properties located in Ring 1 was -14.66%, and the average dollar loss in residential properties less than 75 years old was $15,809. The corresponding losses for Ring 2 were -6.40% and $7,072, while the

Chapter 9: *Impact of Toxic Waste*

comparable impacts for Ring 3 were -5.48% and $5,046. Losses associated with older houses and commercial properties that have a residential component are summarized in Table 7. Thus, the aggregate damages associated with the entire set of 1,586 properties totaled $10,960,637.

TABLE 6 Average Loss Estimates by Ring

	Ring 1	Ring 2	Ring 3	Total
Number of Properties	225	509	484	1,218
Minimum loss	$7,745	$3,141	$2,322	$2,322
Maximum loss	$25,448	$11,301	$8,857	$25,448
Average loss	$15,809	$7,072	$5,046	$7,880
Total	$3,556,917	$3,599,489	$2,442,024	$9,598,430

TABLE 7 Aggregate Losses by Property Type

	Volume	Losses
Vacant lots	207	$152,172
Older houses	55	$270,686
Duplex/triplex	67	$656,898
Residential/commercial	39	$282,452
Total damages	368	$1,362,208

Conclusion

The analysis illustrates that toxic waste landfills have a relatively quick, economically significant, and permanent impact on housing values. The study indicates that a temporary liquidity effect is likely, as evidenced by a reduced volume of sales and an increase in marketing time. At the same time, once housing prices fully adjust to the realities of a contaminated marketplace, the liquidity effect disappears. Thus, houses located near a landfill will begin to sell at a normal pace but at a significantly reduced price. Unfortunately, the ultimate effect is the permanent reduction of real property value within a considerable distance from the contaminated site.

References

Kinnard, W., and Mary Beth Geckler. "The Effects on Residential Real Estate Prices from Proximity to Properties Contaminated with Radioactive Materials." *Real Estate Issues* (Fall/Winter 1991): 25–36.

Kinnard, W., P. Mitchell, G. Beron, and J. Webb. "Market Reaction to an Announced Release of Radioactive Materials: The Impact on Assessable Value." *Property Tax Journal* (September 1991): 283–297.

The Lesson of Love Canal

by Anthony P. Girasole, Jr.

Anthony Girasole, Jr., *grew up in Niagara Falls, N.Y., approximately a quarter mile from the Love Canal site. He has a degree in business administration from the State University of New York at Delhi. Today Girasole is president of Girasole Appraisal Company, Inc., a real estate appraisal and consulting company based in Niagra Falls. He is currently an associate member of the Appraisal Institute pursuing his MAI.*

This article originally appeared in Valuation Insights & Perspectives *(First Quarter 1999).*

If a marketing company completed a name recognition survey, where would Love Canal rank? While most people would recognize the name, would their mental image of Love Canal be accurate? People from all over the country call our company for information about the infamous site, and typically these individuals imagine a desolate, mysterious and dangerous place—a place where the homes are boarded-up, chemicals are running down the streets and "skull and cross bones" signs are posted everywhere. That was never true. But for a time it was close.

"Model City" Becomes Hazardous Dump

Love Canal was just a small part of the vision of William T. Love. In the early 1890s Love had a grandiose dream of building a new city in rural Niagara County, N.Y. It was to be called Model City and would be the envy of the modern world. It would be new and clean, have an efficient layout, and most important, the city would have cheap and abundant electricity that would be generated by the water flowing through Love Canal. The canal was to start on the Niagara River, seven miles east of the world famous Niagara Falls and empty into Lake Ontario.

However, Love's dream was never realized. The acceptance of alternating current (AC) allowed electrical power to be transmitted long distances, eliminating the need for the canal. The small portion of the canal that was built to promote the venture eventually filled with water and lay unused until the 1940s. There is still a Model City in the Town of Lewiston, N.Y., which consists of one road, a couple of businesses, a few homes and a post office.

During World War II the Hooker Chemical Company acquired the property to dispose of its industrial waste. In Niagara County there were many locations used by "midnight dumpers" who would unload wastes anywhere that was convenient. At the time the canal was a good location to dispose of industrial waste, because the area around the canal was still

Chapter 9: *The Lesson of Love Canal*

rural and the clay content in the soil made it an almost ideal site. While there is still no "ideal" site to dispose of hazardous waste, this was better than most other disposal choices at that time.

After WWII, the City of Niagara Falls was growing rapidly and running out of space. The Board of Education acquired much of the area from Hooker Chemical, who inserted a warning in the deed regarding the property's hazardous waste landfill.

The school board acquired the property against the recommendation of their counsel and commenced to build a school. A development progressed through and around the landfill and penetrated the clay cap. Eventually the old canal acted as a "bathtub." The waste seeped from the landfill into the surrounding area. It wasn't until the 1960s that some residents complained of strange odors and chemicals in their basements.

Evacuation and Cleanup Begin

Nothing was done until the late 1970s when the Niagara County Department of Health ordered the area fenced. That was the beginning of the end of this small neighborhood. In 1978, President Jimmy Carter declared an emergency and authorized actions to save lives and property. A few years later, the State of New York started temporary relocation of families with pregnant women and small children. By mid-1980, Congress approved a $20 million bill to relocate residents out of the emergency declaration area and $15 million to purchase 550 homes in the area. In December of 1990, the Superfund program was created to clean up hazardous waste sites across the country.

After the residents who lived in the area were relocated, the State of New York appraised their homes and acquired them. The canal was capped, and a containment system was put into place. The entire area was tested for contamination and several remediation programs were completed. When waste escaped the canal, it traveled slowly across the properties, following natural drainage patterns.

Some of the waste ended up in the drain tile and sump holes of the homes and some made it to the storm sewer lines that led to Black and Cayuga Creeks. These creeks were drained, the creek beds were removed and the soil was treated. It is still in storage bags in Niagara Falls on Occidental Chemical property awaiting permanent disposal.

Love Canal's Redevelopment

On September 27, 1988, Dr. David Axelrod, New York Commissioner of Health, issued the "Habitability Decision, Report on Habitability, Love Canal Emergency Declaration Area." In the report, Axelrod concluded that the government had been overly cautious and included an excessively large area in the evacuation. He indicated that the area to the east of the canal was not fit for residential uses, but the areas to the north and west were clean and suitable for redevelopment. To the south of the canal is a highway.

The area had been desolate since 1980, but now there was a possibility that the area could be returned to the popular neighborhood that it was before.

The Love Canal Area Revitalization Agency (LCARA)

Even growing up in Niagara Falls, I was unaware of Love Canal until the late 1970s when articles started appearing in our local papers. In this industrial town, not much thought was ever given to the consequences of dumping; chemical production was our economic base and the area was growing and doing well.

I became involved first-hand with Love Canal and the Love Canal Area Revitalization Agency (LCARA) at a meeting in 1989 between our company and the director of LCARA. At that meeting, our company was asked to complete a preliminary investigation regarding the sale of the homes deemed habitable. We conducted a study of the housing market in Niagara Falls and gave LCARA suggestions regarding the marketing, timing and pricing of the homes in what is now known as Black Creek Village.

At that time, I was an associate appraiser working for my father, Anthony Girasole, Sr. I had been appraising professionally for just two years. In that first report, we gave LCARA an idea of the potential pricing of the homes and made an initial impact estimation of the stigma of Love Canal on values. We also estimated annual absorption level that the agency could expect.

The director had expected to sell all the 253 homes in two to three years. When we told him it would take over 10 years, he was shocked. Our projections have been upheld by the annual number of sales and that today, after nine years, only six homes remain available.

Rehabilitation and the Appraiser's Role

One very important factor to consider is that this entire redevelopment process has been underwritten by the State of New York and the federal government. If the master plan for the area had not been developed and if LCARA had not paid for the rehabilitation of the homes, this neighborhood would be just a memory.

At the time I became involved in 1989, the entire area was a ghost town. The homes had been vacant for almost 10 years, many had been vandalized and some had deteriorated to the point that rehabilitation was not possible. Only a handful of the residents had stayed and homes that were occupied stood out like flowers in a field of weeds. LCARA rehabilitated each of the homes, and in most cases the entire home was refinished. New roofs, windows, doors, floors, mechanical systems and plumbing fixtures were installed.

Due to the extent of the renovations the homes had to be brought up to current building codes. This meant that the homes sold at a discount in the Love Canal area were far superior in condition compared to the homes in the unaffected areas of the city. No private developer could have accomplished this. In some cases the rehabilitation costs were greater than the sale prices.

Initially the rehabilitation process worked very simply. First, a potential buyer would select a home in the area. Then the LCARA staff would draw up a plan of rehabilitation. Our staff appraisers would inspect the home and use the specifications to estimate the "as completed" value. These inspections were always interesting; we never knew who or what we would find in the homes. Each potential buyer could then purchase the home they had selected at the appraised price. If this sale was agreed upon, a contract would be signed and the rehabilitation would be started.

In the beginning the homes were financed by LCARA-holding mortgages. This worked for a short time until LCARA ran into cash flow prob-

Chapter 9: *The Lesson of Love Canal*

lems. At that point there was good demand for the homes, but no lender would finance the purchase of the homes due to stigma. Eventually the Department of Housing and Urban Development was persuaded by Congressman John LaFalce to insure the loans. Following this success, mortgage money was not a problem and many different lenders and agencies lent in this area. In the mid-1990s, many homes were purchased with affordable housing grants and conventional mortgages.

To estimate the values in the area we used a combination of sales both inside the area and in competing neighborhoods. Most of the homes in Black Creek Village were modest ranches and Cape Cod style homes. Lucky for us, there was an adequate number of sales in the surrounding area.

Changes Affect Value

The most an appraiser can learn from an experience like "Love Canal" is a simple lesson in human behavior; people have short memories. In 1978, when the government decided that there was truly a problem and funded the relocation of the residents, the homes in this area had no value.

With all the press attention at that time, no one was interested in buying homes in this neighborhood. When we became involved in 1989, attention on the area had died down, the State Commissioner of Health had declared part of the area habitable, the homes were being totally renovated and the values were around 80 percent of unaffected areas.

As of 1998, approximately 250 homes had been sold by LCARA, there have been numerous resales and the values are now approximately 90 percent of market value. This has given me a first-hand look at how values are affected by time and changes in perception. As I stated before, I do not think this project would have been feasible without the funding of the government. No private entity could have funded or profited from the redevelopment of this area, considering the millions spent on planning, marketing, promotion and rehabilitation of the homes.

When we initially valued the properties, we assumed two different types of external obsolescence:

There was an overall stigma from being located in the Love Canal area. Most buyers of real estate had heard of all the problems and the possible health implications.

There was also a more localized stigma due to the appearance of the neighborhood. All but a few of the homes had been abandoned for over 10 years; they were obviously vacant. The landscaping was not maintained, many had been vandalized, windows were broken or boarded up and paint was peeling. To drive through the area was like driving through a war zone.

After a majority of the homes had been sold, the nature of the neighborhood had changed and we eliminated the obsolescence factor for the neighborhood appearance. Over time it also became obvious that the market reluctance had diminished and we lessened the overall obsolescence factor gradually.

The Love Canal Legacy

In May of 1999, LCARA will close its doors. This means there will be no more day-to-day management of the neighborhood redevelopment, and all of the homes will have been sold by then. The only property remaining

Valuing Contaminated Properties

with no plan in place will be the area deemed unfit for residential use to the east of the canal. This area is an eerie reminder of what this entire area looked like in 1989.

A private developer who has plans for several different uses purchased the vacant land to the west. A few new homes have been built and in December 1998, ground was broken for a senior assisted living center. As long as no problems occur in the future, this neighborhood will be assimilated back into the fabric of the city. At some point, there will be no distinction between this area and the nearby neighborhoods. Love Canal, however, will be remembered as one of the first nationally known environmental problems and the crisis that created the Superfund program.

The Persistence of Contamination Effects: A Superfund Site Revisited

by Alan Reichert, PhD

The author conducted a previous study in 1994 and published the results in *The Appraisal Journal*.[1] The study was the result of litigation prompted by a class action suit filed on behalf of property owners in Uniontown, Ohio. The study found that beginning in 1988, the period of peak publicity surrounding the hazardous Superfund site, property values within 6,750 feet of the landfill experienced a statistically significant decline in value. The diminution in property values was directly related to proximity to a landfill, with impacts ranging from 5% for the most distant properties to 15% for the closer properties. Measured in 1994 dollars, aggregate damages associated with 1,300 residential properties totaled approximately $9.7 million.[2] The purpose of this research is threefold. Using the same model employed previously, we reestimate damages using two and a half years of additional data to see if damages have changed with the passage of time and, more important, with the introduction of safe drinking water. In addition, the current study employs an alternative model specification to ensure that the damage estimates are not model specific.[3]

The U.S. Environmental Protection Agency (EPA) issued its final remediation plan for Uniontown during 1990, which involves an expensive but potentially effective "pump and treat" approach to the problem. A successful remediation effort that removes the site from the EPA Superfund list could have a significant positive impact on the surrounding housing market. Even though the EPA's onsite remediation plan has not been implemented, significant risk-reducing events, such as the introduction of city water to residents living around the contaminated site, have taken place.

Site Description

Uniontown is a community with a population of approximately 10,000 located in the northeast portion of Ohio. The 30-acre landfill known as the Industrial Excess Landfill (IEL) is located approximately one mile south of the center of Uniontown in close proximity to a large number of

---

Alan Reichert, PhD, is a professor of finance at Cleveland State University in Ohio. He received his BS from Miami University, Oxford, Ohio, and his MS and PhD from Ohio State University, Columbus. His specialties are environmental impact assessment, statistical appraisal models, and commercial banking. Contact: a.reichert@popmail.csuohio.edu.

This article originally appeared in the April 1999 issue of The Appraisal Journal.

---

1. While this article is designed to be self-contained, readers are encouraged to review the earlier article, Alan K. Reichert, "Impact of a Toxic Waste Superfund Site on Property Values," *The Appraisal Journal* (October 1997): 381–392. The previous article contains a more detailed literature review and a more in-depth discussion of the discrete time-space impact model.

2. This excludes damages to nonresidential properties. In December 1994, the jury awarded the defendants a total of $6.7 million in aggregate damages.

3. Virtually all of the reduction in property values took place during 1988. The current study examines market data over the next eight years to see if the housing market has recovered.

residential and commercial properties. (As of 1989 approximately 2,500 people lived within one mile of the site.) The IEL began as a sand and gravel mining operation during the 1950s. From 1966 to when it was ordered closed in 1980, the facility operated as both a municipal and industrial landfill. The landfill accepted a variety of household trash and industrial liquids (latex and organic solvents), sludge, and various solid wastes. The liquid wastes were dumped directly into a large lagoon or mixed with solid wastes.

After a series of fires the County Board of Health banned the dumping of industrial wastes, but the landfill continued to accept residential trash until 1980, when it was permanently closed. It soon became apparent that hazardous waste had begun to contaminate the surrounding groundwater. This posed a major health concern because all of the homeowners were on well water at the time. In addition, significant accumulations of methane gas were discovered in basements near the landfill. During 1984 the IEL was placed on the EPA's Superfund list, and in 1989 a class action suit was filed on behalf of approximately 1,600 property owners. A gas extraction system is currently in operation and an alternative drinking water supply has been made available to local residents. The EPA's onsite remediation plan has not yet been implemented but includes a cap, ground, and surface water treatment as well as dredging of pond and stream sediments at an estimated cost of $18 million, with annual operating and maintenance costs of $440,000.

A great deal of local and national publicity developed about the site. Figure 1 charts the number of local newspaper articles that deal directly with the IEL, beginning in 1983. The number of articles increased dramatically during the 1987–1988 time period and has gradually subsided since then.

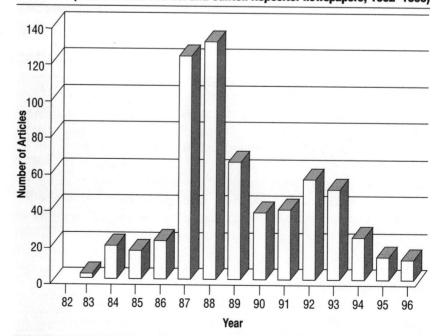

FIGURE 1 Number of Articles per Year on the Industrial Excess Landfill (*Akron Beacon Journal* and *Canton Repositor* newspapers, 1982–1996)

Valuation Theory

The earlier article by this author briefly reviews the relevant literature and discusses the theory of property valuation in depth. This section summarizes several key points relating to property devaluation that are helpful in interpreting both the previous and the current set of results. When negative news such as a major hazardous leak is announced, the market reaction may take several different forms. First, there may be a temporary liquidity effect as sellers are reluctant to immediately adjust their price expectations downward, and as potential buyers attempt to assess the likely long-term impact on market value. Consequently, the market will experience reduced liquidity as evidenced by a significant reduction in the volume of sales transactions and a noticeable increase in average marketing time. Second, a permanent reduction in property values may take place once the market reestablishes a new equilibrium that fully reflects the reduced flow of housing services or increased investment risk. In the case of Uniontown, the reduction in housing services included a lack of safe onsite drinking water and the loss of residential ponds and creeks for fishing, swimming, and play. Increased investment risk was evidenced by a reduction in the ability to obtain mortgage financing.

Both effects were observed in Uniontown. As reported in the earlier study, the number of home sales declined during the period of peak publicity while the average marketing time increased significantly. For example, the average time on the market before public awareness of the hazardous waste problem for the subject area was 25 days less than the average marketing time for the control area. Once the market was informed of this problem, the relative marketing times reversed as subject area properties began to take an average of 35 days longer to sell. This represents a relative slowdown in the housing market in the subject area of 60 days. Further, a new market equilibrium was reached by 1990, with houses in both the subject area and the control once again selling at their prepublicity rate (i.e., approximately 100 days-on-market) but at a significantly lower price.

Methodology and Estimation Model
Control Area

A control area serves as the benchmark with which the price behavior of houses in the subject area is compared. A control group is used to account for various factors, such as changes in interest rates and income levels, which affect housing prices in general. By comparing the subject area with the control area, the effects of these general factors are eliminated. To serve as an effective control area, the region should be located sufficiently far from the landfill to be unaffected by the hazardous waste and should contain housing of the age and types found throughout the subject area. Properties in the control area lie up-grade to the west of the IEL at a distance of 8,000 feet or more. Table 1 provides basic descriptive statistics on several key factors such as age, size, and style for properties located in both the subject and control areas.

Discrete Time-Space Model

This section presents a brief description of the discrete time-space model employed in the original study. The first step was to measure the distance

TABLE 1 Summary Statistics: Subject Area Versus Control Area (1977–1987)

Subject Area

Characteristic	Mean	Minimum	Maximum	Standard Deviation
Price	$68,243	$23,000	$155,000	$16,350
Square footage	1,688	660	3,200	342
Lot size	23,484	6,956	174,350	13,262
Year built	1973	1907	1987	—

Style	Percentage	Bedrooms	Percentage	Baths	Percentage
Ranch	25.9%	One	0.1%	1.0	10.8%
Colonial	33.2%	Two	2.9%	1.5	20.4%
Bi/split	38.6%	Three	53.7%	2.0	24.0%
Other	2.3%	Four	41.3%	2.5	42.0%
		Five	1.8%	3.0+	2.8%

Control Area

Characteristic	Mean	Minimum	Maximum	Standard Deviation
Price	$65,793	$34,000	$118,000	$12,547
Square footage	1,660	1,040	2,600	280
Lot size	20,397	10,440	54,400	6,859
Year built	1977	1962	1987	—

Style	Percentage	Bedrooms	Percentage	Baths	Percentage
Ranch	21.3%	One	0.0%	1.0	0.0%
Colonial	27.0%	Two	0.7%	1.5	22.3%
Bi/split	48.6%	Three	70.3%	2.0	29.1%
Other	0.8%	Four	27.7%	2.5	33.4%
		Five	1.3%	3.0+	3.0%

from each subject property to the landfill and then assign each property into one of four 2,250-foot-wide concentric rings.[4] A categorical variable was used to indicate in which ring a given sale took place and another categorical variable was used to indicate the year of sale. The interaction of the distance variable and the time variable was then used to estimate the average percentage impact for each ring for each year—both before and after the peak publicity surrounding the landfill.

Discrete impact variables are flexible because they make no *a priori* assumptions about the continuation or possible reversal of trends within or between different time periods. In effect, each year-distance ring combination is treated as an independent observation. To reduce the effect of random factors on the annual impact coefficients, the values of the yearly regression coefficients were averaged over both the pre- and post-publicity subperiods. The estimated impact of the IEL for each distance ring is then calculated as the difference between these two average coefficient values. A pooled *F*-test was then conducted on the difference between the means of the two sets of regression coefficients to identify statistically significant shifts.

The earlier study used a Cobb-Douglas exponential log-linear functional form, where the regression coefficients on the continuous variables represent price elasticities and the coefficients on the categorical variables indicate the percentage impact on price for that housing characteristic. The following log-linear model is employed to test this hypothesis.

4. The land surrounding the IEL primarily slopes to the west and southwest. Because very few houses lie to the east of the property, the concentric rings in reality capture housing on only three sides of the IEL (i.e., north, south, and west). The contamination plume travels in all three directions but predominately west. Discussions with homeowners suggest that because the contamination is subterranean, the market views proximity to the IEL from any direction as a significant cause for concern.

$$lnP = b_o + b_1(lnX_1) + b_2(lnX_2) + \ldots + b_n(lnX_n) + a_oD_o + \ldots + a_mD_m + e \quad (1)$$

where

P = Nominal selling price

$X_1..X_n$ = A series of continuous housing characteristics (e.g., square footage of living space, age, lot size)

$D_o..D_m$ = Various categorical (dummy) variables (e.g., style, air conditioning)

b, a = Estimated regression coefficients on the continuous and categorical variables, respectively

e = A random error term

Data

Information on homes sold in the Uniontown area was initially obtained from two multiple listing services (MLS) for the period from January 1977 to May 1994, and later extended through September 1996. The variables used in the model are listed below.

1. *LPRICE* = Selling price (nominal terms)
2. *LAGE* = Age of property at time of sale (years)
3. *LSQFT* = Square feet of living space
4. *FRPL* = Presence of a fireplace (1 or 0)
5. *CAIR* = Presence of central air conditioning (1 or 0)
6. *BSMT* = Presence of a partial or full basement (1 or 0)
7. *POOL* = Presence of an in-ground swimming pool (1 or 0)
8. *BATHS* = Total number of full and half baths
9. *BEDRMS* = Number of bedrooms
10. *NEW* = New house (1 or 0)
11. *LLOTSIZE* = Lot size in square feet
12. *GARAGE* = Size of garage (square feet)
13. *BUNGALOW, BISPLIT, COLONIAL, RANCH* = Style of house; ranch—the base style, bungalow, bi/split level, colonial (1 or 0)
14. *MAJORRD, MINORRD* = Location of property on a high or medium traffic road (1 or 0)
15. *HSCHOOL* = High school district (1 or 0)
16. *QTRXX* = Seasonality (quarter I, II, III, or IV)
17. *CTYWATER* = Presence of city versus well water (1 or 0)
18. *YRXX* = Year of sale (1 or 0 for each of 17 years)
19. *D2250, D4500, D6750, D9000* = Location of the property as measured by one of four concentric circles radiating from the landfill (1 or 0)
20. *Dddyr* = Interaction between year-of-sale and distance from the landfill (1 or 0)

Model Results

Using this discrete time-space model, it was reported in the previous article that property values within 6,750 feet of the landfill experienced a statistically significant decline in value. The diminution in property values was directly related to proximity to the landfill, with impacts ranging from approximately 5% for the most distant properties to 15% for adjacent properties. The main purpose of this article is to determine whether or not the reduction in housing values continues more than 10 years after the initial market reaction. To answer this question, the discrete time-space model employed in the first study is reestimated using two and a half years of more recent housing sales data.

Table 2 presents the results estimated using the discrete time-space model for both the earlier impact period (January 1988–May 1994) and the expanded impact period (January 1988–September 1996). The percentage impacts in the first ring are virtually identical while the negative impact in rings 2 and 3 increased somewhat. For example, the negative impact for Ring 2 increased from 6.40% to 7.26%, which represents a relative increase of 13%. A smaller percentage increase is noted for Ring 3. These larger impact coefficients and the general rise in real estate values in the Uniontown market during the 1994–1996 period caused aggregate damages to increase from $9.7 million to $11.5 million. Examining the regression coefficients on the annual categorical variables over the 1994–1996 period suggests a total appreciation of 8.3%. Adjusting the 1994 damage estimate upward by 8.3% indicates that the same level of damages expressed in 1996 housing dollars would equal $10.5 million, which is still $1 million lower than the level of damages estimated using the updated housing model. Thus, even when adjusted for the rate of inflation in the local market, damages measured in real terms appeared to increase over the more recent sample period.

TABLE 2   Initial Impacts Versus Updated Estimates

Ring	Initial Study (January 1988–May 1994)	Updated Analysis (January 1988–September 1996)
1	-14.66%	-14.58%
2	- 6.40%	-7.26%
3	-5.48%	-5.80%
Aggregate damages:	$9,690,853	$11,537,283

Impact of City Water

While the EPA's onsite remediation plan is not yet underway, approximately 400 homeowners have elected to tap into city water being supplied from Canton, Ohio.[5] Homeowners can hook up for a cost of approximately $5,000. The discrete-time space model includes a variable called *CTYWATER*, which indicates whether the sale took place after the home was connected. One can reasonably argue that access to safe drinking and bathing water would reduce the negative impact of living near a hazardous landfill. The number and percentage of homes that sold during the later impact period with city water, by ring, are as follows:[6]

Ring	Number	Percentage
1	18	32.7%
2	21	12.8%
3	11	6.5%
4	7	5.9%

---

5. The distribution of city water connections by zone is as follows: Zone 1 = 39%; Zone 2 = 41%; Zone 3 = 20%.

6. While the defendants in the litigation paid the fee to have the closest 100 homes placed on city water, the remaining 300 homeowners who elected to hook up at their own expense did so at a cost of approximately $5,000 and suffered the inconvenience of having their front yards dug up to install the access line. The remaining homeowners who elected not to connect undoubtedly considered the cost and inconvenience as well as the ready availability of bottled water.

Chapter 9: *The Persistence of Contamination*

The impact of city water is measured in the regression model by including four dummy variables—one for each ring. The regression coefficients on the first two rings are close to zero with a very low degree of statistical significance. The coefficient for the third ring equals 5.1%, with a significance level of 0.08. The mean housing sales price in Ring 3 between 1988 and 1996 was $95,381. Five percent of $95,381 is $4,864, which is reasonably close to the cost of a city water hook-up. On the other hand, it is surprising that homes closest to the landfill (i.e., rings 1 and 2) experienced no positive impact from access to city water. Apparently the negative stigma effect continues to dominate any potential benefit from city water. On the other hand, one might argue that homes in rings 3 and 4 are sufficiently distant that the stigma effect is considerably less severe or nonexistent, and that access to city water represents a convenience factor that is weakly capitalized by the market. It should be noted that no statistically significant contamination impact was found in Ring 4; yet, the coefficient relating to city water is +3.5%, although it is not statistically significant.

Continuous Trend-Shift Estimation Model

As previously mentioned, a second important objective of this article is to test the validity of the original results to ensure that the discrete time-space model specification previously employed is not driving the results. The alternative model discussed in this section also employs the Cobb-Douglas exponential log-linear functional form. But in contrast to the discrete time-space model, in which annual interaction terms are employed to measure potential impacts, the following alternative specification examines changes in the trend rate of appreciation and the price-distance gradient following 1987. The general form of the estimated equation is as follows:

$$lnP = a_o + a_1 D_o + \ldots + a_m D_m b_o + b_1 (lnX_1) + b_2 (lnX_2) + \ldots + b_n (lnX_n)$$
$$+ b_{n+1} (LTREND) + b_{n+2} (LTRENDPOLL) + b_{n+3} (POLLPER)$$
$$+ b_{n+4} (SDISTANCEB) + b_{n+5} (SDISTBPOLL) + e$$

where,

$P, D_o..D_m, a, b$ and e are defined as before.

The control variables, $X_1..X_n$, represent variables 2–16 included in the discrete time-space model. In addition the model includes the following three time-trend variables and two price-gradient shift variables:

1. *LTREND* = A continuous daily time trend variable measured in natural log form is included to control for housing inflation over the 19-year period.
2. *POLLPER* = A dummy variable that divides the entire time period (1977–1996) into two subperiods: before and after the publicity and market reaction first developed. Thus, *POLLPER* = 1 for the period following 1987 and *POLLPER* = 0 otherwise.
3. *LTRENDPOLL* = A trend-shift variable that allows the trend rate of appreciation in housing prices to change during the pollution period. Hence, *LTRENDPOLL* = (*LTREND*) × *POLLPER*.
4. *SDISTANCEB* = A continuous measure of the distance of each property to the most distant boundary of the subject area, which lies

9,000 feet from the landfill. Thus, properties with a larger *SDISTANCE* measure are located closer to the landfill.

5. *SDISTBPOLL* = A price-distance gradient shift term that is the product of *SDISTANCE* × *POLLPER*.

Model Results

Table 3 presents the results of the continuous trend-shift model. The model generated an R^2 of 85.8%, an *F*-statistic of 250.1, an acceptable Durbin-Watson statistic, plus a statistically significant regression coefficient on all the structural coefficients. (Durbin-Watson is a measure of auto or serial correlation in the estimated error terms. A value of approximately 2.0 would indicate little or no correlation. Auto or serial correlation violates one of the primary assumptions of the time series regression.) The positive and statistically significant coefficient on *SDISTANCEB* indicates that before 1988 a property located farther from the perimeter of the subject area (i.e., closer to the landfill) experienced an increase in property values. This is consistent with the finding produced by the discrete time-space model of a price premium for properties located near the landfill during the prepollution period.

The critical impact coefficient in the continuous trend-shift model is the regression coefficient on *SDISTBPOLL*, which is negative and statistically significant. The effective price-distance gradient relationship during the pollution period is the sum of the coefficient on *SDISTANCEB*

TABLE 3 Continuous Shift-Trend Model Regression Results

Dependent Variable: *LPRICE*   **Number of Observations:** 1,029

Variable	Coefficient	Standard Error	*t*- Statistic	Probability
C	6.6120	0.2206	29.971	0.0000
BEDRMS	0.0244	0.0087	2.7863	0.0054
BATHS	0.0834	0.0098	8.4521	0.0000
LSQFT	0.3377	0.0293	11.523	0.0000
LAGE	-0.1066	0.0091	-11.805	0.0000
NEW	-0.1430	0.0188	-7.6063	0.0000
LLOTSIZE	0.0926	0.0122	7.5730	0.0000
FRPL	0.0451	0.0111	4.0565	0.0001
CAIR	0.0567	0.0077	7.3025	0.0000
GARAGE	0.0361	0.0116	3.0938	0.0020
BSMT	0.0525	0.0147	3.5713	0.0004
BUNGALOW	-0.0915	0.0257	-3.5541	0.0004
BISPLIT	-0.0753	0.0118	-6.3493	0.0000
COLONIAL	-0.0123	0.0027	-4.4917	0.0000
MAJORRD	-0.0306	0.0297	-1.0292	0.3036
MINORRD	-0.0207	0.0146	-1.4164	0.1570
SCHOOL	-0.0304	0.0147	-2.0641	0.0393
POOL	0.0323	0.0211	-2.0641	0.1262
QRT2	0.0135	0.0102	1.3179	0.1878
QRT3	0.0163	0.0110	1.4800	0.1392
QRT4	0.0049	0.0117	0.4181	0.6759
LTREND	0.1180	0.0055	21.162	0.0000
LTRENDPOLL	0.7931	0.0310	25.543	0.0000
POLLPER	-6.5595	0.2671	-24.551	0.0000
SDISTANCEB	0.0089	0.0036	2.4127	0.0160
SDISTBPOLL	-0.0152	0.0039	-3.8718	0.0001

Adjusted R^2:		0.8582	*F*-statistic:	250.05
Standard error of regression:		0.1108	Probability of	
Log likelihood:		816.98	*F*- statistic:	0.000
Durbin-Watson statistic:		1.86		

Estimated using White's heteroskedastic-consistent standard errors and covariance.

(0.008917) and *SDISTBPOLL* (-0.015245), or -0.006328. This negative "net" coefficient indicates that after 1987, a property located farther from the perimeter of the subject area, and hence closer to the landfill, experienced a reduction in value. Thus, instead of commanding a premium, properties close to the landfill began to sell at a discount.[7]

The reduction in property values associated with the landfill is estimated by first calculating the unimpaired value assuming that the positive trend coefficient on *SDISTANCEB* estimated for the prepollution period had remained in effect throughout the post-pollution period. The damage estimate is the difference between the unimpaired value and the forecasted value, which incorporates the downturn in property values (i.e., the impaired or polluted value). Operationally, the unimpaired property value as of October 1996 is forecasted by setting the coefficient on *SDISTBPOLL* equal to zero.

Figure 2 illustrates the distribution of damages by size. The mean loss is estimated to be $8,313, with losses ranging from a low of $0 to a maximum of $20,112. Figure 3 plots the distribution of losses against distance from the landfill. Using $8,313 as the average loss on a total of 1,282 subject properties generates aggregate losses of $10,657,266. This figure is approximately 7.4% lower than the aggregate damage figure of $11,537,283 generated using the discrete time-space model. These two damage estimates are sufficiently close to indicate that the continuation in damages relates to a continuing stigma effect rather than the specific model selected.

7. The regression coefficient on LTENDPOLL is positive and statistically significant, suggesting that housing prices continued to rise throughout the area. This is not surprising, because the housing market nationwide expanded rapidly following the 1990–1991 recession. As noted in the discussion of days-on-market (DOM), the Uniontown market appeared to return to a normal sales volume and average marketing time except that housing located near the landfill continued to sell at a discounted price compared with properties in the control area.

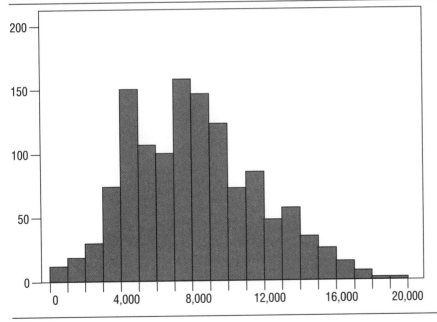

FIGURE 2 Distribution of Damages Estimated Using Continuous Shift-Trend Model

Series:	Damage
Sample:	2446 3727
Observations:	1,282
Mean:	8,313.407
Median:	7,948.084
Maximum:	20,112.10
Minimum:	0.000000
Standard deviation:	3,593.006
Skewness:	0.471554
Kurtosis:	2.838639
Probability:	0.000000

FIGURE 3 Plot of Damages Versus Distance Estimated Using Continuous Shift-Trend Model

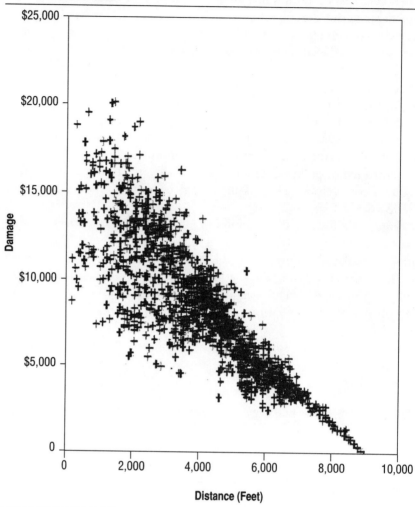

Subperiod Analysis

One limitation of using a single price-distance gradient variable over the entire post-pollution period is that it does not allow for possible changes or reversals in impacts. To adjust for this deficiency, a small modification is made in the model. The post-pollution period is now subdivided into an earlier five-year period (1988–1992) and a later four-year period (1993–1996). This subdivision gives rise to the following new variables, which replace variables 2–5 described in the previous section:

1. *POLL8892* and *POLL9396* = Dummy variables that equal 1 if the sale took place during either 1988–1992 or 1993–1996, respectively. Otherwise, the variables equal 0.
2. *SLTND8892* and *SLTND9396* = Shifts in the trend rate of appreciation, during either 1988–1992 or 1993–1996, respectively. For example, *SLTND8892* = *(lnTREND)* × *POLL8892*.
3. *SDIST8892B* and *SDIST9396B* = The distance from the property to the outer boundary of the subject area during either 1988–1992 or 1993–1996, respectively.

Chapter 9: *The Persistence of Contamination*

The regression results are presented in Table 4. The individual variable coefficients and the overall "goodness-of-fit" statistics are essentially identical to the previous model results. Once again, the key findings are the regression coefficients on the *SDIST8892B* and *SDIST9396B* variables. Both regression coefficients are negative and statisically significant. Note that the absolute value of the regression coefficient for the later period (1993–1996), 9.46E-6, is actually larger than the coefficient for the earlier period (1988–1992), 8.83E-6, although the level of statistical significance is less compared to the earlier period. (The earlier period is slightly longer, which might account for a lower level of statistical significance.) Thus, this adjustment to the model specification provides further evidence consistent with the hypothesis of no recovery in home prices.

Conclusion

This analysis illustrates that in the case of Uniontown, severe hazardous waste contamination had a relatively quick, economically and statistically significant, negative impact on housing values. The study indicates that a

TABLE 4 Continuous Shift-Trend Subperiod Model Regression Results

Dependent variable: *LPRICE*   Number of Observations: 1,027

Variable	Coefficient	Standard Error	*t*- Statistic	Probability
C	6.6101	0.2233	29.5992	0.0000
BEDRMS	0.0212	0.0087	2.43570	0.0150
BATHS	0.0861	0.0098	8.78131	0.0000
LSQFT	0.3442	0.0294	11.7041	0.0000
LAGE	-0.1036	0.0091	-11.2929	0.0000
NEW	-0.1347	0.0188	-7.16845	0.0000
LLOTSIZE	0.0916	0.0121	7.56033	0.0000
FRPL	0.0448	0.0113	3.96527	0.0001
CAIR	0.0575	0.0076	7.37335	0.0000
GARAGE	0.0361	0.0118	3.06042	0.0023
BSMT	0.0513	0.0151	3.39780	0.0007
BUNGALOW	-0.0898	0.0257	-3.49065	0.0005
BISPLIT	-0.0760	0.0117	-6.45362	0.0000
COLONIAL	-0.0120	0.0027	-4.35955	0.0000
MAJORRD	-0.0306	0.0297	-1.02744	0.3045
MINORRD	-0.0223	0.0146	-1.50392	0.1329
SCHOOL	-0.0529	0.0097	-5.43597	0.0000
POOL	0.0360	0.0212	1.69685	0.0900
QRT2	0.0137	0.0102	1.34107	0.1802
QRT3	0.0176	0.0109	1.61814	0.1059
QRT4	0.0095	0.0118	0.80538	0.4208
LTREND	0.1189	0.0057	20.8616	0.0000
SLTND8892	0.6355	0.0583	10.8987	0.0000
SLTND9396	0.9902	0.1415	6.99417	0.0000
POLL8892	-5.2519	0.4947	-10.6161	0.0000
POLL9396	-8.3159	1.2389	-6.71195	0.0000
SDIST8892B	-8.83E-6	3.43E-6	-2.57305	0.0102
SDIST9396B	-9.46E-6	5.77E-6	-1.63766	0.1018
AR(1)	-0.0008	0.0014	-0.60742	0.5437

Adjusted R^2:	0.8570		*F*-statistic:	250.54
Standard Error of Regression:		0.1108	Probability of	
Log likelihood:		817.33	*F*- statistic:	0.000
Durbin-Watson:		1.90		

Estimated using White's heteroskedastic-consistent standard errors and covariance.

temporary liquidity effect is likely, as evidenced by a reduced volume of sales and an increase in marketing time. At the same time, once housing prices fully adjust to the realities of a contaminated marketplace, the liquidity effect disappears. Thus, houses located near a contaminated landfill may begin to sell with normal frequency and in a typical length of time, but at a significantly reduced price. Further, the percentage reduction in property values declines rather rapidly as distance from the landfill increases. For example, for properties within 2,250 feet of the site, the average reduction in value was approximately 15%. For more distant properties out to 6,750 feet, the reduction was only 5.5%. Beyond 6,750 feet, no statistically significant reduction was reported.

During this period, both current and prospective homeowners had the opportunity to hook up to city water and alleviate the most significant health concern associated with the landfill. Further, the degree of publicity concerning the landfill had declined steadily since the 1987–1988 peak publicity period. The housing market within a little more than one mile of the landfill appears to continue to be stigmatized.

For many people, Uniontown, Ohio, and the IEL are one and the same. The regional and national attention focused on the landfill has placed Uniontown "on the map" in a way that will be difficult to erase. While many local residents are skeptical that the on-site remediation plan will ever be implemented, it would be worthwhile to take another look at the housing market following the remediation effort. Further, it would be interesting to survey key components of the Uniontown community regarding its continuing health concerns. As the literature points out, stigma ultimately is a perception problem. Public perceptions are often not logical, and most certainly not easy to reverse.

Chapter 9: *The Persistence of Contamination*

CHAPTER 9 Cross-References

Related article in Chapter 1: Peter J. Patchin, MAI, "Valuation of Contaminated Properties" *The Appraisal Journal* (January 1988), 5–6, 9.

Related articles in Chapter 2: John D. Dorchester, Jr., MAI, CRE, "Environmental Pollution: Valuation in a Changing World" *The Appraisal Journal* (July 1991), 32–34; Albert R. Wilson, "The Environmental Opinion: Basis for an Impaired Value Opinion" *The Appraisal Journal* (July 1994), 68–70; and Albert R. Wilson, "Emerging Approaches to Impaired Property Valuation" *The Appraisal Journal* (April 1996).

Related articles in Chapter 3: Thomas R. Kearns, "Environmental Audits: Real Estate's Newest Transaction Safeguards" *The Appraisal Journal* (July 1991); Steven A. Levine, CERS, CERA, "Environmental Challenges Can Create Work for Real Estate Appraisers" *Valuation Insights & Perspectives* (Third Quarter 1999); and Randall Bell, MAI, "Class VIII—Environmental Conditions," Chapter 8 in *Real Estate Damages: An Analysis of Detrimental Conditions,* Appraisal Institute: 1999, 170–172.

Related articles in Chapter 4: Bill Mundy, MAI, PhD, "Stigma and Value" *The Appraisal Journal* (January 1992); Richard J. Roddewig, "Stigma, Environmental Risk and Property Value: 10 Critical Inquiries" *The Appraisal Journal* (October 1996), 206, 212–213; and Wayne C. Lusvardi, "The Dose Makes the Poison: Environmental Phobia or Regulatory Stigma?" *The Appraisal Journal* (April 2000), 232–235.

Related articles in Chapter 5: Thomas O. Jackson, MAI, "Mortgage-Equity Analysis in Contaminated Property Valuation" *The Appraisal Journal* (January 1998), 261–262; and Richard J. Roddewig, MAI, CRE, "Adjusting Environmental Case Study Comparables by Using an Environmental Scoring System" *The Appraisal Journal* (October 2000).

Related articles in Chapter 6: Albert R. Wilson and Arthur R. Alarcon, SRA, "Lender Attitudes Toward Source and Nonsource Impaired Property Mortgages" *The Appraisal Journal* (October 1997), 300; and Richard J. Roddewig, MAI, CRE and Allen C. Keiter, MAI, "Mortgage Lenders and the Institutionalization and Normalization of Environmental Risk Analysis" *The Appraisal Journal* (April 2001), 306–307.

Related articles in Chapter 7: Jeffrey D. Fisher, PhD, George H. Lentz, PhD, and K.S. Maurice Tse, PhD, "The Affects of Asbestos on Commercial Real Estate: A Survey of MAI Appraisers" *The Appraisal Journal* (October 1993), 329; William N. Kinnard, Jr., CRE and Mary Beth Geckler, "The Effects on Residential Real Estate Prices from Proximity to Properties Contaminated with Radioactive Materials" *Real Estate Issues* (Fall/Winter 1991), 365; Robert W. Hall, CRE, "The Causes of Loss in Value: A Case Study of a Contaminated Property" *Real Estate Issues* (April 1994), 385–386; and Michael L. Robbins, CRE, Michele Robbins Norman, and John P. Norman, "Landfills Aren't All Bad: Considerations for Real Estate Development" *Real Estate Issues* (Fall/Winter 1991), 406.

Related articles in Chapter 8: Michael Greenberg, PhD and James Hughes, PhD, "Impact of Hazardous Waste Sites on Land Use: Tax Assessors' Appraisal" *The Appraisal Journal* (January 1993), 430; and Robert P. Carver, Esq. and Anthony W. Crowell, Esq., "Toxic Tax Assessments: The Ad Valorem Taxation of Contaminated Property" *Real Estate Issues* (Fall 1999).

Related article in Chapter 10: Allan E. Gluck, Donald C. Nanney, and Wayne Lusvardi, "Mitigating Factors in Appraisal & Valuation of Contaminated Property" *Real Estate Issues* (Summer 2000), 529.

Related article in Chapter 11: Ralph W. Holmen, "Current Legal Issues Raised by Environmental Hazards Affecting Real Estate" *Real Estate Issues* (Fall/Winter 1991), 541–543.

Environmental Insurance and Environmental Indemnities and Guarantee Programs

CHAPTER 10

Editor's Introduction
A variety of techniques have been developed to offset some or all of the risks that accompany ownership of contaminated or remediated properties; appraisers often must take these into account when evaluating the environmental situation's impact on value.

Gluck, Nanney, and Lusvardi summarize the array of techniques, including cleanup prior to sale, cost recovery from responsible parties, insurance policies, environmental liens, and private agreements identifying cleanup and risk assumption responsibilities. They then explore the implications of this and the impacts on value that can occur during the course of the entire investigation and remediation life cycle.

Roddewig summarizes the emergence of environmental cleanup and risk insurance, the types of policies, the typical costs and risks covered, and how and when to factor the cost of such insurance into an appraisal.

Finally, this chapter contains a program booklet from the City of Seattle documenting its efforts to stabilize property values and jump-start a real estate market in a neighborhood affected by methane gas that is migrating from a nearby landfill. The city combined a gas containment and extraction effort with a program that guaranteed that residents would obtain the market value of their homes whenever they sold. The Seattle report documents the important role that appraisers and the definition of "market value" played in making the program a success. The Seattle program may be a model for other private and public programs that likely will be created in the future.

Seattle-Kent Good Neighbor Program

Seattle Engineering Department, Gary Zarker, Director

Prepared by Property and Court Services, 650 Dexter Horton Building, Seattle, Washington, 98104-1709 (206) 684-7575

Seattle-Kent Good Neighbor Program—Final report January 1990—Seattle Engineering Department—Gary Zarker. Direcor—Prepared by: Property and Court Services, 650 Dexter Horton Bldg., Seattle, WA 98104-1709

The Seattle-Kent Good Neighbor Program Is a Success Story

The Good Neighbor Program is the story of how a non-traditional approach was successfully used by the Property & Court Services Section of the Seattle Engineering Department to restore the confidence of residents, real estate agents, and potential buyers in the value of houses and the desirability of living in the neighborhoods near the closed Midway Landfill, which had possible environmental problems.

This report presents a comprehensive overview of the Good Neighbor Program, from how it began to its successful conclusion, including figures and charts which show how the program met its goals ahead of schedule and under the projected budget.

Why the Program Was Needed

The City of Seattle operated the Midway Landfill from the mid 1960's until October 1983. During the formal landfill closure process it was discovered that methane gas had migrated off the landfill site and under Interstate 5 via gravel strata in the local geology, emerging in neighborhoods and residences to the southeast.

Methane is non-toxic and odorless. It is the major component of natural gas (94%) used for cooking and heating homes. However, if it is confined in an enclosed space, in just the right proportions to air (5–15%), with an ignition source (a spark), it could pose the potential threat of explosion. Therefore, the decision was made that families would be evacuated if the gas concentration reached 1%. From November 1985 to February 1986, eleven families were evacuated from their homes.

As a result, there was a general perception among residents in the area that their properties and their community had lost all value. Their anger and frustration were clearly expressed at several community meetings at-

Chapter 10: *Seattle-Kent Good Neighbor Program*

tended by as many as 600 residents. Because of extensive negative television and newspaper coverage:

- home purchasers backed out of pending transactions,
- bankers refused to make new loans or to refinance mortgages, and
- real estate agents avoided the area and encouraged potential purchasers to buy homes in other areas.

The City of Seattle Took Swift Action

- To insure the safety of residents, houses were monitored on a regular basis to detect the presence of methane gas, and 11 families were evacuated.
- To prevent further underground migration of methane gas from the landfill, a curtain of inter-connected gas extraction wells was installed around the perimeter of the landfill. Vent-wells were also installed in affected neighborhoods to remove any remaining gas from underground reservoirs.
- To provide accurate and timely information to residents, bankers, real estate agents and house purchasers, an Information Center was located in the community, regular newsletters were distributed throughout the area, and group one-on-one meetings were held.
- To stabilize property values, to rekindle real estate activity, and to restore confidence in the Midway area as a safe and stable family community and a desirable place to live, the City established the Good Neighbor Program.

How the Program Worked

On April 14, 1986, the Mayor and the City Council of Seattle introduced the Good Neighbor Program to the Midway community. The owners of almost 1,000 homes were eligible to sign up to participate under the following guidelines:

- The owner and the City each hired an independent fee appraiser. The average of the appraisals determined the property's Fair Market Value (FMV). If the appraised values were more than 10% apart, a third appraisal was obtained by the City and averaged into the Fair Market Value. The City paid for the appraisals.
- The owner listed the property with a local real estate broker and actively tried to sell the property, without any unusual terms of sale.
- The City reviewed all offers. If the City accepted an offer below the Fair Market Value, it paid the difference to the owner as a subsidy.
- If a property did not sell within 6 months, the City bought the property.
- All payments from the City were "less customary seller's costs," or an equivalent, to keep City purchasers on an equal basis with private purchases.

The program would end either two years after the gas was removed from the neighborhood, or when 10 homes sold for full FMV without any City subsidy.

The Homeowners' Obligations Under the Program

The City designed the program to assure that area residents who had planned or needed to move would realize their full property investment, but not to encourage everybody to relocate. The homeowners' obligations were the same as if they were selling their house in a normal real estate market, including:

- Making structural and cosmetic repairs prior to listing, in order to make the house eligible for financing and appealing to prospective buyers.
- Maintaining the house and yard in a presentable and attractive condition during the listing period.
- Complying with the terms of the listing agreement and making the house readily available for showing to real estate agents and buyers.
- Keeping the property free of liens during the listing period.
- Performing any additional inspections, maintenance and repairs necessary to obtain financing prior to closing.
- Paying all customary seller's closing costs, or an equivalent, including real estate commission, excise tax, recording fees, loan prepayment fees, escrow fees, title insurance, prorations and discount "points." Discount "points" are typically charged by the lender for FHA or VA financing. The "points" are negotiable between the buyer and the seller for an FHA transaction, but the buyer is prohibited from paying any points in for a VA transaction. The City paid an average of about 2 "points." Unfortunately, the City did not charge discount "points" when the City purchased a participant's house. If the City were to offer a program like this again, discount "points" would likely be included as a cost to the participant at the time of the City purchase.

The Participation Agreement was very specific in the homeowners' obligations under the program, and included the terms and conditions contained in the *Good Neighbor Program* booklet, which was a comprehensive guide to the program.

Program Development and Implementation

The Good Neighbor Program was the first of its kind ever undertaken. Therefore it had to be developed and implemented from the ground up. Although this was a considerable task, it was accomplished in a few months. The logistics included:

- Coordinating with the Mayor's Office, City Council, Law Department and Solid Waste Utility.
- Determining what the program should accomplish and establishing how it would operate.
- Creating and preparing the necessary paperwork, including contracts, informational booklets, and legislation.
- Establishing documentation procedures, including an extensive computerized database.
- Hiring additional staff.
- Advertising for, interviewing and selecting consultants.

Chapter 10: *Seattle-Kent Good Neighbor Program*

- Locating an Information Office in the affected community.
- Administering the program, which included extensive meetings with nearly all area residents, the real estate community, lenders, FHA and VA.

A Learning Experience

In retrospect, the program proved to be well conceived and administered. However, when a new program of this scope is combined with the dynamics and pressures of political, community and business interests and concerns, it should come as no surprise that some unexpected situations occurred in which the City was taken advantage of. This was particularly true during the first few months of the program, due to the large number of sign-ups at a time when the City staff was least aware of the potential pitfalls. The two most significant situations were "liberal" Fair Market Value appraisals and excessive repairs required of the City to meet financing standards.

- When the program first began, the appraisal industry defined "Fair Market Value" as the "highest price" at which property would sell. Because of many bank failures, there was considerable congressional pressure on the appraisal industry to correct this definition and establish more uniform appraisal standards. Near the end of the program the appraisal definition was revised to the "most probable price" at which a property would sell. The City staff and consultants estimated that the "highest price" definition resulted in the City paying approximately 5% above the actual market value of the houses during the course of the program.

  As the City staff and consultants became familiar with the appraisers and the houses in the area, it was apparent that certain appraisers were "more liberal" than others. In fact, property owners were actually calling the City asking for the telephone number of a certain appraiser, because they were told by their neighbors that he would give them a "good value."

  These high valuations cost the City extra money, and also contributed to the City purchasing more houses than was expected. This happened because the participants' houses were listed at prices based on FMV, which in many cases was too high. This deterred real estate agents and buyers from making offers. When this pricing problem became apparent, the City staff and consultants evaluated the actual market value of the houses and adjusted listings accordingly.

- Even though program criteria required that any house purchased by the City be in market-ready condition, most of the "Fair Market Value" appraisals did not identify the specific deficiencies which would require repair prior to resale financing. By the time City staff realized there was a problem, and instituted its own inspection process, several houses in poor condition were already in City ownership. Also, property condition standards for FHA and VA financing were revised during the program. These circumstances resulted in the City having to perform significant repairs, such as replacing deteriorated bathrooms and roofs.

  Although the inspections instituted by the City helped to control the repair costs, there continued to be unexpected equipment failures or needed repairs throughout the program for swimming pools and hot tubs, water and sewer lines, and heating, plumbing and electrical systems.

Participants were required to keep their house and property in attractive and presentable condition. Properties were periodically inspected to encourage sellers to comply with the terms and obligations of their participation agreement. A small number of participants did not properly maintain or market their properties, and the City imposed listing extensions. Of the 8 owners who were temporarily suspended from the program, 4 withdrew from further participation.

We attribute the large numbers of early participants not only to the methane problem, but also to the depressed real estate market of the early 1980's. During the depression period many people were unable to sell their house for top dollar and delayed their move or rented out their house while waiting for a more favorable market. For these people the GNP was a windfall opportunity to unload their unwanted house at full market value, and they took advantage of it.

At the beginning of the program the City offered a 5% commission to the selling agency in order to stimulate the interest of the real estate agents. As the program progressed it was obvious that buyers were interested in buying houses in the area and the 5% commission was unnecessary, so the City reduced the selling commission to 3.5%. The listing agency commission was initially 2.5%. In 1988 1/2% was added to the listing agency commission to be used for advertising but was deleted in 1989.

Successful Conclusion of the Program

The gas containment and extraction efforts were very successful. From December 1986 on, there were no more homes with methane gas readings above what is normally found in ambient air: 100 parts per million, or 0.01%. However, to be sure that outside changes in temperature, precipitation, and barometric pressure would not change the gas readings, the City waited until August 1987 to declare victory over the escaped methane. All residents were notified by letter that the Good Neighbor Program would end August 1989, or sooner, if 10 homes sold at full FMV. This was in accordance with the original program criteria.

By March 1988, eleven sales had closed at 100% of Fair Market Value. Notices of a May 6, 1988 signup deadline were again sent to all residents. The number of sales at 100% of FMV has grown to 49.

The Good Neighbor Program successfully accomplished the following during its 26-month course:

- Served nearly 270 residents who utilized the program, stabilizing property values for the area.

- Improved the neighborhood by upgrading houses and their appearance. Many of the houses entered into the program were rentals, which were then sold to occupant-owners who were concerned about pride of ownership. Also, new financing was used for the purchase of most of these houses, which required that the homes be in good condition.

- Re-established a strong real estate market in the neighborhood. Property values appreciated steadily during the program and an average of 10 offers per month were accepted.

- Restored the confidence of residents, purchasers, real estate agents and mortgage lender in the neighborhood. Some families who sold their homes under the program re-purchased within the neighborhood, supporting our belief that neighborhood confidence had been restored.
- Entitled banks and mortgage lenders, including the secondary mortgage market, to the protection of the Good Neighbor Program, although none of the lenders ever exercised this right.
- Operated successfully as the first program of this type by any governmental agency in the nation.
- Completed the program one year ahead of schedule, more than $1,000,000 below the original estimates.

Program Signup and Withdrawal Activities

After the residents' initial interest in the program was satisfied, the number of residents choosing to sell their homes (4 per month) was far below the national average (11.7 per month) for a neighborhood of this type. This low turnover rate indicates the neighborhood is very stable and not adversely affected by the 1985–86 news reports of methane migration. There was a general and continuous downtrend in participation until April 1988 when the announcement was made that ended the program. A surge of late signups occurred in the final month available for residents to enter the program. A large percentage of these last-minute participants eventually withdrew.

The graph below illustrates how many residents signed a Part I agreement in each month of the program and how many of those that signed up in a particular month eventually withdrew from the program.

- 355 residents signed up to participate.
- 86 (nearly 25%) of those residents eventually withdrew.

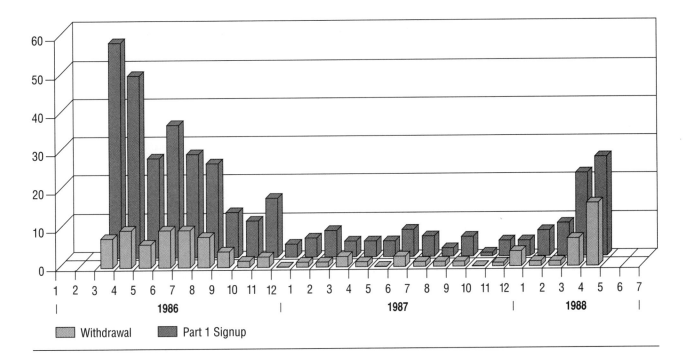

Good Neighbor Program Participation

The graph below illustrates the participation of the 982 eligible property owners:

- 627 (64%) elected not to participate.
- 355 (36%) signed up for the program. However, 86 of these eventually withdrew and remained in their homes.
- 269 (27%) fully participated in the Good Neighbor Program, of which 104 were private sales. The City purchased 165 houses and has resold 164. The 1 City-owned house remaining in the program cannot be sold until a legal dispute is resolved.

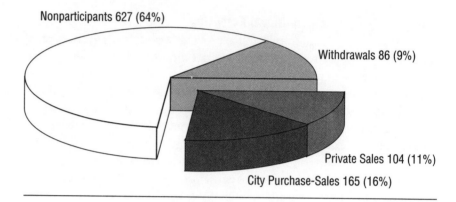

City Subsidies of Private Sales

The City subsidized private sales in the following way: Property owners were required to list their homes for a 6-month period with a real estate company active in the area, and to make a conscientious effort to sell the property. Any offers received by the owner during that period were reviewed by the City. If the City accepted an offer below the appraised Fair Market Value, it paid the difference to the owner as a subsidy.

A total of 104 private sales were completed. Of those, 16 were at 100% of FMV and did not require any subsidy payment.

Year to Year Comparison of City Subsidies	1986	1987	1988	1989	Cumulative Totals
Private Sales	18	49	28	9	104
Fair Market Value	$1,327,559	$4,009,016	$2,261,458	$755,166	$8,443,149
Average FMV	$73,753	$83,853	$80,766	$86,124	$81,184
Total Subsidy	$124,495	$334,558	$55,510	$21,568	$536,131
Average per House	$6,916	$6,828	$1,983	$2,396	$5,155
Subsidy as % of FMV	9.38%	8.16%	2.45%	2.78%	6.35%

The average subsidy payment trended downward throughout the program. Subsidy payments dropped dramatically in 1988 and 1989: 12 of the 37 private sales (35%) during this time period sold at 100% or more of FMV, requiring no City subsidy.

City Purchases and Sales

The City agreed to purchase those houses which did not sell during their 6-month private listing period: 165 houses were bought by the City.

Purchase Activities	1986	1987	1988	1989	Totals
Number Purchased	8	131	19	7	165
Total Purchase Cost	$636,630	$10,055,220	$1,723,494	$599,418	$12,974,762
Average per house	$79,579	$76,757	$90,710	$79,917	$78,635
Sales Activities					
Number Sold	0	67	71	26	164
Purchase Costs		$4,865,654	$5,717,357	$2,310,082	$12,893,093
Sales Revenue		$4,244,424	$5,330,023	$2,199,467	$11,773,914
Return Rate		87%	93%	95%	91%

The average sales price of the 164 houses which have been resold is $79,251, which is 92.77% of the average FMV of $85,431. 25 of the 97 houses sold in 1988 and 1989 closed at 100% or more of Fair Market Value. Overall, purchase offers accepted by the City have averaged nearly 93% of the appraised Fair Market Value.

City Inventory Throughout GNP

The graph below illustrates the weekly status of the inventory of City-owned houses.

- 165 houses were purchased by the City.
- 93 houses were owned by the City in August of 1987, when the City's inventory of available houses peaked.
- 164 (all but 1) City-owned houses have been resold.

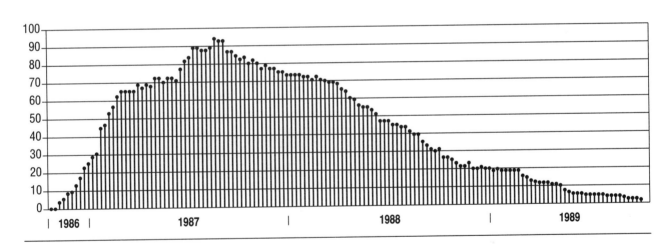

Good Neighbor Houses Sold at Appreciating Values

The graph below illustrates how the sales prices of the GNP houses increased as a percent of Fair Market Value over the course of the program.

During 1986, the first year of the program:

- Private sales averaged 89.9% of FMV.
- There were no City sales.

During 1989, the last year of GNP sales:

- Private sales averaged 98.7% of FMV.
- City sales averaged 95.8% of FMV.

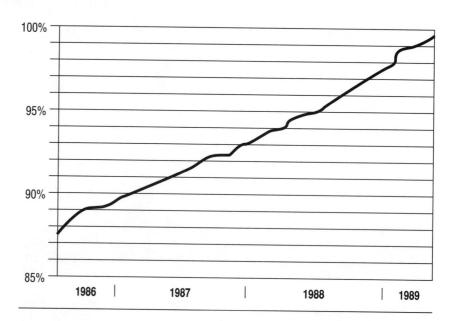

Special Cases

There were other properties subsidized or purchased and resold, as a result of the closure of the Midway Landfill, which are not included in the GNP statistics because they were not within the norms of the program:

- 11 houses were purchased from the families which were evacuated.
- 12 properties were purchased due to Law Department settlements, and from families considered to have suffered a hardship when they lost pending sales due to publicity give to the methane migration.
- 1 house was taken in trade on a City-owned GNP house as a result of constructing the outfall pipe from the Midway Landfill drainage pond. This was a very interesting transaction, and proved to be convenient and cost-effective. The original route would have necessitated purchasing a neighborhood property and removing the house in order to locate the pipe. The remaining vacant lot would have become unbuildable, resulting in an ongoing maintenance obligation for the City.

    These owners were reluctant to sell, but their neighbors approached us and asked that the City purchase their house instead. Further discussion determined this family would be interested in purchasing one of the City-owned Good Neighbor Program houses. A desirable house was soon chosen and their house was traded in. This transaction resulted in a 100% of FMV sale. Additional design revisions made it unnecessary to remove the trade-in house. The house was resold after the pipe was installed, making it possible to recover a substantial portion of the initial costs.
- 1 City-owned house was sold on a real estate contract, which will be paid in full in May of 1992. Due to the age and construction of the house, and because it was located on an extra large subdividable lot, regular institutional financing was not readily available.
- 1 privately-owned house was sold to the West Hill Baptist Church. The accepted sales price and the subsidy amount paid by the City took into consideration rent due for the use of the Church as a Community Information Center during the life of the program.

Chapter 10: *Seattle-Kent Good Neighbor Program*

Good Neighbor Program Costs Compared To The C.I.P. Estimate

The table below compares the actual GNP expenses and participation activity to our totals estimated for the Solid Waste Capital Improvement Program.

Item	Estimate	Actual	Differential
COSTS			
Appraisals	$317,040	$217,790	$99,250
Subsidies	$1,943,160	$536,131	$1,407,029
City Purchases	$13,690,580	$12,974,762	$715,818
Property Management	$457,750	$746,092	($316,158)
Consultants	$217,090	$146,385	$70,705
Administration	$965,000	$1,018,755	($53,755)
Other Administrative Costs	$1,144,590	$1,144,590	-0-
Utilities	0	$86,190	($86,190)
Total Costs	$18,735,210	$16,870,695	$1,864,515
REVENUES			
Sales	$12,553,630	$11,773,914	($779,716)
Rental Income	0	$39,615	$39,615
Total Revenue	$12,553,630	$11,813,529	($740,101)
NET COST	$6,181,580	$5,057,166	$1,124,414
ADDITIONAL EXPENSES AND REVENUES			
"Future Revenue," and "Special Cases" expenses are accounted for separately:			
Future Revenue (estimated)			$104,324
Special Cases (expenses not in GNP statistics, outside program norms)			($228,499)
Estimated Net Adjustment (additional expenses)			($124,175)
ESTIMATED FINAL AMOUNT UNDER BUDGET		$1,000,239	

Outlook and Conclusions

The Property & Court Services Section finished administering the program, except for a few remaining items which will need some attention for a while longer:

- The one remaining City-owned house is involved in litigation, which may drag on for some time.

- There is also an action against the City by a real estate broker who alleges the City owes a commission on a sale which failed.

- Another City-owned house was sold on a 5-year real estate contract. The final transfer of ownership on this house may not be until May of 1992.

- Ongoing landfill impact litigation is requiring substantial document procurement from time to time.

This program has broken new ground. It has been a creative approach to part of an engineering problem that required more than the traditional technical solutions. We take pride in its success: the cost savings from original estimates, the timely conclusion, and the restoration of confidence in neighborhoods around the landfill.

The success of this program is a tribute to the cooperation of everyone involved. The Property and Court Services staff expresses its appreciation to the Mayor, the City Council, the Solid Waste Utility, the Law Department, Engineering Department management, and the other City departments and personnel who contributed their support. Ultimately the success of the program resulted form the cooperation of the real estate agents who believed in the community and promoted houses in the area to prospective buyers. We extend a special thanks to all of them and to the City's real estate consultants, who proved time after time that they were dedicated professionals.

The program has also become a model. We have received inquiries from other parts of the nation where similar problems need to be addressed, and are pleased to share both the experience and success we have had with Seattle's Good Neighbor Program.

Chapter 10: *Seattle-Kent Good Neighbor Program*

APPENDIX Good Neighbor Program Location and Boundary Map

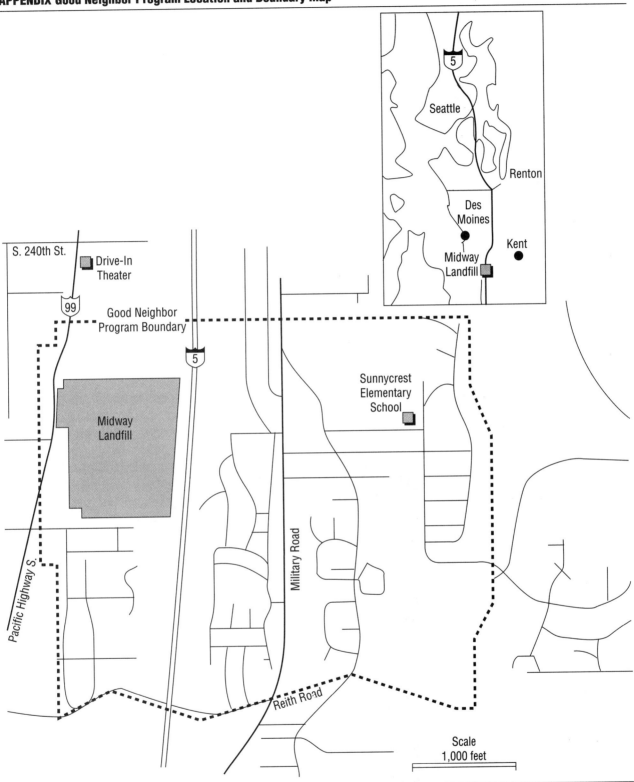

Valuing Contaminated Properties

APPENDIX Newspaper Headlines

Landfill's gas drives family from home

"I am highly suspicious of the landfill. It cries for investigation."
— Dr. Keith Rodaway, pediatrician

Midway home loan turned down by feds

Bankers, realtors unsure of dump's effect on homes

State tells city to pick up pace on landfill gas

Owners question morality of selling

Residents ask for landfill relief

Doctor says more health data needed

Midway Landfill

'Is my house going to blow up?'

Kids, parents, teachers worry about landfill gas

Methane fears seep into school

Landfill gases harm children's ability to learn, parents believe

Probes find methane gas in wide area

Midway Landfill

ATTENTION HOMEOWNERS IN THE MIDWAY LANDFILL AREA!!

Barbara and I have retained the law firm of Oles, Morrison, Rinker, Stanislaw and Ashbaugh to present our claims against the city of Seattle regarding the Midway Landfill. We urge you to join us and your neighbors to do the same. For further information, call us or David L. Ashbaugh or Michele Sales at 623-3427.

Signed John Brumback

APPENDIX Newspaper Headlines

Safeguards sought for Midway real estate

Seattle will buy Midway victim's home

Seattle guarantees Kent family's home will sell

Methane: A claims center

City 'guarantees' home values

'Methane meadows'

Landfill stink means sweet deals, attractive money-back guarantees to budget-minded home buyers

The price is right, should you pay it?

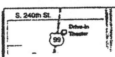

City promises to stablilize landfill property values

Methane gas problem solved

Neighbors toast 'methane zone' sale

First Good Neighbor Program homes sold

Here's where to sign up

Buyer pleased with deal on Midway home

Midway home prices rebounding, city says

Program helped raise values after gas scare

Midway deals . . .

Using the Cost of Environmental Insurance to Measure Contaminated Property Stigma

by Richard J. Roddewig, MAI

Richard J. Roddewig, MAI, *is president of Clarion Associates, Inc., in Chicago and Denver. He codeveloped the Appraisal Institute's seminar,* Environmental Risk and the Real Estate Appraisal Process, *and has taught the seminar nationwide. He is adjunct lecturer of real estate valuation in the Department of Finance at DePaul University, Chicago.*

This article originally appeared in the July 1997 issue of The Appraisal Journal.

Appraisers working on contaminated property assignments are constantly looking for new and more reliable ways to measure the potential stigma that may affect value. When stigma is present, it has an additional effect on value over and above the direct costs of controlling or remediating the contamination or other source of the risk. Not every contaminated property is affected by stigma, but when stigma is present, it is a marketplace reaction to some or all the uncertainties that can accompany ownership of a currently or even previously contaminated property. Among the uncertainties and risks that can contribute to marketplace perceptions of stigma are the following:

- *Uncertainty about the cost of cleanup:* This can vary widely depending on the level of environmental site assessment that has been completed. However, even at sites that have been thoroughly tested and have firm estimates of cleanup costs, there may still be some risk that remediation will be more expensive than even the best estimate.

- *Uncertainty about appropriate cleanup standard:* Federal and state environmental agencies set the cleanup standards for various types of contaminants. However, the fundamental question, "How clean is clean?," is still being answered, and regulators may change the appropriate cleanup standard (even in the middle of remediation programs) as more information is discovered about the environmental or health effects of various types of contaminants.

- *Risk of recontamination:* Even remediated sites can carry some risk of recontamination, especially if the source of the contamination or environmental risk is off site.

- *Risk of off-site migration:* Contaminants can move through the air and by means of surface or groundwater flows. On-site environmental testing and assessment may not always and accurately measure the actual or potential movement of the contaminant off site. And some types of remediation activities, such as groundwater pumping and treating, may, in some instances, inadvertently increase the risk for short-term or long-term contamination of adjacent sites.

- *Risk of heightened public concern:* With contaminated properties, there is often a complex interplay between various "cycles" involving evaluation of health risks, development of remediation techniques, popular press or public media attention, regulatory requirements, and even financial markets.[1] If picked up in the popular press, one new study finding adverse health effects may turn what had formerly been considered by the real estate markets to be a relatively innocuous and controllable contaminant or risk into a perceived serious health or safety risk.

- *Risk of litigation or damage claims:* This can be a big risk and uncertainty for many types of previously or currently contaminated properties. One source of the risk may be the potential for the property to be swept into the federal Superfund program or its state equivalents. Such a program can impose strict, joint, and several liability on all past or present owners or operators for all remediation expenditures and other economic effects caused by the contaminants. Government agencies may sue to recover their investigation and cleanup expenditures. Past, present, or future on-site workers and even nearby neighbors may sue to recover compensation for health-related problems. Neighboring property owners may sue to recover their cleanup costs or seek remuneration for the effect of the environmental risk on the value of their property.

Limitations of the Traditional Approach to Measuring Stigma

Real estate appraisers often measure stigma through case study analysis. Marketplace reactions in similar situations are studied to determine the effect that the various combinations of stigma factors have had on property markets and therefore values.

While such case study work is perfectly appropriate, it has its limitations. The case studies are not usually comparables in the strict sense that term is typically understood by appraisers. There may be substantial differences between the case study property and the appraised property in terms of such factors as type of contaminant, type of use, intensity or degree of contamination or risk, remediation plan or program, regulatory requirements, terms of sale, and location and local marketplace concern about or reaction to the type of contamination. All these differences must be considered by the appraiser in evaluating the case study and applying it to the factual situation at hand. That can be difficult or time consuming, and some appraisers may not be experienced enough to evaluate properly the similarities and differences in arriving at an estimate of the stigma's effect.

The relatively recent development of targeted insurance coverage for owners of contaminated properties creates a new and potentially reliable way for appraisers to measure more directly at least some of that stigma as it applies to the particular property being appraised.

Evolution of Environmental Insurance

The private insurance industry has traditionally been wary of environmental risks. For more than two decades, there has been consternation in the insurance business over the applicability of traditional types of com-

1. For a recent article describing the interplay of these cycles, see Richard J. Roddewig, "Stigma, Environmental Risk and Property Value: 10 Critical Inquiries," *The Appraisal Journal* (October 1996): 375–387.

prehensive general liability insurance policies to environmental contamination situations. The result has been the absolute exclusion of pollution from the coverage of standard liability insurance policies since the mid-1980s.

The insurance industry in recent years, like the lending community, has become more comfortable in gauging the levels of environmental risk associated with owning some types of contaminated property. They have begun to devise formulas to quantify those risks and devise new forms of insurance coverage for many of the risks inherent in owning contaminated properties. Environmental insurance coverage is now available for the following types of risks:

- Cost overruns in approved remediations caused either by changes in regulatory cleanup standards during cleanup or by technical information gathered during the remediation that makes the cleanup more expensive than originally estimated. This is available for properties with known contamination.

- Recontamination or discovery of new contaminants after initial cleanup.

- Future regulatory changes after approval or completion of remediation.

- Claims by third parties for health effects (toxic tort claims) or for effects on property value impacts.

However, these new policies typically do not cover the costs incurred from litigation that may be filed by private citizens to impose a cleanup program on a property, so-called "private enforcement actions." Nor will they typically cover natural resource damage claims, such as damage to animals, aquatic life, or entire ecosystems for which compensation can be required in some types of contamination situations.

These new types of insurance coverage are available to current owners, prospective buyers, and even lenders, and typically come in two policy forms: a "stop loss" policy and a "liability transfer" policy. LandBank, one source for this new form of insurance, describes its policies as follows:

> A Remediation Stop Loss policy insurance covers owners, purchasers and lenders from technical and regulatory risks that may result in remediation cost overruns for planned remediation activities based on known site conditions. Regulatory risks include the potential that a regulatory agency will require more costly remediation than what was planned at the time the insurance policy was purchased. This policy is available for risk-based cleanups, and does not require final remedy approval by a regulatory agency. This stop loss policy is most appropriate at sites with relatively high remediation costs with the potential for significant cost overruns. The term of the project is twice the planned remediation project length. The policy limit attaches over the total estimated remediation cost, which will be based on LandBank's conceptual cost estimate, and a self-insured retention (SIR) of approximately 20% to 50% of the estimated remediation cost...An environmental liability transfer policy covers owners, purchasers and lenders for liability and remediation risks not covered by the Stop Loss Policy. During the remediation process, it provides coverage for remediation costs due to the discovery of previously unknown, additional contamination. During and after the remediation process, it provides coverage for property damage and personal

Chapter 10: *Environmental Insurance and Stigma*

injury claims raised by third parties. After the remediation process is completed, another area of coverage is added: additional remediation for known contamination conditions due to changes in regulatory standards.

In short, a transfer policy covers regulatory risks and third party liability claims resulting from 1) unknown contamination; 2) residual contamination that remains after the site has been granted closure or no further action status by a federal, state or local government agency with jurisdiction over site cleanup requirements; and 3) contamination that is not expected to require remediation.[2]

Marsh & McLennan, another such insurance provider, provides two types of specific products plus custom-tailored insurance plans. Its ENVIROCAP insurance is specifically aimed at protecting the insured against cost overruns in environmental cleanups. Another product, Environmental Protection Insurance Program (EPIP), is available to cover liability during and after cleanup for a multiple-year term and is designed to cover gaps in the coverage of the contractors, engineers, and transport companies involved in site remediation. Custom-tailored packages are available through Marsh & McLennan for mergers and acquisitions involving real property assets and even for the acquisition/disposition of brownfields. Marsh & McLennan describes the availability of their coverage for brownfields as follows:

> Q. How can this program help real estate developers and investors involved with brownfields?
>
> A. After cleaning up a site, Customized Solutions can protect them as well as the new owner. The developer and investor can use this program as an "exit strategy," minimizing future liability and protecting the value of their investment. These policies also are transferable, so they can be used as a marketing tool when selling the property. These programs will respond to third-party bodily injury and property damage caused by contamination including first-party and third-party cleanup costs and defense costs. In this way it can be used to resolve these liability concerns and help facilitate the completion of transactions that otherwise may not close.[3]
>
> Insurance providers custom-tailor the name of the policy type to differentiate it from the competition. For example, Commerce and Industry Insurance Company,[4] a member company of American International Group, offers what it calls "Pollution Legal Liability Select (PLL Select)" a product generally similar in orientation to Marsh & McLennan's EPIP and LandBank's "environmental liability transfer policy."[5]

Using Environmental Insurance Costs to Estimate Stigma

How can appraisers use these new insurance vehicles to measure some of the sources of stigma? One way is to get an actual quote from an insurance provider. But appraisers should understand that insurance companies typically use an underwriter to review and evaluate the contamination and remediation situation to set a price on the policy or set other policy conditions and terms.

An alternative is to undertake an insurance case study by contacting one or more of the companies that provide environmental insurance and getting information from them about recent policies that have been issued, the environmental situation, the coverage, and the cost. Then an appraiser should compare and contrast that other situation to the envi-

2. LandBank; 1990 North California Boulevard, Suite 926; Walnut Creek, California 94596.

3. Marsh & McLennan; 1166 Avenue of the Americas; New York, New York 10036; or 500 West Monroe Street; Chicago, Illinois 60661.

4. Commerce and Industry Insurance Company; 70 Pine Street; New York, New York 10270.

5. For a good description of Commerce and Industry Insurance Company policies, see Janet D. Moylan, "Limiting Loss: Environmental Insurance Helps in Property Redevelopment," *Brownfield News* (February/March 1997): 26.

ronmental conditions at the property being appraised. Finally, an appraiser should make adjustments to the insurance case study situation (perhaps based on conversations with various insurers) to account for likely differences in the way the insurance provider would evaluate the cost of a policy for the property being appraised.

At an American Bar Association seminar in Orlando in 1996, one of the founders of the environmental insurance underwriting program at LandBank was asked to price a policy on a hypothetical case study involving a contaminated property. The hypothetical property was a 96,740-square-foot distribution warehouse facility on a 14.6-acre site. The site was supposedly purchased for $1.75 million by a developer planning to construct a neighborhood shopping center at an additional cost of $8.4 million. The total appraised value of the land and the building after construction is $12 million. Many years ago, a plumbing fixture distribution facility had replated some damaged fixtures located on the site, and a recent on-site environmental investigation revealed that the soil was contaminated by heavy metals, chlorinated solvents, and asbestos. There are also six underground storage tanks on the property, but no groundwater testing had been done.

Each of the seminar panelists played a role in evaluating the prospects for securing a loan and redeveloping the property. The LandBank representative, after undertaking a hypothetical due diligence on the property, indicated a solid "comfort level" with the estimated remediation cost of $800,000, based on the quality of the analysis. Issuing environmental insurance based on the facts as presented in the hypothetical case was distinctly possible. The cost of a stop loss policy was estimated to be 10%–15% of the coverage bought and, in this case, the insurance representative recommended $1.0 million coverage over the $800,000 estimated cleanup cost with a deductible of the first $80,000–$120,000 above the $800,000 estimate. The typical time limit on such a policy would be a two- to five-year remediation period.

The quote for the environmental transfer policy was a one-time $150,000 payment to cover all third-party claims, including toxic tort claims and diminution in property value claims, as well as potential changes in legal standards for cleanup, for a period of five years. This policy could be written to cover lenders and future buyers at no additional cost and could be extended for an additional year or years for 20% of the upfront cost, or $30,000 per year. The legal costs associated with defending against such third-party claims is included in the coverage.

For this shopping center development project, therefore, much of the stigma associated with the environmental situation could be offset at a cost of about $250,000, or about 2.5% of total development costs and only 2.1% of appraised value after construction. When measured against the market price of the warehouse property purchased, the stigma offset by the insurance was almost 15% of market value. Because the coverage lasts only five years, environmental risks beyond that time period are not covered.

The costs of coverage can vary from one insurance carrier to another and from one property situation to the next. Michael McGinn, assistant vice president of insurance brokerage at Marsh & McLennan, states that typical annual premium costs for a *combined* stop loss and environmental transfer policy are 8%–10% of the estimated cleanup costs for total policy coverage up to twice the amount of estimated cleanup cost. Again, this would be coverage for a maximum of five years and possibly renewable in subsequent years.

Conclusion

Analyzing the premium costs of the new types of environmental insurance can help appraisers more accurately estimate some types of stigma on some types of contaminated properties. Because not all risks are covered (for example, the risk of citizen suits seeking enforcement of environmental laws and regulations), the insurance cost may not cover all of the potential stigma. There are also policy limits and deductibles, leaving some of the risk with the property owner. Further, the policies are written for specific terms, usually five years, with "claims made" coverage, leaving some additional risk of stigma for the period after the policy expires. Often, however, such environmental risks diminish significantly as the years pass following remediation. To recover on a property diminution claim, there must be some "environmental condition" as defined in the policy language. A mere marketplace perception of diminished property values, perhaps based on new media attention but unrelated to some actual physical discharge or condition, does not give rise to a policy claim.

On many contaminated properties, these excluded risks may account for some additional stigma not covered by insurance. By adding up the cost of the coverage or discounting the premium costs during the specified coverage period, an appraiser may get a good fix on some or most of the stigma in hard dollar terms. Some insurance companies may be willing to quote rates for a longer term, corresponding to the likely holding period of the typical buyer in the marketplace. The remaining stigma elements, if any, will have to be estimated using the old-fashioned case study method.

Finally, just as an environmental indemnity is only as good as the track record of the guarantor, the relevance of environmental insurance as an offset to stigma will depend much on the experience of insured policy holders in recovering on claims. Since this type of coverage is so new, it is too early for there to be much information about claims payment.

Note: For more information about specific environmental insurance products, contact Reliance (ECS Underwriting); 520 Eagleview Road; Exton, Pennsylvania 19341-0636; and Environmental Warranty; 65 LaSalle Road; West Hartford, Connecticut 06107.

Mitigating Factors in Appraisal & Valuation of Contaminated Real Property

by Allan E. Gluck, Donald C. Nanney, and Wayne C. Lusvardi

Allan Gluck, MAI, is a member of the Appraisal Institute with his own appraisal firm in Los Angeles, California. (Email: agluck@pacbell.net)

Wayne Lusvardi is senior real estate representative, engineering division, Metropolitan Water District of Southern California. Gluck and Lusvardi have significant experience in the appraisal and valuation of contaminated properties. (Email: wlusvardi@mwd.dst.ca.us)

Donald Nanney, Esq., is a partner in the law firm of Gilchrist & Rutter with offices in Los Angeles and Santa Monica, California, and heads the environmental law practice of that firm. Nanney is the author of numerous writings, including the book Environmental Risks in Real Estate Transactions: A Practical Guide (Second Edition), McGraw-Hill, Inc./Executive Enterprises, Inc. (Email: dnanney@grlawyers.com)

The article originally appeared in the Summer 2000 issue of Real Estate Issues. Reproduced with the permission of Real Estate Issues; published and © by the Counselors of Real Estate (a not for profit organization), Chicago, IL. All rights reserved. Further reproduction/distribution is prohibited without the written permission of Real Estate Issues.

The authors are expressing views and concerns of general academic interest, without any reflection as to how they would view any particular property, situation or case. The views and concerns are those of the authors, not necessarily of their companies or firms.

Environmental issues have become a key concern in real property transactions. One particularly difficult issue is the question of how contaminated or formerly contaminated properties should be valued for sale, lease, or financing transactions, as well as to determine loss or damage in litigation cases. The following seemingly simple equation has emerged for valuation of contaminated properties:

$$I = U - C - S$$

Where:

"I" = impaired value

"U" = unimpaired value

"C" = remediation cost

"S" = stigma

This equation has been refined in the literature to break down the cost ("C") factor into three sub-factors, including: 1). the cost to implement an applicable remediation plan; 2). the cost of any applicable use restrictions; and 3). impaired financing costs. Thus, the equation can include more elements, but only as a variation on a theme.

Stigma ("S") can be defined as the incremental loss in value beyond the cost factor due to market perceptions arising from uncertainty and fear associated with the actual or potential presence of contamination.

Unimpaired value ("U") is determined as if there were no contamination, utilizing any of the customary valuation methods: 1). the comparable sales approach (based on recent sales of like properties, with adjustments relevant to the property being appraised); 2). income approach (based on capitalization of income or discounted cash flow); or 3). replacement or reproduction cost.

This equation only refers to the negative or aggravating factors to be deducted from unimpaired value. As a result, mitigating factors that may offset the negatives are often overlooked. Mitigating factors should be considered when using the basic or refined formulas mentioned above, to derive net values.

Both aggravating and mitigating factors generally concern technical and legal aspects of environmental risks and solutions, which likely fall beyond the expertise of an appraiser alone. Thus, it may be necessary to assemble a multi-disciplinary team of environmental consultants, legal counsel, and other relevant professionals to generate the information and analysis necessary to assist an appraiser in placing a value on various aggravating and mitigating factors. The Appraisal Standards Board has approved the use of multi-disciplinary teams for the valuation of contaminated real property, expressly recognizing that appraisers may rely on the professional work of others, as long as each professional acts within the scope of his or her expertise and acknowledges the contributions of the others.[1]

Limiting Costs to Future Owners

A basic premise of value is that it represents the value to a future owner. Contamination affects market value primarily due to environmental liability and costs that may be incurred by future owners. If a future owner may incur little or no cost or loss, there may be little or no reduction in market value.

Cleanup Prior to Sale

In many cases, owners clean up sites before sale, as is the general policy of the major oil companies in selling service station sites. This reduces the uncertainty of cleanup costs, hence mitigating or eliminating possible discounts.

Cost Recovery from Responsible Parties

The market value impact of contamination may be limited by the identification of liable parties, especially those with deep pockets, who may bear remediation costs so that future owners will not be affected or may recover such costs. To illustrate, there may be little or no impact on the value of a property due to contamination from formerly leaking underground storage tanks at a gasoline service station where the responsible parties include a major oil company, but there may be greater impact where the responsible parties are defunct or have limited financial resources.

Environmental laws impose liability on a number of parties. For example, the Comprehensive Environmental Response, Compensation and Liability Act of 1980 (CERCLA), 42 U.S.C. §§ 9601 *et seq.*, generally imposes strict liability on present and past owners and operators of contaminated property, as well as on the generators and transporters responsible for the disposal of hazardous waste, subject to limited defenses. It is therefore appropriate to consider the potential for cost recovery from responsible parties.

According to some commentators, "[g]enerally, anticipated recoveries are not considered in the property value estimate."[2] This may be the case when an appraiser acts alone, without the expertise necessary to estimate cost recoveries, or where estimation would be purely speculative, in which case the appraisal opinion is subject to an important limitation and may *not* reflect economic reality. If possible, cost recovery should be considered in order to enhance the validity of the appraisal.

---

1. See Appraisal Standards Board Advisory Opinion G-9 "Responsibility of Appraisers Concerning Toxic or Hazardous Substance Contamination," dated December 8, 1992; see also, Appraisal Institute Guide Note 8, "The Consideration of Hazardous Substances in the Appraisal Process," as amended January 28, 1994.

2. Colangelo and Miller, *Environmental Site Assessments and Their Impact on Property Value: The Appraiser's Role.* The Appraisal Institute (1995), at p.50.

The cost recovery factor may be considered by a multi-disciplinary team including environmental consultants and counsel who can identify potentially responsible parties and advise as to the extent of their potential liability under applicable legal remedies. The availability of such responsible parties and their ability to bear their liability should also be considered.

Insurance Recovery

The costs of remediation may be covered by liability or property damage insurance. While current forms of commercial general liability insurance policies may contain "absolute" pollution exclusions, coverage may be available under older policies that were in effect when contamination occurred. Furthermore, at some cost, it is possible to purchase insurance specifically addressing environmental risk (*e.g.,* pollution liability coverage, first party property damage insurance without a pollution exclusion, and coverage for costs associated with contamination not discovered during a site assessment by qualified environmental consultants). Stop loss/cost cap insurance may mitigate the risk associated with cost overruns in a remediation program. Costs associated with a leaking petroleum underground storage tank may be covered from a state fund for the cleanup of such sites. Thus, the availability of past or present insurance coverage or similar funding sources should be considered as a mitigating factor, and the advice of qualified insurance professionals and legal counsel may be helpful.

Cleanup by the Government Without Recovery

Due to a perceived threat to public health, a governmental agency may clean up a site at the cost of the public even though there may be no viable responsible parties. For example, remediation of the Ralph Gray Trucking Site in Westminster, California, was undertaken by the U.S. Environmental Protection Agency at a cost of millions of dollars with apparently little prospect for significant cost recovery. The site was used for the disposal of petroleum waste, with the parties known to be responsible for the contamination either no longer in existence or with little resources. The site is occupied largely by a residential tract with the residents benefited by the homeowner's exemption. Thus, the cost of remediation should not be a charge against the value of the homes in that area. To the contrary, not only was the Ralph Gray Trucking Site remediated at no cost to the residents, many homes and yards were renovated at taxpayer cost, a probable windfall to the residents enhancing the appeal and value of the neighborhood as a whole.

Environmental Liens

A governmental agency may seek to recover cleanup costs by imposing a lien against the real property. However, such a lien is a regular priority lien under both CERCLA and the California analogue. Thus, the environmental lien may be wiped out through foreclosure by a senior lienholder, with only partial or no net proceeds remaining for junior lienholders. Several other states, including Connecticut, Louisiana, Maine, Massachusetts, Michigan, New Hampshire, New Jersey, and Wisconsin, have adopted various "superlien" laws pursuant to which an environmental lien may be given priority as of a time earlier than its actual recordation, with the

Chapter 10: *Mitigating Factors*

potential for "priming" otherwise earlier recorded liens. This may alter the valuation analysis in such a state.

Thus, a property may be cleaned up entirely at taxpayers' expense without a viable responsible party or lienable equity in the property. Where governmental cost recovery is frustrated, the value of the cleaned up property could be restored without discount for cleanup cost. In any case, the imposition of an environmental lien would affect the amount of the landowner's equity, not necessarily the value of the cleaned up property itself.

Environmental Risk Allocation by Private Agreement

The potential costs of remediation may be tempered by private agreements, such as through indemnification by the seller or other responsible parties, or by new insurance products as mentioned above. Contaminated properties that may be seemingly unmarketable for sale or lease, or which would otherwise incur a significant discount, can be made viable by such private agreements. Some entrepreneurs have developed alliances with insurance companies and developers to assume environmental risks associated with the acquisition and redevelopment of contaminated property. The value of the property should be restored to the extent that environmental risk has been shifted to such parties, particularly insurers or other creditworthy parties, and away from the property itself.

Environmental Cleanup Not Required or Unlikely

In *SDC/Pullman Partners v. Tolo Inc.* (1997) 60 Cal. App. 4th 37, a landlord sought to require a tenant to remediate toxic materials that were present in the soil at trace levels, not high enough to pose a real increased risk of health problems or to trigger any cleanup order by regulators. The court ruled that the tenant was not obligated to clean up trace or *de minimis* amounts of toxic materials to avoid purely speculative rather than real environmental liability.

The nature and extent of the contamination, the applicable regulatory standards, and the extent of any cleanup obligation should be considered in the valuation process. Where contaminant levels are low or *de minimis*, such that remedial action is not required or is not likely to be required, there should be no remedial cost to present or future owners, and therefore no charge to property value under the cost ("C") factor. Without cost, the remaining factor is market stigma (discussed below).

Time Value of Money

To the extent that remediation costs ("C") will be incurred over a long period of time into the future, it would be inappropriate to deduct the full amount up front in an appraisal. The projected costs should be discounted to present value.

The Uncertainty and Life Cycle of Remediation Costs and Stigma

The costs of remediation are often uncertain. Significant variables include the scope of contamination, the alternative remedial strategies, and the degree of regulatory enforcement. These variables, and associated stigma, may have different impact over time.

Valuation Model v. Life Cycle

The valuation model summarized above operates at only one point in time, whereas the impact of contamination actually changes over time, as to both remedial action cost and stigma factors. Typically, the life cycle of environmental risks, and its costs and discounts, begins with a phase where there is significant fear—possibly irrational—arising from uncertain knowledge of the scope of the problem. When little is known, speculation is rampant, and the emotional impact (stigma) may be greatest at this point in time.

The level of uncertainty frequently changes over time, however, as studies proceed, the contamination is better characterized, the history of the property is ascertained, potentially liable parties are identified, and remedial strategies are developed and effectuated. The unknown becomes known, costs are better defined and fear subsides or becomes contained and focused. (Of course, if it is found that the contamination is more extensive than anticipated, the impact may continue.) The parties often come together to find solutions, including appropriate remedial action, which can allay concerns and reduce the emotional component associated with the impact of the contamination.

Accordingly, the effect of the presence of contamination on value may be reduced over time simply due to changing perceptions as the facts and costs associated with the property are clarified. The outcome may be the redevelopment of the site, in which case the past presence of the contamination may no longer be a factor. For example, when a shopping center is built over a contaminated or formerly contaminated site, the presence of any residual contamination encased beneath the structures might not influence the rents being paid by the tenants, and hence the value of the property may no longer be affected by the presence of the contamination (*i.e.,* if unimpaired value of such an income-producing property is based on the income approach, and if the net income stream is not affected by present or former contamination at the site, the calculation of value could be unaffected).

Remediation Technology

There may be alternative environmental engineering solutions to a given contamination problem, with widely divergent costs. New and more cost-effective cleanup techniques are being developed continually, and as the technology improves, remedial costs could be reduced. The timing requirements for remedial action may also have a significant impact on costs, whether the timing is transaction-driven or imposed by regulators. In general, expedited remedial action usually increases costs greatly. Unless immediate action is required for business reasons or to abate an imminent health hazard, it is usually possible to design more cost-effective remedial measures, spreading out and marginalizing the cost over time. Thus, a wise choice among available remediation options may significantly reduce costs and, concomitantly, mitigate the impact on property value. Of course, the technical advice of qualified environmental consultants is critical to this mitigating factor.

Enforcement and Cleanup Standards

Regulatory standards vary between governmental agencies. Where more than one agency has jurisdiction, remedial action methods and costs may depend on which agency becomes the "lead agency." Moreover, applicable standards may differ based upon the circumstances. Of particular

Chapter 10: *Mitigating Factors*

significance is the potential impact of the contamination on groundwater, especially groundwater that is a source of drinking water. The risks and costs of two otherwise identical sites may be vastly different if the contamination of one affects sources of drinking water but the other does not. Similarly, concern may vary depending upon the natural background level of the contaminant. Accurate estimation of remedial cost should involve the assistance of qualified professionals to assess the risk of exposure to human health or the environment and the remedial standards to be applied by the lead regulatory agency as a result. Remedial costs can be controlled, and hence the impact on property value mitigated by the application of reasonable risk assessment and cleanup standards.

Political Backlash

As indicated by almost daily coverage in the news media during the 1990s, environmental programs have been under attack at federal and state levels, impelled by the perceived adverse impact of environmental regulation on the nation's economic malaise in the early to mid-1990s. The cost of compliance bites harder during recessionary times, especially when the regulations and their enforcement are seen as unfair by the regulated community. Along with other social programs, agencies charged with enforcing environmental laws and regulations have been affected by budget cuts at all levels of government. This political backlash has reduced the real and perceived power of those agencies. Thus, the impact of contamination on property value may be affected by prevailing political forces and the extent to which the applicable agencies are exercising their enforcement powers rigidly or reasonably.

Judicial Backlash

Similarly, after many years of largely unquestioning deference to environmental regulators, the courts in the 1990s began to make decisions curtailing what some judges perceived as excessive application of regulatory authority.

Response of Regulators to the Backlash

Regulators are not insensitive to the backlash, and policies have been modified to make the enforcement of environmental laws more reasonable and consistent among agencies. May "brownfield" initiatives have been adopted to facilitate the cost-effective resolution of environmental problems and to return contaminated sites to productive use. For instance, California's State Water Resources Control Board has adopted an number of initiatives including, significantly, a December 1995 guidance letter to the Regional Boards supporting cessation of remedial action in some cases and, in general, an enhanced consideration of risk assessment-based closure of low-risk sites contaminated by leaking fuel tanks. This represented a major departure from previous views of the threat of leaking USTs, and was based on the Lawrence Livermore National Laboratory report of October 1995 finding that the environmental impact of leaking USTs is not as severe as previously thought, and that natural bioremediation should be a primary remediation tool in most cases once a fuel leak source has been removed. Although this attitude shift has been controversial in some quarters, it has dramatically reduced remedial costs at UST sites around the state as literally hundreds of sites have been closed. Such initiatives may reflect an attempt by regulators to blunt the general political backlash in hopes of avoiding wholesale legislative reversal of environmental laws.

In the face of political and judicial backlash, it is no wonder that the attitude of the regulators has changed. A stronger economy has apparently not reversed that change in attitude. Many regulators realize that cooperative efforts can return idle properties to productive use providing jobs and improving the tax base while still preserving public health. The interested parties, including regulators, tend to work in concert for the efficient remediation of a property, reducing costs where possible and serving both public and private objectives. More reasonable enforcement of environmental laws should have a significant effect on the extent and cost of remedial measures, mitigating the charge to property value.

Stigma
Trend Toward Risk-Assessment

Part of the political backlash has been against the arbitrary application of stringent cleanup standards developed in the abstract seeking zero risk regardless of cost and utilizing unrealistic assumptions such as lifetime exposure to minute levels of pollutants. Now, the trend is toward risk assessment-based decisions focusing on the actual risk posed by a given situation. This significant change in approach can be expected to have a mitigating impact on perceptions, in many cases ameliorating the uncertainty and fear of health risk and potential regulatory requirements, and, hence, reducing the stigma associated with contaminated or formerly contaminated property.

Stigma Diminishes Over Time or May Be Noncompensable

As noted above, customary valuation methods "take a picture" of value as of a given time, whereas the impact of contamination on value actually varies over time. Studies have shown that stigma dissipates, and value eventually returns to, or nearly to, unimpaired value.

Post-cleanup stigma claims appear to be based on the fear that there may be some unknown or residual contamination, or that cleanup standards may become more stringent in the future, leading to additional liability even after sign-off by regulators. Some courts have allowed claims for post-cleanup stigma damages, but other courts have denied or limited such claims. Other cases have considered stigma associated with proximity to contaminated sites or fear of toxic impact from nearby operations. Again, some courts have allowed such claims and other courts have rejected them. Accordingly, it remains controversial whether and under what circumstances post-cleanup or proximity stigma damages are recoverable, and, if recoverable, the extent of the residual damage. Thus, the analysis should include consideration of the law in the applicable jurisdiction. If stigma damages have been rejected as a matter of law, or only narrowly permitted, the application of that factor may be eliminated or mitigated at the time of a property appraisal.

A mechanical application of a stigma discount may be inappropriate. It should be considered in each case whether stigma is a proper factor under the circumstances, and if it is, further consideration should be given to

Chapter 10: *Mitigating Factors*

mitigating factors and approaches, and the manner in which the risk and profit opportunity posed by the stigma element has been or is being allocated between the transaction parties.

Market Factors
Highest and Best Use

The impact of the presence of contamination may also depend on the current or changing "highest and best use" of the property.

In circumstances where the contamination is located in a building, and there is already limited utility to the building, the costs to mitigate the contamination may exceed the contributory value of the improvements, in which case a sound economic alternative may be to remove the improvements, which may cost less than other forms of remedial action, mitigating net remediation costs.

In cases where the land is contaminated, the regulatory stance and market response may be affected by the long-term outlook for the use of the property, so that if the contamination is commonly associated with the anticipated use, its impact on value may be nominal.

If the market perceives that a property can be reused without exacerbating or exposing the contamination, or the anticipated use is consistent with past uses, then liability or stigma may be largely a moot issue. In contrast, if a change in use is anticipated, a change where there is less tolerance for the presence of the contamination than the tolerance existing for the current use, then the presence of the contamination may trigger a significant impact on the value of the property.

Sellers' vs. Buyers' Market

Prevailing economic and market conditions can have a significant impact on the marketability and value of contaminated properties. The 1990s have seen a dramatic swing of the pendulum from the real estate recession to a relatively "hot" economy and real estate market. Many environmentally impacted properties that languished during the recession are now moving in the marketplace. Governmental brownfield initiatives, along with better economic conditions, have helped to stimulate this. In a hot sellers' market, value and price tend to firm up, and buyers tend to be willing to assume more risk with less discount than during gloomy economic times. Thus, the place and time of a transaction in the economic and market cycle is an important factor that may mitigate (or aggravate) the impact of contamination on value and price.

No Uniform Market Price Discount

It is a common misconception that there is a uniform market price discount for contaminated properties. In fact, there are usually few, if any, comparable transactions, as each may represent a unique condition and may reflect a wide geographic range. It may not be possible to draw valid market conclusions from the small sample size. Even if transactions involving comparable property types and environmental conditions are available, the pricing may have been affected by business considerations, such as the need for a particular location, the need to close the second leg of a tax deferred exchange, or private agreements between parties for mitigation of contamination costs. It is therefore necessary in each case to undertake a careful analysis of the applicable method of determining unimpaired value and the various aggravating and mitigating factors that are relevant to a determination of the impairment to value, with the assistance of qualified professionals, as needed.

Legal and Regulatory Exemptions or Defenses

The impact of the presence of contamination may depend, in some circumstances, on limited requirements for investigation or on certain legal limitations and exemptions.

No Duty to Investigate

While certain disclosure duties apply under applicable law, there is no general requirement for a seller to undertake an environmental site assessment prior to sale in order to obtain new knowledge. Nevertheless, environmental site assessments by buyers have become a common feature of real property transactions, particularly when required by lenders, and in some contexts, *e.g.,* for a leased property, existing legal principles may impose on a property owner the duty to inspect and be aware of, and to repair or warn of, dangerous conditions. Also, real estate brokers may have a duty to undertake some investigation. In any case, if the transaction parties are not aware of existing contamination, there would be no impact on market value and price at the time of the transaction. Similarly, in many instances there is no requirement for remediation even when contamination is known to be present, again resulting in little or no potential impact on value.

Condemnation

Some courts have not allowed the presence of contamination to be taken into consideration when determining the value of property that is being condemned, but other courts have ruled that remediation costs or stigma are admissible with respect to determining value in condemnation proceedings. This may also be affected by applicable statutes. For instance, California law expressly excludes consideration of the presence of hazardous substances in determining the appraised value of property being taken by a school district under the power of eminent domain. Instead of a price discount, Calif. Code of Civil Procedure § 1263.740 contemplates that the property will be cleaned up under the procedure set forth in Section 1263.720, using the full fair market value purchase monies, with any excess costs recoverable under Section 1263.730.

Thus, the extent to which loss of value due to contamination may be considered in condemnation proceedings will depend upon the statutes or case law of the applicable jurisdiction.

Homeowner's Exemption

The U.S. EPA has adopted a policy statement establishing a qualified homeowner's exemption declaring that the average homeowner will not be required to conduct or pay for cleanup when residential property is part of a federal Superfund site. This seemingly discretionary policy is, of course, based on the fact that most homeowners would have the benefit of the third-party defense under CERCLA in any event, and it would be decidedly unpopular were the U.S. EPA to begin pursuing homeowners who happen to reside on top of a contaminated region. Similar homeowners' exemptions have been adopted under the laws of some states.

Chapter 10: *Mitigating Factors*

Defenses to Liability

Current and future owners may have defenses to liability under CERCLA and other environmental laws. Thus, the government may have to pursue other responsible parties, if any, for cost recovery (such as former owners or operators, or those who actually disposed of hazardous waste on someone else's property). Even though contamination may nevertheless have to be dealt with by the owner (*e.g.,* to obtain financing), the availability of defenses to liability will enhance the potential for obtaining recovery from other responsible parties.

Thus, to the extent that defenses are available and remedial costs are not legally recoverable from current or future owners, the potential charge to the real property should be mitigated.

Conclusion

It is not enough to deduct mechanically the costs of remediation or regulatory compliance, and any presumed "stigma," in calculating the impact of contamination on the value of real property. The usual valuation model is, at best, simplistic in making short-shrift of relevant mitigating factors (such as those discussed in this manuscript) and may be misleading to the extent that it does not reflect the market devices and legal factors that are frequently present. The valuation of contaminated or formerly contaminated property is a complex undertaking, with a variety of aggravating and mitigating factors. Accurate appraisal requires careful investigation and assessment of such factors, with the assistance of qualified environmental consultants and counsel as to technical and legal aspects. Without a multi-disciplinary team, an appraiser acting alone probably will lack the necessary expertise to render anything but an unimpaired value opinion assuming the absence of contamination. Such an opinion may be of some use, but would not reflect the actual, impaired value of the property, a serious limitation that the appraiser would be obligated to disclose under applicable ethical standards.

Valuing Contaminated Properties

CHAPTER 10 Cross-References

Related article in Chapter 1: Peter J. Patchin, MAI, "Valuation of Contaminated Properties" *The Appraisal Journal* (January 1988), 6, 8–9.

Related article in Chapter 2: John D. Dorchester, Jr., MAI, CRE, "Environmental Pollution: Valuation in a Changing World" *The Appraisal Journal* (July 1991), 38–39.

Related article in Chapter 4: Richard J. Roddewig, "Stigma, Environmental Risk and Property Value: 10 Critical Inquiries" *The Appraisal Journal* (October 1996), 216–217.

Related article in Chapter 5: Scott B. Arens, MAI, SRA, "The Valuation of Defective Properties: A Common Sense Approach" *The Appraisal Journal* (April 1997), 254.

CHAPTER 11

Legal Issues and Valuation in Litigation Settings

Editor's Introduction
Laws and regulations are important to the appraisal of contaminated and remediated properties in many ways. Holmen provides a detailed background briefing in his summary of federal and state Superfund laws, underground storage tank installation and removal regulations, lead-based paint and other types of disclosure requirements, and land use restrictions on the siting of waste disposal facilities. Those types of laws and regulations can directly affect property values.

But much of what we have learned about the propriety or impropriety of techniques for the valuation of contaminated properties has been, and will continue to be, tested in a litigation setting. Some articles in this chapter explain the results of particular cases. Weisheit summarizes the realities of a condemnation case that created a "heated confrontation between classic case law doctrine (on valuation) and the implementation of new environmental legislation." Roddewig summarizes the techniques used by appraisers on both sides and the jury verdict in the Alaska litigation regarding the impact of the Exxon Valdez oil spill on remote and wilderness land values. Simons traces another oil spill litigation case involving a pipeline spill in Virginia, the techniques used by experts in the litigation that ensued, and the innovative settlement that resulted. Friedman summarizes one common type of litigation—a damage claim filed by the owners of a shopping center adjacent to a service station with leaking underground storage tanks. In his summary, he explains the analysis undertaken by the appraisal experts for the oil company defendant.

Finally, both Roddewig and Dorchester discuss a rapidly emerging issue: the new judicial evidentiary criteria for determining whether a real estate appraiser is a qualifying expert and whether the techniques he or she uses in appraising properties affected by contamination or other types of environmental risks are generally accepted in the appraisal community. Dorchester provides additional background information about whether appraisal is an art or a science and how our standards of practice comply with new judicial standards.

Current Legal Issues Raised By Environmental Hazards Affecting Real Estate

by Ralph W. Holmen

Ralph W. Holmen is an attorney in the Office of the General Counsel of the National Association of Realtors®. A member of the American and Chicago Bar Associations, he has been admitted to practice before the U.S. Supreme Court, the Court of Appeals for the Federal Circuit, the U.S. District Court for the Northern District of Illinois and the bar of the State of Illinois.

The article originally appeared in the Fall/Winter 1991 issue of Real Estate Issues. *Reproduced with the permission of* Real Estate Issues; *published and © by the Counselors of Real Estate (a not for profit organization), Chicago, IL. All rights reserved. Further reproduction/distribution is prohibited without the written permission of* Real Estate Issues.

Following two centuries of industrial, commercial, residential and even recreational misuse of America's natural environment and resources, the last several decades have seen significant public concern for protecting the environment from continuing degradation. Federal, state and even local governments have recognized and responded to this concern with a variety of legislative and regulatory programs intended to preserve environmental quality. While much of this effort seeks to ensure clean air and water, a significant amount of environmental regulation seeks to clean up or prevent further contamination of land. Owners, lessors, lessees, buyers, sellers, lenders and brokers of real estate as well as others involved in real estate transactions must cope not only with the health risks and hazards of environmentally affected real estate, but also with laws that govern environmentally contaminated and protected property.

A variety of environmental hazards may affect real estate. Commercial and industrial facilities most often are environmentally contaminated by substances that have been inadvertently or carelessly discharged onto property. These facilities, for example may contain asbestos in the form of insulation or fireproofing materials, or they may overlie abandoned or operational underground storage tanks that are sources of soil or ground-water contamination. Residential properties may be environmentally contaminated by insulation, carpeting or building materials that emit radon, lead, asbestos particles or formaldehyde gas or by materials employed by a previous commercial user. Residential properties also may be environmentally threatened by underground storage tanks and by electromagnetic fields emanating from electric transmission and distribution lines and other power sources. Residential or commercial/industrial properties may be limited in their development by environmental interests in preserving coastal areas, endangered species' habitats or wetlands.

As one might expect, legislative measures adopted to address environmental problems, and the ways in which these laws may affect real estate, are numerous and complex. The purpose of this article therefore is to

Chapter 11: *Current Legal Issues*

identify the most prominent environmental problems addressed by legislative and/or regulatory schemes.

Superfund

Perhaps the most infamous environmental issue affecting real estate originated with the Comprehensive Environmental Response, Compensation and Liability Act of 1980[1] (also known as Superfund or CERCLA) which imposes liability for the costs of cleaning up seriously contaminated property on persons who are or have been involved with the property (often referred to as *potentially responsible parties* or PRPs). PRPs include owners who had no involvement in, control over or even knowledge of the release of environmental contaminants or individuals who acquired the property after it became contaminated but had no knowledge of the contamination at the time of purchase.

The Superfund law is administered and enforced by the U.S. Environmental Protection Agency (USEPA); it empowers USEPA to order the owner of property that has been severely contaminated by hazardous wastes to clean up the site or to conduct the cleanup and secure reimbursement of the cost of doing so from the PRPs. They may be held strictly liable for such costs, which often are of a staggering magnitude measured in millions or tens of millions of dollars.

There are, however, two important exemptions to Superfund liability, both of which are the subject of considerable debate and activity. Superfund exempts from liability persons who, without participating in the management of a facility, hold indicia of ownership primarily to protect a security interest. Although this provision was intended to benefit real estate mortgage lenders, its scope has been narrowed dramatically by judicial interpretation of its language. Court decisions have held a lender to be liable for Superfund cleanup expenses if the lender temporarily becomes the owner of a contaminated property through foreclosure. In addition, in U.S. v. Fleet Factors Corp.[2] the court held that a lender could be liable if it had the *capacity* to influence the property owner's treatment of wastes or contaminants on the property whether or not it exercised that power. Although at least one subsequent court decision reached a contradictory conclusion, lenders understandably have become cautious about making loans secured by real estate unless the environmental condition of the property has been determined. Lenders also have become unwilling or reluctant to foreclose on property which is or may be contaminated. They also hesitate to manage the affairs of a delinquent borrower whose loan is secured by contaminated real estate, for fear of negating the secured lender exemption to Superfund liability.

Several attempts to correct this problem are underway. U.S. Rep. LaFalce (D-NY), Owens (D-Utah) and Weldon (R-PA) and Sen. Garn (R-Utah) have introduced legislative proposals that would (1) expressly prescribe the actions lenders may undertake to protect their collateral without voiding Superfund's secured lender exemption and (2) establish limits on lenders' liability for cleanup costs. In addition, USEPA has released for public comment a rule that describes specifically the extent to which a secured lender may participate in the affairs of a borrower whose loan is secured by contaminated real estate. This proposed rule also itemizes the circumstances under which a lender may foreclose on and liquidate its interest in

1. 42 U.S.C. §§ 9601-9675 (1980).
2. 901 F.2d 1550 (11th Cir. 1990).

a contaminated property without incurring liability for Superfund cleanup expenses. The rule further exempts from liability government entities that involuntarily succeed to ownership or control of contaminated property. This provision is particularly important to the Resolution Trust Corporation (RTC), Federal Deposit Insurance Corporation (FDIC) and other government agencies that are or may become owners of a large inventory of properties previously secured by loans made by failed financial institutions.

Superfund also exempts from liability innocent purchasers, that is, individuals who acquired property without knowing or having any reason to know that the property was contaminated. To establish that one did not have reason to know of the contamination and thus qualify for this exemption, Superfund requires a purchaser to demonstrate that he had undertaken at the time of acquisition, all appropriate inquiry into the previous ownership and uses of the property consistent with good commercial or customary practice. Thus, one must conduct an adequate inspection or examination of the property—often referred to as due diligence—to be entitled to this exemption from liability. Unfortunately, neither the Superfund statute nor its regulations prescribe the nature or extent of the due diligence investigation that would be required. Potential purchasers consequently are uncertain of the degree of inspection that will allow them to claim this exemption for a property that subsequently is discovered to be contaminated.

To fill this void, the American Society for Testing and Materials (ASTM), a private standard-setting organization, has initiated an effort to establish an appropriate standard of investigation that will allow property purchasers to qualify for the exemption. A variety of private and public sector concerns are involved in this effort, including representatives from lending institutions, real state organizations, corporate property owners, and government and environmental consultants. Although the standard ASTM intends to adopt through this process will be voluntary and therefore not bind courts or administrative agencies such as "USEPA, compliance with the standard nevertheless may be viewed as persuasive evidence that the statutory "all appropriate inquiry" requirement has been satisfied. It is anticipated that this standard will be finalized and adopted in 1992. In addition, the legislation introduced by Reps. Owens and Weldon also includes provisions designed to define statutorily the investigation that is necessary to qualify for the innocent landowner exemption to Superfund liability.

Although of great concern to real estate owners, buyers, sellers or lenders, Superfund has virtually no direct application to real estate brokers, agents or other real estate professionals because their activities do not bring them within Superfund's definition of PRPs. Superfund liability applies only to a real estate professional who qualifies as a PRP because he is an owner or operator of a contaminated site, has caused or permitted contaminants to be released on the site or has transported or arranged for the transport of the contaminants to the site. None of these activities, of course, is typical conduct of most real estate professionals.

One reported court case has addressed the potential liability of a real estate broker under Superfund. In Tanglewood East Homeowners v. Charles-Thomas, Inc.,[3] the plaintiffs sued a number of parties involved in the development of a housing subdivision, including the real estate brokerage firm that handled the sale of the homes, to recover costs incurred in cleaning up

3. 849 F.2d 1568 (5th Cir. 1988).

toxic wastes found on the property. The court held that the defendants, including the brokers, could be liable under Superfund as transporters of the contaminating waste because of grading and other related development work. However, this case *does not* provide a basis for imposing Superfund liability on real estate brokers that act solely as brokers and merely market a property. According to this case, only if brokers are involved in property development can they be held liable under Superfund.

State Superfund Laws

Numerous state legislatures have adopted Superfund-like statutes that give states the authority to clean up contaminated sites and claim reimbursement from certain parties for the cleanup costs incurred. Although a variety of permutations and peculiarities exist among the various statutes, most are modeled after Superfund. Like the federal statute, "little Superfund" statutes do not extend liability to real estate professionals who act only in their brokerage capacity.

A number of states have added a twist to their Superfund-like statutory schemes, however. Federal Superfund and similar statutes in at least 21 states allow a lien to be imposed against property for the costs of environmental cleanup. Some statutes extend this lien to other property within the state that is owned by the same party. In 16 states, this lien is an ordinary one, subject to prior liens; however, in five states (Connecticut, Maine, Massachusetts, New Hampshire and New Jersey), the lien is a so-called Superlien, which takes precedence over all other prior liens. In three of these states (Connecticut, Massachusetts and New Jersey), the Superlien acts as a regular priority lien in the case of residential property; nevertheless, in all five states, the lien has first priority over any other security interests in the property that is subject to cleanup.

Underground Storage Tanks

USEPA estimates that there are several million underground storage tanks containing petroleum or hazardous chemicals in the United States. The majority of these tanks and their piping are constructed of unprotected steel; therefore, they are subject to leakage resulting from corrosive decay. Leakage from underground storage tanks can cause fires or explosions, and it can contaminate underground water systems. As a result of concern about the dangers and environmental damage produced by this leakage, Congress in 1984 and again in 1986 acted to regulate underground storage tanks; many states and even some local jurisdictions also have adopted legislation governing these potential environmental hazards.

The objective of federal legislation covering underground storage tanks[4] is to prevent, detect and correct leaks and spills and the corresponding environmental damage they create and to require owners and operators of underground storage tanks to meet certain standards of financial responsibility. Tanks installed after December 1988 must meet standards of construction designed to prevent or resist decay from corrosion and to prevent spills and overflows. Because much tank leakage arises not in the tank itself but in the associated piping, the piping also must meet such standards. In addition, new tanks and piping must be equipped with a leak detection system, and they must be monitored for leaks at least monthly.

4. 42 U.S.C. §§ 6991-6991h and USEPA regulations at 40 C.F.R. Part 280 Subparts A-G (1990).

Existing tanks must be improved by adding corrosion protection and leak detection features that satisfy the requirements for new tanks. The deadline for making these improvements depends on the tank's age; tanks installed before 1965 must meet these requirements sooner than tanks that were installed later. By December 1993, all tanks must be equipped with leak detection systems, and by 1998, all tanks must have corrosion, spill and overflow protection.

In addition to these requirements regarding the quality of tanks and their leakage monitoring systems, USEPA regulations require any suspected or confirmed leak or release and the action taken to correct any damage to be reported to federal or appropriate state authorities.

Closure, or cessation of the use of underground storage tanks, on a temporary or permanent basis, also is regulated by federal law. If use of a tank is to be terminated permanently, the owner of the tank must inspect for and clean up any damage caused by leakage; empty and clean the tank of all remaining liquid, vapors or sludge, and remove the tank or fill it with a stable inactive substance such as sand. If a tank is to be closed temporarily, the leak detection system must be in operation as long as the tank contains materials.

Some underground storage tanks are exempt from these requirements. The most significant exemptions are for farm or residential tanks that hold fewer than 1,100 gallons of motor fuel for noncommercial purposes and tanks that store heating oil for use on the premises. However, even tanks that are exempt from federal regulation may be subject to rigorous state or local regulation.

Property containing underground storage tanks subjects the owner to a plethora of maintenance requirements as well as liability for the environmental damage that leakage from a tank may cause. Owners or potential purchasers of such property therefore must be careful to consider, understand and comply with these requirements.

Lead

Another potentially harmful substance to which many Americans may be exposed in the environment is lead. It enters the human body by inhalation or ingestion and accumulates in the blood, bones and soft tissues. Excessive concentrations of lead in the body can seriously damage the central nervous system, brain, kidneys, red blood cells and in some cases cause death. Children, pregnant women and their fetuses are particularly susceptible to the damaging effects of lead, suffering adverse effects from low concentrations of lead in the body.

Two common sources of lead exposure are residential drinking water and house paint. Lead gets into residential drinking water by leaching from lead-containing pipes or other plumbing materials, including the solder used to join pipes. Although the use of lead and lead-based plumbing materials is now prohibited, may residences contain lead pipes or solder that were installed prior to 1986 when that prohibition was adopted.

Although use of lead-based paint was banned in 1978, a recent government survey shows that it is still contained in many homes built before 1980. It is believed to be a hazard primarily to children who ingest chips of flaking paint. However, the U.S. Department of Health and Human Services and USEPA recently identified house dust tainted with lead paint particles as a major source of lead exposure. Lead-based paint chalks over

Chapter 11: Current Legal Issues

time and may be released into the air from painted surfaces subject to frequent contact, such as window frames and wells. Scraping or sanding paint during remodeling projects also generates lead-paint dust.

The U.S. Department of Housing and Urban Development has established a program for reducing or eliminating lead-based paint in public housing, and USEPA has undertaken efforts to reduce exposure to lead. Among the pieces of legislation introduced in Congress to reduce exposure to lead is a comprehensive bill that will require sellers, lessors and/or real estate brokers to test for and disclose the presence of lead-based paint in residential properties prior to sale.

This recent legislative and regulatory emphasis on the dangers of lead poisoning make it clear that concern about this problem is likely to increase, and owners, lessors, investors and real estate professionals involved with properties that may be the source of lead exposure will be subject to increased regulation.

Disclosure Statutes

Several states have adopted legislation that applies specifically to the environmental condition of property involved in a real estate transaction. The states of California, Connecticut, Illinois, Indiana and Oregon impose disclosure obligations in connection with transactions of certain types of commercial or industrial properties that may be environmentally contaminated. New Jersey has enacted a significantly more rigorous statute, requiring that property containing "industrial establishments" be certified as clean or that any environmental contamination be eradicated, before sale of the property may be completed.

Several states, including Florida, Massachusetts, Montana and New Hampshire, have codified in law the obligation to disclose the presence of or general information about various environmental hazards common to residential properties, such as radon, urea formaldehyde foam insulation, lead paint or underground storage tanks. Two states, Maine and California, have focused specifically on the broker's role in the sale of residential property that potentially may be affected by environmental problems. These states expressly require real estate agents to disclose to buyers of residential properties specific types of information provided by the seller, including known environmental characteristics or problems. In California, a statutorily prescribed form, which includes certain items relating to environmental matters, must be completed by the seller and delivered to the buyer. Maine does not mandate the use of a particular disclosure form but does set forth by regulation those aspects of the property, including specified environmental matters, that must be addressed by such disclosure.

Real estate transaction-invoked environmental disclosure statutes are becoming more widespread, and they are being considered in numerous jurisdictions which have not yet adopted them. Whether such a statute has been enacted, and, if so, its specific requirements should be reviewed by those engaging in real estate transactions.

Common Law Disclosure Responsibility of Real Estate Professionals

In virtually every state, caveat emptor has been discarded even in real estate transactions. As a result, real estate brokers and agents have a statutory, regulatory or common law obligation to disclose any property de-

Valuing Contaminated Properties

fects of which they are aware. Such defects may include environmental problems with the property. Because real estate agents ordinarily lack expertise in technical environmental matters, they often are not aware of the presence of such problems unless they are advised by the seller. Whether an agent has an affirmative obligation to identify actual or suspected environmental problems with the property, in spite of the lack of expertise in technical environmental matters, is not clear. Somewhat surprisingly, few court cases have addressed the broker's duty to discover or disclose environmental problems which may be present on the property.[5-7]

In *Roberts v. Estate of Barbagello*, the court held a real estate firm and its agent liable *not* for failing to disclose the known or suspected presence of an environmental hazard (in this case, urea-formaldehyde foam insulation) but for failing to advise the buyer about the possible effects of the insulation. The court reasoned that this duty was necessary because the broker's failure to disclose the effects of the insulation would "prevent (the buyer) from investigating the insulation in the house prior to signing the agreement of sale or the closing" and that the buyer would investigate if she was advised. The court did not limit this duty to circumstances in which the real estate agent knew or even "should have known" that urea formaldehyde foam insulation was present.

The facts of the Roberts case narrow the apparently wide scope of the court's ruling. The agent had asked the seller about the insulation and had been told that the type of insulation was not known but that it had been blown in. The agent's real estate firm was aware of the following: the Consumer Product Safety Commission's ban against installation of urea formaldehyde foam insulation (which was later invalidated by a federal court); the recommendation of the National Association of Realtors and the local board of Realtors that information about this type of insulation should be provided to buyers; and an advisory of the county health department that specified levels of formaldehyde gas could cause eye, nose and throat irritation. Despite this knowledge, the firm had adopted a policy of *not* providing buyers with information about urea formaldehyde foam insulation. Thus, although the court's decision appears to impose a rather heavy burden on real estate agents to disclose information about hypothetical environmental concerns, the facts of the case suggest that the firm or agent was aware of information that constituted a "red flag" for the presence and the perceived dangers of urea formaldehyde foam insulation.

Brock v. Tarrant also involves an agent's alleged failure to disclose the presence of urea formaldehyde foam insulation in the home. In this case, the *sellers* were aware of the elevated levels of formaldehyde gas in the home and had instituted litigation against those who had sold and installed the insulation. The sellers nevertheless represented to the agent that the property did not require repairs, that it had no structural defects and that the lawsuit (the nature of which was not revealed to the agent) would "definitely not affect" a purchaser's interests. The court in this case held that the agent was not liable because he had no reason to suspect that the sellers' statements were false, and therefore he did not breach the standard of care "to take reasonable steps to avoid disseminating to the buyer false information. (and to) employ a reasonable degree of effort and professional expertise to confirm or refute information from the seller which he knows, or should know is pivotal to the transaction from the buyers perspective."[8]

5. *Roberts v. Estate of Barbagello*, 531 A.2d 1125 (Pa Super. 1987).

6. *Brock v. Tarrant*, 57 Wash. App. 562, 789 P.2d 112 (1990).

7. *Smith v. Renaut*, 564 A.2d 188 (Pa Super. 1989).

8. *Hoffman v. Connall*, 108 Wa. 2d 69, 736 P.2d 242 (1987).

Chapter 11: *Current Legal Issues*

Finally, *Smith v. Renaut* also held that when a real estate agent has no knowledge of the presence of an environmental hazard nor any basis to suspect its presence, he is not liable for failing to disclose information about the hazard. *Smith* involved both termite damage to the property as well as the presence of chlordane, a toxic insecticide that is no longer in use, in the property's well water. The agent was found liable for advising the buyer not to worry about the minor termite damage on the property because there was, in fact, significant termite damage. The court found that the agent was not liable, however, for failing to disclose the presence of chlordane in the well water, because neither the agent nor the seller was aware of this problem, and because the agent made no statement about the condition of the well.

The latter two cases apply essentially the same standard of liability as that employed in cases involving more familiar, non-environmental property defects, That standard requires disclosure of defects such as environmental hazards of which the broker has actual knowledge or a reasonable basis for suspicion. These cases also suggest that a broker may rely on information provided by the seller unless he has a reason to believe that information may be incorrect. Even the Roberts case, when construed narrowly in light of its facts, is consistent with this analysis if one makes the quite reasonable assumption that the owner's statement about the insulation being "blown in" may be considered a "red flag" for the presence of urea formaldehyde foam insulation.

Several commentators have suggested that the proper standard of care concerning environmental matters might be one based on Easton v. Strassburger[9] and would require the broker to perform a reasonable investigation for signs of environmental hazards and disclose the results to the buyer.[10] It also has been suggested by some commentators that a form of the due diligence investigation obligation established by the innocent purchaser exception to Superfund liability ultimately may be applied to brokers and agents in determining their duty to inspect property for environmental flaws. Fairness and reason require that, whatever standard by which brokers and agents are to be judged, they should be expected to identify only those signs of environmental hazards which their training as real estate professionals makes them qualified to recognize.

Whether the broker's duty to inspect for and disclose information about environmental hazards in a particular jurisdiction does, in fact, require the inspection suggested by Easton or is the somewhat more limited duty indicated by Tarrant and Smith, prudent real estate agents are well advised to be prepared to recognize the red flags of common environmental hazards and point them out to clients and customers. As suggested above, such concerns may include radon, urea formaldehyde foam insulation, asbestos, pesticide use, underground storage tanks and lead paint. They also could be extended to other still-to-be identified sources of environmental hazards such as electromagnetic fields emitted by nearby powerlines. Brokers and their agents can limit their exposure by adopting regular practices designed to reveal and disclose to buyers any environmental hazards that may be present.

Land Use Restrictions Imposed for Environmental Purposes

Real estate and real estate transactions may be affected legislation that prevents or limits the use of property, or certain kinds of properties, in

9. 152 Cal. App. 3d 90, 199 Cal. Rptr. 383 (1984).

10. See, Toxic Nightmare of Elm St. Negligence and the Real Estate Broker's Duty in Selling Previously Contaminated Residential Property, 15 B.C. Env. L. Rev. 547 (1988); Environmental Liability of Brokers and Other Parties, 19 Real Est. L.J. 218, 277 (1991); Environmental Problems and Brokers Liability, 3 Nat. Res. And Env. 17 (1988). But to the contrary, see, Home Not-So-Sweet-Home: Real Estate Broker Liability in the Sale of Previously Contaminated Property: Has Broker Liability Gone Too Far? 21 Rutgers L.J. 111 (1989).

order to prevent environmental injury or serve other environmental objectives. Examples of such laws are coastal or beachfront management restrictions that forbid development with a certain proximity to bodies of water, that impose restrictions or procedures on siting waste (hazardous or non-hazardous) disposal or repository facilities or that limit the extent or nature of development and use of areas designated as habitats for endangered species. Perhaps the most pervasive and controversial legislative scheme of this type restricts the use of wetlands.

Wetlands Protection

Federal protection of wetlands arises primarily from Section 404 of the Federal Water Pollution Control Act (also known as the Clean Water Act),[11] which authorizes the U.S. Army Corps of Engineers to issue permits for the discharge of dredged or fill materials into the waters of the United States, including wetlands. Permits issued by the Army Corps of Engineers are subject to the approval of the USEPA. From this authority to issue permits for the development or use of wetlands has emerged an extensive regulatory program.

Wetlands are the familiar areas adjacent to oceans, lakes, rivers and streams, but they also may include areas subject to periodic but not continual inundation. Wetlands serve a number of important and useful ecological functions, including water purification, groundwater supply recharge, flood control and wildlife refuge. Increasing concern about the continued destruction or alteration of wetlands has collided squarely with increasing pressures for development of residential, commercial and industrial areas, roads and other public and private facilities needed to support an expanding American society. President George Bush announced in 1988 a "no net loss" policy applicable to wetlands. This policy encouraged preservation of wetlands or the establishment of new wetlands areas to replace those that were altered or destroyed.

Real estate interests quite obviously are affected by restrictions imposed on development so wetlands areas can be preserved. Questions about the need and appropriateness of such limitations have generated response in several areas:

- In 1989 the Corps of Engineers, USEPA, Soil Conservation Service and the Fish and Wildlife Service jointly adopted the *Federal Manual for Identifying and Delineating Wetlands*. As the title implies, this manual is used to determine the boundaries of wetlands for regulatory purposes. The manual provides for each regulatory agency a uniform means of identifying the presence of wetlands.

  Many property owners and others subject to wetlands regulation have asserted that the 1989 manual inappropriately expands the definition of wetlands, resulting in an expansion of the types of properties that are subject to wetlands limitations and regulation. Hearings were held in 1990 to air concerns about the expansion of wetlands jurisdiction, and at least one lawsuit is challenging the validity of the manual. Revisions have been developed for the manual and are expected to be published for public comment soon. Although these revisions are not yet final, observers believe that they will reduce the scope of the definition of wetlands and the number of property owners subject to the wetlands regulation by the Army Corps of Engineers and USEPA.

11. 33 U.S.C. § 1344.

Chapter 11: *Current Legal Issues*

- Several court cases have raised the issue of whether denial of a wetlands development permit by the Corps of Engineers or USEPA constitutes a "taking" of property which, under the Fifth Amendment, is unconstitutional unless the property owner is compensated. One case, Loveladies Harbor v. United States,[12] held that denial of a permit constitutes a taking of property which requires compensation. That case is on appeal in the Court of Appeals for the Federal Circuit, and an appeal to the U.S. Supreme Court may follow.

- At least two pieces of legislation have been introduced in Congress that seek to eliminate or modify the Section 404 wetlands regulatory program and improve wetlands regulation. Rep. Hayes (D-IL) has proposed a bill that would replace the current regulatory program with a scheme requiring wetlands to be classified according to their value and ecological importance. This bill would permit expedient development of wetlands that provide little or no ecological benefits, and it would require compensation to be paid to owners of wetlands that were too valuable to be altered or destroyed. Rep. Hayes has secured a large number of cosigners for this legislation, and a similar bill may soon be proposed in the Senate.

  Rep. Thomas (D-GA) has proposed a less radical reform plan which would revise existing wetlands regulation by statutorily embracing the "no net loss" policy, providing for wetlands delineation by a rulemaking process, allowing for wetlands mitigation banking in connection with permit applications, requiring mapping of wetlands and methods for assessing their functions and values.

Conclusion

Real estate practitioners, owners, lenders and users can no longer fail to be cognizant of and responsive to legal issues associated with environmental contamination and protection. Today some measure of environmental review or assessment is part of almost every real estate transaction of significant size. The legal concerns discussed in this paper are among the most significant, although undoubtedly other problems and issues will emerge in years to come. Anyone with an interest or involvement in real estate matters will benefit by becoming familiar with the legal aspects of current and yet-to-be identified environmental matters.

12. 21 Cl.Ct. 153 (D.C. Cir. 1990).

Will New Environmental Laws Redefine Just Compensation?

by Bowen P. Weisheit, Sr.

Bowen P. Weisheit, Sr., *is a practicing real estate attorney. Mr. Weisheit holds an AB and a JD degree from the University of Virginia. He has taught courses in real estate appraisal at the college level and is active in the appraisal field.*

This article originally appeared in the January 1992 issue of The Appraisal Journal.

1. Some major examples of this type of legislation include federal laws such as the Comprehensive Environmental Compensation Act (CERCLA 42 U.S.C.S. 9601 et seq., 1980), as amended by the SuperFund Amendments and Reauthorization Act (SARA, 42 U.S.C. Paragraph 9601 et seq., 1986); the Resource Conservation and Recovery Act (RCRA, 42, U.S.C. Paragraph 6901, et seq); the Toxic Substance Control Act (TSCA, 42, U.S.C. Paragraph 2601 et seq.,); the Emergency Planning and Community Right-to-Know Act (EPCRA, 42 U.S.C. Paragraph 11001 et seq.); the Clean Air Act, (42 U.S.C. Paragraph 7401-7642); the Clean Water Act (42 U.S.C. Paragraph 1251 et seq.); State statue examples from the Code of Maryland include the Natural Resources Article (Subtitle 12, Nontidal Wetlands), the Environmental Article (Title 7, Sec 201 et seq.), and the 20 new (1991) environmental laws that amend, add to, and basically establish the state's "SuperFund Bill" to be administered by the Maryland Department of the Environment (MDE).

A partial take condemnation case recently filed by a state roads department contains all of the elements for a heated confrontation between classic case law doctrine and the implementation of new environmental legislation. The conflict is triggered by the rapidly rising tide of hazardous and toxic waste and related cases resulting from the proliferation of federal, state, and local environmental, conservation, toxic control, clean air, clean water, wetlands, and emergency disclosure laws.[1]

The condemnation in the Maryland state roads department case imposes the following conditions.

- A fee and easement taking;
- Damages to the remaining property; and
- Personal liability on the property owner under federal and state environmental laws.

The fee taking and in rem damage to the remainder portions of the condemnation can be addressed in the conventional fair market value manner; however, how should the in personam liability damage to the owner be treated?

Such in personam damage is different from that consistently rejected by the courts in past cases because it arises not from subjective or even objective inquiry, but instead is imposed by the operation of new statutory law itself as it applies to the results of the taking. In other words, an owner's in personam damage now cannot be ignored as a compensable element of the condemnation.

Certainly it is incumbent upon appraisers to address this problem. Perhaps constructive technical advice can be offered to the courts that reflects a concern to avoid inequities previously caused by equating all damage to property market value.

It should be emphasized that while the derivation of in personam damages from new law is unique to each case, elements such as the property

Chapter 11: *New Environmental Laws*

rights of hereditament and devisement and the perpetuation of long-vested, personalized family interests (e.g., graveyards, historic place titles, and gardens) often have been present in condemnation cases. However, they never have been compensated for as such in damage awards. This case law inertia must be overcome if just compensation is to be awarded. It is true that the problem, if seen as a deeper conflict of principle between an inadequate remedy at law on the one hand and the equitable demands of normal definitions of the word "just" on the other, is more complex than it appears. But at least the courts now have a solid new statutory law foundation on which to base an equitable legal decision.

In addition to discussing the state roads department case, this article reviews how the courts came to equate just compensation with market value. This should provide a basis for interpreting the effects of these new laws on just compensation.

The Case

The facts of the case appear to be straightforward. The amount of $9,925 was paid into court under the state's "quick take" condemnation process, as proffered payment in full for the following property rights.

- Fee take of 0.365 acres (of 6.46 acres improved with four houses);
- Perpetual drain easement of 0.021 acres;
- All rights of access to the new highway prohibited except as the state may approve; and
- Perpetual easement to discharge the flow of water from or into the existing waterway—or onto existing ground.

Similarly, the current property use as a residential holding appears ordinary, and

- Includes an owner's residence and three tenant houses;
- Is heavily wooded throughout and is not in a floodplain;
- Has substantial state road frontage on three sides;
- Has county water and sewer available (but are currently unused);
- Is bisected by a stream flowing northeast to southeast through the site; and
- While currently zoned low-density residential, is considered ripe for rezoning.

The taking will, however, be highly damaging to the property because the state plans to

- Remove 304 trees and all natural vegetation screening in the 0.365-acre take area between the residences and the road (125 feet):
- Install an unlined, earth-berm drainage catch basin with a designed depth of nine feet, a volume of over one half million gallons, a discharge pipe of five feet in diameter, and a chain-link fence atop the dam;
- Convert a two-lane state road into a major dual highway designed to handle up to 80,000 vehicles per day within ten years; and
- Install 9.263 acres of new highway so that all runoff from the parking lot and roadbed, whether toxic, polluted, or otherwise, drains

into channelled concrete flues that empty through the catch basin into the small stream that bisects the property between two of the residences.

The Appraisal Problem

In this case, the appraisal may persuade the court that there is a vast discrepancy between the just compensation and the fair market value[2] of the property. It is problematic that the owner of the property will possibly be exposed to an environmental liability and the resultant costs.

As they reach far beyond historic simple property rights such as those of quiet possession, the terms "ownership" and "indicia of ownership" are generating new legal definitions, interpretations, and investigation as a result of environmental liability laws. The efficacy of this judicial exercise, while still evolving, has already potentially included as open to environmental liability all present owners, all past owners, and possibly more distantly related ownership positions such as that of mortgagees in bankruptcy.[3] The inclusion of an exculpatory clause purports to protect innocent owners by providing a forum to prove why they should not be held for SuperFund cleanup costs. However, this construction implies that owners are guilty until proven innocent.[4]

This particular partial take condemnation case should be appealed to the U.S. Supreme Court. It presents a clear example of a situation in which the courts' historic precedent to routinely equate just compensation with fair market value can no longer withstand the demands of innumerable new environmental laws. These laws force recognition of separate in rem real property values and in personam responsibilities as well as the liabilities of real property ownership.

Further, the discrepancy between just compensation and fair market value is readily apparent in this case because the fair market value of the taking plus damage to the remainder interests far exceeds the fair market value of the entire property in the first place (i.e., the before value). This condition can only exist because the damage is not solely to the remaining physical property but affects the owner as well. The damage is thus not only a simple present loss, but a future, ever-increasing source of constant liability.

It is the owner, rather than the property, who is left after the taking with financial responsibility for such contingencies as contamination, dangerous stream bed attractions, storm water discharge damage, and other potentially dangerous health risks to family and tenants from hazardous or toxic waste stream deposits as well as their clean-up costs.

Although the historic market value scenario may be applied to the taking and to the damage to the remaining property, according to this method the owner's new liabilities and responsibilities after the partial taking are not taken into account. Thus, while in theory the damage to the remaining property could be compensated for to the extreme of its entire value, the owner's remaining exposure should not be ignored in the context of a just compensation award.

Damage Theory—Partial versus Total Takes

The niceties of just compensation awards under partial take, in contrast to those under total take, are becoming more apparent. In total take

2. Fair market value is the term used by Maryland State Code of Laws, Real Property Article, Title 12, sec. 12-105.

3. United States v. Maryland Bank and Trust Co., 632 F. Supp. 575. (D. MD. 1986) and United States v. Fleet Factors Corp., 901 F. 2d 1550 (11th circ. May 23, 1990).

4. CERCLA U.S.C.S. 9607 Paragraph 107 (a)(1) and (2) and (b) and (3).

cases, market value remains the most important criterion, with few exceptions made in the name of expediency. In cases in which market value may not be "the best measure of value," (e.g., in a temporary taking case), the court may award the owner speculative operating loss instead of market value in the form of rent.[5]

In partial taking cases, however, a double, triple, or even higher standard of just compensation may develop to cover all facets of loss to the owner, depending on the extent and nature of the taking. Regardless of how feverently this "owner's loss" theory of just compensation is embraced by academicians or even fully recognized by the courts,[6] market value awards appear to reflect the "condemnor's gain" as well as a tendency to settle for less than the owner may deserve. Necessary considerations that result in owner loss may include values attributable to 1) the actual fee/easement take, 2) the resulting damage to the remaining property (an in rem appraisal), and 3) the resulting award necessary to provide for in personam damage to the owner's personal estate resulting from new environmental law liability. Such in personam damage has less to do with property rights than with responsibilities of ownership.

The in personam damages in particular pose the problem. No total take case heard by the Supreme Court has made both in rem (market value) and in personam (owner loss) just compensation awards. However, environmental impact on the questions of damages in partial take cases may cloud the issue enough for in personam damage awards to slip into acceptance under the aegis of the Supreme Court's disclaimer of "not making a fetish of market value."[7]

Nature of Damages

The nature of the damages claimed in this case hinges primarily on careful blending of the usual endemic appraisal techniques with technical procedures associated with the implementation of the new environmental protection laws. The hybrid technique is necessary because the taking itself not only damages the remaining property, but seriously affects the well-being of the owners by forcing liability on them under new laws. These laws admittedly might not be compensable under historically established case law. Many higher courts have asserted their independence from a set formula for establishing just compensation while simultaneously taking market value to be the best criterion, especially when such a value is readily available.[8] Therefore, in personam damages postulate principles not yet accepted as a standard in judging. But these very principles engender the conflict between new legislative law and established case law.

An appraiser who disclaims knowledge of legal ramifications performs a serious disservice to clients. Changes such as these make it necessary for appraisers to become better informed about real estate law.

Origin of Damages

This case's truly distinguishing feature is the devastating effect of the change in property use forced by the state taking. Not until the impact of the take area's new use on the remaining property's use and the accompanying perpetual easements are studied does the full damage pattern become apparent.

By imposing certain risks on the remaining land, the taking effectively eliminates its further present use for normal residential purposes. The prop-

5. *See United States v. Peewee Coal Co.* 344 U.S. 114, 71 S. Ct, 670 (1951)

6. See *Penn Coal Co. v Mahon* 260, U.S. 393, 43, S. Ct. 158 (1922) and *Lynch v. Household Fin. Corp,* 405 U.S. 538 (1972)

7. *United States v. Cors* 337 U.S. 325 (1949)

8. Maryland's constitution follows the Fifth Amendment of the U.S. Constitution requiring just compensation, but the State Code of Laws (see note 2 above) specifically defines the "fair market value" award to be made in condemntion cases. This definition includes "the price... for highest and best use." In some cases this criterion [market value] cannot be used "or because in the circumstances market value furnishes an inappropriate measure of actual value." United States v. General Motors 323 U.S. 373 (1949). "But [the court] has refused to make a fetish even of market value, since it may not be the best measure of value in some cases." United States v. Cors 337 U.S. 325 (1949). Finally and most appropriately in United States v 320.0 Acres of Land, 605 F. 2nd. 762 at 781 (1979), "Just Compensation is not limited to the value of the property as presently used, but includes any additional market value it may command because of the prospects for developing it to the "highest and best use" for which is it suitable." (Emphasis added.)

Valuing Contaminated Properties

erty is currently zoned low-density residential and is located less than 300 yards from a major I-95 interchange, and thus appears ripe for rezoning. (The land use has remained unchanged and the land unbuilt since 1957.)

The property's highest and best use is not its current residential use, but is rather a commercial or light industrial use in keeping with the surrounding environment and the projected land development envelope. Further, a commercial-industrial land use would offer a better opportunity to manage the problems imposed by the taking. Rezoning is now the objectively preferable option for the land. The factual considerations of property value appreciation, neighborhood zoning, and compatible land use in addition to the added implications of the take dictate rezoning. Localities are wont to rely heavily on changes (e.g., economic, physical, and environmental) or mistake to justify rezoning. In *Village of Euclid v. Ambler Reality Co.,*[9] however, the court favored the status quo except when the present zoning "has no foundation in reason and is a mere arbitrary or irrational exercise of power, having no substantial relation to the public, health, morals, safety or public welfare in its property sense."

There is little doubt that a prospective buyer would pay a higher price for the case property than its current and zoned use value. If this were not the case the property would be unsalable after disclosure of the condemnation taking threat. However, a buyer would understand the value of the rezoning to the highest and best use, and could be expected to make a contingent offer and to attempt to bring about the rezoning.[10] Whether property should be rezoned to its highest and best use is a proper issue for the court's consideration in a condemnation case. As the court notes in *United States v. 320.0 Acres of Land,* the impact on value as a result of rezoning to highest and best use should be considered. The court refers generally to *4 Nichols on Eminent Domain,* paragraph 12.322 (1), which provides that "Such likelihood [rezoning] may be considered if the prospect... is sufficiently likely as to have an appreciable influence on present market value."[11] The court also refer to *Wolff v. Commonwealth 1 Cir. 1965,* which states that "The test of course is not either possibly [sic] or probability of rezoning in absolute terms, but the fair market value of the locus in light of the changes as they would appear to the hypothetical willing buyer and seller.... We think that any possibility sufficiently substantial to affect market value must be regarded."[12]

In Rem Damages to the Remaining Property

The in rem damages to the property include landscape alterations, environmental problems, and economic changes.

Landscape Alterations

The changes to the landscape are as follows:

- 304 trees and all vegetation removed, thus causing major aesthetic alterations in the critical take area; and
- Forest screening removed, thus exposing the passing traffic as well as the chain-link fence around the drainage settlement pond.

In addition, physical dangers and installation damage are caused by the following conditions.

- A 1/2 million-gallon drain basin retained by an earthen dam;

---

9. *Village of Euclid v Ambler Realty Co.,* 272 U.S. 365 (1926).
10. See footnote 8, U.S. v. 320 Acres of Land.
11. Ibid.
12. *Wolff v. Commonwealth 1 Cir. 1965,* 841 F. 2nd. 945, 946-7.

- The creation of a dangerous, attractive public nuisance;
- The chain-link fence atop the earthen berm dam;
- The 60-inch discharge pipe and supporting structures;
- The stream bed debris, pollution, and hazardous/toxic waste;
- The probable contamination of the drinking well and clear water spring;
- The severe erosion caused by the enormously increased volume of storm water discharge that changes the course, current, and cross-section of the stream bed; and
- The dumping of water, trash, liquids, metals, debris, dead animals, oil, gas, and grease onto the property.

Environmental Problems

The following environmental problems exist.

- Nontidal wetland legislation violations;
- Hazardous waste contamination of the stream bed through property as well as the drain basin; and
- Potential pollution of spring- and well-water drinking supplies.

Economic Changes

Possible harmful economic consequences to the remaining property are as follows.

- The extent and severity of damages to the remaining property will destroy the current use (low-density residential);
- Rezoning will be difficult as a result of a recently passed zoning law; and
- After disclosure, the property will lose its present use, be unable to be insured or financed for future use, and, without use will become unmarketable until rezoned.

Damage to the remaining property is thus complete; that is, the loss encompasses the difference between the before and after values of the property.

In Personam Damage to Owners

To determine the resulting in personam damages to an owner, the cost-to-cure approach is customarily used. This approach entails consideration of costs to eliminate damage items one by one. The following in personam damages may occur in this case.

- Perpetual risks to health and life of inhabitants, tenants, guests, invitees, and even trespassers. This is because trespassers can be neither insured against after risk disclosure to an insurance company nor avoided. Even outright sale of the property is seriously jeopardized by disclosure.
- Liability for hazardous waste cleanup indefinitely,[13] presumably at least to the extent that it would be necessary to plead and prove an innocent defense.
- Response costs of indefinite duration to treat monitoring, auditing, investigation, and planning as well as other financial considerations.[14]
- Loss of ownership rights such quiet possesion, financing, and hereditaments.

13. See footnote 1,CERCLA and SARA.
14. *See New York v. Exxon Corp.* 633 F. Supp. 609 (S.D. N.Y. 1986), and *General Electric v. Litton,* 715 F. Supp. 949 (W.D. 1989).

Valuing Contaminated Properties

- Loss of viable economic use in the form of rents.

If the cost-to-cure approach were applied to the problem of the at-risk private water and sewer systems currently in use, for example, the cost to cure this damage would be the cost to hook up to the public systems available. This would amount to approximately $20,000 for all four residences.

Unfortunately, this approach is not practicable because such damage items as the dangerous, attractive nuisance aspect of the large runoff basin, the perpetual toxic waste risks to health, or the loss of marketability cannot be eliminated. If, after disclosure, the liability risks cannot be adequately insured against, the only practical alternative is self-insurance (i.e., the owner must have enough funds to meet any possible claims because an insurance company will not issue a policy). Insurance against the following risks must be considered.

- Health risks from hazardous or toxic waste pollutants to family, guests, tenants, invitees, and even trespassers;
- General liabilities caused by such problems as the dangerous, attractive public nuisance; and
- Monitoring costs and ownership cleanup defense, if not liability itself.

The funds necessary to self-insure against these risks are readily calculated by determining the present value amount necessary to provide reasonable protection, as risk increases from years 1 at least through year 10.

A sample capitalization projection to fund the risk in keeping with minimal funding criteria (e.g., bonding) required by the Comprehensive Environmental Compensation and Liability Act (CERCLA) cleanup obligations, may be calculated. The techniques illustrated in Table 1 reasonably indicate the loss in terms of dollars.

TABLE 1 Capitalization Projection to Fund Risk

1) Sum necessary to defray an ultimate potential health risk and general liability exposure of $1,000,000: 6% annual conversion for 10-year exposure basis. Capitalized present value of $1 to be collected later, formula:

$$\frac{1}{Base} = \frac{1}{(1 + interest)^N} = \frac{1}{(1.06)^{10}}$$

$$(1.06) \times (1.06) = (1.06)^2 = 1.1236$$
$$(1.06)^2 \times (1.06)^2 = (1.06)^4 = 1.26247696$$
$$(1.06)^4 \times (1.06)^4 = (1.06)^8 = 1.59384807451$$
$$(1.06)^8 \times (1.06)^2 = (1.06)^{10} = 1.79084769651$$

$$\$1,000,000 \times \frac{1}{1.79084769651} = \$558,395$$

$$\$1,000,000 \times 0.558394777 = \$558,395$$

2) Monitoring costs, etc.

$$\$150,000 \times 0.5583948 = \underline{\$83,759}$$

Total in personam damages = $642,154

Variances in Just Compensation

A final observation addresses a comparison of the difference in the just compensation award depending on whether the take is partial or total. While not based on an appraisal format and not using precise figures, the analysis shown in Table 2 provides an approximate amount of just com-

Chapter 11: *New Environmental Laws*

TABLE 2   Just Compensation: Partial Take versus Total Take

1) Before value	$850,000
2) After value	$380,000
3) Take plus in rem damage to remainder property. Take value ($80,000) plus current use value ($390,000) (found by separate value-in-use appraisal)	$470,000
4) Personal (in personam) loss damage	$640,000

Just Compensation from Condemnor's View

	Under Partial Take	Under Total Take
Taking	$80,000	Before market value
Property in rem damage	$390,000	
Total market value damage	$470,000	$850,000

pensation for both partial and total takes. The figures suggest that the condemnor would do well to proceed with the partial take ($470,000) rather than the total take ($850,000).

These figures do not take into account the in personam damages, however. If the condemnor proceeds with the partial take process, the in personam damages appear readily identifiable and actually imposed by CERCLA. The court would thus award them not as a taking but as damages, for which a precedent has been set in partial take cases anyway. The just compensation award would then be altered to include:

Taking	$80,000
All damages (in rem and in personam)	$1,030,000
Total partial take award	$1,110,000

If the condemnor were to proceed on the total take basis, however, the court would be far less likely to award the in personam losses as well as the before-market value, because no such precedent has been established. The award would therefore be $850,000, which would lead the condemnor to conclude that it would be better to proceed with the total take ($850,000) basis rather than the partial take ($1,110,00) basis.

Just compensation from the condemnee's point of view is shown in Table 3.

If it is true that numbers can be juggled to prove almost anything, the courts may use the new forensic numbers of the environmental statutes to derive a new meaning for just compensation.

TABLE 3 Just Compensation from the Condemnee's View

Under Partial Take — Just Compensation Award		Under Total Take — Just Compensation Award	
Taking	$80,000		
Property damages	$390,000		
	$470,000	Before value	$850,000
Plus personal damages if awarded	$640,000	Plus personal damages if awarded	$640,000
Total	$1,110,000*	Total	$1,490,000**

* Condemnee left with both CERCLA liability and after value

** Condemnee left with CERCLA liability only

Temporary Stigma: Lessons from the Exxon Valdez Litigation

by Richard J. Roddewig, MAI

Richard J. Roddewig, MAI, *is president of Clarion Associates, Inc., in Chicago and Denver. He co-developed the Appraisal Institute's seminar,* Environmental Risk and the Real Estate Appraisal Process *and has taught the seminar nationwide. He is adjunct lecturer of real estate valuation in the Department of Finance at DePaul University, Chicago.*

This article originally appeared in the January 1997 issue of The Appraisal Journal.

Few cases in recent years have been as big, at least in terms of media attention, as the litigation that followed in the wake of the *Exxon Valdez* oil spill in 1989. The approximately 10.8 million gallons of oil released in the spill moved west and south through Prince William Sound and the Gulf of Alaska, oiling in varying degrees about 1,300 miles of Alaska coastline. Intensive cleanup efforts were undertaken by Exxon and others under the supervision of the U.S. Coast Guard during the next four years.

A number of lawsuits were filed in state and federal courts in the wake of the *Exxon Valdez* spill. While many of the most publicized cases did not directly involve real estate valuation issues, a significant, but not very widely publicized, lawsuit in the Alaska state courts did involve claims made by private owners of oiled properties who sought damages for the impact of the spill on the value of their property.[1]

The *Exxon Valdez* litigation was filed at a time when the appraisal profession was finally becoming comfortable with assignments involving valuation of contaminated properties. However, the *Exxon Valdez* litigation raised some cutting-edge issues concerning environmental stigma, temporary impacts of contamination on property markets and values, and the appropriate measures of temporary real estate impacts on properties in remote or limited markets like Prince William Sound.

Stigma: Temporary vs. Permanent Impacts

To understand the context of the real estate aspects of the *Exxon Valdez* litigation, an appraiser must understand the recent rapid evolution of appraisal practice techniques involving the valuation of contaminated property. Over the past two decades, appraisers have learned how to evaluate the impact of a wide variety of environmental risks on property values and real estate markets. Thanks in part to the Appraisal Institute's significant role in providing guidance to the profession on appropriate valuation techniques,[2] appraisers have become more skilled in determining the impact of contamination and other forms of environmental risk on real

1. In re: The *Exxon Valdez*, Superior Court for the State of Alaska, Third Judicial Circuit, 3AN-89-2533. Another piece of the *Exxon Valdez* litigation dealt with damages to state and federal lands.

2. Richard Roddewig, "Stigma, Environmental Risk and Property Value: 10 Critical Inquiries," *The Appraisal Journal* (October 1996): 375–387.

estate values and real estate markets. For an appraiser with little if any prior experience in this practice area, however, or who handles only an occasional assignment involving environmental risk and stigma, the appraisal issues can still be daunting, especially when the stigma caused by the contamination or environmental risk is temporary rather than permanent. In fact, the whole issue of temporary versus permanent impacts on value is becoming increasingly important and sometimes requires appraisers to step outside the neatly defined borders of the three traditional approaches to value in order to handle it.

The appraisal profession has now come to recognize that environmental stigma can indeed be temporary rather than permanent.[3] To understand how some types of environmental stigma can increase, decrease, and even disappear with time, consider the history of the real estate market's response to asbestos. In the 1970s, when health concerns about asbestos first surfaced, some types of commercial real estate were completely stigmatized—the market for them evaporated almost overnight. However, as scientists began to understand the health risks more clearly, technical specialists began to develop quantifiable and cost-effective remediation techniques and monitoring systems to assure existing tenants that asbestos-removal procedures in one part of a building were not contaminating other areas. In addition, lawmakers and regulators began to clarify the legal responsibilities, the marketplace (including lenders) became more knowledgeable and, therefore, more comfortable in dealing with the risks associated with owning property containing asbestos. The result has been a gradual lessening of the stigma (over and above the costs associated with remediation). In fact, today many types of properties containing asbestos may not even be stigmatized and their values may be unaffected by the presence of asbestos.

Points of Agreement and Disagreement Among Exxon Valdez Real Estate Experts

Now that the real estate litigation resulting from the 1989 grounding of the *Exxon Valdez* oil tanker in Prince William Sound has essentially been completed, the appraisal profession can gain some important insights into alternative methodologies for measuring damages caused by "temporary" contamination events. The principal plaintiffs in the real estate litigation were a group of property owners including Native American corporations, native villages, and the Kodiak Island Borough. The principal defendant was Exxon. Both sides retained real estate and other experts to analyze the impact of the spill on real estate markets and measure the damages. While experts on both sides had many disagreements about the impact of the oil spill on real estate markets and even about valuation and market impact methodologies and concepts, there were also some core methodological issues on which they agreed.

- Both sides agreed that the impact of the oil spill on real estate was "temporary." They disagreed on the length of the impact and how to determine its length, however.

- The principal experts on both sides considered it appropriate to classify the affected lands by use and determine damages on a use-by-use basis. They disagreed on the characterization of some of the use

3. See, for example, the discussion in Chapter 6 of the materials for the Appraisal Institute seminar, *Environmental Risk and the Real Estate Appraisal Process.*

categories, amount of acreage in each category, comparables, highest and best use of specific parcels, and, in some categories, land value.

- Both sides attempted to quantify the damages to real estate by determining an imputed economic loss. They disagreed on the characterization of this loss as lost rent or payment for a license to use the land during the oiling and subsequent cleanup.

- Experts on both sides agreed that the economic losses over time could properly be discounted to a present value. They disagreed on the length of the discount period, the appropriate discount rate, and whether the courts or the appraisers should select the appropriate discount rate.

There were other major points of disagreement on methodological and even definitional issues. The case involved such fundamental questions as the meaning of "highest and best use" for property located in a remote and limited real estate market such as that in Prince William Sound and whether "market value" was synonymous with "public interest value" for some of the land affected by the spill. Some of these fundamental disagreements worked their way into Appraisal Journal articles published during the litigation.[4]

Property Owners' Methodology and Conclusions

The principal real estate expert for most of the property owners primarily relied on a comparison of the discounted present value from a 30-year stream of imputed economic rent "before and after" considering the impact of the *Exxon Valdez* oil spill. The difference in the two discounted present values equated to the damages to market value of the oiled properties. Key assumptions and considerations in the discounting model used by the property owners' expert included the following:

- Entire ownership parcels, not just shoreline-related areas, were affected by the spill.

- The duration of the real estate impact is directly related to the physical persistence of the oil on the affected properties as determined by a scientific consultant on which the real estate expert relied.

- The physical persistence of the oil (and, therefore, the duration of the real estate impact) varied from parcel to parcel, depending on the character of the shoreline, the severity of the initial oiling (i.e., light, moderate, or heavy), and the degree and effectiveness of the cleanup. On some heavily oiled shoreline segments, the physical persistence and, therefore, the market impact could last as long as 24 years.

- The annual loss in dollars to the land can be expressed in terms of a lost economic rent even for non-income producing properties.

- Parcels that had only a portion of the length of their shoreline oiled, say, for example, 5,000 feet of a 10,000-foot shoreline, or 50%, were assumed to have lost that same percentage (50%) of their economic rent during the entire period of physical persistence.

- The risks associated with receiving the economic rent on oiled properties was greater than on unoiled properties; therefore, the discount rate should be 400 basis points higher than the appropriate rate for

---

4. Compare Victoria Adams and Bill Mundy, "The Valuation of High-Amenity Natural Land," *The Appraisal Journal* (January 1991): 48 (This paper was written by two of the experts for the property owners.) to Richard J. Roddewig and Gary R. Papke, "Market Value and Public Value: An Exploratory Essay," *The Appraisal Journal* (January 1996): 52 (This paper was written by experts for Exxon.).

unoiled properties not affected by the spill during the period of physical persistence.

- The adverse impact of the spill on economic rent lasts an average of two years longer than the physical persistence of the oil due to "remaining uncertainty," but the difference in the discount rate during those additional two years is only 200 rather than 400 basis points.

- Every oiled parcel suffered a complete market stigma (and, therefore, total loss of imputed economic rent) for one to three years immediately following the oil spill and during the subsequent cleanup.

Exxon's Methodology and Conclusions

The team of experts for Exxon approached the problem in a different way. Both of the firms retained by Exxon actually researched the marketplace to determine the duration of oil spill impacts. One firm compiled information on previous oil spills in North America and elsewhere and developed a methodology for selecting case studies most appropriate to analyze to understand the impact of spills on real estate markets. From an initial list of 43 oil spills, about 13 were selected for further research and analysis and detailed case studies of four spills before and after the *Exxon Valdez* spill were conducted. Two of these spills occurred in Washington state, one in California, and one in Massachusetts. The purpose of these case studies was to gain insights into the real estate marketplace's typical reaction to an oil spill. The case studies selected for detailed analysis involved locations in which an active real estate market existed at the time of the spill. The lessons learned from these active markets could then be applied to the relatively limited and inactive market in Prince William Sound and southcentral Alaska. The case studies resulted in a significant body of market data that answered such questions as the following:

- Does a marketplace indeed shut down after a major oil spill?
- If there is a shutdown, how long does it last?
- Is there any relationship between cleanup efforts and the length of any marketplace impacts from the spill?
- Are only directly oiled properties affected or do market impacts extend to non-oiled properties in proximity to oiled shorelines?
- If non-oiled properties are affected, how far up or down the coast or inland from the spill site does that marketplace impact extend?
- If sales are made at the time the marketplace experiences a spill and begins cleanup, are the prices affected by the spill?

From the case studies, Exxon's experts reached a number of conclusions, including the following:

- There is no automatic direct correlation between physical persistence of oil and real estate impacts.
- If there is any real estate impact following oil spills, it affects directly oiled beachfront property only where use of the property has been impaired and does not extend inland or have a marketwide impact.
- The length and intensity of the cleanup is a significant factor in determining the length of any potential real estate market impact.

- Although there is some evidence of oil spill impact on market values in some of the case studies, "(M)ost of the case study analysis supports a conclusion that oil spills do not adversely affect property values."[5]

Those Exxon experts simultaneously researched and tracked what was happening in the southcentral Alaska land market in the wake of the *Exxon Valdez* spill. They analyzed the numbers of real estate transactions, recordings of warranty deeds and mortgages, changes in local assessed values and State of Alaska estimates of "full value" of property, and value of recorded mortgages. Comparisons were made between oiled and non-oiled property both before and after the spill to determine if the Alaska marketplace itself was showing any impact from the spill. The conclusions of the real estate analysts was that the Alaska marketplace showed neither a temporary nor long-term disruption from the *Exxon Valdez* spill, and most of the indicators showed that market activity and property values actually improved within the portion of the state affected by the spill by comparison to non-oiled areas.

The case study and Alaska market research undertaken by that first group of Exxon real estate experts were used for two purposes in the litigation. First, they provided support to real estate damage calculations by Exxon's other real estate experts. Second, they formed the basis for critical analysis of the property owner's calculation of damages and correction of those damage claims, taking into account the results of the Alaska market research and oil spill case studies for determining such things as the length of stigma impact, amount of shoreline-related property affected by the spill, and discount rates.

An appraisal report was prepared by the second team of Exxon experts. Key considerations in this report included the following:

- Only shoreline-related areas were affected by the spill, not upland (e.g., clifftops or mountaintops) or inland acreage more than one-half mile from shore.

- The duration of the economic impact is lessened by cleanup activities and is not automatically related to the duration of physical persistence of some oils on a property. The removal of oil and curing of visual oiling effects were more important to informed market participants than the physical persistence of scattered remnants of oil in isolated pockets.

- Not all oiled properties suffered economic impairment. A key consideration is whether the oiling interfered with a property's reasonable use.

- The degree of economic impairment is also a function of the highest and best use of the land prior to the spill. Much of the land had only limited use potential even before the spill.

- The annual loss in dollars can be expressed in terms of payment for a temporary nonexclusive real estate license to Exxon to enter and clean the shoreline.

- Licenses in Alaska are typically granted for shorter terms and at a lower annual rate as a percentage of value than are leases.

- Annual economic loss due to impairment of use decreased each year after the spill as a result of Exxon cleanup activities and natural cleans-

5. The Impact of the *Exxon Valdez* Oil Spill on Real Estate Markets," Clarion Associates, Inc., Chicago, May 28, 1993, 190.

ing by winter storms. For example, a heavily oiled property with a near-total impairment of use in 1989 immediately after the spill may have improved to the point that, two years later, impairment was reduced to only 60% and three years later to only 2% in 1992, the last year of cleanup.

- Impairment of use for most parcels did not extend beyond the termination of cleanup activities in 1992, and for all parcels not beyond March 1993, four years after the spill.

Damage Estimates and the Jury's Decision

What were the damage calculations made by both sides and the jury? A variety of property owners filed a series of related cases. The largest damage claims were filed by a group of native corporations and villages that owned property in Prince William Sound and along the Gulf of Alaska. Although their initial property damage claims apparently totaled over $600 million, by the time the actual trial began in July 1994, damage claims by those groups totaled about $93.5 million. Exxon's appraisal expert estimated the total damage claim to be between $2 million and $5 million. Exxon's other real estate experts who investigated the marketplace in southcentral Alaska before and after the spill undertook case study analysis of other oil spills and then adjusted the property owner's damage calculations based on that research. These second experts concluded that when the property owners' methodology was properly adjusted for marketplace factors, the damages were about $5.95 million The jury concluded that the damages totaled about $6.7 million for all plaintiffs combined, including the Kodiak Island property owners.

Lessons of the *Exxon Valdez* Litigation

There are many lessons that are apparent now, and many more will become apparent as time passes. Among the more significant that can now be discerned are the following:

- The nature and purpose of the assignment determine the most appropriate valuation or evaluation technique. A technique perfectly appropriate for the typical appraisal assignment involving uncontaminated residential or commercial property, such as the "before and after" approach, for example, may be inappropriate, and possibly even misleading, in some assignments involving contaminated property or properties affected by environmental stigma.[6]

- Appraisers are trained to deal with market value as of a specific date in time. However, values can change over time, and traditional techniques from typical appraisal assignments may have to be modified to fit the realities of the real estate assignment, especially when the goal is to arrive at an accurate estimate of damages to property during a specific time period.

- Appraisers must look to the marketplace for answers and analyze what the marketplace itself is actually saying. Scientific conclusions about persistence of contaminants do not necessarily correlate with the marketplace's conclusion about the duration of economic impact on real estate.

6. "Stigma" is defined as "an adverse effect on the market's perception of the value of property containing an environmental risk even after cleanup costs have been expended or considered in estimating value." From the *Environmental Risk and the Real Estate Appraisal Process* seminar, 128.

- Estimates of stigma damage can be significantly affected, and possibly overstated or understated, by critical assumptions made about the size of the parcel affected by the contamination situation.

Techniques and solutions developed in unusual appraisal assignments, such as the one faced by the real estate experts in the *Exxon Valdez* litigation, are important to the appraisal profession. They require appraisers to test the adequacy and practical limitations of traditional valuation and analytical tools, devise flexible new tools in the context of basic professional touchstones (such as the definitions of market value and highest and best use), and incorporate those new insights into their professional practice.

Many of the insights gleaned from the *Exxon Valdez* litigation are being incorporated into professional practice by those who have attended the Appraisal Institute's seminar *Environmental Risk and the Real Estate Appraisal Process*, which was prepared by some of the experts involved in that case. Many of the techniques used in the *Exxon Valdez* litigation are discussed, including case studies, before and after approach, analysis of general market data, analysis of tax assessment data, surveys of market participants, hypotheticals, and analogies.[7] I highly recommend this seminar, which offers considerable help to appraisers deciding on the right methodology for measuring temporary environmental stigma.

7. For another look at some of the issues that arose in the *Exxon Valdez* litigation over real estate impacts, see John Dorchester, Jr., "The Exxon Valdez Oil Spill: Property Damage Assessments," *The Valuer and Land Economist*, v. 34, no. 2 (May 1996): 96.

Settlement of an Oil Pipeline Leak with Contaminated Residential Property: A Case Study

by Robert A. Simons

Introduction

Petroleum pipelines transport natural gas, crude oil, and partly and fully refined petroleum products from seaports and domestic oil production areas throughout the United States. According to the Federal Department of Transportation Office of Pipeline Safety (OPS), there were about 2,000 natural gas firms and 300 companies operating petroleum distribution pipelines in 1997, with over two million miles of moderate-to-large (e.g., diameter 8–40) inches) pipelines in service.[1] Unfortunately some pipelines have experienced a chronic weakness in line integrity resulting in pipeline ruptures which have released petroleum product into the environment. Some leaks may be abrupt, while others may go undetected for a long period of time. Under these circumstances, a plume of petroleum product may infiltrate the groundwater, and contaminate drinking water wells. Once contamination has been detected, property values of affected residences can only decrease markedly. The pipeline leaks described in this case study went undetected for several decades.

Because appraisers always consider the arms length of transaction (favorable terms, etc.) the sales in this case study, like any which have inducements or are sold or bought with one party under duress, would normally be discarded. However, the information about the properties in this case study neighborhood reflects the discounted cost of contamination to the responsible party. Thus, it would set an upper boundary on what a free market discount would be.

This study examines how much a negotiated settlement package affects the sales price, under various scenarios, and thus reveals a corporate policy of discounting sales. The case setting considers the effect of petroleum groundwater contamination on the value of rural/ex-urban residential properties on well water, with full information, where a district-wide area is affected.

Robert A. Simons, PhD., is an associate professor of Urban Planning and Real Estate Development at the Levin College of Urban Affairs at Cleveland State University. Research and consulting interests include redevelopment of contaminated land (brownfields), assessment of environmental damages, housing policy, and public real estate issues. (E-mail: roby@urban.csuohio.edu)

The article originally appeared in the Summer 1999 issue of Real Estate Issues. Reproduced with the permission of Real Estate Issues; published and © by the Counselors of Real Estate (a not for profit organization), Chicago, IL. All rights reserved. Further reproduction/distribution is prohibited without the written permission of Real Estate Issues.

---

1. U.S. Department of Transportation, Office of Pipeline Safety (OPS) 1996 Colonial Pipeline Task Force, Final Report January 10, 1997.

Literature Review

Several studies address the effects of petroleum contamination on residential property. A recent investigation regarding residential property value decreases along pipeline easements in suburban Virginia found losses of one percent to two percent for townhouses and up to four percent to five percent for single-family detached homes. These properties were on municipal drinking water and, due to extensive publicity, the market perceived the eventuality of possible repeated discharges.[2] Registered LUST (leaking underground storage tanks) sites in greater Cleveland, Ohio, experienced losses of between 14 percent and 17 percent. Virtually all of these units were on municipal drinking water systems, and all were within 300 feet of a known LUST and/or had actual groundwater contamination.[3]

Page and Rabinowitz found that groundwater contamination had no measurable effect on residential sales price, but their research design was a relatively weak case study approach. Dotzour also found no negative effect on residential property values from groundwater contamination in the Wichita, Kansas, area. However, both of the last two studies mentioned did find negative effects on commercial property.[4]

Des Rosiers *et al* found a five percent to eight percent decrease of residential property values resulting from persistent groundwater contamination in the province of Quebec.[5]

Abdala, Roach, and Epp looked at averting expenditures on the part of the owners of contaminated property as a way to estimate value loss. They concluded that this technique was a "conceptually valid estimate" of the cost to the property owner, and can be easily quantified.[6] The expenses they considered included filtration, bottled water, etc. This last study is germane to the research at hand because this research also evaluates non-market inducements (although they are positive rather than negative), and considers their effect on property value.

BP Pipeline Case Study

The following case study examines the effects of a British Petroleum (BP) pipeline rupture on residential property in Franklin Township, Summit County, Ohio, a suburb of Akron. The case provides a good indication of the extent of property damage that a pipeline leak can have on rural, residential property that is actually contaminated, and where a considerable amount of contamination lingers until the present.

Case Background

Inland Corp. owns a pipeline in northeast Ohio that carries petroleum products. The pipeline is operated by BP. It is a 12-inch line, which replaced a smaller line installed around 1940. The smaller line apparently leaked several times between 1948 and 1962, and attracted the attention of the Ohio EPA and Summit County health department, who were actively working on the case in 1990. Of the 100 homes in the study area that were tested, 13 had detectable levels of hydrocarbon contamination, and six of these had benzene levels above federal standards for municipal water systems. At the time the incident was discovered, all these homes were on well water.

A consent order with the Ohio EPA was signed in 1991, and BP conducted testing to determine the extent of contamination. About this time,

---

2. Robert Simons. (1999). The Effect of Pipeline Ruptures on Non-Contaminated Easement Holding Property. Appraisal Journal July 1999.

3. Robert A. Simons, William Bowen and Arthur Sementelli. (1997). The Effect of Leaking Underground Storage Tanks on Residential Property Value. Journal of Real Estate Research, Vol. 14 no. 1/2 p.29–42; and Robert A. Simons, William Bowen and Arthur Sementelli. (1999). The Effect of LUSTS from Gas Stations on Residential and Commercial Property that is Actually Contaminated, Appraisal Journal, April 1999 p.186–194.

4. William Page and Harvey Rabinowitz (1993). Groundwater Contamination: Its Effects on Property Values and Cities. Journal of the American Planning Association. Vol 59, no 4. pp.473–481, and Mark Dotzour (1997). Groundwater Contamination and Residential Property Values. Appraisal Journal, vol. 65 no 3. pp 279–290.

5. Francois Des Rosiers, Alain Bolduc and Marius Theriault (1997). Environment and Value: Does Drinking Water Affect House Prices. Presentation at the 1997 Meeting of the American Real Estate Society in Sarasota FL.

6. C.W. Abdala, B.A. Roach and D.J. Epp. (1992) Valuing Environmental Quality Changes Using Averting Expenditures. Land Economics. Vol. 68, no. 2 p 163–175.

Chapter 11: *Settlement of Oil Pipeline Leak*

local property owners filed lawsuits. The testing proceeded through 1993, with 19 or more monitoring wells. A more recent OEPA document shows that environmental testing continued through late 1998. An inspection of the site in late 1998 revealed that a number of large green water testing trailers were in place.

Data Gathering Procedures and Analysis

A data set of Summit County property transactions was acquired from the Amerestate Corporation. Based on these actual transaction data, it could be verified that BP Oil Pipeline Co. acquired 41 parcels in the impact area, nearly all since 1993. According to public records, BP still retains ownership of 18 of these homes, and has subsequently sold 23 of them. After deleting double counts, these parcels represent 35 residential properties.

Analysis of BP's Direct Real Estate Transactions in Franklin Township

Figure 1 shows a sale/resale analysis of the 23 properties acquired and resold by BP in the market. Sales data were available for 21 of these residential properties. Before adjusting for carrying costs, market inducements to buyers or appreciation over a holding period averaging 36 months, 19 of these properties decreased in value, and two increased. The two that increased were for properties acquired in the mid-1980s. The average decrease in value was 20.4 percent (between -13.4 percent and -27.2 percent, based on a 95 percent level of confidence). The weighted average decrease was larger, at 27.2 percent. These figures represent the direct loss associated with an oil pipeline leak with groundwater contamination in an area on well water, before accounting for the time value of money.

FIGURE 1   BP Pipeline Leak Sale/Resale Analysis, Summit County, Ohio

Parcel	Resale Amt.	Resale Date	Purchase	Purchase Date	Diff.	% Diff.
1	$100,000	3/19/96	$125,000	7/20/93	-$25,000	-20.0%
2	$104,000	4/25/97	$130,000	8/24/93	-$26,000	-20.0%
3	$108,000	5/31/96	$160,000	8/31/93	-$52,000	-32.5%
4	$100,000	4/26/96	$135,000	4/22/94	-$35,000	-25.9%
5	$88,000	5/13/96	$110,000	10/28/93	-$22,000	-20.0%
6	$122,000	4/23/96	$153,000	4/3/93	-$31,000	-20.3%
7	$90,000	7/18/96	$116,000	10/31/95	-$26,000	-22.4%
8	$75,000	11/26/96	$111,750	5/2/95	-$36,750	-32.9%
9	$80,000	12/1/95	$100,000	12/15/92	-$20,000	-20.0%
10	$75,000	11/22/95	$72,500	10/15/86	$2,500	3.4%
11	$75,000	11/22/95	$93,500	8/23/94	-$18,500	-19.8%
12	$72,000	2/16/96	$90,000	12/15/92	-$18,000	-20.0%
13	$96,000	5/31/96	$120,000	8/24/93	-$24,000	-20.0%
14	$136,000	2/28/96	$460,000	8/9/93	-$324,000	-70.4%
15	$65,500	6/26/96	$82,000	8/22/94	-$16,500	-20.1%
16	$128,000	2/29/96	$160,000	11/17/93	-$32,000	-20.0%
17	$186,000	10/31/95	$240,000	10/22/93	-$54,000	-22.5%
18	$186,000	10/31/95	$240,000	10/22/93	-$54,000	-22.5%
19	$116,000	7/26/96	$145,000	8/31/93	-$29,000	-20.0%
20	$120,000	4/17/96	$87,000	10/29/86	$33,000	37.9%
21	$136,000	3/18/96	$170,000	8/24/93	-$34,000	-20.0%
					(ave. loss)	-20.4%
Total	$2,258,500		$3,100,750		-$842,250	-27.16%
					(weighted ave. loss)	

* In Summit County Tax Book Page 23

Valuing Contaminated Properties

Overall, a reasonable discount for these properties would be 25 percent. These figures should represent market forces on the buyers' side during the most recent round of sales, and a loss-minimizing discounted sales policy on behalf of the seller.

Present Value Analysis of Sales

The sale/resale analysis understates the actual loss because it does not account for the time value of money in holding the properties prior to resale, including those that have not yet been resold. This present value analysis considers the 21 bought and resold properties presented in Figure 1, as well as the remaining 14 houses BP has acquired in the impact area, for a total of 35 residential units. It extends the sales experience of the 21 sold units (the best available information) to the 14 unsold ones, and puts all 35 in the context of time. Including previously unsold units is important because their sales revenues would be included in the analysis, thereby avoiding overstating the loss. Because remediation is still underway, it is assumed that these remaining 14 properties would also be held for three more years, and then resold at a 25 percent discount. For selection of a discount rate, BP's discount rate was assumed to be 12 percent, which reflects the firm's published return on equity over the past nine years.[7]

Figure 2 examines the present value of the loss experienced by BP in these real estate transactions. Based on these assumptions, the present value of the loss would be $1.9 million on a property base value of $4.7 million. This represents a present value loss to BP of just over 40 percent.[8]

Negotiated Settlement

Beyond the direct sale and resale of units, there were another 65 units affected by the pipeline leak. According to a public presentation by BP staff, there was a negotiated settlement between BP and the residents in a specific study area (approximately 100 homes). The deal was facilitated by the Ur-

7. It was decided to use the published return on equity rather than the firm's hurdle rate or target rate because these are not available. The return on equity is an adequate measure of the opportunity cost of capital.

8. This figure was subjected to sensitivity analysis. If the properties were resold faster, in the second year, at only a 10 percent discount, and assuming a discount rate of 18 percent (well above the return to stockholders), the resulting loss is 39 percent, about the same at the figure derived above. If the same sale assumptions are kept, but if BP's discount rate is assumed to be 8 percent, consistent with financing the costs with corporate debt, the overall loss would be 35 percent.

FIGURE 2 Summary: BP Franklin Township Case Study: Present Value of Direct Real Estate Transactions Only

Item	1992	1993	1994	1995	1996	1997	1998	1999	2000	2001	2002
Buy 35 Units	-$350	-$3,178	-$852	-$228	-$87						
Resell 35 Units*				$602	$1,553	$104			$1,200		
Total	-$350	-$3,178	-$852	$374	$1,466	$104	$0	$0	$1,200	$0	$0
Disc. Fac. @ 12%	0.893	0.797	0.712	0.636	0.567	0.507	0.452	0.404	0.361	0.322	0.287
PV/YR	-$313	-$2,533	-$607	$238	$832	$53	$0	$0	$433	$0	$0
Sum of PV	-$1,896										
Base Value (35 Units)	$4,694										
Loss	-40.43%										

Assumptions	Number of Units	All Dollars in Thousands Average Value	Time/Years Duration	Items Excluded from Analysis
Units in Study Area	100	$111.94		Rental Income
Unbought Units*	65	$100.00		Remediation Costs
BP Bought then Resold	21	$147.65		Relocation Expense
BP Bought/Held	14	$113.84		
Discount Rate	0.12		Based on BP's Return on Equity (9 Year Average) of 12%	

* Average Sales Price $100,000

NOTE $1.2 million in sales in the year 2000 is an assumption. See text

Chapter 11: *Settlement of Oil Pipeline Leak*

ban Center at the Levin College of Urban Affairs at Cleveland State University.[9] In addition to paying for remediation of contamination:

- BP offered to buy out, relocate, and compensate those households who wanted to leave for their "pain and suffering." BP was free to resell these homes (the 35 units referred to above).
- BP also offered to give each household a $2,000 grant per year for five years for home improvements (all but three made use of these).
- BP also offered to give each household an indemnification against declining property values for 10 years.

Because this was a negotiated settlement, it helped the residents get on with their lives, and appeared to be well received. The next section analyzes the present value of these market-supporting strategies.

Present Value Analysis of Settlement Package

An analysis of the present value of the overall settlement package between BP and the residents is shown in Figure 3. These figures are assumed to be net to BP, and exclude remediation costs, or any payments to residents for relocation or personal matters. They also exclude rental income to BP from the houses they own and hold. The figures are based on the 35 units presented above, as well as the 65 additional units which BP did not buy, but which received a $2,000 annual maintenance grant for five years, and a guaranteed sales price for 10 years. It was assumed that the 35 homes sold did not receive these non-market supports.[10]

When these other non-market factors are included, the present value of the loss to BP for all 100 units in the study area (a combination of those directly impacted and within the impact area but not contaminated) would

9. Bill Hollis, BP Corp. Public Meeting, Levin College of Urban Affairs, Cleveland State University, April 1997.

10. If a property is sold every ten years, and if there is a 20 percent loss upon sale, then for an average sales price of $100,000, the annual expected expense to cover the losses would be $2,000.

FIGURE 3   Summary: BP Franklin Township Case Study. Present Value of Market Supports to All 100 Units

Item	1992	1993	1994	1995	1996	1997	1998	1999	2000	2001	2002
Buy 35 Units	-$350	-$3,178	-$852	-$228	-$87						
Resell 35 Units				$602	$1,553	$104			$1,200		
Maint. Grants-65 Units		-$130	-$130	-$130	-$130	-$130					
Price Guarantees-65 Units		-$130	-$130	-$130	-$130	-$130	-$130	-$130	-$130	-$130	-$130
Total	-$350	-$3,438	-$1,112	$114	$1,206	-$156	-$130	-$130	$1,070	-$130	-$130
Disc. Fac. @ 12%	0.893	0.797	0.712	0.636	0.567	0.507	0.452	0.404	0.361	0.322	0.287
PV/YR	-$313	-$2,741	-$792	$73	$684	-$79	-$59	-$53	$386	-$42	-$37
Sum of PV	-$2,972										
Base Value (100 Unitts)	$11,194										
Loss	-26.55%										

Assumptions	Number of Units	All Dollars in Thousands Average Value	Time/Years Duration	Items Excluded from Analysis
Units in Study Area	100	$111.94		Rental Income
Unbought Units*	65	$100.00		Remediation Costs
BP Bought then Resold	21	$147.65		Relocation Expense
BP Bought/Held	14	$113.84		
Maintenance Grants	65	$2.00	5	
Price Guarantee**	65	$2.00	10	
Discount Rate	0.12		Based on BP's Return on Equity (9 Year Average) of 12%	

* Average Sales Price $100,000

** Price guarantee based on a 20% loss, sale every 10 years. $100,000 * .20 * .1 = $2,000/Unit/Yr

be just under $3.0 million on a property base of $11.2 million. Thus, the present value of the direct real estate losses and other non-market support activities to BP for the study area in this case, exclusive of remediation, would be -26.5 percent. Because this figure reflects a blend where one-third of the units were directly acquired by the responsible party, and the rest were offered market supports, it is not generalizable beyond this case.

However, those 65 properties in the impact area but not bought by BP received non-market price supports with a present value of $1.1 million, on a property base of $6.5 million. This represents just under 17 percent of the value of these properties, which may be generalizable if a similar settlement package is offered.

Conclusions

This case has analyzed residential sales contaminated by a known pipeline leak where remediation is being undertaken, and the houses are on well water. The case study reveals that single-family homes contaminated by a well-publicized pipeline rupture experienced a loss in real estate value of approximately 25 percent, after the rupture and when remediation is underway. The motivation of the responsible party was an important factor in this analysis. The present value of this reduction in value to the responsible party (exclusive of remediation costs) was 35 percent to 40 percent, depending on the assumptions used.

Secondly, neighboring residential properties within a designated impact area that were not acquired by the responsible party (within the study area but not shown to be directly contaminated) received an array of price supports with a present value equivalent to 17 percent of their market value.

This latter figure is a substantial amount. Further, the settlement terms are not generally available using conventional real estate research methods (e.g., no lien, no responsible party seller, not on a deed registration document). If and when these homes are resold, and if remaining time on these price supports are transferable to new owners, they should be capitalized into the sales price value of the properties.[REI]

Junk Science, Environmental Stigma, Market Surveys, and Proper Appraisal Methodology: Recent Lessons from the Litigation Trenches

by Richard J. Roddewig, MAI

Litigation support assignments sometimes test the limits of acceptable appraisal methodology and practice. Frequently in litigation-related assignments the appraiser is required to follow appraisal standards and methods set out either in statutes, regulations, or prior case decisions. In some areas of the law, eminent domain for example, the statutory, regulatory, and case law precedents are well established. In addition, there is general consistency between jurisdictions as well as between the legal realm and the everyday appraisal world in the manner in which our traditional appraisal methodologies are applied to litigation valuation assignments.[1]

But in many other legal practice areas where judicial rules and precedents coincide with appraisal theory and everyday appraisal practice, the case law is less well developed. Judges and lawyers involved in cases—for example involving the valuation of special-purpose properties, the separation of business value or intangible value from real estate value, and, most recently, the valuation of properties affected by environmental risks and contamination—may find little precedent, unusual appraisal methodology, and procedural questions that must be answered.

Appraisers who work regularly in the legal arena (and even those who do not) need to be aware of some of the appraisal methodological issues arising in recent cases involving determination of damages to real estate, especially damages caused by environmental risks or contamination. This environmental column explores the implications of three recent cases. One involves the general rules concerning the reliability and admissibility of expert testimony. Two cases apply the tests of reliability/admissibility to the utilization of market participant surveys as the basis for estimating the degree of stigma that attaches to property affected by groundwater contamination.

Junk Science and the *Kumho Tire* Extension of the *Daubert* Rule

In March of this year, the U.S. Supreme Court decided *Kumho Tire Company, Ltd., et al., v. Patrick Carmichael.*[2] Although the case involved nei-

Richard J. Roddewig, MAI, is president of Clarion Associates, with offices in Chicago, Denver, and Philadelphia. He codeveloped the Appraisal Institute's seminar, "Environmental Risk and the Real Estate Appraisal Process," and has taught the seminar nationwide. He is a regular contributor to The Appraisal Journal on environmental issues, and is an adjunct lecturer on real estate valuation in the finance department at DePaul University, Chicago.

This article originally appeared in the October 1999 issue of The Appraisal Journal.

1. One of the principal exceptions to this congruity in the eminent domain practice area is the widespread judicial reluctance to accept such standard appraisal methods as the income approach to value or the subdivision development or land residual approaches.

2. *Kumho Tire Company, Ltd., et al. v. Patrick Carmichael,* 119 S. Ct. 1167 (March 23, 1999).

ther real estate nor environmental contamination, it has significant implications for real estate appraisers, not only in cases involving environmental stigma but in all kinds of real estate valuation assignments in litigation.

When the tire on Patrick Carmichael's minivan blew out, resulting in the death of one passenger and injuries to others, Carmichael sued the tire's maker and its distributor. Carmichael and his attorneys retained a tire failure expert who concluded that a design or manufacturing defect caused the blowout and gave a deposition summarizing his conclusion. However, the federal district trial court excluded the expert's testimony, finding that the expert's methodology was not reliable.

In so ruling, the trial court applied the U.S. Supreme Court's previously established test in *Daubert v. Merrell Dow Pharmaceuticals, Inc.*, for evaluating the reliability of an expert's opinion.[3] The earlier *Daubert* decision emphasized that the federal courts have an obligation to serve as "gatekeepers" under the Federal Rules of Evidence, deciding in each case what evidence to let pass through the courtroom doors and into the jury box. *Daubert* specifically stated that the trial judge has the responsibility to decide whether an expert's proposed testimony is both built on a reliable foundation and is "relevant to the task at hand."[4] The *Daubert* court cited some specific factors—testing, peer review, error rates, and "acceptability" in the relevant scientific community—for courts to use in testing the reliability of a particular scientific theory or technique.

The 1993 decision of the Supreme Court in *Daubert* was hailed by many advocates of tort and product liability reform as an important step in keeping "junk science" out of the courtroom and out of the consideration of juries in damage award cases. But the facts of the *Daubert* case dealt with scientific testimony, and there was considerable uncertainty in the legal community (and even in the courts) about the reach of the *Daubert* rule. Did it apply to all types of trial testimony, including that from nontechnical as well as technical and scientific experts?

The Supreme Court's *Kumho Tire* ruling eliminates the uncertainty and extends the *Daubert* ruling to all types of expert testimony "based on 'technical' and 'other specialized' knowledge." The decision was significant enough to be editorialized in many newspapers across the country. As the *Chicago Tribune* stated on April 12, 1999:

> [Prior to the *Kumho Tire* decision] , judges had no control over expert testimony from engineers and other technical—but nonscientific—witnesses. This often left judges exasperated and juries befuddled by all sorts of "expert" witnesses with dubious credentials and conclusions.

Implications for the Appraisal Community

Without a doubt, members of the real estate appraisal community, when testifying as expert witnesses, come within the sweep of the combined *Daubert* and *Kumho Tire* rulings. We certainly are technical experts, with our own specialized knowledge, as evidenced by the educational requirements imposed by both the Appraisal Institute and state appraisal licensing boards.

But the precise sweep of the two Supreme Court rulings for appraisers as expert witnesses is not yet clear, especially in light of the four *Daubert* factors to be considered by judges in exercising their gatekeeper duties.

3. *Daubert v. Merrell Dow Pharmaceuticals, Inc.*, 509 U.S. 579, 113 S. Ct. 2786, 125 L. Ed. 2d 469 (1993). For an earlier commentary on the *Daubert* decision, see Richard W. Hoyt and Robert J. Aalberts, "New Requirements for the Appraisal Expert Witness," *The Appraisal Journal* (October 1997): 342–349.

4. 509 U.S. at 597.

Chapter 11: *Junk Science, Environmental Stigma*

The four core judicial inquiries to be made are reiterated in the *Kumho Tire* decision as follows:

> Whether a theory or technique can be and has been tested;
> Whether the theory or technique has been subjected to peer review and publication;
> Whether a particular technique has a high known or potential rate of error and whether there are standards to control the operation of the technique;
> Whether the theory or technique enjoys "general acceptance" within a "relevant scientific community."

Any and/or all of these factors, as well as any other relevant factor, are to be considered by the trial judge to determine whether the testimony "has a reliable basis in the knowledge and experience of [the relevant] discipline." The *Kumho Tire* court states that the list of four factors is meant to be "helpful" to a trial court but is not "a definitive checklist or test." Because there are so many different kinds of technical experts and disciplines and so many different factual situations in which experts are asked to provide an opinion, one or more of the four factors may not be relevant in a particular case. As an example, the *Kumho Tire* court cites the lack of peer review for a particular theory or technique in a case in which the technical issue is being raised for the first time ever. The Supreme Court was also quick to acknowledge that other factors beyond the four mentioned may also be applied.

In the wake of *Daubert* and *Kumho Tire*, lawyers and courts involved in litigation, where a key issue is the impact of contamination or environmental risks on real estate values, will be testing the reliability of appraisal expert testimony against the tests of reasonableness laid down in those cases. What can we as appraisers tell these lawyers and judges about the *Daubert* and *Kumho Tire* tests of reliability as they apply to real estate appraising, especially appraisals of contaminated property?

1. We can state that the "relevant scientific community"[5] to which we can look for guidance in valuation techniques for contaminated properties is the community of professional real estate appraisers, and especially the Appraisal Institute, the largest such professional organization.

2. As members of the Appraisal Institute, we can state that the relevant theory and techniques for valuing contaminated properties are found within the courses, seminars and publications of the Appraisal Institute, including articles in *The Appraisal Journal* as well as *Valuation Insights and Perspectives*.

3. The courses, seminars, and publications of the Appraisal Institute do go through a process of peer review. Every course and seminar has a development committee that reviews course development proposals and peer-reviews proposed seminar and course content before it is offered to the membership. Through the efforts of the Publications Committee, the Publications Review Subcommittee, the Appraisal Journal Editorial Subcommittee, and the Appraisal Journal Review Panel, an extensive peer review process is undertaken for the organization's publications.

5. While appraisers often debate whether their discipline is an art or a science, in truth it contains a measure of both. And while we often think of "science" in terms of the natural sciences only, the true definition of a science is much broader. *Webster's Ninth New Collegiate Dictionary* includes the following among the various definitions of "science": "1: the state of knowing: knowledge as distinguished from ignorance or misunderstanding 2 a: a department of systematized knowledge as an object of study [the science of theology] b: something (as a sport or technique) that may be studied or learned like systematized knowledge [have it down to a science] c: one of the natural sciences 3 a: knowledge covering general truths or the operation of general laws esp. as obtained and tested through scientific method b: such knowledge concerned with the physical world and its phenomena: NATURAL SCIENCE 4: a system or method reconciling practical ends with scientific laws [culinary science] ...." Our understanding of appraisal as a science best fits with definitions 2a, 3a, and 4.

4. *The Uniform Standards of Professional Appraisal Practice* (USPAP), *The Appraisal of Real Estate*, 11th ed., the other publications of the Appraisal Institute (including articles in *The Appraisal Journal* and *Valuation Insights and Perspectives*), our courses, and our seminars create our "standards" of practice. USPAP contains our general "standards" to control the operation of appraisal "techniques." The Statements on Appraisal Standards, advisory opinions issued by the Appraisal Standards Board, as well as the Supplemental Standards of Professional Appraisal Practice and the Guide Notes to the Standards of Professional Appraisal Practice published by the Appraisal Institute, supplement the general "standards" of practice contained in USPAP, although not in as specific a form as most appraisers would like. When encountering difficult everyday appraisal problems, appraisers turn to the publications, courses, and seminars of the Appraisal Institute for specific instruction on solving appraisal problems and proper application of appraisal methodologies.

But if we are frank, we will also have to tell these lawyers and judges that they will not find answers to all their questions about the appropriateness and reliability of particular valuation techniques in the various professional standards, publications, courses, and seminars for the following reasons.:

1. The valuation of property affected by contamination or environmental risk is a relatively new part of the appraisal discipline that has emerged only in the past 15 years. Techniques and methodologies for determining the impact of environmental risks and stigma on market value are still developing;

2. Given the specialized nature of this appraisal practice area, many appraisers do not have the education, skill, or experience to properly evaluate the impact of contamination on property values and property markets. As a result, neither *The Appraisal of Real Estate*[6] nor the other publications of the profession give this area of practice the attention that the complexity of the valuation issues and methodologies truly demand;

3. The true "scientific community" of contaminated property appraisers may be the relatively small number of appraisers around the country who regularly get involved in this specialized practice area. But since the Appraisal Institute does not organize itself into practice areas for purposes of committee work or publications, that group has no common forum or voice for addressing and resolving issues related to the establishment of acceptable valuation methodologies and their validation and testing;

4. The true "validation and testing" of the techniques for the valuation of properties affected by contamination or environmental risks is not occurring at the Appraisal Institute level but in the courtroom and by reference to the real-world marketplace. In the courtroom, as skilled appraisers on both sides of a particular case review and check the respective data, methods, and analysis used by each side by reference to the marketplace, it is actually the judges, juries, and—most importantly—the marketplace of buyers and sellers of contaminated properties who are testing and validating appraisal techniques for us on a daily basis; and

5. The Appraisal Institute is not currently set up to give sharply focused opinions on specific appraisal practice issues, nor does it pub-

---

6. See *The Appraisal of Real Estate,* 11th ed. (Chicago, Illinois: Appraisal Institute, 1996). The text devotes several pages to a discussion of "environmental liabilities," stigma. This is handled not in the chapters of the book dealing with valuation techniques but in the chapter titled "Neighborhoods and Districts."

lish the results of "review and counseling" committee work in any format that would constitute "precedent" for purposes of appraisers learning from the mistakes of their fellow practitioners.

As a result, while the courts are looking to the appraisal community for guidance on how to resolve methodological disagreements encountered in litigation, the appraisal community is actually looking to judges and juries as well as the marketplace to give it guidance on which techniques pass the test of reasonableness in a marketplace setting.

Using Surveys to Determine Environmental Stigma: Lessons from the Litigation Trenches

Two recent court cases—one in a federal district court in the Southeast, the other in the California state court system—highlight the problems appraisers of contaminated property are beginning to encounter when faced with judicial scrutiny of the reliability of their valuation techniques à la *Daubert* and *Kumho Tire*.[7] Both cases involve alleged diminution in value of a property by contamination migrating from a neighboring property. In both cases, the appraisers first estimated the value of the affected properties uncontaminated and then separately estimated the value considering the impact of the contamination. The differences in the "before and after" values were part of the damages alleged from the contamination. In both cases, the appraisers undertook "surveys" of market participants as part of their process to determine the stigma impact caused by the contamination.

In the first case in the Southeast, the neighboring property and alleged source of the groundwater contamination was subject to a state-imposed remediation program that included a pump and treatment operation. The plaintiff's property was not environmentally pristine; the plaintiff too had contaminated his property and was also subject to a state-imposed remediation plan and program. The court (and the jury) had to distinguish the impact of the neighbor's contamination from the impact of the plaintiff's own contamination on market value in arriving at a conclusion concerning the appropriate damages to award.

The plaintiff's appraiser first estimated the market value of the property as if uncontaminated. The appraiser then concluded that the property was "worthless" when considering the contamination emanating from the neighboring site because lenders would not make loans on a contaminated property. The only basis of his conclusion was a telephone survey of lenders, "limited in scope, limited in depth, and limited in time."

Based on *Daubert* and a review of the plaintiff's expert's survey, the judge ruled that the testimony should have been stricken "because it had little or no probative value in establishing plaintiff's damages and fails to comply with the established rules regarding expert testimony." The judge appears to have two concerns: first, the relative probative value of a survey in establishing value and, second, the content and extent of the survey undertaken by the appraiser.

As to the first point, the probative value of the survey technique, the judge included the following statements in his opinion:

> The record is clear that [the appraiser] totally abandoned the methods of the appraising profession in reaching his second opinion, meaning the property is worthless.

7. Because both cases are still pending, the titles and exact locations of the cases have been withheld pending the outcome of the litigation.

This court is not concerned with what [the appraiser] said, but the lack of a basis for his saying it.

This court is confident that neither [the appraiser] nor any other MAI appraiser has ever given an appraisal to a client and charged a fee when it was based solely [emphasis added] on telephone conversations with bankers.

An expert who supplies nothing but a bottom line supplies nothing of value to the judicial process.

As to the extent and content of the survey, the judge had the following criticisms:

The appraiser kept no notes as to the information that he provided the lenders interviewed.

He did not tell the lenders the exact name and location of the property involved.

He did not tell them that the neighboring property owner that caused the contamination was under a state-imposed remediation program and had acknowledged its responsibility to clean up the property.

Although he told the survey participants that there were two kinds of contamination on the property, one which he characterized as more severe than the other, he made no other differentiation between the two kinds of contamination.

He did not tell them the estimated cleanup costs.

The conversations took less than five minutes, and some less than three minutes.

Most of the lenders contacted were not interested in making loans on any type of contaminated property.

Based on the unreliability and speculative nature of the estimate of value, the judge overturned the jury's damage award and ordered a new trial.

In the second case in the California court system, the judge ruled that the survey results were inadmissible even before the jury had a chance to hear the appraiser's testimony. The appraiser conducted three surveys, one of lenders, another of brokers, and a third of potential buyers of property. The court ruled that all three surveys were inadmissible because the description of the situation provided to each survey respondent was biased and slanted. The judge ticked off the problems with the survey as follows:

Further to indicate that the subject (neighboring) property is the source of groundwater contamination, referencing the Superfund site and the other groundwater contamination issues; and further to state that numerous lawsuits against the present owner by individuals who claim their health has been adversely affected by the subject property, which could be broadened to include the new owner or operator of the property, seem to me to so taint his survey as to make it of absolutely no use and not reliable...

The judge reviewed the survey cards used to solicit opinions and then had the following additional comments:

Well, my concern is that the basis of any valuation opinion, or any other opinion asked for, has to be with matters of a type that are reasonably relied on and that are reasonably trustworthy and have indicia of reliability that would form a reasonable foundation.

[T]his card, or any survey resulting from people who were told that this is the contamination area, that it was the source of groundwater contamination, and the reference to the lawsuits, which is totally speculative ... [is] a scare tactic.

The judge concluded, based on the evidence presented at the trial, that the environmental risks, as summarized on the survey cards read to respondents, had been grossly misstated, and he disallowed the appraiser's income approach and cost approach to value because they were fatally linked to the survey.

> The case here is the use of the survey information by the expert as a foundation for his opinion. Accepting that it may be permissible, the survey data that the court has been provided with so far is not reliable. There is no indication of how the population was chosen. There is no indication that the sampling is representative. We haven't even got to whether acceptable statistical analysis was used.
>
> The fatal flaw seems to me to be whether the questions were clear and (not) misleading, and whether the process was conducted to ensure objectivity. Because the language objectivity contained in card 1 does nothing to ensure objectivity or lack of bias, the design of the survey, I guess, is beyond being suspect. It is just not appropriate.

Implications of Recent Cases for Properly Conducting Stigma Impact Surveys

The two cases from California and the Southeast raise some interesting issues with respect to utilization of surveys as support for conclusions concerning stigma impact. Although the federal district court was fundamentally suspicious of the survey technique as part of a real estate appraisal assignment, neither court went so far as to say surveys were inappropriate techniques.

The first case stands for two points about surveys: first, do not make them the only basis for a stigma conclusion and, second, provide enough information to (and spend enough time with) each survey participant so that they can make an intelligent and reasoned response to the scenario they are being asked to analyze. The second case stands for an even more fundamental principle: Be objective in the presentation of the facts to the survey participants.

The second case vigorously commands appraisers to ensure that the information presented to the potential respondents is complete and unbiased in its description of the factual situation. Rather than emphasize the alleged health risks from the contamination—a "scare tactic" as one of the courts put it— focus on the key real estate market–related facts of the situation. If there is a party that has accepted responsibility for cleanup of the contamination and is part of an approved remediation plan, say so. If there is a "no further action letter" program from the appropriate regulatory agency, or other program to provide assurances to potential buyers or tenants that they will not be responsible for remediation costs, be sure to tell the survey respondents. If the contamination is in groundwater not used for drinking or other domestic purposes and is unlikely to come into contact with property owners, tenants, or employees, state that to the survey respondents. If only a part of the property is affected and the contamination has not interfered with past use or occupancy of the property, make that information a part of the survey form or questionnaire.

The seminal federal court case detailing the factors that determine the reliability of surveys is *Zippo Mfg. Co. v. Rogers Imports, Inc.*:

> The trustworthiness of surveys depends upon foundation evidence that (1) the "universe was properly defined, (2) a representative sample of that universe was selected, (3) the questions to be asked of interviewees were framed in a clear, precise and non-leading manner, (4) sound interview procedures were followed by competent interviewers who had no knowledge of the

litigation or the purpose for which the survey was conducted, (5) the data gathered was accurately reported, (6) the data was analyzed in accordance with accepted statistical principles, and (7) objectivity of the entire process was assured. Failure to satisfy one or more of these criteria may lead to exclusion of the survey."[8]

But even well-conducted, unbiased surveys may have limited utility in courtroom situations. While there is ample appraisal literature on determining environmental stigma by analyzing "comparables" or "case studies" and comparing and adjusting the comparable or case study to the facts and property at hand, there is little in the published appraisal literature on use of surveys to derive an estimate of stigma. For example, what have we really learned from an unbiased, properly conducted survey if 50% of the respondents say they would not get involved as a lender, broker, or buyer but the other 50% say they would? Does that mean there is no market for the property? Of course not. Does it mean that it might take longer to sell the property than the typical property? Not necessarily, because at least 50% of the potential market for any piece of property would not be interested in it for a variety of other reasons such as location, size, condition of improvements, etc. Surveys may have a limited role in some types of assignments involving contaminated property, but collection and analysis of sales and market data will remain the central technique for estimating the stigma impact, if any, that attaches to real property affected by contamination or other forms of environmental risk.

Predictions

Although most real estate appraisers never set foot in the courtroom as an expert witness, many of our fellow practitioners specialize in assignments arising out of litigation. We all need to continue to watch the evolving case law as it deals with determinations of the appropriateness of various techniques for estimating the impact of contamination on market value. In light of the dual decisions of the Supreme Court in the *Daubert* and *Kumho Tire* cases, appraisers, like other technical experts, will increasingly have their opinion testimony scrutinized by the courts to determine if the techniques employed enjoy general acceptance among the community of appraisers.

In fact, whether we like it or not, the Appraisal Institute may be drawn into the courtroom battles. The chairs of various Appraisal Institute committees, such as the Educational Publications Committee, or the organization's course and seminar developers may be called regularly as expert witnesses by parties to litigation, or even the courts themselves, to express their opinions on the propriety of certain appraisal practices and the acceptability of the technique in the relevant appraisal community. In fact, this is already happening in some types of cases.

Someday soon, as a result of the *Daubert* and *Kumho Tire* line of cases, the Appraisal Institute—faced with the seriousness of the stakes in litigation in which it, willingly or unwillingly, may become involved—may have to reevaluate how it determines and legitimates what is acceptable appraisal practice. It may be required to provide an institutional perspective and official position on an appraisal methodology as applied in a specific case. This may result in a whole new way of determining the appropriateness of specific appraiser practice and in a whole new type of Appraisal Institute committee or committee structure. Cases involving

8. *Zippo Mfg. Co. v. Rogers Imports, Inc.*, 216 F. Supp. 670 (S.D.N.Y. 1963).

the determination of the stigma, if any, that applies to properties affected by environmental risks could indeed become the leading edge of a whole new type of "standards of professional practice" for the next century, a set of standards based on precedent and committee decisions in specific cases specifying what is, and what is not, acceptable practice in specific factual situations.

Such a fundamental change in how we determine the acceptable from the unacceptable may be the only logical outcome of the *Daubert* and *Kumho Tire* cases and their progeny. That may indeed be the only logical result—whether we like it or not—for an organization determined to hold itself out as the leader in a discipline and a profession with a Code of Ethics and a set of "scientific" techniques that, when properly applied, should result in a consistent and narrow range of estimates of market value by its members.

Defending an Oil Company Against Litigation for Environmental Contamination (A Case Study)

by Jack P. Friedman, CRE

Jack P. Friedman, PhD, CRE, CPA, *is an author, appraiser, and consultant in Dallas, Texas. He is a member of the Real Estate Issues Editorial Board and current chair of the Dallas/Fort Worth Chapter of The Counselors of Real Estate. E-mail: jackfriedman@prodigy.net*

The article originally appeared in the Winter 1999/2000 issue of Real Estate Issues. Reproduced with the permission of Real Estate Issues; published and © by the Counselors of Real Estate (a not for profit organization), Chicago, IL. All rights reserved. Further reproduction/distribution is prohibited without the written permission of Real Estate Issues.

The author wishes to acknowledge: Sean Higgins, Esq.; Karl Locker, CPA; Joe Milkes, MAI; Jack Harris, PhD; Mark O'Briant, MAI; Suzanne S. Barnhill; and Dan McClellan for their valuable contributions to this case study, and especially to Darrell Grams, Esq., a trial attorney with Brown McCarroll & Oaks Hartline, LLP, Houston, Texas.

The purpose of this case study is to demonstrate real estate consulting issues involved in the defense of a major oil company (OIL) that was sued by the owner of an adjacent neighborhood shopping center (NSC) for environmental damages. The NSC amended its theories many times, with the result that a defense was necessarily multifaceted and complex, providing the material for a unique case study. In this new millennium, real estate matters, especially litigation, will surely increase in complexity. Further, notwithstanding the need for specialization, there are many situations where knowledge in multiple disciplines is useful in providing a study of the facts that were needed for a defense.

The Site

The event occurred in a large and fast-growing suburb of Dallas, Texas. A service station owned by OIL, located on the southeast corner of an important intersection, is surrounded by NSC (*Figure 1*). More than nine years ago, one component of an underground petroleum storage tank system experienced a leak or "release." The release was appropriately reported to the Texas Water Commission (now the Texas Natural Resources Conservation Commission or TNRCC), which added the site to its list of Leaking Petroleum Storage Tanks (LPSTs) and began the monitoring process. OIL drilled monitoring wells on its property and, with permission, on NSC's property. Periodic readings showed the extent of contamination over time.

The Players
NSC

The NSC was initially built in 1977. It was purchased in 1984 by a limited partnership (syndicate) that continues as the current (2000) owner.

The NSC comprises 42 stores, anchored by a supermarket representing the dominant supermarket chain in the area. The supermarket is a 43,000-square-foot store; the total center occupies about 140,000 leas-

FIGURE 1 Site Drawing

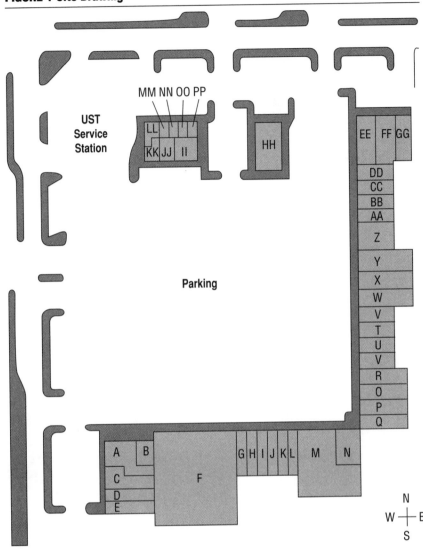

able square feet on almost 14 acres of land. In 1996 the center was refinanced at market rates and favorable terms. In that year, NSC sold a tract of land 164 feet ∞170 feet adjacent to the OIL station, to the south.

Oil

The service station, owned by a major oil company, is temporarily closed, awaiting renovation to become a convenience/fast food/self-service station. The dimensions of its site are approximately 170 feet by 170 feet = 28,900 square feet. It is on a corner.

TNRCC

The TNRCC evaluates the priority and the status of each LPST using codes. These are available on their Web site, www.tnrcc.state.tx.us.[1] Priority codes are as follows:[2]

Priority 1: Emergency level.
Priority 2: Threat to public places, threat to water supply.

1. The TNRCC has informative data and general publications available on its Web site.
2. *Priority levels 1.1 to 1.7:* These range from "explosive levels, or concentrations of vapors that could cause acute health effects" (1.1) to those that are much lower but could still have a health effect or safety concern (1.7). These levels require emergency action.
   Priority levels 2.1 to 2.7: These range from contaminated soils or water that are "exposed and unsecured from public access" and located within 500 feet of "dwellings, playgrounds, parks, day care centers, schools, or similar use facilities" (2.1) to "a public or domestic water supply well that produces from a groundwater zone which is not affected or threatened, located within the known extent of contamination" (2.7).
   Priority levels 3.1 to 3.5: Priority 3 sites range from sites where groundwater is affected within 0.25 and 0.5 miles of a public or domestic water supply well (3.1) to the possibility of affecting a non-community or non-domestic water supply (3.4) or a designated aquifer (3.5).
   Priority level 4.1: Groundwater is affected.
   Priority level 4.2: Groundwater is not affected.

Priority 3: Groundwater is affected, public water supply is a concern.

Priority 4: Groundwater may be affected.

The LPST status is cataloged by the TNRCC in six major areas. Within each area are several steps. The six major areas are as follows:

1. Incident report, issuance of initial directives, receipt of initial response.
2. Various report statuses of Phase II.
3. Various statuses of Phase III report, quarterly monitoring report, and remedial action plan (RAP).
4. Remedial action in progress, quarterly monitoring report overdue or received, review pending.
5. Submission of site closure application, various report statuses of final monitoring.
6. Case closed, referred to another agency or program, or inactive.

Regarding the subject site at the time of the trial, it was rated as "Priority Code 4.1, Groundwater impaired, no apparent threats or impacts to receptors. Status Code 6P, Final concurrence pending documentation of well plugging." In other words, this site had ceased to be a problem before the trial began.

The Action
Closure Letter
The TNRCC issued a "Closure Letter" on February 10, 1998. It stated, "No further corrective action will be necessary." The following criteria were stated in the closure letter:

- Currently the site is an active UST facility and predominately covered with concrete.
- A search indicated no water wells within one-half mile of the site.
- The contaminant plume appears to be confined on site and decreasing in contaminant concentrations.
- The extent of groundwater contamination has been delineated to Category III target levels.
- The shallow groundwater does not appear to have a local beneficial use. Domestic water for this area is provided by a municipal water supply.
- According to the survey, no significant sensitive receptors were affected or identified at the site. Vapor calculations do not indicate a potential problem.

The NSC's Response
The NSC, which had written to the TNRCC requesting that it not close the case, urged TNRCC to reopen the case. The NSC's position was based on finding petroleum products on its site when installing a grease trap for a restaurant (a new tenant, at LL in Figure 1) in 1998, and earlier, in 1996, when digging into the ground to begin construction of a new building on the pad side sold earlier that year just south of the OIL station. The NSC challenged the TNRCC's findings concerning the plume. On Octo-

ber 28, 1999, the TNRCC answered the NSC in a letter providing its reasons for not reopening the case, justified principally by these criteria:

1. Current soil and groundwater concentrations do not exceed theoretical vapor calculations at a known point of exposure.

2. There is no history of phase-separated hydrocarbons at the [OIL] facility.

3. Although the dissolved-phase contaminant plume extends offsite, it appears to be stable. Contaminant concentrations have fluctuated in [OIL] MW-1, however, fluctuations in contaminant concentrations over time are not necessarily abnormal. Plume stability is considered by evaluation of contaminant concentrations both inside and outside the source area. Since no significant increase outside the source area has been seen, it does not appear that the plume itself has increased in extent or should be considered unstable.

4. Soils and groundwater contaminant concentrations do not exceed Construction Worker Protective Levels or Health-Based Target Levels for a Commercial/Industrial site.

5. The site is an active commercial facility which maintains an impervious cover. Future use of the site is expected to remain the same.

6. The impacted shallow groundwater zone does not appear to have any documented local use. No water wells screened within the impacted interval were identified within 0.5 mile radius of the site.

The NSC hired environmental experts to check levels of contaminants. Those findings, their use in the trial, and the rebuttal testimony of OIL's expert are beyond the scope of this case study, which focuses on the business aspects. In short, however, OIL's experts explained and displayed to the court readings from monitoring wells that were taken and reported regularly to the TNRCC.

NSC's Changing Theories

In May 1998, an environmental company hired by NSC's attorneys provided two cost estimates. One, for further testing of soils, was approximately $60,000; the other, for approximately $670,000 was the estimated cost of excavating and removing soil associated with a pad site (approximately 12,000 square feet) adjacent to the OIL station (Figure 1, stores II through PP).

The $670,000 remediation cost for the pad site was then provided to an appraisal firm, which appraised the shopping center at approximately $12 million if clean, in an unsigned report. The appraisers extrapolated the $670,000 amount as though it applied to the entire shopping center and provided an estimated cost to remediate all the land (changing out all the soil) of $27 million plus the cost of rebuilding at $18.5 million (rounded). Thus, in an unsigned appraisal report, the damages were estimated at $45.5 million.

This damage amount was later pared down to $3.1 million by the same appraisal firm, which then considered demolition and rebuilding of the 12,000-square-foot pad building only. Their cost estimate began with $670,000 for soil removal and replacement, inflated to $3.1 million through costs of demolition, rebuilding, releasing space, paying tenants for moving and buyouts, and for lost profits. This time the amount was not extrapolated to the entire center, and the report was signed.

The NSC also engaged, as an expert, a university professor who had co-authored several articles on the effect of contamination on property value.

As time passed, NSC's attorneys dropped both the appraiser and the academic as witnesses, without explanation. Just prior to the trial, the NSC's lawyer stated that the leak had not caused a loss in property value, which may explain why the appraiser was dropped. We don't know why the NSC's complaint was amended and no longer reflected a loss in value.

When the appraiser and academic were dropped, the plaintiff's case for damages shifted to additional past, present, and future management costs associated with monitoring the contamination, plus the cost of active remediation. In response, the defense refocused on these matters.

Although the TNRCC had issued a closure statement, NSC's law firm located an expert who discussed the need to actively bio-remediate the site. This would involve placing rods under the affected pad building. The process is to suck surface air through the ground, using powerful machinery, drawing soil vapors out to be filtered through charcoal drums. The remediation also suggested indoor monitoring of vapors using canisters placed within tenants' buildings. All of this was prepared for execution by the expert's own company over a 30- to 48-month period.

The Defense
Because the NSC modified its charges, OIL's defense became multifaceted and complex. The author prepared a number of documents as part of the defense strategy.

Review of Articles by the Academic
The author drafted a critique of the articles prepared by the academic. Of the commercial properties studied, of particular importance was the lack of relevance to the NSC. One factor was the difference in geographical, neighborhood, and economic characteristics between the area in which these properties were located and the location of the NSC. In addition, the academic's findings for commercial property were not statistically valid, despite an assertion of same in the introduction and summary of the publication. The academic had no expertise in appraisal. Because the academic was dropped as a witness before trial, the draft critique was not finalized.

Review of Other Literature
The author made an extensive review of the literature on the subject of LPSTs with regard to property valuation. Internet searches, beginning with RealSource, provided a start. We sought help through two appraisal forums. A hard-copy bibliography[3] was used to help identify the literature. Footnotes and bibliographies in articles often led to additional literature. The *Journal of Real Estate Literature* was useful in identifying existing publications. *Real Estate Issues Research Digest*, Spring 1999, offered valuable information on existing research, and the Fall/Winter 1991 issue of *Real Estate Issues* (vol. 16, no. 2), a special issue on environmental conditions in real estate, was a rich source of literature.

Draft Appraisal Review
Another preliminary work product was an unsigned draft review of the appraisal under Standard 3 of USPAP. Of special interest to this reviewer was the disparity between the operating expenses stated in the appraisal

3. Compliments of Bill Mundy, CRE.

and those reported in the federal income tax returns. Of greater importance, however, was the appraiser's assumption that the pad building would require demolition. Environmental reports by NSC's experts did not assert the need for demolition. They only provided cost estimates for removing and replacing the soil. Accordingly, the draft appraisal review was critical of the appraiser for leaping from a remediation cost estimate to extensive value diminution. This is not sanctioned by USPAP's Advisory Opinion AO-9 nor by Guide Notes 6 and 8 of the Appraisal Institute. The draft appraisal review was not finalized because the appraiser was withdrawn from the list of testifying experts.

Income and Expense Analysis

We compared the income and expenses of the NSC from its annual income tax returns for the years 1991 through 1998. Charts and graphs were prepared and used at trial to demonstrate NSC's consistently rising rent throughout the period to establish the fact that there was no economic injury to NSC from the LPST.

Charts prepared from the tax returns included exhibits showing gross rental income, all deductible expenses, deductible cash expenses, and cash flow. Rapidly rising rents meant a transformation of the investment from tax shelter status to a cash flow generator.

Current Rent Roll Analysis

Analysis of the NSC's rent rolls showed that the NSC was 94 percent occupied at the time of trial, with only two units vacant out of 42 tenant spaces. The vacancies were not near the OIL station.

Tenant File Review

In an extensive review of tenant files, NSC's leases were abstracted to show that tenants were renewing their leases at higher rents. When a vacancy occurred, the space was re-let at an increased rent.

LPST Site Analysis

A physical review of the subject's city and its neighboring city was prepared that demonstrated that the NSC's situation was not uncommon. There were more than 80 LPSTs on TNRCC's list for each city (except for the subject, none were owned by OIL). We plotted the location of each LPST on a map in preparation for demonstrating to the court how prevalent LPSTs are. A list of shopping centers in both cities was obtained from CACI. Not surprisingly, a number of other shopping centers are neighbors of LPSTs.

To answer a potential question about the effect of LPSTs on real estate activity, we identified several of the LPSTs that were in high-traffic areas. We photographed the surrounding area. Then, using dates on building permit data and ad valorem tax data, we demonstrated the existence of new development, adjacent to LPSTs, that had occurred after the initial leak release. We also identified redevelopment (demolition and rebuilding) and numerous renovations for existing and new tenants. Not surprisingly, there were occurrences of these LPSTs at shopping centers that were "clones" of NSC (same anchor tenant, same age range, same size range).

Lender Survey

To answer the question of whether environmental contamination had an adverse effect on the ability to finance a center, we conducted a survey.

This was not intended to have scientific, statistical validity; it was an effort to understand local lending practices. Of particular interest was that more than half the lenders surveyed (six out of 11) actually make loans on environmentally impaired property. When faced with an environmental impairment, nearly all lenders increase due diligence efforts by requiring at least a Phase I report. If a "no further action" letter or "closure letter" is received from the state agency, all 11 respondents said they would be inclined to approve a loan.

The NSC had been refinanced in 1996 at favorable rates and terms. However, the Phase I report prepared for the refinancing had incorrectly stated that the NSC was not on the TNRCC's list of LPSTs. At trial, NSC's attorney wanted to make an issue that, had the lender been informed, the loan would not have been made or would have been made on less favorable terms. The fact was that the property was successfully refinanced. After receipt of the closure letter, the point would be moot.

Management Survey

In 1999, NSC prepared a log of management discussions held from 1991 through 1998, with the time spent by each employee and the hourly rate for each. A six-digit amount was derived as additional management costs.

To answer the question of whether an additional management fee is charged for managing a contaminated property, we conducted another survey, this one of property managers in the Dallas/Fort Worth area. Interesting findings from this survey were that an additional management fee is justified for property needing remediation, with fees based on three percent to five percent of the money spent for remediation. When remediation is not required, no additional management fee is due. In addition, NSC's general partner/manager charged its limited partners a routine management fee of six percent of the gross rent. This gross rent includes tenant reimbursement in rent. Our study, plus other sources, indicated that four percent of gross rent is the competitive rate for this type of property, indicating that NSC's management charges are more than sufficient.

Ad Valorem Tax Study

The *Texas Property Tax Code* provides relief from ad valorem taxes for environmental impairment (Section 23.14) or in cases of decreased value (Section 22.03). Through tax data, we found that NSC's owners had not challenged their assessment for the current year, and there was nothing to indicate that they had ever appealed the assessment for an environmental reason.

Appraisal

At one point, an appraisal of the NSC was ordered by OIL. Its purpose would be to provide the jury with a second report to refer to in their deliberations. When NSC's attorneys withdrew their appraisers, however, the proposed appraisal no longer had any real significance, so the order was canceled.

Business Judgment

If active remediation were to take place, would stigma result? NSC's bioremediation expert had prescribed a plan for soil treatment as one that would not make too much noise. Still, it would involve running heavy equipment and placing drums or canisters inside and outside the pad building to monitor soil vapors for at least 30 months. Certainly this would not bring business to NSC and could create a stigma (negative public perception). In addition, the TNRCC did not recommend active bioremediation and might not approve it because of the soil type. From a business standpoint, then, these activities could create stigma through their negative visual appearance.

Summary of Consulting Challenges

As to real estate consulting challenges, the activities and skills required include:

- Intense understanding of the literature
- Objective review of appraisal reports
- Survey instrument preparation and survey techniques
- Ability to read and interpret federal income tax returns
- Ability to secure publicly available data for ad valorem taxes and building permits
- Graphic presentation of financial data
- Tenant file review, lease abstracting
- Consideration of management issues

Conclusion

In summary, it took many skills and a great deal of effort and coordination to present the facts accurately for the jury's consideration. Data provided to the jury from an extensive and intensive multifaceted study proved to be effective, and the jury found for OIL._{REI}

The Federal Rules of Evidence and *Daubert*: Evaluating Real Property Valuation Witnesses

by John D. Dorchester, Jr., MAI, CRE

John D. Dorchester, Jr., MAI, CRE, is a former national president of the American Institute of Real Estate Appraisers. His real estate appraisal and consulting business focuses on litigation and litigation support. He has testified in numerous litigation matters including the Exxon Valdez oil spill state cases, the Irvine Company disputes, the Cayuga Indian land claims, and a variety of environmental cases. He provides research and counsel to a number of governmental and private sector clients. Contact: The Dorchester Group, 30598 N. 75th Street, Scottsdale, AZ, 85262. (480) 585-0284, fax(480)585-4871, e-mail: ddorchester@dorchestergroup.com.

This article originally appeared in the July 2000 issue of The Appraisal Journal.

1. The new FRE became effective July 1, 1975 following a 10-year development period. Chief Justice Warren in 1965 appointed an advisory committee to study and draft a comprehensive statement of the rules. After years of debate and controversy, Congress in January 1975 amended proposals transmitted from the Supreme Court, clearing the way for the FRE to become effective in mid-year.
2. *Frye v. United States*, 293 F. 1013, 1014 (D.C. Cir. 1923).
3. *Daubert v. Merrell Dow Pharmaceuticals, Inc.*, 509 U.S. 579 (1993).
4. *Kumho Tire Co. v. Carmichael*, 119 S. Ct. 1167 (1999).
5. *State of Washington v. Copeland*, 922 P.2d 1304 (Wash. 1996).
6. *United States v. Frances Gherini, et al.* United States District Court for Southern California, 1999.
7. Some of these issues are raised in Attacking and Defending the Appraisal Report in Litigation, a seminar of the Appraisal Institute. Also, see Richard J. Roddewig's comments in "Environment and the Appraiser," *Appraisal Journal* (October 1999).

Since the establishment of *Federal Rules of Evidence* (FRE) by Congress in 1975,[1] many questions have arisen regarding what properly qualifies a person as an "expert witness." The earlier Frye case[2] established fundamental tests, but after FRE postdated and superseded the Frye decision, the U.S. Supreme Court added clarifying tests in the *Daubert* decision,[3] subsequently expanded by the court's *Kumho Tire* decision.[4] Since *Daubert*, there have been more than a thousand decisions rendered, but there are still questions of "bright line" (define) distinctions in the qualification of potential witnesses as experts.

The Supreme Court of Washington in a 1996 opinion held that the Frye standard for admission of novel scientific evidence remains the standard of the state, rejecting adoption of *Daubert*. The justices noted that trial judges under *Daubert*, "must analyze opinions involving matters far beyond their knowledge." They also noted that *Daubert* tests have sometimes been considered problematic when considering behavioral and social science-related expert testimony.[5] Prior to the *Kumho Tire* decision, a United States District Court in Los Angeles was one of several that held that the testimony of a real property valuation witness did not fall under the scope of *Daubert* because it did not involve scientific evidence.[6]

Where does content and methodology of the real property valuation witness fall and who should be accepted as an expert witness in real property valuation matters? These issues are the topic of this paper. Examples of common abuses in litigation matters are presented and discussed where quasi-valuation and pseudoscientific methods and concepts are sometimes applied by real property valuation witnesses. Tests are suggested that may lead to bright line determinations of what will qualify expert testimony in real property valuation matters and perhaps provide concepts that may be applied to other fields where technical and specialized knowledge are involved.[7]

Background: The Federal Rules of Evidence

Matters at issue in federal litigation must be approached by expert witnesses in an objective, unbiased fashion, otherwise they may be irrelevant and fail to meet the requirements of FRE Rules 401 and 402. Rule 403 further provides for "exclusion for risk of unfair prejudice, confusion of issues, misleading the jury, or waste of time." Where scientific, technical, or specialized expert witness testimony is involved, the testimony should be applied in keeping with Rule FRE 702, the *Daubert* ruling, and other rules of evidence that may apply. These rules are intended to ensure that juries hear and ultimately consider only admissible material and relevant evidence when deciding issues in a lawsuit. Objectivity requires application of the scientific method where possible.[8] The notion of expertise must relate the services of an expert to relevant evidence that is produced with given norms or standards for the expert work performed and for related testimony.

Rule 702 states, "If scientific, technical, or other specialized knowledge will assist the trier of fact to understand the evidence or to determine a fact in issue, a witness qualified as an expert by knowledge, skill, experience, training or education may testify thereto in the form of an opinion or otherwise." Emphasis should be placed on the words "...will assist the trier of fact..." Those who have written on the topic have stressed that the rule was not established to open the floodgates of potential testimony, but to increase receptivity to expert witness testimony. Rule 702 does not negate Rule 401.

Daubert established that four factors must be considered to determine whether evidence or testimony is scientific knowledge and ultimately reliable. They include whether the technique or method has been tested (thus revealing its fallibility or validity), whether the known error rate of the technique is acceptable, whether the technique or method has been subjected to peer review, and whether the scientific community generally accepts the technique. The U.S. Court of Appeals subsequently explained that these factors were "illustrative rather than exhaustive," and each was not necessarily relevant in every circumstance. Thus, the court may make somewhat liberal interpretations in individual lawsuits. Subsequent opinions apparently now number into the thousands, but the principles have apparently not changed. Focus should be brought upon these principles in judging the work and potential testimony of particular experts.

Real property appraisals, including mass appraisals,[9] require special and technical knowledge and experience, and involve applications of systematic problem solving processes, standards relating to how the process is to be applied, and tests to see whether the process is objective and reasonable. Valuation has a body of knowledge that has been tested, and accepted, by the courts, and the valuation field is subject to well-defined Standards.[10] Scientific tests exist for certain tools applied in real property valuation, and potential error rates can be estimated or quantified.[11] Peer review is commonly accomplished through Ethics and Standards administrative actions under state certification and/or licensing or by actions of professional organizations against their members.[12] The result of these reviews is reflected in courses, seminars, and Standards. Thus, there is a foundation against which the opinions and proposed testimony of real property expert witnesses can be judged, just as is true with other fields in which the federal rules of evidence are applied.

---

8. The scientific method is a process that involves observation, development of a theory, establishment of a hypothesis, and testing. Unfortunately, it does not always distinguish between a fact, a theory, and a hypothesis. The valuation process applies principles of the scientific method as a model, based upon economic principles (particularly substitution) as the hypothesis. The model is widely applied by appraisers and by the marketplace. It is noteworthy that the founders of appraisal practice in the United States referred to the science of appraising in the same sense that they referred to the science of economics.

9. Mass appraisals are valuations that consider many rather than a single property as their subject and are commonly performed in valuation of properties for ad valorem property tax purposes, and have special standards requirements when used in any application. The techniques can be applied in situations requiring analysis of multiple properties.

10. These particularly include the Uniform Standards of Professional Appraisal Practice, discussed later in this paper. Also important is the *Uniform Appraisal Standards for Federal Land Acquisitions* (UASFLA), widely used in the federal jurisdiction.

11. Where statistical processes are applied, multiple regression analysis, time series analyses, and many other procedures provide for analyses of potential errors associated with the process and, for a given data set, are repeatable. The systematic valuation process applied by real property valuers is intended to reduce the range of error and in common market usage, valuations are expected to be competent within a range of tolerance.

12. There are many publications, but not all are peer review quality or have such intent. For example, *Appraisal Journal* articles are reviewed by an Editorial Board prior to publication, but acceptance by the Journal does not signify that there is broad acceptance of the subject matter of the article or approval by the Appraisal Institute. Rather, publication here, as with many other periodicals, provides for new and innovative thought, whether widely accepted at the time of publication or not. Despite the seeming logic of *Daubert's* peer review test, a great deal of published information does not meet the test of stating industry standards or even acceptable practices.

Notwithstanding these qualifications, *Kumho Tire* clearly establishes that scientific knowledge is not a singular hurdle for the expert witness. As with other expert fields, real property valuation has established principles, an advanced educational program of learning and achievement, required evidences of mastery of necessary skills and technical knowledge, and stringent standards for competency, objectivity, and clarity of presentation. Further, education, training, skills demonstration, and experience are not enough—the real property expert must also demonstrate and be prepared to defend the accuracy and reliability of valuation estimates in *every* valuation.

In layman's terms, in order for potential witnesses to qualify as expert witnesses, it is not enough for them to demonstrate that they are expert in some field; they must demonstrate expertise, relevantly and reliably applied, in the particular matter that is the subject of their testimony.[13] The field of expertise must be one for which there are standards by which to judge the relevancy and reliability of the expert's findings. These fields may be broadly categorized as scientific, technical, or specialized knowledge endeavors. Tests established by the U.S. Supreme Court, and permitted under common law, are to be applied to assure compliance with these minimum standards.

Foundational Valuation Discipline Matters

Prior to the Great Depression, real property valuations in the United States were akin to the gunslingers of the Old West: there were few standards, but there were good guys, guys that wore the black hats, and those who served as gun for hire. With the advent of the Great Depression, the National Association of Real Estate Boards allowed the formation of the American Institute of Real Estate Appraisers (Institute) in 1932, and within a year the first *Code of Ethics* was developed for that organization. The central purpose of the Institute was to respond to the period's economic collapse by establishing statements of ethics and standards for valuations so real estate markets and those who depended upon market values could again have confidence in real property valuations.[14] The result was envisioned as a means of reclaiming lost market confidence, establishing more stable future markets, and assuring more reliable real property valuation results.

In the years that followed, little development of appraisal standards occurred until after World War II. A great deal was written about appraisal methodology, but the *Code of Ethics* was considered sufficient for the time. With the passage and funding of programs that called for massive eminent domain actions following the war (urban renewal and the federal highways programs), elements of the Institute's *Code of Ethics* that pertained to Standards were incorporated into valuation manuals and associated procedures for the administration of these programs. Legislators, federal and state agency personnel, litigators, and others took Institute courses to prepare them for administrative and litigation work. Through interaction between government agencies, valuation practitioners, the legal profession, and professional appraisal societies, community standards emerged.

In 1968 the Institute began a major overhaul of its *Code of Ethics*, attempting to expand the area of Standards. The result produced stronger

13. USPAP Standards Rule 1-1(a) states, for example, "In developing a real property appraisal an appraiser must be aware of, understand, and correctly employ those recognized methods and techniques that are necessary to produce a credible appraisal."

14. There are many definitions of market value, but virtually all are built upon the same premise. As used herein, wherever market value is referenced, I will apply the following market value definition: "The amount in cash, or on terms reasonably equivalent to cash, for which in all probability the property would be sold by a knowledgeable owner willing but not obligated to sell to a knowledgeable purchaser who desired but is not obligated to buy. In ascertaining that figure, consideration should be given to all matters that might be brought forward and reasonably be given substantial weight in bargaining by persons of ordinary prudence, but no consideration whatever should be given to matters not affecting market value." Interagency Land Acquisition Conference, Uniform Appraisal Standards for Federal Land Acquisitions (1992) (quoting *United States v. 50 Acres of Land*, 469 U.S. 24, 29 [1984]).

Chapter 11: *Federal Rules of Evidence*

Ethics statements, but less definite statements of Standards. Nonetheless, through the courses and seminars of the Institute, the Society of Real Estate Appraisers, and others, and through the peer review processes of those organizations that had strong Standards/Ethics enforcement practices, stronger de facto valuation Standards began to emerge. For instance, there was a frequent market requirement that Institute MAI-designated appraisers be the only ones who would be acceptable for valuing properties for many banks, insurance companies, developers, mortgage issuers, agencies, and others. The requirement was perceived by users of appraisal services as a better assurance of accurate and capable work. Additionally, there was an ongoing peer review process to reduce the chances of future errors or losses.

During much of this time, although professional societies continued to improve the quality of valuations produced by their members, and advanced the levels of skill and knowledge necessary for professional valuers, the market continued to experience mixed results. Banks, savings and loans, and individual investors often relied upon individuals with even limited real estate experience. They were frequently called upon to testify in litigation matters. A combination of limited rules to qualify experts and the certain states that qualified any owner of real property as an expert witness caused who-do-you-trust contests for juries and courts alike. Unfortunately, many concluded from these experiences that valuations were just an estimate or only someone's opinion, failing to recognize the existing Standards for valuations, which were frequently violated, and the levels of expertise that existed in the valuation discipline.

In the early 1980s, the Institute again undertook a major overhaul in articulating and enforcing its ethics and standards. As the Institute's national president, I appointed the first Appraisal Standards Board in the United States in 1981, and within two years most major valuation organizations had established their own boards or equivalents. By 1985 there was extensive dialog among these organizations. Statements of Standards, which already closely followed the Institute's content and format, began to coalesce. When Congress began investigations of the causes of the nation's financial institutions' collapse in the late-1980s, the professional societies' Standards and Ethics statements became the foundation for appraisal Standards under Title 11 of FIRREA.[15] Subsequently a national Appraisal Standards Board was established and it functions today under the Appraisal Foundation. Its Standards are a refinement of the community standards[16] that had evolved decades earlier.

Because of the importance of real estate to our economy and to individual wealth, every American citizen has a significant financial stake in the health of real estate markets and the avoidance of real estate abuses. This is particularly true within our legal system. This crucial role demanded that a means be developed to distinguish between good appraisals and bad appraisals. Like the gunslinger era, we can still find the gun for hire in real property valuation matters, as is true in other disciplines. Many gunslingers are capable presenters, but good presentations by themselves do not produce credible, reliable, and otherwise qualified expert witnesses by simply applying truth by assertion. A good valuation, then, must first meet established Standards requirements and then be capable of effective presentation by a qualified expert.

15. The Financial Institutions Reform Recovery and Enforcement Act of 1987.

16. Community standards were cited in many early court cases involving real estate valuations. Particularly in the state courts, in the absence of formal industry standards, what was generally recognized in the applicable market area or community was a principal standards test.

To meet these and other public requirements, the Appraisal Standards Board of the Appraisal Foundation implemented the Uniform Standards of Professional Appraisal Practice (USPAP) in April 1987. Standard 1 established standards for performance of real property appraisals and Standard 2 pertains to how they are reported. Standard 3 was established to provide basic rules for real property appraisal reviews. Standards 4 and 5 respectively cover the performance and reporting of consulting (non-valuation) real estate work, and Standard 6 pertains to mass appraisals.[17] These are bound together by a *Code of Ethics* and are periodically supplemented through Statements on Appraisal Standards and by Advisory Opinions. Although USPAP was established initially for certain federal financial transactions, related state licensing and certification programs for appraisers migrated USPAP to all jurisdictional levels, thereby resulting in common "community standards" at national, state, and local levels.[18] Enforcement of Standards is applied through Boards of Appraisal in each state, the District of Columbia, and five territories. Professional appraisal societies also play a key role, with expulsion from membership a possible outcome for violation of ethical conduct or the standards.

Testing the Boundaries of Expertise

During the 1950s and 1960s, there was developing case law relating to appraisals for eminent domain. In general, case law followed the concepts of existing appraisal Standards that were recognized within the real estate valuation profession, but departures occurred in areas where the courts found little precedent or had insufficient information to do otherwise. Reliability of valuation estimates suffered where experts could simply go through the paces of what was typically found in appraisals, but were not held to the tests of available Standards. Many court disputes over valuation revolved around issues of highest and best use, less frequently centering upon underlying appraisal methods, techniques, and theories. Although today's statements of appraisal Standards and the accompanying body of knowledge regarding appraisals have developed significantly over the past three decades, each is now being challenged with new theories, particularly in the field of toxic tort litigation.

Early in the twentieth century, real property valuation was called "the science of appraising." This reflected the roots of valuation theory in classical economics, associated concepts, and methodologies. Significant theoretical and technical writing on appraisal topics appeared in the century's first three decades. With abuses that occurred prior to the 1930s, the horseback appraiser, the repeat sales of the Brooklyn Bridge, and fraudulent valuations to support financial transactions, the Institute's first focus was on ethics because many practitioners believed there was general agreement about methodologies. Most of the principles recognized early in the century still survive, and are at the heart of real property valuation. Sometimes confusing is the argument over whether real property valuation is an art or a science. The field of real property valuation is not alone in this issue. Most types of economic analysis share in the art versus science debate.

The art versus science argument will probably be resolved at the same time we determine whether there is sound associated with the tree falling in a forest with no one around. It is, of course, important to establish a potential expert witness's qualifications, experience, and training for the

---

17. Other USPAP Standards pertain to non-real property valuations. They include the development and reporting of personal property valuations (Standards 7 and 8), and business valuations (Standards 9 and 10).

18. It is important to note that USPAP Standards provide under their Departure Rule that certain sections of the Standards are classified as specific rather than binding requirements. Rather than a relaxation of the Standards, this provision facilitates the application of Standards in a wide array of situations. Stringent requirements are placed upon an appraiser who invokes the Departure Rule, including the burden of proof that the opinions or conclusions produced will be credible given the purpose of the assignment and the use of his or her opinions.

Chapter 11: *Federal Rules of Evidence*

area of proposed testimony. But it is at least equally important to determine what an expert must do when scientific activities are performed and what must be accomplished when such activities are combined with other activities that might be called art. For example, a brain surgeon deals with science in diagnosis, evaluation, and medical decisions. However, interpretations involve an art form (applications of intuition, experience, and judgment) and art is certainly involved for at least portions of surgical procedures. These principles apply to any endeavor that applies scientific procedures. Thus, multiple tests are necessary, not a single characterization such as art or science. In real estate, for example, did the real property valuation expert properly conduct scientific portions of the research and analysis work?[19] If not, the work may fail on this test alone. If properly completed, did the remaining analysis and reasoning *within* applicable Standards produce results that are relevant, appropriate, credible, and reliable given the nature of the litigation? These questions are consistent with the battery of qualifying tests that extend through *Daubert.*

In general, there is sufficient agreement among professionals in the real estate field regarding valuation methods, techniques, and concepts for reliable real property valuations to be performed on a fair and equitable basis, whether for plaintiffs or defendants. Figure 1, for example, charts the real property valuation process. This process is fundamental to individual property valuations and implicit in USPAP. Surgeons' manuals do not say, "Take a knife, open up the patient, take out the bad part, and sew up the patient," but the valuation field has attempted to state its professional process in layman's terms. The result, intended to aid public understanding, belies the extent of skill and knowledge required to accomplish each part of the process.

During the eminent domain era that followed World War II, condemnors and condemnees sometimes sought valuers who would value low or high, depending upon which party they represented. Valuers who engaged in such practices knowingly have been considered unethical since the 1930s, but relatively little weight or focus was given to Standards that existed for judging their expertise in each litigation matter. Today there is common agreement that Standards and related statements of ethics do not permit either liberal or conservative valuations, only reliable ones made in accordance with *generally accepted valuation practices* and related Standards.

Following the establishment of USPAP, there has been a growing movement among some appraisers to redefine the entire process of real property valuation. In terms of *Daubert,* this group would either redefine how USPAP Standards would be met or maintain that they do not apply to their field of expertise. The group is comprised of valuers, economists, statisticians, or others and has undertaken at least three principal points of attack:

1. **Market Value.** Statutory and case law clearly combine to make market value the standard for situations requiring fair, equal, and just measures of value. Market value is the only value type that is capable of performing the role of yardstick in such situations, whether eminent domain, contract or property dispute, or toxic tort matter.[20] Recent cases indicate that some experts appear not so much intent on changing the concept of market value, or its definition, as they are on ignoring it or applying new concepts of the word "market."[21]

19. For example, if an appraiser purports to apply survey research in order to infer some statistical result, were the scientific standards of sampling frame, questionnaire design, survey research conduct, tabulations, and other elements met? If data are eliminated from an appraiser's analysis, what support is offered for their deletion from the analysis model? If a so-called "control group" is selected for comparison, what evidence is offered to establish the market validity of that area's comparability? In short, what scientific principles, if any, can be applied to these processes, and were they applied properly?

20. Other value definitions result in inability to test the validity of valuation estimates in a fair and just context of the open market. For example, assessed value may be based on market value, or it may not. *Investment value* is particular to a given investor and value-in-use applies only to a given user making a particular application of a property. *Intrinsic value* has little meaning unless there is an outside stimulus (such as the market) to quantify the notion of worth. *Going concern value* measures the worth of a business, not its component parts. More than 100 value types have been identified.

21. This is not to say, however, that there is not a continuous, insidious attack on the nature, definition, and/or applicability of market value. See for example the author's paper, "Market Value Is Not an Ideology: The Attack on Market Value Continues Through Public Interest Value and its Family," available through the Appraisal Institute.

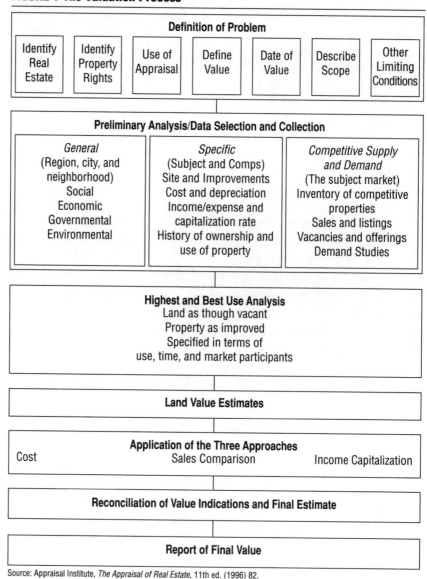

FIGURE 1 The Valuation Process

Source: Appraisal Institute, *The Appraisal of Real Estate*, 11th ed. (1996) 82.

2. **Market Concepts.** For retailers, the market is where their sales come from. The same is true for real estate, whether dealing with purchasers or prospective tenants. Developers, for example, perform market research among larger population groups to discover, quantify, and analyze from that population who might constitute a market for their product (called a "submarket"). The new breed of experts tend to ignore this market concept as too restrictive, instead assuming market data from Miami, Florida (or elsewhere) can be directly applied to any other city or town in the United States. They tend to substitute personal (or client) standards or theories that frequently are crafted to cleverly obscure the fact that they do not deal with relevant market information or processes. Further, these experts commonly rely upon area-wide analyses of groups of properties, where statistical results can be crafted or manipulated, rather than to develop analyses based upon individual properties where validation of the accuracy and reliability of value estimates is possible. These by-

pass a crucial step in the valuation process—validation of the fact that the sales used for comparison also meet the tests of market value.

3. **Market Analysis Methods.** When analyzing the market value of an individual property, the Principle of Substitution applies an important economic concept. Simply stated, it recognizes that buyers can buy land and build a new structure, buy an equally satisfactory substitute property, or put their money into some other form of equivalent investment. The cost approach, sales comparison approach, and income approach are well-recognized applications of this Principle, and are quintessential *Daubert* tests for real property valuations. Each approach relies upon direct market comparison methods, and results in value indications for an individual property. In mass appraising, a universe of properties, or larger groups of sales transactions are used, again to derive individual property value estimates. The new breed of experts commonly uses none of these methods, even though they sometimes claim they do. Instead, they substitute methods that cannot accurately and reliably produce value estimates for individual properties. Hence, they cannot reliably produce market value estimates for larger groups of properties.[22]

Today the courts face a dilemma when confronted by real estate experts. Clearly these potential witnesses should not be the next gunslinger to come through the saloon doors, but how can one know who is entering? What are the requirements for real estate expertise, particularly for real property valuation experts, and how should the tests of current rules of evidence be met?[23] As was usually true for those sitting in the saloon, it is not difficult for the qualified professional to distinguish between the expert and the gun for hire. But, applications of the rules of evidence pertaining to scientific witnesses are still developing and are unclear as they apply to real estate experts. Further, until the courts focus on market value, recognize USPAP, and generally accepted valuation methods in matters pertaining to real property valuation, it will be difficult to even determine generically who a real property valuation expert is, let alone what it is that they should do.

The solution to any puzzle must start somewhere. For real property valuation matters, the beginning is to establish that the appropriate answer for real estate litigation matters involving economic impairment (damage), compensation (eminent domain), or most real estate disputes is a function of the concept of market value. This notion is clearly supported by applicable laws and related real estate litigation precedents. Next, an expert is not determined by credentials or claims alone, but whether the individual in the particular matter can, and does, knowledgeably and competently comply with applicable Standards and apply accepted methods that will result in accurate and reliable market value estimates. By definition, this result is tested at the property level. These tests are logical and empirically supportable in the context of FRE.

An Illustration: Witness Assertions in Toxic Tort Matters

To prepare for evaluations and suggestions that follow, it should be helpful to review sample issues that face the courts where purported real property valuation experts are involved. To establish the situations and related issues that may provide clues regarding identification of expert witnesses

---

22. As an example, an appraiser may apply his or her judgment in the selection of a database of 100 sales from a universe of sales that is vastly larger. From the non-statistical sample, a series of averages are calculated and from these averages statistical inferences are drawn. This form of analysis, which is only one of several that could be cited, carries implied accuracy because of the precision of the calculations, but its failure to properly apply statistical standards, as well as the standards of comparability incorporated into the valuation process, create results that are fatally flawed.

23. For example, FRE 402 requires that evidence which is not relevant is not admissible. FRE 401 defines relevant evidence as "evidence having the tendency to make the existence of any fact that is of consequence to the action more probable or less probable than it would be without the evidence." Finally, FRE 702 provides that "[i]f scientific, technical, or other specialized knowledge will assist the trier of fact to understand the evidence *** a witness qualified as an expert by knowledge, skill, experience, training, or education, may testimony thereto in the form of an opinion or otherwise." The courts have broad discretion to determine relevance and reliability of expert testimony, but these decisions must relate to the particular facts and circumstances of the case.

Valuing Contaminated Properties

and positions they commonly adopt, I will draw from my experiences in the toxic tort litigation field. Because of ongoing litigation matters I will generalize, recognizing that the process of generalization leaves some issues too broad or overstated, but intending to establish foundations that can readily be understood.[24]

My experiences indicate that there is a general theme in how many toxic tort cases are viewed by some experts. Positions commonly stated in their work, which will be commented upon later in this paper, include:

1. Local and national evidence clearly establish that contamination results in a loss of property value. In general, this effect is automatic where contamination is involved and commonly applies in circumstances where no actual physical property damage is present. Further, geographic areas far remote from the property in question can be used for the selection of comparables or for case studies that can be applied as though they were comparables. There is no need to identify or examine cause and effect relationships—contamination and damages go hand in hand.

2. Property value losses may be direct (actual physical damage) or indirect (stigma and other area-wide losses). Damages may be manifested in many ways, but market value effects are not necessarily an important means of quantification.

3. Appraisals of individual properties are too expensive and impractical because of the scale of the damages in larger cases; it is better to look at losses on an area-wide basis, then allocate damage to individual properties.

4. Because individual property appraisals are not involved, no appraisals are necessary; thus, other non-property specific economic and statistical methods may be applied to establish and quantify the amount of property value loss without USPAP considerations. Non-appraisal methods are actually preferred because untainted data required for appraisals may not be available.

5. The Uniform Standards for Professional Appraisal Practice (USPAP) may or may not be applicable to toxic tort damage estimates depending upon what work is provided and the background of the expert. Non-valuation experts need not follow USPAP or generally accepted valuation methods. The Standards are applicable to individual appraisals and to certain aspects of consulting engagements. However, other elements of the analysis and conclusions are outside the scope of USPAP. Specifically excluded from USPAP are estimates of property value loss that are made on an area-wide basis, as contrasted with appraisals of individual properties.

6. Available transaction data for properties in a class area are frequently invalid for comparison purposes in determining property value losses. Sales of properties in contaminated areas (e.g., plume contour or Superfund area) are impacted by the contamination and thus cannot contribute to measures of value loss. Further, such sales may show continuous growth, but cannot show the true growth that would have occurred absent the contaminating conditions.

7. Property values are set and changed by the actions of knowledgeable market participants. These include brokers, lenders, apprais-

24. Portions of the following discussions are taken from a paper presented by the author to the Federal Circuit Bar Association in Washington, D.C. May 20, 1999.

ers, city officials, county officials, experts in the contamination field, and others. Most of the owners, previous buyers, and sellers of properties in a class action lawsuit are not knowledgeable or reasonably informed market participants. Further, many of the buyers and sellers of property class real estate may also suffer from some form of duress. Clearly one would not choose property in a contaminated area over property in a clean area unless one is not knowledgeable or is forced in some way to do so. These perceptions, whether contamination is present or not, create damages that are attributable to trespass, nuisance, and/or stigma even if direct property damage does not occur.

8. For knowledgeable market participants, risk and uncertainty are crucial elements of the market decision. Where there is concern over future uncertainties, even if there were no actual contamination, there is a loss in property value attributable to market perceptions of risk and uncertainty. Thus, market interviews and survey research (opinion polls) are frequently more important than actual sales transactions data in a litigation matter. If interviews indicate that loans are available at all, the loans are made unknowing of the contamination effect.

9. Property damage can be subtle. Special research techniques are required to determine contamination damages. For example, the contaminating condition may have an initial effect of simply reducing market demand; prices begin to lower, owners leave the area, renter occupancies increase, maintenance declines, rental rates drop, crime increases, and long-range patterns are set without a precipitous change in market indicators anywhere in this cycle. The result is economic property damage. It is unnecessary to look for other cause and effect relationships.

10. Data from nearby areas outside a property class are suspect and may be totally unusable for comparisons; the damage from the defendants' actions is broad-reaching and pervasive. Additionally, it is well known that contamination may be present in non-class areas of a contaminated community, and thus prices or other data may already reflect the effects of other contamination.

11. The most effective analysis tools available for analyzing and quantifying damages in toxic tort situations include:

    a. **General economic analysis**—this analysis shows that as the contamination in the property class areas has become known to the public (it is sometimes never really recognized or understood by the residents), the properties in the class areas have fared worse than other elements of the community. General economic differences can be used as units of comparison for direct analysis or sales adjustments.

    b. **Market interviews**—this analysis involves holding interviews with people who evidence knowledge that contamination affects property values, talk to individuals in other market areas, find those who believe that contamination almost certainly causes economic harm, perform surveys that qualify people who have negative reactions to the circumstances or areas involved in the litigation, and perform statistical analyses of their responses. Even limited evidence is sufficient to support a damage assertion. It is not necessary to rely upon market value estimates to do so.

c. **Analogous cases**—these studies entail looking at other market areas, usually in other cities, to ascertain what will happen in a particular situation. To do this, one looks at the literature concerning contamination's effect on property values and reviews a series of case studies from other areas. These will establish the fact that property values losses are frequently much more than what would be estimated from less sophisticated valuation methods. Further, lessons learned from other communities establish direct comparisons for properties in a given litigation area that are similar to comparables of the sales comparison approach.

d. **Multiple regression analysis**—to apply these analyses, one must recognize that regression studies permit more detailed analysis of broader areas. Using regression we can study entire sections of the greater community, or even the community as a whole, to develop a basis for damage estimates. These techniques are widely accepted and avoid the need to make individual property studies, which would be virtually invalid anyway, as discussed above. Regression models must have high explanatory capabilities, but need not produce accurate results if the focus is only on one or more variables used in the process.

e. **Conjoint analysis**—this statistical method emphasizes that it and various other statistical tests apply the tests of *Daubert* and other legal requirements by providing scientific or technical expertise in an unbiased fashion. Although these techniques are not normal and customary valuation techniques, they are normal and customary analysis techniques used in other scientific inquiry and measurement, hence, they meet the necessary legal tests.

f. **Comparative analysis of data and trends**—these studies analyze publicly available sales transactions data (and MLS data where available). Studying these data, one can study averages and the movements of averages over time to establish the relatively lower and slower growth, or absolute declines, in property values in the property class areas. Differences signify damage. (It is possible for such properties to increase in value over time and still be damaged—this arises when their growth is at a slower growth rate than the rate experienced by uncontaminated properties.) A 2% difference translates into over 10% property damage in just five years. Taken over a 50-year economic life, this damage translates into a 170% difference between contaminated and uncontaminated property.

g. **Public opinion polls**—surveys can establish that the market for properties in the property class areas comes from the entire city in which the contamination area is located. Scientific survey research (public opinion polls), among market participants from broad areas or even other communities, can establish differentials between property class areas and other areas of the community. From these differences, one can quantify the extent of loss due to contamination from the defendants. (Although some might refer to this process as contingent valuation, the process will be applied in such a way that we can call it something else, while still not attempting to appraise individual properties.)

    h. **Control groups**—these comparison groups can be applied where other sales comparisons are not available or to supplement those that are. One can establish control groups of properties away from a litigation property or area to use for comparison purposes. It matters not that the control area has only superficial similarities and can be demonstrated to represent different markets. What is important is that the area be far enough removed to avoid possible alleged effects of the litigation situation.

    i. **Matched pairs sales analysis**—because valuation methodology provides for paired sales analysis, a substitute method can be applied. This involves application of a pseudo-comparison approach in which properties with relatively similar physical characteristics, but located in different markets, are used as "comparables." Any differences in price are entirely related to and measure economic harm (damages). The difference of markets and market areas is insignificant because, "all properties that are physically similar should sell for about the same price."

12. Because appraisal methods are unnecessary (and probably inappropriate), there is less (or no) need to focus on a particular date of value. The analysis can be a study of a time period, within which the damage can be observed and quantified. Property damage will be dealt with on an average basis within a property class area and the time frame is less important because the damage is an average over a period which includes a particular date.

13. I hold a PhD and/or professional designation in the real property valuation field:

    a. If I am a PhD or other non-valuer expert, I am not subject to USPAP standards because I am not an appraiser.

    b. If I am an appraiser, USPAP standards may apply, but I can relax or redefine key standards and valuation processes because they are difficult or impossible to apply to large groups of properties at once.

14. These methods and considerations are reasonable and customary for our professional field, and will be supported by other outside experts.

To evaluate the expertise required for reliable valuation or related results and to evaluate positions such as those just summarized, we must first turn our focus to an objective framework in which appropriate analysis can be performed and identify related issues of expertise.

An Objective Framework for Valuers' Analysis of Possible Compensable Toxic Tort Loss

When litigation relating to real property is involved, market value is the appropriate basis for estimating compensable loss; thus, if plaintiffs assert property damage, such damage must be capable of estimation and validation in terms of market value to be valid. (This does not ignore that some litigation may involve fire losses, and thus deal with insurable value, or that a given lawsuit might require identification and application of another type of value than market value because of special circumstances.)

For analysis purposes, it is possible to establish a test hypothesis that "actions of defendants created some degree of property loss that is compensable," and then to develop a work program that focuses on discovery and quantification of any such losses that can be found. This approach forces objective, standards-complying research to ferret out reasonable conclusions by which to judge the test hypothesis. It should reasonably begin a process that meets the evidentiary requirements cited above, but does not ensure compliance. The research and analysis methods selected, and how they are applied, are also crucial.

Valid real estate research must recognize that real estate markets are diverse, somewhat inefficient, and complex. The decision to purchase or sell a given property differs substantially from the aggregate of all buying and selling decisions—i.e., people do not buy and sell because the market acts in a particular way. Instead, they buy and sell for individual motivations and are rarely controlled by the actions of the market at large. Markets values reflect the individual decisions of those who comprise the market for the property or properties in question.

Various indirect analysis methods such as general econometric models may be useful in broader studies to support the possibility of a compensable loss. However, the plaintiffs must be able to provide credible evidence that there is a demonstrable cause and effect relationship between defendant's activities (over time if appropriate) and an economic harm to plaintiffs' properties measurable in market value terms.

The concept of market value is crucial to the court, to the parties in litigation, and to the public at large. Without a recognizable, reliable standard by which to judge monetary damages, any expert's testimony may foster a fraud upon the court, the parties, and the public.[25] Market value has long standing in courts. Its problems largely have been due to failures to apply or uphold the standards of the time, situations for which comparison data are scarce, or attempts to apply market value reasoning in circumstances for which the market value definition does not address all issues at trial. Nonetheless, the market value concept has persevered and is the applicable standard in toxic tort matters.

When market value is involved, USPAP and other professional Standards establish the guidelines that are recognized and applied in the marketplace and are the foundations for Rule 702 and *Daubert* determinations. These Standards have been developed to dissuade untrained individuals and unscrupulous practitioners from misuses of the market value concept, to reduce misunderstandings, and to foster confidence and dependability in matters relating to real estate activities in the United States.[26] The Standards are built upon the principle that market value estimates can be reasonably produced by scientific research and the application of recognized objective technical processes. This does not negate the contribution of judgment, but judgment should be recognized as a process that is used in conjunction with proper research, not as a substitute.

If analysis of research results indicate that some compensable loss has occurred from defendants' actions, it is necessary to quantify that loss so that plaintiffs will receive no less than, nor more than, the compensation

25. For example, where would our standard of measures be with an elastic yardstick, clocks that failed to apply the same time standard, speedometers and odometers that could be set back, or school test scores that could be based on good looks, athletic ability, or judgment?

26. U.S. Standards are similar to those in most other countries. The International Valuation Standards Committee has developed Standards for over 50 nations. It has been determined that, while international Standards are more general, U.S. Standards do not differ in principle.

they are due. Similarly, where no compensable loss is found, it is appropriate for all parties and for the public at large that the absence of compensable damage be properly supported and that no compensation be paid. The process of quantification requires that there be a common standard, or yardstick, not a sliding and indefinite scale.

There is an important distinction between broad economic analyses and those that directly relate to market value. Market value studies must be capable of validation by analysis methods that apply to the field of real estate valuation or appraising. It is common and appropriate for market value studies to include broader economic and area-wide analyses; however, they must be tied to conventional Standards regarding their performance and relevance. The broad studies do not substitute for more direct market value analysis methods.

The valuation process is explained by the Appraisal Institute, the Institute's successor (a merger with the Society of Real Estate Appraisers), in its text and various courses and seminars. The process is observed in various forms worldwide and is built upon the scientific method. Its basic elements are foundations for USPAP Standards 1 and 2. It is incumbent upon an appraiser, identified by USPAP as one who estimates/defines values of identified property interests, to apply the methods that are a part of this process. Where departure is necessary and appropriate, a full disclosure of the facts and circumstances and bases for the departure, are required by Standards.

Real property experts may be divided into a number of professional categories. The application of these categories to the work and proposed testimony of a real estate expert aids in determining what Standards should be applied and how it should be reported:

1. **Appraisal or valuation experts**—those who deal with market value or other defined types of value (if applicable) and the quantification of specific compensable amounts and those who perform other valuation services such as mass appraising or other valuation services. These services must comply with USPAP and other applicable Standards.[27]

2. **Real estate consultant experts**—those who deal with the act or process of providing information, analysis of real estate data, and recommendations or conclusions on diversified problems in real estate, other than estimating value. Their services must comply with USPAP and other applicable Standards. In particular, it is incumbent on the real estate consultant to assure that there is no confusion between valuation and non-valuation services. When valuation services are involved in total or in part, the consultant must also comply with USPAP valuation Standards.[28]

3. **Other experts**—those who do not necessarily meet the USPAP Standards because their services do not fall under either of the first two categories; for example, a cost estimator, a civil engineer, a statistician, an economist, or other person engaged in a specific support role not involving appraising or consulting. Standards for such services may not be set forth in the fashion of USPAP Standards, thus requiring other evidence to comply with evidence rules cited above. Their services may be used by appraisal exerts, in which case under

27. USPAP Standards include Standards 1 and 2 for appraisers, Standard 3 for those who review and critique valuations, and Standard 6 for those who perform mass appraisals. Standards 7 through 10 apply to other types of valuation. Other applicable standards include those imposed as Supplemental Standards by responsible professional societies, applicable standards pertaining to specific statistical or other processes applied, and the like.

28. The reader is reminded that USPAP Standards 1 and 2 relate specifically to valuations, whereas Standards 4 and 5 relate to non-valuation consulting. As provided by the Standards, when engaging in a consultation matter, under the Standards an individual is required to comply with Standards 1 and 2 if the matter also involves valuation as defined by the Standards.

USPAP the appraiser must meet certain requirements in order to place reliance upon the other experts opinions. Clearly, if the other experts' work is incorporated as an estimate of value, the other expert is performing appraisal services and USPAP tests must be applied. Damages or property value loss are estimates of market value and are subject to USPAP.

4. **Dual services experts**—those who may perform two or more of the above categories in any given litigation matter.

When research concerning the test hypothesis posed above indicates that there is insufficient evidence to support an estimate of compensable loss, it is unnecessary to perform property valuations. Individual valuations in large cases would be prohibitively expensive and time consuming and may provide no addition to knowledge. In such cases, the real estate expert may perform market studies and pricing analyses, but the result will be reported as a consulting report under USPAP unless individual property market values are estimated. Conversely, where compensable losses are estimated, appraisal or valuation services must be performed, and generally accepted valuation methods and Standards must be applied.[29]

Damage to property creates a potential property interest. For example, some real estate is sold in fee excepting rights to actual or potential litigation claims against others. However, USPAP cautions against summation approaches in which elements constituting the bundle of rights (or physical components) are valued separately, then summed for an indication of the defined value of the whole. The sum of the parts may not equal the market value of the whole.[30] Similarly, cautions must be exercised in estimating the value of a component without an understanding of the defined value of the whole. Thus, attempts to estimate damages without regard to valuation of the entirety places the estimator in peril of a Standards violation.

Even if the expert asserts that mass appraisal techniques are being applied, validation of the results is necessary. This requires focus on representative evidence regarding relevant market evidence or analysis of market values for individual properties. Mass appraisals result in the valuation of individual properties considered within the mass of properties included in the appraisal. However, depending upon the application, the values derived may not be market values. Further, the process of mass appraising is not one of simply considering many properties at once. Mass appraising is a widely applied valuation discipline with its own standards.[31]

Plaintiff experts customarily have more extensive access to plaintiffs and their properties than defendants' experts, thus allowing plaintiff experts more detailed property and data analysis. For defendant experts to meet the requirements of USPAP or other conventional Standards, it is important that defendant counsel take steps to assist their experts in obtaining necessary information that is otherwise unavailable to the experts. For example, controlled property inspections should be scheduled in sufficient quantities for properties that are essential to analysis. The experts should be afforded access to all relevant discovery materials and should participate in establishing questions for interrogatories and depositions. Rather than signaling that the expert has adopted an advocacy position, these steps can be handled in such a way to preserve the expert's objective, unbiased position.

---

29. It is particularly important to stress the importance of the Departure Rule and the concepts of specific and binding requirements within the Standards. Note also that the appraiser is required by USPAP to "state and explain any permitted departures from specific requirements of STANDARD 1, and the reason for excluding any of the usual valuation approaches." This will include a statement of the rule from which the departure is invoked.

30. There are many examples of this principle. For example, one could not validly estimate the market value of land for commercial purposes and then add an estimated cost of a new residence that failed to develop that highest and best use. (This also violates other economic principles.) Similarly, one could not add the face (market) value of an onerous (non-market) mortgage and a presumed equity value as though the mortgage was at market. The same is true of attempts to add together value estimates of diverse lease interests, each of which is encumbered by special, non-market considerations.

31. Note for example USPAP Standard 6. Also, various standards of the International Association of Assessing Officers cover mass appraisal valuation procedures.

Chapter 11: *Federal Rules of Evidence*

Evaluation of Witness Assertions in Toxic Tort Matters

With the preceding discussion as a foundation, we can summarize points that should be considered in evaluating the competency, relevancy, and appropriateness of real property valuation witnesses and their testimony. The tests apply whether the appraiser has been engaged by the plaintiff or the defendant. To apply our previous example, the following discussion considers the list of 14 pseudo-expert positions itemized above that are sometimes taken in whole, or in part, by some experts in contradiction of Standards or appropriate tests of FRE:

1. Contamination and related toxic tort matters may or may not create a compensable damage. This issue of damages is not one of generalization, regardless of who expresses the opinion. Economic impairment is a function of a particular market's reaction to a situation or event and, as is true with virtually any market situation, the result is dependent upon each particular market. For a witness to carry personal biases that affect the outcome of what purports to be an unbiased opinion is inappropriate and should be guarded against in objective research. For valuation witnesses, biased work violates ethical requirements of the Standards. The use of transactions from geographic areas far remote from the appraisal at hand and case studies from other market areas are no more relevant to the valuation of groups of properties than they are to an individual parcel.

2. Market value is the appropriate yardstick for the quantification of economic impairment to real property that results from causation attributable to a defendant. The market value concept eliminates the need for speculation because market value is the present worth of anticipated future benefits. By deriving accurate and competent market value estimates, whatever the market may think or believe of the future is incorporated into their market transactions. Hence, speculative adjustments are duplicative and incorrect. Many so-called stigma estimates are actually speculations about how future markets may act.

3. Economic impairment is measured at the property level. Where groups of properties are involved, mass appraisal techniques are available and can be performed within the requirements of applicable Standards either for analytical or valuation purposes. Frequently, the class certification process results in larger and more difficult aggregations of diverse submarket areas, often difficult, if not impossible, to value without developing a series of models for the markets they combine. Class certification not based on this consideration does not waive the underlying evidentiary requirements for estimating economic harm. Thus, for larger and more complex class areas, class areas should be organized into smaller, more manageable areas, or it should be recognized that the time for and cost of performing studies required to derive market value estimates will be higher because multiple markets and diverse properties are involved.

4. Non-valuation methods can be effective in analyzing larger areas including multitudes of properties and can supply evidence as to indications that economic harm may or may not have occurred

within defined areas. They cannot, however, derive market value estimates by which to apply the bright line test of economic impairment. When and if non-valuation models can perform valuation tasks, they will be incorporated into valuation methodologies and will have statements of applicable Standards. Despite the apparent persuasiveness of certain statistical procedures, including many applications of hedonic modeling of the acid test, does the method produce a reliable estimate of market value at the property level that can be validated in keeping with Standards.

5. USPAP provides the courts with an extraordinary tool by which expert witnesses and their testimony can be judged. USPAP articulates community standards for real property valuation without regard as to who performs the valuation. Their Standards are applicable to all toxic tort situations in which the issue of economic harm to real property is at issue. Witnesses who attempt to redefine litigation issues for convenience, or for client accommodation, do not meet the public needs of the courts and do not comply with appropriate community Standards.

6. It is true that some market data, as is true with controlled scientific experiments, may be tainted. However, in the world of real estate this does not necessarily mean that the data in such markets should be ignored. If, for example, homes in a given area subject to a contamination event sell for 10% less after the event, why would that fact not be the most important market evidence available after all other things being equal? I have observed a tendency for some experts to reject mostly all market data within a contamination area and to substitute speculative information from other areas that may have little, if any, comparability. This leads to substitution of hypotheses and speculations for factual data.[32]

7. Expert position number 7, like many of their assertions, begins with a statement with which many will agree and progresses to unfounded conclusions. It is not unusual for them to seek the exclusion of factual data by assuming that the market would not act as they did if they knew what the expert knows or thinks. If this premise can be established, the expert is free to engage in hypothesis and speculation, abandoning the real world in which quantifications can be derived. Often the data that the expert attempts to exclude is the best evidence of that expert's error. For example, one expert says a market is not knowledgeable because "it does not have adequate knowledge about a groundwater plume." The expert ignores hundreds of media releases about the contamination, evidence regarding disclosures by sellers and brokers, mailers received by area residents, town hall meetings, and the like. Instead he narrowly defines market knowledge as a function of the arguable location of one or more underground plumes, the actual locations of which are argued by scientists, and assumes that this is the only relevant knowledge even in the face of contrary evidence.

8. Risk and uncertainty are market factors and the market's reaction is reflected in the prices market participants pay for real estate. Using risk and uncertainty as though they were considerations that override and are separate from the market's actions, some experts create hypothetical

32. The reader is again reminded of USPAP Standards Rule 1-1(a) which requires correct employment of "recognized methods and techniques that are necessary to produce a credible appraisal."

prices and price differentials based upon their own assessments of risk and/or uncertainty. Some also attempt to validate their opinions with public surveys. At best, the surveys I have seen in some expert reports are conjectural and speculative. They have not been taken from areas that can validly represent the market(s) involved in particular litigation. Market interviews are important in market studies and the results help to better understand available sales information. However, they do not serve as a substitution for factual data and do not establish market value. Interviews can aid in discovery of market facts and in verifications, such as lending practices and terms.

9. Explanations using logical progressions of subtle damage measures are frequently crafted to use persuasion and speculation that will appeal to a particular audience, but may not have relevance to the real estate markets in question. Logic is important in research and analysis processes, but logic does not substitute for the facts being examined. Further, market preferences of particular submarkets may literally defy logic or the preferences of those who may participate in other submarkets. Objective research requires that the researcher perform studies regardless of personal biases or attitudes and in a way that, if bias is present, it can be overcome. If these tests cannot be met, the expert cannot function as an independent, unbiased expert. (Again, see USPAP SR 1-1[a].)

10. There is no rule that says any data must be absolutely eliminated from some form of consideration. This is a matter of the facts and circumstances at hand. To the contrary, it is important to understand surrounding properties to best understand those in a particular area, such as a litigation class area. The attempt to exclude an analysis of nearby properties is frequently motivated by the expert's desire to seek evidence in a given area, even though that area is not a comparable market area. This practice should raise questions as to the expert's objectivity and the relevance of any area selected for which significant reason for its use cannot be established.

11. Although individual commentary on each of the methods suggested by certain experts is possible, full discussion of each is beyond the scope of this paper. It should be noted that only one of the methods is a generally recognized valuation or mass appraisal method. Multiple regression analysis is an important tool of mass appraisals when properly applied, but common usage by experts does not meet the validation tests of mass appraising. Without proper market validations, the experts cannot produce market value estimates using these methods. Under proper circumstances, many of the methods could be used for market studies, but they do not lend themselves to market value estimation as commonly applied. Further, by inserting many of these methods into the expert's work, confusion can be introduced into the court by focusing on whether the particular method was performed in a proper way rather than whether it was even relevant. In some instances, an expert's seeming mastery of some of the methods is used to implicitly establish bona fides, at least persuasively. They should not be allowed unless they are accurately performed and proved relevant, and unless they will "…assist the trier of fact"[33] in issues before the court.

33. *Fed. R. Evid.* 702.

Valuing Contaminated Properties

12. Markets change over time as a response to many influences. Thus, it is crucial that a date of value is established for when the claims of economic impairment are alleged to begin. Similarly, if the economic effect was likely to have existed over some period of time, that period must also be identified. Cause and effect situations, require that the effect of all other influences be eliminated before the effect of a particular cause can be quantified. For example, general real estate price declines were experienced in the United States in the late 1980s. It would be incorrect to say that all declines in price in a given area are attributable to alleged contamination causes if prices declined in general at the same time because of general economic conditions. Further, averages can be manipulated and their findings can be misleading. Averages do not compensate for failures to resolve cause and effect questions, determination of economic changes that affect specific time periods, or a failure to deal with available facts. Market value is not an average, regardless of whether a valuer considers few or many data examples. In statistics, averages are not determinative of a particular outcome; they are simply tendencies.

13. The curriculum vitae of an expert witness is important and should be judged on content rather than length and form. For real estate experts, it is of less relevance what a particular expert calls himself or herself than whether that individual performs the tasks in a manner that is appropriate and supportable, given the nature of the expert's testimony. Thus, an economist who makes no effort to value particular parcels of real estate should not be qualified as a valuer in that instance and the individual's work should not be interpreted as a valuation. Distinction should be drawn between whether the individual is an expert in some instances and whether he or she is an expert in the particular matters for which the opinions are offered before the court. The highly qualified brain surgeon may be a lousy witness as an auto mechanic and may not even qualify for medical matters pertaining to the eyes, ears, nose, and throat.[34]

14. In helping the court to understand the nature of the expert's services and the purposes for which the testimony is offered, it is essential that the expert be explicit in these matters. "Our professional field," unless clearly identified, is indefinite, unhelpful, and may be misleading. There is no reason why the expert's report cannot be responsive to at least the expert's understandings of the types of *Daubert* and other related tests that will be applied to the expert's work. It is frequently necessary for experts to rely upon the opinions of other experts. When this occurs, the reliance should be disclosed. There should also be a disclosure of the steps taken by the expert making such reliance to validate and to understand the work of the other expert, if any, to assure that the reliance was appropriate, relevant, and proper.[35]

Although these points are brief, risking oversimplification, and there are many circumstances in which defendants' experts may also err, several conclusions can be drawn from the above examples.

---

34. For the new breed experts' position 13b, I mentioned that some experts attempt to avoid USPAP Standards by simply defining them away. USPAP ethics provisions attempt to preclude such practices by prohibiting valuers from producing or distributing false or misleading reports. Accordingly, if the purpose for which a valuation is intended is market value, the size of the work at hand does not provide a basis to avoid the requirements for estimating market value. Thus, a position adopted by the valuer in opposition to this requirement would violate USPAP Standards unless it could be properly qualified under the Standards as a departure.

35. Guide Note 3 of the Appraisal Institute's Supplemental Standards provides professional guidance for reliance on "Reports Prepared by Others." The principles this Guide Note establishes are appropriate to any expert's reliance upon other expert opinions.

1. The FRE address an important need, that of aiding the courts, which are seldom expert in matters that purported experts are offered for testimony, to establish a decision-making process relative to the relevancy and reliability of expert witness testimony.

2. It must be recognized that focus sometimes may be directed away from appropriate FRE tests when experts can demonstrate that they have expertise, but not necessarily for the specific matter for which they are to testify.

3. Because an expert has expertise in a given field should not qualify that expert for testimony without meeting tests appropriate to the particular application of his or her expertise.

4. If an analytical tool evidences a recognized scientific method, this recognition is not an endorsement for use in every analysis situation and does not guarantee that the tool is properly applied.

5. Standards exist in many fields and standards appropriate to the particular litigation should be identified and considered in the witness qualification processes. Where litigation involves real property valuation issues, USPAP has developed a prominent statement of community standards.

6. Market value is a crucial yardstick for real property valuation litigation matters, as it is for many other types of litigation dealing with valuation.

Conclusions

The preceding discussions suggest a number of FRE- and *Daubert*-type tests that can be used to evaluate whether the real estate valuation expert, the expert's work, and the proposed expert's testimony meet necessary litigation requirements. These include:

1. Has the expert reasonably stated the problem being addressed in the context of the particular litigation?

2. Is there a clear and unequivocal identification of the property or properties involved?

3. Is there a full and reliable disclosure of all pertinent facts and circumstances that relate to the valuation or valuation-related issues?

4. Have standards appropriate for the work been identified and have they been reasonably applied?

5. Are terms used by the expert properly identified and defined, including citations by which their meaning and use can be judged by non-experts?

6. Was an appropriate definition of market value cited and has the expert consistently applied generally accepted valuation methods to estimate market value, in keeping with USPAP Standards? If the litigation involves non-market value issues, is an appropriate definition of value included, explained, and justified in accordance with Standards?

7. Is a date of valuation cited, is the date appropriate, and has the expert consistently applied data and analyses that will validly result in a value estimate as of that date? If more than one date, or a series of dates is involved, have the same tests been met?

8. Are the expert's work, report, and related testimony clearly directed to the issues for which the testimony is offered, or do they contain boilerplate, unsupported opinions, and speculation?

9. Can the expert demonstrate proper application of generally accepted valuation methods, including those applicable to scientific procedures applied in the work?

10. Was the scope of work set forth by the expert appropriate for the intended litigation purpose and were all facts discovered during the research period properly disclosed and analyzed?

11. Do the work, report, and testimony evidence an objective attitude of the expert, or does the result reflect bias or accommodation for the client's interest? Although this is ultimately a decision for the trier of fact, the question should be raised by the appraiser throughout his or her work and by the appraiser's client.

12. Does the expert adequately develop and conduct a research program so that reasonable support is developed for conclusions, or do conclusions reflect speculation and conjecture? Are appropriate disclosures made?

13. Are the work and testimony presented in such a way that it would not tend to mislead?

14. Has the expert shown recognition that the work is designed for litigation purposes and that it must be presented in such a fashion that it expresses the expert's best attempt to help the court and to meet reasonable FRE and *Daubert* tests?

15. Do scientific procedures that have associated confidence interval and other tests of accuracy and significance, include these measures and the expert's assessment of the accuracy and reliability of the findings?

16. Are the results reasonable and supported, and are they relevant to the specific determinations for which the expert's testimony is offered?

17. Can the ultimate reliability of the valuer's results be demonstrated and supported by credible market evidence?

Although these tests are stated in the context of valuation witnesses, their essence can be applied to many expert fields. In brief, the expert must perform work in compliance with identifiable Standards, evidence objectivity, clarity of thought and presentation, and demonstrate competency, relevancy, and reliability. Anyone can state an opinion. The expert does so by meeting these tests.

The real property valuation is, to some extent, unique in the since that Standards have been developed for the performance of its experts. Those Standards do not eliminate new and novel concepts and theories, but they do require exposure and testing of those ideas among peers before judges and juries are required to opine upon them. They also provide a foundation for evaluating the testimony of expert witnesses in the context of FRE and *Daubert*.

Some say that Standards are too limiting or that they hinder intellectual freedom. They argue, for example, that market value is a developing concept sometimes requiring a Standards departure from generally accepted valuation practices in particular applications. Some try to force the concept of market value to perform tasks for which it is not intended.[36] Each of these should be viewed with skepticism. To the extent that dynamic forces are present, new applications are found and new methods are introduced, there are established means whereby they can be recognized and approved when they meet the tests of industry Standards. Meanwhile, Standards such as USPAP and related tests such as those offered above, are available to guide the courts in determining who is properly qualified as an expert valuation witness, and based upon the work performed, whether they should be qualified in particular litigation.

36. For example, as the nation emerged from the collapse of savings and loans, many banks and other financial institutions in the early 1980s attempted to require market value appraisals as of future dates. This notion is foreign to the market value definition because of the speculation a future date introduces into the valuation analysis.

Valuing Contaminated Properties

CHAPTER 11 Cross-References

Related article in Chapter 1: Peter J. Patchin, MAI, "Valuation of Contaminated Properties" *The Appraisal Journal* (January 1988), 10.

Related article in Chapter 2: James A. Chalmers, PhD and Scott A. Roehr, "Issues in the Valuation of Contaminated Property" *The Appraisal Journal* (January 1993), 65–66.

Related articles in Chapter 3: Thomas R. Kearns, "Environmental Audits: Real Estate's Newest Transaction Safeguards" *The Appraisal Journal* (July 1991); and Robert V. Colangelo, CPG and Ronald D. Miller, Esq., "Agency Standards and Industry Guidance on Addressing Environmental Hazards," Chapter 2 in *Environmental Site Assessments and Their Impact on Property Value: The Appraiser's Role*, Appraisal Institute: 1995, 151.

Related articles in Chapter 4: Bill Mundy, MAI, PhD, "Stigma and Value" *The Appraisal Journal* (January 1992); Richard J. Roddewig, "Stigma, Environmental Risk and Property Value: 10 Critical Inquiries" *The Appraisal Journal* (October 1996); and Wayne C. Lusvardi, "The Dose Makes the Poison: Environmental Phobia or Regulatory Stigma?" *The Appraisal Journal* (April 2000), 225–226.

Related article in Chapter 7: Michael Rikon, "Electromagnetic Radiation Field Property Devaluation" *The Appraisal Journal* (January 1996), 360–363.

Related article in Chapter 8: Robert P. Carver, Esq. and Anthony W. Crowell, Esq., "Toxic Tax Assessments: The Ad Valorem Taxation of Contaminated Property" *Real Estate Issues* (Fall 1999), 441–451.

Related article in Chapter 10: Allan E. Gluck, Donald C. Nanney, and Wayne Lusvardi, "Mitigating Factors in Appraisal & Valuation of Contaminated Real Property. *Real Estate Issues* (Summer 2000), 536–537.

Fannie Mae Property and Appraisal Analysis: Special Appraisal Considerations

Issued in 1992

Chapter 3. Special Appraisal Considerations
Section 303 Properties Affected by Environmental Hazards

If the real estate broker, the property seller, the property purchaser, or any other party to the mortgage transaction informs the lender that an environmental hazard exists in or on the property or in the vicinity of the property, the lender must disclose that information to the appraiser and note the individual mortgage file accordingly. (We also require the lender to disclose such information to the borrower, and to comply with any state or local environmental laws regarding disclosure.)

When the appraiser has knowledge of any hazardous condition (whether it exists in or on the subject property or on any site within the vicinity of the property)—such as the presence of hazardous wastes, toxic substances, asbestos-containing materials, urea-formaldehyde insulation, radon gas, etc.—he or she must note the hazardous condition on the appraisal report and comment on any influence that the hazard has on the property's value and marketability (if it is measurable through an analysis of comparable market data as of the effective date of the appraisal) and make appropriate adjustments in the overall analysis of the property's value.

We do not consider the appraiser to be an expert in the field of environmental hazards. The typical residential real estate appraiser is neither expected nor required to be an expert in this specialized field. However, the appraiser has a responsibility to note in the appraisal report any adverse conditions that were observed during the inspection of the subject property or information that he or she became aware of through the normal research involved in performing an appraisal.

In rare situations, a particular environmental hazard may have a significant effect on the value of the subject property, although the actual impact is not measurable because the hazard is so serious or so recently discovered that an appraiser cannot arrive at a reliable estimate of market value because there is no comparable market data (such as sales, contract sales, or active listings) available to reflect the impact of the hazard. In such cases, the mortgage will not be eligible for delivery to Fannie Mae.

We will purchase or securitize a mortgage secured by a property that is affected by an environmental hazard if the impact of the hazard is measurable through an analysis of comparable market data as of the effective date of the appraisal and the appraiser reflects in the appraisal report any adverse effect that the hazard has on the value and marketability of the subject property or indicates that the comparable market data reveals no buyer resistance to the hazard. To illustrate: We are frequently asked to address the eligibility of mortgages secured by properties that are located in neighborhoods affected by radon gas or the presence of hazardous wastes. In such situations, we expect the appraiser to reflect any adverse effect or buyer resistance that is demonstrated and measurable through the available comparable market data. Therefore, when a property is located in a neighborhood that has a relatively high level of radon gas or is near a hazardous waste site, we expect the appraiser to consider and use comparable market data from the same affected area because the sales prices of settled sales, the contact sales prices of pending sales, and the current asking prices for active listings will reflect any negative effect on the value and marketability of the subject property.

Although our guidelines expressly require the appraiser to include in the appraisal report comments about any influence that an environmental hazard has on the value and marketability of the property and to make appropriate adjustments to the overall analysis of the value of the property, we expect the lender to oversee the performance of the appraisers it employs. The lender must make the final decision about the need for inspections and the adequacy of the property as security for the mortgage requested. We expect lenders to exercise sound judgment in determining the acceptability of the property. For example, since we require the appraiser to comment on the effect of a hazard on the marketability and value of the subject property, the appraiser would have to note when there is market resistance to an area because of environmental hazards or any other conditions that affect well, septic, or public water facilities. When the lender has reason to believe that private well water that is on or available to a property might be contaminated as the result of the proximity of the well to hazardous waste sites, the lender is exercising sound judgment if it obtains a "well certification" to determine whether the water meets community standards.

Section 402 Neighborhood Analysis

The purpose of the appraiser's neighborhood analysis is to identify the area (based on common characteristics or trends) that is subject to the same influences as the subject property, not to rate or judge the neighborhood. The sales prices of comparable properties in the identified area should reflect the positive and negative influences of the neighborhood. The results of the neighborhood analysis will enable the appraiser to define the area from which to select comparables, to understand market preferences and price patterns, to examine the effect of different locations within the neighborhood, to determine the influence of nearby land uses, and to identify any other value influences affecting the neighborhood.

To perform a neighborhood analysis, the appraiser should collect pertinent data, make a visual inspection of the neighborhood to observe its physical characteristics and boundaries, and identify land uses and any signs that they are changing. Appraisers should extend their search of the subject market area as far as necessary to assure that all significant influences affecting the value of the subject property are reflected in the appraisal report. Appraisers should use their best judgment in determining and describing neighborhood boundaries. The limits of a neighborhood can be identified by various physical characteristics—including, but not limited to, streets, bodies of water, land uses, types of dwellings, etc. The lender's underwriter should review carefully the neighborhood description to confirm that the appraiser used comparables from within the subject neighborhood in his or her analysis.

Chapter 8. Environmental Hazard Assessment

We require an environmental hazard assessment for all new projects that are underwritten as Type B or Type C condominium and Type 2 cooperative projects. (Lenders may pass the costs of performing an environmental hazard assessment on to the project developer or builder or to the owners' association or cooperative corporation for the project.) We will not require a lender to conduct a new environmental hazard assessment if it or the project developer, builder, or construction lender has previously obtained an environmental assessment for the project—as long as the earlier assessment is similar in scope and provides essentially the same information that we require. The lender must include a copy of the assessment in the project submission package it sends to us (or retain it in the individual project file if the project is processed as a Type B project).

Section 801 Types of Environmental Hazard Assessment

There are two types of environmental hazard assessments – a Phase I assessment that lenders can perform (or employ others to perform) by gathering information from various sources to evaluate the environmental soundness of the project and a Phase II assessment that lenders generally hire a qualified environmental consultant to conduct when the Phase I assessment identifies any problems or is inconclusive with regard to any particular hazard. A new condominium or cooperative project (or an existing building that has been converted to a condominium or cooperative project) must be acceptable under either the Phase I assessment or the Phase II assessment.

Section 801.01 Phase I Assessment

A Phase I assessment is principally a screening process that focuses on reviewing the available documentation; interviewing people who are knowledgeable about the site operations; and inspecting the site, the building, and adjoining properties. This assessment enables the lender to quickly determine whether information currently exists to clearly evaluate a property's environmental status.

Lenders must complete and submit the Phase I assessment as part of their project submission package. We do not require a specific form for a Phase I assessment, although we do provide a suggested format (see Exhibit 1). Use of our suggested format (or a similar one) will assure that all the relevant points are addressed in the assessment.

Section 801.02 Phase II Assessment

A Phase II assessment generally provides a more detailed review of the site, including specific physical sampling for each hazard that was not acceptable under the Phase I assessment, and a review of historical records. This assessment generally determines the presence or absence of specific environmental liabilities (such as asbestos or leaking underground storage tanks) or quantifies the extent of an observed or suspected environmental liability (such as soil or ground water contamination). Examples of the kind of testing or sampling that occurs under a Phase II assessment include

- Investigating the status of any enforcement actions related to neighboring properties under the Superfund or Resource, Conservation, and Recovery Acts;
- Testing for underground storage leaks;
- Sampling and analyzing the soil;
- Testing soil or facilities that are suspected as being contaminated by polychlorinated biphenyls; and
- Sampling and analyzing bulk asbestos and developing related abatement and maintenance programs, if necessary.

The specialized nature of the investigations conducted under a Phase II assessment require the knowledge and experience of a qualified consultant. Lenders should use care in choosing firms to perform environmental hazard assessments. A lender should confirm that the consultant it plans to use is not affiliated with the buyer or seller of the property, nor with a firm engaged in business that might present a conflict of interest. The lender should also evaluate whether the consulting firm's personnel have adequate and appropriate education and training to carry out the required duties.

The consultant's report for a Phase II environmental assessment must include a full description of the sampling procedures, the laboratory results, and the consultant's recommendations. The consultant must follow all regulatory standards and good management practices at all times, especially when physical sampling and laboratory analysis are involved. We do not specify an exact format for the consultant's report; any report that is thorough and professionally prepared will be acceptable. We require the consultant to certify in his or her report that the assessment was performed diligently and in accordance with all regulatory and good management standards, and that, to the best of his or her knowledge, the results are complete and accurate. An officer of the consulting firm that performed the work must sign the report. The suggested format included in Exhibit 2 can be used for the lender's Phase II assessment; it should include the consultant's report as an addendum.

We reserve the right to notify a lender that a particular consultant is no longer acceptable to us. We also reserve the right to refuse to accept (at any time) any future environmental assessment, report, warranty, or certification from individual consultants, specific consulting firms, or specific branch offices of consulting firms.

When a Phase II assessment is required to address those hazards identified as being unacceptable under the Phase I assessment, the lender may include the Phase II assessment as part of the project submission package that it submits to obtain our preliminary acceptance of the project or it may wait until after we have completed our preliminary review of the

Addenda: *Fannie Mae Special Appraisal Considerations*

application before it has the consultant conduct the Phase II assessment. When a Phase II assessment is required, we will not issue either a *Conditional Project Acceptance* (Form 1027) or a *Final Project Acceptance* (Form 1028) until we have received and reviewed the Phase II assessment.

Section 802 Unacceptable Environmental Conditions

A property must be acceptable under either the Phase I or the Phase II environmental hazard assessment in order for a new condominium to be an acceptable project under either Type B or Type C project classification or for a new cooperative project to be acceptable under the Type 2 project classification. The existence of one or more unacceptable environmental conditions will generally result in a project being ineligible. However, if the lender believes that the relative risk is minimal or can be managed, it may request our regional office to give special consideration to accepting the project. In some instances, we may accept the project subject to remedial action being taken to reduce or contain the risk.

Examples of unacceptable environmental conditions include, but are not limited to, the following:

- A property that is (or has been) used as a landfill or other solid, hazardous, or municipal waste disposal site;
- A property that is (or has been) used for activity related to the storage of oil, hazardous waste, or other toxic substances — expect that the property may have been used for the storage of small quantities of hazardous substances that are generally recognized as appropriate for residential uses and maintenance of the property;
- A property that is the subject of outstanding environmental or public health litigation or administrative action from private parties or public officials;
- A high-risk neighboring property that has evidence of hazardous waste spills or soil or groundwater contamination on or around its site;
- A property that has documented soil or groundwater contamination and/or a documented tank leak that is leaking at more than 0.05 gallons per hour (which is the National Fire Protection Association's standard);
- A property with soil sampling that has values for metal in excess of the following concentration limits (in parts per million):

chromium :	100 ppm	arsenic:	20 ppm
zinc:	350 ppm	cadmium:	3 ppm
lead:	100 ppm	nickel:	100 ppm
copper:	170 ppm	selenium:	20 ppm

- A property that is contaminated from polychlorinated biphenyls (PBCs);
- A property with soil sampling that has values for other organic materials in excess of the following concentration limits (in parts per million):

Total volatile organics:	1 ppm
Total hydrocarbons:	100 ppm
Total petroleum hydrocarbons:	100 ppm

- A property with groundwater sampling that has values for other organic materials in excess of the following concentration limits (in parts per million):

Total organics (volatiles and base neutrals):	.10 ppm
Total petroleum hydrocarbons:	1.00ppm

- A property with groundwater sampling that has values for metals in excess of the following concentration limits (in parts per million):

Arsenic:	.05 ppm	Lead:	.05 ppm
Boron:	1.00 ppm	Mercury:	.002ppm
Cadmium:	.01 ppm	Selenium:	.01 ppm
Chromium:	.05 ppm	Silver:	.05 ppm

- A property with high radon levels (above 4 picocuries per liter) that can be corrected only through large capital improvements and/or extensive on-going maintenance programs that are beyond the financial or technical abilities of the owners' association or cooperative corporation for the project;
- A property that has conditions representing material violations of applicable local, state, or federal environmental or public health statutes and laws; and
- A property that is contaminated by friable asbestos-containing materials.

Section 803 Remedial Actions

Properties that fail to meet a particular standard may be corrected through remedial actions and then retested. Remedial actions should be undertaken only with the advice and written endorsement of a qualified environmental consultant. All remedial actions must be taken in accordance with all regulatory and good management standards.

Generally, a lender must confirm the completion and effectiveness of remedial action before we will issue a final project acceptance for a specific condominium or cooperative project. However, we will consider issuing a conditional project acceptance before the completion of remedial work under the following conditions:

- A qualified environmental consultant states in writing that remedial work needed to make the property eligible under the environmental standards can be completed within 90 days after we issue our conditional project acceptance (or within any additional time we allow for completion of any repair with moderate rehabilitation work required under our conditional project acceptance); and
- The project's developer or sponsor signs a contract with a qualified firm to perform the remedial work within 90 days after we issue our conditional project acceptance (or within any additional time we allow for completion of any repair or moderate rehabilitation work required under our conditional project acceptance). The project developer or sponsor must provide a performance escrow equal to 150% of the gross contact amount to assure the completion of the remedial work.

Addenda: *Fannie Mae Special Appraisal Considerations*

When we issue a *Conditional Project Acceptance* (Form 1027) before the completion of remedial work, we require a written statement from a qualified consultant when the work is finished, certifying that the job has been satisfactorily completed and that the property meets the environmental eligibility standards.

Valuing Contaminated Properties

EXHIBIT 1 Suggested Format for Phase I Environmental Hazard Assessments

I. Property Log
Project Name:_____

Property Address:_____

Developer/Sponsor Name: _____

Developer/Sponsor Address:_____

Developer/Sponsor Telephone: _____

Lender Name: _____

Lender's Underwriter's Name: _____

Environmental Consultant:_____

Consultant's Firm Name: _____

Consultant's Firm Address: _____

Consultant's Telephone: _____

Date Phase I Assessment Completed:_____

Date Phase II Assessment Completed: _____

II. Summary of Phase I Assessment Results/Recommendations
1. Check applicable result for each hazard, indicating for each "Fail" whether there is a possible remedy or whether a Phase II assessment is needed.

Hazard	Pass	Fail	Possible Remedy	Phase II Requirement
Waste Sites	❑	❑	❑	❑
PCBs	❑	❑	❑	❑
Radon	❑	❑	❑	❑
Underground Storage Tanks	❑	❑	❑	❑
Asbestos	❑	❑	❑	❑
Other (List)				
_____	❑	❑	❑	❑
_____	❑	❑	❑	❑
_____	❑	❑	❑	❑

2. Attach a brief explanation for each hazard that needs a Phase II assessment. List data deficiencies, test results, etc. that require further assessment
3. Attach a brief explanation for each failed hazard that could be corrected by taking remedial actions. Explain what actions are required and how they should be performed.
4. Underwriter's Comments (Attach Phase I Information Checklist): _____
_____

Signature:_____   Date: _____

III. Information Checklist: Information Sources
Check the information sources used to perform the various aspects of the Phase I environmental hazard assessment.
1. Overall Property Description
   - ❑ Building Specifications
   - ❑ Historical Aerial Photos
   - ❑ Current Aerial Photos
   - ❑ Title History
   - ❑ Site Survey
   - ❑ Neighborhood Zoning Maps
   - ❑ Neighborhood Land Use Maps
   - ❑ Other (List)

   - ❑ Lists of Commercial Tenants Previously on Site
   - ❑ Verification of Public Water and Sewer
   - ❑ Interviews with Local Fire, Health, Land Use or Environmental Enforcement Officials

2. Waste Sites
   - ❑ Comprehensive Environmental Response, Compensation, and Liability Information System (CERCLIS) lists or similar state lists of contaminated properties (covering any properties that are within a one-mile radius of the subject property)
   - ❑ State Environmental Protection Agency (EPA) site lists of contaminated properties (covering any properties that are within a one-mile radius of the subject property)
   - ❑ Site Soil and Groundwater Test Results
   - ❑ Other (List)_____

Addenda: *Fannie Mae Special Appraisal Considerations*

EXHIBIT 1 Suggested Format for Phase I Environmental Hazard Assessments *(continued)*

3. Polychlorinated Biphenyls (PCBs)
   - ❏ Utility Transformer Records
   - ❏ Site Survey of Transformers
   - ❏ Site Soil and Groundwater PCB Test Results
   - ❏ Other (List) _____

4. Radon
   - ❏ Water Utility Records
   - ❏ Gas Utility Records
   - ❏ On-Site Radon Test Results
   - ❏ Other (List) _____

5. Underground Storage Tanks
   - ❏ Oil, Motor Fuel, and Waste Oil Systems Reports
   - ❏ Site Soil and Groundwater Tests
   - ❏ Site Tank Survey
   - ❏ Comprehensive Environmental Response, Compensation, and Liability Information System (CERCLIS) lists or similar state lists of contaminated properties (covering any properties that are within a one-mile radius of the subject property)
   - ❏ Other (List) _____

6. Asbestos (Required only if subject property is the conversion of an existing building)
   - ❏ Dated Building Construction/Rehabilitation Specifications
   - ❏ Engineer's/Consultant's Asbestos Report
   - ❏ Other (List) _____

IV. Information Checklist: Evaluation of Specific Hazards

Answer all applicable questions by marking the appropriate box – "Y" for Yes, "N" for No, or "DK" for Don't Know

A. Waste Sites

	Y	N	DK
1. Are there results of physical testing (including on-site sampling of soil and groundwater that meets all regulatory standards and sound industry practice) to show that the property is free of waste contamination and is being operated in an environmentally safe manner?	❏	❏	❏
2. Are there any obvious high-risk neighbors in adjacent properties engaged in producing, storing, or transporting hazardous waste, chemicals, or substances?	❏	❏	❏

Note: If the answer to question 1 is "yes" and the answer to question 2 is "no," stop here because, for underwriting purposes, the property will be acceptable from the standpoint of waste contamination. Otherwise, answer the questions below.

	Y	N	DK
3. Was the site even used for research, industrial or military purposes during the last 30 years?	❏	❏	❏
4. Has any of the site even been leased to commercial tenants who are likely to have used, transported, or disposed of toxic chemicals (such as a dry cleaner, print shop, service station, etc.)?	❏	❏	❏
5. Is water for the building provided by either a private company or a well situated on the property?	❏	❏	❏
6. Does the property or any site within one mile of the property appear on any state or federal list of hazardous waste sites?	❏	❏	❏
7. Is there documented or visible evidence of the handling of dangerous waste on the subject property or on neighboring sites (such as stressed vegetation, stained soil, open or leaking containers, foul fumes or smells, oily ponds, etc.)?	❏	❏	❏

Note: If the answer to any of the questions from 2 Through 7 are "yes" or "don't know," then the property either fails or needs a Phase II assessment conducted. If the answers to all of the questions 2 through 7 are "no," the property, for underwriting purposes, will be acceptable from the standpoint of waste site contamination.

8. Underwriter's Comments: _____
_____

9. Phase I Assessment Results (check one)
   ❏ Pass   ❏ Fail   ❏ Possible Remedy   ❏ Phase II Required

10. Underwriter's Signature and Date: _____

B. Polychlorinated Biphenyls (PCBs)

	Y	N	DK
1. Are there any transformers or capacitors that contain PCBs anywhere on the property?	❏	❏	❏
2. Is there any visible or documented evidence of soil or groundwater contamination from PCBs on the property?	❏	❏	❏

Note: If the answer to the above questions is "no," stop here because, for underwriting purposes, the property will be acceptable from the standpoint of PCB contamination. If the answer to a question is "don't know," stop here since a Phase II assessment is required. Otherwise, answer the questions below.

	Y	N	DK
3. If the answer to question 1 is "yes," are any of the capacitors or transformers inside residential buildings?	❏	❏	❏
4. If the answer to question 1 above is "yes," are any of the transformers or capacitors not clearly marked, not well maintained, or not secure?	❏	❏	❏
5. If the answer to question 1 above is "yes," is there any evidence of leakage on or around the transformers or capacitors?	❏	❏	❏

Valuing Contaminated Properties

EXHIBIT 1 Suggested Format for Phase I Environmental Hazard Assessments (continued)

	Y	N	DK

6. If the answer to question 2 above is "yes," have PCB concentrations of 50 parts per million or greater been found in contaminated soils or groundwater? ❑ ❑ ❑
   Note: If the answers to questions 3 through 6 are all "no," the property, for underwriting purposes, will be acceptable from the standpoint of PCB contamination. Otherwise, the property either fails or needs a Phase II assessment.
7. Underwriter's Comments: _____

_____

8. Phase I Assessment Results (check one)
   ❑ Pass   ❑ Fail   ❑ Possible Remedy   ❑ Phase II Required
9. Underwriter's Signature and Date: _____

C. Radon

	Y	N	DK

1. Is there any evidence that nearby structures have elevated indoor levels of radon or radon progeny? ❑ ❑ ❑
2. Have local water supplies been found to have elevated levels of radon or radium? ❑ ❑ ❑
3. Is the property located on or near sites that are currently, or were formerly, used for uranium, thorium, or radium extraction or for phosphate processing? ❑ ❑ ❑
   Note: If the answers to the above questions are all "yes," a Phase II assessment is required. If the answer to question 2 and 3 is "no," the property, for underwriting purposes, will be acceptable from the standpoint of radon contamination. If the subject property is a conversion of an existing building, go to question 4
4. Were the results of an EPA-approved short-term radon test that was performed in the basement of each of the subject buildings within the last six months at or below four picocuries per liter? ❑ ❑ ❑
   Note: If the answer to this question is "no" or "don't know," a Phase II assessment is required
5. Underwriter's Comments: _____

_____

6. Phase I Assessment Results (check one)
   ❑ Pass   ❑ Fail   ❑ Possible Remedy   ❑ Phase II Required
7. Underwriter's Signature and Date: _____

D. Underground Storage Tanks

	Y	N	DK

1. Is there a current site survey performed by a qualified engineer that indicates the property is free of any underground storage tanks? ❑ ❑ ❑
2. Is there any visible or documented evidence of oil or groundwater contamination on the property? ❑ ❑ ❑
3. Are there any petroleum storage and/or delivery facilities (including gas stations) or chemical manufacturing plants located on adjacent properties? ❑ ❑ ❑
   Note: If the answer to question 1 is "yes," and the answers to questions 2 and 3 are "no," stop here because, for underwriting purposes, the property will be acceptable from the standpoint of underground storage tank contamination. If the answer to questions 2 and 3 is "yes" or "don't know," also stop because the property either fails or needs a Phase II assessment. Otherwise, answer the questions below.
4. Are there any active underground tank facilities on-site that are used for activities such as motor fuel, waste oil, or fuel oil storage? ❑ ❑ ❑
5. If the answer to question 4 is "yes," have these facilities been maintained in accordance with sound industry standards (such as those in the American Petroleum Institute's Bulletins 1621 and 1623 or the National Fire Protection Association's Bulletins 329, 70, 77, etc.)? ❑ ❑ ❑
   Note: If the answer to question 4 is "no," go to question 8 below. If the answer to question 4 is "don't know," stop here because the property either fails or needs a Phase II assessment. If the answer to question 5 is "no" or "don't know," stop here because the property either fails or needs a Phase II assessment. If the answers to questions 4 and 5 are "yes," answer the questions below.
6. If the answer to question 4 is "yes," are any of the tanks more than 10 years old? ❑ ❑ ❑
7. If the answer to question 6 is "yes," have any of the tanks that are more than 10 years old been tested for leaks within the last year using a test approved by the American Petroleum Institute? ❑ ❑ ❑
   Note: If the answer to question 6 is "no," answer the questions below. If the answer to question 6 is "don't know," stop here because the property either fails or needs a Phase II assessment. If the answer to question 7 is "no," answer the questions below. Otherwise, stop here because the property either fails or needs a Phase II assessment.
8. Are there any deactivated underground storage tanks on the property? ❑ ❑ ❑

Addenda: *Fannie Mae Special Appraisal Considerations*

EXHIBIT 1 Suggested Format for Phase I Environmental Hazard Assessments *(continued)*

	Y	N	DK

9. If the answer to question 8 is "yes," were all of the tanks deactivated in accordance with sound industry practices (such as under the American Petroleum Institute's Bulletins 1604 and 2202 or the Nation Fire Protection Association's Bulletin 30)?   ❏ ❏ ❏
Note: If the answer to question 8 is "no" or if the answer to question 9 is "yes," the property, for underwriting purposes, will be acceptable from the standpoint of underground storage tank contamination. If the answer to question 8 is "don't know," or if the answer to question 9 is "no" or "don't know," the property either fails of needs a Phase II assessment.

10. Underwriter's Comments: _____

11. Phase I Assessment Results (check one)
  ❏ Pass   ❏ Fail   ❏ Possible Remedy   ❏ Phase II Required

12. Underwriter's Signature and Date: _____

E. Asbestos (Required only if the project is a conversion of an existing building)

	Y	N	DK

All asbestos-related assessments, testing, remedial action, and maintenance programs must be in compliance with the Environment Protection Agency's document "Guidance for Controlling Asbestos-Containing Materials in Buildings" (EPA 560/5024, 1985).

1. Was the building constructed prior to 1979?   ❏ ❏ ❏
2. Does a site walk-through reveal visible evidence of asbestos?   ❏ ❏ ❏
3. Is there any documented evidence of asbestos?   ❏ ❏ ❏
Note: If the answer to all of the above questions is "no," stop here because, for underwriting purposes, the property will be acceptable from the standpoint of asbestos contamination. If the answer to any of the above questions is "yes" or "don't know," the property either fails or needs a Phase II assessment.

4. Is there an asbestos survey by a certified, independent firm that was performed since 1979?   ❏ ❏ ❏
Note: If the answer to question 4 is "yes," answer the question below. Otherwise, stop because a Phase II assessment is required.

5. Did the survey find the building to be free of both treated and untreated asbestos-containing material?   ❏ ❏ ❏
Note: If the answer to question 5 is "yes," stop here because, for underwriting purposes, the property will be acceptable from the standpoint of asbestos contamination. If the answer to question 5 is "no" or "don't know," the property either fails or needs a Phase II assessment.

6. Underwriter's Comments: _____

7. Phase I Assessment Results (check one)
  ❏ Pass   ❏ Fail   ❏ Possible Remedy   ❏ Phase II Required

8. Underwriter's Signature and Date: _____

F. Additional Hazards (Required only if the project is a conversion of an existing building)

	Y	N	DK

1. Is there any visible or documented evidence of peeling lead paint on the floors, walls, or ceilings of either the unit living areas or the common areas?   ❏ ❏ ❏
Note: If the answer to question 1 is "no," the property, for underwriting purposes, will be acceptable from the standpoint of lead paint contamination; however, answer the questions below related to other hazards. If the answer to question 1 is "yes" or "don't know," the property fails. However, answer the remaining questions since the project may be eligible if remedial actions to remove or cover all peeling lead paint are taken before the lender requests our final project acceptance.

2. Do the unit living areas or common areas contain urea-formaldehyde foam insulation that was installed less than a year ago?   ❏ ❏ ❏

3. If the answer to question 2 is "yes" or "don't know," did the current heating, ventilation, and air conditioning system meet the standards of the American Society of Heating, Refrigerating, and Air Conditioning Engineers when it was installed?   ❏ ❏ ❏
Note: If the answer to question 2 is "no" or the answer to question 3 is "yes," the property, for underwriting purposes, will be acceptable from the standpoint of urea-formaldehyde foam insulation contamination. However, answer the remaining questions. If the answer to question 3 is "no" or "don't know," the property fails. However, answer the remaining questions since the project may be eligible if the lender can demonstrate that the ventilation system meets the American Society of Heating, Refrigerating, and Air Conditioning Engineer's standards before it requests our final project acceptance.

4. Does the local utility providing the drinking water meet current EPA requirements for lead concentration?   ❏ ❏ ❏

5. Underwriter's Comments: _____

6. Phase I Assessment Results (check one)
  ❏ Pass   ❏ Fail   ❏ Possible Remedy   ❏ Phase II Required

7. Underwriter's Signature and Date: _____

Valuing Contaminated Properties

EXHIBIT 2 Suggested Format for Phase II Environmental Hazard Assessments

I. Property Log
Property Name: _____
Property Address: _____

Developer/Sponsor Name: _____
Developer/Sponsor Address: _____

Developer/Sponsor Telephone: _____

Lender Name: _____
Lender's Underwriter's Name: _____

Environmental Consultant: _____
Consultant's Firm Name: _____
Consultant's Firm Address: _____

Consultant's Telephone: _____

Date Phase I Assessment Completed: _____
Date Phase II Assessment Completed: _____

II. Summary of Phase II Assessment Results/Recommendations

1. Check applicable result for each hazard, indicating for each "Fail" where there is a possible remedy. Show "N/A" for any hazard for which there was no Phase II assessment required.

Hazard	Pass	Fail	Possible Remedy
Waste Sites	❏	❏	_____
PCBs	❏	❏	_____
Radon	❏	❏	_____
Underground Storage Tanks	❏	❏	_____
Asbestos	❏	❏	_____
Other (List)_____	❏	❏	_____
_____	❏	❏	_____
_____	❏	❏	_____

2. Attach a brief explanation for each failed hazard that could be corrected by taking remedial actions. Explain what actions are required and how they should be performed._____
_____
_____
_____

3. Underwriter's Comments:_____
   Signature: _____ Date:_____
4. Consultant's Comments (Attach Phase II assessment report): _____
   Signature: _____ Date:_____

Related Discussion from *The Appraisal of Real Estate*, 12th Edition

Environment

Appraisers also analyze land use in light of environmental conditions. Environmental considerations include factors such as

This material originally appeared in Chapter 9 of *The Appraisal of Real Estate*, 12th ed. (Chicago: Appraisal Institute, 2001), 209–216.

- Local climate
- Availability of adequate and satisfactory water supply
- Pattern of drainage
- Quality of air
- Presence of wildlife/endangered species habitats
- Location of earthquake faults and known slide or avalanche zones
- Proximity to streams, wetlands, rivers, lakes, or oceans

Air and water pollution are by-products of increased population and urbanization. Public concern over pollution has prompted political action and legislation to protect the environment. In areas subject to extreme air pollution, regulations may exclude certain industries and limit the volume of traffic; such restrictions impact land use in these jurisdictions. Pollution rights have also become a salable commodity.[1] In locations near natural water sources, industrial uses may be prohibited while recreational uses are promoted. Environmental and climatic advantages and constraints must be analyzed to determine the proper land use for a site. Future land uses must be compatible with the local environment.

A site in a specific location may be influenced by its exposure to sun, wind, or other environmental factors. A very windy location can be disastrous to a resort but beneficial to a fossil-fuel power plant. The sunny side of the street is not always the most desirable for retail shops. In hot climates, the shady side of the street often gets more pedestrian traffic and greater sales, thus producing higher rents and higher land values. Ski resorts almost always have slopes facing north for snow retention, and buildings facing south are desirable.

Analysis of a site's environment focuses on the interrelationships between the appraised site and neighboring properties. The effects of any hazards or

1. The Clean Air Act of 1990 regulated the tonnage of acid-rain emissions that smokestack industries may release in proportion to plant size. Industries that do not use their full legal allowance can transfer or sell their pollution rights to other industries. Since 1993 pollution rights have been sold on both the Chicago Board of Trade and in the off-exchange pollution-rights market.

nuisances caused by neighboring properties must be considered. Of particular importance are safety concerns—e.g., the safety of employees and customers, of occupants and visitors, or of children going to and from school.

A site's value is also influenced by nearby amenities and developments on adjoining sites such as parks, fine buildings, and compatible commercial buildings. The types of structures surrounding the property being appraised and the activities of those who use them can greatly influence site value.

Environmental Liabilities

In recent years the federal government has issued many environmental laws and regulations; state and local governments have added even more. This vast network of regulations defines the natural and man-made conditions that constitute environmental liabilities affecting property values. Natural areas to be protected include wetlands, aquifer replenishment areas, and habitats for endangered or threatened species. Man-made liabilities may be indicated by the presence of leaking underground storage tanks (LUSTs), asbestos, PCBs, or other hazardous materials. The existence of one or more environmental conditions can reduce the value of a property or even create a negative value.

The typical appraiser may not have the knowledge or experience needed to detect the presence of hazardous substances or to measure their quantities. Like buyers and sellers in the open market, the appraiser must often rely on the advice of others. Appraisers are not expected or required to be experts in the detection or measurement of hazardous substances. The role and responsibility of the appraiser in detecting, measuring, and considering environmental substances affecting a property are addressed in Advisory Opinion 9 of USPAP and Guide Note 8 of the Appraisal Institute's Guide Notes to the Standards of Professional Appraisal Practice (see Figure 9.5).

The Property Observation Checklist (Figure 9.6), developed and adopted by the Appraisal Institute in 1995, is consistent with Advisory Opinion 9 and

Figure 9.5 Consideration of Hazardous Substances in the Appraisal Process

Advisory Opinion 9, which was adopted December 8, 1992, addresses the following areas of concern:

- An appraiser who is requested to complete a checklist as part of a process to detect contamination should only respond to those questions that can be answered competently by the appraiser within the limits of his or her particular expertise.
- An appraiser may reasonably rely on the findings and opinions of qualified specialists in environmental remediation and compliance cost estimation.
- An appraiser may appraise an interest in real estate that is or is believed to be contaminated based on the hypothesis that the real estate is free of contamination when 1) the resulting appraisal is not misleading, 2) the client has been advised of the limitation, and 3) the Ethics Rule of USPAP is satisfied.
- The value of an interest in impacted or contaminated real estate may not be measurable by simply deducting the remediation or compliance cost estimate from the estimated value as if unaffected.

Guide Note 8 was adopted January 1, 1991, and amended January 25, 1994. This guide note takes its direction from the Competency Rule of USPAP, which requires appraisers to either

- have the knowledge and experience necessary to complete a specific appraisal assignment competently

or

- disclose their lack of knowledge or experience to the client, take all steps necessary or appropriate to complete the assignment competently, and describe in the report their lack of knowledge or experience and the steps taken to competently complete the assignment

Addenda: *From* The Appraisal of Real Estate

FIGURE 9.6 Property Observation Checklist Form

PROPERTY OBSERVATION CHECKLIST

SCOPE OF ANALYSIS

The Property Observation Checklist is prepared by the appraiser in conjuction with his/her inspection of the subject property in the normal course of an appraisal assignment. In completing the checklist, only visual observations are recorded. The intent of the checklist is to help identify possible environmental factors that could be observable by a non-environmental professional. The appraiser did not search title, interview the current or prior owners, or do any research beyond that normally associated with the appraisal process, unless otherwise stated.

The user of this checklist is reminded that all responses to the questions are provided by an appraiser who is not an environmental professional and is not specifically trained or qualified to identify potential environmental problems; therefore, it should be used only to assist the appraiser's client in determining whether an environmental professional is required. The checklist was not developed for use with single-family residential or agricultural properties.

The appraiser is not liable for the lack of detection or identification of possible environmental factors. The appraisal report and/or the Property Observation Checklist must not be considered under any circumstances to be an environmental site assessment of the property as would be performed by an environmental professional.

GENERAL INSTRUCTIONS

The appraiser should distinguish, as appropriate, between the physical presence of possible environmental factors and the economic effect such factors may have in the marketplace or on the value estimate. In completing the checklist, the appraiser should attach reports, photographs, interview records, notes, public records, etc., as documentation for specific observations. The instructions for each section of the checklist specify the kinds of documentation required.

If, for any reason, this checklist is prepared as a stand-alone document, it must be accompanied by an appropriate statement of assumptions and limiting conditions, as well as the appraiser's signed certification.

TERMINOLOGY AND APPRAISAL STANDARDS

The following checklist terms appear in *The Dictionary of Real Estate Appraisal,* Third Edition (Chicago: Appraisal Institute, 1993) and are specifically referenced in the Property Observation Checklist: *adjoining properties; environmental professional; environmental site assessment;* and *pits, ponds, or lagoons.* Please refer to *The Dictionary of Real Estate Appraisal,* Third Edition, for discussions of these terms.

Please refer to Guide Note 8, "The Consideration of Hazardous Substances in the Appraisal Process," *Guide Notes to the Standards of Professional Appraisal Practice* (Chicago: Appraisal Institute, current edition); Advisory Opinion G-9, "Responsibility of Appraisers Concerning Toxic or Hazardous Substances Contamination," in Addenda to *Uniform Standards of Professional Appraisal Practice* (Washington, D.C.: The Appraisal Foundation, current edition); and other appropriate statements in the professional standards documents for additional information.

© 2001 by the Appraisal Institute. All rights reserved. Appraisal Institute members and affiliates may reproduce this document, providing this copyright is included. All others must obtain permission.

http://www.appraisalinstitute.org/download/

Valuing Contaminated Properties

FIGURE 9.6 Property Observation Checklist Form *(continued)*

SECTION 1	Extent of Appraiser's Inspection of the Property

Describe the appraiser's on-site inspection of the subject property and, as applicable, the adjoining properties:

_____

_____

_____

_____

SECTION 2	Possible Environmental Factors Observed by the Appraiser

Indicate below if any of the following possible environmental factors were observed during the appraiser's visual inspection(s) of the subject property and, as applicable, the adjoining properties. A written description of possible environmental factors should be provided for all questions where "Yes" is checked.

1. Did the appraiser observe an indication of current or past industrial/manufacturing use on the subject property or adjoining properties?

   ○ Yes   ○ No   **If observed, describe below:**

   _____

   _____

2. Did the appraiser observe any containers, storage drums, or disposal devices not labeled or identified as to contents or use on the subject property?

   ○ Yes   ○ No   **If observed, describe below:**

   _____

   _____

3. Did the appraiser observe any stained soil or distressed vegetation on the subject property?

   ○ Yes   ○ No   **If observed, describe below:**

   _____

   _____

4. Did the appraiser observe any pits, ponds, or lagoons on the subject property?

   ○ Yes   ○ No   **If observed, describe below:**

   _____

   _____

5. Did the appraiser observe any evidence of above-ground or underground storage tanks (e.g., tanks, vent pipes, etc.) on the subject property?

   ○ Yes   ○ No   **If observed, describe below:**

   _____

   _____

© 2001 by the Appraisal Institute. All rights reserved. Appraisal Institute members and affiliates may reproduce this document, providing this copyright is included. All others must obtain permission.

http://www.appraisalinstitute.org/download/

Addenda: *From* The Appraisal of Real Estate

FIGURE 9.6 Property Observation Checklist Form *(continued)*

6. Did the appraiser observe any flooring, drains, or walls associated with the subject property that are stained or that emit unusual odors?

◯ Yes   ◯ No   **If observed, describe below:**

_____

_____

7. Did the appraiser observe any water being discharged on or from the subject property?

◯ Yes   ◯ No   **If observed, describe below:**

_____

_____

8. Did the appraiser observe any indication of dumping, burying, or burning on the subject property?

◯ Yes   ◯ No   **If observed, describe below:**

_____

_____

9. Did the appraiser observe any chipped, blistered, or peeled paint on the subject property?

◯ Yes   ◯ No   **If observed, describe below:**

_____

_____

10. Did the appraiser observe any sprayed-on insulation, pipe wrapping, duct wrapping, etc., on the subject property?

◯ Yes   ◯ No   **If observed, describe below:**

_____

_____

11. Did the appraiser observe any transmission towers (electrical, microwave, etc.) on the subject property or adjoining properties?

◯ Yes   ◯ No   **If observed, describe below:**

_____

_____

12. Did the appraiser observe any coastal areas, rivers, streams, springs, lakes, swamps, marshes, or watercourses on the subject property or adjoining properties?

◯ Yes   ◯ No   **If observed, describe below:**

_____

_____

13. Did the appraiser observe any other factors that might indicate the need for investigation(s) by an environmental professional?

◯ Yes   ◯ No   **If observed, describe below:**

_____

_____

© 2001 by the Appraisal Institute. All rights reserved. Appraisal Institute members and affiliates may reproduce this document, providing this copyright is included. All others must obtain permission.

http://www.appraisalinstitute.org/download/

Valuing Contaminated Properties

FIGURE 9.6 Property Observation Checklist Form *(continued)*

SECTION 3	Possible Environmental Factors Reported by Others

Indicate below if in completing this assignment the appraiser was informed—verbally or in writing—of any information concerning possible environmental factors reported by others. "Others" may include the client, the property owner, the property owner's agent, or any other person conveying such information. Documentation should be provided for all instances where "Yes" is checked. If the information was presented verbally, then a written description of the source and circumstance of the communication should be attached to this checklist and/or the appraisal report. Copies of printed reports provided to the appraiser should be attached to this checklist and/or the appraisal report.

14. Has the appraiser been informed about federal- or state-maintained records indicating that environmentally sensitive sites are located on the subject property or adjoining properties?

    ○ Yes   ○ No   **If yes, provide documentation.**

15. Has the appraiser been informed about past or current violations (e.g., liens, government notifications, etc.) of environmental laws concerning the subject property?

    ○ Yes   ○ No   **If yes, provide documentation.**

16. Has the appraiser been informed about past or current environmental lawsuits or administrative proceedings concerning the subject property?

    ○ Yes   ○ No   **If yes, provide documentation.**

17. Has the appraiser been informed about past or current tests for lead-based paint or other lead hazards on the subject property?

    ○ Yes   ○ No   **If yes, provide documentation.**

18. Has the appraiser been informed about past or current tests for asbestos-containing materials on the subject property?

    ○ Yes   ○ No   **If yes, provide documentation.**

19. Has the appraiser been informed about past or current tests for radon on the subject property?

    ○ Yes   ○ No   **If yes, provide documentation.**

20. Has the appraiser been informed about past or current tests for soil or groundwater contamination on the subject property?

    ○ Yes   ○ No   **If yes, provide documentation.**

21. Has the appraiser been informed about other professional environmental site assessment(s) of the subject property?

    ○ Yes   ○ No   **If yes, provide documentation.**

_____
Signature

_____
Name

_____
Date Checklist Signed

_____
State Certification or State License #   State

© 2001 by the Appraisal Institute. All rights reserved. Appraisal Institute members and affiliates may reproduce this document, providing this copyright is included. All others must obtain permission.

http://www.appraisalinstitute.org/download/

Addenda: *From* The Appraisal of Real Estate

Guide Note 8. The checklist provides appraisers conducting property inspections with a uniform, easy-to-use guideline for recording observations about the presence of possible environmental factors. To the extent possible, voluntary use of the checklist limits the appraiser's liability. (Note: the checklist was not developed for single-family residential or agricultural properties.)

Even if there is no reason to believe that the property being appraised is affected by hazardous substances, appraisers are advised to include a standard disclaimer or statement of limiting conditions concerning hazardous substances in their appraisal reports. Such a statement clarifies the normal limits of the appraisal, discloses the appraiser's lack of expertise with regard to hazardous substances, and disclaims responsibility for matters beyond the appraiser's experience. The determination of due diligence remains at issue, even when a disclaimer is used.

Environmental Site Assessments and Environmental Property Assessments

Because of the existence of environmental liability laws and the significant effect that environmental contamination may have on a given property, appraisers and property owners or purchasers should make reasonable inquiries to determine whether there is a likelihood that a particular property may be affected by either apparent or latent environmental conditions. Today this is as common as testing for termites, hidden structural problems, and other factors that may influence value. Most appraisers and property owners are not trained and qualified to make technical assessments, but reasonable examination and inquiry can produce evidence of conditions that are already known to the market.

In most parts of the country, lenders commonly require a specific environmental study before a loan for an income-producing property is processed. While formal studies are less common for single-family residential properties, lenders and secondary markets officials may require studies in Superfund areas and other areas known to have possible environmental contamination to ensure that the condition does not adversely affect the property for which a loan is proposed (see Figure 9.7).

Most environmental site assessments (ESAs) or environmental property assessments (EPRAs) required for real estate transactions are conducted by environmental consultants who are trained to investigate a broad range of environmental issues.

An environmental assessment cannot guarantee that a property is totally free of hazardous substances. An investigation does provide limited legal protection for the innocent purchaser, however, and a reasonable margin of assurance that contamination from hydrocarbons, asbestos, PCBs, or other hazardous substances is unlikely. To guarantee that a property is completely free of contaminants, every building component would have to be examined for asbestos and every cubic foot of soil and groundwater to the earth's core would have to be tested. The science of various environmental conditions and the laws relating to liabilities continue to change as knowledge of and experience with these conditions increase.

Advisory Opinion 9 of USPAP and Guide Note 8 of the Appraisal Institute's Guide Notes to the Standards of Professional Appraisal Practice address the **responsibility of appraisers** in detecting environmental problems. The Property Observation Checklist published by the Appraisal Institute may be used to inspect a property and to record observations about possible environmental factors.

Environmental site assessments (ESAs) and environmental property assessments (EPRAs) are often required for approval of a sale or loan. The extent of an **environmental assessment** may correspond to one of three phases.

environmental property assessment (EPRA): A procedure commonly conducted at commercial and industrial sites to identify potential environmental problems prior to the transfer of the property. EPRAs are performed in phases. A Phase I audit focuses on evidence of potential contamination; a Phase II audit confirms the presence of contamination; and a Phase III audit describes its extent. Also called *environmental survey* or *transactional audit*.

environmental site assessment (ESA): The process by which a person or entity seeks to determine if a particular parcel of real property (including improvements) is subject to recognized environmental conditions. ... An environmental site assessment is both different from and less rigorous than an environmental audit. (American Society for Testing and Materials)

Figure 9.7 Environmental Site Assessments

Many real estate transactions require:

Phase I
- Site visit (interview occupants of the subject and neighboring properties and look for signs of contamination such as stained ground, defoliation, noxious odors, areas of inconsistent surface height or depth, uneven pavement, or the presence of drums or other debris)
- Examination of aerial photographs
- Study of records kept by local, state, and federal environmental agencies
- Review of pertinent regulatory legislation

If a Phase I environmental assessment uncovers evidence of possible contamination or past or present violations of environmental regulations, then:

Phase II
- Invasive sampling of the soil

If contaminants are present, then:

Phase III
- Further invasive sampling of soil to establish the horizontal and vertical extent of soil and groundwater contamination
- Usually a plan for remediation or mitigation is developed, including a timetable and the estimated costs associated with the environmental cleanup.

See Robert V. Colangelo and Ronald D. Miller, *Environmental Site Assessments and Their Impact on Property Value: The Appraiser's Role* (Chicago: Appraisal Institute, 1995), 218–219 and the workbook for the *Environmental Risk and the Real Estate Appraisal Process* seminar (Chicago: Appraisal Institute, 1994), 78–80.

Note: The American Society for Testing and Materials (ASTM) has developed specific standards for such assessments:
- Standard Practice for Environmental Site Assessments: Phase I Environmental Site Assessment Process (Practice 3 1527-93)
- Standard Practice for Environmental Site Assessments: Transaction Screen Process (Practice 1528-93)

Environmentally Impacted Properties

A stigma is an externality that negatively impacts the value of a property or properties in proximity to it. A good way to view stigma in the valuation process is in the application of the cost approach. To calculate the impaired value, one begins with the unimpaired value and deducts the cost to remediate the site and the impact of stigma. The same phenomenon is witnessed in the analysis of a sale of contaminated property. The property sells to a knowledgeable buyer at an impaired price. This price generally consists of two elements:

- First, the buyer's estimate of the of the cost to remediate
- Second, a discount due to uncertainty (stigma)

Totaling the two yields the unimpaired value.

Two sets of risks are associated with environmentally impacted properties. The first set of risks are real or scientifically quantifiable risks, such as the cost to cure or manage the problem. The second set consists of perceived risks (stigma), which vary depending on the following:

- The characteristics of the contamination—i.e., whether it can be concealed, how much it disrupts everyday activities, and what degree of peril is associated with it
- The extent of media exposure
- The nature of the liability (to an individual or entity)

Because an environmental stigma is likely to evoke a reaction from both buyers and lenders, it can result in the effective cessation of mortgage lending for an entire area. Different types of hazardous and toxic materials have different stigmatic effects. Few problems are associated with contained asbestos insulation in buildings, but suspected leakage of a contaminant (i.e., a plume) into the groundwater can stigmatize property greatly even if the contaminant is absent from the ground under the property being appraised.

The appraisal of real property impacted by environmental contamination and any accompanying stigma is an area of ongoing investigation and appraisal scholarship subject to an ever-changing legal environment. Appraisers must be mindful of their liability when performing assignments involving properties subject to environmental contamination and possible stigma, and they must also recognize the special expertise required in such situations. Currently a diverse array of techniques are being used to value contaminated properties, and the evolution of a standardized approach to the challenges presented by such assignments is unlikely.

Further Reading: Bill Mundy, "Stigma and Value," *The Appraisal Journal* (January 1992); William N. Kinnard, Jr., and Elaine M. Worzala, "How North American Appraisers Value Contaminated Property and Associated Stigma," *The Appraisal Journal* (July 1999); Richard Roddewig, "Stigma, Environmental Risk, and Property Value: 10 Critical Inquiries," *The Appraisal Journal* (October 1996); and Richard Roddewig, "Classifying the Level of Risk and Stigma Affecting Contaminated Property," *The Appraisal Journal* (January 1999).

Standard on the Valuation of Properties Affected by Environmental Contamination

Approved July 2001 by International Association of Assessing Officers

1. Scope

This standard provides information and guidance concerning the effect of environmental contamination on the valuation of property for assessment purposes. The standard includes definitions of types of environmental contamination that may affect value, discusses types of impact on value, and lists numerous considerations of which the assessor should be aware. The standard is divided into several sections, including a glossary and a bibliography. Unless otherwise indicated, statutes and regulations referred to in this standard are from the United States.

2. Introduction

Environmental factors are increasingly important in property valuation as the market has become more aware of the potentially detrimental effects of chemical, radiation, noise, and other contaminants on air, water (surface water and groundwater), soil, and overall environment. In certain cases, especially when incomplete information is available on the effects of a contaminant, the market may overreact, and prices may be depressed more than is rational. In other cases, knowledge about a particular contaminant is so new or limited that there is a virtual absence of market data, and effects on value are difficult to ascertain. The property owner (taxpayer) may tend to press for a lower assessment in many of these cases. However, the market often recognizes that contaminated properties can be redeemed and redeveloped into valued assets. In fact, there is a growing national, state, and local effort to revitalize urban brownfields.

To deal with all of these issues, to respond effectively to appeals and value property equitably, it is important for the assessing officer to become knowledgeable about contaminants and their effect on property values. As courts, for example, in California (*Redevelopment Agency of City of Pomona v. Thrifty Oil Co.* [1992]) and Georgia (*Stafford v. Bryden County Board of Education* [1995]), have noted, the general environmental condition of a property requiring remediation is a relevant factor in valuation.

The Standard on the Valuation of Properties Affected by Environmental Contamination, adopted by the Executive Board of the International Association of Assessing Officers (IAAO), represents the IAAO's position on the issues addressed therein. Copyright 2001 International Association of Assessing Officers, 130 East Randolph, Suite 850, Chicago, IL 60601; www.iaao.org.

To understand the effect of environmental contaminants on property value, the assessor must have some background knowledge on this subject. In addition to merely recognizing contaminating substances, the assessor must understand the potential for changes in lists of substances or conditions currently thought to produce contamination. The current state of detection, monitoring, and cleanup technology must be recognized. Public awareness is a somewhat intangible factor that nevertheless may affect value. Finally, the state of current and proposed federal, state, or local regulations and court decisions can greatly affect the marketability and value of property. At least twenty-four states enacted voluntary cleanup legislation between 1988 and 1995, bringing the current total to more than thirty.

2.1 Changes in Lists and Definitions of Hazardous Substances or Other Contaminants

Lists and characteristics of substances that are hazardous, as well as amounts of substances considered harmful, change frequently as new information becomes available. Information on specific hazardous waste is often available from state or local environmental agencies. The International Association of Assessing Officers (IAAO) maintains a searchable online bibliography that includes materials relating to pollution and property value. See also the bibliography at the end of this standard.

The assessor should also pay close attention to court cases on environmental issues, many of which involve federal courts and have the potential to affect value in new areas as new contaminants are implicated. A list of many pertinent federal regulatory acts and current court cases is found in appendices A and B, respectively. Additional court cases are synopsized in the *Assessment Journal,* and many are on file in the IAAO library.

2.2 Technology and Public and Private Sector Money

Both currently available and new technologies have the potential to influence the effect of contaminants on value positively or negatively. Technology that permits safe, efficient, and inexpensive cleanup of contaminants tends to minimize any decrease in property value. Often, cleanup costs are prohibitively expensive, given current technology, but new developments may dramatically improve cleanup operations. However, new technology may also make it possible to detect quantities or types of contamination that were previously undetectable. In addition, as more contaminants are identified, new, more restrictive regulations may be written. Thus, a "clean" property may suddenly have a major problem that affects value. The assessor should keep abreast of regulations and technological advances.

Because costs may change with technological advances, the assessor should follow developments and may wish to obtain estimates of cleanup costs independent from those provided by the property owner. This step is no different from providing independent appraisals to defend values on appeal. In most circumstances, however, cost information provided by the taxpayer can be corroborated through regulatory agencies; several courts require further independent estimates. Enormous sums, well in excess of several billion, are now available for remediation and brownfield revitalization efforts. Public/private sector commitments may eliminate sites that had been viewed as environmentally lost properties. As one Tennessee court has observed, the effect certain conditions have in the mind of the buying public may be critical (*State of Tennessee v. Brandon* [1994]).

Addenda: *Standard on Valuation*

2.3 Public Awareness and Perception

The public can be aware of certain contaminants but uninformed about others. Residential buyers would typically give some consideration to asbestos in a house; they would also probably be concerned if the house were located near a nuclear power plant. They may not, however, be particularly aware of radon gas, especially if they are moving from an area where this substance is rare. They may be aware of, but not concerned with, the potential effects of electromagnetic radiation from proximity to overhead power distribution lines because the effect of this contaminant is currently under debate in the scientific community. The potential exists, however, that electromagnetic radiation or some other, yet unknown, substance will be found harmful, and values of various properties could be affected suddenly.

Public overreaction may create a gap between cost to cure and decline in value. Even though it may cost $10,000 to cure a particular problem, the potential sale price may decline initially by $20,000. The assessor might view this as a form of functional or economic obsolescence, or perhaps as a negative locational influence. However, the initial overreaction may not properly reflect value and usually does not reflect value after resolution of environmental problems. The assessor, therefore, needs to compute the present value of residual future value after cleanup and must endeavor to explain the valuation process and concepts to the taxpayer (see section 8.2 and the definition of "residual value" in the glossary).

2.4 Government Regulations

Federal, state and provincial, and local agencies regulate hazardous substances and other contaminants and respond to violations. The principal organization in the United States is the Environmental Protection Agency (EPA), which administers the Comprehensive Environmental Response, Compensation, and Liability Act of 1980 (CERCLA), as amended by the Superfund Amendment and Reauthorization Act of 1986 (SARA). Many state or local agencies are also involved. Often, local requirements are more stringent than federal requirements. The assessor should maintain periodic contact with these various agencies to stay current with all regulations and changes.

United States federal environmental regulatory acts are subject to congressional review and amendment. Changes that are promulgated through this process may affect value, and the assessor should remain aware of such changes.

In Canada, the Canadian Environmental Protection Act, the Fisheries Act, and the Waste Management Act are pertinent federal statutes. Provinces may enact additional legislation. Appraisers are subject to a "positive duty to investigate" responsibility.

Properties may be located within designated contaminated areas, known as "Superfund" sites. Values of such properties may be affected differently from values of equally contaminated properties outside a designated site. Within Superfund sites, there generally is greater certainty about the extent of contamination. Depending on severity and projected cleanup timetable and costs, the effect on value may be positive or negative. However, as one New Jersey decision notes, such costs are site specific and should not be presumed by considering other, allegedly comparable properties (*Badische Corp. v. Town of Kearny* [1996]). Accurate mapping of areas of contamination is vital to understanding potential effects on value (see section 5.2).

The present and anticipated status of environmental discharge permits held by a taxpayer may also affect property value. A discharge permit has value to a company and may offset the negative effects of environmental considerations, if permit requirements can be easily met. A property with a discharge permit is usually more valuable than a similar property without such a permit because the permit may be necessary for the company to be able to operate as expected.

Rights to pollute are similar to permits and have value. For example, the Clean Air Act provides "tradable allowances," which are exchangeable between facilities and permit one property to raise pollutant discharges if another reduces its pollutants. Property with such rights will be more resistant to decline in market value caused by environmental contamination, provided such contamination is related to the specific rights. Rights to pollute constitute salable, although intangible, assets that may contribute to the value of property (see section 7.4 and "offsets" in the glossary).

It is important to realize that EPA regulations tend to focus on significant problems. Virtually any property could be considered contaminated given sufficient investigation. It is necessary to differentiate between contamination problems already discounted by the market and those from extraordinary influences that result in additional loss of value.

Some naturally occurring contaminants may be present in an area. Presence of contaminants at their natural "baseline" levels in generally not sufficient for the EPA to require cleanup. However, the presence of such contaminants may affect value; if so, the effect should be considered as due to locational, not environmental, influences.

3. Definitions

3.1 Contamination

In assessment usage, contamination is any recognized physical or nonphysical environmental influence that must be considered to determine value. Contamination may take various forms including physical, aesthetic, and perceptual. Contamination is recognized through federal, state, or local agencies that regulate environmental contamination. Contaminants not recognized by the various regulatory agencies (such as light pollution) may produce locational influences on value.

3.1.1 Physical Contaminants

Physical contaminants are substances present in, on, or near a subject property in measurable quantities and identified as having a harmful environmental impact (see section 3.2). Some substances are deemed hazardous because they are ignitable, corrosive, toxic, or reactive.

Substances not accepted by the regulatory community as harmful should not be considered physical contaminants. The market may still respond to these substances, however, and value may change. However, because the change would result from only a perception, the contaminant would not be defined as physical.

3.1.2 Nonphysical Contaminants

Contaminants, such as intrusive light, that have no tangible, physical substance are considered nonphysical. These take many forms and must be considered as "real" as physical contaminants because they may affect property value. For example, proximity to noise sources often diminishes utility and therefore property value. Another example is electromagnetic radiation originating from nearby power lines or radio wave transmission devices.

Also included would be prevailing market perceptions of substances or situations. For example, toxic substances may have been completely cleansed from a property. However, the stigma attached to this property may not immediately disappear, and value may be affected by this non-physical condition. The assessor should watch for additional (post-cleanup) efforts (such as new wells) by property owners or public agencies because these often lessen the stigma and result in a more rapid recovery of value.

3.2 List of Contaminants

The substances listed in Table 1 or associated perceptual issues may affect value and should be considered in the valuation process. Many of these are specific to certain types of property and would not need to be looked for in every case. Each contaminant must be considered in its potential for physical, nonphysical, or perceptual effect. Although the list of contaminants shown in Table 1 is not comprehensive, examples are given of suspect industries and situations in addition to selected physical substances.

3.3 Examples of Special Situations

Some environmental contamination situations that have become particularly important or widespread are discussed in greater detail in this section. In evaluating the effect of these conditions on market value, consideration should be given to public perception and fear, which may affect values in the marketplace. However, appraisers should not make assumptions about market effects without market data. Numerous studies have been done on the market effects of asbestos, contamination, electromagnetic towers, radiation, landfills, noise, public fear, traffic, and other environmental factors. Appraisers should be aware of these studies.

3.3.1 Underground Storage Tanks (USTs)

These are tanks typically used for storage of liquids, usually petroleum products. Although such tanks are termed "underground," the Resource Conservation and Recovery Act (RCRA) states that a tank will meet this

TABLE 1

Acid rain	Intrusive light
Air contaminants	Lead paint
Airborne substances, indoors	Mining byproducts
Airport noise	Nitrates
Asbestos	Noise—airport, road traffic
Carbon black	Noxious odors
Chlorine and related compounds	Nuclear material and industry
Diminished quality of drinking water	Oil refinery
Dioxin	Organic and inorganic compounds
Dry-cleaning fluids and solvents	PCBs
Empty containers that previously stored hazardous materials	Pesticides, herbicides, and other agricultural chemicals
Fertilizer	Pipelines
Floodwater	Power lines and microwave sources
Fluorine and related compounds	Radon
Formaldehyde	Suspect industries
Heavy metals, including lead and mercury	Underground storage tanks
Industrial byproducts	

classification if more than 10 percent of the volume of the tank and associated piping is underground. Contamination may occur from tank leaks or from spills during the filling of the tank. Depending on substances involved as well as soil and bedrock characteristics, contamination may spread to adjoining areas. Wells and other water resources may be contaminated. Secondary air pollution may result from fumes released by evaporation of leaking substances. Additional toxic substances may result from chemical reactions between leaking substances or between these substances and the environment contacted. In this situation, cleanup may be more difficult and costly.

Maps are usually available to show areas where groundwater has been contaminated by the spread of substances leaking from USTs (see sections 5.2 and 10). Petroleum products are not regulated under "Superfund" authority; rather, liability is governed by separate, special statutes.

3.3.1.1 Change in Commercial Industrial Property Value

Property value may change for several reasons as a result of contamination from leaks from USTs. Direct loss of income may occur, for example, if oil is stored to be used or sold by a business as part of its operation. Property components may need to be dug up and replaced, and contaminated soil removed. Property owners may be liable for fines or cleanup of adjacent property and affected groundwater and other water resources. Even after cleanup is completed, owners may be liable for additional cleanup of contamination not discovered initially. Often costs exceed initial estimates and affect marketability of property and income streams for a long time.

In some areas, governmental agencies have established insurance funds to protect existing properties with USTs from future liability. When these programs are available, certification of current tank conditions will be provided to the owner. Such certification, as well as availability of this type of insurance, may increase the value of properties with these tanks. Large insurance deductibles may offset this gain.

3.3.1.2 Effect on Residential Property Value

The EPA has not enforced environmental regulations with respect to residential property. For this reason there has been little direct effect on residential property value from USTs (or other environmental contamination problems). However, residential property value may be affected because of proximity to commercial or industrial properties. There is also a potential for significant future impact, which would occur if regulations were extended to include residential property. The assessor should be aware of developments in this area.

3.3.2 Asbestos and Other Insulating Materials

Insulating material containing asbestos or urea-formaldehyde creates potential contamination problems that often affect value. Although asbestos has not been used for many years, older structures often contain the material. This substance is dangerous when deterioration allows the asbestos to enter the living areas of a structure. It is particularly dangerous when it is in "friable" condition. It is far less of a threat when it has been encapsulated.

Urea-formaldehyde foam insulation (UFFI) has not been in general use for several years, so the formaldehyde level is typically below hazardous thresholds, and the insulation does not have to be removed. Energy-efficient homes may be suspect, however, even if recently constructed. Formaldehyde byproducts can also enter indoor air from glues used in wood particle and carpeting products. Concentrations are usually minimal, and public response is usually relatively mild, indicating little effect on value.

3.3.3 Lead Paint and Products

Lead is a heavy metal that is found in paint, especially in older structures, and in pipes and some solder used to join lead or copper pipes. Dust or chips of lead paint may contaminate living areas. Where lead is in contact with drinking water, contamination will result. Lead paint usually requires a replacement with less toxic paint; piping may also need replacement with polyvinyl chloride (PVC) or copper with non-lead solder connections.

Because public awareness of lead contamination is high, property value is affected by cleanup costs and the stigma associated with lead. There is probably less of a stigma associated with lead than with other, more exotic forms of contamination.

3.3.4 Radon

Radon is a naturally occurring radioactive gas released during decay of radioactive elements generally found in granitic rock. In recent years, public awareness of this substance and associated risks has grown. Because the substance is denser than air, it may accumulate in basements and lower portions of structures. Often, ventilation or air exchange systems can be constructed to remove the gas and cure the problem. Energy-efficient structures, especially underground homes, are particularly susceptible because underground construction often restricts exchange of indoor and outdoor air. In some localities, favorable radon test results may increase market value.

Radon is common in certain, typically mountainous, areas of the United States and uncommon in most other areas. If detected in trivial concentrations, foundations or crawl space sealants or improved ventilation will usually eliminate the problem, adding only minor costs. The effects of stigma are not usually present. At least twenty-one states require disclosure of radon to prospective purchasers.

3.3.5 Nuclear Facilities

Nuclear facilities use, store, or dispose of radioactive material. These facilities include power plants, private and governmental research sites, hospitals, and disposal sites, as well as equipment used to transport radioactive material. Proximity of property to nuclear power plants and other nuclear facilities is likely to produce negative value effects. Aside from the obvious risks of nuclear accidents, additional risks are associated with decommissioning, waste disposal, and contaminated areas. To some extent, the problems are no different from those associated with proximity to conventional heavy industry. However, because radioactive waste often remains toxic for a very long time and tends to be more difficult to dispose of, a greater stigma may result. Finally, current radioactivity research indicates more risk from less exposure than was previously believed. Nuclear facilities with little current effect on value may someday be considered heavily contaminated, and values may decline.

Valuing Contaminated Properties

Although proximity to a nuclear power plant may reduce the value of adjoining properties through the stigma alone, this concern does not reduce the value of the plant itself. Most regulatory commissions require public utilities to provide buffer zones around nuclear power plants, If the cost of the buffer zone property is included in the rate base, the capitalized earning indicator reflects the value of the buffer zone. No deduction or discount should be made in the cost approach because of the buffer zone requirement. If there is actual contamination of the buffer zone, this would affect land values inside the zone. Also, because the total amount of land is fixed, less land will be available outside the zones for other purposes, which may raise land costs elsewhere.

Regulatory bodies generally require public utilities to make annual payments into dedicated nuclear plant decommissioning trust funds. When these payments are deducted as expenses, the capitalized earnings indicator reflects the impact of the present value of the decommissioning costs on the unitary value (when the plant is part of the unit and a unit value is estimated). No further adjustments are necessary. Whatever influence the stigma may have on plant value is reflected in the unitary value of the operating utility.

Groundwater or surface water dispersal from seepage of radioactive material is common and may affect value far from the original contamination site.

Regardless of potential or actual contamination, an operating nuclear power plant represents a valuable property, and future cleanup costs are mandated and should be reflected in the income stream used to determine value.

Enterprises not normally associated with the nuclear industry may use radioactive material in significant quantities. As awareness of this use increases, values may be affected. For example, the most common user of radioactive (and other toxic) material close to residential areas is often a hospital. Proximity may affect value through the stigma or real contamination.

3.3.6 Air Pollution

Air becomes polluted when contaminants are released into the atmosphere or when nontoxic substances react with other substances or light to produce contaminants. The degree to which values are affected by air pollution depends on the economic cost to escape the pollution. For example, air pollution may occur equally throughout a major center. Because of distance to alternative work sites or other costs of doing business, it may be noncompetitive or undesirable to locate in less polluted locations. In this case, the effect of air pollution will be constant and already accounted for in the market. No additional adjustment will be necessary, unless regulatory agencies mandate reduction of pollution. Added expenses will then affect the income stream and reduce market value in the short run. These same expenses may, however, improve industry competitiveness in the long run or have no effect if competition is among similar industries all having to deal with the same level of pollution and with the same regulations.

3.3.7 Noise Pollution

Noise pollution includes unwanted sound generated by airports, road traffic, and heavy industry. Effects should be considered similar to other

Addenda: *Standard on Valuation*

locational and neighborhood desirability influences and may be incurable economic obsolescence. However, data on the market effects are essential before any conclusions can be drawn.

3.3.8 Toxic Substances in the Home

Many toxic substance are used in the home, including insecticides, mothballs, motor oils, antifreeze, wood preservatives, rust removers, polishes, batteries, deodorizers, degreasers, weed killer, drain cleaners, disinfectants, pool chemicals, paints, hobby products, bleaches, nail polish remover, and car wax. In addition, residential construction may involve lead and other toxic substances, or products that break down and release such substances. Particleboard, carpet glue, and certain insulation may release formaldehyde, for instance.

Fortunately, many of these toxic substances are not structural, but transient, being removed from property when transfer of ownership occurs. However, residuals may be left behind along with toxic substances related to construction materials. Ultimately, the market will determine how much these factors influence value, the presumption being that additional functional or economic obsolescence may be recognized if buyers pay less for properties with contamination. Aside from construction-related materials and residual contamination, however, the presence of transient materials should be ignored. These could be viewed as management factors, with "good" home managers keeping fewer toxic materials. Assuming typical management, it would be unnecessary to investigate the owner's practices in determining value.

3.3.9 Surface Water and Groundwater Quality Requirements

Most property uses require availability of adequate water supplies. This is true for optimum use of residential property, where tests showing contamination may become locational factors and may influence value. Water quality is also important in agricultural uses, where crops or livestock cannot otherwise be maintained, and the income-producing capability of the land can be affected (Food Security Act of 1985).

Water quality can be affected by factors as diverse as industrial point source contamination, faraway groundwater contamination, excessive rainfall resulting in flooding or siltation, runoff from land to which agricultural chemicals and fertilizers have been applied, and infiltration of salt water in coastal areas. The effect on present and future productivity of the land must be determined. If problems can be cured, income-producing capacity may be restored, and the present value of this future worth can be computed. Water quality problems are similar to other problems related to agricultural land, such as slope, water availability, and erosion. These problems may alter the income-producing capability of the land, thus changing its value. Environmental contamination problems must be differentiated from management problems in determining value.

One of the problems associated with groundwater contamination relates to the liability of commercial property located above spreading groundwater contamination. Provided the property in question did not contribute to the contamination, current EPA rules do not hold this property liable for cleanup costs. Lender may still be reluctant, however, to provide financing, and unfavorable financing arrangements may affect value. In addition, there is some conflict between federal statutes and EPA rules, and assessors should be alert for new developments in this volatile area. Local regulations or statutes may also lead to liability. Residential property is less subject to liability, but financing considerations and stigma may still affect value.

If groundwater contamination does not directly influence the water supply of the subject property, it is not appropriate to adjust value to reflect complete cleanup. The utility of the property should be the primary concern and will rarely be affected if adequate clean water can be assured.

3.3.10 Waste Disposal Facilities and Practices

Facilities for waste disposal include incinerators, landfills, and associated transfer sites. Although intended to remediate pollution, these facilities are focal points for pollution and may become sites from which air or groundwater contamination can spread. The assessor may be required to value the disposal facility itself or any surrounding property. In either case, additional monitoring costs and effects of the stigma may affect value. The disposal of medical waste and other highly publicized substances in such facilities can add to the stigma. However, studies have shown that, in many cases, the value of property near landfills is unaffected. Market trends must be observed to determine if values are actually affected.

Waste disposal practices can contribute to the degree of value loss. For example, establishments that have used dry-cleaning solvents and other chemicals are often suspect as potential sources of contamination because of former improper disposal practices. Although these practices may not have violated any laws or regulations in force at the time of disposal, hazardous chemicals may have entered the surrounding environment through soil contamination, leading to groundwater contamination. Present levels of contamination may violate current environmental statutes. Because sites may have been abandoned or the contaminating business may no longer exist on the original site, accurate historical maps (Sanborn maps used for fire insurance purposes are often available) and chain of ownership information should be referenced in determining areas of possible contamination. Values of nearby properties may be affected; adverse financing effects are possible.

3.3.11 Illegal Drug Manufacture—Effect on Property Value

Illegal drugs are often manufactured in small, mobile units, often in remote areas. Typically, little effort is made to dispose of toxic materials properly, which often are byproducts of illegal drug manufacture. These materials may contaminate adjacent properties or be disposed of indiscriminately and contaminate property never involved in the production of the drugs.

Although the chemicals used in illegal drug manufacture may not be more toxic than those produced by many legitimate industries, discovery is made more difficult by the impracticality of tracking down anyone with specific knowledge about the contamination of a given site. Even if the manufacturers could be found and were cooperative, they would have had no incentive to keep track of or determine the exact nature of byproducts, so little precise information is likely to be forthcoming.

Cleanup will therefore be more costly and less successful. Because of added uncertainty, prospective buyers will be more reluctant, and the value of the property may suffer—possibly out of proportion to the actual cost of cleanup.

Also, the remote nature of many manufacturing sites may make access difficult, further reducing the likelihood of adequate cleanup. Time lag between contamination and discovery is likely to be significant, leading to increased chances for dispersal of contaminants from the original location and even less successful cleanup.

3.4 Testing

The assessor should not rely solely on statements of the property owner estimating the loss in value due to environmental contamination problems. Results of independent (private or governmental) testing and governmental certification of a site as contaminated should be reported as proof of contamination. To help determine the actual effect on value, files of test results should be maintained so that comparable levels of contamination can be treated comparably. Test reports should include information on the extent of the problem regarding adjacent property, water contamination, and so on. Soil characteristics should also be included. The burden of providing test results and proving contamination is on the taxpayer attempting to demonstrate the effect on value.

4. Impact on Value—General Areas of Impact

The basic provisions of regulations requiring cleanup of contaminated properties assign the costs to responsible parties. Where this cannot be done, the chain of title is followed to establish liability. CERCLA, as amended by SARA, allows certain exceptions. For example, the current owner would not be held liable, provided that before purchasing the property this owner made all appropriate inquiries without discovering existing contamination.

Contamination can range from mild, requiring minimal cleanup costs and having little, if any, effect on value, to severe, with virtually no use of the property possible for the present or the foreseeable future and with prohibitive costs to correct the problem. The degree to which contamination affects the present and future utility of the property must be established.

When regulations require the same improvement to be made by all in an industry, the effect is uniform, and costs become part of the typical expenses of the business. Often, extra costs for pollution are part of start-up or development costs associated with a new facility and, in this case, will not reduce property value. In any other situation requiring plant improvements, costs may be amortized over expected life and computed in terms of present worth; in this way, high costs incurred in the year of installation will not be weighted improperly. These principles would apply, for instance, if additional air pollution control equipment were required to meet new standards.

Many states offer partial or full property tax exemptions (and other cost-related tax credits or state-funded financing) to industry for equipment and improvements used to control pollution. At least two states (Idaho and New Jersey) provide an incentive for remediation by allowing remediated land to retain part of any lower value it was assigned to reflect contamination. Exemptions of this type reduce the effective costs of dealing with contamination and reduce the impact of cleanup on both the income stream and property value. Sixteen states not only have voluntary cleanup programs but also provide financial assistance and tax credits to attract business development. Eleven states have negotiated Superfund agreements with the EPA that permit site remediation plans, issue no further action letters, and the like. Several states have adopted a variety of flexible approaches to revitalizing blighted properties.

4.1 Concepts of Value

Two concepts of value that must be considered in reference to environmentally distressed property are the unencumbered value and the value in use of the property.

The unencumbered value is the value that the property would have if no adjustment were made for any environmental encumbrance. This value can be obtained using standard appraisal methods. There is a tendency to discount this value based on costs related to remediating or isolating environmental contamination. Fully deducting the costs may overstate the decline in value because the value in use concept would then be ignored. Value in use suggests that a property which is still in use, or which can be used in the near future, has a value to the owner. This would be true even if costs to cure the environmental problems exceed the nominal, unencumbered value. The value in use will most nearly reflect the market value of the property (see discussion of costs versus value in section 4.2).

4.2 Costs

The first cost associated with environmental contamination is the cost of discovering the presence or extent of any problem. To enable the new owner to use the "innocent landowner" defense (see section 4.4.4), and as a preliminary step in establishing cleanup costs, an environmental assessment report must be obtained before purchase.

The cost to cure a particular problem must be determined, but may overstate or understate the effect on value. For example, property may be able to maintain an income stream while costs are incurred, and costs may be amortized over a longer period. This will increase debt, but not affect present worth on a dollar-for-dollar basis. Costs may often be amortized over expected improvement life, and the present worth of the costs computed. Costs are often not fully recognized when contamination is discovered. Difficulty in estimating costs is greater in certain types of environmental problems, groundwater contamination being more difficult than soil contamination. If initial estimates are low and additional or ongoing expenses are involved, the effect on value may be greater. Alternatively, costs may result in capital improvement; a more efficient, less polluting system may be installed, and residual property value may increase. The potential for either decreasing or increasing value must be recognized (see "residual value" in glossary).

The cost to cure a contamination problem includes all costs necessitated by and associated with the cleanup. These can include costs for physical cleanup, monitoring, legal fees, and ongoing costs. Complete cleanup may be impossible; costs to control contamination may be substituted for

Addenda: *Standard on Valuation*

costs to cure the problem. Many states (including Illinois and Minnesota) permit remediation to a certain defined level of "clean" that depends upon the new use intended for the property.

Whenever possible, costs should be determined from the market. It is often possible to obtain comparable costs for cleanup of similar situations. Files of cleanup cost information should be developed and maintained. Often, information outside the particular jurisdiction or region may be necessary. In determining costs, it is important to recognize that higher costs will be incurred if the EPA is involved because its overhead must be absorbed by those liable for the cleanup. This factor can alter the baseline costs determined from comparable cleanup situations.

4.2.1 Cost of Physical Cleanup

Actual costs must be ascertained. Estimates provided by a property owner may be overstated. For example, regulatory agencies may grant permission to use less expensive alternatives, such as isolation rather than cleanup. Deferrals may be granted, and these allow more time for cleanup and reduce current costs, although the present value of the property may also be reduced.

4.2.2 Continued Costs of Monitoring

The costs of testing and monitoring may be added to the expenses; thus the costs are subtracted from the income of property subject to cleanup. These costs may be substantial and should be established or predicted from evidence provided by the property owner and regulatory authority.

4.2.3 Legal Costs

The contaminated property may incur legal costs in dealings with regulatory agencies and other potentially responsible parties. In addition, lawsuits may be filed by other affected property owners or by third parties seeking to share their own liability.

Ordinarily legal costs can be viewed as part of management and not as an influence on property value. Legal costs associated with contamination may be considered part of the cost to cure the problem. However, to be considered, these costs must exceed costs of customary legal advice. The potential for litigation or pending litigation may affect marketability and value by deterring prospective buyers.

4.2.4 Ongoing Costs

Final costs are often unknown before completion of cleanup. These costs often exceed original estimates, especially when future, more stringent regulations are anticipated. In addition, perceived or actual risks remaining after completion of cleanup may result in higher insurance costs and reduced ability to use the property as security for loans. Certain types of costs may be amortized over a period corresponding to anticipated improvement life or the time to implement the cure.

4.2.5 Indirect Costs

These can include anything that affects the property's income-producing ability during or after the cleanup. For example, tenants may not be able to live in a rental unit during lead paint removal. Another income restriction would occur if one portion of an industrial plant could not be used because of toxic contamination, and an intermediate product manufactured in that area could no longer be created on site. Additional expenses could be incurred, and the plant's earning could suffer accordingly. Although this impact would be somewhat transient, it should be included in the same manner as other costs (see sections 4.2 and 7.4).

As the field of environmental law matures, cleanup costs will become easier to predict. Private insurance companies may become more willing to provide coverage. Insurance costs, which appear prohibitive today, may become more reasonable, and the cleanup could have less effect on value.

4.3 Financing

Financing is known to affect property value. The impact is particularly significant when favorable or unfavorable financing is obtained because the market has already accepted the influence of typical financing costs.

In the case of environmentally contaminated properties, two types of financing effects need to be considered: the ability of a prospective buyer to finance the purchase of the property and the terms for financing the actual costs to cure contamination problems. If prospective buyers cannot obtain typical financing due to the problem, the cash equivalency value of the property will be diminished. If terms for financing the costs to cure problems are poor, additional liability or unfavorable debt will reduce buyer income anticipation and thereby reduce market value (see section 5.4). (Additional information on financing adjustments is found in IAAO 1990 and Gloudemans 1999). Many lenders, particularly in Region 5 EPA (which includes Illinois, Indiana, Michigan, Minnesota, and Wisconsin) are developing innovative programs to help finance blighted land revitalization. However, lender approaches may differ from region to region.

4.4 Liability

Liability for costs associated with environmental contamination often lies with property owners. Liability may affect the use of the property and its future sale and may contribute to any stigma (see section 4.5). The EPA will assume liability only in the event that no other potentially responsible party can be discovered; even then the EPA will usually hold the property owner liable for some portion of the cleanup cost (unless the owner qualifies under the "innocent landowner" defense).

Alaska, Massachusetts, and Michigan provide for joint and several liability. However, Arkansas, California, Illinois, Maryland, and Ohio have recently adopted proportionate liability. Colorado, Indiana, Michigan, Minnesota, and Ohio have limited liability for nonresponsible owners and prospective buyers. Illinois, Indiana, Minnesota, and Ohio have extended that protection to commercial lenders. Thus, the effect of liability on value may be more or less pronounced, depending on state actions.

4.4.1 Use of Property

The highest and best use of property that has suffered contamination may be altered. Contamination of farmland, for example, may make it impossible to grow edible crops. Industrial contamination may make production as originally established impossible. When determining the highest and best use of the property, it is important to recognize that current use may need to be modified or abandoned. However, seldom is property so contaminated that the highest and best use indicates no value. Very rarely, where contamination is extreme, but proper soil conditions exist and regulatory permits can be obtained, the property may still be used as a toxic waste disposal site. Even this represents use and value. This particular use is limited, however, because the EPA is authorized to require corrective action to remove or remediate contaminants that have leached into soil or groundwater.

The use of property is further affected by environmental permits, which, in effect, grant property the "right to pollute." This right has value as an asset and can sometimes be traded between facilities. These rights can increase property value and are further described in the Clean Air Act and in many state and local laws.

4.4.2 Selling Contaminated Property

Buyer reluctance often focuses as much on the potential for additional undisclosed problems as on contamination already known and discounted. To facilitate a sale, the seller may be required to include indemnity as a contingency for future liability. This provision often reestablishes a market—and a market value—where none seemingly existed. However, in cases of severe contamination, with ongoing cleanup anticipated, the seller may not be able to obtain a bond or provide indemnification for the full amount of the anticipated costs. In these cases, a sale may not be possible or the sale price may have to be reduced, although the property may retain a value in use (see section 4.1. and 7.4). As the Washington Board of Tax Appeals held in *Salmon Bay Terminals v. Noble* (1996), the sale of a contaminated property should be given weight because it indicates the risks associated with that property.

4.4.3 Who May Be Liable?

Liability for cleanup of contamination nominally rests with current and past owners of the property, as well as the generators or transporters of hazardous substances, or the party responsible for the contamination, typically the current user. However, if insolvency occurs, liability can be transferred to the entities listed below:

- Current owner or operator
- Previous owners or operators at the time of contamination
- Foreclosing entity or a secured creditor
- Lessors or lessees
- Trustees
- Corporate officers/stockholders
- Parent corporations

The "Superfund" becomes available as a source of cleanup funds only if no other responsible party can be found or where immediate cleanup action must be taken by the EPA, as in an emergency situation. In this case, the EPA can seek to recover costs from the above parties.

EPA regulations exempt lending institutions and other creditors from liability in most foreclosures, provided that these lenders were not directly involved in the management of the contaminated property and do not actively manage the property or contribute to the contamination once they take ownership. Under these regulations, governmental jurisdictions that take involuntary ownership of property as a result of unpaid taxes are exempt from direct cleanup cost liability. However, these jurisdictions may still be named in third-party lawsuits and may be liable for cleanup of additional contamination occurring after acquisition of the property.

The courts are somewhat divided on the liability issue. One recent court decision found that, in most cases, parent companies may not be held responsible for their subsidiaries' hazardous waste cleanup liabilities (*Joslyn Manufacturing Co. v. T.L. James & Co.* [1990]). Other decisions, including *State of Idaho v. Bunker Hill Co. and Gulf Resources* (1986), have held that parent companies are liable for a subsidiary's actions.

4.4.4 Innocent Landowner

Under CERCLA (see glossary), section 107(b)(3) and 101(35)(B), it is established that current owners may be considered "innocent" and not responsible or liable for contamination under certain circumstances. Such "innocence" would be established if, after making all appropriate inquiries into the condition of the property (exercising due diligence), the current owner had no reason to know of the existence of contamination prior to purchase of the property and had not contributed to the contamination. Presumably, regulatory agencies would incur curative costs (this is the purpose of the "Superfund") unless other responsible parties can be found. Value may still be affected because marketability could be reduced until the problem is corrected.

This issue is far from certain, although the assessor should be aware that CERCLA liability has been upheld by several courts (for example, *United States v. Olin Corp.* [1997], *Continental Tile Co. v. Peoples Gas Light and Coke Co.* [1997], and *Raytheron Co. v. McGraw Edison Co.* [1997]) to apply retroactively to hazardous disposals occurring before its enactment. To the contrary, several courts have insulated current owners from liability for mere passive migration of contaminants (for example, *ABB Industrial Systems, Inc. v. Prime Tech, Inc.* [1997], *United States v. CMDG Realty* [1997], *Joslyn Manufacturing Co. v. T.L. James & Co.* [1990], and *United States v. Cordova Chemical Co.* [1997]).

4.4.5 Indemnification Agreements

In an indemnification agreement, the seller agrees to retain responsibility for current and future costs related to environmental contamination. This is usually done in the form of a bond or contractual agreement that would provide for contamination-related costs. If agreements of this type become typical in an area or for a particular class of property, their effect will automatically be capitalized into the market value of the property, and further adjustment will be necessary only if terms vary from typical (similar to financing adjustments—see section 4.3).

4.5 Stigma

Stigma is an intangible factor, which may not be measurable in terms of cost to cure, but may affect market value, at least as determined through the sales comparison (market) approach. It may be seen as a blight or perceived blemish or stain on a property resulting from real or perceived risk associated with the property. Where contamination problems are not obvious, the stigma is likely to be overstated, and value effects may be minimal.

4.5.1 Reduced Market Value

A stigma may make property less desirable, even though complete cleanup has been accomplished. This creates a situation similar to obsolescence because, if the market will pay less for a once contaminated, but now restored property, the value of the property has been diminished. Effects of this nature may be transitory, declining over time or perhaps after additional restorative efforts are demonstrated. For example, even though the water from a previously contaminated well now meets all environmental standards and passes all tests, property value may be reduced until the seller builds a new well in a different location or establishes an independent, alternative water supply.

Stigma can also affect property neighboring previously contaminated areas, especially if regulatory agencies declare the neighboring property to be in a "border zone." The stigma in these cases may, however, be overstated because value is often not demonstrably affected despite the presence of nearby contaminated sites.

Any adverse effect of stigma must be supported by the marketplace. Where sales data, expert testimony, appraisal analysis, and case studies have been accepted into evidence, stigma-related reductions were found appropriate by courts in Michigan (*Sweepster Inc. v. Secco Township* [1997]), Minnesota (*Alomor Corp. v. County of Hennepin* [1997]), and New Jersey (*Custom Distribution Services Inc. v. City of Perth Amboy* [1997]).

4.5.2 Stigma versus Cost to Cure

Because of the intangible nature of the stigma attached to a contamination problem, the effect on value may be out of proportion to the cost to cure the problem. If the property owner makes no attempt to overcome the stigma, however, and thereby accepts a lower price for the property, this price may not accurately reflect market value. Similar problems, in comparison with curative costs, should be reviewed in determining effect on value. Appraised values should be adjusted to reflect typical costs of overcoming the stigma. However, in some markets, time alone may reduce or eliminate the stigma. If this appears to be the case, the assessor may wish to treat stigma as a type of time adjustment and ignore additional costs incurred.

5. Specific Factors Influencing Value

Specific conditions or characteristics relating to contamination must be established for each property. These factors and their impact on value are often quite different from property to property. Courts in Florida (*Finklestein v. Dept. of Transportation* [1995]), Georgia (*Hammond v. City of Warner Robbins* [1997]), Illinois (*Techalloy Co., Inc. v. Property Tax Appeal Board* [1997]), Iowa (*Bockeloo v. Board of Review of City of Clinton* [1995]), Massachusetts (*Reliable Electric Finishing Co. v. Board of Assessors* [1991]), and Ohio (*Vopelgesang v. CECOS International, Inc.* [1993]) have all held that the mere allegation of unmarketability is not enough. Loss or diminution of value must be proven by market data.

5.1 Extent and Nature of Contamination

The property owner must provide clear documentation for the nature and extent of environmental contamination. Accurate and detailed maps must be included as part of this documentation. Without information, property must be valued as if uncontaminated. Some contamination, such as air pollution, may be universal throughout a jurisdiction. In all other cases, contamination should be viewed as a special circumstance, particular to a property. The contaminated property must be compared to typical, unencumbered property, and differences established. To be granted special consideration affecting value, the owner must substantiate the contamination through an independent party (typically, an engineering firm testing for contaminants or a regulatory agency). Evidence is the key. Where it is particularly strong, it has been possible (albeit rare) under extraordinary circumstances in Pennsylvania (*Monroe County Board of Assessors v. Miller* [1990]), Michigan (*Comercia Bank Detroit v. Metamora Township* [1987]), and Minnesota (*Westling v. County of Mille Lacs* [1998]) even to find that a property has a zero or nominal value.

5.2 Type and Location of Property

Location of property can make a significant difference in the amount of utility lost due to environmental contamination. For example, the amount of contamination that may be tolerated in an industrial plant located fifty miles from the nearest population center may be considerably greater than contamination from a source within an urban center or in a largely residential suburban area. The remote plant would stand to lose little value. It is not enough, therefore, to establish the extent of contamination; locational influences must also be determined and evaluated.

Accurate hazard maps are necessary to understand fully the extent of environmental contamination (see example in section 10). These are often available from regulatory agencies. A valuable, and often overlooked, source of maps and other information is a local historical society. These organizations often maintain maps dating back to the founding of a locality. Information about previous land use can be most informative during an attempt to ascertain the extent of environmental contamination. Maps, such as Sanborn maps, created years ago for fire insurance purposes, often contain this kind of information as well.

5.3 Demand for Alternative Uses

Often industrial contamination results in closure of all or part of a plant for cleanup. After cleanup the site may no longer be amenable to the original use. Other uses must then be considered. The demand for these uses in a particular area must be evaluated. If other uses are apparent and in demand, there will be less effect on marketability and value.

5.4 Presence of Assumable Financing

The loss in value is often less if assumable financing is available. For obvious reasons, lenders may not be willing to offer financing at all or at acceptable terms once contamination is disclosed. Assumable financing eliminates this problem.

5.5 Liquidity Problems Caused by Lack of Marketability

Capital that cannot be liquidated quickly tends to be less valuable. The period during which curative efforts will be made must be established. This will help define the extent of liquidity problems, which may also be affected by associated stigma (see section 4.5).

5.6 Availability of Bond to Pay Cleanup

Existence of bonding improves marketability of property and diminishes the effect of environmental contamination on value. However, in cases of severe contamination, the seller may be unable to obtain such a bond because it may be difficult to give necessary assurances that solvency can be maintained and cleanup costs provided.

5.7 State and Regional Environmental Regulations

Zoning regulations have restricted property use for many years. Similarly, local or regional environmental regulations may restrict use of property and thereby affect value by reducing utility. Environmental assessments are often required by various agencies to evaluate potential problems.

6. Approaches to Value

Valuing contaminated properties is complex because circumstances are different for each affected property and because sufficient comparable sales may be unavailable or difficult to obtain. Nevertheless, as in all other types of property valuation, three approaches to value are recognized and should be used. Highest and best use must be established so unencumbered value can be found. Adjustments can then be market-justified and made.

6.1 Sales Comparison Approach

The sales comparison approach to value requires property to be appraised via a comparison with similarly affected properties recently sold. When adequate data exist for similarly affected properties, this approach is considered the most objective and supportable. Court decisions in California (Firestone Tire and Rubber v. County of Monterey [1990]), New Hampshire (Appeal of Great Lakes Container Corp. [1985]), and Minnesota (Westling v. County of Mille Lacs [1998]) have given serious consideration to the sales comparison approach, and it is possible to find, as the Washington Tax Tribunal did, that a particular property in its present condition is not marketable (Bamford v. Brown [1992]).

The sales comparison approach requires sufficient sales of similar properties. As in the general sales comparison approach when data on comparable contaminated properties are limited, the assessor should expand strata, the period from which sales are drawn, and geo-economically defined areas. However, appropriate adjustments must be made to ensure that proper comparability is achieved.

Rather than relying only on the limited data available for similarly contaminated property, sales of similar uncontaminated property can also be used. In this way a benchmark, unencumbered value can be established for the subject property, after which adjustments can be made for the contamination. Such adjustments should be based on the cost to cure (properly discounted or amortized), imposed limitations on use, increased insurance and financing costs, and potential liability.

6.2 Cost Approach

The cost approach is based on the premise that the market value of an improved parcel is equal to the market value of the land plus the current construction costs of the improvement less accrued depreciation. The cost approach is often applicable in cases of environmental contamination, provided the present worth of direct and indirect costs is calculated and used and provided adjustments are made for overestimation or underestimation of costs and impact. The cost approach, however, may ignore the value-in-use concept and thereby overstate the impact of costs to cure contamination problems (see section 4.1). There have been decisions in Florida (*Roden v. Estech* [1987]), Massachusetts (*Reliable Electric Finishing Co. v. Board of Assessors* [1991]), Minnesota (*Nicollet Restoration, Inc. v. County of Hennepin* [1992]), and Pennsylvania (*B.P. Oil, Inc. v. Board of Assessment Appeal of Jefferson County* [1993]) that have focused on the cost approach.

6.2.1 Cost to Cure as Functional or Economic Obsolescence

The cost to cure a problem reduces the utility of property and should be considered a form of functional or economic obsolescence of improvements. This would then be added to the accrued depreciation because current replacement cost new would be based on the assumption of a typical, presumably clean, environment.

Cost to cure includes all expenses associated with a cleanup, including some that may not be mandated but that reduce stigma (see section 4.5). Cost to cure must be recognized, but it is usually not appropriate to subtract such costs on a dollar-for-dollar basis, as an owner's expenditures are not conclusive of value (*Inmar Associates v. Borough of Carlstadt* [1988]; *Alladin, Inc. v. Blackhawk County* [1997]). However, there have been decisions in California (*Mola Development Corp. v. Orange County Assessment Appeals Board No. 2* [2000]), Illinois (*Manufacturer's Life Insurance Co. v. DuPage County Board of Review* [1994]), New York (*Commerce Holding Co. v. Board of Assessors* [1996]), and New Jersey (*University Plaza Realty Corp. v. City of Hackensack* [1993]) that have employed a dollar-for-dollar offset. Great care should be taken in this regard to gauge and interpret the marketplace adequately. In some cases it may be appropriate to treat these costs as capital improvements, to be depreciated over the useful life of the property or the improvements (if their life is shorter).

6.2.2 Specialized Costs

Contamination-related legal and insurance expenses, above those that would be typical for ordinary operation, must be considered. In addition, provision should be made for the cost of discovery of contamination and future monitoring to watch for recurrence of contamination (see section 4.2.2).

6.3 Income Approach

The income approach to value estimates property value by determining the present value of the projected typical income stream for the type of property. Income-producing properties are the most common property type influenced by environmental regulations and subject to contamination. Often, the greatest and most easily measured effect is on the ability of the property to continue to generate income. For this reason, the income approach is often the most suitable approach for contaminated properties.

The income approach is also effective in dealing with the situation that occurs when even the present worth of the cost to cure a problem far exceeds the replacement cost of the property. Courts have held that there is a "value in use" to the owner even where no other market exists, "so long as the owner continued to operate the facility" (*Inmar Associates v. Borough of Carlstadt* [1988]). The Utah Supreme Court has recently adopted a similar view of value in use as establishing current value (*Schmidt v. Utah State Tax Commission* [1999]). Value in use, however, may be impaired by temporary closure or loss of customers. For this reason, some adjustment in income stream and income-determined value is likely.

6.3.1 Capitalization Rates

Properly developed income capitalization rates, derived from the market and including both debt and equity components, can be used to determine the value of contaminated properties. The capitalization rate is based on the equity yield rate, mortgage terms, and anticipated future appreciation or depreciation. Mortgages may be unobtainable and future appreciation not applicable in some cases. This leaves equity yield as the major capitalization rate component (Patchin 1988). In developing this rate, the presumption must be that the property is still capable of producing income. Adjusted rates may be developed for property not currently producing income, but expected to do so at a predictable level at a predictable time in the future. The capitalization rate must reflect the difference between comparable contaminated and uncontaminated properties. Increasing the capitalization rate to reflect added risk has been employed by courts and tribunals in Massachusetts (*Woburn Services Inc. v. Board of Assessors of City of Woburn* [1996]), North Carolina (*Camel City Laundry Co. v. Forsyth County Board of Equalization and Review* [1994]), and Washington (*Northwest Cooperage, Inc. v. Ridder* [1990]).

6.3.2 Income Stream

Use of market rental data assumes that the property is still in use (or will be shortly) and is capable of commanding rent. When these conditions are met, market rental data should be obtained for establishing the base capitalization rate. The income stream must be modified to account for the cost to cure the contamination problem and any loss of utility. Modification should be based on the amortized present worth of actual costs, recognizing that permissible alternatives may limit costs to those necessary to satisfy the regulatory agency, not necessarily the full cost to cure the problem. Further income modification may be necessary to account for more expensive substitute processes or materials that can no longer be manufactured on site. Adjustments to reflect temporary closure or loss of customers must also be considered (see section 4.2.5). Expenses must be taken into account, and income and rate adjustments made accordingly. Expenses must be those typical to cure a particular problem and include the amortized present worth of the cost to cure the contamination, including discovery, legal expenses, monitoring, and the amortized present worth of any cost to eliminate stigma. Some expenses should be taken immediately; others, amortized over time.

Physical plant changes may ultimately improve operation. For example, in the course of replacing or adding electronic scrubbing devices to remove particulates from discharged air, a more efficient incineration system might be installed. Future costs may be lower than if the original system had been left intact. Costs involved and subsequent adjustments to the income stream should be considered (at least partially) as capital improvements, and both increases and reductions in these costs should be factored into value. Economic incentives to reduce air pollution must also be considered (Clean Air Act).

Preliminary estimates may differ from the actual costs to cure problems. Additional, undisclosed problems may be found, especially as improved technology with increased detection sensitivity is developed. Some contaminants, such as asbestos, however, are often more easily treated than many initial estimates assume. However, unproven problems must be treated as unknown costs. Impact on value should not be anticipated. It must be proven by objective data collected from the marketplace.

Ongoing monitoring is often expensive. Inflation will increase costs, which often are incurred over lengthy periods. These factors should be included when modified income streams are developed. It is important to note, however, that all allowable costs should be considered, while not ignoring the principle of future benefits, which may give the property present worth in anticipation (*Appeal of Great Lakes Container Corp.* [1985]).

Expenses (costs) that are allowable should include those that can be documented as actual, current, or reliably anticipated. Expenses to be used should be based on current cleanup mandates, not ones that are invoked only upon sale of property or change in use, as is sometimes the case. Documentation provided by the property owner should be verified through environmental regulatory agencies.

6.4 Alternative Approaches to Value

Because of difficulties in establishing comparative market data and correctly adjusting a contaminated property's income stream, certain nontraditional valuation methods have been examined as possible means of valuing contaminated property. An example of an alternative procedure is use of "contingent valuation methods" (CVM), in which survey methods are employed to investigate and determine values. Although not specifically endorsed in this standard, such alternative methods should be investigated when absence of reliable information lessens the applicability of more conventional techniques. Finally, one Minnesota decision (*Hubbard Milling Co. v. County of Blue Earth* [1994]) sanctioned a reduction of cost to cure from all three of the traditional approaches to value.

7. Other Considerations
7.1 Proof of Contamination

Proof of contamination and associated expenses should be required before value is adjusted for such consideration.

7.1.1 Burden of Proof on Taxpayer

Often, detailed technical information privately held by the property owner is the only evidence of contamination. If the owner wants contamination information to be taken into account in developing an assessed value, the owner should provide the necessary financial information, including a balance sheet of costs. Proof that less costly alternatives are not acceptable to the regulatory agency should also be provided. The assessor is encouraged to approach the taxpayer cooperatively on this subject to demonstrate that the goal is to achieve fair and equitable value, not to penalize for environmental considerations (see section 7.2). The taxpayer always will have been required to obtain an environmental assessment report. Much useful information can be derived from this document.

7.1.2 Certification
Certification or verification of contamination should be available from involved federal, state or provincial, or local agencies. This should be required from the property owner before consideration for environmental contamination is given.

7.1.3 Alternative Solutions
Less costly solutions or partial solutions are often available and may be acceptable to regulators. Often, these involve isolating contamination with fencing or protective covering. Management of the contamination, rather than complete remediation, may be permitted. Costs for a partial solution will be lower and should be reviewed to be sure that effect on value is not overstated. Partial solutions may have a negative effect if prospective buyers perceive the problem as not yet solved or as insolvable , with a potential impact on future income.

7.2 Assessment Practices versus Environmental Policy
Jurisdictions have sometimes argued that assessment practices which respond to contamination with lower value in effect reward environmental regulation violators, shifting taxes to other, arguably more environmentally sound properties, which retain higher values. The argument has been made that the effect of contaminants on value should be ignored to penalize the polluter.

One approach One approach that attempts to Courts have generally disagreed with this reasoning, arguing instead that assessment of property is an independent function, which, to be uniform, must be undertaken without regard for public policy issues in other areas, for example, the environment (see *Inmar v. Carlstadt* [1988]). The assessor should be concerned with interpreting the market and establishing the most accurate market value for the property in question. Just as it is inappropriate to value the person (higher value for rich, lower for poor), so, too, it is inappropriate to conduct or support environmental policy with altered assessments or by ignoring the effect of these policies on value. The expenses associated with environmental policy should be viewed as part of the cost of doing business (although these may exceed ordinary costs). These expenses affect the income stream and, therefore, the value of the property. For assessment purposes, the issue becomes one of obsolescence rather than management.

One approach that attempts to balance all of these policy, valuation, and assessment issues is that employed in Washington as a result of the decision in *Weyerhauser v. Easter* (1995). In Washington, the property owner must prove the existence of contamination, a requirement for cleanup dictated by a government flat or business necessity, a reasonably certain cost of remediation, and a formal cleanup plan and timetable.

7.3 When is Value Affected?
The period during which value is affected must be established. This should be related to the time when expenses are clearly incurred or definitely to

be incurred. The shorter the period, the less the probable effect on value because disruption to the income stream is less pronounced, and perception of the property as "clean" will occur sooner. The period of impact can also be important because it may be inappropriate for the assessor to take into account costs that are incurred later than a certain date (perhaps January 1 or some other "assessment date"). In such a case, adjustment of value for contamination may have to wait until the next assessment year.

7.4 Intrinsic Value of Property

Does a property have remaining value that exists even when the cost to cure the problem exceeds apparent market value? If not, it would be appropriate to assign zero value to property in such a case. The question that needs to be answered to decide this issue is that of utility. If the property can be used, value must exist. With use comes market demand, at least at some point in time.

To determine value in use, several factors should be reviewed, including current income stream, predicted future income stream, demand for alternative uses, and cost to modify operation for alternative uses.

The concept of value in use appears to conflict with the concept of value in exchange, which statutes in many jurisdictions require be assessed. However, many recent court decisions have held that property that has use has value, even though a traditional market may not be immediately apparent.

Property is often permitted to pollute to a certain extent. Acceptable amounts of pollution are defined in permits granted by regulatory agencies. These "rights" to pollute enable a business to operate when no operation would be possible if zero pollution were required. This then contributes to the income-producing ability of the business and enhances its value. Both the "rights" and the business will therefore have value (see section 2.4 and 4.4.1).

7.5 Failure to Pay Taxes

Although not strictly an assessment issue, a related issue is the response of the assessing jurisdiction if taxes owing go unpaid. Usually, in property with value, all or part of the delinquent taxes would be recouped upon confiscation and sale by the jurisdiction. In the case of severely contaminated property, however, the ability to sell the property may be so limited that delinquent taxes will not be recovered. In addition, the jurisdiction will now own the property and may risk liability for costs to cure the contamination problem if the original owner or contaminator (or any other potentially responsible party) is insolvent and if additional contamination or even active management occurs while the jurisdiction is the owner. However, provided that the governmental entity has not caused or contributed to the contamination, under CERCLA (as amended by SARA in 1986), "the term owner or operator does not include a unit of state or local government which acquired ownership or control involuntarily through bankruptcy, tax delinquency, abandonment, or their circumstances in which the government involuntarily acquires title by virtue of its function as a sovereign."

The EPA has regulations restricting the degree of liability in cases of foreclosure by private or governmental entities. However, these regulations do not protect if the entity is actively managing or contributing to the contamination. It is also permissible for states to have stricter laws than those established at the federal level. These would take precedence and must be understood to determine potential liability fully. Regardless of the liability issue, the jurisdiction may be unable to sell the property to satisfy the tax lien without remediation of contamination.

8. Summary of Considerations

The valuation of contaminated properties requires the assessor to ascertain all of the components of value, as if the property were unencumbered, and then to determine appropriate adjustments. Market reaction and high immediate costs may overstate impact on value and reduce the usability of the comparable sales and cost approaches to value. Additional reliance should be placed on the income approach, with costs discounted and treated as part of the income stream. Some costs will result in improved operations, and these costs should be treated like any capital expenditures. The principles of current use and future value apply in these cases, as does the principle of value in use. However, some adjustment to value is likely and should be considered.

8.1 Current Use

If some use exists, value must exist; property should be valued as if uncontaminated, and the present worth of amortized costs, which do not increase future efficiency and value, should be deducted. Debt and equity components may be increased to account for increased risk.

8.2 Future Value

If no present use exists, there may still be value, based on expectations of future value after cleanup. The present value of residual future value after cleanup must be determined.

8.3 Adjustments to Value

Courts have tended to reject arguments that cleanup costs remain with people rather than property. Most rulings find that the assessor must determine the most accurate value for the property. This would not allow value determinations that disregard the influence of contamination. The conclusion is that the assessor does not have a role to support environmental policy. In interpreting the market, the assessor must respond to all measurable influences on value; environmental contamination is one such influence.

9. Public Relations

As with all other aspects of assessment, effective communication with all parties is critical. The effect of environmental contamination on value must be discussed knowledgably with representatives from the affected property, concerned regulatory agency officials, other governmental officials, and the public. Skills and methods are discussed in the *Standard on Public Relations* (2001). Issues include discussion of the assessment process as it relates to the individual taxpayer and uncontaminated properties within the jurisdiction.

9.1 Assessment Process

Both political and legal ramifications must be understood. The assessor should be proactive in seeking meetings with the owner of the contaminated property and with governmental officials involved with this property. Meeting with the owner makes cooperation in obtaining needed cost and other information more likely. An appeal may be less likely if the owner believes that pertinent facts have been carefully reviewed and taken into consideration. The owner must be allowed to present all pertinent information. An appropriate explanation must be given for value decisions. If there is a suspicion of contamination at the time of assessment, a contract specifying all determinable information should be developed. This will help protect the jurisdiction from future liability.

Various governmental officials within the jurisdiction may wish preferential treatment to be given or withheld. A city manager may be concerned that a business employing many residents is about to be lost and may hope to stave off this possibility with a lower assessment. Environmentally concerned citizenry may wish to penalize a polluter further by means of an unchanged or higher assessment. Public hearings and explanations are important for all parties.

9.2 Effect on Other Taxpayers in Jurisdiction

Tax shifts may result from lower assessments for properties with newly discovered environmental contamination. If these are large industrial properties, the jurisdiction may lose much value, and this can result in tax shifts to uncontaminated property or even loss of revenue to governmental units (such as schools and cities). The relationship between the assessment process and the generation of revenue and distribution of taxes should be discussed with the public, as well as with representatives from governmental units. The assessor's role in providing fair market value for all property, regardless of other considerations, should be emphasized, but the reality of tax effects should be analyzed and made public to avoid loss of credibility.

10 Example of Map of Contaminated Area

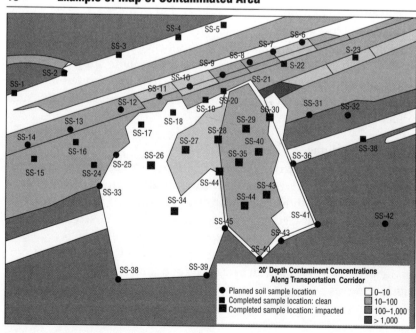

Addenda: *Standard on Valuation*

11. Glossary
All terms are defined in accordance with usage in this standard.

CERCLA
The Comprehensive Environmental Response, Compensation, and Liability Act of 1980 as amended by the Superfund Amendment and Reauthorization Act (SARA) of 1986; known as the "Superfund" and administered by the EPA.

Cost to cure
Cost or expense of cleaning up environmental contamination. Cleanup would result in levels of contamination that met standards of regulatory agencies. Complete cleanup may not be required, if contamination can be isolated. Costs include future monitoring and costs to reduce stigma (*see* **Stigma**). In many cases complete cure is impossible, and cost to cure is actually cost to control.

Electromagnetic radiation
Waves emitted by various sources, including power lines, radio transmitters, and microwave sources. Value of property may be affected by proximity to sources.

Environmental assessment
A report showing the results of investigation into environmental contamination. This report is often required by the EPA and other regulatory agencies to establish the extent of contamination suspected. "Phase I" or more extensive "Phase II" assessments may be required (*see* **Phase I and II reports**).

Environmental containment
Any tangible substance or intangible occurrence that may degrade property, resulting in decreased utility or having an effect on value (*see also* **Physical contaminant** and **Nonphysical contaminant**).

EPA
United States Environmental Protection Agency

Formaldehyde
Chemical constituent of certain insulating materials and glues. May enter air and become contaminant.

Hazardous substances
Any substance designated under various federal acts as toxic or hazardous, including hazardous solid waste, toxic air pollutants, and imminently hazardous chemicals and mixtures. This term does not include petroleum and natural gas products or synthetic fuel gas.

Hazardous waste
A solid waste that may pose a present or potential hazard to health or to the environment. This includes any solid waste that is ignitable, corrosive, toxic; infectious, or reactive.

Indemnification

Bonds established to provide security against future costs resulting from previously existing contamination. This is usually provided by the seller to facilitate a sale of contaminated property.

Innocent landowner

A landowner who purchased property subsequent to contamination, but who had no knowledge of and did not contribute to the contamination. The landowner must have made all "appropriate inquiries" into the property prior to purchase. If qualified, the "innocent landowner" is not liable under CERCLA.

Intrinsic value

Value that remains when cost to cure a contamination problem exceeds original market value (*see* **Value in use**).

Liability

Responsibility for cleanup costs associated with environmental contamination. This usually rests with the party originally responsible for the condemnation, but may transfer to the current owner.

NAPL

Nonaqueous-phase liquids—liquid contaminants often trapped in soil or bedrock.

National Priorities List (NPL)

The list of sites determined to pose enough risk to become "Superfund" sites.

Nonphysical contaminant

Any recognized contaminant that does not consist of any tangible, physical substance.

Offsets

Environmental permits allow certain amounts of air pollutants to be released into the environment. If an industry wishes to expand, it may first be required to reduce its current level of emissions, so that the expanded plant will not emit more air pollution than did the original plant. A company may also trade air pollution allowances with another company to facilitate expansion of the first company.

Phase I and II reports

Phase I reports include historical information about the subject property and the neighborhood, and a review of pertinent government records to determine any prior violation pertaining to hazardous wastes or substances. This report requires physical inspection of the property. Phase II reports are required when potential problems are identified in the Phase I study. Phase II is an in-depth study of groundwater, air, soil, and improvements to determine existence of any hazardous waste or substance, or other contaminants (*see* **Environmental assessment**).

Physical containment
A substance recognized as hazardous by the EPA or local or regional authorities (*see* **Hazardous substances**).

Radon
Radioactive gas, which may enter structures from beneath the ground and contaminate air.

Remediation
The act or process of eliminating environmental contamination on, in, or under property to restore the property to an uncontaminated state.

Residual value
The value of the property after cleanup of environmental contamination. This may be more or less than the original value depending on counterbalancing effects of stigma and improvements to plant efficiency.

Stigma
An unfavorable perception, which may influence value, that continued contamination remains after cleanup has been effectuated.

Toxics
Recognized hazardous substances in the environment.

Tradable allowances
See **Offsets**

Treatment, storage, and disposal facility (TSDF)
Business that treats, stores, and disposes of hazardous waste. Regulated by the Resource Conservation and Recovery Act (RCRA).

Underground storage tank (UST)
Any tank and associated piping that has more than 10 percent of its volume underground. If leaking, these tanks are known as LUSTs.

Unencumbered value
The value of property without consideration of any detrimental environmental contamination.

Value in use
The ability of property to generate income or otherwise retain some value or use to the owner, regardless of the presence of contamination and even with related expenses exceeding the apparent market value of the property.

Bibliography

American Bankers Association. 1990. *ABA guide to the environmental liabilities of fiduciaries.* Washington, DC. American Bankers Association.

Cameron, Trudy Ann. 1991. Interval estimates of non-market resources values from referendum contingent valuation surveys. *Land Economics* 67(4):413–21.

Diskin, Barry A., Joel B. Haynes, and Michael A. McElveen. 1990. Lender perceptions of value influences of asbestos contamination in income-producing buildings. *Assessment Digest* 12(6):10–15.

Dybvig, Larry O. 1991. Legal liability and toxic real estate. *Canadian Appraiser* 35(2): 25–31.

Ferruggia, Frank. 1991. Valuation of contaminated property: New Jersey's *Inmar* decision. *Assessment Digest* 13(2):2–6.

Ferruggia, Frank. 1997. Stigma and market value: *Woburn Services, Inc. v. Board of Assessors of the City of Woburn, Massachusetts. Journal of Property Tax Management* 9(2):1–8.

Galvin, David, and Sally Toreff. 1986. Toxics on the home front. *Sierra* 71(5):44–48.

Garippa, John E., and Seth Davenport. (January 13) 1992. Environmental contamination: A legal perspective on its effects on property values. *State Tax Notes:* 13:50–57.

Gloudemans, Robert J. 1999. *Mass appraisal of real property.* Chicago: International Association of Assessing Officers.

Groves, Roger. 1990. Do America's state cases answer the question: How should you value contaminated properties? From a paper presented at 10th Annual Legal Seminar. Grenelefe, FL: International Association of Assessing Officers.

Guidotti, G.L., and Phillip Jacobs. 1993. *American Journal of Public Health* 83(2):233–39.

Harrison, George. 1998. Environmental considerations in mortgage lending. *Appraisal Review and Mortgage Underwriting Journal* 17(1):70–81.

International Association of Assessing Officers (IAAO). 1990. *Property appraisal and assessment administration.* Chicago: IAAO.

International Association of Assessing Officers (IAAO). 2001. *Standard on public relations.* Chicago: IAAO.

Jaconetty, Thomas A. 1996. Stigma, phobia, and fear. Their effect on valuation. *Assessment Journal* 3(1):51–67.

Jaconetty, Thomas A. 1999. Revitalizing urban brownfields—A national, state, and local effort to reclaim blighted properties. *Assessment Journal* 6(4):56–67.

Kempner, Jonathan. (February 16) 1990. National Multi Housing Council, *Environmental Update* 1–4 + glossary. 202/659–3381.

Kinnard, William N., Jr., Sue Ann Dickey, and Mary Beth Geckler. 1994. Fear and property value: Opinion survey results vs. market sales evidence. *Conference Proceedings,* Sixtieth Annual Conference on Assessment Administration, Seattle, October 16–19, 1994, 171–88. Chicago: International Association of Assessing Officers.

Lusvardi, Wayne C. 2000. The dose makes the poison: Environmental phobia or regulatory stigma? *The Appraisal Journal* 68(2):184–94.

Mitchell, Phillip S. 2000. Estimating economic damages to real property due to loss of marketability, rentability, and stigma. *The Appraisal Journal* 68(2):162–70.

Mundy, Bill. 1992. The impact of hazardous and toxic material on property value: Revisited. *The Appraisal Journal* 60(4):463–71.

Mundy, Bill, Dave McLean, and John A. Kilpatrick. 1999. The brownfield challenge. *Valuation Insights & Perspectives* 4(1):14–16, 18, 45.

Patchin, Peter J. 1988. Valuation of contaminated properties. *The Appraisal Journal* 56(1): 7–16.

Patchin, Peter J. 1994. Contaminated properties and the sales comparison approach. *The Appraisal Journal* 62(3):402–9.

Peters, Bill Thomas. 1990. The cost of cleanup and its impact on property values. *Assessment Digest* 12(6):2–9.

Rinaldi, Anthony J. 1991. Contaminated properties—Valuation solutions. *The Appraisal Journal* 59(3):377–81.

Simons, Robert. 1994. How clean is clean? *The Appraisal Journal* 62(3):424–38.

Smart, Miles M., and David L. Wynes. 1990. The impact of environmental conditions on real property. *Assessment Digest* 12(6):22–25.

Wilson, Albert R. 1990. Environmental risk valuation and evaluation. Part IV—A valuation model for environmental risk. *Focus* 2(3):17–24.

Wilson, Albert R. (1994) The environmental opinion: Basis for an impaired value opinion. *The Appraisal Journal* 62(3):410–23.

Addenda: *Standard on Valuation*

Appendix A
United States Federal Environmental Regulatory Acts

Comprehensive Environmental Response, Compensation, and Liability Act (CERCLA)
Creates liability for the cleanup of sites contaminated with hazardous substances. Provides "Superfund" for cleaning contaminated sites for which no responsible party can be found. Also specifies liability for potentially responsible parties.

Clean Air Act (CAA)
Provides national air quality standards and regulations.

Clean Water Act (CWA)
Regulates quality of water and point source pollution of waterways.

Food Security Act of 1985
Regulates water quality and requires erosion control.

Fungicide and Rodenticide Act (FIFRA)
Regulates fungicide and rodenticides.

Resource Conservation and Recovery Act (RCRA)
Regulates solid and hazardous waste management and underground storage tanks containing petroleum products.

Superfund Amendments and Reauthorization Act (SARA)
Strengthened authority to effect cleanup of contaminated sites. Created "innocent landowner" defense.

Toxic Substances Control Act (TSCA)
Regulates toxic materials.

Appendix B
Pertinent Court Cases

ABB Industrial Systems, Inc. v. Prime Tech, Inc., 120 F.3d 351 (2nd Cir. 1997).

Alladin, Inc. v. Blackhawk County, 562 N.W.2d 608 (1997).

Alomor Corp. v. County of Hennepin, 566 N.W.2d 696 (1997).

Appeal of Camel City Laundry Co. II, 472 S.E.2d 402 (1994).

Appeal of Great Lakes Container Corp., 126 N.H. 167, 489 A.2d 134 (1985).

Badische Corp. v. Town of Kearny, 14 N.J. Tax 219 (1994), 672 A.2d 186 (1995), 288 N.J.Super. (App.Div. 1996).

Bamford v. Brown, Nos. 39962-39966 (Wash. Bd. Tax Appeals 1992).

Bielat, et al. v. Macomb Twp., Michigan Tax Tribunal, Docket No. 93707, et al. (1987).

Bockeloo v. Board of Review of City of Clinton, 529 N.W.2d 278 (1995).

B.P. Oil, Inc. v. Board of Assessment Appeal of Jefferson County, 159 Pa.Cmwlth. 414, 633 A.2d 124 (1993).

Camel City Laundry Co. v. Forsyth County Board of Equalization and Review, 115 N.C.App. 469, 444 S.E.2d 689 (1994).

Comercia Bank—Detroit v. Metamora Twp., Michigan Tax Tribunal, Docket No. 103325 (1987).

Commerce Holding Co. v. Board of Assessors, 216 A.D. 466, 628 N.Y.S.2d 186 (1995) and 88 N.Y.2d 724, 649 N.Y.S.2d 932, 673 N.E.2d 127 (1996).

Community Consultants, Inc. v. Bedford Twp., 3 MITTR 593 (1985).

Continental Tile Co. v. Peoples Gas Light and Coke Co., 959 F.Supp. 893 (N.D. Ill. 1997).

Custom Distribution Services, Inc. v. City of Perth Amboy, 1997 W.L. 795825 (Bankr. D. N.J. 1997).

Finklestein v. Dept. of Transportation, 656 So.2d 921 (1995).

Firestone Tire & Rubber Company v. County of Monterey, 223 Cal.App.3d 382, 272 Cal.Rptr. 745 (6 Dist. 1990).

GAF Corp. v. Borough of South Bound Brook, 112 N.J. 593 (1988).

Hammond v. City of Warner Robbins, 224 Ga.App. 684, 482 S.E.2d 422 (Ga.App. 1997).

Hubbard Milling Co. v. County of Blue Earth, Nos. C4-93-641-R, C6-93-642 (Minn. Tax Ct. 1994).

Inmar Associates v. Borough of Carlstadt, 112 N.J. 593, 549 A.2d 38 (N.J. 1988).

Joslyn Manufacturing Co. v. T.L. James & Co., 893 F.2d 80 (5th Cir. 1990).

Mola Development Corp. v. Orange County Assessment Appeals Board No. 2, 80 Cal.App. 4th 309, 95 Cal. Rptr.2d 546 (2000).

Manufacturer's Life Insurance Co. v. DuPage County Board of Review, Nos. 90-2290-C-3 and 91-3218-C-3 (1994).

Monroe County Board of Assessors v. Miller, 131 Pa.Cmwlth. 538, 570 A.2d 1386 (1990).

Murray Pacific Corp. v. Brown, No. 38037 (Wash. Bd. Tax Appeals 1990).

Nicollet Restoration, Inc. v. County of Hennepin, No. T.C. 12361 (4th Dist. 1992).

Northwest Cooperage Company, Inc., v. Ridder, Wash. Board of Tax Appeals, Docket Nos. 36278-36280 (1990).

Peterson v. Amherst, N.H. Slip Opinion, Docket No. 1239-81 (1982).

Raytheron Co. v. McGraw Edison Co., 979 F.Supp. 858 (E.D. Wis. 1997).

Redevelopment Agency of City of Pomona v. Thrifty Oil Co., 4 Cal.App. 4th 469, 5 Cal. Rptr.2d 687 (1992).

Reliable Electric Finishing Co. v. Board of Assessors, 410 Mass. 381, 573 N.E.2d 959 (1991).

Roden v. Estech, 508 So.2d 728 (1987).

Salmon Bay Terminals v. Noble, Nos. 45939-45940 (1996).

Schmidt v. Utah State Tax Commission, 1999 Utah 48, 980 P.2d 690 (1999).

Stafford v. Bryden County Board of Education, 219 Ga.App. 750, 466 S.E.2d 637 (1995).

State of Idaho v. Bunker Hill Co. & Gulf Resources, 635 F.Supp. 655 (D. Idaho, 1986).

Addenda: *Standard on Valuation*

State of Tennessee v. Brandon, 878 S.W.2d 224 (Tenn.App. 1994).

Sweepster Inc. v. Seco Township, 225 Mich.App. 497, 571 N.W.2d 553 (1997).

Techalloy Co., Inc. v. Property Tax Appeal Board, 291 Ill.App. 3d 86, 683 N.E.2d 206 (1997).

United States v. CMDG Realty, 96 F.3d 706 (3rd Cir. 1997).

United States v. Cordova Chemical Co., 113 F.3d 572 (6th Cir. 1997).

United States v. Olin Corp., 107 F.3d 1506 (11th Cir. 1997).

University Plaza Realty Corp. v. City of Hackensack, 12 N.J. Tax 354 (1992), aff'd 264 N.J. Super. 353, 624 A.2d 1000 (1993), cert. den. 134 N.J. 481, 634 A.2d 527 (1993).

Vopelgesang v. CECOS International, Inc., 85 Ohio App. 3d 339, 619 N.E.2d 1072 (1993).

Westling v. County of Mille Lacs, 543 N.W.2d 91 (Minn. 1996).

Westling v. County of Mille Lacs, 588 N.W.2d 815 (Minn. 1998).

West Orange v. Goldman's Estate, 2 N.J. Tax 582 (1981).

Weyerhauser v. Easter, 126 Wash.2d 370, 894 P.2d 1290 (1995).

Woburn Services Inc. v. Board of Assessors of City of Woburn, Nos. 212519, 212521, 212523-212531 (Mass. App. Tax Board 1996).

Wyckoff Company v. Carol Belas, Kitsap County Assessor, Docket No. 39107 (1991).

Guide Note 8: The Consideration of Hazardous Substances in the Appraisal Process

Introduction

The consideration of environmental forces along with social, economic and governmental forces is fundamental to the appraisal of real property. Although appraisal literature has long recognized environmental forces as major determinants of value, the focus has been on the consideration of climatic conditions, topography and soil, the surrounding neighborhood, accessibility, and proximity to points of attraction. These environmental forces are readily apparent to a member of the general public who is not specifically trained as an expert in observing these forces. There is, however, a growing need to give special consideration to the impact of hazardous substances on the valuation of real property.

The growing need to consider hazardous substances is a recent trend stemming from the creation and identification of new hazards, recent federal and state legislation enacted to control and place responsibility for these hazards, and an increasing public awareness of the problems resulting from these hazards.

The presence of hazardous substances can significantly impact value. In some cases the property may have a "negative" value if remediation cost is greater than the property value after any necessary clean up.

For the purpose of this guide note the term "hazardous substances" covers any material within, around or near a property that may have a negative impact on its value. Accordingly, the principles discussed in this guide note apply equally to hazardous substances that may be contained within the property and external hazardous substances.

The purpose of this guide note is to provide guidance in the application of the Uniform Standards of Professional Appraisal Practice ("USPAP") to the appraisal of real property affected by or potentially affected by hazardous substances and, in particular, to the consideration of such hazards in the appraisal process. It is not the purpose of this guide note to provide technical instructions or explanations concerning the detection or measurement of the effect of hazardous substances.

Addenda: *Guide Note 8*

Competency

The Competency Provision of the Uniform Standards of Professional Appraisal Practice requires the appraiser to have the knowledge and experience necessary to complete a specific appraisal assignment competently or alternatively to disclose the lack of knowledge or experience to the client, take all steps necessary or appropriate to complete the assignment competently and describe in the report the lack of knowledge or experience and the steps taken to competently complete the assignment.

The Competency Provision is of particular importance in the appraisal of real property that may be affected by hazardous substances. Most appraisers do not have the knowledge or experience required to detect the presence of hazardous substances or to measure the quantities of such material. The appraiser, like the buyers and sellers in the open market, typically relies on the advice of others in matters that require special expertise.

There is nothing to prevent a professional appraiser from becoming an expert in other fields, but the real estate appraiser is neither required, nor expected, to be an expert in the special field of the detection and measurement of hazardous substances. This guide note therefore addresses the problem of hazardous substances from the viewpoint of the appraiser who is not qualified to detect or measure the quantities of hazardous substances.

For an appraisal which develops an opinion of the effects on value of hazardous substances, most appraisers would require the professional assistance of others. For an appraisal with no separate accounting for the possible effects on value of known hazardous substances, the appraiser would not require the professional assistance of others. These alternatives are further discussed below.

The appraiser may accept an assignment involving the consideration of hazardous substances without having the required knowledge and experience in this special field, provided the appraiser discloses such lack of knowledge and experience to the client prior to acceptance of the assignment, arranges to complete the assignment competently and describes the lack of knowledge or experience and the steps taken to competently complete the assignment in the report. This may require association with others who possess the required knowledge and experience or reliance on professional reports prepared by others who are reasonably believed to have the necessary knowledge and experience. If the appraiser draws conclusions based upon the advice or findings of others, the appraiser must believe that the advice or findings are made by persons who are properly qualified. (See Guide Note 6, Reliance on Reports Prepared by Others.) It is suggested that the client, not the appraiser, choose and hire any qualified environmental professionals.

In some cases, an appraiser may be asked to complete a checklist which lists specific contaminants and questions the appraiser's knowledge of each. This is addressed in USPAP Advisory Opinion AO-9 entitled "Responsibility of Appraisers Concerning Toxic or Hazardous Substance Contamination," which states, "If an appraiser is requested to complete a checklist as part of the process for recognizing contamination, the appraiser should only respond to those questions that can be answered competently by the appraiser within the limits of his or her particular expertise in this area."

Valuing Contaminated Properties

Basis for Proper Valuation

In developing an appraisal based in part on the findings of others with respect to the existence and effects of hazardous substances, the appraiser must correctly employ those recognized methods and techniques that are necessary to produce a credible appraisal. The loss of value attributable to hazardous substances is sometimes measurable using the same methods and techniques that are used to measure depreciation from other causes. In other cases, more specialized techniques are indicated. However, in some cases even environmental professionals cannot agree on the level of clean up required, the appropriate method of that clean up, or the cost.

The appraiser is cautioned that the value of a property impacted by hazardous substances may not be measurable simply by deducting the typical remediation cost, or discovery cost from the total value, as if "clean." The possibility of other changes affecting value, such as a change in highest and best use, marketability, and stigma should be considered. In any analysis the appraiser should concentrate on developing an opinion of the effect on value caused by the hazardous substances.

S.R. 2-3 and S.R. 5-3 require the appraiser to include, within each written report, the name of each individual providing significant professional assistance. Accordingly, environmental engineers, inspectors and other professionals who prepare reports, furnish advice or make findings that are used in the appraisal process must be named in the certification.

The appraiser may accept an assignment that would exclude the consideration of hazardous substances, provided that: the resulting appraisal is not misleading; the client has been advised of the limitation; and the report is qualified to reflect this limitation.

When there are no known hazardous substances it is recommended, as a matter of standard practice, that the appraiser issue a disclaimer or limiting condition to the effect that the appraisal is predicated on the assumption that hazardous substances do not exist. If the property being appraised is not known[1] to be affected by hazardous substances and there is no reason to believe that it may be so affected, the issuance of such a disclaimer of limiting condition would not be considered to limit the scope of the appraisal. If the property being appraised is known to be affected by hazardous substances, or if there is reason to believe that it may be so affected, the appraiser cannot exclude the consideration of such materials without limiting the scope of the appraisal. In such appraisals, the appraiser must take great care to make sure that the limitation is not misleading. The known or suspected existence of hazardous substances must be disclosed.

If a property is known to be affected by hazardous substances, or if there is reason to believe that a property may be so affected, it may serve a valid and useful purpose to obtain an appraisal of the property, excluding the consideration of hazardous substances. Such an appraisal could be required as the logical starting point in a study of the impact of hazardous substances or in connection with legal proceedings. Whatever the purpose, such an appraisal must be properly qualified to prevent its misuse and must not be misleading. The valuation of property, as if unaffected by hazardous substances that are known to be present or are suspected of being present, would be predicated on an extraordinary assumption and therefore subject to S.R. 2-1(c) without exception. S.R. 2-1(c) requires

---

1. Knowledge is being defined here to mean obvious to the untrained person or specifically communicated through a reasonably reliable source.

that each written or oral real estate appraisal report must clearly and accurately disclose any extraordinary assumption, hypothetical condition, or limiting condition that directly affects the appraisal and indicate its impact in value. The validity of and reason for making the extraordinary assumption should also be disclosed. Similarly, S.R. 2-2(a) (xi), S.R. (b), (xi), and S.R. (c) (xi) require that the report clearly identify and explain any permitted departure from the requirements of Standard 1.

In limited assignments such as discussed above, the requirements of the Departure Provision, S.R. 2-1(c), S.R. 2-2(a) (xi), S.R. 2-2(b), (xi), and S.R. 2-2(c) (xi)) may be satisfied by including a suitable disclosure or limiting condition, an appropriate statement of purpose and properly qualified conclusions in the report. For purposes of illustration, assume that a property known to contain friable asbestos is to be appraised in accordance with the client's instructions, as if unaffected by asbestos. The report for such an appraisal would require a limiting condition, an appropriate statement of purpose and qualified conclusions similar in content to the following example.

> In accordance with the client's instructions, the value opinion reported herein reflects the total value of the subject property, as if unaffected by asbestos. It is reported that asbestos is present within the subject property. The presence of asbestos may have a negative influence on the value of the subject property, but the consideration of the effects of asbestos on the value of the subject property is beyond the purpose and scope of this appraisal. The appraiser cautions against the use of this appraisal without knowledge of the intended purpose and limited scope of the appraisal.

In addition to an appropriate limiting condition such as shown above, there should be an appropriate statement of purpose and the conclusion should be properly qualified, as illustrated below.

> The purpose of this appraisal is to develop an opinion of the market value of the subject property, as if unaffected by asbestos, as of January 1, 19XX.
> The appraiser's final opinion of the market value of the subject property, as if unaffected by asbestos, as of January 1, 19XX.

The limiting condition(s) should be stated in the letter of transmittal, if any, the body of the report, and whenever the report conclusion is stated.

Standard Disclaimers and Statements of Limiting Conditions

As previously mentioned, it is recommended practice, even in the appraisal of property where there is no reason to believe that the property is affected by hazardous substances, to include a standard disclaimer or statement of limiting conditions that pertains specifically to hazardous substances in the appraisal report. Such statements are not required by the Standards of Professional Appraisal Practice, and they are not intended to limit the scope of the appraisal to something less than would otherwise be required. Rather, they are intended to clarify the normal limits of the appraisal, disclose the appraiser's lack of expertise with respect to hazardous substances, and disclaim the appraiser's responsibility for matters beyond the appraiser's level of expertise.

The following examples are offered for illustration only.

> Unless otherwise stated in this report, the existence of hazardous substances, including without limitation asbestos, polychlorinated biphenyl, petroleum

Valuing Contaminated Properties

leakage, or agricultural chemicals, which may or may not be present on the property were not called to the attention of nor did the appraiser become aware of such during the appraiser's inspection. The appraiser has no knowledge of the existence of such materials on or in the property unless otherwise stated. The appraiser, however, is not qualified to test for such substances. The presence of such hazardous substances may affect the value of the property. The value opinion reported herein is predicated on the assumption that no such hazardous substances exist on or in the property or in such proximity thereto which would cause a loss in value. No responsibility is assumed for any such hazardous substances, or for any expertise or knowledge required to discover them.

Because the appraiser's value opinion is based on assessment of what a knowledgeable buyer would pay a knowledgeable seller, the appraiser needs to be aware of the steps that knowledgeable buyers and sellers now take in the market place. Under federal and most state laws, the owner of a piece of property which is contaminated and from which there is a release or threatened release, may be held liable for the cost of corrective action. Under federal and state laws, an "innocent purchaser" may avoid this liability. In order for a purchaser to qualify for the "innocent purchaser" defense, the purchaser must establish that it undertook all proper investigation of the property and the purchaser's knowledge. This has come to mean, at a minimum, that the purchaser of commercial, industrial or vacant property must conduct at least a "Phase I" investigation of the property prior to acquisition. Such an investigation entails a review of the property, its history, and available government records to determine if there is reason to believe that it may contain contamination. If a properly conducted Phase I investigation finds no likelihood of contamination, it should be sufficient to establish the "innocent purchaser" defense. If the potential for contamination is disclosed in the Phase I report, further investigation, often characterized as Phase II or Phase III investigations should be able to determine with a reasonable degree of scientific certainty whether the property is affected by contamination, and if it is, what the possible remedies and costs may be. Given the accepted practice in the marketplace, the appraiser may wish to qualify his or her appraisal as follows:

If the appraiser has been provided with a Phase I, Phase II, or Phase III report finding no evidence of possible contamination:

"The client has provided an environmental assessment for the property performed by "XXX". According to the (date of report) report describing that assessment no adverse hazardous substances were found on the subject property. The reader of this appraisal report is urged to review the entire environmental assessment for specific detail."

If no Phase I report has been prepared or provided to the appraiser and the appraiser has no reason to suspect the existence of hazardous substances, the appraiser may wish to state specifically that:

"The appraiser has not reviewed a Phase I report of examination and such an examination is customary in the transfer of commercial, industrial or vacant real estate. The appraisal is based on an assumption of a Phase I report indicating no contamination."

Of course, if a Phase I, Phase II, or Phase III report indicates the possibility of contamination, that must be noted together with the amount of further investigation that is required by customary business practice as well as necessary to establish the "innocent purchaser" defense (such further investigation must reveal the absence of contamination to establish the "innocent purchase" defense). A statement similar to the following is suggested:

> "The client has provided a Phase XX environmental assessment for the property performed by "XXXX". According to the (date of report) report describing that assessment the following hazardous substances are found on the subject property. The reader of this appraisal report is urged to review the entire environmental assessment for specific detail. A Phase XX environmental assessment is suggested."

There is no suggestion that the preceding statements or any other disclaimers or limiting conditions would be appropriate in all jurisdictions and circumstances. Appraisers are advised to consult their own legal counsel for assistance in developing individualized language for limiting conditions statements. Such statements may be considered in determining the extent of the appraiser's liability, if any, in connection with hazardous substances, and in determining whether the appraiser is eligible for errors and omissions liability insurance in connection with appraisals involving the consideration of hazardous substances. If the appraiser becomes aware of any information not previously disclosed by the client regarding possible hazardous substances affecting the subject, the appraiser should inform the client in writing of the possibility of the existence of a hazardous substance prior to the completion of the report.

The appraiser should note in the report any evidence of hazardous substances that is observed during the inspection of the subject property or becomes known to the appraiser through the normal research involved in performing the appraisal which would lead the appraiser to believe that hazardous substances may be present in or on the subject property, or is at variance with information or descriptions provided by others.

Unacceptable Practices

In the appraisal of property that requires the consideration of hazardous substances, but where the appraiser does not have the knowledge or experience required to detect the presence of such hazards, to measure the quantities of such hazards or to quantify the impact these hazards may have on value, the following practices are unacceptable.

1. Failure to disclose to the client the appraiser's lack of knowledge and experience with respect to the detection and measurement of hazardous substances (See Competency Provision).

2. Failure to take the necessary steps to complete the assignment competently such as personal study by the appraiser, association with another appraiser who has the required knowledge and experience or obtaining the professional assistance of others who possess the required knowledge and experience (See Competency Provision).

In the appraisal of property affected by hazardous substances, but where the purpose of the appraisal is to develop an opinion of value as if unaffected by hazardous substances, the following practice is unacceptable.

3. Failure to include in the report a qualification that reflects the limited scope of the appraisal, a limiting condition that clearly reveals

Valuing Contaminated Properties

the fact that the property is appraised as if unaffected by hazardous substances, an appropriate statement of purpose and properly qualified conclusions (See Departure Provision, S.R. 2-1(c), S.R. 2-2(a) (viii) and (xi), S.R. (b), (viii) and (xi), and S.R. (c) (viii) and (xi) .

4. Failure to report known hazardous substances affecting the property (See S.R. 2-1(b), S.R. 2-2(a), S.R. 2-2(b) and S.R. 2-2(c)).

In the appraisal of property affected by hazardous substances, if the appraiser relies upon the findings of other professionals with respect to the presence of, and the probable effect of, hazardous substances, the following practice is unacceptable.

5. Failure to acknowledge the professional assistance of others and to name the persons providing the assistance in the certification (See S.R. 2-3 and S.R. 5-3).

[Please note: Guide Notes to the Standards of Professional Appraisal Practice are an integral part of the Standards document. Guide Notes illustrate how the requirements of the Standards should be applied. They should not be considered without referring to the Standards of Professional Appraisal Practice.]

Advisory Opinion 9 (AO-9). Responsibility of Appraisers Concerning Toxic or Hazardous Substance Contamination

This communication by the Appraisal Standards Board (ASB) does not establish new standards or interpret existing standards. Advisory Opinions are issued to illustrate the applicability of appraisal standards in specific situations and to offer advice from the ASB for the resolution of appraisal issues and problems.

The Issue:

Federal and state legislation has been enacted to control environmentally toxic or hazardous substances and assign responsibility for any resulting contamination. How do the *Uniform Standards of Professional Appraisal Practice* (USPAP) apply to the appraisal of property considering:

1. recognition of contamination,
2. remediation and compliance cost estimation, and
3. value opinions of interests in impacted real estate?

Advice from the ASB on the Issue:

Honesty and professional competency are common threads throughout USPAP. The professional competency of an appraiser should not be presumed to include the knowledge or experience of a professional surveyor, architect, engineer, title lawyer, or other specialist. An appraiser that professes or implies such expertise but lacks the requisite qualifications is misleading the client, users of the appraisal report, and the public. Such misleading conduct is prohibited by the Ethics Rule of USPAP. However, an appraiser may reasonably rely on the findings and opinions of a properly qualified specialist and may work in concert with other professionals in multidisciplinary groups assembled to address a contaminated parcel of real estate.

Recognition of Contamination

An appraiser is a trained and experienced observer of real estate, but recognizing, detecting, or measuring contamination is often beyond the scope of the appraiser's expertise. The appraiser becomes aware of contamination through disclosure by the client and known facts prior to the acceptance of an appraisal assignment or through the normal observation and research conducted during an appraisal assignment. If an appraiser is requested to complete a checklist as part of the process for recognizing contamination, the appraiser should respond only to those questions that can be answered competently by the appraiser within the limits of his or her particular expertise in this area. In each situation, the Competency Rule of USPAP outlines the responsibilities of the appraiser.

Remediation and Compliance Cost Estimation

Remediation and compliance cost estimation involves knowledge and experience beyond that of most appraisers. These estimates are typically provided by environmental consulting specialists who are properly versed in federal and state environmental requirements and are qualified to assess and measure the materials and/or methods appropriate for remediation or compliance. Other professionals who deal with legal liabilities and business operations may also be involved in the cost estimate process. An appraiser may reasonably rely on the findings and opinions of qualified specialists in environmental remediation and compliance cost estimation.

Value Opinions of Interests in Impacted Real Estate

Many clients employ experts in various disciplines separately and simultaneously and make business decisions on the basis of the results of findings from the various experts. These clients may request an appraiser to appraise real estate that is or may be contaminated under the hypothetical condition that the real estate is free of contamination. An appraiser may appraise interests in real estate that is or is believed to be contaminated under the hypothetical condition that the real estate is free of contamination when the resulting appraisal is not misleading, the client has been advised of the limitation, and the Ethics Rule of the USPAP is satisfied. To avoid confusion in the marketplace, the Ethics Rule requires a clear and accurate disclosure of the factual contamination problem as well as a statement of the validity of and useful purpose for the hypothetical condition that the real estate is not affected.

When qualified specialists have documented the existence of contamination and estimated the costs of remediation or compliance, an appraiser may be in a position to develop an opinion of "as is" value and should be aware of, understand, and correctly employ those recognized methods and techniques necessary to produce a credible appraisal. The value of an interest in impacted or contaminated real estate may not be measurable simply by deducting the remediation or compliance cost estimate from the opinion of value as if the property is unaffected. Other factors may influence value, including any positive or negative impact on marketability (stigma) and the possibility of change in highest and best use.

Multidisciplinary Solutions

Some appraisers have already developed a specialization in the appraisal of interests in contaminated real estate through association with environ-

Addenda: *Advisory Opinion 9*

mental engineers, environmental lawyers, and related professionals in a multidisciplinary group. This type of association is commendable, provided that each of the professionals involved remains within the limits of the expertise associated with his or her profession and acknowledges the contributions of the other professionals in any specific reports that rely in part on the work of others.

This Advisory Opinion is based on presumed conditions without investigation or verification of actual circumstances. There is no assurance that this Advisory Opinion represents the only possible solution to the problems discussed or that it applies equally to seemingly similar situations.

Approved December 8, 1992
Revised September 16, 1998.

Bibliography by Topic

General Articles

Access EPA. Washington, D.C.: Information Access Branch, Information Management and Services Division, USEPA (updated annually).

American Society of Real Estate Counselors. *Real Estate Issues: Environmental Conditions in Real Estate*, vol. 16, no. 2 (Fall/Winter 1991).

_____ *Seminar on Toxic Contamination in Real Estate* (November 1989), statement by speaker—David Houston, CRE.

Ames, R. "Appraising Environmentally Sensitive Land." *Real Estate Appraiser and Analyst* (Winter 1984).

Armfield. "Casualty Loss Valuation." *The Appraisal Journal* (1982).

Appraisal Institute. "Environmental Risk and the Real Estate Appraisal Process." Seminar. Chicago, Illinois: Appraisal Institute, 1994: 128.

_____ *Hidden Factors: Environmental Risk Evaluation and the Real Estate Appraiser.* Chicago, Illinois: Appraisal Institute, 1992. Videotape.

_____ *Measuring the Effects of Hazardous Materials Contamination on Real Estate Value: Techniques and Applications.* Papers and proceedings of the 1991 Appraisal Institute Symposium, Philadelphia, Pennsylvania (1992).

Arens, Scott B., MAI, SRA. "The Valuation of Defective Properties: A Common Sense Approach." *The Appraisal Journal* (October 1992): 143–148.

Arnold, James R. "Appraising and Valuing Contaminated Properties." *ALI-ABA Course Materials Journal*, vol. 16, no. 4 (1991).

Atkinson, Steve. "Toxic Hazards Can Be Dangerous to a Development's Health." *Real Estate Review* (Summer 1986).

Bell, Randall, MAI. "Class VIII—Environmental Conditions." Chapter 8 in *Real Estate Damages: An Analysis of Detrimental Conditions.* Chicago, Illinois: The Appraisal Institute, 1999: 122–142.

_____ "The Impact of Detrimental Conditions on Property Values." *The Appraisal Journal* (October 1998): 380–391.

_____ "Quantifying Diminution in Value Due to Detrimental Conditions: An Application to Environmentally Contaminated Properties." *Environmental Claims Journal* (October 1996): 135.

Bennett. "Home Sweet Home—Or Is It? Environmental Issues in Residential Setting." *Toxic Law Reporter* (1991).

Bennett, M.J. "Environmental Issues in Residential Real Estate Transactions." *Environmental Watch* (Fall 1991).

Bond, Sandy G. and Paul J, Kennedy. "The Valuation of Contaminated Land: New Zealand and United Kingdom Practice Compared." Paper presented at the European Real Estate Society Conference, Maastricht, Netherlands (June 1998).

Bond, Sandy, G., William N. Kinnard, Jr., Elaine W. Worzala, and Steven D. Kapplin. "Market Participants' Reactions Toward Contaminated Property in New Zealand and the U.S.A." *Journal of Property Valuation and Investment*, vol. 16, no. 3 (1998): 251–272.

Campanella, Joseph A. "Commercial Property Values and Toxic Sites." *The California Lawyer* (May 1990).

Chalmers. "Valuation of Contaminated Property." ABA working paper (1992).

Chalmers and Adams. "Quantifying Contamination's Effects on Residential Property Values." *Environmental Compliance and Litigation Strategy* (1995).

Chalmers and Beatty. "Environmental Hazards Devastate Property Values." *Real Estate Valuation* (1994).

Chalmers, James A. and Thomas O. Jackson. "Risk Factors in the Appraisal of Contaminated Property." *The Appraisal Journal* (January 1996): 44–58.

Chalmers, James A., PhD and Scott A. Roehr. "Issues in the Valuation of Contaminated Property." *The Appraisal Journal* (January 1992): 28–41.

Chan, Nelson. "How Australian Appraisers Assess Contaminated Land." *The Appraisal Journal* (October 2000): 432–440.

Christensen, B. "Can Pollution Contaminate Value?" *The Real Estate Appraiser and Analyst* (Fall/Winter 1987).

Clayton. "Rational Expectations, Market Fundamentals, and Housing Price Volatility." *Real Estate Economics* (1996).

Colangelo, Robert V., CPG and Ronald D. Miller, Esq. *Environmental Site Assessments and Their Impact on Property Value: The Appraiser's Role*. Chicago, Illinois: The Appraisal Institute, 1995.

Craig, David W., MAI, CRE. "The Environmentally Impacted Property Assignment: The Best Approach is a Good Defense." *Valuation, Insights & Perspectives* (First Quarter 1999).

D'Arge. "A Practical Guide to Economic Valuation of the Natural Environment." 35. *Rocky Mt. Mineral Law Inst.*, Ch. 5 (1989).

Derbes, Max J., Jr., CRE. "Environmental Counseling Cases." *Real Estate Issues* (Fall/Winter 1991).

Dilmore, Gene, MAI, SREA. "Appraising Houses." *The Real Estate Appraiser*. Chicago: Illinois: Society of Real Estate Appraisers, July–August 1974: 21–32.

Dorchester, John D., Jr., MAI, CRE. "Environmental Pollution: Valuation in a Changing World." *The Appraisal Journal* (July 1991): 289–302.

Downey, James P. "Environmental Cleanup Actions, the Valuation of Contaminated Properties, and Just Compensation for Affected Property Owners." *Journal of Law Use & Environmental Law* (1993).

Environmental Risk and the Real Estate Appraisal Process. Chicago, Illinois: Appraisal Institute Seminar.

Federal Highway Administration, U.S. Department of Transportation. *The Effects of Contamination on the Market Value of Property* (1993).

Gale, Charles M., Esq. "Common Environmental Myths, When Selling, Buying, or Leasing Real Property." *Los Angeles Business Journal* (October 5, 1992).

Garippa, John E. and Seth I. Davenport. "The Market Value of Industrial Property in New Jersey." *Journal of Property Tax Management* (1996).

Gatzlaff and Tirtiroglu. "Real Estate Market Efficiency: Issues and Evidence." *Journal of Real Estate Literature* (1995).

Gladstone, Robert A. "Contaminated Property: A Valuation Perspective." *Toxic Laws Reporter* (November 1991): 798–802.

Gluck, Allan E., Donald C. Nanney, and Wayne Lusvardi. "Mitigating Factors in Appraisal & Valuation of Contaminated Real Property." *Real Estate Issues* (Summer 2000): 22–29.

Goodman, Gary A. and Dennis P. Harkawik. "Handling Transactions Involving Environmentally Contaminated Property." *Real Estate Review* (Spring 1991).

Hall, Robert W., CRE. "The Cause of Loss in Value: A Case Study of a Contaminated Property." *Real Estate Issues* (April 1994): 23–27.

Haney, Richard L., Jr. "Adverse Environmental Conditions: Their Impacts on Real Estate Values." *Journal of Real Estate Research*, vol. 7, no. 3 (Summer 1992).

Harrington, J.T. "Addressing Environmental Hazards: Considerations for Appraisers." *Environmental Watch* (Spring 1990).

International Association of Assessing Officers. *Standard on the Valuation of Property Affected by Environmental Contamination*. Chicago, Illinois, 1992.

Jackson, Thomas O., MAI. "The Effect of Previous Environmental Contamination on Industrial Real Estate Prices." *Appraisal Journal* (April 2001).

_____ "Investing in Contaminated Real Estate." *Real Estate Review* (Winter 1997).

Kaine, Timothy M. "Local Environmental Regulations and Property Value." *Tenth Annual IAAO Legal Seminar*, Grenelefe, Florida (November 15, 1990).

Kinnard, William N., Jr. "Current Techniques and Procedures for Dealing with the Effects of Property Contamination." *1990 SREA Symposium*, San Antonio, Texas (September 13, 1990).

Kinnard, William N., Jr. "Measuring the Effects of Contamination on Property Values." *Environmental Watch*, vol. IV, no. 4 (Winter 1992).

_____ *Property Valuation: A Primer on Proximity Impact Research*. Paper presented at Executive Enterprises Conference on Electric and Magnetic Fields, Washington, D.C. (December 1993).

_____ *What Appraisers Can Do and Must Do to Estimate the Impact of Contamination on Property Value*. Paper presented at American Bar Association Meeting, New York, New York (March 1993).

Kinnard, William N., Jr. and Gail L. Beron. "Bibliography." *The Impact of a Release of Radioactive Materials on Sales Prices of Proximate Residential Properties*. Storrs, Connecticut: Real Estate Counseling Group of Connecticut, December 1987.

Kinnard, William N., Jr., MAI, SRA, PhD and Elaine W. Worzala, PhD. "How North American Appraisers Value Contaminated Property and Associated Stigma." *The Appraisal Journal* (July 1999): 269–279.

Kline, Stephen M. "Valuing Contaminated Property: New and Unfamiliar Territory." *Journal of Technical Valuation* (August 1991).

Kopstein, Melvyn J. "Toxic Waste: Properties Devaluation: Question of Degree." *Expert-at-Law* (March–April 1990).

Marks, J.V., E.B. Campbell, T.C. Phillips, S.D. Weyhing, and R.L. Nichols. "Impact of Environmental Hazards on the Valuation Process." Educational program presented at annual meeting of the American Institute of Real Estate Appraisers, Chicago, April 1988 (Chicago, Illinois: First Tape, Inc., 1988) Audio recording.

Marx, Ron D. "This ELF Could Be the Next Giant in Environmental Hazards." *Econ: The Environmental Magazine for Real Property Hazards* (November 1993).

McCallion, Kenneth F. "A Survey of Approaches to Assessing Damages to Contaminated Private Property." *Fordham Environmental Law Report* (1992).

McMahan, John. "Environmental Hazards and Real Estate." *Real Estate Issues*, 14 (Spring/Summer 1989).

Miller, R.D. "Exploring Possible Environmental Hazards: Serving Clients' Needs." *Environmental Watch* (Fall 1990).

Milligan, Peter A. "Contaminated Land or Toxic Real Estate: Lessons from Ontario." *Journal of Property Tax Management*, vol. 16, no. 3 (Winter 1995).

Mundy, Bill, MAI, PhD. "Effect of Contamination on Real Estate Values." *Insider* (February 28, 1990).

_____ "Impact of Contaminants on Real Property Marketability and Value." Unpublished paper (November 1989).

_____ "The Impact of Hazardous Materials on Property Value." *The Appraisal Journal* (April 1992): 155–162.

_____ "The Impact of Hazardous Materials on Property Value: Revisited." *The Appraisal Journal* (October 1992): 463–471.

_____ "The Income Approach and Environmentally Impaired Property: A Response." *Environmental Watch* (Fall 1994).

_____ "Summary of Methodologies for Measuring Impaired Property Value." *Environmental Analysis and Valuation Seminar*. Seattle, Washington (March 1992).

_____ "Valuing Contaminated Property." *JARPA: Journal of Applied Real Property Analysis*, vol. 1, no. 1 (1997).

Neal, L.A. "Taking on Environmental Hazards." *Real Estate Appraiser and Analyst* (Summer 1987).

Nelson, R.D. and J.L. Messer. "Valuing Larger, Older Industrial Buildings." *Real Estate Appraiser and Analyst* (Spring 1990).

Ness, Shirley A. "Environmental Hazards in Real Estate." *Commercial Industrial Real Estate Journal* (July/August 1988).

Neumann, H. Denis. "Identifying Hazardous Wastes." *The M&E Appraiser*, American Society of Appraisers (Spring 1990).

Neustein, Richard A., MAI, SRA. "Estimating Value Diminution by the Income Approach." *Appraisal Journal* (April 1992): 283–287.

Nolan, J.M., Jr. and F.S. Blakeslee. "Environmental Auditing—For Compliance or Conviction? The DOJ Guidelines." *Environmental Watch* (Spring 1992).

Olson, Ralph K. "Hazardous Waste Sites." *The Appraisal Journal* (April 1989).

O'Malley, R.A. and J.C. Schuman. "Warning: Environmental Hazards." *Real Estate Appraiser and Analyst* (Fall 1989).

Parks, David C. *Environmental Management for Real Estate Professionals*. Chicago: Institute of Real Estate Management, 1992.

Patchin, Peter J., MAI. "Contaminated Properties and the Sales Comparison Approach." *The Appraisal Journal* (July 1994): 402–409.

———. "The Valuation of Contaminated Properties." *The Appraisal Journal* (January 1988): 7–16.

———. "Valuing Contaminated Properties: Case Studies." *Measuring the Effects of Hazardous Materials Contamination on Real Estate Values: Techniques and Applications.* Chicago, Illinois: Appraisal Institute, 1992.

Perla, Stanley R. "New Impairment Standard." *The E&Y Kenneth Leventhal Real Estate Journal* (July 1995).

Phillips, Beverly S., Peter D. Bowes, and John Reiss. "Environmental Issues and Diminution of Value: A Case Study." *Environmental Watch* (Winter 1994).

Popper, F. "Environmental Impact and Public Response." *Environment*, vol. 27, no. 2 (March 1985).

"Publicized Hazards Reports Affect Market Perception." *Environment Watch*, 3.89, vol. II, no. 1.

Randall, Alan, Berry C. Ives, and Clyde Eastman. "Bidding Games for Valuation of Aesthetic Environmental Improvements." *Journal of Environmental Economics and Management*, vol. 1 (1974).

Rinaldi, Anthony J., MAI, ASA. "Contaminated Properties—Valuation Solutions." *The Appraisal Journal* (July 1991): 377–381.

Roddewig, Richard J., MAI, CRE. "Adjusting Environmental Case Study Comparables by Using an Environmental Scoring System." *The Appraisal Journal* (October 2000): 371–374.

———. "Choosing the Right Analytical Tool for the Job." *The Appraisal Journal* (July 1998): 320–327.

Samsal. "An Introduction to the Valuation of Contaminated Property." *Assessment Journal* (1994).

Scagnelli, John M. "The Impact of Environmental Contamination on Market Value." *Environmental Compliance & Litigation Strategy* (April 1995).

Seattle Engineering Department, Gary Zarker, director. "Seattle-Kent Good Neighbor Program: Final Report January 1990."

Simons, Robert, PhD. "How Clean is Clean?" *The Appraisal Journal* (July 1994): 424–438.

Skov, Iva Lee Marie. "Does Pollution Affect Residential Property Values?" Unpublished PhD dissertation, University of Southern California (1976).

Smart, Miles M. and David L. Wynes. "The Impact of Environmental Conditions on Real Property." *Assessment Digest* (November/December 1990).

Stuard, Eugene, IFAC. "Appraising Contaminated Properties." *Appraisal Review* (Winter 1995).

Sullivan, Thomas F. P. *Environmental Information Sources*, 5th ed. Rockville, Maryland: Government Institutes, Inc., 1995.

———. *Environmental Regulatory Glossary.* 6th ed. Rockville, Maryland: Government Institutes, Inc., 1993.

Sullivan, Thomas F. P. and Richard F. Hill. *Environmental Information Sources.* Rockville, Md.: Government Institutes, Inc., September, 1996.

Svoboda, Robert S. "Valuation Case Studies Involving Environmental Issues." *15th Annual IPT Conference*, Reno, Nevada (June 23, 1991).

Syms, Paul. "Contaminated Land: Identification, Assessment, and Valuation." RECGA working paper (1997).

Thompson, Donald N. *The Economics of Environmental Pollution.* Cambridge, Massachusetts: Winthrop Publishers, Inc., 1973.

Weber. "The Valuation of Contaminated Land." *Journal of Real Estate Research* (1997).

Willard, Jane M. "Environmental Consultants: Assessments and Reports." *Environmental Watch*, vol. V, no. 1 (Spring 1992).

Wilson, Albert R. "Emerging Approaches to Impaired Property Valuation." *The Appraisal Journal* (April 1996): 155–170.

———. "Environmentally Encumbered Value Opinion Development." *Methodologies for Valuation of Real Property Impacted by Pollution from Hazardous and Toxic Materials*, a seminar prepared and presented by The Real Estate Counseling Group of America, Inc., Orlando, Florida (February 28, 1991).

———. "Environmentally Impaired Valuation: A Team Approach to a Balance Sheet Presentation." *Technical Report.* Chicago, Illinois: The Appraisal Institute, 1992.

Wilson, Donald C. "Highest and Best Use: Preservation Use of Environmentally Significant Real Estate." *The Appraisal Journal* (January 1996): 76–86.

Zaddack. "Real Estate Applications for GIS: A Review of Existing Conditions and Future Opportunities." *Real Estate Issues* (1998).

Appraisal Standards

Appraisal Institute. *Guide Notes to The Standards of Professions Appraisal Practice, Guide Note 6—Reliance on Reports Prepared by Others.* Chicago, Illinois: Appraisal Institute, 1991.

_____ *Guide Notes to The Standards of Profession Appraisal Practice, Guide Note 8—The Consideration of Hazardous Substances in the Appraisal Process.* Chicago, Illinois: Appraisal Institute, 1991.

Federal National Mortgage Association (Fannie Mae). "Uniform Residential Appraisal Report (Form 1004)." Washington, D.C.: Fannie Mae, 1993.

"Final Report on the Task Force on Appraisers' Environmental Responsibility." *Environmental Watch* (Summer 1993).

Martin, Danny J. "The New URAR and Environmental Hazards." *The Appraisal Journal* (January 1995): 47–52.

Roddewig, Richard J., MAI, CRE. "Contaminated Properties and Guide Note 8: Questions, Answers, and Suggestions for Revision." *The Appraisal Journal* (January 1998): 99–105.

Rudolph, Patricia. "Will Bad Appraisals Drive Out Good?" *The Appraisal Journal* (July 1994).

Inspections, Disclosures, Environmental Site Assessments, and Remediation

American Society for Testing and Materials. *Standard Practice for Environmental Site Assessments: Transaction Screen Process* (May 1993).

_____ *ASTM Standards on Environmental Site Assessments for Commercial Real Estate* (Philadelphia, 1993).

Appraisal Institute. *Environmental Site Assessments and Their Impacts on Property Value: The Appraiser's Role* (1995).

_____ Property Observation Checklist. Chicago: Appraisal Institute, 1993.

_____ *Standards of Professional Appraisal Practice of the Appraisal Institute.* Chicago, Illinois: Appraisal Institute, 1994.

"Bioremediation Under the Resource Conservation and Recovery Act." *Natural Resources & Environment* (Winter 1995).

BNA. *Environmental Due Diligence Guide* (April 1994): 29.

Caban, James N. "Business Transactions: A Guide Through the Wilderness." *Natural Resources & Environment* (Summer 1990).

Coffay, Edmund P., III. "The Revised URAR: Clarifying the Appraiser's Role in Reporting Environmental Hazards." *Environmental Watch* (Summer 1993).

Danis, Gary F. and Mary T. Zdanowicz. "Deciding How Clean is Clean: A Risky Business." *Environmental Permitting* (Winter 1994–95).

"Department of Interior, 43CFR Part 11, Natural Resource Damage Assessments, Notice of Proposed Rulemaking." *Federal Register*, vol. 56, no. 82 (April 29, 1991): 19752–19773.

Dunmire, Thea D. "Environmental Redlining: Phase I Auditing Concerns in Real Estate Transactions." *Tenth Annual IAAO Legal Seminar*, Grenelefe, Florida (November 15, 1990).

"Environmental Liability of Brokers and Other Parties." 19 *Real Estate Law Journal* 218, 277 (1991).

"Environmental Problems and Brokers Liability." 3 *Natural Resources and Environment* 17 (1988).

Ethier, William H. "The ASTM Standards on Environmental Assessments for Commercial Real Estate." *Environmental Watch* (Spring 1994).

Foreman, R.L. "Elements of Damage Estimates for Contaminated Real Estate." *Environmental Watch* (October 1989).

Hageman, Ronda K. "An Assessment of the Value of Natural Hazards Damage Reduction in Dwellings Due to Buildings Codes: Two Case Studies." *Natural Resources Journal*, vol. 23, (1983).

Heath, Jenifer S. "Remedial Strategies Should Enhance Property Value." Technical Paper (86), Woodward-Clyde Consultants.

"Home, Not-So-Sweet Home: Real Estate Broker Liability in the Sale of Previously Contaminated Property: Has Broker Liability Gone Too Far?" 2 *Rutgers Law Journal* 111 (1989).

Hudnut, Wiliam H., III. "New Strategies for Old Buildings and Abandoned Land." *Urban Land* (June 1997).

Kearns, Thomas R. "Environmental Audits: Real Estate's Newest Transaction Safeguards." *The Appraisal Journal* (July 1991): 348–352.

Kuhle, James L., James R. Webb, and Eric Mahler. "An Overview of the Contaminated Site Regulatory Framework, the Site Assessment Process and Parameters Affecting Site Cleanup Costs." *Journal of Real Estate Research*, vol. 7, no. 3 (Summer 1992).

Lendy, Terry. "Environmental Site Assessment 101: A Crash Course in REALTORS on Phase I Site Assessments." *Illinois Realtor* (March 1994).

Levine, Steven A., CERS, CERA. "Environmental Challenges Can Create Work for Real Estate Appraisers." *Valuation, Insights & Perspectives* (Third Quarter 1999): 30–32.

_____ "The Residential Real Property Disclosure Act." *Illinois Bar Journal*, vol. 82 (October 1994).

Morrin, James R. "Controlling the Environmental Audits." March 1989.

Naleid, David S. "Zen and the Art of Feasibility Study Costing." *Federal Environmental Restoration Conference and Exhibitions.* Washington, D.C.: Federal Environmental Restoration Conference and Exhibitions, 1992.

Pamukcu, Sibel, J. Kenneth Wittle, and Charles H. Titus. "Electrokinetics: Emerging Technology for In Situ Soil Remediation." *Federal Environmental Restoration Conference and Exhibitions.* Washington, D.C.: Federal Environmental Restoration Conference and Exhibitions, 1992.

Peavy, Howard S., et al. *Environmental Engineering* (New York: McGraw-Hill Book Company, 1985).

Russell, Milton E., William Colglazier, and Mary English. *Hazardous Waste Remediation: The Task Ahead.* Knoxville, Tennessee: Waste Management Research and Education Institute, 1991.

Salvesen. "Contamination and the Reuse of Land." *Urban Land* (1993).

"Toxic Nightmare on Elm Street: Negligence and the Real Estate Broker's Duty in Selling Previously Contaminated Residential Property." 15 *Boston College Environmental Law Review* 547 (1988).

Wildavsky, Aaron. *But, Is It True? A Citizen's Guide to Environmental Health and Safety Issues.* Cambridge, Massachusetts: Harvard University Press, 1995.

Wilson, Albert R. "The Environmental Opinion: Basis for an Impaired Value Opinion." *The Appraisal Journal* (July 1994): 410–423.

Woodring, Jeannie. "Three Steps to Property Cleanup." *Alaska Business Monthly* (June 1994).

Stigma

Brion, D. "An Essay on LULU, NIMBY and the Problem of Distributive Justice." *Boston College Environmental Affairs*, vol. 15 (1988).

Cabot, Howard Ross. "Post-Remediation 'Stigma' Damages." *For the Defense* (May 1995).

Clark-McGlennon, Associates. *Negotiating to Protect Your Interests: A Handbook on Siting Acceptable Hazardous Waste Facilities in New England*, prepared for New England Regional Commission (November 1980).

Closser, Bruce M., MAI, SRA. "Fuel-Oil Contamination of a Residence: a Case Study in Stigma." *Appraisal Journal* (July 2001).

Dear, Michael. "Understanding and Overcoming the NIMBY Syndrome." *Journal of the American Planning Association*, vol. 58, no. 3 (Summer 1992).

Eliot-Jones, Michael. *Bixby Ranch: Some Observations on Plaintiff's Expert's Appraisal of Post-Clean-Up 'Stigma'.* San Francisco, California: Foster Associates, 1995.

_____ "Stigma Damages and the Bad Address." Unpublished paper (1996).

_____ *'Stigma' in Light of Bixby Ranch, DeSario, and T&E Industries.* San Francisco, California: Foster Associates, 1995.

_____ "Valuation of Post-Cleanup Property: The Economic Basis for Stigma Damages." *Bureau of National Affairs Toxic Law Reporter* (February 1995): 944–945.

"Emerging Trend: Stigma Damages." *Real Estate/Environmental Liability News* (1995).

Guidotti, Tee L. "The Cancer Non-Epidemic of County 20: Case Study of An Epidemiological Mistake." *Public Health Review*, 1991/92; 19:179–190.

Guidotti, Tee L. and Philip Jacobs. "The Implications of an Epidemiological Mistake: A Community's Response to a Perceived Excess Cancer Risk." *American Journal of Public Health*, vol. 83 (1993): 233–239.

Hogin, Bradley R. "Post-Cleanup Stigma Claims: The Latest from the War Over Hazardous Waste." *Toxic Law Reporter* (February, 1995).

Jaconetty, Thomas, "Stigma, Phobias, and Fear: Their Effect on Valuation." *Assessment Journal*, vol. 3, no. 1 (January/February 1996).

Kamenir-Reznik and Ehrlich. "Minimizing Damages in Environmental Contamination Cases: Cleanup Costs, Diminution in Value, and the Emergence of Stigma." *Real Estate Environmental Liability News* (November 3, 1995).

Keil, Katherine. "Measuring the Impact of the Discovery and Cleaning of Identified Hazardous Waste Sites on House Values." *Land Economics*, 71 (1995).

Keil, Katherine A. and Katherine T. McClain. "House Prices During Siting Decision Stages: The Case of an Incinerator from Rumor Through Operation." *Journal of Environmental Economics and Management* (March 1995): 241–255.

Kimball, J.R. and W.C. Weaver. "Evaluating the Impact of Solid-Waste Transfer Stations." *The Appraisal Journal* (January 1983).

Kinnard, William N., Jr. "Analyzing the Stigma Effect of Proximity to Hazardous Materials Site." *Environmental Watch* (December 1989): 4–7.

_____ "Stigma and Property Values: A Summary and Review of Research and Literature." Paper presented at the Appraisal Institute Symposium, Washington, D.C. (June 1997).

Kleindorfer, Paul and Peter J. Knez. "A Compensation Mechanism for Siting Noxious Facilities: Theory and Experimental Design." *Journal of Environmental Economics and Management*, vol. 14 (1987): 371–383.

Lusvardi, Wayne C. "The Dose Makes the Poison: Environmental Phobia or Regulatory Stigma?" *The Appraisal Journal* (April 2000): 184–194.

Melius, J. "Facility Siting and Health Questions: The Burden of Health Risk Certainty." *Environmental Law Report*, vol. 15, no. 10242 (August 1985).

Mitchell, Phillip S., PhD. "Estimating Economic Damages to Real Property Due to Loss of Marketability, Rentability, and Stigma." *The Appraisal Journal* (April 2000).

Moore, Cassandra Chromes. *Haunted Housing: How Toxic Scare Stories Are Spooking the Public Out of House and Home.* Washington, D.C.: Cato Institute, 1997.

Muldowney and Harrison. "Stigma Damages: Property Damage and the Fear of Risk." *Defense Counsel Journal* (October 1995).

Mundy, Bill, MAI, PhD. "Contamination, Fear and Industrial Property Transactions." Professional Report, Washington D.C.: Society of Industrial and Office Realtors (May/June 1993).

_____ "Stigma Influences on Value." *Methodologies for Valuation of Real Property Impacted by Pollution from Hazardous and Toxic Materials.* A seminar presented and prepared by The Real Estate Counseling Group of America, Inc., Orlando, Florida (February 28, 1991).

_____ "Stigma and Value." *Appraisal Journal* (January 1992): 7–13.

Patchin, Peter J., MAI. "Contaminated Properties Stigma Revisited." *The Appraisal Journal* (April 1991): 167–172.

"Property Devaluation from Off-Site Environmental Hazards." *Environmental Strategies for Real Estate*, vol. 2, no. 8. Boston, Massachusetts: Warren, Gorham Lamont, May 1995.

Richards. "An Analysis of the Impact of Contamination and Stigma on the Valuation of Commercial Property Investments." University of Reading, PhD Thesis (1997).

Roddewig, Richard J., MAI, CRE. "Classifying the Level of Risk and Stigma Affecting Contaminated Property." *The Appraisal Journal* (January 1999): 98–102.

_____ "Stigma, Environmental Risk and Property Value: 10 Critical Inquiries." *The Appraisal Journal* (October 1996): 375–387.

Weber, Bruce R. "Stigma: Quantifying Murphy's Law." *Urban Land* (June 1988).

Weigman, Gutteling, Boer and Houwen. "Newspaper Coverage of Hazards and the Reactions of Readers." *Journalism Quarterly* (1979).

Wilson, Albert R. "Proximity Stigma?" Unpublished Paper (2001).

Wise and Pfeifenberger. "The Enigma of Stigma: The Case of the Industrial Excess Landfill." *Toxic Law Reporter* (1994).

Asbestos

Adams and Baker. "Sale or Lease of Asbestos-Contaminated Buildings: Legal and Marketplace Issues." *National Asbestos Council Journal* (1986).

American Institute of Real Estate Appraisers. *Asbestos: Basic Information for Appraisers*, 2d ed. Chicago, Illinois: American Institute of Real Estate Appraisers, 1990.

Asbestos Abatement Services, Inc. *The AASI Bulletin.* Washington, D.C.: Quarterly.

"Asbestos: Basic Information for Appraisers." Research Department, *AIREA* (1988).

"Asbestos and Carcinogenicity." *Science*, vol. 249 (August 24, 1990).

"Asbestos, Carcinogenicity, and Public Policy." *Science*, vol. 248 (May 18, 1990).

Associated Press. "Ex-Asbestos Giant Faces New Court Challenges." *The Los Angeles Times* (January, 19, 1993): Business Section 1.

Barsky, Neil. "Assessment Cut on Office Building Due to Asbestos." *The Wall Street Journal* (January 23, 1991): B2.

Bell, Randall, MAI. "The Impact of Asbestos on Real Estate Values." *Right of Way* (October 1994): 10–21.

Bible, Douglas S., Marshall F. Graham, and Michael T. Newman. "Travis Square: A Study of ACM Removal in a Class A Office Building." *Environmental Watch* (Winter 1991).

Brittandall, Gerald. "Identifying and Resolving Asbestos Problems." *Journal of Property Management*, Bulletin 371 (May/June 1985): 41.

Dewees, Donald N. *Controlling Asbestos in Buildings: An Economic Investigation.* Washington D.C.: Resources for the Future, 1986.

Bibliography

Dorsey, T.A. "Asbestos and Appraisers." *Real Estate Appraiser and Analyst* (Summer 1988).

Environmental Protection Agency. "Assessing Asbestos Exposure in Public Buildings." Washington, D.C.: Office of Toxic Substances, May 1988.

_____ "EPA Study of Asbestos-Containing Materials in Public Buildings: A Report to Congress." Washington, D.C., February 1988.

_____ "Guidance for Controlling Asbestos-Containing Materials in Buildings." Washington, D.C.: Office of Pesticides and Toxic Substances, June 1985.

_____ "Managing Asbestos in Place: A Building Owner's Guide to Operations and Maintenance Programs for Asbestos-Containing Materials." Washington, D.C.: Office of Pesticides and Toxic Substances (July 1990).

"Fiberboard, Insurers Settle Asbestos Suit for Record $3 Billion." *Los Angeles Times* (August 31, 1993): Business Section 1.

Fineman, S.J. "Asbestos and the Appraiser." *Appraisal Journal* (April 1987).

Fisher, Jeffrey D., PhD, George H. Lentz, PhD, and K.S. Maurice Tse, PhD. "Effects of Asbestos on Commercial Real Estate: A Survey of MAI Appraisers." *The Appraisal Journal* (October 1993): 587–599.

_____ "Valuation of Effects of Asbestos on Commercial Real Estate." *The Journal of Real Estate Research*, vol. 7, no. 3 (Summer 1992).

Harvard University. *Summary of Symposium on Health Aspects of Exposure to Asbestos in Buildings.* Cambridge, Massachusetts: Energy and Environmental Policy Center, John F. Kennedy School of Government, Harvard University, 1989.

Hillman, Chris. "Asbestos and the Closing Table: Taking the Discount–Taking on the Problem." *Management and Operations* (September 1989).

Kirkland, Janis L. "What's Current in Asbestos Regulation." *University of Richmond Law Review*, vol. 23 (Spring 1989).

Koehn, Michael F., Paul W. MacAvoy, and Harindra De Silva. "Market Responses to Asbestos in Buildings." *Journal of Real Estate and Financial Economics* (September 1990).

Lenz, George H. "Asbestos and the Value of Commercial Real Estate." *The MGIC Newsletter* (March/April 1989): 2.

Mansfield, Richard H., III. "Disclosure of Asbestos, Who Is Responsible?" *Legal Line* (April 1992): 36–37.

McGraw-Hill, Inc. "Owners Get Tax Refund Due to Asbestos." *The Appraisal Journal* (July 1992): 427–428.

McIntosh, Will. "Study of the Southern State Office Building: The Effect of ACMs on Rents and Marketability in a Healthy Market." *Environmental Watch.* Chicago, Illinois: Appraisal Institute, Winter 1991.

Minter, Nancy L. "Asbestos in Buildings." *Urban Land* (January 1990).

Mossman, B.T., J. Bigon, M. Corn, A. Seaton, and J.B.L. Gee. "Asbestos: Scientific Developments and Implications for Public Policy." *Science*, vol. 247 (January 19, 1990).

Mundy, Bill, MAI, PhD. "The Impact of Asbestos on a Commercial Property." *Environmental Watch* (June 1989).

"Perilous Particle: Tiny Asbestos Fibers Pose a Health Threat to Workers." *The Wall Street Journal* (June 8, 1972).

Ragas, Wade R. and R. Dunbar Argote. "Valuation of Office Buildings with ACMs Using DCF Analysis." *Environmental Watch.* Chicago, Illinois: Appraisal Institute, Winter 1991.

Ramsland, Maxwell O., Jr. "An Asbestos Assessment Model: A Valuation Methodology for Appraisers." *Environmental Watch* (Spring 1990).

_____ "Asbestos: Risk and the Remediation Process." *Technical Report.* Chicago, Illinois: Appraisal Institute, 1992.

_____ "A Case Study from 'Asbestos: Risk and the Remediation Process'." Originally presented at the 1991 Appraisal Institute Symposium and published in *Measuring the Effects of Hazardous Materials Contamination on Real Estate Values: Techniques and Applications.* Chicago, Illinois: The Appraisal Institute, 1992.

Rosen, Kenneth A. and Frederick D. Morris. "Finally, Something Good Comes from Asbestos Contaminations." *The Real Estate Finance Journal* (Spring 1995).

Shenkman, Martin M. "Asbestos: What You Really Should Know." *Real Estate Insight* (March 1989).

Spengler, John D., et al. *Summary of Symposium on Health Aspects of Exposure to Asbestos in Buildings.* Cambridge, Massachusetts: Harvard University Energy and Environmental Policy Center, August 1989.

Tenenbaum, Wayne A. "The Effect of Asbestos on Market Value: A Suggested Methodology." *14th Annual IPT Conference* (June 1990).

Troen, Mark L., CRE. "Asbestos: How You Frame the Issue Does Make a Difference." *Real Estate Issues* (Fall/Winter 1991).

United Press International. "New Attitudes and Litigation Over Asbestos." *Los Angeles Times* (September 22, 1993), Business Section, 7.

United States Environmental Protection Agency (EPA). *EPA Study of Asbestos-Containing Materials in Public Buildings.* Washington, D.C.: U.S. Government Printing Office, 1988.

Wilson, Albert R. "Probable Financial Effect of Asbestos Removal on Real Estate." *The Appraisal Journal* (July 1989): 378–391.

Wilson, A.R., J.T. Harrington, and S.M. Raterman. "The Impact of Asbestos on Appraising." Education program presented at annual meeting of the American Institute of Real Estate Appraisers, Chicago, April 1988. Chicago, Illinois: First Tape, Inc., 1988. Audio recording.

Lead and Heavy Metals

Anderson, Eugene R. "Lead Paint and 'Sick Building Syndrome' Liability Claims." *The Real Estate Finance Journal* (Summer 1995).

Chatterjee, Samar and Herman H. Moore. "Remediation of Mercury Contaminated Soils/Mixed Wastes." *Federal Environmental Restoration Conference and Exhibitions.* Washington, D.C.: Federal Environmental Restoration Conference and Exhibitions, 1992.

Farr, Walter G. "The Impact of Childhood Lead Poisoning on Affordable Housing." *The Real Estate Finance Journal* (Winter 1995).

Ford, D.A. and M. Gilligan. "The Effect of Lead Paint Abatement Laws on Rental Property Values." *AREUEA Journal* (Spring 1988).

Franklin. "Getting the Lead Out." *Real Estate Valuation* (1996).

Hunsperger, Wayne L. "Heavy Metal Pollution and Residential Property Damages." *Environmental Watch*, vol. VI, no. 3 (Fall 1993).

Keenan, R. Mark. "Important Points About Lead Paint Removal." *The Real Estate Finance Journal* (Summer 1995).

Kelly, Donald E. "Getting the Lead Out: New Regulations Require Disclosure and Evaluation." *Valuation, Insights & Perspectives* (First Quarter 1997): 33–35.

Witkin and Desiderio. "Getting the Lead Out: Federal Regulations Analyzed Regarding Disclosure of Lead-Based Paint Hazards." *Real Estate/Environmental Liability News* (1997).

LUSTs

American Institute of Real Estate Appraisers. *Underground Storage Tanks: Basic Information for Appraisers* (December 1988).

Donovan, Brian and Pat O'Connor. "Underground Storage Tank Update." *Plant Engineering* (June 1989).

"Environmental Hazards: Research Report on Underground Storage Tanks." *Southern California Chapter of AIREA* (1988).

"How the New Underground Storage Tank Law Affects Lender Liability." Seminar, McBride, Baker & Coles Environmental Practice Group & EPS Environmental Services, Inc. (December 6, 1994).

Rosenwinkel, Karen and Michael J. Maher. "Lesson in L.U.S.T.—Cleaning Up Leaking Underground Storage Tanks." *Illinois Bar Journal* (March 1993).

Sementelli, Arthur and Robert Simons. "Regulation of Leaking Underground Storage Tanks: Policy Enforcement and Unintended Consequences." *Economic Development Quarterly* (August 1997).

Simons, Robert A. and Rudy R. Robinson, III. *Negative Proximity Influence of Leaking Underground Storage Tanks/Toxic Neighbors on Residential Property: Issues of Information and Measurement.* Paper presented at Annual Meeting of the American Real Estate Society, Hilton Head, South Carolina (April 1995).

Simons, Robert A., PhD and Arthur Sementelli. "Liquidity Loss and Delayed Transactions with Leaking Underground Storage Tanks." *The Appraisal Journal* (July 1997): 255–260.

Simons, Robert A., PhD, William M. Bowen, PhD, and Arthur J. Sementelli, PhD. "The Effect of Leaking Underground Storage Tanks on Residential Property Value." *Journal of Real Estate Research*, vol. 14, no. _ (1997): 29–42.

_____ "The Effects of LUSTs from Gas Stations on Residential and Commercial Property That Is Actually Contaminated." *Appraisal Journal* (April 1999): 186–194.

_____ "The Effect of Underground Storage Tanks on Residential Property Values in Cuyahoga County, Ohio." *The Journal of Real Estate Research*, vol. 14, no. _ (1997).

_____ "The Price and Liquidity Effects of UST Leaks from Gas Stations on Adjacent Contaminated Property." *The Appraisal Journal* (April 1999): 186–194.

EMFs, Radon, and Radiation

American Council on Science and Health. *Health Effects of Low-Level Radiation.* New York: American Council on Science and Health, 1989.

Appraisal Institute, Research Department. "Radon: Basic Information for Appraisers." Rev. ed. Chicago, Illinois: American Institute for Real Estate Appraisers, March 1990.

Ball, Thomas A. *A Study of the Economic Effects of High Voltage Electrical Transmission Lines on the Market Value of Real Property.* Tempe, Arizona: Salt River Project, 1989.

Baumbach, Charles. "EMF Radiation and the Increased Awareness of Real Estate Markets." *Environmental Watch* (Winter 1993).

Beasley, Ben. "High Voltage Power Lines: Impact on Nearby Property Values." *Right of Way* (February 1991).

Beauregard, Conseil Eur. *Final Report: Assessment of the Impacts of the Hydro Line River Crossing...On the Residents of the Immediate Region.* Hydro Quebec, Environmental Vice–Presidency, 1990.

Blomquist, Glenn. "The Effect of Electrical Utility Power Plant Location on Area Property Value." *Land Economics* (February 1974): 97–100.

Bolton, David R., MAI. "Properties Near Power Lines and Valuation Issues: Condemnation or Inverse Condemnation?" Paper presented to the Annual Conference Institute on Planning, Zoning and Eminent Domain, Dallas, Texas (November 17–19, 1993).

Brodeur, Paul. "Annals of Radiation: The Hazards of Electromagnetic Fields." *The New Yorker* (June 12, 19, & 26, 1989) later published as *Currents of Death: Power Lines, Computer Terminals and the Attempt to Cover Up Their Threat to Your Health.* New York: Simon and Shuster, 1989.

Buesing, Robert H. "Condemnation for Electric Transmission Lines: Meeting the Challenge of Adequate Proof." *Probate & Property* (May/June 1994).

California Energy Commission. *High Voltage Transmission Lines* (July 1992).

Callanan, Judith and R.V. Hargreaves. "The Effect of Transmission Lines on Property Values: A Statistical Analysis." New Zealand, 1995.

Clark, Louis E., Jr., MAI and F.H. Treadway, Jr., MAI. *Impact of Electric Power Transmission Line Easements on Real Estate Values* (American Institute of Real Estate Appraisers, 1972).

Cohen, B.L. "Radon." Education program presented at annual meeting of the American Institute of Real Estate Appraisers, Chicago, April 1988. Chicago: First Tape, Inc., 1988. Audio Recording.

Cole, Leonard. *Element of Risk: The Politics of Radon.* Washington, D.C.: AAAS Press, 1993.

Colwell, Peter. "Power Lines and Land Value." *Journal of Real Estate Research* (Spring 1990).

Colwell, Peter and K. Foley. "Electric Transmission Lines and the Selling Price of Residential Property." *The Appraisal Journal* (October 1979).

Cowger, John R., Steven C. Bottemiller, and James M. Cahill. "Transmission Line Impact on Residential Property Values." *Right of Way* (September/October 1996).

Delaney, Charles J. *Valuation Impacts for Residential Property Proximate to High Voltage Power Lines: A New Environmental Concern?* Baylor University, Department of Real Estate (Spring 1991). Unpublished manuscript.

Delaney, C. and D. Timmons. "High Voltage Power Lines: Do They Affect Residential Property Value?" *Journal of Real Estate Research,* vol. 7, no. 3 (Summer 1992).

Economics Consultants Northwest. *Garrison-West High Voltage Transmission Line Social Monitoring Study.* Montana Department of Natural Resources & Conservation, and Bonneville Power Administration, 1990.

Electric Power Research Institute. "Socioeconomic Impacts of Power Plants." Palo Alto, California: February 1982.

Faucett Associates. Jack. *Evaluation of Power Plant Externalities: A Land Use Approach.* Maryland Department of Natural Resources, U.S. Department of Commerce, National Technical Information Source (NTIS), Annapolis, Maryland (January 1976).

Florig, H. Keith and M. Granger Morgan. "Measurements of Housing Density Along Transmission Lines." *Bioelectromagnetics,* vol. 9 (1988).

Furby, Lita, Robin Gregory, Paul Slovic, and Baruch Fischoff. "Electric Power Transmission Lines, Property Values, and Compensation." *Journal of Environmental Management,* 27 (1988).

Hamilton, Stanley W. and Gregory M. Schwann. "Do High Voltage Electric Transmission Lines Affect Property Value?" *Land Economics* (November 1995).

Health Physics Society. "Radiation Risk in Perspective." *Poison Statement.* McLean, Virginia: Health Physics Society, 1996.

Ignelzi, Patrice C. "Successfully Conducting Transmission Line Impact Assessments of Property Values." *Transmission Lines in Residential Neighborhoods: Issues in Siting and Environmental Planning.* Edison Electric Institute, Portland, Oregon (October 12–13, 1989).

Ignelzi, Patrice C. and Thomas Priestly. *A Methodology for Assessing Transmission Line Impacts in Residential Communities,* Edison Electric Institute, Washington, D.C. (June 1989).

_____ *A Statistical Analysis of Transmission Line Impacts in Six Neighborhoods.* Albany, California: Pacific Consulting Services, February 1991. Two volumes.

Kinnard, William N., Jr. "The Effect of High-Voltage Overhead Transmission Lines on Sales Prices and Market Values of Nearby Real Estate: An Annotated Bibliography and Evaluative Analysis." *Transmission Lines in Residential Neighborhoods: Issues in Siting and Environmental Planning.* Edison Electric Institute, Portland, Oregon (October 12–13, 1989).

_____ "Impact of High Voltage Transmission Lines on Property Values." *Journal of Property Tax Management,* vol. 1, no. 4, (Summer 1990).

_____ *Patterns of Property Value Impacts from Proximity to High-Voltage Transmission Lines: Analytical Update.* Paper presented at Edison Electric Institute Conference, Duluth, Minnesota (August 1992).

_____ "Tools and Techniques for Measuring the Effects of Proximity to Radioactive Contamination on Single-Family Residential Sales Prices." *Measuring the Effects of Hazardous Materials Contamination on Real Estate Values: Techniques and Applications.* Chicago, Illinois: Appraisal Institute, 1992.

Kinnard, William N., Jr., Sandy Bond, Paul M. Syms, and Jake W. DeLottie. "Effects of Proximity to High-Voltage Transmission Lines on Nearby Residential Property Values: An International Perspective on Recent Research." Paper presented at the 1997 International Conference of the American Real Estate and Urban Economics Association, Berkeley, California (May 1997).

Kinnard, William N., Jr., CRE and Sue Ann Dickey. "A Primer on Proximity Impact Research: Residential Property Values Near High-Voltage Transmission Lines." *Real Estate Issues* (April 1995).

Kinnard, William N., Jr., CRE, and Mary Beth Geckler. "The Effects on Residential Real Estate Prices from Proximity to Properties Contaminated with Radioactive Materials." *Real Estate Issues* (Fall/Winter 1991): 25–36.

Kinnard, William N., Jr, P. Mitchell, G. Beron, and J. Webb. "Market Reaction to an Announced Release of Radioactive Materials: The Impact on Assessable Value." *Property Tax Journal* (September 1991).

Kinnard, William N., Jr., Mary Beth Geckler, and Jake W. DeLottie. *Effects of Proximity to High-Voltage Power Lines on Nearby Residential Property: An International Perspective.* Paper prepared by the Chartered Surveyors' Educational Channel Television Education Network, Ltd., Royal Institution of Chartered Surveyors, London, England (August 1996).

_____ "Post-1992 Evidence of EMF Impacts on Nearby Residential Property Values." Paper presented at the 1997 Annual Conference of the American Real Estate Society, Sarasota, Florida (April 1997).

Kinnard, William N., Jr., Jeffrey B. Kinnard, and John K. Geckler. *The Effect of High-Voltage Overhead Transmission Lines on Sales Prices and Market Values of Nearby Real Estate: An Annotated Bibliography and Evaluative Analysis.* Storrs, Connecticut: Real Estate Counseling Group of Connecticut, September 1988.

Kinnard, William N., Jr., Phillip S. Mitchell, and James R. Webb. "The Impact of High-Voltage Overhead Transmission Lines on the Value of Real Property." Paper presented at the American Real Estate Society Annual Conference, Arlington, Virginia (April 1989).

Kroll, Cynthia A. *Property Valuation: A Primer on Proximity Impact Research.* Paper presented at the Conference on Electric and Magnetic Fields, San Francisco, California (February 8, 1994).

Kroll, Cynthia A. and Thomas Priestley. *The Effects of Overhead Transmission Lines on Property Values: A Review and Analysis of the Literature.* A report prepared for the Siting and Environmental Planning Task Force, Edison Electric Institute, Piedmont, California (December 1991).

Kung, Hsiang-te and Charles F. Seagle. "Impact of Power Transmission Lines on Property Values: A Case Study." *The Appraisal Journal* (July 1992).

Mitchell, Phillip S. and William N. Kinnard, Jr. "Statistical Analysis of High-Voltage Overhead Transmission Line Construction on the Value of Vacant Land." *Valuation,* vol. 40, no. 1 (June 1996).

Morris, K.B. "Radon Gas Nature's Inverse Condemnation." *The Appraisal Journal* (July 1986).

Payne, B.A., S. Jay Olshansky, and T.E. Segel. "The Effects on Property Values of Proximity to a Site Contaminated with Radioactive Waste." *Natural Resources Journal,* vol. 27 (Summer 1987).

_____ "The Effects on Residential Property Values of Proximity to a Site Contaminated with Radioactive Waste." *Waste Management Conference*. Tucson, Arizona, (March 24, 1985). Presented by Argonne National Laboratory, Illinois.

Pease, Craig M. and James J. Bull. "Do Electromagnetic Fields Cause Cancer?" in the University of Texas Biology 301C [electronic bulletin board] 1996—[cited January 15, 1998]. Available: http://www.utexas.edu/courses/bio301c/Topics/EMG/Text.html.

Porter, Jeffrey R. and Carolyn S. Langer. "Electromagnetic Fields: Courts Deal with EMF's Effect on Property Values." *Massachusetts Lawyer's Weekly* (February 27, 1995).

"Power Lines Raise Fears in Home Buyers." *The New York Times*, Section 10 (July 11, 1993).

"Power Lines Short-Circuit Sales, Homeowners Claim." *The Wall Street Journal* (December 8, 1993).

"Power Struggle—High-Tension Lines Creating Tension Among Some Buyers." *New York Newsday* (August 14, 1994).

Priestly, Thomas. *Perceived Impacts of Electric Transmission Facilities: A Review of Survey-Based Studies*, vol. 1.: Research Summaries and Evaluation (Edison Electric Institute, March 1992).

_____ *Perceived Impacts of Electric Transmission Facilities: A Review of Survey-Based Studies,* vol. 2 (Edison Electric Institute, March 1992).

_____ "Perceptions of Transmission Lines in Residential Neighborhoods: Results of a California Case Study." *Transmission Lines in Residential Neighborhoods: Issues in Siting and Environmental Planning*. Edison Electric Workshop, Portland, Oregon (October 12–13, 1989).

Priestly, Thomas and Gary Evans. *Perceptions of Transmission Lines in Residential Neighborhoods: A Case Study in Vallejo, California*. South California Edison Company (1990).

Rauch, Gregory B. and David W. Fugate. "EMF: A Techno-Environmental Issue of the 1990s." *Journal of Environmental Law & Practice*.

Reed, Richard A. "Fear and Lowering Property Values in New York: Proof of Consequential Damages from 'Cancerphobia' in the Wake of *Criscuola v. Power Authority of the State of New York*." *New York State Bar Journal* (March/April 1994).

Reese, L. "Radon and the Energy-Efficient House." *The Appraisal Journal* (July 1981).

Rhodeside & Harwell, Inc. *Perceptions of Power Lines: Residents' Attitudes*. Richmond, Virginia: Virginia Power Company, 1988.

_____ (Andrew A. White, Statistical Consultant), *Transmission Line Impact on Property Values*. Richmond, Virginia: Virginia Power Company, June 1992.

Rikon, Michael. "Electromagnetic Radiation Field Property Devaluation." *The Appraisal Journal* (January 1996): 87–90.

Rigdon, Glenn J. "138 kV Transmission Lines and the Value of Recreational Land." *Right of Way* (December 1991).

Sewell, E. Larry. *230 kV Transmission Lines: Impact Study on Real Estate Marketability*. Sarasota, Florida: Sewell, Valentich, Tillis & Thatcher, 1989.

Taubes, Gary. "Fields of Fear." *The Atlantic Monthly* (November 1994).

Treffer, B.E. "Radon Gas May Seep Into Your Liability." *Real Estate Appraiser and Analyst* (Spring 1987).

United States Environmental Protection Agency. *Statewide Radon Survey*. Washington D.C.: EPA, 1990.

University of California at Berkeley. "Electrophobia: Overcoming Fear of EMFs." *Wellness Letter* (November 1994).

U.S. Department of Energy, National Institute for Occupational Safety and Health, and National Institute of Environmental Health Sciences. *EMF in the Workplace*. Washington, D.C.: U.S. Government Printing Office, 1996.

Wellman, Juliana B. "The Threat of EMF Litigation and the Case for Sound Science." *The Litigation Journal* (Fall 1993).

Wertheimer, N. and E. Leeper. "Electrical Wiring Configurations and Childhood Cancer." *American Journal of Epidemiology*, vol. 109, no. 3 (March 1979).

Soil and Groundwater

Abdalla, C.W., B. Roach and D. Epp. "Valuing Environmental Quality Changes Using Averting Expenditures: An Application to Groundwater Contamination." *Land Economics*, 68 (May 1992).

Ashengrau, Ozonoff, Paulu, Coogan, Vezina, Heeren, and Zhang. "Cancer Risk and Tetrachloroethyene Contaminated Drinking Water in Massachusetts." *Archives of Environmental Health* (1998).

Bendix. "Let the Buyer Beware: Toxics Underfoot." *Experts-at-Law* (1990).

Bergstrom, Boyle, Job, and Kealy. "Assessing the Economic Benefits of Ground Water for Environmental Policy Decisions." *Water Resources Bulletin* (1996).

Colten. "A Historical Perspective on Industrial Wastes and Groundwater Contamination." *The Geographical Review* (undated, appears to be from the 1960s).

Dotzour, Mark, PhD. "Groundwater Contamination and Residential Property Values." *The Appraisal Journal* (July 1997): 279–290.

Environmental Protection Agency. "EPA Policy Toward Owners of Property Containing Contaminated Aquifers." *Environmental Due Diligence Guide* (1996).

Fitzgerald. "Accord Close in Groundwater Contamination Case." *Editor & Publisher* (1995).

Girasole, Anthony P., Jr. "The Lesson of Love Canal." *Valuation, Insights, & Perspectives* (First Quarter 1999): 9–13.

Glaser and Cherches. "Local Government's Role in Groundwater Cleanup." *Public Management* (1992).

Hawley. "Assessment of Health Risk from Exposure to Contaminated Soil." *Risk Analysis* (1985).

"Human Health Based Guidance Levels for the Ingestion of Contaminants in Drinking Water and Soil." Arizona Dept. of Environmental Quality (June 1992).

Kinnard, William N., Jr., Mary Beth Geckler, and Jake W. DeLottie. "The Effect of Varying Levels of Negative Publicity on Single-Family Property Values: A Case Study of Soil Contamination." *Assessment Journal*, vol. 3, no. 5 (September/October 1996).

Kinnard, William N., Jr., Jake W. DeLottie, Mary Beth Geckler, and Benjamin H. Noble. *The Impact of Widespread, Long-Term Soil Contamination on Residential Property Values: A Case Study.* Paper presented at the Annual Meeting of the American Real Estate Society, Hilton Head, South Carolina (April 1995).

Lunz, Robert, MAI, CRE. "Groundwater Contamination and Real Estate Value: How What Is Below Affects What Is Above." *U.S. Water News* (October 1989).

Malone, Patricia and Richard Barrows. "Groundwater Pollution's Effects on Residential Property Values, Portage County, Wisconsin." *Journal of Soil and Water Conservation* (March–April 1990).

Nash, G.J. "Appraisal of Commercial Real Estate with Toxic Soil Contamination: Discounted Cash Flow Strategies." *Environmental Watch* (Fall 1990).

O'Neil and Raucher. "The Costs of Groundwater Contamination." *Journal of Soil and Water Conservation* (1990).

Page, William and Harvey Rabinowitz. "Groundwater Contamination: Its Effects on Property Values and Cities." *Journal of the American Planning Association* (Autumn 1993).

Quadri, Claire Garrison. "A Primer on Groundwater Contamination and Movement." *Journal of Environmental Law & Practice.*

Rosiers, Francois Des, Alain Bolduc, and Marius Theriault. "Environment and Value: Does Drinking Water Affect House Prices?" Presentation at the 1997 Meeting of the American Real Estate Society in Sarasota, Florida.

"Termite Control Pesticides May Linger in Air and Soil." *Environmental Watch* (1989).

Natural Gas and Oil

Campbell, Brad, Ed Kern, and Dean Horn. *Impact of Oil Spillage from World War II Tanker Sinkings.* Massachusetts Institute of Technology, Department of Ocean Engineering (January 1977).

Dorchester, John D., MAI, CRE. "The Exxon Valdez Oil Spill: Property Damage Assessments." *The Valuer and Land Economist*, vol. 34, no. 2 (May 1996).

Flower, Patrick and Wade Ragas. "The Effects of Refineries on Neighborhood Property Values." *Journal of Real Estate Research*, vol. 9, no. 3 (1994).

Friedman, Jack P., CRE. "Defending An Oil Company Against Litigation for Environmental Contamination (A Case Study)." *Real Estate Issues* (Winter 1999/2000): 33–39.

Kinnard, William N., Jr. *The Impact of Proximity to High-Pressure Natural Gas Pipelines on Single-Family Residential Property Values.* Paper presented at the 1993 Annual Meeting of the American Real Estate Society, Key West, Florida (April 1993).

Kinnard, William N., Jr., Sue Ann Dickey, and Mary Beth Geckler. "Natural Gas Pipeline Impact on Residential Property Values: An Empirical Study of Two Market Areas." *Right of Way* (June/July 1994).

Klein, L.A. and K.L. Golub. "Appraising Petroleum Terminals—A 15 Year Retrospective." *Real Estate Appraiser and Analyst* (Fall 1989).

Mead, Walter J. and Phillip E. Sorensen. "The Economic Cost of the Santa Barbara Oil Spill." *Santa Barbara Oil Symposium.* Sponsored by the National Science Foundation and the Marine Science Institute at the University of California at Santa Barbara (December 16–18, 1970).

National Ocean Service, National Oceanic and Atmospheric Administration. *Assessing the Social Costs of Oil Spills: The AMOCO CADIZ Case Study* (July 1983).

Ragas, Wade R. and Patrick C. Flower. "Petroleum Refineries—Can Larger Site Buffers Limit Adjacent Property Value Impacts?" Professional Report on the Society of Industrial and Office Realtors (October 1994).

_____ "Refineries and Neighborhood Property Values." *Technical Report 1018.* College Station, Texas: Texas A&M University, April 1994.

Roddewig, Richard J., MAI, CRE. "Temporary Stigma: Lessons from the Exxon Valdez Litigation." *The Appraisal Journal* (January 1997): 96–101.

Simons, Robert, PhD. "The Effect of Pipeline Ruptures on Noncontaminated Residential Easement-Holding Property in Fairfax County." *The Appraisal Journal* (July 1999).

_____ "Settlement of an Oil Pipeline Leak with Contaminated Residential Property: A Case Study." *Real Estate Issues* (Winter 1999/2000): 46–52.

Toma, Darrell M. "The Effects of Pipelines on Agricultural Land Values." *Right of Way* (October 1983).

U.S. Department of Transportation, Office of Pipeline Safety (OPS). *1996 Colonial Pipeline Task Force, Final Report* (January 10, 1997).

Noise and Traffic

Allen, Gary R. "Highway Noise, Noise Mitigation, and Residential Property Values." *Transportation Research Record,* No. 812 (1981).

Allen, W. Bruce and David E. Boyce. "Impact of High Speed Rapid Transit Facility on Residential Property Values." *High Speed Ground Transportation Journal,* vol. 8, no. 2 (Summer 1974).

Cantrell, W.F., E.D. Crook and L.S. Pipkin. "Noise. We Have Heard it Before." *Real Estate Appraiser and Analyst* (Fall 1983).

Bell, Randall, MAI. "The Impact of Airport Noise on Residential Real Estate." *Appraisal Journal* (July 2001).

Bornis, Sanford R. "Mieszkowski and Saper's Estimate of the Effects of Airport Noise on Property Values: A Comment." *Journal of Urban Economics,* vol. 9, no. 1 (January 1981).

Crowley, Ronald W. "A Case Study of the Effects of an Airport on Land Value." *Journal of Transport Economics and Policy,* vol. VII, no. 2 (May 1973).

Frankel, Marvin. "Airport Noise and Residential Property Values: Results of a Survey Study." *The Appraisal Journal* (January 1991): 96–110.

_____ "The Impact of Aircraft Noise on Residential Property Markets." *Illinois Business Review,* vol. 45, no. 5 (October 1988).

Gamble, Hays B., Owen H. Sauerlander, and C. John Langley. "Adverse and Beneficial Effects of Highways on Residential Property Values." *Transportation Research Record,* no. 508 (1974).

Gautrin, Jean-Francois. "An Evaluation of the Impact of Aircraft Noise on Property Values with a Simple Model of Urban Land Rent." *Land Economics* (February 1975).

Hall, Fred L., Barbara E. Breston, and S. Martin Taylor. "Effects of Highway Noise on Residential Property Values." *Transportation Research Record,* no. 686 (1978).

Hall, Fred L. and Douglas Welland. "The Effect of Noise Barriers on the Market Value of Adjacent Residential Properties." *Transportation Research Record,* no. 1143 (1987).

Harvey, Milton E., John W. Frazier, and Mindaugas Matulionis. "Cognition of a Hazardous Environment: Reactions to Buffalo Airport Noise." *Economic Geography,* vol. 55, no. 4 (October 1979).

Hirschman, Ira and Michael Henderson. "Methodology for Assessing Local Land Use Impacts of Highways." *Transportation Research Record,* no. 1274 (1990).

Hughes, William T. and C.F. Sirmans. "Traffic Externalities and Single-Family House Prices." Unpublished paper, College of Business Administration, Louisiana State University (March 1992).

Hyde, James V., Jr. "The Appraiser's Approach to Noise Damage." *The Real Estate Appraiser* (November/December 1976).

Kamerud, Dana B. and Calvin R. vonBuseck. "The Effects of Traffic Sound and Its Reduction on House Prices." *Transportation Research Record,* no. 1033 (1985).

Langdon, F.J. "Noise Nuisance Caused by Road Traffic in Residential Areas: Part III." *Journal of Sound and Vibration,* vol. 49, no. 2 (1976).

Langley, C. John, Jr. "Adverse Impacts of the Washington Beltway on Residential Property Values." *Land Economics,* vol. 52, no. 1 (February 1976).

_____ "Time-Series Effects of a Limited-Access Highway on Residential Property Values." *Transportation Research Record,* no. 812 (1981).

Lewis, Harold J. "The Appraisal of Highway Noise Damages." *The Appraisal Journal* (October 1977).

McGough, B.C. "Methodology for Highway Impact Studies." *The Appraisal Journal* (January 1968).

Mieszkowski, Peter and Arthur M. Saper. "An Estimate of the Effects of Airport Noise on Property Values." *Journal of Urban Economics,* vol. 5, no. 4 (October 1978).

Nelson, Jon P. "Airport Noise, Location Rent, and the Market for Residential Amenities." *Journal of Environmental Economics and Management,* vol. 6 (1979): 320–331.

_____ *Aircraft Noise and the Market for Residential Housing: Empirical Results for Seven Selected Airports.* Washington, D.C.: Department of Transportation, Research and Special Programs Administration, September 1978.

_____ "Airports and Property Values: A Survey of Recent Evidence." *Journal of Transport Economics and Policy*, vol. XIV, no. 1 (January 1980).

_____ "Highway Noise and Property Values. A Survey of Recent Evidence." *Journal of Transport Economics and Policy*, vol. 16, no. 2 (May 1982).

Nelson, Jon P. and Joseph J. Seneca. "Housing Values, Census Estimates, Disequilibrium, and the Environmental Cost of Airport Noise: A Case Study of Atlanta." *Journal of Environmental Economics and Management* (1985): 169–178.

Nelson, Roland D. and Laurence G. Allen. "Expressway Proximity Damages to Residential Property." *Right of Way*, vol. 30, no. 1 (February 1983).

Palmquist, Raymond B. "Impact of Highway Improvements on Property Values in Washington State." *Transportation Research Record*, no. 887 (1982).

Pennington, G., N. Topham, and R. Ward. "Aircraft Noise and Residential Values Adjacent to Manchester International Airport." *Journal of Transport Economics and Policy*, vol. XXIV, no. 1 (January 1990).

Plessas, D. "Airport Noise: Some Analytical and Policy Perspectives." *Land Economics*, XLVIV (1973).

Taylor, S.M., B.E. Breston, and F.L. Hall. "The Effect of Road Traffic Noise on House Process." *Journal of Sound and Vibration*, vol. 80, no. 4 (February 1982).

Walters, A.A. "Airports—An Economic Study." *Journal of Transport Economics and Policy*, vol. XII, no. 2 (May 1978).

West, Robert J. "Statistical Interference: An Aviation Easement Analysis." *Real Estate Issues*, vol. 13, no. 1 (Spring/Summer 1988).

Wieand, K. "Air Pollution and Property Values: A Study of the St. Louis Area." *Journal of Regional Sciences*, vol. 13, no. 91 (1973).

Wigle, W.G. "The Effect of Urban Expressways on Adjacent Land Values." *Right of Way* (February 1975).

Air and Water

Anderson, R. and T. Crocker. "Air Pollution and Residential Property Values." *Urban Land*, vol. 8, no. 171 (1971).

Bledel, Irene. "The Market for Indoor Air Quality." *Urban Land* (June 1995).

Compilation of Air Pollutant Emission Factors (AP-42), 1999, EPA.

Deyak and Smith. "Residential Property Values and Air Pollution: Some New Evidence." *Quarterly Review of Economics and Business* (1974).

Diamond, Mark. "Indoor Pollution: The Horsemen Cometh." *The Real Estate Finance Journal* (Winter 1995).

Egar, Francis J. "Air Pollution and Property Values in the Hartford Metropolitan Region." Unpublished PhD dissertation, Fordham University (1973).

Freeman, A. Myrick, III. "Air Pollution and Property Values: A Methodological Comment." *Review of Economics and Statistics* vol. 53, no. 415 (1971).

_____ "On Estimating Air Pollution Control Benefits from Land Value Studies." *Journal of Environmental Economics and Management* (May 1974).

Housel, J.M. "UFFI: A Potential Health Hazard in Residential Housing." *Real Estate Appraiser and Analyst* (Spring 1983).

Kilpatrick, Brown and Rogers. "The Performance of Exterior Insulation Finish Systems and Property Values." *The Appraisal Journal* (1999).

Kirshner, D. and Deboral Moore. "The Effect of San Francisco Bay Water Quality on Adjacent Property Values." *Journal of Environmental Management*, vol. 27 (1989): 263–274.

Lansink, B.J. "UFFI and Value." *Real Estate Appraiser and Analyst* (Summer 1984).

Pomento, Joe. "Clean Air-Clean Water: At What Cost?" *Aqueduct* (Metropolitan Water District of Southern California, November 1, 1998).

Ridker, Ronald G. and John A. Henning. "The Determinants of Residential Property Values with Special Reference to Air Pollution." *The Review of Economics and Statistics* (May 1967).

Rosiers, Francois Des, Alain Bolduc, and Marius Theriault. "Environment and Value: Does Drinking Water Affect House Prices." Presentation at the 1997 Meeting of the American Real Estate Society in Sarasota, Florida.

Smith, V. Kerry, and Timothy A. Deyak. "Measuring the Impact of Air Pollution on Property Values." *Journal of Regional Science* (July 1986).

Landfills

American Bar Association, Urban, State and Local Government Section Land Use, Planning and Zoning Committee. 1995 Annual Report of the Subcommittee on Land Use and Waste Disposal. "Land Use Implications of Waste Disposal Regulation: Recent Developments."

Ankney, Barry R. "Appraisal Report: Harvard Landfill Site." *Ninth Annual IAAO Legal Seminar.* New Orleans, Louisiana: November 8 and 9, 1989.

Barlaz, Morton A., et al. "Mass Balance Analysis of Anaerobically Decomposed Refuse." *Journal of Environmental Engineering* 115 (December 1989).

_____ "Methane Production from Municipal Refuse: A Review of Enhancement Techniques and Microbial Dynamics." *Critical Reviews in Environmental Control* 19 (1990).

Bleich, Donald H., M. Chapman Findlay, III, and G. Michael Phillips. "An Evaluation of the Impact of a Well-Designed Landfill on Surrounding Property Values." *The Appraisal Journal* (April 1991).

Bookter, Todd J. and Robert K. Ham. "Stabilization of Solid Waste in Landfills." *Journal of Environmental Engineering Division, ASCE* 108 (December 1982).

Carother, Andre. "Living Next to the Landfill: The Coming of Age of Sumter County." *Real Estate Appraiser and Analyst* (Spring 1989).

Cartee, Charles P. "A Review of Sanitary Landfill Impacts on Property Values." *The Real Estate Appraiser and Analyst* (Spring 1989).

Coughlin, R., H. Newburger, and C. Seigner. *Perceptions of Landfill Operations Held by Nearby Residents.* Philadelphia, PA: Regional Science Research Institute, Discussion Paper Series, no. 65, 1973.

Dabaie, Michael. "Keeping the Country in Countryside." *Waste Age* (March 1995).

Dunphy, R.T. and B.C. Lin. "A Battle for Local Landfills." *Real Estate Appraiser* (December 1991).

Entreken, H.C. "Appraisal of a Class III Landfill." *The Appraisal Journal* (October 1987).

Foreman, R.L., J. Pestinger, and W.L. Hunsperger. "Landfills and Their Effect Upon Value." Educational program presented at annual meeting of the Appraisal Institute, Seattle, August 1991. Largo, Florida: Convention Recordings International. Inc., 1991. Audio recording.

Gamble, Hays B. and Roger H. Downing. "Effects of Sanitary Landfills on Property Values and Residential Development." *Solid and Liquid Wastes: Management, Methods and Socioeconomic Considerations* (The Pennsylvania Academy of Science, 1984).

Gamble, Hays B., R.H. Downing, J.S. Shortle, and D.J. Epp. "Effects of Solid Waste Disposal Sites on Community Development and Residential Property Values." *Final Report for Bureau of Solid Waste Management*, Dept. of Environmental Resources, Commonwealth of Pennsylvania (Institute for Research on Land and Water Resources, Pennsylvania State University, November 1982).

Garippa, John E. and Kenneth R. Kosco. "The Development Law of Landfill Valuation." *Journal of Property Tax Management*, vol. 6, no. 4 (Spring 1995): 1–15.

Goldberg, L., et al. *The Effects of Solid Waste Disposal Sites on Property Values.* Washington, D.C.: U.S. Environmental Protection Agency, 1972.

Guntermann, Karl. "Sanitary Landfills, Stigma and Industrial Land Values." *Journal of Real Estate Research*, vol. 10, no. 5 (1995).

Ham, Robert K. "Landfill Gas, Leachate, and Related Problems."

_____ "Sanitary Landfill State-of-the-Art." Paper presented at *2nd International Landfill Symposium*, Sardinia, Italy (1989).

Ham, Robert K. and Morton A. Barlaz. "Measurement and Prediction of Landfill Gas Quality and Quantity." Paper presented at *ISWA International Symposium "Process, Technology, and Environmental Impact of Sanitary Landfills."* Cagliari, Sardinia, Italy.

Harper, Stephen R. and Frederick G. Pohland. "Landfills: Lessening Environmental Impacts." *Civil Engineering* 58 (November 1988).

Havlicek, Joseph Jr., Robert Richardson, and Lloyd Davies. "Measuring the Impacts of Solid Waste Disposal Site Location on Property Values." *University of Chicago Urban Economics Report No. 65* (November 1971; unpublished c. 1972).

Hunsperger, Wayne L. "Methane Seepage from a Nearby Landfill: Its Effect on Commercial Real Estate." *Environmental Watch* (Fall 1991).

Hwang and Rudzitis. "The External Costs of Sanitary Landfills." *Journal of Environmental Systems* (1977).

Magnuson, Anne. "New Uses for Old Landfills." *Waste Age* 22, (April 1991).

Massey, D. *Attitudes of Nearby Residents Toward Establishing Sanitary Landfills.* Washington, D.C.: U.S. Environmental Protection Agency, 1978.

Mollard, Beth. "Former Landfill Site Offers Low Price, Special Problems." *Business First, Columbus* 7 (February 11, 1991).

Nealon, George and David L. Hansen. "A New Public Works Complex on an Old Landfill." *Public Works* 122 (April 1991).

Nelson, Arthur C., John Genereux, and Michell Genereux. "Price Effects of Landfills on "House Values." *Land Economics*, vol. 68, no. 4 (November 1992).

Pestinger and Gambill. "Home Values Stabilized After Landfill Gas Scare." *International Right of Way Association* (December 1990).

Pierson, John. "Landfills Become Parks as Refuse Goes Green." *The Wall Street Journal* (December 31, 1990).

Reichert, Alan K., M. Small, and S. Mohanty. "The Impact of Landfills on Residential Property Value." *Journal of Real Estate Research*, vol. 7, no. 3 (1992).

Repa, Edward W. "Clean Air Act: Requirements for Landfills." *Waste Age* (April 1995).

"Report of the Subcommittee on Land Use and Solid Waste." *The Urban Lawyer*, vol. 23, no. 4 (Fall 1991).

Robbins, Michael, CRE, Michele Robbins Norman, and John P. Norman. "Landfills Aren't All Bad: Considerations for Real Estate Development." *Real Estate Issues* (Fall/Winter 1991): 11–19.

Rudzitis, G. and E.G. Hwang. "The External Costs of Sanitary Landfills." *Journal of Environmental Systems* vol.7, no. 4 (1977–1978): 301–308.

Seppa, Nathan. "Reactor Landfills Studied." *Wisconsin State Journal* (September 20, 1990).

Tchobanoglous, George, et al. *Sold Wastes Engineering Principles and Management Issues*. New York: McGraw-Hill Book Company, 1977.

Thompson, Stephanie. "Landfill Turned into Park." *American City and County* 106 (January 1991).

Treadaway. "Landfills Become Landscapes: The American Park Revolution." *Right of Way* (1989).

Weinstein, Bernard L. and Harold T. Gross. *The Economic Impacts of the Skyline Landfill on Ferris, Texas*. Center for Economic Development and Research, University of North Texas, March 1990.

Wilson, David G., ed. *Handbook of Solid Waste Management*. New York: Van Norstrand Reinhold Company, 1977.

Wilson, Sandy. "A Landfill by Any Other Name May Be a Development Site." *The Business Journal, Milwaukee* 7 (April 9, 1990).

Nuclear Facilities

Abkowitz, Mark D., Moses Karakouzian, and James A. Cardle. "Developing an Impact Analysis System for the Transport of High-Level Nuclear Wastes." *Transportation Research Record*, no. 1264 (1990).

Beron, Gail L. "Measuring the Effects of Proximity to a Uranium Processing Facility." *Measuring the Effects of Hazardous Materials Contamination on Real Estate Values: Techniques and Applications*. Chicago, Illinois: Appraisal Institute, 1992.

Bjornstad, David J. and David P. Vogt. "Some Comments Relating to Model Specification on 'Effects of Nuclear Power Plants on Residential Property Values.' " *Journal of Regional Science*, vol. 24, no. 1 (1984).

Capitol Region Planning and Development Agency. "Adverse Housing Related Impacts on Viability of Neighborhoods Due to the Three Mile Island Accident." Report to the Pennsylvania Department of Community Affairs, Bureau of Policy Planning (August 21, 1980).

Chalmers, J.D., K. Pijawka, K. Branch, P. Bergmann, and J. Flynn. "Socioeconomic Impacts of Nuclear Generating Stations: Summary Report." *Nuclear Regulatory Commission* (CR-2750), Washington, D.C. (1982).

Folland and Hough. "Nuclear Power Plants and the Value of Agricultural Land." *Land Economics* (1991).

Galster, George C. "Nuclear Power Plants and Residential Property Values: A Comment on Short-Run vs. Long-Run Considerations." *Journal of Regional Science*, vol. 26, no. 4 (1986).

Gamble, Hays B. and Roger H. Downing. *Effects of the Accident at Three Mile Island on Residential Property Values and Sales*. Institute for Research on Land and Water Resources, Pennsylvania State University. Prepared for U.S. Nuclear Regulatory Commission (NUREG/CR-2063) (1981).

_____ "A Reply to 'Nuclear Power Plants and Residential Property Values: A Comment on Short-Run vs. Long-Run Considerations.' " *Journal of Regional Science*, vol. 24, no. 1 (1984).

_____ "Some Comments Relating to Model Specification on 'Effects of Nuclear Power Plants on Residential Property Values.' ": Reply." *Journal of Regional Science*, vol. 24, no. 1 (1984).

Gamble, Hays B. and Roger H. Downing. "Effects of Nuclear Power Plants on Residential Property Values." *Journal of Regional Science* vol. 22, no. 4 (1982).

Gamble, Hays B., R.H. Downing, and O.H. Sauerlender. "Effects of Nuclear Power Plants on Community Growth and Residential Property Values." Pennsylvania State University, Prepared for U.S. Nuclear Regulatory Commission (NUREG/CR-0454) (April 1979).

Griffin, C.R. and Daniel R. Vellenga. *Homeowner Attitudes Toward Purchasing and Living in the Near Proximity to a Nuclear Facility*. Paper presented at annual conference of American Real Estate Society, Key West, Florida (April 17, 1993).

Hageman, Rhonda K. "Nuclear Waste Disposal: Potential Property Value Impacts." *Natural Resources Journal* (October 1982): 789–810.

Hoyt, Richard W., R. Keith Schwer, and William Thompson. "A Note on Homebuyer Attitudes Toward a Nuclear Repository." *The Journal of Real Estate Research*, vol. 7, no. 2 (Spring 1992).

Kinnard, William N., Jr., Phillip S. Mitchell, and Gail L. Beron. "The Market Impact of a Release of Radioactive Materials on Local Housing Values: An Econometric Study." *Journal of Property Tax Management* (Summer 1990).

Kinnard, William N., Jr., Phillip S. Mitchell, Gail L. Beron, and James R. Webb. "Market Reactions to an Announced Release of Radioactive Materials: The Impact on Assessable Value." *Property Tax Journal*, vol. 10, no. 3 (September 1991).

Miller, N. "A Geographical Information System-Based Approach to the Effects of Nuclear Processing Plants on Surrounding Property Values: The Case of the Fernald Settlement Study." Working Paper, University of Cincinatti (March 31, 1992).

Nelson, Jon P. "Three Mile Island and Residential Property Values: Empirical Analysis and Policy Implications." *Land Economics* (August 1981): 363–372.

Pijawka, D. and J. Chalmers. "Impact of Nuclear Generating Plants on Local Areas." *Economic Geography* (January 1983).

Rankin, William L. and Barbara D. Melber. *Public Perceptions of Nuclear Waste Management Issues*. Seattle, Washington: Battekke Memorial Institute Human Affairs Research Centers, 1980.

Shearer, Don Paul. *Three Mile Island Nuclear Accident Community Impact Study on Real Estate*. Greater Harrisburg Boards of Realtors, Inc., TMI Impact Study Committee (1978).

Slovic, Lichtenstein, and Fischoff. "Images of Disaster: Perception and Acceptance of Risks from Nuclear Power." *Energy and Risk Management*. Foodman & Rowe, eds. London: Academic Press, 1979.

Twark, Richard D., Raymond W. Eyerly, and Roger H. Downing. *The Effect of Nuclear Power Plants on Residential Property Values: A New Look at Three Mile Island* (Environmental Resources Research Institute, University Park, Pennsylvania: Pennsylvania State University, September 1990).

Webb, James R. "Nuclear Power Plants: Effects on Property Values." *The Appraisal Journal* (April 1980): 230–235.

Brownfields, Hazardous Waste Facilities, and Superfund Sites

Arnold, Alvin L., ed. "Hazardous Waste and Real Estate Transactions." *The Mortgage and Real Estate Executive's Report* (January 1, 1987).

Austrian, Ziona and Henning Eichler. "1993 Urban Brownfields Site Survey: Preliminary Analysis." Working Paper, Cleveland State University, Ohio (April 1993).

Bacharch, Kenneth M. and Alex J. Zautra. "Assessing the Impact of Hazardous Waste Facilities: Psychological, Politics and Environmental Impacts Statements" in Lebovits, et al. (eds.). *Advances in Environmental Psychology, Volume 6: Exposure to Hazardous Substances: Psychological Parameters*. Hillsdale, New Jersey: Lawrence Erlbaum Associates, 1984.

Bacow, Lawrence S. and James R. Milkey. "Overcoming Local Opposition to Hazardous Waste Facilities: The Massachusetts Approach." *Harvard Environmental Law Review*, vol. 6 (1982): 265–305.

Baker, Brian P. *Land Values Surrounding Waste Disposal Facilities*. Department of Agricultural Economics, New York State College of Agricultural and Life Sciences, Cornell University (October 1982).

———— *Perception of Hazardous Waste Disposal Facilities and Residential Real Property Values*. Department of Agricultural Economics, Cornell University, Report A.E. Res. 87–17 (July 1987).

Baker, Jean B., M.D., M.P.H., et al. "A Health Study of Two Communities Near the Stringfellow Waste Disposal Site." *Archives of Environmental Health*, vol. 43, no. 5 (September/October 1988).

Baker, Mary Dunn. "Property Values and Potentially Hazardous Waste Production Facilities: A Case Study of the Kanawha Valley, West Virginia." The Florida State University, PhD Dissertation (1986).

Baker, Greenland, Mendelein, and Marmon. "Stringfellow Waste Disposal Site." *Archives of Environmental Health* (1988).

Brown, Johnine J. "Superfunds and Superleins: Super Problems for Secured Lenders." *BNA's Banking Report*, vol. 50, no. 14 (April 4, 1988).

Campanella, Joseph A. "Valuation of Environmentally Impaired Assets." Paper presented to Conference on Brownfields Redevelopment, Washington, D.C. (March 23, 1995).

Centaur Associates and U.S. Environmental Protection Agency, Office of Waste and Waste Management. *Siting of Hazardous Waste Management Facilities and Public Opposition*, document SW-809 (1979).

Colton, C.E. and D. Mulville-Friel. "Property Transfer Site Histories: Hazardous Material Generation and Disposal Practices (Part I)." *Environmental Watch* (Spring 1991).

_____ "Property Transfer Site Histories: Hazardous Waste Material Generation and Disposal Practices (Part II)." *Environmental Watch* (Spring 1991).

Cooney, Deborah, Jocelyn Seitzman, Charles Bartsch, and Carol Andress. *Revival of Contaminated Industrial Sites: Case Studies*. Washington, D.C.: Northeast-Midwest Institute, 1992.

Edelstein, Michael R. "Toxic Exposure and the Inversion of the Home." *Journal of Architectural Planning and Research* 3 (1986).

Eliot-Jones, Michael. "Commercial Property Values and Toxic Sites." *Topics in Environmental Economics* (1992).

_____ "Rents and Proximity to Toxic Sites." *Spectrum Economics*. San Francisco, California (1991).

_____ *Toxic Sites, Property Values Liquidity*. San Francisco, California: Foster Associates, 1991.

Farkas, Alan L. "Overcoming Public Opposition to the Establishment of New Hazardous Waste Disposal Sites." *Capital University Law Review*, vol. 9 (1980): 451–465.

Fisher, Jeffrey D., William Goolsby, William N. Kinnard, Jr., and Bill Mundy. "The Impact of Hazardous and Toxic Materials on Property Values." Unpublished paper. Seattle, Washington: Real Estate Counseling Group of America, Inc., March 1991.

Fitchen, Janet M. "When Toxic Chemicals Pollute Residential Environments: The Cultural Meanings of Home and Homeownership." *Human Organization* 48, (Winter 1989).

Forcade, Bill S. "Public Participation in Siting." *Hazardous Waste Management in Whose Backyard?* M. Hearthill, ed. Boulder, Colorado: Westview Press, 1984.

Hazardous Waste Management in Whose Backyard? M. Hearthill, ed. Boulder, Colorado: Westview Press, 1984.

Geltman. "Recycling Land: Encouraging the Redevelopment of Contaminated Property." *NR&E* (1996).

Greenberg, Michael R. and Richard F. Anderson. *Hazardous Waste Sites: The Credibility Gap*. New Brunswick, New Jersey: Center for Urban Policy Research, 1984.

Greenberg, Michael, PhD, Richard Anderson, and Kirk Rosenburger. "Social and Economic Effects of Hazardous Waste Management Sites." *Hazardous Waste*, vol. 1, no. 3 (1984): 387–395.

Greenberg, Michael, PhD. "The Impact of Hazardous Waste Superfund Sites on the Value of Houses Sold in New Jersey." *Annals of Regional Science*, vol. 26 (1992).

Griffin, C.R. "Assessing the Impact on Housing Prices of the Environmental Hazard of Rocky Flats, Colorado." Paper presented at the Annual Meeting of the American Real Estate Society, Sarasota, Florida (April 11, 1991).

Hernandez, Jennifer L., Kimberley M. McMorrow, and Laurie G. Ballenger. "Joining the National Brownfields Bandwagon: New Options in Contaminated Property Redevelopment." *Land Development* (National Association of Home Builders, Fall 1996).

Holznagel, Bernd. "Negotiation and Mediation: The Newest Approach to Hazardous Waste Facility Siting." *Environmental Affairs*, vol. 13 (1986): 329–378.

Hunsperger, Wayne L. "Case Example: Impact of Hazardous Waste Material on Appraisal." *Focus: The Bulletin of Environmental Risk Evaluation and Management* (February 1, 1991).

Hurwitz. "Liability Lessons from Love Canal." *National Underwriter* (1984).

Institute for Environmental Studies, University of North Carolina. *Costs and Benefits to Local Governments Due to the Presence of a Hazardous Waste Management Facility and Related Compensation Issues* (March 1985).

Jackson, Thomas C. and Steven M. Jawetz. "Superfund and Real Estate Development." *Land Development* (Winter 1995).

Johnston. "Public Concerns and Issues: Siting Hazardous Waste Facilities." *International Right-of-Way Association* (1990).

Kaas, Bridgen and Lee. "Brownfields: Where the Market Makes Green." *NR&E* (1998).

Ketkar, Kusum. "Hazardous Waste Sites and Property Values in the State of New Jersey." *Applied Economics*, vol. 24: 647–659.

Kinnard, William N., Jr. "Approaches to Valuation of Properties Impacted by Pollution from Hazardous and Toxic Materials." *Methodologies for Valuation of Real Property Impacted by Pollution from Hazardous and Toxic Materials*. A seminar prepared and presented by The Real Estate Counseling Group of America, Inc., Orlando, Florida (February 28, 1991).

_____ "Measuring Locational Obsolescence: Proximity to Hazardous Materials Sites." *Silver Anniversary Professional Seminar on Appraisal of Distressed Properties*. International Association of Assessing Officers, Montreal, Quebec, Canada, (October 13, 1990).

Kinnard, William N., Jr., Mary Beth Geckler, and John K. Geckler. "Are Residential Property Values Impacted by Proximity to Alleged or Perceived Hazards to Human Health and Safety?" *Journal of Property Tax Management* (Fall/Winter 1995).

Kleindorfer, P.R. "Compensation and Negotiation in the Siting of Hazardous Waste Sites." *Sci. Total Environ.* The Netherlands, vol. 51 (1986).

Kohlhase, Janet. "The Impact of Toxic Waste Sites on Housing Values." *Journal of Urban Economics*, vol. 30 (1991).

Lautenberg, Sandra. "The Effect of Abandoned Hazardous Waste Dump Sites on Land Use and Values in Edison, New Jersey." Unpublished paper. New Brunswick, New Jersey: Department of Urban Planning and Policy Development, 1982.

Lawson, Jeffrey T. and Barbara H. Cane. *Hazardous Waste and the Real Estate Transaction: A Practical and Theoretical Guide* (for the technical consultant, real estate attorney, business person, investor, or anyone involved in buying and selling land). National Symposium, Management of Uncontrolled Hazardous Waste Sites, Washington, D.C., November 29–December 1, 1982.

Mason, Anthony. *Risk Perception in Communities on the Industrial Margin*. New Brunswick, New Jersey: Rutgers University Department of Geography, PhD thesis, 1989.

Mazur, Allan. *A Hazardous Inquiry: The Rashomon Effect at Love Canal*. Cambridge, Massachusetts: Harvard University Press, 1998.

McClelland, Gary H., William D. Schulze, and Brian Jurd. "The Effect of Risk Beliefs on Property Values: A Case Study of a Hazardous Waste Site." *Risk Analysis,* vol. 10, no. 4 (December, 1990).

McGregor, Gregor I. "Landowner Liability for Hazardous Waste." *The Journal of Real Estate Development,* 4 (Winter 1989).

Mitchell, Robert and W.H. Desvouges. "The Value of Avoiding a LULU: Hazardous Waste Disposal Sites." *Review of Economics and Statistics*, 68: 293–299.

Montague. "The Connection Between Brownfields and Waterway Sediments." *Brownfield News* (1998).

Mundy, Bill, MAI, PhD. "Hazardous Waste: Contamination, Fear and Industrial Property Transactions." *Professional Report.* Washington, D.C.: Society of Industrial Realtors, May/June 1993.

Mundy, Bill, MAI, Dave McLean, and John Kilpatrick. "The Brownfield Challenge." *Valuation, Insights & Perspectives* (First Quarter 1999).

Nijman, Jennifer T. "CERCLA's Secured Creditor Exemption: Back to the Future." *Illinois Bar Journal* (February 1995).

Page, William and Harvey Rabinowitz. "Potential for Redevelopment of Contaminated Brownfield Sites." *Economic Development Quarterly*, vol. 8, no. 4 (1994).

Pettit, C.L. and Charles Johnson. "The Impact on Property Values of Solid Waste Facilities." *Technical Bulletin 86-1 for the National Solid Waste Management Association* (January 31, 1986). Also in *Waste Age* (April 1987): 97–102.

Phillips, B.S. "Examining a Nonhazardous Liquid Solidification and Disposal Facility." *Environmental Watch* (Summer 1992).

Phillips, Kenneth W. "Creative Cost Recovery and CERCLA Limitations." *The Real Estate Finance Journal* (Summer 1995).

Price, Joe R. *The Impact of Solid Waste Management Facilities on Surrounding Real Estate Values*. West Palm Beach, Florida: Callaway & Price, Inc., 1989.

Public Interest Economics Foundation. *Benefits of Regulating Hazardous Waste Disposal: Land Values as an Estimator* (executive summary). Office of Policy Analysis, U.S. Environmental Protection Agency, Washington, D.C. (June 1984).

Reichert, Alan K., PhD. "Impact of a Toxic Waste Superfund Site on Property Values." *The Appraisal Journal* (October 1997): 381–392.

_____ "The Persistence of Contamination Effects: A Superfund Site Revisited." *The Appraisal Journal* (April 1999): 126–135.

Reid, Tex Ann, Edward M. Clar, Anthony M. Diecidue, and Mark F. Johnson. "Assessing a Municipality's Ability to Pay Superfund Cleanup Costs." *Federal Environmental Restoration Conference and Exhibitions.* Washington, D.C.: Federal Environmental Restoration Conference and Exhibitions, 1992.

Roddewig, Richard J., MAI, CRE. "EPA's Brownfield Initiative: Will It Improve the Market for Contaminated Properties?" *Valuation, Insights, & Perspectives* (Third Quarter 1997): 46–52.

Rosenblatt, Fred and Martha Brand. "Handling Hazardous Wastes: A Case Study." *Real Estate Outlook.* Boston, Massachusetts: Warren, Gorham and Lamont, Spring 1988.

Schmalensee, Richard, Ramachandra Ramanathan, Wolfhard Ram, and Dennis Smallwood. *Measuring External Effects of Solid Waste Management.* Institute for Policy Analysis, California NTIS Report, U.S. Environmental Protection Agency (PB-243 407) (March 1975).

Schultze, W., G. McClelland, M. Doane, E. Balisteri, R. Boyce, B. Hurd, and R. Simenauer. *An Evolution of Public Preferences for Superfund Site Cleanup: A Preliminary Assessment.* Washington, D.C.: U.S. Environmental Protection Agency/Office of Policy, Planning and Evaluation, March 1995.

Silverman, Gerald B. "Love Canal: A Retrospective." *Environmental Reporter* (Bureau of National Affairs, Inc.), vol. 20, no. 20, Part II (September 15, 1989).

Simons, Robert, PhD. "Cost Minimizing and Land Acquisition Strategies for Residential Lot Redevelopment in the City of Cleveland: A Case Study of the Glenville Neighborhood." Prepared for the City of Cleveland, Department of Community Development (December 1992).

Smith, Martin A., F.M. Lynn, and R.N. Andrews. "Economic Impacts of Hazardous Waste Facilities." *Hazardous Waste and Hazardous Materials* (1986).

Smith, Lynn, Andrews, Olin, and Maurer. "Costs and Benefits to Local Government Due to Presence of a Hazardous Waste Management Facility and Related Compensation Issues." University of North Carolina, working paper (1985).

Smith, V. Kerry and W.H. Desvouges. "Asymmetries to the Valuation of Risk and the Siting of Hazardous Waste Disposal Facilities." *American Economic Review* (May 1986).

_____ "The Value of Avoiding a LULU: Hazardous Waste Disposal Sites." *The Review of Economics and Statistics,* vol. 68 (1986): 293–299.

Smolen, Gerald E. et al. "Economic Effects of Hazardous Chemical and Proposed Radioactive Waste Landfills on Surrounding Real Estate Value." *The Journal of Real Estate Research* (Summer 1992).

Smolen, Gerald E., Gary Moore, and Lawrence V. Conway. "Economic Effects of Hazardous Waste Landfills on Surrounding Real Estate Values in Toledo, Ohio." *Journal of Real Estate Research* (1991).

_____ "Hazardous Waste Landfill Impacts on Local Property Values." *The Real Estate Appraiser* (April 1992).

Steinberg, Robert E. "Real Estate Transactions and the 1986 Superfund Amendments, Part I." *The Journal of Real Estate Development* (Spring 1987).

_____ "Real Estate Transactions and the 1986 Superfund Amendments, Part II." *The Journal of Real Estate Development* (Spring 1987).

Stever, Danold W. *Law of Chemical Regulation and Hazardous Waste.* New York: Clark Boardman Company, 1988—update annually.

Swartzman, Daniel, Kevin Croke, and Sheri Swibel. "Reducing Aversion to Living Near Hazardous Waste Facilities Through Compensation and Risk Reduction." School of Public Health, University of Illinois at Chicago, published in *Journal of Environmental Economics and Management* (1985).

"Your Property's Value Could Rise Dramatically If It's Located Near a Hazwaste Facility!" *Waste Age* (August 1985).

Welch, R.E. "Caution: Hazardous Material on Site." *Real Estate Appraiser* (May 1991).

White, J.M., ed. *Measuring the Effects of Hazardous Materials Contamination on Real Estate Values: Techniques and Applications.* Research Department *Technical Report.* Chicago, Illinois: Appraisal Institute, 1992.

Zeiss, Chris and James Atwater. "Waste Facility Impacts on Residential Property Values." *Journal of Urban Planning and Development* vol. 115 (1989): 123–134.

Mortgages and Mortgage Lenders

Adams, Victoria and Bill Mundy. "Attitudes and Policies of Lending Institutions Toward Environmental Impairment." *Environmental Watch* (6:4, 1993).

Bibliography

Arnold, Alvin L., ed. "Protecting Lenders from Hazardous Waste Liability." *The Mortgage and Real Estate Executives Report* (February 1, 1991).

Bernet, Richard G. "The Bankers' Act (SB 41): Added Protection for Purchasers of Real Property or Simply More Work for Environmental Consultants?" *ISBA Real Property* (March 1994).

Branff. "Damned if You Do and Damned if You Don't: A Last Plea for a Rational Approach to Lender Liability under CERCLA." *The Digest of Environmental Law* (1992).

Buonicore, Anthony J. "Environmental Liabilities in Financing Real Estate." *The Real Estate Finance Journal* 5 (Summer 1989).

"CERCLA Lender Liability: How Lenders Can Protect Themselves Under the Current Law." *Environmental Developments* (August 1994).

"FDIC Instructs Banks and Thrifts to Limit Environmental Liability." *Environmental Watch* (1993).

Ferguson, Jerry T. and Phyllis S. Myers. *Managing the Hazardous Waste Risk of Landlords and Lenders*. Paper presented at the Annual Meeting of the American Real Estate Society, Hilton Head, South Carolina (April 1995).

Gibson, Jeremy. "Lender Safe Harbor for Underground Storage Tank Liabilities Proposed by EPA." *Environmental Insights* (June 1994).

Harrington, J.T. "Lender Liability Under Superfund: The Saga Continues as EPA Steps In." *Environmental Watch* (Spring 1991).

Healy, Patricia R. and John J. Healy, Jr., MAI. "Lenders' Perspectives on Environmental Issues." *The Appraisal Journal* (July 1992): 394–398.

International Association of Assessing Officers. "Standard on the Valuation of Property Affected by Environmental Contamination." (August 1992).

Jackson, Thomas O., MAI. "Mortgage-Equity Analysis in Contaminated Property Valuation." *The Appraisal Journal* (January 1998): 46–55.

Jackson, Thomas O., Mark E. Dobroski, and Trevor E. Phillips. "Analyzing Contaminated Real Estate in a Changing Market." *The Journal of Real Estate Finance* (Fall 1997).

James, Walter D., III. "Financial Institutions and Hazardous Waste Litigation: Limiting the Exposure to Superfund Liability." *Natural Resources Journal* (Spring 1988).

Jones. "Watch Out for the Hidden Threat." *Mortgage Banking* (1988).

Kinnard, William N., Jr., MAI, SRA, PhD and Elaine W. Worzala, PhD. *Attitudes and Policies of Institutional Investors and Lenders Toward On-Site and Nearby Property Contamination*. Paper presented at American Real Estate Society Annual Meeting, South Lake Tahoe, California (March 1996).

_____. "Evolving Attitudes and Policies of Institutional Investors and Lenders Toward On-Site and Nearby Properties Contamination." Paper presented at *The Cutting Edge* Conference sponsored by the Royal Insitution of Chartered Surveyors, Bristol, England (1996).

_____. "Investor and Lender Reactions to Alternative Sources of Contamination." *Real Estate Issues* (August 1997).

Miller, Canfield, Paddock, and Stone Environmental Practice Group. "Lender Environmental Liability: EPA Rules Create New Guidelines for Secured Lenders." (1992).

Lentz and Wang. "Residential Appraisal and the Lending Process: A Survey of the Issue." *Journal of Real Estate Research* (1998).

Reilly, Mary Anne. "EPA, Congress Moving Toward Lender Liability Rule Under CERCLA." *Hazmat World* (December 1990): 14–15.

Roddewig, Richard J., MAI, CRE, and Allan C. Keiter, MAI. "Mortgage Lenders and the Institutionalization and Normalization of Environmental Risk Analysis." *The Appraisal Journal* (April 2001): 119–125.

Ryan, Daniel F. "Lender's View of Hazardous Substances and Appraiser Responsibility." *The Real Estate Appraiser and Analyst* (Fall 1989).

Urban Land Institute. "Mortgage Industry Suffering from Fears of Environmental Problems." *Land Use Digest*, vol. 28, no. 8 (1995).

Wilson, Albert R. and Arthur R. Alarcon, SRA. "Lender Attitudes Toward Source and Nonsource Impaired Property Mortgages." *The Appraisal Journal* (October 1997): 396–400.

Worzala, Elaine M. and William N. Kinnard, Jr., CRE. "Investor & Lender Reactions to Alternative Sources of Contamination." *Real Estate Issues* (August 1997): 42–48.

Tax Assessment

Airst. "Fair Assessment for Contaminated Properties." *Urban Land* (1994).

Carver, Robert, Esq. and Anthony W. Crowell, Esq. "Toxic Tax Assessments: The Ad Valorem Taxation of Contaminated Property." *Real Estate Issues* (Fall 1999): 10–19.

Dent, John C., Jr. "Environmental Regulations and Their Impact on Ad Valorem Taxation." *Tenth Annual IAAO Legal Seminar*, Grenelefe, Florida (November 15, 1990).

Dunmire, Thea D. "Real Estate Tax Valuations: Factoring in Environmental Impacts." *Environmental Finance* (1992): 461–472.

Ferruggia, Frank E. "Valuation of Contaminated Property: New Jersey's *Inmar* Decision." *Assessment Digest* (March/April 1991).

Garippa, John E. and Seth I. Davenport. "The Effects of Environmental Contamination on Property Values for Tax Assessment Purposes." *15th IPT Annual Conference*, Reno, Nevada (June 26, 1991).

Greenberg, Michael, PhD and James Hughes, PhD. "Impact of Hazardous Waste Sites on Land Use: Tax Assessors' Appraisal." *The Appraisal Journal* (January 1993): 42–51.

_____ "Impact of Hazardous Waste Sites on Property Value and Land Use: Tax Assessors' Appraisal." *The Appraisal Journal* (January 1993).

Keen, Bonnie H. "Tax Assessment for Contaminated Property: Tax Breaks for Polluters?" *Environmental Affairs*, vol. 19 (1992).

Peters, Bill Thomas. "How the Cost of Cleanup, Liability Factors, and Governmental Regulation of Hazardous Wastes Impacts Property Values for Purposes of Ad Valorem Taxation." *Ninth Annual IAAO Legal Seminar*, New Orleans, Louisiana (November 9, 1989).

White, Mark A. "The Environmental Impact on Valuation." Virginia Association of Assessing Officers, 39th Annual Property Assessment Program, Charlottesville, Virginia (July 20–22, 1994).

Wilson, Albert R. "Preparing an Assessed Value Appeal for Environmentally Impaired Property." *Environmental Watch* (Fall 1992).

Wilson, Albert R., Maxwell Ramsland, Thomas Wihelmy, and Roger Groves. "Ad Valorem Taxation and Environmental Devaluation Part I: An Overview of the Issues and Processes." *Journal of Property Tax Management* (Summer 1993): 1–32.

Environmental Insurance and Environmental Indemnities and Guarantee Programs

Brown. "Confronting Environmental Liabilities in the Purchase of Industrial Property." *Chicago Bar Association Record* (1987).

Champion International Corporation. *Champion Property Value Guarantee Program Guidelines, Solid Solutions for Solid Waste* (1989).

Ewing, Thomas F. "Hamilton, Ohio: Guarantees Near a Landfill." *New York Times* (July 8, 1990): Section 1, p. 27.

Grayson, E. Lynn, Esq. "Strategies to Minimize Environmental Liabilities in Real Estate Transactions." Presented at *Environmental Issues Associated with Real Estate* program, ISBA Regional Office, Chicago, Illinois (March 24, 1995).

Hall, Evelyn. "EIL Is Poised for Growth." *Best's Review—Property & Casualty* (April 1995).

Moylan, Janet D. "Limiting Loss: Environmental Insurance Helps in Property Redevelopment." *Brownfield News* (February/March 1997).

Oldham, Morris M. "Environmental Liability: Plan Now to Avoid Trouble Later." *Real Estate Focus: A Perspective on Real Estate* (Fall 1994).

Ragas, Wade R. *Housing Price Indemnification Program: Research Report*. University of New Orleans Real Estate Market Data Center (September 1990).

Roddewig, Richard J., MAI, CRE. "Using the Cost of Environmental Insurance to Measure Contaminated Property Stigma." *The Appraisal Journal* (July 1997): 304–308.

Solid Waste Agency of Northern Cook County (SWANCC). *Home Value Guarantee Plan* (1990).

Ziess, Chris and James Atwater. "Property-Value Guarantees for Waste Facilities." *Journal of Urban Planning and Development* (1989).

Legal Issues and Litigation

Anaya, William J., Esq. "The New Generation of Responsible Property Transfer Disclosure Laws: An Alternative." *Real Estate/Environmental Liability News*, vol. 1, no. 11 (March 29, 1990).

Berger, C. Jaye. *Hazardous Substances in Buildings: Liability, Litigation, and Abatement* (John Wiley & Sons, 1992).

Bleicher. "Redefining the CERCLA Liability of Former Owners, Tenants and Operators." *Toxic Law Reporter* (1992).

Bibliography

Browner, Carol M., administrator, U.S. Environmental Protection Agency. Statement before the Commerce, Trade, and Hazardous Materials Subcommittee, Committee on Commerce, U.S. House of Representatives (March 16, 1995).

Comprehensive Environmental Response, Compensation and Liability Act, 40 CFR Part 300, National Oil and Hazardous Substance Pollution Contingency Plan; Final Rule (March 8, 1990).

Dorchester, John D., MAI, CRE. "The Federal Rules of Evidence and *Daubert*: Evaluating Real Property Valuation Witnesses." *The Appraisal Journal* (July 2000): 290–306.

Dunmire, Thea D. "An Overview of Federal EPA Laws and Regulations Which Impact Real Property." *Tenth Annual IAAO Legal Seminar*. Grenelefe, Florida (November 15, 1990).

Dushoff, Jay and Denise Henslee. "When Eminent Domain 'Working Rules' Don't Work." *The Appraisal Journal* (July 1991): 429–435.

Eaton, J.D. *Real Estate Valuation in Litigation*, 2d ed. Chicago, Illinois: The Appraisal Institute, 1995.

Edelstein, Michael R. "Disabling Communities: The Impact of Regulatory Proceedings." *Journal of Environmental Systems* (1986).

"Environmental Liability of Brokers and Other Parties." 19 *Real Estate Law Journal* 218, 277 (1991).

"Environmental Problems and Brokers Liability." 3 *Natural Resources and Environment* 17 (1988).

Foster, Kenneth R., David E. Bernstein, and Peter W. Huber. *Phantom Risk: Scientific Risk and the Law*. Cambridge, Massachusetts: Massachusetts Institute of Technology Press, 1993.

Friedman, Jack P., CRE. "Defending An Oil Company Against Litigation for Environmental Contamination (A Case Study)." *Real Estate Issues* (Winter 1999/2000): 33–39.

Gerber, Ellen JoAnne. "Industrial Property Transfer Liability: Reality versus Necessity." *Cleveland State Law Review*, vol. 40 (1992).

Government Institutes, Inc., *Environmental Law Handbook*. 12th ed. (Rockville, Maryland).

_____ *Environmental Statutes*. Rockville, Maryland, 1993.

Groves, Roger M. "Do America's State Cases Answer the Question: How Should You Value Contaminated Properties? Sorry." *Tenth Annual IAAO Legal Seminar*, Grenelefe, Florida (November 15, 1990).

Gwin, Jay and Judon Fambrough. *The Effect of Environmental Law in Real Estate Transactions*, a technical report of the Real Estate Center (College Station, Texas: Texas A&M University, January 1990).

Harr, Jonathon. *A Civil Action*. New York: Vintage Books, 1995.

Holmen, Ralph W. "Current Legal Issues Raised by Environmental Hazards Affecting Real Estate." *Real Estate Issues* (Fall/Winter 1991): 37–43. "Home, Not-So-Sweet Home: Real Estate Broker Liability in the Sale of Previously Contaminated Property: Has Broken Liability Gone Too Far?" 2 *Rutgers Law Journal* 111 (1989).

Hoyt, Richard M. and Robert J. Aalberts. "Implications of the *Kuhmo Tire* Case for Appraisal Expert Witnesses." *The Appraisal Journal* (January 2001).

_____ "New Requirements for the Appraisal Expert Witness." *Appraisal Journal* (October 1997).

Inderbitzin, Sarah L. "Taking the Burden Off the Buyer: A Survey of Hazardous Waste Disclosure Statutes." *The Environmental Lawyer*, vol. 1, no. 2.

Jessup, Deborah Hitchcock. *Guide to State Environmental Programs*, 3rd ed. Washington, D.C.: The Bureau of National Affairs, Inc., 1994.

Kabat, Thomas E., MAI, CCIM, Randi L. Firus, MA, and Suzanne M. Stuckwisch, MBA, MS. "The Financial Consultant's Role in the Proof of Environmental Damages." in Roman L. Weil, et al. "Litigation Services Handbook: The Role of the Financial Expert." 3d edition. New York: John Wiley & Sons, Inc.

Mays, Richard H. "Environmental Laws: Impact on Business Transactions." *A Practical Guide with Forms*. Washington, D.C.: The Bureau of National Affairs, Inc., 1992.

McLain, Wallis E., Jr. *U.S. Environmental Laws*. Washington, D.C.: The Bureau of National Affairs, Inc., 1991.

McMurray, Robert I. and David Pierce. "Environmental Remediation and Eminent Domain." *ALI–ABA Eminent Domain Seminar* (January 1992): 105–146.

National Property Law Digests, Inc. *Digest of Environmental Law* Bethesda, Maryland.

_____ *The Digest of Environmental Law of Real Property* Washington, D.C.: Bi-monthly.

Phillips, Kenneth W. "Innocent Landowner Loses Big." *The Real Estate Finance Journal* (Spring 1995).

Robinson, Nicholas A. *Environmental Regulation of Real Property Law.* New York: Law Journal Seminars-Press, 1993.

Ruskin, William H. "Value Protection: An Alternative to Litigation." *Toxic Law Reporter,* vol. 5, no. 14 (September 5, 1990).

Ruyak, Matthew. "CERCLA Update: Recent Court Decisions Interpreting Liability Provisions." *The Newsletter of Conservation Law* (March/April 1995).

Securities and Exchange Commission. *Staff Accounting Bulletin 92,* 17CFR Part 211, (SAB 92) 58 FR 32843 (June 14, 1993).

Seyer, David V. "Sources of Environmental Liability in Appraisals." *Tenth Annual IAAO Legal Seminar.* Grenelefe, Florida (November 15, 1990).

Stimson, James A., Jeffrey J. Kimmel, and Sara Thurin Rollin. *Guide to Environmental Laws from Premanufacture to Disposal.* Washington, D.C.: the Bureau of National Affairs, Inc., 1993.

Toxic Laws Reporter. Washington, D.C.: Bureau of National Affairs, November 20, 1991.

Vale and Cline. "Stigma and Property Contamination—Damnum Absque Injuria." *Tort and Insurance Law Journal* (1998).

Vanderver, Timothy A., Jr. *Clean Air Law and Regulation.* Washington, D.C.: The Bureau of National Affairs, Inc., 1992.

Weil, Roman L., Michael J. Wagner, and Peter B. Frank. "Litigation Services Handbook: The Role of the Financial Expert." 3d edition. New York: John Wiley & Sons, Inc.

Weisheit, Bowen P., Sr. "Will New Environmental Laws Redefine Just Compensation?" *The Appraisal Journal* (January 1992): 59–67.

Wise, Kenneth T., M. Alexis Maniatis, Paul R. Ammann, and Gayle S. Koch. "Filling the GAAP: An Approach to Improve SEC Disclosure of Environmental Liabilities." *Journal of Environmental Law & Practice.*

Risk-Based Assessment

Crone and Voith. "Risk and Return within the Single Family Housing Market." *Real Estate Economics* (1999).

Hammit, Belsky, Levy, and Graham. "Residential Building Codes, Affordability, and Health Protection: A Risk-Tradeoff Approach." Harvard University working paper (1998).

Harrison, Henry S. "Environmental Risk Screening." *REEA Journal* (Spring 1990).

Heath, Jenifer S. "Superfund Risk Assessments and PRPs: Status of the Prohibition." Technical Paper (63), Woodward-Clyde Consultants.

Kasperson, Renn, Slovic, Brown, Emel, Goble, Kasperson, and Ratick. "The Social Amplifications of Risk." *Risk Analysis* (1988).

Kraus and Slovic. "Taxonomic Analysis of Perceived Risk: Modeling Individual and Group Perceptions within Homogeneous Hazard Domains." *Risk Analysis* (1988).

Lewis, H.W. *Technologic Risk.* New York: W.W. Norton, 1990.

Long, F.A. and Glenn E. Schwietzer, eds. "Risk Assessment at Hazardous Waste Sites." *ACS Symposium Series 204.* Washington, D.C.: American Chemical Society, 1982.

Machlin, Jennifer L. and Tomme R. Young. *Managing Environmental Risk: Real Estate and Business Transactions.* New York: Clark Boardman Company, 1991.

Manning, Christopher A. "Managing Environmental Risk and Investment Opportunities to Maximize Shareholder Wealth." *Journal of Real Estate Research,* vol. 7, no. 3 (Summer 1992).

Meyer and Weiand. "Risk and Return to Housing, Tenure Choice, and the Value of Housing in an Asset Pricing Context." *Real Estate Economics* (1996).

Runge, C. "Risk Assessment and Environmental Benefits Analysis." *Natural Resources Journal,* vol. 23 (1983).

Slovic. "Trust, Emotion, Sex, Politics, and Science: Surveying the Risk-Assessment Battlefield." Chapter 12 of *Environment, Ethics and Behavior,* Bazerman, et al., eds. San Francisco: The New Lexington Press, 1997.

Slovic, Fischoff, and Lichtenstein. "Characterizing Perceived Risk." Chapter 5 of *Perilous Progress: Managing the Hazards of Technology,* Kates, et al., eds. (Boulder, Colorado: Westwood Press, 1985).

VanDoran, Peter. *Chemicals, Cancer and Choices: Risk Reduction Through Markets.* Washington, D.C.: Cato Institute, 1999.

Vidich, Charles. "Calculating the Risk of Purchasing Toxic Real Estate." Paper presented at 1991 Annual Conference, American Real Estate Society, Sarasota, Florida (April 12, 1991).

Wilson, Albert R. "Appraisal Practice Concerning Environmental Risks." *Focus,* vol. 2, no. 2 (November 1, 1989).

_____ "Calculation of an Extraordinary Risk Premium." *Focus,* vol. 5, no. 2 (January 2, 1992).

_____ "Environmental Risk Evaluation." *Focus* (March 30, 1990).

_____ *Environmental Risk: Identification and Management.* Chelsea, Michigan: Lewis Publishers, 1991.

_____ "A Valuation Model for Environmental Risk." *Focus* (January 15, 1990).

Regression Analysis, Hedonic Modeling, Contingent Valuation and Survey Methods

Adamowicz, Louviere, and Williams. "Combining Revealed and Stated Preference Methods for Valuing Environmental Amenities." *Journal of Environmental Economics and Management* (1994).

Ball, M. "Recent Empirical Work on the Determinants of Relative House Prices." *Urban Studies,* vol. 10, no. 213 (1973).

Brookshire, Thayer, Schulze, and d'Arge. "Valuing Public Goods: A Comparison of Survey and Hedonic Approaches." *The American Economic Review* (March 1982).

Brown and Gregory. "Why the WTA-WTP Disparity Matters." *Ecological Economics* (1999).

Case, Bradford and Charles M. Quigley. *Statistical Analysis of Sales Data to Verify Appraisal Information.* Working Paper no. 88–150. Berkeley, California: Center for Real Estate and Urban Economics, October 1988.

Chambers, Chambers, and Whitehead. "Contingent Valuation of Quasi-Public Goods: Validity, Reliability, and Application to Valuing a Historic Site." *Public Finance Review* (1998).

Clark, David and Leslie Nieves. "An Interregional Hedonic Analysis of Noxious Facility Impacts on Local Wages and Property Values." Working Paper, Marquette University, Milwaukee, Wisconsin (1993).

Compensable Value Determination (*CV/CJ/PD, methodological criteria*) *Federal Register,* 59–5 (January 7, 1994).

Cummings, Ronald G., David S. Brookshire, and William D. Schulze. *Valuing Public Goods, The Contingent Value Method.* Totowa, N.J.: Rowman & Allanheld Publishers, 1986.

Dilmore. "Appraising with Regression Analysis: A Pop Quiz." *The Appraisal Journal* (October 1997).

Green, Kreiger, and Agarwal. "Adaptive Conjoint Analysis: Some Caveats and Suggestions." *Journal of Marketing Research* (May 1991).

Green and Srinivasan. "Conjoint Analysis in Marketing: New Developments with Implications for Research and Practice." *Journal of Marketing* (October 1990).

Halstead, John M. "Measuring the Non-Market Value of Massachusetts Agricultural Land: A Case Study." *Northeast Journal of Agricultural and Resource Economics,* vol. 14 (1983).

Harrison, David, Jr. and James H. Stock. "Hedonic Housing Values, Local Public Goods, and the Benefits of Hazardous Waste Cleanup." Discussion Paper E-84-09, Harvard University Energy and Environmental Policy Center, Cambridge, Massachusetts: November 1984.

Huber, Wittink, Fiedler, and Miller. "The Effectiveness of Alternative Preference Elicitation Procedures in Predicting Choice." *Journal of Marketing Research* (February 1993).

Isakson. "The Review of Real Estate Appraisals Using Multiple Regression Analysis." *Journal of Real Estate Research* (1998).

James, Steven E. and James H. Schaarsmith. "Use of Decision Science Techniques in Management of Environmental Financial Risks." *Journal of Environmental Law & Practice.*

Kiel, Katherine A. and Katherine T. McClain. "The Effect of An Incinerator Siting on Housing Appreciation Rates." *Journal of Urban Economics,* 37(3): 311–23.

Kinnard, William N., Jr. *Fear (As a Measure of Damages) Strikes Out: Two Case Studies Comparisons of Actual Market Behavior with Opinion Survey Research.* Paper presented at American Real Estate Society Annual Conference, Santa Barbara, California (April 1994).

Kinnard, William N., Jr., Sue Ann Dickey, and Mary Beth Geckler. "Fear and Property Value: Opinion Survey Results vs. Market Sales Evidence." Paper presented at the IAAO 1994 Annual Conference, Seattle, Washington (October 1994).

Kinnard, William N., Jr., P. Mitchell, G. Beron, and J. Webb. *Patterns of Real Estate Market Behavior Around the Feed Materials Production Center, Fernald, Ohio, December 1982–February 1987: A Quantitative Analysis and Evaluation of Changes in the Levels and Trends of Market Indicators of Property Values.* Storrs, Connecticut: Real Estate Counseling Group of Connecticut, Inc., October 1987.

Kroll and Smith. "The Buyers Response Techniques—A Framework for Improving Comparable Selection and Adjustment in Single Family Appraising." *Journal of Real Estate Research* (1988).

Mendelsohn, Hellerstein, Huguenin, Unsworth, and Brazee. "Measuring Hazardous Waste Damages with Panel Models." *Journal of Environmental Economics and Management* (1992).

Michaels, R. and V. Smith. "Market Segmentation and Valuing Amenities with Hedonic Models: The Case of Hazardous Waste Sites." *Journal of Urban Economics,* vol. 28 (1990).

Valuing Contaminated Properties

Mitchell, Robert Cameron and Richard T. Carson. "Using Surveys to Value Public Goods: The Contingent Valuation Method." *Resources for the Future* (1988).

Mundy, Bill, MAI. PhD. "Analog Research: Market Evidence of Impaired Property Sales and Case Studies." *Environmental Analysis and Valuation Seminar*. Seattle, Washington (March 1992).

Pace and Barry. "Quick Computation of Spatial Autoregressive Estimators." *Geographical Analysis* (July 1997).

_____ "Sparse Spatial Autoregressions." *Statistics and Probability Letters* (1997).

Rich, Peter R. and L. Joe Moffitt. "Benefits of Pollution Control on Massachusetts Housatonic River: A Hedonic Pricing Approach." *Water Resources Bulletin*, vol. 18, no. 6 (December 1982).

Roddewig, Richard J., MAI, CRE. "Junk Science, Environmental Stigma, Market Surveys, and Proper Appraisal Methodology: Recent Lessons from the Litigation Trenches." *The Appraisal Journal* (October 1999): 447–453.

Roe, Boyle, and Teisl. "Using Conjoint Analysis to Derive Estimates of Compensating Variation." *Journal of Environmental Economics and Management* (1996).

Slovic, Paul. "Perception of Risk." *Science* (vol. 236, 1987).

Smith, V. Kerry and W.H. Desvouges. "An Empirical Analysis of the Economic Value of Risk Changes." *Journal of Political Economy* vol. 95, no. 11 (1987).

Syms, Paul. "Perceptions of Risk in the Valuation of Contaminated Land." *The Journal of Property, Valuation and Investment*, vol. 15, no. 1 (1997).

Thayer, Mark A. "Contingent Valuation Techniques for Assessing Environmental Impacts: Further Evidence." *Journal of Environmental Economics and Management*, vol. 8.

Thayer, M., H. Albers, and M. Rahmatian. "The Benefits of Reducing Exposure to Waste Disposal Sites: A Hedonic Housing Value Approach." *Journal of Real Estate Research* (Summer 1992).

U.S. Department of Commerce. *Report of the NOAA Panel on Contingent Valuation*. Washington, D.C.: National Oceanographic and Atmospheric Administration, January 1993. (Published in *Federal Register*, vol. 58, no. 10, January 15, 1993).

Wildavsky, Aaron. "No Risk is the Highest Risk of All." *American Science* (vol. 67, 1979).

Willumsen, Maria, Robert D. Cruz, and William G. Vogt. *Modeling and Simulation*, vol. 20, Part 1, University of Pittsburgh School of Engineering. Proceedings of the 20th Annual Pittsburgh Conference (May 4–5, 1989).

Wittink and Cattin. "Commercial Use of Conjoint Analysis: An Update." *Journal of Marketing* (July 1989).

Wolverton. "Empirical Investigation into the Limitations of the Normative Paired Sales Adjustment Method." *Journal of Real Estate Research* (1998).

Miscellaneous

Adams, Victoria and Bill Mundy. "Environmentally Impaired Properties and the SIOR." *SIOR Professional Report* (Fall 1995).

Anderson, Orell C., MAI. "Environmental Contamination: An Analysis in the Context of the DC Matrix." *Appraisal Journal* (July 2001).

Bate, Roger, ed. *What Risk?* Oxford, England: Butterworth-Heimemann, 1997.

Breyer, Stephen. *Breaking the Vicious Circle: Toward Effective Risk Regulation*. Cambridge, MA: Harvard University Press, 1993.

Campanella, Joseph A. "Valuing Partial Losses in Contamination Cases." *The Appraisal Journal* (April 1984): 301–304.

DeLong, James V. "A Civil Action or A Civil Fiction?" *Competitive Enterprise Institute* (January 1999)– *www.cei.org/civilaction.html.*

Edelstein, Michael R. *Contaminated Communities: The Social and Psychological Impacts of Residential Toxic Exposure*. Boulder, Colorado: Westview Press, 1988.

Eliot-Jones, Michael. "Real Estate Value and Toxic Sites." *The Digest of Environmental Law* (July 1992): 89–92.

Gots, Ronald E. *Toxic Risks: Science, Regulation and Perception*. Ann Arbor, Michigan: Lewis Publishers, 1993.

Gould, Jay. *Quality of Life in American Neighborhoods, Levels of Affluence, Toxic Waste and Cancer Mortality in Residential Zip Code Areas*. Boulder, Colorado: Westview Press, 1986.

Rabe, Barry G. *Fragmentation and Integration in State Environmental Management*. Washington, D.C.: The Conservation Foundation, 1986.

Sanders, Michael V. "Post-Repair Diminution in Value from Geotechnical Problems." *The Appraisal Journal* (January 1996).

Slutsker, Gary. "Paratoxicology." *Forbes* (January 8, 1990): 303.

"Staff Accounting Bulletin 93." *Federal Register*, vol. 58. Washington, D.C.: Department of the Treasury, Office of the Comptroller of the Currency, June 14, 1993: 32843.

Starfield, Lawrence E. "The 1990 National Contingency Plan—More Detail and More Structure, but Still a Balancing Act." *Environmental Law Reporter* (1990).

United Church of Christ, Commission for Racial Justice. *Toxic Waste and Race in the United States*. New York: United Church of Christ, 1987.

"Answering the Critics." *Waste Age* (July 1980).

Watson, K. "Measuring and Mitigating Socio-Economic Environmental Impacts of Constructing Energy Projects: An Emerging Regulatory Issue." *Natural Resources Lawyer*, vol. 10 (1977).

Wilson, Albert R. and Raymond S. Bovaird. "Topovalue Mapping: A Visual-analytical Approach to Real Property Evaluation." *Focus* (May 31, 1990).